S0-AXY-463

Rest easy and save!

Look for the Signs Along the Way

When selecting a place to dine while traveling, look for Official Appointment restaurants that display the AAA Approved sign. It's the only sign you need to be assured of an enjoyable dining experience.

As a member, you already know the AAA sign indicates quality establishments. So, when you don't have advance dining reservations, look for the AAA Approved sign along the way, for a meal you'll long remember!

Michigan & Wisconsin

Published by:
AAA Publishing
1000 AAA Drive
Heathrow, FL 32746-5063
Copyright AAA 2003

Send Written Comments to:
AAA Member Comments
1000 AAA Drive, Box 61
Heathrow, FL 32746-5063

Advertising Rate and Circulation Information
Call: (407) 444-8280

Printed in the USA by Quebecor World, Buffalo, NY

 Printed on recyclable paper. Please recycle whenever possible.

Stock #4616

Michigan & Wisconsin

TourBook Navigator

Follow our simple guide to make the most of this member benefit 9-25

Comprehensive City Index

■ Michigan

■ Wisconsin

Featured Information

Have you ever celebrated when you've seen your exit sign?

 Every day should come with a smile. And at Hampton®, we're committed to making you smile. That's why we offer our **Stay and Save**™ rates for AAA members. That's 10% off the best available room rates when you book a room with your AAA card. And with over 1,000 locations nationwide, we're sure to be close to wherever you're traveling. Plus, we'll make sure you start the day right with our free breakfast bar and leave completely satisfied. It's why we have our 100% Satisfaction Guarantee. It's also why you get both Hilton HHonors® hotel points and airline miles for each stay. So book your next trip at Hampton today. Just call **1-800-456-7793** for reservations.

We're with you all the way.

hilton.com

doubletree.com

embassysuites.com

Check in with your card.
Cash in on great savings.

Stay with the Hilton family of hotels and enjoy our
Stay and Save™ rates with your AAA membership.
We offer members a special discounted AAA rate at
over 700 AAA-approved locations in the US. Choose
from conveniently located properties ranging

hiltongardeninn.com

 from luxury resorts to value-priced
accommodations with all the amenities.
Show Your Card & Save® at any
participating hotel in the Hilton family. To make
advance reservations, call our dedicated AAA number
at **1-877-655-5694** or your local AAA travel office.

homewoodsuites.com

6

Crossword Puzzle

ACROSS

2 (umbrella)
4 (beach)
5 (camera)
8 (suitcase/sun)
9 (suitcase)
11 (sunglasses)
12 (map)
13 (truck)
14 (tent)

DOWN

1 (car)
3 (FLORIDA AAA 12B license plate)
6 (mountains)
7 (barn)
10 (music)

Which two are the same?

Towty is a trademark of AAA

WHAT YOU SAVE ON RAMADA'S RATES, SPEND ON FILM.

How far can you get on a vacation? Wherever you go in Michigan and Wisconsin, low rates at

ADD'L $5 OFF | Ramada® hotels plus an additional $5 off your AAA rate can take you further.* When you're not taking in the sights, you can take it easy in a comfortable room. And enjoy amenities like HBO and a pool.** But bring your camera. With the money you save, you can capture a lot of memories. For reservations or more information, visit us online or call today.

RAMADA®
A very good place to be.℠

RAMADA.COM or 1.800.2 RAMADA
Ask for promo code S3A to receive your AAA discount.**

Trust the AAA TourBook® guide for objective travel information. Follow the pages of the TourBook Navigator to thoroughly understand this unique member benefit.

Making Your Way Through the AAA Listings

Attractions, lodgings and restaurants are listed on the basis of merit alone after careful evaluation, approval and rating by one of our full-time, professionally trained Tourism Editors. Annual evaluations are unannounced to ensure that our Tourism Editors see an establishment just as our members would see it.

Those lodgings and restaurants listed with an (fyi) icon have not gone through the same evaluation process as other rated properties. Individual listings will typically denote the reason why this icon appears. Bulleted recreational activity listings are not inspected but are included for member information.

An establishment's decision to advertise in the TourBook guide has no bearing on its evaluation or rating. Advertising for services or products does not imply AAA endorsement.

How the TourBook is
Organized

Geographic listing is used for accuracy and consistency. This means attractions, lodgings and restaurants are listed under the city in which they physically are located—or in some cases under the nearest recognized city. The Comprehensive City Index located in the back of the book contains an A-to-Z list of cities. Most listings are alphabetically organized by state or province, city, and establishment name. A color is assigned to each state or province so that you can match the color bars at the top of the page to switch from ❶ Points of Interest to ❷ Lodgings and Restaurants.

Destination Cities and Destination Areas

The TourBook guide also groups information by destination city and destination area. If a city is grouped in a destination vicinity section, the city name will appear at its alphabetical location in the book, and a handy cross reference will give the exact page on which listings for that city begin. Maps are placed at the beginning of these sections to orient you to the destinations.

❸ Destination cities, established based on government models and local expertise, are comprised of metropolitan areas plus nearby vicinity cities.

Destination areas are regions with broad tourist appeal. Several cities will comprise the area.

All information in this TourBook guide was reviewed for accuracy before publication. However, since changes inevitably occur between annual editions, we suggest you contact establishments directly to confirm prices and schedules.

Points of Interest Section

Orientation maps
near the start of each Attractions section show only those places we call points of interest. Coordinates included with the city listings depict the locations of those cities on the map. A GEM symbol (🏵) accents towns with "must see" points of interest which offer a *Great Experience for Members*. And the black ovals with white numerals (**22** for example) locate items listed in the nearby Recreation Areas chart.

Destination area maps
illustrate key travel areas defined by local travel experts. Communities shown have listings for AAA approved attractions.

National park maps
represent the area in and around the park. Some campground sites and lodges spotted on the maps do not meet AAA/CAA criteria, but are shown for members who nevertheless wish to stay close to the park area.

Walking or self-guiding tour maps
correspond to specific routes described in TourBook guide text.

City maps
show areas where numerous points of interest are concentrated and indicate their location in relation to major roads, parks, airports and other landmarks.

Lodgings & Restaurants Section

Destination area maps
illustrate key travel areas defined by local travel experts. Communities shown have listings for AAA-RATED® lodgings and/or restaurants.

Spotting maps
show the location of lodgings and restaurants. Lodgings are spotted with a black background (**22** for example); restaurants are spotted with a white background (**23** for example). Spotting map indexes have been placed immediately after each map to provide the user with a convenient method to identify what an area has to offer at a glance. The index references the map page number where the property is spotted, indicates if a property is an Official Appointment and contains an advertising reference if applicable. It also lists the property's diamond rating, high season rate range and listing page number.

Downtown/city spotting maps
are provided when spotted facilities are very concentrated. GEM points of interest also appear on these maps.

Vicinity spotting maps
spot those properties that are outside the downtown or city area. Major roads, landmarks, airports and GEM points of interest are shown on vicinity spotting maps as well. The names of suburban communities that have AAA-RATED® accommodations are shown in magenta type.

Featured Information Section

Driving distance maps
are intended to be used only for trip-distance and driving-time planning.

Sample Attraction Listing

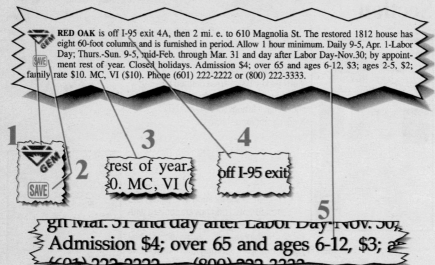

RED OAK is off I-95 exit 4A, then 2 mi. e. to 610 Magnolia St. The restored 1812 house has eight 60-foot columns and is furnished in period. Allow 1 hour minimum. Daily 9-5, Apr. 1-Labor Day; Thurs.-Sun. 9-5, mid-Feb. through Mar. 31 and day after Labor Day-Nov.30; by appointment rest of year. Closed holidays. Admission $4; over 65 and ages 6-12, $3; ages 2-5, $2; family rate $10. MC, VI ($10). Phone (601) 222-2222 or (800) 222-3333.

1

2

3 rest of year. 0. MC, VI (

4 off I-95 exit

5 gh Mar. 31 and day after Labor Day-Nov. 30, Admission $4; over 65 and ages 6-12, $3; a (601) 222-2222   (800) 222-3333

1 This attraction is of exceptional interest and quality and therefore has been designated a AAA GEM—offering a *Great Experience for Members.*

2 Participating attractions offer AAA/CAA, AAA MasterCard or AAA Visa cardholders a discount off the attraction's standard admission; members should inquire in advance concerning the validity of the discount for special rates. Present your card at the admission desk. A list of participating points of interest appears in the Indexes section of the book. The SAVE discount may not be used in conjunction with other discounts. Attractions that already provide a reduced senior or child rate may not honor the SAVE discount for those age groups. All offers are subject to change and may not apply during special events, particular days or seasons or for the entire validity period of the TourBook. Shopping establishments preceded by a SAVE icon also provide discounts and/or gift with purchase to AAA/CAA members; present your card at the mall's customer service center to receive your benefit.

3
AX=American Express	DS=Discover	MC=MasterCard
CB=Carte Blanche	JC=Japan Credit Bureau	VI=VISA
DC=Diners Club		

Minimum amounts that may be charged appear in parentheses when applicable.

4 Unless otherwise specified, directions are given from the center of town, using the following highway designations: I (interstate highway), US (federal highway), Hwy. (Canadian highway), SR (state route), CR (county road), FM (farm to market road), FR (forest road), MM (mile marker).

5 Admission prices are quoted without sales tax. Children under the lowest age specified are admitted free when accompanied by an adult. Days, months and age groups written with a hyphen are inclusive. Prices pertaining to points of interest in the United States are quoted in U.S. dollars; prices for Canadian province and territory points of interest are quoted in Canadian dollars.

Bulleted Listings: Casino gambling establishments are visited by AAA personnel to ensure safety; casinos within hotels are presented for member information regardless of whether the lodging is AAA approved. Recreational activities of a participatory nature (requiring physical exertion or special skills) are not inspected. Wineries are inspected by AAA Tourism Editors to ensure they meet listing requirements and offer tours. All are presented in a bulleted format for informational purposes.

Attraction Partners

Show Your Card & Save

AAA. Every Day.

These Show Your Card & Save® partners provide the listed member benefits. Admission tickets that offer greater discounts may be available for purchase at the local AAA/CAA club. A maximum of six tickets is available at the discount price.

SeaWorld/Busch Gardens

SAVE Save at SeaWorld, Busch Gardens, Sesame Place, Water Country USA and Adventure Island

SAVE Save 10% on general admission

Six Flags Adventure Parks

SAVE Save $4 per adult on general admission at the gate

SAVE Save $12 per adult on general admission at the gate each Wednesday

SAVE Save 10% on selected souvenirs and dining (check at main gate for details)

Universal Orlando

SAVE Save $4 on a 2-day/2-park pass or $5 on a 3-day/2-park pass at Universal Orlando's theme parks (savings apply to tickets purchased at the gate)

SAVE Save 10% on select dining and souvenirs at both Universal Orlando theme parks and at all Universal CityWalk Orlando restaurants (except Emeril's)

Universal Studios Hollywood

SAVE Save $3 on a 1-day Universal Hollywood pass (savings applies to tickets purchased at the gate)

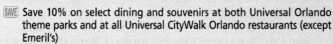

SAVE Save 10% on selected dining and souvenirs at Universal Studios Hollywood and Universal CityWalk

Gray Line

SAVE Save 10% on sightseeing tours of 1 day or less

Restaurant Partners

Landry's Seafood House, The Crab House, Joe's Crab Shack

SAVE Save 10% on food and non-alcoholic beverages at Landry's Seafood House, The Crab House and Joe's Crab Shack and 10% on merchandise at Joe's Crab Shack. Savings applicable to AAA/CAA members and up to six people

Hard Rock Cafe

SAVE Save 10% on food, beverage, and merchandise at all U.S., Canada, and select international locations

Visit aaa.com to discover all the great Show Your Card & Save® restaurants in your area.

Sample Lodging Listing

1. $\text{\small AAA}$ or $\text{\small CAA}$ indicates our Official Appointment (OA) lodgings. The OA program permits properties to display and advertise the $\text{\small AAA}$ or $\text{\small CAA}$ emblem. We highlight these properties with red diamonds and classification. Some OA listings include special amenities such as free continental breakfast; early check-in/late check-out; free room upgrade or preferred room, such as ocean view or poolside (subject to availability); free local phone calls; and free daily newspaper. This does not imply that only these properties offer these amenities. The $\text{\small AAA}$ or $\text{\small CAA}$ sign helps traveling members find accommodations that want member business.

   ▼▼▼ ▼▼▼ or ▼▼▼◆▼▼▼ The number of diamonds—not the color—informs you of the overall level of quality in a lodging's amenities and service. More diamond details appear on page 16.

   Classic Resort Large-scale Hotel or Classic Resort Large-scale Hotel: Diamond ratings are applied in the context of lodging type, or classification. See pages 22-23 for details about our Lodging Classifications and Subclassifications.

Member Values

Official Appointment properties guarantee members a minimum 10% discount off the standard room rates published in TourBook guides or the lowest public rate available at the time of booking for the dates of stay, for standard rooms.

AAA's Show Your Card & Save® chain partners provide AAA's best rates and a satisfaction guarantee to our members: Select from Best Western, Choice Hotels, Hyatt Hotels, Days Inn, most Hilton brands, La Quinta Inn and most Marriott brands. Individual properties appearing in the TourBook guides have been evaluated and approved by AAA. Reservations can be made by calling the AAA member toll-free reservation number 866-AAA-SAVE (have your membership card available), or refer to page 20 for details and a complete listing of participating lodging chains.

Establishments offer a minimum senior discount of 10% off the listed rates. This discount is available to members 60 or older.

Many properties offer discounts to members even though the lodgings do not participate in a formal discount program. The ASK is another reminder to inquire about available discounts when making your reservations or at check-in.

Discounts normally offered at some lodgings may not apply during special events or holiday periods. Special rates and discounts may not apply to all room types.

To obtain published rates or discounts, you must identify yourself as a AAA or CAA member, request AAA rates when making reservations and have written confirmation sent to you. The SAVE or senior discount may not be used in conjunction with other discounts. At registration, show your membership card and verify the room rate.

The rates listed for approved properties are provided to AAA by each lodging and represent the regular (rack) rate for a standard room. Printed rates, based on rack rates and last room availability, are rounded to the nearest dollar. Rates do not include taxes and discounts. U.S. rates are in U.S. dollars; rates for Canadian lodgings are in Canadian dollars.

2 Rate Lines

Shown from left to right: dates the rates are effective; meal plan provided with rates (see Meal Plan Indicators-if no plan noted, rate includes room only); rates for 1 person or 2 persons; extra person charge (XP); and any applicable family plan indicator.

Rates Guaranteed

AAA/CAA members are guaranteed that they will not be charged more than the maximum regular rate printed in each rate range for a standard room. Rates may vary within the range depending on season and room type. Listed rates are based on last standard room availability. Rates for properties operating as concessionaires for the National Park Service are not guaranteed due to governing regulations.

Exceptions

Lodgings may temporarily increase room rates, not recognize discounts or modify pricing policies during special events. Examples of special events range from Mardi Gras and Kentucky Derby (including pre-Derby events) to college football games, holidays, holiday periods and state fairs. Although some special events are listed in AAA/CAA TourBook guides, it is always wise to check, in advance, with AAA travel professionals for specific dates.

Discounts

Member discounts will apply to rates quoted, within the rate range, applicable at the time of booking. Special rates used in advertising, and special short-term, promotional rates lower than the lowest listed rate in the range, are not subject to additional member discounts.

3 Meal Plan Indicators

The following types of meal plans may be available in the listed room rate:

AP = American Plan of three meals daily
BP = Breakfast Plan of full hot breakfast
CP = Continental Plan of pastry, juice and another beverage
ECP = Expanded Continental Plan, which offers a wider
      variety of breakfast items
MAP = Modified American Plan of two meals daily
See individual listing "Terms" section for additional meal plans that may be offered.

> Check-in times are shown in the listing only if they are after 3 p.m.; check-out times are shown only if they are before 10 a.m.

4 Family Plan Indicators

F = Children stay free
D = Discounts for children
F17 = Children 17 and under stay free (age displayed will reflect property's policy)
D17 = Discount for children 17 and under

5 Lodging Locators

Black ovals with white numbers are used to locate, or "spot," lodgings on maps we provide for larger cities.

6 Unit Types

Unit types, amenities and room features preceded by the word "Some" indicate the item is available on a limited basis, potentially within only one unit.

7 Lodging Icons

A row of icons is included with each lodging listing. These icons represent the member values, member services, and facilities offered by that lodging. See page 19 for an explanation of each icon.

The Lodging Diamond Ratings

AAA Tourism Editors evaluate and rate each lodging based on the overall quality, the range of facilities and the level of services offered by a property. The size, age and overall appeal of an establishment are considered as well as regional architectural style and design.

While guest services are an important part of all diamond ratings, they are particularly critical at the four and five diamond levels. A property must provide a high level of service, on a consistent basis, to obtain and support the four and five diamond rating.

These establishments typically appeal to the budget-minded traveler. They provide essential, no-frills accommodations. They meet the basic requirements pertaining to comfort, cleanliness, and hospitality.

These establishments appeal to the traveler seeking more than the basic accommodations. There are modest enhancements to the overall physical attributes, design elements, and amenities of the facility typically at a modest price.

These establishments appeal to the traveler with comprehensive needs. Properties are multifaceted with a distinguished style, including marked upgrades in the quality of physical attributes, amenities and level of comfort provided.

These establishments are upscale in all areas. Accommodations are progressively more refined and stylish. The physical attributes reflect an obvious enhanced level of quality throughout. The fundamental hallmarks at this level include an extensive array of amenities combined with a high degree of hospitality, service, and attention to detail.

These establishments reflect the characteristics of the ultimate in luxury and sophistication. Accommodations are first-class. The physical attributes are extraordinary in every manner. The fundamental hallmarks at this level are to meticulously serve and exceed all guest expectations while maintaining an impeccable standard of excellence. Many personalized services and amenities enhance an unmatched level of comfort.

The lodging listings with fyi in place of diamonds are included as an "information only" service for members. The icon indicates that a property has not been rated for one or more of the following reasons: too new to rate; under construction; under major renovation; not evaluated; or may not meet all AAA requirements. Those properties not meeting all AAA requirements are included for either their member value or because it may be the only accommodation available in the area. Listing prose will give insight as to why the fyi designation was assigned.

Guest Safety
Room Security

In order to be approved for listing in AAA/CAA TourBook guides for the United States and Canada, all lodgings must comply with AAA's guest room security requirements.

In response to AAA/CAA members' concern about their safety at properties, AAA-RATED® accommodations must have dead-bolt locks on all guest room entry doors and connecting room doors.

If the area outside the guest room door is not visible from inside the room through a window or door panel, viewports must be installed on all guest room entry doors. Bed and breakfast properties and country inns are not required to have viewports. Ground floor and easily accessible sliding doors must be equipped with some other type of secondary security locks.

Tourism Editors view a percentage of rooms at each property since it is not feasible to evaluate every room in every lodging establishment. Therefore, AAA cannot guarantee that there are working locks on all doors and windows in all guest rooms.

Fire Safety

Because of the highly specialized skills needed to conduct professional fire safety inspections, AAA/CAA Tourism Editors cannot assess fire safety.

Properties must meet all federal, state and local fire codes. Each guest unit in all U.S. and Canadian lodging properties must be equipped with an operational, single-station smoke detector. A AAA/CAA Tourism Editor has evaluated a sampling of the rooms to verify this equipment is in place.

For additional fire safety information, read the page posted on the back of your guest room door, or write:

National Fire Protection Association
1 Batterymarch Park / P.O. Box 9101 / Quincy, MA 02269-9101

Golden Passports

Golden Passports, available in two types, offer a significant savings to individuals who meet certain guidelines.

Citizens or permanent residents of the United States who are 62 and older can obtain Golden Age Passports for a one-time $10 fee. Proof of age is required.

Golden Access Passports are free to citizens or permanent residents of the United States (regardless of age) who are medically blind or permanently disabled.

Both cover entrance fees for the holder and accompanying private party to all national parks, historic sites, monuments, battlefields, recreation areas and wildlife refuges within the U.S. national park system, plus half off camping and other fees. Apply in person at a federally operated area where an entrance fee is charged.

National Parks Pass

The National Parks Pass, valid for 1 year from the month of purchase, allows unlimited admissions to all U.S. national parks. The $50 pass covers all occupants of a private vehicle at parks where the entrance fee is per vehicle. At parks with individual entry fees, the pass covers the pass holder, spouse, parents and children.

As a result of a partnership with the National Park Service, AAA members may purchase the pass for $48, either through AAA's internet site (www.aaa.com) or by visiting a participating AAA office. Members may also phone the National Park Foundation at (888) 467-2757. Non-members may purchase the pass through AAA for the full $50 price.

For an upgrade fee of $15, a Golden Eagle hologram sticker can be added to a National Parks Pass. The hologram covers entrance fees not just at national parks, but at any federal recreation area that has an admission fee. Valid for the duration of the National Parks Pass to which it is affixed, the Golden Eagle hologram is available at National Park Service, Fish and Wildlife Service and Bureau of Land Management fee stations.

Access for Mature Travelers and Travelers with Disabilities

Qualified properties listed in this guide are shown with symbols indicating they meet the needs of the hearing-impaired or offer some accessible features for mature travelers or travelers with disabilities.

Hearing Impaired

Indicates a property has the following equipment available for hearing-impaired travelers: TDD at front desk or switchboard; visual notification of fire alarm, incoming telephone calls, door knock or bell; closed caption decoder; text telephone or TDD for guest room use; telephone amplification device, with shelf or electric outlet next to guest room telephone.

Accessible Features

Indicates a property has some accessible features meeting the needs of mature travelers and travelers with disabilities. Lodging establishments will provide at least one guest room meeting the designated criteria as well as accessible restrooms and parking facilities. Restaurants provide accessible parking, dining rooms and restrooms.

AAA/CAA strongly urges members to call the property directly to fully understand the property's exact accessibility features. Some properties do not fully comply with AAA/CAA's exacting accessibility standards but may offer some design standards that meet the needs of some guests with disabilities.

AAA/CAA does not evaluate recreational facilities, banquet rooms, or convention or meeting facilities for accessibility.

Service Animals

No fees or deposits, even those normally charged for pets, may be charged for service animals. Service animals fulfill a critical need for their owners—they are *not* pets.

The Americans With Disabilities Act (ADA) prohibits businesses that serve the public from discriminating against persons with disabilities. Some businesses have mistakenly denied access to persons who use service animals. ADA, a federal mandate, has priority over all state and local laws, as well as a business owner's standard of business, which might bar animals from the premises. Businesses must permit entry to guests and their service animals, as well as allow service animals to accompany guests to all public areas of a property. A property is permitted to ask whether the animal is a service animal or a pet, and whether the guest has a disability. The property may not, however, ask questions about the nature of the disability, the service provided by the animal or require proof of a disability or certification that the animal is a service animal.

What The Lodging Icons Mean

Member Values
(see p. 14)

AAA or **AAA** Official Appointment

SAVE Offers minimum 10% discount or lowest public rate *(see p. 14)*

SAVE Show Your Card & Save lodging partners

A$K May offer discount

S/D Offers senior discount

fyi Informational listing only

Member Services

✈ Airport transportation

🛏 Pets allowed

🍴 Restaurant on premises

🍴⁺ Restaurant off premises (walking distance)

24🍴 24-hour room service

🍸 Cocktail lounge

🛈 Child care

Accessibility Features
(see p. 18)

♿M Accessible features

♿ Roll-in showers

👂 Hearing impaired

Leisure Activities

🎲 Full service casino

🏊 Pool

🏋 Health club on premises

🏋 Health club off premises

⊗ Recreational activities

In-Room Amenities

⊠ Designated non-smoking rooms

🅰C No air conditioning

📺 No TV

📺 No cable TV

VCR VCR

🎦 Movies

DATA PORT Data port/modem line

☎ No telephones

🧊 Refrigerator

📱 Microwave

☕ Coffee maker

Availability

If an in-room amenity is available only on a limited basis (in one or more rooms), the term "SOME UNITS" will appear above those icons.

SOME UNITS
♿M 👂 VCR 🎦 ☕ / ⊠ DATA PORT 🧊 /

Additional Fees

Fees may be charged for some of the services represented by the icons listed here. The word "FEE" will appear below each icon when an extra charge applies.

SOME UNITS
♿M 👂 VCR 🎦 ☕ / ⊠ DATA PORT 🧊 /
FEE FEE   FEE

Preferred Lodging Partners

SAVE UP TO 50% ON OVER 1,500,000 ROOMS - When contacting one of the partners listed, you will be given AAA's best rates for your dates of stay. Your valid membership card must be presented at check-in.

SATISFACTION GUARANTEE - If you are not satisfied with any part of your stay, you must provide the property the opportunity to correct the situation during your stay. If the matter cannot be resolved, you will be entitled to recompense for a portion of, or your entire, stay. Satisfaction guarantee varies by chain.

Select the chain you want and have your membership card available when making a reservation and checking in.

| Visit | Over 1,100 AAA Offices | Click | aaa.com | Call | 866-AAA-SAVE |

Making Reservations

When making reservations, you must identify yourself as a AAA or CAA member. Give all pertinent information about your planned stay. Ask about the lodging's pet policy, or the availability of any other special feature that is important to your stay. Request written confirmation to guarantee: type of room, rate, dates of stay, and cancellation and refund policies. At registration, show your membership card. Note: Age restrictions may apply.

Confirm Deposit, Refund and Cancellation Policies

Most establishments give full deposit refunds if they have been notified at least 48 hours before the normal check-in time. Listing prose will note if more than 48 hours notice is required for cancellation. However, when making reservations, confirm the property's deposit, cancellation and refund policies. Some properties may charge a cancellation or handling fee.

When this applies, "cancellation fee imposed" will appear in the listing. If you cancel too late, you have little recourse if a refund is denied.

When an establishment requires a full or partial payment in advance, and your trip is cut short, a refund may not be given.

When canceling reservations, phone the lodging immediately. Make a note of the date and time you called, the cancellation number if there is one, and the name of the person who handled the cancellation. If your AAA/CAA club made your reservation, allow them to make the cancellation for you as well so you will have proof of cancellation.

Review Charges for Appropriate Rates

When you are charged more than the maximum rate listed in the TourBook guide for a standard room, question the additional charge. If management refuses to adhere to the published rate, pay for the room and submit your receipt and membership number to AAA/CAA within 30 days. Include all pertinent information: dates of stay, rate paid, itemized paid receipts, number of persons in your party, the room number you occupied, and list any extra room equipment used. A refund of the amount paid in excess of the stated maximum will be made if our investigation indicates that unjustified charging has occurred.

Get the Room You Reserved

When you find your room is not as specified, and you have written confirmation of reservations for a certain type of accommodation, you should be given the option of choosing a different room or finding one elsewhere. Should you choose to go elsewhere and a refund is refused or resisted, submit the matter to AAA/CAA within 30 days along with complete documentation, including your reasons for refusing the room and copies of your written confirmation and any receipts or canceled checks associated with this problem.

How to Get the Best Room Rates

You'll find the best room rate if you book your reservation in advance with the help of a travel professional or agent at your local AAA/CAA office.

If you're not yet ready to make firm vacation plans or if you prefer a more spontaneous trip, take advantage of the partnerships that preferred hotel chains have arranged with AAA. Phone the toll-free number on the previous page that has been set up exclusively for members for the purpose of reserving with these Show Your Card & Save® chain partners.

Even if you were unable to make a reservation, be sure to show your membership card at the desk and ask if you're being offered the lowest rate available for that time. Many lodgings offer reduced rates to members.

Lodging Classifications

AAA Tourism Editors evaluate lodgings based on classification, since all lodging types by definition do not provide the same level of service and facilities. Thus, hotels are rated in comparison to other hotels, resorts to other resorts—and so on. A lodging's classification appears beneath its diamond rating in the listing.

Large-scale Hotel
A multistory establishment with interior room entrances. A variety of guest unit styles is offered. Public areas are spacious and include a variety of facilities such as a restaurant, shops, fitness center, spa, business center, or meeting rooms.

Small-scale Hotel
A multistory establishment typically with interior room entrances. A variety of guest unit styles is offered. Public areas are limited in size and/or the variety of facilities available.

Motel
A one- to three-story establishment typically with exterior room entrances facilitating convenient access to parking. The standard guest units have one bedroom with a bathroom and are typically similar in décor and design throughout. Public areas are limited in size and/or the variety of facilities available.

Country Inn
Similar in definition to a bed and breakfast, but usually larger in scale with spacious public areas and offers a dining facility that serves at least breakfast and dinner.

Bed & Breakfast
Small-scale properties emphasizing a high degree of personal touches that provide guests an "at home" feeling. Guest units tend to be individually decorated. Rooms may not include some modern amenities such as televisions and telephones, and may have a shared bathroom. Usually owner-operated with a common room or parlor separate from the innkeeper's living quarters, where guests and operators can interact during evening and breakfast hours. Evening office closures are normal. A continental or full, hot breakfast is served and is included in the room rate.

Condominium
Vacation-oriented or extended-stay, apartment-style accommodations that are routinely available for rent through a management company. Units vary in design and décor and often contain one or more bedrooms, living room, full kitchen, and an eating area. Studio-type models combine the sleeping and living areas into one room. Typically, basic cleaning supplies, kitchen utensils and complete bed and bath linens are supplied. The guest registration area may be located off-site.

Cabin/Cottage

Vacation-oriented, small-scale, freestanding houses or cabins. Units vary in design and décor and often contain one or more bedrooms, living room, kitchen, dining area, and bathroom. Studio-type models combine the sleeping and living areas into one room. Typically, basic cleaning supplies, kitchen utensils, and complete bed and bath linens are supplied. The guest registration area may be located off-site.

Ranch

Typically a working ranch with an obvious rustic, Western theme. In general, equestrian-related activities are featured, but ranches may include other animals and activities as well. A variety of guest unit styles is offered in a family-oriented atmosphere.

Vacation Home

Vacation-oriented or extended-stay, large-scale, freestanding houses that are routinely available for rent through a management company. Houses vary in design and décor and often contain two or more bedrooms, living room, full kitchen, dining room, and multiple bathrooms. Typically, basic cleaning supplies, kitchen utensils, and complete bed and bath linens are supplied. The guest registration area may be located off-site.

Lodging Subclassifications

The following are subclassifications that may appear along with the classifications listed above to provide a more specific description of the lodging.

Casino

Extensive gambling facilities are available such as blackjack, craps, keno, and slot machines. **Note:** This subclassification will not appear beneath its diamond rating in the listing. It will be indicated by a dice icon and will be included in the row of icons immediately below the lodging listing.

Classic

Renowned and landmark properties, older than 50 years, well-known for their unique style and ambience.

Historic

These properties are typically over 75 years of age and exhibit many features of a historic nature with respect to architecture, design, furnishings, public record, or acclaim. Properties must meet one of the following criteria:
- Maintained the integrity of the historical nature
- Listed on the National Register of Historic Places
- Designated a National Historic Landmark
- Located in a National Register Historic District

Resort

Recreation-oriented, geared to vacation travelers seeking a specific destination experience. Travel packages, meal plans, theme entertainment, and social and recreational programs are typically available. Recreational facilities are extensive and may include spa treatments, golf, tennis, skiing, fishing, or water sports, etc. Larger resorts may offer a variety of guest accommodations.

Sample Restaurant Listing

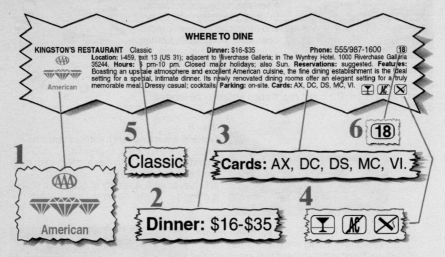

WHERE TO DINE

KINGSTON'S RESTAURANT Classic   **Dinner:** $16-$35   **Phone:** 555/987-1600 ⑱

Location: I-459, exit 13 (US 31); adjacent to Riverchase Galleria; in The Wynfrey Hotel. 1000 Riverchase Galleria 35244. **Hours:** 5 pm-10 pm. Closed major holidays; also Sun. **Reservations:** suggested. **Features:** Boasting an upscale atmosphere and excellent American cuisine, the fine dining establishment is the ideal setting for a special, intimate dinner. Its newly renovated dining rooms offer an elegant setting for a truly memorable meal. Dressy casual; cocktails **Parking:** on-site. **Cards:** AX, DC, DS, MC, VI.

American

5 Classic

3 Cards: AX, DC, DS, MC, VI.

6 ⑱

1 American

2 Dinner: $16-$35

4

---

1   or   indicates our Official Appointment (OA) restaurants. The OA program permits properties to display and advertise the   or   emblem. We highlight these properties with red diamonds and cuisine type. The   or   sign helps traveling members find restaurants that want member business.

  or   The number of diamonds—not the color—informs you of the overall level of quality for food and presentation, service and ambience.

A cuisine type is assigned for each restaurant listing. AAA currently recognizes more than 90 different cuisine types.

2 Prices represent the minimum and maximum entree cost per person. Exceptions may include one-of-a-kind or special market priced items.

3 AX = American Express
CB = Carte Blanche   DS = Discover   MC = MasterCard
DC = Diners Club   JC = Japan Credit Bureau   VI = VISA

4 These three icons are used in restaurant listings. When present, they indicate: the presence of a cocktail lounge, the lack of air conditioning, and/or that the restaurant has a designated non-smoking section or is entirely smoke-free.

5 If applicable, restaurants may be further defined as:

Classic—renowned and landmark properties, older than 25 years, known for unique style and ambience.

Historic—properties must meet one of the following criteria:
- Listed on the National Register of Historic Places
- Designated a National Historic Landmark
- Located in a National Register Historic District

6 These white ovals with black numbers serve as restaurant locators and are used to locate, or "spot," restaurants on maps we provide for larger cities.

The Restaurant Diamond Ratings

AAA Tourism Editors are responsible for determining a restaurant's diamond rating based on established criteria.

These criteria were established with input from AAA trained professionals, members, and restaurant industry experts. They are purposely broad to capture what is typically seen throughout the restaurant industry at each diamond rating level.

These establishments appeal to a diner seeking good, wholesome, no-nonsense eating at an affordable price. They typically provide simple, familiar, and unadorned foods served in a sensible, casual or self-service style. Often quick service and family oriented.

Examples include coffee shops, diners, cafeterias, short order, and modest full service eateries.

These establishments provide for dining needs that are increasingly complex, but still reasonably priced. They typically exhibit noticeable efforts in rising above the ordinary in many aspects of food, service and decor. Service is typically functional yet ambitious, periodically combining informal style with limited self-service elements. Often well-suited to traditional, special occasion, and family dining.

Examples include a varied range of specific concept (theme) and multi-purpose establishments.

These establishments impart an increasingly refined and upscale, adult-oriented experience. This is the entry level into fine dining. Creative and complex menus offer a blend of traditional and trendy foods. The service level is typically semi-formal with knowledgeable and proficient staff. Routinely these restaurants appeal to the diner in search of an experience rather than just a meal.

Examples include high-caliber, chic, boutique, and conventional restaurants.

These establishments impart a luxurious and socially refined experience. This is consistent fine dining. Menus typically reflect a high degree of creativity and complexity, featuring elaborate presentations of market-driven or traditional dishes. A cultured, professional, and highly proficient staff consistently demonstrates a profound desire to meet or exceed guest expectations. Restaurants of this caliber are geared to individuals with an appetite for an elite, fine-dining experience.

Examples include dining rooms associated with luxury lodgings, or exclusive independent restaurants often found in metropolitan areas.

Often renowned, these establishments impart a world-class and opulent, adult-oriented experience. This is "haute cuisine" at its best. Menus are often cutting edge, with an obvious dedication to use of only the finest ingredients available. Even the classic dishes become extraordinary under the masterful direction of highly acclaimed chefs. Presentations are spectacular, reflecting impeccable artistry and awareness. An expert, formalized staff continuously anticipates and exceeds guest expectations. Staff members' unfailing attention to detail appears effortless, well-rehearsed and unobtrusive. Undoubtedly, these restaurants appeal to those in search of the ultimate dining experience.

Examples include renowned dining rooms associated with luxury lodgings, or exclusive independent restaurants often found in metropolitan areas.

The restaurants with [fyi] in place of diamonds are included as an "information only" service for members. These listings provide additional dining choices but have not yet been evaluated.

Savings for all Seasons

Hertz rents Fords and other fine cars. ® REG. U.S. PAT. OFF. © HERTZ SYSTEM INC., 1999/2004-96

No matter the season, Hertz offers AAA members exclusive discounts and benefits.

Operating in 140 countries at over 7,000 locations, Hertz makes traveling more convenient and efficient wherever and whenever you go. Hertz offers AAA members discounts up to 20% on car rentals worldwide.

To receive your exclusive AAA member discounts and benefits, mention your AAA membership card at time of reservation and present it at time of rental. In addition, to receive a free one car class upgrade, in the United States mention PC# 929714, in Canada mention PC# 929725 and in Puerto Rico mention PC# 929736 at the time of reservation. Offer available through 12/31/04.

For reservations and program details, call your AAA travel office or the Hertz/AAA Desk at **1-800-654-3080**.

Look for the Signs Along the Way

Whyen selecting a place to dine while traveling, look for Official Appointment restaurants that display the AAA Approved sign. It's the only sign you need to be assured of an enjoyable dining experience.

As a member, you already know the AAA sign indicates quality establishments. So, when you don't have advance dining reservations, look for the AAA Approved sign along the way, for a meal you'll long remember!

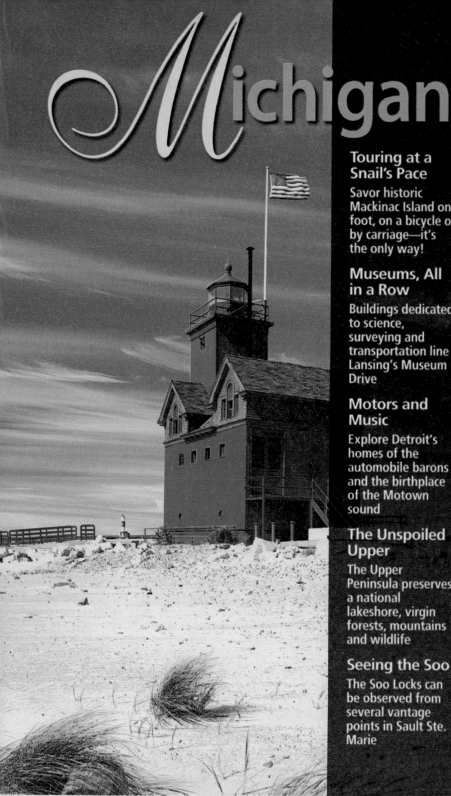

Michigan

Touring at a Snail's Pace

Savor historic Mackinac Island on foot, on a bicycle or by carriage—it's the only way!

Museums, All in a Row

Buildings dedicated to science, surveying and transportation line Lansing's Museum Drive

Motors and Music

Explore Detroit's homes of the automobile barons and the birthplace of the Motown sound

The Unspoiled Upper

The Upper Peninsula preserves a national lakeshore, virgin forests, mountains and wildlife

Seeing the Soo

The Soo Locks can be observed from several vantage points in Sault Ste. Marie

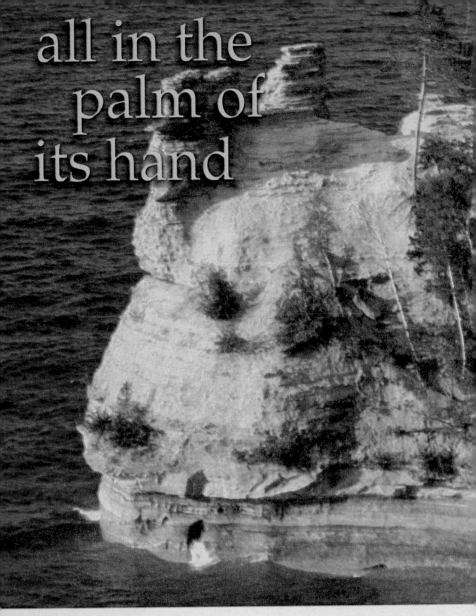

all in the palm of its hand

Mitten-shaped Michigan greets visitors with a hearty wave hello.

When exploring the Wolverine State, start at the base of the thumb, where Henry Ford's jumpy Model-T turned Detroit into the world's best known assembly line.

Head to the pinkie, where Sleeping Bear Dunes National Lakeshore is lapped by Lake Michigan, only one of the truly "great" lakes bordering the state. Lining the lakes are more than 100 lighthouses that illuminate the way for American and Canadian ships.

Near the heel of the hand is Holland, a town proud of its Dutch heritage. On any given day you can see shopkeepers scrubbing the cobblestone sidewalks and crafting wooden shoes.

Between the thumb and forefinger is Frankenmuth, which has a decidedly German flavor. Melodies ring through the streets from the 35 bells of the Glockenspiel Tower.

And at the fingertip, Mackinac Bridge, the longest suspension bridge in the world, connects Colonial-style Mackinaw City to the Upper Peninsula, where more than 150 cascading waterfalls, includings pectacular Tahquamenon Falls, delight spectators. Here boats chug through Soo Locks and steep cliffs are dubbed Pictured Rocks.

Spend some time in Michigan; you'll find it carries a bit of everything in its hand.

Ever since Charles King drove the first "horseless carriage" down the streets of Detroit in 1896, Michigan has been synonymous with motoring. Henry Ford and Ransom E. Olds hopped on the wagon, so to speak, and before long, "merry Oldsmobiles" and "Tin Lizzies" came to represent a freedom not previously known to travelers—putting Michigan on the map and making millionaires of many.

Ford's assembly line concept made mass production of automobiles possible, bringing great wealth to auto barons. Visit Henry Ford's Fair Lane mansion in Dearborn to get a glimpse of how the Fords spent their earnings. If the house itself isn't enough to make your jaw drop, Clara Ford's formal rose garden should do it. It once was attended by 20 full-time gardeners.

Take a tour of Edsel and Eleanor Ford's sprawling estate in Grosse Pointe Shores. On its 87 acres is the Play House given to daughter Josephine on her seventh birthday. Constructed in mock-Tudor style and in three-fourths scale, the cottage is every little girl's dream—and is probably more expensive than most *real* houses.

Hit the Road, Jack

The automobile remains the most convenient form of travel, and there's no better means of visiting some of Michigan's smaller towns.

Take to the highway and explore Holland. Be sure to arrive in May, when millions of colorful tulips bloom during the spring festival. Slip into a pair of wooden shoes, clomp around the town's adorable restored downtown and check out the wee Dutch village surrounding De Zwaan windmill.

If you prefer sausage and sauerkraut, cruise to Frankenmuth, which sports a Bavarian architectural flair. You'll think you're smack in the middle of Munich when you hear the Glockenspiel Tower's twinkling bells. Sneak a smooch under the Holz-Brücke covered bridge before heading to giant Bronner's Christmas Wonderland, rumored to be the world's largest Christmas store. With a showroom bigger than a football field, the talk may be true.

Heading north, you'll reach Mackinaw City. Costumed guides at Fort Michilimackinac, built by the French in 1715, reenact life during Colonial days by launching cannons on Lake Huron's shore, cutting logs with crosscut saws, peddling furs and singing French songs.

Father Jacques Marquette establishes the first settlement at Sault Ste. Marie.
1668

The Treaty of Paris awards land that includes future Michigan territory to the United States.
1783

Lansing becomes the new state capital, succeeding Detroit.
1847

The Soo Locks are completed, marking the first continuous shipping route between lakes Superior and Huron.
1855

1837
Statehood is granted.

1881
Fires ravage the "thumb" of the state, causing hundreds of deaths and the devastation of the lumber industry.

Michigan Historical Timeline

By Bridge or Ferry

With most of Michigan surrounded by those "great" lakes, bridges provide another handy way to get around. For starters, take the Mackinac Bridge from Michigan's Lower Peninsula to the rugged Upper Peninsula (U.P.). The bridge, affectionately termed "Big Mac," stretches across the Straits of Mackinac, where lakes Michigan and Huron meet.

How about lunch in Canada? Drive over the Detroit River on the Ambassador Bridge, which links Detroit and Windsor, Ontario. Impress friends back home with your fancy international itinerary.

To get to peaceful Mackinac Island, you'll have to take a ferry, catamaran or plane. Once you're there, ride in a horse-drawn carriage, bike or stroll—but leave your car behind, since no automobiles are allowed on this little island. Browse the boutiques in downtown's gingerbread-laced buildings, sampling homemade fudge at one of many candy shops. Even if locals call you a "fudgie" (tourist), the chocolatey goodness will make make up for it! Next, take a tour of the 1887 Grand Hotel, a beautiful white Victorian building with a sweeping 600-foot-long veranda topped by a sky-blue ceiling.

Outdoorsy folks will love Isle Royale National Park, off the western tip of the U.P. in Lake Superior; a ferry or floatplane can escort you. This roadless island is home to historic lighthouses, shipwrecks, ancient copper mining sites and lots of spots to see moose and wolves.

A unique mode of transit exists on the U.P.—the Soo Locks, which allow ships to navigate the rapids between lakes Huron and Superior. You can take a boat tour through the locks to experience a 21-foot lift to the level of Lake Superior. Adjacent St. Marys Rapids are a frothy, delightful sight.

And there's more—from a space center in Jackson to a stop on the Underground Railroad in Kalamazoo to Greenfield Village in Dearborn, where the Wright brothers tinkered with the airplane. Michigan will encourage you to gas up the ol' Chevy and put the "pedal to the metal."

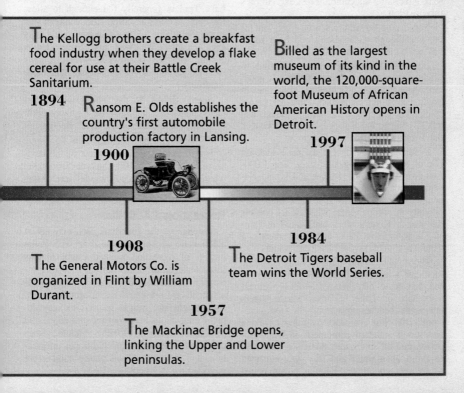

The Kellogg brothers create a breakfast food industry when they develop a flake cereal for use at their Battle Creek Sanitarium.

1894

Ransom E. Olds establishes the country's first automobile production factory in Lansing.

1900

Billed as the largest museum of its kind in the world, the 120,000-square-foot Museum of African American History opens in Detroit.

1997

1908

The General Motors Co. is organized in Flint by William Durant.

1984

The Detroit Tigers baseball team wins the World Series.

1957

The Mackinac Bridge opens, linking the Upper and Lower peninsulas.

Recreation

You've gotta hand it to Michigan. Complete with three national forests, one national park and two national lakeshores—not to mention four Great Lakes and nearly a hundred state parks from Bald Mountain to Sleepy Hollow—it's no wonder the state packs a punch when it comes to recreation options.

Water Watch

Perhaps the coolest outdoor activity here—literally—is donning wet suit and tanks to go **scuba diving** at one of more than 3,000 shipwrecks littering 38,000 square miles of Michigan's Great Lakes bottomlands. Largely dating to the last quarter of the 19th century, the wrecks are remarkably well-preserved due to the fresh and—here's the key—*extremely* cold waters of lakes Huron, Michigan and Superior. Depths range from 20 to 150 feet, and visibility varies from excellent to muddy.

Some ships worth looking for: the *Bermuda*, an 1880s schooner resting only 25 feet below the surface in Murray Bay, off Munising; and the skeletal *Michael Groh*, which met its fate on a Lake Superior sandbar in November 1895. Of more recent vintage is the *Cedarville*, a 700-foot ore carrier that sank intact after succumbing to Lake Huron's fury in 1966.

Non-diving adventurers aren't left out of the fun, though: **Glass-bottomed boat tours** can be chartered in Munising.

Downed ships aren't all you'll find in Michigan's many waterways; **fishing** is good, too. Along Lake Michigan's shoreline at South Haven and Saugatuck there are plenty of charters targeting coho salmon, which can top 25 pounds. For walleye, float your boat in the Tittabawassee River or Saginaw Bay.

Landlubbers can opt to try their luck on one of several fishing platforms. The 1,000-foot North Pier in St. Joseph and Grand Haven's South Pier are both renowned as perch hangouts. Near Rockford, a deck built specifically to accommodate wheelchairs borders the Rogue River's west bank. And at Lansing's Riverfront Park and Trail there's a water-level dock favored by local anglers.

Those who would rather swing a paddle than cast a line will find ideal conditions for **sea kayaking** off Pictured Rocks National Lakeshore on Lake Superior, whose waters lap sandy beaches and richly layered sandstone cliffs. But even in top-skirted kayaks a wet suit is standard equipment on frigid Superior, and all small-craft boaters are advised to avoid open water and stay well-informed of weather conditions. Popular put-in points

include Sand Point, Miners Beach, the Munising Municipal Boat Ramp and Grand Island Landing. Twelvemile Beach Campground and Grand Marais Marina are at the park's east end.

Should you prefer rubbing shoulders with the big ships, board an authentic ferry steamer in Ludington for a Lake Michigan **cruise** with an "ocean liner" feel. Or head to Sault Ste. Marie, where 2-hour tours through the Soo Locks put you right alongside enormous freighters.

In addition to its border lakes, Michigan has many inviting interior waterways offering myriad **boating** options, from low-key **canoeing** on the Au Sable River, near Roscommon, to high-speed **water skiing** at Haughton Lake, the state's largest inland body of water.

Shore Leave

You can enjoy Michigan's wealth of water from a distance, too. **Climb** the dunes to a sweeping view of Lake Michigan at Sleeping Bear Dunes National Lakeshore. Or **hike** in sight of five waterfalls in the Ottawa National Forest's Black River Harbor area. Within Huron-Manistee National Forest, the Jewell Lake Trail is generally flat enough to allow for easy lakeside ambling. And **walkers** will enjoy Sault Ste. Marie's waterfront Locks Park Historic Walkway and Silver City's .5-mile elevated boardwalk, which follows the Presque Isle River and passes still more waterfalls.

Scenic drives do the job as well. Especially pretty are the lakeside highway north of Muskegon State Park and Bessemer's Black River National Forest Scenic Byway.

But to really get an overview of the landscape, visit Tower Hill, outside Bridgman, where perfectly placed winds lure **hang gliders** into the sky year-round.

Recreational Activities

Throughout the TourBook, you may notice a Recreational Activities heading with bullet listings of recreation-oriented establishments listed underneath. Since normal AAA inspection criteria cannot be applied, these establishments are presented for information only. Age, height and weight restrictions may apply. Reservations are often recommended and sometimes required. Visitors should phone or write the attraction for additional information, and the address and phone number are provided for this purpose.

Fast Facts

POPULATION: 9,938,444.

AREA: 56,804 square miles; ranks 23rd.

CAPITAL: Lansing.

HIGHEST POINT: 1,979 ft., Mount Arvon.

LOWEST POINT: 572 ft., Lake Erie.

TIME ZONE(S): Eastern/Central. DST.

MINIMUM AGE FOR DRIVERS: 17.

MINIMUM AGE FOR GAMBLING: 21.

SEAT BELT/CHILD RESTRAINT LAWS: Seat belts required for driver and front-seat passengers, and all rear-seat passengers ages 4-16; child restraints required for under 4.

HELMETS FOR MOTORCYCLISTS: Required.

RADAR DETECTORS: Permitted.

FIREARMS LAWS: Vary by state or county. Contact local law enforcement agencies or the Michigan Department of State Police, Central Records, Firearms Unit, 7150 Harris Dr., Lansing, MI 48913.

HOLIDAYS: Jan. 1; Martin Luther King Jr. Day, Jan. (3rd Mon.); Presidents Day, Feb. (3rd Mon.); Memorial Day, May (last Mon.); July 4; Labor Day, Sept. (1st Mon.); Veterans Day, Nov. 11; Thanksgiving; Dec. 25.

TAXES: Michigan's statewide sales tax is 6 percent. Local options allow taxes ranging from 1.5 to 6 percent on lodgings in convention hotels and lodging taxes of up to 5 percent at other facilities. An additional 2 percent tax is charged in metropolitan areas.

STATE INFORMATION CENTERS: Centers are maintained all year on I-94 at New Buffalo; on I-69 at Coldwater; on US 23 at Dundee; on US 2 at Ironwood; on US 2 in Iron Mountain; on US 41S in Marquette; on US 41 in Menominee; on I-75N in St. Ignace; on I-75 at the south end of the International Bridge at Sault Ste. Marie; on I-94 at Water Street in Port Huron; on US 127 at a rest area 1 mile north of Clare; on SR 108 in Mackinaw City; and on I-75 at Monroe.

FURTHER INFORMATION FOR VISITORS:
Travel Michigan
Michigan Economic Development Corporation
P.O. Box 30226
Lansing, MI 48909
(888) 784-7328

RECREATION, FISHING & HUNTING INFORMATION:
Department of Natural Resources
P.O. Box 30028
Lansing, MI 48909
(517) 373-0908 (fishing information)
(517) 373-9453 (hunting information)

NATIONAL FOREST INFORMATION:
U.S. Forest Service
310 W. Wisconsin Ave., Suite 500
Milwaukee, WI 53203
(414) 297-3693
(877) 444-6777 (reservations)

©2002 NAVIGATION TECHNOLOGIES

4060-A

© AAA

![GEM logo] **Points of Interest Offering A**
Great Experience for Members

Baldwin (F-2)

SHRINE OF THE PINES—The beauty and versatility of the white pine—the state tree—is seen in handmade furnishings and decorative pieces created by one man and fittingly displayed in a log cabin. See p. 45.

Battle Creek (I-3)

BINDER PARK ZOO—Exotic animals are displayed in natural settings. See p. 46.

Dearborn (L-4)

HENRY FORD MUSEUM & GREENFIELD VILLAGE—American ingenuity is the theme that links collections of inventions, vehicles and buildings. See p. 63.

Detroit (H-5)

THE DETROIT INSTITUTE OF ARTS—Collections feature artwork spanning several centuries. See p. 55.

Fayette (C-4)

HISTORIC FAYETTE TOWNSITE—Fayette is a preserved 1867 town that thrived along with the iron industry for nearly 25 years. See p. 67.

Flint (H-4)

ALFRED P. SLOAN MUSEUM—Regional history topics ranging from archeology to automobiles are covered. See p. 68.

Frankenmuth (G-5)

BRONNER'S CHRISTMAS WONDERLAND—It's Christmas all year at this gigantic showroom of yuletide trappings. See p. 69.

Gaylord (E-4)

CALL OF THE WILD MUSEUM—Lifelike sounds of animals and birds permeate this specimen-filled museum. See p. 70.

Grand Rapids (H-2)

GERALD R. FORD MUSEUM—Learn about the private and public sides of one of our nation's presidents. See p. 71.

VAN ANDEL MUSEUM CENTER OF THE PUBLIC MUSEUM OF GRAND RAPIDS—In addition to heritage and manufacturing exhibits, this museum features a full-scale reproduction of an 1890s street, complete with shops. See p. 72.

Hickory Corners (H-3)

GILMORE CAR MUSEUM—Antique barns stable a diverse collection of classic vehicles. See p. 74.

Isle Royale National Park (A-1)

ISLE ROYALE NATIONAL PARK—Truly a natural wilderness, this wooded island with wildlife is a U.S. Biosphere Reserve. See p. 77.

Jackson (I-4)

MICHIGAN SPACE AND SCIENCE CENTER—Apollo, *Challenger* and Mercury are some of the space flight subjects explored at this center. See p. 78.

Kalamazoo (I-2)

KALAMAZOO AVIATION HISTORY MUSEUM (AIR ZOO)—Vintage flying aircraft, aviation equipment and a museum are highlights. See p. 79.

Mackinac Island (C-6)

FORT MACKINAC—Original buildings constructed in the 18th and 19th centuries still overlook the Straits of Mackinac. See p. 83.

Mackinaw City (D-3)

COLONIAL MICHILIMACKINAC—Reconstructed buildings are telling reminders that this site was occupied by the French, the British and American Indians. See p. 84.

HISTORIC MILL CREEK—One of the oldest industrial complexes in the Great Lakes region is on this site. See p. 85.

Midland (G-4)

HERBERT H. DOW HISTORICAL MUSEUM—The life of the founder of the Dow Chemical Co. is depicted. See p. 88.

Negaunee (B-3)

MICHIGAN IRON INDUSTRY MUSEUM—Exhibits focus on the importance of iron to area development. See p. 91.

Pictured Rocks National Lakeshore

PICTURED ROCKS NATIONAL LAKESHORE—Dunes and cliffs that tower above Lake Superior are the focal point of this park, where recreation opportunities abound. See p. 94.

Rochester (K-5)

OAKLAND UNIVERSITY'S MEADOW BROOK HALL—Built in the Tudor style, this 1920s mansion is the showpiece of the campus along with its counterpart, a miniature playhouse. See p. 64.

Royal Oak (K-5)

DETROIT ZOOLOGICAL PARK—A short drive outside the Detroit city limits will take you to the continents of the world and the animals that inhabit them. See p. 64.

Saginaw (G-5)

JOHNNY PANTHER QUESTS—Get a close-up view of the wildlife and habitats of the Saginaw Valley water system. See p. 97.

St. Joseph (I-1)

CURIOUS KIDS' MUSEUM—A world of fantasy and fact awaits children here. See p. 98.

Sault Ste. Marie (B-6)

SOO LOCKS BOAT TOURS—The workings of the locks between lakes Superior and Huron are explained through narrated tours. See p. 100.

Whitefish Point (A-5)

GREAT LAKES SHIP-WRECK MUSEUM—Ship disasters—including the wreck of the *Edmund Fitzgerald*—are recalled with artifacts, photographs and film presentations. See p. 105.

West Bloomfield (K-4)

HOLOCAUST MEMORIAL CENTER—This center is dedicated to perpetuating the memory of the Holocaust. See p. 65.

RECREATION AREAS	MAP LOCATION	CAMPING	PICNICKING	HIKING TRAILS	BOATING	BOAT RAMP	BOAT RENTAL	FISHING	SWIMMING	PETS ON LEASH	BICYCLE TRAILS	WINTER SPORTS	VISITOR CENTER	LODGE/CABINS	FOOD SERVICE
NATIONAL PARKS *(See place listings)*															
Isle Royale (A-1) 571,790 acres in Lake Superior.		•	•	•	•			•					•	•	•
NATIONAL FORESTS *(See place listings)*															
Hiawatha 893,348 acres in the Upper Peninsula.		•	•	•	•	•		•	•	•	•	•	•		
Huron-Manistee 964,711 acres in the northern part of the Lower Peninsula.		•	•	•	•	•	•	•	•	•	•	•	•		
Ottawa 986,518 acres in the Upper Peninsula.		•	•	•	•	•		•	•	•	•	•	•		
NATIONAL LAKESHORES *(See place listings)*															
Pictured Rocks (A-4) 70,822 acres along Lake Superior n.e. of Munising.		•	•	•	•	•		•	•	•			•		
Sleeping Bear Dunes (E-2) 71,105 acres along Lake Michigan n. of Frankfort.		•	•	•	•	•		•	•	•		•	•		
STATE															
Albert E. Sleeper (F-5) 723 acres 5 mi. n.e. of Caseville on SR 25.	❶	•	•	•				•	•	•		•			
Algonac (H-6) 1,307 acres 2 mi. n. of Algonac on SR 29.	❷	•	•	•	•	•		•		•		•			
Aloha (D-4) 106 acres 9 mi. s. of Cheboygan on SR 33.	❸	•	•		•	•		•	•	•					
Bald Mountain (J-5) 4,637 acres 7 mi. n. of Pontiac off SR 24. Shooting range.	❹		•	•	•	•	•	•	•	•	•	•		•	•
Baraga (B-2) 53 acres 1 mi. s. of Baraga on US 41.	❺	•	•					•	•	•			•		
Bay City (G-4) 1,300 acres 5 mi. n. of Bay City on SR 247. Nature center.	❻	•	•	•				•	•	•			•	•	
Bewabic (B-2) 315 acres 4 mi. w. of Crystal Falls on US 2. Tennis.	❼	•	•	•	•			•	•	•		•			
Brighton (K-2) 4,913 acres 3 mi. w. of Brighton on Main St. (Brighton Rd.), then s. on Chilson Rd. Horse rental.	❽	•	•	•	•	•	•	•	•	•	•	•		•	•
Brimley (B-5) 151 acres 1 mi. e. of Brimley on SR 221.	❾	•	•		•	•		•	•	•					
Burt Lake (D-3) 405 acres .5 mi. s.w. of Indian River on SR 68.	❿	•	•	•	•	•	•	•	•	•				•	•
Charles Mears (F-1) 50 acres 1 mi. n. of Pentwater off US 31 Bus. Rte.	⓫	•	•	•				•	•	•					•
Cheboygan (D-4) 932 acres 4 mi. e. of Cheboygan on US 23.	⓬	•	•	•				•	•	•		•		•	

RECREATION AREAS

	MAP LOCATION	CAMPING	PICNICKING	HIKING TRAILS	BOATING	BOAT RAMP	BOAT RENTAL	FISHING	SWIMMING	PETS ON LEASH	BICYCLE TRAILS	WINTER SPORTS	VISITOR CENTER	LODGE/CABINS	FOOD SERVICE
Clear Lake (D-4) 290 acres 9 mi. n. of Atlanta off SR 33.	13	•	•	•	•	•	•	•	•	•		•		•	
Dodge No. 4 (K-4) 136 acres 6 mi. w. of Pontiac off SR 59. Playground.	14		•		•	•		•	•	•		•			•
Fayette (C-4) 711 acres in Fayette off SR 183. Historic.	15	•	•	•	•	•	•	•	•	•			•	•	
Fisherman's Island (D-2) 2,942 acres 3 mi. s.w. of Charlevoix off US 31.	16	•	•	•				•	•	•					
F.J. McLain (A-2) 417 acres 8 mi. w. of Calumet on SR 203. *(See Hancock p. 72)*	17	•	•	•				•	•	•		•		•	
Fort Custer (I-3) 3,033 acres 8 mi. w. of Battle Creek on SR 96.	18	•	•	•	•	•		•	•	•	•	•		•	•
Fort Wilkins (A-3) 700 acres 1 mi. e. of Copper Harbor on US 41. Historic. Cross-country skiing. *(See Copper Harbor p. 51)*	19	•	•	•	•	•	•	•	•	•	•	•	•	•	•
Grand Haven (H-1) 48 acres 1 mi. w. of Grand Haven off US 31. *(See Grand Haven p. 70)*	20	•	•		•			•	•	•					•
Harrisville (E-5) 107 acres 1 mi. s. of Harrisville on US 23.	21	•	•	•	•				•	•					
Hartwick Pines (E-4) 9,672 acres 7 mi. n.e. of Grayling on SR 93. Historic. Cross-country skiing. *(See Grayling p. 72)*	22	•	•	•				•		•	•	•	•	•	
Highland (K-3) 5,524 acres 2 mi. e. of Highland off SR 59. Cross-country skiing; horse rental.	23	•	•	•	•			•	•	•	•	•		•	
Holland (H-2) 142 acres 7 mi. w. of Holland on US 31.	24	•	•		•	•		•	•	•					•
Holly (J-3) 7,670 acres 12 mi. n.w. of Pontiac off I-75.	25	•	•	•	•	•		•	•	•	•	•		•	
Indian Lake (B-4) 567 acres 5 mi. w. of Manistique on SR 442.	26	•	•	•	•	•	•	•	•	•				•	
Interlochen (E-2) 187 acres 1 mi. s. of Interlochen on SR 137.	27	•	•	•	•	•		•	•	•				•	•
Ionia (H-3) 4,085 acres 2 mi. w. of Ionia on SR 66. Hunting; snowmobiling; playground.	28	•	•	•	•	•		•	•	•	•	•		•	•
Island Lake (K-3) 3,466 acres 4 mi. s.e. of Brighton off US 23.	29		•	•	•	•		•	•	•	•			•	•
J.W. Wells (C-3) 694 acres 2 mi. s. of Cedar River on SR 35. Cross-country skiing.	30	•	•	•	•			•	•	•		•		•	
Lake Gogebic (B-1) 361 acres 12 mi. n.e. of Marenisco on SR 64. *(See Ottawa National Forest p. 93)*	31	•	•		•	•		•	•	•			•		
Lake Hudson (I-4) 2,650 acres 6 mi. s.e. of Hudson on SR 156.	32	•	•		•	•		•	•	•					
Lakeport (H-6) 565 acres 10 mi. n. of Port Huron on SR 25.	33	•	•	•	•			•	•	•				•	•
Leelanau (D-2) 1,300 acres 7 mi. n. of Northport on SR 201. Hunting; playground.	34	•	•	•	•	•		•	•	•					
Ludington (F-1) 5,202 acres 8 mi. n. of Ludington on SR 116. Cross-country skiing; nature center. *(See Ludington p. 82)*	35	•	•	•	•	•	•	•	•	•	•	•	•	•	•
Maybury (L-3) 944 acres w. of Detroit on I-96 to I-275N, then 5 mi. w. on Eight Mile Rd. Horse rental, working farm. *(See Northville p. 64)*	36		•	•				•		•	•	•	•		
Metamora-Hadley (J-4) 683 acres 10 mi. s. of Lapeer off SR 24.	37	•	•	•	•	•		•	•	•				•	•
Mitchell (F-3) 334 acres 4 mi. w. of Cadillac on SR 115. Museum.	38	•	•	•	•	•		•	•	•			•	•	•
Muskegon (G-2) 1,165 acres 4 mi. w. of North Muskegon on Memorial Dr.	39	•	•	•	•	•		•	•	•		•		•	•
Muskellunge Lake (B-5) 217 acres 31 mi. w. of Whitefish Point on H-58 at Deer Park.	40	•	•	•	•	•		•	•	•				•	
Newaygo (G-2) 257 acres 8 mi. w. of Morley off US 131 following signs.	41	•		•	•			•		•					
North Higgins Lake (E-4) 429 acres 7 mi. w. of Roscommon via US 127 and Military Rd.	42	•	•	•	•	•		•	•	•		•	•		
Onaway (D-4) 158 acres on Black Lake 7 mi. n.w. of Onaway on SR 211.	43	•	•	•	•	•		•	•	•					
Orchard Beach (F-1) 201 acres 2 mi. n. of Manistee on SR 110.	44	•	•	•				•	•					•	
Ortonville (J-5) 4,875 acres 4 mi. n.e. of Ortonville on SR 15. Shooting range.	45	•	•	•	•	•		•	•	•	•	•	•	•	•
Otsego Lake (E-3) 62 acres 7 mi. s. of Gaylord off I-75.	46	•	•		•	•		•	•	•				•	•

RECREATION AREAS

RECREATION AREAS	MAP LOCATION	CAMPING	PICNICKING	HIKING TRAILS	BOATING	BOAT RAMP	BOAT RENTAL	FISHING	SWIMMING	PETS ON LEASH	BICYCLE TRAILS	WINTER SPORTS	VISITOR CENTER	LODGE/CABINS	FOOD SERVICE
Petoskey (D-3) 305 acres at Petoskey off SR 119. *(See Petoskey p. 94)*	47	•	•	•	•			•	•			•			
P.H. Hoeft (D-4) 301 acres 5 mi. n.w. of Rogers City on US 23. Cross-country skiing; Huron dunes. *(See Rogers City p. 96)*	48	•	•	•	•			•	•	•		•		•	
Pinckney (L-2) 10,201 acres 4 mi. s.w. of Pinckney via SR 36. Cross-country skiing; horse rental.	49	•	•	•	•	•		•	•	•	•	•			•
P.J. Hoffmaster (G-1) 1,043 acres 10 mi. n.w. of Grand Haven off US 31. Cross-country skiing; nature center. *(See Grand Haven p. 70)*	50	•	•	•				•	•	•		•	•		•
Pontiac Lake (K-4) 3,700 acres 8 mi. w. of Pontiac on SR 59. Archery and rifle ranges, horse rental.	51	•	•	•	•	•	•	•	•	•		•			•
Porcupine Mountains Wilderness (A-1) 63,000 acres 3 mi. w. of Silver City on SR 107. Scenic. Cross-country skiing. *(See Silver City p. 100)*	52	•	•	•	•	•	•	•	•		•	•	•	•	•
Port Crescent (F-5) 569 acres 5 mi. s.w. of Port Austin on SR 25. Cross-country skiing.	53	•	•	•				•	•	•		•			
Proud Lake (K-3) 3,614 acres 4 mi. s.e. of Milford off I-96. Cross-country skiing.	54	•	•	•	•	•	•	•	•	•		•			
Rifle River (F-4) 4,329 acres 6 mi. s.e. of Rose City on Rose City Rd.	55	•	•	•	•	•	•	•	•	•		•			
Saugatuck Dunes (H-2) 889 acres 1 mi. n. of Saugatuck off US 31. Cross-country skiing.	56		•	•					•	•		•			
Seven Lakes (J-3) 1,730 acres 1 mi. w. of Holly off US 23. Cross-country skiing, hunting; playground.	57	•	•	•	•	•	•	•	•	•		•			•
Silver Lake (F-1) 3,400 acres on Silver Lake 7 mi. w. of Mears via US 31. Off-road vehicle area. *(See Mears p. 88)*	58	•	•	•	•	•		•	•			•			
Sleepy Hollow (H-4) 2,860 acres 15 mi. n.e. of Lansing off US 127. Cross-country skiing, hunting; playgrounds.	59	•	•	•	•	•	•	•	•	•		•		•	•
South Higgins Lake (F-3) 962 acres 8 mi. s.w. of Roscommon off US 127. Cross-country skiing.	60	•	•	•	•	•	•	•	•	•		•			
Sterling (I-5) 1000 acres e. of I-75 on the n. edge of Monroe on State Park Rd. Cross-country skiing.	61	•	•	•	•	•		•	•	•		•			
Straits (B-5) 181 acres 1 mi. s.w. of St. Ignace on US 2.	62	•	•					•		•			•		
Tahquamenon Falls (B-5) 40,000 acres 12 mi. w. of Paradise on SR 123. Scenic. Cross-country skiing. *(See Paradise p. 93)*	63	•	•	•	•	•		•	•	•		•			•
Tawas Point (F-5) 183 acres 3 mi. e. of East Tawas off US 23.	64	•	•	•				•	•				•		
Traverse City (E-2) 45 acres 3 mi. e. of Traverse City on US 31.	65	•	•	•				•	•				•		
Twin Lakes (A-2) 175 acres 25 mi. s. of Houghton on SR 26.	66	•	•	•	•	•		•	•				•		
Van Buren (I-1) 400 acres 4 mi. s. of South Haven off I-196.	67	•	•					•	•						•
Van Riper (B-3) 1,044 acres 3 mi. w. of Champion on US 41.	68	•	•	•	•	•		•	•				•	•	
Walter J. Hayes (I-4) 654 acres 9 mi. w. of Clinton off US 12.	69	•	•					•	•					•	•
Warren Dunes (I-1) 1,950 acres on Lake Michigan 3 mi. s.w. of Bridgman via Red Arrow Hwy. Cross-country skiing. *(See Bridgman p. 48)*	70	•	•	•				•	•	•		•	•		•
Waterloo (L-1) 19,962 acres 7 mi. w. of Chelsea off I-94. Cross-country skiing; horse rental, geology center.	71	•	•	•	•	•	•	•	•	•	•	•	•		•
Wilderness (D-3) 8,500 acres 11 mi. w. of Mackinaw City on Wilderness Park Dr.	72	•	•	•	•	•		•	•	•		•		•	
Wilson (F-3) 36 acres 1 mi. n. of Harrison on US 127 Bus. Rte.	73	•	•		•	•		•							
Yankee Springs (H-2) 5,014 acres 8 mi. e. of Bradley off A-42 following signs.	74	•	•	•	•	•	•	•	•	•	•	•		•	•
Young (D-3) 563 acres 2 mi. n.w. of Boyne City on SR 75.	75	•	•					•	•				•	•	•
OTHER															
Ella Sharp (I-4) 562 acres 2 mi. s. of Jackson on 4th St. Golf (18 holes), tennis; driving range. *(See Jackson p. 78)*	76		•	•				•		•		•			•
Fitzgerald (H-3) 78 acres 2 mi. w. of Grand Ledge on SR 43.	77		•	•	•			•	•				•	•	

RECREATION AREAS

	MAP LOCATION	CAMPING	PICNICKING	HIKING TRAILS	BOATING	BOAT RAMP	BOAT RENTAL	FISHING	SWIMMING	PETS ON LEASH	BICYCLE TRAILS	WINTER SPORTS	VISITOR CENTER	LODGE/CABINS	FOOD SERVICE
Fox Memorial (H-3) 35 acres 1 mi. n. of Potterville off SR 100.	78		•	•				•	•			•			
Genesee (G-5) 4,540 acres 6 mi. n.e. of Flint off I-475 exit 13. (See Flint p. 68)	79	•	•	•	•	•	•	•	•	•	•	•	•		•
Hudson Mills (L-2) 1,600 acres 12 mi. n.w. of Ann Arbor via US 23 and N. Territorial Rd. Cross-country skiing; nature trails.	80		•	•	•			•		•	•	•	•		•
Indian Springs (K-4) 2,300 acres 5 mi. s.w. of Clarkston on White Lake Rd. Golf (18 holes); nature trails.	81		•	•						•	•	•	•		•
John Henes (C-3) 45 acres 2.5 mi. n.e. of Menominee off SR 35.	82		•	•				•				•			
Kensington (K-3) 4,350 acres 35 mi. n.w. of Detroit via I-96. Cross-country skiing; farm, nature trails.	83		•	•	•	•	•	•	•	•	•	•	•		•
Lake Erie (I-5) 1,590 acres near Gibraltar on W. Jefferson. Golf (18 holes); marina, wave pool.	84		•	•	•	•	•	•	•	•	•	•	•		•
Lower Huron (I-5) 1,200 acres 5 mi. s. of Belleville via Huron River Dr. to Waltz Rd. Cross-country skiing; nature trails, pool.	85		•	•				•	•	•	•	•	•		•
Metro Beach (K-6) 770 acres 3 mi. e. of Mount Clemens via Metropolitan Pkwy. (Sixteen Mile Rd.). Cross-country skiing; nature trails.	86		•	•	•	•		•	•	•	•	•	•		•
Stony Creek (K-5) 4,460 acres near Utica on 26-Mile Rd. Cross-country skiing, golf (18 holes); nature trails.	87		•	•	•	•	•	•	•	•	•	•	•		•
Sunken Lake Campground (D-5) 160 acres 5 mi. s. of Posen on SR 65, 1 mi. w. on Maple Ln., then 2 mi. n. on Leer Rd.	88	•	•	•	•	•		•	•	•	•				
Willow Metropark (I-5) 1,525 acres 4 mi. n.w. of Flat Rock on Willow Rd. Cross-country skiing, golf (18 holes), tobogganing; paddle boats, pool.	89		•	•	•			•	•	•	•	•	•		•

Michigan Temperature Averages
Maximum / Minimum
From the records of the National Weather Service

	JAN	FEB	MAR	APR	MAY	JUNE	JULY	AUG	SEPT	OCT	NOV	DEC
Detroit	32/19	34/20	43/28	58/39	68/48	79/59	83/63	82/62	74/55	63/45	48/34	35/24
Grand Rapids	30/16	33/16	42/24	57/36	69/45	79/56	83/60	82/58	74/51	63/41	46/31	34/21
Houghton Lake	26/9	28/8	37/16	53/30	65/40	75/50	79/54	77/53	68/46	58/37	42/27	30/15
Marquette	25/12	26/13	34/20	48/32	59/41	70/50	75/57	74/57	65/49	56/41	40/29	29/18
Sault Ste. Marie	22/6	24/7	32/15	47/29	59/38	70/47	75/52	73/53	64/46	55/38	39/26	27/13

Points of Interest

ACME (E-3) pop. 4,332, elev. 604'

MUSIC HOUSE MUSEUM is 1.5 mi. n. of SR 72 at 7377 US 31N. The late 19th-century farm complex includes re-creations of a general store, saloon, lyric theater and candy store. Music boxes, nickelodeons and organs are featured in period displays. Entrance is by guided tour only. Allow 2 hours minimum. Tours are offered Mon.-Sat. 10-4, Sun. noon-4, May-Oct.; phone for holiday hours. Admission $8; ages 6-15, $2.50. DS, MC, VI. Phone (231) 938-9300.

ADA (H-3) pop. 9,882, elev. 664'

ALTICOR CORPORATION VISITOR CENTER is 5 mi. e. of I-96 via SR 21 at 7575 Fulton St. E. Alticor is the parent company of Amway. The center offers interactive displays and audiovisual presentations about product manufacturing and the history of the company. Allow 1 hour minimum. Mon.-Fri. 8:30-noon and 1-5. Free. Under 16 must be with an adult. Phone (616) 787-6701.

ADRIAN (I-4) pop. 21,574, elev. 812'

An industrial city on the Raisin River, Adrian has an impressive historic district centered on Dennis and State streets. The 79 houses in the district exemplify the evolution of architectural styles in the area, from the Greek and Gothic revivals of the 1830s to Italianate to the Queen Anne-style houses that became popular after the Civil War. The houses are all privately owned.

The Croswell Opera House, 129 E. Maumee St., is an example of the utilitarian architecture prevalent after the Civil War. It has been offering musicals, plays, lectures and operas since 1866; phone (517) 264-7469.

Lenawee County Chamber of Commerce: 202 N. Main St., Suite A, Adrian, MI 49221; phone (517) 265-5141.

Shopping areas: Adrian Mall, at the junction of US 223 and SR 52, has Elder-Beerman, JCPenney and Sears.

ALBION (I-3) pop. 9,144, elev. 950'

WHITEHOUSE NATURE CENTER is e. on Erie St. then s. on Hannah St. to the Albion College campus. The 135-acre outdoor education facility offers five self-guiding nature trails through a variety of natural and man-made habitats. The interpretive building houses a small observation room with live exhibits; tour brochures are available. Guided tours are available by appointment.

Allow 1 hour minimum. Building open daily 10:30-4:30; closed major and college holidays. Trails open daily dawn-dusk. Free. Phone (517) 629-0582.

ALLENDALE (H-2) pop. 11,555, elev. 657'

In downtown Allendale, visitors will find the Engine House No. 5 Museum, 6610 Lake Michigan Dr., which displays firefighting equipment and memorabilia; phone (616) 895-4347.

VETERANS GARDEN OF HONOR is just off SR 45 (Lake Michigan Dr.) on 68th St. The memorial, dedicated to U.S. veterans, features eight life-size statues placed in a circle surrounding an 18-foot-tall obelisk. Seven soldiers represent the seven U.S. wars, and a female statue honors female veterans. Daily dawn-dusk. Free. Phone (616) 895-6295.

ALMA (G-3) pop. 9,275, elev. 730'

Alma is near the geographical center of the Lower Peninsula. It is the home of Alma College, a private liberal arts college.

Gratiot Area Chamber of Commerce: 110 W. Superior St., P.O. Box 516, Alma, MI 48801-0516; phone (989) 463-5525.

ALPENA (E-5) pop. 11,304, elev. 594'

Settled in 1840 at the head of Thunder Bay, Alpena served the booming lumber enterprises in the late 19th century. It is a center for industry and recreational boating, diving, fishing, snowmobiling, cross-country skiing and hunting. Diving and fishing charters are popular in nearby Lake Huron. The remains of approximately 80 shipwrecks are in the area of Thunder Bay, making Alpena an excellent diving location. The area also is home to a number of lighthouses.

Limestone quarries remain important in the region. North and west of the city is an area of natural sinkholes created by the settling of the limestone crust into caverns formed by subterranean streams. Some of the sinkholes are more than 150 feet deep.

Island Park and Alpena Wildlife Sanctuary, US 23N at the Thunder Bay River, offers nature trails, bird and wildlife viewing and fishing.

An 8-mile bicycling and hiking path winds through the city's parks and beaches.

Convention and Visitors Bureau of Thunder Bay Region: 235 W. Chisholm St., Alpena, MI 49707; phone (989) 354-4181 or (800) 425-7362.

JESSE BESSER MUSEUM is at 491 Johnson St. The museum is a regional center for the art, history and science of northeastern Michigan. Displays include a re-created 1890s street with period shops, Michigan wildlife paintings, sculpture, American

Indian artifacts and lumbering, agricultural and industrial equipment. Historical structures are outside. Changing exhibits and a planetarium are featured.

Allow 1 hour minimum. Tues.-Sat. 10-5, Sun. noon-4; closed major holidays. Planetarium shows Sun. at 2. Museum $3; over 60 and ages 5-17, $2. Planetarium $1. Phone (989) 356-2202.

ANN ARBOR (L-2) pop. 114,024, elev. 766′

"Kaw-GOOSH-kaw-nick, kaw-GOOSH-kaw-nick"—the chant of a gristmill resounding through the woods along Allen's Creek about 1824 allegedly furnished the local American Indians with the name for the hamlet that grew up around the mill. The less phonetically inclined settlers preferred Ann Arbor, referring to a grape arbor and the first pioneers' wives, Ann Allen and Ann Rumsey.

While only a mere upstart of 13 years and with fewer than 2,000 residents, Ann Arbor bid for and was granted the University of Michigan. Civic foresight paid off. Since its move from Detroit in 1837 the university has been the primary influence in the growth and life of the city. Research and development industries also contribute significantly to the economy.

Ann Arbor Area Convention and Visitors Bureau: 120 W. Huron St., Ann Arbor, MI 48104; phone (800) 888-9487.

Shopping areas: Kerrytown is a complex of specialty shops housed in three renovated historic buildings next to Farmer's Market on N. Fifth Avenue. Marshall Field's, Jacobson's, JCPenney and Sears can be found at Briarwood Mall, I-94 and State Street.

THE ANN ARBOR HANDS-ON MUSEUM is at 220 E. Ann St. The museum is housed in a historic former firehouse and features more than 250 interactive exhibits. In one area, visitors can learn about the human body, see how the skeleton moves and measure heart rate, reaction time and flexibility.

The natural world exhibit includes a working beehive and displays relating to the properties of light and optics. A water wall explores hydraulics. Visitors are offered the opportunity to make a hot air balloon take flight, check out an ambulance, see a tornado form, hear a whisper from across the room or encase themselves in giant soap bubbles. Computers enable users to manipulate a robot arm or play 3-D tic-tac-toe. Also featured are traveling exhibits and a preschool gallery. Allow 2 hours minimum.

Mon.-Sat. 10-5, Sun. noon-5; closed major holidays. Admission $7; over 65, students with ID and ages 2-17, $5. MC, VI. Phone (734) 995-5439.

UNIVERSITY OF MICHIGAN is e. on Huron St. to State St. The university has long since outgrown the original 40 acres that were donated to aid the selection of Ann Arbor as the school's new home. The grounds now cover more than 2,800 acres. Highlights include the Gothic buildings of the Law

Quadrangle at State Street and S. University Avenue, the Power Center for the Performing Arts and the Natural Science Museum. Michigan Stadium, one of the largest college stadiums in the country, seats nearly 105,000.

The university has two carillons. Burton Memorial Tower, on the central campus, houses the 55-bell Baird Carillon; the bells are played Mon.-Fri. noon-12:30. A 60-bell carillon in Lurie Tower on the north campus is open to visitors and is played Mon.-Fri. 1-1:30, Sun. 1:15-2. Weekly concerts are offered Mon. at 7 p.m., mid-June through July 31. Carillons are closed during exams and university vacations. Phone (734) 764-4636 for general campus information or (734) 764-2539 for Burton Memorial and Lurie towers.

Among the facilities on the North Campus are engineering research laboratories and the School of Music building, designed by Eero Saarinen. The School of Music offers free recitals and concerts. The medical center's six hospitals serve more than a million patients annually.

Exhibit Museum of Natural History is at Geddes and Washtenaw aves. The museum has a planetarium and exhibits about dinosaurs, prehistoric life, fossils, minerals, anthropology, astronomy, biology and Michigan wildlife. Museum open Mon.-Sat. 9-5, Sun. noon-5. Planetarium shows Sat. every hour 11:30-3:30, Sun. 1:30-3:30. Museum accepts donations. Planetarium $3. Phone (734) 764-0478 or (734) 763-6085.

Kelsey Museum of Archaeology is at 434 S. State St. Displays feature pottery, glass, statues and other artifacts excavated at the university's Mediterranean and Near Eastern digs. Tues.-Fri. 9-4, Sat.-Sun. 1-4; closed holidays. Free. Phone (734) 764-9304.

Matthaei Botanical Gardens is e. of US 23 at 1800 N. Dixboro Rd. Exotic plants from around the world bloom in the conservatory all year. Along the outdoor nature trails are changing seasonal displays. Conservatory open daily 10-4:30. Grounds open daily 8-dusk. Conservatory admission $3; ages 5-18, $1; free to all Mon. until 1. Grounds free. Phone (734) 998-7060.

Museum of Art is at 525 S. State St. at S. University Ave. The collection includes Western art from the sixth century to the present, Near and Far Eastern art, African art and a collection of prints and drawings. The museum also offers changing exhibitions, concerts, family programs and other events. Tues.-Sat. 10-5 (also Thurs. 5-9), Sun. noon-5; closed major holidays. Donations. Phone (734) 764-0395.

Nichols Arboretum is next to the University of Michigan central campus at 1610 Washington Heights Rd. From the James D. Reader, Jr. Urban Environmental Education Center, visitors can follow nature trails through grounds containing more than 400 labeled tree species. A peony garden blooms in early June. Self-guiding tour brochures are available.

Grounds open daily dawn-dusk. Guided tours are available at 2 on the third Sun. of each month. Education center open Sat.-Sun. 1-4, Feb.-Nov. Free. Phone (734) 998-9540.

Phoenix Memorial Laboratory is on the North Campus at 2301 Bonisteel Blvd. The laboratory is devoted to researching peaceful uses for atomic energy. Allow 1 hour minimum. Guided tours are offered by appointment Mon.-Fri. 9-3. Free. Phone (734) 764-6220.

William L. Clements Library is at 909 S. University Ave. The library houses notable collections of Americana, original manuscripts, maps and rare books about the Revolution and Civil War. Exhibits open Mon.-Fri. 1-4:45. Reading room open Mon.-Fri. 9-11:45 and 1-4:45. Free. Phone (734) 764-2347.

AUBURN HILLS—*see Detroit p. 62.*

AUGUSTA (I-3) pop. 899, elev. 790′

The Barn Theatre, 1 mile west on SR 96, is the home of the oldest professional resident summer theater in Michigan, which presents Broadway plays and musicals. Numerous alumni of the theater company are now stars in theater, film and television. Housed in a renovated dairy barn, the theater presents shows mid-May to mid-September; phone (269) 731-4121.

FORT CUSTER NATIONAL CEMETERY is 1 mi. e. on SR 96 to 15501 Dickman Rd. The 770-acre portion of Fort Custer was dedicated as a national cemetery in 1981. Allow 30 minutes minimum. Daily dawn-dusk. Free. Phone (269) 731-4164.

BAD AXE (F-5) pop. 3,462, elev. 765′

SANILAC PETROGLYPHS HISTORIC STATE PARK is 13 mi. s. on SR 53, 3.5 mi. e. on Bay City/Forestville Rd., then .5 mi. s. on Germania Rd. The park contains the Sanilac Petroglyphs, a series of American Indian rock carvings on sandstone. The 300- to 1,000-year-old carvings consist of figures that resemble animals, birds and humans. A mile-long nature trail winds around the site. Allow 30 minutes minimum. Wed.-Sun. 11:30-4:30, Memorial Day-Labor Day. Free. Phone (989) 269-7186.

BALDWIN (F-2) pop. 1,107, elev. 841′

A railroad junction in earlier days, Baldwin offers access to the numerous lakes and streams of the surrounding Huron-Manistee National Forests *(see place listing p. 75).*

Lake County Chamber of Commerce: 911 Michigan Ave., P.O. Box 130, Baldwin, MI 49304; phone (231) 745-4331 or (800) 245-3240.

SHRINE OF THE PINES is 2 mi. s. on SR 37. The shrine was created by Raymond W. Oberholzer as a memorial to the white pine. He hand-chiseled furnishings from

tree stumps and roots gleaned from virgin stands of white pine that were cut in the late 1800s.

Oberholzer scraped the roots with broken glass and wire brushes, then rubbed each piece by hand with handmade sandpaper, natural resin and deer hide. From these pieces he fashioned beds, chairs, chandeliers and candlesticks; particularly impressive is a table with drawers, carved from a 700-pound stump. The furnishings are housed in a log hunting lodge in a wooded park on the banks of the Pere Marquette River. A nature trail meanders through the pines.

Allow 30 minutes minimum. Mon.-Sat. 10-6, Sun. 1:30-6, May 15-Oct. 15. Last tour begins 30 minutes before closing. Admission $3.75; over 54, $3; ages 13-18, $2; ages 6-12, $1; family rate (parents and children under 18) $10. Phone (231) 745-7892.

BARAGA (A-2) pop. 1,285, elev. 621′

HANKA HOMESTEAD MUSEUM is 7 mi. w. of US 41 on Arnheim Rd., following signs. The century-old Finnish farming homestead is restored to its 1920s appearance. Guided tours of the farm and its outbuildings are available. Allow 1 hour minimum. Tues., Thurs., Sat.-Sun. noon-4 and by appointment, Memorial Day-Aug. 31; by appointment Sept. 1 to mid-Oct. Donations. Phone (906) 353-6239.

THE SHRINE OF THE SNOWSHOE PRIEST is 3.5 mi. s. on US 41. The six-story structure includes a 35-foot-tall brass statue featuring Bishop Frederic Baraga, a Catholic priest who moved to the Great Lakes region in 1830 and devoted his life to American Indians. He earned his nickname because he traveled by snowshoe up to 700 miles to visit the tribes. The statue overlooks Keweenaw Bay. Allow 30 minutes minimum. Mon.-Sat. 9-8, Sun. 10-6. Admission $3; ages 10-18, $1. Phone (906) 524-7021.

BATTLE CREEK (I-3) pop. 53,364, elev. 819′

In 1894 two brothers named Kellogg, experimenting in the kitchens of the Battle Creek Sanitarium, developed a flake cereal. From this modest beginning grew the Kellogg Co., the Post Division of Kraft-General Foods Corp. and the Ralston Purina Co., which have made Battle Creek the breakfast food center of the nation.

Battle Creek residents' progressive attitudes are manifested in other issues. In the decades before the Civil War the city was an abolitionist stronghold and an overt station on the Underground Railroad. Thus the names Kellogg and Post are no more important than that of Sojourner Truth. An ex-slave, this tall, persuasive woman carried her crusade for truth and freedom from tiny rooms to President Lincoln's office. She came to Battle Creek in 1858 and died in 1883; her grave is in Oak Hill Cemetery at South Avenue and Oak Hill Drive. Statues in Monument Park and Linear Park honor her work.

Residents find respite from industrial and commercial activities in city parks. Bailey Park and C.O. Brown Stadium, between Capital Avenue and the Battle Creek River, are the scenes of national amateur baseball tournaments. South of town on Goguac Lake, landscaped Willard Park offers water sports and picnicking. Linear Park extends across much of the city, offering 17 miles of landscaped walkways highlighted by gazebos, boardwalks and bridges, which provide opportunities for jogging, bicycling, walking and picnicking.

Guided tours are offered of the SAVE Historic Adventist Village, 482 Van Buren St. The religious community features restored and re-created 19th-century buildings; phone (269) 965-3000.

Greater Battle Creek/Calhoun County Visitor and Convention Bureau: 77 E. Michigan Ave., Suite 100, Battle Creek, MI 49017; phone (269) 962-2240 or (800) 397-2240.

Shopping areas: Lakeview Square, east on Beckley Road from I-94 and Capital Avenue, has almost 100 stores, including Marshall Field's, JCPenney and Sears. McCamly Place offers specialty stores and restaurants in a high-rise complex on W. Jackson Street.

ART CENTER OF BATTLE CREEK is at 265 E. Emmett St. Changing exhibits of works by regional and national artists as well as art of other cultures are on display. Works by 20th-century Michigan artists and craftsmen, classes and workshops also can be seen. Tours are provided by reservation. Tues.-Sat. 10-5 (also Thurs. 5-7), Sun. 1-4; closed holidays. Free. Phone (269) 962-9511.

GEM BINDER PARK ZOO is 3 mi. s. of I-94 exit 100, at 7400 Division Dr. The zoo has SAVE wooden boardwalks and a conservation adventure station with hands-on activities. Exotic animals live in a natural park setting. Visitors can board a train to tour the safari-style habitat of Wild Africa. Camel rides are offered most weekends. Food is available.

Allow 2 hours minimum. Mon.-Fri. 9-5, Sat. and holidays 9-6, Sun. 11-6, late Apr. to mid-Oct. Last admission 30 minutes before closing. Admission (includes safari train) $8.50; over 65, $7.50; ages 2-10, $6.50. Camel ride $2. DS, MC, VI. Phone (269) 979-1351.

Miller Children's Zoo features a life-size dinosaur replica, a petting area, a miniature train and domestic animal exhibits. Miniature train $2.

SAVE **KELLOGG BIRD SANCTUARY** is 8 mi. n.w. on SR 89 following signs to 12685 E. C Ave., between 40th St. and E. Gull Lake Dr. An experimental facility of Michigan State University, the area is inhabited by birds of prey, wild ducks, geese, swans, peacocks, pheasants and other upland species. The sanctuary has displays and an observation deck. Allow 1 hour, 30 minutes minimum. Daily 9-8, Apr.-Oct.; 9-5, rest of year. Admission

$3; over 64, $2; ages 2-12, $1. Phone (269) 671-2510.

KELLOGG'S CEREAL CITY USA is off I-94 to exit 98B, n. to Michigan Ave., then w. to 171 Michigan Ave. The family attraction celebrates Will Kellogg's accidental creation of the cereal industry. Exhibits focus on trivia, advertising, marketing and history of breakfast cereal. A simulated cereal production line, a historical time line, four theaters and an interactive Cereal City are included. Food is available. Allow 2 hours minimum.

Mon.-Fri. 9:30-5, Sat. 9:30-6, Sun. 11-5, early June-late Aug.; Tues.-Fri. 10-4, Sat. 10-5, Sun. noon-5, late Mar.-early June and late Aug.-early Nov.; Sat. 10-5, Sun. noon-5, rest of year. Closed Jan. 1, Thanksgiving and Dec. 24-25. Admission $7.95; over 64, $6.50; ages 3-12, $4.95. AX, DS, MC, VI. Phone (269) 962-6230.

LEILA ARBORETUM is at W. Michigan Ave. at 20th St. A 72-acre tract of ornamental trees and shrubs, the arboretum is known for its collection of mature conifers and perennial demonstration beds. Daily dawn-dusk. Free. Phone (269) 969-0270.

BAY CITY (G-5) pop. 36,817, elev. 594′

Bay City is a major distribution point for the industrial and agricultural wealth of east-central Michigan. Many domestic and foreign freighters pass through the city's busy port, and boat races are often held on the river. Shipping and commerce have been the foundation of Bay City's prosperity since the demise of its lumber industry around 1900. Mansions built by the lumber barons can be seen along the tree-shaded residential streets in the city's three historic districts.

The Saginaw River and Saginaw Bay provide ample recreational opportunities. Bay City State Recreation Area (see Recreation Chart) is 5 miles north on SR 247 on the Lake Huron shore.

Bay Area Convention and Visitors Bureau: 901 Saginaw St., Bay City, MI 48708; phone (888) 229-8696.

HISTORICAL MUSEUM OF BAY COUNTY is at 321 Washington Ave. Displays, which trace the development of Bay County, include period rooms and exhibits pertaining to agriculture, maritime history, American Indian culture, the fur trade and the lumber, shipbuilding and shipping industries. Allow 1 hour minimum. A research library also is included. Museum open Mon.-Fri. 10-5, Sat.-Sun. noon-4. Library open Tues.-Thurs. 1-5. Free. Phone (989) 893-5733.

SAGINAW BAY VISITORS CENTER is 3 mi. n. in Bay City State Recreation Area. Permanent and changing exhibits depict life in the wetlands. A 15-minute multimedia presentation about wetlands development is offered. The paved Frank N. Anderson Nature Trail leads to Tobico Marsh, a 1,700-acre refuge for more than 100 species of birds and migratory waterfowl.

In addition to nature trails, observation towers and a 300-foot boardwalk, the wetlands contain a fishing pier. Visitors can walk to the marsh from the center. The center also includes a bird observation room and a wet lab. Programs are available; phone for schedule. Allow 30 minutes minimum. Tues.-Sun. noon-5. Admission $4 per private vehicle. Phone (989) 667-0717.

BEAVER ISLAND (B-4)

About 30 miles offshore in Lake Michigan, Beaver Island is the largest island of the Beaver Archipelago. The French established the island's first settlement but abandoned it in 1603. The arrival of the Mormons in 1847, led by tyrannical king and politician James Jesse Strang, aroused resentment on the mainland, leading to dissolution of the colony by force in 1856. The island was eventually settled by Irish fishermen.

The island is popular for fishing and hunting. A museum occupies an 1850 print shop built by the Mormons. St. James, the former Mormon capital and a pleasant vacation spot, is accessible from Charlevoix *(see place listing p. 49)* by boat or plane.

BELLEVILLE—*see Detroit p. 62.*

BENZONIA (E-2) pop. 519

BENZIE AREA HISTORICAL MUSEUM is 1 blk. w. of US 31 on River Rd. Housed in a century-old church, the museum contains displays about the farmers, fishermen, lumberjacks and sailors who tamed the northern Michigan wilderness. Allow 1 hour minimum. Tues.-Sat. 10-4, May-Dec.; closed holidays. Admission $2; ages 5-18, 50c. MC, VI. Phone (231) 882-5539.

GWEN FROSTIC PRINTS is 2 mi. w. of US 31 on River Rd. A small wooden building is within a 285-acre wildlife sanctuary on the Betsie River. Carvings of wild birds and animals are among the collection and works of Gwen Frostic, an artist and poet specializing in nature themes. Presses make prints from original blocks Mon.-Fri. 9-5:30. A nature library is available. Tours are given by reservation. Allow 30 minutes minimum. Daily 9-4:30,

May-Oct.; Mon.-Sat. 9-4:30, rest of year. Free. Phone (231) 882-5505.

BERRIEN SPRINGS (I-2)
pop. 1,862, elev. 671'

1839 COURTHOUSE MUSEUM is at Old US 31 and Union St. An 1870 sheriff's residence, an 1830s log house, a re-created county jail and the 1860 county office building are included. The 1839 courthouse contains local history exhibits and a courtroom restored to its original appearance. Allow 1 hour minimum. Tues.-Fri. 9-4, Sat.-Sun. 1-5. Free. Phone (269) 471-1202.

WINERIES
- **Lemon Creek Fruit Farm and Winery** is off I-94 exit 16, n. 2.5 mi. to Lemon Creek Rd., then 6 mi. e. to 533 Lemon Creek Rd. Mon.-Sat. 9-6, Sun. noon-6, May-Nov. Phone (269) 471-1321.

BESSEMER (B-1) pop. 2,148, elev. 1,437'

BLACK RIVER NATIONAL FOREST SCENIC BYWAY (CR 513) follows the winding course of the Black River to Lake Superior. The scenic 11-mile drive passes five waterfalls, which range from 25 to 40 feet high and are accessible by well-marked trails. Black River Harbor, at the end of Black River Drive, has picnicking and camping areas and a playground *(see the AAA Great Lakes CampBook)*; phone (906) 932-1330.

BLOOMFIELD HILLS—*see Detroit p. 62.*

BRIDGEPORT (G-4) pop. 7,849, elev. 610'

JUNCTION VALLEY RAILROAD is 2 mi. s. on Dixie Hwy. Two-mile train rides are offered on a railroad built to one-quarter size. Trains wind past buildings and across bridges built to scale. Visitors may depart the train at a park equipped with picnic tables and a playground and return on a later train. Special excursions are scheduled during the Halloween season. Food is available.

Allow 1 hour minimum. Mon.-Sat. 10-6, Sun. 1-6, mid-May through Labor Day; Sat.-Sun. 1-5, day after Labor Day-early Oct. Phone for holiday schedules. Fare $5; over 65, $4.75; ages 2-12, $4.25. Additional charge for special excursions. Phone (989) 777-3480.

BRIDGMAN (I-1) pop. 2,428

Hang gliders are a familiar sight in the sky south of Bridgman. Prevailing winds from Lake Michigan and a 240-foot vertical drop afforded by Tower Hill have made nearby Warren Dunes State Park *(see Recreation Chart)* a popular all-year locale for the sport. Flights more than an hour long have been recorded.

BRIMLEY (B-5) elev. 655′

CASINOS

• **Bay Mills Casino** is at 11386 W. Lakeshore. Daily 24 hours. Phone (906) 248-3701 or (906) 248-3720.

BUCHANAN (I-1) pop. 4,681, elev. 732′

BEAR CAVE is 4 mi. n. on Red Bud Tr. to 4085 Bear Cave Rd. The 150-foot-long tufa rock cave is accessible by a 40-foot winding stairway. A taped narration guides visitors past unique geological formations, among them the 250,000-year-old Kansan Boulder. The cave maintains a constant temperature of 58 F; suitable clothing is advised. Walkways are narrow, and visitors also should be aware that the cave contains bats. Allow 30 minutes minimum. Daily 10-4, Memorial Day-Labor Day. Admission $3; ages 5-11, $1.50. Phone (269) 695-3050.

WINERIES

• **Tabor Hill Winery** is at 185 Mt. Tabor Rd. Tours available noon-4:30; closed Jan. 1 and Dec. 25. Phone (800) 283-3363.

CADILLAC (F-3) pop. 10,000, elev. 1,292′

Begun as a lumber camp in 1871, Cadillac was named for the founder of Detroit, Antoine de la Mothe Cadillac. The rolling terrain of the Huron-Manistee National Forests *(see place listing p. 75)* and the proximity of Cadillac and Mitchell lakes have made the town a popular recreational center.

Cadillac Area Visitors Bureau: 222 Lake St., Cadillac, MI 49601; phone (231) 775-0657 or (800) 225-2537.

SAVE **JOHNNY'S WILD GAME AND FISH PARK** is w. on I-55, s. on CR 3, then e. on 46½ Mile Rd. The park houses a variety of wild and domestic game animals in a natural setting. Visitors can feed and pet deer, goats, birds and other animals. Trout fishing and fish cleaning also are available. Allow 30 minutes minimum. Daily 10-6, Memorial Day-Labor Day. Admission $4.50; over 55, $4.25; ages 3-14, $4. Phone (231) 775-3700.

CALUMET (A-2) pop. 879, elev. 1,202'

CALUMET THEATRE is at 340 Sixth St. A variety of scheduled theater events are offered. The building opened in 1900 for stage performances and for a time was used as a motion picture theater. The theater is now used for concerts and stage performances. Tours are offered. Allow 30 minutes minimum. Tues.-Sat. 11-2, late May to mid-Sept.; closed holidays. Admission $4; ages 6-12, $2. Self-guiding tours $2. Phone (906) 337-2610.

COPPERTOWN MINING MUSEUM is on Red Jacket Rd., 2 blks. w. of US 41. A co-operating site of Keweenaw National Historical Park, Coppertown traces the evolution of mines and mining through displays of mining equipment. A simulated mine at the entrance provides a glimpse of the miner's world. Allow 30 minutes minimum. Mon.-Sat. 10-5, late May-early Oct. (also Sun. 12:30-4, July-Aug.). Admission $3; national parks pass holders $2; ages 12-18, $1. Phone (906) 337-4354.

CAMBRIDGE JUNCTION (I-4)

A nostalgic Irishman who settled in the rolling region around Cambridge Junction dubbed it Irish Hills. The significance of the junction, however, predated the area's name: Two major turnpikes from Detroit and Monroe converge en route to Chicago.

North of US 12 and west of SR 50 is Michigan International Speedway, the site of NASCAR and Indy-car races during the summer.

WALKER TAVERN HISTORIC SITE is at jct. US 12 and SR 50. The history of Michigan's stagecoach era is presented through exhibits, audiovisual presentations and walking tours. The tavern is an 1840s clapboard house that was used as a stagecoach stop on the Detroit to Chicago path. Picnicking is permitted. Wed.-Sun. 10-4, Memorial Day-Labor Day. Free. Phone (517) 467-4414.

CASPIAN (B-2) pop. 997

IRON COUNTY MUSEUM is 1.5 mi. s. of US 2 on SR 189, then e. on CR 424 to Museum Rd. Several outdoor complexes depict life in the late 1800s. Exhibits examine the lumber industry, farming, mining, transportation and domestic life. Among the 22 structures are an 1890 train depot, the Caspian Mine Headframe Mining Memorial, a logging camp and the home of Carrie Jacobs-Bond, composer of such tunes as "I Love You Truly" and "End of a Perfect Day."

An arts complex features two galleries: the Renaissance-style home of Brandon Giovanelli and the Bernhardt Collection, which includes works by Simmi Knox, a presidential portrait artist. The Lee Leblanc Memorial Art Gallery features one of the largest collections of wildlife art by a single artist in the United States. Mon.-Sat. and holidays 9-5, Sun. 1-5, June-Aug.; Mon.-Sat. 10-4, Sun. 1-4 in

May and Sept. Admission $5; ages 5-18, $2.50. Phone (906) 265-2617 or (906) 265-3942.

CHARLEVOIX (D-3) pop. 2,994, elev. 592'

Its early history linked to the stormy affairs of the Mormon monarchy on Beaver Island *(see place listing p. 47)*, Charlevoix is an enterprising resort center. Lakes Michigan and Charlevoix offer excellent beaches and opportunities for boating. Round Lake, lying between the two, provides the city with its fine yacht harbor. The city offers band shell musical entertainment during July and August.

Charlevoix is on US 31, a scenic route that follows the shore between Traverse City and Petoskey.

Beaver Island Boat Co., 103 Bridge Park Dr., offers ferry service to Beaver Island; phone (231) 547-2311.

Charlevoix Area Chamber of Commerce: 408 Bridge St., P.O. Box 358, Charlevoix, MI 49720; phone (231) 547-2101.

CHEBOYGAN (D-4) pop. 5,295, elev. 600'

The crew members of the Coast Guard icebreaker *Mackinaw* make Cheboygan their home port. Specialized construction fits the ship for rescue towing as well as icebreaking; it is credited with extending the shipping season on the Great Lakes by 6 weeks. When in port, the *Mackinaw* is docked on the Cheboygan River; visitors are welcome.

This industrial and resort city is surrounded by some of Michigan's largest lakes. Mullett and Burt lakes, both noted for bass and muskellunge, are part of the historic inland waterway. The waterway became a major transportation link in the late 19th century after a lock was built at Cheboygan. Traffic consists of pleasure boaters, who can still cruise as far as Conway.

One of the Great Lakes' largest cattail marshes, a nesting site for 54 bird species, can be viewed from a boardwalk in Gordon Turner Park at the north end of Huron Street. The Mackinac Bridge and Round and Bois Blanc islands also can be seen from the boardwalk and from the nearby fishermen's walkway.

Cheboygan Area Chamber of Commerce: 124 N. Main St., P.O. Box 69, Cheboygan, MI 49721; phone (231) 627-7183 or (800) 968-3302.

CHEBOYGAN COUNTY HISTORICAL SOCIETY MUSEUM is at 404 S. Huron St. at the corner of Court St. The 2-story brick structure, with an attached county jail, was built in 1882 and served as the sheriff's home until 1969. The house's parlor, kitchen, schoolroom and bedrooms are re-created in period style. The Spies Heritage Hall contains logging, railroad, veterans' and marine displays.

A flower garden, country store, schoolroom and a 19th-century furnished log cabin are on the grounds. Allow 30 minutes minimum. Mon.-Fri. 1-4, May 1-Oct. 5; otherwise by appointment. Admission $2, under 18 free. Phone (231) 627-9597, or (231) 627-5448 for appointments.

THE OPERA HOUSE is at 403 N. Huron St. The Victorian theater was constructed in 1877, rebuilt following a fire in 1888 and restored in 1984. Mary Pickford, Annie Oakley and Marie Dressler were among the theater's actors and entertainers; it now is a focal point for local entertainment. It is open for guided tours Tues.-Fri. 1-4, June-Sept. Admission $1. Phone (231) 627-5432 or (231) 627-5841 for box office.

CHESTERFIELD—*see Detroit p. 62.*

CHRISTMAS (B-4) elev. 619′

CASINOS
- **Christmas Kewadin Casino** is on SR 28. Daily 24 hours. Phone (906) 387-5475.

COLDWATER (I-3) pop. 12,697

From cabin to inn to village was the early progression of Coldwater, on the Chicago Turnpike, a primary east-west transportation route. By the 1880s the city had assumed its present character as a trading and supply center.

 # Do you know the facts?

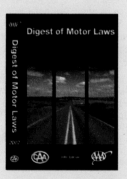

AAA publishes the Digest of Motor Laws to assist traveling motorists. Filled with facts and information, this one-of-a-kind compilation includes a comprehensive description of the laws that govern motor vehicle registration and operation in the United States and Canada. This sixty-eighth edition guide has a new, easy-to-read format with graphics, state-by-state tax summary tables and detailed information on occupant protection laws, driver licensing laws, automated enforcement laws and motor vehicle fees and taxes.

You can easily locate various licensing and motor laws governing the states in which you are traveling. In addition to vehicle registration and operation laws, the Digest contains information and facts about alcohol laws, traffic safety laws and more.

Call your local club or 1-877-AAA-BOOK to obtain a copy of the Digest.

The book retails for $13.95.

Branch County Chamber of Commerce: 20 Division St., Coldwater, MI 49036; phone (517) 278-5985.

TIBBITS OPERA HOUSE is at 14 S. Hanchett St. The theater opened in 1882 to house the many performers and theater companies that played Coldwater en route between Chicago and Detroit. Its excellent acoustics and sophisticated backstage equipment were widely acclaimed. The renovated French-Victorian building presents a variety of concerts and art exhibitions.

A professional summer stock series and a children's series are offered June through August. Community and youth productions are presented the rest of the year. Theater tours, including the backstage area and the art gallery, are available on request. Mon.-Fri. 9-5. Free. Phone (517) 278-6029.

CONCORD (I-3) pop. 1,101, elev. 940′

MANN HOUSE MUSEUM is .2 mi. s. of SR 60 at 205 Hanover St. The 1884 house contains Mann family heirlooms dating from 1840 and depicts family life in the Midwest during the Victorian period. A carriage house and Victorian and herb gardens are on the grounds. Tours are available. Allow 30 minutes minimum. Wed.-Sun. 10-3, Memorial Day-Labor Day. Free. Phone (517) 524-8943.

COOPERSVILLE (G-2) pop. 3,910

COOPERSVILLE AREA HISTORICAL SOCIETY AND MUSEUM is at 363 Main St. This former railroad depot contains such area artifacts as a train collection and antique furniture as well as re-creations of a local drugstore and the interior of a one-room schoolhouse. An exhibit is dedicated to Del Shannon, a member of the Rock and Roll Hall of Fame and a Coopersville native. An additional building contains a sawmill exhibit. Guided tours are available by request. Allow 30 minutes minimum. Tues. 2-8, Sat. 10-4; Sun. 2-5. Free. Phone (616) 837-6978.

COPPER HARBOR (A-3) elev. 621′

Tales of copper lying on the lakeshore first drew explorers, then miners, to the remote Keweenaw Peninsula. The deposits proved scant, and Copper Harbor lost its vitality as its mines, timber and port activity successively dwindled.

Michigan's northernmost community is a popular summer vacation spot. Boat trips to Isle Royale National Park *(see place listing p. 77)* are available mid-May to late September. Lake Superior and the surrounding woodlands can be viewed along the 9.5-mile Brockway Mountain Drive, which runs west from Copper Harbor and rejoins SR 26 about 10 miles east of Eagle Harbor.

The Astor House Museum at US 41 and SR 26 contains antique dolls, American Indian relics and local historic artifacts. The Estivant Pines, a grove of 100-foot-tall white pines, some 500 years old, grow along the Montreal River. *Also see Upper Peninsula p. 105.*

DELAWARE COPPER MINE TOUR is 12 mi. s. on US 41. Visitors can take a 45-minute underground walking tour into a mid-1800s copper mine where veins of copper can be seen. The mine temperature averages 45 F; warm clothing is recommended. Allow 1 hour minimum. Guided tours depart every 20 minutes daily 10-5:15, July-Aug. Self-guiding tours are available daily 10-5, mid-May through June 30 and Sept. 1 to mid-Oct. Admission $8.50; ages 6-12, $4.50. Phone (906) 289-4688.

FORT WILKINS STATE PARK is 1 mi. e. on US 41. The 700-acre park contains the restored buildings of Fort Wilkins, the Army post established in 1844 to protect copper miners. The fort had no hostilities and was finally abandoned in 1870. Refurbished officers' quarters and other buildings also are visited; wildflower and historical exhibits also are included. From late June to late August costumed staff members portray life at the fort in the 1800s.

Allow 1 hour minimum. Daily 8-dusk, Memorial Day to mid-Oct. Park admission $4 per private vehicle. Round-trip fare to the lighthouse $12; under 12, $7. Phone (906) 289-4215. *See Recreation Chart and the AAA Great Lakes CampBook.*

Copper Harbor Lighthouse is reached by a boat departing from the Copper Harbor Marina, .5 mi. w. on SR 26. Visitors can see the 1866 Copper Harbor Lighthouse, the 1848 lighthouse keeper's house and a 1933 steel light tower. Transportation to the lighthouse is by narrated cruise. Guided tours are offered. Boats depart the harbor daily 10-5 on the hour, July-Aug.; at 10, noon, 2 and 4, May-June and in Sept. Fare $12; under 12, $7. AX, DS, MC, VI. Phone (906) 289-4966 for the marina, or (906) 289-4215 for Fort Wilkins.

DEARBORN—*see Detroit p. 63*

DELTON (H-2) elev. 935′

BERNARD HISTORICAL MUSEUM is at 7135 W. Delton Rd. Displays housed in a 1930s hospital include historic artifacts and items used in the hospital. An 1873 schoolhouse, a 1900 country store and a blacksmith shop are nearby. A re-created seamstress cottage with sewing machines and domestic artifacts is featured. Also on the grounds are a working windmill, a marked nature trail, a red barn with farm equipment and handmade tools, and a small house that once served as a residence for visiting medical professionals. Allow 1 hour minimum. Daily 1-5, July-Aug.; Sun. 1-5 in June and Sept. Donations. Phone (269) 623-2077.

Detroit

One of the world's greatest automobile manufacturing cities, Detroit is an international symbol of America's productive might. The spirit of Detroit—the automobile and the assembly line—has spread around the globe, profoundly changing the lives of millions of people.

The French settled the city in 1701 and called it *d'etroit* or city "of straits," referring to the 27-mile Detroit River that connects lakes Erie and St. Clair. The Detroit River, a segment of the international border between the United States and Canada, marks the only point where Canada lies directly south of the United States. A remnant of the early settlement is Ste. Anne de Detroit Catholic Church. Its original log chapel was built in 1701.

Strategically located, Detroit was the objective of several major campaigns during the struggle for supremacy between the French and British. During the Revolutionary War the community served as Northwest headquarters for the British. The settlement took on new life following the War of 1812; the launching in 1818 of the first steam vessel on the Great Lakes and the subsequent expansion of shipbuilding and commerce helped to assure the future prosperity of the city.

However, at the turn of the 20th century Detroit was still a tree-shaded small town busily engaged in making stoves, beer and carriages. This serenity was broken by Henry Ford's creation, a practical vehicle propelled by power generated from within itself, the wheezing, sputtering Model T. Detroit was never the same.

With the growth of the automobile industry the town burst its river-hugging confines and absorbed surrounding communities. To augment local manpower for the assembly lines, Detroit turned to Europe for help and soon became one of the largest cities in the United States.

While still recovering from rapid growth and expansion, the city has recast its image. Although such tags as the Motor City are foremost in outsiders' minds, Detroit residents are eager to point out that the port of Detroit is one of the world's busiest inland ports and ranks high in customs collection. The Detroit area is a great steel center and a leader in the manufacture of pharmaceuticals, office equipment, paint, rubber products, salt and more than half the garden seed used throughout the country.

A polyglot community pulled together by high aspirations and hard work, Detroit has many sports and cultural activities. The city boasts a civic center complex, the Renaissance Center, a sports arena on the riverfront, an excellent park system and numerous theaters, museums and galleries.

The Detroit Civic Center covers 75 acres along the downtown riverfront. The center includes Cobo

Conference/Exhibition Center, phone (313) 877-8111; Cobo Arena, phone (313) 983-6616; Joe Louis Arena, phone (313) 983-6606; and Renaissance Center, phone (313) 568-5600.

Approaches

By Car

Interstate highway systems provide speedy access to Detroit from the north, south and west. I-75 enters Detroit from the south and the north; SR 10 also enters from the north. Approaching from the west and the northeast is I-94; also entering from the west is I-96. From the east, Canadian Hwy. 401 becomes SR 3 when entering Detroit from Windsor, Ontario, via the toll bridge, and SR 3B when entering via the toll tunnel.

Getting Around

Street System

City planners originally patterned Detroit after Washington, D.C., but abandoned this plan during its rapid growth. Instead, planners superimposed the basic grid system on Detroit's downtown streets. The result is confusing to drivers; since most of the downtown streets are one-way, a detailed map is necessary. Detroit's freeway system provides access to points within the city. Rush hours, 7-9 and 4-6:30, should be avoided.

Parking

Metered parking is minimal in downtown Detroit; most of the 8,000 meters are in the fringe areas. To compensate for this, Detroit has many municipal and privately operated parking lots and garages. Rates range from approximately $1 to $2.50 for the first hour and average 50c to 85c for each additional hour. Some offer flat daily rates of $3.50 to $8, with reduced fees for evenings and during events.

Public Transportation

Considering the confusing maze of downtown streets and the hectic pace of traffic, Detroit's Department of Transportation might be the answer to getting from one place to another with a minimum of frustration. Bus fare is generally $1.25, plus 25c for each transfer and 25c when leaving the city limits (exact fare only). For schedules and routes phone (313) 933-1300.

For those who would like to ride in a different style, antique red and brass trolleys run from Times Square to the Renaissance Center Mon.-Fri. 7-6, Sat.-Sun. 10-6, May-Nov. (weather permitting). An English double-decker trolley travels the same route Memorial Day to Labor Day. Hours are extended during events and shortened during winter months. The fare is 50c each way; phone (313) 224-6449.

The automated People Mover, a 2.9-mile elevated light-rail system, operates through the central business

(continued on p. 55)

The Informed Traveler

City Population: 951,270

Elevation: 635 ft.

WHOM TO CALL

Emergency: 911

Police (non-emergency): (313) 267-4600

Time: (313) 472-1111

Hospitals: Detroit Receiving Hospital, (313) 745-3600; Harper Hospital, (313) 745-8040; Henry Ford Hospital, (313) 916-2600; Hutzel Hospital, (313) 745-7555; St. John Detroit Riverview Hospital, (313) 499-4000.

WHERE TO LOOK

Newspapers

The two daily newspapers—*News* and *Free Press*—are supplemented with a variety of weekly papers.

Radio

Detroit radio station WWJ (950 AM) is an all-news/weather station; WDET (101.9 FM) is a member of National Public Radio.

Visitor Information

Maps, brochures, calendars of events, lists of sightseeing companies and hotel location maps are available from the visitors bureau. Write Detroit Metro Convention and Visitors Bureau, 211 W. Fort St., Suite 1000, Detroit, MI 48226; phone (313) 202-1800 or (800) 338-7648.

TRANSPORTATION

Air Travel

Major commercial airlines have regularly scheduled flights to the Detroit Metropolitan Airport, 21 miles west of downtown. Allow approximately 45 minutes travel time to the airport. Van service from downtown hotels to the airport is available daily by reservation. The one-way cost is $19. For information phone Commuter Express, (888) 854-6700.

Rental Cars

Car rental companies may be found at the airport. Hertz, (800) 654-3131, offers discounts to AAA members. Check the local telephone directory for listings of other agencies.

Rail Service

Amtrak Stations are at 11 W. Baltimore Ave. in the New Center area and in Dearborn near Michigan Avenue and Greenfield. They provide train service to various parts of the country; phone (800) 872-7245.

Buses

Greyhound Lines Inc. serves Detroit. The terminal is at 1001 Howard St.; for information about fares and schedules phone (800) 231-2222.

Taxis

Taxis operate on a meter system; the basic charge is $1.40, plus $1.40 per mile. There is no extra charge for additional riders. The two largest companies are Checker Cab, (313) 963-7000, and City Cab, (313) 833-7060. For a complete list of taxi services check the telephone directory.

Boats

Detroit, one of the world's busiest inland freight ports, is linked by 25 steamship companies to more than 40 countries worldwide. Vessels ranging from ocean-going freighters to private craft dock in Detroit's well-protected harbor.

district, including the Civic Center, Mon.-Thurs. 7 a.m.-11 p.m., Fri. 7 a.m.-midnight, Sat. 9 a.m.-midnight, Sun. noon-8. Hours are extended during events. The fare is 50c, under 5 free, and must be in exact change or tokens. For more information phone (313) 962-7245.

What To See

CHARLES H. WRIGHT MUSEUM OF AFRICAN AMERICAN HISTORY is at 315 E. Warren Ave. Exhibits include Mae Jemison's NASA flight suit, a replica of Dr. Martin Luther King's Birmingham jailhouse door, and numerous other artifacts. Two galleries feature changing exhibits. A research library and archives contain materials relating to African and American history. Food is available.

Allow 1 hour minimum. Wed.-Sat. 9:30-5, Sun. 1-5; closed major holidays. Admission $5; under 18, $3. Phone (313) 494-5800.

DETROIT HISTORICAL MUSEUM is at 5401 Woodward Ave. at Kirby Ave. The museum depicts lifestyle changes of the typical American from 1701 to the 1900s. Reconstructions of early streets, historic model railroads and period automobiles trace Detroit's growth from Indian settlement to the present. Films and educational programs are offered.

Allow 1 hour minimum. Tues.-Fri. 9:30-5, Sat.-Sun. 10-5; closed major holidays except Easter. Admission $5; senior citizens and ages 12-18, $2.50; free to all Wed. Phone (313) 833-1805.

THE DETROIT INSTITUTE OF ARTS is at 5200 Woodward Ave. at Farnsworth Ave. Exhibits trace the development of art from ancient to modern times. Notable are the 17th-century Dutch and Flemish paintings, the William Hearst Collection of armor, the Tannahill Collection of impressionist paintings, the Pre-Columbian Native American Art exhibit, the G. Mennen Williams collection of African art and Diego Rivera's Detroit industry murals. Guided tours are available.

Films are shown Friday through Monday evenings; programs and concerts also are presented. Allow 1 hour, 30 minutes minimum. Galleries open Wed.-Fri. 10-4 (also Fri. 4-9), Sat.-Sun. 10-5; closed holidays. Tours are given Wed.-Sat. at 1, Sun. at 1 and 2:30. Admission $4, ages 6-17, $1. Phone (313) 833-7900.

DETROIT PUBLIC LIBRARY is at 5201 Woodward Ave. at Kirby Ave. The Italian Renaissance building features white Vermont marble. Murals by Edwin H. Blashfield and Gari Melchers, painted-glass windows designed by Frederick J. Wiley, mosaic panels depicting Shakespeare's "Seven Ages of Man" and Pewabic tiles adorn the interior. The Burton Historical Collection in the rare book room also is of interest. The National Automotive History Collection is open limited hours. Library open Tues.-Wed. noon-8, Thurs. 10-6; closed holidays. Free. Phone (313) 833-1000.

DETROIT SCIENCE CENTER is at 5020 John R. St. at Warren Ave. in the midtown cultural center. The hands-on science center features an IMAX theater and a digital dome planetarium. Physics-related programs are presented on the Science Stage, and electrical demonstrations are the focus in the Sparks Theater. Exhibit laboratories explore matter and energy; waves and vibration; life sciences; and mechanics and motion. Classrooms offer hands-on activities about applied, earth, life, physical and space sciences.

Allow 2 hours minimum. Mon.-Fri. 9:30-5, Sat.-Sun. 10:30-6, June-Aug.; Mon.-Fri. 9:30-3, Sat. 10:30-6, Sun. noon-6, rest of year. Closed major holidays. Admission $7; over 60 and ages 2-12, $6. IMAX theater and planetarium $4 extra. Parking $3. AX, MC, VI. Phone (313) 577-8400.

GRAND CIRCUS PARK is at Adams and Woodward aves. This park has defined the northern limit of the downtown area since the 1860s. There are two notable statues and a fountain, illuminated in summer, that honor Thomas Edison. Trolley car rides to Grand Circus Park leave from the Renaissance Center, Cobo Conference/Exhibition Center and Cobo Arena (see Getting Around, Public Transportation). Daily 24 hours. Free.

MOTOWN HISTORICAL MUSEUM is at 2648 W. Grand Blvd. The Motown sound of the early 1960s originated in this old brick house that now houses the museum. Such entertainers as Marvin Gaye, Smokey Robinson, Diana Ross and the Supremes, and Stevie Wonder got their starts here under the direction of Motown Records founder Berry Gordy Jr. The renovated galleries contain a variety of musical instruments, photographs, artifacts and the original Studio A and control room.

Tues.-Sat. 10-6, Sun.-Mon. noon-6; otherwise by appointment. Closed major holidays. Admission $7; under 13, $4. Phone (313) 875-2264.

OLD MARINERS' CHURCH is at 170 E. Jefferson Ave. Built in 1849, the church originally stood on Woodward Avenue. It was moved to its present location in 1955 to make way for the construction of the civic center. The interior of the stone Gothic Revival church incorporates 19th-century nautical design into Christian symbolism. A blessing of the fleet and memorial service commemorating those who have died at sea is held the second Sunday in March.

On the Sunday closest to Nov. 10 a memorial service is held for the crew of the Edmund Fitzgerald, which sank in Lake Superior in 1975. Guided tours are available by request; reservations are required. Donations. Phone (313) 259-2206.

PEWABIC POTTERY is at 10125 E. Jefferson Ave. The ceramics museum, gallery, workshop and studio offers changing contemporary exhibits. A collection of historic work by Mary Chase Perry

Destination Detroit

Detroit Zoological Park, Royal Oak. Perched on a tall, nearly-natural cliff, resident lions scope out the happenings in the rest of the zoo. (See listing page 64)

*I*t's the Motor City. Motown's hometown. And an inland port on par with some of the world's busiest.

*B*ut diverse Detroit is much more than an industrial hub. Also assembled here are cultural diversions, professional sports teams and a wealth of sites embracing wonders of progress and reminders of the past.

The Detroit Institute of Arts, Detroit. Vincent Van Gogh's "Self-Portrait with Straw Hat" is one of many prestigious works of art on display at the museum. (See listing page 55)

See Vicinity map page 58

*P*laces included in this AAA Destination City:

Waterford •

West Bloomfield •

Walled Lake •

Farmington Hills

96

Novi •   102

Northville •   Livonia •

14   Plymouth •

275

23   94

Belleville   275

Charles H. Wright Museum of African American History, Detroit. Outstanding African Americans are honored here, and archives preserve past lessons. (See listing page 55)

Henry Ford Museum & Greenfield Village, Dearborn. Is it 1920? Tunes from a banjo mingle with the swish of the paddlewheel on the *Suwanee*, which takes guests around a peaceful lagoon. (See listing page 63)

See Downtown Inset page 58

Automotive Hall of Fame, Dearborn. Walter P. Chrysler and Henry Ford were among the hall's first inductees; recent honorees include Joe Girard, who holds the world record for one-on-one retail automobile sales—18 in one day! (See listing page 63)

Stratton, Pewabic's founder, also is displayed. Mon.-Sat. 10-6; closed holidays. Free. Phone (313) 822-0954.

CASINOS

- **MGM Grand** is at 1300 John C. Lodge. Daily 24 hours. Phone (313) 393-7777. *See color ad p. 61.*

- **Motor City Casino** is at 2901 Grand River Ave. Daily 24 hours. Phone (313) 237-7711 or (877) 777-0711. *See color ad p. 61.*

What To Do

Sightseeing

Various tours encompassing the city and its environs are available; the most economical is by bus. Gray Line Bus Tours, based at 1301 E. Warren Ave., makes regularly scheduled visits to many of the city's points of interest. Phone (313) 870-5012.

Boat Tours

[SAVE] **DIAMOND JACK'S RIVER TOURS** departs from docks at both Hart Plaza and Bishop Park in Wyandotte *(see place listing p. 65).* Passengers ride on a former Mackinac Island ferry for a 2-hour narrated cruise. The Detroit trip passes historic and modern buildings, shipyards and downtown Windsor, Ontario, as well as under the Ambassador Bridge and around Belle Isle. The Wyandotte trip focuses on nature and wildlife. Food is available.

Allow 2 hours, 30 minutes minimum. Cruises depart from Hart Plaza or Bishop Park Thurs.-Sun. at 1 and 3:30, mid-June through Labor Day. Fare for either trip $14; senior citizens $12; ages 6-16, $10. Parking is available in nearby garages; fees vary. Phone (313) 843-7676. *See ad p. 60.*

Sports and Recreation

Sports enthusiasts can watch the Detroit Tigers **baseball** team at Comerica Park, (313) 962-4000, and the Lions **football** team at Ford Field, (313) 262-2000 or (800) 616-7627. The Palace of Auburn Hills is the home of the Detroit Pistons **basketball** team; phone (248) 377-0100. The 2001-02 Stanley Cup champion Red Wings **hockey** team challenges rivals in the Joe Louis Arena; phone (313) 983-6606. Since Detroit sports are popular, tickets should be ordered at least a month before the scheduled date of the event.

Harness racing can be enjoyed at Northville Downs, (248) 349-1000; Hazel Park Harness Raceway, (248) 398-1000; and Windsor Raceway in Windsor, Ontario, (313) 961-9545 or (519) 969-8311.

Note: Policies concerning admittance of children to pari-mutuel betting facilities vary. Phone ahead for information.

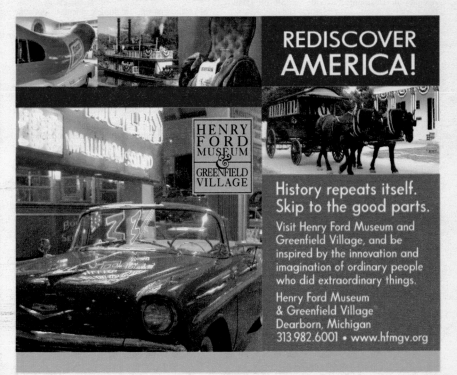

Several public courses offer **golf** in Detroit: Chandler Park, 12801 Chandler Park Dr., (313) 331-7755; Palmer Park, Woodward at Seven Mile Road, (313) 883-2525; Rackham, 10100 W. Ten Mile Rd. in Huntington Woods, (248) 543-4040; Rogell, at Seven Mile and Berg roads, (313) 578-8006; and Rouge Park, 11701 Burt Rd., (313) 837-5900.

Swimming is permitted at Belle Isle and at the mile-long Metropolitan Beach Metropark; phone (313) 224-1100. Twelve other metro parks have playgrounds and facilities for swimming, golfing, **boating, ice skating, picnicking** and nature study. Many parks have courts for **tennis** and **shuffleboard** in addition to winter recreation facilities.

Shopping

From an automobile right off the assembly line to an ice cream cone from a vendor; from imported, pewter-topped, glazed beer steins to poodle shampoos—all these and much more can be purchased in Detroit. The Stores of Renaissance Center are popular with shoppers.

Suburban shopping centers contain many major department store chains and smaller specialty shops and theaters. Among the largest malls are Eastland, at SR 102 (Eight Mile Road) and Kelly Road; Fairlane, at SR 39 (Southfield) and US 12 (Michigan Avenue) in Dearborn; Lakeside, at SR 59 (Hall Road) and Schoenherr in Sterling Heights; Northland, north of SR 102 at SR 10 (Northwestern Highway); The Somerset Collection and Somerset North, at Big Beaver (Sixteen Mile Road) and Coolidge in Troy; Southland, at Eureka and Pardee roads in Taylor; Twelve Oaks Mall, off I-96 Novi Road exit in Novi; and Westland, at Wayne Road and Warren Avenue.

Bass Pro Shops Outdoor World, in [SAVE] Great Lakes Crossing Mall at 4500 Baldwin Rd. in Auburn Hills, features a waterfall, 30,000-gallon aquarium, wildlife exhibits and sporting demonstrations; phone (248) 209-4200. The mall features more than 200 stores, restaurants and entertainment facilities.

Theater and Concerts

The industrial side of Detroit is tempered by the city's notable cultural offerings. The Detroit Symphony plays a full season of concerts, including children's concerts at Orchestra Hall; phone (313) 576-5111. Throughout the year the following theaters offer a variety of stage presentations, including concert artists, drama, opera and dance: Fox Theatre, (313) 471-3200; the Masonic Temple, (313) 832-2232; and the Music Hall Center for the Performing Arts, (313) 963-7622.

Detroit ranks high in sales of theater tickets. Professional repertory, including first-run and off-Broadway productions, can be enjoyed at the Fisher Theater at 3001 W. Grand Blvd.; phone (313) 872-1000. Theater and cabaret performances are offered at the Detroit Repertory Theatre; phone (313) 868-1347.

Other area theaters offer concerts and plays sponsored by the drama departments of the University of Detroit-Mercy, (313) 993-1130, and Wayne State University, (313) 577-2960 or (313) 577-2972. Among the area's popular suburban theaters are the Meadowbrook Music Festival, (248) 475-5668; the New Pine Knob Music Theatre, (248) 377-0100; the Palace of Auburn Hills, (248) 377-0100; and the Freedom Hill Amphitheatre, 14900 Metropolitan Pkwy. in Freedom Hill County Park, Sterling Heights, (586) 268-5100.

Several first-run multiple cinemas dot the suburbs. Local newspapers carry complete information concerning concerts, theater, movies and other events.

Special Events

Summers in Detroit, though at times hot and humid, are celebrated with a variety of events. Festivities begin with Flower Day at Eastern Market in May.

In late June and early July, Detroit and Windsor, Ontario, share the International Freedom Festival ,considered to be the largest transborder festival in North America. The two holidays celebrated are Canada Day, July 1, and Independence Day, July 4.

Sports events, concerts, fireworks, parades and cultural arts and craft shows take place during the weeklong celebration.

Detroit's Riverfront festivals celebrate the city's heritage. In July hydroplane races are held on the Detroit River, and Indy cars are featured at the Grand Prix in August.

The Michigan State Fair follows in late August. For music lovers the Montreux Detroit Jazz Festival is presented over Labor Day weekend. Initiating the holiday season is the Michigan Thanksgiving Day Parade on Thanksgiving Day. Fantasyland is held in nearby Lincoln Park from late November through Christmas Eve. The Christmas Carnival in December rounds out the year's events.

The Detroit Vicinity

AUBURN HILLS (K-5) pop. 19,837, elev. 975′

SAVE **WALTER P. CHRYSLER MUSEUM** is off I-75 exit 78, then 1.3 mi. e. to One Chrysler Dr. Interactive displays and vignettes relate the history of Walter P. Chrysler and the Chrysler Corporation. Seventy cars, including restored classics, muscle cars, trucks and race cars, are on display. Visitors may watch three 7-minute films in the theater. Allow 30 minutes minimum. Tues.-Sat. 10-6, Sun. noon-6; closed holidays. Admission $6; over 61 and ages 6-12, $3: Chrysler employees and retirees free. AX, MC, VI. Phone (888) 456-1924.

BELLEVILLE (I-5) pop. 3,997, elev. 670′

YANKEE AIR MUSEUM is off I-94 exit 190, 1 mi. n. to Tyler Rd., 1 mi. w. to Beck Rd., then .8 mi. n. to the Willow Run Airport gate. The museum features a number of displays describing the history of the Willow Run B-24 Liberator production facilities as well as rooms dedicated to the history of flight and women in flight. Nearly 25 aircraft can be seen, including a Boeing B-52D Stratofortress. Allow 30 minutes minimum. Mon.-Sat. 10-4, Sun. noon-4, Apr.-Dec.; closed holidays. Admission $7; over 64, $4; ages 5-12, $3. Phone (734) 483-4030.

BLOOMFIELD HILLS (K-5) pop. 3,940

In 1819 Judge Amasa Bagley cleared land for a tavern and a farm on what was to become known as Bagley's Corner. It remained an agricultural center until about 1900 when city dwellers from Detroit began to buy acreage for estates. In 1932 the name was changed to Bloomfield Hills.

Among the wealthy who were attracted to this quiet community during the first decade of the 20th century were the publisher of *The Detroit News*, George G. Booth, and his wife, Ellen Scripps Booth. Their estate, Cranbrook, has become a notable cultural and educational center.

CRANBROOK EDUCATIONAL COMMUNITY is on Woodward Ave. (SR 1). The 315-acre campus includes a graduate art school and lower, middle and upper schools. Architect Eliel Saarinen designed many of the buildings. The fountains and statuary include works by sculptor Carl Milles.

SAVE **Cranbrook Art Museum** is at 39221 Woodward Ave. (SR 1). Changing displays of contemporary art and faculty and student artwork are the focus of the museum's collection. Traveling exhibitions are featured throughout the year. Allow 1 hour minimum. Tues.-Sun. 11-5 (also Fri. 5-9); closed major holidays. Admission $5, over 65 and students with ID $3. Phone (248) 645-3323.

SAVE **Cranbrook House and Gardens** is at 380 Lone Pine Rd. Designed by Albert Kahn, the Arts and Crafts-style house is situated on 40 acres that include formal plantings, woods, sculpture, fountains, pine walks and two lakes. Allow 1 hour minimum. House tours Thurs. at 11 and 1:15, Sun. at 3, June-Oct. Gardens daily 10-5, May-Aug.; daily 11-3, in Sept.; Sat.-Sun. 11-3 in Oct. House $10; over 65, $8. Gardens $5, over 65 and students with ID $4, under 5 free. Phone (248) 645-3147.

SAVE **Cranbrook Institute of Science** is at 39221 Woodward Ave. (SR 1). This museum of science and natural history has a large mineral collection, planetarium, laser light shows, observatory, bat area and changing exhibits.

Allow 2 hours minimum. Daily 10-5 (also Fri. 5-10). Laser shows Fri. at 7 p.m. and 9 p.m., Sat.-Sun. at 2 and 4. Planetarium shows Fri. at 8 p.m., Sat.-Sun. at 11:30. Admission $7; over 64 and ages 2-12, $5. Planetarium shows extra $3; over 64 and ages 2-12, extra $1.50. Laser shows extra $3, under 4 free. DS, MC, VI. Phone (248) 645-3200.

CHESTERFIELD (K-6) pop. 37,405

LIONEL VISITORS CENTER is off I-94 exit 243, then 2 mi. w. on 23 Mile Rd. Tours are offered of the operating model train display in the visitor center. Following a 10-minute videotape presentation, visitors have access to the interactive exhibit featuring up to 16 trains operating simultaneously on more than 1,000 feet of track. Other operating models also are shown.

Allow 1 hour minimum. Tours are given Wed.-Thurs. at 10, 3 and 4, Fri. at 10, 1:30 and 2:30, Sat. at 9, 10, 11 and noon; closed major holidays. Free. Reservations are required. Phone (810) 949-4100.

DEARBORN (L-4) pop. 97,775, elev. 604'

While its giant neighbor Detroit absorbed adjoining townships, Dearborn—itself created from the merger of Fordson and Dearborn—did not lose its identity. It had a giant of its own, Henry Ford, who put Dearborn on the map by putting the nation on wheels.

Dearborn Chamber of Commerce: 15544 Michigan Ave., Dearborn, MI 48126; phone (313) 584-6100.

SAVE **AUTOMOTIVE HALL OF FAME** is at 21400 Oakwood Blvd. adjacent to the Henry Ford Museum. Plaques and memorabilia are dedicated to the men and women of the automotive industry. Honorees include designers, educators, inventors, journalists, manufacturers, race car drivers and automotive association members. A transportation display, library and archives also are available.

Allow 1 hour, 30 minutes minimum. Daily 10-5, Memorial Day-Oct. 31; Tues.-Sun. 10-5, rest of year. Closed Jan. 1, Thanksgiving and Dec. 25. Admission $6; over 62, $5.50; ages 5-12, $3. Phone (313) 240-4000.

DEARBORN HISTORICAL MUSEUM is at 21950 Michigan Ave. and 915 Brady St. The museum includes two buildings of the original United States Government Arsenal. An exhibit annex has farm equipment, wagons and buggies. The commandant's quarters and the McFadden-Ross House date from the early 1800s and contain period furnishings. The Richard Gardner House, built in 1831 and furnished in period, belonged to the family of Henry Ford's childhood friend Richard Gardner. Allow 30 minutes minimum. Mon.-Sat. 9-5, May-Oct.; 1-5, rest of year. Closed holidays. Free. Phone (313) 565-3000.

SAVE **HENRY FORD ESTATE—FAIR LANE** is on the campus of the University of Michigan-Dearborn at 4901 Evergreen Rd. Tours of the mansion and powerhouse are given. The Fords entertained such luminaries as Charles Lindbergh, the Duke of Windsor and President Herbert Hoover in their spacious mansion. The powerhouse, the combined creation of Ford and Thomas Edison, gave the estate the independence to produce its own power, heat and light. Gardens and trails are on the grounds. Food is available.

Allow 1 hour, 30 minutes minimum. Tours depart Mon.-Sat. at 10, 11, 1, 2 and 3, Sun. every 30 minutes 1-4:30, Apr.-Dec.; Mon.-Fri. at 1, Sun. every 30 minutes 1-4:30, rest of year. Closed Jan. 1, Easter, Thanksgiving and Dec. 24-25. Admission $8; over 62, $7; ages 5-12, $5. Phone (313) 593-5590.

GEM **HENRY FORD MUSEUM & GREEN-FIELD VILLAGE** is at 20900 Oakwood Blvd. at Village Rd. The museum and village serve as a 93-acre monument to American innovation and enterprise. Documenting nearly 3 centuries of technological and cultural change, the museum's collections encompass communications, transportation, industry, agriculture and domestic life.

The museum includes the Rosa Parks bus; the chair that Abraham Lincoln sat in when he was assassinated; a folding camp bed used by George Washington during the Revolutionary War; the limousine in which John F. Kennedy was assassinated; Edgar Allan Poe's writing desk; and the Weinermobile. "Heroes in the Sky" is a 40,000-square-foot exhibition with 15 historic aircraft and related displays.

Exhibits in Greenfield Village span more than 300 years of history, with an emphasis on American resourcefulness. The 81-acre site includes steam locomotives, a steamboat, costumed interpreters and artisans as well as 90 houses—once owned by Noah Webster, the Wright brothers and Henry Ford. "Journey of the Model T" allows visitors to ride in a Model T. The boyhood farmstead of Harvey Firestone operates as a working 1880s farm.

An IMAX theater is housed in the visitor center. Events with historic and seasonal themes are held throughout the year. Light clothing and comfortable shoes are recommended. Food is available.

Allow a full day. Mon.-Sat. 9-5, Sun. noon-5; closed Thanksgiving and Dec. 25. **Note:** Greenfield Village is undergoing renovations and will re-open in June 2003. Museum admission $14; over 61, $13; ages 5-12, $10. Village admission $18; over 61, $17; ages 5-12, $12. IMAX $10; over 61, $9; under 12, $8.50. AX, DS, MC, VI. Phone (313) 982-6001 or (800) 835-5237 (outside 313 area code). *See color ad p. 59.*

FARMINGTON HILLS (K-4) pop. 82,111

MARVIN'S MARVELOUS MECHANICAL MUSEUM is at 31005 Orchard Lake Rd. Displays include antique slot and pinball machines and other mechanical memorabilia and video games, including nickelodeons, vintage neon signs and magic show posters. Mon.-Thurs. 10-9, Fri.-Sat. 10 a.m.-11 p.m., Sun. 11-9. Free. Phone (248) 626-5020.

GROSSE POINTE SHORES (L-6)

pop. 2,823, elev. 586'

SAVE **EDSEL & ELEANOR FORD HOUSE** is 1.5 mi. e. from I-94 Vernier/8 Mile exit, then 1 mi. n. on Lake Shore Rd. The 60-room house, styled after houses in the Cotswold area of England, was built 1926-29 by the Ford Motor Co. executive and his wife. The estate was constructed to accommodate their family as well as their extensive fine and decorative arts collections and landscaped grounds. Twenty of the rooms are shown on guided tours that begin with a 15-minute videotape presentation in the Activities Center.

Allow 2 hours minimum. Tours are given on the half-hour Tues.-Sat. 10-4, Sun. noon-4, Apr.-Dec.; Wed.-Sat. 1-4, rest of year. Admission $6; over 59, $5; ages 6-12, $4. Phone (313) 884-4222.

LIVONIA (L-4) pop. 100,545, elev. 638'

GREENMEAD HISTORICAL PARK is at jct. Eight Mile and Newburgh rds. at 20501 Newburgh Rd. Tours of up to nine historical buildings are offered. Picnic facilities are available on the 95-acre farm site. Allow 2 hours minimum. Grounds open daily dawn-dusk. Tours of historic buildings Sun. 1-4, May-Oct. and in Dec. Closed holiday weekends. Admission $2; under 18, $1. Phone (248) 477-7375.

NORTHVILLE (L-3) pop. 6,459, elev. 829'

MAYBURY WORKING FARM is on Eight Mile Rd., 5 mi. w. of I-275 in Maybury State Park *(see Recreation Chart)*. Animals, seed displays and crops can be seen on this working farm. A petting area includes such farm animals as horses, rabbits and chickens. The farm offers a variety of events; phone for schedule. Farm open daily 10-7. Park open 8-dusk. Park admission $4 per private vehicle. Phone (248) 349-8390.

NOVI (L-4) pop. 47,386, elev. 909'

MOTORSPORTS MUSEUM AND HALL OF FAME is inside the Novi Expo Center at the s.w. corner of I-96 and Novi Rd. The museum exhibits motorized race vehicles including stock cars, boats, trucks, motorcycles and Indy cars. Racing videotapes, uniforms and memorabilia also are on display. Visitors can try slot car racing. Allow 1 hour minimum. Daily 10-5, Memorial Day-Labor Day; Thurs.-Sun. 10-5, rest of year. Closed Easter and Dec. 25. Admission $4; over 60 and under 12, $2. Slot cars are extra. MC, VI. Phone (248) 349-7223.

PLYMOUTH (L-3) pop. 9,022, elev. 741'

Plymouth was founded in 1867 by a group of settlers from Plymouth, Mass. Their Colonial influence can still be seen in the town's architecture.

Plymouth Community Chamber of Commerce: 386 S. Main St., Plymouth, MI 48170; phone (734) 453-1540.

SAVE **PLYMOUTH HISTORICAL MUSEUM** is 1 blk. n. of Kellogg Park at 155 S. Main St. The history of early Plymouth is reflected through permanent and changing exhibits. A gallery houses Main Street shops and offices and reflects the many trades and professions of 19th-century Plymouth. Other highlights include an Abraham Lincoln exhibit, the Victorian Rooms exhibit and the Then and Now hands-on center. A library and archives also are available.

The 15,000-square-foot museum has what is said to be the only Alter car, an automobile built in Plymouth 1916-17. An extensive collection of Daisy air rifles, once manufactured in Plymouth, also is

displayed. Allow 1 hour minimum. Wed.-Thurs. and Sat.-Sun. 1-4. Admission $3, students with ID $1; family rate $7. Phone (734) 455-8940.

PONTIAC (K-4) pop. 66,337, elev. 933'

Pontiac was established in 1818 where the Pontiac Trail crossed the Clinton River. Settlers began pouring in, and by the 1880s the city entertained a major wagon and carriage making industry. In a sense, it still does: What began as the Pontiac Spring Wagon Works is known as General Motors. The Pontiac Division of General Motors perpetuates the name of the great Ottawa Indian chief who reputedly spent his summers at nearby Orchard Lake.

A number of municipal parks and more than 400 nearby lakes that arc around the western side of the city offer outdoor recreation.

Greater Pontiac Area Chamber of Commerce: 30 N. Saginaw, Suite 404, Pontiac, MI 48342; phone (248) 335-9600.

ROCHESTER (K-5) pop. 10,467, elev. 745'

Although on the fringe of metropolitan Detroit, Rochester lies among wooded hills—an apt home for Oakland University.

Rochester Area Chamber of Commerce: 71 Walnut, Suite 110, Rochester, MI 48307; phone (248) 651-6700.

GEM **OAKLAND UNIVERSITY'S MEADOW BROOK HALL** is 3 mi. e. via Walton Blvd., then .3 mi. s. on Adams Rd. on the SAVE eastern campus of Oakland University. This 80,000-square-foot, 100-room 1920s Tudor Revival-style mansion was once the residence of Matilda Dodge Wilson and lumber broker Alfred G. Wilson. It boasts a two-story ballroom, 24 fireplaces, hand-carved paneling, sculptured ceilings and many original furnishings and works of art.

Knole Cottage, also on the premises, is a brick six-room playhouse that was built for the Wilson's daughter. It is furnished in the same style as Meadow Brook Hall.

Allow 1 hour, 30 minutes minimum. Guided tours Mon.-Sat. on the half-hour 10:30-3:30, Sun. at 11:30 and 3:30, Memorial Day-Labor Day; Mon.-Sat. at 1:30, Sun. at 1:30, 2:30 and 3:30, rest of year. Closed most holidays. Admission $8; over 61, $6; ages 5-12, $4. Prices slightly higher during events. Knole Cottage $1 extra. Phone (248) 370-3140.

ROYAL OAK (K-5) pop. 60,062, elev. 661'

GEM **DETROIT ZOOLOGICAL PARK** is at 8450 W. Ten Mile Rd. at Woodward Ave. One of the most modern zoos in the country, it features spacious, open exhibits. Designed to simulate natural environments, habitats are laid out over 125 acres of landscaped grounds. Highlights are a 4-acre great ape complex, a snow monkey area with a hot spring, a reptile house, a free-flight aviary and penguin and polar bear exhibits.

A miniature railroad carries passengers across the grounds. A hands-on learning center also is available. The Wildlife Interpretive Gallery features art and an indoor butterfly and hummingbird garden. Picnicking is permitted. Food is available.

Allow 4 hours minimum. Daily 9-5, Apr.-Oct.; 10-4, rest of year. Closed Jan. 1, Thanksgiving and Dec. 25. Admission $8; over 62 and ages 2-12, $6. Parking $4. AX, MC, VI. Phone (248) 398-0900.

NATIONAL SHRINE OF THE LITTLE FLOWER is at jct. SR 1 and 12 Mile Rd. at 2123 Roseland Ave. The shrine became known through the radio broadcasts of its pastor, Father Charles E. Coughlin, now deceased. A striking feature is the 90-foot crucifixion tower, girded by four crosses; below the figure is a carving of the last words of Christ.

The church is built of granite and limestone interspersed with stone blocks from America's states and territories; on each is carved the state name and flower. Guided tours are available by appointment. Allow 30 minutes minimum. Mon.-Fri. 6 a.m.-7 p.m., Sat.-Sun. 6 a.m.-7:30 p.m. Free. Phone (248) 541-4122.

WALLED LAKE (K-3) pop. 6,713

COE RAIL SCENIC TRAIN is at the Railroad Depot at 840 N. Pontiac Tr. One-hour train rides in vintage cars are offered through scenic Walled Lake and West Bloomfield. Trips depart Sun. at 1 and 2:30, late Apr.-late Oct. Fare $9; over 65 and ages 2-10, $8. Phone (248) 960-9440.

WATERFORD (K-4) pop. 73,150

DRAYTON PLAINS NATURE CENTER is at jct. US 24 (Dixie) and Hatchery Rd., following signs to 2125 Denby Dr. An interpretive center displays mounted animals in re-creations of their natural habitats. The surrounding grounds encompass 137 acres along the Clinton River and feature 4 miles of marked trails. Allow 30 minutes minimum. Grounds open dawn-dusk. Interpretive center open Mon.-Fri. 11-5, Sat. 11-4, Sun. noon-4. Closed major holidays. Donations. Phone (248) 674-2119.

WEST BLOOMFIELD (K-4) pop. 64,862

HOLOCAUST MEMORIAL CENTER is on the Jewish Community Campus at 6602 W. Maple Rd., at the corner of Drake Rd. The center documents the history of the Holocaust with exhibits, videotape presentations, photographs, dioramas and a memorial flame. The Morris and Emma Schaver Library and Archives is dedicated to the study of the Holocaust and Jewish history, culture and genealogy. Outside the memorial center is the Bernard Maas Garden of the Righteous.

Sun.-Thurs. 10-3:30, Fri. 9-noon, Sept.-June; Sun.-Thurs. 10-3:30, rest of year. Closed holidays. Guided tours are offered Sun. and Wed. at 1. Reservations are required for tours. Donations. Phone (248) 661-0840.

WYANDOTTE (I-6) pop. 28,006, elev. 590'

THE FORD-MacNICHOL HOME/WYANDOTTE MUSEUM is at 2610 Biddle Ave. The 1896 Victorian house includes original fixtures, furnishings, wallpaper and woodwork. The lower level houses a museum that chronicles the development of the town from an Indian village through the 19th century. A Christmas open house is held during the first two weekends in December. Allow 1 hour minimum. Mon.-Fri. noon-4, first Sun. of the month 2-5; closed holidays. Admission $1; over 60, 50c; under 12, 25c. Phone (734) 324-7297.

This ends listings for the Detroit Vicinity.
The following page resumes the alphabetical listings
of cities in Michigan.

DOUGLAS (H-1) pop. 1,214

Before a bridge linked the towns of Douglas and Saugatuck *(see place listing p. 98)*, the only way across the Kalamazoo River was by a hand-cranked, chain-powered ferry. Despite the presence of a bridge, the ferry continued until recently to operate as it had since the 1830s, carrying pedestrians and bicyclists between the two towns daily.

In keeping with the town's quaint atmosphere and charm, no fast food restaurants can be found. On area beaches, rockhounds can find septarian nodules. When halved and polished, these concretions display an endless array of designs.

SS *KEEWATIN* is moored off CR A2 (Blue Star Hwy.) at the Kalamazoo River s. of the Saugatuck-Douglas Bridge. One of the last of the classic steamships, it was built in Scotland in 1907 for the Canadian Pacific Railway's upper Great Lakes passenger route. Now a marine museum, the 350-foot coal-burning vessel is maintained and preserved as it was during its 57 years of service on the lakes. Daily 10:30-4:30, Memorial Day weekend-Labor Day. Admission $7.50; ages 6-12, $3.50. MC, VI. Phone (269) 857-2464.

DOWAGIAC (I-2) pop. 6,147, elev. 772'

SOUTHWESTERN MICHIGAN COLLEGE MUSEUM is e. on SR 62 from SR 51, then .2 mi. s. to 58900 Cherry Grove Rd., following signs. The museum explores science, technology and regional history through hands-on exhibits, artifacts and pictures. Allow 30 minutes minimum. Tues.-Sat. 10-5 (also Wed. 5-8); closed holidays. Free. Phone (269) 782-1374.

DRUMMOND ISLAND (B-6) pop. 500

Part of the rocky Manitoulin archipelago that separates Georgian Bay and the North Channel from the rest of Lake Huron, Drummond Island lies off the eastern tip of the Upper Peninsula at the mouth of the St. Marys River.

Anglers, boaters, hunters and vacationers are drawn to this cliffbound, deeply indented wilderness isle. Its woodlands harbor deer, grouse and rabbits; duck hunting is particularly good. From the bays and inlets come bass, northern pike, yellow perch and walleye. Hiking in the summer and snowmobiling in the winter are favorite pastimes along the forest trails. Dolomite quarries augment the economy. The island is accessible by automobile ferry from De Tour Village on SR 134.

When the treaty ending the War of 1812 ousted the British from Mackinac Island, they reestablished their garrison on the southwest promontory of Drummond Island, despite the fact that the boundary through the archipelago was still indefinite. British attempts to obtain the island failed, and in 1828 the Union Jack was lowered.

The Drummond Island Historical Society Museum, 10 miles from the ferry on the northwest end of the island, contains rocks and minerals, American Indian artifacts, furniture and written accounts of the island's history. Phone (906) 493-5746.

DRYDEN (H-5) pop. 815

SEVEN PONDS NATURE CENTER is at 3854 Crawford Rd. Various natural communities—Earl's Prairie, glacial lakes, an herb garden, wetlands, a wildflower garden and a butterfly garden—are accessible by 6 miles of trails contained within 323 acres. Maps are available at an interpretive center. Allow 1 hour minimum. Tues.-Sun. 9-5; closed Jan. 1, Thanksgiving, day after Thanksgiving and Dec. 25. Admission $3; under 12, $1. Phone (810) 796-3200.

DURAND (H-4) pop. 3,933, elev. 796'

MICHIGAN RAILROAD HISTORY MUSEUM AND DURAND UNION STATION is at 200 Railroad St. Railroad artifacts are on display, and a library houses abundant literature about railroads. Tues.-Fri. 11-4, Sat.-Sun. 1-5; closed holidays. Donations. Phone (989) 288-3561.

EAST LANSING (H-4) pop. 46,525

Primarily residential, East Lansing complements the governmental and industrial emphasis of Lansing *(see place listing p. 79)*, which it abuts. The creation of Michigan Agricultural College in 1855 spurred the town's growth; since then East Lansing's development has paralleled that of the school, which became Michigan State University.

MICHIGAN STATE UNIVERSITY is e. on Grand River Ave. (SR 43), following signs. The school is the nation's pioneer land-grant university. From three buildings in a field of stumps near the Red Cedar River, it has grown to a 5,320-acre educational complex with one of the largest enrollments in the country. The university's housing complex lodges more than 20,000 students and student families.

Among the noteworthy features of the main campus are the library, containing more than 4 million volumes; the Kellogg Center for Continuing Education, which also is a laboratory for training in hotel, restaurant and institutional management; the Munn Ice Arena; the Breslin Student Events Center; and the seasonal displays of the Beal Botanical Garden, established in 1873. The Wharton Center for Performing Arts, on the eastern side of campus, offers backstage tours Sun. at 2. Phone (517) 355-4458 for general campus information, (517) 432-2000 for the Wharton Center, or (517) 432-9508 for campus tour information.

Abrams Planetarium is on the Michigan State University campus. The planetarium offers a variety of exhibits about astronomy and features a Digistar II projector. It is recommended that preschool children only attend the family show. Exhibit hall open Mon.-Fri. 8:30-noon and 1-4:30. Planetarium shows Fri.-Sat. at 8 p.m., Sun. at 4. Family show Sun. at

2:30. Exhibit hall and planetarium closed in Aug. Exhibit hall free. Planetarium shows $3; over 64 and students with ID $2.50; under 12, $2. Ticket sales begin 30 minutes prior to show times. Phone (517) 355-4676.

Beaumont Tower is on the Michigan State University campus. On the site of one of the Michigan Agricultural College's original buildings, the tower contains a 49-bell carillon.

Kresge Art Museum is on the Michigan State University campus. Noted for its comprehensive collections of art from many cultures; the museum contains exhibits spanning more than 5,000 years of art history. Changing exhibits are presented. Tours are available by appointment. Mon.-Wed. and Fri. 10-5, Thurs. 10-8, Sat.-Sun. noon-5, Sept.-May; Tues.-Fri. 11-5, Sat.-Sun. noon-5, June-July. Closed major holidays. Free. Phone (517) 355-7631 or (517) 353-9834.

MSU Museum is on campus opposite the library. Three floors display permanent and changing natural and cultural history exhibits. The museum features full dinosaur skeletons and audiovisual presentations. Tours are available. Allow 30 minutes minimum. Mon.-Fri. 9-5, Sat. 10-5, Sun. 1-5; closed major holidays. Donations. Limited metered parking is available. Parking permits are sold in the museum store and at the visitor counter. Phone (517) 355-2370, or (517) 432-1472 for tours.

Television Studio (WKAR-TV) is in the MSU Communication Arts and Sciences Building at Wilson and Red Cedar rds. The studio contains three studios and complete facilities for live programming and student training. Tours are available by appointment. Mon.-Fri. 9-noon and 1-4. Free. Phone (517) 432-3120, ext. 364.

EAST TAWAS (F-5) pop. 2,951, elev. 588'

East Tawas, a resort community on Tawas Bay, offers opportunities for exploring the woodlands of nearby Huron-Manistee National Forests *(see place listing p. 75)*. Fishing is good, particularly for perch, salmon, trout and walleye. Recreational opportunities also are available at Tawas Point State Park *(see Recreation Chart and the AAA Great Lakes CampBook)*.

ELK RAPIDS (E-3) pop. 1,700, elev. 587'

GUNTZVILLER'S SPIRIT OF THE WOODS MUSEUM is 2 mi. s. on US 31. The museum houses collections of American Indian artifacts and dioramas displaying both common and unusual North American animals and fish. Arrowheads, pipes, ceremonial pieces, bows and moccasins are exhibited, while beavers, otters, deer, bison, bears and minks are among the animals shown in natural settings. Collections of early hunting and fishing gear also are displayed.

Allow 1 hour minimum. Mon.-Sat. 9-6, Sun. 11-4, June-Aug.; Mon.-Sat. 9-5, rest of year. Closed Dec. 25. Admission $3; over 64 and students with

ID $2; ages 6-12, $1; two adults $5. DS, MC, VI. Phone (231) 264-5597.

ESCANABA (C-3) pop. 13,140, elev. 598'

The logging industry's hunger for the seemingly inexhaustible stands of Upper Peninsula pine spurred the establishment of Escanaba in the early 1800s. Its excellent deepwater harbor at the mouth of the Escanaba River on Little Bay de Noc also attracted the attention of the various iron enterprises; therefore the town continued to flourish once the virgin forests were depleted.

Second growth forests are the basis for paper and lumber industries. The only ore port on Lake Michigan, Escanaba still ships several million tons of iron ore every year. North of town lies Hiawatha National Forest *(see place listing p. 73)*.

An especially scenic highway is the section of US 2 that extends 143 miles—about 50 of them along the Lake Michigan shore—between Escanaba and St. Ignace *(see place listing p. 98)*. Also see *Upper Peninsula p. 105*.

Delta County Area Chamber of Commerce: 230 Ludington St., Escanaba, MI 49829; phone (906) 786-2192 or (888) 335-8264.

DELTA COUNTY HISTORICAL MUSEUM is in Ludington Park at the e. end of Ludington St. Displays chronicle the development of Delta County and the Upper Peninsula. Items include logging, railroad, shipping, military and household artifacts. A 1905 motor launch powered by a one-cylinder engine also is on display. Allow 30 minutes minimum. Daily 9-5, June-Aug.; 1-4, in Sept. Free. Phone (906) 786-3428.

Sand Point Lighthouse is next door to the Delta County Historical Museum. Restored to its original 1867 appearance, the tower adjoins the keeper's house, furnished in period. Winding stairs lead to the tower's observation deck. Allow 30 minutes minimum. Daily 9-5, June 1-Labor Day; 1-4, day after Labor Day-Sept. 30. Admission $1; under 14, 50c; family rate $3. Phone (906) 786-3763.

FARMINGTON HILLS—*see Detroit p. 63.*

FAYETTE (C-4)

HISTORIC FAYETTE TOWNSITE is off SR 183 in Fayette State Park *(see Recreation Chart)*. The preserved industrial community was founded in 1867 by Jackson Iron Co. manager Fayette Brown. The community thrived after the furnaces began smelting charcoal iron, but when the operation ceased in 1891, the site was abandoned. A self-guiding walking tour begins at the interpretive museum. Along the walk are views of the cliffs and of Lake Michigan.

Museum buildings open daily 9-dusk, mid-June through Labor Day; 9-5, mid-May to mid-June and day after Labor Day to mid-Oct. Park open daily 24 hours. Admission $4 per private vehicle. Phone (906) 644-2603.

FENNVILLE (H-2) pop. 1,459, elev. 664'

WINERIES

- **Fenn Valley Vineyards** is at 6130 122nd Ave. Mon.-Sat. noon-5, Sun. 1-5.; closed Jan. 1, Easter, Thanksgiving and Dec. 25. Phone (269) 561-2396.

FLINT (H-4) pop. 124,943, elev. 800'

From its inception Flint has been associated with transportation. In its early days the site was an important river crossing on the Pontiac Trail, one of the network of Indian routes that crisscrossed the wilderness. The logging boom created the need for katydids—two-wheeled log-hauling contrivances—in addition to road carts and wagons; Flint soon became a major center for their manufacture.

The city's subsequent carriage-making industry quickly gained international repute. Flint remains one of the world's largest manufacturers of carriages of the horseless variety and was where General Motors originated.

Flint Area Convention and Visitors Bureau: 519 S. Saginaw St., Flint, MI 48502; phone (810) 232-8900 or (800) 253-5468.

Shopping areas: Genesee Valley Center Mall, off I-75 at the junction of Miller and Linden roads, offers Marshall Field's, JCPenney and Sears as well as specialty stores and restaurants.

[SAVE] **THE CHILDREN'S MUSEUM** is at 1602 W. Third Ave. The hands-on learning center has exhibits related to science, technology and the arts. Children should be accompanied by an adult. Allow 2 hours minimum. Mon.-Sat. 10-5, Sun. noon-5; closed major holidays. Admission $3; over 60, $2.50; under 1 free. MC, VI. Phone (810) 767-5437.

[SAVE] **CROSSROADS VILLAGE AND HUCKLE-BERRY RAILROAD** is off I-475 exit 13, following signs to 6140 Bray Rd. in the Genesee Recreation Area. The restored 1860-80 Genesee County community features 33 historic structures, including an operating blacksmith shop, cider mill, sawmill, gristmill, general store, school and several residences. Carousel, Ferris wheel and children's amusement rides are available at an additional charge. Food is available.

Huckleberry Railroad is a steam train with open and closed antique passenger cars pulled by a steam powered Baldwin locomotive. It departs from Crossroads Depot for 45-minute trips through the recreation area.

Allow 4 hours minimum. Tues.-Fri. 10-3, Sat.-Sun. 11-5:30, May 12-June 14; Tues.-Fri. 10-5, Sat.-Sun. and holidays 11-5:30, June 15-Aug. 25; Sat.-Sun. 11-5:30 in Sept. Phone for holiday season hours. Closed Thanksgiving and Dec. 24-25. Admission (includes village and train or boat ride) $10; over 59, $9; ages 3-12, $7. Holiday rates vary; phone ahead. MC, VI. Phone (810) 736-7100 or (800) 648-7275.

Genesee Belle is docked inside Crossroads Village. Visitors can take 45-minute sightseeing cruises on Mott Lake. The paddlewheeler departs hourly Tues.-Fri. 12:30-3:30, Sat.-Sun. 1-4, Mother's Day-Labor Day. Admission (includes village and boat ride) $10; over 59, $9; ages 3-12, $7. AX, MC, VI. Phone (810) 736-7100 or (800) 648-7275.

FLINT CULTURAL CENTER is off I-475 exit 8A to 817 E. Kearsley St. The campus includes an art institute, gallery, planetarium, museum, auditorium, youth theater and music center.

[GEM] [SAVE] **Alfred P. Sloan Museum** is at 1221 E. Kearsley St. The museum has a variety of permanent and changing exhibits, highlighting fur trading and pioneer life to lumbering, carriage manufacturing and the General Motors automobile boom. The Buick Gallery displays vintage and experimental prototype automobiles. A Discovery Center features hands-on science displays. Mon.-Fri. 10-5, Sat.-Sun. noon-5; closed holidays. Admission $5; over 55, $4; ages 4-11, $3. MC, VI. Phone (810) 237-3450.

Flint Institute of Arts is at 1120 E. Kearsley St. African, American, Asian, European, impressionist and contemporary art is on display. Tues.-Sat. 10-5, Sun. 1-5; closed holidays. Free. Phone (810) 234-1695.

[SAVE] **Longway Planetarium** is at 1310 E. Kearsley St., across from Whiting Auditorium. The projector reproduces the night sky on a 60-foot dome. Family programs are offered throughout the year; phone for information. Traveling exhibits also are featured. Star shows Sat.-Sun. at 1 and 2:30. Laser light shows Fri.-Sat. evenings; phone ahead for schedule. Admission $5; over 55 and under 12, $4. MC, VI. Phone (810) 237-3400 or (877) 477-8277.

GENESEE RECREATION AREA is 6 mi. n.e. off I-475 exit 13. Covering 4,540 acres along the Flint River, the recreation area contains beaches, bicycle paths, a boat launch, a campground, fishing sites, hiking and horse trails, picnic areas and a recreational vehicle area. After sunset from Memorial Day through Labor Day colored lights play upon Stepping Stone Falls, the spillway of the dam that impounds 600-acre Mott Lake. Free. Phone (810) 736-7100. *See Recreation Chart.*

FRANKENMUTH (G-5) pop. 4,838

Pastors in Bavaria, concerned over the religious life of Lutheran immigrants and their American Indian neighbors, sent a colony to the United States to demonstrate their faith on a day-to-day basis. Fifteen Franconians from Bavaria arrived in the Saginaw Valley in 1845 and named their settlement Frankenmuth, meaning "courage of the Franconians."

The Indian tribe soon moved elsewhere, but the Bavarian heritage remained and was reinforced by other arrivals from Germany. For many years after 1900 German remained the principal language of the community. The Old World atmosphere is still evident in the architecture.

The 35-bell automatic carillon in the Bavarian Inn's Glockenspiel Tower plays selected melodies followed by a presentation of carved wooden figures depicting the legend of the Pied Piper of Hamelin. Nearby is a replica of the 19th-century Holz-Brücke—Frankenmuth's wooden covered bridge that spans the Cass River.

Frankenmuth Chamber of Commerce and Convention and Visitors Bureau: 635 S. Main St., Frankenmuth, MI 48734; phone (800) 386-8696.

Shopping areas: In the center of the business district is School Haus Square. Originally the St. Lorenz Lutheran School, it now houses 25 specialty shops. River Place Shopping Area, 925 S. Main St., features 30 shops and a nightly laser light show. *See color ad p. 294.*

BRONNER'S CHRISTMAS WONDERLAND is 1 mi. s. at 25 Christmas Ln. More than 50,000 Christmas ornaments, lights and decorations—including nativity scenes ranging from tiny hand-carved figures to life-size scenes, animated figures and more than 260 artistically decorated Christmas trees—are displayed. A multi-image presentation offers historical information, and a spectacular outdoor light display is featured every evening. The Bronner's Silent Night Memorial Chapel is open daily. Food is available.

Allow 1 hour, 30 minutes minimum. Mon.-Sat. 9-9, Sun. noon-7, June-Dec.; Mon.-Sat. 9-5:30 (also Fri. 5:30-9), Sun. noon-5:30, rest of year. Closed Jan. 1, Easter, Thanksgiving and Dec. 25; shorter hours on Good Friday and Dec. 24 and 31. Free. Phone (989) 652-9931 or (800) 255-9327. *See color ad.*

FRANKENMUTH HISTORICAL MUSEUM is at 613 S. Main St. Permanent and changing exhibits depict the area's German ancestry and history from American Indian mission days. Mon.-Fri. 10:30-5, Sat. 10-5, Sun. noon-5, June 1-Labor Day; Mon.-Fri. 10:30-7 (also Fri. 7-8 p.m.), Sat. 10-8, Sun. 11-7, day after Labor Day-Dec. 31. Admission $1; under 13, 50c. Phone (989) 652-9701.

FRANKENMUTH RIVERBOAT TOURS is at 445 S. Main St. The tour company offers 45-minute sightseeing cruises on the Cass River. The captain of the *Riverview Queen* narrates Cass River folklore and history. Allow 1 hour minimum. Departures daily on the half-hour, 11:30-4:30 and at 6 and 7, June 1-Labor Day; at 12:30, 2:30, 4:30 and 6 in May and day after Labor Day-Oct. 31 (weather permitting). Fare $6; ages 3-12, $3. Phone (989) 652-8844.

MICHIGAN'S OWN INC.—MILITARY AND SPACE MUSEUM is at 1250 Weiss St. The museum honors Michigan's veterans of the nation's six foreign wars. Included are displays about the famed World War I Polar Bears, an army unit based in northern Russia at the end of the war. Visitors can see the uniforms of the state's Medal of Honor recipients as well as the uniforms and flight suits of Michigan's astronauts.

Another exhibit is dedicated to Michigan's POWs and MIAs from the Vietnam and Persian Gulf wars. Mon.-Sat. 10-5, Sun. 11-5, Mar.-Dec. Admission $3; over 64, $2; ages 6-18, $1. Phone (989) 652-8005.

FRANKFORT (E-1) pop. 1,513, elev. 585'

High bluffs surround the natural harbor of Frankfort, one of northwest Michigan's busiest ports. Beach lovers are drawn to the area's sandy shores, and the city's natural harbor, yacht facilities and launching ramp accommodate boating and fishing. North of the city off SR 22 is the Point Betsie Lighthouse, near the entrance to Sleeping Bear Dunes National Lakeshore (see place listing p. 100).

Some think that Jesuit explorer and missionary Pere Jacques Marquette died at the mouth of Betsie Bay in 1675; a marker and wooden cross signify the supposed site. It is generally believed that he died near Ludington (see place listing p. 81), about 50 miles south.

GAYLORD (E-4) pop. 3,681, elev. 1,348'

In the center of the northern end of the Lower Peninsula, Gaylord is one of the highest incorporated communities in Michigan. The Black, Manistee, Pigeon and Sturgeon rivers and the North Branch of the Au Sable River all rise nearby and flow in different directions.

A sister city to Pontresina, Switzerland, Gaylord maintains the atmosphere of an Alpine village. Buildings of Swiss-style architecture line Main and surrounding streets. An average of nearly 150 inches of snow falls on the town and nearby ski slopes and cross-country trails each year. A Swiss essence also pervades community activities throughout the year.

Gaylord Area Convention and Tourism Bureau: 101 W. Main St., P.O. Box 3069, Gaylord, MI 49734; phone (989) 732-6333 or (800) 345-8621.

CALL OF THE WILD MUSEUM is e. on Main St., then .2 mi. s. to 850 S. Wisconsin Ave. More than 150 lifelike North American wild animals and game birds are displayed. Beavers, elk and polar bears appear in re-created natural settings, complete with sound effects. Allow 1 hour minimum. Daily 8:30 a.m.-9 p.m., mid-June through Labor Day; 9:30-6, rest of year. Closed Jan. 1, Thanksgiving and Dec. 25. Admission $6; over 62, $5.50; ages 5-13, $4. DS, MC, VI. Phone (989) 732-4336.

GERMFASK (B-4) pop. 491

During the lumberjack era Germfask was on the old tote road from Manistique to Seney, 8 miles north. Named by combining the initials of the town founders, the settlement was referred to as the dump because logs were dropped into the Manistique River to be floated to the mill. Also see Upper Peninsula p. 105.

SENEY NATIONAL WILDLIFE REFUGE headquarters entrance is about 2 mi. n. on SR 77. The refuge encompasses 95,000 acres west of the village. More than 200 species of birds as well as beavers, black bears, coyotes, minks, muskrats, otters and white-tailed deer inhabit the refuge. Large numbers of Canada geese breed at the refuge, which also has one of the highest concentrations of nesting loons in the state.

In addition, the refuge shelters nesting populations of bald eagles, ospreys, sandhill cranes and trumpeter swans. Hunting and fishing are permitted in certain areas; check with the refuge office for regulations.

Visitors can follow a 1.5-mile self-guiding walking trail daily dawn-dusk and an unpaved 7-mile self-guiding driving tour route daily dawn-dusk, May 15-Oct. 15. The best times to drive the route or hike the trail are early morning and evening. An orientation slide program is shown at the visitor center, which also includes a touch table and other exhibits. Visitor center open daily 9-5, May 15-Oct. 15. Refuge office open Mon.-Fri. 8-4. Free. Phone (906) 586-9851, ext. 15.

GRAND HAVEN (G-2) pop. 11,168, elev. 603'

At the mouth of the Grand River, Grand Haven benefits equally from its busy port and from the tourists attracted to the beaches, bayous, rolling dunes and wooded hills along Lake Michigan, Spring Lake and Ferrysburg. According to geologists, this is one of the few areas where singing sand is found. When walked upon the tiny sand particles emit a peculiar musical whistle.

Popular beach areas include Grand Haven State Park (see Recreation Chart and the AAA Great Lakes CampBook), 1 mile west, and P.J. Hoffmaster State Park, 10 miles northwest off US 31 (see Recreation Chart). Grand Haven's waterfront features shopping and dining areas and a 2.5-mile boardwalk along the Grand River. The city also has an open-air Farmers Market and Harbourfront Place, a renovated historic piano factory building containing shops and restaurants.

A large musical fountain on Dewey Hill at the waterfront combines light, water and music in nightly concerts held at dusk, Memorial Day through Labor Day and weekends in May and September. During the holiday season it appears as a 40-foot nativity scene and offers evening performances during December.

Trolley car routes through Grand Haven, Spring Lake and Ferrysburg offer convenient access to area attractions and a pleasant way to tour the town. The trolleys operate from Memorial Day through Labor Day. For views from the water there are sailing charters on Lake Michigan and riverboat cruises on the Grand River and Spring Lake. Peak fall color is early to mid-October.

Grand Haven/Spring Lake Visitors Bureau: One S. Harbor Dr., Grand Haven, MI 49417; phone (616) 842-4499 or (800) 303-4096.

HARBOR STEAMER EXCURSION BOAT is docked at Chinook Pier, 301 N. Harbor Dr. The paddle-wheel riverboat escorts visitors on narrated 1- and 1.5-hour scenic cruises of the Grand Haven harbor, Grand River and Spring Lake. Tours depart Tues.-Sat. at 1:30, 3 and 5, Sun. at 3 and 5, June

1-Labor Day. Fare for 1-hour trip $8; ages 5-17, $5. Fare for 1.5-hour trip $10; ages 5-17, $7. Phone (616) 842-8950.

TRI-CITIES HISTORICAL MUSEUM is at Harbor Dr. and Washington St. Displays about the railroad, shipping and lumber industries as well as exhibits about area pioneers and local history are in an original 1868-70 train depot. Allow 1 hour minimum. Tues.-Sat. 10-9:30, Sun. noon-9:30, Memorial Day weekend-Labor Day; Tues.-Fri. 10-5, Sat.-Sun. noon-4, rest of year. Donations. Phone (616) 842-0700.

GRAND RAPIDS (H-2)
pop. 197,800, elev. 610′

Grand Rapids is a vigorous manufacturing, cultural and convention center. It owes its development and its name to the rapids of the Grand River, a place of gathering and exchange since Louis Campau established a trading post in 1826. The water power and transportation afforded by the river and the abundance of wood from the forests made the growth of the furniture industry almost inevitable. By 1900 the city was renowned as a producer of quality office furniture, a reputation it still maintains.

DeVos Place on Monroe Avenue includes large convention and exhibit halls. Also downtown, the Calder sculpture "La Grande Vitesse" pays homage to the rapids *(vitesse).* In contrast are the stolid lines of a reconstructed covered bridge that spans the Thornapple River at Ada, east of Grand Rapids via SR 21.

In the Heritage Hill historic district is the three-story Voigt House Victorian Museum. Built in the late 19th century, the opulent house retains the original furnishings of the Voigt family; phone (616) 456-4600. In nearby Lowell the James C. Veen Observatory is open to the public the second and last Saturdays of each month, weather permitting, April through October; phone (616) 897-7065 after 7:30 p.m. for status.

Broadway shows and performances by the Grand Rapids Ballet, Opera Grand Rapids and the Grand Rapids Symphony are presented at DeVos Performance Hall, on Monroe Avenue N.W. The Grand

Rapids Civic Theatre, 30 N. Division Ave., presents community theatrical performances. Concerts and sporting events are held at the Van Andel Arena, 130 W. Fulton St.

Grand Rapids/Kent County Convention and Visitors Bureau: 140 Monroe Center N.W., Grand Rapids, MI 49503; phone (616) 459-8287 or (800) 678-9859. *See ad.*

BLANDFORD NATURE CENTER is at 1715 Hillburn Ave. N.W. The center is surrounded by 143 acres of fields, forests, ponds and streams. On the grounds are several self-guiding trails. A visitor center has a wildlife care program. Allow 1 hour minimum. Mon.-Fri. 9-5, Sat.-Sun. 1-5; closed holidays. Free. Phone (616) 453-6192.

FISH LADDER SCULPTURE is n. on the Grand River at jct. Leonard and Front sts. The concrete, five-step environmental ladder was built by a local artist to assist salmon in jumping over a 6-foot dam to reach their spawning grounds. Although the leaping fish can be viewed at any time, the best time to see them scale the aquatic steps is late Sept.-late Oct. Daily 24 hours. Free. Phone (800) 678-9859.

 FREDERIK MEIJER GARDENS is n.e. of jct. I-96 exit 38 and E. Beltline at 1000 E. Beltline N.E. The 125-acre gardens and sculpture park contains perennial, American, Victorian, shade and arid gardens as well as seasonal displays in a greenhouse and tropical plants in the Lena Meijer Conservatory, a five-story glass enclosure. A 30-acre outdoor sculpture park boasts more than 100 bronze sculptures by artists of international renown. Most notable is a 24-foot-tall Leonardo da Vinci horse by Nina Akamu. A butterfly exhibit takes place March through April.

Allow 1 hour minimum. Mon.-Sat. 9-5 (also Thurs. 5-9, June-Aug.), Sun. noon-5; closed Jan. 1 and Dec. 25. Admission $7; over 64, $6; ages 5-13, $3.50. Phone (616) 957-1580 or (888) 957-1580.

GERALD R. FORD MUSEUM is off US 131 exit 85B at 303 Pearl St. N.W. The triangular building has a glass wall that mirrors downtown from the west bank of the

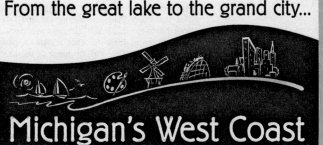

Grand River. Displays portray both the private life and public career of President Ford. Exhibits include a re-creation of the Ford Paint & Varnish Company where the future president worked as a boy as well as information about the October 1973 vice-presidential confirmation hearings when Ford served as House Minority Leader.

Visitors also can take a holographic tour of the White House, observe foreign policy procedures in the White House Situation Room and view the nomination of Ford at the Republican National Convention in 1976. Allow 1 hour minimum. Daily 9-5; closed Jan. 1, Thanksgiving and Dec. 25. Admission $4; over 62, $3; under 16 free. Phone (616) 451-9263.

SAVE **THE GRAND RAPIDS ART MUSEUM** is at 155 Division St. N. Housed in the renovated 1910 Federal Building that served as post office and courthouse, the museum features works from Alexander Calder, Richard Diebenkorn, Childe Hassam and Max Pechstein. Collections include 19th- and 20th-century prints, paintings, photographs, sculptures and decorative arts. A children's gallery features hands-on art and color displays. Tues.-Sun. 11-6 (also Fri. 6-9 p.m.); closed holidays. Admission $5, senior citizens and college students with ID $2; ages 6-17, $1; free to all Fri. after 5. Phone (616) 831-1000 or (616) 831-1001.

GRAND RAPIDS CHILDREN'S MUSEUM is at 11 Sheldon Ave. N.E. Colorful play areas are both recreational and educational. Children can make bubbles, create poems on a large magnetic wall or paint. Hands-on and seasonal exhibits also are presented. Allow 1 hour, 30 minutes minimum. Mon.-Sat. 9:30-5 (also Thurs. 5-8), Sun. noon-5, Memorial Day-Aug. 31. Closed Labor Day, Thanksgiving and Dec. 25. Admission $4, under 2 free. Admission Thurs. 5-8, $1. MC, VI. Phone (616) 235-4726.

SAVE **JOHN BALL ZOO** is at jct. I-196 and SR 45. One of the largest zoos in the state, it houses 1,000 animals from many parts of the world. Of particular interest are the nocturnal animals, snake house, aquarium and children's zoo. Allow 1 hour minimum. Daily 10-6, mid-May through Labor Day; 10-4, rest of year. Admission $4; over 62 and ages 5-13, $2.50; free to all Dec.-Feb. Phone (616) 336-4300 or (616) 336-4301.

VAN ANDEL MUSEUM CENTER OF THE PUBLIC MUSEUM OF GRAND RAPIDS is at 272 Pearl St. N.W. Exhibits depict the heritage and manufacturing traditions of Grand Rapids and include a partially operational reconstruction of an early 20th-century furniture factory. The museum also houses a 76-foot finback whale skeleton as well as an operational Spillman carousel. Visitors can walk through a re-creation of a downtown street in 1890s Grand Rapids. The street includes a theater, a department store, nine other shops and the sounds and sights of the times. Food is available.

Allow 2 hours minimum. Mon.-Sat. 9-5, Sun. noon-5; closed Jan. 1, Easter, Thanksgiving and Dec. 25. Admission $6; senior citizens $5; ages 3-17, $2.50. Carousel ride $1. Phone (616) 456-3977.

The Roger B. Chaffee Planetarium is within the Van Andel Museum Center. Equipped with technical sound, laser and videotape projection equipment, the dome sky theater features performances related to space technology. Phone (616) 456-3663.

GRAYLING (E-3) pop. 1,952, elev. 1,132'

Grayling is on the Au Sable River in one of the Lower Peninsula's leading recreation regions. Although the game fish for which it was named no longer inhabits nearby rivers, the town remains a starting point for trout fishing, canoeing, hunting, cross-country skiing and snowmobiling expeditions. Canoeing is especially popular; canoes, supplies and guides are available in the community.

In spring the rare Kirtland warbler nests in a restricted area east of Grayling. This tiny, elusive songbird winters in the Bahamas. Guided tours of the area are offered by the Department of Natural Resources from mid-May through July 4.

Grayling Visitors Bureau: P.O. Box 217, Grayling, MI 49738; phone (800) 937-8837.

HARTWICK PINES STATE PARK is 7 mi. n.e. on SR 93. The park contains stands of virgin pine and hemlock. The Michigan Forest Visitor Center, a chapel and reproductions of a kitchen, mess hall and workshop from an early logging camp and sawmill are on the grounds. A museum contains displays depicting the state's 19th-century logging industry.

Park open daily 8 a.m.-10 p.m. Visitor center and park buildings open daily 9-7, Labor Day to mid-Oct.; Sat.-Sun. 9-4, rest of year. Admission $4 per private vehicle. Phone (989) 348-7068. *See Recreation Chart and the AAA Great Lakes CampBook.*

GROSSE POINTE
SHORES—*see Detroit p. 63.*

HANCOCK (A-2) pop. 4,323, elev. 607'

Among the many groups of Europeans who settled the Upper Peninsula during the mid-1800s copper boom were Finnish farmers and Cornish miners. Traces of their influence remain. A pasty, the meat pie that often was the lunch of the tough Cornish miners, can still be found. Suomi College in Hancock is the only college in the country founded by Americans of Finnish descent.

Like its sister city Houghton *(see place listing p. 75),* Hancock depends on tourism and commerce along the Keweenaw Waterway. Created by dredging Portage Lake and cutting a canal to Lake Superior, the waterway bypasses the dangerous waters off Keweenaw Point. Rockhounds can find agates along the beach at F.J. McLain State Park, north on

SR 203 *(see Recreation Chart and the AAA Great Lakes CampBook)*. Also north, on US 41, is the Lookout-Historic Monument, which provides fine views of the waterway. *Also see Upper Peninsula p. 105.*

QUINCY MINE HOIST is 1 mi. n. on US 41. A guided tour takes visitors to the seventh level of the mine, about 400 feet underground. The mine houses what is believed to be the largest steam-powered hoist ever manufactured. Weighing 880 tons and occupying a four-story hoist house, it could lift 13 tons of ore in an ore car at 36.4 miles per hour. Structures reflect the site's appearance 1846-1945.

Mon.-Sat. 8:30-7, Sun. 12:30-5, mid-June to late Aug.; Mon.-Sat. 9:30-5, Sun. 12:30-5, late Apr. to mid-June and late Aug.-early Nov. Hours vary; phone ahead. Admission $12.50; senior citizens $11.50; ages 6-12, $7. Phone (906) 482-3101.

HARBOR BEACH (F-6) pop. 1,837, elev. 610′

FRANK MURPHY MEMORIAL MUSEUM is at 142 S. Huron Ave. A collection of historical items relating to the politician—who served as an associate justice of the Supreme Court, mayor of Detroit, governor-general of the Philippines, governor of Michigan and U.S. attorney general—are housed in the Murphy family home. Guided tours are given Thurs.-Mon. 10-4, Memorial Day-Labor Day; closed major holidays. Admission $2; ages 5-12, $1. Phone (989) 479-3363.

HARBOR SPRINGS (D-3) pop. 1,567

On the north shore of Little Traverse Bay, Harbor Springs is both a center for winter recreation and a summer resort. SR 119, a scenic lakeshore drive through the tunnel of trees, passes through Harbor Springs as it travels north to Cross Village.

Harbor Springs Chamber of Commerce: 368 E. Main St., P.O. Box 37, Harbor Springs, MI 49740; phone (231) 526-7999.

HARRIS (C-3) pop. 1,895, elev. 790′

CASINOS

- **Chip-in Island Resort and Casino** is at W399 US 2/41. Write P.O. Box 35, Harris, MI 49845. Daily 24 hours. Phone (906) 466-2941 or (800) 682-6040.

HASTINGS (H-3) pop. 7,095, elev. 790′

[SAVE] **HISTORIC CHARLTON PARK VILLAGE MUSEUM AND RECREATION AREA** is 2 mi. s. on SR 37, then 4 mi. e. on SR 79, following signs. Encompassing more than 300 acres, the complex includes a re-created turn-of-the-20th-century rural Midwestern village and a recreation area with nature trails, picnic areas, playgrounds, a beach and a boat launch. The village contains 16 buildings—among them a carpenter/cooper shop, blacksmith shop, schoolhouse, print shop, general store, barbershop, hardware store, church, town hall and residences.

The museum, which focuses on the Civil War, is furnished in period and contains displays of such items as clocks, firearms, tools and Civil War artifacts. Farm implements are housed in a separate building.

Village and museums daily 8:30-4:30, Memorial Day-Labor Day. Recreation area daily 8 a.m.-9 p.m., Memorial Day-Labor Day. Free. Admission charged for special events. Phone (269) 945-3775.

HERMANSVILLE (C-3) elev. 887′

IXL HISTORICAL MUSEUM is s. from US 2 to First St., then 2.5 blks. w. to IXL Dr. and W. River St. The museum is housed in the offices of the Wisconsin Land & Lumber Company, once the largest hardwood flooring plant in the country. Begun in the 1880s, the brand name was derived from the phrase "I excel." Museum exhibits contain late 19th-century furnishings and office equipment; tools and equipment used in the early lumber era; and the second-story living quarters of the owners and company executives.

Allow 1 hour minimum. Daily 12:30-4, Memorial Day-Labor Day. Admission $2, students with ID $1. Phone (906) 498-2181.

HESSEL (B-5) elev. 603′

CASINOS

- **Kewadin Hessel** is 17 mi. e. on SR 134, then 4 mi. n. on Three Mile Rd. Sun.-Thurs. 9 a.m.-1 a.m., Fri.-Sat. 9 a.m.-2 a.m., May-Oct.; Sun.-Thurs. 9 a.m.-midnight, Fri.-Sat. 9 a.m.-1 a.m., rest of year. Phone (906) 484-2903.

HIAWATHA NATIONAL FOREST

Elevations in the forest range from 580 ft. at Lake Michigan to 960 ft. next to Lake Superior in Munising, Grand Island. Refer to AAA maps for additional elevation information.

With shorelines on lakes Huron, Michigan and Superior, the two portions of the Hiawatha National Forest embrace 893,348 acres of Upper Peninsula and feature the only Great Lakes lighthouses in the national forest system. The broad western unit extends southward from Munising to Rapid Rivers and includes Big Bay de Noc and Little Bay de Noc. The eastern unit reaches from St. Ignace *(see place listing p. 98)* north to Whitefish Bay.

The forest also manages Government Island, one of Les Cheneaux Islands *(see place listing p. 81)*, which offers an unspoiled environment for boating and other outdoor activities. Grand Island National Recreation Area near Munising is adjacent to Pictured Rocks National Lakeshore.

Recreational opportunities in the forest include hunting for black bears, deer, grouse, turkeys and rabbits; fishing for bass, pike, trout and walleye; cross-country skiing and snowmobiling; camping;

canoeing along canoe routes and boating on more than 400 lakes; and hiking or bicycling along miles of trails. Visitors may enjoy a drive along the Lake Superior shoreline on the Whitefish Bay scenic byway.

West of Munising near the town of Christmas are the Bay Furnace ruins, the remains of an 1870s iron furnace. Forest daily 24 hours. Furnace daily dawn-dusk. Free. For further information contact the Forest Supervisor, 2727 N. Lincoln Rd., Escanaba, MI 49829; phone (906) 786-4062. *See Upper Peninsula, Recreation Chart and the AAA Great Lakes CampBook.*

HICKORY CORNERS (H-3) elev. 967'

▼▲ GILMORE CAR MUSEUM is at 6865 Hickory Rd. More than 140 antique, classic and high performance cars show the development of the automobile. American models include Cadillac, Checker, Duesenberg, Ford, Packard and Pierce-Arrow, while Alfa-Romeo, Bentley, BMW, Ferrari, Jaguar, Porsche and Rolls Royce represent European models. Vehicles are exhibited in nine restored antique barns on 90 landscaped acres.

An interpretive center resembling a 1932 Shell filling station displays a 1950 Shell Ford pickup truck, nostalgic signs, tools, photographs, equipment and collections of hood ornaments and car badges. Allow a full day. Daily 10-5, first Sat. in May-last Sun. in Oct. Admission $7; over 62, $6; ages 7-15, $4. MC, VI. Phone (269) 671-5089.

HOLLAND (H-2) pop. 35,048, elev. 612'

Settled by Dutch immigrants in 1847, Holland retains the essence of a Dutch town. Millions of blooming tulips in the parks and neighborhoods provide a spectacular floral display during May.

Seven miles west on Lake Michigan is Holland State Park *(see Recreation Chart and the AAA Great Lakes CampBook).*

Holland Area Convention and Visitors Bureau: 76 E. Eighth St., Holland, MI 49423; phone (800) 506-1299.

Shopping areas: Holland Outlet Center, at US 31 and James Street next to Dutch Village *(see attraction listing),* offers more than 50 factory outlet stores. Westshore Mall, also next to Dutch Village on US 31, features specialty stores as well as JCPenney, Sears and Younker's department stores. More than 100 shops and galleries highlight the downtown area.

[SAVE] CAPPON HOUSE AND SETTLERS HOUSE MUSEUM is at 228 W. 9th St. The Cappon House, built in 1874 in the Italianate and Victorian styles, was the family residence of Isaac Cappon, a Dutch immigrant who was the city's first mayor. A nursery, kitchen, parlor and sitting room are furnished in period with many original furnishings. Displays in the tiny Settlers House reflect the hardships early settlers faced. Both homes are on the National Register of Historic Places.

Allow 30 minutes minimum. Wed.-Sat. 1-4, June-Oct.; Fri.-Sat. 1-4, rest of year. Closed holidays. Admission to both houses $3; over 65 and ages 6-17, $2; family rate $7. Phone (616) 392-6740 or (888) 200-9123.

DE KLOMP WOODEN SHOE AND DELFTWARE FACTORY is at 12755 Quincy St. at US 31 next to Veldheer Tulip Gardens. Self-guiding tours of the premises allow visitors to see craftspeople demonstrate wooden shoe carving and the making of blue and white delftware. Allow 30 minutes minimum. Daily 8 a.m.-9 p.m., in May; Mon.-Fri. 8-6, Sat.-Sun. 9-5, rest of year. Phone ahead for demonstration schedule. Free. Phone (616) 399-1900.

[SAVE] DUTCH VILLAGE is 1 mi. n. of SR 21 on US 31. The village features canals, gardens, windmills, museums, a film, klompen dancers, carving exhibits, a Frisian farmhouse and children's rides. Food is available. Allow 2 hours minimum. Daily 9-5, mid-Apr. to mid-Oct. Admission $7; ages 3-11, $5. AX, DS, MC, VI. Phone (616) 396-1475.

[SAVE] THE HOLLAND MUSEUM is at 31 W. 10th St. Exhibits focus on the early Dutch settlement and development of the city of Holland and include a room from a Dutch fisherman's cottage. Dutch decorative arts and historical collectibles also are featured. Allow 1 hour minimum. Mon. and Wed.-Sat. 10-5 (also Thurs. 5-8), Sun. 2-5. Closed major holidays. Admission $3; family rate $7. MC, VI. Phone (616) 392-9084 or (888) 200-9123.

VELDHEER TULIP GARDENS, 3 mi. n. on US 31 at Quincy St., displays more than 275 varieties of tulips and daffodils during the main flowering season in May in a setting of windmills, drawbridges and canals. A wide selection of bulbs and flowering plants replaces the flowers for the remainder of the year. Daily 8-dusk, in May; Mon.-Fri. 8-6, Sat.-Sun. 9-5 in Apr. and June-Dec.; Mon.-Fri. 9-5, rest of year. Admission $5; ages 3-13, $3. DS, MC, VI. Phone (616) 399-1900.

WINDMILL ISLAND is at Seventh St. and Lincoln Ave. The island is an unusual 30-acre park. Canals, a drawbridge, miniature Dutch village and extensive spring tulip gardens surround the park's main feature, a 1780s operating windmill brought from the Netherlands. Called De Zwaan, the mill produces a fine graham flour. The post house is a replica of a 14th-century Netherlands wayside inn.

A slide presentation is presented all year, and klompen dancing is presented in summer. May through October organ concerts are presented hourly and guided tours are offered. Allow 2 hours minimum. Mon.-Sat. 9-6, Sun. 11:30-6 in May and July-Aug.; Mon.-Sat. 10-5, Sun. 11:30-5 in June and Sept.; Mon.-Fri. 10-4, Sat. 9-4, Sun. 11:30-4, in Oct. Admission $6; ages 5-12, $3. Phone (616) 355-1030.

HOUGHTON (A-2) pop. 7,010, elev. 637'

Houghton shares its multinational origins, copper mining heritage and guardianship of the Keweenaw Waterway with nearby Hancock *(see place listing p. 72)*. The Portage Lake Vertical Lift Bridge links the two cities. Mineralogical interests are served at Michigan Technological University.

The city is the mainland headquarters of Isle Royale National Park *(see place listing p. 77)*. Boat service is available between Houghton and the park June to mid-September. Float plane service is available mid-May through September. *Also see Upper Peninsula p. 105.*

Keweenaw Tourism Council: 326 Shelden Ave., P.O. Box 336, Houghton, MI 49931; phone (800) 338-7982.

A.E. SEAMAN MINERAL MUSEUM is on the fifth floor of the Electrical Energy Resources Center at Michigan Technological University. Displays include copper and silver specimens native to the Upper Peninsula, fluorescent minerals, natural and copper crystals and a simulated iron-manganese cave. Guided tours are offered by appointment. Metered parking is available on Townsend Drive (I-41). Mon.-Fri. 9-4:30 (also Sat. noon-4, July-Sept.); closed university holidays. Schedule may vary; phone ahead. Donations. Phone (906) 487-2572.

HOUGHTON LAKE (F-3) pop. 3,749

Sportsmen and vacationers have replaced the loggers and commercial anglers who once were the vital elements of Houghton Lake. The village is the core of a year-round resort area that borders the lake of the same name. Michigan's largest inland lake, Houghton Lake is 10 miles long and 6 miles wide with a 32-mile shoreline.

Although summer brings boaters and water skiers and winter attracts snow skiers, fishing knows no season. Ice fishing for bluegill, crappie and walleye is popular, and snowmobile trails are prevalent.

Houghton Lake Chamber of Commerce: 1625 W. Houghton Lake Dr., Houghton Lake, MI 48629; phone (989) 366-5644 or (800) 248-5253.

HURON CITY (F-6)

In 1871 and 1881 catastrophic forest fires twice destroyed Huron City, dashing its hopes of becoming a prosperous lumber center. It was reconstructed after these disasters only to be abandoned a short time later when the wells dried up. Not quite a ghost town, Huron City is owned by the William Lyon Phelps Foundation, which operates the remaining buildings as a museum.

[SAVE] **HURON CITY MUSEUMS** are on SR 25. The area consists of several restored buildings—a general store, log cabin, church, carriage shed, inn, U.S. Life Saving Station, barns and an information center—containing a variety of artifacts. The House of Seven Gables is a restored 1881 Victorian mansion with original furnishings. Thurs.-Mon. 10-5,

July 1-Labor Day. Combination buildings and mansion admission $10; over 62, $8; ages 10-15, $5. Buildings or mansion admission $6; over 63, $5; ages 10-15, $3. Phone (989) 428-4123.

HURON-MANISTEE NATIONAL FORESTS

Elevations in the forest range 580 ft. around Lake Michigan to 1,407 ft. at Briar Hills north of Harrietta. Refer to AAA maps for additional elevation information.

In the northern part of the Lower Peninsula, Huron-Manistee National Forests extend over 964,711 acres. Through the Huron National Forest flows the Au Sable River, once heavily used to float logs to the sawmills at East Tawas and Oscoda. The river provides electricity generated by the dams along its course.

The forests offer a variety of outdoor recreational opportunities, including hunting for the morel mushroom in the spring, swimming in lakes Huron and Michigan in the summer and cross-country skiing in the winter. Trout fishing is excellent in many lakes and streams as well as in the Au Sable River. The Au Sable, Manistee, Pine and Pere Marquette rivers in the Manistee National Forest are favorites of canoeists; from mid-May to early September a permit is required to canoe on the Pine and Pere Marquette rivers.

The Nordhouse Dunes are spread across a mile of undeveloped shoreline along Lake Michigan in the Manistee National Forest. The dunes provide opportunities for solitude and seasonal deer hunting. The Loda Lake Wildflower Sanctuary offers a 1-mile trail through marsh, forest and orchard. A 11.5-mile trail offers hiking along the Manistee River and connects to the North Country Trail via a wooden suspension bridge across the river. Together the trails make a 22-mile loop.

The River Road Scenic Byway, in the Huron National Forest, runs 22 miles along the south bank of the Au Sable River. The byway provides vistas of tree-banked reservoirs and offers views of bald eagles, spawning salmon, the Canoeists Memorial and the Lumberman's Monument. Part of the Shore-to-Shore Hiking-Riding Trail also traverses the forest. The North Country Trail offers snowshoeing, camping, backpacking and hiking in the Manistee National Forest.

The Lumberman's Monument, a bronze statue depicting early loggers, overlooks the river valley 10 miles northwest of East Tawas. A visitor center at the monument houses interpretive displays that explore the rich logging legacy of the Au Sable River.

The forests are open daily 24 hours. Information and maps of the Huron National Forest can be obtained at district offices in Oscoda and Mio. Offices in Baldwin, Cadillac and Manistee provide information on the Manistee National Forest; phone (800) 821-6263.

Some areas require a vehicle pass; contact the Huron-Manistee National Forests Headquarters, 1755 S. Mitchell St., Cadillac, MI 49601; phone (231) 775-2421 or (800) 821-6263. *See Recreation Chart and the AAA Great Lakes CampBook.*

INDIAN RIVER (D-4) pop. 2,008

Today's and yesterday's highways intersect at the heart of the inland waterway in Indian River: I-75 crosses the inland waterway that was once used by Indians to avoid the Straits of Mackinac. Nearby Burt Lake State Park offers recreational opportunities *(see Recreation Chart and the AAA Great Lakes CampBook).*

Indian River Chamber of Commerce: 3435 S. Straits Hwy., P.O. Box 57, Indian River, MI 49749; phone (231) 238-9325 or (800) 394-8310.

THE CROSS IN THE WOODS is 1 mi. w. of I-75. Said to be the world's largest crucifix, the 55-foot-high cross weighs 21 tons and is made from one California redwood tree. The 13-acre site has an outdoor church, flower gardens and several shrines. A museum features more than 500 nun and priest dolls dressed in the costumes of different religious orders. Allow 30 minutes minimum. Church open daily dawn-dusk. Museum open daily 9-5, Apr.-Oct. Donations. Phone (231) 238-8973 or (231) 238-8722.

INTERLOCHEN (E-2) elev. 849'

The northern Michigan village of Interlochen is headquarters for the Interlochen Center for the Arts, which includes Interlochen Arts Camp, Interlochen Arts Academy and Interlochen Public Radio. Founded in 1928, the camp enrolls students in music, art, dance and drama for 8 weeks each summer. During the winter students participate in academics and fine arts at the academy.

The 1,200-acre campus includes two large outdoor concert halls, a theater, an art gallery, an indoor auditorium, a chapel/recital hall and a complex of buildings that contains classrooms and studios. For further information contact the Interlochen Center for the Arts, P.O. Box 199, Interlochen, MI 49643; phone (231) 276-7200.

Interlochen Area Chamber of Commerce: P.O. Box 13, 2120 M-137, Interlochen, MI 49643; phone (231) 276-7141.

IRISH HILLS (I-4)

In the verdant, rolling region of the same name, Irish Hills has many lakes and is a popular vacation center. Recreational facilities are available at nearby Walter J. Hayes State Park *(see Recreation Chart and the AAA Great Lakes CampBook).*

MYSTERY HILL is on US 12 opposite Walter J. Hayes State Park. Twenty-minute guided tours are offered through exhibits that seem to defy the laws of gravity, such as water running uphill. A 19-hole miniature golf course and radio-controlled race cars are also offered. Daily 11-7, Memorial Day-Labor

Day; Sat.-Sun. 11-7, day after Labor Day-Sept. 30 Admission $5; ages 4-12, $4. Phone (517) 467-2517.

ST. JOSEPH'S SHRINE is 3 mi. e. of SR 50 on US 12. The shrine sits at the site of an early religious settlement established in the late 1790s by Father Gabriel Richard, minister to the Potawatomi Indians. The church is a combination of the original fieldstone chapel, erected by Irish settlers in the mid-1840s, and a 1929 addition. On the grounds are a life-size crucifixion group and outdoor Stations of the Cross overlooking Iron Lake. Church open daily 8-dusk. Grounds open daily 24 hours. Free. Phone (517) 467-2183.

STAGECOACH STOP, U.S.A. is at 7203 US 12. The re-created 19th-century village contains a general store, trading post, saloons, print shop, ice cream parlor and a bank. More than 10,000 antiques are displayed. There are sawmill demonstrations as well as a wild country train ride, petting zoo, playground, picnic area and children's rides. Staged gunfights and magic shows take place daily. Food is available.

Tues.-Fri. noon-5:30, Sat.-Sun. 10:30-6:30, Memorial Day-Labor Day; closed Tues. following a Mon. holiday. Admission $10; over 65, $8; ages 4-11, $6. AX, DS, MC, VI. Phone (517) 467-2300.

IRON MOUNTAIN (B-2) pop. 8,154

Iron Mountain was established in 1879 following the discovery of rich iron deposits. The mines continued to operate into the 1940s. *Also see Upper Peninsula p. 105.*

Tourism Association of the Dickinson County Area: 600 S. Stevenson St., Iron Mountain, MI 49801; phone (906) 774-2945 or (800) 236-2447.

(SAVE) **CORNISH PUMPING ENGINE AND MINING MUSEUM** is 2 blks. w. of US 2 on Kent St. The museum features one of the largest steam engines built in North America. Displays of mining equipment and artifacts relate the history of mining in the eastern Menominee Range. A World War I glider exhibit also is on display. Mon.-Sat. 9-5, Sun. noon-4, Memorial Day-Labor Day; otherwise varies. Admission $4; over 62, $3.50; ages 10-18, $2. Combination admission with the Menominee Range Historical Foundation Museum $7; over 62, $6; ages 10-18, $3. Phone (906) 774-1086.

(SAVE) **IRON MOUNTAIN IRON MINE** is 8 mi. e. of US 2. The mine, which operated 1877-1945, produced some 21,625,000 tons of ore. Guided tours by rail include demonstrations of mining machinery. Visitors should wear warm clothing. Daily 9-5, Memorial Day to mid-Oct. Admission $7; ages 6-12, $6. Phone (906) 563-8077.

(SAVE) **MENOMINEE RANGE HISTORICAL FOUNDATION MUSEUM** is at 300 E. Ludington St. The museum depicts local history from American Indian habitation to the present through chronological displays and re-created period rooms. Mon.-Sat.

10-4, May-Sept. Admission $4; over 62, $3.50; ages 10-18, $2. Combination admission with the Cornish Pumping Engine and Mining Museum $7; over 62, $6; ages 10-18, $3. Phone (906) 774-4276.

IRONWOOD (B-1) pop. 6,293, elev. 1,500'

Largest city in the Gogebic Range, Ironwood grew with the iron mining boom of the 1880s. It is the main trading, lumber and winter recreation center of the region. An imposing local landmark is the 52-foot colored fiberglass statue of Hiawatha, on Houk Street. *Also see Upper Peninsula p. 105.*

Western Upper Peninsula Convention and Visitors Bureau: 648 W. Cloverland Dr., P.O. Box 706, Ironwood, MI 49938; phone (906) 932-4850.

BLACK RIVER NATIONAL FOREST SCENIC BYWAY—*see Bessemer p. 47.*

RECREATIONAL ACTIVITIES
Skiing

- **Big Powderhorn** is off US 2 to Powderhorn Rd. N. Write N. 11375 Powderhorn Rd., Bessemer, MI 49911. Daily 9-4, mid-Nov. to early Apr. Phone (906) 932-4838.

- **Blackjack** is 6 mi. e. on US 2 to Blackjack Rd., Bessemer, MI 49911. Daily 9-4, early Dec.-late Mar. Phone (906) 229-5115 or (888) 906-9835.

- **Indianhead/Bear Creek** is 2 mi. w. on US 2. Write 500 Indianhead Rd., Wakefield, MI 49968. Daily 9-4, late Nov.-early Apr. Phone (800) 346-3426.

- **Mount Zion** is at 4946 Jackson Rd. Ironwood, MI 49938. Daily 9-4, Dec. 16-Mar 1. Phone (906) 932-3718.

ISHPEMING (B-3) pop. 6,686, elev. 1,434'

In accordance with its name, which is thought to mean heaven, the Marquette iron range city of Ishpeming has become a well-known ski center. Organized skiing began in Ishpeming in 1887, when three Norwegians formed a ski club that eventually grew into a national ski association. *Also see Upper Peninsula p. 105.*

Ishpeming-Negaunee Chamber of Commerce: 661 Palms Ave., Ishpeming, MI 49849; phone (906) 486-4841.

SAVE **U.S. NATIONAL SKI HALL OF FAME AND MUSEUM** is on US 41 between Second and Third sts. at 610 Palms Ave. The greats of American skiing are honored here. The development of the sport is shown through photographs, antique grooming equipment, a cable car, trophies and other memorabilia. An 18-minute orientation videotape also is available.

Allow 1 hour minimum. Mon.-Sat. 10-5; closed Jan. 1, Easter, Thanksgiving and Dec. 25. Admission $3; over 55, $2.50; students with ID $1; under 10 free. MC, VI. Phone (906) 485-6323.

ISLE ROYALE NATIONAL PARK (A-1)

Elevations in the park range from 600 ft. at Lake Superior to 1,394 ft. at Mt. Desor. Refer to AAA maps for additional elevation information.

Northwest of the Upper Peninsula, Isle Royale is the largest island in Lake Superior. Dedicated as a national park in 1946, the main island is about 45 miles long and 8.5 miles across at the widest point. The park boundary extends 4.5 miles offshore. A rugged coastline and numerous crags and ridges add to the park's beauty; 99 percent of the island is wilderness.

Although the soil is only a few inches to a few feet deep, Isle Royale is covered with dense growths of spruce and balsam fir softened by carpets of wildflowers. Beavers, loons, wolves, moose, red foxes and snowshoe hares are abundant in the park. The island is an important research site and is designated as a U.S. Biosphere Reserve.

General Information and Activities

The park is open mid-April through October, with full services from mid-June through Labor Day. The park's 165 miles of trails are rocky and often wet and slippery; proper footwear should be worn when hiking. Visitors planning hiking trips should write for information. Camping is based on a first come-first served basis and is free. Permits are required and are available at ranger stations. Campfires are prohibited at most campgrounds, so visitors should bring self-contained fuel stoves; check with park headquarters or ranger stations.

All surface drinking water must be boiled for 2 minutes or filtered with a .4-micron filter before consumption. Chemical purification will not kill the tapeworm eggs that may exist in the water. No medical facilities are available on Isle Royale.

Swimming in the park is undesirable due to low water temperatures in Lake Superior (35-60 F). Swimming is allowed in the inland lakes; however, there are no lifeguards or beaches. Scuba diving should be attempted only by experienced divers; charters are available. Though a license is not necessary for fishing in the park's inland lakes and streams, Michigan state fishing regulations apply. Only artificial lures are permitted on inland waters. A Michigan state license is required for fishing in Lake Superior's waters. Guides are available for fishing trips.

Travel in the park is on foot or by boat. Boats and motors can be rented and gasoline purchased at Rock Harbor Lodge from late May to mid-September and at Windigo from early June to mid-September. The marina at Rock Harbor Lodge is open from mid-May to mid-September.

Transportation to the park is by boat or seaplane; reservations are recommended. Boat service to the island is available from Copper Harbor aboard the

Isle Royale Queen III mid-May through Sept. 29. Crossings take 4.5 hours one way. Boat service is available from Houghton aboard the park-owned *Ranger III* mid-May to mid-September. Crossings take 6 hours one-way. From Grand Portage, Minn., service is available from the *Wenonah* mid-June to early September; or *Voyageur II* mid-May through October. Crossings to Windigo take 1.5 hours one way, while the voyage to Rock Harbor takes 7 hours one way.

Float plane service also is available from Houghton mid-May to late September. Schedules and information for all vessels can be obtained from park headquarters. *See Upper Peninsula, the Recreation Chart and the AAA Great Lakes CampBook.*

WARNING— Crossing Lake Superior to the park in a craft less than 20 feet long is not advised. Private outboards, canoes, kayaks and boats up to 20 feet long may be transported on the *Ranger III* out of Houghton. Gasoline is available on the island but may not be carried on private boats.

ADMISSION is $4 per day, under 12 free. There are costs for transportation to the park.

PETS are not permitted in the park, including 4.5 miles offshore and on private or commercial vessels going to the park.

ADDRESS inquiries to park headquarters at Isle Royale National Park, 800 E. Lakeshore Dr., Houghton, MI 49931-1869, or phone (906) 482-0984. Reservations for Rock Harbor Lodge or housekeeping cabins should be made with National Park Concessions Inc., Mammoth Cave, KY 42259-0027, (502) 773-2191, or from mid-May to mid-September with Rock Harbor Lodge, P.O. Box 605, Houghton, MI 49931-0605, (906) 337-4993.

Points of Interest

Beginning some 4,000 years ago, the park was mined for copper—evidence that the island might have been the source of much of the copper used by early American Indians. The metal has been found throughout the Ohio and Mississippi valleys. Mining activity also took place in the late 1800s on Isle Royale.

GREENSTONE RIDGE AND MINONG TRAILS generally follow the prominent ridges after which they are named. The Greenstone Ridge Trail permits access to points at either end of the island.

MOUNT FRANKLIN is reached by a scenic hike from the head of Tobin Harbor or by trail from Rock Harbor.

MOUNT OJIBWAY is reached by a 1.7-mile hike from Daisy Farm Campground. The peak affords a view of the surrounding countryside.

ROCK HARBOR LIGHTHOUSE is 6 mi. by launch from Rock Harbor Lodge. The restored 1855 lighthouse is reached by a .3-mile trail from the Edisen Fishery.

JACKSON (I-4) pop. 36,316, elev. 942'

Although the Republican Party itself was founded in Ripon, Wis., in 1854, Jackson played host to the party's first formal meeting. The city also was one of the key stops on the Underground Railroad. Some of the houses that served as way stations and sanctuaries still can be seen. Today diversified industry and transportation services anchor Jackson's economy. With 188 lakes, the area offers plenty of recreational opportunities.

Jackson County Convention and Visitors Bureau: 6007 Ann Arbor Rd., Jackson, MI 49201; phone (517) 764-4440 or (800) 245-5282.

Shopping areas: Jackson Crossing Mall, at the junction of US 127 and I-94, features Kohl's, Sears and Toys R Us; Westwood Mall, at Michigan Avenue and Brown Street, features Elder-Beerman and JCPenney.

[SAVE] **CASCADES AT SPARKS FOUNDATION COUNTY PARK** is s.w. of city limits at jct. Brown and Denton sts. The park occupies 465 acres and contains the Illuminated Cascades—a giant waterfall and six fountains over which water tumbles in continually changing patterns. There also is a small museum depicting the history of Cascades Falls, two golf courses, tennis courts, a picnic area, lagoons, paddleboats, batting cages and a miniature golf course.

Park open daily until 11 p.m. Illuminated Cascades can be seen 7:30-11 p.m., Memorial Day-Labor Day. Park free. Admission to Cascades $3, under 6 free. Phone (517) 788-4320.

ELLA SHARP PARK is 2 mi. s. on 4th St. The largest park in the city, it covers 562 partially wooded acres. On the grounds are athletic fields, bicycle and jogging paths, cross-country ski trails, an 18-hole golf course, a driving range, a miniature golf course, picnic areas, nature trails and a swimming pool. Food is available. Daily 24 hours. Free. Phone (517) 788-4343. *See Recreation Chart.*

[SAVE] **Ella Sharp Museum** is at 3225 4th St. The museum provides a look at 19th-century farmstead life. It includes a Victorian house; a pioneer log house; a barn with 1800s carriages, sleighs and farm implements; a woodshop; an 1885 one-room schoolhouse; and a country store complex featuring a print shop and doctor's office. The museum also features modern art exhibition galleries. Guided tours of the Victorian house are included. Food is available.

Tues.-Fri. 10-4, Sat.-Sun. 11-4; closed major holidays. Last tour begins 30 minutes before closing. Museum $4; over 55 and students with ID $3; ages 5-18, $2; family rate (2 adults and 2 children under 18) $10. DS, MC, VI. Phone (517) 787-2320.

[GEM] **MICHIGAN SPACE AND SCIENCE CENTER** is on the Jackson Community College campus at 2111 Emmons Rd. A striking [SAVE] gold geodesic dome houses the *Apollo 9* command module, a memorial to the space shuttle

Challenger, space suits, satellites, a moon rock, the Astrotheatre, an infinity room, a model of the Hubble Space Telescope and a Mars PathFinder exhibit. Other displays deal with past and future space voyages, black holes and a space capsule into which visitors may climb. There are several interactive computer exhibits. Outside is an 85-foot Mercury Redstone rocket as well as rocket engines and missiles. Picnic facilities are available.

Allow 1 hour minimum. Tues.-Sat. 10-5, Sun. noon-5, May-Oct.; Tues.-Sat. 10-5, rest of year. Closed Jan. 1, Thanksgiving and Dec. 25. Last tour begins 1 hour before closing. Admission $4, over 60 and students with ID $2.75, under 5 with parent free. DS, MC, VI. Phone (517) 787-4425.

KALAMAZOO (I-2) pop. 77,145, elev. 792′

Springs bubbling up in the riverbed are said to have been the inspiration for Kalamazoo's catchy name, an American Indian word meaning "place where the water boils." Whatever its origin, Kalamazoo has enlivened many a poem and song.

Produce from the nearby vegetable-growing region and the diverse yields of many industries provide the basis of Kalamazoo's economy. Western Michigan University and other schools contribute to the city's cultural life. River Oaks Park and Bronson Park are sites for numerous festivals.

Kalamazoo County Convention and Visitors Bureau: 346 W. Michigan St., P.O. Box 1169, Kalamazoo, MI 49007; phone (269) 381-4003.

 KALAMAZOO AVIATION HISTORY MUSEUM (AIR ZOO) is off I-94 exit 78, .7 mi. s. on Portage Rd., then .5 mi. e. to 3101 E. Milham Rd. Museum exhibits include rare planes dating from pre-World War II, most of which still fly, and several aircraft used in Korea and Vietnam. Among the collection of more than 70 vintage aircraft are a Curtiss P-40 and four Grumman Cats. Flying demonstrations are held daily at 2, May through September (weather permitting).

Among the displays are several functioning aircraft engines, a USMC jeep, memorabilia and more than 100 model aircraft. Highlights include the Guadalcanal Memorial Museum; Simulation Station, which features Hudson full-motion flight simulators and trainers; and the Michigan Aviation Hall of Fame. Videotape presentations are shown continuously. Guided tours of the restoration center are available. Rides in a 1929 Ford Tri-Motor are available May through October.

Allow 1 hour, 30 minutes minimum. Mon.-Sat. 9-6, Sun. noon-6, June-Aug.; Mon.-Sat. 9-5; Sun. noon-5, rest of year. Closed Jan. 1, Easter, Thanksgiving and Dec. 24-25. Admission $10; over 60, $8; ages 6-15, $5. AX, DS, MC, VI. Phone (269) 382-6555.

KALAMAZOO INSTITUTE OF ARTS is at 314 S. Park St. The complex combines galleries, a school, a library and an auditorium in a contemporary structure. Displayed in the galleries are permanent and temporary exhibits of 20th-century American art, European prints and works from Michigan artists. Tues.-Sat. 10-5 (also Thurs. 5-8), Sun. noon-5, Sept.-July; Tues.-Sat. 10-5, rest of year. Closed major holidays. Donations. Phone (269) 349-7775.

KALAMAZOO NATURE CENTER is at 7000 N. Westnedge Ave. The area's natural history is illustrated through an interactive exhibit at the center, which is situated on a 1,000-acre preserve. Visitors can enjoy nature trails and an 11-acre arboretum with a hummingbird and butterfly garden. A sun/rain room features tropical birds, geckos and tropical fish. A restored pioneer homestead is open during special events, and a petting farm is operated May through September. Tours are available by appointment.

Nature center and grounds Mon.-Sat. 9-5, Sun. and holidays 1-5; closed Jan. 1, Thanksgiving and Dec. 24-25. Admission $4.50; over 54, $3.50; ages 4-13, $2.50. Phone (269) 381-1574.

KALAMAZOO VALLEY MUSEUM is at 230 N. Rose St. on the Arcadia Commons Campus of the Kalamazoo Valley Community College. Permanent exhibits include a 2,500-year-old mummy and science and history galleries that house interactive exhibits, photographs and artifacts. Mini-missions simulate a trip to Mars in the Challenger Learning Center. The Digistar II Planetarium and Theater also are available.

Mon.-Sat. 9-5 (also Wed. 5-8), Sun. 1-5; closed major holidays. Phone for program schedules. Challenger admission $3. Planetarium admission $3. Museum free. Under 12 must be accompanied by an adult in the Challenger center. Under 6 are not permitted. Phone (269) 373-7990.

WINERIES

• **Peterson & Sons Winery** is s. off I-94 exit 85, following signs to 9375 E. P Ave. Mon. and Fri.-Sat. 10-6, Sun. noon-6; closed major holidays. Phone (269) 626-9755.

LANSING (H-3) pop. 119,128, elev. 843′

Lansing became the permanent state capital in 1847 more by default than design. Weary of wrangling and unable to suggest a better place, the legislature—amid laughter because the chosen site then consisted of one log cabin and a sawmill—gave the honor to Lansing. Because proponents of renaming the new capital Michigan or Michigamme reached a similar impasse, Lansing it remained.

Once the decision was made, the town began to grow. By the time it was incorporated in 1859, there were some 4,000 enterprising residents, an increasing number of small industries, a new brick Capitol and two newspapers that provided more political entertainment than news.

The real industrial flowering of the city is credited to R.E. Olds, whose buggy was one of the first practical motor vehicles. By the early 1900s Lansing was a leading maker of automobiles and gasoline engines. Although its economy is more diversified, Lansing is still a stronghold of the automotive industry. The atmosphere of manufacturing and government is leavened with that of education by Michigan State University and its many points of interest *(see East Lansing p. 66)*.

Greater Lansing Convention and Visitors Bureau: 1223 Turner St., Suite 200, Lansing, MI 48906; phone (888) 252-6746 or (800) 648-6630.

CARL G. FENNER NATURE CENTER is at 2020 E. Mount Hope Ave. The center has 4 miles of nature trails, an herb garden, a butterfly garden and a visitor center building with reptiles, amphibians, native birds and environmental displays. Picnicking is permitted.

Grounds daily 8-dusk. Visitor center Tues.-Fri. 9-4, Sat.-Sun. 11-5, mid-Mar. through Nov. 30; Sat.-Sun. 11-5, rest of year. Closed Jan. 1, Easter, Thanksgiving, day after Thanksgiving, and Dec. 22-25 and 29-31. Free. Phone (517) 483-4224.

 IMPRESSION 5 SCIENCE CENTER is at 200 Museum Dr. Housed in a renovated century-old building with original wood floors and brick walls, the hands-on museum has a chemistry lab and displays about energy, water, chemistry, simple mechanics, medicine and physics. Allow 2 hours minimum. Mon.-Sat. 10-5; closed major holidays and Dec. 24. Admission $5; over 62 and ages 3-17, $3.50. AX, DS, MC, VI. Phone (517) 485-8116.

MICHIGAN LIBRARY AND HISTORICAL CENTER COMPLEX is at 717 W. Allegan St. The museum has displays about state history from prehistoric times to the late 20th century. Twenty-six permanent galleries and a temporary exhibit area feature a three-story relief map; a re-created, walk-through copper mine; a one-room schoolhouse; a 1920s street scene; and a large diorama. The center also houses the state library and archives. Museum open Mon.-Fri. 9-4:30, Sat. 10-4, Sun. 1-5; closed holidays. Free. Phone (517) 373-3559 for the museum, (517) 373-1300 for the library or (517) 373-1408 for the archives.

MICHIGAN WOMEN'S HISTORICAL CENTER & HALL OF FAME is at 213 W. Main St. Rotating exhibits call attention to the lives, history and achievements of Michigan women. An art gallery features the work of outstanding artists and photographers, while the Michigan Women's Hall of Fame honors those who have made significant contributions to the state. Allow 30 minutes minimum. Wed.-Fri. noon-5, Sat. noon-4, Sun. 2-4; closed major holidays. Admission $2.50; over 60, $2; ages 5-18, $1. MC, VI. Phone (517) 484-1880.

MUSEUM OF SURVEYING is .2 mi. w. on Michigan Ave., then .2 mi. s. to 220 S. Museum Dr. The museum houses a collection of historical land surveying artifacts. Educational programs, archives and a videotape library also are available. Allow 30 minutes minimum. Mon.-Fri. 9-4; closed major holidays. Free. Phone (517) 484-6605.

POTTER PARK ZOO is at 1301 S. Pennsylvania Ave. Primates, lions, penguins, snow leopards, rhinoceroses, reptiles, farm animals and birds live at the zoo. Pony rides are offered in summer, and light shows are presented late November through December. Picnicking is permitted. Food is available. Allow 1 hour minimum. Park open daily 9-5. Buildings open daily 10-5. Admission $5; over 59, $3; ages 3-15, $1. Parking $2; oversized vehicles Sat.-Sun. $5. Phone (517) 483-4222.

R.E. OLDS TRANSPORTATION MUSEUM is .2 mi. w. on Michigan Ave., then .2 mi. s. to 240 Museum Dr. Artifacts and documents trace the history of area transportation from 1883 to the present. Antique vehicles and automotive memorabilia as well as aircraft, bicycles and carriages are displayed. Automobiles exhibited range from the first Oldsmobile, built in 1897 to contemporary vehicles. Guided tours are available by request.

Allow 30 minutes minimum. Tues.-Sat. 10-5, Sun. noon-5, May-Oct.; Tues.-Sat. 10-5, rest of year. Closed most holidays. Admission $4; over 60, ages 6-17 and students with ID $2; family rate $8. MC, VI. Phone (517) 372-0422 or (517) 372-0529.

STATE CAPITOL is at Capitol and Michigan aves. One of the first state capitols designed to resemble the U.S. Capitol, it was dedicated in 1879 and since has been restored to reflect that period. Tours lasting 45 minutes are offered every 30 minutes Mon.-Fri. 9-4, Sat. 10-3. Free. Phone (517) 373-2353.

LELAND (E-2) pop. 2,033, elev. 656′

The village of Leland, bordered by Lake Michigan to the west and Lake Leelanau to the east, is a popular departure point for lake cruises and fishing charters. Settled in 1853, Leland was named by the many sailors who used the harbor. On the harbor is Fishtown, a collection of shops, galleries and art studios in a rustic fishing village setting.

Passenger ferry service is available to the North and South Manitou islands *(see Sleeping Bear Dunes National Lakeshore p. 100)* by Manitou Island Transit. Daily service is provided to South Manitou Island, while transportation to North Manitou Island is available daily July 1 to mid-Aug.; Wed., Fri. and Sun., June 1-15; Wed. and Fri.-Mon., June 16-30. Reservations are recommended. Tours of South Manitou Island also are available. Phone (231) 256-9061.

LEELANAU HISTORICAL MUSEUM is at 203 E. Cedar St. Permanent and changing historical displays document the settlement and development of the Leelanau peninsula. Traditional and folk arts exhibits also are included. Allow 30 minutes minimum. Mon.-Sat. 10-4, Sun. 1-4, mid-June through Labor Day; Fri.-Sat. 1-4 and by appointment, rest of year. Closed holidays. Admission $1; ages 5-11, 50c. VI. Phone (231) 256-7475.

WINERIES

• **Good Harbor Vineyards** is 3 mi. s. on SR 22. Mon.-Sat. 11-6, Sun. noon-6, mid-May through day before Labor Day; Mon.-Sat. 11-5, Sun. noon-5, Labor Day-Oct. 30; Sat. 11-5, Nov.-Dec. Phone (231) 256-7165.

LES CHENEAUX ISLANDS (B-6)

The many bays and channels *(cheneaux)* created by the 36 wooded islands that dot Lake Huron off the south shore of the eastern Upper Peninsula account for the islands' name as well as their popularity. This is one of the most scenic snowmobiling, boating and fishing areas in the state. Government Island is maintained as an uninhabited isle by the Hiawatha National Forest *(see place listing p. 73).*

The islands can be reached from both Hessel and Cedarville. An information center on SR 134 at Cedarville is open Mon.-Fri. 9-5.

Les Cheneaux Area Welcome Center: P.O. Box 10, Cedarville, MI 49719; phone (906) 484-3935 or (888) 364-7526.

LIVONIA—*see Detroit p. 64*

LUDINGTON (F-1) pop. 8,357, elev. 593′

Ludington is a popular fishing center and port on the eastern shore of Lake Michigan at the mouth of the Pere Marquette River. Freighters and pleasure craft find safe deepwater harborage in Pere Marquette Lake. Chinook, coho and king salmon can be caught in Lake Michigan and in the Pere Marquette River.

The SS *Badger*, operated by the Lake Michigan Carferry Service, offers 4-hour cruises and automobile ferry service from Ludington to Manitowoc, Wis. For information and fares phone (800) 841-4243. *See color ad p. 81 & p. 144.*

The huge illuminated cross that overlooks the harbor marks the spot where Pere Jacques Marquette is thought to have died in 1675. Eight miles north on SR 116, Ludington State Park *(see Recreation Chart and the AAA Great Lakes CampBook)* borders both Lake Michigan and Hamlin Lake and offers fine beaches, dunes and a visitor center.

Ludington Area Convention and Visitors Bureau: 5827 US 10W, Ludington, MI 49431; phone (231) 845-5430 or (800) 542-4600.

SAVE **HISTORIC WHITE PINE VILLAGE** is 2 mi. s. via Pere Marquette Hwy. to Iris Rd., then w. 1.5 mi. to 1687 S. Lakeshore Dr. This reconstructed community of 22 1850-1950 buildings overlooks Lake Michigan. Included are a blacksmith shop, courthouse, hardware store, fire hall, chapel and schoolhouse along with music, logging and maritime museums. Self-guiding tours are available. Picnicking is permitted.

Allow 1 hour, 30 minutes minimum. Tues.-Sat. 11-5, Apr.-Oct. Admission $5; over 59, $4.50; ages 6-17, $4; family rate (parents or grandparents and children under 18) $15. Admission is slightly higher during events. MC, VI. Phone (231) 843-4808.

MACKINAC ISLAND (C-6) pop. 523

American Indians called it Michilimackinac, or "Great Turtle," but time and usage have shortened the island's name to Mackinac (MACK-i-naw). This limestone outcrop became a frontier outpost in 1780, when the English moved the old French garrison on the mainland to the more strategic island.

It remained the stronghold of the Straits of Mackinac for 115 years.

The island is 3 miles long and 2 miles wide with high cliffs fronting the shore. Ravines, natural bridges, caves and strange rock formations can be found. Arch Rock and Sugar Loaf are scenic points. Mackinac Island State Park is particularly attractive in mid-June when the lilacs bloom.

The island can be reached by boat from St. Ignace or Mackinaw City *(see place listings p. 98 and p. 84).* Summer sports facilities include a yacht harbor and golf courses. Pets must be physically restrained at all times. Accommodations are available from mid-May to late October and mid-December to March.

Ferry service from St. Ignace to Mackinac Island operates from early May through October. For schedules and prices, contact Arnold Mackinac Island Ferry, (906) 847-3351 or (800) 542-8528. *See color ad p. 83.* SAVE Shepler's Mackinac Island Ferry, (906) 643-9440, (231) 436-5023 or (800) 828-6157. See color ad p. 84; or Star Line Mackinac Island Hydro-Jet Ferry, (906) 643-7635 or (800) 638-9892. *See color ad.*

Once on the island, transportation is by horse-drawn carriage, bicycle or saddle horse; no motorized vehicles are permitted, except for a public utilities truck, a fire truck and an ambulance. For this reason, SR 185, which rims the island, is possibly the only state highway in the nation on which a motor vehicle accident has never occurred. Bicycles may be brought over on the ferry or rented on the island.

Mackinac Island Chamber of Commerce: Main St., P.O. Box 451, Mackinac Island, MI 49757; phone (906) 847-3783 or (800) 454-5227.

CARRIAGE TOURS depart from the center of the shopping district on Main St. Narrated tours (lasting 1 hour, 45 minutes) visit Mackinac Island's scenic and historic points of interest, including Arch Rock, Fort Mackinac, Governor's Mansion, the Grand Hotel, Skull Cave and Surrey Hill. Daily 9-5, mid-June through Labor Day; 9-3, mid-May to mid-June and day after Labor Day-Oct. 31. Fare $16; ages 4-11, $7.50. Phone (906) 847-3307.

EARLY MISSIONARY BARK CHAPEL is in Marquette Park. The church is a reconstruction patterned after chapels built on the island in the late 1600s. The original was erected by early Jesuit missionaries. Daily 9:30-5, mid-May to mid-Oct. Free. Phone (906) 847-3328.

FORT MACKINAC is on a bluff overlooking the harbor. The restored 18th- and 19th-century British and American military outpost is preserved as a museum. All the buildings are original; their history is interpreted through period settings, audiovisual presentations and the children's discovery room. Costumed guides offer reenactments, military music and cannon and rifle firings. Food is available.

Daily 9:30-6, mid-June to late Aug.; otherwise varies, early May to mid-June and late Aug.-early Oct. Admission $9; ages 6-17, $5.75 (admission June 14-Aug. 24 includes Dr. Beaumont Museum, Benjamin Blacksmith Shop, Biddle House, Mission Church and McGulpin House). Combination admission with Colonial Michilimackinac and Historic Mill Creek *(see Mackinaw City p. 84)* $18; ages 6-17, $10.50; annual family pass $49. MC, VI. Phone (906) 847-3328 or (231) 436-4100.

Benjamin Blacksmith Shop is on Market St. Demonstrations using original 19th- and 20th-century blacksmith equipment are offered. Daily 11-6, mid-June to late Aug.

Biddle House is on Market St. The house contains early 19th-century furnishings. Domestic craft demonstrations are offered. Daily 11-6, mid-June to late Aug.

Dr. Beaumont Museum is on Fort St. Housed in the restored 1820 American Fur Company Store, the museum is dedicated to Dr. William Beaumont, who pioneered studies of the human digestive system. His medical instruments are on display and are explained by costumed interpreters. Daily 11-6, mid-June to late Aug.

McGulpin House is on Fort St. An example of French-Canadian architecture, the house may have been one of the buildings brought to Mackinac Island from Fort Michilimackinac, established in 1780. Daily 11-6, mid-June to late Aug.

Mission Church is 1 mi. e. on Huron St. The church is the first Protestant work of the American Indians at Fort Mackinac and is said to be the oldest surviving church in the state. It was built in 1829 by local residents in the New England Colonial style and contains an antique organ. Allow 30 minutes minimum. Daily noon-4, mid-June to late Aug.

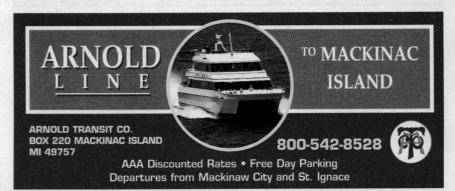

MACKINAW CITY (D-3) pop. 859, elev. 591'

First a guardian of the Straits of Mackinac, now a destination for thousands of northbound vacationers, Mackinaw City was once a trading post established by early French settlers; the post became Fort Michilimackinac in 1715. During the ensuing decades the strategically situated garrison was held successively by the French, the British, the Indians, then the British again. The British moved the fort to Mackinac Island 1780-81.

The city is connected to the Upper Peninsula by way of the Mackinac Bridge. One of the longest suspension spans in the world, it stretches for 5 miles. Built in 1957, it provided a convenient means of transportation between the two peninsulas. The toll is $1.50.

Mackinaw Area Visitors Bureau: 10300 US 23, P.O. Box 160, Mackinaw City, MI 49701; phone (231) 436-5664 or (800) 666-0160. *See color ad p. 85 & p. 334.*

Shopping areas: Mackinaw Crossing, at 248 S. Huron Ave., is a shopping, dining and entertainment complex containing a five-screen movie theater, restaurants, stores and courtyards. Varied shops line Central Avenue (Main Street).

 COLONIAL MICHILIMACKINAC is on the site of Fort Michilimackinac. The fort comprises 27 acres. Built by the French in 1715, it was occupied by British forces 1761-1781. Among the reconstructed buildings are a priest's house, a guardhouse, blockhouses, barracks, a storehouse, a blacksmith shop, a French church and a British trader's house.

Costumed reenactments, an audiovisual program and exhibits illustrate the history of the fort. Other programs include blacksmithing and cooking demonstrations, musket and cannon firings, a Colonial wedding and dance, an American Indian encampment, an archeological tunnel exhibit and the arrival of French voyageurs. Archeological excavations are conducted daily mid-June through Labor Day.

Allow 2 hours minimum. Daily 9-6, mid-June to late Aug.; otherwise varies, early May to mid-June and late Aug.-early Oct. Admission $9; ages 6-17,

$5.75. Combination admission with Fort Mackinac (*see Mackinac Island p. 83*) and Historic Mill Creek $18; ages 6-17, $10.50; annual family pass $49. DS, MC, VI. Phone (231) 436-4100.

HISTORIC MILL CREEK is 3 mi. s.e. on US 23. This is the site of an 18th-century industrial complex believed to be the oldest in the Great Lakes region. A water powered sawmill built about 1790 provided lumber for construction on Mackinac Island. Archeological evidence of the sawmill, a dam and several houses was discovered in 1972 by a Cheboygan high school history teacher.

Demonstrations of sawmill operations are given daily. Interpretive nature trails lead to scenic overlooks, including a view of the Mackinac Bridge and a beaver colony. There is a 12-minute audiovisual orientation. Food is available.

Daily 9-5, mid-June to late Aug.; 9-4, early May to mid-June and late Aug.-early Oct. Admission $7.50; ages 6-17, $4.50. Combination admission with Fort Mackinac (*see Mackinac Island p. 83*) and Colonial Michilimackinac $18; ages 6-17, $10.50; annual family pass $49. DS, MC, VI. Phone (231) 436-4100.

MACKINAC BRIDGE MUSEUM is at 231 E. Central Ave. Memorabilia and artifacts pertain to the history and construction of the Mackinac Bridge. A film about the bridge is presented continuously. Food is available. Allow 30 minutes minimum. Daily 8 a.m.-midnight, May-Oct. Free. Phone (231) 436-5534.

MANISTEE (F-2) pop. 6,586, elev. 598′

As early as 1790 French and English fur traders inhabited the area that the Chippewa called Manistee, "spirit of the woods." The 19th-century logging frenzy ensured that the name would outlive the woods, yet the people—mainly Swedes and Norwegians—who came to shear the timber stayed to develop the city.

The port handles the deluge of fruit grown in the area. Vast brine deposits make Manistee a primary producer of salt.

Manistee Area Chamber of Commerce: 50 Filer St., Suite 224, Manistee, MI 49660; phone (800) 288-2286.

Self-guiding tours: Relics of the logging era, many ornate Victorian mansions line the residential streets, and refurbished buildings can be found in the commercial section. Walking tour brochures are available at the chamber of commerce and the Lyman Building.

MANISTEE COUNTY HISTORICAL MUSEUM is at 425 River St. Historical exhibits are housed in the old A. H. Lyman Company store. Displays include the fittings of an 1885 drugstore and general store, photographs and exhibits of Civil War and pioneer memorabilia. Allow 1 hour minimum. Mon.-Sat. 10-5, June-Sept.; Tues.-Sat. 10-5, rest of year. Closed holidays except July 4. Admission $2; family rate $5. Phone (231) 723-5531.

Water Works Building is at 540 W. First St. Built in 1882, it houses marine and logging exhibits. Allow 30 minutes minimum. Tues.-Sat. 10:30-4:30, mid-June to late Aug. Donations. Phone (231) 723-5531.

CASINOS

- **Little River Casino** is at 2700 Orchard Hwy. Daily 24 hours. Phone (231) 723-1535. *See color ad.*

MANISTIQUE (B-4) pop. 3,583, elev. 613′

Manistique provides access to the 300 lakes and numerous streams of the Lake Superior State Forest and 135 miles of maintained snowmobile trails. The bridge carrying SR 94 across the Manistique River is unusual in that its floor is below river level.

Palms Book State Park, 12 miles northwest, is best known for Kitch-iti-ki-pi, a clear, cold spring 200 feet wide and 40 feet deep. Seven miles southwest via US 2 and SR 149 is the state fish hatchery that introduced the coho salmon into Michigan waters to counteract the invasion of alewives that followed the opening of the St. Lawrence Seaway.

A scenic portion of US 2 passes through Manistique on its way from Escanaba *(see place listing p. 67)* to St. Ignace *(see place listing p. 98)*. About one-third of the distance follows the shore of Lake Michigan. *Also see Upper Peninsula p. 105.*

Schoolcraft County Chamber of Commerce: 1000 W. Lake Shore Dr., Manistique, MI 49854; phone (906) 341-5010.

CASINOS

- **Kewadin Casino** is 4.5 mi. e. on US 2. Daily 24 hours, May-Oct.; 8 a.m.-3 a.m., rest of year. Phone (906) 341-5510.

MARQUETTE (B-3) pop. 19,661, elev. 636′

First settled in 1849 as a shipping center, Marquette was named for the French missionary and explorer Father Jacques Marquette. Surrounded by the rugged Laurentian Uplands on the southern shore of Lake Superior, the city is heralded as the medical, shopping and political center of the Upper Peninsula. The wooden dome at Northern Michigan University's Great Lakes Sports Training Center offers football, soccer and an Olympic training facility.

Marquette is the western terminus of a scenic 42-mile drive that is US 41 for a few miles south, then SR 28 along the lakeshore to Munising *(see place listing p. 90)*. *Also see Upper Peninsula p. 105.*

Marquette Country Convention and Visitors Bureau: 2552 US 41W, Suite 300, Marquette, MI 49855; phone (906) 228-7749 or (800) 544-4321.

Self-guiding tours: Walking tour maps of historic Marquette can be purchased at the Marquette County History Museum, 213 N. Front St., Marquette, MI 49855; phone (906) 226-3571.

MARQUETTE COUNTY HISTORY MUSEUM is at 213 N. Front St. Visitors can see pioneer artifacts and mining and lumber displays. Mon.-Fri. 10-5 (also third Thurs. of the month 5-9), Sat. 11-4, June-Aug.; closed holidays. Admission $3, students with ID $1, under 13 free. Phone (906) 226-3571.

MARQUETTE MARITIME MUSEUM is at 300 Lakeshore Blvd. Displays in an 1890s water works building chronicle the maritime heritage of Marquette and Lake Superior. Displays include boats and models, three lighthouse lenses, children's hands-on exhibits, photographs and charts. A film is shown continuously. The dockside offices of Marquette's first commercial fishing and passenger freight companies are re-created, and a replica of a fishing shanty contains items related to sport fishing. A Coast Guard lighthouse is adjacent to the museum; guided tours of the lighthouse and grounds are available.

Allow 30 minutes minimum. Daily 10-5, Mar.-Oct. Admission $3; K-12, $2. Lighthouse grounds

tour $3; K-12, $2. Combination ticket $5; K-12, $3. MC, VI. Phone (906) 226-2006.

PRESQUE ISLE PARK is n. of the city. This 328-acre wooded peninsula juts into Lake Superior. The park offers picnic facilities and rock hunting; facilities include an outdoor pool with a waterslide. Nature trails wind throughout the park and are used for bog walks in the summer and snowshoeing and cross-country skiing in winter. Allow 30 minutes minimum. Daily 7 a.m.-11 p.m. Free. Phone (906) 228-0460.

THE UPPER PENINSULA CHILDREN'S MUSEUM is at 123 W. Baraga Ave. Interactive exhibits were designed with input from local children and families. Subjects range from reptiles and forests to trains and planes. Allow 1 hour minimum. Mon.-Sat. 10-6 (also Fri. 6-8 p.m.), Sun. noon-5; closed Jan. 1, Thanksgiving and Dec. 25. Admission $4.50; ages 2-17, $3. Phone (906) 226-3911.

MARSHALL (I-3) pop. 7,459, elev. 898′

In 1846 near the site of Triangle Park, an event occurred that bore nationwide import. Adam Crosswhite, a Marshall resident, was seized by agents of the Kentucky slaveholder from whom he had escaped 2 years earlier. The townsfolk sprang to his defense, sending the slave hunters home without him and providing the Crosswhite family with passage to freedom in Canada.

Sued by the former slave owner, the Marshall abolitionists lost. The Crosswhite case was instrumental in the creation of the 1850 Fugitive Slave Act, which in turn contributed to tensions that became the Civil War.

A historic houses tour held the first weekend after Labor Day focuses on one of Marshall's hallmarks: an unusual number of excellent, well-preserved examples of Greek and Gothic revival, Italianate and Queen Anne architecture. Their survival resulted in part from the dashing of two 19th-century dreams: Marshall failed to become the capital, and the railroad boom collapsed. Foresight has since supplanted chance, and the structures are carefully protected.

Marshall Area Chamber of Commerce: 424 E. Michigan Ave., Marshall, MI 49068; phone (269) 781-5163 or (800) 877-5163.

Self-guiding tours: A map detailing a tour of Marshall is available at local shops and inns, the chamber of commerce and the Honolulu House.

SAVE **HONOLULU HOUSE** is off Fountain Cir. to 107 N. Kalamazoo Ave. The home was built in 1860 by a chief justice of the Michigan Supreme Court who later became U.S. Consul to Hawaii. A blend of Victorian styling and island living, the house was strongly influenced by his Hawaiian house. A raised veranda, a pagoda-capped tower and rooms featuring elaborate 15-foot ceilings hand-painted in high Victorian style are highlights of the house, now a museum. Daily noon-5, May-Sept.; Thurs.-Sun. noon-5 in Oct. Admission $5; senior citizens and ages 12-18, $4; under 5 free. Phone (269) 781-8544.

MEARS (G-1)

MAC WOOD'S DUNE RIDES is 9 mi. w. of US 31 on Silver Lake. Guides take passengers on 40-minute scenic rides over 8 miles of shifting sand dunes. Daily 9:30-8:30, May 1-early Oct. Fare $12.50; under 12, $8. Phone (231) 873-2817.

SILVER LAKE STATE PARK is off US 31 to Hart or Shelby exit, then 7 mi. w. following signs. The park encompasses 3,400 acres, approximately 1,800 of which are covered in sweeping sand dunes. The dunes can be explored in off-road vehicles in the northern portion of the park or on foot in the center section. Silver Lake is a good place for swimming, fishing or boating. Little Sable Point Lighthouse, built in 1873, overlooks a scenic portion of Lake Michigan.

Daily 9 a.m.-10 p.m., Memorial Day-Labor Day; 9-8, Apr. 1-day before Memorial Day and day after Labor Day-Oct. 31. Day pass $4; off-road permit (to drive on dunes) $16.25. Phone (231) 873-3083. *See Recreation Chart.*

RECREATIONAL ACTIVITIES

Jeep Tours (Self-driving)

- **Sandy Korners Jeep Tours** is off US 31 Hart exit, then 2 mi. w., following signs to 1762 N. 24th Ave. Daily 10-8:30, May-Oct. Phone (231) 873-5048.

MIDLAND (G-4) pop. 41,685, elev. 610′

The development of Midland from a lumber town into a handsome, well-planned and culturally active city is entwined with the growth of the Dow Chemical Co. Large brine deposits precipitated the establishment of the company in Midland.

The Alden B. Dow Home and Studio, 315 Post St., integrates organic textures, geometric angles and rich colors with the natural surroundings. The building was designed by Dow, who apprenticed with Frank Lloyd Wright. Tours are given by appointment; phone (989) 839-2744.

The Tridge, a three-legged pedestrian bridge, is at the confluence of the Tittabawasee and Chippewa rivers. The Pere Marquette Rail-Trail provides 22 miles of paved hiking trails between the Tridge and Coleman. The riverfront area also features picnic facilities, walking trails, an outdoor concert park and a farmers' market.

Midland County Convention and Visitors Bureau: 300 Rodd St., Suite 101, Midland, MI 48640; phone (989) 839-9522 or (888) 464-3526.

CHIPPEWA NATURE CENTER is 3.5 mi. s.w. at 400 S. Badour Rd. More than 1,000 acres of woods, fields, ponds, rivers and wetlands as well as hiking and cross-country skiing trails are featured. A museum has interactive exhibits, a library, a restored 1870s farm, an 1880s log school house, a sugarhouse and an arboretum of Michigan trees and shrubs.

Allow 2 hours minimum. Visitor center open Mon.-Fri. 8-5, Sat. 9-5, Sun. 1-5; holiday hours vary. Closed Thanksgiving and Dec. 25. Grounds open daily dawn-dusk. Donations. Phone (989) 631-0830.

DOW GARDENS is next to Midland Center for the Arts at 1809 Eastman Ave. On display are 600 species of flowers and shrubs on 100 landscaped acres. Allow 1 hour minimum. Daily 9-dusk; closed Jan. 1, Thanksgiving and Dec. 25. Admission $3; ages 6-17, $1. Phone (989) 631-2677 or (800) 362-4874.

HERBERT H. DOW HISTORICAL MUSEUM is w. on W. Main St. to 3200 Cook Rd. Displays chronicle the life of the founder of Dow Chemical Co., Herbert H. Dow, who conducted his pioneering chemical experiments in a nearby shed. The museum is housed in a replica of a gristmill. Exhibits include Dow's first office and his father's workshop. A 12-minute videotape presentation features a miniature image of Dow explaining his contributions to chemistry.

Next to the mill is a replica of the 1890 Midland Chemical Co., Dow's first manufacturing plant. A laboratory, steam engine and chemical tank help convey the humble beginnings of the Dow Chemical Co. Allow 1 hour, 30 minutes minimum. Wed.-Sat. 10-4, Sun. 1-5; closed holidays. Admission $2; ages 5-12, $1; family rate $5. Phone (989) 832-5319.

Bradley Home Museum & Carriage House is at 3200 Cook Rd. The 1874 Victorian house contains Victorian furnishings, fixtures and costumes. The Carriage House exhibits 15 horse-drawn vehicles, blacksmithing equipment and related items. Allow 30 minutes minimum. Wed.-Sat. 10-4, Sun. 1-5; closed holidays. Free with admission to Dow Historical Museum. Phone (989) 832-5319.

MIDLAND CENTER FOR THE ARTS is 2 mi. s. of US 10 at Eastman and W. St. Andrews rds. Concerts, plays and musicals are presented here. The center contains a museum with displays about science, technology, health, hands-on discovery, art and history. The Art Midland galleries and Midland Historical Society exhibits also can be seen. Guided tours are available. Allow 1 hour minimum. Daily 10-6; closed major holidays. Free. Phone (989) 631-5930.

MIO (E-4) pop. 2,016

Surrounded by the Huron-Manistee National Forests *(see place listing p. 75)* and with the Au Sable River nearby, Mio is a popular departure point and equipment rental center for fishing and canoeing expeditions. In spring the rare Kirtland Warbler nests in protected areas south of Mio near Mack Lake. Guided tours of the nesting area leave from the U.S. Forest Service station; phone (989) 826-3331, (989) 826-3252 or (800) 800-6133.

OUR LADY OF THE WOODS SHRINE is 1.5 blks. w. of SR 33 on SR 72. Visitors can see replicas of Roman Catholic shrines. Daily dawn-dusk, Memorial Day-Labor Day; by appointment rest of year. Free. Phone (989) 826-5509.

MONROE (I-5) pop. 22,076, elev. 590'

One of the oldest communities in the state, Monroe was founded in 1780 by the French at the site of an American Indian village where the River Raisin enters Lake Erie. The settlement, originally called Frenchtown, was the scene of the River Raisin Massacre in 1813 during the War of 1812. Gen. George Custer lived in Monroe for many years before his Army service. A 1920 bronze statue of Custer titled "Sighting the Enemy" is on the southwest corner of N. Monroe Street and W. Elm Avenue.

Shipping and industry support the city. The Vietnam War Memorial is off I-75 exit 15, then one-fourth mile west on SR 50 in Heck Park. The memorial is similar to the one in Washington, D.C., and lists the names of Monroe County soldiers.

Monroe County Convention and Tourism Bureau: 106 W. Front St., P.O. Box 1094, Monroe, MI 48161; phone (734) 457-1030 or (800) 252-3011.

Self-guiding tours: A tour of the historic Navarre-Anderson Trading Post Complex, 3775 N. Custer, is offered weekends Memorial Day through Labor Day.

Shopping areas: Frenchtown Square Mall, a half mile north on US 125 at 2121 N. Monroe St., includes Elder-Beerman, JCPenney and Sears among its stores. Horizon Outlet Center at I-75 exit 11 and LaPlaisance Road offers more than 70 factory outlet stores.

MONROE COUNTY HISTORICAL MUSEUM is at 126 S. Monroe St. Exhibits in the old post office building focus on the family of Gen. George A. Custer as well as on area history. The museum also contains local maps, Victorian furnishings and displays about American Indian and French pioneer history.

Allow 1 hour minimum. Daily 10-5, May-Sept.; Wed.-Sun. 10-5, rest of year. Closed Jan. 1, Easter, Thanksgiving and Dec. 25. Admission June-Aug. $2; ages 7-17, $1. Phone (734) 240-7780.

NAVARRE-ANDERSON TRADING POST AND MARTHA BARKER COUNTRY STORE MUSEUM are 5 mi. w. on Elm St. to 3775 and 3815 N. Custer Rd. Said to be the oldest wooden residence in the state, the trading post retains a bullet reputedly fired during the War of 1812. It is furnished as it appeared in 1797. The Martha Barker Country Store Museum, housed in a 1860s schoolhouse, contains items dating from 1900-10. Wed.-Sun. 1-5,

Memorial Day-Labor Day. Free. Phone (734) 240-7780.

RIVER RAISIN BATTLEFIELD VISITOR CENTER is off I-75 exit 14 to 1403 E. Elm Ave. Displays depict the Battle of the River Raisin, one of the largest engagements of the War of 1812. Exhibits include dioramas, maps and mannequins. A 15-minute auditorium presentation explains the major turning points of that war. The center also provides information about Monroe County. Allow 30 minutes minimum. Daily 10-5, Memorial Day-Labor Day; Sat.-Sun. 10-5, rest of year. Closed major holidays. Donations. Phone (734) 243-7136 or (734) 240-7780.

MOUNT PLEASANT (G-3)
pop. 25,946, elev. 761'

Originally known as Ojibway Besse, Mount Pleasant was a hunting ground for the Chippewa Indians. Magnificent pine and hardwoods destined the town to become a major lumber center. Mount Pleasant is home to Central Michigan University, founded in 1892, and the Saginaw Chippewa Indian Tribe on the Isabella Indian Reservation.

Horse racing takes place at Mount Pleasant Meadows May through September; phone (989) 773-0012.

Note: Policies concerning admittance of children to pari-mutuel betting facilities vary. Phone ahead for information.

Mount Pleasant Area Convention and Visitors Bureau: 114 E. Broadway, Mount Pleasant, MI 48858; phone (800) 772-4433.

Shopping areas: Loafers Glory Village of Yesteryear, about 15 miles west at 431 Main St. in Blanchard, is an early 1800s building that comprises several shops featuring antiques, crafts and food.

THE MUSEUM OF CULTURAL AND NATURAL HISTORY is in Rowe Hall on Bellows St. on the Central Michigan University campus. Displays explore human and natural history through exhibits and dioramas; among the displays are lumber exhibits, Civil War artifacts and handmade tools and implements as well as American Indian art. Dioramas feature mammals, birds and fish native to Michigan. The skeletal remains of an American mastodon also can be seen. Allow 1 hour minimum. Mon.-Fri. 8-5. Free. Phone (989) 774-3829.

CASINOS
- **Soaring Eagle Casino** is at 6800 Soaring Eagle Blvd. Daily 24 hours. Phone (888) 732-4537. *See color ad p. 388.*

RECREATIONAL ACTIVITIES
Canoeing
- **Chippewa River Outfitters** is 2 mi. w. on Broomfield Rd., then .3 mi. n. to 3763 S. Lincoln Rd., Mount Pleasant, MI 48858. Other activities are offered. Daily 10-8, mid-Apr. to mid-Oct.; by

appointment rest of year. Phone (989) 772-5474 or (888) 775-6077.

MUNISING (B-4) pop. 2,539, elev. 626'

Munising's harbor is protected from the brunt of Lake Superior's gales by Grand Island; the town is guarded on the landward side by a ring of sharply rising hills. A number of waterfalls cascade down the slopes within the city limits. Grand Island is a national recreation area; Munising also provides access to Hiawatha National Forest *(see place listing p. 73)* and is the eastern gateway to Pictured Rocks National Lakeshore *(see place listing p. 94)*.

The city is the eastern terminus of a scenic section of SR 28 that skirts the shore of Lake Superior to US 41 and Marquette *(see place listing p. 87)*. *Also see Upper Peninsula p. 105.*

Alger County Chamber of Commerce: 501 SR 28E, P.O. Box 405, Munising, MI 49862; phone (906) 387-2138.

PICTURED ROCKS CRUISES depart from Municipal Pier. Cruises, which cover 37 miles and last 2 hours, 40 minutes, follow the colorful rock formations that rise sharply from Lake Superior to heights of 200 feet. Cruises depart daily on the hour 9-5, July 1-late Aug.; at 9, 11, 1, 3 and 5, late Aug.-early Sept.; at 10 and 2, late May to mid-June and early Sept.-early Oct. (weather permitting). Fare $25; ages 6-12, $10. Phone (906) 387-2379. *See ad p. 91.*

SHIPWRECK TOURS is at 1204 Commercial St. Passengers ride in a glass-bottom boat for narrated tours of three Lake Superior shipwrecks. Additional highlights include views of the South Lighthouse and an original settlement on Grand Island. Two-hour cruises depart daily at 10 and 1, June 1-Oct. 7

(also at 4, July-Aug.). Fare $22; ages 6-12, $9. MC, VI. Phone (906) 387-4477. *See ad.*

MUSKEGON (G-1) pop. 40,105, elev. 599'

Formerly known as the Lumber Queen of the World, Muskegon produced 665 million board feet of lumber in 1888 alone. Although the languishing of the logging boom severely affected the town, the excellence of its harbor and success in attracting new enterprises prospered it. Muskegon is the largest city on the eastern shore of Lake Michigan, with a diversified mix of industry, tourism, culture and recreational activities comprising its economy.

More than 3,000 acres of recreational land balance Muskegon's industrial image. Pere Marquette Park occupies the southern flank of the channel; Muskegon State Park *(see Recreation Chart)* is to the north. The lakeside highway leading north from Muskegon State Park is an especially scenic drive.

The Muskegon River offers fishing for walleyed pike, boating and canoeing; numerous lakes and streams are restocked yearly. Hundreds of anglers line the channel and breakwater walls on Lake Michigan during the perch and salmon runs.

Muskegon Area Convention and Visitors Bureau: 610 Western Ave., Muskegon, MI 49440; phone (231) 724-3100 or (800) 250-9283.

GILLETTE SAND DUNE VISITOR CENTER is in P.J. Hoffmaster State Park, 3 mi. w. off US 31 Pontaluna exit. Hands-on exhibits, displays and a multimedia presentation illustrate the history and ecology of sand dunes and plant and animal life. Nature trails lead from the center to observation decks.

Center open Tues.-Sat. 10-5, Sun. noon-5, Memorial Day-Labor Day; Tues.-Thurs. and Sun. 12:30-4:30, Fri.-Sat. 10-4:30, day after Labor Day-Nov. 30. Park open daily 8 a.m.-10 p.m., Apr.

1-early Nov.; 8-6:30, rest of year. Park admission $4 per vehicle (includes visitor center). Phone (231) 798-3573.

GREAT LAKES NAVAL MEMORIAL AND MUSEUM is on the south side of the channel at 1346 Bluff St. The focus of the memorial is the USS *Silversides*, a restored, much-decorated World War II submarine. Guided tours through the sub's compartments explain how sailors lived and worked despite cramped quarters. Allow 30 minutes minimum. Daily 10-5:30, June-Aug.; Mon.-Fri. 1-5:30, Sat.-Sun. 10-5:30 in May and Sept.; Sat.-Sun. 10-5:30 in Apr. and Oct. Admission $5.25; ages 12-18, $4.25; over 62, $3.75; ages 5-11, $3.25. Phone (231) 755-1230.

MICHIGAN'S ADVENTURE AMUSEMENT PARK is 8 mi. n. via US 31 Russell Rd. exit. The park has 47 rides, including six roller coasters. A large water park has 20 slides, three wave pools and two play areas. Amusement park open daily at 11, mid-May through Labor Day. Water park open daily at noon. Closing times for both parks vary; phone ahead. Closed Aug. 27-30. Admission $23, under 3 free. Phone (231) 766-3377.

MUSKEGON COUNTY MUSEUM is at 430 W. Clay Ave. Displays describe Michigan's lumber industry and fur trade. Hands-on science and health displays as well as exhibits relating to American Indians also are offered. Mon.-Fri. 9:30-4:30, Sat.-Sun. 12:30-4:30; closed major holidays. Free. Phone (231) 722-0278 or (888) 843-5661.

MUSKEGON MUSEUM OF ART is at 296 W. Webster Ave. Works of such American artists as Ralph Albert Blakelock, Winslow Homer, Edward Hopper and James Abbot McNeill Whistler are displayed. John Steuart Curry's "Tornado Over Kansas" also can be seen. A European collection has objects ranging from ancient glass to contemporary art. Guided tours are available by appointment. Tues. noon-4, Thurs. noon-8, Wed. and Fri. 10-4, Sat. 9-5, Sun. noon-5; closed major holidays. Free. Phone (231) 720-2570.

NAUBINWAY (B-5) elev. 595'

SAVE **GARLYN ZOOLOGICAL PARK** is 6 mi. e. on US 2. A variety of animals, including wolves, bears, camels, cougars, otters and wallabies, live in a wooded park setting. Daily 11-7, Apr.-Oct.; Sat.-Sun 11-5, Nov. 1-Dec. 25. Admission $5.50; ages 4-16, $4.50; family rate $20. AX, DS, MC, VI. Phone (906) 477-1085.

NEGAUNEE (B-3) pop. 4,576, elev. 1,400'

Negaunee, the first mining city on the Marquette Range, was brought into being in 1844 by a group of explorers who were led to the ore beds by an Indian chief from the Keweenaw country. *Also see Upper Peninsula p. 105.*

 MICHIGAN IRON INDUSTRY MUSEUM is 3 mi. e. off US 41E to Maas St., e. to Forge Rd. then w. to 73 Forge Rd. The museum overlooks the Carp River and the site of the first iron forge in the Lake Superior region. Through exhibits and audiovisual displays the museum presents the history of Michigan's iron ranges and the people who worked them. "The Yankee," an 1860s locomotive from the Jackson Mine, is on display. Allow 1 hour, 30 minutes minimum. Daily 9:30-4:30, May-Oct. Free. Phone (906) 475-7857.

NEWBERRY (B-5) pop. 2,686, elev. 788'

OSWALDS BEAR RANCH is 4 mi. n. on SR 123 to Four Mile Corner, then 4.5 mi. w. to 13814 CR 407. Twenty-three American black bears are raised and kept on the 80-acre ranch. Visitors may view them in re-created natural habitats. Allow 30 minutes minimum. Daily 10-8, Memorial Day weekend-Labor Day; 10-6, day after Labor Day-Sept. 30. Admission $10 per private vehicle. Phone (906) 293-3147.

TAHQUAMENON LOGGING MUSEUM is 1.5 mi. n. on SR 123. The complex, situated on 29 acres, includes a museum with logging memorabilia, a cook shack and a circa 1900 log cabin. A slide presentation also is offered. Allow 1 hour minimum. Daily 9-5, Memorial Day-Labor Day. Admission $3; ages 6-12, $1.50. Phone (906) 293-3700.

NILES (I-2) pop. 12,204, elev. 659'

Because the banners of France, England, Spain and the United States have flown successively over this region, Niles is called the City of Four Flags. Its position as a stop on the 1830s Detroit-to-Chicago stagecoach route encouraged industrial and commercial development. Among Niles' natives are Montgomery Ward, Ring Lardner and the Dodge brothers of automobile fame.

Four Flags Area Council on Tourism: 321 E. Main St., P.O. Box 1300, Niles, MI 49120; phone (269) 684-7444.

FERNWOOD BOTANIC GARDEN AND NATURE CENTER is off US 31N (St. Joseph Valley Pkwy.) exit 7 to 13988 Range Line Rd. The 105-acre nature preserve offers gardens, woodland trails and prairie. A visitor center includes gallery shows, exhibits and a fern conservatory. Food is available. Allow 2 hours minimum. Tues.-Sat. 10-6, Sun. noon-6, May-Oct.; Tues.-Sat. 10-5, Sun. noon-5, rest of year. Admission $5; over 65, $4; ages 13-18, $3; ages 6-12, $2. Phone (269) 695-6491.

FORT ST. JOSEPH MUSEUM is at 508 E. Main St. The museum, located in the carriage house of the 1882 Chapin home, contains more than 10,000 historic items, including Sioux and Potawatomi Indian relics, artifacts from the site of Fort St. Joseph and Sitting Bull pictographs. Allow 30 minutes minimum. Wed.-Sat. 10-4. Free. Phone (269) 683-4702.

NORTH MUSKEGON (G-2)
pop. 4,031, elev. 621'

RECREATIONAL ACTIVITIES

Skiing (cross-country)
• **Muskegon Winter Sports Complex** is in Muskegon State Park. Write P.O. Box 5085,

North Muskegon, MI 49445. Other activities are offered. Lodge open daily 10-10, Dec.-Mar. Phone (231) 744-9629.

NORTHPORT (D-2) pop. 648

The coastal community of Northport lies in the northern end of the Leelanau Peninsula. The town is noted for its sandy beaches and spectacular sunsets. Several area wineries offer tours and tastings. Leelanau State Park *(see Recreation Chart)* is 7 miles north on SR 201. The Grand Traverse Lighthouse and Museum offers tours.

Leelanau Peninsula Chamber of Commerce: 5046 S. West Bay Shore Dr., Suite G, Suttons Bay, MI 49682; phone (231) 271-9895.

NOVI—*see Detroit p. 64.*

ONTONAGON (A-2) pop. 1,769, elev. 605'

Named Place of the Bowl by American Indians due to the shape of the river's mouth, Ontonagon was visited frequently from the 1600s to the mid-1800s by voyageurs and Jesuits. All who came took note of a huge copper boulder that measured 50 inches by 41 inches. American Indians believed the boulder to be the mediator between them and the Great Spirit. Publication of the discovery of copper led to an influx of prospectors and settlers on Lake Superior. Within the county that shares Ontonagon's name are 45 waterfalls. *Also see Upper Peninsula p. 105.*

Ontonagon County Chamber of Commerce: P.O. Box 266, Ontonagon, MI 49953; phone (906) 884-4735.

ONTONAGON COUNTY HISTORICAL MUSEUM is at 422 River St. Artifacts reflect the history of the county. Exhibits include photographs, Finnish items, logging and mining equipment and a replica of the Ontonagon copper boulder, which was recorded in 1843 as weighing 3,708 pounds. Tours of an on-site lighthouse are by appointment. Mon.-Fri. 9-5, Sat. 10-4. Admission $2, under 16 free. Phone (906) 884-6165.

OSCODA (E-5) pop. 992

Oscoda is a resort community, offering access to the Huron-Manistee National Forests (see place listing p. 75).

Fishing and canoeing on the Au Sable River are especially popular. The town also is a major sport fishing center for Lake Huron, with chinook salmon and lake and brown trout the main catches.

Oscoda-Au Sable Chamber of Commerce: 4440 N. US 23, Oscoda, MI 48750; phone (989) 739-7322 or (800) 235-4625.

SAVE **PADDLEWHEEL RIVER BOAT TRIPS** depart Foote Dam, 7 mi. w. on W. River Rd. on the Au Sable River. The 19-mile, round-trip cruise, which provides a narrative about historic and scenic points of interest, lasts approximately 2 hours.

The Au Sable River Queen of Oscoda, featuring a cocktail bar and glass-enclosed decks, leaves daily at noon and 3, Memorial Day weekend, late June-late Aug. and Sept. 1-Labor Day; at 1, day after Memorial Day-late June, in late Aug. and day after Labor Day-late Sept. Fall color tours offered Mon.-Fri. at noon and 2:30, Sat.-Sun. at 10:30, 1 and 3:30, fourth weekend in Sept.-third weekend in Oct.

Fall color tour fare $13; over 60, $11.75 (Mon.-Thurs.); ages 5-12, $6. Regular tour fare $10; over 60, $9; ages 5-12, $5. Reservations are required for fall color tours and are recommended for regular tours. AX, DC, DS, MC, VI. Phone (989) 739-7351, or (989) 728-3131 after 6 p.m.

OSSINEKE (E-5) pop. 1,059, elev. 604′

At the mouth of the Devil River and the site of an American Indian village in 1839, Ossineke was named for a native word, wawsineke, meaning "image stones," which referred to a prominent landmark. The pair of boulders were thought to encase the spirit of Chief Shinggabaw, who had promised to return there after death.

When a rival tribe removed the sacred stones during a raid, the waters of Thunder Bay are said to have destroyed the raiders and returned the stones to their original site at the village. An angler later used the boulders to anchor fishing nets; the stones now repose at the bottom of Lake Huron.

DINOSAUR GARDENS PREHISTORICAL ZOO is on US 23S. Nature trails, a miniature golf course and life-size reproductions of prehistoric creatures are in a 40-acre forest. Allow 1 hour minimum. Daily 9-6, Memorial Day-Labor Day. Admission $5; ages 6-11, $4; under 6, $3. Phone (989) 471-5477.

OTTAWA NATIONAL FOREST

Elevations in the forest range from 602 ft. at Lake Superior, Black River Harbor to 1,826 ft. at Wolfe Mountain. Refer to AAA maps for additional elevation information.

In the Upper Peninsula, the 986,518 acres of the Ottawa National Forest are intermingled with approximately 606,300 acres of state, county and privately owned land. Included are Lake Gogebic State Park (see Recreation Chart and the AAA Great Lakes CampBook) near Marenisco and the Sylvania Wilderness and the Sturgeon Gorge Wilderness.

In excess of 50,000 acres in the forest remain as a federally designated wilderness, with pristine lakes and old growth trees. More than 35 waterfalls within the forest are accessible by woodland trails. Those falls that can be reached by road include Potawatomi Conglomerate, Gorge, Sandstone and Rainbow on the Black River north of Ironwood and Bessemer; the Agate Falls observation deck west on SR 28 near Trout Creek; and Bond Falls via Bond Falls Road.

More than 500 named lakes and more than 2,700 miles of rivers and streams yield varieties of panfish and trout. Fishing for coho salmon and rainbow trout is good on Lake Superior. Hunting for deer, bears and small game is permitted. Snowmobiling, snowshoeing, cross-country skiing and ice fishing are popular winter sports.

The J.W. Toumey Forest Nursery in Watersmeet supplies seed and tree stock to Great Lakes state forests; guided and self-guiding tours are offered on request. The Ottawa National Forest Visitor Center, US 2 and US 45 in Watersmeet, has exhibits, an interpretive trail, audiovisual programs and scheduled naturalist-conducted activities; phone (906) 358-4724.

For further information contact the Forest Supervisor, Ottawa National Forest, E6248 US 2, Ironwood, MI 49938; phone (906) 932-1330. See Recreation Chart and the AAA Great Lakes CampBook.

PARADISE (B-5) pop. 4,191, elev. 615′

The town's name is derived from a conversation between two of Paradise's pioneer developers who were commenting about the area's natural beauty. "This is a regular paradise," one said, and the name stuck. Snowmobilers and cross-country skiers enjoy the recreational facilities provided by the state and national forests that surround the village. Also see Upper Peninsula p. 105.

TAHQUAMENON FALLS STATE PARK is 12 mi. w. on SR 123. The 40,000-acre park includes two falls on the Tahquamenon River. The Upper Falls are nearly 50 feet high and 200 feet wide at the crest. The Lower Falls, divided by an island, are a series of rapids and cascades.

The Upper Falls also can be reached by regularly scheduled boat service. The park offers a variety of recreational opportunities. Allow 30 minutes minimum. Daily 8 a.m.-10 p.m. Admission $4 per private vehicle. Phone (906) 492-3415. *See Recreation Chart.*

PAW PAW (I-2) pop. 3,363, elev. 739′

WINERIES

- **St. Julian Winery** is off I-94 exit 60 at 716 S. Kalamazoo St. Mon.-Sat. 9-5:30, Sun. noon-5:30, July 1-Labor Day; Mon.-Sat. 9-5, Sun. noon-5, rest of year. Closed Jan. 1, Easter, Thanksgiving and Dec. 25. Phone (269) 657-5568.

- **Warner Vineyards** is off I-94 exit 60 at 706 S. Kalamazoo St. Mon.-Sat. 10-5, Sun. noon-5. Phone (269) 657-3165 or (800) 756-5357.

PETOSKEY (D-3) pop. 6,080, elev. 636′

Petoskey is a resort center on Little Traverse Bay. On the bottom of the bay at a depth of 34 feet, an 11-foot figure of Christ serves as the Skin Divers' Shrine. Rockhounds crowd the Petoskey State Park *(see Recreation Chart and the AAA Great Lakes CampBook)* and Magnus Park in spring, sorting through winter's debris for Petoskey stones. The remains of an extinct coral that inhabited the shallow waters of 350 million years ago,

the stones were designated Michigan's state stone in 1965.

Fishing in Little Traverse Bay and area rivers and lakes yields bass, blue gill, lake and rainbow trout, perch, salmon and walleye. A number of scenic drives can be enjoyed in the other seasons: The lakeshore routes along US 31 west through Charlevoix then south to Traverse City *(see place listing p. 102)* and SR 119 north through Harbor Springs *(see place listing p. 73)* to Cross Village are particularly enjoyable. Closer to town, US 131 and Walloon Lake Drive provide a pleasant loop.

Petoskey/Harbor Springs/Boyne Country Visitors Bureau: 401 E. Mitchell St., Petoskey, MI 49770; phone (231) 348-2755 or (800) 845-2828. *See ad.*

Shopping areas: The Gaslight Shopping District along Lake, Howard and Bay streets offers more than 60 shops. Some shops are closed in the winter. Shopping is also available in the Bay Harbor Marina District.

LITTLE TRAVERSE HISTORY MUSEUM is on the waterfront at Bayfront Park. Housed in an 1892 railroad depot, the museum features exhibits from the area's Odawa Indian, pioneer and Victorian past as well as exhibits about Ernest Hemingway, Civil War author Bruce Catton and the area's lumber and resort industries. Allow 30 minutes minimum. Mon.-Sat. and holidays 10-4, Memorial Day-Labor Day; Tues.-Sat. and holidays 10-4, day after Labor Day-Dec. 31; Tues.-Sat. 10-4, May 1-day before Memorial Day. Admission $1, under 18 free. Phone (231) 347-2620.

▼ GEM PICTURED ROCKS NATIONAL LAKESHORE (A-4)

Pictured Rocks National Lakeshore extends 40 miles along Lake Superior from Grand Marais to Munising *(see place listing p. 90).* The Pictured Rocks cliffs rise to 200 feet above the lake, a spectacular example of the erosive action of waves, wind and ice. The Grand Sable Dunes expose part of a glacial deposit up to 200 feet high. Five square miles of dunes that once edged an ancient predecessor of Lake Superior top the banks by another 100 feet.

Lake Superior and the many inland lakes and streams harbor a variety of fish. Fishing is excellent in spring and fall; a Michigan license is required. Summer months offer swimming, hiking, picnicking, backpacking and a scenic boat ride along the Pictured Rocks.

Twenty-one miles of cross-country ski trails, abundant off-trail skiing and a yearly snowfall approaching 200 inches accommodate winter sports enthusiasts. Snowshoeing and ice fishing are popular activities.

Park rangers conduct campfire programs and guided walks in summer. Drive-in camping areas are at Hurricane River, Little Beaver Lake and Twelvemile Beach; roads to these areas are closed by snow from November through April. Back-country permits are required and may be obtained at park visitor centers; the fee is $15. Advance reservations are accepted. The fee for drive-in camping is $10 per night and is on a first come-first served basis. Phone (906) 387-3700.

The Hiawatha National Forest/Pictured Rocks National Lakeshore Visitor Information Center, SR 28 and CR-H58 in Munising, is open daily 8-6, mid-June to mid-Sept.; Mon.-Sat. 9-4:30, rest of year; phone (906) 387-3700. The unstaffed Munising Falls Interpretive Center at the beginning of Sand Point Road is open daily, May-Oct. The Grand Sable Visitor Center, CR-H58 just west of Grand Marais, is open daily, late May-Labor Day; phone (906) 494-2660.

The Grand Marais Maritime Museum and Ranger Station on Coast Guard Point in Grand Marais usually is open July 1-Labor Day but hours vary. Park headquarters on Sand Point Road near Munising is open Mon.-Fri. 8-4:30. The park is open daily 24 hours. For more information contact Pictured Rocks National Lakeshore, P.O. Box 40, Munising, MI 49862; phone (906) 387-2607. *Also see Upper Peninsula p. 105 and the Recreation Chart.*

PICTURED ROCKS begin 5 mi. n.e. of Munising. These cliffs, from Longfellow's "The Song of Hiawatha," are notable for their rich color and interesting formations. Except for Miners Castle, they are accessible only by boat or on foot. Pictured Rocks Cruises offers 2.5-hour tours of the formations leaving from Munising *(see place listing p. 90).*

PINCONNING (F-4) pop. 1,386, elev. 596'

Once an important railhead during the lumber era, Pinconning serves the surrounding agricultural and dairy region and is known as the cheese capital of Michigan. It also is known for perch and walleye fishing on Saginaw Bay.

Pinconning Area Chamber of Commerce: P.O. Box 856, Pinconning, MI 48650; phone (989) 879-2816.

[SAVE] **DEER ACRES STORYBOOK AMUSEMENT PARK** is 3 mi. s. on SR 13. Sculptured, life-size Mother Goose characters are the focus of the park, which includes a playground. Deer and other animals may be hand fed. Other amusements are train, antique car and safari rides, a moon walk, a Ferris wheel and a merry-go-round. Picnicking is permitted. Food is available.

Allow 1 hour minimum. Mon.-Fri. 10-6, Sat.-Sun. 10-7, mid-May through Labor Day; Sat.-Sun. 10-5, day after Labor Day to mid-Oct. Admission $9; over 62, $8; ages 3-12, $7. Fee $1.50 per ride or 10 rides for $12. DS, MC, VI. Phone (989) 879-2849.

PLYMOUTH—*see Detroit p. 64.*

PONTIAC—*see Detroit p. 64.*

PORT AUSTIN (F-5) pop. 737, elev. 604'

Named for P.C. Austin in 1839, Port Austin is at the tip of Michigan's thumb. The town is known for its picturesque sunrises and sunsets on Lake Huron.

[SAVE] ***MISS PORT AUSTIN* PERCH PARTY BOAT** departs from the Port Austin State Dock, 8787 Lake St. Perch fishing trips lasting 4.5 hours are available on the 20-passenger *Miss Port Austin*. Bait is provided; fishing poles are available for $2. A valid state fishing license is required for those over 17; 1-day licenses are available at local bait and tackle shops. Soft-soled shoes are recommended.

Trips depart Mon., Wed. and Sat.-Sun. at 7:30 and 2:30, Fri. at 7:30, July-Aug.; Sat. at 7:30 and 2:30, Wed. and Sun. at 7:30, May-June and in Sept. Fare $30, over 55 and family rate (Mon.-Fri.) $25 per person. Phone (989) 738-5271.

PORT HURON (H-6) pop. 32,338, elev. 596'

Linked by the Blue Water International Bridge with Sarnia, Ontario, at the point where Lake Huron empties into the St. Clair River, Port Huron is the center of the St. Clair River manufacturing district. It is one of the oldest settlements in the state, dating from 1686 when the French built Fort St. Joseph to guard against possible British incursions into their fur trade. The first permanent colony, however, was not established until 1790.

The fact that Thomas Edison spent his youth in Port Huron seems to reflect the city's proclivity for electrical pioneering. One of the earliest electrical utilities was formed in 1844. The 1891 railway tunnel, built beneath the St. Clair River to accommodate double-decker trains, is considered to have been the first electrified underwater tunnel.

Some of Port Huron's popular parks are Lakeside Park, with opportunities for swimming and picnicking, and Lighthouse Park, which surrounds Fort Gratiot Lighthouse, one of the oldest working lighthouses on the Great Lakes. Tours are available by appointment in summer. Another popular spot is Pine Grove Park, where the Huron, the last commissioned lightship, is docked.

Blue Water Area Convention and Visitors Bureau: 520 Thomas Edison Pkwy., Port Huron, MI 48060; phone (810) 987-8687 or (800) 852-4242.

Shopping areas: Birchwood Mall, north on SR 25 at Keewahdin Road, features 90 specialty stores as well as Marshall Field's, JCPenney, Sears, Target and Younker's. Horizon Outlet Center, west on Range Road at I-94 exit 269, offers 33 factory outlet shops. Main Street Port Huron offers more than 70 specialty shops, restaurants and art galleries along an 11-block historic area concentrated on Huron Avenue between Quay Street and McMorran Boulevard.

HURON LIGHTSHIP MUSEUM is in Pine Grove Park. Built in 1920, the lightship was used until it was decommissioned in 1970. It is believed to be the only lightship on the Great Lakes and has been certified a National Treasure. Allow 30 minutes minimum. Wed.-Sun. 1-4:30, Apr.-Dec.; closed major holidays. Admission $3; over 54 and ages 7-17, $2. Combination admission with Port Huron Museum and Thomas Edison Depot Museum $5; over 54 and ages 7-17, $3. AX, MC, VI. Phone(810) 984-9768.

SAVE **PORT HURON MUSEUM** is at 1115 Sixth St. Displays—which include American Indian relics and marine items, a pioneer log house, Thomas Edison memorabilia and fine arts—trace 300 years of local history. Allow 30 minutes minimum. Wed.-Sun. 1-4:30; closed holidays. Admission $3; over 54 and ages 7-17, $2. Combination admission with *Huron* Lightship Museum and Thomas Edison Depot Museum $5; over 54 and ages 7-17, $3. AX, MC, VI. Phone (810) 982-0891.

SAVE **Thomas Edison Depot Museum** is at 1115 Sixth St. Housed in the Fort Gratiot Railroad Station where Thomas Edison worked, the museum features re-created period displays, hands-on activities that focus on his inventions and a vintage baggage car that contains a mock-up of Edison's first laboratory. A videotape presentation also is offered. Allow 30 minutes minimum. Daily 1-4:30 (also Fri. 4:30-8), Memorial Day-Labor Day; Wed.-Sun. 1-4:30, rest of year. Closed major holidays. Admission $3; over 54 and ages 7-17, $2. Combination admission with Port Huron Museum and *Huron* Lightship Museum $5; over 54 and ages 7-17, $3. AX, MC, VI. Phone (810) 982-0891.

PORT SANILAC (G-6) pop. 658

Until 1857 when Port Sanilac was allegedly renamed for a well-known Wyandotte Indian chief, this locale was called Bark Shanty Point, a name stoutly defended in one issue of the village's newspaper, the *Bark Shanty Times.*

No editors, reporters, printers or editorial policies complicated the production of the paper, which was known throughout the region. Everyone who came through the general store/post office simply wrote news or commentary on a sheet of newsprint paper kept on the counter. Once thoroughly perused, the edition was bound and filed, and a new one was begun.

SAVE **SANILAC COUNTY HISTORICAL MUSEUM AND VILLAGE** is at 228 S. Ridge Rd. (SR 25). The 1875 Loop-Harrison House, a restored Victorian house, contains most of its original furnishings. Also on display are medical instruments; antique glassware; marine, military and American Indian artifacts; and the original Bark Shanty post office cancellation stamp.

On the grounds are a dairy museum, with relics of the industry; the restored late 19th-century Banner Cabin, furnished in period; Huckins School; a general store; and a carriage barn that contains exhibits relating to the fishing, blacksmithing and lumber industries as well as carriages and a theater.

Allow 1 hour minimum. Wed.-Fri. 11-4:30, Sat.-Sun. noon-4:30, mid-June to early Sept. Admission $5; over 55, $4; ages 5-12, $2. Phone (810) 622-9946.

PRESQUE ISLE (D-5) pop. 1,691

Presque Isle, on the eastern shore of Grand Lake, is a supply center for the surrounding resort area. Three miles north is Presque Isle Harbor, an active lumber port in the mid-1800s, with a full marina facility.

OLD LIGHTHOUSE PARK AND MUSEUM stands on the northern arm of land enclosing the harbor. Built in 1840, it was replaced in 1870 by the current lighthouse a mile north on the tip of the peninsula. The tower and keeper's house are restored. A 3,425-pound bronze bell, larger than the Liberty Bell, is on display. Allow 30 minutes minimum. Old and new lighthouses open daily 9-6, mid-May to mid-Oct. Fee to climb new lighthouse tower $2.50. Admission for both lighthouses (includes museum) $2.50; ages 6-12, $1. Phone (989) 595-9917 for new lighthouse, or (989) 595-6979 for old lighthouse.

ROCHESTER—*see Detroit p. 64.*

ROCKLAND (B-2) pop. 324, elev. 1,093′

OLD VICTORIA is 4 mi. s.w. on a paved road near the Victoria dam. This is a restored late 19th-century company town. The original settlement was established by miners from Cornwall, England, who came to work the copper mines. The mines opened 1847-49 and operated until 1921 when they fell victim to low copper prices and competition from open pit mines in the West.

Guided tours explain the history of the village and its decline. Three houses and a sauna and barn are open to the public. Hiking trails and picnic facilities are available. Daily 11:30-3:30, Memorial Day to mid-Oct. Donations. Phone (906) 886-2617.

ROGERS CITY (D-5) pop. 3,322, elev. 655′

Rogers City's principal industry is readily apparent: Possibly the world's largest open limestone quarry—more than 3 miles long and nearly 2 miles across at its widest point—extends southeastward from the city limits. Worked continuously since 1912, the quarry is expected to produce into the 21st century. Operations can be seen from the rim of the pit at Quarry View; except in winter, the docking and loading of the huge freighters are visible from Harbor View.

Established during the 1870s lumber boom, Rogers City remains the largest community in Presque Isle County. P.H. Hoeft State Park *(see Recreation Chart and the AAA Great Lakes CampBook)* is 5 miles northwest on US 23 and includes a section of Huron dunes. Ocqueoc Falls, the largest falls in the Lower Peninsula, is 12 miles west of Rogers City off SR 68. A 7-mile self-guiding trail originates there.

Rogers City Chamber of Commerce: 292 S. Bradley Hwy., P.O. Box 55, Rogers City, MI 49779; phone (989) 734-2535, or (800) 622-4148.

PRESQUE ISLE COUNTY HISTORICAL MUSEUM is at 176 W. Michigan Ave. Exhibits about maritime and local history are in the restored Bradley House. Three floors are furnished in the style of the 1920s, while others re-create a general store and a Victorian sitting room. Displays include American Indian artifacts as well as carpentry, farming, household and lumber-related items. Tues.-Sat. noon-4, June-Oct. Donations. Phone (989) 734-4121.

ROSCOMMON (E-4) pop. 1,133, elev. 1,123'

A resort area and starting point for canoe trips down the Au Sable River, Roscommon is near both North Higgins Lake and South Higgins Lake state parks *(see Recreation Chart and the AAA Great Lakes CampBook).*

CIVILIAN CONSERVATION CORPS MUSEUM is at the entrance of North Higgins Lake State Park. Housed in replica barracks, the museum showcases the accomplishments of the men who helped "put Americans back to work." Many photographs were donated by CCC alumni. Two original buildings used during the 1930s are on the grounds. Picnic areas and hiking trails are available. Trail maps are available for self-guiding tours.

Allow 30 minutes minimum. Daily 11-4, Memorial Day-Labor Day. An interpreter is on-site Thurs.-Mon. Admission $4 per private vehicle. Phone (989) 821-6125.

MICHIGAN FIREMEN'S MEMORIAL is 2.5 mi. s. on CR 18, then .5 mi. e. on Robinson Rd. The 12-foot bronze statue was created by Detroit's Edward Chesney. Daily 8-6, May-Nov. Free.

ROYAL OAK—*see Detroit p. 64.*

SAGINAW (G-5) pop. 61,799, elev. 592'

When the Saginaw Valley was shorn of its pine forests, the once busy lumber center of Saginaw turned to the processing and shipping of shorter crops such as beans and sugar beets. Tourism contributes heavily to the economy.

The city's Celebration Square is home to attractions and parks, including the Lucille E. Andersen Memorial Garden, Ezra Rust Drive, which adorns the top of the city's 20-million-gallon underground reservoir; phone (989) 759-1362.

Saginaw County Convention and Visitors Bureau: 1 Tuscola St., Suite 101, Saginaw, MI 48607; phone (989) 752-7164 or (800) 444-9979.

HISTORICAL SOCIETY OF SAGINAW COUNTY is at 500 Federal Ave. The renovated 1897 post office building was designed in French chateau style and sports a spiral staircase and corner towers. Permanent and changing exhibits trace the social and industrial development of the Saginaw Valley. Allow 1 hour minimum. Guided tours are available by appointment. Mon.-Sat. 10-4:30, Sun. 1-4:30; closed holidays. Admission $1; ages 5-18, 50c. Phone (989) 752-2861.

JAPANESE CULTURAL CENTER AND TEA HOUSE is at the corner of Ezra Rust Dr. and S. Washington Ave. The center offers insights into Japanese culture and the ritual and ceremony of the tea service. Saginaw's ties with Tokushima, its sister city in Japan, were the impetus for the establishment of the Friendship Garden; many of the trees, bridges and stones used in the garden came from Japan. Following a tour of the garden, tea and sweets are served. Every second Saturday at 2 a full tea ceremony is offered.

Allow 1 hour minimum. Gardens open Tues.-Sat. 9-8, June-Sept.; 9-4, Apr.-May and Oct.-Nov. Tea House open Tues.-Sat. noon-4, May 30-Dec. 1. Gardens free. Tea House tour $3. Full tea ceremony $6. Phone (989) 759-1648.

JOHNNY PANTHER QUESTS departs from various points in the Saginaw River valley. Personalized boat tours through the Shiawassee National Wildlife Refuge put visitors up close to bald eagles, beavers, deer and their natural habitats. Tours can be customized depending on size of party and preferred destination. A jacket is recommended for afternoon cruises. Daily dawn-dusk. Tours $40-$100 per person. Reservations are required. Phone (810) 653-3859.

MARSHALL M. FREDERICKS SCULPTURE MUSEUM is in the Arbury Fine Arts Center at 7400 Bay Rd. (SR 84) on the Saginaw Valley State University campus. The museum houses hundreds of original plaster models that span the career of the noted sculptor. Free-standing sculptures, reliefs, portraits and drawings by Fredericks are exhibited. Photographs show finished bronze and stone sculptures now exhibited around the world. An adjacent sculpture garden and fountain also feature works by the sculptor. Allow 1 hour minimum. Tues.-Sun. 1-5; closed holidays. Free. Phone (989) 964-7125.

SAGINAW ART MUSEUM is at 1126 N. Michigan Ave. Housed in the 1904 Georgian-revival Ring Mansion, the museum has a permanent collection of art by E. Irving Couse and a children's hands-on gallery. Major collections include 19th- and 20th-century American art, and collections of Asian art, landscapes, contemporary prints, plaster sculpture by John Rogers and textiles. The garden is landscaped to its original design. Allow 1 hour minimum. Tues.-Sat. 10-5, Sun. 1-5; closed holidays. Donations. Phone (989) 754-2491.

SAGINAW CHILDREN'S ZOO is at jct. SRs 13/46 at 1730 S. Washington Ave. The zoo features a hand-carved carousel, a walk-through butterfly exhibit, a train, pony rides and timber wolf and monkey exhibits. Allow 1 hour, 30 minutes minimum.

Mon.-Sat. 10-5 (also Wed. 5-8), Sun. 11-6, May-Aug.; Sat. 10-5, Sun. 11-6 in Sept. Closed Feb. 14, Easter, Oct. 31 and Dec. 25. Admission $4.50; over 65 and ages 3-12, $3.50. Phone (989) 759-1408.

ST. IGNACE (B-5) pop. 2,678, elev. 592′

St. Ignace's strategic location on the north shore of the Straits of Mackinac was quickly recognized by explorers. The town was founded in 1671 when Father Jacques Marquette established a mission; a fortress was built shortly thereafter. In 1701 the garrison moved to Detroit and St. Ignace's military importance became a thing of the past; by 1706 so was the mission.

St. Ignace, on the Upper Peninsula, is joined to the Lower Peninsula by the 5-mile-long Mackinac Bridge, which links the town with Mackinaw City. Each Labor Day morning thousands participate in the Mackinac Bridge Walk, from St. Ignace to Mackinaw City.

Ferry service to Mackinac Island is available at the harbor from early April until ice forms on the Straits of Mackinac, usually in October.

Scenic US 2, heading west from St. Ignace, winds down to the sand dunes and up into the wooded hills along Lake Michigan to Escanaba (see place listing p. 67). Castle Rock, 4 miles north, was an ancient lookout of the Algonquin Indians and offers a scenic view. Also see Upper Peninsula p. 105.

St. Ignace is the site of what is reportedly the world's largest all-category auto show on the last Saturday in June.

St. Ignace Area Chamber of Commerce: 560 N. State St., St. Ignace, MI 49781; phone (906) 643-8717 or (800) 338-6660. See color ad p. 335.

FATHER MARQUETTE NATIONAL MEMORIAL is .2 mi. n.w. of the bridge via US 2; exit in the Marquette unit of Straits State Park. The memorial honors Jacques Marquette, the French explorer who established the state's first European settlements at Sault Ste. Marie and St. Ignace. Interpretive trails through the 52-acre park provide panoramic views of the straits and Mackinac Bridge. Picnicking is permitted. Allow 1 hour minimum. Park open daily 24 hours. Admission $4 per private vehicle. Phone (906) 643-8620.

FORT DE BAUDE INDIAN MUSEUM is at 334 N. State St. Built on the site of the original fort, the museum houses displays and dioramas depicting the lives of the area's early inhabitants. Local beadwork, stonework and weapons are displayed. Daily 9-9, Memorial Day to mid-Sept. Admission $5; ages 6-17, $3. Phone (906) 643-6622.

SAVE **MARQUETTE MISSION PARK AND MUSEUM OF OJIBWA CULTURE** is at 500 N. State St. The park is the presumed site of Father Jacques Marquette's grave. A statue honoring him, an interpretive kiosk about his life and a re-created Victorian garden are on the grounds. The site has yielded important archeological finds—most dating back to the Huron, Ottawa and French settlements of the late 1600s. The museum, housed in a restored 19th-century Jesuit church, is dedicated to the Ojibwa—the original inhabitants of the upper Great Lakes region.

Displays include artifacts, some dating to 6000 B.C., and reproductions relating to the Ojibwa culture. A typical Ojibwa family is portrayed in an 8-minute videotape. Allow 30 minutes minimum. daily 10-8, July 1-Labor Day; Mon.-Sat. 11-5, Sun. 1-5, Memorial Day-June 30 Admission $2; ages 6-12, $1; family rate $5. Phone (906) 643-9161.

CASINOS

• **Kewadin Shores Casino** is at 3039 Mackinac Tr. Daily 24 hours. Phone (906) 643-7071 or (800) 539-2346.

ST. JOSEPH (I-1) pop. 8,789, elev. 591′

In 1833 Newberryport was renamed St. Joseph after the St. Joseph River bordering the peninsular city along with Lake Michigan. Originally St. Joseph grew as a stopping place for travelers between Chicago and Detroit. Today there are more than 75 specialty shops as well as a variety of beaches and parks.

Self-guiding tours: Historic walking tour information can be obtained from St. Joseph Today, 413 State St., St. Joseph, MI 49085; phone (269) 982-0032.

GEM **CURIOUS KIDS' MUSEUM** is at 415 Lake Blvd. Curiosity and learning is encouraged through hands-on exhibits. Each exhibit SAVE comes with its own costumes for young visitors to wear. Children can serve customers in their own diner; type their names in braille; and pick apples from simulated trees, follow the crop through processing and then sell apple-related products at a market stand. Allow 2 hours minimum. Mon.-Sat. 10-5, Sun. noon-5, June 1-Labor Day. Admission $5, under 1 free. Phone (269) 983-2543.

KRASL ART CENTER is at 707 Lake Blvd. Three galleries and an outdoor sculpture collection contain folk art, traditional art and works by regional artists. Traveling exhibitions from such major museums as the Smithsonian Institution and Detroit Institute of Arts also are included. Allow 30 minutes minimum. Mon.-Sat. 10-4, Sun. 1-4, Memorial Day-Labor Day; Fri. 10-1, rest of year. Closed holidays. Free. Phone (269) 983-0271.

SAUGATUCK (H-1) pop. 1,065

The dunes along Lake Michigan and the pretty countryside around Lake Kalamazoo helped make Saugatuck a well-known art colony. Along with its sister city, Douglas (see place listing p. 66), the town also is a popular resort.

STAR OF SAUGATUCK **BOAT CRUISE** departs from 716 Water St. The 1.2- to 1.5-hour narrated tour aboard the 150-passenger stern-wheeler travels down the Kalamazoo River to Lake Michigan. Cruises depart daily at 11, 1, 3 and 5, Memorial Day weekend and July 1-Labor Day; Mon.-Fri. and Sun. at 1 and 3, Sat. at 1, 3 and 5, early May-day before Memorial Day weekend; Mon.-Fri. at 1 and 3, Sat.-Sun. at 11, 1, 3 and 5, day after Memorial Day-June 30; Mon.-Fri. at 1 and 3, Sat. at 11, 1, 3 and 5, Sun. at 1 and 3, day after Labor Day-Sept. 30; Mon. at 11 and 1, Fri.-Sun. at 1 and 3 in Oct. Fare $13; ages 3-12, $7. Phone (269) 857-4261.

SAULT STE. MARIE (B-6)
pop. 16,542, elev. 617'

The oldest town in the state, Sault Ste. Marie was first visited by a European about 1620 when the French *voyageur* Étienne Brulé passed through the area on his way to the Lake Superior region. The first Jesuit missionaries, Isaac Jogues and Charles Raymbault, arrived about 1641; the first mission was established in 1668 by fathers Jacques Marquette and Claude Dablon, who named the town in honor of the Virgin Mary.

The French and British competed for the profitable fur trade in the upper Great Lakes. The Treaty of Paris established the Michigan Territory as part of America, and in 1820 a treaty with the Chippewa Indians brought the area and its inhabitants under government regulation. Fort Brady was built shortly thereafter and trade increased. The first American lock was built in 1855, and later sailors and travelers began referring to the town as the Soo. Railroad and highway bridges link the city with its Canadian twin, Sault Ste. Marie, Ontario.

The rapids of the St. Marys River, which drop some 21 feet from Lake Superior to Lake Huron, are the reason for the town's greatest attraction, the Soo Locks. Four locks on the U.S. side bypass this beautiful barrier. More than 95 million tons of freight pass through the Soo every year.

Parkland parallels the locks; in the upper park are three observation platforms and a Corps of Engineers information center. Originating at the information center, the Locks Park Historic Walkway follows the waterfront for about a mile. It links many historic attractions and four main points of interest: the Locks Overlook; Plank Alley, site of the original business district; Fort Brady, site of both French and American forts; and the Johnston Homestead, a preserved neighborhood. *Also see Upper Peninsula p. 105.*

Sault Area Convention and Visitor's Bureau: 2650 I-75 Business Spur, Sault Ste. Marie, MI 49783; phone (906) 632-3366 or (800) 647-2858.

MUSEUM SHIP *VALLEY CAMP* is e. of the Soo Locks at 501 E. Water St. Walk-in tours of the retired Great Lakes freighter include the pilot house, captain's quarters, the Marine Museum and an aquarium. Also on board are two lifeboats recovered from the *Edmund Fitzgerald*, a freighter that sank with all hands during a storm on Lake Superior in 1975.

Daily 9-9, July-Aug.; 10-6, mid-May through June 30 and Sept. 1 to mid-Oct. Last admission 1 hour before closing. Admission $8; ages 6-16, $4. Phone (888) 744-7867.

[SAVE] **RIVER OF HISTORY MUSEUM** is at 209 E. Portage Ave. on the first floor of the restored Federal Building. Exhibit galleries chronicle more than 8,000 years of St. Marys River history. The river valley's development is traced from the Anishnabeg (Chippewa) Indians—the area's first settlers—through the lucrative 18th-century French fur trade to modern industrial and environmental issues. An audio system re-creates such sounds of history as the excavation of locks and canals that brought maritime commerce to the river in the mid-19th century.

Allow 30 minutes minimum. Mon.-Sat. 10-5, Sun. noon-5, May 15-Oct. 15. Phone for holiday schedule. Admission $5; over 55, $3.50; ages 8-16, $2.50; family rate $15 (five or more members). Phone (906) 632-1999.

SOO LOCKS BOAT TOURS depart from two locations, 515 and 1157 E. Portage Ave. Two-hour narrated tours take visitors through the Soo Locks and alongside the giant ships. A live narration explains the operation and the history of the locks, St. Marys Rapids, Algoma Steel Plant, waterfronts of twin Saults and other sights. A sunset dinner cruise along the St. Marys River (including a locks tour) is available. A lighthouse cruise passes U.S. and Canadian lighthouses in Whitefish Bay.

Locks tours depart daily 9-6:40, July-Aug.; 9-5:30, June 21-June 30; 9-4:30, mid-May through June 20 and Sept.-Oct. Fare for locks tour $17.50; ages 13-18, $15.50; ages 4-12, $8. Reservations are recommended for dinner and lighthouse cruises. DS, MC, VI. Phone (906) 632-6301 or (800) 432-6301. *See color ad p. 99.*

TOWER OF HISTORY is e. of Soo Locks at 326 E. Portage Ave. The 21-story structure offers a panoramic view of the locks, the St. Marys River and rapids, and the city's historical sites. The tower has artifacts and a videotape show depicting the history of the Great Lakes and Sault Ste. Marie. The ride to the top is by elevator. Allow 1 hour minimum. Daily 10-6, mid-May to mid-Oct. Last admission 1 hour before closing. Admission $4; ages 6-16, $2. Phone (906) 632-3658 or (888) 744-7867.

CASINOS

- **Kewadin Casino**, .7 mi. e. on Marquette St. to 2186 Shunk Rd. Daily 24 hours. Phone (906) 632-0530 or (800) 539-2346.

SHELBY (G-2) pop. 1,914

Orchards and asparagus farms form a backdrop for this small western Michigan town.

SHELBY MAN-MADE GEMSTONES is n. of Shelby Rd. at 1330 Industrial Dr. Visitors can see gem-producing equipment and gems that are made on the premises. An audiovisual presentation about artificial gem making is offered. Allow 30 minutes minimum. Mon.-Fri. 9-5:30, Sat. noon-4; closed holidays and Dec. 25-Jan. 1. Free. Phone (231) 861-2165.

SILVER CITY (A-1)

In 1872 hopeful miners fanned out across the Silver City countryside searching for the source of the silver nuggets sold to traders by local Indians. Little mining was done; by 1876 the few tunnels were abandoned. *Also see Upper Peninsula p. 105.*

PORCUPINE MOUNTAINS WILDERNESS STATE PARK is 3 mi. w. on SR 107. The 63,000-acre park is one of the few remaining large wilderness areas in the Midwest. Camping, skiing and backpacking are popular activities, and natural history programs are offered. Lake of the Clouds Scenic Overlook, on an escarpment high above the lake at the western end of SR 107, offers an excellent view. Wilderness panoramas can also be enjoyed from Summit Peak scenic site.

A .75-mile elevated boardwalk with viewing platforms along the Presque Isle River guides visitors past several waterfalls. Interpretive programs are available in summer; phone ahead for schedule. The Wilderness Visitor Center is open daily 10-6, late May to mid-Oct. Park open daily 24 hours. Admission $4 per private vehicle. Phone (906) 885-5275. *See Recreation Chart and the AAA Great Lakes CampBook.*

SLEEPING BEAR DUNES NATIONAL LAKESHORE (E-2)

Sleeping Bear Dunes National Lakeshore lies along 35 miles of the Lower Peninsula's northwestern shore and includes the Manitou Islands. The name is derived from a Ojibway Indian legend that tells of a bear and her two cubs forced to swim across Lake Michigan to escape a forest fire. The mother reached the shore safely and climbed to the top of a dune to await the cubs, who lagged behind and never arrived. She still maintains her vigil in the form of a dark hill of sand atop a plateau, while the errant cubs have become the North and South Manitou islands.

The dunes are the product of several glacial assaults that ended 11,000 years ago. The glaciers left a legacy of rock, sand and silt as they melted. Rugged bluffs rise as high as 480 feet above the lake. Among the dunes are ghost forests, the bleached remains of trees that were once covered by advancing dunes, then exposed as the sand moved on. The 7-mile Pierce Stocking Scenic Drive, open mid-May to mid-October, provides access to the high dunes of Sleeping Bear Plateau and affords views from the bluffs overlooking the lake.

Fishing and canoeing are popular on the Platte and Crystal rivers and adjoining lakes, as are hiking and cross-country skiing on the park's 55 miles of marked trails. On South Manitou Island is a lighthouse, the wreck of the Liberian freighter *Francisco Morazan* and the Valley of Giants—a virgin white-cedar forest. North Manitou Island, 15,000 acres of wilderness, attracts backpackers. The islands are accessible by passenger ferry from Leland *(see place listing p. 81).*

The Maritime Museum at the Sleeping Bear Point Coast Guard Station, 1 mile west of Glen Haven, has displays depicting the maritime history of the area; it is open daily, Memorial Day through Labor Day. The visitor center and park headquarters, on SR 72 in Empire, has exhibits about the region's natural history and a slide program about the park. The center is open daily, but is closed during off-season holidays.

Admission is $7 per week. For further information contact the Superintendent, Sleeping Bear Dunes National Lakeshore, 9922 Front St., Empire, MI 49630; phone (231) 326-5134. *See Recreation Chart and the AAA Great Lakes CampBook.*

SOO JUNCTION (B-5)

[SAVE] **TOONERVILLE TROLLEY AND RIVERBOAT TOUR TO TAHQUAMENON FALLS** is 2 mi. n. of SR 28 to CR 381. Tour 1 is a 6.5-hour narrow-gauge train trip and riverboat ride to the Tahquamenon River. A nature trail leads to the falls. Tour 2, offered in the summer, is a wilderness train ride to the river and back lasting approximately 1 hour, 45 minutes. Tour 1 departs Mon.-Thurs. at 10:30, mid- to late June; Mon.-Sat. at 10:30, July 1-Aug. 24; Wed.-Sat. at 10:30, Aug. 25-early Oct. Tour 2 departs Fri.-Sat. at noon, mid- to late June; Tues.-Sat. at noon, July 1-Aug. 24 and Labor Day weekend.

Tour 1 fare $28; ages 6-15, $13. Tour 2 fare $12; ages 6-15, $6. DS, MC, VI. Phone (906) 876-2311 or (888) 778-7246.

SOUTH HAVEN (H-1) pop. 5,021, elev. 589′

Greater South Haven Area Chamber of Commerce: 300 Broadway, South Haven, MI 49090; phone (269) 637-5171.

[SAVE] **MICHIGAN MARITIME MUSEUM** is off I-196 exit 20, then w. to 260 Dyckman Ave. Exhibits tell about the people who built and used boats on the Great Lakes and about changes in fishing history. U.S. Coast Guard exhibits also are displayed. Daily 10-5, Sun. noon-5; closed major holidays. Admission $2.50; over 62 and ages 5-12, $1.50. Phone (269) 637-8078 or (800) 747-3810.

SUTTONS BAY (E-2) pop. 589

Suttons Bay is surrounded by fragrant orchards and vineyards; several nearby wineries offer tours and tastings. Farm markets and antique shops can be found along SR 22 between Suttons Bay and Northport.

Suttons Bay Chamber of Commerce: 104 Broadway, P.O. Box 45, Suttons Bay, MI 49682; phone (231) 271-5077.

CASINOS

• **Leelanau Sands Casino** is at 2521 N.W. Bayshore Dr. Fri.-Sat. 8 a.m.-3 a.m., Sun.-Thurs. 8 a.m.-2 a.m. Phone (231) 271-4104 or (800) 922-2946. *See color ad p. 103.*

TECUMSEH (I-4) pop. 8,574, elev. 795'

TECUMSEH AREA HISTORICAL MUSEUM is at 302 E. Chicago Blvd. The museum is housed in Tecumseh's first Catholic church, which was built in 1913 by local farmers with stones from their fields. Displays include 19th-century dresses, Civil War items, arrowheads, old quilts and the surveying equipment used to lay out the town in 1824. Changing exhibits also are featured. Allow 30 minutes minimum. Wed.-Sat. 10-2; closed holidays. Free. Phone (517) 423-2374.

TIPTON (I-4)

HIDDEN LAKE GARDENS is 8 mi. w. of SR 52 on SR 50. The 755-acre garden is part of Michigan State University and has a greenhouse complex displaying plants from arid, tropical and temperate climates. There also are gardens, natural and developed landscapes, an all-America display, a lake, a picnic area, several hiking trails and a 6-mile scenic drive. There are thousands of labeled trees, shrubs and flowers and a display of dwarf and unusual evergreens. Daily 8-dusk, Apr.-Oct.; 8-4, rest of year. Admission $3, Apr.-Oct. $2, rest of year. Phone (517) 431-2060.

TRAVERSE CITY (E-2)
pop. 14,532, elev. 589'

Old orchards found when the lumber mill village of Traverse City was expanding during the late 1800s might have pointed the way for the future. By the time the timber was exhausted, the town was the center of a flourishing cherry-growing region. Several wineries contribute to the area's growing wine industry.

The city's setting at the base of Grand Traverse Bay makes it a busy resort in all seasons. Winter sports are widely available. In summer the bay provides good sailing and fishing. Traverse City State Park *(see Recreation Chart and the AAA Great Lakes CampBook)* is 2 miles east. The area has more than 30 golf courses, including courses designed by Jack Nicklaus, Arnold Palmer and Gary Player.

Particularly picturesque among the area's many scenic drives is the 36-mile trip on SR 37 through Old Mission Peninsula, which splits the bay into two long, narrow arms. It is especially lovely when the cherry trees bloom in mid-May and when leaves take on their fall colors, beginning in September. The tip of the peninsula, marked by a lighthouse, is equidistant from the Equator and the North Pole. At Old Mission is a reconstructed Indian mission originally built in 1836. Another scenic route along the lakeshore is US 31 between Traverse City and Petoskey, then SR 119 to Cross Village.

Traverse City Convention and Visitors Bureau: 101 W. Grandview Pkwy., Traverse City, MI 49684-2252; phone (800) 872-8377.

CLINCH PARK is at jct. Cass St. and Grandview Pkwy. The park contains a zoo of native wildlife, an aquarium displaying native game fish and a sandy beach. A steam train circles the park Memorial Day weekend through Labor Day. Daily 9:30-5:30, Memorial Day weekend-Labor Day; 10-4, mid-Apr. through day before Memorial Day weekend and day after Labor Day-Oct. 31. Admission $3; ages 5-12, $1.50. Train ride $1; ages 5-12, 50c. Phone (231) 922-4904.

Madeline is berthed at the Clinch Marina, jct. Cass St. and Grandview Pkwy. Tours are offered of this 92-foot replica of an 1845 schooner. Tours daily 8 a.m.-9 p.m. when docked, June-Sept. Donations. Reservations are required. Phone (231) 946-2647.

DENNOS MUSEUM CENTER is at 1701 E. Front St. on the campus of Northwestern Michigan College. Permanent and changing art exhibits in the galleries include the Discovery Gallery, offering hands-on art, science and technological exhibits; and the Inuit Art Gallery, featuring an extensive collection of Eskimo art. Allow 1 hour minimum. Mon.-Sat. 10-5, Sun. 1-5. Admission $4; under 13, $2; family rate $10. Phone (231) 995-1055.

WINERIES

• **Chateau Chantal Winery** is 12 mi. n. on SR 37 to 15900 Rue de Vin. Mon.-Sat. 11-8, Sun. noon-5, June 15-Labor Day; Mon.-Sat. 11-7, Sun. noon-5, day after Labor Day-Oct. 31; Mon.-Sat. 11-5, Sun noon-5, rest of year. Tours daily at 1, 2 and 3, June 1-Labor Day. Phone (231) 223-4110 or (800) 969-4009.

• **Chateau Grand Traverse** is 8.5 mi. n. on SR 37 at 12239 Center Rd. Mon.-Sat. 10-7, Sun. noon-6, Memorial Day-Labor Day; Mon.-Sat. 10-6, Sun. noon-6, May 1-day before Memorial Day and day after Labor Day-Oct. 31; Mon.-Sat. 10-5, Sun. noon-5, rest of year. Phone (231) 223-7355.

Precautions Can Save A Vacation!

*T*ravelers are faced with the task of protecting themselves while in a strange environment. Although there is no way to guarantee absolute protection from crime, the experts–law enforcement officials–advise travelers to take a proactive approach to securing their property and ensuring their safety.

- Make sure the hotel desk clerk does not announce your room number; if he/she does, quietly request a new room assignment.

- Ask front desk personnel which areas of town to avoid and what, if any, special precautions should be taken when driving a rental car (some criminals target tourists driving rental cars).

- Never open the door to a stranger; use the peephole and request identification. If you are still unsure, call the front desk to verify the identity of the person and the purpose of his/her visit.

- Carry money separately from credit cards or use a "fanny pack." Carry your purse close to your body and your wallet in an inside coat or front trouser pocket. Never leave luggage unattended, and use your business address, if possible, on luggage tags.

- Beware of distractions staged by would-be scam artists, especially groups of children that surround you, or a stranger who accidentally spills something on you. They may be lifting your wallet.

- If using an automatic teller machine (ATM), choose one in a well-lit area with plenty of foot traffic, such as one at a grocery store. Law enforcement officials suggest that machines inside establishments are generally safer to use.

- Use room safes or safety deposit boxes provided by the hotel. Store all valuables out of sight, even when you are in the room.

- Law enforcement agencies consider card-key (electronic) door locks the most secure.

UPPER PENINSULA

That the Upper Peninsula is part of Michigan at all was the result of the unpopular compromise that won Michigan its statehood. The crucial issue at stake was the sole proprietorship of a strip of territory along the Michigan-Ohio border that included the city of Toledo. The bitterly fought Toledo War (contested in Congress with blazing words, not in Toledo with bullets) resulted in Michigan's ceding that land to Ohio in exchange for statehood.

Michigan somewhat grudgingly accepted the Upper Peninsula—then considered a barren wasteland—as a consolation prize. Hardly a Michigander today would have it any other way. In terms of natural resources alone the raw deal turned out to be a steal. When Michigan became a state in 1837, the Upper Peninsula's fabulous deposits of pure copper were already being uncovered; the deposits were, however, not news to American Indians, who had mined the metal thousands of years before.

In 1957 the slender strand of the Mackinac Bridge anchored the Upper Peninsula to the Lower, making the U.P.—as locals call it—easily accessible from the south. Recreation and tourism have since helped alleviate some of the region's economic slack.

Known now for its unspoiled beauty rather than its industrial scars, the Upper Peninsula is a popular haven for outdoors enthusiasts. State and national forests cover much of the land; Isle Royale National Park (see place listing p. 77) and Pictured Rocks National Lakeshore (see place listing p. 94) preserve some of the rugged peninsula's most impressive terrain. Aspen, birch, fir, maple and spruce trees shelter such animals as black bears, Eastern timber wolves, white-tailed deer and moose.

The Porcupine Mountains in the west have a large stand of virgin hemlock and one of the largest relatively undisturbed northern hemlock hardwood forests west of New York's Adirondack Mountains. Recreational opportunities range from swimming to skiing, with almost legendary popularity in fishing.

The following places in the Upper Peninsula are listed separately under their individual names: Bessemer, Calumet, Caspian, Copper Harbor, Escanaba, Fayette, Germfask, Hancock, Hiawatha National Forest, Houghton, Iron Mountain, Ironwood, Ishpeming, Isle Royale National Park, Manistique, Marquette, Munising, Negaunee, Ontonagon, Paradise, Pictured Rocks National Lakeshore, Rockland, St. Ignace, Sault Ste. Marie, Silver City, Soo Junction and Whitefish Point.

WALLED LAKE—see Detroit p. 65.

WATERFORD—see Detroit p. 65.

WATERLOO (L-1) pop. 3,069

Plentiful game attracted many of the Great Lakes Indian tribes to Waterloo, an area of low hills and marshes that divides the headwaters of the westward-flowing Grand River from the eastbound Huron River. Waterloo is in the midst of Waterloo State Recreation Area (see Recreation Chart and the AAA Great Lakes CampBook).

GERALD E. EDDY DISCOVERY CENTER is at 16345 McClure Rd. in the Waterloo State Recreation Area, exit 157 off I-94, following signs. Hands-on exhibits and 17 miles of walking trails are featured. A slide presentation discusses the geology of Earth and of Michigan. Allow 1 hour minimum. Tues.-Sun. 9-5. Park admission $4 per private vehicle. Discovery Center free. Phone (734) 475-3170.

SAVE **WATERLOO AREA FARM MUSEUM AND DEWEY SCHOOL** is 3 mi. n. to 9998 Waterloo-Munith Rd. Several restored buildings comprise the complex: two barns, a corn crib, schoolhouse, Victorian farmhouse, granary, workshop, icehouse, milk cellar, windmill and log house. Displays of tools, clothing, furnishings and decorations depict 19th-century farm life. Guides in period garb lead tours. Allow 1 hour minimum. Wed.-Sun. 1-5, June-Aug.; tours by appointment in Sept. Last tour leaves 30 minutes before closing. Admission $3; over 62, $2.50; ages 5-18, $1. Phone (517) 596-2254.

WEST BLOOMFIELD—see Detroit p. 65.

WHITEFISH POINT (A-5)

GEM **GREAT LAKES SHIPWRECK MUSEUM** is at 18335 N. Whitefish Point Rd. The museum features a restored lighthouse keeper's quarters. Displays include artifacts, including the bell of the Edmund Fitzgerald, and pictures of shipping disasters. A theater offers a short videotape presentation about the Edmund Fitzgerald, and a boardwalk extends to Lake Superior. Allow 30 minutes minimum. Daily 10-6, May 15-Oct. 15. Admission $8; under 13, $5; family rate $22.50. MC, VI. Phone (906) 635-1742. See color ad p. 85.

Whitefish Point Light Station is at jct. SR 123 and Whitefish Point Rd. The light station began operation in 1849 and is the oldest working lighthouse on Lake Superior. Overlooking the graveyard of the Great Lakes, it marks the critical turning point for all ships leaving and entering Lake Superior.

WHITEHALL (G-1) pop. 2,884, elev. 599′

WHITE RIVER LIGHT STATION MUSEUM is w. off US 31 to White Lake Dr. exit, w. on S. Shore Dr. to Murray Rd., then s. to 6199 Murray Rd. This 1875 lighthouse displays photographs, paintings and marine artifacts. Allow 30 minutes minimum. Tues.-Fri. 11-5, Sat.-Sun. noon-6, June-Aug.; Sat.-Sun. noon-6, Memorial Day weekend and in Sept. Admission $2; ages 10-18, $1. Phone (231) 894-8265.

WILLIAMSBURG (E-3) elev. 732'

CASINOS

- **Turtle Creek Casino** is at 7741 SR 72E, Williamsburg, MI 49690. Daily 24 hours. Phone (231) 267-9546 or (888) 777-8946. *See color ad p. 103.*

WYANDOTTE—*see Detroit p. 65.*

YPSILANTI (I-5) pop. 22,362, elev. 720'

When the youthful Greek revolutionary general Demetrios Ypsilanti held the entire Turkish Army at bay and escaped without losing even one of his 300 soldiers, he had no idea that his bravery would cause a muddy but energetic village in the wilds of southeastern Michigan to become his namesake in 1832. This city on the Huron River is an industrial center and the home of Eastern Michigan University, Riverside Park and the noted Water Tower.

The city's 40-block historic district, centered around Huron Street, contains some 700 restored buildings in the Greek Revival, Gothic Revival, Italianate, Second Empire, Queen Anne and Tudor Revival architectural styles.

Ypsilanti Area Convention and Visitors Bureau: 106 W. Michigan Ave., Ypsilanti, MI 48197; phone (734) 483-4444.

WIARD'S ORCHARDS & COUNTRY FAIR is 4 mi. s. of I-94 exit 183 (Huron St.) following signs to 5565 Merritt Rd. The property has been run by the Wiard family since 1853. Nearly 200 acres contain apple orchards, a pumpkin patch and a cider mill. Activities (which may vary due to the seasonal nature of farm operations) include picking your own fruits, petting animals, riding ponies and exploring a hay barn. A recurring country fair features a haunted barn, monster maze and hay rides. Food is available.

Mon.-Fri. 10-6, mid-Sept. through Oct. 31. Country fair Sat.-Sun. 10-6, mid-Sept. to late Oct. Closed holidays. Orchards free. Country fair (includes rides) $8.25. Phone (734) 482-7744.

YPSILANTI AUTOMOTIVE HERITAGE COLLECTION AND MILLER MOTORS HUDSON is at 112 E. Cross St. Housed in the last Hudson dealership, the museum contains more than 35 original and restored cars, from a copy of the Tucker Torpedo to an original Kaiser. Corvairs, Chevy IIs and Hudsons also are on display, along with Hudson memorabilia. Mon.-Fri. 1:30-5:30, Sat. 9-5, Sun. noon-5; closed holidays. Donations. Phone (734) 482-5200.

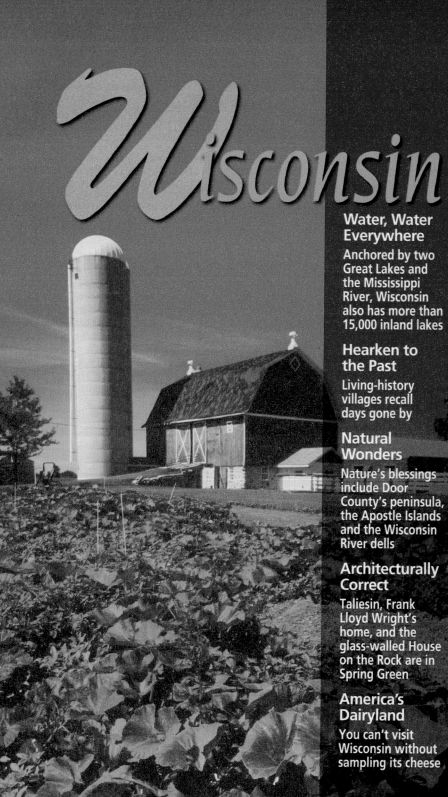

Wisconsin

Water, Water Everywhere

Anchored by two Great Lakes and the Mississippi River, Wisconsin also has more than 15,000 inland lakes

Hearken to the Past

Living-history villages recall days gone by

Natural Wonders

Nature's blessings include Door County's peninsula, the Apostle Islands and the Wisconsin River dells

Architecturally Correct

Taliesin, Frank Lloyd Wright's home, and the glass-walled House on the Rock are in Spring Green

America's Dairyland

You can't visit Wisconsin without sampling its cheese

say "cheese"

I n America's Dairyland, there are lots of reasons to say "cheese."

Smiles, rest and relaxation are a way of life in the communities along the Door County peninsula. Although square in the Midwest, you'll experience the flavor of New England in a rugged landscape peppered with fishing villages, farms, lighthouses and sand beaches.

The state's biggest city, Milwaukee, reflects a decidedly German heritage. Key players in its development—such sudsy names as Miller, Pabst and Schlitz—are sure to elicit a grin or two.

Noted architect Frank Lloyd Wright left his mark in the middle of the state. The Richland Center native brought his visions to life in such cities as Madison and Spring Green.

Affectionately called "cheeseheads," fans of the Green Bay Packers (the oldest team in the NFL) cheer wildly and beam like Cheshire cats.

Stretching along the western border is the St. Croix River, a recreational hot spot with scenic gorges, rock formations and waterfalls.

And like sprinkled Parmesan, the intriguing Apostle Islands top the state.

The national lakeshore features more lighthouses than any other national park.

For a sampling of the old days, visit living-history farms and villages in Cassville, Eagle and New Glarus, where things ahven't changed much since the 19th century.

Wisconsin. It's whey more than dairy.

Milk Wisconsin for all it's worth, and you end up with more than just cheese.

Sure, the state earned its nickname as America's Dairyland by being a leader in dairy production. However, it's also a big processor of snap beans, sweet corn, hay, oats and potatoes. It manufactures much of the nation's mining machinery, x-ray equipment and power cranes. And its economy thrives on a booming tourism business—which is no small wonder, given the seemingly endless number of things you can do.

Take steps into the past. A replica of the log cabin in which "Little House" books author Laura Ingalls Wilder was born is in Pepin. Historic lighthouses line the Door Peninsula. Costumed interpreters perform daily chores around the 360-acre grounds of the 1851 Wade House in Greenbush.

Explore another culture. A strong Norwegian influence embraces Blue Mounds. Scandinavian customs prevail on Washington Island, the country's oldest Icelandic settlement. New Glarus, often called "Little Switzerland," reflects a decidedly Swiss heritage. German, Danish, Polish and Finnish homesteads are among the more than 65 preserved buildings at the 1870s rural village in Eagle.

Awakening the Senses

Admire great architecture. Massive fireplaces, waterfalls and a windowed room that juts out over Wyoming Valley are among the wonders of The House on the Rock, south of Spring Green. Richland Center native Frank Lloyd Wright designed buildings in Madison and Spring Green. The State Capitol in Madison shows a Roman Renaissance flair. A 40-foot circular stairway winds among five floors of the 1854 Octagon House in Watertown.

Give your palate a treat. Sip apple, cherry and grape wines in Algoma, Barneveld, Carlsville, Cedarburg and Prairie du Sac. Taste brewery samples in the city made famous for beer: Milwaukee. Nibble on cheese in Monroe and Rudolph. Savor cranberry refreshments made from berries cultivated in marshes around Manitowish Waters and Warrens.

Play the slots and scream out "Bingo!" Casinos in Baraboo, Carter, Green Bay and Keshena invite you to test your luck. Gamble on the greyhounds at a park in Kenosha.

Learn about locomotives. You can ride the rails through the St. Croix River Valley in Osceola and the lake country of Spooner,

Wisconsin Historical Timeline

French explorer Jean Nicolet leads an expedition ashore near Green Bay.
1634

Jacques Marquette and Louis Joliet leave De Pere on their historic journey to the Mississippi River.
1673

Wisconsin becomes the nation's 30th state.
1848

Following the Treaty of Paris, the U.S. takes ownership of the Wisconsin territory.
1783

1816
The establishment of Fort Howard at Green Bay and Fort Crawford at Prairie du Chien opens the region to settlement.

1867
Architect Frank Lloyd Wright is born in Richland Center.

where a former train depot holds railroad memories. Iron horses from the steam and diesel eras also are preserved at museums in Green Bay and North Freedom.

Focus on other transportation. Aircraft are showcased at an Oshkosh museum. Classic automobiles beg to be admired in Hartford. Maritime vessels are centerpieces at museums in Gills Rock, Sturgeon Bay and Superior. Circus wagons have a big-top home in Baraboo.

Remember veterans. Museums and parks in Madison, Neillsville, Oshkosh and Waupaca pay tribute to those who served in conflicts.

Trees, Caves and Wildlife

Trace the papermaking trade. The "Lumberjack Special" steam-powered train carries visitors from the historic depot in Laona to Camp Five Museum Complex, where logging relics and an audiovisual presentation detail the history of an industry that feeds off 15 million acres of forestland. Tours of paper mills in Wisconsin Rapids guide you through to the finished product.

Get back to nature. Rose-colored cliffs punctuate the weathered caves and hollows at Apostle Islands National Lakeshore. The glacial phenomena of Devil's Lake State Park and Kettle Moraine State Forest are a sight to behold. River tours wander among unusual rock formations and caverns in Wisconsin Dells.

Confront a local legend. The folksy myth of the Hodag, a creature once said to have inhabited the forests around Rhinelander, is kept very much alive in the area.

Study native wildlife. Cruises departing from Hazelhurst and Horicon bring you face-to-face with all kinds of creatures. Birdwatchers gather on the shores of St. Croix National Scenic Riverway and in a Waupun refuge.

Catch a great view. On a clear day, you can see practically forever from the lofty vantage point atop Granddad Bluff, which towers 600 feet above La Crosse.

When it comes to family fun, America's Dairyland may just be the cream of the crop.

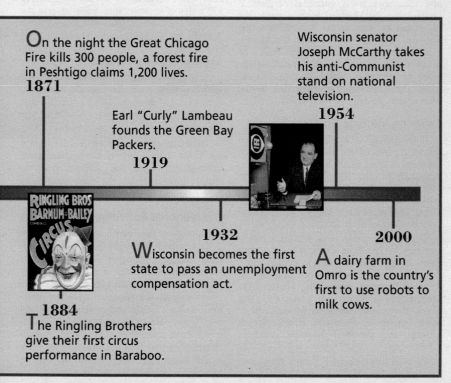

On the night the Great Chicago Fire kills 300 people, a forest fire in Peshtigo claims 1,200 lives.
1871

Wisconsin senator Joseph McCarthy takes his anti-Communist stand on national television.
1954

Earl "Curly" Lambeau founds the Green Bay Packers.
1919

1932
Wisconsin becomes the first state to pass an unemployment compensation act.

2000
A dairy farm in Omro is the country's first to use robots to milk cows.

1884
The Ringling Brothers give their first circus performance in Baraboo.

Recreation

With 15,000 inland lakes and 25,000 miles of waterways—plus borders touching lakes Michigan and Superior, the Brule, St. Croix and Menominee rivers and the mighty Mississippi—Wisconsin is an H_2O utopia.

Sailing enthusiasts float through the steely waters of Chequamegon and Sturgeon bays, while **windsurfers** unfurl sails of their own around the southern tip of Lake Winnebago and at Kohler-Andrae State Park, on the shores of Lake Michigan.

Break the surface during a **scuba diving** trip along Apostle Islands National Lakeshore, or explore the shipwrecks lining "death's door," the nautical passage between Door County and Washington Island.

Such lazy rivers as the Apple, Chippewa and Namekagon are prime territory for **tubing.** Moderate currents enhance the **canoeing** experience on the Baraboo, Crystal, La Crosse, Oconto, St. Croix, Upper Bois Brule and Wisconsin rivers. The winding Kickapoo—dubbed the "crookedest river in the world"—is navigable its entire length.

Challenging rapids result in irresistible **kayaking** on the Flambeau, Grant, Ontonagan and Tomahawk rivers. Stretches of class V rapids make the Montreal River a great spot for expert kayakers to put their skills to the test. Although the waters around the Apostle Islands are more placid, paddlers won't be disappointed. Rugged sea caves riddling the bases of sandstone cliffs beckon you to explore. For **white-water rafting,** take on the Menominee, Peshtigo or Wolf rivers.

Differing Vantage Points

If thoughts of lofty heights don't leave you quivering, Wisconsin delivers thrills. **Rock climbing** in Devil's Lake State Park, near Baraboo, leads you atop 500-foot bluffs around the lake for which the park is named. **Hang gliders** who launch from similar bluffs shouldering the Upper Mississippi River Valley enjoy a memorable perspective of the area.

Once you've taken advantage of a bird's-eye view of the land, check it out up close from **hiking** and **horseback riding** trails. You'll find facilities for both activities at Wildcat Mountain State Park, southeast of Ontario, and at several state forests, including Black River, near Black River Falls; Brule River, in Brule; Flambeau River, east of Draper; and Governor Knowles, west of Grantsburg.

On-road **bicycling** trails paint a fitting picture of the varied landscape. The 22-mile High Falls Tour, which weaves through Marinette County, passes the cascade of Veterans Falls and the glimmering waters of High Falls Reservoir. Take your bike over an original covered bridge on the 30-mile trail that begins at Cedar Creek Park in Cedarburg, or pedal through the stone railroad tunnels of the 32-mile Elroy-Sparta Trail.

For off-road excitement, **mountain biking** trails cater to cyclists of all abilities. The Boulder Junction Area Trail System, or B.A.T.S., covers 10 mostly easy miles around Boulder Junction. Skilled riders favor the tough Washburn Lake trails, near Rhinelander, or the wild and jarring experience afforded by the Swiss-cheeselike terrain of Kettle Moraine State Forest, much of which only extreme adventurists would like.

"Snow" Much Fun

During winter, the groomed trails at many state parks entice **cross-country skiers** and **snowshoers.** Some of the more extensive systems trek through Governor Dodge State Park, north of Dodgeville; Mirror Lake State Park, southwest of Lake Delton; and Newport State Park, northeast of Ellison Bay. Nearly 120 miles of snowmobiling trails traverse the northern and southern units of Kettle Moraine State Forest. Quadruple your fun on the 480-plus miles of trails in Northern Highland-American Legion State Forest.

Among the popular **downhill skiing** and **snowboarding** areas are Cascade Mountain, southwest of Portage; Devil's Head, near Merrimac; Trollhaugen, in Dresser; and Whitecap Mountain, west of Montreal.

Trout and salmon **fishing** is excellent in the Great Lakes. For northern pike, bass, muskellunge, perch and walleye, head to smaller lakes and streams. Many state parks have **camping** facilities.

Recreational Activities

Throughout the TourBook, you may notice a Recreational Activities heading with bulleted listings of recreation-oriented establishments listed underneath. Since normal AAA inspection criteria cannot be applied, these establishments are presented only for information. Age, height and weight restrictions may apply. Reservations often are recommended and sometimes are required. Visitors should phone or write the attraction for additional information; the address and phone number are provided for this purpose.

Fast Facts

POPULATION: 5,363,675.

AREA: 56,154 square miles; ranks 26th.

CAPITAL: Madison.

HIGHEST POINT: 1,953 ft., Timm's Hill.

LOWEST POINT: 581 ft., Lake Michigan.

TIME ZONE(S): Central. DST.

MINIMUM AGE FOR DRIVERS: 18; 16 with drivers education.

MINIMUM AGE FOR GAMBLING: 18; 21 if alcohol is served on the premises.

SEAT BELT/CHILD RESTRAINT LAWS: Seat belts required for driver and all passengers; child restraints required for under 4.

HELMETS FOR MOTORCYCLISTS: Required for those under 18 or when operating with a learner's permit.

RADAR DETECTORS: Permitted.

FIREARMS LAWS: Vary by state and/or county. Contact Wisconsin State Police Headquarters, 4802 Sheboygan Ave., Madison, WI 53707; phone (608) 266-3212.

HOLIDAYS: Jan. 1; Martin Luther King Jr. Day, Jan. (3rd Mon.); Presidents' Day, Feb. (3rd Mon.); Memorial Day, May (last Mon.); July 4; Labor Day, Sept. (1st Mon.); Columbus Day, Oct. (2nd Mon.); Veterans Day, Nov. 11; Thanksgiving; Dec. 25.

TAXES: Wisconsin's statewide sales tax is 5 percent, with local options for an additional increment of 0.5 percent, plus a lodgings tax.

STATE INFORMATION CENTERS: Centers are in Madison at 201 W. Washington Ave., in Grant County on US 151/61, at Beloit and La Crosse off I-90, at Hudson and Kenosha off I-94, near Genoa City on US 12, at Superior on US 2, at Hurley on US 51, in Prairie du Chien at 211 S. Main St., in Marinette on US 41 and in Chicago, Ill., at 52 W. Adams St. Madison center open Mon.-Fri. 8-4:30. Chicago center open Mon.-Fri. 7:30-6. Other centers open daily 8-6, June 1-Labor Day; 8-4 (except Superior 9-5), day after Labor Day-Oct. 31. Beloit, Hudson, Hurley, Kenosha and La Crosse open Tues.-Sat. 8-4, Nov.-Apr.

FURTHER INFORMATION FOR VISITORS:

Wisconsin Department of Tourism
P.O. Box 7976
Madison, WI 53707-7976
(608) 266-7621
(800) 432-8747

FISHING AND HUNTING REGULATIONS:
Wisconsin Department of Natural Resources
P.O. Box 7921
Madison, WI 53707
(608) 266-2621

NATIONAL FOREST INFORMATION:
U.S. Forest Service, Eastern Region
310 W. Wisconsin Ave., Suite 500
Milwaukee, WI 53203
(414) 297-3693
(877) 444-6777 (for reservations)

©2002 NAVIGATION TECHNOLOGIES

Wisconsin Orientation

NOT INTENDED FOR DRIVING.
SEE APPROPRIATE AAA SHEET MAP.

Only places listed in the Attractions section appear on this map.

⚑ See AAA GEM Attractions

🔺 See Chart of Recreation Areas

Miles

41

4081-A

© AAA

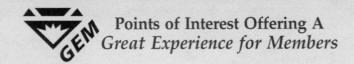

Points of Interest Offering A
Great Experience for Members

Apostle Islands National Lakeshore (A-3)

APOSTLE ISLANDS NATIONAL LAKESHORE—Surrounded by the waters of Lake Superior, the Apostle Islands were early fur-trading outposts; the lakeshore is now visited for recreational pursuits. See p. 121.

SIGHTSEEING CRUISES—The Apostle Islands are explored by a variety of narrated cruises; area geology, history and legends are related, and stops might include nature hikes or visits to lighthouses or a restored fish camp. See p. 121.

Baraboo (G-5)

CIRCUS WORLD MUSEUM—Step right up, ladies and gentlemen, for big-top circus performances, parades, a circus museum and a collection of handcrafted circus wagons; don't forget the elephant rides! See p. 124.

DEVIL'S LAKE STATE PARK—Bordered on three sides by quartzite cliffs, Devil's Lake is part of the Ice Age National Scientific Reserve; the park is a favorite for hiking, swimming and camping. See p. 124.

THE INTERNATIONAL CRANE FOUNDATION—Guided tours of this world center for the study and preservation of cranes introduce visitors to a variety of crane species; an overlook, chick exercise yard, and nature trails through restored wetlands, prairies and savannas add to the understanding of these creatures. See p. 124.

Blue Mounds (I-5)

CAVE OF THE MOUNDS—Uncovered by a 1939 quarry blast, this National Natural Landmark boasts crystallized rock formations and shimmering underground pools. See p. 126.

Cassville (I-3)

GOVERNOR NELSON DEWEY HOMESITE—The home of Wisconsin's first governor has been reconstructed to reflect the lifestyle of the Dewey family; the agricultural estate is reminiscent of a Virginia plantation. See p. 128.

STONEFIELD STATE HISTORIC SITE—The site consists of Stonefield, the farm estate of Wisconsin's first governor; the State Agricultural Museum, where farm machinery helps trace the state's agricultural history; and a turn-of-the-20th-century village where everyday life of that period still goes on. See p. 127.

Eagle (I-7)

OLD WORLD WIS-CONSIN—This 576-acre state historic site depicts 19th-century Wisconsin through representations of a rural cross-

roads village, Yankee farmsteads and African-American settlements; costumed interpreters recreate pioneer life. See p. 159.

Green Bay (E-8)

NATIONAL RAILROAD MUSEUM—All aboard for a chance to see more than 70 locomotives and rolling stock, including "The Big Boy," said to be the world's largest steam locomotive. See p. 135.

Greenbush (G-7)

WADE HOUSE & WESLEY JUNG CARRIAGE MUSEUM—This restored stagecoach inn includes a smithy, a smokehouse and a residence typical of the 1850s, with costumed interpreters conducting tours and performing daily chores; the carriage museum contains a collection of horse-and-buggy era vehicles. See p. 135.

Laona (D-7)

LUMBERJACK SPECIAL AND CAMP FIVE MUSEUM COMPLEX TOUR—A steam-powered train takes visitors from the Laona depot to the museum complex, where they can visit a logging museum, an active blacksmith shop, an old country store and a nature center; other options include a forest tour by surrey and a wildlife tour on a pontoon boat. See p. 140.

Madison (H-6)

WISCONSIN STATE CAPITOL—The 1917 Roman Renaissance structure has a white granite dome topped by a bronze statue; guided tours cover the rotunda, the Supreme Court and the state's Senate and Assembly chambers. See p. 143

WISCONSIN VETER-ANS MUSEUM—Dedicated to the Wisconsin residents who served their country in military service from the Civil War to the Persian Gulf War, the museum features lifelike dioramas utilizing actual military equipment in realistic settings. See p. 143.

Manitowoc (F-8) 8)

RAHR-WEST ART MUSEUM—In a Victorian mansion, the museum contains period furnishings, dolls, and ivory and porcelain objects. See p. 144.

WISCONSIN MARITIME MU-SEUM—Shipping on the Great Lakes from the days of three-masted schooners to today's vessels is depicted through maps, nautical equipment and models; a highlight is an exhibit about the World War II submarines built in Manitowoc. See p. 144.

Milwaukee (H-8)

MILWAUKEE ART MUSEUM—More than 20,000 works of art ranging from Frank Lloyd Wright to German Expressionism are housed inside this lakefront museum. See p. 153.

MILWAUKEE COUNTY ZOO—The zoo's collections, grouped by continent in settings that resemble their natural habitats, can be seen close-up courtesy of a zoomobile tour; sea lion and raptor shows and a working dairy farm are highlights. See p. 154.

MILWAUKEE PUBLIC MUSEUM—The museum interprets the world's natural and cultural heritage through such displays as life-size dinosaurs, the streets of old Milwaukee and environmental exhibits about rain forests, Africa and Latin America. See p. 155.

MITCHELL PARK HORTICULTURAL CONSERVATORY—"THE DOMES"—The conservatory's three domes have individual motifs: One features tropical plants; another, the world's deserts; and the third has five themed floral shows each year. See p. 155.

New Glarus (I-5)

SWISS HISTORICAL VILLAGE—The Swiss heritage of New Glarus is depicted here in 14 buildings, replicas of the first structures built by the community's 19th-century Swiss settlers; a hall of history traces Swiss immigration to America. See p. 163.

Oshkosh (F-7)

EAA AIRVENTURE MUSEUM—More than 95 historic aircraft, a hangar and an airport typical of the early days of air travel are part of this complex; come during the summer for flights in a restored 1929 airplane or open-cockpit bi-plane. See p. 165.

Prairie du Chien (H-3)

VILLA LOUIS—This Victorian mansion and several outbuildings were built by a pioneering family prominent in the business of fur trading; the opulent furnishings include a fine collection of decorative arts. See p. 167.

St. Croix Falls (D-1)

INTERSTATE STATE PARK—Wisconsin's oldest state park is well-known for its scenic beauty and for the Old Man of the Dalles, a rock outcropping along the St. Croix River. See p. 169.

Spring Green (H-4)

THE HOUSE ON THE ROCK—This multi-level house perched on a precipice overlooking the Wyoming Valley has a glass-walled room extending out over the valley, waterfalls and an observation deck; other buildings house a variety of eclectic collections. See p. 172.

Watertown (H-6))

OCTAGON HOUSE— The 1854 house has five antique-filled floors as well as a 40-foot circular stairway; a late 19th-century barn contains farm-related exhibits. See p. 176.

Wausau (E-5)

LEIGH YAWKEY WOODSON ART MUSEUM—In addition to its permanent collection, the Woodson, housed in an English Tudor-style building, presents changing exhibitions both inside the museum and outdoors in its landscaped, parklike gardens. See p. 177.

Wisconsin Dells (G-5)

DELLS BOAT TOURS—Boat tours through the Upper and Lower dells of the Wisconsin River cruise past sandstone cliffs, canyons, and erosion-carved islands and rock formations. See p. 179.

RECREATION AREAS

	MAP LOCATION	CAMPING	PICNICKING	HIKING TRAILS	BOATING	BOAT RAMP	BOAT RENTAL	FISHING	SWIMMING	PETS ON LEASH	BICYCLE TRAILS	WINTER SPORTS	VISITOR CENTER	LODGE/CABINS	FOOD SERVICE
NATIONAL FORESTS *(See place listings)*															
Chequamegon-Nicolet 1,518,138 acres. North-central and northeastern Wisconsin. Horse rental.		•	•	•	•	•		•	•	•	•	•			•
NATIONAL LAKESHORES *(See place listings)*															
Apostle Islands (A-5) 69,372 acres off northern Wisconsin's Bayfield peninsula in Lake Superior.		•	•	•	•	•	•	•	•	•	•	•			
NATIONAL RIVERWAYS *(See place listings)*															
St. Croix (E-1, B-2) 252 mi. from Cable to Prescott.		•	•	•	•	•		•	•	•	•		•		
STATE															
Amnicon Falls (A-2) 825 acres 10 mi. s.e. of Superior on US 2. Scenic.	**1**	•	•	•				•		•					
Big Bay (A-4) 2,358 acres e. of Bayfield on Madeline Island via ferry.	**2**	•	•	•				•	•	•					
Big Foot Beach (I-7) 271 acres 2.5 mi. s. of Lake Geneva on SR 120.	**3**	•	•	•	•			•	•	•			•		
Black River (F-4) 67,000 acres. *(See Black River Falls p. 125)*	**4**	•	•	•	•			•	•	•		•			
Blue Mound (H-5) 1,124 acres off US 18/151 in Blue Mounds. Scenic. Cross-country skiing. *(See Blue Mounds p. 126)*	**5**	•	•	•					•	•		•	•		•
Bong (I-8) 4,515 acres 4 mi. s. of Kansasville on SR 142. Horse rental.	**6**	•	•	•	•	•		•	•	•		•	•		
Browntown-Cadiz Springs (I-5) 644 acres 1 mi. e. of Browntown off SR 11.	**7**		•	•	•			•	•	•					
Brule River (B-3) 40,367 acres at Brule.	**8**	•	•	•				•		•		•			
Brunet Island (D-3) 1,032 acres 1 mi. n. of Cornell off SR 27. Historic.	**9**	•	•	•	•	•		•	•	•		•			
Buckhorn (G-5) 2,507 acres 13 mi. n. of Mauston on CRs Q and G.	**10**	•	•	•	•	•		•	•	•			•		
Copper Falls (B-4) 2,483 acres 2 mi. n.e. of Mellen on SR 169. Nature programs.	**11**	•	•	•				•	•	•		•			•
Council Grounds (D-5) 462 acres 2 mi. n.w. of Merrill on SR 107.	**12**	•	•	•	•	•		•	•	•		•	•		•

RECREATION AREAS

	MAP LOCATION	CAMPING	PICNICKING	HIKING TRAILS	BOATING	BOAT RAMP	BOAT RENTAL	FISHING	SWIMMING	PETS ON LEASH	BICYCLE TRAILS	WINTER SPORTS	VISITOR CENTER	LODGE/CABINS	FOOD SERVICE
Devil's Lake (H-5) 10,000 acres 3.5 mi. s. of Baraboo on SR 123. Scenic. *(See Baraboo p. 124)*	13	•	•	•	•	•		•	•	•			•		•
Flambeau River (C-4) 89,914 acres 5 mi. e. of Draper on SR 70.	14	•	•	•	•	•		•	•	•			•		
Governor Dodge (H-5) 5,029 acres 3 mi. n. of Dodgeville on SR 23. Nature programs. Scenic. Bridle trails. *(See Dodgeville p. 130)*	15	•	•	•	•	•	•	•	•	•	•		•		•
Governor Knowles (C-1) 19,185 acres 5 mi. w. of Grantsburg on SR 70. Bridle trails.	16		•	•	•	•		•	•	•			•		
Harrington Beach (G-8) 636 acres 2 mi. e. of Belgium on CR O. Nature trails.	17	•	•	•				•	•	•			•		•
Hartman Creek (F-6) 1,323 acres 6 mi. w. of Waupaca on SR 54. Nature programs.	18	•	•	•	•			•	•	•			•		
High Cliff (F-7) 1,145 acres 3 mi. s. of Sherwood off SR 55. Nature programs.	19	•	•	•	•	•		•	•	•			•		
Horicon Marsh (G-7) 11,000 acres n. of Horicon. *(See Horicon p. 136)*	20		•	•	•	•		•			•	•	•		
Interstate (D-1) 1,377 acres .5 mi. s. of US 8 on US 35. Scenic. Nature programs. *(See St. Croix Falls p. 169)*	21	•	•	•	•	•		•	•	•			•		
Kettle Moraine North (G-8) 28,910 acres. Nature programs. Bridle trails, horse rental. *(See Campbellsport p. 127)*	22	•	•	•	•	•		•	•	•	•		•		•
Kettle Moraine South (I-7) 18,391 acres at Eagle. Nature programs. Bridle trails.	23	•	•	•	•			•	•	•	•		•		
Kohler-Andrae (G-8) 879 acres 6 mi. s.e. of Sheboygan off US 141. Nature programs.	24	•	•	•				•	•	•			•		•
Lake Kegonsa (H-6) 343 acres 10 mi. s. of Madison off CR N.	25	•	•	•	•	•		•	•	•			•		
Lake Wissota (E-3) 1,062 acres 5 mi. e. of Chippewa Falls on SR 29. Nature programs. Horse rental.	26	•	•	•	•	•	•	•	•	•			•		
Merrick (F-2) 322 acres 2 mi. n.w. of Fountain City off SR 35.	27	•	•	•	•	•		•	•	•			•		
Mill Bluff (G-4) 1,258 acres 4 mi. n.w. of Camp Douglas off I-90.	28		•	•					•	•					
Mirror Lake (G-5) 2,057 acres 4 mi. s.w. of Lake Delton on SR 23. Nature programs.	29	•	•	•	•	•	•	•	•	•			•		
Nelson Dewey (I-3) 756 acres 1.2 mi. n.w. of Cassville on CR VV. *(See Cassville p. 127)*	30	•	•	•						•					
New Glarus Woods (I-5) 350 acres 1.5 mi. s. of New Glarus via SR 69 on CR NN.	31	•	•	•						•	•				
Newport (D-9) 2,368 acres n.e. of Ellison Bay via SR 42. Cross-country skiing.	32	•	•	•				•	•	•		•	•	•	
Northern Highland-American Legion (C-5) 220,455 acres 3 mi. w. of Eagle River on SR 70. Nature programs.	33	•	•	•	•	•	•	•	•	•			•		
Pattison (B-2) 1,374 acres 10 mi. s. of Superior on SR 35. Nature programs.	34	•	•	•				•	•	•		•	•		
Peninsula (D-9) 3,763 acres .25 mi. n. of Fish Creek. Nature programs. Nature trails. Golf, tennis.	35	•	•	•	•	•	•	•	•	•	•	•	•		•
Perrot (F-3) 1,300 acres 1 mi. n. of Trempealeau off SR 35. Nature programs. Historic.	36	•	•	•	•			•		•		•	•		
Pike Lake (H-7) 678 acres 2 mi. e. of Hartford on SR 60.	37	•	•	•				•	•	•					
Point Beach (F-8) 2,903 acres 6 mi. n.e. of Two Rivers. Nature programs.	38	•	•	•				•	•	•		•	•	•	•
Potawatomi (E-9) 1,226 acres 2 mi. n.w. of Sturgeon Bay on CR M. Downhill and cross-country skiing, snowmobiling.	39	•	•	•				•		•		•	•		
Rib Mountain (E-5) 941 acres 4 mi. s.w. of Wausau on CR N. Nature trails. *(See Wausau p. 177)*	40	•	•	•						•			•		•
Roche A Cri (G-5) 411 acres 2 mi. n. of Friendship on SR 13.	41	•	•	•						•					
Rock Island (D-9) 912 acres on Rock Island via ferry. Historic.	42	•	•	•	•			•	•	•				•	
Rocky Arbor (G-5) 226 acres 2 mi. n.w. of Wisconsin Dells off I-90.	43	•	•	•						•					

RECREATION AREAS

	MAP LOCATION	CAMPING	PICNICKING	HIKING TRAILS	BOATING	BOAT RAMP	BOAT RENTAL	FISHING	SWIMMING	PETS ON LEASH	BICYCLE TRAILS	WINTER SPORTS	VISITOR CENTER	LODGE/CABINS	FOOD SERVICE
Tower Hill (H-5) 77 acres 3 mi. s.e. of Spring Green on SR 23.	44	•	•	•	•	•	•	•		•					
Whitefish Dunes (E-9) 863 acres 10 mi. n.e. of Sturgeon Bay via SR 57.	45		•	•				•	•	•			•		•
Wildcat Mountain (G-4) 3,526 acres 3 mi. s.e. of Ontario off SR 33. Bridle trails.	46	•	•	•	•		•	•	•	•		•			
Willow River (E-1) 2,843 acres 7 mi. n.e. of Hudson. Nature programs.	47	•	•	•				•	•	•		•	•		•
Wyalusing (H-3) 2,596 acres 7 mi. s.e. of Prairie du Chien on US 18 and SR 35, then 5 mi. w. on CR C. Scenic. Nature programs. *(See Prairie du Chien p. 167)*	48	•	•	•	•	•		•		•		•	•		•
Yellowstone (I-5) 771 acres 7 mi. n.w. of Argyle on CR N.	49	•	•	•	•	•	•	•	•	•					•
OTHER															
Blackhawk Lake Recreation Area (H-4) 2,200 acres 3.5 mi. n. of Cobb via SR 80, then e. on CR BH. Cross-country skiing.	50	•	•	•	•	•		•	•	•		•			
Carson (E-3) 135 acres. Cross-country skiing. No motor vehicles. *(See Eau Claire p. 131)*	51			•				•		•		•	•		
Eau Galle Lake (E-1) n.w. of Spring Valley via CR CC (Van Buren Rd.). Ice fishing, snowmobiling; bridle trails.	52	•	•	•	•	•		•	•	•		•			
Glacier Hills (H-7) 140 acres 10 mi. w. of Richfield on Freiss Lake Rd. Nature programs. Cross-country skiing.	53	•	•	•				•	•	•		•		•	
Goose Island (G-3) 3 mi. s. of La Crosse on SR 35, then 2.5 mi. w. on CR GI. Cross-country skiing.	54	•	•	•	•	•		•		•		•			
Homestead Hollow (H-8) 105 acres 20 mi. n. of Milwaukee on US 41.	55		•	•				•					•		
Pine View (G-4) 200 acres on the Fort McCoy Base, 6 mi. e. of Sparta. Miniature golf; canoe rental.	56	•	•	•	•			•		•		•		•	
Ridge Run (H-7) 140 acres on University Dr. in West Bend. Nature trails.	57		•	•				•		•		•			
Sandy Knoll (G-8) 267 acres 1 mi. n.w. on SR 28, then 1 mi. e. on Wallace Lake Rd. Cross-country skiing, snowmobiling.	58		•	•				•	•	•		•			
Shawano Lake (E-7) 6,062 acres 3 mi. n.e. of Shawano via SR 29 on CR H. Cross-country skiing, golf, snowmobiling, tennis; bridle trails.	59	•	•		•	•	•	•	•	•		•	•	•	•

Wisconsin Temperature Averages
Maximum / Minimum
From the records of the National Weather Service

	JAN	FEB	MAR	APR	MAY	JUNE	JULY	AUG	SEPT	OCT	NOV	DEC
Green Bay	24 / 7	27 / 9	37 / 20	54 / 33	66 / 43	76 / 53	81 / 58	79 / 56	70 / 48	60 / 39	42 / 26	29 / 13
La Crosse	25 / 7	30 / 10	40 / 22	58 / 37	69 / 49	78 / 58	83 / 62	82 / 61	72 / 52	62 / 42	43 / 28	30 / 14
Madison	25 / 8	29 / 11	39 / 21	56 / 34	67 / 45	77 / 55	81 / 59	80 / 57	71 / 48	61 / 39	43 / 26	30 / 14
Milwaukee	27 / 11	30 / 15	39 / 23	55 / 35	65 / 43	75 / 54	80 / 59	80 / 59	71 / 51	61 / 41	44 / 28	31 / 17

Points of Interest

ALGOMA (E-9) pop. 3,357, elev. 600'

Algoma began with a sawmill and store in the 1850s. The community, on the shore of Lake Michigan, is a popular recreation center, offering opportunities for anglers, boaters and hikers.

Algoma Area Chamber of Commerce: 1226 Lake St., Algoma, WI 54201; phone (920) 487-2041 or (800) 498-4888.

WINERIES

• **Von Stiehl Winery**, 115 Navarino St. Tastings daily 9-5:30, July-Aug.; 9-5, May-June and Sept.-Oct.; 11-5, Nov.-Dec.; 11-4, rest of year. Tours daily May-Oct. Phone (920) 487-5208 or (800) 955-5208.

APOSTLE ISLANDS NATIONAL LAKESHORE (A-3)

The Apostle Islands lie offshore from Bayfield Peninsula in Lake Superior. Thought to number only 12 by the missionaries who named them, the Apostle Islands in fact number 22. The islands range in size from 3 acres to 14,000 acres. All but Madeline Island *(see place listing p. 141)* are within the national lakeshore, which also includes a 12-mile strip of shoreline on the peninsula.

The Apostles are the result of the ice age, when huge ice sheets gouged channels into the bedrock and then left piles of debris in their wake. As the glaciers retreated, the islands were exposed, revealing rose-colored cliffs that the lake's waters since have shaped into twisted formations, caves and hollows.

Fur trading began here as early as the 17th century, and commercial fishing and logging continue around the islands today. For the early traders the islands offered plentiful game and refuge from the lake's storms. Later developers harvested such resources as timber and sandstone. The latter became the brownstone used extensively in buildings in Chicago and other Midwestern cities in the late 19th century.

By the turn of the 20th century, wealthy city dwellers had transformed the remote islands into a fashionable retreat, building summer cottages on Madeline Island. This idyllic period ended with the Depression.

Once again sugar maple, birch, balsam fir, red pine and an array of wildflowers blanket the islands, and with the new forest are renewed populations of deer, bears and a variety of birds.

Stockton Island, the largest island in the lakeshore, has the most extensive trail system and such facilities as docks, campgrounds and a regular camper shuttle service from the mainland. Recreational activities on the other islands vary and can include hiking, camping, sailing, kayaking and fishing. Lake Superior rarely is warm enough for swimming, and the area's treacherous weather can make canoeing and boating hazardous.

There are scheduled ranger programs on some of the islands, including Raspberry and Stockton. For additional information write the Superintendent, Apostle Islands National Lakeshore, Route 1, Box 4, Bayfield, WI 54814; phone (715) 779-3397. *See Recreation Chart and the AAA Great Lakes CampBook.*

HOKENSON FISHERY HISTORIC SITE is in the Apostle Islands at Little Sand Bay. This complex of buildings was used for more than 30 years by the Hokenson Brothers Fishery. During the summer, guided tours describe the tools and techniques of the rigorous family occupation. A visitor center displays historic artifacts and lakeshore exhibits. Picnicking is permitted. Allow 1 hour minimum. Grounds open year-round. Visitor center and tours daily 9:30-4, Memorial Day-Labor Day; Fri.-Sun. 9:30-4, day after Labor Day-Sept. 30. Free. Phone (715) 779-7007.

SIGHTSEEING CRUISES depart from Bayfield Dock. The Grand Tour is a narrated cruise past the 22 Apostle Islands as well as the historic Raspberry Island and Devils Island lighthouses and the Devils Island Sea Caves. Other cruises include stops at Manitou Island and Stockton Island, and several include stops to tour island lighthouses. A camper shuttle service to many of the islands also is available. Inquire about weather policies.

Allow 3 hours minimum. Grand Tour departs daily (weather permitting) at 10, mid-May to mid-Oct. Grand Tour $24.95; ages 6-12, $13.95. Reservations are recommended. MC, VI. Phone (715) 779-3925 or (800) 323-7619.

VISITOR CENTER is at 4th St. and Washington Ave. in Bayfield. The Apostle Islands are detailed in exhibits, a movie and publications. Maps, weather information and a schedule of naturalist programs also are available. Daily 8-6, Memorial Day weekend-Labor Day; 8-5, day after Labor Day-late Oct.; Mon.-Fri. 8-4:30, rest of year. Little Sand Bay Information Center, off SR 13, offers similar services to visitors early June-late Sept. Phone (715) 779-3397.

APPLETON (F-7) pop. 70,087, elev. 714'

The largest of the five cities along the Fox River, Appleton and its neighboring communities make up the third largest metropolitan area in Wisconsin. Early settlers and French explorers quickly learned the economic value of the "water highway" that tumbles from Lake Winnebago toward Green Bay.

As the lumber industry became established in the mid-19th century, many mills were built along the river's shores. Now known as "Paper Valley," the area supports numerous paper mills and related industries. With the construction of a hydroelectric station in 1882, Appleton became the first city in North America to generate its electricity with water power.

The city is home to Wisconsin's first coeducational institution of higher learning, Lawrence University, which is noteworthy for the Henry M. and Ruth B. Wriston Art Center at Alton and Law streets. "Metamorphosis," a sculpture in Houdini Plaza, is the city's tribute to magician and Appleton native Harry Houdini. Sen. Joe McCarthy, a fervent anti-communist during the 1950s, also hailed from Appleton; a bust of McCarthy is displayed at the county courthouse.

The diverse cultural population lends a distinct ethnic flavor to the area. Descendants of the original New England settlers mingle with Dutch, German, Polish and Vietnamese immigrants.

Fox Cities Convention & Visitors Bureau: 3433 W. College Ave., Appleton, WI 54914; phone (920) 734-3358 or (800) 236-6673. *See color ad.*

Shopping areas: Fox River Mall, 1 block off US 41 on Wisconsin Avenue, has more than 180 stores, including Dayton's, JCPenney, Sears and Younkers. Vande Walle's Candies, 400 Mall Dr., offers self-guiding tours through its candy-manufacturing areas.

FOX CITIES CHILDREN'S MUSEUM is at 100 W. College Ave. An art workshop and a fire engine are among 18 hands-on exhibits for children, infants and toddlers. Special programs teach children about science, art, safety and other cultures. The Amelia Bubolz Doll Collection features some 1,000 dolls dating from 1850 to the present. Allow 1 hour minimum. Mon.-Fri. 9-5, Sat. 10-5, Sun. noon-5, Memorial Day-Labor Day; Tues.-Fri. 9-5, Sat. 10-5, Sun. noon-5, rest of year. Admission $4; under 1 free. MC, VI. Phone (920) 734-3226.

THE GORDON BUBOLZ NATURE PRESERVE is 1.5 mi. n. of CR 41 on CR A. This privately maintained reserve covers 775 acres and provides 8 miles of trails for year-round outdoor activities. Six trails range from a half-mile to 4.5 miles in length and accommodate cross-country skiers in winter. Abundant wildlife, including more than 150 species of birds, can be seen at the refuge. Exhibits at the nature center describe the seasonal changes of indigenous plants and animals. Picnicking is permitted.

Allow 1 hour minimum. Preserve daily dawn-dusk; nature center Tues.-Fri. 8-4:30, Sat. 11-4:30, Sun. 12:30-4:30. Donations. Fee for cross-country skiing. Phone (920) 731-6041.

[SAVE] **HEARTHSTONE HISTORIC HOUSE MUSEUM** is at 625 W. Prospect Ave. Hearthstone is said to have been the first house in the world to be lit by a central hydroelectric station using the Edison System. Hands-on electrical exhibits and working models are featured. The restored 1882 structure contains period furniture, intricate woodwork and original light switches designed by the Edison Co. Five of the nine fireplaces are decorated with Minton tiles. Changing exhibits with a Victorian theme are presented. Allow 1 hour minimum.

Tues.-Fri. 10-4, Sun. 1-4. Admission $4; ages 7-17, $2. An additional fee is charged during the Christmas season. Phone (920) 730-8204.

[SAVE] **OUTAGAMIE MUSEUM** is at 330 E. College Ave. Displays represent the region's social, technological and economic history. The Tools of Change exhibit includes a Model-T Ford, an 1896 wire weaving loom, a 1920s newspaper composing room, a 19th-century paper shop, a 1930s burglar-proof bank and a 1940s physician's office. Allow 1 hour, 30 minutes minimum. Mon.-Sat. 10-5, Sun. noon-5, June-Aug.; Tues.-Sat. 10-5, Sun. noon-5, rest of year. Closed major holidays. Admission (includes Houdini Historical Center) $4; over 65, $3.50; ages 5-17, $2; family rate $10. MC, VI. Phone (920) 735-9370 or (920) 733-8445.

Houdini Historical Center displays items once owned by magician Harry Houdini. The collection includes videotape clips, photographs, posters, handcuffs, leg irons and lock picks. Allow 1 hour minimum. Phone (920) 733-8445.

ASHIPPUN (H-7) elev. 858'

HONEY ACRES MUSEUM is 2 mi. n. on SR 67. The history and techniques of beekeeping are preserved at Honey Acres, which has been owned by a family of beekeepers and honey packers since 1852. A 20-minute multimedia presentation and various displays highlight pollination and the enemies of the bee. Visitors can taste five varieties of honey and four varieties of mustard and view an active beehive. A nature trail is on the grounds.

Allow 30 minutes minimum. Mon.-Fri. 9-3:30, Sat.-Sun. noon-4, mid-May through Oct. 31; Mon.-Fri. 9-3:30, rest of year. Closed holidays. Free. Phone (920) 474-4411.

ASHLAND (B-4) pop. 8,620, elev. 660'

Whether Fourth of July festivities on Madeline Island inspired Asaph Whittlesey to establish a new town is uncertain, but on July 5, 1854, he arrived on the southeast shore of Chequamegon Bay of Lake Superior, built a cabin and founded Ashland. Once his cabin was complete, Whittlesey opened negotiations with the railroad in Chicago to provide an outlet for the area's timber, brownstone and iron ore.

The railroad, completed in 1877, combined with Ashland's natural harbor, soon made the community a thriving port; millions of tons of iron ore and timber were shipped annually. Legacies of this prosperous period are the distinctive facades of preserved, early 20th-century commercial buildings in the Main Street Historic District.

Although the area's commercial resources are important, its other resources—local parks, national forests and Lake Superior—have made Ashland an active recreation center. Trout, walleye, perch, salmon, northern pike and muskellunge thrive in Lake Superior and inland lakes and streams. Deepwater charter and sailboat excursions can be arranged in Ashland.

Prentice Park, 100 acres at the west edge of town, is a refuge for deer, ducks and swans; camping, hiking and picnicking are available. Band concerts take place at Memorial Park Thursday evenings in the summer.

Ashland is part of a statewide network of well-groomed snowmobile trails, which include the Tri-County Trail and the Mount Valhalla Recreational Area in Chequamegon-Nicolet National Forest *(see place listing p. 128).* A map outlining area snowmobile touring loops and cross-country ski trails is available from the chamber of commerce.

Ashland Area Chamber of Commerce: 805 W. Lakeshore Dr., P.O. Box 746, Ashland, WI 54806; phone (715) 682-2500 or (800) 284-9484.

NORTHERN GREAT LAKES VISITOR CENTER is 2.5 mi. w. on US 2 to CR G. A 30-minute multi-image, musical presentation chronicles area history, highlighting the cultural heritage of the region. Also at the center are exhibits, videotape presentations, nature trails and archives. Allow 1 hour minimum. Visitor center daily 9-6, June-Oct.; 9-5, rest of year. Archives Tues.-Fri. 1-4:30. Free. Phone (715) 685-9983.

AUGUSTA (E-3) pop. 1,186, elev. 972'

DELL'S MILL is 3 mi. n. on SR 27, then w. on CR V. The flour and feed mill served the community for 137 years. Although no major commercial milling has been done since the building was converted to a museum in 1968, the machinery still is in working order and a small amount of milling continues to take place. Visitors can tour the five-story 1864 structure to observe how the water-powered parts—including 3,000 feet of belting and 175 pulleys—interact. Allow 1 hour minimum. Daily 10-5, May-Oct. Admission $7; ages 6-18, $3.50; ages 3-5, $1.50. Phone (715) 286-2714.

BABCOCK (F-5) elev. 975'

SANDHILL WILDLIFE AREA is on CR X. Automobile and hiking trails with observation towers permit visitors to view the woods and wide marshes of this 9,500-acre wildlife refuge, home to ferns, ducks, bison, deer, beavers and other native flora and fauna. Allow 2 hours minimum. Park open daily dawn-dusk. Automobile trails open daily, mid-Apr. through Oct. 31; also mid-Dec. to mid-Mar. for cross-country skiing. Free. Phone (715) 884-2437.

BAILEYS HARBOR (D-9) elev. 595'

During a fierce storm in 1848, Captain Justice Bailey found a safe port for his schooner on the Lake Michigan coast. Baileys Harbor, as the place came to be known, is the oldest village in Door County. The scenic harbor, notched into the Door Peninsula, is a popular vacation center. A half-mile north, the Ridges Sanctuary offers hiking trails in a natural wildlife area where wildflowers and species of native orchids can be seen from May to September. Tours are conducted during the summer and early fall.

Nearby recreational activities include salmon and trout fishing, bicycling, sea kayaking, windsurfing, snowmobiling and cross-country skiing. The Cana Island Lighthouse, about 4 miles northeast of Baileys Harbor via CR Q, was built in 1851; phone (920) 743-5958 Memorial Day-late Oct. *See Door County p. 130.*

BARABOO (G-5) pop. 10,711, elev. 879'

The river, the nearby mountains of purplish quartzite and the trim little city of Baraboo all took their name from the French trader Baribault, whose post stood here in the early 19th century. Another name is almost synonymous with Baraboo—Ringling. Fond memories of a circus boat they had seen in Iowa spurred five sons of a German harness-maker to present their first "Classic and Comic Concert Company" show in 1882.

From 1884 to 1918 Baraboo was home of their enterprise, which ultimately became Ringling Bros. and Barnum & Bailey Circus. Many old circus buildings have been converted to industrial and commercial uses.

Baraboo Area Chamber of Commerce: 600 W. Chestnut St., P.O. Box 442, Baraboo, WI 53913; phone (608) 356-8333 or (800) 227-2266.

CIRCUS WORLD MUSEUM is at 550 Water St., following signs. Preserving more than 50 acres of the original winter quarters of the Ringling Brothers, the museum celebrates the history of the American circus. Throughout the summer season the museum offers big-top circus performances, a daily circus parade, demonstrations of historic circus operations, concerts and exhibits, including what is described as the world's largest collection of circus wagons.

Allow 4 hours minimum. Daily 9-6, mid-May through Labor Day; Mon.-Sat. 10-4, Sun. 11-4, rest of year. Closed Jan. 1, Easter, Thanksgiving, Dec. 24-25 and 31. Admission mid-May through Labor Day $14.95; over 64, $12.95; ages 5-11, $7.95. Admission day after Labor Day-late Oct. $7; over 64, $6; ages 5-11, $3.50. Admission rest of year $5; over 64, $4; ages 5-11, $2.50. AX, DS, MC, VI. Phone (608) 356-8341 or (866) 693-1500. *See color ad p. 179.*

DEVIL'S LAKE STATE PARK is 3.5 mi. s. on SR 123. Devil's Lake, spring fed and having no visible outlet, is bounded on three sides by the quartzite cliffs of the Baraboo Range. Bear, Lynx and Eagle Indian mounds were created by ancient tribes. The 10,000-acre park is one of several units of the Ice Age National Scientific Reserve, which is under development. Naturalist programs and exhibits explain the glacial phenomena of the area.

Park open daily 6 a.m.-11 p.m. Admission per private vehicle $10, state residents $5. Annual permit $30, state residents $20. Phone (608) 356-8301. *See Recreation Chart and the AAA Great Lakes CampBook.*

THE INTERNATIONAL CRANE FOUNDATION is 5.2 mi. n. on US 12, then 1.2 mi. e. on Shady Lane Rd.; from I-90/94 exit 92, 1.5 mi. s. on US 12, then 1.2 mi. e. on Shady Lane Rd. This center is dedicated to the study, propagation and preservation of endangered species of cranes and the protection of their wetland and grassland habitats.

The foundation maintains a collection of cranes for breeding and reintroduction into the wild. Visitors can see rare whooping cranes, young crane chicks in their exercise yard and an art exhibit. Nature trails that wind through restored wetlands, prairies and savannas also are on the grounds. Self-guiding and guided tours are available. Open daily 9-5, Apr. 15-Oct. 31. Guided 90-minute tours are given daily at 10, 1 and 3, June-Aug.; Sat.-Sun. at

10, 1 and 3, Apr. 15-May 30 and Sept.-Oct. Admission $7; over 61, $6; ages 5-11, $3.50. DS, MC, VI. Phone (608) 356-9462.

MID-CONTINENT RAILWAY MUSEUM— *see North Freedom p. 163.*

SAUK COUNTY HISTORICAL MUSEUM is at 531 4th Ave. Housed in a 1903 mansion, the museum displays American Indian and pioneer relics, Civil War equipment, household furnishings, toys, textiles and genealogical records. Tues.-Sat. noon-5. Admission $4; ages 13-17, $2. Phone (608) 356-1001.

CASINOS

- Ho-Chunk Casino and Bingo, S3214A Hwy. 12. Daily 24 hours. Phone (800) 746-2486.

BARNEVELD (H-5) pop. 1,088

WINERIES

- **Botham Vineyards and Winery** is off US 18/151; take CR K 1.7 mi. s. to Langberry Rd., then .2 mi. w. to 8180 Langberry Rd. Wed.-Sun. 10-5, early Apr.-late Dec.; Sat.-Sun. 10-5 in Mar. Phone (608) 924-1412.

BAYFIELD (A-3) pop. 611, elev. 607'

Mansions of locally quarried brownstone—the same brownstone seen on the elegant townhouses of Chicago and New York—grace the side streets of Bayfield, once the main shipping point for the popular building material. The town now relies on fishing, fruit crops and the annual throng of summer vacationers.

Sightseeing cruises among the Apostle Islands *(see Apostle Islands National Lakeshore p. 121)* and ferry service to Madeline Island *(see place listing p. 141)*, both offshore in Lake Superior, depart from Bayfield. In the winter a motorized windsled offers transportation to the island until the lake freezes and cars can travel on an ice highway.

The area affords good hunting, fishing, skiing, snowmobiling, boating and sailing. Deepwater fishing trips leave the pier daily; a fishing license is required.

Bayfield Chamber of Commerce: 42 S. Broad St., P.O. Box 138, Bayfield, WI 54814; phone (715) 779-3335 or (800) 447-4094.

LAKE SUPERIOR BIG TOP CHAUTAUQUA is 3.5 mi. s. on SR 13, then 1 mi. w. on Ski Hill Rd. at the foot of Mount Ashwabay. Concerts, plays and illuminated historical musicals are presented under a big-top canvas tent. Food is available. Allow 2 hours, 30 minutes minimum. Show times Tues.-Thurs. at 7:30 p.m., Fri.-Sat. at 8:15 p.m., early June-Labor Day. Reserved seats $18; ages 1-12, $8. General admission $12; ages 1-12, $4. Some big-name acts cost more. MC, VI. Phone (715) 373-5552 or (888) 244-8368.

BEAVER DAM (H-6) pop. 15,169, elev. 872'

A trading and manufacturing center, Beaver Dam serves the surrounding dairy region. The Dodge County Historical Society, in an 1890 Romanesque library at 105 Park Ave., houses more than 4,000 items relating to city and county history; phone (920) 887-1266. Nearby Beaver Dam Lake is noted for good fishing.

Beaver Dam Area Chamber of Commerce: 127 S. Spring St., Beaver Dam, WI 53916; phone (920) 887-8879.

BELMONT (I-4) pop. 871, elev. 1,063'

Belmont held high hopes for growth and prominence when it served as the first capital of the Wisconsin Territory in 1836. But representatives who convened there objected so vehemently to the site that the governor agreed to move the capital to a location upon which the majority could agree. After a long dispute Madison was selected, although at the time it existed only on paper.

With little other reason to thrive, Belmont declined. The *coup de grace* was the removal of the railroad to a point 3 miles distant; most of the town moved with it, leaving Old Belmont and its vacant capitol complex to molder. Contemporary Belmont is an agricultural village.

FIRST CAPITOL STATE HISTORIC SITE is 3 mi. n.w. on CR G. Two restored buildings stand on the site where the first territorial legislature met in 1836. In the Council House the legislature drafted many laws and fixed the permanent government seat in Madison. The lodging house contains displays about Wisconsin's early territorial government and history. Picnicking is permitted at the Belmont Mound. Daily 10-4, mid-June through Labor Day. Schedule may vary; phone ahead. Free. Phone (608) 987-2122.

BELOIT (I-6) pop. 35,775, elev. 745'

The agent for New England Emigrating Co. must be credited with having a silver tongue, for nearly the entire town of Colebrook, N.H., moved to this site on the Rock River in 1837. Determined to sustain "science and religion and all the adjuncts that contribute to the elevation of society," the cultured arrivals promptly established a church and chartered Beloit College in 1846.

The college and light industry are the lifeblood of the city. The Beloit College campus also is the site of more than two dozen American Indian mounds. Wright Museum of Art on the Beloit College campus, exhibits Oriental art, graphics and sculpture.

Other points of interest in town include the Near East Side and Bluff Street historic districts, which contain rare 19th-century cobblestone houses, and Neese Performing Arts Theatre, on Bushnell Street, which presents theater, dance and other performing arts events. Pohlman Field is the site of all home games for Beloit's minor-league baseball team.

Beloit Convention and Visitors Bureau: 1003 Pleasant St., Beloit, WI 53511; phone (608) 365-4838 or (800) 423-5648.

Self-guiding tours: Walking tour brochures about local historic districts are available from the convention and visitors bureau.

SAVE **THE ANGEL MUSEUM** is at 656 Pleasant St. (US 51). Housed in a renovated historic church built by Italian immigrants, the museum features more than 6,000 angels from the Berg Angel Collection as well as nearly 500 black angels donated by Oprah Winfrey. Allow 1 hour minimum. Tues.-Sat. 10-4, Sun. 1-4, June-Aug.; Tues.-Sat. 10-4, Feb.-May and Sept.-Dec. Closed holidays. Admission $5; over 62 and ages 12-18, $4; ages 5-11, $3. MC, VI. Phone (608) 362-9099.

LOGAN MUSEUM OF ANTHROPOLOGY is at 700 College St. in Memorial Hall on the Beloit College campus. The 1869 building houses a highly regarded collection of more than 225,000 artifacts, including Paleolithic art, jewelry from ancient civilizations, pre-Columbian ceramics and American Indian beadwork, baskets and clothing. A two-story glass cube allows visitors to see the pieces as well as watch the ongoing conservation and cataloging of objects. Allow 30 minutes minimum. Tues.-Sun. 11-4; closed Thanksgiving and college holidays. Free. Phone (608) 363-2677.

BLACK RIVER FALLS (F-3)

pop. 3,618, elev. 809'

Canoeing on the Black River, hunting, fishing and winter sports are among the attractions offered by Black River Falls. However, the cascade for which the town is named is now tamed by an upstream power dam. One of the first sawmills in Wisconsin was built here in 1819; the city was a busy logging center throughout the 19th century.

Black River Falls Area Chamber of Commerce: 120 N. Water St., Black River Falls, WI 54615; phone (715) 284-4658 or (800) 404-4008.

BLACK RIVER STATE FOREST is e. on US 12. Comprising 67,000 acres primarily in Jackson County, the forest lies in the former bed of a glacial lake. Hunting is permitted in season. Daily 6 a.m.-11 p.m. Admission per private vehicle $10, state residents $5. Annual permit $30, state residents $20. Fees are charged for camping, bicycling and cross-country skiing. Phone (715) 284-1406. *See Recreation Chart and the AAA Great Lakes CampBook.*

BLUE MOUNDS (I-5) pop. 708, elev. 1,296'

Serving as landmarks for Winnebago Indians and lead miners following the ore veins from Galena, Ill., two blue hills, the highest in southern Wisconsin, attracted Ebenezer Brigham in 1828. Using nothing more than a windlass, rope and tub, Brigham extracted more than 4 million pounds of lead from the ground. With his establishment of a smelting furnace, the town of Blue Mounds took shape.

When the Black Hawk War threatened, settlers built Fort Blue Mounds, which successfully defended the town during an ambush by Sac Indians. The fort later helped supply the troops who drove Black Hawk out of the state. A bronze plaque now commemorates the site.

Mt. Horeb Area Chamber of Commerce: 100 S. First St., P.O. Box 84, Mt. Horeb, WI 53572; phone (608) 437-5914 or (888) 765-5929.

BLUE MOUND STATE PARK is off US 18/151. The 1,124-acre park's centerpiece is 1,716-foot Blue Mound, the highest point in southern Wisconsin. According to legend, Winnebago treasure is buried in the mound. The summit offers views of the Baraboo Range and Wisconsin River Valley. Park open daily 6 a.m.-11 p.m. Office open daily 8-4:30. Admission per private vehicle $10, state residents $5. Annual permit $30, state residents $20. MC, VI. Phone (608) 437-5711. *See Recreation Chart and the AAA Great Lakes CampBook.*

CAVE OF THE MOUNDS is off US 18/151 on Cave of the Mounds Rd. This National Natural Landmark has theatrical lighting enhancing a variety of brilliantly colored stalactites, stalagmites and underground pools. A short film explains the history of the cave and its formation. Guided 1-hour tours follow concrete walkways through the cave, which maintains a uniform temperature of 50 F. The grounds also offer rock gardens and picnic areas. Food is available in summer.

Tours depart every 15 min. daily 9-7, Memorial Day weekend-Labor Day; on the hour Mon.-Fri. 10-4, every 30 min. Sat.-Sun. 9-5, day after Labor Day-Nov. 15 and Mar. 15-day before Memorial Day weekend; on the hour Sat.-Sun. 10-4, rest of year. Admission $12; over 65, $11; ages 5-12, $6. DS, MC, VI. Phone (608) 437-3038.

LITTLE NORWAY is off US 18/151 between Mount Horeb and Blue Mounds; exit Cave of the Mounds Rd. and follow signs to CR JG. This farmstead, known as Nissedahle ("Valley of the Elves"), was built by Norwegian settlers in the mid-1800s and houses pioneer furnishings, arts and crafts. On the grounds is a replica of a stave church built in Norway for the 1893 World's Columbian Exposition. Costumed guides conduct 45-minute tours.

Daily 9-7, July-Aug.; 9-5, May-June and Sept.-Oct. Admission $10; over 62, $8; ages 6-12, $3. MC, VI. Phone (608) 437-8211.

BOULDER JUNCTION (C-5) elev. 1,648'

Boulder Junction offers access to the woodlands and lakes of the surrounding Northern Highland-American Legion State Forest *(see Recreation Chart and the AAA Great Lakes CampBook).* Recreational activities include hiking, boating, cross-country skiing and bicycling. Fishing for muskellunge is particularly rewarding in the area, which bills itself as the "Musky Capital of the World." There are nearly 200 lakes within a 9-mile radius of Boulder Junction. The forest is a major producer of seedling pines for state reforestation programs.

Boulder Junction Chamber of Commerce: 5352 Park St., P.O. Box 286 B, Boulder Junction, WI 54512; phone (715) 385-2400 or (800) 466-8759.

BRODHEAD (I-5) pop. 3,180, elev. 792'

Edward Brodhead, chief engineer of the Milwaukee and Minnesota Railroad, is credited with having brought the railroad into the treeless sand prairie where the town began in 1856. Ancient trails already crossed the area, known to American Indians as the halfway point between the Mississippi and Lake Michigan. Both American Indians and European settlers once collected sap from the hard maples lining the Sugar River to make maple syrup and sugar.

The First Brigade Band, organized in 1857, achieved considerable popularity. Enlisted in the Civil War, the six-horse bandwagon followed Union general William T. Sherman on his Atlanta campaign and marched in the grand review in Washington, D.C., at the war's end.

The 23-mile Sugar River Trail, built on an abandoned railroad bed, follows the meandering river from Brodhead to New Glarus *(see place listing p. 163).*

Brodhead Chamber of Commerce: 602 E. 2nd Ave., P.O. Box 16, Brodhead, WI 53520; phone (608) 897-8411.

Self-guiding tours: Brodhead's Exchange Square and North Residential historic districts can be explored on a self-guiding walking tour. Maps are available from Brodhead Historical Museum in the old railroad depot on SR 11; phone (608) 897-2639 or (608) 897-2549.

BURLINGTON (I-7) pop. 9,936, elev. 790'

Burlington is most noted for being the home of the Burlington Liars' Club. This organization encourages the telling of tall tales in the classic country manner. Contributors from all over the world have promoted the tradition since 1929, when the first competition gained national attention. The tradition continues as scores of tall-tale tellers vie for first place each January 1. Visitors can explore the "Tall Tale Trail," a trail through town where tall tales can be heard at several locations.

St. Francis Retreat Center, 2 miles northeast on CR W between SRs 11 and 36, contains gardens and picturesque grottoes open to visitors year-round. Another popular Burlington attraction is the dramatic offerings of the Haylofters from May through October at Malt House Theatre, the oldest community theater group in Wisconsin. Free water-skiing performances by the Aquaducks are offered at Fischer Park on Browns Lake Saturday at 6:30, Memorial Day through Labor Day. Burlington, home to the Nestle Co., has been designated by the state legislature as "Chocolate City USA."

Burlington Area Chamber of Commerce: 112 E. Chestnut St., P.O. Box 156, Burlington, WI 53105; phone (262) 763-6044.

CABLE (B-3) elev. 1,370′

The Cable vicinity is a popular year-round vacation area in northwest Wisconsin set in the heart of Chequamegon-Nicolet National Forest. Fine hunting and fishing are available along more than 150 lakes. More than 300 miles of mapped and marked trails, stretching from Hayward to Delta, are available for mountain bicyclists. Hiking trails surround the area.

Cable Area Chamber of Commerce: P.O. Box 217, Cable, WI 54821; phone (715) 798-3833 or (800) 533-7454.

CABLE NATURAL HISTORY MUSEUM is .2 mi. e. on CR M. Exhibits about northern Wisconsin wildlife include displays of native animals and birds mounted in natural settings. A summer lecture series is offered the first Wednesday evening in July through the last Wednesday in August at the community center on CR M.

Tues.-Sat. 10-4, Sun. 11-3, June-Aug.; Tues.-Sat. 10-4, rest of year. Junior naturalist programs are offered Tues.-Wed. 10-noon, mid-June to mid-August. Closed holidays. Free. Phone (715) 798-3890.

RECREATIONAL ACTIVITIES
Skiing
- **Telemark Ski Area** is n. on US 63, e. on CR M, then 2 mi. s. on Telemark Rd. Write 42225 Telemark Rd., Cable, WI 54821. Other activities are offered. Daily Nov.-Apr. Phone (715) 798-3999.

CAMBRIDGE (H-6) pop. 1,101, elev. 855′

Founded in the mid-1800s, Cambridge has long been a popular vacation spot for Chicagoans and other city dwellers lured to the spring-fed waters of nearby Lake Ripley. Ripley Park, on the lake's western shore, encompasses sandy beaches and a swimming area. The Cambridge area also is popular with cross-country skiers and hikers. The Glacial Drumlin Bike Trail, which follows the path of the 19th-century Chicago & Northwestern Railway, provides a winding, 47-mile-long scenic trail for bicyclists. Hiking and mountain biking trails, canoeing and picnicking are available.

Cambridge is noted for its salt-glazed pottery, antiques and artwork displayed in historic buildings along its Victorian-style Main Street.

Cambridge Chamber of Commerce: 102 W. Main St., P.O. Box 572, Cambridge, WI 53523; phone (608) 423-7559 or (608) 423-3780.

CAMERON (D-2) pop. 1,546, elev. 998′

PIONEER VILLAGE MUSEUM is 1.5 mi. w. on CR W (Museum Rd.). The pioneer street setting features 28 old buildings, including a train depot, church, general store, town hall, smithy, farmstead and late 19th-century house. Most display buildings are furnished in period. Five display buildings house additional items relating to the county's settlement. An exhibit hall contains 40 display cases with historic artifacts. Thurs.-Sun. 1-5, June 1-Labor Day. Admission $4; under 13, $2. Phone (715) 458-2841 or (715) 458-2080.

CAMPBELLSPORT (G-8)
pop. 1,913, elev. 1,062′

KETTLE MORAINE STATE FOREST is 7 mi. e. on SR 67. Geological formations in the area were created by glaciers more than 20,000 years ago. Visitors can take a self-guiding automobile tour that features glacial eskers, kames and kettles. Henry Reuss Ice Age Visitor Center provides information about the forest's geological history. Recreational activities include boating, camping, fishing, hiking, horseback riding, mountain biking, swimming, cross-country skiing and snowmobiling. Picnicking is permitted.

Allow 3 hours minimum. Park and Mauthe Lake Recreation Area open daily 6 a.m.-11 p.m. Long Lake Recreation Area open daily 6 a.m.-11 p.m., May 1-second week in Oct. Admission per private vehicle $10, state residents $5. Annual permit $30, state residents $20. Phone (262) 626-2116 Mon.-Fri. or (920) 533-8322. *See Recreation Chart.*

CARLSVILLE (E-8)

WINERIES
- **Door Peninsula Winery** is on SR 42. Daily 9-6. Tours daily on the hour 10-4; otherwise varies. Phone (920) 743-7431 or (800) 551-5049. *Also see Door County p. 130.*

CARTER (D-7) elev. 1,525′

CASINOS
- **Potawatomi Bingo and Northern Lights Casino** is on SR 32. Casino opens daily at 9; closing hours vary. Closed major holidays. Phone (715) 473-2021 or (800) 487-9522.

CASSVILLE (I-3) pop. 1,085, elev. 622′

In the 1830s the Mississippi River community of Cassville was among several towns that vied for the status of territorial capital. It lost, but continued its existence as grain port and trading center for the surrounding farms.

Cassville Car Ferry, which departs from the Prime Street landing, makes trips across the Mississippi River to Turkey River Landing, near Millville, Iowa. The ferry operates May through October. Phone (608) 725-5180.

 STONEFIELD STATE HISTORIC SITE is 1.2 mi. n.w. on CR VV, next to Nelson Dewey State Park *(see Recreation Chart and the AAA Great Lakes CampBook)*. The first of the site's three parts is Stonefield, the reconstructed home of Nelson Dewey, Wisconsin's first governor. The second part, the State Agricultural Museum, exhibits farm tools and machinery, manufacturers' models and domestic items tracing the evolution of agriculture and rural life from frontier days.

A covered bridge leads to the third section, a turn-of-the-20th-century village. More than 30 reconstructed buildings are furnished in period and include a bank, saloon, newspaper office, smithy and general store; shopkeepers and craftsmen are stationed throughout the site.

Allow 2 hours minimum. Tues.-Sun. 10-5, July-Aug.; 10-4, May-June and in Sept.; Sat.-Sun. 10-4 in Oct. Last admission 1 hour before closing. Admission $8; over 64, $7.20; ages 5-12, $4. MC, VI. Phone (608) 725-5210.

Governor Nelson Dewey Homesite is at 12195 CR VV. The Gothic Revival home of Wisconsin's first governor has been reconstructed on the site. The original red brick house burned in 1873, but the doors, walls and millwork that remained intact were used in the reconstruction. Books and personal belongings of the Dewey family are displayed. The 2,000-acre estate was one of the few Midwestern farms planned in the manner of a Virginia plantation. Tours are given daily 10:30, 2 and 4, Memorial Day weekend-early Oct. Last tour begins 1 hour before closing.

CEDARBURG—see Milwaukee p. 159.

CHEQUAMEGON-NICOLET NATIONAL FOREST

Elevations in the forest range from 600 ft. at Lake Superior to 1,860 ft. near Twin Lake. Refer to AAA maps for additional elevation information.

In north-central and northeastern Wisconsin, the Chequamegon-Nicolet National Forest comprises 1.5 million acres in four separate regions. The Chequamegon (she-Wa-ma-gon) area covers 856,938 acres east, south and northwest of Park Falls on SRs 182 and 13; the Nicolet (nik-oh-LAY) area totals 661,200 acres east of Rhinelander and is accessible via several major highways.

More than 800 lakes dot the Chequamegon forest, where tree species include maple, aspen, pine, spruce, balsam, oak and birch. Licensed hunting and fishing are available in season. The Chippewa, Flambeau, Jump, St. Croix and Yellow rivers provide good canoeing in the spring and early summer. Muskellunge fishing is excellent.

An extensive 200-mile trail system threads through the Chequamegon, where a 40-mile segment of the Ice Age National Scenic Trail follows the terminal moraines of the last glaciers. Providing a system of loops used for cross-country skiing as well as hiking, the Rock Lake National Recreation Trail passes near Cable. Maps of snowmobile and cross-country ski trails are available at the forest supervisor headquarters.

The North Country National Scenic Trail traverses 60 miles of the northern part of the forest, roughly between Mellen and Iron River. Part of this route crosses the Rainbow Lake and Porcupine Lake wildernesses. Together covering about 11,000 acres of glaciated, lake-dotted woodlands, the wilderness areas offer an opportunity to experience a Northern hardwood forest free of development.

Primitive trails thread through the Nicolet region's three wilderness areas: Whisker Lake Wilderness Area, 8 miles west of Florence on SR 70, containing Riley and Whisker lakes; Blackjack Springs Wilderness Area, 8 miles east of Eagle River on SR 70, containing spring ponds; and the 22,000-acre Headwaters Wilderness Area, 8 miles east of Three Lakes on SR 32 and FR 2183.

With 1,200 lakes, 1,100 miles of trout streams and more than 400 spring ponds, the Nicolet forest also offers good fishing; there is hunting for deer, bears and upland game in season. Canoeing on the Wolf and Peshtigo rivers provides white-water excitement, while the Oconto, Pine, Popple and Wisconsin rivers are gentler.

The Great Divide Scenic Byway (SR 77) provides visitors with some of the most picturesque scenery in Wisconsin. The portion of this route between Hayward and Glidden is punctuated by several highlands known as the Penokee Range. The byway takes its name from the ridges that form the Great Divide, which separates waters flowing north to Lake Superior from waters flowing south to the Mississippi River.

There are more than 45 developed campgrounds in the combined forests; campsites are available on a first-come, first-served basis, but a limited number may be reserved in advance. For reservations, phone (877) 444-6777 daily 10-8.

For information about Chequamegon campgrounds and facilities, contact the forest headquarters at 1170 4th Ave. S., Park Falls, WI 54552; phone (715) 762-2461, or TTY (715) 762-5701, Mon.-Fri. 8-4:30. For information about facilities in the Nicolet forest, contact the forest office at 68 S. Stevens St., Rhinelander, WI 54501; phone (715) 362-1300, or TTY (715) 362-1383, Mon.-Fri. 8-4:30. Information also is available from district ranger offices in Eagle River, Florence, Glidden, Hayward, Lakewood, Laona, Medford, Park Falls and Washburn. See Recreation Chart and the AAA Great Lakes CampBook.

CHIPPEWA FALLS (E-2)
pop. 12,925, elev. 848'

That several locally made beverages have attained critical acclaim is credited to the purity of Chippewa Falls' ground water. It was not the clear water, however, that first attracted settlement to the banks of the Chippewa in 1837, but the vast white-pine forests and the river's potential for producing power.

With the passing of the logging era, attention turned to serving the local farmers, generating electricity for use throughout the region and developing diversified industry—including brewing and spring water bottling. Chippewa Water Co., which still operates today, was founded in 1880 by Thaddeus Pound—former Wisconsin lieutenant governor and grandfather of poet Ezra Pound.

Impounded by the Chippewa Falls dam, Lake Wissota provides fishing and other recreational activities. Lake Wissota State Park *(see Recreation Chart and the AAA Great Lakes CampBook)* is on the east shore. The Chippewa Rose Society Garden, Jefferson Avenue and Bridgewater, is among Wisconsin's largest.

Chippewa Falls Area Chamber of Commerce: 10 S. Bridge St., Chippewa Falls, WI 54729; phone (715) 723-0331 or (888) 723-0024.

IRVINE PARK is .5 mi. n. on SR 124. The 364-acre park contains a zoo with native animals that are best viewed mid-April through September, though the park is open all year. Cross-country skiing trails, hiking trails and picnic facilities are on the grounds.

The park also includes Glen Loch Dam and Overlook, a museum housing antique machinery and farm implements, an old log house and an old schoolhouse. Christmas Village is open Thanksgiving through Jan. 1. For further information contact the Parks and Recreation Department, 109 E. Spruce St., Chippewa Falls, WI 54729. Park open daily 7 a.m.-dusk. Free. A fee is charged for use of the swimming pool. Phone (715) 723-3890 or (715) 723-0051.

LEINENKUGEL BREWERY TOURS is on SR 124 at 1 Jefferson Ave. Guided 30-minute tours detail the brewing process. Displays depict the history of brewing in the area. Tastings are available. Guided tours are given Mon.-Sat. 9:30-4, Sun. 11:30-3, Memorial Day-Labor Day; Mon.-Sat. 9:30-4, rest of year. Closed holidays. Free. Reservations are recommended. Phone (715) 723-5557.

COON VALLEY (G-3) pop. 714, elev. 735′

In a valley laced with numerous springs and surrounded by high bluffs, Coon Valley lies in a landscape forever captured in the books of Hamlin Garland, who grew up on a farm in nearby West Salem *(see place listing p. 178)*. Reminiscent of the valleys of Norway, the ravines in the Coon Valley area attracted Norwegian and Bohemian immigrants beginning in 1849.

The hills around the village are among the highest along US 14/61. Between the bluffs are tobacco and dairy farms run by descendants of the village's original settlers.

[SAVE] **NORSKEDALEN NATURE & HERITAGE CENTER** is 3 mi. n.e. via CRs P and PI. The 400-acre educational and research area offers nature trails, a museum, an arboretum, a visitor center and a restored 1890s pioneer homestead. Skumsrud Heritage Farm, south of Norskedalen off US 14/61, offers self-guiding tours through 12 historic buildings. Weekly programs are offered Sundays at 2.

Special events are featured throughout the year. Guided tours of the homestead are available. Picnicking is permitted. Pets are not allowed.

Allow 1 hour minimum. Mon.-Fri. 9-4, Sat. 10-4, Sun. noon-4, Apr. 15-Oct. 31; Mon.-Fri. 10-4, Sun. noon-4, rest of year. Homestead open daily 10-3:30, Apr. 15-Oct. 31. Last tour begins 30 minutes before closing. Skumsrud open Mon.-Fri. 11-4, Sat. 10-4, Sun. noon-4, June-Aug. Admission (including Skumsrud) $4; ages 5-17, $2; family rate $10. MC, VI. Phone (608) 452-3424.

COUDERAY (C-3) pop. 96, elev. 1,265′

THE HIDEOUT is 6 mi. n. on CR CC. The stone lodge, Al Capone's northwoods hideout in the 1920s, includes a massive fireplace, spiral staircases, a machine-gun tower, a blockhouse and furnishings. Food is available. Guided tours are offered daily on the hour noon-6, Memorial Day weekend-Labor Day; Fri.-Sun. noon-5, May 1-day before Memorial Day weekend and day after Labor Day-last weekend in Sept. Admission $9.50; ages 7-12, $4.50. MC, VI. Phone (715) 945-2746.

DANBURY (C-2) elev. 947′

FORTS FOLLE AVOINE HISTORICAL PARK is 2.5 mi. w. on CR U from jct. SR 35. This 80-acre living history site includes reconstructions of an Ojibwe Indian village and fur trading posts that flourished along the Yellow River 1802-04. Costumed interpreters provide guided tours of the park, which includes museum displays, archeological exhibits, a research library and hiking trails. Allow 1 hour minimum. Tours depart on the hour Wed.-Sun. 9-5, June-Sept. Admission $5; ages 6-11, $4; family rate $9.50. MC, VI. Phone (715) 866-8890.

DE PERE (F-7) pop. 20,559, elev. 595′

De Pere originally was called "Rapides des Pères" for the Jesuits who established the first mission in the state in 1669. From this point explorers Jacques Marquette and Louis Joliet departed on their voyage of discovery. Tours of the St. Joseph National Shrine are free and can be arranged at St. Norbert Abbey, 1016 N. Broadway; phone (920) 337-4300.

WHITE PILLARS is at 403 N. Broadway. Built in 1836 and remodeled in 1912, this building once housed the first bank offices in Wisconsin. It is now home to the De Pere Historical Society and its Historical Museum. An extensive collection includes rare documents, photographs and archives. Allow 30 minutes minimum. Mon.-Fri. noon-4; closed holidays. Donations. Phone (920) 336-3877.

DICKEYVILLE (I-4) pop. 1,043, elev. 955′

DICKEYVILLE GROTTO is on US 61 and SR 35. Made of colorful bits of stone, glass and shell from around the world, the grotto was built 1925-30 by Father Mathias Wernerus as an expression of unity between religion and patriotism. Allow 30 minutes minimum. Grotto open daily 24 hours. Guided tours daily 11-4, June-Aug.; Sat.-Sun. 11-5 in May and Sept.-Oct. Donations. Phone (608) 568-3119.

DODGEVILLE (I-4) pop. 4,220, elev. 1,249′

Along with Mineral Point *(see place listing p. 162)*, Dodgeville was a metropolis of the lead-mining region during the 1820s and 1830s. The town bears the name of Henry Dodge, a colorful frontiersman who pioneered the mining industry, figured prominently in the defeat of Black Hawk and served as the first territorial governor of Wisconsin and later as a U.S. senator.

Dodgeville Chamber of Commerce: 178 ½ N. Iowa St., Suite 201, Dodgeville, WI 53533; phone (608) 935-5993.

GOVERNOR DODGE STATE PARK is 3 mi. n. on SR 23. This unglaciated area contains scenic rock formations, which can be seen from the network of hiking and riding trails. During the summer park naturalists conduct nature hikes and evening programs. Daily 6 a.m.-11 p.m. Admission per private vehicle $10, state residents $5. Annual permit $30, state residents $20. Phone (608) 935-2315. *See Recreation Chart and the AAA Great Lakes CampBook.*

SAVE **MUSEUM OF MINERALS AND CRYSTALS** is 4 mi. n. on SR 23. More than 3,000 rock, mineral and crystal specimens were collected mostly from Africa, Australia, Brazil, England and Mexico. The collection includes material from the mines of southwestern Wisconsin and other parts of the United States. Notable samples in their raw state include a 90-pound quartz crystal from Arkansas, a 315-pound Brazilian agate and a 215-pound amethyst geode.

Fluorescent material is displayed in a black-lit room. Among the museum's special exhibits is a gemstone picture of Man O' War. Horseback riding is available. Allow 1 hour minimum. Daily 9-5, June-Aug.; 9-4, Apr.-May and Sept.-Oct. Admission $4; over 64, $3.50; ages 6-18, $3. Two-hour horseback rides $30; 1-hour rides $16; 45-minute rides $12. Trail pass $3. DS, MC, VI. Phone (608) 935-5205.

DOOR COUNTY (E-9)

Door County stretches northeast from Sturgeon Bay to the tip of the Door Peninsula. Wisconsin's most conspicuous feature extends like the spout of a teapot into Green Bay and Lake Michigan. The waters on either side of the 75-mile-long peninsula have carved much of its rocky shoreline into caves, arches and cliffs. The overall effect is that this rugged landscape—dotted with fishing villages, farms and orchards—resembles New England more than the Midwest.

Despite its scenic allure, the treacherously narrow channel between the peninsula's end and its outlying rocky islands was feared by American Indians and trappers. They named the channel *porte des morts,* or death's door, from which the peninsula and county take their names.

According to legend 17th-century French fur traders first ran afoul of the strait when Robert La Salle's ship *Griffin* sank. To circumvent the straits and the tedious trip around the peninsula, traders followed the American Indians' portage at Sturgeon Bay, which allowed easier passage to the important trade route at the head of Green Bay.

Fur trading dominated the area for 200 years, and it was not until the 19th century that Moravians, Scandinavians and other immigrants settled the peninsula. Around the turn of the 20th century wealthy city dwellers discovered the region's charms, transforming rustic villages into resorts.

Much of the peninsula caters to vacationers. Sailing on the surrounding waters, hiking and golf in one of the nearby state parks, as well as such cultural activities as summer theater and concerts, are area draws. Historic lighthouses, cherry blossoms and the sand beaches along Lake Michigan further accentuate the allure.

The following places on the Door Peninsula are listed separately under their individual names: Baileys Harbor, Carlsville, Egg Harbor, Ephraim, Fish Creek, Gills Rock, Sturgeon Bay and Washington Island *(see place listings).*

Door County Chamber of Commerce: 1015 Green Bay Rd., P.O. Box 406, Sturgeon Bay, WI 54235; phone (920) 743-4456 or (800) 527-3529 for a vacation planning guide.

EAGLE —*see Milwaukee p. 159.*

EAGLE RIVER (C-6) pop. 1,443, elev. 1,628′

Eagle River is in an all-year resort area. The Eagle chain of lakes, consisting of 28 navigable lakes, is one of the best known boating and fishing areas in northern Wisconsin. At 611 Sheridan Street is the Trees for Tomorrow Environmental Education Center, which has a self-guiding demonstration forest trail; phone (715) 479-6456.

The U.S. Forest Service maintains about 40 miles of cross-country ski trails in nearby Chequamegon-Nicolet National Forest *(see place listing p. 128);* there also are 600 miles of groomed trails in the area.

Eagle River Area Chamber and Visitors Center: 116 S. Railroad St., P.O. Box 1917, Eagle River, WI 54521; phone (715) 479-6400 or (800) 359-6315.

Shopping areas: Antiques and arts and crafts can be found on Wall Street and in the surrounding area.

EAST TROY (I-7) pop. 3,564, elev. 860′

EAST TROY ELECTRIC RAILROAD MUSEUM is at 2002 Church St. Historical exhibits chronicle the role the electric railroad played in the advancement of transportation. Visitors may take an 11-mile ride from East Troy to a farmer's market in Mukwonago aboard a restored trolley car. Guided tours are available. Allow 1 hour, 30 minutes minimum. Daily 11:30-4, Memorial Day-last weekend in Oct. Train departs every 45 min. Admission $9; ages 3-11, $5. MC, VI. Phone (262) 642-3263.

EAU CLAIRE (E-3) pop. 61,704, elev. 796'

Relations with Eau Claire's upstream neighbor, Chippewa Falls *(see place listing p. 128)*, were not always amicable in the days when rival logging companies from both towns drove their cuts down the *eau claire* ("clear water") of the Chippewa River. A number of midnight log drives and battles took place before cooperation supplanted warfare. When the timber was exhausted, Eau Claire, like Chippewa Falls, turned to diversified manufacturing.

Eau Claire's position at the confluence of the Chippewa and Eau Claire rivers enhances its status as a gateway to the resort areas of northwestern Wisconsin. Outdoor activities, such as bicycling, hiking, fishing and skiing, abound throughout the year.

Chippewa Valley Convention & Visitors Bureau: 3625 Gateway Dr., Suite F, Eau Claire, WI 54701; phone (715) 831-2345 or (888) 523-3866.

Shopping areas: Oakwood Mall, at US 53 and Golf Road, has more than 100 stores, including Dayton's, JCPenney and Sears.

CARSON PARK is a 135-acre peninsula on Half Moon Lake. A quarter-scale railroad is among the park's highlights. Hank Aaron started his professional baseball career at the park with the Eau Claire Bears; a sculpture of Aaron is in front of Carson Park Stadium. Many sports events and recreational activities are held at the park. Daily 4 a.m.-11 p.m. Free. Phone (715) 839-5032. *See Recreation Chart.*

SAVE **Chippewa Valley Museum** is in Carson Park. Regional history exhibits range from prehistoric times to the early 1900s. Displayed are Ojibwe Indian artifacts, agricultural and early industrial exhibits, a working early 20th-century ice cream parlor and a 21-room doll house. An 18-minute multimedia production is offered.

The 1880 Sunnyview School and 1860s Lars Anderson log house on the museum grounds are furnished in period. Allow 1 hour minimum. Daily 10-5, Memorial Day weekend-Labor Day; Tues.-Sun. 1-5, rest of year. Closed Jan. 1, Thanksgiving and Dec. 24-25. Admission $4; ages 3-18, $1.50. Phone (715) 834-7871.

Paul Bunyan Logging Camp and Interpretive Center features a re-created 1890s logging camp. Artifacts are displayed in the cook shanty, bunkhouse, barn, smithy and shed. The Interpretive Center introduces visitors to the logging industry by means of a movie, an exhibit room, a tall tales room and a forest history exhibit. Daily 10-4:30, first Mon. in Apr.-first Mon. in Oct. Admission $3; ages 5-17, $1.50. MC, VI. Phone (715) 835-6200.

EGG HARBOR (E-9) pop. 250, elev. 635'

Although some sources credit Increase Claflin, the first settler of Door County, with naming the town for a nest of duck eggs, one legend claims the "Battle of the Eggs" gave Egg Harbor its name. A group of Green Bay men supposedly sailed into the harbor in 1825 and engaged in an egg-throwing fight when they reached the townsite.

From mid-June to mid-August, Birch Creek Music Performance Center, a performing arts school and concert venue 3 miles east via CR E, presents symphony, percussion/steel band and big band performances in an early 1900s barn adapted as a concert hall; phone (920) 868-3763. *Also see Door County p. 130.*

ELKHORN (I-7) pop. 7,305, elev. 996'

A busy industrial community, Elkhorn traditionally has been associated with the manufacture of band instruments. Joseph Philbrick Webster, a popular composer during the Civil War era, wrote "Lorena" and "The Sweet Bye and Bye" while living in Elkhorn.

Elkhorn Area Chamber of Commerce: P.O. Box 41, Elkhorn, WI 53121; phone (262) 723-5788.

SAVE **WEBSTER HOUSE MUSEUM** is at 9 E. Rockwell St. Built in 1836 as the local land office during Wisconsin's territorial years, the house was moved from the public square to its present site in 1840. It was home of composer Joseph Webster until his death in 1875 and contains some of his memorabilia, as well as American Indian, Civil War and Victorian items and a 400-piece mounted bird collection. Costumed interpreters depict the Civil War era. Guided tours are available by appointment.

Allow 1 hour minimum. Wed.-Sat. 1-5, mid-May to mid-Oct. Admission $5; ages 6-12, $2; family rate $15. Phone (262) 723-4248.

EPHRAIM (D-9) pop. 353, elev. 710'

Founded in 1853 by Moravians from Norway, Ephraim is a resort village. A monument to the Moravian founders overlooks the harbor. South of town is Peninsula State Park. *See Recreation Chart and Door County as well as Fish Creek in the AAA Great Lakes CampBook.*

The 1848 Goodletson Cabin, on Moravia St., offers a glimpse into how families lived during the era. Guided walking tours of Ephraim's historic district are offered Monday, Wednesday and Friday at 10:30, mid-June through Labor Day, departing from Anderson Barn Museum, Anderson Lane. For further information contact the Ephraim Foundation, Box 165, Ephraim, WI 54211; phone (920) 854-9688.

THE ANDERSON STORE is .5 mi. n. on SR 42. The restored 1858 general store displays typical retail items of the period as well as antiques, tools and possessions of Ephraim's settlers. Allow 30 minutes minimum. Mon.-Sat. 10:30-4, mid-June through Labor Day; Fri.-Sat. 10:30-4, day after Labor Day to mid-Oct. Admission (includes Pioneer Schoolhouse) $2. Phone (920) 854-9688.

PIONEER SCHOOLHOUSE is 1.5 mi. e. of SR 42 on Moravia St. Built in 1880, the school was in operation until 1949. Exhibits include artifacts, photographs and costumes of local origin. Mon.-Sat. 10:30-4, mid-June through Labor Day; Fri.-Sat. 10:30-4, day after Labor Day-second weekend in Oct. Admission (includes the Anderson Store) $2. Phone (920) 854-9688.

ERIN—*see Milwaukee p. 160.*

EVANSVILLE (I-6) pop. 4,039, elev. 893'

Reports of prime agricultural land drew New Englanders from New York and Vermont during the 1840s to "The Grove," so named for the abundant forest edging part of the prairie belt settlement. The early economy of Evansville rested on wheat but was replaced by tobacco during the Civil War era. The need to market agricultural produce gave rise to a host of processing plants, including a sawmill and gristmill on Allen's Creek.

With the arrival of the railroad in 1864, tobacco warehouses and other commercial enterprises clustered around the tracks. On the main line of the North Western Railroad, the city became Wisconsin's largest shipping point for wool and a major distribution center for livestock during the mid-19th century.

Evansville's development is reflected in its wide range of architecture, spanning more than 125 years. The 22-block historic district has many unaltered structures in such diverse styles as Greek Revival, Italianate, Late Picturesque, Neoclassic and Prairie. Along the shores of Lake Leota are park and recreational facilities. An 18-hole golf course is nearby.

Evansville Chamber of Commerce: 30 W. Main St. P.O. Box 51, Evansville, WI 53536; phone (608) 882-5131.

Self-guiding tours: A brochure describing residential and commercial structures in Evansville's historic district can be obtained at the library, 39 W. Main St., and the City Hall, 31 S. Madison St.; phone (608) 882-2260.

FISH CREEK (D-9) elev. 583'

A huge castellated cliff rising above Green Bay dominates Fish Creek's western waterfront. Sheltered coves provide the finest natural harbors on this side of the peninsula, augmented by the town's marina.

North of the village in Peninsula State Park (*see Recreation Chart and the AAA Great Lakes CampBook*) is the restored Eagle Bluff Lighthouse. From mid-June through November the American Folklore Theatre, (920) 854-6117, presents original musical productions at Peninsula State Park Amphitheatre; performances are at various Door County town halls through October.

The Peninsula Players, (920) 868-3287, the oldest resident professional summer stock company in the country, performs a variety of comedy, music and drama at Theatre in a Garden Tuesday through Sunday evenings, late June to mid-October. *Also see Door County p. 130.*

FOND DU LAC (G-7) pop. 42,203, elev. 765'

The French traders who first visited this region referred to it as the *fond,* or "far end," of Lake Winnebago, Wisconsin's largest freshwater lake; hence the name Fond du Lac. In 1835 Wisconsin's first judge and later territorial governor, James D. Doty laid out the town in hopes of it becoming the state capital; it lost to Madison in 1848.

Today mansions of industrial barons line Division Street. Fond du Lac offers a diversity of industry and business, including the world headquarters for Mercury Marine, and Giddings and Lewis/Thyssen, a supplier of industrial automation products and machine tools.

Fond du Lac Area Convention & Visitors Bureau: 19 W. Scott St., Fond du Lac, WI 54935-2342; phone (920) 923-3010 or (800) 937-9123.

Self-guiding tours: Fond du Lac County's Talking Country Roads audiotape tour spans the history of the area from the ice age to a front porch view of Horicon National Wildlife Refuge. A "Talking House" tour of some 24 historic houses and sites enables visitors to hear information about 13 stops on the route by tuning in a radio frequency. Contact the convention and visitors bureau for information.

Shopping areas: Downtown Main Street offers specialty shops including antiques, gourmet coffee, stained glass and quilting shops. Kristmas Kringle Shoppe, at 1330 S. Main Street at the entrance to the city, features a large assortment of glass ornaments, trees, animated figures and collectibles displayed in a Bavarian village setting.

A variety of shops can be found in Fond du Lac Plaza, at the entrance to Lakeside Park (see attraction listing). Forest Mall, off US 41 at Johnson Street, has more than 60 stores, including JCPenney, Kohls, Sears and Younkers department stores. More than 60 outlet stores, including Bugle Boy, Lands End and Oshkosh B'Gosh, are featured at Prime Outlet Center, off US 41.

[SAVE] **GALLOWAY HOUSE AND VILLAGE AND BLAKELY MUSEUM** is on the s. city limits at 336 Old Pioneer Rd.; from US 41 exit n. on SR 175, then e. on Pioneer Rd., following signs. Made up of more than 25 buildings from the turn of the 20th century, the village includes a church, courtroom, general store, law office, one-room schoolhouse, operating gristmill, photo studio, post office, printshop, railroad depot, smithy, toy shop and vet office. Guides and audiotape recordings are in most buildings.

Galloway House is an elaborate 30-room mansion constructed in 1847 to resemble an Italianate villa. Blakely Museum exhibits a collection of American Indian artifacts, pioneer relics, early industrial tools and machines, dolls, paintings, prints and photographs.

Allow 1 hour, 30 minutes minimum. Daily 10-5, Memorial Day weekend-Labor Day; Sat.-Sun. 10-5, day after Labor Day-Sept. 30. Admission $6.50; under 18, $3.50; preschoolers free; family rate $15; half-price to all Memorial Day. Under 12 must be with an adult. Phone (920) 922-6390 or (800) 937-9123.

LAKESIDE PARK is on the n. end of Main St. The 400-acre park on Lake Winnebago contains a white-tailed deer enclosure, miniature train rides, a carousel, gardens, covered wooden bridges, a lighthouse and a scenic drive. Aqua bikes and canoes can be rented. Boats can launch from 24 launch ramps. Park open daily 7 a.m.-11 p.m. Lighthouse open daily 8-dusk (weather permitting), Apr. 15-Oct. 15. Free. Phone (800) 937-9123.

ST. PAUL'S EPISCOPAL CATHEDRAL is at 51 W. Division St. The interior features German woodcarvings and stained-glass windows from European and American studios. A 1-hour guided tour is available by reservation. Office open Tues.-Fri. 9-4. Donations. Guided tour $2. Phone (920) 921-3363.

FORT ATKINSON (I-7)
pop. 11,621, elev. 790'

American Indian effigy mounds are numerous in the Fort Atkinson area. Panther Intaglio, west on SR 106 at 1236 Riverside Dr., is of interest: Rather than forming a mound on the site, Indians dug an effigy into the earth. The Fireside Restaurant and Playhouse is an entertainment complex offering theatrical and musical productions.

Fort Atkinson Area Chamber of Commerce: 244 N. Main St., Fort Atkinson, WI 53538; phone (920) 563-3210 or (888) 733-3678.

HOARD HISTORICAL MUSEUM AND NATIONAL DAIRY SHRINE'S VISITORS CENTER is at 407 Merchants Ave. (US 12). The Hoard House contains exhibits about the Black Hawk War and collections of American Indian artifacts, mounted birds, historic clothing and textiles, 19th-century tools, Civil War exhibit room and library and decorative arts. The 1841 Dwight Foster House is the restored pioneer home of one of Fort Atkinson's founders. The oldest dwelling in town, the house is furnished with original pieces from the 1840-70 period.

The National Dairy Shrine's Visitors Center chronicles the history of dairy farming and offers a multimedia presentation about dairying. Allow 1 hour minimum. Tues.-Sat. 9:30-4:30, Sun. 11-3, June 1-Labor Day; Tues.-Sat. 9:30-3:30, day after Labor Day-Dec. 31 and Jan. 18-May 31. Free. Phone (920) 563-7769.

GILLS ROCK (D-9) elev. 594'

DOOR COUNTY MARITIME MUSEUM AT GILLS ROCK is just n. of jct. SR 42 and Wisconsin Bay Rd. This museum on the tip of the Door Peninsula chronicles the area's fishing heritage with exhibits including shipwreck artifacts, navigational instruments, antique motors and models. The Hope, a restored commercial tugboat, is featured. Guided tours are offered. Allow 30 minutes minimum. Daily 10-4, Memorial Day weekend to mid-Oct. Admission (includes guided tour) $4; ages 5-17, $1; family rate $9 (two adults and children under 18). MC, VI. Phone (920) 854-1844.

GRAFTON—see Milwaukee p. 160.

GRANTSBURG (C-1) pop. 1,369, elev. 940'

Named after General Ulysses S. Grant's victory at Vicksburg, the village of Grantsburg was incorporated in 1886. One resident of notable stature was Gust Anderson, local marshal and lamplighter, who stood 7 1/2 feet tall. A wooden statue of "Big Gust" is in front of the community center on Pine Street.

CREX MEADOWS WILDLIFE AREA is .5 mi. n. on CR D, following signs. This state wildlife management area includes more than 30,000 acres of wetlands, brush prairie and forests. Some 270 species of birds have been observed in the area, including blue herons, bald eagles, Canada geese, ospreys, sandhill cranes and migrating waterfowl. Spring and fall are peak migration times. A visitor center offers maps, brochures, an herbarium and wildlife exhibits. A brochure for a 24-mile, self-guiding driving tour is available outside the center. A wildlife education center also is on the grounds. Picnicking is permitted.

Allow 1 hour, 30 minutes minimum. Daily 24 hours. Visitor center open Mon.-Fri. 8-4:30, Sat.-Sun. 10-4, Apr. 1-Nov. 1; Mon.-Fri. 8-4:30, rest of year. Donations. Phone (715) 463-2896.

GREEN BAY (E-8) pop. 102,313, elev. 604'

Green Bay, at the head of its namesake bay, has two claims to fame that no other town in the state can match: its longevity and the Green Bay Packers. Permanent settlement began in 1669 when Father Allouez established a mission. By the time the United States assumed dominance in 1816, the town—a major fur trading and military post—had changed hands three times.

In 1850 Norwegian Otto Tank came to Green Bay to serve as a Moravian missionary to about 50 families of farmers. Bringing with him a large amount of development capital, Tank bought 800 acres of land along the west bank of the Fox River and parceled them out to members of his religious colony. The Moravians built a lumber mill and steel foundry—the first industrial stirrings in Green Bay.

Christ Church (Episcopal), at Cherry and Madison streets, was established in 1829. It is the oldest permanent church site in the state. Phone (920) 432-0042 for information.

In addition to its success as a paper- and cheese-producing and shipping center, the enthusiasm generated by the Green Bay Packers, the oldest professional football team in the National Football League, helps keep the old town young. The team was founded in 1919.

Green Bay Area Visitor & Convention Bureau: 1901 S. Oneida St., P.O. Box 10596, Green Bay, WI 54307; phone (920) 494-9507, (800) 236-3976 or (888) 867-3342.

Shopping areas: Bay Park Square, south of Lambeau Field on Oneida Street, houses more than 60 stores, including Elder-Beerman, Kohl's, Montgomery Ward, Old Navy and ShopKo. Port Plaza Mall, in downtown's City Centre, features more than 100 stores, including Boston Store, JCPenney and Younkers.

BAY BEACH AMUSEMENT PARK AND WILDLIFE SANCTUARY is at the n. end of Irwin St. A small amusement park is combined with a 700-acre urban wildlife sanctuary featuring nature programs, wildlife exhibits and cross-country ski trails. A nature center has interactive exhibits, including a two-story forest with native habitats. Nocturnal animals,

a family of timber wolves and a deer habitat also can be seen. Picnicking is permitted.

Amusement park open daily 10-9, May 26-Aug. 19; daily 10-6, Aug. 20-26; Sat.-Sun. 10-6, May 5-20 and Labor Day-Sept. 23. Sanctuary open daily 8-7:30, mid-Apr. to mid-Sept.; 8-4:30, rest of year. Free; individual ride tickets 20c (some rides require more than one ticket). Phone (920) 391-3671.

GREEN BAY BOTANICAL GARDEN is at 2600 Larsen Rd. Thirty acres of landscaped grounds include a four seasons garden with magnolias, crab apples, lilacs and perennials; a contemporary rose garden with shrub and English varieties; an American perennial garden; a children's garden; and a woodland garden featuring plants and wildflowers native to Wisconsin. Daily 9-5, May-Oct.; Mon.-Fri. 9-4, rest of year. Admission $3; ages 5-12, $1. Phone (920) 490-9457.

GREEN BAY PACKER HALL OF FAME is opposite Lambeau Field in the Brown County Expo Centre complex at 855 Lombardi Ave. The hall of fame features a wide variety of Packers memorabilia, including mementos chronicling the team's history through NFL championships and Super Bowl victories, as well as interactive and historical displays. Game highlights are available for viewing. Allow 2 hours minimum. Daily 9-5; closed Easter, Thanksgiving and Dec. 25. Admission $8; over 62, $6; ages 6-11, $5. DS, MC, VI. Phone (920) 499-4281 or (888) 442-7225.

SAVE **HAZELWOOD HISTORIC HOUSE** is at 1008 S. Monroe Ave. Overlooking the Fox River, the 10-room Greek Revival home was the residence of Morgan L. Martin, a prominent politician, businessman, attorney and judge for 60 years. The home, which contains many items belonging to the family, depicts the 1890s period. Guided tours are given Mon. and Wed.-Fri. 10-2, Sat.-Sun. 1-4, June-Aug.; Sat.-Sun. 1-4 in May, and Dec. 14-23 and 27-29. Admission $4; senior citizens $3.50; ages 6-12, $2.50. Phone (920) 437-1840.

SAVE **HERITAGE HILL STATE PARK** is e. of the Fox River at jct. Webster Ave. and SR 172. A 40-acre complex of furnished historical buildings is grouped in four theme areas. The La Baye Area includes a 1762 fur trader's cabin, a chapel, a log sugaring house and a reproduction of Wisconsin's first courthouse.

The Small Town Heritage Area contains the 1835 Baird Law Office; a town hall; print shop; smithy; firehouse; the 1803 Tank Cottage, one of Wisconsin's oldest standing houses; and the 1842 Beaupre Place, a Greek Revival house that served as the center of social life in Green Bay for nearly 30 years.

The Fort Howard Area consists of a hospital, officers' quarters, school and company mess in use during the 1830s. The Agricultural/Ethnic Heritage Area contains a Belgian farmhouse, log barns, a stone summer kitchen, a cheese factory and a chapel. A schedule of events is available from the park. Living-history presentations take place at the museum buildings daily.

Allow 2 hours minimum. Tues.-Sat. 10-4:30, Sun. noon-4:30, Memorial Day weekend-Labor Day. Admission $7; over 62, $6; ages 5-19, $5. MC, VI. Phone (920) 448-5150 or (800) 721-5150.

NATIONAL RAILROAD MUSEUM is at 2285 S. Broadway, .2 mi. e. of Ashland Ave. via Cormier on the Fox River. The museum houses more than 70 locomotives and rolling stock from the steam and diesel eras. Highlights include Eisenhower's World War II command train and "The Big Boy," said to be the world's largest steam locomotive. A reception center has an exhibit hall and theater featuring an audiovisual presentation. A 1.5-mile ride on a standard-gauge train is included in admission. On the grounds, a 65-foot tower overlooks the Fox River. Picnic facilities are available.

Allow 2 hours minimum. Daily 9-5. Guided tours are given daily at 10:30 and 1:30, Memorial Day weekend-Labor Day. Train rides available May-Sept. Closed Jan. 1, Thanksgiving and Dec. 25. Admission May-Sept. $7; over 62, $6; ages 6-15, $5; family rate $20. Admission rest of year $5; over 62, $4; ages 6-15, $3. DS, MC, VI. Phone (920) 437-7623.

NEVILLE PUBLIC MUSEUM OF BROWN COUNTY is at 210 Museum Pl. Six galleries are devoted to art, history and science. Major traveling exhibits complement art, natural science, history and technology exhibits and changing displays of local art and artifacts. Particularly noteworthy is the exhibit "On the Edge of the Inland Sea," which traces 12,000 years of northeast Wisconsin's development.

Allow 2 hours minimum. Tues.-Sat. 9-4 (also Wed. 4-9), Sun. noon-4. Closed Jan. 1, Thanksgiving and Dec. 25; closes at 12:30 Good Friday, Dec. 24 and Dec. 31. Donations. Phone (920) 448-4460.

NEW ZOO AND REFORESTATION CAMP is off US 41 exit 176, 2.5 mi. w. on CR B, then 1 mi. n. on CR IR to 4418 Reforestation Rd. The zoo features 1,600 acres of trails, trout ponds and animal exhibits. Animals are shown in their natural habitats. The Wisconsin Trails exhibit features bears, wolves, lynxes, foxes and game birds. The Prairie Grasslands Area is home to prairie dogs, buffaloes, elk, cranes and swans; lions, baboons, snow monkeys and penguins live in the International Trail section. A children's area offers the opportunity to feed goats and reindeer. Food is available.

Allow 1 hour, 30 minutes minimum. Daily 9-6, Apr.-Oct.; 9-4 in Mar. and Nov.-Dec. Admission $2; senior citizens and ages 2-16, $1; family rate $5. Phone (920) 434-7841.

ONEIDA NATION MUSEUM is 5 mi. w. on SR 54 from US 41 exit, then 5 mi. s. on CR E and just w. on CR EE. This museum has displays and hands-on exhibits tracing the history and culture of the Oneida Indian Nation as it moved from New York

to Wisconsin. Two nature trails are on the grounds. Guided tours are available by appointment. Picnicking is permitted. Allow 1 hour minimum. Tues.-Fri. 9-5, Sat. 10-5, June-Aug.; Tues.-Fri. 9-5, Feb.-May and Sept.-Dec. Admission $2; senior citizens and under 18, $1. MC, VI. Phone (920) 869-2768.

CASINOS

- **Oneida Bingo & Casino** is at 2020/2100 Airport Dr. Daily 24 hours. Phone (920) 497-8118 or (800) 238-4263.

GREENBUSH (G-8)

WADE HOUSE & WESLEY JUNG CARRIAGE MUSEUM is off SR 23 at Plank Rd. The Wade House stagecoach inn, built in 1850 along the plank road that linked Sheboygan and Fond du Lac, has been restored. Settings include the taproom, ballroom, dining room, bedrooms and kitchens. Other restored buildings on the 360-acre state historic site include a smokehouse and smithy. Costumed interpreters conduct tours and can be seen performing such daily chores as cooking, weaving, spinning and blacksmithing.

Wesley Jung Carriage Museum has about 120 carriages, wagons and sleighs dating 1870-1915. Horse-drawn carriage rides are included with admission. Site open Tues.-Sun. 9-5, May-Oct. Last admission is 1 hour before closing. Admission $10; over 64, $9; ages 5-12, $5; family rate (2 adults and children under 18) $27. MC, VI. Phone (920) 526-3271.

HARTFORD—*see Milwaukee p. 160.*

HAYWARD (C-3) pop. 2,129, elev. 1,192'

NATIONAL FRESH WATER FISHING HALL OF FAME is at jct. SR 27/CR B. Housed in a building designed to resemble a muskellunge, the museum includes an observation deck in the mouth of the giant fish. Five other buildings on 6 acres of landscaped grounds display more than 400 specimens of fish from around the world, as well as angling equipment, trophies and other items.

Allow 1 hour minimum. Daily 10-5, June-Sept.; 10-4:30, Apr. 15-May 30 and in Oct. Last admission 30 minutes before closing. Admission $5; over 65, $4.50; ages 10-17, $3.50; under 10, $2.50. MC, VI. Phone (715) 634-4440.

WILDERNESS WALK is 3 mi. s. on SR 27. The 35-acre park features live animals in natural habitats, an animal nursery and the Old West Town. Food is available. Picnicking is permitted. Allow 1 hour minimum. Daily 10-4:30, mid-May through Labor Day. Last admission is 1 hour before closing. Admission $6; over 62, $5.50; ages 2-11, $4.50. MC, VI. Phone (715) 634-2893.

HAZELHURST (C-5) elev. 1,595'

WILDERNESS CRUISES depart 7 mi. w. off US 51 on CR Y, then 3 mi. w. on Willow Dam Rd. Two-hour and 2.5-hour narrated boat tours through the scenic Willow Flowage area are offered. Sights include wildlife, islands, coves and nearly 100 miles of undeveloped shoreline. Lunch and dinner cruises also are available. Sightseeing cruises depart Tues.-Sun., July-Aug. and in Sept.; Tues., Thurs. and Sat.-Sun. in June. Fare $9.95; ages 3-10, $5.95. Reservations are required. DS, MC, VI. Phone (715) 453-3310 or (800) 472-1516.

HORICON (H-7) pop. 3,775, elev. 886′

The Horicon area presents visitors with many sightseeing opportunities. Tours of John Deere Horicon Works, 300 N. Vine St., are offered by appointment; phone (920) 485-4411.

Horicon Chamber of Commerce: 319 E. Lake St., Suite 101, P.O. Box 23, Horicon, WI 53032; phone (920) 485-3200.

BLUE HERON TOURS, INC. departs from the bridge at SR 33. Narrated 1-hour pontoon boat tours explore Horicon Marsh, a wetland inhabited by more than 260 species of birds. A 2-hour birding tour also is available May through September. Canoe and kayak rentals are available April through September. Marsh tour departs daily at 1, May-Sept; Mon.-Fri. at 1, in Oct. Sat.-Sun. departures vary in Oct.; phone ahead. Marsh tour $9; ages 12-15, $5.50; ages 4-11, $4.50. Birding tour $17; ages 12-15, $10; ages 4-11, $8. Reservations are required for birding tour. MC, VI. Phone (920) 485-4663.

HORICON MARSH WILDLIFE AREA is at N7725 SR 28. The southernmost third of the Horicon Marsh, a 11,000-acre state-owned area, is primarily used for recreation. Activities include nature study, fishing, hunting, canoeing, hiking, birdwatching and photography. Naturalist programs on the weekends in the spring and fall also are offered. Allow 1 hour minimum. Daily dawn-dusk. Park office daily 8-4:30. Free. Phone (920) 387-7860. *See Recreation Chart.*

HUDSON (E-1) pop. 8,775, elev. 669′

Founded by fur traders on the St. Croix River in the 1840s, Hudson developed into a prosperous steamboat and lumbering center within 20 years. Evoking the Victorian era are renovated historic buildings in Hudson's downtown and residential areas. The stately houses along Third and Vine streets formerly were the showplaces of wealthy merchants and lumber barons.

Phipps Center for the Arts, First and Locust streets, presents theatrical productions, concerts, art exhibitions and other cultural programs. Lakefront Park along the St. Croix River offers fishing, boating and swimming. Just outside of town is Willow River State Park *(see Recreation Chart and the AAA Great Lakes CampBook).*

Hudson Area Chamber of Commerce & Tourism Bureau: 502 Second St., Hudson, WI 54016; phone (715) 386-8411 or (800) 657-6775.

Self-guiding tours: Maps outlining walking, bicycling and driving tours of historic Hudson are available at the chamber of commerce and tourism bureau.

OCTAGON HOUSE, 1004 Third St., represents architectural styles of the 1850s. It contains dolls and period furnishings. The carriage house has a smithy and a display devoted to the town's early settlers. A country store exhibit and a collection of early farm machinery are displayed in the garden house. Guided tours are available.

Allow 30 minutes minimum. Tues.-Sat. 11-4, Sun. 2-4:30, May-Oct. and the 3 weeks after Thanksgiving; closed holidays. Last tour departs 30 minutes before closing. Admission $3; over 64 and ages 13-19, $2; ages 5-12, $1. Phone (715) 386-2654.

HURLEY (B-4) pop. 1,818, elev. 1,502′

Begun as an iron-mining and logging town around 1884, Hurley enjoyed more than 30 years of prosperity and high living—its main street once was studded with 76 saloons and taverns along a five-block stretch.

The town's colorful past is celebrated in several books, including Pulitzer Prize-winner Edna Ferber's "Come and Get It." The movie version of Ernest Hemingway's novel "Adventures of a Young Man" was filmed in Hurley. A museum in the old county courthouse, Iron Street and 3rd Avenue, contains relics recalling Hurley's mining and ogging heritage; phone (715) 561-2244.

Summer adventurers can try out miles of hiking, mountain bicycling and all-terrain vehicle trails. During winter, skiers can visit Whitecap Mountain in nearby Ironbelt. Hurley also is a convenient base for exploring Iron County's 450 miles of snowmobile trails.

Hurley Area Chamber of Commerce: 316 Silver St., Hurley, WI 54534; phone (715) 561-4334, or (715) 561-3866 for recorded information.

JANESVILLE (I-6) pop. 59,498, elev. 804′

Soldiers returning home from the Black Hawk War were the first to promote Janesville's fertile valley on the Rock River. One who heard their praise was pioneer and visionary Henry F. Janes, who arrived in 1836, became the town's first postmaster and started a ferry and tavern. In 1892 George Parker opened Parker Pen Co., and 1919 brought the arrival of General Motors Corp., which became the town's largest employer. Guided tours of the GM plant at 1000 Industrial Ave. are offered by appointment; phone (608) 756-7681.

Several accomplished women hail from Janesville. Carrie Jacobs Bond, one of the first female songwriters to become published, wrote "A Perfect Day," which sold more than 5 million copies in 10 years. During the 19th century, Frances Willard became the national president of the Women's Christian Temperance Union and a relentless suffragist.

A resident of nearby Johnstown, poet Ella Wheeler Wilcox sent the public stampeding to the bookstores after her "Poems of Passion" was printed by a progressive publisher.

Free water-skiing shows are performed at Traxler Park on Wednesday and Sunday evenings in summer.

Janesville Area Convention & Visitors Bureau: 51 S. Jackson St., Janesville, WI 53545; phone (608) 757-3171 or (800) 487-2757.

Self-guiding tours: The Janesville Historic Commission has identified six residential and four downtown commercial historic districts. Brochures describing each district and the Janesville Heritage self-guiding tour map are available from the Janesville Historic Commission, 200 W. Milwaukee, P.O. Box 5005; phone (608) 755-3107.

HELEN JEFFRIS WOOD MUSEUM CENTER is at 426 N. Jackson St. Housed in the 1912 Prairie-style home of Stanley Dexter Tallman, the Rock County Historical Society museum offers temporary and traveling exhibits and educational programs. Facilities include the Lincoln-Tallman Restorations visitor and ticketing center (*see attraction listing*) and a children's interactive area. Daily 9-4 during exhibitions; phone for schedule. Closed major holidays. Admission $3.50; over 61, $3; grades K-12, $2.50. Phone (608) 756-4509 or (800) 577-1859.

[SAVE] **THE LINCOLN-TALLMAN RESTORATIONS** is at 440 N. Jackson St., on US 14 Bus. Rte., 2 blks. n.e. of jct. US 51. The 26-room Italian Villa-style house was built by William Morrison Tallman, a wealthy attorney and abolitionist from New York. When the house was built 1855-57, it had such conveniences as running water, a communication system, central heating, plumbing and gas lighting. Abraham Lincoln was a weekend guest in 1859.

Tours are given daily on the hour 9-4, June-Sept.; Sat.-Sun. 9-4, rest of year. Closed major holidays. Christmas tours are offered Nov. 20-Dec. 31. Admission $8; over 61, $7.50; grades K-12, $4. MC, VI. Phone (608) 756-4509.

ROTARY GARDENS is .7 mi. w. of I-90 via SR 11, then .7 mi. s. at 1455 Palmer Dr. Fifteen acres of internationally-themed botanical gardens surround a 2-acre pond. A footpath, boardwalk and Japanese bridge connect the 16 gardens. The Rath Environmental Center houses the administrative office. Special events and programs take place throughout the year. Allow 1 hour minimum. Gardens open daily dawn-dusk. Office Mon.-Fri. 8:30-4:30, Sat.-Sun. and holidays 10-6. Donations. Phone (608) 752-3885.

KAUKAUNA (F-8) pop. 12,983, elev. 712′

Five gallons of rum was the price paid for the parcel of land that created Kaukauna in 1793, in the first deeded transaction executed in Wisconsin. On the portage that bypassed the long rapids of the Fox River, the community developed into a busy trading and milling center. The same cascade that once hampered travel long since has been tamed for industrial use.

Fox Cities Convention and Visitors Bureau: 3433 W. College Ave., Appleton, WI 54914; phone (920) 734-3358 or (800) 236-6673.

1000 ISLANDS ENVIRONMENTAL CENTER is at 1000 Beaulieu Ct. The 350-acre center features an indoor exhibition of mounted animals from Africa, Asia and North America. The collection includes antelopes, lions, polar bears, rhinoceroses, tigers and zebras. Bald eagles, deer, ducks, herons and owls can be seen on the grounds. Nature trails wind along the Fox River and through the woods. Snowshoes can be rented. Picnicking is permitted. Allow 2 hours minimum. Mon.-Fri. 8-4, Sat.-Sun. 10-3:30; closed holidays. Free. Phone (920) 766-4733.

[SAVE] **GRIGNON MANSION** is 1 mi. n.e. on Augustine St. Built in 1837, the mansion has been restored and features some of its original furnishings. An orchard and gardens are on the grounds. Guided tours are available. Allow 30 minutes minimum. Tues.-Sat. 10-4, Sun. noon-4, holidays by appointment. Admission $4; over 64, $3.50; ages 5-17, $2; family rate $10. Phone (920) 766-3122.

KENOSHA (I-8) pop. 90,352, elev. 611′

Wisconsin's southernmost Lake Michigan port, Kenosha is an important manufacturing city. Residential streets shaded by elms and oaks hint of the town's settlement by New Englanders in 1835. Municipal parks line much of the lakefront. The area is headquarters to such firms as Snap-on Tools, G. eblanc Corp. and Jockey International, Inc.

Self-guiding tours are available at the international headquarters of the Society for the Preservation and Encouragement of Barber Shop Quartet Singing in America in Harmony Hall, overlooking the lake at 6315 3rd Ave.; phone (262) 653-8440. Guided tours of the Civil War Museum on the Carthage College campus are offered by appointment; phone (262) 551-5801.

Greyhound racing is available year-round at Dairyland Greyhound Park, I-94 and SR 158; phone (262) 657-8200 or (800) 233-3357.

Note: Policies concerning admittance of children to pari-mutuel betting facilities vary. Phone for information.

Kenosha Area Convention & Visitors Bureau: 812 56th St., Kenosha, WI 53140; phone (262) 654-7307 or (800) 654-7309.

Shopping areas: The Original Outlet Mall, I-94 and SR 50 exit 344, has some 100 stores, including such brand-name outlets as Eddie Bauer, Pfaltzgraff and Sony. Nike, Oshkosh B'Gosh, Polo/Ralph Lauren and Timberland are just four of the nearly 70 stores that can be found at Prime Outlets at Kenosha, I-94 and SR 165 exit 347.

SAVE **BRISTOL RENAISSANCE FAIRE** is at 12550 120th Ave.; take I-94 s. to exit 347, w. to Frontage Rd., then 2 mi. w., following signs. This site depicts a 16th-century English village; costumed performers provide entertainment on 16 stages and in the streets. Visitors experience the food, games and crafts of Elizabethan England. Highlights include Queen Elizabeth I and her court, jousting, falconry demonstrations, sword fighting, juggling and the Kids Kingdom.

Allow a full day. Sat.-Sun. 10-7, June 29-Aug. 25. Admission $16.50; over 54 and students with ID $15.50; ages 5-12, $8.50. MC, VI. Phone (847) 395-7773.

KENOSHA PUBLIC MUSEUM is at 5500 First Ave. in HarborPark. A two-story atrium cuts through the center of this museum, an architectural representation of the glacier that sculpted Wisconsin during the Ice Age. Natural history exhibits include pottery, fossils, dioramas and the Schaefer mammoth, excavated in Kenosha County. An art gallery features works by Marc Chagall, Salvador Dali, Joan Miro, Pablo Picasso and Auguste Renoir. Self-guiding tours are available. Allow 1 hour minimum. Tues.-Sat. 9-5, Sun.-Mon. noon-5; closed major holidays. Free. Phone (262) 653-4140.

KESHENA (E-7) pop. 1,394, elev. 825'

CASINOS

• **Menominee Casino Bingo Hotel**, 1.5 mi. s. on SR 47/55. Daily 24 hours; closed noon Dec. 24-noon Dec. 25. Phone (715) 799-3600 or (800) 343-7778.

KEWAUNEE (F-9) pop. 2,806, elev. 672'

Although the growth of Chicago and the development of the railroads foiled Kewaunee's plan to become a major Lake Michigan shipping center, the town still is a busy port. Both commercial and sport fishing boats depart from its harbor.

Kewaunee Chamber of Commerce: 308 N. Main St., P.O. Box 243, Kewaunee, WI 54216; phone (920) 388-4822 or (800) 666-8214.

Self-guiding tours: A booklet detailing a walking tour of 43 homes and a school in Kewaunee's Marquette Historic District is available from the Kewaunee County Historical Museum and Old Jail in Court House Square.

KEWAUNEE COUNTY HISTORICAL MUSEUM AND OLD JAIL is in Court House Sq. at Vliet and Dodge sts. Housed in the 1876 former sheriff's house and jail wing, the museum displays area relics and antiques. Notable are a large basswood carving, "Custer's Last Stand," and four life-size carvings of Father Marquette and American Indians, depicting his landing in 1674. Allow 30 minutes minimum. Daily noon-4, Memorial Day weekend-Labor Day. Donations. Phone (920) 388-7176 or (920) 388-3858.

KOHLER (G-8) pop. 1,926, elev. 680'

Kohler is a planned, landscaped, incorporated village surrounding the factories of Kohler Co., manufacturers of plumbing and leisure products, engines and generators. The model village has won national recognition for its architecture.

KOHLER DESIGN CENTER is at 101 Upper Rd. The center includes a ceramic art gallery, archives, relics from its early factory and village and a theater. A multi-level product showroom features designer bathrooms and kitchens. A 2.5-hour factory tour is available. Allow 1 hour minimum. Design center open Mon.-Fri. 9-5, Sat.-Sun. and holidays 10-4; closed Thanksgiving and Dec. 25. Factory tour offered Mon.-Fri. at 8:30. Free. Under 14 are not permitted on factory tours, and reservations are required. Phone (920) 457-3699.

WAELDERHAUS is reached from I-43 exit 126 (Kohler Memorial Dr.), w. on SR 23 to Highland Dr., then 1.25 mi. s. This house employs a style of architecture found in Bregenzerwald, Austria. Waelderhaus is a replica of the John M. Kohler house. Allow 1 hour minimum. Guided tours are given daily at 2, 3 and 4; closed major holidays. Free. Phone (920) 452-4079.

LAC DU FLAMBEAU (C-5)
pop. 1,646, elev. 1,609'

The village of Lac du Flambeau lies in the center of the 144-square-mile Lac du Flambeau Chippewa Indian Reservation. Said to be the world's most concentrated lake region, the Lac du Flambeau country was named "the Lake of the Flaming Torch" after an old American Indian custom of catching fish by the light of flares.

Lac du Flambeau Chamber of Commerce: 14075 Gauthier Ln., Lac du Flambeau, WI 54538; phone (715) 588-3346 or (877) 588-3346.

GEORGE W. BROWN, JR. OJIBWE MUSEUM & CULTURAL CENTER is 2 blks. s. of SR 47 on Peace Pipe Rd., just s. of the Indian Bowl. A collection of American Indian artifacts dates to the mid-18th century. A four-seasons display demonstrates Indian activities, clothing and living arrangements. Of interest is a 24-foot dugout canoe discovered off the shores of Strawberry Island and thought to be 200 years old. Guided tours are available.

Allow 1 hour minimum. Mon.-Sat. 10-4 or by appointment, May-Oct.; Tues.-Thurs. 10-2, rest of year. Admission $3; over 54 and ages 5-15, $2. MC, VI. Phone (715) 588-3333.

RECREATIONAL ACTIVITIES
Fishing

• **Lac Du Flambeau Tribal Fish Hatchery** is at the lower end of Pokegama Lake. Daily May-Aug. Phone (715) 588-3303.

LA CROSSE (G-2) pop. 51,818, elev. 640'

On the Mississippi River where the Black and La Crosse rivers meet, La Crosse was founded in 1842 as an American Indian trading post. Serious development began a decade later, when settlers from New York, Ohio and Vermont established sawmills and gristmills and spurred the arrival of the railroad. The Easterners were joined by German and Norwegian immigrants attracted by the extensive pine groves.

La Crosse was faced with a crippling depression when the La Crosse and Milwaukee Railroad Co. went bankrupt in 1857. However, when the Civil War closed river traffic on the Mississippi below the Ohio River, La Crosse provided a major link with the East, thus ensuring the town's economic recovery. A railroad bridge erected over the Mississippi in 1876 precipitated a dramatic increase in trade and manufacturing, as the network of railroads radiating from La Crosse found new markets.

The city lies on a scenic route that follows the Mississippi. The route consists of SR 35, which heads southeast to La Crosse, and US 53, which runs northwest to its junction with SR 54/35. Overseeing all river traffic is a 25-foot carved wooden American Indian in Riverside Park at the base of State Street near the downtown area. The park is the docking site for the steamboats *The American Queen* and *The Mississippi Queen*. Lock and Dam No. 7, a U.S. Army Corps of Engineers project 5 miles north of La Crosse, has an observation deck.

Goose Island County Park *(see Recreation Chart and the AAA Great Lakes CampBook)* offers developed recreational facilities and a wildlife refuge. During the winter downhill and cross-country skiing are available in the area.

Tours of the University of Wisconsin-La Crosse campus are available; phone (608) 785-8067. The university's art gallery exhibits works by prominent artists September through May. Cultural events also take place at Viterbo College.

La Crosse Area Convention & Visitors Bureau: Riverside Park, 410 Veterans Memorial Dr., La Crosse, WI 54601; phone (608) 782-2366 or (800) 658-9424.

Self-guiding tours: A self-guiding tour devoted to buildings of architectural and historical significance in downtown La Crosse begins at the Hixon House and Museum *(see attraction listing).*

Shopping areas: Valley View Mall, I-90 exit 4 on US 16, has more than 85 stores, including Dayton's, JCPenney and Sears.

GRANDAD BLUFF is 2 mi. e. on Main St. Towering about 600 feet above the city, the summit offers a panoramic view. On clear days you can see three states—Iowa, Wisconsin and Minnesota. The bluff can be visited daily 6 a.m.-11 p.m.

THE HIXON HOUSE AND MUSEUM is at 429 N. 7th St. The mid-19th-century Italianate house reflects an affluent lifestyle. Original contents include Oriental rugs, ceramics from Europe and the Orient and furniture of the Victorian period. A self-guiding tour devoted to buildings of architectural and historical significance in downtown La Crosse begins at the Hixon House. Guided museum tours are available. Daily 1-5, Memorial Day-Labor Day. Admission $5; under 12, $3; family rate $12. Phone (608) 782-1980.

LA CROSSE QUEEN departs at the n. end of Riverside Park, 3 blks. w. of US 53 off State St. An authentic paddlewheeler offers 90-minute narrated sightseeing cruises on the Mississippi River. Weekend brunch, dinner and lunch cruises and some 3-hour cruises also are available. Sightseeing cruises depart daily May-Oct.; phone for schedule. Sightseeing fare varies; phone ahead. Reservations are required for meal cruises. MC, VI. Phone (608) 784-2893 or (608) 784-8523.

MYRICK PARK ZOO is at 2000 La Crosse St. (SR 16). The park contains a small collection of domestic and wild animals and birds, as well as picnic areas, children's amusement rides, a wading pool and nature trails. Daily 8-7:45, May-Aug.; 8-3, Sept.-Oct. Park free. Fee charged for rides. Phone (608) 789-7190.

PUMP HOUSE REGIONAL ARTS CENTER is 1 blk. w. of US 53 at 119 King St. Built in the Romanesque Revival style, the 1880 waterworks building now houses a performing arts theater and fine-arts galleries with changing exhibits by local and regional artists. Allow 30 minutes minimum. Tues.-Sat. noon-5. Donations. Phone (608) 785-1434.

RIVERSIDE MUSEUM is at the base of State St. in Riverside Park. The history of LaCrosse is chronicled through historic photographs and a videotape presentation. The museum displays an extensive collection of American Indian artifacts. Riverboat history is emphasized. Allow 30 minutes minimum. Daily 10-5, Memorial Day weekend-Labor Day. Donations. Phone (608) 782-1980.

SWARTHOUT MUSEUM is in the Main Library at 9th and Main sts. Changing exhibits relate to local history, including such topics as early social customs, American Indians, transportation, river life, agriculture, industry and commerce. Allow 30 minutes minimum. Tues.-Fri. 10-5, Sat.-Sun. 1-5; closed major holidays. Donations. Phone (608) 782-1980.

LAKE GENEVA (I-7) pop. 7,148, elev. 864'

This noted year-round resort is on spring-fed Geneva Lake. At the western end of the lake is Fontana, occupied in the late 1800s by the Potawatomi village of Chief Big Foot. Recreational facilities include beaches, boat ramps, golf courses, excursion boats, a greyhound racing facility, hang-gliding, hot-air balloon rides, parasailing and horseback riding.

Note: Policies concerning admittance of children to pari-mutuel betting facilities vary. Phone for information.

Lake Geneva also has hiking, snowmobile and cross-country ski trails. In winter Lake Geneva is host to legions of downhill skiers and ice skaters. Big Foot Beach State Park is 2.5 miles south of Lake Geneva (*see Recreation Chart and the AAA Great Lakes CampBook*).

Lake Geneva Area Convention & Visitors Bureau: 201 Wrigley Dr., Lake Geneva, WI 53147-2004; phone (262) 248-4416 or (800) 345-1020.

SAVE **GENEVA LAKE CRUISE LINE** departs from the Riviera Docks. Sightseeing trips on Geneva Lake are offered aboard restorations or replicas of historic yachts. Mail boat, luncheon, dinner, ice cream social and Sunday brunch cruises also are available. One-hour Geneva Bay tours depart daily at 10, 11:15, 12:30, 1:45, 3 and 4:15, mid-June to late Aug.; at 11 and 3:15, late Aug.-late Oct.; at 11, 1 and 3:45, May 1 to mid-June. Two-hour full lake tours depart daily at 12:35 and 2:50, mid-June to late Aug.; at 12:45, late Aug.-late Oct.

Geneva Bay tour $13.75; over 62, $12.75; ages 13-17, $10.75; ages 4-12, $7.95. Full lake tours $17.25; over 62, $16.25; ages 13-17, $13.25; ages 4-12, $9.95. Reservations are required for cruises longer than 1 hour. Phone (262) 248-6206 or (800) 558-5911.

LAKE MILLS (H-7) pop. 4,843, elev. 857′

Archeologists theorize that Aztalan, 3 miles east of Lake Mills on CR B, then right on CR Q, was the northernmost city of the Middle Mississippian Phase Indians, a culture influenced by the Aztecs in Mexico. Established 1075-1175, a 21-acre stockaded village once was occupied by about 500 Aztalan Indians. The Aztalans had a settled farming culture characterized by pyramidal mounds, complex pottery and crafts, and cannibalism.

After the Black Hawk War ended in 1836, settlers flooding into the area founded the second village of Aztalan at the junction of two stagecoach roads just northwest of the stockade. By 1842, the pioneer town had evolved into an industrial center, with Jefferson County's first post office, two hotels, a brickyard and five small factories. Aztalan's demise came in 1859, after the railroad bypassed the town.

Truncated mounds and stockade sections of the ancient Indian village are identified with markers in Aztalan State Park, quarter-mile south of the Aztalan Museum (*see attraction listing*).

Lake Mills Area Chamber of Commerce: 322 N. Main St., P.O. Box 125, Lake Mills, WI 53551-0125; phone (920) 648-3585.

AZTALAN MUSEUM is 3 mi. e. on CR B at jct. CR Q, next to Aztalan State Park. The only remaining building from the 1830s pioneer village of Aztalan, this former Baptist church houses a collection of Aztalan and Woodland Indian artifacts, as well as

exhibits, maps and documents relating to Aztalan and early Lake Mills.

Four log cabins on the 4-acre site date from the mid- to late 1800s: The Pettey cabin has furnishings of the 1840s, the Zickert house is outfitted with items from the late 19th century and the Bornell cabin is furnished as an early 20th-century store. A two-story granary houses a collection of antique tools. A log cabin church built in the 1850s and the contents of a one-room, red-brick schoolhouse also are displayed.

Allow 1 hour minimum. Thurs.-Sun. noon-4, mid-May to late Sept.; other times by appointment. Admission $3; ages 7-18, $1. Phone (920) 648-4632 or (920) 648-4496.

LAND O'LAKES (B-6) elev. 1,709′

Heart of the region of the same name, the attractive village of Land O'Lakes is surrounded by some 135 lakes. To the west, the Cisco chain of 17 lakes forms the second longest chain in Wisconsin. Lac Vieux Desert, east of town, is the source of the Wisconsin River. A popular resort center, the region offers summer and winter sports.

Land O'Lakes Chamber of Commerce: 6484 SR 45N, P.O. Box 599, Land O'Lakes, WI 54540; phone (715) 547-3432 or (800) 236-3432.

LAONA (D-7) elev. 1,580′

Laona is a lumbering and vacation center providing access to the varied recreational opportunities available in Chequamegon-Nicolet National Forest (*see place listing p. 128*).

Laona Chamber of Commerce: P.O. Box 229, Laona, WI 54541; phone (715) 674-3007.

GEM **LUMBERJACK SPECIAL AND CAMP FIVE MUSEUM COMPLEX TOUR** is on US 8 jct. SR 32. Steam-powered train rides SAVE aboard the Laona and Northern Railway's "Lumberjack Special" travel from the historic depot in Laona to the Camp Five Museum Complex. At the complex a logging museum contains logging relics from the river and railroad eras through the gasoline era, an active blacksmith and harness shop, transportation and agricultural displays, a lumber company money collection and an audiovisual presentation about logging history.

The complex also includes an early 20th-century country store, animal corral and a nature center with a videotape presentation about the workings of a steam engine. A 30-minute forest tour by surrey and a hayrack/pontoon boat ride along banks of wild rice and through a bird refuge are available.

Allow 2 hours minimum. Museum open Mon.-Sat. 11-4, mid-June to late Aug. Trains depart at 11, noon, 1 and 2. Fall color tours are offered Sept. 20 and 27 and Oct. 4. Museum, surrey ride and train $15; ages 13-17, $10; ages 4-12, $5; family rate $40. Hayrack/pontoon ride $2.50; ages 4-12, $1.25. MC, VI. Phone (715) 674-3414 or (800) 774-3414.

MADELINE ISLAND (A-4)

Madeline Island is east of the Bayfield Peninsula in Lake Superior. The largest of the Apostle Islands group *(see Apostle Islands National Lakeshore p. 121)*, Madeline has a permanent population of fewer than 200 residents. The island was the focus of some of the earliest trading, missionary activity and commercial fishing in the interior of North America. It is possible that Etienne Brule visited the region as early as 1622 in his attempt to find the mythical Northwest Passage to China and the East Indies.

The French explorers Radisson and Groseilliers explored Madeline in 1659. Trading posts were established by the French in 1693 and by the British in 1793. La Pointe became headquarters for a post of the American Fur Co. in 1816. It currently serves the thousands of summer visitors to the island. Big Bay State Park *(see Recreation Chart)* is on the east shore of the island. Just across the lagoon is Big Bay Town Park.

Ferries operate between Bayfield *(see place listing p. 124)* and the island town of La Pointe daily from April to early December (weather permitting). They run about every 30 minutes during the peak season, mid-June to early October. Fares vary according to season; phone (715) 747-2051. In the winter a motorized windsled offers transportation to the island until the lake freezes and cars can travel on an ice highway.

Tours of the island, offered by Madeline Island Bus Tours, depart several times daily, mid-June through Labor Day, from the Madeline Island Ferry Lines office near the ferry landing; phone (715) 747-2051 or (715) 747-6801.

Madeline Island Chamber of Commerce: 274 Middle Rd., P.O. Box 274, La Pointe, WI 54850; phone (715) 747-2801 or (888) 475-3386.

Shopping areas: During the summer Woods Hall Craft Shop, 3 blocks south of the ferry landing, features craftspersons displaying their wares.

MADELINE ISLAND HISTORICAL MUSEUM is 1 blk. from the ferry landing in La Pointe. Surrounded by a log stockade, this state historic site consists of an American Fur Co. warehouse, the island jail, a barn and the old Sailors' Home. Exhibits depict American Indian life, the expeditions of French *voyageurs*, the arrival of the fur traders and the development of the fishing and logging industries in the Chequamegon Bay region. Changing exhibits depict tourism in the early 1900s. A 23-minute film also is available.

Daily 9-5, Memorial Day weekend-first weekend in Oct. Last admission 30 minutes before closing. Admission $5.50; over 64, $4.95; ages 5-12, $2.75; family rate $15. MC, VI. Phone (715) 747-2415.

MADISON (H-6) pop. 208,054, elev. 845'

Madison existed only as a plan when it was selected as the territorial capital in 1836. By 1838 there was one inn and a general store, and construction had just begun on the Capitol. The going was slow, and the legislature, weary of cold, crowded and bedless accommodations, repeatedly threatened to move the capital elsewhere.

With the completion of the statehouse, Wisconsin's attainment of statehood and the establishment of the University of Wisconsin in 1848, the city began to assume some of its present character. Madison is a thriving center for business, government, education and recreation.

Much of the recreation is available on more than 18,000 acres of lake surface within or just outside the city limits. The "Four Lakes of Madison" are Mendota, Monona, Wingra and Waubesa. Mendota, about 8 miles long, is the largest. From Picnic Point, a narrow spit jutting into Lake Mendota, there is a spectacular view of the city.

The city center is on an eight-block-wide isthmus between lakes Mendota and Monona. By ordinance, the city's skyline is dominated by the 2,500-ton dome of the state Capitol. Capitol Square is connected to the university campus by State Street Mall, a tree-lined shopping district with import shops, ethnic restaurants and crafts studios. The Madison Civic Center, housing three performing arts theaters and Madison Art Center, is in the middle of the mall at 211 State St.

The Unitarian Church at 900 University Bay Dr. is an especially noteworthy example of Frank Lloyd Wright's architectural style. Wright intended its ascending triangular forms to symbolize unity and prayer. The Dane County Expo Center is the scene of sports events and expositions. The Madison Kodiaks play professional hockey at the center. The Madison Black Wolf play minor-league baseball at Warner Park.

Greater Madison Convention & Visitors Bureau: 615 E. Washington Ave., Madison, WI 53703; phone (608) 255-2537 or (800) 373-6376.

Shopping areas: Madison has two major malls: East Towne at I-90/94 and US 151, which has 100 stores, and West Towne at Gammon and Mineral Point roads, which has more than 100 stores. Anchor stores are Boston Store, JCPenney, Sears and Younkers.

CAVE OF THE MOUNDS—
see Blue Mounds p. 126.

HENRY VILAS ZOO is on Lake Wingra via W. Washington Ave., then .5 mi. w. on Drake St. Founded in 1911, the park contains 150 species of animals, including 17 that are endangered. Prairie dogs and miniature horses are among the residents of a children's zoo, which includes interactive exhibits and feeding stations. Picnicking is permitted.

Grounds open daily 9:30-5; closed afternoons Jan. 1, Martin Luther King Jr. Day, Thanksgiving, day after Thanksgiving and Dec. 24-25 and 31. Children's zoo open daily 10-4:45, Memorial Day weekend-Labor Day. Free. Phone (608) 266-4732.

MADISON ART CENTER is in Madison Civic Center at 211 State St. The galleries contain three floors of changing exhibits of modern and contemporary art, including paintings, sculpture and photographs. Tues.-Fri. 11-5 (also Fri. 5-9), Sat. 10-9, Sun. 1-5; closed holidays. Free. Phone (608) 257-0158.

MADISON CHILDREN'S MUSEUM is at 100 State St. across from the State Capitol. This educational and cultural museum is designed for children up to age 8. Exhibits include Dig Into Dinosaurs, the Shadow Room, First Feats: Celebrating the Early Years and Let's Grow. Additional hands-on exhibits change periodically. Allow 1 hour minimum. Daily 9-4, Memorial Day-Labor Day; Tues.-Sat. 9-4, Sun. noon-4, rest of year. Closed holidays. Admission $4, under 1 free; free to all first Sun. of the month. MC, VI. Phone (608) 256-6445.

MONONA TERRACE COMMUNITY AND CONVENTION CENTER is 2 blks. e. of Capitol Sq. at 1 John Nolen Dr. Frank Lloyd Wright proposed this civic center on the shores of Lake Monona in 1938. The building was completed in 1997 after nearly 60 years of debate. The 250,000-square-foot complex bears Wright's signature style of dramatic open spaces, circular forms and expansive views of the outdoors.

A photograph exhibition of Wright's work and the Madison Sports Hall of Fame are included. A rooftop garden includes a memorial to Otis Redding, who died in a Lake Monona plane crash in 1967. Food is available. Center open daily 8-5. Guided tours are offered daily at 1. Center free. Tours $3; under 18, $2. MC, VI. Phone (608) 261-4000.

OLBRICH BOTANICAL GARDENS is at 3330 Atwood Ave. This oasis on the shores of Lake Monona includes 16 acres of specialty gardens, a botanical center, a conservatory and a Thai pavilion. The rose garden has more than 125 varieties and 700 individual rose bushes, while the rock garden features hardier flora. Other gardens display herbs, hostas, perennials, wildflowers and annuals. A 50-foot-high glass conservatory simulates a rainforest atmosphere and contains tropical plants, bamboo arbors, a waterfall, palm trees and free-flying birds.

Guided tours are available by appointment, and flower shows, concerts and special events are offered throughout the year. Allow 2 hours minimum.

Gardens open daily 8-8, Apr.-Sept.; 9-4, rest of year. Conservatory open Mon.-Sat. 10-4, Sun. 10-5. Closed Jan. 1, Thanksgiving and Dec. 25. Gardens and Thai pavilion admission free. Conservatory $1, under 6 free; free to all Wed. and Sat. 10-noon except during special exhibits. Phone (608) 246-4550.

THE UNIVERSITY OF WISCONSIN is w. of downtown. Opened in 1848 with 20 students, the university now occupies a 1,000-acre campus. The Kohl Center Arena, on campus, is home to the university's basketball and hockey teams. A campus assistance and visitor center is in the "Old Red Gym" at 716 Langdon St. The center is open Mon.-Fri. 8-6, Sat. 10-3, Sun. 11-3; hours vary during university breaks and holidays. Phone (608) 263-2400.

Elvehjem Museum of Art is at 800 University Ave. The museum houses a permanent collection of more than 16,000 artworks dating from 2300 B.C. to the present. Noteworthy holdings include American and western European paintings, sculpture, prints and drawings as well as ancient and Asian art. Other highlights are regular changing exhibits and the Kohler Art Library, with more than 100,000 volumes. Tues.-Fri. 9-5, Sat.-Sun. 11-5; closed Jan. 1, Thanksgiving and Dec. 24-25. Free. Phone (608) 263-2246.

Geology Museum is in Weeks Hall at Charter and W. Dayton sts. Mineral, rock and fossil exhibits include the skeletons of a 33-foot-long duck-billed dinosaur and a Wisconsin mastodon. Additional highlights include a 6-foot rotating globe and a walk-through model of a limestone cave. Mon.-Fri. 8:30-4:30, Sat. 9-1; closed holidays. Free. Phone (608) 262-1412 or (608) 262-2399.

University of Wisconsin Madison Arboretum is at 1207 Seminole Hwy. Covering 1,260 acres along Lake Wingra, the arboretum displays natural plant and animal communities native to Wisconsin, including flowering trees, shrubs and a renowned lilac collection. Pets are not allowed. Guided tours are offered on weekends and by appointment. Daily 7 a.m.-10 p.m.; closed holidays. Free. Phone (608) 263-7888.

Washburn Observatory is at 1401 Observatory Dr. Objects can be viewed through a 15-inch telescope. Astronomers are available to answer questions. Open in clear weather every Wed. at 9 p.m., June-Aug.; first and third Wed. at 9 p.m., Sept.-Oct. and April-May; first and third Wed. at 7:30 p.m., Nov.-Mar. Closed holidays. Free. Phone (608) 262-9274.

WISCONSIN HISTORICAL MUSEUM is at 30 N. Carroll St. on Capitol Sq. Permanent and changing exhibits illustrate Wisconsin's history from prehistoric times and territorial days to social issues and the 20th century. Allow 1 hour minimum. Tues.-Sat. 9-4; closed major holidays. Donations. Phone (608) 264-6557 to schedule a tour.

WISCONSIN STATE CAPITOL is on Capitol Sq. This impressive example of Roman Renaissance architecture was built in 1917. The white granite dome is topped by Daniel Chester French's "Wisconsin," a gilded bronze allegorical statue. Guided tours of the rotunda, the governor's conference room, the Supreme Court of Wisconsin and the Senate and Assembly chambers include commentary about the building's history and the artworks in the various rooms.

Allow 1 hour minimum. Building open Mon.-Fri. 8-6, Sat.-Sun. and holidays 8-4. Tours are given daily on the hour Mon.-Sat. 9-11 and 1-4, Sun. on the hour 1-3. Free. Phone (608) 266-0382.

WISCONSIN VETERANS MUSEUM is downtown at 30 W. Mifflin St. The site is dedicated to the men and women of Wisconsin who served in America's conflicts from the Civil War to the Persian Gulf War. Several dioramas portray historical events using figures of military personnel in re-created environments ranging from steamy jungles to snow-covered forests. The 19th Century Gallery houses exhibits recounting events of the Civil War and Spanish American War; it features a diorama dramatizing the Battle of Antietam.

Visitors can view displays illustrating the Mexican Border Campaign, World War I, World War II, the Korean War, the Vietnam War and the Persian Gulf War in the 20th Century Gallery. This area includes dioramas depicting the Battle of the Bulge in Europe and jungle warfare in Papua New Guinea. Three aircraft are suspended from the gallery ceiling: a Sopwith "Camel" biplane from World War I, a P-51 "Mustang" from World War II and a "Huey" helicopter from the Vietnam War.

Also displayed are scale models of 19th- and 20th-century military ships and 17 bronze figures that personify Wisconsin veterans. Allow 1 hour minimum. Mon.-Sat. 9-4:30, Sun. noon-4, Apr.-Sept.; Mon.-Sat. 9-4:30, rest of year. Closed holidays. Free. Phone (608) 267-1799.

MANITOWISH WATERS (B-5) elev. 1,640'

A year-round vacation center, Manitowish Waters is in the Northern Highland-American Legion State Forest (see Recreation Chart and the AAA Great Lakes CampBook). The waters that inspired the town's name consist of a 10-lake chain. The area offers water sports, tennis, golf, riding and archery in summer and cross-country skiing, ice fishing and snowmobiling in winter.

Cranberry tours depart from North Lakeland Discovery Center, US 51 to CR W, every Friday at 10, mid-July to mid-October. A videotape is shown and cranberry refreshments are served. For further information contact the chamber of commerce.

Manitowish Waters Chamber of Commerce: US 51 and Airport Rd., P.O. Box 251, Manitowish Waters, WI 54545; phone (715) 543-8488 or (888) 626-9877.

MANITOWOC (F-8) pop. 34,053, elev. 595'

Manitowoc, an American Indian name meaning "the abode of the Great Spirit Manitou," is a leading industrial and shipping center. Its harbor at the mouth of the Manitowoc River has made it an important port since the early 1830s. Hundreds of ships, including submarines, have been built at local shipyards since the schooner *Citizen* was launched in 1848; Burger Boat shipyard still is in operation.

Distinguished as one of the world's largest producers of aluminum ware, the city balances its commercial enterprises with refuges for both animals and nature lovers. Collins Marsh Wildlife Refuge, 16 miles west of Manitowoc on CR JJ, is a natural haven for wildfowl; it is open May through October on a limited basis.

The SS *Badger*, operated by the Lake Michigan Carferry Service, offers 4-hour cruises and car-ferry service from Manitowoc to Ludington, Mich. For information and fares phone (888) 643-3779. Several charter fishing associations also operate out of the town. *See color ad p. 81 & below.*

Manitowoc Visitor & Convention Bureau & Visitor Information Center: 4221 Calumet Ave., P.O. Box 966, Manitowoc, WI 54221-0966; phone (920) 683-4388 or (800) 627-4896.

Shopping areas: In nearby Mishicot, 7 miles north via CR B at 315 Elizabeth St., is the Old School House, which contains 12 shops. Particularly noteworthy are the Frances Hook Room, which displays paintings and figurines, and the Rockwell Center. The latter contains one of the country's largest collections of Norman Rockwell paintings, plates and artwork and offers slide presentations; phone (920) 755-2291.

PINECREST HISTORICAL VILLAGE is 3 mi. w. of I-43 via CR JJ to Pine Crest Ln. The village, which depicts rural life in Manitowoc County from the 1850s to the early 1900s, contains a collection of restored buildings relocated to this 60-acre site. Structures include three log houses, a smokehouse, cheese factory, bank, church, law office, school, blacksmith shop, harness shop, saloon, general store, dress shop, firehouse, town hall and train depot with a caboose and an 1887 engine.

Allow 1 hour minimum. Daily 9-5, July 1-Labor Day; 9-4, May-June; 10-4, day after Labor Day-third Sun. in Oct. Admission $6; ages 6-17, $4; family rate $15. Phone (920) 684-5110 or (920) 684-4445.

RAHR-WEST ART MUSEUM is at 610 N. 8th St. Housed in a Victorian mansion, the museum contains period furnishings, Chinese ivory, dolls and porcelain objects. An art gallery presents changing exhibits. Mon.-Fri. 10-4 (also Wed. 4-8), Sat.-Sun. 11-4; closed holidays. Free. Phone (920) 683-4501.

WISCONSIN MARITIME MUSEUM is off I-43 exit 152, 4 mi. e. on US 10, then 1 mi. s. to 75 Maritime Dr. Exhibit galleries depict the history of shipping on the Great Lakes. Model ships range from an 1847 three-masted schooner to present-day vessels. Maps, charts and nautical equipment also are displayed. Of note is an exhibit about submarine building during World War II. Special events take place during the year.

Allow 2 hours minimum. Daily 9-6, Memorial Day weekend-Labor Day; daily 9-5, rest of year. Closed Jan. 1, Easter, Thanksgiving and Dec. 25. Admission $5; ages 6-12, $4. Combination ticket with submarine tour $7; ages 6-12, $5; family rate $20 (two adults and two children under 18). DS, MC, VI. Phone (920) 684-0218.

The Submariners Memorial USS *Cobia* is docked in the Manitowoc River next to the museum. The *Cobia* is a World War II submarine of the same class as those built at the Manitowoc shipyards during the war. Allow 1 hour minimum. Guided tours are given daily 9-6, Memorial Day weekend-Labor Day; daily 9-5, Apr. 1-day before Memorial Day weekend and day after Labor Day-Oct. 31; Mon.-Sat. 9-5, Sun. 11-5, rest of year. Admission is only with a combination ticket from the Wisconsin Maritime Museum.

MARINETTE (D-8) pop. 11,749, elev. 597'

Wisconsin's "Queen City" was named after Queen Marinette, a woman of French and Chippewa Indian extraction. With her husband, William Farnsworth, she operated a fur-trading post during Marinette's early years. From 1830 to 1930 the city was regarded as the white pine producing center of the world. In all, more than 10 board feet of logs were floated down the Menominee River when the sawmills were in operation.

Wood products still figure in the economy of Marinette, but diversified industry and retail merchandising are now the principal support of this port at the mouth of the Menominee River. The city also serves as a trade center for the surrounding area in Marinette County, which encompasses 250 lakes, 50 trout streams and numerous waterfalls.

Marinette Area Chamber of Commerce: 601 Marinette Ave., P.O. Box 512, Marinette, WI 54143; phone (715) 735-6681 or (800) 236-6681.

MARINETTE COUNTY HISTORICAL MUSEUM is downtown on US 41 in Stephenson Island Park. The museum houses early farming and logging tools and hand-carved miniatures of logging operations. American Indian items as well as furniture and other household items also are displayed. Stephenson Island Park offers picnic facilities, a playground and a boat ramp. Allow 1 hour minimum. Tues.-Sat. 10-4:30, Sun. noon-4, Memorial Day weekend-Labor Day; otherwise by appointment. Admission $2; ages 13-18, $1. Phone (715) 732-0831.

MARSHFIELD (E-5) pop. 18,800, elev. 1,276'

Marshfield once was a railroad hub with 50 trains stopping daily as hotels were crowded with passengers awaiting connections to go "out West" or "back East." In the early days of the Marshfield Clinic, one of the country's largest medical clinics, physicians rode the trains to serve patients in smaller outlying communities.

Hiking, bicycling, camping and swimming are popular during summer. In winter Marshfield provides ample opportunity for cross-country skiing, snowmobiling and hunting. Marshfield Super Speedway is host to stock car races; phone (715) 384-8325.

Marshfield Visitors & Promotion Bureau: 700 S. Central Ave., P.O. Box 868, Marshfield, WI 54449; phone (715) 384-3454 or (800) 422-4541.

NEW VISIONS GALLERY is 8 blks. n. of SR 13 in the Marshfield Clinic. Permanent displays include posters by Marc Chagall, West African sculpture, Japanese prints, Haitian paintings, Australian aboriginal art and original prints by modern artists. Temporary exhibits change every 6 to 8 weeks. Allow 1 hour minimum. Mon.-Fri. 9-5:30, Sat. 11-3; closed holidays. Free. Phone (715) 387-5562.

WILDWOOD PARK & ZOO is at 1800 S. Central Ave., 1 blk. w. of SR 13. Home to more than 200 animals and birds, the 60-acre park offers picnic facilities, tennis courts, a swimming pool, nature trails, a nine-hole Frisbee golf course and cross-country skiing areas. Allow 1 hour minimum. Park open daily 6 a.m.-10:30 p.m. Zoo open daily 8-7:30, early May to late Sept.; 8-6, late Sept. to mid-Oct.; Mon.-Sat. 8-3, rest of year. Closed Jan. 1, Thanksgiving, Dec. 24-25 and 31. Free. Phone (715) 384-4642.

MELLEN (B-4) pop. 835, elev. 1,240′

South of Copper Falls State Park *(see attraction listing)* and surrounded by the wooded hills of the Penokee Mountain Range, Mellen is a lumbering town as well as an eastern gateway to Chequamegon-Nicolet National Forest *(see place listing p. 128)*. The red and black granite quarried in the area is used widely for monuments and buildings.

Mellen Area Chamber of Commerce: 125 E. Bennett Ave., P.O. Box 193, Mellen, WI 54546; phone (715) 274-2330.

COPPER FALLS STATE PARK is 2 mi. n.e. on SR 169. The 2,483-acre park is named for falls where the Bad River flows over the edge of the Keeweenawan traprock into a canyon. Starting at the log footbridge that spans the river, a self-guiding nature trail leads to several observation points. Loon Lake, near the park entrance, has a sand beach for swimming as well as a canoe launch and access to hiking trails with waterfalls.

The Bad and Tyler Forks rivers contain rainbow, brown and brook trout. In winter the park has six cross-country ski trail loops. Daily 6 a.m.-11 p.m. Admission per private vehicle $10, state residents $5. Annual permit $30, state residents $20. Phone (715) 274-5123. *See Recreation Chart and the AAA Great Lakes CampBook.*

MENOMONIE (E-2) pop. 14,937, elev. 794′

Menomonie began as a lumber mill settlement on the Red Cedar River in 1830. Almost 50 years later the town's lumber corporation had become one of the largest in the world. Dairying later replaced lumbering as the city's economic mainstay.

Several 19th-century attractions downtown recall the days of the early lumber barons. Near Lake Menomin stand the 1868 John Holly Knapp House and the 1846 Wilson Place, stately Victorian mansions of the founders of Knapp Stout & Co. At Wilson Circle, Wilson Place, now a museum depicting the early settlement era, was the estate of Sen. James H. Stout, founder of the University of Wisconsin-Stout in Menomonie.

Of humbler origin is the home of Caddie Woodlawn, the subject of the award-winning children's book "Caddie Woodlawn" by Carol Ryrie Brink. A memorial park, 8 miles south on SR 25, contains the pioneer girl's home and provides picnic facilities.

Bordering the Red Cedar River along the western city limits is the Red Cedar State Park Trail for bicyclists, hikers and cross-country skiers. Lake Menomin offers boating, and the Red Cedar River provides good fishing. Hoffman Hills State Park, 9 miles northeast, has 8 miles of trails. During the summer the Ludington Guard Band performs every Tuesday evening at 8 in the Wilson Park band shell.

Menomonie Area Chamber of Commerce: 700 Wolske Bay Rd., Suite 200, Menomonie, WI 54751; phone (715) 235-9087 or (800) 283-1862.

[SAVE] **THE MABEL TAINTER MEMORIAL BUILDING** is at 205 Main St. Built in 1889, the Moorish-style building contains a public reading room, meeting rooms and an ornate Victorian theater. Decorated with mahogany, oak, Italian marble and polished brass, the theater features an unusual organ with 1,597 pipes and 25 stops. Performing arts programs, an exhibit gallery and daily historic guided tours also are featured.

Allow 1 hour minimum. Tours are given daily on the hour 1-4, except when theater is in use; closed Easter and Dec. 25. Admission $5; over 61, $4; ages 6-12, $3. MC, VI. Phone (715) 235-0001.

[SAVE] **RUSSELL J. RASSBACH HERITAGE MUSEUM** is at 1820 Wakanda St. in Wakanda Park. The museum features Victorian rooms, an interactive bank robbery exhibit, a children's discovery area and historical displays including Civil War memorabilia. Wed.-Sun. 10-5, Memorial Day-Labor Day; Wed.-Sun. noon-4, rest of year. Closed July 4 and Dec. 25. Admission $4; over 65, $3; ages 12-17, $2; ages 6-11, $1; family rate $12. Phone (715) 232-8685.

MILTON (I-7) pop. 5,132, elev. 875′

Joseph Goodrich, an abolitionist from New York, fostered the growth of Milton when he established a stagecoach inn in 1844 on the site of three well-traveled trails. That same year marked the founding of Milton College, which closed in 1982. The former campus now accommodates a museum and visitor center as well as antique and craft shops. Milton is a leading manufacturer of electronic medical instruments. Agribusiness also supports the community.

Milton Area Chamber of Commerce: P.O. Box 222, Milton, WI 53563; phone (608) 868-6222.

[SAVE] **MILTON HOUSE MUSEUM** is at 18 S. Janesville St. Built by Joseph Goodrich in 1844, the six-sided house was the first poured-concrete building in the United States. A guided tour includes the house, a 20-room former stagecoach inn, an Underground Railroad tunnel, an 1837 log cabin and a country store. Also featured is a miniature replica of the original inn. Allow 1 hour minimum. Daily 10-5, Memorial Day-Labor Day; Sat.-Sun. 10-5, May 1-day before Memorial Day. Admission $5; over 61 and ages 13-17, $4; ages 5-12, $2. Phone (608) 868-7772.

AAA Travel ... for Those On the Go.

Going on a trip? Whether you let AAA handle the planning or do it yourself, trust us to steer you right with reliable information and valuable guidance. We'll help you:

- Choose the best **travel route**, whether it's scenic, direct, or somewhere in between.
- Select **accommodations**, from pampered luxury to clean and practical.
- Explore your **dining** options, whether it's a night on the town to a bite on the run.
- Get the inside scoop on **attractions**, from neon lights to natural sights.

Prefer personal assistance? Enjoy the complimentary services of a AAA/CAA auto travel professional at your local club office or by phone. Just tell us what you have in mind and we'll design your route, book your reservations, and offer you exclusive travel materials to enhance your trip.

Rather do it yourself? Choose from a flexible array of travel resources. Use *Traveler*, the Internet TripTik on aaa.com, to create your ultimate route, complete with driving distances and stops at AAA Approved hotels, restaurants, and attractions. Book your stays using the Online TourBook. And explore your destination using detailed TourBook guides and handy sheet maps.

Whichever way you go ... go with AAA Travel! Contact your nearest AAA/CAA service office to speak with a travel professional and pick up valuable travel materials. Or, access AAA's renowned travel services online at www.aaa.com!

Travel With Someone You Trust®

Milwaukee

During the 19th century immigrants from more than 30 European countries flocked to Milwaukee, bringing with them their skills, arts and cuisines. Germans were the largest group; as the decades passed their *gemütlichkeit* (hospitality) assumed Italian, Polish, Scandinavian, Irish and other national overtones.

Milwaukee's watery surroundings, while a boon to its eventual development as a river port, posed a few problems during its early years. A fierce rivalry developed over the question of payment for the Milwaukee River bridges that connected the two villages of Juneautown and Kilbourntown. The Great Bridge War was settled by the legislature in 1845, but not before both factions angrily had torn down every bridge and the residents of Juneautown had trained a loaded cannon on Kilbourntown.

The new city of Milwaukee witnessed the arrival of the Forty-eighters, refugees from unsuccessful revolutionary movements against German monarchies in 1848. This intellectual minority launched the city into new cultural and political directions, endowing the city with theaters, music societies, athletic clubs and Freethinker groups. They also established a reform tradition that later gave rise to Milwaukee's distinctive brand of socialism.

During the last half of the 19th century, the reference to Milwaukee as the German Athens was hardly an exaggeration. Only the Polish and Irish populations came close in number. English was almost never heard in some neighborhoods, especially on the northwest side. By the late 1870s Milwaukee had six daily newspapers published in German.

Public schools zealously enforced their requirement that German be taught from kindergarten on. Ever-popular were family picnics at such open-air beer gardens as the Schlitz Palm Garden. By the end of the century, however, German cultural allegiances had begun to fade. The decision of the Stadt Theater, pride of Milwaukee's German culture, to alternate plays in German and English was an indisputable sign of changing times.

In reality Milwaukee's northern European heritage never disappeared. Its influence survived, despite such setbacks as World War I's repressive effect on the German community and Prohibition's nearly fatal blow to the city's brewing industry. The period following World War II brought massive development.

Milwaukee is the state's largest city, its primary commercial and manufacturing center and one of its busiest ports, as well as a major grain market. Called the "machine shop of America," Milwaukee ranks among the nation's principal industrial cities and is a leader in the production of equipment for the generation and distribution of electrical power. Factories also manufacture motorcycles, mining machinery and combustion engines.

But what really has made Milwaukee famous is beer. Though other industries have dethroned the king since 1889, the brewing industry remains synonymous with the city. Besides the ubiquitous smell of malt in the air, associations with brewing are everywhere. Wealthy brewers and other industrialists built lavish houses, some of which have been converted to public museums. One of the nation's largest breweries has its headquarters in Milwaukee.

Although modern steel and glass high rises occupy much of the downtown area, Milwaukee's European heritage is evident in the design of some of the city's noteworthy buildings and residences. The blue-domed Annunciation Greek Orthodox Church, a magnificent example of Byzantine architecture, came from the drawing board of Frank Lloyd Wright.

City Hall and Pabst Theater, both built in the 1890s in the Flemish Renaissance style, have been preserved carefully. Residents also embrace the return of a few old German cafes and beer gardens, where zither music is played and sauerbraten is served with the suds.

Approaches

By Car

From the north I-43 provides controlled access into downtown Milwaukee. I-94 affords direct access to the downtown area from Chicago and other southern points. From the west I-94 is the controlled-access highway into the city. Bypassing the metropolitan area to the south and west, I-894 provides the best connection for the I-94 through corridor.

Getting Around

Street System

Lake Michigan flanks the city on the east, and Wisconsin Avenue is the main downtown east-west thoroughfare. The Milwaukee River divides the downtown area into approximately equal east and west sections; I-94 is the approximate dividing line between north and south street addresses. Streets are numbered in ascending order west of the Milwaukee River and continue well into the suburbs to the Milwaukee County line.

The official unposted speed limit is 25 mph; other limits are posted. Rush hours are 7-9 a.m. and 3:30-6 p.m. Right turns are permitted on red unless otherwise posted.

Parking

Private commercial lots are scattered throughout the downtown area and near the airport. Lot rates are $2-$3 per hour and $4-$10 for all-day parking. Private lots within four blocks of the Midwest Express Center and Bradley Center provide parking for functions at the centers.

(continued on p. 152)

The Informed Traveler

City Population: 596,974

Elevation: 740 ft.

Sales Tax: The sales tax in Milwaukee is 5.6 percent. There also is a 9 percent tax on hotel rooms, a 3 percent tax on car rentals and a .25 percent tax on food and beverage purchases.

WHOM TO CALL

Emergency: 911

Police (non-emergency): (414) 933-4444

Time: (414) 844-1414

Weather: (414) 936-1212

Hospitals: Columbia Hospital, (414) 961-3300; Froedtert Memorial Lutheran Hospital, (414) 805-3000; St. Francis Hospital, (414) 647-5000; St. Luke's Medical Center, (414) 649-6000; St. Mary's Hospital, (414) 291-1000; Sinai Samaritan Medical Center, (414) 219-2000.

WHERE TO LOOK

Newspapers

The morning daily *Milwaukee Journal/Sentinel* is Milwaukee's major newspaper.

Radio

Milwaukee radio station WTMJ (620 AM) is an all-news/weather/sports station; WUWM (89.7 FM) is a member of National Public Radio.

Visitor Information

Information is available at the Greater Milwaukee Convention and Visitors Bureau, 400 W. Wisconsin Ave., Milwaukee, WI 53203, Mon.-Fri. 8-5, Sat. 9-2, Memorial Day-Labor Day; Mon.-Fri. 8-5, rest of year. Phone (414) 273-7222 or (800) 554-1448.

Visitor centers are at General Mitchell International Airport, (414) 747-4808, Mon.-Fri. 7:30 a.m.-9:30 p.m., Sat. 9-6, Sun. 1-9:30; and at the Midwest Express Center, 400 W. Wisconsin Ave., (414) 908-6205, Mon.-Fri. 8-5.

TRANSPORTATION

Air Travel

General Mitchell International Airport, 8 miles south via I-94 East, is served by several major domestic and international passenger carriers. Transportation to and from the airport by taxi takes about 20 minutes. One-way fares range from $15 to $20. The Milwaukee County Transit System operates buses to and from the airport from all points on its system via transfers from 5 a.m. to 12:30 a.m.; the fare is $1.35. Phone (414) 344-6711.

Rental Cars

Hertz, at the airport, (414) 747-5200 or (800) 654-3080, offers discounts to AAA members. For listings of other agencies check the telephone directory.

Rail Service

Amtrak, 433 W. St. Paul Ave., provides railroad passenger service to the city; phone (414) 271-0840, or (800) 872-7245 for reservations.

Buses

The Greyhound Lines Inc. terminal is at 606 N. James Lovell St.; phone (414) 272-2156 or (800) 231-2222.

Taxis

All taxis in Milwaukee use the meter system. The fare is $3 for the first mile, $1.50 for each additional mile and 50c for each additional person. Taxis can be ordered by phone or hired at taxi stands at most major hotels. Yellow Cab is the city's major taxi service; phone (414) 271-1800.

Public Transport

The Milwaukee County Transit System, 1942 N. 17th St., operates 22-hour service throughout Milwaukee County and eastern Waukesha County. The fare is $1.35; ages 6-11, 65c. Exact fare is required. For schedule and route information daily 6 a.m.-10 p.m. phone (414) 344-6711.

Destination Milwaukee

Milwaukee has a lot to offer visitors-from art museums to a variety of parks, gardens and nature centers.

Sightseeing is at its best here; horse-and-carriage tours, cruises and scenic drives are offered. The young and young-at-heart can enjoy an impressive zoo, an enormous ice-skating facility and a clown hall of fame.

Milwaukee Public Museum. Ocean exhibits give visitors a fish-eyed view of underwater life. (See listing page 155)

Pabst Mansion, Milwaukee. Stained-glass windows and ornamental ironwork adorn this 37- room mansion built for beer baron Capt. Frederick Pabst. (See listing page 155)

West Bend

Saukville   Port Washington

Cedarburg   Grafton

Hartford

Erin

Milwaukee

Oconomowoc

See Downtown map page 152

Waukesha

Eagle

Old World Wisconsin, Eagle. See what life in 19th-century Wisconsin entailed at this 576-acre state historic site, which includes Yankee farmsteads. (See listing page 159)

Places included in this AAA Destination City:

What To See

AMERICA'S BLACK HOLOCAUST MUSEUM is at 2233 N. 4th St. Historical exhibits, a video presentation and a live commentary follow the struggle of African-Americans through slavery and the battle for civil rights. Self-guiding and guided tours are available. Allow 1 hour minimum. Mon.-Tues. and Thurs.-Sat. 9-5, Sun. noon-5; closed major holidays. Admission $5; senior citizens, $4; students with ID $3. AX, DS, MC, VI. Phone (414) 264-2500.

BASILICA OF ST. JOSAPHAT is at 569 W. Lincoln Ave. Built in 1901 by Polish immigrants, this Romanesque basilica was designed after St. Peter's in Rome and features one of the largest domes in the world. The interior is noted for its hand-carved marble pulpit, ornate stained glass, murals and gilded plasterwork. Guided tours are available by appointment. Allow 30 minutes minimum. Mon.-Fri. 9-4; closed holidays. Masses are open to the public Sat. at 4:30, Sun. at 8, 10 and noon. Donations. Phone (414) 645-5623.

SAVE **BETTY BRINN CHILDREN'S MUSEUM** is at 929 E. Wisconsin Ave. in the Miller Pavilion at O'Donnell Park. Designed specifically for children under 11, the museum offers hands-on exhibits, interactive programs, activities and workshops. Exhibits include A Trading Place; WBB-TV; Toys by Us; Sound All Around; My Body Works; Let's Play Railway; and Betty's Busy Backyard, a play area for children under 3. Allow 1 hour minimum. Mon.-Sat. 9-5, Sun. noon-5, June-Aug.; Tues.-Sat. 9-5, Sun. noon-5, rest of year. Closed major holidays. Admission $4; under 1 free. DS, MC, VI. Phone (414) 390-5437.

CENTRAL UNITED METHODIST CHURCH is on Wisconsin Ave. at 639 N. 25th St. Noted for its revolutionary architecture based on energy efficiency, the church building is partially underground with an earth-covered roof. Prairielike landscaping is incorporated in the overall design; a large bell tower collects solar energy. Mon.-Fri. 9-3:30. Free. Phone (414) 344-1600.

SAVE **DISCOVERY WORLD—THE JAMES LOVELL MUSEUM OF SCIENCE, ECONOMICS AND TECHNOLOGY** is at 815 N. James Lovell St. More than 150 hands-on exhibits explore science, technology and economics. Shows demonstrating scientific principles are offered on weekends. Allow

1 hour minimum. Daily 9-5; closed July 4, Thanksgiving and Dec. 25. Admission $5.50; over 59, $5; ages 4-17, $4. DS, MC, VI. Phone (414) 765-9966.

SAVE **THE INTERNATIONAL CLOWN HALL OF FAME** is at 161 W. Wisconsin Ave., Suite LL700, in Grand Avenue Mall. Dedicated to the preservation and advancement of clown art, the museum displays clown clothing, shoes, props and memorabilia. Paintings and videotaped presentations of clowns can be seen. Clown shows are scheduled periodically; phone ahead. Guided tours are available. Allow 1 hour, 30 minutes minimum. Mon.-Fri. 10-4; closed Jan. 1, Memorial Day, Labor Day, Thanksgiving and Dec. 25. Admission $2, under 6 free. Additional fee for clown shows. MC, VI. Phone (414) 319-0848.

MILWAUKEE CITY HALL is at 200 E. Wells St. Built in 1895 in the Flemish Renaissance style, the building is noted for its stained-glass windows, ornately carved woodwork and stenciled ceilings in the Common Council Chamber and anteroom. Guided tours are available by appointment when council is not in session. Open Mon.-Fri. 8-4; closed major holidays. Free. Phone (414) 286-2266.

MILWAUKEE COUNTY HISTORICAL CENTER is at 910 N. Old World 3rd St. The city's past is preserved through permanent and changing exhibits. Displays chronicle Milwaukee's early settlers; the city's ethnic heritage; military history, including the Civil War and World War I; and panorama painters. There also is a slide presentation about the history of Milwaukee. Allow 1 hour minimum. Mon.-Fri. 9:30-5, Sat. 10-5, Sun. 1-5; closed holidays. Free. Phone (414) 273-8288.

MILWAUKEE COUNTY WAR MEMORIAL COMPLEX includes five sites throughout the city. This living memorial to Milwaukee's war dead consists of a performing arts center, three museums and a war memorial center. The Marcus Center for Performing Arts, 929 N. Water St., is the setting for concerts, plays and other cultural productions of the Milwaukee Symphony Orchestra, the Florentine Opera, the Milwaukee Ballet Company and First Stage Milwaukee Theater for Children as well as touring Broadway shows. Tours of the complex are available by appointment. Phone (414) 273-7121 or (414) 273-7206 for the box office and tour reservations.

The Charles Allis Art Museum is at 1801 N. Prospect Ave. at the corner of E. Royall Pl. The museum occupies a Tudor-style mansion built in 1909 by Charles Allis, the first president of Allis-Chalmers Co. Spanning 2,000 years, the collection includes Chinese, Greek, Japanese, Korean, Persian and Roman art objects; fine American, English and French period furniture; Renaissance bronze objects; and landscapes by major 19th- and 20th-century French and American painters.

Allow 30 minutes minimum. Wed.-Sun. 1-5; closed holidays. Docent-guided tours are available Sun. 2-4. Admission $5, over 62 and students $3, under 13 free. Phone (414) 278-8295.

GEM **Milwaukee Art Museum** is at 700 N. Art Museum Dr. Visitors enter the lakefront museum through Quadracci Pavilion, a 90-foot-high reception hall designed by Spanish architect Santiago Calatrava. Soaring above the white marble and glass pavilion is the Burke Brise Soleil, a winglike sunscreen that serves as a moving sculpture.

The museum was established in 1888 and houses more than 20,000 works dating from antiquity to the 20th century. Particularly notable are the collections of the old masters; 19th- and 20th-century European and American art, including products of

German Expressionism and the American Ash Can School; and works by modern artists. The museum also features collections of Haitian art, American decorative arts and folk art and the Prairie School archives of Frank Lloyd Wright. A suspended pedestrian bridge links the museum to downtown Milwaukee at Wisconsin Avenue.

Allow 2 hours minimum. Tues.-Sun. 10-5 (also Thurs. 5-8); closed Jan. 1, Thanksgiving and Dec. 25. Admission $6, over 64 and students with ID $4, under 12 free with adult. Special exhibitions $6. AX, MC, VI. Phone (414) 224-3200.

Villa Terrace Decorative Arts Museum is at 2220 N. Terrace Ave. Of 16th-century Italian Renaissance style, this 1923 villa was designed by architect David Adler. From the house, terraces cascade down a bluff to a formal garden at beach level. Exhibits of 15th- through 20th-century decorative arts include Spanish, Dutch and Italian paintings, English porcelains and wrought-iron works by Milwaukee blacksmith Cyril Colnik. Allow 30 minutes minimum. Wed.-Sun. 1-5. Admission $5, over 62 and students $3, under 13 free. Phone (414) 271-3656.

MILWAUKEE COUNTY ZOO is 6 mi. w. on US 18 between US 45 and SR 100 at 10001 W. Bluemound Rd. The zoo represents one of the country's largest, most comprehensive collections. More than 2,000 animals are displayed in five continental groupings and in natural habitat settings giving the illusion that predator and prey are together. Among the exhibits are Humboldt penguins, sea lions and polar bears that can be seen from an underwater viewing area.

The Apes of Africa features lowland gorillas and bonobos. The Wolf Woods exhibit is home to young timber wolves. Koalas can be seen in the Australian Building. The Aquatic and Reptile Center features endangered Chinese alligators, Caribbean iguanas and a 23,000-gallon Pacific Coast aquarium. The Oceans of Fun Show, which takes place daily (weather permitting), is a 20-minute educational show featuring California sea lions and harbor seals. The Raptor Bird Show is presented daily, Memorial Day weekend-Labor Day.

Other highlights include a close-up educational tour in zoomobiles, rubber-tired trackless trains; 20 minute "Animals in Action" programs; Heritage Farm, an educational dairy complex; a petting zoo; and a miniature train. Stroller and wheelchair rentals and food are available.

Allow 3 hours minimum. Zoo open Mon.-Sat. 9-5, Sun. and holidays 9-6, May-Sept.; daily 9-4:30, rest of year. Zoomobiles, petting zoo and miniature train daily Memorial Day weekend-Labor Day; Sat.-Sun. in spring and fall. Animal in Action show daily 10:30-3 (weather permitting). Admission Apr.-Oct. $9; over 59, $8; ages 3-12, $6. Admission rest

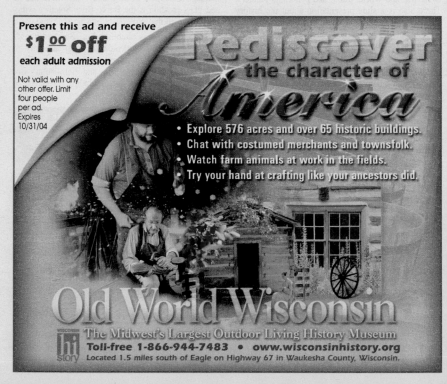

of year $7.50; over 59, $6; ages 3-12, $4.50. Zoomobile $1.50; ages 2-12, $1. Miniature train $2; ages 2-12, $1. Parking $6. DS, MC, VI. Phone (414) 771-3040. *See ad p. 153.*

MILWAUKEE PUBLIC MUSEUM is at 800 W. Wells St. More than 6.2 million specimens include what is said to be the world's largest dinosaur skull. Natural and cultural history are the focus of such walk-through exhibits as Temples, Tells and Tombs, a display of artifacts from ancient Mediterranean civilizations. The Tribute to Survival exhibit provides an overview of North American Indian history and culture.

Visitors to the museum can walk through a Costa Rican rain forest and the turn-of-the-20th-century streets of Old Milwaukee. A glass-enclosed tropical garden showcases butterflies and moths from around the world. Cultural celebrations and changing exhibits are offered throughout the year at the museum, which houses the Humphrey IMAX Dome Theater. Guided tours and food are available.

Daily 9-5; closed July 4, Thanksgiving and Dec. 25. Admission $6.75; over 59, $5.50; ages 3-17, $4.50. IMAX movies are additional. MC, VI. Phone (414) 278-2702, or (414) 319-4629 for IMAX information.

MITCHELL PARK HORTICULTURAL CONSERVATORY—"THE DOMES" is off I-94 exit 309B, just w. on St. Paul Ave., then .7 mi. s. on 27th St. to 524 S. Layton Blvd. Three glass domes, each seven stories high and 140 feet in diameter, house a variety of exotic gardens.

The Arid Dome features plants from the world's deserts, such as cactuses, succulents, palms and grasses. More than 750 species of plants, including orchids, thrive in the Tropical Dome; birds, lizards and frogs also inhabit this rain forest-like environment. Five themed floral displays each year are presented in the Show Dome; the displays of lilies and poinsettias are spectacular at Easter and Christmas. Picnicking is allowed with a permit.

Allow 1 hour, 30 minutes minimum. Daily 9-5. Admission $4.50; ages 6-17 and the physically impaired $3. Free to Milwaukee County residents with ID Mon. 9-11:30. Phone (414) 649-9800, or (414) 649-4954 for a picnic permit.

[SAVE] **PABST MANSION** is at 2000 W. Wisconsin Ave. This 37-room Flemish Renaissance mansion was built in 1892 for beer baron Capt. Frederick Pabst. The building is highlighted by carved wood, stained-glass windows, nine bedrooms, 14 fireplaces and ornamental ironwork. Guided tours are available. Tours depart on the hour Tues.-Sat. 10-3:30, Sun. noon-3:30; closed major holidays. Admission $7; over 62 and students with ID $6; ages 6-17, $3. Prices may vary during special events. MC, VI. Phone (414) 931-0808.

THE PATRICK AND BEATRICE HAGGERTY MUSEUM OF ART is on the e. mall of the Marquette University campus at 13th and Clybourn sts. More than 4,000 works of art include Renaissance, Baroque and modern paintings; sculpture, prints and photographs; and Asian, tribal and decorative arts. Traveling exhibits also are featured. Allow 1 hour minimum. Mon.-Sat. 10-4:30 (also Thurs. 4:30-8), Sun. noon-5; closed Jan. 1, Easter, Thanksgiving and Dec. 25. Free. Phone (414) 288-1669.

PETTIT NATIONAL ICE CENTER is s. of I-94 exit 306 at 500 S. 84th St. The 200,000-square-foot ice skating facility houses a 400-meter speedskating oval and two full-size rinks for hockey, figure skating and short-track speedskating. The center is the official U.S. Olympic training facility for long-track speedskating. Various competitions and events take place annually, and the ice is open to the public several times daily. Warm clothing is recommended. Guided tours are available by appointment only.

Allow 30 minutes minimum. Daily 8 a.m.-9 p.m. Phone for public skating times. Spectators free except during special events. Guided tours $3; over 61 and under 13, $2. Skating $6; over 61 and under 13, $5. Skate rentals $2.50. MC, VI. Phone (414) 266-0100.

ST. JOAN OF ARC CHAPEL is at 601 N. 14th St. on Central Mall on the campus of Marquette University. This 15th-century French chapel stood in the Rhone River Valley for more than 500 years. Falling into disrepair after the French Revolution, the chapel was transported in 1927 to a Long Island estate and reconstructed stone by stone by John Russell Pope, one of America's leading architects.

In 1965 it again was reconstructed laboriously at Marquette University. Incorporated within the structure is the Joan of Arc Stone, before which the saint supposedly prayed.

An outstanding example of Gothic architecture, the small stone building contains items from the 11th to 15th centuries; four stained-glass windows were designed by Charles J. Connick. Part of the floor is the tomb of the Companion of Bayard, a French knight. Mon.-Sat. 10-4, Sun. noon-4; closed major holidays. Free. Phone (414) 288-6873.

SCHLITZ AUDUBON NATURE CENTER is 1 mi. e. of I-43 exit 82A at 1111 E. Brown Deer Rd. This 225-acre nature center and sanctuary on the shores of Lake Michigan, once the home of wagon horses, has about 6 miles of trails through fields, into forests, along ponds and marshlands and down to the lakeshore. Clump planting has provided attractive habitats for native animal and bird species, and a 60-foot observation tower offers views of Lake Michigan and the surrounding countryside.

An interpretive building contains natural history displays; brochures are available for self-guiding trails. Hiking, snowshoeing and cross-country skiing are popular recreational activities. Center and trails open Tues.-Sun. 9-5; closed Jan. 1, Thanksgiving and Dec. 25. Admission $4; over 61 and ages 2-12, $2. MC, VI. Phone (414) 352-2880.

UNIVERSITY OF WISCONSIN-MILWAUKEE encompasses 90 acres on Downer Ave. Founded in 1885 as the Milwaukee Normal School, UWM now has an enrollment of more than 22,000 students. The university's programs in architecture and urban planning are considered among the best in the country. The Institute of Visual Arts offers contemporary exhibitions at several sites on campus; phone (414) 229-5070 for information.

American Geographical Society Collection is at 2311 E. Hartford Ave. in the Golda Meir Library. An exceptional collection of material relates to geography, exploration, map making, earth science and history. Highlights include maps, globes and geography-related books, including many rare items. Mon.-Fri. 8-5. Free. Phone (414) 229-6282.

WHITNALL PARK is at 5879 S. 92nd St. One of the largest municipal parks in the nation, the 660-acre grounds encompass an 18-hole golf course, an archery range, a variety of all-year recreational facilities, picnic areas, nature trails, an environmental education center and botanical gardens. In winter the park is popular for cross-country skiing and sledding. Park open daily dawn-dusk. Free. Phone (414) 425-7303.

Boerner Botanical Gardens is at 5879 S. 92nd St. Trees, shrubs and flowers are displayed through formal and informal gardens. The rose garden has more than 3,000 rose plants of 500 varieties; each year more than 11,000 annuals are planted for seasonal floral exhibitions. Particularly noteworthy are the perennial and herb gardens, as well as the tulip display and the crab apple collection, which is one of the largest in North America.

The Garden House contains art exhibits. Formal gardens open daily 8-dusk, mid-Apr. to late Nov. Garden House open daily 8-7, May-Sept.; 8-4 in Apr.; Mon.-Sat. 8-4, rest of year. Gardens free. Parking $3.50 May-Sept.; special events and holidays $4. Phone (414) 425-1130.

Wehr Nature Center is in the center of the park at 9701 W. College Ave. Natural history displays are featured at the center, which includes a 30-acre prairie restoration site and more than 5 miles of nature trails in its surrounding woodlands and wetlands. Seasonal hikes and lectures are conducted by naturalists. Daily 8-4:30; closed Thanksgiving and Dec. 24-26. Donations; fee for special events. Parking (May-Sept.) $2.50. Phone (414) 425-8550.

WILLIAM F. EISNER MUSEUM OF ADVERTISING is at 208 N. Water St. The museum is a component of the Milwaukee Institute of Art & Design. The development of graphic design and its relationship to advertising is explained with an interactive video and exhibits, an educational center and a simulated radio station. Allow 30 minutes minimum. Tues.-Sat. 11-5; closed major holidays. Admission $4.50; over 55, $2.50; under 12 free with adult. AX, DS, MC, VI. Phone (414) 847-3290.

What To Do

Sightseeing

Boat Tours

EDELWEISS CRUISE DINING departs from Riverfront Plaza; take the I-794 Plankinton Ave. exit, 6 blks. n. to Kilbourne Ave., then 1 blk. to 1110 Old World 3rd St. Visitors can enjoy lunch, dinner, brunch and hors d'oeuvre cruises through downtown Milwaukee via the river and the harbors of Lake Michigan. The 2-hour cruises depart Thurs.-Sun. at 1 and 3, Apr.-Oct., rain or shine. Schedule may vary. Fare $15-$59. Reservations and full payment are required; no refunds within 72 hours of departure. AX, DS, MC, VI. Phone (414) 272-3625.

IROQUOIS HARBOR CRUISES departs between the Michigan and Clybourn St. bridges on the w. bank of the Milwaukee River at 505 N. Riverwalk Way. Narrated 75-minute cruises include such sights as the international shipping docks, breakwater, lighthouse and harbor entrance. Food is available. Trips depart daily at 1 (also Sat.-Sun. at 3), late June-Labor Day. Fare $11.50; over 59, $11; ages 12-17, $9; one child under 12 free with adult (each additional child $8). MC, VI. Phone (414) 294-9450.

Bus and Limousine Tours

Several public and private charter transportation companies offer sightseeing tours that explore the city. Customized tours devoted to Milwaukee's industrial, cultural, civic and residential sights are available, often complemented by lunch or dinner.

Carriage Tours

Horse-drawn carriages offer a memorable means of transportation through downtown and along the shores of Lake Michigan. Shamrock Coach & Carriage, (414) 272-6873, provides nightly service (weather permitting).

Driving Tours

A scenic drive extends from the downtown area at Lincoln Memorial Drive, north to SR 32 through beautiful parks and past the lakeside mansions of the early brewers to Brown Deer Road. North Lake Drive along the bluffs is particularly attractive.

Industrial Tours

MILLER BREWING CO. is at 4251 W. State St. A guided tour of the facility includes a theater presentation, visits to the packaging and shipping centers, the brew house and the historic caves where beer barrels were cooled in the 1800s. Miller products can be sampled by guests over 21 with ID following the 1-hour guided tour that includes stairs and 4 blocks of walking. Strollers are not permitted on the tour. Tours depart the visitor center Mon.-Sat. Tour times and holiday schedules vary; phone ahead. Free. Phone (414) 931-2337 or (414) 931-2467.

Walking Tours

Brochures outlining historic walking tours of Milwaukee's east, west and south sides are available at the Greater Milwaukee Convention and Visitors Bureau as well as at visitor centers throughout the city *(see The Informed Traveler box)*. Campus tours are available at the University of Wisconsin-Milwaukee, (414) 229-2222, and at Marquette University, (414) 288-7302.

Historic Milwaukee Inc. offers guided walking tours that concentrate on the city's historical and architectural heritage. Ninety-minute tour options include Milwaukee's skywalk system, the Riverwalk, the city's historic German and Polish neighborhoods, mansions along Lake Drive, and historic districts such as Walker's Point, the Third Ward and Yankee Hill; phone (414) 277-7795.

Sports and Recreation

Milwaukee sports fans enthusiastically support their professional teams. **Baseball** fans make their pilgrimage to Miller Park, where the beloved Brewers play from April through September; phone (414) 902-4000. Almost before the last baseball game's hot dog can be digested, the NBA's Milwaukee Bucks begin **basketball** exhibition games. Regular season games are played until April at Bradley Center, 1001 N. 4th St.; phone (414) 227-0400 or (414) 227-0500. The Marquette University Golden Eagles also play at Bradley Center; phone (414) 227-0400 or (414) 288-7127.

Three indoor sports fill the calendar at Bradley Center. The Milwaukee Wave play indoor **soccer** November through April; phone (414) 227-0400. The Milwaukee Admirals compete with other teams of the International **Hockey** League October through April; phone (414) 227-0550 or (414) 227-0400. The Milwaukee Mustangs play professional indoor football April through August; phone (414) 227-0400.

Spectators are outdoors again in the spring and the fall to watch fierce **rugby** matches at Veterans Park. The Milwaukee Rampage play professional outdoor soccer April through August at Uihlein Soccer Park on Good Hope Road; phone (414) 358-2655. National championship **automobile races** are held at the State Fair Park, (414) 453-8277, and Hales Corners Speedway, (414) 425-7252, from May through September. **Sailboat races** skirt Lake Michigan's shoreline, off N. Lincoln Memorial Drive, weekends during the summer.

The lakefront also is the playground of anglers, sailors and swimmers during the warm months. **Swimming** is possible at five beaches with lifeguards and dressing facilities: Bradford Beach, 2400 N. Lincoln Memorial Dr.; Doctor's Park Beach, 1870 E. Fox Ln.; Grant Beach, 100 Hawthorne Ave.; McKinley Beach, 1750 N. Lincoln Memorial Dr.; and South Shore Beach, 2900 S. Shore Dr. For those who cannot adjust to Lake Michigan's chilly waters, there are 20 more tepid public pools. Sailors with their own **boating** craft may use the launch ramps at Grant Park, Riverfront, McKinley Marina and South Shore Yacht Club for a fee.

Fishing in Lake Michigan can reward anglers with prize catches of salmon and trout as big as 30 pounds. Full- and half-day charters are offered by numerous companies; check the telephone directory.

Tennis is available at 30 county parks; many courts are lighted. Court use is free, though a $3.50 fee is charged for reservations; phone (414) 257-8030. North Shore Elite Fitness and Racquet Club, (414) 351-2900, at 5750 N. Glen Park Rd., is one of several clubs that offers indoor tennis courts. Lawn bowling is popular at Lake and Dineen parks; instruction and equipment are available during the summer.

About two-thirds of the **golf** courses in the Milwaukee vicinity are 18-hole courses. Brown Deer Golf Course, (414) 352-8080, 7835 N. Green Bay Rd., is home to the PGA Greater Milwaukee Open and is open to the public. The county also maintains par-three and regulation 18-hole courses and an 18-hole pitch-and-putt course. In the winter, the Currie Park Golf Dome, 3535 N. Mayfair Rd., offers an indoor driving range; phone (414) 453-1742.

The Milwaukee County Park System offers a variety of public facilities among its 140 parks, including beaches, swimming pools, golf courses, tennis courts, soccer fields, **hiking** trails and the 90-mile Oak Leaf Trail, a paved path for **bicycling,** inline skating and jogging that encircles the city. Many county parks also are equipped for winter sports. For information about county park facilities phone (414) 257-4575.

Although Milwaukee's winters are somewhat formidable, the lure of various winter sports entices even the frostbite-prone outdoors. The park department floods more than 30 sites for **ice skating.** The premier site, however, is Pettit National Ice Center *(see attraction listing p. 155)*. Wilson Park Center also offers indoor skating.

Whitnall County Park has a ski tow for **downhill skiing,** and Brown Deer, Currie, Dretzka and Grant parks have trails for **cross-country skiing.** Old World Wisconsin *(see Eagle p. 159)* and Schlitz Audubon Nature Center *(see attraction listing p. 155)* also provide cross-country ski trails.

Favorite weekend destinations for Milwaukee residents include Kettle Moraine State Forest *(see Recreation Chart and Campbellsport p. 127)*, the greyhound tracks in Kenosha and Delavan, and any of the 60 inland lakes in the metropolitan area.

Note: Policies concerning admittance of children to pari-mutuel betting facilities vary. Phone for information.

Shopping

In the heart of Milwaukee, a legacy of cobblestone streets and ethnic specialty shops blend gracefully with the skywalks and covered malls that characterize the modern emporiums. The city's centerpiece is Grand Avenue Mall, a four-block multilevel marketplace on Wisconsin Avenue between N.

4th Street and the Milwaukee River that incorporates the historic Plankinton Arcade. It is anchored by Boston Store and encloses more than 130 shops and eateries.

Such marketplaces as Grand Avenue Mall have not displaced Milwaukee's traditional shopping areas. Just below one of the mall's skywalks is Old World 3rd Street, between Wells and Juneau avenues, where late 19th-century buildings house specialty stores along a cobblestone street. Some shops include Ambrosia Chocolate Company, Usinger's famous sausage, the Wisconsin Cheese Mart, Spice House and others offering Hummel figurines, furniture and crafts.

Across the Milwaukee River in East Town, the elegant shops along Jefferson Street include George Watts' china and crystal and those offering antiques, furnishings and other items. Two other colorful east-side neighborhoods are Brady Street, between Farwell Avenue and Marshall Street, steeped in Old World tradition, and Downer Avenue, between E. Webster and E. Park. Antiques enthusiasts can browse along three floors of antiques and collectibles at Milwaukee Antique Center, 341 N. Milwaukee St.

An archway welcomes shoppers to Milwaukee's Historic Third Ward, the city's original commercial district. Renovated warehouses and factories now house art galleries, antique stores, restaurants, specialty shops and performing arts centers along streets lined with old-fashioned street lights. Downtown, the Milwaukee River and Lake Michigan form the boundaries for the Ward's 17-block shopping area.

Cedar Creek Settlement *(see Cedarburg p. 159)* offers a delightful step back in time. Stonewood Village, 17700 W. Capitol Dr. in Brookfield, markets Colonial wares.

Shopping centers in the metropolitan area are Bayshore, 5900 N. Port Washington Rd.; Brookfield Square, 95 N. Moorland Rd.; Mayfair Mall, 2500 N. Mayfair Rd.; Northridge, 7700 W. Brown Deer Rd.; and Southridge, 5300 S. 76th St. The stores generally are open Mon.-Fri. 10-9, Sat. 10-6, Sun. noon-5.

Theater and Concerts

Milwaukee boasts several nationally acclaimed performing arts companies. The Marcus Center for the Performing Arts, 929 N. Water St., is home to many of these, including the Florentine Opera Company, Milwaukee Ballet Company and the Milwaukee Symphony Orchestra. The Milwaukee Symphony Orchestra's regular season is early September through June; phone (414) 273-7206 or (888) 612-3500.

Free Rainbow Summer concerts and other cultural offerings are presented at the Marcus Center for the Performing Arts' riverfront tent stage on summer afternoons. The park department also sponsors less well-known groups in free concerts at various parks during the summer.

The Milwaukee Repertory Theater performs a variety of dramatic productions at 108 E. Wells St. from mid-September to mid-May; phone (414) 224-9490. Since the restoration of the late 19th-century Victorian Pabst Theater at 144 E. Wells St., the grand old theater presents musical and theatrical productions ranging from Broadway shows to chamber music and other concerts. Tours of the theater are offered Saturday at 11:30; phone (414) 286-3663. The Ko-Thi Dance Co. is among the groups performing at the Pabst Theater.

The Helfaer Theater, (414) 288-7504, at 13th and Clybourn on the Marquette University campus, presents quality theater and concert offerings. The Milwaukee Riverside Theater, (414) 224-3000, at 116 W. Wisconsin Ave., presents touring Broadway shows and musical artists. Marcus Amphitheater on the Summerfest Grounds at 200 N. Harbor Dr. features concerts; phone (414) 273-2600.

Musicals and operettas are staged by the Skylight Opera Theater, which performs at the Broadway Theatre Center, 158 N. Broadway; phone (414) 291-7800. The Broadway Theatre Center also is home to the Milwaukee Chamber Theatre, which stages both classical and contemporary works, phone (414) 276-8842, and Theater X, an experimental theater group.

The events sections of the city's newspaper carries current information about local cultural activities. Visitors also can contact the Milwaukee Convention and Visitors Bureau for an update; phone (800) 554-1448.

Special Events

Annual events begin in January with the U.S. International Snow Sculpting Competition. The regular sports calendar includes the *Milwaukee Journal/ Sentinel* Sports Show, which draws crowds to the Midwest Express Center in mid-March.

State Fair Park in the suburb of West Allis plays host to several automobile races throughout the year, including the PPG CART Miller 225 the weekend after Memorial Day and the NASCAR/ Diehard 250 in late June. The Greater Milwaukee Open Golf Tournament takes place in early July.

Supreme among Milwaukee's cultural events are the Lakefront Festival of the Arts in June and Summerfest, held from late June to early July. Riverfest, also in June, offers 10 city blocks of music, food and fireworks along the river. Ethnic festivals include the Polish Fest and the Asian Moon Festival in June and the Fiesta Italiana, Bastille Days and German Fest in July.

The Great Circus Parade, considered the only one of its kind in the country, offers bands, costumed units, animals and the Ringling Bros. circus wagons, also in July. Rainbow Summer at the Performing Arts Center includes noon and evening musical performances on the riverfront June through August. The same months offer sailboat races, held every weekend off North Lincoln Memorial Drive.

Big-name entertainment is prominent in August among the festivities that surround the Wisconsin State Fair. Also in August are the African World Festival, the Irish Fest and Mexican Fiesta. Indian Summer, Arabian Fest and Oktoberfest take place in September. More than 50 ethnic groups gather in mid-November for the Holiday Folk Fair, which salutes Old World culture.

Colorful floats and other displays launch yuletide festivities at the Christmas Parade, traditionally held in November.

Each season of the year is celebrated with a spectacular flower show at Mitchell Park Horticultural Conservatory—"The Domes." Waves of color and fragrance treat the senses during the Spring Flower Show, late March to mid-May, and the Summer Flower Show, held from June to mid-September. The Fall Flower Show takes place from late September to mid-November. The Christmas Flower Show is held from Thanksgiving to early January, and the Winter Flower Show, held mid-January to mid-March, closes the season.

The Milwaukee Vicinity

CEDARBURG (H-8) pop. 10,908, elev. 778′

Thanks to the water power provided by Cedar Creek and an abundant supply of limestone, Cedarburg had become a busy milling, textile, quarrying and industrial center by the 1850s. The original center of activity was New Dublin, later renamed Hamilton, southeast of the present downtown section. Now designated a historic district, Hamilton includes the 1853 Concordia Mill and several other historic stone buildings.

The 1855 Cedarburg Mill, used as a refuge for families during the Great Indian Scare of 1862, still stands near the Columbia Road bridge over Cedar Creek. One of the last two surviving covered bridges in the state crosses Cedar Creek about 3 miles north via CR NN and Covered Bridge Road. The other spans the Crystal River in Waupaca *(see place listing p. 176)*.

Lime Kiln Park, on Green Bay Road in nearby Grafton, features restored lime kiln chimneys and a picturesque dam. The park, on the Milwaukee River, offers a picnic area and a canoe launch. Landmark Tours provides guided tours of Cedarburg and Ozaukee County; phone (262) 375-1426.

Cedarburg Chamber of Commerce: Washington Ave. and Spring St., P.O. Box 104, Cedarburg, WI 53012; phone (262) 377-9620.

Self-guiding tours: Several brochures describing Cedarburg's historic district and outlining a walking tour are available from the chamber of commerce. A cassette tape costing $5 also describes a walking tour; the tape is available from the Cedarburg Cultural Center, W62 N546 Washington Ave.; phone (262) 375-3676.

Shopping areas: Hidden treasures can be found in the numerous antiques shops lining Washington Avenue in the historic district. Cedar Creek Settlement, Washington Avenue and Bridge Road, offers some 30 shops and cafes surrounding the five-story Cedarburg Mill.

THE BREWERY WORKS is at W62 N718 Riveredge Dr. An 1843 brewery has been converted into the art studios of sculptor Paul J. Yank and the

Ozaukee County Art Center. Working artisans sometimes can be seen. Allow 1 hour minimum. Wed.-Sun. 1-4; closed Jan. 1, Thanksgiving and Dec. 25. Donations. Phone (262) 377-8230 or (262) 377-7220.

CEDAR CREEK SETTLEMENT is downtown at jct. Bridge Rd. and Washington Ave. at N70 W6340 Bridge Rd. Built in 1864 and in operation until 1969, the old Wittenberg Woolen Mill was restored in the early 1970s to house nearly 30 retail establishments, including Cedar Creek Winery. Mon.-Sat. 10-5, Sun. 11-5. Free. Phone (800) 827-8020.

WINERIES

- [SAVE] **Cedar Creek Winery** is at jct. Bridge Rd. and Washington Ave. at N70 W6340 Bridge Rd. Mon.-Sat. 10-5, Sun. 11-5; closed Jan. 1, Easter, Thanksgiving and Dec. 25. Phone (262) 377-8020 or (800) 827-8020.

EAGLE (I-7) pop. 1,707, elev. 947′

[GEM] **OLD WORLD WISCONSIN** is 1 mi. s. on SR 67. This 576-acre state historic site consists of 67 preserved and furnished buildings erected by 19th-century immigrants. Displayed are a rural crossroads village of the 1870s; Yankee farmsteads; and an African-American pioneer site. Costumed interpreters explain the story of immigration to Wisconsin and each ethnic group's role.

A 15-minute orientation film about 19th-century Wisconsin is offered on the lower level of Ramsey Barn Visitor Center. A 2.5-mile tour is required to see the entire museum; if walking, allow 4 to 6 hours and wear comfortable shoes. Tram service is available. Seasonal events take place some weekends. The 5-mile Aldo Leopold Environmental History Trail includes interpretive signs about the area's heritage and habitats.

On winter weekends Old World Wisconsin is open for cross-country skiing, conditions permitting. Trails vary from about three-quarters of a mile to 4.3 miles in length. Sleigh rides also are offered. The complex also is open selected dates in December for Christmas tours; phone for hours and prices. Food is available.

Complex open Wed.-Sun. 10-5, May 1-June 17 and Labor Day-Oct. 31; Tues.-Sun. 10-5, June 18-day after Labor Day. Last admission is 1 hour before closing; tickets purchased after 3 p.m. also are good for an additional day. Admission $13; over 64, $11.90; ages 5-12, $7.50; family rate (2 adults and children under 18) $30. MC, VI. Phone (262) 594-6300. *See color ad p. 154.*

ERIN (H-7)

HOLY HILL is 8 mi. w. on SR 167. This national shrine to Mary, Help of Christians is staffed by Discalced Carmelites. The order was formed in the late 16th century and is based upon a life of prayer, for which the 1,340-foot-high wooded retreat is particularly suited. Settlers erected a 15-foot oak cross and chapel on the summit in the early 19th century.

The log chapel evolved into a Romanesque church, a national shrine to the Virgin Mary and a monastery for the 17 friars who staff the shrine. A tower affords picturesque views. Allow 1 hour minimum. Daily 6 a.m.-5 p.m. Donations. Phone (262) 628-1838.

GRAFTON (H-8) pop. 10,312, elev. 757'

SAVE **THE FAMILY FARM** is at 328 W. Port Washington Rd. A 46-acre restored turn-of-the-20th-century farmstead comprises five historic buildings and livestock including goats, chickens, donkeys, horses, rabbits, pigs, cows and a llama. Antique farm implements are displayed. A nature walk, horse-drawn rides and food are available. Allow 1 hour minimum. Wed.-Sat. 9-4, Sun. 11-4, mid-May through Sept. 30; Tues.-Fri. 9-4, Sat. 9-5, Sun. 11-5 in Oct. Admission $6.25; over 61, $5.25; ages 2-12, $3.75. Horse-drawn rides $1. MC, VI. Phone (262) 377-6161.

HARTFORD (H-7) pop. 10,905, elev. 988'

Pike Lake State Park, 2 miles east on SR 60, offers a variety of recreational activities year-round, including camping, picnicking, hiking, fishing, swimming and cross-country skiing. *See Recreation Chart and the AAA Great Lakes CampBook.*

Hartford Area Chamber of Commerce: P.O. Box 270305, Hartford, WI 53027; phone (262) 673-7002.

WISCONSIN AUTOMOTIVE MUSEUM is at 147 N. Rural St. More than 90 antique and classic automobiles are exhibited, including Austin-Americans, Fords, Hudsons, Metzes, Wisconsin-built Nashes and the locally manufactured Kissel. Also displayed are motorcycles, single-cylinder farm engines, automotive relics, outboard motors, gas pumps and a 250-ton steam locomotive.

Allow 1 hour minimum. Mon.-Sat. and holidays 10-5, Sun. noon-5, May-Sept.; Wed.-Sat. 10-5, Sun. noon-5, rest of year. Closed Jan. 1, Easter, Thanksgiving and Dec. 24-25 and 31. Admission $6; over 61 and students with ID $5; ages 8-15, $2.50. Phone (262) 673-7999.

OCONOMOWOC (H-7) pop. 12,382, elev. 869'

Surrounded by lakes and easily accessible from Milwaukee, Chicago and other cities, Oconomowoc was a wealthy resort in the late 19th century. The most fashionable people of the period built their elaborate summer cottages on the nearby lakes. Many of these houses remain and lend their charm to this popular vacation community.

Oconomowoc Convention & Visitors Bureau: 174 E. Wisconsin Ave., Oconomowoc, WI 53066; phone (800) 524-3744.

Self-guiding tours: The historic houses around Fowler Lake can be viewed on a self-guiding 2-mile-long walking tour. Maps are available from the chamber of commerce.

OCONOMOWOC AND LAKE COUNTRY MUSEUM is at 103 W. Jefferson St. The history of Oconomowoc and the Lake Country area is depicted in permanent and temporary exhibits and special events. Displays include a model train, railroad memorabilia and World War II artifacts. Representations of local architecture include a Victorian home, dentist's office, barbershop, print shop, general store, bank and a medical clinic. A theater has a 20-minute videotape presentation about area history. Fri.-Sun. 1-5, early May-Dec. 31; other times by appointment. Donations. Phone (262) 569-0740.

PORT WASHINGTON (G-8)
pop. 10,467, elev. 668'

Patriotic fervor was hardly the reaction of Ozaukee County farmers when the governor ordered all able-bodied citizens to enroll for service during the Civil War. On Nov. 10, 1862, an angry mob stampeded Port Washington's courthouse and destroyed the draft rolls.

Lest their point of view go unacknowledged, they later seized the small cannon ordinarily used for Fourth of July celebrations and positioned it on the south bluff overlooking the harbor. The rebels were no match for government troops, however, who sailed into the harbor by night and easily subdued the small army.

Port Washington is a fishing and yachting center on Lake Michigan distinguished by many pre-Civil War houses, including the 19th-century Eghart House, 316 Grand Ave. On a hill overlooking the downtown area is St. Mary's Church, a much-photographed Gothic church built in 1882. Upper Lake Park offers a fine vantage point for viewing the harbor, where coal carriers regularly deposit huge supplies to fuel the waterfront power plant.

Numerous charter boats operate from the marina during the summer and fall; fishing for trout as well as coho and chinook salmon is popular all year.

Port Washington Chamber of Commerce: 126 E. Grand Ave., P.O. Box 514, Port Washington, WI 53074; phone (262) 284-0900 or (800) 719-4881.

SAUKVILLE (H-8) pop. 4,068, elev. 771'

[SAVE] **OZAUKEE COUNTY PIONEER VILLAGE** is at 4880 CR I. A collection of 1800s Wisconsin buildings is preserved. Ranging from a log hay barn, smokehouse and residence to a trading post, smithy and railroad station, the structures represent a cross section of frontier architecture. All are furnished in period. Costumed guided tours are available. Allow 1 hour minimum. Sat.-Sun. noon-5, Memorial Day weekend to mid-Oct. Admission $4; over 55 and ages 12-18, $3; ages 5-11, $1. Special events $5. Phone (262) 377-4510.

WAUKESHA (H-8) pop. 64,825, elev. 867'

Waukesha takes its name from an American Indian word meaning "by the Little Fox." Although the Fox River has been important in the city's steady industrial growth, it was the many mineral springs and their purported curative powers that brought Waukesha its fame as the elegant "Saratoga of the West" during the late 19th century. Plants bottling carbonated beverages are the only vestiges of those halcyon days.

Another small reminder of past notoriety is a marker in Cutler Park honoring a local citizen who safely transported the first slave through Wisconsin to Canada. Waukesha was an important station on the Underground Railroad and an abolitionist stronghold; the *American Freeman* was published in the town 1844-48.

Waukesha is an industrial and college town serving the surrounding dairying and farming area. Colleges include Carroll College, University of Wisconsin-Waukesha and Waukesha County Technical College. Frame Park, the largest of seven municipal parks, is noted for its formal garden.

Waukesha Area Convention & Visitors Bureau: 2240 N. Grandview Blvd., Suite 2, Waukesha, WI 53188; phone (262) 542-0330 or (800) 366-8474.

WAUKESHA COUNTY MUSEUM is at 101 W. Main St. at East Ave. Exhibits relate to the area's pioneers, its earthen mounds, American Indian culture and Civil War history. A replica of an 1830s fur trader's cabin is included. A research center specializing in family and local history is open to the public. Allow 30 minutes minimum. Museum open Tues.-Sat. 10-4:30. Research center Tues. and Fri-Sat. 10-noon and 12:30-4:30, Thurs. 12:30-4:30.

Closed holidays. Museum admission by donation. Research Center $3. Phone (262) 521-2859.

WEST BEND (G-8) pop. 28,152, elev. 906'

West Bend, a busy industrial community on the Milwaukee River, has its name appearing in homes worldwide on small appliances and kitchenware. Outdoor recreation abounds throughout the more than 650 acres of city park land. Challenging terrain makes the area popular with cyclists and hikers. Sledding and skiing keep adventure seekers busy in winter.

Riverfront Parkway, a trail that winds along the Milwaukee River through West Bend, can be enjoyed by joggers, walkers or those on bicycles. In addition to the scenic beauty of the trail is a series of sculptures at the river's edge.

West Bend Area Chamber of Commerce: 735 S. Main St., P.O. Box 522, West Bend, WI 53095; phone (262) 338-2666 or (888) 338-8666.

LIZARD MOUND COUNTY PARK is 4 mi. n. on SR 144, then .2 mi. e. on CR A. The internationally known archeological site is named after its most prominent effigy mound, which is shaped like a gigantic lizard. Between A.D. 400 and 1200, the American Indians built the mounds to cover their burial and ceremonial sites.

Designed in animal, bird and geometric shapes, the 31-acre park's 25 mounds and earthworks are among the best preserved in Wisconsin. A self-guiding tour, nature trail and picnic facilities are available. Allow 1 hour minimum. Daily dawn-dusk, April-Oct. Free. Phone (262) 335-4445.

OLD COURTHOUSE SQUARE MUSEUM is at 320 S. 5th Ave. This restoration of the 1889 Romanesque-revival courthouse contains a variety of permanent and temporary exhibits centering on local history. Adjacent to the museum is the restored 1886 jailhouse and home of the county sheriff. Wed.-Fri. 10-4, Sun. 1-4. Free. Phone (262) 335-4678.

WEST BEND ART MUSEUM is at 300 S. 6th Ave. Permanent and changing displays showcase the work of locally, regionally and nationally known artists. The museum features hundreds of works by Carl von Marr, an internationally recognized painter from the area. An elaborate doll house also is exhibited. Allow 1 hour minimum. Wed.-Sat. 10-4:30, Sun. 1-4:30; closed holidays. Free. Phone (262) 334-9638.

The previous listings were for the Milwaukee Vicinity.
This page resumes the alphabetical listings of cities in Wisconsin.

MINERAL POINT (I-4)
pop. 2,617, elev. 1,041'

Some of the early surface miners who came to Mineral Point in search of "mineral," or lead, were so obsessed that they lived in the holes they were digging—and provided the source for Wisconsin's nickname, "The Badger State." Beginning in 1830 they were joined by Cornish miners skilled in hard-rock mining.

Their English heritage survives in the town's stone houses, colorful stories and traditional pasties (PAST-ees), saffron cakes and tea biscuits. The name of Shake Rag Street stems from the Cornish wives' custom of waving rags to summon their men working on the opposite hillside.

Lately Mineral Point has become a center for arts and handicrafts, with some of the buildings in the restored areas devoted to studio space.

Mineral Point Chamber of Commerce: 225 High St., Mineral Point, WI 53565; phone (608) 987-3201 or (888) 764-6894.

Self-guiding tours: Maps outlining a driving tour and a walking tour of Mineral Point's historical and architectural attractions can be obtained at the chamber of commerce.

PENDARVIS STATE HISTORIC SITE is at 114 Shake Rag St. On the site are 10 carefully restored stone and log houses built by Cornish lead miners in the 1840s; six of the structures are open to the public and furnished in period. Also displayed are old tools and mining equipment. The Pendarvis site offers information about a self-guiding tour of nearby Merry Christmas Mine Hill, where visitors can see mining history by viewing abandoned mine shafts and "badger holes."

Guided tours daily; phone ahead for schedule. Last tour begins 1 hour before closing. Fee $8; over 65, $7.20; ages 5-12, $4. MC, VI. Phone (608) 987-2122.

MINOCQUA (C-5) elev. 1,603'

Calling itself the "Island City," Minocqua is in the Lakeland area, which has more than 3,200 lakes. The region is known for fishing and boating in summer and cross-country skiing and snowmobiling in winter. Minocqua Winter Park, 6 miles west on SR 70 and 6 miles south on Squirrel Lake Road, offers 75 miles of groomed cross-country trails.

Northern Lights Playhouse in Minocqua presents Broadway musicals and comedies nightly from Memorial Day weekend through mid-October; phone (715) 356-7173.

Minocqua-Arbor Vitae-Woodruff Area Chamber of Commerce: 8216 US 51S, P.O. Box 1006, Minocqua, WI 54548; phone (715) 356-5266 or (800) 446-6784.

CIRCLE M CORRAL is 2.5 mi. w. of US 51 on SR 70. This amusement park offers children's rides, water games and a waterslide, go-carts, bumper boats, train rides, pony rides, miniature golf, horseback riding, batting cages and video games. Food is available. Daily 10-5, mid-May to late Sept. Admission free; prices for activity packages start at $5. MC, VI. Phone (715) 356-4441.

PECK'S WILDWOOD WILDLIFE PARK AND NATURE CENTER is 2 mi. w. of US 51 on SR 70. More than 500 varieties of birds and tame wildlife live in the 25-acre park. Visitors can walk among deer and pet baby animals. Nature programs are offered daily, and a nature walk, "Explore and Learn" area and a timber wolf and bald eagle presentation also are featured. Picnicking is permitted. Boat rides and food are available. Daily 9-5:30, June 1-Labor Day; 9-4:30 in May and day after Labor Day to mid-Oct. Admission $8; ages 2 months-11 years, $5.50. MC, VI. Phone (715) 356-5588.

MONROE (I-5) pop. 10,843, elev. 1,050'

Monroe and its environs are known as the Swiss cheese capital of the United States. Many inhabitants are of Swiss descent, and old customs prevail at certain festivals. Some of the shops on the business square that surrounds the red brick courthouse have ornate Swiss-style facades. Of note is the Old Methodist Church, designed by Milwaukee architect E. Townsend Mix in 1869.

The Alp and Dell Cheese Factory, north on SR 69, offers free tours of its factory; phone (608) 328-3355.

Monroe Chamber of Commerce: 1505 9th St., Monroe, WI 53566; phone (608) 325-7648.

NEENAH-MENASHA (F-7)
pop. 40,838, elev. 753'

The twin cities of Neenah and Menasha meet at the junction of Nicolet Boulevard and Abbey Avenue, on the island separating the two channels through which Lake Winnebago empties into the Fox River. Although they have separate governments, the cities share many civic and industrial enterprises, including their reputation as Wisconsin's papermaking center.

It was the possibility of water power that spurred the birth of the two villages in the 1840s. Neenah was incorporated in 1873. A year later Menasha was established and awarded the charter to develop the water power for the area.

Fox Cities Convention and Visitors Bureau: 3433 W. College Ave., Appleton, WI 54914; phone (920) 734-3358 or (800) 236-6673.

BERGSTROM-MAHLER MUSEUM is at 165 N. Park Ave. on Lake Winnebago. Displays include antique and modern glass paperweights, Germanic glass and changing exhibitions. Allow 1 hour minimum. Tues.-Fri. 10-4:30, Sat. 9-4:30, Sun. 1-4:30; closed holidays except Easter. Donations. Phone (920) 751-4658.

DOTY GRAND LOGGERY is at Lincoln and Fifth sts. in Doty Park. This replica of the home of James Doty, second territorial governor, contains American Indian artifacts, belongings of the Doty family and other historical items. Allow 30 minutes minimum. Daily noon-4, June-Aug. Donations. Phone (920) 751-4614.

NEILLSVILLE (F-4) pop. 2,731, elev. 977'

The Wisconsin Pavilion from the 1964-65 New York World's Fair is at 1200 E. Division St. It contains the radio station WCCN and a cheesehouse. Visitors can observe the radio station through windows. A replica of the world's largest cheese, weighing 34,500 pounds, and Chatty Belle, an enormous mechanical talking cow, are on the grounds.

Neillsville Area Chamber of Commerce: 106 W. Division St., P.O. Box 52, Neillsville, WI 54456; phone (715) 743-6444 or (888) 252-7594.

THE HIGHGROUND is 4 mi. w. on US 10. A 140-acre veterans memorial park features monuments to soldiers of World War I, World War II and the Wisconsin veterans of the Vietnam War. Memorials dedicated to female veterans, POWs, MIAs and Native American veterans also are on the premises. A replica of the Liberty Bell also is on the grounds. A half-million acres of Wisconsin woodland and glacial moraine are visible from the memorial's plaza.

Picnicking is available. For additional information write The Highground, P.O. Box 457, Neillsville, WI 54456-0457. Allow 1 hour minimum. Daily 24 hours. Donations. Phone (715) 743-4224.

NEW GLARUS (I-5) pop. 2,111, elev. 859'

Impelled by economic adversity in Switzerland, 118 emigrants from the canton of Glarus settled New Glarus in 1845. "Little Switzerland," as the community often is called, remains essentially Swiss in character. Emblems of the Swiss cantons adorn buildings and street signs. Dairying and cheesemaking brought New Glarus its prosperity.

New Glarus also is a popular departure point for the Sugar River State Trail, a 23-mile hiking, bicycling and snowmobiling route leading to Brodhead.

New Glarus Chamber of Commerce: P.O. Box 713, New Glarus, WI 53574-0713; phone (608) 527-2095 or (800) 527-6838.

CHALET OF THE GOLDEN FLEECE is at 618 2nd St. Modeled after a Swiss Bernese mountain chalet, the 1937 house museum is furnished with many items from Switzerland and other parts of the world. The interior woodwork is particularly impressive. Guided tours are available. Allow 1 hour minimum. Daily 10-4:30, June-Aug.; 10-4 in May and Sept.-Oct. Admission $5; ages 6-17, $2. Phone (608) 527-2614.

SWISS HISTORICAL VILLAGE is at 612 7th Ave. Fourteen buildings on the landscaped grounds include a firehouse, smithy, log church, butcher shop, tool shed, general store, print shop, Swiss bee house and cheese factory. A log cabin and schoolhouse are original. The Hall of History contains displays tracing Swiss immigration to America and the settlement of the New Glarus area. Allow 1 hour, 30 minutes minimum. Daily 10-4, May-Oct. Last tour begins 30 minutes before closing. Admission $6; ages 6-13, $2. Phone (608) 527-2317.

NEW LONDON (F-7) pop. 7,085, elev. 758'

New London, on the Wolf River near its junction with the Embarrass River, witnessed the booming days when great log drives traveled down both streams. Agribusiness and timber-related industries employ much of the area's population. The area offers numerous recreational opportunities, including cross-country skiing, snowmobiling, whitewater rafting and fishing.

The New London Heritage Historical Village, just east of Mill Street at 900 Montgomery St., consists of five historical buildings—a log cabin, an octagon-shaped house, a chapel, a school and a railroad depot—all moved to the site. The village is open limited weekends June through August and by appointment; phone (920) 982-5186 or (920) 982-8557.

New London Area Chamber of Commerce: 301 E. Beacon Ave., New London, WI 54961; phone (920) 982-5822.

MOSQUITO HILL NATURE CENTER is 2 mi. s. of CR S from jct. SR 54 at N3880 Rogers Rd. Several miles of nature trails wind through the center's 430 acres along the Wolf River, and an interpretive building has natural history displays and an outdoors observation deck. A butterfly house also is available. Snowshoeing along marked trails can be enjoyed during the winter months; phone ahead for trail conditions. Tues.-Fri. 8-4:30, Sat.-Sun. 10-3. Butterfly house Wed. and Sat.-Sun. 11-3, July-Aug. Closed holidays. Donations. Phone (920) 779-6433.

NEW LONDON PUBLIC MUSEUM is on US 45 at 406 S. Pearl St. The museum contains American Indian and African artifacts, minerals, fossils, shells, displays about the extinct passenger pigeon and regional historical items. Regular changing exhibits are featured. Allow 1 hour minimum. Tues.-Fri. 10-5 (also Tues. 5-8), Sat. 9-2, Labor Day-Memorial Day; Mon.-Fri. 9-5, rest of year. Closed holidays. Free. Phone (920) 982-8520.

NICOLET NATIONAL FOREST—

see Chequamegon-Nicolet National Forest p. 128.

NORTH FREEDOM (H-5) pop. 649, elev. 867'

SAVE **MID-CONTINENT RAILWAY MUSEUM** is w. on W. Walnut St. Vintage trains take passengers on a 50-minute ride along a former branch line of the Chicago and North Western Railroad. The museum includes an 1894 depot, a wooden water tower, restored locomotives and railroad cars and equipment displays. A winter ride runs the third weekend in February; an autumn color train ride takes place the first two weekends in October; and Santa Claus Express is offered Thanksgiving weekend. A dinner train ride also is available. Picnicking is permitted.

Museum open daily 9:30-5, mid-May through Labor Day; Sat.-Sun. 9:30-5, day after Labor Day to mid-Oct. Trains depart at 10:30, 12:30, 2 and 3:30, mid-May to Labor Day. Passengers should arrive at least 15 minutes prior to departure. Museum free. Train fare $11; over 62, $10; ages 3-12, $6. Caboose rides $13; ages 3-12, $7. AX, DS, MC, VI. Phone (608) 522-4261.

OCONOMOWOC—*see Milwaukee p. 160.*

OCONTO (E-8) pop. 4,708, elev. 590′

The Oconto that attracts duck hunters and anglers to its favorable Green Bay location once was the burial site of an ancient Copper Culture people. The discovery of the burial site, now a park on Mill Street, revealed that they had populated the area more than 4,000 years ago.

Modern by comparison is the West Main Street Historic District, a three-block area lined with elegant houses marking the period when lumber was supreme in Oconto. Among the houses dating 1860-1928 is one that belonged to Edward Scofield, the last of Wisconsin's lumberman governors. The first church built by the Christian Science denomination is at Chicago and Main streets.

Oconto Area Chamber of Commerce: 110 Brazeau Ave., P.O. Box 174, Oconto, WI 54153; phone (920) 834-2255.

BEYER HOME MUSEUM is at 917 Park Ave. The 1868 Victorian house is furnished to reflect the 1890s. A museum annex on the grounds contains Old Main Street and its shops, a cabin, Copper Culture artifacts and displays of Oconto County history. A barn/carriage house houses tools and historic vehicles, including two antique electric cars. Allow 1 hour minimum. Tours are given Mon.-Sat. 10-4, Sun. noon-4, June 1-Labor Day. Admission $3; ages 6-18, $1; family rate $7. Phone (920) 834-6206.

OSCEOLA (D-1) pop. 2,421, elev. 809′

On the bluffs of the St. Croix River, Osceola was a popular stop for late 19th-century excursion steamboats. Passengers disembarked to follow a boardwalk to scenic Cascade Falls. Visitors today can duplicate that hike along a path leading to the waterfall. Interstate State Park, known for its cliffs, potholes and hiking trails, is a short drive north (*see St. Croix Falls p. 169*).

Osceola Chamber of Commerce: 114 Depot Rd., P.O. Box 251, Osceola, WI 54020; phone (715) 755-3300 or (800) 947-0581.

[SAVE] **OSCEOLA & ST. CROIX VALLEY RAILWAY** departs from 114 Depot Rd. Scenic 50- and 90-minute narrated excursions aboard restored diesel-powered trains take passengers along the St. Croix River Valley separating Wisconsin from Minnesota. Trips depart Sat.-Sun. at 11, 1 and 2:30, Memorial Day weekend-late Oct. Fare $10-$13; over 62, $9-$12; ages 5-15, $5-$7; family rate $25-$38. AX, DS, MC, VI. Phone (715) 755-3570 or (800) 711-2591.

OSHKOSH (F-7) pop. 62,916, elev. 755′

Oshkosh is an important manufacturing center on the west shore of Lake Winnebago at the mouth of the upper Fox River. Because the Fox and its tributaries could transport logs from far to the north and because nearby lakes Poygan and Butte des Morts provided natural storage facilities, the lumbering boom lasted longer in Oshkosh than in other central Wisconsin sawmill towns.

Streets inches deep in sawdust elicited the nickname "Sawdust City" and probably contributed to the fact that the downtown area was destroyed by fire five times 1859-75. After the last conflagration, rebuilding was done with brick.

A noted Oshkosh resident, Helen Farnsworth Mears, won national acclaim for her sculpture "Genius of Wisconsin," now at the Capitol in Madison. More than 240 acres of municipal parks and the University of Wisconsin-Oshkosh enhance the community. Campus tours are offered; phone (920) 424-1234.

A swimming beach, marina and children's zoo are among the recreational facilities available at Menominee Park, open daily May through October. Also featured is Little Oshkosh, a playground complete with castles, mazes, tunnels and a fire truck.

A collection of nativity scenes, including one made by German POWs in World War II, is displayed at the United Methodist Church on Algoma Boulevard. Viewing is available during church office hours; phone (920) 231-2800.

Oshkosh Convention & Visitors Bureau: 525 W. 20th Ave., Oshkosh, WI 54902; phone (920) 303-9200 or (877) 303-9200.

Shopping areas: The Aviation Plaza, 2185 S. Koeller, has the Miles Kimball Warehouse. The CCA Candle Outlet is at 1122 S. Koeller. Prime Outlets, US 41 and SR 44, offers more than 60 outlet stores.

EAA AIRVENTURE MUSEUM is at 3000 Poberezny Rd., .25 mi. s.e. of jct. US 41/SR 44. A collection of more than 95 full-size aircraft includes home-built sport planes, gliders, barnstormers, helicopters, racers and aerobatic planes as well as antique, military, solar-powered and ultralight aircraft. Hangar X! is a hands-on exhibit for children.

The museum also has a multimedia exhibit as well as models, engines, propellers, components and cutaways to show structural design. Allow 1 hour, 30 minutes minimum. Mon.-Sat. 8:30-5, Sun. 10-5; closed Jan. 1, Easter, Thanksgiving and Dec. 25. Airplane rides are available May-Oct. (weather permitting). Admission $8; over 61, $7; ages 8-17, $6.50; family rate $21. Aircraft rides $25-$50. Phone (920) 426-4818. *See color ad p. 164.*

GRAND OPERA HOUSE is at 100 High Ave. The restored 1883 Victorian theater offers concerts, plays and community events. Allow 30 minutes minimum. Box office hours Mon.-Fri. 11-6, Sat. 10-3. Guided tours are available by appointment. Admission $2. MC, VI. Phone (920) 424-2355 for tours and information, or (920) 424-2350 for tickets.

MENOMINEE PARK ZOO is in Menominee Park at the corner of Hazel St. and Merritt Ave. This small zoo displays a variety of animals in cages. Recreational activities are available in the vicinity. Allow 1 hour minimum. Daily 9-7:30, May-Sept. Admission $1, children 50c. Phone (920) 236-5082.

MILITARY VETERANS MUSEUM is in the City Center Complex on Pearl Ave. Memorabilia represents all branches of U.S. military service—Air Force, Army, Coast Guard, Marines and Navy—and all major wars from the American Revolution to the Persian Gulf. Exhibits include Jeeps from World War II, Korea and Vietnam; ships logs from the USS *California* dated Dec. 7, 1941; weapons; women's service uniforms; and an original *New York Herald* newspaper article announcing President Lincoln's assassination.

Allow 1 hour minimum. Mon.-Sat. and holidays noon-5, Sun. noon-3. Free. Phone (920) 426-8615.

OSHKOSH PUBLIC MUSEUM is at 1331 Algoma Blvd. A collection of exhibits represents the people and history of the Lake Winnebago Region. The 8-foot-tall Apostles Clock, created by German immigrant Mathias Kitz in 1895, is a prized example of Wisconsin folk art. Allow 1 hour minimum. Tues.-Sat. 9-5, Sun. 1-5; closed holidays. Donations. Phone (920) 424-4730 or (920) 424-4731.

PAINE ART CENTER AND GARDENS is at 1410 Algoma Blvd. The Tudor Revival great house was designed in the 1920s for local lumber baron Nathan Paine and his wife. The center features period rooms, decorative arts, sculpture and American and French 19th-century paintings. Changing exhibitions supplement the permanent collections. Four acres of themed gardens surround the art center.

Allow 1 hour, 30 minutes minimum. Tues.-Sun. 11-4; closed holidays. Admission $5; over 59, $2.50; students with ID $2; under 12 free. MC, VI. Phone (920) 235-6903.

PEPIN (F-2) pop. 878, elev. 688'

Charles Ingalls acquired a small tract of land near Pepin in 1863, where he built his "Little House in the Big Woods." His daughter, author Laura Ingalls Wilder, was born there in 1867. A replica of the log cabin is on the site at Little House Wayside—north of town off CR CC. The "beautiful lake" about which she wrote is scenic Lake Pepin, which still attracts nature lovers.

Pepin Visitor Information Center: P.O. Box 277, Pepin, WI 54759; phone (715) 442-3011.

PEPIN HISTORICAL MUSEUM is at 306 Third St. Items pertain to the history of Pepin County as well as memorabilia of Laura Ingalls Wilder, author of the "Little House" books. A kitchen and bedroom are furnished in period. Allow 1 hour minimum. Daily 10-5, May 15-Oct. 15. Donations. Phone (715) 442-3011.

PESHTIGO (E-8) pop. 3,357, elev. 600'

On Oct. 8, 1871, Chicago was not the only community in flames. About 270 miles to the north was a forest area that had been plagued for days with small fires in the dry woodlands. On that October day winds whipped the small blazes into great ones; towns were leveled and more than 1,200 people perished. In Peshtigo alone 800 residents died.

A monument to the dead is in the Peshtigo Fire Cemetery. The Peshtigo Fire Museum, containing local items relating to the tragedy, is on Oconto Avenue; phone (715) 582-3422. The Peshtigo Wildlife Area, about 6 miles southeast on CR BB, is primarily a waterfowl habitat and refuge.

Peshtigo Chamber of Commerce: P.O. Box 36, Peshtigo, WI 54157; phone (715) 582-0327.

PLATTEVILLE (I-4) pop. 9,989, elev. 968′

On hillsides where dairy cattle now graze, miners once burrowed for lead. Platteville was settled in 1827, following John Rountree's discovery of "mineral" nearby. Rountree had the small mining town designed in the 1820s by an English architect who incorporated features of his native village of Yorkshire into the town plan.

Although some lead and zinc still are mined, cheese production is a more common industry. The town is a trading center for the surrounding agricultural and dairying region. Platteville also has the University of Wisconsin-Platteville.

Platteville Chamber of Commerce: 275 US 151W, Platteville, WI 53818; phone (608) 348-8888.

SAVE **THE MINING MUSEUM** is at 385 E. Main St. The development of lead and zinc mining in the area is traced through dioramas, models, relics and photographs. A guided tour includes a walk into the Bevans Lead, an 1845 lead mine 50 feet underground; a visit to the hoist house; and a train ride around the museum grounds in ore cars pulled by a 1931 mine locomotive. Changing exhibits are offered in the Rountree Gallery.

Allow 1 hour, 30 minutes minimum. Guided tours daily 9-5, May-Oct. Gallery Mon.-Fri. 11-4. Hours vary rest of year. Closed holidays. Museum admission (including the Rollo Jamison Museum) $7; over 64, $6.30; ages 5-15, $3. Gallery free. Phone (608) 348-3301.

Rollo Jamison Museum is next to the Mining Museum at 405 E. Main St. Exhibits include carriages, farm implements, tools, a tavern/general store, a kitchen and parlor, musical instruments and mechanical music boxes. Daily 9-5, May-Oct.; schedule varies, rest of year. Phone (608) 348-3301.

PORTAGE (G-6) pop. 9,728, elev. 798′

In 1673 Jacques Marquette and Louis Joliet were probably the first Europeans to make the portage between the Fox and Wisconsin rivers, thus linking the Great Lakes with the Mississippi River. This junction rapidly developed into an important trade route. By 1835 the portage had become a plank road, which was replaced by a canal in the 1870s.

The town of Portage grew up around Fort Winnebago, which was built to protect the stream of commerce. Jefferson Davis, a young West Point lieutenant, was assigned in 1829 to cut logs for the barracks. He later became president of the Confederacy.

Modern and attractive, Portage acknowledges its origins with several restorations and the Marquette Trail, a hiking trail that follows the Fox River from the Governor's Bend Locks to the Fort Winnebago Surgeon's Quarters. The city attends to the present by serving the surrounding farming and dairying area.

Portage Area Chamber of Commerce: 139 W. Cook St., Portage, WI 53901; phone (608) 742-6242 or (800) 474-2525.

SAVE **FORT WINNEBAGO SURGEON'S QUARTERS RESTORATION** is 2 mi. e. on SR 33. Built at old Fort Winnebago by François LeRoi, a fur trader and portaging businessman, the restored 1819-24 building contains period furnishings, historic documents and original plans for the fort. At the site is the 1850 Garrison School, furnished with antique desks, McGuffey readers and mannequins in period costumes. Allow 1 hour minimum. Daily 10-4, May 15-Oct. 15. Admission $3.50; over 64, $3; ages 4-12, $1.50. Phone (608) 742-2949.

SAVE **HISTORIC INDIAN AGENCY HOUSE** is .2 mi. e. on SR 33, then .5 mi. n. along the canal. The house was built in 1832 by the U.S. government for John Kinzie, agent to the Ho-Chunk (Winnebago) Indians, and his wife, Juliette. The structure has been restored and furnished in period and has a visitor center. Guided tours are available. Allow 1 hour minimum. Mon.-Sat. 10-4, Sun. 11-4, May 15-Oct. 15; by appointment rest of year. Admission $3.50; over 63, $3; ages 4-14, $1.50. Phone (608) 742-6362.

PORT WASHINGTON—see Milwaukee p. 160.

POYNETTE (H-6) pop. 2,266, elev. 852′

Poynette is the southeastern terminus of a scenic stretch of I-94, which follows the Wisconsin River and ends at the junction with I-90.

Poynette Chamber of Commerce: P.O. Box 625, Poynette, WI 53955; phone (608) 635-2425.

MacKENZIE **ENVIRONMENTAL EDUCATION CENTER** is 2 mi. e. on CRs CS and Q off US 51. This Department of Natural Resources facility includes a wildlife exhibit with live animals native to Wisconsin, a model forest nursery, a fire tower and an arboretum. The center also has logging and conservation museums, hiking trails and picnic facilities. Allow 2 hours minimum. Grounds open daily dawn-dusk. Exhibits open daily 8-4, May 1 to mid-Oct.; Mon.-Fri. 8-4, rest of year. Free. Phone (608) 635-8110.

PRAIRIE DU CHIEN (H-3)
pop. 6,018, elev. 635′

Dating from 1673, when Jacques Marquette and Louis Joliet reached this site at the confluence of the Mississippi and Wisconsin rivers, Prairie du Chien is pre-dated only by Green Bay. Its name, French for "prairie of the dog," refers to the American Indian chief Alim, whose name meant "dog." The oldest part of the town is on St. Feriole Island in the Mississippi.

Prairie du Chien became a flourishing fur market soon after the French explorers' visit, attracting American Indians from the remote upper reaches of the Mississippi and Wisconsin rivers, as well as traders and settlers. From 1685 to 1831 four forts were built and occupied at various times by French, British and American forces. It was at Fort Crawford that Jefferson Davis and Zachary Taylor were stationed.

Prairie du Chien is the southeastern terminus of an especially scenic route that follows the Mississippi River. The route consists of SR 35 running north to La Crosse, then US 53 to its junction with SR 54 and SR 54/35.

Prairie du Chien Chamber of Commerce: 211 S. Main St., P.O. Box 326, Prairie du Chien, WI 53821; phone (608) 326-8555 or (800) 732-1673.

FORT CRAWFORD MUSEUM is at 717 S. Beaumont Rd. Located in the hospital of the second Fort Crawford built 1829-33, the museum chronicles area history, including the American Indian treaties, the first and second Fort Crawford and the Blackhawk War and the Civil War. Local collections and exhibits related to Prairie du Chien history also are displayed.

Other highlights include a reconstructed pharmacy of the 1890s, dioramas illustrating the progress of surgery, and models of the human body depicting functions of the various systems and organs. The work that Dr. William Beaumont did on the digestive system while at Fort Crawford in the early 19th century also is featured. Allow 1 hour minimum. Daily 10-5, May-Oct. Admission $4; over 55, $3.25; ages 5-12, $2.25. Phone (608) 326-6960.

 VILLA LOUIS is 1 mi. n.w. at 521 N. Villa Louis Rd. on St. Feriole Island. This state historic site was the estate of Col. H.L. Dousman, fur trader and agent of John Jacob Astor's American Fur Co., and his son Louis Dousman, an art collector and horse breeder. The present mansion, named for the younger Dousman, was built in 1870 on an ancient American Indian mound. This Victorian-style mansion replaced a house called House on the Mound, built in 1843 by the elder Dousman.

The house contains one of the finest collections of Victorian decorative arts in the country. Almost all the furnishings, artworks, china, glass, silver and books belonged to the Dousman family and were used 1843-1913. Next to the mansion are the icehouse, preserve house and office. The Fur Trade Museum on the grounds has exhibits about the fur trade of the upper Mississippi River Valley. Tours are conducted by costumed guides.

Allow 1 hour, 30 minutes minimum. Tues.-Sun. 9-5, mid-May to late Oct.; Wed.-Sun. 9-5, rest of year. Tours are given on the hour 10-4. Last tour begins 1 hour before closing. Tour $8.50; over 65, $7.50; ages 5-12, $4.50; family rate (2 adults and children under 18) $23. MC, VI. Phone (608) 326-2721.

WYALUSING STATE PARK is 7 mi. s.e. on US 18 and SR 35, then 5 mi. w. on CR C. The 2,596-acre park encompasses the spot where Father Jacques

Marquette and Louis Joliet discovered the Mississippi River. On Sentinel Ridge, 520 feet above the Mississippi, are prehistoric mounds said to be the most valuable undepleted group in existence. Interesting rock formations, bluffs and lookouts are found throughout the park. Camping, picnicking and hiking are popular.

Daily 6 a.m.-11 p.m. Admission per private vehicle $10, state residents $5. Annual permit $30, state residents $20. Phone (608) 996-2261. *See Recreation Chart and the AAA Great Lakes CampBook.*

PRAIRIE DU SAC (H-5)
pop. 3,231, elev. 767′

Prairie du Sac and its neighbor Sauk City, on the high-bluffed west bank of the Wisconsin River, share a colorful historical character, Aguston Haraszthy. Arriving in 1841 with flamboyant attire, an international perspective and high ideals, the Hungarian nobleman fostered free thought in the Wisconsin wilderness. He also established some of the first vineyards in this fertile area before moving on to California, where his vineyards became the foundation of the wine industry.

The towns constitute the eastern terminus of a scenic route that follows SR 60 along the Wisconsin River and ends in Prairie du Chien. The river provides fishing and canoeing opportunities; bald eagles roost along the banks of the river during the winter.

Sauk-Prairie Area Chamber of Commerce: 207 Water St., Suite D, Sauk City, WI 53583; phone (608) 643-4168 or (800) 683-2453.

Self-guiding tours: Brochures describing a walking tour of Prairie du Sac's historic homes and businesses are available from the chamber of commerce.

WINERIES

• **Wollersheim Winery** is .2 mi e. on SR 60, then .7 mi. s. on SR 188. Guided tours are given daily at 10:15, 11:15, 12:15, 1:15, 2:15, 3:15 and 4:15; closed Jan. 1, Easter, Thanksgiving and Dec. 25. Tastings are available daily 10-5. Phone (608) 643-6515 or (800) 847-9463.

RACINE (I-8) pop. 81,855, elev. 626′

Heavily industrialized Racine occupies a promontory jutting into Lake Michigan. Bisected by the winding Root River, it has many residential areas and about 900 acres of parkland. Like many Wisconsin cities, it is multinational in makeup, but the emphasis is Danish. West Racine is often dubbed "Kringleville" for its bakeries specializing in Danish kringle.

A powerful orator promoting women's suffrage, Olympia Brown came to Racine in 1880 to take over the ministry of a Universalist church. Later she devoted herself completely to the suffrage issue, becoming president of the Wisconsin Suffrage

Association. When the 19th Amendment was passed in 1920, Olympia, at the age of 85, was the only suffragist to have participated in the movement from beginning to end.

Racine's architectural legacy includes five buildings designed by Frank Lloyd Wright, among them the landmark SC Johnson Wax Administration Center at 1525 Howe St. The great workroom with its lily-pad columns is still in use today. Guided tours of the facility are offered on Friday at 11 and 1:15, departing from the Golden Rondelle Theater. Reservations are required; phone (262) 260-2154.

Downtown Racine is the sight of Reefpoint Marina, with some 1,000 boat slips and Racine Civic Centre Festival Park.

Racine County Convention & Visitors Bureau: 14015 Washington Ave., Sturtevant, WI 53177. Phone (262) 884-6400 or (800) 272-2463.

Shopping areas: The Regency Mall, I-94 exit 335 on US 11, includes Boston Store, JCPenney, Sears and Younkers among its 115 stores. The shops in Market Square, I-94 at 7 Mile Road, feature antiques and collectibles.

CHARLES A. WUSTUM MUSEUM OF FINE ARTS is at 2519 Northwestern Ave. (SR 38). The museum contains a permanent collection and offers several annual exhibitions of national, regional and local artists. The 13-acre grounds also accommodate the Racine Theater Guild; phone (262) 633-4218. Museum open Mon.-Sat. 11-5 (also Mon. and Thurs. 5-9), Sun. 1-5; closed holidays and during exhibition changes. Donations. Phone (262) 636-9177.

RACINE HERITAGE MUSEUM is at 7th and Main sts. Exhibits detail Racine's manufacturing innovations, inventions and cultural heritage. Allow 30 minutes minimum. Museum open Tues.-Fri. 9-5 (also Thurs. 5-8), Sat.-Sun. 1-5. Archives open Tues. and Sat. 1-4, Thurs. 5-7. Closed holidays. Donations. Phone (262) 636-3926.

RACINE ZOOLOGICAL PARK is at 2131 N. Main St. (park in lot off Wisconsin St.). This 32-acre park on the shore of Lake Michigan is home to 250 animals, including the endangered orangutan, African penguin, red wolf and white rhinoceros. Animal Crackers Jazz Series concerts are offered selected Wednesday evenings during the summer. Allow 1 hour minimum. Park open daily 9-8, Memorial Day-Labor Day; 9-4, rest of year. Donations. Phone (262) 636-9189.

REEDSBURG (G-4) pop. 7,827, elev. 876'

SAVE   **MUSEUM OF NORMAN ROCKWELL ART** is 1 blk. s. of SR 33 at 227 S. Park St. Nearly 4,000 original magazine covers, advertisements and illustrations by Norman Rockwell are displayed. Mon.-Sat. 9-5, Sun. 10-5, June-Sept.; hours vary, rest of year. **Note:** The museum is closed for renovations until spring 2003; phone ahead to verify schedule. Admission $6; over 64, $5; ages 13-18, $3. DS, MC, VI. Phone (608) 524-2123.

RHINELANDER (C-5) pop. 7,735, elev. 1,553'

Rhinelander had its beginning in the 1880s during the days of the pioneer lumber industry. Besides lumber, the area's forests yielded the Hodag, a creature that became the town's most popular legend. Finally exposed as a hoax composed of wood and oxhides, the Hodag myth is kept alive in local symbols and also can be seen at the Rhinelander Logging Museum *(see attraction listing)*.

Within a radius of 12 miles are 232 lakes, 11 trout streams and two rivers offering nearly every type of water sport. More than 1,000 miles of snowmobile trails near Rhinelander are open to the public. The region also is noted for its scenic hiking, mountain bicycling and Nordic ski trails.

The Consolidated Industrial Forest, 12 miles east of the city near US 8 and US 45, offers an 11-mile driving tour that demonstrates forest management techniques; it is open daily, June through September. Booklets can be obtained at the forest entrance, .2 mile west of US 8 and US 45 at the Consolidated Monico Timberlands' office and at the Rhinelander Chamber of Commerce.

Nicolet College, on CR G and Oneida Avenue, is noted for its architecture, which blends into the surrounding woods. Free tours are given Mon.-Fri. 8-3 by appointment; phone (715) 365-4410.

Rhinelander Area Chamber of Commerce: US Bus. Rte. 8W and Sutliss Ave., P.O. Box 795, Rhinelander, WI 54501; phone (715) 365-7464 or (800) 236-4386.

THE RHINELANDER HISTORICAL SOCIETY MUSEUM is at 9 S. Pelham St. Housed in a restored 1894 boarding house, the museum portrays area history from the turn of the 20th century to the present. Mon.-Fri. 10-4 or by appointment, June-Aug.; Tues. 10-4, rest of year. Donations. Phone (715) 369-3833.

RHINELANDER LOGGING MUSEUM is in Pioneer Park at jct. US Bus. Rte. 8/CR G. This reproduction of an 1870s logging camp features the Sioux Line Depot, built in 1892, loggers' living quarters, a cook's shack, schoolhouse, smithy and all the tools of their respective trades. Displays include a narrow-gauge engine built in 1879 and a replica of the Hodag. Allow 1 hour minimum. Daily 10-5, Memorial Day-Labor Day. Donations. Phone (715) 369-5004.

RICHLAND CENTER (H-4)
pop. 5,114, elev. 736'

Richland Center was settled in 1849. It is the birthplace of Frank Lloyd Wright, whose fine early work is represented by the A.D. German Warehouse. Another noted resident was Ada James, an avid suffragette. Upon learning of Wisconsin's ratification of the 19th Amendment, James quickly put her 76-year-old father on the first train to Washington to present the ratification papers before any other state could secure the honor.

In an unglaciated corner of Wisconsin, Richland Center is surrounded by countryside characterized by fruit orchards, hardwood trees, steep hills, deep valleys and unusual rock formations. A natural bridge is in a county park 9 miles north on SR 80 near Rockbridge. Scenic SR 60 follows the Wisconsin River south from Richland Center.

Richland Area Chamber of Commerce: 174 S. Central Ave., P.O. Box 128, Richland Center, WI 53581-0128; phone (608) 647-6205 or (800) 422-1318.

Self-guiding tours: A map outlining a historical and architectural tour of Richland Center is available at the chamber of commerce.

Shopping areas: Richland Center offers numerous antique shops including Treasures in the Bakery, 155 E. Seminary St.

RIPON (G-7) pop. 6,828, elev. 932′

Ripon began as an experiment in communal living called Ceresco, established in 1849 by 200 followers of the 19th-century socialist philosopher Charles Fourier. On the west edge of town stands one of the longhouses of the commune, which disbanded in 1851.

The Republican Party was founded in Ripon in 1854 at a local political meeting, which originally was called in order to organize against the extension of slavery. Alvan E. Bovay, a local lawyer and prominent Whig, proposed the party name. Four months later the name "Republican" formally was adopted at a state party convention in Jackson, Mich.

Ripon College, established in 1851, occupies a 250-acre campus on the highest hill in the city. A highlight of the college is C.J. Rodman Center for the Arts, with two Anthony Van Dyck portraits and changing exhibits. Free guided tours of the campus can be arranged; phone (920) 748-8364.

Ripon Area Chamber of Commerce: 214 Jefferson St., P.O. Box 305, Ripon, WI 54971; phone (920) 748-6764.

Self-guiding tours: Brochures outlining walking tours of the city are available from the chamber of commerce.

SAVE **LARSON'S FAMOUS CLYDESDALES** is 4 mi. s. on SR 49, then 1.6 mi. e. on Reeds Corner Rd. A 90-minute behind-the-scenes guided tour and show about Clydesdales includes performances by the horses, explanations of their history and how they are prepared for show and judged. The barn, where Clydesdale colts can be seen and petted, is open after the program. Video cameras are prohibited. Shows are scheduled Mon.-Sat. at 1, May-Oct. Admission $10; under 12, $5. Reservations are recommended. Phone (920) 748-5466.

LITTLE WHITE SCHOOL HOUSE is on Blackburn St. This mid-19th-century schoolhouse was the birthplace of the Republican Party. Allow 30 minutes minimum. Daily 10-4, June-Aug.; Sat.-Sun. 10-4 in May and Oct. or by appointment. Donations. Phone (920) 748-6764.

RUDOLPH (F-5) pop. 423, elev. 1,139′

DAIRY STATE CHEESE CO. is at SR 34 and CR C. An observation area and a multimedia presentation about cheesemaking are offered. Mon.-Fri. 8-5:15, Sat. 8-5, Sun. 9-noon. Free. Phone (715) 435-3144.

GROTTO GARDENS AND WONDER CAVE is on SR 34. The site includes the Shrine of Peace and Our Lady of Lourdes Shrine and Museum, which contains pictures, plans and tools depicting the history of the grounds. The lush gardens of St. Phillips Church contain several other shrines and St. Jude's Chapel, constructed entirely of hand-cut logs. The .2-mile-long Wonder Cave contains 26 shrines depicting the life and teachings of Jesus.

Daily 10-5, Memorial Day weekend-Labor Day; by appointment rest of year. Wonder Cave $2.50; ages 12-17, $1.25; ages 6-11, 25c. Grotto Gardens by donation. Phone (715) 435-3120.

ST. CROIX FALLS (D-1)
pop. 2,033, elev. 884′

St. Croix Falls is a center for outdoor recreation in the scenic valley of the St. Croix River. Long noted for excellent lake and stream fishing, the area is gaining popularity as a winter playground.

Two state fish hatcheries are easily accessible from St. Croix Falls. On River Street downtown, the St. Croix Falls Fish Hatchery stocks brook and brown trout. Osceola Fish Hatchery, 7 miles south on CR S, breeds all of the state's rainbow trout.

Polk County Information Center: 710 US 35S, St. Croix Falls, WI 54024; phone (715) 483-1410 or (800) 222-7655.

GEM **INTERSTATE STATE PARK** is .5 mi. s. of US 8 on US 35. The oldest of Wisconsin's state parks, it lies along the east side of the Dalles of the St. Croix River, a scenic gorge carved by glacial meltwater out of ancient bedrock. The canyon walls rise to a height of 200 feet above the river. On the other side of the river is Minnesota's Interstate Park. The Old Man of the Dalles, a strange rock formation, and potholes formed by the swirling current of glacial meltwaters are located in the park.

The area is one of nine units that make up the Ice Age National Scientific Reserve. A 20-minute film about the reserve is shown in the Ice Age Interpretive Center, near the park entrance off SR 35.

Naturalist programs are offered Memorial Day weekend-Labor Day. The park has several hiking trails, and the lake offers a beach and bathhouse. Boat trips through the Dalles of the St. Croix River leave Taylors Falls, Minn., daily May 1 to mid-Oct. Park open daily 6 a.m.-11 p.m. Interpretive center open daily 8:30-4:30, Memorial Day-Labor Day; hours vary, rest of year. Admission per private vehicle $10, state residents $5. Annual permit $30, state residents $20. Phone (715) 483-3747. *See Recreation Chart and the AAA Great Lakes CampBook.*

ST. CROIX NATIONAL SCENIC RIVERWAY (E-1, B-2)

Reaching from northern Wisconsin to the St. Croix's juncture with the Mississippi River just south of Minneapolis-St. Paul, the St. Croix National Scenic Riverway is a 252-mile river reserve. The Upper St. Croix River and its tributary, the Namekegon River, were among the original eight rivers designated as National Wild and Scenic Rivers in 1968. Four years later the Lower St. Croix River from St. Croix Falls to Prescott was added to the system by the National Park Service.

For hundreds of years the St. Croix was an important link between the Mississippi and Lake Superior. Besides being a major waterway, the St. Croix possessed marshes, pools and rapids that provided a wealth of food and fur for the Chippewas who once lived in this area. Beaver, otter and other pelts became the currency of a profitable trade with the French.

During the 17th and 18th centuries the river rang with the raucous songs of *voyageurs* as they paddled their loaded canoes up the St. Croix and down the Brule River to Lake Superior and eventually to Fort William. By the mid-19th century a new sound was heard, as logs thundered down the St. Croix from the sawmills strung along its banks.

Other than the development along its lower portion and the legacy of dams, the river retains much of its pristine nature. Both the Namekegon and St. Croix begin as narrow streams winding through forests, marshes and wide valleys. When the two rivers join, the riverway becomes wider, deeper and slower, making the area popular for small powerboats and canoes. The last segment below St. Croix Falls becomes wider and more civilized yet, marked by towns and pleasure craft.

General Information and Activities

The upper reaches of the St. Croix Riverway are canoe waters, with only a few rapids and none classified as white water. The canoeing season generally begins in May and ends in September; outfitters can be found in Trego, Webb Lake and other towns on the riverway.

Canoe-access primitive camping predominates. Along the Wisconsin-Minnesota border several state forests and parks offer developed campsites, hiking and cross-country skiing.

Bass and muskellunge can be found along the entire riverway; trout are found in the headwaters. Anglers favor the upper reaches. Otters and such birds as osprey compete with the anglers for fish. The presence of these and other animals and waterfowl draw both birdwatchers and hunters. Fishing and hunting licenses are required within the riverway.

The proximity to urban areas and the river's width and placidity make the lower reaches below St. Croix Falls a popular area for boaters, water skiers and sailors. Highlights in this area include the scenic gorge in Interstate State Park *(see St. Croix Falls p. 169)* and the Apple River, which joins the St. Croix and is one of the most popular rivers in the state for tubing.

ADDRESS inquiries to the Superintendent, St. Croix National Scenic Riverway, P.O. Box 708, St. Croix Falls, WI 54024; phone (715) 483-3284.

Points of Interest

NAMEKAGON VISITOR CENTER is in Trego on US 63. Animal tracks and a handmade birch bark canoe are among the exhibits, which focus on logging, the riverway, fur trade and wildlife. Thurs.-Mon. 8-4:30, Memorial Day weekend-Labor Day. Hours may vary; phone ahead. Phone (715) 635-8346.

ST. CROIX VISITOR CENTER is in St. Croix Falls at Hamilton and Massachusetts aves. The center has exhibits about logging, the area's Scandinavian immigrants and regional geology, as well as a slide program, movie and information about the riverway. Daily 8:30-5, May-Sept.; Mon.-Fri. 8:30-4:30, rest of year. Phone (715) 483-3284, ext. 638.

SAUKVILLE—*see Milwaukee p. 161.*

SHAWANO (E-7) pop. 8,298, elev. 822′

Shawano has grown from a lumber boom town to a retail trade center for the region's small farms. Shawano is among Wisconsin's leading dairy counties.

With its rolling hills beckoning cross-country skiers and its miles of snowmobile trails, Shawano is popular for winter recreation. Ice fishing as well as summer water sports are available on the Wolf River and Shawano Lake *(see Recreation Chart).* The Navarino Nature Center, 15 miles south on CR K, offers bicycling and nature trails and cross-country skiing in winter.

Two former railroad corridors, now serving as recreational trails, pass through Shawano. The Mountain Bay and the Wiouwash state trails are open to hikers all year and to other recreational users seasonally; a fee is charged. Phone (715) 526-9150 for information.

Shawano Area Chamber of Commerce: 213 E. Green Bay St., P.O. Box 38, Shawano, WI 54166; phone (715) 524-2139 or (800) 235-8528.

SHEBOYGAN (G-8) pop. 50,792, elev. 625′

Although the audible thunder of the falls 3 miles up the Sheboygan River may have inspired the American Indian term (Shawb-wa-way-going—"rumbling underground") for this location, the town means sausage and cheese to many people because of its industries. Sheboygan also is an active

Lake Michigan port; in addition to its savories, it produces and distributes steel, furniture, clothing and leather goods. It also is a major retail trade center for the surrounding dairying region.

Scenic drives along the lakeshore include Broughton Drive, and Lakeshore Drive and North 3rd Street. Lake Michigan offers good boating and fishing; other recreational pastimes are available at nearby Kohler-Andrae State Park *(see Recreation Chart and the AAA Great Lakes CampBook).*

Sheboygan County Convention and Visitors Bureau: 712 Riverfront Dr., Suite 101, Sheboygan, WI 53081-4665; phone (920) 457-9495 or (800) 457-9497.

JOHN MICHAEL KOHLER ARTS CENTER is at 608 New York Ave. Visual and performing arts are presented in a restored house and gallery. Folk art exhibitions are displayed and a theater presents stage, dance and concert productions. An interactive exhibit offers a chance for children to explore various aspects of art; phone for schedule to the interactive exhibit. Center open Mon.-Fri. 10-5 (also Tues. and Thurs. 5-8), Sat.-Sun. 10-4; closed major holidays. Free. Phone (920) 458-6144.

SHEBOYGAN COUNTY HISTORICAL SOCIETY MUSEUM is at 3110 Erie Ave. The museum includes an 1850s Victorian mansion, an 1860s log house furnished with pioneer items, an early 20th-century barn that houses farm tools and machinery used by early settlers, and an 1867 cheese factory.

Other exhibits highlight American Indian history, ice harvesting, immigration, the circus, sports, maritime history and early agriculture. Allow 1 hour minimum. Tues.-Sat. 10-5, Apr.-Oct.; Tues.-Sat. noon-7, Sun. noon-5, Thanksgiving-Dec. 15. Admission $3; ages 7-12, $1. Phone (920) 458-1103.

SHEBOYGAN INDIAN MOUND PARK is just s. of Panther Ave. at 5000 S. 9th St. American Indian burial mounds in the park are shaped like panthers and deer. Dating from A.D. 500 to 1000, this is one of the few mound groups still intact. A nature trail leads to the lush valley of Hartman Creek, where both upland and lowland plant communities are identified. Self-guiding tours daily 10-10. Free. Phone (920) 459-3444.

SHELL LAKE (C-2) pop. 1,309, elev. 1,241′

[SAVE] **MUSEUM OF WOODCARVING** is at jct. SR 63/CR B. The collection of Joseph Barta's hand-carved wood figurines depicts such Biblical events as The Last Supper. Barta created the 400 miniature and 100 life-size figures over a span of 30 years, using oak, poplar, walnut and basswood. Allow 30 minutes minimum. Daily 9-6, May-Oct. Admission $4.50; under 12, $2.50. Phone (715) 468-7100.

SPARTA (G-4) pop. 8,648, elev. 793′

Sparta calls itself "the bicycling capital of the world" and is home to the western end of the

Elroy-Sparta State Trail. Running through Kendall, the 32-mile bicycling trail was the nation's first to be converted from an abandoned railroad bed. For maps and information, phone (608) 463-7109 May through Oct.

[SAVE] **THE DEKE SLAYTON MEMORIAL SPACE & BICYCLE MUSEUM** displays artifacts, documents and photographs related to the Sparta native's career as an aviator and astronaut, as well as exhibits related to the history of the bicycle. The exhibits are on the second floor of the Monroe County Museum at 200 W. Main St.; phone (608) 269-0033.

Six miles east of Sparta is Fort McCoy, the state's only U.S. Army installation. Two recreation areas on the base are open to the public: Pine View offers camping, hiking, boating, swimming, fishing and hunting. For information, phone (608) 388-3517. Whitetail Ridge is a winter facility for downhill and cross-country skiing, snow-tubing and snowmobiling. For information, phone (608) 388-4498.

SPOONER (C-2) pop. 2,653, elev. 1,065′

A railroad junction during the lumbering era, Spooner was named after John Coit Spooner, a railroad attorney elected to the U.S. Senate in 1885 and 1897. Spooner is now a popular resort in the wooded lake country of northwestern Wisconsin. More than 900 lakes attract tourists to Washburn County. A float trip down the Namekagon River is a popular pastime; landings are in Trego, 5 miles north of Spooner at the junction of US 53 and US 63, and on CR K, 10 miles north of Spooner.

Washburn County Tourist Information Center: 122 N. River St., Spooner, WI 54801; phone (715) 635-9696 or (800) 367-3306.

Self-guiding tours: The Spooner Heritage Walking Tour showcases some of the city's oldest homes and businesses. Also on the tour are the sites of Spooner's first school and church services. The tour guidebook can be obtained from the tourist information center.

GOVERNOR TOMMY G. THOMPSON STATE FISH HATCHERY is .5 mi. w. of US 63 on SR 70 to 951 W. Maple St. Said to be the world's largest muskellunge-rearing facility, the hatchery also produces Northern pike and walleye. A visitor center is on the premises. Guided tours are given Mon.-Fri. at 10 and 2, May 1-Labor Day. Free. Phone (715) 635-4147.

RAILROAD MEMORIES MUSEUM is at 424 Front St. behind the post office parking lot. This museum in the former Chicago and Northwestern Depot displays 11 rooms of railroad memorabilia including tools used by track workers, firemen and brakemen; headlights; lanterns; uniforms; railroad logos; office equipment; and promotional materials from various railroads. A library and video room are offered. Allow 30 minutes minimum. Daily 10-5, Memorial

Day-Labor Day. Admission $3; ages 6-12, 50c. Phone (715) 635-3325 or (715) 635-2752.

WISCONSIN GREAT NORTHERN RAILROAD is at 426 N. Front St. Round-trip sightseeing excursions travel from Spooner to Trego and Springbrook. The historic train features a 1940 locomotive with restored cars from 1912 and 1918. Dinner trains and special events are offered. Allow 3 hours minimum.

Sightseeing trips depart from the Spooner depot daily at 1 and 4 (also Tues.-Sat. at 10 a.m.), June 30-Oct. 7; Sat.-Sun. at 1 and 4, May 5-June 24; Sat.-Sun. at 10, 12:30 and 3, Oct. 13-28. Schedule may vary; phone ahead. Reservations are recommended. Fare $8-$15, ages 3-12, $5-$10. Phone (715) 635-3200 or (888) 390-0412 in Wisc.

SPRING GREEN (H-4) pop. 1,444, elev. 729′

Frank Lloyd Wright chose this farming community on the Wisconsin River as the site for his home, Taliesin, and for his architectural school. As a result, Spring Green has a great concentration of Wright-influenced structures. In contrast to Wright's break with tradition, Spring Green's American Players Theatre bases its reputation on its adherence to the classics.

Across the river is Tower Hill State Park *(see Recreation Chart and the AAA Great Lakes CampBook)*. The restored Civil War shot tower is the last vestige of the town of Helena, a busy river port and railhead that once contended for the status of territorial capital.

Spring Green Area Chamber of Commerce/ Visitors Council: E5028 SR 14, P.O. Box 142, Spring Green, WI 53588; phone (608) 588-2054 or (800) 588-2042.

FRANK LLOYD WRIGHT'S TALIESIN is 3 mi. s. on SR 23. The noted architect's primary home and studio was designed in 1902 out of sandstone and native oak. Wright continued to enhance the site throughout his life. Included on the grounds are a school, small theater, living and dining rooms, drafting studios, a gallery containing furniture Wright designed, artwork from his Asian collection and photograph murals and models of buildings he designed.

The visitor center, designed by Wright in 1953, overlooks the Wisconsin River and the Taliesin site. The center is the origin of Taliesin's various guided tours, including the Hillside Studio & Theater tour, which gives an introduction to Wright and his work. Phone for information about Taliesin's various other tours. Food is available.

Allow 1 hour minimum. Visitor center open daily 8:30-5:30, May-Oct. Hours may vary; phone ahead. Hillside tours depart daily on the hour 10-4. Tour fees $10-$70. Reservations are required for tours of the Wright home. Phone (608) 588-7900.

THE HOUSE ON THE ROCK is 9 mi. s. on SR 23. Designed and built by Alex Jordan Jr. beginning in the early 1940s, this multilevel house stands atop chimneylike Deer Shelter Rock, 450 feet above the Wyoming Valley. The house is a modern architectural wonder with pools of running water, waterfalls, massive fireplaces and a room of windows jutting out over the valley. Among the furnishings are Oriental art objects, stained-glass lamps and bronze statuary.

The view from the observation deck stretches 30 miles; the Infinity Room, extending 218 feet out over the valley below, also offers an excellent view through some 3,264 panes of glass. A 350-foot-long overhead walkway connects the gatehouse to the house.

The Cannon Building houses a gigantic cannon and two revolving carousels of bisque dolls; the Doll Building displays one of the world's largest collections of wooden dollhouses. The Circus Building has circus paraphernalia. Heritage of the Sea features a 200-foot-long sculpture of an octopus struggling with a whaling expedition.

The Oriental Building contains ancient Oriental art. The Mill House has paperweights, mechanical banks and other items. The Armor Room displays medieval European and Asian armor; the Gun Room features dueling pistols and blunderbusses; and the Crown Jewel Room has replicas of the jewelry kept in the Tower of London.

The Music of Yesterday Museum houses a collection of animated, automated musical machines and a giant carousel, reputed to be the world's largest, illuminated with more than 20,000 lights and carrying 269 hand-crafted creatures. The Organ Building features three of the world's largest theater organ consoles and a 45-foot-high perpetual motion clock.

The Streets of Yesterday re-creates a 19th-century gas-lit Main Street with old houses, a sheriff's office and carriage house.

Self-guiding tours take 2 to 4 hours. Strollers are not permitted. The entire complex is open daily 9-7, mid-Mar. through the last full weekend in Oct.; closed Thanksgiving and Dec. 24-25. Holidays tours are conducted daily 9-6, early Nov.-early Jan. Last admission 1 hour before closing. Fee to the complex $19.50; ages 7-12, $11.50; ages 4-6, $5.50. Fee for holiday tours $12.50; ages 7-12, $7.50; ages 4-6, $3.50. DS, MC, VI. Phone (608) 935-3639, ext. 123.

SPRING VALLEY (E-2)
pop. 1,189, elev. 1,100′

CRYSTAL CAVE is 1 mi. w. on SR 29. Passageways carved by an underground river and thousands of cave formations can be seen. Allow 1 hour minimum. Guided 1-hour tours depart daily 9-5:30, every 30 minutes, May 15-Labor Day; daily 9:30-4:30, day after Labor Day-Oct. 31; Sat.-Sun. 9:30-4:30, Apr. 1-May 14. Admission $8.50; ages 4-12, $4.50. DS, MC, VI. Phone (715) 778-4414 or (800) 236-2283.

STEVENS POINT (E-6)
pop. 24,551, elev. 1,084'

Stevens Point was founded by George Stevens as a trading post on the Wisconsin River in 1838. Since its incorporation as a city in 1859, Stevens Point has fostered many industries including Worzalla Publishing; Herrschners, a needlecraft distribution center; Sentry Insurance; and the Stevens Point Brewery.

For recreation there are 11 swimming lakes and 19 public parks in or around Stevens Point; lakes DuBay and Emily and Sunset Lake are particularly popular. Rainbow Falls Amusement Park in Plover features five waterslides and a wave pool. In winter cross-country skiers glide along more than 36 miles of trails that lace the surrounding countryside, and downhill skiers enjoy the two nearby slopes.

The University of Wisconsin-Stevens Point campus offers a wealth of activities at minimal or no cost. "E Pluribus Unum," a mosaic mural on the wall of the College of Natural Resources, depicts the university and its environs using 25 tons of tiled panels.

Stevens Point Area Convention & Visitors Bureau: 340 Division St. N., Stevens Point, WI 54481; phone (715) 344-2556, or (800) 236-4636 in Iowa, Wis., upper Mich. and Minneapolis.

MUSEUM OF NATURAL HISTORY is in the Albertson Learning Resources Center of the University of Wisconsin-Stevens Point. Exhibits include a large collection of preserved birds and bird eggs as well as other wildlife displays. The museum features minerals, dinosaur fossils, exhibits about ecosystems and two African savanna dioramas. Allow 1 hour minimum. Mon.-Fri. 9-4 (also Mon. 4-7), Sat. 10-3, Sun. 1-4, Sept. 4 to mid-May; Mon.-Fri. 9-4, rest of year. Hours may vary during semester breaks and in summer. Free. Phone (715) 346-2858.

SCHMEECKLE RESERVE is on Northpoint Dr. The 275-acre wildlife preservation area offers natural history programs. Bicycling and hiking trails are available. A visitor center and the Wisconsin Conservation Hall of Fame are on the grounds. Daily 8-5. Free. Phone (715) 346-4992.

STURGEON BAY (E-9) pop. 9,437, elev. 922'

Where once a tedious portage was necessary to avoid the 100-mile voyage around the tip of the Door Peninsula, boats and giant freighters easily ply the ship canal between Green Bay and Lake Michigan. Sturgeon Bay, named for its fine natural harbor, is one of the largest shipbuilding ports on the Great Lakes. Boat tours leading south through the canal to Lake Michigan and north into Green Bay are available daily, July and August, at the municipal dock.

Sturgeon Bay also processes the ruby yield of Door County's cherry orchards, the most extensive in the state. Some 3,000 acres of cherry trees produce from 8 to 20 million pounds of fruit annually.

The trees bloom in late May, carpeting the peninsula in blossoms; harvest occurs from mid-July to early August.

During the annual chinook salmon spawning run each fall, as many as 500 anglers attack the waters daily in Sturgeon Bay Harbor in search of the 20- to 40-pound fish. Abundant winter recreation opportunities are available, including cross-country skiing and snowmobiling. The slopes at Potawatomi State Park *(see Recreation Chart and the AAA Great Lakes CampBook)* are lighted for nighttime skiing. *Also see Door County p. 130.*

COLLECTOR SHOWCASE is 3 mi. n. at 3910 SR 42/57. Displays include toys, dolls, some 1,000 Barbie dolls and more than 500 old Marshall Fields' animated Christmas window mechanicals. Thirty-five vintage automobiles are exhibited in historically appropriate settings. Daily 9-4, Memorial Day weekend to mid-Oct. Admission $2.50; under 13, $1. Phone (920) 743-6788.

DOOR COUNTY HISTORICAL MUSEUM is at 4th and Michigan sts. A wildlife diorama, pioneer items and an early firehouse are among the exhibits. Allow 1 hour minimum. Daily 10-4:30, May-Oct. Donations. Phone (920) 743-5809.

[SAVE] **DOOR COUNTY MARITIME MUSEUM** is on the waterfront at 120 N. Madison Ave. Exhibits span the nautical history of Door County from early American Indian canoes to post-World War II bulk carriers. The museum features a model ship gallery, a small craft workshop, a lighthouse exhibit, an art gallery and vintage outboard motors and marine engines. The pilot house from a Great Lakes ore carrier is displayed, and a nuclear ballistic submarine periscope offers a bay area view. Daily 9-6, Memorial Day-Labor Day; 10-5, rest of year. Admission $6.50; ages 5-17, $3; family rate $16. MC, VI. Phone (920) 743-5958.

[SAVE] **THE FARM** is 4 mi. n. on SR 57. The 40-acre rural environment includes various farm buildings, a pioneer homestead and farm animals, including young animals that can be held and fed. Particularly noteworthy are the nature cabin, with displays about the natural attractions of Door County, and the woodshed, with farm tools and utensils. There also are milking demonstrations, nature trails and vegetable, flower and herb gardens. Picnicking is permitted.

Allow 1 hour minimum. Daily 9-5, Memorial Day weekend to mid-Oct. Admission $7; over 62, $5.80; ages 4-13, $3.50. MC, VI. Phone (920) 743-6666.

MILLER ART MUSEUM is in the Door County Public Library at 107 S. 4th Ave. Permanent and changing exhibits include paintings and graphics by Door County and other Midwestern artists. The main gallery also serves as a community center for musical programs and a winter lecture series about the arts. Allow 30 minutes minimum. Mon.-Thurs. 10-8, Fri.-Sat. 10-5; closed holidays. Donations. Phone (920) 746-0707.

SCENIC AIRPLANE RIDES depart from the Door County Cherryland Airport, 1 mi. s. on SR 42/57, then 1.5 mi. n. on Park Dr. Air tours of the Door Peninsula are offered by Orion Flight Services, Inc. A 172 Cessna high-wing aircraft cruises at 1,000 feet and provides excellent views of beaches, state parks, fruit orchards, resorts, Green Bay and Lake Michigan. Four different tours range from 15 minutes to 1 hour. Up to three passengers can be accommodated.

Mon.-Sat. 8-5 (also Fri.-Sat. 5-7), Sun. 10-5, Memorial Day-late Oct. Fare $30-$129, depending on length of flight; under 2 free. Reservations are recommended and there is a two-person minimum per flight. AX, DS, MC, VI. Phone (920) 743-6952.

SUPERIOR (A-2) pop. 27,368, elev. 638′

By the millions of tons, ore, grain and coal pour through the great port at Superior-Duluth. This excellent deepwater harbor at the head of Lake Superior ranks among the nation's leading ports in tonnage. Along the 28 miles of shoreline in Superior are shipyards, grain elevators, many heavy industries and some of the world's largest docks.

The campus of the University of Wisconsin-Superior and a number of parks are part of the municipal geography. Billings Park, at the west end of 21st Street, includes many lagoons and gardens.

Scenic Amnicon Falls highlights nearby Amnicon Falls State Park. Pattison State Park, south of the city, offers varied summer and winter recreation and has the highest waterfall in the state. *See Recreation Chart and the AAA Great Lakes CampBook.*

Superior also boasts one of the largest municipal forests in the country. The 4,500-acre Superior Municipal Forest offers 17 miles of trails for cross-country skiing and hiking. The Tri-County Corridor provides a snowmobile and all-terrain vehicle trail through the city of Superior. The trail allows travel through Wisconsin from Canada, Minnesota and Michigan.

Superior/Douglas County Chamber of Commerce and Convention & Visitors Bureau: 205 Belknap St., Superior, WI 54880; phone (715) 392-2773 or (800) 942-5313.

BARKER'S ISLAND is at US 2/53. Accessible from the mainland, the island combines a 420-slip marina with a shopping village, an 18-hole miniature golf course, playground, picnic area, beach and the SS *Meteor* Maritime Museum *(see attraction listing).* Charters are available for fishing, sailing and harbor cruises. Phone (715) 392-2773.

FAIRLAWN MANSION AND MUSEUM is off US 2/53 to 906 E. 2nd St. The 42-room Victorian mansion is styled after a French chateau. Overlooking Lake Superior and Barker's Island, Fairlawn was built in 1890 for the family of Martin Pattison, a late 19th-century lumber and mining baron and the second mayor of Superior. The first-floor rooms are restored, showing the lavish use of carved wood, marble, silver trim, brass and English tile and Victorian paintings.

Exhibits throughout the house recall the prosperity and elegance of Superior's early boomtown days, as well as Fairlawn's 42-year history as a children's home. Guided tours are available. Allow 1 hour minimum. Daily 9-5, Memorial Day-Labor Day; hours vary, rest of year. Closed Jan. 1, Easter, Thanksgiving and Dec. 25. Admission $7; over 62 and students $5.50; ages 6-12, $5. Phone (715) 394-5712.

SS *METEOR* MARITIME MUSEUM is on US 2/53 on Barker's Island. The Great Lakes vessel was used during the late 19th and early 20th centuries and now contains a museum. Ship tours are offered. Daily 9-5, mid-May to mid-Oct. Admission $5, over 62 and students with ID $3.50; ages 6-12, $3. Phone (715) 392-5742.

VISTA FLEET/SUPERIOR-DULUTH HARBOR CRUISES depart from the Barker's Island Dock, jct. US 2/SR 13. Passengers can enjoy a narrated sightseeing tour of the Superior-Duluth Harbor aboard the *Vista King.* The tour passes by some of the world's largest grain elevators, Great Lakes freighters, ore docks and the open span of the Aerial Lift Bridge. Lunch, dinner and moonlight cruises are available aboard the *Vista Star* and depart from the D.E.C.C. Dock in Duluth, Minn. *(see attraction listing in AAA North Central TourBook).*

Cruises depart daily, mid-May to mid-Oct. Sightseeing fare $10; ages 3-11, $5. AX, DS, MC, VI. Phone (715) 394-6846 or (218) 722-6218.

TOMAHAWK (D-5) pop. 3,770, elev. 1,450′

The joining of the Somo, Spirit and Tomahawk rivers with the Wisconsin abetted Tomahawk's early growth as a lumber town and continues to enhance its popularity as an all-year North Woods resort area. Game fish, deer and small game are abundant. Eleven local parks provide opportunities for picnicking and other outdoor activities. The Hiawatha Trail, a 6.6-mile bicycle, hiking and snowmobile trail, begins in Tomahawk and extends northward to Lake Nokomis.

Water ski shows are held 3 nights a week mid-June through August at Kwahamot Bay. Winter sports activities include snowmobiling, cross-country skiing and ice fishing.

Tomahawk Regional Chamber of Commerce: 208 N. 4th St., P.O. Box 412, Tomahawk, WI 54487; phone (715) 453-5334 or (800) 569-2160.

TWO RIVERS (F-9) pop. 12,639, elev. 587′

As it has been since the 1830s, the harbor at Two Rivers is the home of an important commercial fishing fleet. Light, diversified industry augments the economy. Point Beach State Forest *(see Recreation Chart and the AAA Great Lakes CampBook)* lies along Lake Michigan north of town.

Woodland Dunes Nature Center, west off SR 310, is a bird-banding station, wildlife research area and wildflower sanctuary in a woodland and meadow habitat with hiking trails and nature displays; phone (920) 793-4007.

HAMILTON WOOD TYPE AND PRINTING MUSEUM is at 1619 Jefferson St. Housed in a 1926 Hamilton factory, this museum preserves an extensive collection of 19th- and 20th-century wood type and printing equipment, much of it in working condition and used in visitor demonstrations. Exhibits include hand-operated printing presses, artisan tools, cutting patterns, rare type specimen catalogs and printing memorabilia. Allow 30 minutes minimum. Mon.-Sat. 9-5, Sun. 1-5; closed Dec. 25. Free. Phone (920) 794-6272.

VIROQUA (G-4) pop. 4,335, elev. 1,280′

Following the initial wave of Eastern settlers, Norwegian immigrants successfully introduced tobacco farming and dairying into the region around Viroqua. Arriving by covered wagon in 1853 was Jeremiah McLain Rusk, who served in Congress for 6 years and as governor for three successive terms.

VERNON COUNTY HISTORICAL MUSEUM is at 410 S. Center Ave. County history is depicted through displays about pioneer farming, Civil War items and genealogical material. Tours are available by appointment. Tues.-Sun. noon-4, May 15-Sept. 15; Tues.-Thurs. noon-4 or by appointment, rest of year. Closed major holidays. Donations. Phone (608) 637-7396.

WARRENS (F-4) pop. 286, elev. 1,024′

CRANBERRY MUSEUM is 4 mi. e. on CR EW. Hands-on exhibits, an 18-minute videotape and other displays describe how cranberries are cultivated and harvested. Demonstrations illustrate packaging procedures as well as various uses of the product. Allow 1 hour minimum. Daily 9-4, Apr.-Oct. Admission $5; over 55, $4.50; ages 6-12, $3.50. MC, VI. Phone (608) 378-4878.

WASHINGTON ISLAND (D-9)

Six miles off the tip of the Door Peninsula, Washington Island is surrounded by the waters of Lake Michigan and Green Bay. More than 200 years ago Potawatomi Indians inhabited the island. The tribe later almost was destroyed by a sudden, severe squall that swamped the canoes of a war party as they crossed what is now known as Death's Door Strait, en route to the mainland.

The island's population is predominantly Scandinavian and constitutes the oldest Icelandic settlement in the United States. It is reached by daily ferry service from the Northport Pier, 2 miles east of Gills Rock on SR 42; phone (920) 847-2546. Narrated sightseeing tram trips of the island are offered; tours depart the Washington Island dock.

Passenger excursion service to Rock Island State Park *(see Recreation Chart)* also is offered late May to mid-October. *Also see Door County p. 130.*

Washington Island Chamber of Commerce: R.R. 1, Box 222, Washington Island, WI 54246; phone (920) 847-2179.

JACOBSEN'S MUSEUM is 6 mi. n. of the ferry dock on Little Lake. A cedar log building houses American Indian artifacts, antiques, rocks and fossils gathered on the island. Allow 30 minutes minimum. Daily 10-4, Memorial Day weekend to mid-Oct. Admission $1, under 12 free. Phone (920) 847-2213.

WASHINGTON ISLAND FARM MUSEUM is 5.4 mi. n. of the ferry dock on Jackson Harbor Rd. The museum provides a detailed look at Washington Island's farming history. Items displayed include horse-drawn farm equipment, log buildings, tools, a weaving loom and historic photographs. A blacksmith shop also is on the property. Daily 10-6, late June to mid-Oct. Donations. Phone (920) 847-2156.

WATERFORD (I-8) pop. 4,048, elev. 949'

GREEN MEADOWS FARM is 3 mi. w. on SR 20. This working farm has more than 200 farm animals. A 2-hour guided tour includes tractor-drawn hay rides, pony rides, a petting farm, milking demonstrations followed by hands-on experience, and, in October, pumpkin picking. Tours Tues.-Sat. 10-noon, mid-June to late Aug.; Mon.-Fri. 10-noon, Sat.-Sun. 10-2 in Oct. Admission $9, under 2 free. Phone (262) 534-2891.

WATERTOWN (H-6) pop. 21,598, elev. 825'

Watertown has been essentially industrial since its founding in the 1830s, when New Englanders harnessed the rapids of the Rock River to produce power for their sawmills, wagonworks and other factories. Many of the first arrivals were German intellectuals fleeing political conditions in the fatherland after the 1848 revolution.

One of these was Carl Schurz, who entered local politics on the new Republican ticket and ultimately became minister to Spain under President Abraham Lincoln. It is his wife, however, who is remembered: While living in Watertown in 1856, Margarethe Meyer established what is considered to be the nation's first kindergarten. She was a student of Fredrich Froebel, the renowned German pioneer of infant education.

Watertown Area Chamber of Commerce: 519 E. Main St., Watertown, WI 53094; phone (920) 261-6320.

OCTAGON HOUSE is at 919 Charles St. This 1854 dwelling includes five floors furnished with antiques. The house contains a central 40-foot circular stairway. What is considered to have been the nation's first kindergarten, furnished in period, also is on the grounds. A

late 1800s barn, moved from the old Watertown-Milwaukee Plank Road, houses farm implements and exhibits.

Allow 1 hour, 30 minutes minimum. Daily 10-4, Memorial Day-Labor Day; 11-3, May 1-day before Memorial Day and day after Labor Day-Oct. 31. Admission $5.50; over 65, $5; ages 6-17, $3; family rate (2 adults and children under 18) $15. Phone (920) 261-2796.

WAUKESHA—*see Milwaukee p. 161.*

WAUPACA (F-6) pop. 5,676, elev. 868'

The resort community of Waupaca, near a chain of 22 lakes to the southwest, supposedly was named after Sam Waupaca, a Potawatomi chief credited with persuading his braves not to massacre the white settlers in the area. The chief collapsed and died at the conclusion of the speech.

Waupaca is a popular departure point for canoe and launch trips through the spring-fed lakes and along Crystal River; canoe rentals are available locally. The area's well-stocked trout streams, also filled with pickerel, bass and small pan fish, are extremely popular with anglers.

Nearby Hartman Creek State Park *(see Recreation Chart and the AAA Great Lakes CampBook)* has developed recreational facilities, including snowmobile trails that connect with 288 miles of groomed trails and 150 miles of club trails throughout Waupaca County.

Near the property of The Red Mill, 3 miles south on CR K, are the quaint Chapel in the Woods and one of the two surviving covered bridges in Wisconsin *(see Cedarburg p. 159).* The old mill, built in 1855, has a 24-foot waterwheel, one of the largest in America. Friday night band concerts are performed in the summer in the Gay '90s bandstand in City Square.

Waupaca Area Chamber of Commerce: 221 S. Main St., Waupaca, WI 54981; phone (715) 258-7343 or (888) 417-4040.

***CHIEF WAUPACA* STERNWHEELER CRUISE** is at Clear Water Harbor, 3.7 mi. s.w. of US 10 on CR QQ. Narrated 90-minute cruises travel the Waupaca Chain o' Lakes. Brunch cruises also are available. Two-hour tours also are available aboard the *Lady of the Lakes* motor yacht. Cruises depart daily at 11:30, 1, 2:30 and 4, Memorial Day weekend-Labor Day; Sat.-Sun. at 1, weekend after Labor Day-last weekend in Oct. Sightseeing fare $6.95; ages 3-12, $3.95. Phone (715) 258-2866.

WISCONSIN VETERANS MUSEUM is 4 mi. s.w. of US 10 on CR QQ in Marden Memorial Center of the Wisconsin Veterans Home. Dedicated to veterans of all wars, this museum displays memorabilia and weapons from nations involved in those wars. Allow 30 minutes minimum. Daily 8-4. Free. Phone (715) 258-5586.

WAUPUN (G-7) pop. 10,718, elev. 894'

Waupun sometimes is called the "City of Sculpture." Statues, presented to the city by the late industrialist Clarence Shaler, include the first bronze casting of James Earl Fraser's "End of the Trail." "The Recording Angel," by Lorado Taft, stands in the Forest Mound Cemetery.

Shaler himself was a sculptor; some of his works include "Dawn of Day" on the City Hall terrace, "The Pioneers" in Wilcox Park and "Doe and Fawn" at Rock River Country Club. Others include "Pioneer Woman" and "The Citadel" as well as two of his other sculptures found on the campus of Ripon College in Ripon *(see place listing p. 169)*.

Waupun Chamber of Commerce: 121 E. Main St., Suite A, Waupun, WI 53963; phone (920) 324-3491.

HORICON MARSH is entered e. of town on SR 49. The marsh occupies 32,000 acres of wetlands and uplands. The northern 21,000 acres, accessible from SR 49, are a national wildlife refuge; the southern third, accessible from SR 28 at Horicon, is state-owned *(see Horicon p. 136)*. During the mid-April migration as many as 20,000 Canada geese use the marsh as a stopover point.

Fall migration from mid-September to mid-November brings more than 1 million birds through the marsh. Mallards, redheads, ruddy ducks and blue-wing teals nest during the summer; egrets, herons, muskrats, coots and deer also are common. A self-guiding auto tour winds through 3.2 miles of the national refuge; maps are available at the Mayville visitor center. Hiking trails are in the northwest corner on the east side and in the southern portion. The 34-mile Wild Goose State Trail runs from Fond du Lac to SR 60 south of Juneau.

The Horicon Marsh Parkway makes a 30-mile loop of the entire Horicon Marsh and offers numerous overlooks; follow the signs from Horicon. For additional information write W4279 Headquarters Rd., Mayville, WI 53050. Hiking trails open dawn-dusk. Free. Phone (920) 387-2658 or (920) 387-7860.

MARSH HAVEN NATURE CENTER is adjacent to the Horicon Marsh on SR 49. A 30-foot-tall observation tower, theater, wildlife dioramas, art exhibits and a display of live birds are housed at the center, which offers information about American Indian history, glaciers, trees and tools. Picnicking is permitted. Mon.-Fri. 10-4, Sat.-Sun. and holidays 9-5, mid-May to mid-Nov. Admission $1; under 13, 50c. Phone (920) 324-5818.

WAUSAU (E-5) pop. 38,426, elev. 1,204'

No longer considered far away (Wausau means "far away place"), Wausau ranks among the state's major industrial centers. This busy Wisconsin Valley city began as a sawmill settlement called Big Bull Falls. After the timber supply was depleted, farming and diversified manufacturing sustained the economy. Marathon County continues to be one of the nation's leading producers of cheddar cheese and ginseng.

Glimpses of the town's past can be seen in the Andrew Warren Historic District, a 10-block area of Wausau that preserves more than 60 historic buildings.

Wausau/Central Wisconsin Convention & Visitors Bureau: 10204 Park Plaza, Suite B, Mosinee, WI 54455; phone (715) 355-8788 or (888) 948-4748.

Shopping areas: Cedar Creek Factory Stores, US 51 exit 185, offer outlet shopping. Dealers display antiques at Rib Mountain Antique Mall, 3300 Eagle Ave. Wausau Center, 3rd and Washington streets, features more than 60 stores, including JCPenney, Sears and Younkers.

DELLS OF THE EAU CLAIRE PARK is 17 mi. e. on CR Z, then n. on CR Y to the Eau Claire River. Trails crisscross the 192-acre park, noted for its unusual rock formations. Daily 7:30 a.m.-11 p.m., May-Oct. Free. Phone (715) 261-1550. *See the AAA Great Lakes CampBook.*

LEIGH YAWKEY WOODSON ART MUSEUM is at 700 N. 12th St. Housed in a Tudor-style building, the museum presents changing exhibitions by national and international artists. Highlights include wildlife paintings and sculptures, decorative art and a large outdoor sculpture garden. Birds in Art, presented each fall, is recognized as one of the finest exhibitions of bird paintings and sculpture, in the world. Allow 1 hour minimum. Tues.-Fri. 9-4, Sat.-Sun. noon-5; closed holidays. Free. Phone (715) 845-7010.

MARATHON COUNTY HISTORICAL MUSEUM is at 403 McIndoe St. The first floor preserves the 1900 neoclassical house of Cyrus Yawkey, a wealthy lumberman. Ionic columns and elaborate door and window frames mark the entrance. The living room, music room, dining room and den are furnished in period. The basement contains a model railroad display. A library and exhibit area are adjacent to the house. Tues.-Thurs. 9-4:30, Sat.-Sun. 1-4:30; closed holidays. Donations. Phone (715) 842-5750.

RIB MOUNTAIN STATE PARK is near the jct. US 51/CR N. Rising to 1,940 feet, Rib Mountain is one of the highest points in Wisconsin. The park has hiking trails, an observation tower with two observation decks offering a view of the scenic Wisconsin River valley, camping sites, a 170-seat amphitheater and one of the Midwest's finest ski areas. Daily 6 a.m.-11 p.m. Admission per private vehicle $10, state residents $5. Annual permit $30, state residents $20. Phone (715) 842-2522. *See Recreation Chart and the AAA Great Lakes CampBook.*

WEST BEND—*see Milwaukee p. 161.*

WEST SALEM (G-3) pop. 4,540, elev. 746'

When the railroad was laid a mile south of Neshonoc in 1858, the village's population of Easterners and Norwegians packed up and moved to West Salem near the tracks. Thomas Leonard, West Salem's founder, had offered the railroad free land if it would build a station in West Salem rather than in one of the neighboring towns. The railroad accepted Leonard's offer, ensuring the town's growth. Historic Salem, 99 Jefferson St., is Leonard's 1859 home.

This farm trade center became best known for its creamery, capable of producing a million pounds of butter annually. Emerging from this rural environment was one of Wisconsin's foremost authors, Hamlin Garland. Deeply influenced by his childhood on the frontier, Garland set his autobiographical "Middle Border" books and some dozen short stories in the coulee area around La Crosse.

HAMLIN GARLAND HOMESTEAD is at 357 W. Garland St. The house has been restored as a memorial to the winner of 1921 Pulitzer Prize. Of particular note is the upstairs study where Garland did much of his writing. Allow 30 minutes minimum. Guided tours Mon.-Sat. 10-4:30, Sun. 1-4:30, Memorial Day weekend-Labor Day; by appointment rest of year. Admission $1; ages 6-18, 50c; family rate $2.50. Phone (608) 786-1399 or (608) 786-1675.

PALMER-GULLICKSON OCTAGON HOUSE is at 360 N. Leonard St. Built in 1856, the eight-sided house displays original Victorian furnishings. Allow 30 minutes minimum. Guided tours Mon.-Sat. 10-4:30, Sun. 1-4:30, Memorial Day weekend-Labor Day; by appointment rest of year. Admission $1; ages 6-18, 50c; family rate $2.50. Phone (608) 786-1675 or (608) 786-1399.

WISCONSIN DELLS (G-5)
pop. 2,418, elev. 899'

Believed by the early Winnebago Indians to be the path of a giant serpent, considered a bane by 19th-century log drivers, and a fascination to geologists and photographers—the scenic dells of the Wisconsin River are the state's foremost natural attraction. The river has cut a channel through soft sandstone to a depth of 150 feet and, for a distance of 15 miles, has carved the rock into fantastic forms. A dam separates the river into the Upper and Lower dells.

In 1856 the center of population and business of the region was the flourishing town of Newport. Then the railroad decided to build its bridge 2 miles north, and Newport ceased to exist almost overnight. Several buildings were moved to the new site, called Kilbourn City. To publicize the geologic novelty of the dells, Kilbourn City was renamed Wisconsin Dells in 1931.

In addition to countless summer recreational opportunities, Wisconsin Dells offers varied winter diversions, including 610 miles of snowmobile trails. Devil's Lake and Mirror Lake state parks *(see Recreation Chart and Baraboo and Lake Delton in the AAA Great Lakes CampBook)* offer cross-country ski trails, and four downhill ski areas are within a 20-mile radius.

Wisconsin Dells Visitor & Convention Bureau: 701 Superior St., Wisconsin Dells, WI 53965; phone (608) 254-8088 or (800) 223-3557.

DELLS ARMY DUCKS is off I-90 exit 92, then n. on US 12 to 1550 Wisconsin Dells Pkwy. Passengers board amphibious vehicles for 1-hour land and water tours through the Lower Dells glacial area of the Wisconsin River region. Among the formations seen are the Sugar Bowl & Grotto Island, Twin Ink Stand and Lone Rock. A tour of the Upper Dells aboard the *Mark Twain* features such sites as Black Hawk Island, Chapel Gorge and Chimney Rock. Daily 9-6, May-Oct. Fare $16; ages 6-11, $8.50. DS, MC, VI. Phone (608) 254-6080.

[SAVE] **DELLS AUTO MUSEUM** is at 591 Wisconsin Dells Pkwy. Displays include antique automobiles, Indianapolis pace cars, license plates, a doll collection, toys and antique clothing. The museum specializes in antique convertibles. Allow 30 minutes minimum. Daily 9-9, mid-April through Labor Day; Sat.-Sun. 10-5, day after Labor Day-Oct. 31. Admission $4.50; senior citizens $3.25; ages 6-12, $2.25. Phone (608) 254-2008 or (608) 221-1964.

DELLS BOAT TOURS depart from the center of town at the Upper Dells Landing on SR 13/16/23, and from the Lower Dells Landing at jct. US 12 and SR 13/16/23. The trips offer guided sightseeing tours through the Upper and Lower dells of the Wisconsin River. The 2-hour Upper Dells tour includes sandstone cliffs, rock formations and stops at Witches Gulch and Stand Rock to walk along nature trails. The 1-hour, non-stop Lower Dells cruise goes past unusual rock formations, caverns and the Rocky Islands. Tickets are available at booths throughout the Dells area.

Boats depart daily every 30-45 minutes 9-6, June-Aug.; less frequently in Apr.-May and Sept.-Oct. Fare for 2-hour Upper Dells tour $17.75; ages 6-11, $9. Fare for 1-hour Lower Dells tour $14.75; ages 6-11, $7.50. Combination Upper and Lower Dells tour $24.75; ages 6-11, $13. AX, MC, VI. Phone (608) 254-8555.

FAMILY LAND is 1 mi. s. on US 12. This 35-acre water park offers 29 waterslides, a wave pool, double speedslide, flume slides, inner tube ride, water playground, skeeter and bumper boats, miniature golf, the Huck's Lagoon interactive water-play site and the Demon's Drop and Dragon's Tail rides. Allow 4 hours minimum. Daily 9-7, Memorial Day weekend-Labor Day. Admission (includes Bay of Dreams) $23.95, under 3 free. AX, DS, MC, VI. Phone (608) 254-7766.

Bay of Dreams is adjacent to Family Land. Open year-round, this indoor water park features a Mayan-themed adventure river, a children's pirate ship and one of the longest and tallest waterslides in the nation. Daily 9-7, Memorial Day weekend-Labor Day. Park opens at 10:30 a.m. rest of year; closing times vary. Admission Memorial Day weekend-Labor Day (includes Family Land) $23.95, under 3 free. Admission rest of year Mon.-Thurs. $14.95; Fri.-Sun., holidays and spring break $19.95. AX, DS, MC, VI. Phone (608) 254-7766.

SAVE **H.H. BENNETT STUDIO & HISTORY CENTER** is at 215 Broadway. Personal photographs, equipment and an interactive exhibit area explain the life and contributions of Henry Hamilton Bennett to the photography industry. Self-guiding and guided tours are available. Allow 1 hour, 30 minutes minimum. Daily 10-5, May-Oct. Admission $5; over 64 and students with ID $4.50; ages 5-12, $2.50; family rate $13.50. MC, VI. Phone (608) 253-3523 or (866) 944-7483.

LOST CANYON is 3.5 mi. s. on US 12, then .5 mi. e. on Canyon Rd. Horse-drawn wagons leaving every 15 minutes tour the sandstone formations in the canyon. The walls of the canyon reach 80 feet in height. Picnic facilities are available. Allow 30 minutes minimum. Daily 8:30-dusk, mid-May through Labor Day; 10-6, day after Labor Day-Oct. 31. Admission $6.75; ages 4-11, $3.50. MC, VI. Phone (608) 254-8757.

SAVE **NOAH'S ARK, AMERICA'S LARGEST WATERPARK** is 1.5 mi. s. on US 12 and SR 23. The park features 36 water slides, including Point of No Return, Paradise Lagoon, Black Thunder, The Lazy River and Adventure River. Two wave pools, four children's water-play areas, bumper boats and miniature golf also are offered. Special events are featured daily. Food is available. Picnicking is permitted. Allow 6 hours minimum. Daily 9-8, Memorial Day weekend-Labor Day. All-day pass $26.99; over 55, $21.59; under 3 free. DS, MC, VI. Phone (608) 254-6351.

ORIGINAL WISCONSIN DUCKS INC. is 1 mi. s. on US 12 and SR 23. One-hour land and water tours aboard green and white vehicles cover 8.5 miles of the Wisconsin River, Lake Delton and scenic wilderness trails. Daily 8-7, June-Aug.; 9-5 in May; 9-4, Sept.-Oct.; 10-4 in Apr. Fare $16.75; ages 6-11, $9. DS, MC, VI. Phone (608) 254-8751.

SAVE **RIPLEY'S BELIEVE IT OR NOT!** is downtown at 115 Broadway. The museum displays bizarre and unusual items and relates events of the type featured in the well-known comic strip. Videotape displays throughout the two-story building describe other strange items discovered by Ripley. Allow 1 hour minimum. Daily 9 a.m.-midnight, June-Aug.; 10-8, mid-Apr. through May 31 and Sept. 1 to mid-Oct.; schedule varies, rest of year. Admission $7.95; ages 5-12, $5.95. DS, MC, VI. Phone (608) 253-7556.

RIVERVIEW PARK AND WATERWORLD is .2 mi. s. on US 12. The park offers amusement rides and racing vehicles, including Grand Prix cars and high-speed go-carts. Waterworld has two speed slides, three curved waterslides, a rapids tube ride, a children's pool and a wave pool. Allow 4 hours minimum. Opens daily at 10 a.m., Memorial Day weekend-Labor Day. Closing times for park and water rides vary from 5 to 11 p.m. Individual rides $3-$4. All-day pass for water activities $11.99. All-day pass for "you-drive" rides and other activities $17.99; under 5, $9.99. DS, MC, VI. Phone (608) 254-2608.

SAVE **STORYBOOK GARDENS** is at 1500 Wisconsin Dells Pkwy. The gardens contain a petting zoo and life-size statues that depict nursery rhyme characters. Miniature train rides also are featured. Daily 9:30-5, late May-Labor Day (weather permitting). Admission $8.99, under 2 free. DS, MC, VI. Phone (608) 253-2391.

SAVE **TOMMY BARTLETT'S ROBOT WORLD AND EXPLORATORY** is 3 mi. s. on US 12 at 560 Wisconsin Dells Pkwy. This playground for the imagination includes virtual-reality exhibits, simulators, mirrors, puzzles, holograms and hands-on activities. The original Russian space station MIR also is displayed. Daily 8 a.m.-10 p.m., Memorial Day weekend-Labor Day; 10-4, rest of year. Admission $11.13, over 64, $8.90, under 6 free. DS, MC, VI. Phone (608) 254-2525.

SAVE **TOMMY BARTLETT THRILL SHOW** is 3 mi. s. on US 12 at 560 Wisconsin Dells Pkwy. A live outdoor entertainment show features professional water skiers, daredevil performers, a comedy juggler and an evening laser show fireworks finale. Shows daily at 1, 4:30 and 8:30, June 28-Labor Day; at 4:30 and 8:30, Memorial Day weekend-June 27. Admission $11.13, over 64, $8.90, under 6 on lap free. Upgraded seating is available. DS, MC, VI. Phone (608) 254-2525.

SAVE **WAX WORLD OF THE STARS** is on SR 13/16/23 at 105 Broadway. More than 100 life-like figures of famous individuals, both real and fictional, are displayed. Allow 30 minutes minimum. Daily 8 a.m.-11 p.m., Memorial Day weekend-Labor Day; 10-6, May 1-day before Memorial Day weekend and day after Labor Day to mid-Oct. Admission $6.95; ages 5-12, $4.95. DS, MC, VI. Phone (608) 254-2184.

WISCONSIN DEER PARK is 1 mi. s. on US 12. This 28-acre wildlife area is home to more than 100 deer of many varieties. Visitors may feed and pet the deer. Allow 1 hour minimum. Daily 9-7, Memorial Day-Labor Day; 10-4, day after Labor Day to mid-Oct. Admission $6.50; ages 4-11, $4.75. MC, VI. Phone (608) 253-2041.

WISCONSIN OPRY is .2 mi. s. of I-90/94 exit 92 on US 12. Country music by local and national professionals is showcased. Allow 2 hours minimum. Mon.-Sat. at 8 p.m. (dinner at 6 p.m.), some Sun. at 3 and 8 p.m., Memorial Day weekend-late Sept. Admission Mon.-Sat. $27.50, including meal; $15, without meal. Admission Sun. $29, including meal; $18, without meal. Phone (608) 254-7951 for schedule information.

RECREATIONAL ACTIVITIES
Fishing

- **B & H Trout Fishing** is 7 mi. n. to 3640 SR 13. Daily 6 a.m.-9 p.m. Phone (608) 254-7280.

- **Beaver Springs Fishing Park** is at 600 Trout Rd. Daily 9-8. Phone (608) 254-2735.

WISCONSIN RAPIDS (F-5)
pop. 18,435, elev. 1,028'

Wisconsin Rapids, on the Wisconsin River, is in the center of the world's largest inland cranberry-producing area. Cranberry harvests take place from early September through October.

Some of the nation's largest manufacturers of business papers came after the river's rapids were harnessed to provide water power. Stora Enso North America, formerly Consolidated Papers, offers guided tours of its papermaking facilities; phone (715) 422-3789 for reservations. Tours of the Port Edwards Mill of Georgia-Pacific/Wisconsin, 100 Wisconsin River Dr., are available during the summer.

Wisconsin Rapids Municipal Zoo at 1911 Gaynor Ave. is open from Memorial Day-Labor Day; a petting zoo, playground and picnic facilities are available. The area's historical background is described at South Wood County Historical Society Museum, 540 3rd St. S.; phone (715) 423-1580.

Wisconsin Rapids Area Convention & Visitors Bureau: 1120 Lincoln St., Wisconsin Rapids, WI 54494-5229; phone (715) 423-1830 or (800) 554-4484.

Self-guiding tours: Three historic walking tours in Wisconsin Rapids all have the Wisconsin River as their focal point. Brochures can be obtained from the convention and visitors bureau.

WOODRUFF (C-5) elev. 1,618'

Once a roistering settlement whose establishments provided for the pleasures of loggers in from the woods, Woodruff now caters to outdoors enthusiasts and vacationers enjoying the nearby forest and lake country. The area boasts one of the largest concentrations of freshwater lakes in the world. Old logging trails are groomed in the winter for cross-country skiing and snowmobiling, while bicyclists and hikers use them in the summer.

A unit of the Chequamegon-Nicolet National Forest *(see place listing p. 128)* and the Northern Highland-American Legion State Forest *(see Recreation Chart and the AAA Great Lakes CampBook)* flank the community.

Minocqua-Arbor Vitae-Woodruff Area Chamber of Commerce: 8216 US 51S, P.O. Box 1006, Minocqua, WI 54548; phone (715) 356-5266 or (800) 446-6784.

ART OEHMCKE STATE FISH HATCHERY is .7 mi. s.e. on SR 47, then 1.5 mi. e. on CR J. Muskellunge, northern pike, walleye and suckers are produced at the facility; more than 100 million fish can be hatched annually. Hatchery operations are best viewed May through June. Aquarium displays are featured. Allow 1 hour minimum. Mon.-Fri. 8-4. Guided tours are offered Mon.-Fri. at 11 and 2, day after Memorial Day-day before Labor Day. Free. Phone (715) 358-9213.

Fairytale Destinations.

Trust AAA to take you there.

Storybook lands. Magical worlds.

Enchanted voyages to paradise.

Whatever your dream,

there's a Disney vacation for you.

And when you book select vacation

packages through AAA Travel, you

can enjoy exclusive benefits

and great values.

Your fairytale is just a phone call away.

Call or visit your local AAA Travel office today.

Walt Disney World.

Disneyland.
RESORT
IN CALIFORNIA

Disney CRUISE LINE.

Ships' Registry: the Bahamas
As to Disney artwork, logos and properties: ©Disney K7888194

CST# 1022229-50

Look for the
Signs of Approval

When you're on the road, look for lodgings that display the AAA Approved sign. It's your sign that the property works hard to win AAA member business. In fact, these properties offer AAA members great room rates*.

When you see AAA Approved signs, you know you've arrived.

See TourBook Navigator, page 14, for complete details.

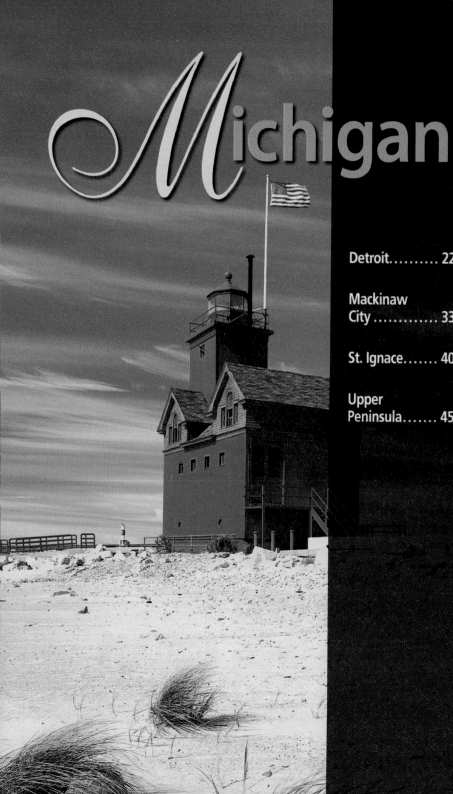

Michigan

ACME pop. 4,332

──────── WHERE TO STAY ────────

GRAND TRAVERSE RESORT & SPA

	1P	2P	XP	
6/15-8/16	1P: $211-$256	2P: $211-$256	XP: $15	F18
4/27-6/14	1P: $134-$179	2P: $134-$179	XP: $15	F18
4/1-4/26 & 8/17-3/31	1P: $103-$152	2P: $103-$152	XP: $15	F18

Phone: (231)938-2100

Resort / Large-scale Hotel

Location: On US 31, 0.5 mi n of jct SR 72. 100 Grand Traverse Village Blvd 49610. Fax: 231/938-5494. **Facility:** Extensive recreational facilities are featured at this resort, which is on spacious, manicured grounds. 658 units. 460 one-bedroom standard units, some with efficiencies and/or whirlpools. 122 one-, 56 two- and 20 three-bedroom suites, some with kitchens and/or whirlpools. 3-17 stories, interior/exterior corridors. **Parking:** on-site. **Terms:** check-in 4 pm, 3 day cancellation notice-fee imposed, package plans - seasonal & weekends, $9 service charge. **Amenities:** video games, voice mail, irons, hair dryers. *Some:* dual phone lines, honor bars. **Dining:** Trillium, see separate listing. **Pool(s):** 2 heated outdoor, 2 heated indoor. **Leisure Activities:** saunas, whirlpools, paddleboats, fishing, cross country skiing, snowmobiling, ice skating, recreation programs, bicycles, hiking trails, jogging, playground, basketball, volleyball. *Fee:* charter fishing, golf-54 holes, 9 tennis courts (5 indoor, 9 lighted), massage, game room. **Guest Services:** gift shop, valet laundry, area transportation. **Business Services:** conference facilities, business center. **Cards:** AX, DC, DS, MC, VI.

SOME UNITS

(ASK) (S/D) ♿ ❙❙ 🍸 🏋 🏊 🐾 ✕ 📹 📠 💻 / ✕ 📼 🔌 🛏 / FEE

HOLIDAY INN EXPRESS HOTEL & SUITES

	1P	2P	XP	
6/14-8/23 [ECP]	1P: $89-$209	2P: $89-$209	XP: $6	F19
8/24-10/18 [ECP]	1P: $79-$209	2P: $79-$209	XP: $6	F19
10/19-3/31 [ECP]	1P: $69-$209	2P: $69-$209	XP: $6	F19
4/1-6/13 [ECP]	1P: $69-$149	2P: $69-$149	XP: $6	F19

Phone: (231)938-2600

Small-scale Hotel

Location: Jct US 31 and SR 72, 0.5 mi sw. Located in a commercial area. 3536 Mount Hope Rd 49610 (PO Box 177). Fax: 231/938-0945. **Facility:** 81 one-bedroom standard units, some with whirlpools. 3 stories, interior corridors. *Bath:* combo or shower only. **Parking:** on-site. **Amenities:** dual phone lines, voice mail, irons, hair dryers. **Pool(s):** heated indoor. **Leisure Activities:** whirlpool. *Fee:* game room. **Guest Services:** valet laundry. **Business Services:** meeting rooms. **Cards:** AX, DC, DS, MC, VI. *(See color ad card insert & p 439)*

SOME UNITS

(ASK) (S/D) ❙❙ ♿ 🏊 📹 📠 / ✕ 🔌 🛏 💻 /

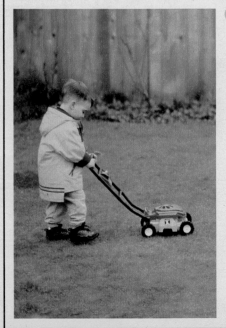

SLEEP INN AND SUITES

Phone: (231)938-7000

AAA SAVE

6/24-8/31 [ECP]	1P: $109-$199	2P: $109-$199	XP: $5	F18
9/1-10/31 [ECP]	1P: $69-$119	2P: $69-$119	XP: $5	F18
4/1-6/23 & 11/1-3/31 [ECP]	1P: $59-$109	2P: $59-$109	XP: $5	F18

Location: Jct US 31 and SR 72, 0.5 mi sw. Located in a commercial area. 5520 US 31 N 49610. Fax: 231/938-7001. Small-scale Hotel **Facility:** 74 units. 73 one-bedroom standard units. 1 one-bedroom suite. 3 stories, interior corridors. *Bath:* combo or shower only. **Parking:** on-site. **Terms:** check-in 4 pm, cancellation fee imposed. **Amenities:** safes (fee). *Some:* irons, hair dryers. **Pool(s):** heated indoor. **Leisure Activities:** whirlpool, exercise room. **Guest Services:** coin laundry. **Business Services:** meeting rooms. **Cards:** AX, CB, DC, DS, MC, VI. **Special Amenities:** free continental breakfast and free local telephone calls. *(See color ad p 449)*

SOME UNITS

🔊🕹️ 🍴 👨‍🦽 🚷 🏊 🐾 DATA PORT / ✕ 🛗 🖥️ 💻 /

-------- **WHERE TO DINE** --------

TRILLIUM

AAA

Continental

Dinner: $17-$30

Phone: 231/938-2100

Location: On US 31, 0.5 mi n of jct SR 72; in Grand Traverse Resort & Spa. 100 Grand Traverse Village Dr 49610. **Hours:** 6 pm-10 pm; hours vary in season. Closed: Sun. **Reservations:** suggested. **Features:** The busy restaurant is popular for its fantastic, 16th-floor view of the bay and its surroundings. Such dishes as rack of lamb are well-presented and tasty. Utilizing fresh ingredients, the menu represents regional specialties. Dressy casual; cocktails. **Parking:** on-site. **Cards:** AX, DC, DS, JC, MC, VI.

👨‍🦽 🍽️ ✕

ADA pop. 9,882

-------- **WHERE TO DINE** --------

THORNAPPLE/THE BISTRO

American

Lunch: $7-$10   **Dinner:** $15-$26   **Phone:** 616/676-1233

Location: Corner of Fulton and Ada St SE. 445 Thornapple Village Dr SE. **Hours:** 11:30 am-10 pm, Fri-11 pm, Sat 5 pm-11 pm. Closed: Sun. **Reservations:** suggested. **Features:** A family friendly restaurant with unique menu items. Start your meal with crispy portabella fries, complete with banana catsup, and then choose from specialty pizza or a variety of fish, meat and vegetarian entrees. Casual dress; cocktails. **Parking:** on-site. **Cards:** AX, DC, DS, MC, VI.

🍽️ ✕

ADRIAN pop. 21,574

-------- **WHERE TO STAY** --------

CARLTON LODGE

Phone: 517/263-7000

All Year   1P: $90-$160   XP: $8   F

Location: Jct M-52 and US 223, 3 mi w on US 223. 1629 W Maumee St 49221. Fax: 517/263-7000. **Facility:** 98 Small-scale Hotel units. 96 one-bedroom standard units. 2 one-bedroom suites. 2 stories, interior corridors. **Parking:** on-site. **Terms:** [ECP] meal plan available. **Amenities:** high-speed Internet (fee), voice mail, irons, hair dryers. **Pool(s):** heated indoor/outdoor. **Leisure Activities:** exercise room. **Guest Services:** valet laundry. **Business Services:** meeting rooms. **Cards:** AX, DC, DS, MC, VI.

SOME UNITS

ASK 🅿️ 🐾 🐾 DATA PORT / ✕ 🛗 💻

HOLIDAY INN EXPRESS

Phone: 517/265-5700

All Year [ECP]   1P: $89   2P: $89   XP: $8   F18

Location: Just w of jct US 223 and M-52. 1077 W US 223 49221. Fax: 517/265-5700. **Facility:** 60 one-bedroom Small-scale Hotel standard units. 3 stories, interior corridors. *Bath:* combo or shower only. **Parking:** on-site. **Amenities:** voice mail, irons, hair dryers. *Some:* CD players. **Leisure Activities:** exercise room. **Guest Services:** valet laundry. **Cards:** AX, CB, DC, DS, JC, MC, VI.

SOME UNITS

ASK 🍴 🅿️ 🐾 DATA PORT / ✕ VCR 🛗 🖥️ /

SUPER 8 MOTEL

Phone: (517)265-8888

All Year   1P: $64   2P: $64   XP: $8   F16

Location: Just w of jct US 223 and M-52. 1091 W US 223 49221. Fax: 517/265-8888. **Facility:** 51 one-bedroom Small-scale Hotel standard units. 2 stories, interior corridors. *Bath:* combo or shower only. **Parking:** on-site. **Terms:** age restrictions may apply, [CP] meal plan available. **Guest Services:** valet laundry. **Cards:** AX, DS, MC, VI.

SOME UNITS

ASK 🔊🕹️ 👨‍🦽 🅿️ 🐾 DATA PORT / ✕ 🛗 🖥️ /

ALBION pop. 9,144

──── WHERE TO STAY ────

DAYS INN
[SAVE]
♦♦♦ ♦♦♦
Small-scale Hotel
DC, DS, MC, VI.

				Phone: (517)629-9411
1/1-3/31 [CP]	1P: $66	2P: $71	XP: $5	F18
4/1-12/31 [CP]	1P: $61	2P: $66	XP: $5	F18

Location: I-94, exit 121. 27644 C Dr N 49224 (PO Box 865). **Fax:** 517/629-8960. **Facility:** 102 one-bedroom standard units, some with whirlpools. 2 stories (no elevator), interior corridors. **Parking:** on-site. **Terms:** small pets only. **Amenities:** hair dryers. *Some:* dual phone lines. **Pool(s):** heated indoor. **Leisure Activities:** limited exercise equipment. **Guest Services:** coin laundry. **Business Services:** meeting rooms. **Cards:** AX,

SOME UNITS
[icons]

ALGONAC pop. 4,613

──── WHERE TO STAY ────

LINDA'S LIGHTHOUSE INN
♦♦♦ ♦♦♦
Bed & Breakfast

			Phone: (810)794-2992
5/15-10/15 [BP]	1P: $95-$135	2P: $95-$135	

Location: I-94, exit 243, 14 mi e. 5965 Pointe Tremble Rd (M-29) 48001. **Fax:** 810/794-2992. **Facility:** Smoke free premises. 4 one-bedroom standard units, some with whirlpools. 2 stories (no elevator), interior corridors. *Bath:* combo or shower only. **Parking:** on-site. **Terms:** open 5/15-10/15, check-in 4 pm, 7 day cancellation notice, small pets only ($15 extra charge). **Amenities:** video library. **Leisure Activities:** whirlpool, boat dock, fishing, bicycles, horseshoes. **Guest Services:** TV in common area. **Cards:** MC, VI.

SOME UNITS
[icons]

ALLEGAN pop. 4,050

──── WHERE TO STAY ────

CASTLE IN THE COUNTRY B & B
♦♦♦♦
Historic Bed
& Breakfast

		Phone: 269/673-8054
All Year [BP]	2P: $105-$185	XP: $10

Location: M-40 S, 6 mi s. Located in a quiet, rural area. 340 M-40 S 49010. **Fax:** 269/686-0058. **Facility:** Some guest rooms at this 1906 Queen Anne-style home on five acres of farmland have Italian-tile fireplaces and whirlpool tubs. Designated smoking area. 5 units. 4 one-bedroom standard units, some with whirlpools. 1 one-bedroom suite with whirlpool. 3 stories (no elevator), interior corridors. *Bath:* combo or shower only. **Parking:** on-site. **Terms:** check-in 4 pm, 2 night minimum stay - weekends, 7 day cancellation notice. **Amenities:** video library. *Some:* CD players. **Leisure Activities:** recreation programs, hiking trails, basketball. **Guest Services:** gift shop, complimentary evening beverages. **Business Services:** meeting rooms, fax. **Cards:** MC, VI.

[icons]

ALLEN PARK —*See Detroit p. 243.*

ALMA pop. 9,275

──── WHERE TO STAY ────

DAYS INN
[SAVE]
♦♦ ♦♦
Motel
(See color ad card insert)

				Phone: (989)463-6131
4/1-6/30 [CP]	1P: $49-$150	2P: $49-$150	XP: $7	F13
7/1-12/31 [CP]	1P: $49-$99	2P: $49-$99	XP: $7	F13
1/1-3/31 [CP]	1P: $45-$79	2P: $45-$79	XP: $7	F13

Location: Jct SR 27 and 46. 7996 Alger Rd 48801. **Fax:** 989/463-2456. **Facility:** 49 one-bedroom standard units. 2 stories (no elevator), exterior corridors. **Parking:** on-site. **Terms:** cancellation fee imposed. **Amenities:** hair dryers. **Pool(s):** heated indoor. **Leisure Activities:** sauna. **Cards:** AX, CB, DC, DS, MC, VI.

SOME UNITS
[icons]

ALPENA pop. 11,304

—————— **WHERE TO STAY** ——————

40 WINKS MOTEL
Motel

All Year   1P: $42-$45   2P: $42-$49
Phone: 989/354-5622
XP: $5   F12
Location: 1 mi s on US 23. 1021 State St 49707. Fax: 989/358-8839. **Facility:** 16 one-bedroom standard units. 1 story, exterior corridors. **Parking:** on-site. **Terms:** package plans. **Cards:** AX, DS, MC, VI.

SOME UNITS

DAYS INN SAVE
Small-scale Hotel

All Year [CP]   2P: $80-$125
Phone: (989)356-6118
XP: $5   F18
Location: 2.5 mi w of jct US 23. 1496 Hwy 32 W 49707. Fax: 989/356-4208. **Facility:** 76 one- and 1 two-bedroom standard units, some with efficiencies and/or whirlpools. 1-2 stories (no elevator), interior corridors. *Bath:* combo or shower only. **Parking:** on-site, winter plug-ins. **Amenities:** safes (fee), irons, hair dryers. **Pool(s):** heated indoor. **Leisure Activities:** sauna, whirlpool, exercise room. **Guest Services:** coin laundry. **Business Services:** meeting rooms. **Cards:** AX, CB, DC, DS, JC, MC, VI. **Special Amenities:** free continental breakfast. *(See color ad card insert)*

SOME UNITS

DEW DROP INN SAVE
Motel

5/1-10/31   1P: $42-$46   2P: $42-$52
Phone: (989)356-4414
XP: $5   F12
4/1-4/30 & 11/1-3/31   1P: $38-$42   2P: $38-$48   XP: $5   F12
Location: 1 mi n of hospital on US 23. 2469 French Rd 49707. **Facility:** 14 one-bedroom standard units. 1 story, exterior corridors. *Bath:* shower only. **Parking:** on-site, winter plug-ins. **Cards:** AX, DS, MC, VI. **Special Amenities:** free local telephone calls.

SOME UNITS

HOLIDAY INN SAVE
Small-scale Hotel

All Year   1P: $79-$99   2P: $79-$99
Phone: (989)356-2151
XP: $10   D18
Location: 1 mi n on US 23. 1000 Hwy 23 N 49707. Fax: 989/356-2151. **Facility:** 148 one-bedroom standard units. 2 stories, interior corridors. **Parking:** on-site, winter plug-ins. **Amenities:** voice mail, irons, hair dryers. *Fee:* video games, high-speed Internet. **Dining:** 6:30 am-2 & 5-10 pm, Sat 6:30 am-10 pm, Sun 6:30 am-9 pm, cocktails. **Pool(s):** heated indoor. **Leisure Activities:** sauna, whirlpool, putting green, indoor recreation area, exercise room. *Fee:* game room. **Guest Services:** valet and coin laundry. **Business Services:** conference facilities. **Cards:** AX, CB, DC, DS, MC, VI. *(See color ad below)*

SOME UNITS

FEE

—————— **WHERE TO DINE** ——————

JOHN A LAU SALOON & STEAKHOUSE
American

Lunch: $5-$9   **Dinner:** $12-$18   **Phone:** 989/354-6898
Location: Located in the old town section. 414 N 2nd Ave 49707. **Hours:** 11:30 am-11 pm, Sun 4 pm-9 pm. Closed major holidays. **Features:** Housed in the oldest historic salon in Alpena, this microbrewery offers a varied menu of standard bar favorites such as hamburgers as well as a number of daily specials. Casual dress; cocktails. **Parking:** on-site and street. **Cards:** AX, DS, MC, VI.

SPINNAKERS
American

Lunch: $5-$9   **Dinner:** $10-$17   **Phone:** 989/354-8900
Location: 1 mi s on US 23. 1100 State Ave 49707. **Hours:** 11 am-8 pm; hours may vary seasonally. Closed major holidays; also Sun. **Reservations:** suggested; in season. **Features:** Overlooking the beach, this nautically themed restaurant specializes in locally caught seafood such as perch and whitefish as well as offering a variety of steaks. Casual dress; cocktails. **Parking:** on-site. **Cards:** AX, DC, DS, MC, VI.

ANN ARBOR pop. 114,024

―――― **WHERE TO STAY** ――――

BELL TOWER HOTEL
Phone: (734)769-3010

4/1-12/19 [CP]   1P: $153-$263   2P: $171-$281   XP: $18
1/2-3/31 [CP]   1P: $157   2P: $175   XP: $18
Small-scale Hotel   **Location:** just e. Located on MSU Campus. 300 S Thayer St 48104. Fax: 734/769-4339. **Facility:** 66 units. 58 one-bedroom standard units. 8 two-bedroom suites. 3-4 stories, interior corridors. *Bath:* combo or shower only. **Parking:** on-site (fee) and valet. **Terms:** open 4/1-12/19 & 1/2-3/31, check-in 4 pm. **Amenities:** dual phone lines, voice mail, irons, hair dryers. *Some:* safes, honor bars. **Guest Services:** valet laundry. **Business Services:** meeting rooms. **Cards:** AX, DC, DS, MC, VI.

SOME UNITS

BEST WESTERN EXECUTIVE PLAZA
Phone: (734)665-4444

SAVE

All Year [ECP]   1P: $59-$129   2P: $59-$129   XP: $10   F17
Location: I-94, exit 172, just e. 2900 Jackson Rd 48103. Fax: 734/665-5558. **Facility:** 163 units. 161 one-bedroom standard units, some with whirlpools. 2 one-bedroom suites with efficiencies and/or whirlpools. 2-4 stories, interior/exterior corridors. **Parking:** on-site. **Terms:** 14 day cancellation notice. **Amenities:** voice mail, irons, hair dryers. **Pool(s):** heated indoor/outdoor. **Leisure Activities:** sauna, whirlpool, exercise room.
Small-scale Hotel   *Fee:* game room. **Guest Services:** valet and coin laundry. **Business Services:** conference facilities.
Cards: AX, DC, DS, MC, VI.

SOME UNITS

CANDLEWOOD SUITES
Phone: (734)663-2818

All Year   1P: $55-$107
Location: I-94, exit 175 (Ann Arbor/Saline Rd), just e on Eisenhower Rd. 701 Waymarket Way 48103.
Small-scale Hotel   Fax: 734/663-6750. **Facility:** 124 units. 96 one-bedroom standard units with efficiencies. 28 one-bedroom suites ($69-$161) with efficiencies. 3 stories, interior corridors. *Bath:* combo or shower only. **Parking:** on-site. **Terms:** small pets only. **Amenities:** video library, CD players, dual phone lines, voice mail, irons, hair dryers. **Guest Services:** sundries. **Cards:** AX, CB, DC, DS, JC, MC, VI.

SOME UNITS

COURTYARD BY MARRIOTT
Phone: (734)995-5900

AAA **SAVE**

All Year [BP]   1P: $104-$124   2P: $114-$129
Location: I-94, exit 177 (State St), just n, then just e on Victor's Way. 2803 Boardwalk St 48104. Fax: 734/995-2937.
Facility: 160 units. 120 one-bedroom standard units. 40 one-bedroom suites ($114-$149). 4 stories, interior corridors. **Parking:** on-site. **Terms:** cancellation fee imposed, [CP] & [ECP] meal plans available, 16% service charge. **Amenities:** video games (fee), voice mail, irons, hair dryers. *Some:* dual phone lines.
Small-scale Hotel   **Pool(s):** heated indoor. **Leisure Activities:** whirlpool, exercise room. **Guest Services:** valet and coin laundry. **Business Services:** conference facilities. **Cards:** AX, CB, DC, DS, MC, VI. **Special Amenities:** free newspaper.
(See color ad below)

SOME UNITS

CROWNE PLAZA HOTEL AND RESORT ANN ARBOR   Phone: (734)761-7800
▼▼▼▼▼ All Year   1P: $144-$184   2P: $144-$184
Location: I-94, exit 177 (State St), just n, then just w. 610 Hilton Blvd 48108. Fax: 734/761-1040. **Facility:** 198 one-
Small-scale Hotel bedroom standard units. 3 stories, interior corridors. **Parking:** on-site. **Amenities:** video games (fee), dual
phone lines, voice mail, irons, hair dryers. **Pool(s):** heated indoor. **Leisure Activities:** sauna, whirlpool, ex-
ercise room. **Guest Services:** gift shop, valet laundry. **Business Services:** conference facilities, business center. **Cards:** AX,
CB, DC, DS, JC, MC, VI.

SOME UNITS
ASK SD ⑪ ⌘ ⇲ ⊠ ⑭ DATA PORT ⊑ /⊠ ⊟ /

THE DAHLMANN CAMPUS INN   Phone: (734)769-2200
▼▼▼▼ All Year   1P: $175-$225   2P: $195-$245   XP: $20
Location: At E Huron and State sts. Located adjacent to Dahlmann Campus. 615 E Huron St 48104.
Large-scale Hotel Fax: 734/769-6222. **Facility:** 208 units. 198 one-bedroom standard units. 10 one-bedroom suites ($250-
$375). 15 stories, interior corridors. **Parking:** on-site. **Terms:** check-in 4 pm, 60 day cancellation notice.
Amenities: irons, hair dryers. Some: high-speed Internet, safes, honor bars. **Pool(s):** heated outdoor. **Leisure Activi-
ties:** saunas, exercise room. **Guest Services:** gift shop, valet laundry. **Business Services:** meeting rooms. **Cards:** AX, DC, DS,
MC, VI.

SOME UNITS
⑪ ⑭ ⌘ ⇲ DATA PORT /⊠ VCR ⊟ /

EXTENDED STAY AMERICA   Phone: (734)332-1980
▼▼▼ ▼▼▼ All Year   1P: $55   2P: $59
Location: I-94, exit 177 (State St), just nw. 1501 Briarwood Circle Dr 48108. Fax: 734/332-1998. **Facility:** 112 one-
Small-scale Hotel bedroom standard units with efficiencies. 3 stories, interior corridors. Bath: combo or shower only. **Parking:**
on-site. **Terms:** cancellation fee imposed, weekly rates available. **Amenities:** voice mail. **Guest Services:**
coin laundry. **Cards:** AX, CB, DC, DS, MC, VI.

SOME UNITS
⑪⊹ ⊑M ⌕ ⌘ ⑭ DATA PORT ⊟ ⊞ ⊑ /⊠ /

FAIRFIELD INN BY MARRIOTT   Phone: (734)995-5200
ⒶⒶⒶ SAVE All Year [ECP]   1P: $79-$119   2P: $89-$129
Location: I-94, exit 177 (State St), just n, then e on Victor's Way. 3285 Boardwalk St 48108. Fax: 734/995-5394.
▼▼▼▼ **Facility:** 110 one-bedroom standard units. 4 stories, interior corridors. **Parking:** on-site. **Terms:** cancellation
Small-scale Hotel fee imposed. **Amenities:** video games (fee), irons. **Pool(s):** heated indoor. **Leisure Activities:** whirlpool.
Guest Services: valet laundry. **Cards:** AX, CB, DC, DS, MC, VI. **Special Amenities: free continental
breakfast and free newspaper.** (See color ad p 190)

SOME UNITS
SD ⑪⊹ ⇲ ⑭ DATA PORT /⊠ /

HAMPTON INN-NORTH   Phone: (734)996-4444
SAVE All Year   1P: $79-$99   2P: $89-$109
Location: US 23, exit 41 (Plymouth Rd), just nw. 2300 Green Rd 48105. Fax: 734/996-0196. **Facility:** 130 one-
bedroom standard units. 4 stories, interior corridors. **Parking:** on-site. **Terms:** 3 day cancellation notice,
▼▼▼ ▼▼▼ [ECP] meal plan available, small pets only ($25 fee). **Amenities:** voice mail, irons, hair dryers. **Pool(s):**
heated indoor. **Leisure Activities:** whirlpool, exercise room. **Guest Services:** valet and coin laundry. **Busi-
Small-scale Hotel ness Services:** meeting rooms. **Cards:** AX, CB, DC, DS, MC, VI.

SOME UNITS
SD ⌂ ⑪⊹ ⊑M ⌘ ⇲ ⑭ DATA PORT ⊑ /⊠ ⊟ ⊞ /

HAMPTON INN-SOUTH   Phone: (734)665-5000
SAVE All Year [ECP]   1P: $79-$179   2P: $79-$179   XP: $10   F18
Location: I-94, exit 177 (State St), just ne. 925 Victor's Way 48108. Fax: 734/665-8452. **Facility:** 149 one-bedroom
standard units. 4 stories, interior corridors. **Parking:** on-site. **Amenities:** voice mail, irons. **Pool(s):** heated
indoor. **Leisure Activities:** whirlpool, exercise room. **Guest Services:** valet and coin laundry. **Business
Small-scale Hotel Services:** meeting rooms. **Cards:** AX, CB, DC, DS, MC, VI. (See color ad below)

SOME UNITS
SD ⑪⊹ ⌘ ⇲ ⑭ DATA PORT ⊑ /⊠ ⊟ ⊞ /

HAWTHORN SUITES

Phone: (734)327-0011

All Year [BP]   1P: $85-$165

Small-scale Hotel

Location: US 23, exit 41 (Plymouth Rd), just sw. 3535 Green Rd 48105. Fax: 734/327-6109. **Facility:** 82 units. 21 one-bedroom standard units with efficiencies. 40 one- and 21 two-bedroom suites ($125-$225) with kitchens. 3 stories, interior corridors. *Bath:* combo or shower only. **Parking:** on-site. **Terms:** small pets only ($150 fee). **Amenities:** video library (fee), voice mail, irons, hair dryers. **Pool(s):** heated indoor. **Leisure Activities:** whirlpool, exercise room, sports court. **Guest Services:** sundries, valet and coin laundry, area transportation. **Business Services:** meeting rooms. **Cards:** AX, CB, DC, DS, JC, MC, VI.

HOLIDAY INN EXPRESS HOTEL & SUITES

Phone: (734)761-2929

All Year   1P: $99-$149   2P: $99-$149

Small-scale Hotel

Location: I-94, exit 177 (State St), just n, then w. 600 Hilton Blvd 48108. Fax: 734/761-2997. **Facility:** 107 one-bedroom standard units. 4 stories, interior corridors. *Bath:* combo or shower only. **Parking:** on-site. **Terms:** cancellation fee imposed, [CP] meal plan available. **Amenities:** video games (fee), dual phone lines, voice mail, irons, hair dryers. **Pool(s):** heated indoor. **Leisure Activities:** whirlpool. **Guest Services:** valet and coin laundry. **Business Services:** meeting rooms. **Cards:** AX, CB, DC, DS, JC, MC, VI.

SOME UNITS

HOLIDAY INN NORTH CAMPUS

Phone: (734)769-9800

All Year   1P: $89-$129   2P: $89-$129

Small-scale Hotel

Location: US 23, exit 41 (Plymouth Rd), just sw. 3600 Plymouth Rd 48105. Fax: 734/761-1290. **Facility:** 223 one-bedroom standard units. 2-5 stories, interior corridors. **Parking:** on-site. **Amenities:** high-speed Internet (fee), dual phone lines, voice mail, irons, hair dryers. **Pool(s):** heated indoor/outdoor. **Leisure Activities:** whirlpool, 2 tennis courts, exercise room, basketball, volleyball. *Fee:* game room. **Guest Services:** valet and coin laundry, area transportation. **Business Services:** conference facilities. **Cards:** AX, CB, DC, DS, JC, MC, VI. *(See color ad below)*

SOME UNITS

MICROTEL INN & SUITES

Phone: (734)997-9100

All Year [CP]   1P: $52-$62   2P: $52-$62

Small-scale Hotel

Location: US 23, exit 41 (Plymouth Rd), just sw. 3610 Plymouth Rd 48105. Fax: 734/997-9012. **Facility:** 83 one-bedroom standard units. 3 stories, interior corridors. *Bath:* combo or shower only. **Parking:** on-site. **Terms:** 2 night minimum stay - seasonal, 3 day cancellation notice-fee imposed, weekly rates available. **Amenities:** voice mail, hair dryers. **Leisure Activities:** 2 tennis courts, basketball. **Cards:** AX, CB, DC, DS, JC, MC, VI.

SOME UNITS

MOTEL 6 - 1247

Phone: 734/665-9900

5/22-10/11	1P: $49-$59	2P: $55-$65	XP: $3 F17
10/12-3/31	1P: $47-$57	2P: $53-$63	XP: $3 F17
4/1-5/21	1P: $41-$51	2P: $47-$57	XP: $3 F17

Motel

Location: I-94, exit 177 (State St), just s, then just w on Airport Rd. 3764 S State St 48108. Fax: 734/665-2202. **Facility:** 109 one-bedroom standard units. 1 story, exterior corridors. *Bath:* combo or shower only. **Parking:** on-site. **Terms:** small pets only. **Pool(s):** outdoor. **Cards:** AX, CB, DC, DS, MC, VI.

SOME UNITS

QUALITY INN & SUITES
Phone: (734)971-2000

AAA SAVE
▼▼ ▼▼
Small-scale Hotel

All Year   1P: $65   2P: $75
Location: US 23, exit 37B, just w. 3750 Washtenaw Ave 48104. Fax: 734/971-1149. **Facility:** 103 units. 93 one-bedroom standard units, some with whirlpools. 10 one-bedroom suites ($109). 3 stories, interior corridors. **Parking:** on-site. **Terms:** 3 day cancellation notice. **Amenities:** irons, hair dryers. **Dining:** 11 am-10 pm. **Pool(s):** outdoor. **Business Services:** meeting rooms. **Cards:** AX, DC, MC, VI. **Special Amenities:** free continental breakfast and free local telephone calls.

SOME UNITS

[icons]

RED ROOF INN
Phone: (734)996-5800

AAA SAVE
▼▼ ▼▼
Motel

5/23-9/13   1P: $56-$69   2P: $61-$74   XP: $5   F18
4/1-5/22 & 9/14-3/31   1P: $49-$69   2P: $54-$74   XP: $5   F18
Location: US 23, exit 41 (Plymouth Rd), just nw. 3621 Plymouth Rd 48105. Fax: 734/996-5707. **Facility:** 108 one-bedroom standard units. 2 stories, exterior corridors. *Bath:* combo or shower only. **Parking:** on-site. **Terms:** small pets only. **Amenities:** video games, voice mail. **Cards:** AX, CB, DC, DS, MC, VI. **Special Amenities:** free local telephone calls and free newspaper.

SOME UNITS

[icons]

RESIDENCE INN BY MARRIOTT
Phone: (734)996-5666

SAVE
▼▼ ▼▼
Small-scale Hotel

7/1-9/30 [BP]   1P: $99-$139   2P: $139-$179
4/1-6/30 & 10/1-3/31 [BP]   1P: $89-$119   2P: $129-$169
Location: I-94, exit 177 (State St), just ne. 800 Victor's Way 48108. Fax: 734/996-1919. **Facility:** 114 units. 78 one- and 36 two-bedroom standard units with kitchens. 2-3 stories, interior/exterior corridors. *Bath:* combo or shower only. **Parking:** on-site. **Terms:** pets ($125 fee). **Amenities:** dual phone lines, voice mail, irons, hair dryers. **Pool(s):** heated outdoor. **Leisure Activities:** whirlpool, exercise room, sports court. **Guest Services:** valet and coin laundry. **Business Services:** meeting rooms. **Cards:** AX, CB, DC, DS, JC, MC, VI.

SOME UNITS

[icons]

SHERATON INN-ANN ARBOR
Phone: (734)996-0600

▼▼ ▼▼
Small-scale Hotel

All Year   1P: $89-$109
Location: I-94, exit 177 (State St), just ne. 3200 Boardwalk 48108. Fax: 734/996-8136. **Facility:** 197 one-bedroom standard units, some with whirlpools. 6 stories, interior corridors. *Bath:* combo or shower only. **Parking:** on-site. **Terms:** age restrictions may apply, 14 day cancellation notice. **Amenities:** dual phone lines, voice mail, irons, hair dryers. **Fee:** video games, high-speed Internet. **Pool(s):** heated indoor/outdoor. **Leisure Activities:** sauna, whirlpool, exercise room. **Guest Services:** sundries, valet laundry, area transportation. **Business Services:** conference facilities, business center. **Cards:** AX, CB, DC, DS, JC, MC, VI. *(See color ad below)*

SOME UNITS

[icons]

WEBER'S INN

Phone: (734)769-2500

All Year   1P: $125-$280   2P: $135-$280   XP: $10   F18
Location: I-94, exit 172, just n. 3050 Jackson Rd 48103. Fax: 734/769-4743. **Facility:** 158 one-bedroom standard units, some with whirlpools. 4 stories, interior corridors. *Bath:* combo or shower only. **Parking:** on-site. **Terms:** check-in 4 pm, cancellation fee imposed, package plans. **Amenities:** video games (fee), voice mail, safes, irons, hair dryers. *Some:* CD players. **Dining:** restaurant, see separate listing. **Pool(s):** heated indoor.
Small-scale Hotel
Leisure Activities: sauna, whirlpool, sun deck, indoor recreation area, adjacent hiking & jogging trails, exercise room. *Fee:* game room. **Guest Services:** valet laundry. **Business Services:** meeting rooms. **Cards:** AX, CB, DC, DS, JC, MC, VI. **Special Amenities:** free continental breakfast and free newspaper. *(See ad below)*

SOME UNITS

——— WHERE TO DINE ———

AMADEUS CAFE PATISSERIE   **Lunch:** $6-$10   **Dinner:** $10-$17   **Phone:** 734/665-8767

Hungarian

Location: Between Main St and Fourth Ave; downtown. 122 E Washington 48104. **Hours:** 11:30 am-10 pm, Fri & Sat-11 pm, Sun 11 am-3 pm. Closed major holidays; also Mon. **Reservations:** accepted. **Features:** This cozy, European style restaurant features Polish and Central European cuisine, and fabulous pastry creations. The Hungarian combination plate is a fine example of a distinctive recipe prepared with care and fresh ingredients. Casual dress; cocktails; entertainment. **Parking:** street.

CHINA GATE   **Lunch:** $5-$6   **Dinner:** $7-$11   **Phone:** 734/668-2445

Chinese

Location: Center. 1201 S University 48104. **Hours:** 11 am-10 pm. Closed major holidays. **Features:** Nestled in the downtown area near the University of Michigan Campus, this Chinese restaurant offers a predictable menu including Szechuan, Hunan, Mandarin and Taiwanese dishes. Casual dress. **Parking:** street. **Cards:** MC, VI.

THE CHOP HOUSE   **Dinner:** $12-$40   **Phone:** 734/669-9977

Steak House

Location: Downtown. 322 S Main St 48104. **Hours:** 5 pm-midnight, Fri & Sat-11 pm, Sun 4 pm-9 pm. Closed major holidays. **Features:** The perfect place for that special dinner; trendy, yet refined. The restaurant serves an excellent selection of steak, seafood and poultry, and features an extensive wine list. This is a venue to be seen in. Cocktails. **Parking:** on-site. **Cards:** AX, DS, MC, VI.

DANIEL'S ON LIBERTY   **Dinner:** $19-$31   **Phone:** 734/663-3278

Regional American

Location: Just w from Main St, at W Liberty and Second. 326 W Liberty 48103. **Hours:** 5:30 pm-9:30 pm. Closed major holidays; also Mon. **Reservations:** suggested. **Features:** Secretly hidden near the downtown area, this restored 1870 residential Victorian home offers a wide variety of American regional cuisine. The spacious yet intimate dining room sets the stage for such seasonal delicacies as diver scallops, fesh pan-smeared salmon, wild game and signature sourdough bread. As a grand finale, unique pastries are offered with artistic flair. Dressy casual; cocktails. **Parking:** on-site. **Cards:** AX, DC, DS, MC, VI.

DON CARLOS MEXICAN RESTAURANTE   **Lunch:** $6-$8   **Dinner:** $8-$14   **Phone:** 734/572-0050

Mexican

Location: US 23, exit 37A (Washtenaw Ave), 0.3 mi e. 4890 Washtenaw Ave 48108. **Hours:** 11:30 am-10 pm, Mon-9 pm, Fri & Sat-11 pm, Sun noon-9 pm. Closed major holidays. **Reservations:** accepted. **Features:** Colorful paintings add to the upbeat, festive look of this casual restaurant. Fajitas, chiles rellenos and lots of burrito creations are among the Mexican dishes on the menu. Try the luncheon buffet, and sample it all. Casual dress; cocktails. **Parking:** on-site. **Cards:** AX, DC, DS, MC, VI.

THE EARLE   **Dinner:** $12-$18   **Phone:** 734/994-0211

Provincial French

Location: Just w of Main St; downtown. 121 W Washington St 48104. **Hours:** 5:30 pm-10 pm, Fri-midnight, Sat 6 pm-midnight. Closed major holidays; also Sun. **Reservations:** accepted. **Features:** Provincial French and Italian cuisine are the specialties of this cellar level restaurant. Candlelight and live jazz music fill this space with warmth and energy, serving as a popular escape from the hustle and bustle of the outside world. Dressy casual; cocktails. **Parking:** street. **Cards:** AX, DS, MC, VI.

GANDY DANCER   **Lunch:** $8-$14   **Dinner:** $16-$26   **Phone:** 734/769-0592

American

Location: Jct State and Fuller sts. 401 Depot St 48104. **Hours:** 11:30 am-3:30 & 4:30-10 pm, Fri-11 pm, Sat 4:30 pm-11 pm, Sun 10 am-1:30 & 3:30-9 pm. Closed: 12/25. **Reservations:** suggested. **Features:** Located near the University of Michigan Campus, this restored 1886 railroad depot with its beautifully appointed dining room features stained glass windows and red oak ceilings. The menu offers a tempting selection of fresh seafood specialties including shrimp fettuccine verde, potato encrusted whitefish, and crab stuffed rainbow trout. Casual dress; cocktails. **Parking:** valet and street. **Cards:** AX, DC, DS, MC, VI.

GRATZI   **Lunch:** $8-$12   **Dinner:** $15-$20   **Phone:** 734/663-6387

Italian

Location: Downtown. 326 S Main St 48104. **Hours:** 11:30 am-10 pm, Fri & Sat-11:30 pm, Sun 4 pm-9 pm. Closed major holidays. **Reservations:** accepted. **Features:** Housed in a former theater space, this dramatic restaurant comes complete with bold trompe l'oeil affects and larger than life framed mirrors. Regional Itailian cuisine such as veal, seafood and pastas are presented with flair. Dressy casual; cocktails. **Parking:** street. **Cards:** AX, CB, DC, DS, MC, VI.

GRIZZLY PEAK BREWING COMPANY   **Lunch:** $8-$10   **Dinner:** $9-$14   **Phone:** 734/741-7325

American

Location: Center. 120 W Washington St 48104. **Hours:** 11 am-11 pm, Fri & Sat-midnight, Sun noon-11 pm. Closed major holidays. **Features:** Copper kettles dominate the front windows of this local microbrewery that specializes in handcrafted beers, and as much attention has been placed into the continental menu that serves both daily specials and bar favorites. Cocktails. **Parking:** on-site and street. **Cards:** AX, MC, VI.

JONATHON B PUB   **Lunch:** $5-$10   **Dinner:** $5-$20   **Phone:** 734/668-7500

American

Location: I-94, exit 177 (State St), just n; in Briarwood Mall near JC Penney. 468 Briarwood Cir 48108. **Hours:** 11 am-11 pm, Fri & Sat-midnight, Sun noon-8 pm. Closed major holidays. **Features:** This small chain location features an English pub menu and decor. They serve gigantic portions of fish & chips and their shepherd's pie is also terrific. Casual dress; cocktails. **Parking:** on-site. **Cards:** AX, DS, MC, VI.

KAI GARDEN

Chinese

Lunch: $8-$10   **Dinner:** $8-$10   **Phone:** 734/995-1786
Location: Just s of jct W Huron and S Main sts; downtown. 116 S Main St 48104. **Hours:** 11 am-10 pm, Fri & Sat-11 pm, Sun noon-10 pm. Closed major holidays. **Features:** Underneath the surface of this quiet and unassuming restaurant, which serves a menu of contemporary Chinese-American favorites, is the second menu. Focusing on authentic Cantonese and Taiwanese food, the "little menu," as regulars call it, offers adventureous diners such choices as Fried Taro with Duck; Shang -Tun Fired Chicken and Pig's Ear. Casual dress; cocktails. **Parking:** street. **Cards:** DC, DS, MC, VI.

LA DOLCE VITA

Bakery/Desserts

Dinner: $6-$8   **Phone:** 734/669-9977
Location: Downtown. 322 S Main St 48104. **Hours:** 5 pm-midnight, Fri & Sat-1 am, Sun 4 pm-11 pm. Closed major holidays. **Features:** Squeezed between Gratzi and The Chop House, this after-dinner restaurant is reminiscent of a beautifully appointed living room. Overstuffed chairs, coffee tables, intimate lighting and a fireplace make for the perfect place to relax and enjoy house-made desserts and an extensive designer drink menu. A well ventilated downstairs cigar bar is a popular hang out for aficionados. Dressy casual; cocktails. **Parking:** street. **Cards:** AX, DS, MC, VI.

MEDITERRANO

Mediterranean

Lunch: $8-$14   **Dinner:** $10-$21   **Phone:** 734/332-9700
Location: I-94, exit 177 (State St), just n; corner of State St and Eisenhower. 2900 S State St 48104. **Hours:** 11 am-10 pm, Fri-11 pm, Sat noon-11 pm, Sun noon-10 pm. Closed major holidays. **Features:** The theme is decidedly Greek in the cozy dining room, which is decorated with colorful landscapes and statues of mythological figures. The summer patio resembles a gazebo. Such dishes as Moroccan sea bass are colorful and tasty. Casual dress; cocktails. **Parking:** on-site. **Cards:** AX, MC, VI.

METZGER'S GERMAN RESTAURANT

German

Lunch: $6-$9   **Dinner:** $12-$15   **Phone:** 734/668-8987
Location: I-94, exit 169; in Baxter's Plaza. 305 N Zeeb Rd 48103. **Hours:** 11 am-10 pm, Sun-8 pm. Closed major holidays. **Reservations:** accepted. **Features:** After enjoying a brief retirement, the owners have returned to a new location at the request of their many friends and fans. The comfortable dining room features brief glimpses of local and personal history culled over the years that this restaurant has been serving fine German cuisine. Dressy casual; cocktails. **Parking:** on-site. **Cards:** AX, MC, VI.

PAESANO'S RESTAURANT

Italian

Lunch: $7-$10   **Dinner:** $12-$22   **Phone:** 734/971-0484
Location: US 23, exit 37B (Washtenaw Ave), 0.3 mi w. 3411 Washtenaw Ave 48104. **Hours:** 11 am-11 pm, Fri-midnight, Sat noon-midnight, Sun noon-10 pm. Closed major holidays. **Reservations:** accepted. **Features:** This contemporary restaurant bustles with festive action. The menu runs the gamut of Italian specialties, sampling preparations of veal, seafood and chicken. Pasta is made in many varieties, such as lasagna and fettuccine. Salads are innovative and tasty. Casual dress; cocktails. **Parking:** on-site. **Cards:** AX, DC, DS, MC, VI.

WEBER'S RESTAURANT

American

Lunch: $7-$10   **Dinner:** $13-$27   **Phone:** 734/665-3636
Location: I-94, exit 172, just n; in Weber's Inn. 3050 Jackson Rd 48103. **Hours:** 6:30 am-10:30 pm, Fri-11 pm, Sat 8 am-11 pm, Sun 8 am-9:30 pm. Closed: 12/25. **Reservations:** suggested. **Features:** Prime rib, fresh fish, pasta and lobster are among dishes on the menu of this established restaurant, an area fixture since the late 1930s. You will find a well illuminated, comfortable dining room, and pleasing cuisine. Dressy casual; cocktails; entertainment. **Parking:** on-site. **Cards:** AX, DC, DS, JC, MC, VI. *(See ad p 194)*

ZINGERMAN'S DELI

Deli/Subs
Sandwiches

Lunch: $5-$8   **Dinner:** $5-$8   **Phone:** 734/663-3354
Location: Jct Detroit and Kingsley sts; downtown. 422 Detroit St 48104. **Hours:** 7 am-10 pm. Closed major holidays. **Features:** It's not unusual to see long line ups outside of this widely popular deli/gourmet grocery. A wide selection of made-to-order sandwiches are prepared using house-made bread and imported meats and cheeses. A wide variety of gourmet groceries are also available. Casual dress. **Parking:** street. **Cards:** AX, MC, VI.

AUBURN pop. 2,011

—— WHERE TO STAY ——

SUPER 8 MOTEL

Small-scale Hotel

Phone: 989/662-7888
All Year   1P: $47-$67   2P: $57-$77
Location: US 10, exit Garfield Rd. Located in a commercial area. 4955 S Garfield Rd 48611. Fax: 989/662-7607. **Facility:** 73 units. 61 one-bedroom standard units, some with whirlpools. 12 one-bedroom suites ($84-$119), some with whirlpools. 3 stories (no elevator). **Parking:** on-site, winter plug-ins. **Terms:** [CP] meal plan available. **Amenities:** *Some:* irons, hair dryers. **Pool(s):** heated indoor. **Leisure Activities:** sauna, whirlpool, exercise room. **Guest Services:** coin laundry, airport transportation (fee)-Tri-City Airport. **Cards:** AX, DS, MC, VI.

SOME UNITS

AUBURN HILLS —See Detroit p. 243.

AU GRES pop. 1,028

——— WHERE TO STAY ———

BEST WESTERN PINEWOOD LODGE　　　　　　　　　　　　　　　　**Phone:** 989/876-4060

SAVE　　5/1-10/31　　　　　　　　　1P: $79　　　　　　2P: $84
　　　　　4/1-4/30 & 11/1-3/31　　　　1P: $69　　　　　　2P: $74
Small-scale Hotel　**Location:** Just w on US 23. 510 W US 23 48703. Fax: 989/876-4290. **Facility:** 30 one-bedroom standard units, some with whirlpools. 1 story, interior corridors. **Parking:** on-site, winter plug-ins. **Terms:** cancellation fee imposed, [CP] meal plan available, pets ($10 fee). **Amenities:** irons, hair dryers. **Pool(s):** heated indoor. **Leisure Activities:** whirlpool, exercise room. *Fee:* game room. **Guest Services:** gift shop, coin laundry. **Cards:** AX, DS, MC, VI.

SOME UNITS

AUGUSTA pop. 899

——— WHERE TO STAY ———

——— *The following lodgings were either not evaluated or did not* ———
meet AAA rating requirements but are listed for your information only.

BROOK LODGE HOTEL AND CONFERENCE RESORT　　　　　　　　**Phone:** 269/731-2200

[fyi]　　Did not meet all AAA rating requirements for locking devices in some guest rooms at time of last evaluation
Resort Cottage　on 01/15/2002. **Location:** Jct SR 89 (West Michigan Ave), 1.5 mi n. Located in rural area. 6535 N 42nd St 49012. Facilities, services, and decor characterize a mid-range property.

YARROW　　　　　　　　　　　　　　　　　　　　　　　　　**Phone:** 269/731-2090

[fyi]　　Did not meet all AAA rating requirements for room decor/ambiance at time of last evaluation on 01/17/2002.
Resort　　**Location:** Jct SR 89 (West Michigan Ave), 3.3 mi n. Located in rural area. 10499 N 48th St 49012. Facilities, services,
Small-scale Hotel　and decor characterize a mid-range property.

BAD AXE pop. 3,462

——— WHERE TO STAY ———

BAD AXE HOTEL & RESORT　　　　　　　　　　　　　　　　　　**Phone:** 989/269-3930

　　　　All Year　　　　　　　　　1P: $55-$89
　　　　Location: 1 mi n; downtown. 898 N Van Dyke Rd 48413. Fax: 989/269-3849. **Facility:** 38 one-bedroom standard
Small-scale Hotel　units, some with whirlpools. 2 stories, interior corridors. **Parking:** on-site. **Terms:** cancellation fee imposed, weekly rates available, small pets only. **Amenities:** irons, hair dryers. **Leisure Activities:** sauna, whirlpool, exercise room. *Fee:* game room. **Business Services:** meeting rooms. **Cards:** AX, DS, MC, VI.

SOME UNITS

BARAGA pop. 1,285

——— WHERE TO STAY ———

BEST WESTERN BARAGA LAKESIDE INN　　　　　　　　　　　　**Phone:** (906)353-7123

SAVE　　6/1-10/14 & 12/16-3/31　　1P: $75-$84　　　2P: $79-$99　　　XP: $5　　　F16
　　　　4/1-5/31 & 10/15-12/15　　1P: $65-$69　　　2P: $69-$99　　　XP: $5　　　F16
　　　　Location: On US 41, 0.8 mi s of SR 38. Located on the shores of Keweenaw Bay. 900 US 41 S 49908 (PO Box 873).
Large-scale Hotel　Fax: 906/353-7799. **Facility:** 36 one-bedroom standard units, some with whirlpools. 3 stories, interior corridors. **Parking:** on-site, winter plug-ins. **Amenities:** irons, hair dryers. **Pool(s):** heated indoor. **Leisure Activities:** sauna, whirlpool, marina, fishing, snowmobiling. **Guest Services:** gift shop. **Business Services:** meeting rooms. **Cards:** AX, CB, DC, DS, MC, VI.

SOME UNITS

CARLA'S LAKE SHORE MOTEL & RESTAURANT　　　　　　　　　**Phone:** 906/353-6256

　　　　All Year　　　　　　　　　1P: $38-$45　　　2P: $52-$58　　　XP: $5　　　F12
　　　　Location: 6 mi n on US 41. Located opposite the bay. 49908 (Rt 1, Box 233). **Facility:** 10 one-bedroom standard
Motel　　units. 1 story, exterior corridors. *Bath:* combo or shower only. **Parking:** on-site. **Terms:** 7 day cancellation notice, pets ($5 extra charge). **Leisure Activities:** sauna, snowmobiling. **Cards:** AX, DS, MC, VI.

SOME UNITS

SUPER 8 MOTEL　　　　　　　　　　　　　　　　　　　　　　　**Phone:** (906)353-6680

　　　　7/1-10/31 [ECP]　　　　　1P: $54　　　　　2P: $59　　　XP: $5　　　F12
　　　　12/15-3/31 [ECP]　　　　　1P: $53　　　　　2P: $58　　　XP: $5　　　F12
　　　　4/1-6/30 & 11/1-12/14 [ECP]　1P: $49　　　　　2P: $54　　　XP: $5　　　F12
Small-scale Hotel　**Location:** 1 mi w on SR 38. Located opposite from a casino. 790 Michigan Ave 49908. Fax: 906/353-7246.
Facility: 40 one-bedroom standard units. 2 stories (no elevator), interior corridors. **Parking:** on-site, winter plug-ins. **Terms:** pets ($5 extra charge). **Leisure Activities:** snowmobiling. **Cards:** AX, CB, DC, DS, MC, VI.

SOME UNITS

BATTLE CREEK pop. 53,364

——— WHERE TO STAY ———

AMERIHOST INN & SUITES
Phone: (269)565-0500

(AAA) (SAVE)

▽▽▽▽▽

Small-scale Hotel

6/1-9/1 [ECP]   1P: $88-$98   2P: $95-$105
4/1-5/31 & 9/2-3/31 [ECP]   1P: $82-$95   2P: $88-$98
Location: I-94, exit 98B, 4 mi n, then 0.5 mi w. 182 W Van Buren 49017. Fax: 269/565-0501. **Facility:** 62 one-bedroom standard units, some with whirlpools. 2 stories (no elevator), interior corridors. *Bath:* combo or shower only. **Parking:** on-site. **Terms:** 10 day cancellation notice. **Amenities:** voice mail, safes (fee), irons, hair dryers. **Pool(s):** heated indoor. **Leisure Activities:** whirlpool, exercise room. **Guest Services:** valet laundry. **Business Services:** meeting rooms. **Cards:** AX, CB, DC, DS, MC, VI. **Special Amenities:** free continental breakfast and free newspaper.

SOME UNITS

(icons) /X/

BATTLE CREEK INN
Phone: (269)979-1100

(AAA) (SAVE)

▽▽▽▽

Motel

All Year [CP]   1P: $64-$70   2P: $70-$78   XP: $8   .F18
Location: I-94, exit 97, just s. 5050 Beckley Rd 49015. Fax: 269/979-1899. **Facility:** 212 one-bedroom standard units, some with kitchens and/or whirlpools. 2 stories (no elevator), interior/exterior corridors. **Parking:** on-site. **Terms:** check-in 4 pm. **Amenities:** voice mail. **Dining:** 6:30 am-2 & 5-10 pm, cocktails. **Pool(s):** heated outdoor, heated indoor. **Leisure Activities:** whirlpool, putting green, exercise room. *Fee:* game room. **Guest Services:** valet and coin laundry. **Business Services:** meeting rooms. **Cards:** AX, DC, DS, MC, VI. **Special Amenities:** free continental breakfast and free local telephone calls. *(See color ad below)*

SOME UNITS

(icons) /X 🔒 📺/

BATTLE CREEK QUALITY INN

Phone: (269)964-3000

All Year 1P: $59-$99 2P: $69-$129 XP: $7 F18
Location: I-94, exit 104, just se. 11081 E Michigan Ave 49014. Fax: 269/963-9915. **Facility:** 93 units. 89 one-bedroom standard units. 4 one-bedroom suites ($79-$199). 2 stories, interior corridors. **Parking:** on-site.
Terms: weekly rates available, [ECP] meal plan available, package plans. **Amenities:** safes. *Some:* irons, hair dryers. **Pool(s):** heated indoor. **Leisure Activities:** whirlpool. *Fee:* game room. **Guest Services:** valet and coin laundry. **Business Services:** meeting rooms. **Cards:** AX, CB, DC, DS, MC, VI. **Special Amenities:** free continental breakfast and free local telephone calls. *(See color ad p 198)*

Small-scale Hotel

SOME UNITS

BAYMONT INN & SUITES-BATTLE CREEK

Phone: (269)979-5400

4/1-10/30 [ECP] 1P: $72 2P: $80
10/31-3/31 [ECP] 1P: $59 2P: $65
Location: I-94, exit 97, just sw. 4725 Beckley Rd 49015. Fax: 269/979-3390. **Facility:** 87 units. 86 one-bedroom standard units, some with whirlpools. 1 one-bedroom suite with kitchen. 3 stories, interior corridors. *Bath:* combo or shower only. **Parking:** on-site. **Terms:** 30 day cancellation notice-fee imposed, pets (1st floor, in smoking units). **Amenities:** video games, voice mail, irons, hair dryers. **Pool(s):** heated indoor. **Leisure Activities:** whirlpool. **Guest Services:** valet and coin laundry. **Business Services:** fax (fee). **Cards:** AX, DC, DS, MC, VI. **Special Amenities:** free continental breakfast and free newspaper.

Small-scale Hotel

SOME UNITS

COMFORT INN

Phone: (269)965-3201

6/1-10/1 [ECP] 1P: $79-$119 2P: $79-$119 XP: $10 F18
4/1-5/31 & 10/2-3/31 [ECP] 1P: $69-$99 2P: $69-$99 XP: $10 F18
Location: I-94, exit 97, just n. 2590 Capital Ave SW 49015. Fax: 269/965-0740. **Facility:** 99 one-bedroom standard units, some with whirlpools. 2 stories, interior corridors. *Bath:* combo or shower only. **Parking:** on-site. **Terms:** check-in 4 pm. **Amenities:** dual phone lines, voice mail, irons, hair dryers. *Fee:* video games, high-speed Internet. **Pool(s):** heated indoor. **Leisure Activities:** exercise room. *Fee:* game room. **Guest Services:** valet laundry. **Business Services:** meeting rooms, business center. **Cards:** AX, CB, DC, DS, MC, VI.

Small-scale Hotel

SOME UNITS

DAYS INN

Phone: (269)979-3561

4/1-9/30 [CP] 1P: $45-$49 2P: $49-$89 XP: $4 F18
10/1-3/31 [CP] 1P: $35-$42 2P: $39-$59 XP: $4 F18
Location: I-94, exit 97. 4786 Beckley Rd 49017. Fax: 269/979-1400. **Facility:** 84 units. 83 one-bedroom standard units, some with whirlpools. 1 one-bedroom suite. 1 story, exterior corridors. **Parking:** on-site. **Terms:** check-in 4 pm, 2-3 night minimum stay - seasonal, package plans, small pets only ($25 extra charge). **Guest Services:** valet laundry. **Business Services:** meeting rooms. **Cards:** AX, CB, DC, DS, MC, VI. *(See color ad card insert)*

Motel

SOME UNITS

FAIRFIELD INN BY MARRIOTT

Phone: 269/979-8000

4/1-9/1 1P: $94-$139 2P: $94-$139
9/2-3/31 1P: $79-$109 2P: $79-$109
Location: I-94, exit 97, 0.3 mi sw. Located in a quiet area. 4665 Beckley Rd 49015. Fax: 269/979-3341. **Facility:** 74 one-bedroom standard units, some with whirlpools. 3 stories, interior corridors. *Bath:* combo or shower only. **Parking:** on-site. **Terms:** check-in 4 pm, cancellation fee imposed, [CP] meal plan available. **Amenities:** dual phone lines, voice mail, irons, hair dryers. **Pool(s):** small heated indoor. **Leisure Activities:** whirlpool, exercise room. **Guest Services:** valet and coin laundry. **Business Services:** meeting rooms. **Cards:** AX, DC, DS, MC, VI. *(See ad below)*

Small-scale Hotel

SOME UNITS

HAMPTON INN

Phone: (269)979-5577

All Year 1P: $65-$85 2P: $70-$90
Location: I-94, exit 97, 0.3 mi e. 1150 Riverside Dr 49015. Fax: 269/979-1041. **Facility:** 64 one-bedroom standard units. 3 stories, interior corridors. *Bath:* combo or shower only. **Parking:** on-site. **Terms:** [ECP] meal plan available. **Amenities:** voice mail, irons, hair dryers. **Pool(s):** small heated indoor. **Leisure Activities:** whirlpool. **Guest Services:** valet laundry. **Cards:** AX, CB, DC, DS, MC, VI.

Small-scale Hotel

SOME UNITS
FEE

MCCAMLY PLAZA HOTEL
▼▼▼▼   All Year   1P: $149   2P: $159   **Phone:** (269)963-7050   XP: $10   F18
Location: Center. 50 Capital Ave SW 49017. Fax: 269/963-4335. **Facility:** 239 units. 236 one-bedroom standard
Large-scale Hotel   units. 3 one-bedroom suites. 16 stories, interior corridors. *Bath:* combo or shower only. **Parking:** on-site (fee)
and valet. **Terms:** small pets only. **Amenities:** video games (fee), voice mail, honor bars, irons, hair dryers.
Dining: Porter's Steak House, see separate listing. **Pool(s):** heated indoor. **Leisure Activities:** saunas, whirlpool, exercise
room. **Guest Services:** valet laundry, area transportation. **Business Services:** conference facilities, business center. **Cards:** AX,
CB, DC, DS, MC, VI.

SOME UNITS
(ASK) 🔊 🐾 ❓ 🍴 24 🖥 📠 🔛 🏊 ✕ 📷 💾 💻 / ✕ VCR /

MOTEL 6 - 1149
▼   5/22-8/31   1P: $37-$47   2P: $43-$53   **Phone:** 269/979-1141
       9/1-3/31   1P: $33-$43   2P: $39-$49   XP: $3   F17
Motel   4/1-5/21   1P: $31-$41   2P: $37-$47   XP: $3   F17
Location: I-94, exit 97, just sw. 4775 Beckley Rd 49015. Fax: 269/979-1733. **Facility:** 76 one-bedroom standard
units. 2 stories (no elevator), exterior corridors. *Bath:* combo or shower only. **Parking:** on-site. **Terms:** small pets only. **Pool(s):**
outdoor. **Guest Services:** coin laundry. **Cards:** AX, CB, DC, DS, MC, VI.

SOME UNITS
🔊 🐾 🍴 ♿ ✕ 🏊 📷 💾 / ✕ /

——— WHERE TO DINE ———

CLARA'S ON THE RIVER   **Lunch:** $7-$16   **Dinner:** $7-$18   **Phone:** 269/963-0966
▼▼ ▼▼   **Location:** Near McCamly Pl; downtown. 44 N McCamly St 49017. **Hours:** 11 am-10 pm, Fri & Sat-midnight, Sun
       10 am-10 pm. Closed: 11/27, 12/25. **Reservations:** suggested; weekends. **Features:** This refurbished train
American   depot is appointed with stained glass, old wood and antiques. The lengthy menu includes a little bit of
everything—from burgers and steak to seafood and enchiladas. The emphasis is on fun, rather than fine,
family dining. Cocktails. **Parking:** on-site. **Cards:** AX, DC, DS, MC, VI.
♿ 🍷 ✕

FINLEY'S AMERICAN RESTAURANT   **Lunch:** $4-$8   **Dinner:** $9-$20   **Phone:** 269/968-3938
▼   **Location:** I-94, exit 97, 2 mi n on Capital Ave, 0.3 mi e. 140 E Columbia Ave 49015. **Hours:** 11 am-10 pm, Fri &
    Sat-11 pm. Closed: 11/27, 12/25. **Features:** A busy restaurant that is packed most evenings, so expect a
American   short wait when you arrive. Finley's is famous for their award-winning baby back ribs that are so tender,
the meat falls off the bone. Casual dress; cocktails. **Parking:** on-site. **Cards:** AX, DC, DS, MC, VI.
✕

HIGHNOON   **Lunch:** $11-$15   **Dinner:** $18-$25   **Phone:** 269/962-3355
(AAA)   **Location:** Downtown. 17 W Michigan Ave 49017. **Hours:** 11:30 am-1 & 5-9 pm, Fri & Sat 5 pm-10 pm. Closed
major holidays. **Reservations:** suggested. **Features:** Self-proclaimed "cowboy cuisine" is served
▼▼▼▼   at this trendy spot in downtown Battle Creek. Mixing canela scented foie gras with house specialties such
American   as brown sugar cured strip loins add a decidedly French twist to the Southwest menu. Dressy casual.
Parking: on-site. **Cards:** AX, CB, DC, DS, MC, VI.
🍷 ✕

PORTER'S STEAK HOUSE   **Lunch:** $5-$12   **Dinner:** $10-$25   **Phone:** 269/963-9686
▼▼▼ ▼▼▼   **Location:** Center; in McCamly Plaza Hotel. 50 Capital Ave SW 49017. **Hours:** 6:30 am-2 & 5:30-10 pm, Fri &
     Sat-11 pm. **Reservations:** suggested. **Features:** A full service dining room situated on the 16th
Steak House   floor of the McCamly Plaza Hotel. The specialty is real beef for hearty appetites. Both the beef and dessert
selections are presented tableside on rolling carts. Casual dress; cocktails. **Parking:** on-site (fee) and
valet. **Cards:** AX, CB, DC, DS, JC, MC, VI.
♿ 🍷 ✕

WATERFRONT RESTAURANT   **Lunch:** $5-$10   **Dinner:** $7-$30   **Phone:** 269/962-7622
(AAA)   **Location:** I-94, exit 97, 2 mi n on Capital Ave, 0.3 mi w. 315 W Columbia Ave 49015. **Hours:** 11 am-9 pm, Sat from
4 pm. Closed major holidays; also Sun. **Reservations:** suggested; weekends. **Features:** A casual dining
▼▼ ▼▼   retreat with floor to ceiling windows for panoramic views of the adjacent lake. Lunch buffet is popular with
American   the retired circle and the dinner menu featuring steaks and seafood always packs in the locals. Cocktails.
Parking: on-site. **Cards:** AX, DS, MC, VI.
♿ 🍷 ✕

BAY CITY pop. 36,817

────── WHERE TO STAY ──────

AMERICINN OF BAY CITY
Phone: (989)671-0071

| | 5/1-8/31 [CP] | 1P: $69-$119 | 2P: $69-$119 | XP: $5 | F17 |
| | 4/1-4/30 & 9/1-3/31 [CP] | 1P: $59-$99 | 2P: $59-$99 | XP: $5 | F17 |

Location: I-75, exit 164. 3915 Three Mile Rd 48706. Fax: 989/671-0311. **Facility:** 65 one-bedroom standard units. 2 stories (no elevator), interior corridors. *Bath:* combo or shower only. **Parking:** on-site. **Amenities:** voice Small-scale Hotel mail, irons. **Pool(s):** heated indoor. **Leisure Activities:** sauna, whirlpool. **Guest Services:** coin laundry. **Business Services:** meeting rooms. **Cards:** AX, CB, DC, DS, MC, VI. **Special Amenities:** free continental breakfast and free local telephone calls. *(See color ad below & p 289)*

SOME UNITS

BAY MOTEL
(AAA) [SAVE]
Motel

Phone: (989)684-4100

4/1-10/31	1P: $30-$55	2P: $60-$85	XP: $5	F
11/1-3/31	1P: $25-$40	2P: $40-$55	XP: $5	F

Location: Jct I-75 and US 10, 1.8 mi e on SR 25, then 0.5 mi s on SR 13. Located in a commercial area. 910 S Euclid Ave 48706. **Facility:** 18 one-bedroom standard units. 1 story, exterior corridors. *Bath:* combo or shower only. **Parking:** on-site. **Terms:** 7 day cancellation notice, weekly rates available. **Cards:** AX, CB, DC, DS, JC, MC, VI. **Special Amenities: free local telephone calls and preferred room (subject to availability with advanced reservations).**

SOME UNITS

[S] [i+] [⊠] [▯] / [⊠] /

BEST VALUE INN & SUITES
(AAA) [SAVE]
Small-scale Hotel

Phone: 989/686-0840

6/1-3/31	1P: $55-$60	2P: $60-$70	XP: $10	F12
4/1-5/31	1P: $45-$50	2P: $60-$65	XP: $10	F12

Location: Jct I-75 and SR 84, exit 160 (Saginaw Rd). 6285 W Side Saginaw Rd 48706. Fax: 989/686-0840. **Facility:** 70 one-bedroom standard units, some with whirlpools. 2 stories (no elevator), interior corridors. **Pool(s):** heated outdoor. **Leisure Activities:** sauna, whirlpool, exercise room. **Guest Services:** valet laundry. **Business Services:** meeting rooms. **Cards:** AX, DS, MC, VI. **Special Amenities: early check-in/late check-out and free local telephone calls.**

SOME UNITS

[S] [i+] [≈] [⊠] [⊠] [▭] / [⊠] [DATA PORT] [▯] /

CLEMENTS INN
▼▼ ▼▼
Bed & Breakfast

Phone: (989)894-4600

All Year [ECP]	1P: $75-$195	2P: $75-$195	XP: $25	D18

Location: 1 mi e on SR 25. 1712 Center Ave 48708. Fax: 989/891-9442. **Facility:** Smoke free premises. 6 units. 5 one-bedroom standard units, some with whirlpools. 1 one-bedroom suite ($125-$195) with kitchen and whirlpool. 3 stories (no elevator), interior corridors. *Bath:* combo or shower only. **Parking:** on-site. **Terms:** check-in 4 pm, 7 day cancellation notice-fee imposed, no pets allowed (owner's pet on premises). **Amenities:** video library, voice mail, hair dryers. **Cards:** AX, DC, DS, MC, VI.

SOME UNITS

[⊠] [VCR] [DATA PORT] / [▯] [▭] [▭] /

DELTA MOTEL
(AAA) [SAVE]
Motel

Phone: (989)684-4490

All Year	1P: $35	2P: $40

Location: Jct I-75 and US 10, 1.8 mi e on SR 25, 0.8 mi s on SR 13. Located in a commercial area. 1000 S Euclid Ave 48706. Fax: 989/684-4490. **Facility:** 19 one-bedroom standard units. 1 story, exterior corridors. *Bath:* combo or shower only. **Parking:** on-site, winter plug-ins. **Terms:** small pets only. **Amenities:** irons, hair dryers. **Cards:** AX, DS, MC, VI.

SOME UNITS

[S] [🛏] [i+] [⊠] [▯] [▭] / [⊠] /

EUCLID MOTEL
(AAA) [SAVE]
Motel

Phone: (989)684-9455

All Year	1P: $36-$46	2P: $46-$56	XP: $6	F12

Location: Jct I-75 and US 10, 1.8 mi e on SR 25, 0.8 mi n on SR 13. Located in a commercial area. 809 N Euclid Ave 48706. Fax: 989/686-6440. **Facility:** 36 one-bedroom standard units. 1 story, exterior corridors. **Parking:** on-site, winter plug-ins. **Terms:** weekly rates available, [CP] meal plan available. **Pool(s):** heated outdoor. **Leisure Activities:** playground, basketball. **Cards:** AX, CB, DC, DS, JC, MC, VI. **Special Amenities: early check-in/late check-out and free continental breakfast.** *(See ad p 201)*

SOME UNITS

[S] [i+] [≈] [⊠] / [⊠] [▯] /

FAIRFIELD INN
[SAVE]
▼▼ ▼▼
Small-scale Hotel

Phone: (989)667-7050

All Year	1P: $65-$85	2P: $70-$90

Location: 1 mi e of SR 13. Located at the Bay City Mall. 4015 E Wilder Rd 48706. Fax: 989/667-7050. **Facility:** 64 one-bedroom standard units. 3 stories, interior corridors. *Bath:* combo or shower only. **Parking:** on-site. **Terms:** [ECP] meal plan available. **Amenities:** irons. **Pool(s):** heated indoor. **Leisure Activities:** heated whirlpool. **Guest Services:** valet laundry. **Business Services:** meeting rooms. **Cards:** AX, CB, DC, DS, MC, VI.

SOME UNITS

[S] [i+] [&] [≈] [⊠] [DATA PORT] / [⊠] [▯] [▭] /

HOLIDAY INN
▼▼ ▼▼
Large-scale Hotel

Phone: (989)892-3501

All Year	1P: $74-$110	2P: $74-$110	XP: $10	F17

Location: Center line on I-75 business loop, SR 15 and 25; downtown. 501 Saginaw St 48708. Fax: 989/892-9342. **Facility:** 100 one-bedroom standard units. 4 stories, interior corridors. *Bath:* combo or shower only. **Parking:** on-site. **Terms:** check-in 4 pm. **Amenities:** irons, hair dryers. **Pool(s):** heated indoor. **Leisure Activities:** sauna, whirlpool. **Guest Services:** complimentary laundry. **Business Services:** meeting rooms. **Cards:** AX, CB, DC, DS, JC, MC, VI.

SOME UNITS

[ASK] [S] [🛏] [i+] [&] [≈] [⊠] [▭] / [⊠] /

——— **WHERE TO DINE** ———

BERGER'S FAMILY RESTAURANT
▼▼
American

Lunch: $4-$6   **Dinner:** $8-$11   **Phone:** 989/686-0224

Location: Jct I-75 and SR 84, 0.5 mi s. 6519 W Side Saginaw Rd 48706. **Hours:** 10 am-11 pm, Sun noon-8 pm; to 7:30 pm in winter. **Features:** Owned and operated through four generations of the same family, this established restaurant is a local favorite for fish, steak, sandwiches and delicious homemade pie. Attractive painted mirrors are among decor touches that enhance the dining room. Casual dress; cocktails. **Parking:** on-site. **Cards:** DS, MC, VI.

CHAR HOUSE
(AAA)
▼▼
American

Lunch: $4-$9   **Dinner:** $9-$25   **Phone:** 989/893-5881

Location: On SR 15, 1.5 mi s of SR 25. 432 Tuscola Rd 48708. **Hours:** 8 am-9 pm, Fri & Sat-10 pm. Closed: 11/27, 12/24, 12/25. **Reservations:** suggested. **Features:** Tried-and-true American staples—steak, seafood, chops and chicken—are at the heart of the family-oriented restaurant's menu. A nautical theme is prevalent in the comfortable dining room, which is decorated with some shipwreck memorabilia. Breakfast anytime. Casual dress; cocktails. **Parking:** on-site. **Cards:** AX, DS, MC, VI.

[⊠]

HEREFORD & HOPS

American

Lunch: $8-$18   **Dinner:** $8-$18   **Phone:** 989/891-4677

Location: Center. 804 E Midland St 48708. **Hours:** 11 am-11 pm, Fri & Sat-1 am, Sun noon-8 pm. Closed: 12/25. **Reservations:** accepted. **Features:** Patrons of the brew pub and restaurant can grill their own steaks, kebabs or catch of the day on the charcoal grill. The Friday night fish fry is also popular. Casual dress; cocktails. **Parking:** on-site. **Cards:** AX, DS, MC, VI.

KRZYSIAK'S HOUSE RESTAURANT
Polish

Lunch: $3-$5   **Dinner:** $7-$15   **Phone:** 989/894-5531

Location: 2.3 mi s on SR 13, 0.5 mi e on Cass Ave. 1605 S Michigan Ave 48708. **Hours:** 6:30 am-9 pm, Fri & Sat-10 pm, Sun-8 pm. Closed: 5/26, 12/25. **Reservations:** suggested; weekends. **Features:** Lively and upbeat, the friendly restaurant is a favorite for family dining. The menu meshes the cuisines of Poland and America. The seafood buffet on Friday and Saturday evenings draws a good crowd. Colorful hand-painted murals decorate the walls. Casual dress; cocktails. **Parking:** on-site. **Cards:** AX, DC, MC, VI.

THE LANTERN
American
DC, DS, MC, VI.

Lunch: $4-$8   **Dinner:** $10-$19   **Phone:** 989/894-0772

Location: 3 blks n; on the river. 1019 N Water St 48706. **Hours:** 11 am-9 pm, Fri-10 pm, Sat noon-10 pm, Sun 10 am-8 pm. Closed: 1/1, 12/25. **Features:** Overlooking the Saginaw River. Serving beef and seafood dishes, and a handful of surprises, such as Jamaican jerk-style ribs. Popular buffet and outdoor dining in season. The atmosphere is livliest on weekends. Casual dress; cocktails. **Parking:** on-site. **Cards:** AX, CB,

---
The following restaurant has not been evaluated by AAA but is listed for your information only.

LINDEN HOF
[fyi]

Phone: 989/686-2209

Not evaluated. **Location:** 201 N Euclid Ave 48706. **Features:** This well established restaurant has been popular with families in the area for many years.

Look For Savings

When you pick up a AAA TourBook® guide, look for establishments that display a bright red AAA logo, SAVE icon, and Diamond rating in their listing. These Official Appointment establishments place a high value on the patronage they receive from AAA members. And, by offering members great room rates*, they are willing to go the extra mile to get your business.

So, when you turn to the AAA TourBook guide to make your travel plans, look for the establishments that will give you the special treatment you deserve.

See TourBook Navigator section, page 14, for complete details.

BAY HARBOR

THE INN AT BAY HARBOR   **Phone:** (231)439-4000

◆◆◆ SAVE   5/11-10/26 & 12/11-3/21 [BP]   1P: $145-$810   2P: $145-$810   XP: $15   F12

▽▽▽▽   **Location:** On US 31; center. 3600 Village Harbor Dr 49770. Fax: 231/439-4904. **Facility:** Designated smoking area. 136 units. 89 one-bedroom standard units, some with efficiencies and/or whirlpools. 40 one- and two-bedroom suites with whirlpools, some with efficiencies. 6 stories, interior corridors. *Bath:* combo or shower

Resort   only. **Parking:** on-site and valet. **Terms:** open 5/11-10/26 & 12/11-3/21, check-in 4 pm, 2 night minimum stay

Large-scale Hotel - weekends, 10 day cancellation notice-fee imposed, 5% service charge. **Amenities:** dual phone lines, voice mail, irons, hair dryers. *Fee:* video games, high-speed Internet. *Some:* CD players. **Dining:** 2 restaurants, 8 am-10 pm; to 9 pm off season, cocktails. **Pool(s):** heated outdoor. **Leisure Activities:** whirlpool, snowmobiling, recreation programs in season, jogging, exercise room, spa. *Fee:* charter fishing, golf-45 holes, bicycles, game room. **Guest Services:** gift shop, valet and coin laundry, area transportation. **Business Services:** conference facilities. **Cards:** AX, DC, DS, MC, VI. *(See color ad below)*   SOME UNITS

🍽 🍸 🛄 ♿ 🏊 ✂ ✕ 🎥 [DATA PORT] 🛏 🖥 / 📺 /

---------- **WHERE TO DINE** ----------

SAGAMORE'S
▼▼▼◆◆◆
American
Dinner: $18-$22   **Phone:** 231/439-4059
Location: On US 31; center; in The Inn at Bay Harbor. 3600 Village Harbor Dr 49770. **Hours:** 5:30 pm-10 pm. **Reservations:** suggested. **Features:** This stunningly elegant dining room's elegant French doors look out over the bay at the receding ships. Specializing in regional cuisine, the chef pairs classics such as whitefish with an international palate of flavors. Dressy casual; cocktails. **Parking:** on-site and valet.
Cards: AX, DC, DS, MC, VI.

🍽️ ❌

BAY VIEW pop. 1,000

---------- **WHERE TO STAY** ----------

COACH HOUSE INN   **Phone:** (231)347-8281
(AAA) SAVE
▼▼▼
Motel

6/1-9/3	1P: $59-$99	2P: $59-$99
11/1-3/31	1P: $39-$99	2P: $39-$99
9/4-10/31	1P: $59-$79	2P: $39-$79
4/1-5/31	1P: $39-$59	2P: $39-$59

Location: Center. 1011 N US 31 49770. Fax: 231/347-1828. **Facility:** 21 one-bedroom standard units. 1 story, exterior corridors. *Bath:* combo or shower only. **Parking:** on-site. **Terms:** cancellation fee imposed, package plans - seasonal, pets ($10 extra charge). **Cards:** AX, CB, DC, DS, MC, VI. **Special Amenities:** free continental breakfast and free local telephone calls.

SOME UNITS
⑤🅳 🛏️ 🛁+ / ❌ 🗄️ /

COMFORT INN   **Phone:** (231)347-3220
(AAA) SAVE
▼▼▼
Small-scale Hotel

All Year [ECP]	1P: $50-$190	2P: $60-$200	XP: $10 F18

Location: Jct US 31 and SR 119. Located in a quiet area. 1314 US 31 N 49770 (1314 US 31 N, PETOSKEY). Fax: 231/347-9191. **Facility:** 65 units. 64 one-bedroom standard units, some with whirlpools. 1 one-bedroom suite ($125-$300) with kitchen and whirlpool. 2 stories (no elevator), interior corridors. **Parking:** on-site, winter plug-ins. **Terms:** check-in 4 pm. **Amenities:** voice mail, irons, hair dryers. **Cards:** AX, DC, DS, MC, VI. **Special Amenities:** free continental breakfast and free newspaper. *(See color ad p 402)*

SOME UNITS
⑤🅳 🛏️ 🛁+ 📺 🖥️ 🗄️ / ❌ 🗄️ 📷 /

STAFFORD'S BAY VIEW INN   **Phone:** (231)347-2771
▼▼▼◆◆◆
Small-scale Hotel

6/13-10/26 & 1/4-3/31 [BP]		2P: $135-$175	XP: $20 D18
4/1-6/12 & 10/27-1/3 [BP]		2P: $118-$138	XP: $20 D18

Location: 0.5 mi n on US 31. 2011 Woodland Ave 49770. Fax: 231/347-3413. **Facility:** Smoke free premises. 31 units. 18 one-bedroom standard units. 13 one-bedroom suites ($135-$280), some with whirlpools. 3 stories, interior corridors. *Bath:* combo or shower only. **Parking:** on-site. **Terms:** 7 day cancellation notice-fee imposed, package plans - seasonal & weekends. **Amenities:** *Some:* irons, hair dryers. **Leisure Activities:** bicycles. **Guest Services:** TV in common area, gift shop. **Business Services:** meeting rooms. **Cards:** AX, DS, MC, VI.

ASK 🍽️ ❌ 🅦 ☎️

TERRACE INN   **Phone:** (231)347-2410
▼▼
Small-scale Hotel

6/1-10/31	1P: $78-$108	2P: $78-$108
11/1-3/31	1P: $49-$108	2P: $78-$108
4/1-5/31	1P: $49-$108	2P: $49-$108

Location: Center; follow signs off US 31. 1549 Glendale 49770 (PO Box 266, PETOSKEY). Fax: 231/347-2407. **Facility:** Smoke free premises. 43 units. 42 one-bedroom standard units. 1 one-bedroom suite ($99-$159) with whirlpool. 3 stories (no elevator), interior corridors. *Bath:* combo or shower only. **Parking:** street. **Terms:** check-in 4 pm, cancellation fee imposed, [ECP] & [MAP] meal plans available, package plans. **Leisure Activities:** cross country skiing, bicycles. **Guest Services:** TV in common area. **Cards:** AX, MC, VI.

SOME UNITS
ASK ⑤🅳 🍽️ ❌ 🅦 ☎️ / 🅐🅒 /

---------- **WHERE TO DINE** ----------

LA SENORITA
▼▼▼
Mexican
Lunch: $5-$7   **Dinner:** $7-$12   **Phone:** 231/347-7750
Location: Jct US 31 and SR 119. 1285 US 31 N 49770. **Hours:** 11 am-10 pm, Fri & Sat-11 pm, Sun noon-10 pm; to midnight Fri & Sat 5/29-9/4. Closed: 4/20, 11/27, 12/25. **Features:** Casual dining. Warm atmosphere with Mexican knickknacks throughout. Good variety of reasonably priced Mexican dishes, snacks and salad. Mesquite cooked items. Smoking permitted in the lounge only. Casual dress; cocktails. **Parking:** on-site. **Cards:** AX, DC, DS, MC, VI.

🍽️ ❌

SCHELDE'S
▼▼▼
American
Lunch: $5-$10   **Dinner:** $10-$17   **Phone:** 231/347-7747
Location: Just n of jct US 31 and SR 119. 1315 US 31 N 49770. **Hours:** 11 am-10 pm. Closed: 11/27, 12/24, 12/25. **Features:** The menu comprises traditional, wholesome preparations of chicken, steak, fish, ribs and pasta. The family-oriented restaurant, decorated with knickknacks from the past, is homey and relaxed. Portion sizes are ample and food is reasonably priced. Casual dress; cocktails. **Parking:** on-site.
Cards: AX, DS, MC, VI.

❌

BELLEVILLE —See Detroit p. 246.

BENTON HARBOR pop. 11,182

---------- **WHERE TO STAY** ----------

BEST WESTERN T.C. INN & SUITES   **Phone:** (269)925-1880
SAVE
▼▼▼ ◆◆◆
Small-scale Hotel

All Year [CP]	1P: $59-$89	2P: $69-$99

Location: I-94, exit 29, just n to Mall Dr, then just w. 1598 Mall Dr 49022. Fax: 269/925-1880. **Facility:** 52 one-bedroom standard units. 2 stories, interior corridors. **Parking:** on-site. **Terms:** cancellation fee imposed, pets (in limited units). **Pool(s):** heated indoor. **Leisure Activities:** whirlpool. **Cards:** AX, CB, DC, DS, MC, VI.

SOME UNITS
⑤🅳 🛏️ 🛁+ 🏊 📺 🗄️ / ❌ 🗄️ 📷 /

COMFORT SUITES

SAVE

⬙⬙⬙⬙
Small-scale Hotel

Phone: (269)925-8800

All Year [ECP]   1P: $89   2P: $99   XP: $10   F18
Location: I-94, exit 29, just s. 1825 Meadowbrook Rd 49022. Fax: 269/925-8700. **Facility:** 62 one-bedroom standard units, some with whirlpools. 3 stories, interior corridors. *Bath:* combo or shower only. **Parking:** on-site. **Terms:** cancellation fee imposed, weekly rates available. **Amenities:** high-speed Internet (fee), dual phone lines, voice mail, irons, hair dryers. **Pool(s):** heated indoor. **Leisure Activities:** sauna, whirlpool, exercise room. **Guest Services:** valet and coin laundry. **Business Services:** meeting rooms, business center. **Cards:** AX, CB, DC, DS, JC, MC, VI.

SOME UNITS

⬛🅢ᴅ ⬛ 🅶ᴹ ⬛ 🛬 ⬛ ✕ ⬛ 📷 ⬛ 🄳🄰🅃🄰🄿🄾🅁🅃 ⬛ ⬛ ⬛ ⬛ / ✕ /

COURTYARD BY MARRIOTT

SAVE

⬙⬙⬙⬙
Small-scale Hotel

Phone: (269)925-3000

6/1-8/31   1P: $99-$149   2P: $99-$149
9/1-3/31   1P: $69-$129   2P: $69-$129
4/1-5/31   1P: $69-$99   2P: $69-$99
Location: I-94, exit 29, just n to Mall Dr, then just w. 1592 Mall Dr 49022. Fax: 269/925-8796. **Facility:** 98 one-bedroom standard units, some with whirlpools. 2 stories (no elevator), interior corridors. **Parking:** on-site. **Terms:** [BP] meal plan available. **Amenities:** video games (fee), voice mail, irons, hair dryers. **Pool(s):** heated indoor/outdoor. **Leisure Activities:** whirlpool, exercise room. **Guest Services:** valet and coin laundry. **Business Services:** meeting rooms, business center. **Cards:** AX, DC, DS, JC, MC, VI.

SOME UNITS

🅢ᴅ 🍴 🛬 📷 🄳🄰🅃🄰🄿🄾🅁🅃 ⬛ / ✕ 📼 ⬛ ⬛ /

HOLIDAY INN EXPRESS

⬙⬙⬙
Small-scale Hotel

Phone: 269/927-4599

6/1-8/31   1P: $99-$199   2P: $99-$199   XP: $10   F18
4/1-5/31   1P: $89-$159   2P: $89-$159   XP: $10   F18
9/1-3/31   1P: $69-$159   2P: $69-$159   XP: $10   F18
Location: I-94, exit 29, just s. 2276 Pipestone Rd 49022. Fax: 269/927-4699. **Facility:** 79 one-bedroom standard units, some with whirlpools. 3 stories, interior corridors. *Bath:* combo or shower only. **Parking:** on-site. **Terms:** [CP] & [ECP] meal plans available. **Amenities:** dual phone lines, voice mail, irons, hair dryers. **Pool(s):** heated indoor. **Leisure Activities:** whirlpool, exercise room. **Guest Services:** valet laundry. **Business Services:** meeting rooms. **Cards:** AX, DC, DS, MC, VI.
(See color ad card insert)

SOME UNITS

🄰🅂🄺 🅢ᴅ 🍴 ⬛ 🦮 🛬 📷 🄳🄰🅃🄰🄿🄾🅁🅃 ⬛ / ✕ ⬛ ⬛ /

MOTEL 6 - 1141

⬙⬙
Motel

Phone: 269/925-5100

5/22-8/31   1P: $37-$47   2P: $43-$53   XP: $3   F17
9/1-11/1   1P: $35-$45   2P: $41-$51   XP: $3   F17
11/2-3/31   1P: $32-$42   2P: $38-$48   XP: $3   F17
4/1-5/21   1P: $29-$39   2P: $35-$45   XP: $3   F17
Location: I-94, exit 29, just nw. 2063 Pipestone Rd 49022. Fax: 269/934-8404. **Facility:** 88 one-bedroom standard units. 1 story, exterior corridors. **Parking:** on-site. **Terms:** small pets only. **Pool(s):** small outdoor. **Guest Services:** coin laundry. **Cards:** AX, CB, DC, DS, MC, VI.

SOME UNITS

🅢ᴅ 🐾 🍴 🅶ᴹ 🛬 📷 🄳🄰🅃🄰🄿🄾🅁🅃 / ✕ /

RAMADA INN

⬙⬙⬙
Small-scale Hotel

Phone: (269)927-1172

6/16-9/15   1P: $99   2P: $99
9/16-3/31 [BP]   1P: $49   2P: $59
4/1-6/15   1P: $49   2P: $59
Location: I-94, exit 28, just sw. 798 Ferguson Dr 49022. Fax: 269/927-1198. **Facility:** 118 one-bedroom standard units, some with whirlpools. 5 stories, interior corridors. **Parking:** on-site. **Terms:** cancellation fee imposed, [MAP] meal plan available, pets ($25 deposit, $5 extra charge). **Amenities:** voice mail, irons, hair dryers. **Pool(s):** heated indoor. **Leisure Activities:** whirlpool, exercise room. *Fee:* game room. **Guest Services:** valet laundry. **Business Services:** meeting rooms. **Cards:** AX, DS, MC, VI.

SOME UNITS

🄰🅂🄺 🐾 🍴 🍷 🛬 ✕ 📷 🄳🄰🅃🄰🄿🄾🅁🅃 ⬛ / ✕ ⬛ ⬛ /

RED ROOF INN

🅰🅰🅰 **SAVE**

⬙⬙
Motel

Phone: (269)927-2484

5/25-9/13   1P: $41-$66   2P: $46-$71   XP: $5   F18
4/1-5/24 & 9/14-3/31   1P: $36-$56   2P: $41-$61   XP: $5   F18
Location: I-94, exit 29, just n, then just w. 1630 Mall Dr 49022. Fax: 269/927-1805. **Facility:** 108 one-bedroom standard units. 2 stories, exterior corridors. **Parking:** on-site. **Terms:** small pets only. **Amenities:** video games (fee), voice mail. **Cards:** AX, CB, DC, DS, MC, VI. **Special Amenities:** free local telephone calls and free newspaper.

SOME UNITS

🐾 🍴 🅶ᴹ 🦮 📷 🄳🄰🅃🄰🄿🄾🅁🅃 / ✕ ⬛ ⬛ /

─────── **WHERE TO DINE** ───────

HACIENDA MEXICAN RESTAURANT   **Lunch:** $6-$12   **Dinner:** $6-$12   **Phone:** 269/927-4593

⬙⬙⬙
Mexican

Location: I-94, exit 29, 0.5 mi n, 0.5 mi w. 1599B Mall Dr 49022. **Hours:** 11 am-10 pm, Fri & Sat-11 pm. Closed: 11/27, 12/25. **Reservations:** accepted. **Features:** Delicious dishes—such as sizzling steak and shrimp fajitas—are served in generous portions. Cheerful colors of stucco, pottery and sombreros brighten the decor. Casual dress; cocktails. **Parking:** on-site. **Cards:** AX, MC, VI.

🍷 ✕

BIG RAPIDS pop. 10,849

―――― WHERE TO STAY ――――

HOLIDAY INN HOTEL & CONFERENCE CENTER
AAA SAVE
▼▼▼▼▼
Large-scale Hotel
All Year   2P: $94-$104   XP: $10   F18
Phone: (231)796-4400
Location: US 131, exit 139, 1.3 mi e on SR 20. Located at Ferris State University. 1005 Perry St 49307. Fax: 231/796-0220. **Facility:** 118 one-bedroom standard units, some with whirlpools. 4 stories, interior corridors. **Parking:** on-site. **Terms:** check-in 4 pm. **Amenities:** irons, hair dryers. **Dining:** 6:30 am-10 pm, Fri-11 pm, Sat 7 am-11 pm, cocktails. **Pool(s):** heated indoor. **Leisure Activities:** sauna, whirlpool. *Fee:* golf-18 holes. **Guest Services:** gift shop, valet laundry. **Business Services:** conference facilities. **Cards:** AX, CB, DC, DS, MC, VI. *(See color ad below)*

SOME UNITS

SUPER 8 MOTEL
▼▼▼ ▼▼▼
Small-scale Hotel
All Year [CP]   1P: $58-$65   2P: $63-$70   XP: $5   F12
Phone: (231)796-1588
Location: I-131, exit 139, 1.4 mi e on SR 20. 845 Water Tower Rd 49307. Fax: 231/796-1588. **Facility:** 52 one-bedroom standard units, some with whirlpools. 2 stories (no elevator), interior corridors. *Bath:* combo or shower only. **Parking:** on-site. **Terms:** check-in 4 pm, cancellation fee imposed. **Amenities:** hair dryers. *Some:* irons. **Pool(s):** heated indoor. **Leisure Activities:** whirlpool. **Guest Services:** coin laundry. **Business Services:** meeting rooms. **Cards:** AX, CB, DC, DS, MC, VI.

SOME UNITS

BIRCH RUN pop. 1,653

―――― WHERE TO STAY ――――

COMFORT INN
SAVE
▼▼▼▼▼
Small-scale Hotel
4/1-12/30 [ECP]   1P: $79-$169   2P: $79-$169   XP: $10   F18
12/31-3/31 [ECP]   1P: $59-$149   2P: $59-$149   XP: $10   F18
Phone: (989)624-7777
Location: I-75, exit 136, just e. 11911 Dixie Hwy 48415. Fax: 989/624-7273. **Facility:** 99 units. 93 one-bedroom standard units, some with whirlpools. 6 one-bedroom suites with whirlpools. 3 stories, interior corridors. *Bath:* combo or shower only. *Some:* irons. **Pool(s):** small heated indoor. **Leisure Activities:** whirlpool, exercise room. *Fee:* game room. **Guest Services:** valet and coin laundry. **Business Services:** meeting rooms, business center. **Cards:** AX, CB, DC, DS, JC, MC, VI.

SOME UNITS

COUNTRY INN & SUITES BY CARLSON
AAA SAVE
▼▼▼▼▼
Small-scale Hotel
All Year [ECP]   2P: $79-$149
Phone: (989)624-8000
Location: I-75, exit 136, just w; at entrance to outlets at Birch Run. Located across from an outlet mall. 12112 S Beyer Rd 48415. Fax: 989/624-8080. **Facility:** 71 units. 61 one-bedroom standard units, some with whirlpools. 10 one-bedroom suites ($109-$149). 3 stories, interior corridors. *Bath:* combo or shower only. **Parking:** on-site. **Amenities:** irons, hair dryers. **Pool(s):** small heated indoor. **Leisure Activities:** whirlpool. **Business Services:** meeting rooms. **Cards:** AX, CB, DC, DS, MC, VI. *(See color ad p 243)*

SOME UNITS

HAMPTON INN
SAVE
▼▼▼▼▼
Small-scale Hotel
4/1-8/31 [ECP]   1P: $69-$119   2P: $69-$119
9/1-3/31 [ECP]   1P: $59-$99   2P: $59-$99
Phone: (989)624-2500
Location: I-75, exit 136, just e. 12130 Tiffany Blvd 48415. Fax: 989/624-2501. **Facility:** 89 one-bedroom standard units, some with whirlpools. 3 stories, interior corridors. **Terms:** check-in 4 pm. **Amenities:** voice mail, irons, hair dryers. **Pool(s):** heated indoor. **Leisure Activities:** whirlpool, exercise room. *Fee:* game room. **Guest Services:** valet and coin laundry. **Business Services:** meeting rooms. **Cards:** AX, CB, DC, DS, JC, MC, VI.

SOME UNITS
FEE   FEE

HOLIDAY INN EXPRESS

AAA [SAVE]

Small-scale Hotel

Phone: (989)624-9300

All Year [ECP]   1P: $79-$110

Location: I-75, exit 136, just e. 12150 Dixie Hwy 48415. Fax: 989/624-2053. **Facility:** 95 one-bedroom standard units, some with whirlpools. 3 stories, interior corridors. *Bath:* combo or shower only. **Parking:** on-site. **Terms:** check-in 4 pm. **Amenities:** irons, hair dryers. **Pool(s):** heated indoor. **Leisure Activities:** whirlpool, exercise room. *Fee:* game room. **Guest Services:** coin laundry. **Business Services:** meeting rooms. **Cards:** AX, DC, DS, MC, VI.

SOME UNITS

(icons)

SUPER 8 MOTEL

AAA [SAVE]

Small-scale Hotel

Phone: (989)624-4440

6/1-12/31 [CP]	1P: $55-$70	2P: $55-$70	XP: $5 F12
4/1-5/31 & 1/1-3/31 [CP]	1P: $40-$65	2P: $40-$65	XP: $5 F12

Location: I-75, exit 136, just e. 9235 E Birch Run Rd 48415. Fax: 989/624-9439. **Facility:** 109 one-bedroom standard units, some with whirlpools. 2 stories, interior corridors. **Parking:** on-site, winter plug-ins. **Amenities:** *Some:* irons. **Leisure Activities:** sauna, whirlpool. *Fee:* game room. **Guest Services:** valet laundry. **Business Services:** meeting rooms. **Cards:** AX, DC, DS, JC, MC, VI. **Special Amenities:** free continental breakfast and free local telephone calls.

SOME UNITS

(icons)

BIRMINGHAM —*See Detroit p. 247.*

BLANCHARD

———— WHERE TO STAY ————

SUPER 8 OF EDMORE

Small-scale Hotel

Phone: (989)427-8888

4/1-9/30 [ECP]	1P: $70-$100	2P: $70-$100	XP: $5 F16
10/1-3/31 [ECP]	1P: $60-$100	2P: $60-$100	XP: $5 F16

Location: On SR 46; center. 1106 E Main St 48829 (1106 E Main St, EDMORE). Fax: 989/427-8411. **Facility:** 51 units. 46 one-bedroom standard units. 5 one-bedroom suites ($79-$160), some with whirlpools. 2 stories, interior corridors. *Bath:* combo or shower only. **Parking:** on-site. **Terms:** weekly rates available, 8% service charge. **Amenities:** hair dryers. **Pool(s):** heated indoor. **Leisure Activities:** whirlpool, steamrooms, exercise room. *Fee:* game room. **Guest Services:** coin laundry. **Business Services:** meeting rooms. **Cards:** AX, CB, DC, DS, MC, VI.

SOME UNITS

(icons)

BLISSFIELD pop. 3,223

———— WHERE TO STAY ————

H. D. ELLIS INN

Bed & Breakfast

Phone: (517)486-3155

All Year [BP]   1P: $90   2P: $110   XP: $10

Location: Just w of town on US 223. 415 W Adrian St 49228. Fax: 517/486-3155. **Facility:** Smoke free premises. 4 one-bedroom standard units. 2 stories, interior corridors. *Bath:* combo or shower only. **Parking:** on-site. **Terms:** check-in 4 pm, 7 day cancellation notice, weekly rates available. **Cards:** AX, MC, VI.

SOME UNITS

(icons)

———— WHERE TO DINE ————

HATHAWAY HOUSE   Historic

AAA

American

Lunch: $6-$14   **Dinner:** $16-$26   **Phone:** 517/486-2141

Location: 0.3 mi w of town on US 223. 424 W Adrian St 49228. **Hours:** 11:30 am-9 pm, Fri & Sat-10 pm, Sun noon-8 pm. Closed: 1/1, 12/24, 12/25; also Mon. **Reservations:** suggested. **Features:** You'll find several inviting period dining rooms in this 1851 Greek revival mansion. The menu lists imaginatively prepared soups, salads, seafood, beef, and poultry. Try the broiled whitefish, its delicate flavors will please you. Casual dress; cocktails. **Parking:** on-site. **Cards:** DS, MC, VI.

(icons)

MAIN STREET STABLE & TAVERN   Historic

American

Lunch: $6-$20   **Dinner:** $6-$20   **Phone:** 517/486-2144

Location: 0.3 mi w of town on US 223; adjacent to Hathaway House. 116 N Main St 49228. **Hours:** 11:30 am-10 pm, Fri & Sat-midnight, Sun 11 am-9 pm. Closed: 1/1, 12/25. **Features:** This rustic restored carriage house is a fitting spot for meal and a drink. The menu offers light fare—snacks, soup, sandwiches and salad as well as entrees from salmon to steak. The banana cream pie is to die for. Casual dress; cocktails. **Parking:** on-site. **Cards:** AX, DS, MC, VI.

(icon)

BLOOMFIELD HILLS —*See Detroit p. 248.*

BOYNE CITY pop. 3,500

——— **WHERE TO STAY** ———

BOYNE CITY MOTEL
Phone: 231/582-6701

◆◆◆ ◆
Motel

Property failed to provide current rates
Location: On SR 75, just ne. Located in a residential area. 110 N East St 49712. Fax: 231/582-3193. **Facility:** 19 one-bedroom standard units. 2 stories (no elevator), exterior corridors. *Bath:* combo or shower only. **Parking:** on-site, winter plug-ins. **Leisure Activities:** playground, basketball. **Cards:** AX, CB, DC, DS, MC, VI.

SOME UNITS

〔⊪〕 〔🎥〕 〔DATA PORT〕 / 🗙 📶 🖰 /

WATER STREET INN
Phone: 231/582-3000

(AAA) [SAVE]
◆◆◆◆
Condominium

9/3-12/31	1P: $85-$200	2P: $85-$200	XP: $10 F12
6/1-9/2	1P: $95-$190	2P: $85-$125	XP: $10 F12
4/1-5/31 & 1/1-3/31	1P: $85-$125	2P: $85-$125	XP: $10 F12

Location: Center. 240 Front St 49712. Fax: 231/582-3001. **Facility:** 27 one-bedroom suites with whirlpools, some with efficiencies or kitchens. 3 stories, exterior corridors. **Parking:** on-site. **Terms:** 3 day cancellation notice-fee imposed. **Amenities:** video library (fee). *Some:* irons. **Leisure Activities:** snowmobiling. **Guest Services:** coin laundry. **Cards:** AX, MC, VI. **Special Amenities:** free local telephone calls and preferred room (subject to availability with advanced reservations).

SOME UNITS

〔S/D〕 〔⊪〕 〔VCR〕 〔🎥〕 🖰 🖰 🖭 / 🗙 /

——— **WHERE TO DINE** ———

——— *The following restaurant has not been evaluated by AAA* ———
but is listed for your information only.

RED MESA GRILL
Phone: 231/582-0049

〔fyi〕

Not evaluated. **Location:** Downtown. 117 Water St 49712. **Features:** The menu displays a mix of Cajun, Creole and Mexican dishes.

BOYNE FALLS pop. 370

——— **WHERE TO STAY** ———

DEER LAKE BED & BREAKFAST
Phone: (231)582-9039

◆◆◆◆
Bed & Breakfast

All Year [BP] 1P: $85-$105 2P: $95-$115 XP: $15
Location: Jct US 131 and CR C48, 0.8 mi w, then 2.2 mi s. Located in a quiet, rural area. 00631 E Deer Lake Rd 49712 (00631 E Deer Lake Rd, BOYNE CITY). Fax: 231/582-5385. **Facility:** This B&B offers lake views and tastefully furnished accommodations; two rooms have private balconies. Smoke free premises. 5 one-bedroom standard units. 2 stories (no elevator), interior corridors. *Bath:* shower only. **Parking:** on-site. **Terms:** 2 night minimum stay - weekends, 10 day cancellation notice. **Amenities:** irons, hair dryers. **Leisure Activities:** paddleboats, sailboats, horseshoes, volleyball. **Guest Services:** TV in common area. **Cards:** DS, MC, VI.

〔S/D〕 〔🗙〕 🗙 〔W〕

BREVORT

——— **WHERE TO STAY** ———

CHAPEL HILL MOTEL
Phone: 906/292-5534

◆◆◆
Motel

6/16-9/15 & 12/16-3/31	1P: $44-$49	2P: $49-$54	XP: $5
4/1-6/15 & 9/16-12/15	1P: $35	2P: $35-$39	XP: $5

Location: Center. Located in a semi-commercial area. 4422 W US 2 49760. **Facility:** 26 units. 25 one- and 1 two-bedroom standard units. 1 story, interior/exterior corridors. *Bath:* combo or shower only. **Parking:** on-site, winter plug-ins. **Terms:** cancellation fee imposed, small pets only ($5 extra charge). **Pool(s):** heated outdoor. **Leisure Activities:** snowmobiling, playground. **Cards:** DC, MC, VI.

SOME UNITS

🐾 🛋 〔🎥〕 🖭 / 🗙 🗲 🖰 🖰 /

BRIDGEPORT pop. 7,849

——— **WHERE TO STAY** ———

BAYMONT INN & SUITES-FRANKENMUTH/BRIDGEPORT
Phone: (989)777-3000

(AAA) [SAVE]
◆◆◆ ◆◆
Small-scale Hotel

All Year [CP] 1P: $59 2P: $59
Location: I-75, exit 144A. 6460 Dixie Hwy 48722. Fax: 989/777-2070. **Facility:** 100 units. 98 one-bedroom standard units, some with whirlpools. 3 stories, interior corridors. *Bath:* combo or shower only. **Parking:** on-site. **Terms:** pets ($10 extra charge, in limited rooms). **Amenities:** video games, voice mail, irons, hair dryers. **Pool(s):** heated indoor. **Leisure Activities:** whirlpool, exercise room. **Guest Services:** coin laundry. **Cards:** AX, CB, DC, DS, MC, VI. **Special Amenities:** free continental breakfast and free newspaper.

SOME UNITS

〔S/D〕 🐾 〔⊪〕 〔🗲〕 🛋 〔🎥〕 〔DATA PORT〕 🖭 / 🗙 🖰 🖰 /

DAYS INN-FRANKENMUTH/BRIDGEPORT
Phone: (989)777-1611

SAVE

8/1-11/30 [ECP]   1P: $65-$120   2P: $65-$120   XP: $5   F17
4/1-7/31 & 12/1-3/31 [ECP]   1P: $55-$85   2P: $55-$85   XP: $5   F17

Small-scale Hotel

Location: I-75, exit 144B. 6379 Dixie Hwy 48722. **Fax:** 989/777-6650. **Facility:** 123 one-bedroom standard units, some with whirlpools. 4 stories, interior corridors. **Parking:** on-site, winter plug-ins. **Amenities:** safes (fee), hair dryers. *Some:* dual phone lines, irons. **Pool(s):** heated indoor. **Leisure Activities:** sauna, whirlpool, exercise room. **Guest Services:** coin laundry. **Business Services:** meeting rooms. **Cards:** AX, CB, DC, DS, MC, I.V/tq;rr *(See color ad card insert)*

SOME UNITS

HEIDELBERG INN MOTEL
Phone: (989)777-2195

AAA SAVE

All Year   1P: $35-$50   2P: $40-$65   XP: $5   F10

Motel

Location: I-75, exit 144A, 1 mi s. Located in a semi-rural location, next to a bowling alley. 6815 Dixie Hwy 48722. **Fax:** 989/777-8324. **Facility:** 14 one-bedroom standard units. 1 story, exterior corridors. *Bath:* shower only. **Parking:** on-site. **Terms:** weekly rates available, [ECP] meal plan available. **Cards:** AX, DC, MC, VI.

SOME UNITS

KNIGHTS INN
Phone: (989)777-2582

AAA SAVE

6/1-11/30   1P: $37-$70   2P: $40-$80   XP: $6   F18
4/1-5/31 & 12/1-3/31   1P: $33-$49   2P: $37-$55   XP: $6   F18

Motel

Location: I-75, exit 144B. Located in a commercial area. 6361 Dixie Hwy 48722. **Fax:** 989/777-9546. **Facility:** 111 one-bedroom standard units. 1 story, exterior corridors. *Bath:* combo or shower only. **Parking:** on-site. **Terms:** weekly rates available, [CP] meal plan available, small pets only. **Cards:** AX, DS, MC, VI. **Special Amenities:** free continental breakfast and free local telephone calls.

SOME UNITS

——— WHERE TO DINE ———

——— *The following restaurant has not been evaluated by AAA* ———
but is listed for your information only.

FREEWAY FRITZ
Phone: 989/777-8730

[fyi]

Not evaluated. **Location:** I-75, exit 144 (Dixie Hwy), just s. 6560 Dixie Hwy 48722. **Features:** This fast-food restaurant serves Frankenmuth-style chicken dinner and snacks. Also at this location are several other food outlets and a gift shop.

BRIDGMAN pop. 2,428

——— WHERE TO DINE ———

HYERDALL'S CAFE   **Lunch:** $5-$7   **Dinner:** $8-$12   **Phone:** 269/465-5546

American

Location: I-94, exit 16, 1 mi n. 9673 Red Arrow Hwy 49106. **Hours:** 7 am-9 pm. Closed major holidays; also Mon. **Reservations:** accepted. **Features:** This is a small town, main street cafe that has been operating since 1927. Caters to the families and couples looking for fresh home cooking with items like chicken, fish, chops and steak. **Parking:** on-site.

BRIGHTON pop. 6,701

——— WHERE TO STAY ———

COURTYARD BY MARRIOTT
Phone: (810)225-9200

SAVE

All Year   1P: $74-$96   XP: $10   F18

Small-scale Hotel

Location: I-96, exit 145 (Grand River S), just ne. 7799 Conference Center Dr 48114. **Fax:** 810/225-2028. **Facility:** 90 units. 88 one-bedroom standard units, some with whirlpools. 2 one-bedroom suites ($109-$121). 3 stories, interior corridors. *Bath:* combo or shower only. **Parking:** on-site. **Terms:** [BP] meal plan available, package plans, 18% service charge. **Amenities:** video games (fee), dual phone lines, voice mail, irons, hair dryers. **Pool(s):** heated indoor. **Leisure Activities:** whirlpool, exercise room. **Guest Services:** valet and coin laundry. **Business Services:** meeting rooms.

SOME UNITS

HOLIDAY INN EXPRESS HOTEL & SUITES
Phone: (810)225-4300

All Year [ECP]   1P: $99-$159   2P: $99-$159   XP: $10   F16

Small-scale Hotel

Location: I-96, exit 145 (Grand River S). Located in Towne Square Shopping Plaza. 8079 Challis Dr 48116. **Fax:** 810/225-0250. **Facility:** 107 units. 72 one-bedroom standard units, some with efficiencies. 35 one-bedroom suites, some with whirlpools. 2 stories, interior corridors. *Bath:* combo or shower only. **Parking:** on-site. **Amenities:** video games, dual phone lines, voice mail, irons, hair dryers. **Pool(s):** heated indoor. **Leisure Activities:** whirlpool, exercise room. *Fee:* game room. **Guest Services:** valet and coin laundry. **Business Services:** meeting rooms, business center. **Cards:** AX, CB, DC, DS, JC, MC, VI.

SOME UNITS

——— WHERE TO DINE ———

LU & CARL'S   **Lunch:** $8-$12   **Dinner:** $10-$15   **Phone:** 810/229-9660

AAA

American

Location: I-96, exit 145 (Grand River S), downtown. 100 W Main St 48116. **Hours:** 11 am-midnight, Thurs-Sat to 2 am. Closed major holidays. **Features:** Dog lovers will particularly enjoy this bright and airy restaurant that pays homage to man's best friend. A varied menu offers both daily specials and traditional favorites. Casual dress; cocktails. **Parking:** street. **Cards:** AX, DC, MC, VI.

BRIMLEY

─── WHERE TO STAY ───

BAY MILLS RESORT & CASINO　　　　　　　　　　　　　　　　**Phone:** (906)248-3701
♦♦♦♦ ♦♦♦♦　　6/15-10/15　　　　1P: $79-$89　　　2P: $79-$89　　　XP: $15　　　F17
　　　　　　4/1-6/14 & 10/16-3/31　1P: $59-$69　　　2P: $59-$69　　　XP: $15　　　F17
Resort　　**Location:** From the end of SR 221, 2 mi w. Located on the water's edge. 11386 W Lakeshore Dr 49715.
Large-scale Hotel **Fax:** 906/248-3720. **Facility:** 142 units. 137 one-bedroom standard units, some with whirlpools. 5 one-bedroom suites ($140-$190) with whirlpools. 2 stories, interior corridors. *Bath:* combo or shower only.
Parking: on-site. **Terms:** cancellation fee imposed, package plans - seasonal. **Amenities:** hair dryers. **Leisure Activities:** cross country skiing, snowmobiling. **Fee:** golf-18 holes. **Guest Services:** gift shop. **Business Services:** conference facilities.
Cards: AX, DS, MC, VI. *(See color ad p 424)*
SOME UNITS
🎲 ASK S🅳 🍴 🍸 ✕ ➖ / ✕ 🛄 📷 /

WILLABEE'S MOTEL　　　　　　　　　　　　　　　　　　**Phone:** 906/248-3090
♦♦♦♦ ♦♦♦♦　　10/16-3/31　　　　1P: $66-$72　　　2P: $66-$72　　　XP: $8　　　F18
Motel　　　6/16-10/15　　　　1P: $64-$72　　　2P: $64-$72　　　XP: $8　　　F18
　　　　　　4/1-6/15　　　　　1P: $55-$62　　　2P: $55-$62　　　XP: $8　　　F18
Location: At the end of SR 221. Located along the banks of the river. 9903 W 6 Mile Rd 49715 (PO Box 386).
Fax: 906/248-3169. **Facility:** 36 units. 35 one- and 1 two-bedroom standard units. 2 stories (no elevator), exterior corridors. *Bath:* combo or shower only. **Parking:** on-site. **Terms:** 3 day cancellation notice. **Leisure Activities:** boat dock, fishing, snowmobiling.
Cards: AX, DS, MC, VI.
SOME UNITS
🍴 🍸 ♿ ✕ 📠 / ✕ 🛄 /

BROOKLYN pop. 1,176

─── WHERE TO STAY ───

CHICAGO STREET INN　　　　　　　　　　　　　　　　　**Phone:** (517)592-3888
♦♦♦ ♦♦♦　　All Year [BP]　　　1P: $85-$155　　　2P: $85-$155　　　XP: $20
Historic Bed　**Location:** Jct Chicago and Main sts (M-50), just w; downtown. 219 Chicago St 49230. **Fax:** 517/592-9025.
& Breakfast　**Facility:** Smoke free premises. 6 one-bedroom standard units, some with whirlpools. 3 stories (no elevator), interior corridors. *Bath:* combo or shower only. **Parking:** on-site. **Terms:** check-in 4 pm, cancellation fee imposed. **Cards:** AX, MC, VI.
SOME UNITS
ASK S🅳 🍴 ✕ 🕿 🛄 / VCR 📷 /

SUPER 8 MOTEL　　　　　　　　　　　　　　　　　　　**Phone:** 517/592-0888
♦♦♦♦ ♦♦♦　　5/1-9/30　　　　　1P: $66-$130　　　2P: $66-$130　　　XP: $5　　　F17
　　　　　　4/1-4/30 & 10/1-3/31　1P: $58-$120　　　2P: $58-$120　　　XP: $5　　　F17
Small-scale Hotel **Location:** Jct SR 50 and SR 124; downtown. 155 Wamplers Rd 49250 (PO Box 687). **Fax:** 517/592-0880.
Facility: 52 units. 48 one-bedroom standard units, some with kitchens and/or whirlpools. 4 one-bedroom suites ($102-$130) with whirlpools. 2 stories (no elevator), interior corridors. *Bath:* combo or shower only. **Parking:** on-site. **Terms:** [CP] meal plan available, small pets only ($5 extra charge). **Amenities:** *Some:* irons, hair dryers. **Guest Services:** coin laundry. **Business Services:** conference facilities. **Cards:** AX, DC, DS, MC, VI.
SOME UNITS
ASK S🅳 🐾 ♿ 🅼 ♿ 🎥 / ✕ 🛄 📷 /

BRUCE CROSSING

─── WHERE TO DINE ───

GRAMMA GROOTER'S　　**Lunch:** $5-$12　　　**Dinner:** $5-$12　　　**Phone:** 906/827-3413
♦♦♦　　**Location:** 0.5 mi e. Hwy 28 E 49912. **Hours:** 6 am-10 pm. Closed: 11/27, 12/24, 12/25. **Features:** Families
American　gather in the cozy log building to enjoy ample portions of home-style fare. The popular skillet breakfasts are served all day. The menu delivers a little bit of everything—from sandwiches and salad to chicken, fish and steak dinners. Casual dress; cocktails. **Parking:** on-site. **Cards:** MC, VI.
🍸 ✕

BYRON CENTER pop. 3,777

─── WHERE TO STAY ───

AMERIHOST INN-GRAND RAPIDS SOUTH　　　　　　　　　**Phone:** 616/827-9900
AAA SAVE　　All Year [ECP]　　　1P: $73　　　　2P: $78
♦♦♦♦ ♦♦♦♦　**Location:** US 131, exit 76. Located in a business park. 7625 Caterpillar Ct SW 49548. **Fax:** 616/827-9998.
Small-scale Hotel **Facility:** 61 one-bedroom standard units, some with whirlpools. 2 stories, exterior corridors. *Bath:* combo or shower only. **Parking:** on-site. **Terms:** 30 day cancellation notice. **Amenities:** voice mail, safes (fee), irons, hair dryers. **Pool(s):** heated indoor. **Leisure Activities:** sauna, whirlpool, exercise room. **Guest Services:** valet laundry. **Business Services:** meeting rooms. **Cards:** AX, CB, DC, DS, JC, MC, VI. **Special Amenities:** free continental breakfast and free newspaper.
SOME UNITS
S🅳 ♿ 🏊 ✕ 🎥 📠 ➖ / ✕ 🛄 📷 /

CADILLAC pop. 10,000

─────── **WHERE TO STAY** ───────

BEST WESTERN OF CADILLAC

AAA SAVE

Small-scale Hotel

	1P:	2P:	XP:	
5/23-10/16 [CP]	1P: $109	2P: $109	XP: $5	F17
10/17-3/31 [CP]	1P: $79	2P: $79	XP: $5	F17
4/1-5/22 [CP]	1P: $78	2P: $78	XP: $5	F17

Phone: (231)775-2458

Location: On SR 55, 0.5 mi w of jct SR 115. Located in a semi-commercial area. 5676 E M55 49601 (PO Box 668). Fax: 231/775-8383. **Facility:** 66 one-bedroom standard units. 1 story, exterior corridors. **Parking:** on-site, winter plug-ins. **Terms:** 7 day cancellation notice-fee imposed, pets ($5 extra charge). **Amenities:** irons, hair dryers. **Dining:** 7 am-10 pm, Sun 8 am-6 pm; breakfast hours vary off season, cocktails. **Pool(s):** heated indoor. **Leisure Activities:** sauna, whirlpool, 2 tennis courts, snowmobiling. **Fee:** off-site golf privileges, bowling. **Business Services:** conference facilities. **Cards:** AX, DS, MC, VI. **Special Amenities:** early check-in/late check-out and free continental breakfast.

SOME UNITS

DAYS INN

SAVE
Small-scale Hotel

	1P:	2P:	XP:	
All Year [CP]	1P: $79-$99	2P: $79-$99	XP: $5	

Phone: (231)775-4414

Location: On SR 115, 0.5 mi n of SR 55. Located next to an amusement park. 6001 M-115 49601. Fax: 231/779-0370. **Facility:** 60 one-bedroom standard units. 2 stories (no elevator), interior corridors. **Parking:** on-site, winter plug-ins. **Amenities:** safes (fee), irons, hair dryers. **Pool(s):** heated indoor. **Leisure Activities:** whirlpool, snowmobiling. **Guest Services:** valet laundry. **Business Services:** meeting rooms. **Cards:** AX, CB, DC, DS, MC, VI. *(See color ad card insert)*

SOME UNITS

ECONO LODGE

AAA SAVE
Small-scale Hotel

	1P:	2P:	XP:	
5/30-8/31	1P: $65-$85	2P: $65-$85	XP: $7	F17
9/1-9/30	1P: $55-$75	2P: $55-$75	XP: $7	F17
4/1-5/29 & 10/1-3/31	1P: $50-$65	2P: $50-$70	XP: $7	F17

Phone: (231)775-6700

Location: Jct SR 55 and 115. Located on the main highway. 2501 Sunnyside Dr 49601. Fax: 231/775-8828. **Facility:** 31 one-bedroom standard units. 2 stories (no elevator), interior/exterior corridors. **Parking:** on-site, winter plug-ins. **Leisure Activities:** snowmobiling. **Cards:** AX, DS, MC, VI.

SOME UNITS

HAMPTON INN

SAVE
Small-scale Hotel

	1P:	2P:
All Year	1P: $79-$99	2P: $89-$99

Phone: (231)779-2900

Location: US 131, exit 177, 1 mi n. 1650 S Mitchell St 49601. Fax: 231/779-0846. **Facility:** 120 one-bedroom standard units. 4 stories, interior corridors. **Parking:** on-site. **Terms:** 2 night minimum stay - seasonal, [CP] & [ECP] meal plans available. **Amenities:** video games, dual phone lines, voice mail, irons, hair dryers. **Pool(s):** heated indoor. **Leisure Activities:** whirlpool, snowmobiling. **Guest Services:** valet laundry. **Business Services:** meeting rooms. **Cards:** AX, CB, DC, DS, MC, VI.

SOME UNITS

FEE

HOLIDAY INN EXPRESS

AAA SAVE
Small-scale Hotel

	1P:	2P:	XP:
6/21-9/3	1P: $99-$119	2P: $99-$119	XP: $10
4/1-6/20 & 9/4-1/3	1P: $79-$119	2P: $79-$119	XP: $10
1/4-3/31	1P: $79-$99	2P: $79-$99	XP: $10

Phone: 231/779-4656

Location: US 131, exit 177, 0.7 mi n. Located in a semi-rural area. 7642 S Business US 131 49601. Fax: 231/779-4642. **Facility:** 70 one-bedroom standard units. 3 stories, interior corridors. **Bath:** combo or shower only. **Parking:** on-site. **Terms:** [CP] meal plan available. **Amenities:** dual phone lines, voice mail, irons, hair dryers. **Pool(s):** heated indoor. **Leisure Activities:** whirlpool, snowmobiling, exercise room. **Guest Services:** valet and coin laundry. **Business Services:** meeting rooms. **Cards:** AX, CB, DC, DS, MC, VI.

SOME UNITS

MCGUIRES RESORT

Phone: (231)775-9947

5/10-8/10	1P: $89-$189	2P: $99-$189	XP: $20 F18
8/11-10/12	1P: $79-$169	2P: $89-$189	XP: $20 F18
10/13-3/31	1P: $69-$159	2P: $89-$189	XP: $20 F18
4/1-5/9	1P: $69-$149	2P: $79-$149	XP: $20 F18

(AAA) (SAVE)

Resort
Large-scale Hotel

Location: US 131, exit 177, 0.7 mi n, then 0.5 mi w. Located in a semi-rural area. 7880 Mackinaw Tr 49601. **Fax:** 231/775-9621. **Facility:** A variety of rooms, some with patios, is offered at this resort set on spacious grounds. 122 units. 119 one-bedroom standard units, some with whirlpools. 3 one-bedroom suites, some with whirlpools. 2-3 stories (no elevator), interior/exterior corridors. *Bath:* combo or shower only. **Parking:** on-site. **Terms:** check-in 4 pm, 7 day cancellation notice, package plans, pets ($15 extra charge, in smoking units). **Amenities:** irons, hair dryers. **Dining:** 2 restaurants, 7 am-10 pm, Sun-8 pm; to 9 pm 9/15-5/15, cocktails. **Pool(s):** heated indoor. **Leisure Activities:** sauna, whirlpool, snowmobiling, tobogganing, ski shop, exercise trail, basketball, horseshoes, shuffleboard, volleyball. *Fee:* golf-27 holes, 2 lighted tennis courts, cross country skiing, cross country skis & snowshoes, game room. **Guest Services:** gift shop, valet laundry. **Business Services:** conference facilities. **Cards:** AX, DC, DS, MC, VI. **Special Amenities:** free local telephone calls. *(See color ad p 212)*

SOME UNITS

[amenity icons]   FEE   FEE

SUNSET SHORES RESORT

Phone: (231)876-3700

All Year   1P: $139-$169

Condominium

Location: US 131, exit 176, 2.3 mi nw on SR 115, then 1.1 mi ne. Located on the waters edge. 1246 Sunnyside Dr 49601 (PO Box 154). **Facility:** Smoke free premises. 22 units. 12 two- and 10 three-bedroom suites with kitchens. 3 stories (no elevator), interior corridors. **Parking:** on-site, winter plug-ins. **Terms:** 7 day cancellation notice. **Amenities:** voice mail. *Some:* irons. **Leisure Activities:** boat dock, fishing, snowmobiling. **Guest Services:** complimentary laundry. **Cards:** DS, MC, VI.

[amenity icons]

WHERE TO DINE

HERMANN'S EUROPEAN CAFE & INN

Lunch: $7-$11   **Dinner:** $17-$22   **Phone:** 231/775-9563

(AAA)

American

Location: Center. 214 N Mitchell St 49601. **Hours:** 11 am-9:30 pm, Fri & Sat-10 pm. Closed: 1/1, 11/27, 12/25; also Sun & 12/24 for dinner. **Features:** The Austrian chef-owner prepares an interesting array of European dishes, such as schnitzel, wild boar, pork loin and apple strudel. Couples favor the quiet restaurant for moderately upscale fine dining. Attentive servers provide good follow-up. Casual dress; cocktails. **Parking:** street. **Cards:** DS, MC, VI.

[icon]

LAKESIDE CHARLIES

Lunch: $5-$7   **Dinner:** $10-$17   **Phone:** 231/775-5332

American

Location: Jct SR 55 and 115. 301 S Lake Mitchell 49601. **Hours:** 11:30 am-9 pm, Fri & Sat-10 pm, Sun-8 pm; 11:30 am-10 pm, Fri & Sat-11 pm, Sun-8 pm 6/1-9/6. Closed: 11/27, 12/25. **Reservations:** suggested. **Features:** Overlooking Lake Mitchell, the restaurant has three dining rooms decorated with hunting and fishing memorabilia and various antiques. The focus of the menu is on beef and seafood. The basic ice cream fudge sundae is hard to beat. Casual dress; cocktails. **Parking:** on-site. **Cards:** AX, DS, MC, VI.

[icons]

CALUMET pop. 879

WHERE TO STAY

AMERICINN OF CALUMET

Phone: (906)337-6463

7/1-10/31 & 1/1-3/31 [ECP]	1P: $78	2P: $83	XP: $5 F12
4/1-6/30 & 11/1-12/31 [ECP]	1P: $73	2P: $78	XP: $5 F12

Small-scale Hotel

Location: US 41; just w of Visitors Center. Located next to Mine St Station Complex. 56925 S Sixth St 49913. **Fax:** 906/337-4990. **Facility:** 68 units. 66 one-bedroom standard units, some with whirlpools. 2 one-bedroom suites ($83-$138), some with whirlpools. 2 stories (no elevator), interior corridors. *Bath:* combo or shower only. **Parking:** on-site, winter plug-ins. **Terms:** 5 day cancellation notice. **Amenities:** hair dryers. *Some:* irons. **Pool(s):** heated indoor. **Leisure Activities:** sauna, whirlpool, snowmobiling. *Fee:* game room. **Guest Services:** coin laundry. **Business Services:** meeting rooms. **Cards:** AX, DC, DS, MC, VI.

SOME UNITS

[amenity icons]

CANTON —See Detroit p. 249.

CARP LAKE

WHERE TO DINE

The following restaurant has not been evaluated by AAA but is listed for your information only.

GOLDIES CAFE

Phone: 231/537-4089

[fyi]

Not evaluated. **Location:** Just e of US 31; center. 6492 Paradise Tr 49718. **Features:** On Paradise Lake, the restaurant presents a menu of home-style specialties. Diners can request inside or deck seating.

CASCADE —See also GRAND RAPIDS.

WHERE TO STAY

BAYMONT INN-GRAND RAPIDS AIRPORT

Phone: (616)956-3300

All Year   1P: $67   2P: $99   XP: $10   F18

(AAA) (SAVE)

Small-scale Hotel

Location: I-96, exit 43B, just e. Located in a commercial area. 2873 Kraft Ave SE 49512. **Fax:** 616/956-5561. **Facility:** 102 one-bedroom standard units. 3 stories, interior corridors. **Parking:** on-site. **Terms:** weekly rates available, [ECP] meal plan available, package plans. **Amenities:** video games, voice mail, irons, hair dryers. **Guest Services:** valet and coin laundry. **Business Services:** meeting rooms. **Cards:** AX, CB, DC, DS, MC, VI. **Special Amenities:** free continental breakfast and free newspaper.

SOME UNITS

COUNTRY HEARTH SUITES

Phone: (616)940-1777

▼▼ ▼▼▼

Small-scale Hotel

All Year   1P: $55-$85   2P: $55-$85

Location: I-96, exit 43B, just e. Located in a commercial area. 2985 Kraft Ave SE 49512. Fax: 616/940-9809. **Facility:** 40 one-bedroom standard units. 2 stories, interior corridors. **Parking:** on-site. **Terms:** [CP] meal plan available, pets ($10 fee, $20 deposit, in designated units). **Amenities:** irons, hair dryers. **Guest Services:** valet and coin laundry. **Cards:** AX, DC, MC, VI.

(ASK) (S/D) 🐕 (¶¶+) (🍴+) 🖥 (DATA PORT) 🖨 🖳 🖵
FEE

COUNTRY INN & SUITES BY CARLSON

Phone: (616)977-0909

▼▼▼ ▼▼▼

Small-scale Hotel

All Year   1P: $65-$85   2P: $70-$90

Location: I-96, exit 43B, just e on SR 11. Located next to a shopping center. 5399 28th St 49512. Fax: 616/977-0909. **Facility:** 61 units. 51 one-bedroom standard units. 10 one-bedroom suites. 3 stories, interior corridors. *Bath:* combo or shower only. **Parking:** on-site. **Terms:** [ECP] meal plan available, small pets only (in smoking units). **Amenities:** voice mail, irons, hair dryers. **Pool(s):** heated indoor. **Leisure Activities:** whirlpool. **Guest Services:** valet laundry. **Cards:** AX, CB, DC, DS, MC, VI. **(See color ad p 243)**

SOME UNITS

(ASK) (S/D) 🐕 (¶¶+) (&M) 🖥 🌀 🏊 (🍴+) 🎬 (DATA PORT) 🖳 / ✕ 🖨 🖵 /
FEE

CROWNE PLAZA HOTEL GRAND RAPIDS

Phone: (616)957-1770

▼▼▼ ▼▼▼

Large-scale Hotel

All Year   1P: $134-$168   2P: $134-$168   XP: $18   F18

Location: I-96, exit 43B, 0.3 mi e on SR 11. Located in a commercial area. 5700 28th St SE 49546 (5700 28th St SE, GRAND RAPIDS). Fax: 616/957-0629. **Facility:** 320 units. 316 one-bedroom standard units. 4 one-bedroom suites ($275-$300). 5 stories, interior corridors. *Bath:* combo or shower only. **Parking:** on-site. **Terms:** check-in 4 pm, cancellation fee imposed. **Amenities:** video games, voice mail, irons, hair dryers. *Some:* high-speed Internet. **Pool(s):** heated indoor/outdoor. **Leisure Activities:** sauna, whirlpool, exercise room. **Guest Services:** gift shop, valet and coin laundry, area transportation. **Business Services:** conference facilities, business center. **Cards:** AX, CB, DC, DS, JC, MC, VI.

SOME UNITS

(ASK) (S/D) ✈ (¶¶) 🍷 🖥 🌀 🏊 ✕ 🎬 (DATA PORT) 🖳 / ✕ 🖨 🖵 /

DAYS INN AIRPORT

Phone: (616)949-8400

(AAA) (SAVE)
▼▼ ▼▼
Small-scale Hotel

All Year [ECP]   1P: $59-$89   2P: $65-$95   XP: $6   F18

Location: I-96, exit 43B, just e on SR 11. Located opposite Meijer's Shopping Center. 5500 28th St SE 49512. Fax: 616/949-9021. **Facility:** 140 one-bedroom standard units. 2 stories, interior corridors. **Parking:** on-site. **Amenities:** voice mail, hair dryers. *Some:* irons. **Pool(s):** heated indoor. **Leisure Activities:** sauna, whirlpool, exercise room. **Guest Services:** valet and coin laundry, airport transportation-Gerald R Ford International Airport. **Business Services:** meeting rooms. **Cards:** AX, DC, DS, MC, VI.

(See color ad card insert)

SOME UNITS

(S/D) ✈ (¶¶+) 🏊 ✕ 🎬 🖳 / ✕ (DATA PORT) 🖨 🖵 /

EXEL INN OF GRAND RAPIDS

Phone: (616)957-3000

(AAA) (SAVE)
▼▼ ▼▼
Small-scale Hotel

6/1-9/30 [CP]   1P: $44-$60   2P: $50-$66   XP: $6   F18
4/1-5/31 & 10/1-3/31 [CP]   1P: $40-$52   2P: $46-$58   XP: $6   F18

Location: I-96, exit 43A, 0.5 mi w on SR 11. Located in a commercial area. 4855 28th St SE 49512 (4855 28th St SE, GRAND RAPIDS). Fax: 616/957-0194. **Facility:** 109 one-bedroom standard units, some with whirlpools. 2 stories (no elevator), interior corridors. **Parking:** on-site. **Terms:** small pets only. **Amenities:** irons, hair dryers. **Leisure Activities:** exercise room. **Guest Services:** coin laundry. **Cards:** AX, CB, DC, DS, MC, VI.
Special Amenities: early check-in/late check-out and free continental breakfast. *(See color ad p 300)*

SOME UNITS

(S/D) 🐕 (¶¶+) 🎬 (DATA PORT) 🖳 / ✕ 🖨 🖵 /

HAMPTON INN

Phone: (616)956-9304

(SAVE)
▼▼ ▼▼▼
Small-scale Hotel

All Year [ECP]   1P: $81-$89   2P: $86-$94

Location: I-96, exit 43A, 0.5 mi w on SR 11. Located in a commercial area, next to a movie theater. 4981 28th St SE 49512 (4981 28th St SE, GRAND RAPIDS). Fax: 616/956-6617. **Facility:** 119 one-bedroom standard units. 2 stories, interior corridors. **Parking:** on-site. **Terms:** small pets only. **Amenities:** video games, voice mail, irons. **Pool(s):** outdoor. **Leisure Activities:** exercise room. **Guest Services:** valet laundry. **Business Services:** meeting rooms. **Cards:** AX, DC, DS, MC, VI. **(See color ad p 301)**

SOME UNITS

(S/D) 🐕 (¶¶+) 🌀 🏊 🎬 (DATA PORT) 🖳 / ✕ 🖨 /

LEXINGTON HOTEL SUITES

Phone: (616)940-8100

(AAA) (SAVE)
▼▼ ▼▼
Small-scale Hotel

All Year [ECP]   1P: $79-$89   2P: $86-$96   XP: $7   F17

Location: I-96, exit 43B, just e on SR 11. Located next to Meijer's Shopping Center. 5401 28th St Ct SE 49546 (5401 28th St Ct SE, GRAND RAPIDS). Fax: 616/940-0914. **Facility:** 121 one-bedroom standard units. 3 stories, interior corridors. **Parking:** on-site. **Amenities:** voice mail, irons, hair dryers. **Pool(s):** heated indoor. **Leisure Activities:** whirlpool, exercise room. **Guest Services:** coin laundry, airport transportation-Gerald R Ford Airport. **Business Services:** meeting rooms. **Cards:** AX, DC, DS, JC, MC, VI.

SOME UNITS

(S/D) ✈ (¶¶+) 🏊 🎬 (DATA PORT) 🖨 🖳 🖵 / ✕ /

RED ROOF INN

Phone: (616)942-0800

(AAA) (SAVE)
▼▼ ▼▼
Motel

All Year   1P: $48-$61   2P: $54-$67   XP: $6

Location: I-96, exit 43A, 0.3 mi w on SR 11. Located in a busy commercial area. 5131 28th St 49512 (5131 28th St, GRAND RAPIDS). Fax: 616/942-8341. **Facility:** 107 one-bedroom standard units. 2 stories, exterior corridors. *Bath:* combo or shower only. **Parking:** on-site. **Amenities:** video games, voice mail. **Cards:** AX, CB, DC, DS, MC, VI. **Special Amenities: free local telephone calls and free newspaper.**

SOME UNITS

(¶¶+) 🖥 🎬 (DATA PORT) / ✕ /

—— WHERE TO DINE ——

The following restaurant has not been evaluated by AAA —— but is listed for your information only.

NOTO'S   Phone: 616/493-6686

Not evaluated. **Location:** I-96, exit 43B, 1.5 mi e on SR 11. 6600 28th St SE 49546. **Features:** The upscale restaurant serves steak, chops and seafood with fine Italian wines and homemade-style desserts.

CASEVILLE pop. 888

—— WHERE TO DINE ——

BAY WINDOW   **Lunch:** $4-$6   **Dinner:** $6-$16   Phone: 989/856-2676

Location: Center. 6750 Main St 48725. **Hours:** 6 am-8 pm, Sat & Sun-9 pm. Closed: 11/27, 12/25.
Features: Burgers, steak, seafood and pasta make up the bulk of the family restaurant's classic menu. An outdoorsy decor, with fish and wildlife, punctuates the relaxed dining room. The summer patio is popular in season. For dessert, have a slice of homemade pie. Casual dress. **Parking:** street. **Cards:** DS, MC, VI.
American   ⊠

SHAKERS   **Lunch:** $4-$7   **Dinner:** $4-$7   Phone: 989/856-2663
Location: Center. 6685 Main St 48725. **Hours:** 8 am-8 pm, Fri & Sat-10 pm. Closed major holidays.
Features: A bright red and white roadside diner that along with an ice cream bar serves such favorites as
American   hamburgers and sandwiches. Casual dress. **Parking:** on-site.   ⊠

CEDARVILLE

—— WHERE TO STAY ——

CEDARVILLE INN   Phone: 906/484-2266
         6/26-9/1 [CP]   1P: $99-$139   2P: $99-$139   XP: $10   F18
         9/2-3/31 [CP]   1P: $79-$109   2P: $79-$109   XP: $10   F18
Motel   4/1-6/25 [CP]   1P: $79-$99   2P: $79-$99   XP: $10   F18
Location: On SR 134, just w of SR 129. Located on the main highway. 106 W M-134 49719 (PO Box 189).
Fax: 906/484-3066. **Facility:** 49 one-bedroom standard units, some with whirlpools. 2 stories (no elevator), interior corridors.
Parking: on-site, winter plug-ins. **Terms:** package plans, 9% service charge, pets (in limited units). **Amenities:** video library
(fee). *Some:* irons, hair dryers. **Pool(s):** heated indoor. **Leisure Activities:** whirlpool, snowmobiling, exercise room. *Fee:* game
room. **Guest Services:** coin laundry. **Business Services:** meeting rooms. **Cards:** AX, DC, DS, MC, VI.

SOME UNITS
(ASK) ⧅ 🛁 🍽 🛬 ⊠ 📽 [DATA PORT] 🖥 / ⊠ [VCR] 📞 📷 /
FEE

CENTRAL LAKE pop. 990

—— WHERE TO DINE ——

MURPHY'S LAMPLIGHT INN   **Dinner:** $9-$19   Phone: 231/544-6443
Location: On SR 88; center. 2535 N Main St 49622. **Hours:** 5 pm-9 pm; hours may vary seasonally. Closed:
Mon-Wed 11/1-5/31. **Reservations:** suggested. **Features:** Hand-cut steaks and fresh local seafood are the
Steak & Seafood   menu's focus. Fireplaces, artwork and pottery lend to the turn-of-the-20th-century atmosphere of the dining
room. Finish off your meal with a slice of delicious Kentucky Derby pie or a hot fudge sundae. Cocktails.
Parking: on-site. **Cards:** AX, DS, MC, VI.   🍸 ⊠

CHARLEVOIX pop. 2,994

─── **WHERE TO STAY** ───

SLEEP INN   **Phone:** (231)547-0300
SAVE   6/17-9/3 [ECP]   1P: $125   2P: $135   XP: $10   F16
                4/1-6/16 & 9/4-3/31 [ECP]   1P: $80   2P: $90   XP: $10   F16
♦♦♦ ♦♦♦   **Location:** 1 mi n on US 31. Located in a commercial area. 800 Petoskey Ave 49720. Fax: 231/547-3995. **Facility:** 62
Small-scale Hotel one-bedroom standard units. 3 stories, interior corridors. *Bath:* combo or shower only. **Parking:** on-site.
                Terms: 2 night minimum stay - weekends, cancellation fee imposed, pets ($25 deposit). **Amenities:** *Some:*
CB, DC, DS, MC, VI. irons. **Pool(s):** heated indoor. **Leisure Activities:** whirlpool. **Business Services:** meeting rooms. **Cards:** AX,

SOME UNITS
Ⓢ🅳 🛏 🕽➕ 🖥 ➿ 🎦 📠 / ✕ 📺 /

WEATHERVANE TERRACE INN & SUITES   **Phone:** (231)547-9955
ⒶⒶⒶ **SAVE**   All Year   1P: $55-$239   2P: $55-$239   XP: $5   F17
♦♦♦ ♦♦♦   **Location:** Just off US 31; at Harbor Bridge. Located in a commercial area. 111 Pine River Ln 49720.
Motel   Fax: 231/547-0070. **Facility:** 68 units. 41 one-bedroom standard units, some with efficiencies and/or whirl-
                pools. 27 one-bedroom suites ($85-$239), some with efficiencies, kitchens and/or whirlpools. 2-3 stories, ex-
                terior corridors. *Bath:* combo or shower only. **Parking:** on-site, winter plug-ins. **Terms:** check-in 4 pm, 7 day
                cancellation notice-fee imposed, [ECP] meal plan available. **Amenities:** video library (fee), irons, hair dryers.
Pool(s): heated outdoor. **Leisure Activities:** whirlpool. **Business Services:** meeting rooms. **Cards:** AX, DC, DS, MC, VI.
Special Amenities: free continental breakfast and free local telephone calls. *(See color ad below)*

SOME UNITS
🕽➕ ➿ 📼 🎦 📠 🖬 📠 / ✕ 📺 /

Weathervane Terrace Inn & Suites

Email: wvane@freeway.net   www.weathervane-chx.com

Suites w/ Lake Michigan views, jacuzzis & fireplaces

Standard rooms with refrigerators & VCRs

FREE deluxe continental breakfast

Hot tub spa tower & swimming pool

1/2 block to downtown shopping & dining

Golf courses & ski resorts nearby

Special package rates available

800-552-0025 · 231-547-9955

111 Pine River Lane, Charlevoix, Michigan 49720

GREY GABLES INN

♦♦♦ American

Dinner: $13-$20 **Phone:** 231/547-9261

Location: Just e of US 31. 308 Belvedere Ave 49720. **Hours:** 5 pm-10 pm, Fri & Sat-11 pm. **Closed:** Sun & Mon. **Reservations:** suggested. **Features:** Pork chops, veal, lobster, prime-graded meat and pasta are among the dishes on the restaurant's varied menu. Well-prepared whitefish is a house specialty. Seating is offered in four rooms of the Victorian house. In-house desserts are tempting. Casual dress; cocktails. **Parking:** street. **Cards:** AX, MC, VI.

🍸 ✕

STAFFORD'S WEATHERVANE RESTAURANT

♦♦♦ American

Lunch: $7-$12 **Dinner:** $15-$39 **Phone:** 231/547-4311

Location: US 31 at Pine River Bridge; downtown. 106 Pine River Ln 49720. **Hours:** 11 am-3 & 4:30-10 pm. **Closed:** 12/25. **Reservations:** accepted. **Features:** Weathervane scallops and planked whitefish stand out on a menu of mostly steak and seafood selections. The nautical theme is evident in the dining room decor, as well as in the seagull-shaped roof of the building itself. Families are welcomed. Casual dress; cocktails. **Parking:** on-site. **Cards:** AX, DS, MC, VI.

🍸 ✕

CHARLOTTE pop. 8,389

COMFORT INN

SAVE

♦♦♦ Small-scale Hotel

			Phone: (517)543-7307
5/2-10/31 [ECP]	1P: $79-$99	2P: $79-$99	XP: $5 F12
4/1-5/1 & 11/1-3/31 [ECP]	1P: $69-$99	2P: $69-$99	XP: $5 F12

Location: I-69, exit 61 (Lansing Rd), 0.5 mi e. 1302 E Packard Hwy 48813. **Fax:** 517/543-7311. **Facility:** Smoke free premises. 61 one-bedroom standard units, some with whirlpools. 3 stories, interior corridors. *Bath:* combo or shower only. **Parking:** on-site. **Terms:** 7 day cancellation notice. **Amenities:** voice mail, irons, hair dryers. **Pool(s):** heated indoor. **Guest Services:** coin laundry. **Business Services:** meeting rooms. **Cards:** AX, CB, DC, DS, MC, VI.

SOME UNITS
🅂🄳 🄼 🐾 🎥 📠 💻 / ✕ 🛗 🖵 /

HOLIDAY INN EXPRESS & SUITES

AAA SAVE

♦♦♦ Small-scale Hotel

			Phone: (517)541-5000
All Year	1P: $79-$150	2P: $79-$150	XP: $7

Location: I-69, exit 60, just e on SR 50. Located adjacent to Meijer Shopping Mall. 500 Meijer St 48813. **Fax:** 517/541-0000. **Facility:** Smoke free premises. 67 one-bedroom standard units, some with whirlpools. 3 stories, interior corridors. *Bath:* combo or shower only. **Parking:** on-site. **Terms:** [CP] meal plan available. **Amenities:** dual phone lines, voice mail, irons, hair dryers. **Pool(s):** heated indoor. **Leisure Activities:** whirlpool, exercise room. **Guest Services:** coin laundry. **Business Services:** meeting rooms. **Cards:** AX, CB, DC, DS, JC, MC, VI. **Special Amenities:** free continental breakfast and free local telephone calls.

SOME UNITS
🅂🄳 🄼 🐾 🎥 📠 / ✕ 🛗 🖵 💻 /

SUPER 8 MOTEL

AAA SAVE

♦♦ Resort Small-scale Hotel

			Phone: (517)543-8288
5/1-3/31 [ECP]	1P: $54-$60	2P: $63-$70	XP: $10 F12
4/1-4/30 [ECP]	1P: $42-$45	2P: $45-$50	XP: $10 F12

Location: I-69, exit 60, just w on SR 50. 828 E Shepherd St 48813. **Fax:** 517/543-8481. **Facility:** 50 one-bedroom standard units, some with whirlpools. 2 stories, interior corridors. **Parking:** on-site. **Terms:** small pets only. **Business Services:** meeting rooms. **Cards:** AX, DC, DS, MC, VI. **Special Amenities:** free continental breakfast and free local telephone calls.

SOME UNITS
🎲 🅂🄳 🛏 🎥 📠 / ✕ 🛗 🖵 /

THE GAVEL

♦ American

Lunch: $4-$6 **Dinner:** $8-$10 **Phone:** 517/543-1620

Location: I-69, exit 61 (Lansing Rd), jct of Lansing Rd and Cochran St; downtown. 112 S Cochran 48813. **Hours:** 7 am-9:30 pm, Fri-11 pm. **Closed** major holidays; also Sun. **Features:** Wide storefront windows are a good spot for people watching at this neighborhood eatery. Casual dress; cocktails. **Parking:** street. **Cards:** AX, MC, VI.

🄼 🍸 ✕

CHEBOYGAN pop. 5,295

BEST WESTERN RIVER TERRACE MOTEL

AAA SAVE

♦♦♦ Motel

			Phone: (231)627-5688
	1P: $68-$137	2P: $88-$147	XP: $10 F12
4/1-6/19 & 9/1-3/31	1P: $48-$98	2P: $58-$137	XP: $10 F12

Location: 1 mi s on SR 27. 847 S Main St 49721. **Fax:** 231/627-2472. **Facility:** 53 one-bedroom standard units, some with whirlpools. 2 stories (no elevator), interior/exterior corridors. **Parking:** on-site. **Amenities:** voice mail, irons, hair dryers. **Pool(s):** heated indoor. **Leisure Activities:** whirlpool, boat dock, exercise room. **Cards:** AX, CB, DS, MC, VI. **Special Amenities:** early check-in/late check-out. *(See color ad p 218)*

SOME UNITS
🛗📶 🐾 ✕ 🎥 📠 💻 / ✕ /

BIRCH HAUS MOTEL

AAA **SAVE**

Motel

	1P: $30-$45	2P: $40-$55	**Phone: (231)627-5862**
All Year [CP]	1P: $30-$45	2P: $40-$55	XP: $5 F12

Location: On US 23, 0.8 mi nw. 1301 Mackinaw Ave 49721. **Facility:** 13 units. 12 one- and 1 two-bedroom standard units. 1 story, exterior corridors. **Parking:** on-site, winter plug-ins. **Terms:** cancellation fee imposed, small pets only ($5 extra charge). **Leisure Activities:** snowmobiling. **Cards:** AX, DS, MC, VI. **Special Amenities:** free continental breakfast and free local telephone calls.

SOME UNITS

🐕 📹 🔒 / ✕ /

CONTINENTAL INN

Phone: 231/627-7164

Motel

Property failed to provide current rates

Location: At jct US 23 and SR 27. 613 N Main St 49721. Fax: 231/627-8753. **Facility:** 42 units. 22 one- and 20 two-bedroom standard units. 2 stories, exterior corridors. *Bath:* combo or shower only. **Parking:** on-site. **Terms:** open 5/1-10/15. **Amenities:** hair dryers. **Pool(s):** heated outdoor. **Cards:** AX, CB, DC, DS, MC, VI.

SOME UNITS

🍴 ♿ 🏊 📠 / ✕ 🔒 🖥 /
FEE FEE

DAYS INN

SAVE

Small-scale Hotel

	1P:	2P:	**Phone: (231)627-3126**
6/27-8/31 [CP]	1P: $49-$150	2P: $49-$150	XP: $5 F21
4/1-6/26 & 9/1-3/31 [CP]	1P: $42-$98	2P: $42-$98	XP: $5 F21

Location: On SR 27, 1.3 mi s. 889 S Main St 49721. Fax: 231/627-2889. **Facility:** 42 one-bedroom standard units, some with whirlpools. 2 stories (no elevator), interior corridors. **Parking:** on-site, winter plug-ins. **Terms:** 3 day cancellation notice. **Amenities:** voice mail, hair dryers. **Leisure Activities:** boat dock, fishing. **Cards:** AX, CB, DC, DS, MC, VI. *(See color ad card insert)*

SOME UNITS

🆂 🍴 ⌂M 📠 / ✕ 🔒 🖥 🖥 /

PINE RIVER MOTEL

AAA **SAVE**

Motel

		2P:	**Phone: 231/627-5119**
6/16-9/30		2P: $45-$65	XP: $5 F12
10/1-3/31		2P: $30-$60	XP: $5 F12
4/1-6/15		2P: $30-$50	XP: $5 F12

Location: 0.5 mi e on US 23. 102 Lafayette 49721. **Facility:** 15 one-bedroom standard units. 1 story, exterior corridors. *Bath:* combo or shower only. **Parking:** on-site, winter plug-ins. **Terms:** 3 day cancellation notice, weekly rates available, package plans, pets ($10 extra charge). **Leisure Activities:** snowmobiling. **Cards:** DS, MC, VI. **Special Amenities:** free local telephone calls and preferred room (subject to availability with advanced reservations).

SOME UNITS

🆂 🐕 🍴 📹 / ✕ 🔒 /

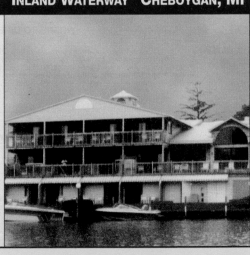

------ **WHERE TO DINE** ------

THE BOATHOUSE   **Lunch:** $6-$9   **Dinner:** $14-$19   **Phone:** 231/627-4316
♦♦♦ ♦♦♦
                    Location: Center. 106 Pine St 49721. **Hours:** 11 am-10 pm, Sat from 4 pm, Sun-8 pm. **Closed:** 12/25; also
                    Mon-Wed in winter. **Reservations:** suggested. **Features:** Representative of menu selections is the flavorful
American   honey-pecan walleye, which is sauteed in honey and sprinkled with pecans. The converted former
                    boathouse was built by a Purple Gang member in the 1930s to run whiskey from Canada during
Prohibition. Casual dress; cocktails. **Parking:** on-site. **Cards:** AX, DC, DS, MC, VI.

HACK-MA-TACK INN   Historic   **Dinner:** $19-$29   **Phone:** 231/625-2919
△△△
                    Location: 3.3 mi s on SR 27, 0.3 mi e on US 33, then 2 mi sw, follow signs. 8131 Beebe Rd 49721. **Hours:** Open
♦♦♦ ♦♦♦   5/1-10/15; 5 pm-10 pm. **Features:** This historic 1894 log lodge overlooks the Cheboygan River, sitting
American   amid a mature cedar, pine and birch setting. Rustic appointments, a moosehead mounted on a stone
                    fireplace, a canoe and racing boat hanging from the log rafters all add to the ambience. Prime rib and
                    whitefish are house specialties. Casual dress; cocktails. **Parking:** on-site. **Cards:** AX, DC, DS, MC, VI.

CHELSEA pop. 4,398

------ **WHERE TO STAY** ------

CHELSEA COMFORT INN & CONFERENCE CENTER   **Phone:** 734/433-8000
[SAVE]   All Year   1P: $89-$129   2P: $89-$129   XP: $10   F17
                    Location: I-94, exit 159, just n. 1645 Commerce Park Dr 48118. Fax: 743/433-9565. **Facility:** 84 units. 82 one- and
♦♦♦♦♦   2 two-bedroom standard units, some with whirlpools. 3 stories, interior corridors. *Bath:* combo or shower only.
Small-scale Hotel   **Parking:** on-site. **Terms:** cancellation fee imposed, [CP] & [ECP] meal plans available. **Amenities:** dual
                    phone lines, voice mail, irons, hair dryers. **Pool(s):** heated indoor. **Leisure Activities:** whirlpool, exercise
DC, DS, MC, VI.   room. **Guest Services:** valet laundry. **Business Services:** conference facilities, business center. **Cards:** AX,

SOME UNITS

HOLIDAY INN EXPRESS   **Phone:** 734/433-1600
♦♦♦♦   All Year [ECP]   1P: $79-$109   2P: $79-$109   XP: $8   F18
                    Location: I-94, exit 159, 0.3 mi n. 1540 Commerce Park Dr 48118. Fax: 734/433-1600. **Facility:** 65 one-bedroom
Small-scale Hotel   standard units. 3 stories, interior corridors. *Bath:* combo or shower only. **Parking:** on-site. **Amenities:** dual
                    phone lines, voice mail, irons, hair dryers. *Some:* CD players. **Pool(s):** heated indoor. **Leisure Activi-
ties:** exercise room. **Guest Services:** valet laundry. **Cards:** AX, CB, DC, DS, JC, MC, VI.

SOME UNITS

------ **WHERE TO DINE** ------

THE COMMON GRILL   **Lunch:** $8-$12   **Dinner:** $16-$22   **Phone:** 734/475-0681
♦♦♦♦
                    Location: I-94, exit 159, 2 mi n. 112 S Main St 48118. **Hours:** 11 am-10 pm. Closed major holidays; also Mon.
American   **Features:** This busy eatery has a trendy look and an imaginative menu. They serve American food, and
                    use exotic spices to give it a new twist. The owner constantly searches the markets of such cities as Los
                    Angeles and San Francisco, to bring back fresh new recipes. Casual dress; cocktails. **Parking:** on-site.
Cards: AX, MC, VI.

CHESANING pop. 2,548

------ **WHERE TO STAY** ------

COLONIAL MOTEL   **Phone:** (989)845-3292
△△△ [SAVE]   4/1-10/31   1P: $48-$54   2P: $68-$130   XP: $10   F12
                    11/1-3/31   1P: $45-$51   2P: $58-$99
♦♦♦ ♦♦♦   **Location:** 0.5 mi e on SR 57. 9475 E M-57 48616. Fax: 989/845-3230. **Facility:** 14 one-bedroom standard units,
Motel   some with whirlpools. 1 story, exterior corridors. **Parking:** on-site. **Terms:** 3 day cancellation notice-fee im-
                    posed, [CP] meal plan available. **Cards:** DS, MC, VI. **Special Amenities: free continental breakfast and
                    free local telephone calls.**

SOME UNITS

------ **WHERE TO DINE** ------

CHESANING HERITAGE HOUSE   Historic   **Lunch:** $7-$14   **Dinner:** $11-$21   **Phone:** 989/845-7700
♦♦♦ ♦♦♦
                    Location: Center. 605 W Broad St 48616. **Hours:** 11 am-9 pm, Fri & Sat-10 pm, Sun noon-9 pm. **Closed:**
American   12/24, 12/25. **Features:** In the historic district, the 1908 Southern-style home boasts three glassed-in
                    porches and loads of cozy charm. Menu selections include ample portions of seafood, tenderloin, prime rib
DS, MC, VI.   and pork specialties. Service is friendly and efficient. Casual dress; cocktails. **Parking:** on-site. **Cards:** AX,

CLARE pop. 3,000

CLARKSTON —See Detroit p. 250.

CLAWSON —See Detroit p. 250.

COLDWATER pop. 12,697

―――― WHERE TO STAY ――――

CHICAGO PIKE INN   **Phone:** 517/279-8744
▼▼▼▼   All Year [BP]   1P: $100-$195   2P: $100-$195   XP: $20
           Location: I-69, exit 13, 0.8 mi w. 215 E Chicago St (US 12) 49036. Fax: 517/278-8597. **Facility:** Stained-glass windows are among the vintage details at this 1903 Victorian inn, which also boasts latter-day conveniences.
Historic Bed   Designated smoking area. 8 units. 7 one-bedroom standard units, some with whirlpools. 1 one-bedroom suite
& Breakfast   ($165-$195). 2 stories (no elevator), interior corridors. *Bath:* combo or shower only. **Parking:** on-site.
Terms: age restrictions may apply, 7 day cancellation notice-fee imposed. **Leisure Activities:** bicycles. **Guest Services:** gift
shop. **Cards:** AX, DS, MC, VI.

SOME UNITS

⊠ / ⟨AC⟩ ⟨VCR⟩ 🛢 🖵 /

HOLIDAY INN EXPRESS   **Phone:** (517)279-0900
▼▼▼▼   All Year [ECP]   1P: $79-$129   2P: $79-$129   XP: $6   F19
           Location: I-69, exit 13, just sw. 630 E Chicago St 49036. Fax: 517/278-3775. **Facility:** 80 units. 76 one-bedroom
Small-scale Hotel   standard units, some with whirlpools. 4 one-bedroom suites. 3 stories, interior corridors. *Bath:* combo or
           shower only. **Parking:** on-site. **Amenities:** dual phone lines, voice mail, irons, hair dryers. **Pool(s):** heated
indoor. **Leisure Activities:** whirlpool, exercise room. **Guest Services:** valet and coin laundry. **Business Services:** meeting
rooms. **Cards:** AX, DC, DS, MC, VI. *(See color ad below & card insert)*

SOME UNITS

⟨ASK⟩ 🆂🅳 ⟨&M⟩ ⟨&⟩ 🏊 ⟨🎥⟩ ⟨DATA PORT⟩ / ⊠ 🛢 🖵 /
                                                          FEE

RAMADA INN   **Phone:** (517)278-2017
⟨AAA⟩ ⟨SAVE⟩   All Year   1P: $59-$199   2P: $59-$199   XP: $6   F18
▼▼▼ ▼▼▼   **Location:** I-69, exit 13, 0.3 mi w on E Chicago St (US 12), just n on N Michigan Ave, then just e. 1000 Orleans Blvd
           49036. Fax: 517/279-7214. **Facility:** 128 units. 90 one-bedroom standard units, some with whirlpools. 38 one-
Small-scale Hotel   bedroom suites ($79-$199), some with kitchens and/or whirlpools. 2 stories, interior corridors. **Parking:** on-
           site. **Terms:** cancellation imposed, small pets only. **Amenities:** voice mail, safes, irons, hair dryers.
Dining: 6:30 am-11 & 5-9 pm, Sun-noon, cocktails. **Pool(s):** heated indoor. **Leisure Activities:** whirlpool,
exercise room. **Fee:** game room. **Guest Services:** coin laundry. **Business Services:** meeting rooms, fax (fee). **Cards:** AX, CB,
DC, DS, JC, MC, VI. **Special Amenities:** early check-in/late check-out and free local telephone calls.

SOME UNITS

🆂🅳 ⟨🛏⟩ ⟨🍴⟩ ⟨🍸⟩ 🏊 ⊠ ⟨🎥⟩ ⟨DATA PORT⟩ 🖵 / ⊠ 🛢 🖵 /
                                           FEE   FEE

RED ROOF INN
▼▼ ▼▼ ▼▼
Small-scale Hotel

Phone: (517)279-1199
All Year [CP]　　　　1P: $49-$89　　　2P: $49-$89　　XP: $6　　　　F18
Location: I-69, exit 13, just e. 348 S Willowbrook 49036. **Fax:** 517/279-0869. **Facility:** 65 one-bedroom standard units. 3 stories, interior corridors. *Bath:* combo or shower only. **Parking:** on-site, winter plug-ins. **Amenities:** voice mail. **Guest Services:** valet laundry. **Cards:** AX, DC, DS. *(See color ad p 221)*

SOME UNITS

(ASK) (S🄳) (🚗M) (🖥️) (🐾) (DATA PORT) / (✕) /

SUPER 8 MOTEL
(AAA) (SAVE)
▼▼ ▼▼
Small-scale Hotel

Phone: (517)278-8833
All Year　　　　　1P: $55-$60　　　2P: $65-$75　　XP: $7　　　　F12
Location: I-69, exit 13, 0.3 mi w on US 12 (E Chicago St), just n on N Michigan Ave, then just e. 600 Orleans Blvd 49036. **Fax:** 517/278-2347. **Facility:** 58 one-bedroom standard units, some with whirlpools. 2 stories, interior corridors. *Bath:* combo or shower only. **Parking:** on-site. **Terms:** small pets only. **Cards:** AX, CB, DC, DS, MC, VI. **Special Amenities:** free continental breakfast and free local telephone calls.

SOME UNITS

(🛏️) (🚗M) (🖥️) (🐾) (DATA PORT) / (✕) (🍴) (📷)
FEE FEE

────── WHERE TO DINE ──────

CARNEGIE'S
▼▼ ▼▼
American

Lunch: $5-$8　　　　**Dinner:** $10-$15　　　　**Phone:** 517/278-9775
Location: I-69, exit 13, 1.5 mi w on US 12 (E Chicago St), 0.4 mi s on Divison St. 32 Railroad St 49036. **Hours:** 11 am-10 pm, Fri & Sat-11 pm. Closed major holidays; also Sun. **Features:** Railroad memorbilia is housed along the walls and in the ceiling rafters of this converted train station. The continental menu offers a wide range of food from burgers to daily specials. Casual dress; cocktails. **Parking:** on-site. **Cards:** MC, VI.

(🍴) (✕)

COMSTOCK PARK pop. 10,674—See also GRAND RAPIDS.

────── WHERE TO STAY ──────

SWAN INN
▼▼ ▼▼
Small-scale Hotel

Phone: 616/784-1224
All Year　　　　　1P: $45-$65　　　2P: $50-$80　　XP: $3　　　　F12
Location: Jct I-96 and Alpine Ave, 3 mi n on SR 37. Located in a semi-commercial area. 5182 Alpine Ave 49321. **Fax:** 616/784-6565. **Facility:** 38 one-bedroom standard units, some with efficiencies or kitchens (no utensils). 2 stories, exterior corridors. *Bath:* combo or shower only. **Parking:** on-site, winter plug-ins. **Terms:** [AP] meal plan available, small pets only. **Pool(s):** heated outdoor. **Guest Services:** coin laundry. **Business Services:** meeting rooms. **Cards:** AX, DC, DS, MC, VI.

SOME UNITS

(🛏️) (🍴) (🏊) (🐾) / (✕) (🍴) (📷) (💻) /

COOPERSVILLE pop. 3,910

────── WHERE TO STAY ──────

AMERIHOST INN-COOPERSVILLE
(AAA) (SAVE)
▼▼ ▼▼ ▼▼
Small-scale Hotel

Phone: (616)837-8100
All Year [ECP]　　　1P: $79-$99　　　2P: $85-$105　　XP: $6　　　F17
Location: I-96, exit 16, just n. 1040 O'Malley Dr 49404. **Fax:** 616/837-5179. **Facility:** 59 one-bedroom standard units, some with whirlpools. 2 stories, interior corridors. *Bath:* combo or shower only. **Parking:** on-site. **Terms:** 7 day cancellation notice. **Amenities:** safes, irons, hair dryers. **Pool(s):** heated indoor. **Leisure Activities:** sauna, whirlpool, exercise room. **Business Services:** meeting rooms. **Cards:** AX, DC, DS, JC, MC, VI. **Special Amenities:** free continental breakfast and free newspaper.

SOME UNITS

(S🄳) (🚗M) (🖥️) (🏊) (✕) (🐾) (DATA PORT) (💻) / (✕) (🍴) (📷) /

COPPER HARBOR

────── WHERE TO STAY ──────

LAKE FANNY HOOE RESORT & CAMPGROUND
▼▼ ▼▼
Motel

Phone: 906/289-4451
All Year　　　　　1P: $65-$80　　　2P: $65-$80　　XP: $7　　　　F12
Location: Just s on Manganese Rd. Located in a quiet area. 505 Second St 49918 (PO Box 31). **Fax:** 906/289-4450. **Facility:** 17 units. 14 one-bedroom standard units with efficiencies. 3 cabins. 2 stories (no elevator), exterior corridors. *Bath:* combo or shower only. **Parking:** on-site. **Terms:** 7 day cancellation notice-fee imposed, pets ($5 extra charge). **Leisure Activities:** rental boats, rental canoes, rental paddleboats, boat dock, fishing, cross country skiing, snowmobiling, hiking trails. **Fee:** game room. **Guest Services:** gift shop, coin laundry. **Cards:** AX, DS, MC, VI.

SOME UNITS

(🛏️) (🍴) (✕) (🎿) (🐾) (📞) (📷) / (✕) (💻) /

NORLAND MOTEL
▼▼
Motel

Phone: 906/289-4815
Property failed to provide current rates
Location: 2 mi e on US 41; beyond entrance to Fort Wilkins State Park. Located in a quiet area. US 41, F #172 49918 (Box 49). **Fax:** 906/289-4815. **Facility:** Smoke free premises. 8 one-bedroom standard units, some with efficiencies. 1 story, exterior corridors. *Bath:* combo or shower only. **Parking:** on-site. **Terms:** open 5/15-10/15, pets ($5 extra charge). **Leisure Activities:** boat dock, fishing, hiking trails.

SOME UNITS

(🛏️) (✕) (✕) (🎿) (🐾) (📞) (📷) (💻) / (📷) /

────── WHERE TO DINE ──────

TAMARACK INN
(AAA)
▼▼
American

Lunch: $4-$7　　　　**Dinner:** $8-$16　　　　**Phone:** 906/289-4522
Location: Jct US 41 and SR 26. 512 Gratiot 49918. **Hours:** Open 6/10-10/10; 8 am-9 pm. **Features:** In the heart of the small, remote town, the casual restaurant is a nice spot for a relaxed meal. Menu offerings include broasted chicken, prime rib and fresh whitefish and trout from Lake Superior. Wait times are typically short, even during summer. **Parking:** on-site. **Cards:** MC, VI.

(🍴) (✕)

CROSS VILLAGE pop. 100

——— WHERE TO DINE ———

LEGS INN
AAA
Polish
Lunch: $5-$8   Dinner: $8-$17   Phone: 231/526-2281
Location: At end of M-119; center. 6425 Lake Shore Dr 49723. **Hours:** Open 5/14-10/17; noon-10 pm; closing hours vary 5/14-6/30 & 9/1-10/17. **Features:** More than 100 varieties of beer and wine complement authentic entrees of Polish and American cuisine. The historic stone and timber landmark is decorated with distinctive driftwood furniture. The outdoor patio and gardens overlook the lake. Casual dress; cocktails. **Parking:** on-site. **Cards:** DS, MC, VI.

DAVISON pop. 5,536

——— WHERE TO STAY ———

COMFORT INN OF DAVISON
AAA SAVE
Small-scale Hotel
Phone: (810)658-2700
All Year   1P: $69-$125   2P: $74-$125   XP: $10   F18
Location: I-69, exit 145, just n on SR 15, then e. Located in a quiet area. 10082 Lapeer Rd 48423. **Fax:** 810/658-2640. **Facility:** 67 one-bedroom standard units, some with whirlpools. 2 stories (no elevator), interior corridors. *Bath:* combo or shower only. **Parking:** on-site. **Terms:** age restrictions may apply, [ECP] meal plan available. **Amenities:** video library (fee), irons, hair dryers. **Pool(s):** heated outdoor. **Guest Services:** valet laundry. **Business Services:** meeting rooms. **Cards:** AX, CB, DC, DS, JC, MC, VI. **Special Amenities:** free continental breakfast and free newspaper.

SOME UNITS

——— WHERE TO DINE ———

ITALIA GARDENS
Italian
Lunch: $7-$10   Dinner: $8-$11   Phone: 810/653-6899
Location: I-69, exit 145, 1 mi n on SR 15. 1141 S State Rd 48423. **Hours:** 11 am-9 pm, Fri & Sat-11 pm, Sun noon-8 pm. Closed major holidays. **Features:** The small restaurant serves up many favorite entrees such as spaghetti, ribs, manicotti and pizza. The casually upscale dining room features a modern Italian theme, which is evident in the stone columns and candle-topped pedestal tables. Casual dress; beer & wine only. **Parking:** on-site. **Cards:** AX, DC, DS, MC, VI.

DEARBORN —See Detroit p. 250.

Camper
Sweet Camper

*Travel With Someone
You Trust®*

*I*f camping is where your heart is, then **AAA's CampBook® guides** are for you. With information about campgrounds throughout North America, **CampBooks** provide campers valuable details on camping facilities. From rate information to site descriptions to recreational activities, these guides give campers all the information they need before hitting the trail.

To get your **CampBook guide**, call or visit your local AAA office today.

Destination Detroit
pop. 951,270

Motor in. Sail out. And shop till you drop. Detroit offers it all.

Depending on the season, you could root for the home team with some of hockey's proudest fans. Catch a concert. Or just enjoy one of the many amenities that make this symbol of America's might a mighty fine place to play.

Detroit skyline. Commerce and culture mingle in this vibrant riverside metropolis.

Hydroplane Races, Detroit River. Sleek boats scream across the river, attracting thousands to this summer event. (See mention page 62)

See Vicinity map page 228

P*laces included in this AAA Destination City:*

Greektown District, Detroit.
Opa! Centered on Monroe Street, the historic area boasts Victorian-era commercial buildings housing boutiques, small groceries, restaurants and excellent pastry shops.

Comerica Park, Detroit.
Tigers resting on the scoreboard roar to celebrate home runs at the home of Detroit's major league baseball team. (See mention page 59)

See Downtown map page 226

Eastern Market, Detroit.
Any local knows that this outdoor farmer's market is the place to shop on Saturday mornings. (See mention page 60)

Downtown
Detroit
Lodging & Dining

1942-A

Downtown Detroit

This index helps you "spot" where approved accommodations and restaurants are located on the corresponding detailed maps. Lodging rate ranges are for comparison only and show the property's high season; rates are per night, unless only weekly (W) rates are available. Restaurant rate range is for dinner, unless only lunch (L) is served. Turn to the listing page for more detailed rate information and consult display ads for special promotions.

Spotter/Map Page Number	OA	DOWNTOWN DETROIT - Lodgings	Diamond Rating	Rate Range High Season	Listing Page
1 / p. 226		Hotel St. Regis	◆◆◆	$130-$142	237
2 / p. 226		The Inn on Ferry Street	◆◆◆	$139-$209	237
3 / p. 226	AAA	**Comfort Inn-Downtown Detroit**	◆◆	$79-$179 [SAVE]	236
4 / p. 226	AAA	**The Atheneum Suite Hotel & Conference Center**	◆◆◆◆	$185-$950 [SAVE]	236
5 / p. 226	AAA	**Shorecrest Motor Inn** - see color ad p 237	◆◆	$74-$104 [SAVE]	237
6 / p. 226		Holiday Inn Express & Suites Detroit Downtown	◆◆◆	$179	236
7 / p. 226		Detroit Downtown Courtyard by Marriott	◆◆◆	$169	236
8 / p. 226		Detroit Marriott Renaissance Center	◆◆◆	$189	236
9 / p. 226		Hotel Pontchartrain	◆◆◆	$119-$169	237
		DOWNTOWN DETROIT - Restaurants			
1 / p. 226		Cuisine	◆◆◆	$20-$30	238
2 / p. 226		Twingo's	◆◆	$8-$12	240
3 / p. 226		Whitney Restaurant	◆◆◆	$19-$35	240
4 / p. 226		Traffic Jam & Snug	◆◆	$10-$18	240
5 / p. 226		Majestic Cafe	◆◆	$7-$18	239
6 / p. 226		Union Street	◆◆	$8-$16	240
7 / p. 226		Roma Cafe	◆◆	$13-$18	240
8 / p. 226		Mario's	◆◆	$12-$35	239
9 / p. 226		Carl's Chop House	◆◆	$14-$26	238
10 / p. 226		Classics Buffet	◆◆	$30	238
11 / p. 226	AAA	**Iridescence Restaurant**	◆◆◆◆	$24-$65	239
12 / p. 226		Johnny Rockets	◆	$3-$6	239
13 / p. 226		Sala Thai	◆	$6-$9	240
14 / p. 226		Courthouse Brasserie	◆◆	$19-$32	238
15 / p. 226		Cyprus Taverna	◆◆	$6-$18	238
16 / p. 226		Intermezzo	◆◆	$16-$35	239
17 / p. 226		Pegasus Taverna Restaurant	◆	$7-$24	240
18 / p. 226		Blue Nile Ethiopian Cafe	◆◆	$11-$14	238
19 / p. 226		Fishbone's Rhythm Kitchen Cafe	◆◆	$5-$25	238
20 / p. 226		Loco Bar & Grill	◆	$5-$17	239
21 / p. 226		Opus One	◆◆◆	$20-$39	239
22 / p. 226		American Coney Island	◆	$2-$8	238
23 / p. 226		Lafayette Coney Island	◆	$2-$6	239
24 / p. 226		Caucus Club	◆◆	$11-$22	238
25 / p. 226	AAA	**Hollywood Brown Derby**	◆◆◆	$20-$40	239
26 / p. 226	AAA	**Mexican Village Restaurant**	◆	$6-$16	239
27 / p. 226		Evie's Tamales	◆	$6-$7	238
28 / p. 226		Armando's	◆	$6-$26	238

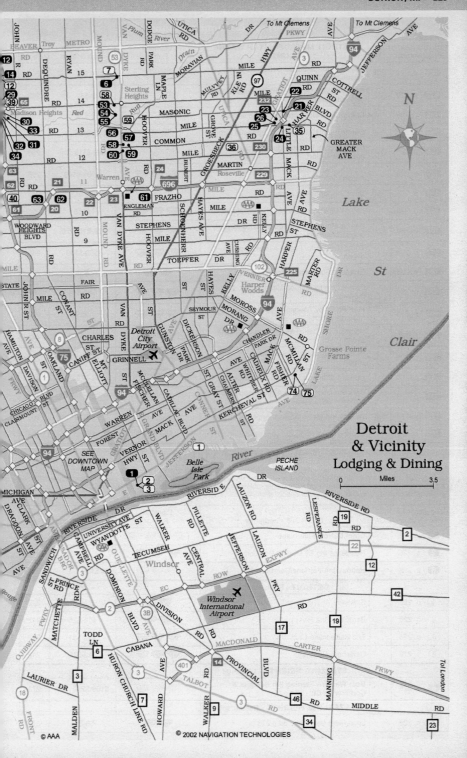

Detroit
& Vicinity
Lodging & Dining

© 2002 NAVIGATION TECHNOLOGIES

✈ Airport Accommodations

Spotter/Map Page Number	OA	DETROIT METROPOLITAN WAYNE COUNTY	Diamond Rating	Rate Range High Season	Listing Page
141 / p. 228	AAA	Baymont Inn & Suites Detroit-Airport, opposite airport	▽▽	$79-$89 SAVE	265
132 / p. 228	AAA	Best Western Gateway International Hotel, opposite airport	▽▽▽	$79-$89 SAVE	265
136 / p. 228	AAA	Clarion Barcelo' Hotel, opposite airport	▽▽▽	$59-$79 SAVE	265
143 / p. 228	AAA	Comfort Inn Metro Airport, opposite airport	▽▽	$65-$169 SAVE	266
135 / p. 228	AAA	Courtyard by Marriott-Metro Airport, opposite airport	▽▽▽	$69-$119 SAVE	266
129 / p. 228		Crowne Plaza Hotel and Resort Detroit Metro Airport, opposite airport	▽▽▽	$109-$149	266
144 / p. 228	AAA	Days Inn, opposite airport	▽▽	$69-$79 SAVE	266
147 / p. 228		Detroit Airport Marriott Hotel, at the airport	▽▽▽	$159	266
137 / p. 228	AAA	Detroit Marriott Romulus at Metro Airport, opposite airport	▽▽▽	$79-$169 SAVE	266
142 / p. 228		DoubleTree Hotel Detroit Airport, opposite airport	▽▽▽	$89-$149	266
138 / p. 228		Extended Stay America, opposite airport	▽▽	$55	266
134 / p. 228		Fairfield Inn by Marriott-Metro Airport, opposite the terminal	▽▽▽	$84-$94	267
140 / p. 228		Four Points by Sheraton Detroit Metro Airport, opposite airport	▽▽▽	$89	267
133 / p. 228		Hampton Inn-Detroit Metro Airport, opposite airport	▽▽	$68-$125	267
139 / p. 228		Hilton Suites-Detroit Metro Airport, opposite airport	▽▽▽	$79-$190	268
145 / p. 228	AAA	Howard Johnson Inn, opposite airport	▽▽	$69-$79 SAVE	268
131 / p. 228	AAA	Park Inn-Detroit Metro Airport, opposite airport - see ad p 463	▽▽	$80 SAVE	268
128 / p. 228	AAA	Quality Inn Metro Airport, opposite airport	▽▽	$59-$119 SAVE	268
146 / p. 228		Super 8 Motel-Romulus, opposite airport	▽▽	$59-$71	268

Detroit and Vicinity

This index helps you "spot" where approved accommodations and restaurants are located on the corresponding detailed maps. Lodging rate ranges are for comparison only and show the property's high season; rates are per night, unless only weekly (W) rates are available. Restaurant rate range is for dinner, unless only lunch (L) is served. Turn to the listing page for more detailed rate information and consult display ads for special promotions.

Spotter/Map Page Number	OA	DETROIT - Lodgings	Diamond Rating	Rate Range High Season	Listing Page
1 / p. 228	AAA	Omni Detroit Riverplace	▽▽▽▽	$139-$159 SAVE	240
2 / p. 228		Residence Inn By Marriott-Dearborn	▽▽▽	$134	242
3 / p. 228	AAA	Holiday Inn Fairlane/Dearborn	▽▽▽	$129 SAVE	240
		DETROIT - Restaurants			
1 / p. 228		Sindbad's At The River	▽▽	$9-$18	242
2 / p. 228		Baron's on the River	▽▽	$16-$26	242
3 / p. 228		The Rattlesnake Club	▽▽▽	$17-$31	242
4 / p. 228		Giovanni's Ristorante	▽▽▽	$12-$18	242
		STERLING HEIGHTS - Lodgings			
6 / p. 228	AAA	Best Western Sterling Inn Banquet & Conference Ctr - see ad p 273	▽▽▽	$109-$209 SAVE	273
		STERLING HEIGHTS - Restaurant			
7 / p. 228		Loon River Cafe - see ad p 273	▽▽	$6-$15	274

Spotter/Map Page Number	OA	TROY - Lodgings	Diamond Rating	Rate Range High Season	Listing Page
9 / p. 228		Troy Marriott	◆◆◆	$209-$229	276
10 / p. 228	AAA	**Drury Inn**	◆◆	$109-$139 SAVE	275
11 / p. 228		Residence Inn by Marriott	◆◆◆	$143-$169	276
12 / p. 228		Holiday Inn-Troy	◆◆◆	$69-$125	275
13 / p. 228	AAA	**Red Roof Inn-Troy**	◆◆	$55-$69 SAVE	276
14 / p. 228		Courtyard by Marriott	◆◆◆	$69-$169	275
		TROY - Restaurants			
10 / p. 228		The Capitol Grille	◆◆◆	$20-$30	276
11 / p. 228		P.F. Chang's China Bistro	◆◆	$10-$15	277
12 / p. 228	AAA	**Mon Jin Lau**	◆◆◆	$12-$22	276
13 / p. 228		Priya	◆◆	$10-$20	277
14 / p. 228		Anitas Kitchen	◆	$7-$10	276
15 / p. 228		Shield's of Troy	◆	$5-$10	277
		BIRMINGHAM - Lodgings			
17 / p. 228		Holiday Inn Express Birmingham - see ad p 247	◆◆◆	$89-$199	247
18 / p. 228	AAA	**The Townsend Hotel**	◆◆◆◆	$289 SAVE	247
		BIRMINGHAM - Restaurants			
22 / p. 228	AAA	**Big Rock Chop House**	◆◆◆	$9-$35	247
23 / p. 228		Peabody	◆◆	$8-$15	248
24 / p. 228		Forte'	◆◆	$18-$25	248
25 / p. 228		220	◆◆	$15-$25	247
26 / p. 228		Rugby Grille	◆◆◆◆	$25-$40	248
		ROSEVILLE - Lodgings			
21 / p. 228		Comfort Inn	◆◆◆	Failed to provide	269
22 / p. 228	AAA	**Holiday Inn Express & Suites**	◆◆◆	$99-$109 SAVE	269
23 / p. 228	AAA	**Georgian Inn**	◆◆◆	$70-$123 SAVE	269
24 / p. 228	AAA	**Baymont Inn & Suites Detroit-Roseville -** see color ad p 241	◆◆◆	$69-$89 SAVE	269
25 / p. 228		Microtel Inn & Suites	◆◆	$50-$80	269
26 / p. 228		Extended StayAmerica	◆◆	$55	269
		ROSEVILLE - Restaurants			
35 / p. 228		Pearl City	◆	$7-$10	269
36 / p. 228	AAA	**Mr. Paul's Chophouse**	◆◆◆	$10-$23	269
		MADISON HEIGHTS - Lodgings			
29 / p. 228	AAA	**Best Western Troy-Madison Inn**	◆◆	$69-$109 SAVE	260
30 / p. 228		Fairfield Inn by Marriott	◆◆	$59-$99	260
31 / p. 228		Econo Lodge	◆	$47-$50	260
32 / p. 228		Residence Inn by Marriott-Madison Heights	◆◆◆	$125-$161	260
33 / p. 228	AAA	**Red Roof Inn**	◆◆	$52-$71 SAVE	260
34 / p. 228		Hampton Inn - see color ad p 260	◆◆◆	$104-$109	260

Spotter/Map Page Number	OA	**MADISON HEIGHTS - Restaurants**	Diamond Rating	Rate Range High Season	Listing Page
(39) / p. 228		Big Fish Seafood Bistro	◆◆	$7-$24	261
(40) / p. 228		Boodle's Restaurant	◆◆	$9-$28	261
		ROYAL OAK - Lodgings			
(37) / p. 228	AAA	**Travelodge**	◆	$45-$70 SAVE	270
		ROYAL OAK - Restaurants			
(43) / p. 228		Memphis Smoke	◆	$7-$15	270
(44) / p. 228		D'Amato's Neighborhood Restaurant	◆◆	$10-$20	270
(45) / p. 228		Royal Oak Brewery	◆◆	$8-$12	270
(46) / p. 228		Lepanto	◆◆◆	$18-$25	270
(47) / p. 228		Wood-Ruff's	◆◆◆	$14-$22	270
(48) / p. 228		Pronto! 608	◆◆	$4-$8	270
		SOUTHFIELD - Lodgings			
(40) / p. 228		Homestead Studio Suites Hotel-Detroit/Southfield	◆◆◆	$84-$104	271
(41) / p. 228		Embassy Suites Detroit-Southfield	◆◆◆	Failed to provide	271
(42) / p. 228	AAA	**Red Roof Inn-Southfield**	◆	$59-$83 SAVE	271
(43) / p. 228		Hilton Inn-Southfield	◆◆◆	$69-$159	271
(44) / p. 228		Hampton Inn-Southfield	◆◆◆	$79-$109	271
(45) / p. 228		Courtyard by Marriott-Southfield	◆◆◆	$64-$169	270
(46) / p. 228		Southfield Marriott Hotel	◆◆◆	$89-$189	272
(47) / p. 228		Holiday Inn-Southfield	◆◆	$94-$111	271
(48) / p. 228		Ramada Limited & Suites	◆◆	$79-$99	271
(49) / p. 228		Westin Hotel Southfield-Detroit	◆◆◆◆	$99-$270	272
(50) / p. 228		Ramada Inn-Southfield	◆◆	$89-$109	271
		SOUTHFIELD - Restaurants			
(51) / p. 228		Beverly Hills Grill	◆◆	$12-$20	272
(52) / p. 228		Joe Muer's Grill	◆◆	$19-$27	272
(53) / p. 228	AAA	Il Posto Ristoronte	◆◆◆	$18-$28	272
(54) / p. 228		New Seoul Restaurant	◆◆	$9-$20	272
(55) / p. 228		C A Muer's Merriwether	◆◆	$14-$30	272
		WARREN - Lodgings			
(53) / p. 228	AAA	**Hampton Inn-Warren/Sterling Heights**	◆◆◆	$99 SAVE	279
(54) / p. 228		Candlewood Suites-Detroit Warren	◆◆◆	$71-$107	278
(55) / p. 228		Fairfield Inn by Marriott	◆◆	$59-$99	279
(56) / p. 228		Hawthorn Suites Ltd	◆◆◆	$89-$189	279
(57) / p. 228	AAA	**Baymont Inn & Suites Detroit-Warren Tech Center -** see color ad p 241	◆◆◆	$74-$84 SAVE	278
(58) / p. 228		Courtyard by Marriott-Warren	◆◆◆	$119-$129	278
(59) / p. 228	AAA	**Residence Inn by Marriott**	◆◆◆	$80-$116 SAVE	280
(60) / p. 228		Four Points by Sheraton Hotel & Suites Detroit North	◆◆◆	$109-$199	279
(61) / p. 228		Holiday Inn Express	◆◆◆	$119-$139	280
(62) / p. 228	AAA	**Comfort Suites**	◆◆◆	$69-$259 SAVE	278

Spotter/Map Page Number	OA	**WARREN - Lodgings (continued)**	Diamond Rating	Rate Range High Season	Listing Page
63 / p. 228	AAA	Red Roof Inn-Warren	◇◇	$53-$77 SAVE	280
		WARREN - Restaurants			
58 / p. 228		Andiamo Italia Ristorante	◇◇◇	$12-$24	280
59 / p. 228		Michelle's Restaurant & Sweetheart Bakery	◇◇	$7-$10	280
		FARMINGTON HILLS - Lodgings			
66 / p. 228		Fairfield Inn by Marriott	◇◇◇	$94-$129	255
67 / p. 228	AAA	**Comfort Inn-Farmington Hills**	◇◇	$84-$109 SAVE	255
68 / p. 228		Courtyard by Marriott	◇◇◇	$109	255
69 / p. 228		Candlwood Suites	◇◇◇	Failed to provide	255
70 / p. 228	AAA	**Red Roof Inn-Farmington Hills**	◇	$55-$74 SAVE	256
71 / p. 228		Holiday Inn Farmington Hills	◇◇◇	$75-$129	255
72 / p. 228	AAA	**Radisson Suite Hotel Farmington Hills** - see color ad p 241	◇◇◇	$97 SAVE	256
		FARMINGTON HILLS - Restaurants			
66 / p. 228	AAA	**Family Buggy Restaurant**	◇◇	$9-$15	256
67 / p. 228		Hong Hua	◇◇◇	$10-$25	256
68 / p. 228		Tribute	◇◇◇◇	$65-$85	256
		NOVI - Lodgings			
75 / p. 228		Country Inn & Suites By Carlson - see color ad p 243	◇◇◇	$105	262
76 / p. 228		Hilton Novi	◇◇◇	$79-$199	262
		NOVI - Restaurant			
71 / p. 228		New Ah Wok	◇◇	$8-$12	263
		NORTHVILLE - Lodgings			
79 / p. 228		Ramada Limited of Novi	◇◇	Failed to provide	261
80 / p. 228		Hampton Inn	◇◇◇	$69-$109	261
		LIVONIA - Lodgings			
83 / p. 228		Embassy Suites Hotel	◇◇◇	$89-$169	258
84 / p. 228	AAA	**AmeriSuites (Detroit/Livonia)**	◇◇◇	$79-$149 SAVE	257
85 / p. 228		Courtyard by Marriott	◇◇◇	$59-$124	258
86 / p. 228	AAA	**Fairfield Inn Detroit/Livonia**	◇◇◇	$79-$89 SAVE	258
87 / p. 228		TownePlace Suites	◇◇◇	$69-$89	259
88 / p. 228	AAA	**Holiday Inn Livonia-West** - see color ad p 258	◇◇◇	$99-$149 SAVE	259
89 / p. 228		Residence Inn Detroit-Livonia	◇◇◇	$94-$124	259
90 / p. 228	AAA	**Livonia Marriott**	◇◇◇	$89-$159 SAVE	259
91 / p. 228	AAA	**Best Western Laurel Park Suites**	◇◇◇	$79-$109 SAVE	258
92 / p. 228	AAA	**Comfort Inn**	◇◇◇	$89-$99 SAVE	258
		LIVONIA - Restaurants			
78 / p. 228		Sweet Lorraine's Cafe & Bar	◇◇	$8-$12	259
79 / p. 228	AAA	**Family Buggy Restaurant**	◇◇	$9-$15	259
80 / p. 228		Depalmas Ristorante	◇◇	$10-$20	259

Spotter/Map Page Number	OA	PLYMOUTH - Lodgings	Diamond Rating	Rate Range High Season	Listing Page
95 / p. 228	AAA	Red Roof Inn-Plymouth	▽▽ ▽▽	$49-$73 SAVE	263
96 / p. 228	AAA	Quality Inn Plymouth Clocktower - see color ad p 226	▽▽ ▽▽	$99-$139 SAVE	263
		DEARBORN - Lodgings			
99 / p. 228		TownePlace Suites	▽▽ ▽▽ ▽▽	$99-$139	254
100 / p. 228		Courtyard by Marriott-Dearborn	▽▽ ▽▽ ▽▽	Failed to provide	250
101 / p. 228	AAA	The Ritz-Carlton, Dearborn	▽▽ ▽▽ ▽▽ ▽▽	$125-$1500 SAVE	254
102 / p. 228		Extended Stay America	▽▽ ▽▽	$79	251
103 / p. 228	AAA	Hyatt Regency Dearborn - see color ad p 250	▽▽ ▽▽ ▽▽	$99-$209 SAVE	253
104 / p. 228		Hampton Inn Dearborn	▽▽ ▽▽ ▽▽	$99-$140	251
105 / p. 228	AAA	Red Roof Inn-Dearborn	▽▽ ▽▽	$56-$83 SAVE	254
106 / p. 228	AAA	The Dearborn Inn, A Marriott Hotel	▽▽ ▽▽ ▽▽	$79-$199 SAVE	250
		DEARBORN - Restaurants			
83 / p. 228		Kabob Village	▽▽ ▽▽	$6-$10	254
84 / p. 228		Ritz-Carlton, The Grill	▽▽ ▽▽ ▽▽ ▽▽	$25-$40	255
85 / p. 228		Kiernan's Steak House	▽▽ ▽▽	$10-$18	254
86 / p. 228		Ristorante Ciao	▽▽ ▽▽	$11-$20	255
87 / p. 228	AAA	Annam Restaurant Vietnamien	▽▽ ▽▽ ▽▽	$10-$15	254
88 / p. 228		La Shish	▽▽ ▽▽	$8-$14	255
89 / p. 228		BD's Mongolian Barbeque	▽▽	$14	254
90 / p. 228		LaPita	▽▽ ▽▽	$10-$14	254
91 / p. 228	AAA	Richter's Chalet	▽▽ ▽▽	$7-$17	255
92 / p. 228		Early American Room	▽▽ ▽▽ ▽▽	$18-$26	254
		CANTON - Lodgings			
109 / p. 228		Motel 6 - 1070	▽▽	$47-$63	249
110 / p. 228	AAA	Baymont Inn & Suites Detroit-Canton - see color ad p 241	▽▽ ▽▽ ▽▽	$64-$79 SAVE	249
111 / p. 228		Extended StayAmerica-Canton	▽▽ ▽▽	$55	249
112 / p. 228		Days Inn - *see color ad card insert*	▽▽ ▽▽	$55-$75	249
113 / p. 228		Super 8 Motel-Canton	▽▽ ▽▽	$54-$89	249
114 / p. 228		Holiday Inn Express Hotel & Suites - see color ad card insert	▽▽ ▽▽ ▽▽	$89	249
115 / p. 228		Fairfield Inn by Marriott	▽▽ ▽▽	$61-$79	249
		ALLEN PARK - Lodgings			
118 / p. 228	AAA	Best Western Greenfield Inn - see color ad p 251	▽▽ ▽▽ ▽▽	$95-$135 SAVE	243
119 / p. 228	AAA	Holiday Inn Express & Suites - see color ad card insert, p 252	▽▽ ▽▽ ▽▽	$110-$130 SAVE	243
		LINCOLN PARK - Lodgings			
122 / p. 228	AAA	Sleep Inn Inn & Suites - see color ad p 253	▽▽ ▽▽ ▽▽	$89-$110 SAVE	257
		TAYLOR - Lodgings			
125 / p. 228		Quality Inn & Suites	▽▽ ▽▽ ▽▽	$69-$89	274
		ROMULUS - Lodgings			
128 / p. 228	AAA	Quality Inn Metro Airport	▽▽ ▽▽	$59-$119 SAVE	268

Spotter/Map Page Number	OA	ROMULUS - Lodgings (continued)	Diamond Rating	Rate Range High Season	Listing Page
129 / p. 228		Crowne Plaza Hotel and Resort Detroit Metro Airport	◆◆◆	$109-$149	266
130 / p. 228		Hilton Garden Inn-Detroit Metro Airport - see ad p 267	◆◆◆	$69-$139	267
131 / p. 228	AAA	**Park Inn-Detroit Metro Airport**	◆◆	$80 SAVE	268
132 / p. 228	AAA	**Best Western Gateway International Hotel**	◆◆◆	$79-$89 SAVE	265
133 / p. 228		Hampton Inn-Detroit Metro Airport	◆◆	$68-$125	267
134 / p. 228		Fairfield Inn by Marriott-Metro Airport	◆◆	$84-$94	267
135 / p. 228	AAA	**Courtyard by Marriott-Metro Airport**	◆◆◆	$69-$119 SAVE	266
136 / p. 228	AAA	**Clarion Barcelo' Hotel**	◆◆◆	$59-$79 SAVE	265
137 / p. 228	AAA	**Detroit Marriott Romulus at Metro Airport**	◆◆◆	$79-$169 SAVE	266
138 / p. 228		Extended Stay America	◆◆	$55	266
139 / p. 228		Hilton Suites-Detroit Metro Airport - see ad p 267	◆◆◆	$79-$190	268
140 / p. 228		Four Points by Sheraton Detroit Metro Airport	◆◆◆	$89	267
141 / p. 228	AAA	**Baymont Inn & Suites Detroit-Airport -** see color ad p 241	◆◆	$79-$89 SAVE	265
142 / p. 228		DoubleTree Hotel Detroit Airport	◆◆◆	$89-$149	266
143 / p. 228	AAA	**Comfort Inn Metro Airport**	◆◆	$65-$169 SAVE	266
144 / p. 228	AAA	**Days Inn**	◆◆	$69-$79 SAVE	266
145 / p. 228	AAA	**Howard Johnson Inn**	◆◆	$69-$79 SAVE	268
146 / p. 228		Super 8 Motel-Romulus	◆◆	$59-$71	268
147 / p. 228		Detroit Airport Marriott Hotel	◆◆◆	$159	266
		ROMULUS - Restaurants			
95 / p. 228		Leonardo's Pizzeria & Ristorante	◆◆	$6-$10	268
96 / p. 228		Merriman Street Grill	◆◆	$6-$10	268
		SOUTHGATE - Lodgings			
150 / p. 228		Comfort Suites	◆◆◆	$89-$189	273
151 / p. 228	AAA	**Baymont Inn & Suites Detroit-Southgate -** see color ad p 241	◆◆◆	$64-$79 SAVE	273
152 / p. 228		Holiday Inn Southgate Heritage Center	◆◆◆	$99	273
153 / p. 228	AAA	**Cross Country Inn -** see color ad p 236	◆◆	$47-$63 SAVE	273
		BLOOMFIELD HILLS - Restaurants			
18 / p. 228		Beau Jack's Food & Spirits	◆◆	$7-$17	248
19 / p. 228		Andiamo Italia West	◆◆◆	$16-$25	248
		CLAWSON - Restaurant			
29 / p. 228		Clawson Steak House	◆◆	$15-$25	250
		WEST BLOOMFIELD - Restaurant			
32 / p. 228		The Lark	◆◆◆◆	$55-$70	281
		FERNDALE - Restaurants			
62 / p. 228		Maria's Front Room	◆◆	$14-$17	256
63 / p. 228		Assaggi Mediterranean Bistro	◆◆◆	$18-$26	256
		GROSSE POINTE FARMS - Restaurants			
74 / p. 228		Lucy's Tavern On The Hill	◆◆	$5-$19	257
75 / p. 228		The Hill Seafood and Chop House	◆◆◆	$15-$25	257

DOWNTOWN DETROIT   (See map p. 226; index p. 227)

-------- WHERE TO STAY --------

THE ATHENEUM SUITE HOTEL & CONFERENCE CENTER
Phone: (313)962-2323   **4**
(AAA) [SAVE]   All Year   1P: $185-$950   2P: $185-$950   XP: $20   F18

Location: At corner of Brush Ave and Lafayette Blvd; downtown. Located in Greektown. 1000 Brush Ave 48226.
Fax: 313/962-2424. **Facility:** Murals of Trojan warriors dominate the lobby of this luxury hotel; guest rooms
feature mahogany case goods and baths with glass-block accents. 174 units. 21 one-bedroom standard
Large-scale Hotel units. 153 one-bedroom suites, some with whirlpools. 10 stories, interior corridors. **Parking:** on-site (fee) and
valet. **Terms:** 3 day cancellation notice, package plans - weekends. **Amenities:** CD players, dual phone
lines, voice mail, safes, honor bars, irons, hair dryers. **Dining:** Fishbone's Rhythm Kitchen Cafe, see separate listing. **Leisure
Activities:** exercise room. **Guest Services:** valet laundry, area transportation-downtown area. **Business Services:** conference
facilities, business center. **Cards:** AX, CB, DC, DS, JC, MC, VI.

SOME UNITS
[S/D] [✈] [¶] [24†] [⊤] [&M] [🚭] [📺] [DATA PORT] [💻] / [✕] [🔒] /
FEE

COMFORT INN-DOWNTOWN DETROIT
Phone: (313)567-8888   **3**
(AAA) [SAVE]   All Year   1P: $79-$179   2P: $79-$179   XP: $10   F18

Location: I-375, exit E Jefferson Ave, 0.5 mi e. 1999 E Jefferson Ave 48207. Fax: 313/567-5842. **Facility:** 78 one-
bedroom standard units, some with whirlpools. 3 stories, interior corridors. *Bath:* combo or shower only.
Parking: on-site. **Terms:** [CP] meal plan available, pets ($200 deposit). **Amenities:** voice mail, hair dryers.
Small-scale Hotel   *Fee:* video games, safes. *Some:* irons. **Leisure Activities:** exercise room. **Guest Services:** valet and coin
laundry. **Cards:** AX, DC, DS, MC, VI. **Special Amenities: free continental breakfast and free news-**
paper.

SOME UNITS
[S/D] [🐾] [¶†] [&] [📺] [DATA PORT] [💻] / [✕] [🔒] [🖥] /

DETROIT DOWNTOWN COURTYARD BY MARRIOTT
Phone: (313)222-7700   **7**
[SAVE]   All Year   1P: $169   2P: $169

Location: In Millender Center. Located opposite Renaissance Center. 333 E Jefferson Ave 48226. Fax: 313/222-6509.
Facility: 260 units. 255 one-bedroom standard units. 5 one-bedroom suites ($300). 21 stories, interior corri-
dors. *Bath:* combo or shower only. **Parking:** on-site (fee) and valet. **Terms:** 19% service charge.
Large-scale Hotel   **Amenities:** dual phone lines, voice mail, irons, hair dryers. *Fee:* video games, high-speed Internet. **Pool(s):**
heated indoor. **Leisure Activities:** sauna, whirlpool, jogging. *Fee:* 2 tennis courts, massage. **Guest Serv-**
ices: gift shop, valet laundry, tanning facility. **Business Services:** conference facilities, PC. **Cards:** AX, CB, DC, DS, JC,
MC, VI.

SOME UNITS
[¶] [⊤] [🚭] [🏊] [✈] [✕] [📺] [DATA PORT] [💻] / [✕] [🔒] [🖥] /

DETROIT MARRIOTT RENAISSANCE CENTER
Phone: (313)568-8000   **8**
[SAVE]   All Year   1P: $189   2P: $189
Location: Downtown. Renaissance Center 48243. Fax: 313/568-8146. **Facility:** 1298 units. 1246 one-bedroom
standard units. 52 one-bedroom suites ($295). 73 stories, interior corridors. *Bath:* combo or shower only.
Parking: on-site (fee) and valet. **Amenities:** video games, dual phone lines, voice mail, safes, irons, hair
Large-scale Hotel   dryers. **Leisure Activities:** *Fee:* massage. **Guest Services:** gift shop, valet laundry. **Business Services:**
conference facilities, business center. **Cards:** AX, CB, DC, DS, JC, MC, VI.

SOME UNITS
[¶] [🐾] [&] [🚭] [✈] [📺] [DATA PORT] [💻] / [✕] [🔒] /

HOLIDAY INN EXPRESS & SUITES DETROIT DOWNTOWN
Phone: (313)887-7000   **6**
[✈✈✈]   All Year   1P: $179   2P: $179
Location: At corner of Washington Blvd and Michigan. 1020 Washington Blvd 48226. Fax: 313/965-4307.
Large-scale Hotel   **Facility:** 252 units. 240 one-bedroom standard units. 12 one-bedroom suites. 17 stories, interior corridors.
Bath: combo or shower only. **Parking:** valet. **Terms:** 3 day cancellation notice-fee imposed, [CP] meal plan
available, package plans - weekends, small pets only ($25 fee). **Amenities:** video games (fee), voice mail, irons, hair dryers.
Pool(s): heated indoor. **Leisure Activities:** exercise room. **Guest Services:** valet laundry. **Business Services:** meeting
rooms.

SOME UNITS
[ASK] [S/D] [🐾] [¶†] [&] [🏊] [📺] [DATA PORT] [💻] / [✕] [🔒] /
FEE

(See map p. 226)

HOTEL PONTCHARTRAIN   Phone: (313)965-0200   **9**
All Year   1P: $119-$169   2P: $119-$169
Large-scale Hotel   **Location:** Opposite Cobo Hall. 2 Washington Blvd 48226. **Fax:** 313/965-9464. **Facility:** 413 units. 401 one-bedroom standard units, some with whirlpools. 12 one-bedroom suites. 25 stories, interior corridors. *Bath:* combo or shower only. **Parking:** on-site (fee) and valet. **Terms:** 15% service charge. **Amenities:** video games, high-speed Internet, voice mail, irons, hair dryers. **Pool(s):** heated outdoor. **Leisure Activities:** saunas, steamroom, exercise room. **Guest Services:** gift shop, valet and coin laundry. **Business Services:** conference facilities, business center. **Cards:** AX, DC, DS, MC, VI.

SOME UNITS
(ASK) (SO) (+ FEE) (🖥) (🏊) (🗙) (🎬) (DATA PORT) (☕) / (🗙) (📶)

HOTEL ST. REGIS   Phone: (313)873-3000   **1**
4/1-12/31   1P: $130-$142   2P: $130-$142
1/1-3/31   1P: $130-$142
Small-scale Hotel   **Location:** W Grand Blvd and Cass. 3071 W Grand Blvd 48202. **Fax:** 313/873-2574. **Facility:** 221 units. 204 one-bedroom standard units, some with whirlpools. 17 one-bedroom suites ($199-$249), some with efficiencies (no utensils) and/or whirlpools. 6 stories, interior corridors. *Bath:* combo or shower only. **Parking:** on-site and valet. **Terms:** [AP], [BP] & [CP] meal plans available. 18% service charge. **Amenities:** dual phone lines, voice mail, irons, hair dryers. **Leisure Activities:** exercise room. **Guest Services:** gift shop, valet laundry. **Business Services:** conference facilities. **Cards:** AX, CB, DC, DS, MC, VI.

SOME UNITS
(ASK) (SO) (🍴) (Y) (&) (🎬) (DATA PORT) (☕) / (🗙) (📶) (🖥) /

THE INN ON FERRY STREET   Phone: (313)871-6000   **2**
All Year [ECP]   1P: $139-$209   2P: $139-$209   XP: $10   F12
Historic   **Location:** Jct Woodward and Ferry aves, just e. 84 E Ferry St 48202. **Fax:** 313/871-1473. **Facility:** 42 units. 36 one-bedroom standard units, some with whirlpools. 5 one- and 1 two-bedroom suites ($189-$209), some with whirlpools. 2-3 stories (no elevator), interior corridors. *Bath:* combo or shower only. **Parking:** on-site.
Small-scale Hotel   **Terms:** check-in 4 pm, cancellation fee imposed, weekly rates available. **Amenities:** CD players, dual phone lines, voice mail, irons, hair dryers. **Guest Services:** valet laundry, area transportation. **Business Services:** meeting rooms. **Cards:** AX, CB, DC, DS, JC, MC, VI.

SOME UNITS
(ASK) (SO) (🍴) (&M) (&) (DATA PORT) (☕) / (🗙)

SHORECREST MOTOR INN   Phone: (313)568-3000   **5**
(AAA) (SAVE)   All Year   1P: $74-$104   2P: $74-$104
(▽▽▽▽)   **Location:** Just e of Renaissance Center. 1316 E Jefferson Ave 48207. **Fax:** 313/568-3002. **Facility:** 54 one-bedroom standard units. 2 stories, exterior corridors. *Bath:* combo or shower only. **Parking:** on-site.
Motel   **Terms:** weekly rates available. **Amenities:** *Some:* hair dryers. **Dining:** 6 am-3 pm, Sat & Sun from 7 am. **Guest Services:** valet laundry. **Cards:** AX, CB, DC, DS, MC, VI. **Special Amenities:** early check-in/late check-out and preferred room (subject to availability with advanced reservations).

(See color ad below)

(+ FEE) (🍴) (🎬) (DATA PORT) (📶)

(See map p. 226)

————— WHERE TO DINE —————

AMERICAN CONEY ISLAND Lunch: $2-$8 Dinner: $2-$8 Phone: 313/961-7758 ㉒
▼▼
American

Location: At corner of Griswold; downtown. 114 W Lafayette 48226. **Hours:** 24 hours. **Features:** Stretch limousines still idle at 3 am in front of the famous hot dog and chili compound. The restaurant does a fine job with its steamed buns, spicy chili, onions, mustard and natural casings that snap when bitten. The decor is red, white and blue. Casual dress; beer only. **Parking:** street.

☒

ARMANDO'S Lunch: $5-$12 Dinner: $6-$26 Phone: 313/554-0666 ㉘
▼▼
Mexican

Location: Between Clark and Scotten. 4242 W Vernor 48209. **Hours:** 10:30 am-1:30 am, Fri & Sat-3:30 am. Closed: 11/27, 12/25. **Reservations:** accepted. **Features:** This local favorite offers a menu largely of Mexican dishes with specialty cuisine from Cuba, Guatemala and other Latin American countries. Casual dress; cocktails. **Parking:** on-site. **Cards:** AX, MC, VI.

☒

BLUE NILE ETHIOPIAN CAFE Dinner: $11-$14 Phone: 248/547-6699 ⑱
▼▼ ▼▼
Ethiopian

Location: At corner of Monroe and Beaubien sts; downtown in Greektown. 508 Monroe St 48226. **Hours:** 5 pm-10 pm, Sat-11 pm. Closed major holidays. **Features:** Not for the unadventerous, the Blue Nile will introduce you to traditional cuisine of Ethiopia and the manner in which it is eaten. Casual dress; cocktails. **Parking:** on-site. **Cards:** AX, DS, MC, VI.

☒

CARL'S CHOP HOUSE Lunch: $6-$15 Dinner: $14-$26 Phone: 313/833-0700 ⑨
▼▼ ▼▼
American

Location: 1 mi nw. 3020 Grand River Ave 48201. **Hours:** 11:30 am-11 pm, Fri & Sat-midnight, Sun 10:30 am-10 pm. Closed: 12/25. **Reservations:** suggested. **Features:** Reputed to have the best relish tray in Detroit, this local favorite made its reputation on serving quality meat and a secret zip sauce. Casual dress; cocktails. **Parking:** on-site and valet. **Cards:** AX, CB, DC, DS, MC, VI.

▣ ☒

CAUCUS CLUB Lunch: $9-$18 Dinner: $11-$22 Phone: 313/965-4970 ㉔
▼▼ ▼▼
American

Location: In Penobscot Building. 150 W Congress 48226. **Hours:** 11:30 am-8 pm, Fri-10 pm. Closed major holidays; also Sat & Sun. **Reservations:** suggested. **Features:** Low lighting and attractive antiques give the clublike dining room a sophisticated ambience. Standard favorites—such as seafood, barbecue pork ribs, Dover sole and fresh perch—are well-prepared, consistent and appropriately seasoned. Dressy casual; cocktails. **Parking:** on-site (fee) and valet. **Cards:** AX, DC, DS, MC, VI.

▣ ☒

CLASSICS BUFFET Lunch: $16 Dinner: $30 Phone: 313/237-7711 ⑩
▼▼ ▼▼
American

Location: In Motor City Casino. 2901 Grand River Ave 48201. **Hours:** 10:30 am-4:30 & 5-4 am, Fri 10:30 am-4 & 5-1:30 am, Sat & Sun 2 am-5 pm & 5:30-4 am. **Features:** With such a large and varied selection it will be hard to know where to start. The all-you-can-eat seafood buffet on Friday is quickly becoming legendary for its seemingly endless supply of crab legs. Casual dress; beer only. **Parking:** on-site and valet. **Cards:** AX, CB, DC, DS, JC, MC, VI.

☒

COURTHOUSE BRASSERIE Lunch: $12-$15 Dinner: $19-$32 Phone: 313/963-8887 ⑭
▼▼ ▼▼
American

Location: Brush St at Gratiot. 1436 Brush St 48226. **Hours:** 11:30 am-2:30 & 5-10 pm, Sat from 5 pm, Sun 4:30 pm-8 pm. Closed: 11/27, 12/25. **Reservations:** accepted. **Features:** Ring the doorbell to enter the eatery, which serves classic cuisine in a 10-table serene, elegant room. Dishes are distinctively presented works of art. Try the sauteed chicken breast with a mushroom white sauce or the perfectly poached salmon. Dressy casual; cocktails. **Parking:** on-site. **Cards:** AX, DC, DS, MC, VI.

☒

CUISINE Dinner: $20-$30 Phone: 313/872-5110 ①
▼▼▼▼
French

Location: Jct 2nd St and Lothrop Rd. 670 Lothrop Rd 48202. **Hours:** 4 pm-10 pm, Sun-7 pm. Closed major holidays; also Mon. **Reservations:** accepted. **Features:** Hidden from view behind the Fisher Theatre, the chef/owner of this upscale converted house has turned French-American cuisine completely on its head. Using premium ingredients and boundless creativity, even classically prepared dishes such as beef Rossini find a new and exciting life when paired with seared foie gras, a potato-daikon cake and topped with black truffle demi glace. Dressy casual; cocktails. **Parking:** valet and street. **Cards:** AX, DC, MC, VI.

▣ ☒

CYPRUS TAVERNA Lunch: $5-$7 Dinner: $6-$18 Phone: 313/961-1550 ⑮
▼▼ ▼▼
Greek

Location: At corner of Monroe St and St. Antoine; downtown in Greektown. 579 Monroe 48226. **Hours:** 11 am-2 am, Fri & Sat-4 am. Closed: 11/27, 12/25. **Features:** The restaurant, tastefully decorated with Greek murals and art. A local favorite for great spinach pie and lamb; mouthwatering Cypriot specialties, such as koupes; minced meat in bulgur casing; and a coriander-fragrant braised pork dish called afelia. Casual dress; cocktails. **Parking:** street. **Cards:** AX, DC, DS, MC, VI.

☒

EVIE'S TAMALES Lunch: $6-$7 Dinner: $6-$7 Phone: 313/843-5056 ㉗
▼▼
Mexican

Location: Corner of Bagley and 24th; in Mexicantown. 3454 Bagley 48216. **Hours:** 8 am-6 pm, Sun-3 pm. Closed major holidays. **Features:** Dine in at the tiny, cozy restaurant, or pick up the perfectly seasoned and nearly grease-free steamed corn-husk-wrapped pork and cornmeal delights by the bag for carryout. Another flavorful Mexican selection is the chicken enchilada suiza. Casual dress. **Parking:** street.

☒

FISHBONE'S RHYTHM KITCHEN CAFE Lunch: $6-$13 Dinner: $5-$25 Phone: 313/965-4600 ⑲
▼▼ ▼▼
Cajun

Location: At corner of Brush Ave and Lafayette Blvd; downtown; in The Atheneum Suite Hotel & Conference Center. 400 Monroe St 48226. **Hours:** 6:30 am-midnight, Fri & Sat-2 am, Sun from 10:30 am. Closed: 11/27, 12/25. **Features:** This restaurant boasts a loud and lively crowd eager to dine on such New Orleans Cajun specialties as whiskey barbecue ribs, chicken and seafood gumbo. Casual dress; cocktails. **Parking:** on-site (fee). **Cards:** AX, DC, DS, MC, VI.

▣ ☒

(See map p. 226)

HOLLYWOOD BROWN DERBY   Dinner: $20-$40   Phone: 877/847-8471   ㉕
⬥⬥⬥
▽▽▽▽
Steak & Seafood

Location: On SR 10; in MGM Grand Casino. 1300 John C Lodge 48226. **Hours:** 6 pm-11 pm, Fri & Sat-midnight, Sun 11 am-3 & 6-11 pm. **Reservations:** required. **Features:** Set just off the bustling casino floor, this fine eatery presents a sophisticated clubby atmosphere with cherrywood walls, fine chandeliers, velvety red high back chairs and white linen tabletops. The faces of Hollywood are skillfully etched into the glass throughout the dining room. The menu features well-prepared prime steak, chops and fresh seafood that are beautifully presented on fine china. Tableside preparations are also featured and are skillfully done by the talented service staff. Dressy casual; cocktails; entertainment. **Parking:** on-site (fee) and valet. **Cards:** AX, CB, DC, DS, JC, MC, VI.   &M 🍸 ✕

INTERMEZZO   Lunch: $13-$20   Dinner: $16-$35   Phone: 313/961-0707   ⑯
▽▽ ▽▽
Italian

Location: Between Gratiot and Madison near Music Hall and the new opera house; in Harmonie Park. 1407 Randolph St 48226. **Hours:** 11 am-2:30 pm, Tues-Thurs 11 am-4 & 5-10 pm, Fri & Sat-11 pm. Closed major holidays; also Sun except for seasonal theater events. **Reservations:** suggested. **Features:** The restaurant's seasonal menu outlines dishes prepared with care and presented with style. Much of the pasta is made on the premises, and the tasty biscotti is baked fresh twice a week. The atmosphere is eclectic, yet casually sophisticated. Casual dress; cocktails. **Parking:** valet and street. **Cards:** AX, DC, DS, MC, VI.   &M 🍸 ✕

IRIDESCENCE RESTAURANT   Dinner: $24-$65   Phone: 313/237-7711   ⑪
⬥⬥⬥
▽▽▽ ▽▽▽
Asian

Location: In Motor City Casino. 2901 Grand River Ave 48201. **Hours:** 5 pm-midnight. **Reservations:** suggested. **Features:** Located in the former site of a Wonder Bread factory, this upscale and richly appointed restaurant will make everyone feel like a high roller. While specializing in steak and seafood such as lobster tail, Dover sole and a Delmonico with wild mushrooms and au gratin potatoes, the signature Kaboom dessert is not to be missed. Dressy casual; cocktails. **Parking:** on-site and valet. **Cards:** AX, CB, DC, DS, JC, MC, VI.   &M ✕

JOHNNY ROCKETS   Lunch: $3-$6   Dinner: $3-$6   Phone: 313/471-3446   ⑫
▽▽
American

Location: Fox Theater Office Center; located across from Commerce Park. 2239 Woodward Ave 48226. **Hours:** 11 am-9 pm, Wed & Thurs-11 pm, Fri & Sat-midnight. Closed major holidays. **Features:** Located across from Comerica Park, this 1950s retro diner serves a variety of hamburgers and other comfort foods in a loud, nostalgia-filled atmosphere. Casual dress. **Parking:** street. **Cards:** AX, MC, VI.   ✕

LAFAYETTE CONEY ISLAND   Lunch: $2-$6   Dinner: $2-$6   Phone: 313/954-8198   ㉓
▽▽
American

Location: At corner of Griswold. 118 W Lafayette 48226. **Hours:** 24 hours. Closed: 12/25. **Features:** Stretch limousines still idle at 3 am in front of the famous hot dog and chili compound. The restaurant does a fine job with its steamed buns, spicy chili, onions, mustard and natural casings that snap when bitten. The decor reflects a diner style. Casual dress; beer only. **Parking:** street.

LOCO BAR & GRILL   Lunch: $5-$17   Dinner: $5-$17   Phone: 313/965-3737   ⑳
▽▽
Tex-Mex

Location: At Lafayette and Beaubien; downtown. 454 E Lafayette 48226. **Hours:** 11 am-midnight, Fri-2 am, Sat & Sun noon-2 am. Closed major holidays. **Reservations:** accepted. **Features:** The rough-and-tumble cowboy bar serves up tasty renditions of Tex-Mex cuisine, with a large selection of hot sauces and beer. Sink your teeth into zippy enchiladas, quesadillas, tacos, chunky salsa and spicy Mexican sausage with rice and beans. Casual dress; cocktails. **Parking:** on-site (fee) and street. **Cards:** AX, DC, DS, MC, VI.   ✕

MAJESTIC CAFE   Lunch: $5-$11   Dinner: $7-$18   Phone: 313/833-0120   ⑤
▽▽ ▽▽
American

Location: Between Alexandrine and Canfield. 4140 Woodward 48202. **Hours:** 11 am-2 am, Sat & Mon from 4:30 pm, Sun from 11:30 am. Closed major holidays. **Reservations:** suggested; weekends. **Features:** Big, bright windows and cool, faux-Miro murals lend to the casually upscale feel of the dining room. The spicy menu falls somewhere between Midwest and Middle Eastern. Symphony and cultural crowds frequent the reserved restaurant before shows. Casual dress; cocktails. **Parking:** on-site. **Cards:** AX, DC, MC, VI.   🍸 ✕

MARIO'S   Lunch: $7-$15   Dinner: $12-$35   Phone: 313/832-1616   ⑧
▽▽ ▽▽
Italian

Location: 1.5 mi n of Civic Center. 4222 2nd Ave 48201. **Hours:** 11:30 am-11 pm, Fri-midnight, Sat 4 pm-midnight, Sun 2 pm-11 pm. Closed: 12/25. **Reservations:** suggested. **Features:** Dark and romantic, you will almost expect to see Old Blue Eyes himself at this local institution, famous for its 1960s style Italian dishes and ambience. Casual dress; cocktails. **Parking:** street. **Cards:** AX, DC, MC, VI.   🍸 ✕

MEXICAN VILLAGE RESTAURANT   Lunch: $6-$16   Dinner: $6-$16   Phone: 313/237-0333   ㉖
⬥⬥⬥
▽▽
Mexican

Location: At jct Bagley and 18th sts. 2600 Bagley 48216. **Hours:** 11 am-11 pm, Fri & Sat-2 am. Closed major holidays. **Features:** In business since 1943, the restaurant is an established favorite for fajitas, burritos, nachos and combination plates. White stucco arches, paintings depicting Mexican history and colorful decorations add to the lively ambience of the dining room. Casual dress; cocktails. **Parking:** on-site. **Cards:** AX, DC, MC, VI.   🍸 ✕

OPUS ONE   Lunch: $10-$19   Dinner: $20-$39   Phone: 313/961-7766   ㉑
▽▽▽▽
American

Location: Corner of E Lerned St and St. Antoine. 565 E Larned St 48226. **Hours:** 11:30 am-10 pm, Fri-11 pm, Sat 5 pm-11 pm. Closed major holidays; also Sun. **Reservations:** suggested. **Features:** Much like the wine of the same name, this restaurant is quietly opulent and meticulous in detail. An extensive wine list which includes its namesake, fresh preparations of seafood, fowl and beef and a renown dessert tray make this an enjoyable experience. Dressy casual; cocktails; entertainment. **Parking:** on-site and valet. **Cards:** AX, DC, DS, MC, VI.   🍸 ✕

(See map p. 226)

PEGASUS TAVERNA RESTAURANT   **Lunch:** $6-$20   **Dinner:** $7-$24   **Phone:** 313/964-6800   ⑰
▽▽▽
Greek
Location: In Greektown area; downtown. 558 Monroe St 48226. **Hours:** 11 am-midnight, Fri & Sat-2 am, Sun 10:30 am-midnight. Closed: 11/27, 12/25. **Features:** Located in Greektown, this restaurant offers couples intimate booth seating and a wide selection of authentic Greek dishes and dessert to choose from. Casual dress; cocktails. **Parking:** on-site. **Cards:** AX, DC, DS, JC, MC, VI.   ⎣M⎦ 🍷 ✕

ROMA CAFE   **Lunch:** $8-$12   **Dinner:** $13-$18   **Phone:** 313/831-5940   ⑦
▽▽▽ ▽▽▽
Italian
Location: At jct Via Roma (Riopelle) and Erskine; near Eastern Market area. 3401 Riopelle 48207. **Hours:** 11 am-10:30 pm, Sat-midnight. Closed major holidays; also Sun. **Reservations:** suggested. **Features:** Homemade pasta and a flavorful house meat sauce add to the great taste of such dishes as spaghetti and lasagna. Attractive prints and a hand-carved bar decorate the appealingly unpretentious dining room. Tuxedoed servers are friendly and efficient. Casual dress; cocktails. **Parking:** on-site. **Cards:** AX, DC, MC, VI.   🍷 ✕

SALA THAI   **Lunch:** $6-$9   **Dinner:** $6-$9   **Phone:** 313/567-8424   ⑬
▽▽▽
Thai
Location: E of I-375; in Lafayette Park Plaza. 1541-1543 E Lafayette 48207. **Hours:** 11 am-9 pm, Fri-10 pm, Sat noon-10 pm, Sun 3 pm-8 pm. Closed major holidays. **Features:** The bright, pretty restaurant serves first-rate renditions of sweet, sour and spicy Southeast Asian cuisine. Scrumptious are the chicken satay with peanut sauce and the lime- and chili-scented tom yum soup. Service is friendly and well-timed. Casual dress. **Parking:** on-site. **Cards:** AX, DS, MC, VI.   ✕

TRAFFIC JAM & SNUG   **Lunch:** $8-$12   **Dinner:** $10-$18   **Phone:** 313/831-9470   ④
▽▽▽ ▽▽▽
American
Location: W Canfield at 2nd; 2 blks w of Woodward Ave, then 2 blks s of Forest. 511 W Canfield 48201. **Hours:** 11 am-10:30 pm, Fri-midnight, Sat noon-midnight. Closed major holidays; also Sun. **Features:** On the end of a cobblestone street of restored turn-of-the-20th-century Victorian mansions, the restaurant serves complex and creative preparations, such as the smoked turkey Reuben with sauerkraut and melted Swiss cheese on a potato roll. Casual dress; cocktails. **Parking:** no self-parking. **Cards:** MC, VI.   ⎣M⎦ 🍷 ✕

TWINGO'S   **Lunch:** $6-$10   **Dinner:** $8-$12   **Phone:** 313/832-3832   ②
▽▽▽ ▽▽▽
American
Location: Jct Cass Ave and Prentis St. 4710 Cass Ave 48201. **Hours:** 11 am-11 pm, Fri & Sat-midnight. Closed major holidays. **Reservations:** suggested. **Features:** Reminiscent of a Paris cafe, this two story eclectic space offers a small menu of French influenced entrees and a wide variety of soups and sandwiches. Casual dress; wine only. **Parking:** on-site (fee) and street. **Cards:** AX, DC, DS, MC, VI.   ⎣M⎦ 🍷 ✕

UNION STREET   **Lunch:** $8-$14   **Dinner:** $8-$16   **Phone:** 313/831-3965   ⑥
▽▽▽ ▽▽▽
American
Location: Between Alexandrine and Canfield. 4145 Woodward Ave 48201. **Hours:** 11 am-10 pm, Sat 4 pm-2 am. Closed major holidays; also Sun. **Features:** Loud, noisy and fun, the energetic restaurant is a hangout for students and professionals. Seafood bisque, pasta with flavorful sauces and fiery foods, such as ribs slathered with hot sauce, are representative of menu choices. Servers are upbeat. Casual dress; cocktails. **Parking:** on-site (fee) and street. **Cards:** AX, DC, MC, VI.   ⎣M⎦ ✕

WHITNEY RESTAURANT   Historic   **Lunch:** $12-$30   **Dinner:** $19-$35   **Phone:** 313/832-5700   ③
▽▽▽▽
American
Location: Between Mack and Warren aves. 4421 Woodward Ave 48201. **Hours:** Mon 6 pm-9 pm, Tues 11 am-2 & 6-9 pm, Wed & Thurs 11 am-2 & 5-9 pm, Fri-10 pm, Sat 5 pm-10 pm, Sun-8 pm. Closed major holidays. **Reservations:** suggested. **Features:** The chef uses fresh ingredients in creative preparations of contemporary cuisine. In a restored 1894 Victorian mansion, the restaurant exudes elegant charm. Stained glass windows, lovely woodwork and a hand-laid mosaic tile floor enhance the decor. Dressy casual; cocktails. **Parking:** valet and street. **Cards:** AX, CB, DC, DS, MC, VI.   ⎣M⎦ 🍷 ✕

DETROIT pop. 951,270   (See map p. 228; index p. 230)

———— WHERE TO STAY ————

HOLIDAY INN FAIRLANE/DEARBORN   **Phone:** (313)336-3340   ❸
◇◇◇ SAVE
▽▽▽▽
Small-scale Hotel
All Year   1P: $129   2P: $129
Location: Just w of Southfield Frwy at jct Ford Rd. 5801 Southfield Service Dr 48228. Fax: 313/336-7037. **Facility:** 347 units. 342 one-bedroom standard units, some with whirlpools. 5 one-bedroom suites. 2-6 stories, interior corridors. **Parking:** on-site. **Amenities:** dual phone lines, voice mail, irons, hair dryers. **Dining:** 6 am-2 & 5-10 pm, Sat & Sun from 7 am, cocktails. **Pool(s):** heated outdoor, heated indoor. **Leisure Activities:** whirlpools, exercise room, sports court. **Guest Services:** gift shop, valet laundry. **Business Services:** conference facilities, business center. **Cards:** AX, DC, DS, MC, VI. **Special Amenities:** free newspaper.

SOME UNITS
🅢🅓 ⑪ ⎣M⎦ 🕿 🏊 ✕ 🐾 ⎡DATA PORT⎦ 🖥 / ✕ 📠 /

OMNI DETROIT RIVERPLACE   **Phone:** (313)259-9500   ❶
◇◇◇ SAVE
▽▽▽▽
Small-scale Hotel
All Year   1P: $139   2P: $159
Location: 1.5 mi on E Jefferson Ave, 4 blks s on McDougall; downtown. 1000 River Pl 48207. Fax: 313/259-3744. **Facility:** Many rooms at this elegant riverfront hotel offer water views. 108 units. 99 one-bedroom standard units. 9 one-bedroom suites, some with whirlpools. 5 stories, interior corridors. **Parking:** on-site. **Terms:** 12% service charge. **Amenities:** dual phone lines, voice mail, safes, honor bars, irons, hair dryers. **Dining:** Baron's on the River, see separate listing. **Pool(s):** heated indoor. **Leisure Activities:** saunas, whirlpool. *Fee:* 2 tennis courts, croquet court, massage. **Guest Services:** valet laundry, area transportation (fee), tanning facility. **Business Services:** meeting rooms. **Cards:** AX, DC, DS, MC, VI.

SOME UNITS
🅢🅓 ⑪ 🍷 🏊 🕊 ✕ 🐾 ⎡DATA PORT⎦ 🖥 / ✕ ⎡VCR⎦ /
FEE

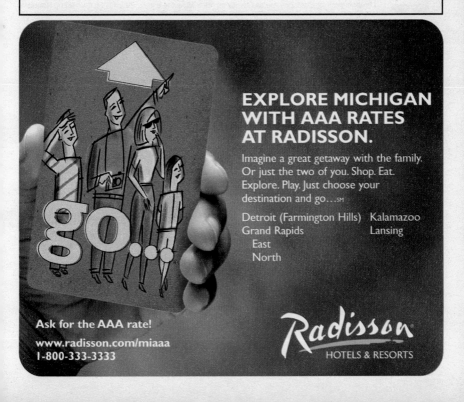

(See map p. 228)

RESIDENCE INN BY MARRIOTT-DEARBORN — Phone: (313)441-1700 ②
All Year [BP]　　　　　　1P: $134　　　　　2P: $134
Location: Just n of Southfield Frwy at jct Ford Rd. 5777 Southfield Service Dr 48228. Fax: 313/441-4144. **Facility:** 128 one-bedroom standard units with kitchens, some with whirlpools. 2 stories, exterior corridors. *Bath:* combo or shower only. **Parking:** on-site. **Terms:** pets ($100 fee, $7 extra charge). **Amenities:** dual phone lines, voice mail, irons, hair dryers. **Pool(s):** heated outdoor. **Leisure Activities:** whirlpool, exercise room, sports court. **Guest Services:** valet and coin laundry. **Cards:** AX, CB, DC, DS, MC, VI.

Small-scale Hotel

SOME UNITS

——— WHERE TO DINE ———

BARON'S ON THE RIVER　　　Lunch: $6-$14　　　Dinner: $16-$26　　　Phone: 313/259-9500 ②
Location: 1.5 mi on E Jefferson Ave, 4 blks s on McDougall; downtown; in Omni Detroit Riverplace. 1000 River Place 48207. **Hours:** 7 am-2 & 5-10 pm, Fri-Sun to 10:30 pm. **Reservations:** accepted. **Features:** Enormous portions of aged prime Angus beef—as well as chops, seafood and pasta dishes—make up the dinner menu, while scaled-down lunch selections include meatloaf, pot pie and sandwiches. The atmosphere is
American
casual and clublike. Patio views are great. Dressy casual; cocktails. **Parking:** valet. **Cards:** AX, CB, DC, DS, MC, VI.

GIOVANNI'S RISTORANTE　　　Lunch: $8-$13　　　Dinner: $12-$18　　　Phone: 313/841-0122 ④
Location: Between Schaefer and Fort. 330 S Oakwood Blvd 48217. **Hours:** 11 am-9 pm, Fri-10 pm, Sat 4 pm-10 pm. Closed major holidays; also Sun & Mon. **Reservations:** suggested. **Features:** A local favorite; the
Italian
restaurant prepares Italian favorites. Dressy casual; cocktails. **Parking:** on-site. **Cards:** AX, DC, MC, VI.

THE RATTLESNAKE CLUB　　　Lunch: $9-$16　　　Dinner: $17-$31　　　Phone: 313/567-4400 ③
Location: 1.5 mi on E Jefferson Ave, 4 blks s on McDougall; downtown. 300 River Pl 48207. **Hours:** 11:30 am-10 pm, Fri-11 pm, Sat 5:30 pm-11 pm. Closed major holidays; also Sun. **Reservations:** accepted.
American
Features: Trendy and cutting edge, this riverside restaurant located in Detroit's river place area, offers sophisticated American cuisine geared toward the hip and lively. Dressy casual; cocktails. **Parking:** valet
and street. **Cards:** AX, DC, DS, JC, MC, VI.

SINDBAD'S AT THE RIVER　　　Lunch: $5-$8　　　Dinner: $9-$18　　　Phone: 313/822-7817 ①
Location: From jct E Jefferson Ave and Marquette, follow Marquette e to St. Clair. 100 St. Clair 48214. **Hours:** 11 am-11 pm, Fri & Sat-1 am. Closed major holidays. **Features:** On the banks of the Detroit River, the
Steak & Seafood
restaurant has been an area institution for casual dining and great waterfront views since 1949. The menu centers on a good selection of seafood and steaks. Outdoor dining is popular during pleasant weather.
Casual dress; cocktails. **Parking:** valet. **Cards:** AX, DC, DS, MC, VI.

The Detroit Vicinity

ALLEN PARK pop. 29,376   (See map p. 228; index p. 234)

―――― WHERE TO STAY ――――

BEST WESTERN GREENFIELD INN
Phone: (313)271-1600   **118**

Small-scale Hotel

All Year   1P: $95-$125   2P: $105-$135
Location: At jct I-94 and Oakwood Blvd, 2 mi from Greenfield Village. 3000 Enterprise Dr 48101. Fax: 313/271-1600. **Facility:** 209 one-bedroom standard units. 3 stories, interior corridors. **Parking:** on-site. **Terms:** package plans - seasonal & weekends, pets ($100 deposit, small dogs only). **Amenities:** video library (fee), dual phone lines, voice mail, safes, irons, hair dryers. **Dining:** 6 am-10 pm, Fri & Sat-11 pm 6/1-8/31, cocktails. **Leisure Activities:** sauna, whirlpool, exercise room. **Guest Services:** valet and coin laundry, area transportation-within 5 mi. **Business Services:** meeting rooms, PC, fax. **Cards:** AX, DC, MC, VI. **Special Amenities: early check-in/late check-out and free newspaper.** *(See color ad p 251)*

SOME UNITS

HOLIDAY INN EXPRESS & SUITES
Phone: (313)323-3500   **119**

Small-scale Hotel

All Year [ECP]   1P: $110-$130   2P: $110-$130
Location: I-94, exit 206, jct Oakwood Blvd. 3600 Enterprise Dr 48101. Fax: 313/323-3553. **Facility:** 121 units. 92 one-bedroom standard units, some with whirlpools. 29 one-bedroom suites, some with whirlpools. 3 stories, interior corridors. *Bath:* combo or shower only. **Parking:** on-site. **Terms:** package plans, pets (dogs only). **Amenities:** high-speed Internet, dual phone lines, voice mail, safes, irons, hair dryers. **Pool(s):** heated indoor. **Leisure Activities:** whirlpool, exercise room. **Guest Services:** valet and coin laundry. **Business Services:** meeting rooms. **Cards:** AX, CB, DC, DS, MC, VI. **Special Amenities: free continental breakfast and free local telephone calls.** *(See color ad card insert & p 252)*

SOME UNITS
FEE

AUBURN HILLS pop. 19,837

―――― WHERE TO STAY ――――

AMERISUITES (DETROIT/AUBURN HILLS)
Phone: (248)475-9393

Small-scale Hotel

All Year   1P: $99   2P: $99   XP: $10   F17
Location: I-75, exit 79 (University Dr), just w, then just n. 1545 Opdyke Road 48326. Fax: 248/475-9399. **Facility:** 128 one-bedroom standard units. 6 stories, interior corridors. *Bath:* combo or shower only. **Parking:** on-site. **Terms:** [ECP] meal plan available, small pets only. **Amenities:** voice mail, irons, hair dryers. *Some:* dual phone lines. **Pool(s):** heated indoor. **Leisure Activities:** exercise room. **Guest Services:** valet and coin laundry. **Business Services:** meeting rooms. **Cards:** AX, DS, MC, VI. **Special Amenities: free continental breakfast and free newspaper.**

SOME UNITS

CANDLEWOOD SUITES

Phone: 248/373-3342

All Year — 1P: $89

Location: I-75, exit 79 (University Dr), just w, then 0.4 mi n. 1650 N Opdyke Rd 48326. Fax: 248/373-4523. Small-scale Hotel. **Facility:** 110 units. 96 one-bedroom standard units with efficiencies. 14 one-bedroom suites with kitchens. 3 stories, interior corridors. **Parking:** on-site. **Terms:** weekly rates available. **Amenities:** video library, CD players, dual phone lines, voice mail, irons, hair dryers. **Leisure Activities:** exercise room. **Guest Services:** sundries. **Cards:** AX, CB, DC, DS, JC, MC, VI.

SOME UNITS

COMFORT SUITES OF AUBURN HILLS

Phone: (248)370-0200

	1P	2P	XP	
6/1-8/31	$109-$199	$109-$199	$10	F18
4/1-5/31 & 9/1-3/31	$99-$189	$99-$189	$10	F18

Location: I-75, exit 79 (University Dr), just w, then just n. 1565 N Opdyke Rd 48326. Fax: 248/370-0980. **Facility:** 63 units. 53 one-bedroom standard units, some with whirlpools. 10 one-bedroom suites ($99-$199), some with whirlpools. 3 stories, interior corridors. *Bath:* combo or shower only. **Parking:** on-site. **Terms:** [ECP] meal plan available. **Amenities:** voice mail, irons, hair dryers. *Some:* dual phone lines. **Pool(s):** heated indoor. **Leisure Activities:** whirlpool. **Guest Services:** valet laundry. **Business Services:** meeting rooms. **Cards:** AX, CB, DC, DS, MC, VI.

SOME UNITS

COURTYARD BY MARRIOTT-AUBURN HILLS

Phone: (248)373-4100

All Year — 1P: $59-$154

Location: I-75, exit 79 (University Dr), just w, then just n. 1296 Opdyke Rd 48326. Fax: 248/373-1885. **Facility:** 148 units. 138 one-bedroom standard units. 10 one-bedroom suites ($134-$154). 2-3 stories, interior corridors. *Bath:* combo or shower only. **Parking:** on-site. **Terms:** cancellation fee imposed, package plans - weekends. **Amenities:** voice mail, irons, hair dryers. **Dining:** 6:30-10 am, Sat & Sun 8 am-noon. **Pool(s):** heated indoor. **Leisure Activities:** whirlpool, exercise room. **Guest Services:** valet and coin laundry. **Business Services:** meeting rooms. **Cards:** AX, DC, DS, JC, MC, VI. **Special Amenities:** early check-in/late check-out and preferred room (subject to availability with advanced reservations).

SOME UNITS

EXTENDED STAYAMERICA-AUBURN HILLS

Phone: (248)373-1335

All Year — 1P: $65 — 2P: $65

Location: I-75, exit 79 (University Dr), just w, just s on Opdyke Rd, then just e. 1180 Doris Rd 48326. Fax: 248/373-1354. **Facility:** 113 one-bedroom standard units with efficiencies. 3 stories, interior corridors. *Bath:* combo or shower only. **Parking:** on-site. **Terms:** cancellation fee imposed, weekly rates available. **Amenities:** voice mail, hair dryers. **Guest Services:** sundries, valet and coin laundry. **Cards:** AX, CB, DC, DS, MC, VI.

SOME UNITS

FAIRFIELD INN BY MARRIOTT-AUBURN HILLS

Phone: (248)373-2228

All Year — 1P: $59-$89 — 2P: $69-$99 — XP: $10 — F18

Location: I-75, exit 79 (University Dr), just w, then s. 1294 Opdyke Rd 48326. Fax: 248/373-2228. **Facility:** 134 one-bedroom standard units. 3 stories, interior/exterior corridors. *Bath:* combo or shower only. **Parking:** on-site, winter plug-ins. **Terms:** cancellation fee imposed, weekly rates available, [CP] meal plan available. **Amenities:** irons. **Pool(s):** heated outdoor. **Guest Services:** valet laundry. **Cards:** AX, CB, DC, DS, MC, VI.

SOME UNITS

HAMPTON INN

Phone: (248)370-0044

All Year [ECP] — 1P: $114 — 2P: $114

Location: I-75, exit 79 (University Dr), just w, then just n. 1461 N Opdyke Rd 48326. Fax: 248/370-9590. **Facility:** 124 one-bedroom standard units. 3 stories, interior corridors. **Parking:** on-site. **Amenities:** dual phone lines, voice mail, irons, hair dryers. **Pool(s):** heated outdoor. **Leisure Activities:** exercise room. **Guest Services:** valet laundry. **Business Services:** meeting rooms, business center. **Cards:** AX, DC, DS, MC, VI.

SOME UNITS

HILTON SUITES AUBURN HILLS

Phone: (248)334-2222

All Year — 1P: $95-$199 — 2P: $95-$199 — XP: $15 — F18

Location: I-75, exit 79 (University Dr), just w, then 0.5 mi s on Opdyke Rd, just e. 2300 Featherstone Rd 48326. Fax: 248/322-2300. **Facility:** 224 one-bedroom suites. 5 stories, interior corridors. *Bath:* combo or shower only. **Parking:** on-site, winter plug-ins. **Amenities:** video games (fee), dual phone lines, voice mail, irons, hair dryers. *Some:* high-speed Internet. **Pool(s):** heated indoor. **Leisure Activities:** sauna, whirlpool, exercise room. **Guest Services:** gift shop, area transportation. **Business Services:** conference facilities, business center. **Cards:** AX, CB, DC, DS, MC, VI.

SOME UNITS

HOLIDAY INN SELECT-AUBURN HILLS

Phone: (248)373-4550

All Year — 1P: $89-$169 — 2P: $89-$169 — XP: $10 — F16

Location: I-75, exit 79 (University Dr). 1500 Opdyke Rd 48326. Fax: 248/373-8220. **Facility:** 190 units. 188 one-bedroom standard units, some with whirlpools. 2 one-bedroom suites. 8 stories, interior corridors. *Bath:* combo or shower only. **Parking:** on-site. **Terms:** check-in 4 pm, cancellation fee imposed, package plans - weekends. **Amenities:** voice mail, irons, hair dryers. **Pool(s):** heated indoor. **Leisure Activities:** sauna, whirlpool, exercise room. **Guest Services:** valet and coin laundry, area transportation. **Business Services:** conference facilities, business center. **Cards:** AX, CB, DC, DS, MC, VI.

SOME UNITS

HOMESTEAD STUDIO SUITES HOTEL-DETROIT/AUBURN HILLS

Phone: (248)340-8888

Small-scale Hotel

All Year   1P: $89-$99   2P: $94-$104
Location: I-75, exit 79 (University Dr), 0.9 mi e. 3315 University Dr 48326. Fax: 248/340-8622. **Facility:** 134 one-bedroom standard units with efficiencies. 3 stories, interior corridors. *Bath:* combo or shower only. **Parking:** on-site, winter plug-ins. **Terms:** pets ($75 deposit). **Amenities:** voice mail, irons. **Guest Services:** sundries, valet and coin laundry. **Cards:** AX, CB, DC, DS, JC, MC, VI.

SOME UNITS

STAYBRIDGE SUITES

Phone: (248)322-4600

Small-scale Hotel

All Year   1P: $135   2P: $135
Location: I-75, exit 79 (University Dr), just w, then just s. on Opdyke Rd, just e. 2050 Featherstone Rd 48326. Fax: 248/322-4700. **Facility:** 118 units. 58 one-bedroom standard units with efficiencies. 38 one- and 22 two-bedroom suites with efficiencies. 3 stories, interior corridors. *Bath:* combo or shower only. **Parking:** on-site. **Terms:** [ECP] meal plan available, pets ($75 fee). **Amenities:** video library (fee), high-speed Internet, dual phone lines, voice mail, irons, hair dryers. **Pool(s):** heated outdoor. **Leisure Activities:** exercise room, sports court. **Guest Services:** sundries. **Business Services:** meeting rooms, business center. **Cards:** AX, DC, DS, MC, VI.

SOME UNITS

WELLESLEY INN & SUITES (DETROIT/AUBURN HILLS)

Phone: (248)335-5200

Small-scale Hotel

1/1-3/31 [ECP]   1P: $80-$99   2P: $80-$99   XP: $10   F17
4/1-12/31 [ECP]   1P: $75-$94   2P: $75-$94   XP: $10   F17
Location: I-75, exit 79 (University Dr), just w, then 0.5 mi s on Opdyke Rd, just e. 2100 Featherstone Rd 48326. Fax: 248/335-5800. **Facility:** 139 units. 68 one-bedroom standard units with efficiencies. 71 one-bedroom suites with efficiencies. 3 stories, interior corridors. *Bath:* combo or shower only. **Parking:** on-site. **Terms:** pets ($50 deposit). **Amenities:** video games (fee), voice mail, irons, hair dryers. **Pool(s):** heated outdoor. **Leisure Activities:** exercise room. **Guest Services:** valet and coin laundry. **Business Services:** meeting rooms. **Cards:** AX, DC, DS, JC, MC, VI. **Special Amenities:** free continental breakfast and free newspaper.

SOME UNITS

WINGATE INN

Phone: (248)334-3324

Small-scale Hotel

All Year [ECP]   1P: $75-$129   2P: $75-$129   XP: $10   F
Location: I-75, exit 79 (University Dr), just w, then 0.5 mi s on Opdyke Rd, just e. 2200 Featherstone Rd 48326. Fax: 248/334-2057. **Facility:** 102 one-bedroom standard units, some with whirlpools. 4 stories, interior corridors. **Parking:** on-site. **Terms:** 7 day cancellation notice. **Amenities:** video games, high-speed Internet, voice mail, safes, irons, hair dryers. **Pool(s):** heated indoor. **Leisure Activities:** whirlpool, exercise room. **Guest Services:** valet laundry. **Business Services:** meeting rooms, business center. **Cards:** AX, CB, DC, DS, MC, VI.

SOME UNITS

———— WHERE TO DINE ————

BIG BUCK BREWERY & STEAKHOUSE

Lunch: $7-$29   **Dinner:** $7-$29   **Phone:** 248/276-2337

Steak House

Location: I-75, exit 79 (University Dr), just w, then just s. 2550 Takata Dr 48326. **Hours:** 11 am-11 pm, Fri-midnight, Sat noon-midnight, Sun noon-10 pm. Closed major holidays. **Features:** The Big Buck Brewery and Steakhouse produces fine brews, bound to please the beer connoisseur, and features the finest "Sterling Silver" certified premium USDA choice beef, for steak that is guaranteed to be tender, juicy and flavorful or your money back. Casual dress; beer only. **Parking:** on-site. **Cards:** AX, DC, DS, MC, VI.

FRAN O'BRIEN'S MARYLAND CRAB HOUSE

Lunch: $7-$15   **Dinner:** $9-$25   **Phone:** 248/332-7744

American

Location: I-75, exit 79 (University Dr), just w, 1 mi s. 621 S Opdyke Rd 48342. **Hours:** 11 am-10 pm, Sat 3 pm-11 pm, Sun 3 pm-9 pm. Closed major holidays. **Features:** Located in a shopping plaza, a short distance from the Pontiac Silverdome, this modest nautically themed restaurant is popular with the post and pre game crowd. Casual dress; cocktails. **Parking:** on-site. **Cards:** AX, MC, VI.

LELLI'S INN OF AUBURN HILLS

Lunch: $8-$15   **Dinner:** $10-$25   **Phone:** 248/373-4440

Northern Italian

Location: I-75, exit 79 (University Dr), then 0.5 mi s. 885 N Opdyke Rd 48326. **Hours:** 11 am-10 pm, Fri & Sat-11 pm, Sun noon-9 pm. Closed major holidays. **Reservations:** suggested. **Features:** A Detroit legend in a new location overlooking the Pontiac Silverdome. Still serving the filet mignon and shrimp Lelli that made the original restaurant famous, Lelli's Inn is perfect for special occasions. Dressy casual; cocktails. **Parking:** on-site. **Cards:** AX, DC, MC, VI.

RANGOLI INDIAN CUISINE

Lunch: $5-$8   **Dinner:** $7-$12   **Phone:** 248/377-3800

Indian

Location: I-75, exit 79 (University Dr), 1 mi n on Opdyke Rd, then 0.5 mi s. 3055 E Walton Blvd 48326. **Hours:** 11 am-2:30 & 5-9:30 pm, Fri-10:30 pm, Sat 11:30 am-3 & 5-10 pm, Sun 11:30 am-3 & 5-9 pm. Closed major holidays. **Reservations:** accepted. **Features:** Named for a type of traditional Indian Folk painting, this attractive restaurant showcases India's widely varied regional cuisines. Expert waiters will help guide you through the extensive menu. Casual dress. **Parking:** on-site. **Cards:** AX, DS, MC, VI.

BELLEVILLE pop. 3,997

——— WHERE TO STAY ———

COMFORT INN

SAVE

Small-scale Hotel

All Year [ECP]   1P: $55-$129   2P: $59-$129   **Phone:** (734)697-8556   XP: $5   F17
Location: I-94, exit 190 (Belleville Rd), just s. 45945 S I-94 Service Dr 48111. Fax: 734/697-8513. **Facility:** 64 one-bedroom standard units, some with whirlpools. 2 stories, interior corridors. *Bath:* combo or shower only. **Parking:** on-site. **Terms:** 14 day cancellation notice, pets (with prior approval). **Amenities:** voice mail, safes, irons, hair dryers. **Pool(s):** small heated indoor. **Leisure Activities:** whirlpool. **Guest Services:** coin laundry. **Business Services:** meeting rooms. **Cards:** AX, CB, DC, DS, JC, MC, VI.

SOME UNITS

HAMPTON INN

(AAA) SAVE

Small-scale Hotel

All Year   1P: $89-$99   2P: $89-$99   **Phone:** (734)699-2424   XP: $5   F18
Location: I-94, exit 190 (Belleville Rd), just w. 46280 N I-94 Service Dr 48111. Fax: 734/699-7340. **Facility:** 90 one-bedroom standard units. 3 stories, interior corridors. *Bath:* combo or shower only. **Parking:** on-site. **Terms:** [ECP] meal plan available. **Amenities:** dual phone lines, voice mail, irons, hair dryers. **Pool(s):** heated indoor. **Leisure Activities:** whirlpool, exercise room. **Guest Services:** valet and coin laundry, airport transportation-Detroit Metro Willow Run Airport. **Business Services:** fax (fee). **Cards:** AX, DC, DS, MC, VI. **Special Amenities:** free continental breakfast and free local telephone calls.

SOME UNITS

HOLIDAY INN EXPRESS HOTEL & SUITES

(AAA) SAVE

Small-scale Hotel

All Year [ECP]   1P: $89-$99   2P: $89-$99   **Phone:** (734)857-6200   XP: $5   F18
Location: I-94, exit 190 (Belleville Rd), just w. 46194 N I-94 Service Dr 48111. Fax: 734/857-6229. **Facility:** Smoke free premises. 108 one-bedroom standard units, some with whirlpools. 3 stories, interior corridors. *Bath:* combo or shower only. **Parking:** on-site. **Amenities:** dual phone lines, voice mail, irons, hair dryers. **Pool(s):** heated indoor. **Leisure Activities:** saunas, whirlpool, steamrooms, exercise room. **Guest Services:** valet and coin laundry, airport transportation-Willow Run Airport. **Business Services:** meeting rooms. **Cards:** AX, DC, DS, MC, VI. **Special Amenities:** free continental breakfast and free newspaper. *(See color ad card insert & below)*

SOME UNITS

RED ROOF INN METRO AIRPORT

(AAA) SAVE

Motel

All Year   1P: $49-$69   2P: $55-$75   **Phone:** (734)697-2244   XP: $6   F18
Location: I-94, exit 190 (Belleville Rd). 45501 N I-94 Expwy, Service Dr 48111. Fax: 734/697-4384. **Facility:** 112 one-bedroom standard units. 2 stories, exterior corridors. *Bath:* combo or shower only. **Parking:** on-site. **Terms:** small pets only. **Amenities:** video games. **Cards:** AX, CB, DC, DS, MC, VI. **Special Amenities:** free local telephone calls and free newspaper.

SOME UNITS

SUPER 8 MOTEL

Small-scale Hotel

All Year [ECP]   1P: $57   2P: $63   **Phone:** (734)699-1888   XP: $6   F12
Location: I-94, exit 190 (Belleville Rd), just s. 45707 S I-94 Service Dr 48111. Fax: 734/699-3596. **Facility:** 63 one-bedroom standard units, some with whirlpools. 3 stories, interior corridors. **Parking:** on-site. **Terms:** weekly rates available, pets ($20 extra charge). **Amenities:** safes. **Business Services:** fax (fee). **Cards:** AX, CB, DC, DS, MC, VI.

SOME UNITS

──────── WHERE TO DINE ────────

BAYOU GRILL
▼▼▼ ▼▼▼
Cajun

Lunch: $8-$12   **Dinner:** $12-$16   **Phone:** 734/697-2300
Location: I-94, exit 190, jct of Main St and 4th Ave; downtown. 404 Main St 48111. **Hours:** 11 am-11 pm, Sat from 2 pm, Sun noon-9 pm. Closed major holidays. **Features:** Using a wide range of Cajun and Creole ingredients such as crawfish, andouille sauage and shrimp, this Mardi Gras-themed restaurant can be loud and boisterous at times but does faithfully recreate authentic Cajun dishes. Casual dress; cocktails.
Parking: on-site. **Cards:** AX, MC, VI.
⊠

DOS PESOS RESTAURANT
▼
Mexican

Lunch: $5-$7   **Dinner:** $7-$11   **Phone:** 734/697-5777
Location: I-94, exit 190 (Belleville Rd), just s; in shopping plaza. 11800 Belleville Rd 48111. **Hours:** 11 am-9:30 pm, Fri & Sat-10:30 pm. Closed major holidays; also Sun. **Features:** Nestled in a small shopping plaza, this casual Mexican eatery serves modestly prepared Mexican fare including unique renditions of flautas, quesadillas and enchiladas. Casual dress; cocktails. **Parking:** on-site. **Cards:** MC, VI.
&M ⊠

BIRMINGHAM pop. 19,291   (See map p. 228; index p. 231)

──────── WHERE TO STAY ────────

HOLIDAY INN EXPRESS BIRMINGHAM   **Phone:** (248)646-7300   **17**
▼▼▼▼
Small-scale Hotel

All Year   1P: $89-$199   2P: $89-$199
Location: On SR 1, jct Woodward Ave and Maple Rd; center. 34952 Woodward Ave 48009. **Fax:** 248/646-4501. **Facility:** 124 units. 123 one-bedroom standard units. 1 one-bedroom suite with kitchen. 2-5 stories, interior/exterior corridors. *Bath:* combo or shower only. **Parking:** on-site. **Terms:** [ECP] meal plan available, small pets only. **Amenities:** dual phone lines, voice mail, irons, hair dryers. **Fee:** video games, safes. *Some:* high-speed Internet. **Leisure Activities:** exercise room. **Guest Services:** valet laundry. **Business Services:** meeting rooms. **Cards:** AX, CB, DC, DS, JC, MC, VI. *(See ad below)*

°SOME UNITS
(ASK) (S/D) (🐾) (🍽) (⛨) (🎮) (DATA PORT) (🔌) (💻) / (⊠) (📷) /

THE TOWNSEND HOTEL   **Phone:** (248)642-7900   **18**
(AAA) (SAVE)
▼▼▼ ▼▼▼
Small-scale Hotel

6/2-9/1   1P: $289   2P: $289
4/1-6/1 & 9/2-3/31   1P: $269   2P: $269
Location: Center. 100 Townsend St 48009. **Fax:** 248/645-9061. **Facility:** An elegant hotel close to downtown stores. 151 units. 145 one-bedroom standard units. 4 one- and 2 two-bedroom suites ($355-$1400), some with kitchens. 6 stories, interior corridors. *Bath:* combo or shower only. **Parking:** valet. **Terms:** check-in 4 pm, cancellation fee imposed. **Amenities:** video games, CD players, high-speed Internet, dual phone lines, voice mail, safes, honor bars, irons, hair dryers. **Dining:** Rugby Grille, see separate listing. **Leisure Activities:** *Fee:* massage. **Guest Services:** valet laundry, area transportation (fee). **Business Services:** meeting rooms, business center. **Cards:** AX, CB, DC, DS, MC, VI. **Special Amenities: free newspaper and free room upgrade (subject to availability with advanced reservations).** Affiliated with A Preferred Hotel.

SOME UNITS
(S/D) (🔌) (🍽) (24?) (🍸) (⛨) (🌀) (🏋) (🎮) (DATA PORT) / (⊠) (🔌) (💻) /
FEE   FEE

──────── WHERE TO DINE ────────

220
▼▼ ▼▼
American

Lunch: $10-$15   **Dinner:** $15-$25   **Phone:** 248/645-2150   **25**
Location: Center. 220 Merrill St 48009. **Hours:** 11 am-11 pm, Thurs-midnight, Fri & Sat-1 am. Closed major holidays; also Sun. **Features:** Paying homage to the inventor of the light bulb, this comfortable "see and be seen" restaurant offers a creative Italian-Continental menu featuring risotto, pasta, veal chops and a variety of fish dishes. A walk-down martini-cigar bar is popular with the often boisterous cell phone set.
Dressy casual; cocktails. **Parking:** street. **Cards:** AX, DC, MC, VI.
&M 🍸 ⊠

BIG ROCK CHOP HOUSE
(AAA)
▼▼ ▼▼
Steak & Seafood

Lunch: $8-$19   **Dinner:** $9-$35   **Phone:** 248/647-7774   **22**
Location: 1 mi e of SR 1 (Woodard Ave), s on Maple Rd. 245 S Eton St 48009. **Hours:** 11 am-midnight. Closed major holidays; also Sun. **Reservations:** required. **Features:** A sophisticated interpretation of the microbrewery-steakhouse concept, the Big Rock serves some very fine beef cooked the way meat lovers like it. There is award winning beer to sample, and even a cigar and martini lounge upstairs for the connoisseurs of those particular pleasures. All the above, combined with a whimsical flying buffalo, make for an above average dining experience. Semi-formal attire; cocktails. **Parking:** on-site and valet.
Cards: AX, DC, DS, MC, VI.
&M 🍸 ⊠

(See map p. 228)

FORTE'   **Lunch:** $15-$20   **Dinner:** $18-$25   **Phone:** 248/594-7300   24
Location: Downtown. 201 S Old Woodward Ave 48009. **Hours:** 11:30 am-2 & 5-10 pm, Thurs-Sat to 11 pm. Closed major holidays; also Sun. **Reservations:** accepted. **Features:** A loud and trendy "see and be
American   seen" bar overlooks the elegant and somewhat eclectic dining room. A mix of styles ranging through French, Mediterranean and California fuse into a menu that offers everything from tapas to brick-oven roasted rosemary rubbed chicken breast. Dressy casual; cocktails. **Parking:** valet and street. **Cards:** AX, DC, DS, MC, VI.

PEABODY   **Lunch:** $6-$10   **Dinner:** $8-$15   **Phone:** 248/644-5222   23
Location: At Woodward Ave and Maple Rd. 34965 Woodward Ave 48009. **Hours:** 11 am-10:30 pm. Closed major holidays; also Sun. **Features:** At this well known local eating and drinking establishment you will find a
American   friendly, yet dressy tavern atmosphere. Great food, is served up in generous portions, by a congenial staff that delivers what you order quickly. Casual dress; cocktails. **Parking:** on-site. **Cards:** AX, CB, DC, DS,
MC, VI.

RUGBY GRILLE   **Lunch:** $10-$20   **Dinner:** $25-$40   **Phone:** 248/642-7900   26
Location: Center; in The Townsend Hotel. 100 Townsend St 48009. **Hours:** 6:30 am-midnight, Fri & Sat-1 am. Closed: 12/25. **Reservations:** suggested. **Features:** Evocative of an English Country Club, the waiters
American   avoid the snootiness and, with a little panache, concentrate on preparing such traditional favorites such as Steak Tartar, Chateau-Briand for two and Cherries Jubilee at your table side. Dressy casual; cocktails.
Parking: valet. **Cards:** AX, CB, DC, DS, JC, MC, VI.

BLOOMFIELD HILLS pop. 3,940 (See map p. 228; index p. 235)

——— WHERE TO STAY ———

KINGSLEY HOTEL & SUITES   **Phone:** 248/644-1400
AAA [SAVE]   **All Year**   1P: $149   2P: $149   XP: $10   F18
Location: On SR 1 (Woodward Ave), just s of jct Long Lake Rd. 39475 Woodward Ave 48304. **Fax:** 248/644-5449.
Facility: 150 units. 142 one-bedroom standard units. 8 one-bedroom suites ($159-$199), some with whirl-
Small-scale Hotel   pools. 2-4 stories, interior corridors. **Parking:** on-site. **Terms:** cancellation fee imposed, package plans.
Amenities: dual phone lines, voice mail, irons, hair dryers. **Dining:** 6 am-midnight, cocktails, also, Northern Lakes Seafood Company, see separate listing. **Pool(s):** heated indoor. **Leisure Activities:** whirlpool, exercise room. **Guest Services:** gift shop, valet laundry, area transportation-within 5 mi. **Business Services:** conference facilities.
Cards: AX, DC, DS, JC, MC, VI. **Special Amenities:** free local telephone calls and free newspaper.

SOME UNITS

——— WHERE TO DINE ———

ANDIAMO ITALIA WEST   **Lunch:** $13-$17   **Dinner:** $16-$25   **Phone:** 248/865-9300   19
Location: Maple and Telegraph rds. 6676 Telegraph Rd 48301. **Hours:** 11 am-11 pm, Fri-midnight, Sat 4 pm-midnight, Sun 3 pm-9 pm. Closed major holidays. **Reservations:** suggested. **Features:** Andiamo Italia
Italian   West features traditional Italian dishes such as ravioli and lasagna, prepared using authentic recipes, high quality ingredients, and accented with an exquisite Parmesan cheese. The spacious dining room, with its
upscale artwork, and comfortable furnishings is an ideal setting for an intimate dinner. Dressy casual; cocktails. **Parking:**
on-site and valet. **Cards:** AX, MC, VI.

BEAU JACK'S FOOD & SPIRITS   **Lunch:** $5-$9   **Dinner:** $7-$17   **Phone:** 248/626-2630   18
Location: Just w of jct US 24 (Telegraph Rd). 4108 W Maple Rd 48302. **Hours:** 11:30 am-10:30 pm, Fri & Sat-11:30 pm, Sun 4 pm-9 pm. Closed major holidays. **Features:** The rustic restaurant, relaxed in its
American   sports tavern decor, encourages laid-back dining. Menu choices range from burgers and steaks to seafood and stir-fry. A pianist further adds to the boisterous and noisy atmosphere Thursdays through Saturdays.
Casual dress; cocktails; entertainment. **Parking:** on-site. **Cards:** AX, MC, VI.

FOX & HOUNDS RESTAURANT   **Lunch:** $7-$18   **Dinner:** $14-$30   **Phone:** 248/644-4800
Location: On SR 1, just s of jct Long Lake Rd. 39560 N Woodward Ave 48304. **Hours:** 11 am-3 & 5-10 pm, Sat 5 pm-11 pm, Sun 4 pm-9 pm. Closed major holidays. **Reservations:** suggested. **Features:** Tudor style
Steak & Seafood   architecture and an Olde English atmosphere set the stage for traditional fish and fowl dishes as well as desserts made at the on-site bakery. Casual dress; cocktails; entertainment. **Parking:** valet. **Cards:** AX,
DS, MC, VI.

NORTHERN LAKES SEAFOOD COMPANY   **Lunch:** $8-$15   **Dinner:** $19-$30   **Phone:** 248/646-7900
Location: On SR 1 (Woodward Ave), just s of jct Long Lake Rd; in Kingsley Hotel & Suites. 39495 Woodward Ave 48304. **Hours:** 11 am-2:30 & 5-11 pm, Fri & Sat-midnight, Sun 10 am-2 & 5-9 pm. Closed major holidays.
Seafood   **Reservations:** suggested; weekends. **Features:** This popular restaurant features a comfortable dining room decorated with marine accents, like light globes that include a glass octopus. They serve generous
portions of deliciously prepared fish, shrimp and lobster. Their special "martini menu" includes a spectacular selection of variations on the basic drink that you can enjoy, like olives stuffed with blue cheese or anchovies. It is a great place for that special family dinner. Casual dress; cocktails. **Parking:** on-site and valet. **Cards:** AX, DC, DS, MC, VI.

CANTON pop. 76,366   (See map p. 228; index p. 234)

———— WHERE TO STAY ————

BAYMONT INN & SUITES DETROIT-CANTON   **Phone:** (734)981-1808   **110**
All Year [ECP]   1P: $64-$79   2P: $64-$79
Location: I-275, exit 25, just w on SR 153 (Ford Rd). Located behind White Castle. 41211 Ford Rd 48187.
Fax: 734/981-7150. **Facility:** 98 one-bedroom standard units. 3 stories, interior corridors. **Parking:** on-site.
Terms: small pets only. **Amenities:** video games, voice mail, irons, hair dryers. **Guest Services:** valet and
Small-scale Hotel coin laundry. **Business Services:** fax (fee). **Cards:** AX, CB, DC, DS, MC, VI. **Special Amenities:** free con-
tinental breakfast and free newspaper. *(See color ad p 241)*
SOME UNITS

DAYS INN   **Phone:** (734)721-5200   **112**
All Year [ECP]   1P: $55-$75   2P: $55-$75   XP: $5   F12
Location: I-275, exit 22, just e on US 12 (entry at Wendy's). 40500 Michigan Ave 48188. **Fax:** 734/721-8814.
Facility: 84 one-bedroom standard units, some with whirlpools. 2 stories, exterior corridors. **Parking:** on-site.
Terms: 5 day cancellation notice. **Amenities:** video games (fee), hair dryers. **Pool(s):** outdoor. **Guest Serv-**
Motel   **ices:** valet laundry. **Cards:** AX, CB, DC, DS, MC, VI. *(See color ad card insert)*
SOME UNITS

EXTENDED STAYAMERICA-CANTON   **Phone:** (734)844-6725   **111**
All Year   1P: $55   2P: $55
Location: I-275, exit 25, just w on SR 153 (Ford Rd), then just s. 2000 Haggerty N 48187. **Fax:** 734/844-6726.
Small-scale Hotel   **Facility:** 104 one-bedroom standard units with efficiencies. 3 stories, interior corridors. *Bath:* combo or
shower only. **Parking:** on-site. **Terms:** cancellation fee imposed, weekly rates available. **Amenities:** dual
phone lines, voice mail. **Guest Services:** coin laundry. **Business Services:** meeting rooms. **Cards:** AX, CB, DC, DS, MC, VI.
SOME UNITS

FAIRFIELD INN BY MARRIOTT   **Phone:** (734)981-2440   **115**
1/1-3/31 [ECP]   1P: $61-$79   2P: $61-$79
4/1-12/31 [ECP]   1P: $56-$71   2P: $56-$71
Location: I-275, exit 25, just w on SR 153 (Ford Rd). 5700 Haggerty Rd 48187. **Fax:** 734/981-2440. **Facility:** 133
Small-scale Hotel   one-bedroom standard units. 3 stories, interior/exterior corridors. *Bath:* combo or shower only. **Parking:** on-
site. **Terms:** [CP] meal plan available. **Amenities:** irons. **Pool(s):** outdoor. **Guest Services:** valet laundry.
Cards: AX, CB, DC, DS, MC, VI.
SOME UNITS

HOLIDAY INN EXPRESS HOTEL & SUITES   **Phone:** (734)721-5500   **114**
All Year   1P: $89   2P: $89   XP: $10   F18
Location: I-275, exit 22, just e. 3950 Lotz Rd 48188. **Fax:** 734/721-1300. **Facility:** 81 one-bedroom standard
Small-scale Hotel   units, some with whirlpools. 3 stories, interior corridors. *Bath:* combo or shower only. **Parking:** on-site.
Amenities: video games (fee), dual phone lines, voice mail, irons, hair dryers. **Pool(s):** small heated indoor.
Leisure Activities: whirlpool, exercise room. **Guest Services:** valet laundry. **Business Services:** meeting rooms, business
center. *(See color ad card insert)*
SOME UNITS

MOTEL 6 - 1070   **Phone:** 734/981-5000   **109**
5/22-8/31   1P: $47-$57   2P: $53-$63   XP: $3   F17
9/1-3/31   1P: $44-$54   2P: $50-$60   XP: $3   F17
4/1-5/21   1P: $39-$49   2P: $45-$55   XP: $3   F17
Motel   **Location:** I-275, exit 25, just w on SR 153 (Ford Rd). 41216 Ford Rd 48187. **Fax:** 734/981-5432. **Facility:** 107 one-
bedroom standard units. 1 story, exterior corridors. *Bath:* combo or shower only. **Parking:** on-site. **Terms:** small pets only.
Pool(s): outdoor. **Business Services:** fax (fee). **Cards:** AX, CB, DC, DS, MC, VI.
SOME UNITS

SUPER 8 MOTEL-CANTON   **Phone:** (734)722-8880   **113**
All Year [CP]   1P: $54-$89   2P: $59-$89   XP: $6   F18
Location: I-275, exit 22, just e on US 12, then just s. 3933 Lotz Rd 48188. **Fax:** 734/722-8880. **Facility:** 70 one-
Small-scale Hotel   bedroom standard units, some with whirlpools. 3 stories, interior corridors. **Parking:** on-site. **Terms:** weekly
rates available. **Amenities:** safes (fee). **Business Services:** fax (fee). **Cards:** AX, CB, DC, DS, MC, VI.
SOME UNITS

———— WHERE TO DINE ————

THAI BISTRO   **Lunch:** $6-$12   **Dinner:** $6-$12   **Phone:** 734/416-2122
Location: I-275, exit 25 (Ford Rd), 2 mi w, jct Canton Center Rd. 45620 Ford Rd 48187. **Hours:** 11:30 am-2:30 &
5-9 pm, Fri-10 pm, Sat 5 pm-9 pm. Closed major holidays; also Sun. **Features:** Tucked away in a strip
Thai   mall, this modest but pleasant dining serves up a strong menu of Thai specialties. Using fresh ingredients
and stellar sauces, the chef/owner faithfully recreates the flavors of Thailand. Casual dress; beer only.
Parking: on-site. **Cards:** AX, DC, DS, MC, VI.

CLARKSTON pop. 1,000

———— WHERE TO DINE ————

THE CLARKSTON UNION **Lunch:** $6-$8 **Dinner:** $13-$20 **Phone:** 248/620-6100
▼▼ ▼▼ **Location:** Downtown. 54 S Main St 48346. **Hours:** 11 am-10 pm, Fri & Sat-11 pm, Sun-9 pm. Closed major
holidays. **Features:** Savor hearty, homemade comfort foods in a resurrected 1840s church. An extensive
American selection of European and American microbrewed beer complements a limited offering of pub-type food. A
nice variety of tea and gourmet coffee are also available. Casual dress; cocktails. **Parking:** on-site.
Cards: AX, DS, MC, VI.

CLAWSON pop. 12,732   (See map p. 228; index p. 235)

———— WHERE TO DINE ————

CLAWSON STEAK HOUSE **Lunch:** $10-$15 **Dinner:** $15-$25 **Phone:** 248/588-5788 (29)
▼▼ ▼▼ **Location:** I-75, exit 65, 1 mi w, jct 14 Mile and Rochester rds. 56 S Rochester Rd 48017. **Hours:** 11 am-11 pm, Fri
& Sat-midnight. Closed major holidays; also Sun. **Reservations:** accepted. **Features:** Reminiscent of a
Steak House 1950's supper club, the mauve dining room has been popular with locals of all ages for over 40 years.
Wednesday through Saturday live music is featured after 8 pm while diners enjoy traditional steak house
favorites. Dressy casual; cocktails. **Parking:** on-site and valet. **Cards:** AX, CB, DC, DS, MC, VI.

DEARBORN pop. 97,775   (See map p. 228; index p. 234)

———— WHERE TO STAY ————

COURTYARD BY MARRIOTT-DEARBORN **Phone:** 313/271-1400 (100)
▼▼▼▼ Property failed to provide current rates
Location: SR 39 (Southfield Frwy), exit Ford Rd, just e, then s. 5200 Mercury Dr 48126. **Fax:** 313/271-1184.
Small-scale Hotel **Facility:** 147 units. 137 one-bedroom standard units. 10 one-bedroom suites. 2 stories, interior corridors.
Bath: combo or shower only. **Parking:** on-site. **Amenities:** high-speed Internet, dual phone lines, voice mail,
irons, hair dryers. **Pool(s):** small heated indoor. **Leisure Activities:** whirlpool, exercise room. **Guest Services:** coin laundry.
Business Services: meeting rooms, fax (fee). **Cards:** AX, DC, DS, MC, VI.
SOME UNITS

THE DEARBORN INN, A MARRIOTT HOTEL **Phone:** (313)271-2700 (106)
(AAA) (SAVE) All Year 1P: $79-$199 2P: $79-$199
▼▼▼▼ **Location:** SR 39 (Southfield Frwy), exit Oakwood Blvd, 1 mi w. 20301 Oakwood Blvd 48124. **Fax:** 313/271-7464.
Facility: 222 units. 215 one-bedroom standard units. 3 one- and 4 three-bedroom suites ($209). 2-4 stories,
Historic interior/exterior corridors. *Bath:* combo or shower only. **Parking:** valet. **Terms:** check-in 4 pm.
Small-scale Hotel **Amenities:** high-speed Internet, dual phone lines, voice mail, irons, hair dryers. **Dining:** 2 restaurants, 6:30
am-11 pm, cocktails, also, Early American Room, see separate listing. **Pool(s):** heated outdoor. **Leisure Ac-
tivities:** 2 tennis courts, exercise room. **Guest Services:** gift shop, valet laundry, area transportation-within
3 mi. **Business Services:** meeting rooms, business center. **Cards:** AX, CB, DC, DS, JC, MC, VI. **Special Amenities:** free newspaper and preferred room (subject to availability with advanced reservations).
SOME UNITS
FEE

(See map p. 228)

EXTENDED STAY AMERICA
▼▼ ▼▼
Small-scale Hotel
All Year   1P: $79   2P: $79   **Phone:** (313)336-0021   102
Location: SR 39 (Southfield Pkwy) between exits Ford Rd and Michigan Ave, just w of jct Service and Hubbard Drives. Located adjacent to shopping mall. 260 Towne Center Dr 48126. **Fax:** 313/336-0052. **Facility:** 93 one-bedroom standard units with efficiencies. 4 stories, interior corridors. *Bath:* combo or shower only. **Parking:** on-site.
Terms: cancellation fee imposed, weekly rates available. **Amenities:** dual phone lines, voice mail. **Guest Services:** coin laundry.
Cards: AX, CB, DC, DS, MC, VI.

SOME UNITS

HAMPTON INN DEARBORN
SAVE
▼▼ ▼▼
Small-scale Hotel
7/2-3/31 [ECP]   1P: $99-$140   2P: $109-$140   **Phone:** (313)436-9600   104
4/1-7/1 [ECP]   1P: $97-$140   2P: $107-$140
Location: Off SR 39 (Southfield Frwy), exit Michigan Ave, just w. 20061 Michigan Ave 48124. **Fax:** 313/436-8345. **Facility:** 119 one-bedroom standard units. 4 stories, interior corridors. **Parking:** on-site. **Amenities:** video games, voice mail, irons, hair dryers. **Pool(s):** heated indoor. **Leisure Activities:** exercise room. **Guest Services:** valet and coin laundry. **Business Services:** meeting rooms. **Cards:** AX, CB, DC, DS, MC, VI.

SOME UNITS

(See map p. 228)

HYATT REGENCY DEARBORN

 All Year — 1P: $99-$209 — Phone: (313)593-1234 — **103**

XP: $25 — F18

Location: Jct SR 39, 0.3 mi w on Michigan Ave, 0.3 mi n on Evergreen Rd, then e on Fairlane Rd. Located opposite Ford Motor Co. World Headquarters. Fairlane Town Center 48126. Fax: 313/593-3366. **Facility:** The lobby's cast glass, stainless steel, beech wood and dramatic lighting suggest modern elegance. 772 units. 741 one-bedroom standard units. 31 one-bedroom suites, some with whirlpools. 13 stories, interior corridors. *Bath:* combo or shower only. **Parking:** on-site and valet. **Terms:** cancellation fee imposed. **Amenities:** voice mail, irons, hair dryers. *Some:* fax. **Dining:** 3 restaurants, 6:30 am-10 pm, Fri-Sun to midnight, cocktails, nightclub. **Pool(s):** heated indoor. **Leisure Activities:** sauna, whirlpool, exercise room. **Guest Services:** gift shop, valet laundry, airport transportation (fee)-Detroit Metro Airport. **Business Services:** conference facilities, business center. **Cards:** AX, CB, DC, DS, JC, MC, VI.

Large-scale Hotel

(See color ad p 250)

(See map p. 228)

RED ROOF INN-DEARBORN
Phone: (313)278-9732 • 105
(AAA) (SAVE)
All Year 1P: $56-$76 2P: $63-$83 XP: $7 F18
Location: Jct US 12 and 24. 24130 Michigan Ave 48124. Fax: 313/278-9741. **Facility:** 111 one-bedroom standard units. 2 stories, exterior corridors. *Bath:* combo or shower only. **Parking:** on-site. **Terms:** small pets only. **Amenities:** video games, voice mail. **Cards:** AX, CB, DC, DS, MC, VI. **Special Amenities:** free local telephone calls and free newspaper.
Motel

THE RITZ-CARLTON, DEARBORN
Phone: (313)441-2000 • 101
(AAA) (SAVE)
All Year 1P: $125-$1500 2P: $125-$1500 XP: $15 F18
Location: SR 39 (Southfield Frwy), between Ford Rd and Michigan Ave exits, on Service Dr. 300 Town Center Dr 48126. Fax: 313/441-2051. **Facility:** Marble floors and wood paneling in the lobby give this hotel a refined, traditional ambience. 308 units. 295 one-bedroom standard units. 13 one-bedroom suites ($339-$1500). 11 stories, interior corridors. *Bath:* combo or shower only. **Parking:** on-site and valet. **Terms:** 15% service charge, pets ($200 deposit). **Amenities:** video games (fee), CD players, dual phone lines, voice mail, safes, honor bars, irons, hair dryers. **Dining:** Ritz-Carlton, The Grill, see separate listing, entertainment. **Pool(s):** heated indoor. **Leisure Activities:** saunas, whirlpool, tennis & racquetball privileges, exercise room. *Fee:* massage. **Guest Services:** gift shop, valet laundry, area transportation-within 5 mi. **Business Services:** conference facilities, business center. **Cards:** AX, DC, DS, JC, MC, VI. **Special Amenities:** early check-in/late check-out and free newspaper.
Large-scale Hotel

TOWNEPLACE SUITES
Phone: (313)271-0200 • 99
(SAVE)
All Year 1P: $99-$139 2P: $99-$139
Location: SR 39 (Southfield Frwy), exit 7 (Ford Rd), just e, then 0.8 mi n. 6141 Mercury Dr 48126. Fax: 313/271-3177. **Facility:** Smoke free premises. 148 units. 126 one-bedroom standard units with kitchens. 22 two-bedroom suites with kitchens. 3 stories, interior corridors. *Bath:* combo or shower only. **Parking:** on-site. **Terms:** pets ($100 deposit, $5 extra charge). **Amenities:** high-speed Internet (fee), dual phone lines, voice mail, irons, hair dryers. **Pool(s):** heated outdoor. **Leisure Activities:** horseback riding, exercise room, sports court. **Guest Services:** sundries, valet and coin laundry. **Business Services:** business center. **Cards:** AX, DC, DS, JC, MC, VI.
Small-scale Hotel

—— **WHERE TO DINE** ——

ANNAM RESTAURANT VIETNAMIEN
Lunch: $10-$15 Dinner: $10-$15 Phone: 313/565-8744 • 87
(AAA)
Location: Jct US 24 (Telegraph Rd) and 12 (Michigan Ave). 22053 Michigan Ave 48124. **Hours:** 11 am-2:30 & 5-9 pm, Fri-11 pm, Sat from 5 pm. Closed major holidays; also Sun. **Reservations:** accepted. **Features:** Named for ancient Vietnam, this small, tastefully decorated and designed space offers a representative menu of authentic dishes such as Pho. Extraordinary flavors and colourful presentations are emphasized through subtle use of seasonings and mini bouquets of fresh herbs. Dressy casual; wine only. **Parking:** street. **Cards:** AX, MC, VI.
Nouvelle Vietnamese

BD'S MONGOLIAN BARBEQUE
Lunch: $7-$11 Dinner: $14 Phone: 313/792-9660 • 89
Location: Jct US 24 (Telegraph Rd) and 12 (Michigan Ave), 0.3 mi e. 22115 Michigan Ave 48124. **Hours:** 10:30 am-10:30 pm, Fri & Sat-11:30 pm, Sun 11 am-10 pm. Closed major holidays. **Features:** A busy, popular, sometimes loud, and always informal dining spot that features a do-it-yourself stir fry. Make up your own combination, and they cook it for you. There is also a varied salad bar. Casual dress; cocktails. **Parking:** on-site. **Cards:** AX, DS, MC, VI.
Mongolian

EARLY AMERICAN ROOM
Dinner: $18-$26 Phone: 313/271-2700 • 92
Location: SR 39 (Southfield Frwy), exit Oakwood Blvd, 1 mi w; in The Dearborn Inn, A Marriott Hotel. 20301 Oakwood Blvd 48124. **Hours:** 5:30 pm-10 pm, Sun 10 am-2 pm. Closed: Mon-Wed. **Reservations:** accepted. **Features:** Located in the first airport hotel in the country, this traditional and elegant dining room features attentive service and a creative menu that changes seasonally. Dressy casual; cocktails. **Parking:** on-site and valet. **Cards:** AX, CB, DC, DS, MC, VI.
American

KABOB VILLAGE
Lunch: $6-$10 Dinner: $6-$10 Phone: 313/581-0055 • 83
Location: Downtown. 13823 Michigan Ave 48126. **Hours:** 11 am-11 pm. Closed major holidays. **Features:** All your Middle Eastern favorites such as chicken and lamb kabobs, tabbouleh and humus are found at this bright and comfortable eatery. Casual dress. **Parking:** on-site. **Cards:** AX, MC, VI.
Lebanese

KIERNAN'S STEAK HOUSE
Lunch: $8-$15 Dinner: $10-$18 Phone: 313/565-4260 • 85
Location: 1.3 mi w of jct SR 39 on US 12. 21931 Michigan Ave 48124. **Hours:** 11 am-11 pm, Sat from 5 pm, Sun 4 pm-9 pm. Closed major holidays. **Reservations:** suggested. **Features:** As its name suggests, the restaurant focuses on steakhouse fare: veal, pork, chicken, seafood and, of course, beef. Silk lampshades and subtle illumination add to the romantic ambience of the tavern-like dining room. Servers are friendly and attentive. Casual dress; cocktails. **Parking:** on-site and valet. **Cards:** AX, DS, MC, VI.
American

LAPITA
Lunch: $6-$7 Dinner: $10-$14 Phone: 313/565-7482 • 90
Location: On US 12, between Outer Dr and Military Rd; 1 mi e of jct US 24 (Telegraph Rd). 22435 Michigan Ave 48124. **Hours:** 10 am-11 pm, Sun 11 am-10 pm. Closed: 11/27, 12/25. **Features:** The comfortable restaurant specializes in Middle Eastern cuisine, such as chicken and lamb kabobs, tabbouleh and hummus. Wall murals depict such scenes as people riding horses, a woman carrying a basket of bread, towering palm trees and a mosque. Casual dress. **Parking:** on-site. **Cards:** AX, DC, DS, MC, VI.
Ethnic

(See map p. 228)

LA SHISH
▼▼▼
Ethnic

Lunch: $7-$9 **Dinner:** $8-$14 **Phone:** 313/562-7200   88

Location: Jct SR 39 (Southfield Frwy), 1.3 mi w. 22039 Michigan Ave 48124. **Hours:** 10 am-11 pm, Fri & Sat-midnight. Closed: 11/27, 12/25. **Features:** If you haven't tried Lebanese cuisine, here's your opportunity. Among the authentic Middle Eastern selections are seafood entrees and such delicious kabobs as the lamb. The flat bread is fresh and flavorful. Service is friendly and attentive. Casual dress; cocktails.
Parking: on-site. **Cards:** AX, DC, DS, MC, VI.   ⊠

RICHTER'S CHALET
ⒶⒶⒶ
▼▼
German

Lunch: $4-$8 **Dinner:** $7-$17 **Phone:** 313/565-0484   91

Location: Jct US 24 (Telegraph Rd) and 12 (Michigan Ave), just e. 23920 Michigan Ave 48124. **Hours:** 11 am-8:30 pm, Fri-9 pm, Sat 3 pm-9 pm, Sun noon-7 pm. Closed: 7/4, 11/27, 12/24, 12/25; also Mon. **Features:** The cozy restaurant offers a menu of authentic German dishes—such as potato pancakes, Wiener schnitzel and sauerbraten—with a handful of American dishes also described. Light background music and Bavarian appointments set the tone in the dining room. Casual dress. **Parking:** on-site. **Cards:** MC, VI.   ⊠

RISTORANTE CIAO
▼▼▼
Italian

Lunch: $11-$20 **Dinner:** $11-$20 **Phone:** 313/274-2426   86

Location: 1.3 mi w of jct SR 39 and US 12 (Michigan Ave), just s. 1024 Monroe 48124. **Hours:** 11 am-2 & 5-11 pm, Sat from 5 pm. Closed major holidays; also Sun. **Reservations:** suggested. **Features:** Evoking images of the Tuscan countryside, this cozy and candlelit restaurant is well known for its creative preparations of Italian favorites. Dressy casual; wine only. **Parking:** street. **Cards:** AX, DS, MC, VI.   ⚫M ⊠

RITZ-CARLTON, THE GRILL
▼▼▼▼
Continental

Lunch: $12-$18 **Dinner:** $25-$40 **Phone:** 313/441-2000   84

Location: SR 39 (Southfield Frwy), between Ford Rd and Michigan Ave exits, on Service Dr, in The Ritz-Carlton, Dearborn. 300 Town Center Dr 48126. **Hours:** 6 am-2:30 & 6-10 pm, Fri & Sat-11 pm. **Reservations:** suggested. **Features:** Nestled in the Ritz Carlton hotel, this elegant restaurant, reminiscent of an English country club, offers impeccable service and creative takes on a continental menu that features classics such as Steak Tartare, Muscovy Duck Breast and Dover Sole. Dressy casual; cocktails. **Parking:** on-site and valet. **Cards:** AX, CB, DC, DS, JC, MC, VI.   ♿M 🍸 ⊠

FARMINGTON HILLS pop. 82,111   (See map p. 228; index p. 233)

─── WHERE TO STAY ───

CANDLWOOD SUITES
▼▼▼
Small-scale Hotel

Phone: 248/324-0540   69

Property failed to provide current rates

Location: I-696, exit I-96 east/I-275 S/M-5, just s to MI-5 N, then 2 mi n to 12 Mile Rd, 1.3 mi s on 12 Mile Rd, then 0.3 mi s on Halsted Rd. 37555 Hills Tech Dr 48331. **Fax:** 248/324-0541. **Facility:** 127 units. 94 one-bedroom standard units with efficiencies. 33 one-bedroom suites with efficiencies. 4 stories, interior corridors. **Parking:** on-site. **Terms:** small pets only ($150 deposit). **Amenities:** video library, CD players, voice mail, irons, hair dryers. **Leisure Activities:** exercise room. **Cards:** AX, CB, DC, DS, JC, MC, VI.
SOME UNITS
🐾 ♿M 🅿️ 📼 📶 ⊞ 🖥️ 💻 / ⊠ /

COMFORT INN-FARMINGTON HILLS
ⒶⒶⒶ SAVE
▼▼ ▼▼
Small-scale Hotel

Phone: (248)471-9220   67

All Year [ECP] 1P: $84-$109 2P: $84-$109 XP: $8   F12
Location: I-696, exit 5, just n, then just e. 30715 W 12 Mile Rd 48334. **Fax:** 248/471-2053. **Facility:** 136 units. 130 one-bedroom standard units. 6 one-bedroom suites ($149). 4 stories, interior corridors. *Bath:* combo or shower only. **Parking:** on-site. **Amenities:** voice mail, irons, hair dryers. **Guest Services:** valet laundry. **Business Services:** meeting rooms, fax (fee). **Cards:** AX, DC, DS, MC, VI. **Special Amenities:** free continental breakfast and free local telephone calls.
SOME UNITS
🆂🅳 🍽️ 🍸 🛁 📶 🗃️ 💻 / ⊠ ⊞ /
FEE

COURTYARD BY MARRIOTT
SAVE
▼▼▼
Small-scale Hotel

Phone: (248)553-0000   68

All Year [BP] 1P: $109
Location: I-696, exit 5, just w. 31525 12 Mile Rd 48334. **Fax:** 248/553-7630. **Facility:** 202 units. 158 one-bedroom standard units, some with whirlpools. 44 one-bedroom suites ($129), some with whirlpools. 3 stories, interior corridors. **Parking:** on-site. **Terms:** 21 day cancellation notice-fee imposed. **Amenities:** voice mail, irons, hair dryers. *Fee:* video games, high-speed Internet. **Pool(s):** heated indoor. **Leisure Activities:** saunas, whirlpool, exercise room. **Guest Services:** valet and coin laundry, area transportation. **Business Services:** conference facilities. **Cards:** AX, DS, MC, VI.
SOME UNITS
🆂🅳 🍽️ 🍸 🛁 🏊 ⊠ 📶 🗃️ 💻 / ⊠ ⊞ /

FAIRFIELD INN BY MARRIOTT
SAVE
▼▼▼
Motel

Phone: (248)442-9800   66

All Year [ECP] 1P: $94-$129
Location: I-696, exit 5, just n, then just e on 12 Mile Rd, then just s. 27777 Stansbury Blvd 48334. **Fax:** 248/442-9563. **Facility:** 91 one-bedroom standard units, some with whirlpools. 3 stories, interior corridors. *Bath:* combo or shower only. **Parking:** on-site. **Terms:** [CP] meal plan available. **Amenities:** video games, voice mail, irons, hair dryers. **Pool(s):** heated indoor. **Leisure Activities:** whirlpool, exercise room. **Guest Services:** valet and coin laundry. **Cards:** AX, CB, DC, DS, JC, MC, VI.
SOME UNITS
🍽️ ♿M 🛁 📶 🗃️ / ⊠ /

HOLIDAY INN FARMINGTON HILLS
▼▼▼
Small-scale Hotel

Phone: (248)477-4000   71

All Year 1P: $75-$129 2P: $75-$129 XP: $15   F18
Location: I-275, exit 165 (SR 5/Grand River Ave), 1 mi e, then just s. 38123 W 10 Mile Rd 48335. **Fax:** 248/476-4570. **Facility:** 262 one-bedroom standard units, some with whirlpools. 3-5 stories, interior corridors. **Parking:** on-site. **Terms:** cancellation fee imposed, [AP] & [BP] meal plans available, package plans. **Amenities:** video games, voice mail, irons, hair dryers. **Pool(s):** heated outdoor, heated indoor. **Leisure Activities:** sauna, whirlpool, putting green, exercise room. *Fee:* game room. **Guest Services:** gift shop, valet and coin laundry. **Cards:** AX, CB, DC, DS, JC, MC, VI.
SOME UNITS
ASK 🆂🅳 🍽️ 🍸 🛁 🏊 ⊠ 📶 🗃️ 💻 / ⊠ 📼 ⊞ /
FEE FEE

(See map p. 228)

RADISSON SUITE HOTEL FARMINGTON HILLS
Phone: (248)477-7800   **72**

All Year [BP]   1P: $97   2P: $97

Location: I-96/275 and SR 102, exit 165 (Grand River Ave), just s to Halsted Rd. 37529 Grand River Ave 48335. Fax: 248/478-3799. **Facility:** 137 units. 132 one-bedroom standard units. 5 one-bedroom suites, some with whirlpools. 4 stories, interior corridors. *Bath:* combo or shower only. **Parking:** on-site. **Terms:** [AP] meal plan available. **Amenities:** video games, voice mail, irons, hair dryers. **Dining:** 6:30-9:30 am, 11-2 & 5-10 pm, Sat & Sun 8 am-11 & 5-10 pm, cocktails. **Pool(s):** heated indoor. **Leisure Activities:** sauna, whirlpool, exercise room. *Fee:* game room. **Guest Services:** valet laundry. **Business Services:** meeting rooms. **Cards:** AX, CB, DC, DS, JC, MC, VI. *(See color ad p 241)*

AAA [SAVE]   Small-scale Hotel

SOME UNITS

RED ROOF INN-FARMINGTON HILLS
Phone: (248)478-8640   **70**

5/25-10/25	1P: $55-$69	2P: $60-$74	XP: $5 F18
10/26-3/31	1P: $51-$65	2P: $56-$70	XP: $5 F18
4/1-5/24	1P: $49-$65	2P: $54-$70	XP: $5 F18

Location: I-96/275 and M-5, exit 165 (Grand River Ave), just w. 24300 Sinacola Ct 48335. Fax: 248/478-4842. **Facility:** 108 one-bedroom standard units. 2 stories, exterior corridors. *Bath:* combo or shower only. **Parking:** on-site. **Amenities:** video games, voice mail. **Cards:** AX, CB, DC, DS, MC, VI. **Special Amenities:** free local telephone calls and free newspaper.

AAA [SAVE]   Motel

SOME UNITS

------ WHERE TO DINE ------

FAMILY BUGGY RESTAURANT
Lunch: $7-$9   Dinner: $9-$15   Phone: 248/553-9090   **66**

Location: I-696, exit 5, 1 mi n. 29335 Orchard Lake Rd 48334. **Hours:** 11 am-9 pm, Fri & Sat-10 pm. Closed: 1/1, 11/27, 12/25. **Features:** Antique furnishings and decorations give you the feeling that you've slipped into yesteryear. The homey, family-oriented restaurant is a comfortable place in which to enjoy such reliable favorites as smothered chicken breast and barbecue ribs. Casual dress. **Parking:** on-site. **Cards:** MC, VI.

AAA   American

HONG HUA
Lunch: $7-$9   Dinner: $10-$25   Phone: 248/489-2280   **67**

Location: I-696, exit 5 (Orchard Lake Rd), just n. 27925 Orchard Lake Rd 48334. **Hours:** 11 am-10:30 pm, Fri & Sat-midnight, Sun noon-midnight. Closed major holidays. **Reservations:** accepted. **Features:** An exacting eye for detail is evident in this upscale, white table-clothed Cantonese restaurant. Everything from the "floral" arrangements of carved vegetables to the fresh fish kept in aerated freshwater tanks in the kitchen speak volumes about the 120-item menu. Offering such specialties such as shark's fin and bird's nest soups as well as fresh abalone, the menu also pays a brief nod to hot and spicy Szechuan style and does offers more traditional Chinese-American fare. Dressy casual; cocktails. **Parking:** on-site. **Cards:** AX, DC, DS, MC, VI.

Cantonese

TRIBUTE
Dinner: $65-$85   Phone: 248/848-9393   **68**

Location: I-696, exit 5, just n, then just w. 31425 W 12 Mile Rd 48334. **Hours:** 5:30 pm-9 pm. Closed major holidays; also Sun & Mon. **Reservations:** required. **Features:** This restaurant will get your attention as you enter and are greeted by a pleasant and charming hostess. The extensive wine racks on the way to your table will tempt your patience. The dining room ambience is surrounded with high banquette booths and an elegant open drape between the two main dining rooms. A nightly seven-course vegetable or the special degustation menu is a popular item that may be your choice among the several entree offerings. An exceptional dining experience. Semi-formal attire; cocktails. **Parking:** valet. **Cards:** AX, DC, DS, MC, VI.

Nouvelle French

FERNDALE pop. 22,105   (See map p. 228; index p. 235)

------ WHERE TO DINE ------

ASSAGGI MEDITERRANEAN BISTRO
Lunch: $12-$15   Dinner: $18-$26   Phone: 248/584-3499   **63**

Location: Jct Woodward Ave and 9 Mile Rd, just w. 330 W 9 Mile Rd 48220. **Hours:** 11 am-2 & 5-10 pm, Fri & Sat-11 pm, Sun 4 pm-9 pm. Closed major holidays; also Mon. **Reservations:** accepted. **Features:** Using fresh herbs and vegetables grown in its own kitchen garden, this storefront restaurant highlights an innovative menu that mixes and matches Mediterranean styles such as French, Spanish, Greek and Lebanese dishes, regardless of national borders. Dressy casual; wine only. **Parking:** valet and street. **Cards:** AX, DC, DS, MC, VI.

Mediterranean

MARIA'S FRONT ROOM
Dinner: $14-$17   Phone: 248/542-7378   **62**

Location: Jct Woodward Ave and 9 Mile Rd, just w. 215 W 9 Mile Rd 48220. **Hours:** 5 pm-9 pm, Tues-Sat to 10 pm. Closed major holidays; also Sun. **Reservations:** accepted. **Features:** A long, narrow storefront location, this unassuming restaurant comes complete with red and white table cloths and candles stuck in chianti bottles. Focusing on simple Italian dishes such as spaghetti alla puttanesca and pizzas, this restaurant also features the only house-made wine in Michigan. Casual dress; wine only. **Parking:** street. **Cards:** AX, DS, MC, VI.

Italian

FLAT ROCK pop. 8,488

——— **WHERE TO STAY** ———

SLEEP INN
Phone: (734)782-9898

[SAVE]

[diamond diamond diamond]

Small-scale Hotel

4/1-10/31   1P: $65-$70   2P: $65-$70
11/1-3/31   1P: $55-$60
Location: I-75, exit 29 (Gibraltar Rd), just e. 29101 Commerce Dr 48134. Fax: 734/783-5029. **Facility:** 62 one-bedroom standard units. 3 stories, interior corridors. *Bath:* combo or shower only. **Parking:** on-site. **Terms:** weekly rates available, [CP] meal plan available. **Pool(s):** heated indoor. **Leisure Activities:** whirlpool, exercise room. **Guest Services:** valet laundry, area transportation (fee). **Cards:** AX, DC, DS, MC, VI.

SOME UNITS

[icons] FEE

GROSSE POINTE FARMS pop. 9,764   (See map p. 228; index p. 235)

——— **WHERE TO DINE** ———

THE HILL SEAFOOD AND CHOP HOUSE   **Lunch:** $15-$25   **Dinner:** $15-$25   **Phone:** 313/886-8101   [75]

[diamond diamond diamond]

Steak & Seafood

Location: Downtown. 123 E Kercheval Ave 48236. **Hours:** 11 am-3 & 5-10 pm, Fri & Sat-11 pm. Closed major holidays; also Sun. **Reservations:** accepted. **Features:** A country club atmosphere exudes through this comfortable and subtly upscale space. Simple and classic dishes such as Dover sole meuniere are prepared from the freshest fish while the 20 ounce rib chop is prepared with a light bourbon-butter sauce. Dressy casual; cocktails. **Parking:** valet and street. **Cards:** AX, DC, DS, MC, VI.

[icons]

LUCY'S TAVERN ON THE HILL   **Lunch:** $5-$19   **Dinner:** $5-$19   **Phone:** 313/640-2020   [74]

[diamond diamond diamond]

American

Location: Downtown. 115 Kercheval Ave 48236. **Hours:** 11 am-10 pm, Fri & Sat-midnight, Sun 2 pm-11 pm. Closed: 11/27, 12/25. **Features:** Lucy's is a popular local drinking and dining establishment, featuring a cozy, friendly pub-like atmosphere and sophisticated tavern style meals. Try one of their scrumptious steaks complemented with tasty waffle fries and your favorite beer or wine. Casual dress; cocktails. **Parking:** street. **Cards:** AX, DS, MC, VI.

[icons]

LAKE ORION pop. 2,715

——— **WHERE TO STAY** ———

BEST WESTERN PALACE INN
Phone: (248)391-2755

[AAA] [SAVE]

[diamond diamond diamond]

Small-scale Hotel

4/1-8/31 & 3/1-3/31   1P: $80-$90   2P: $80-$90
9/1-2/29   1P: $70-$80   2P: $70-$80
Location: I-75, exit 81 (Lapeer Rd), 3.3 mi n. 2755 N Lapeer Rd 48360. Fax: 248/391-9722. **Facility:** 76 one-bedroom standard units, some with whirlpools. 2 stories, interior/exterior corridors. *Bath:* combo or shower only. **Parking:** on-site. **Terms:** 7 day cancellation notice, weekly rates available, [ECP] meal plan available, small pets only ($25 fee). **Amenities:** voice mail, irons, hair dryers. **Pool(s):** heated indoor. **Leisure Activities:** whirlpool, exercise room. *Fee:* game room. **Guest Services:** valet and coin laundry. **Business Services:** meeting rooms, business center. **Cards:** AX, CB, DC, DS, MC, VI. **Special Amenities:** free continental breakfast and free newspaper.

SOME UNITS

[icons]

LINCOLN PARK pop. 40,008   (See map p. 228; index p. 234)

——— **WHERE TO STAY** ———

SLEEP INN INN & SUITES
Phone: (313)381-5600   [122]

[AAA] [SAVE]

[diamond diamond diamond]

Small-scale Hotel

All Year [ECP]   1P: $89-$110   2P: $89-$110   XP: $10   F18
Location: I-75, exit 41 (Southfield Hwy). Located in front of the railway tracks. 1805 John Papelas Dr 48146. Fax: 313/381-5900. **Facility:** 82 one-bedroom standard units, some with whirlpools. 3 stories, interior corridors. *Bath:* combo or shower only. **Parking:** on-site. **Amenities:** dual phone lines, voice mail, safes (fee), irons, hair dryers. **Pool(s):** heated indoor. **Leisure Activities:** sauna, exercise room. **Guest Services:** coin laundry. **Business Services:** meeting rooms. **Cards:** AX, CB, DC, DS, JC, MC, VI. *(See color ad p 253)*

SOME UNITS

[icons] FEE

LIVONIA pop. 100,545   (See map p. 228; index p. 233)

——— **WHERE TO STAY** ———

AMERISUITES (DETROIT/LIVONIA)
Phone: (734)953-9224   [84]

[AAA] [SAVE]

[diamond diamond diamond]

Small-scale Hotel

All Year [ECP]   1P: $79-$129   2P: $129-$149   XP: $10   F17
Location: I-275, exit 169A, just w on 7 Mile Rd. 19300 Haggerty Rd 48152. Fax: 734/953-9225. **Facility:** 128 one-bedroom standard units. 6 stories, interior corridors. *Bath:* combo or shower only. **Parking:** on-site. **Terms:** small pets only. **Amenities:** video games, voice mail, irons, hair dryers. *Some:* dual phone lines. **Pool(s):** heated indoor. **Leisure Activities:** exercise room. **Guest Services:** coin laundry. **Business Services:** meeting rooms, business center. **Cards:** AX, DC, DS, JC, MC, VI. **Special Amenities:** free continental breakfast and free newspaper.

SOME UNITS

[icons]

(See map p. 228)

BEST WESTERN LAUREL PARK SUITES
Phone: 734/464-0050 **91**

All Year   1P: $79-$109

Location: I-275, exit 170, just e, then just s. Located across from Laurel Park Mall. 16999 S Laurel Park Dr 48154. Fax: 734/464-5869. **Facility:** 124 one-bedroom standard units, some with whirlpools. 2 stories (no elevator), interior corridors. **Parking:** on-site. **Terms:** cancellation fee imposed, [ECP] meal plan available, small pets only ($50 deposit). **Amenities:** video games, voice mail, irons, hair dryers. **Pool(s):** heated outdoor. **Leisure Activities:** exercise room. **Guest Services:** valet laundry. **Business Services:** meeting rooms. **Cards:** AX, DC, DS, MC, VI. **Special Amenities: free continental breakfast and free newspaper.**

SOME UNITS

COMFORT INN
Phone: (734)458-7111 **92**

All Year [ECP]   1P: $89-$99   2P: $89-$99

Location: I-96, exit 176, just n on Middlebelt Rd. 29235 Buckingham Ave 48154. Fax: 734/458-1530. **Facility:** 112 one-bedroom standard units, some with whirlpools. 3 stories, interior corridors. **Parking:** on-site. **Terms:** 14 day cancellation notice-fee imposed, weekly rates available. **Amenities:** video games, irons, hair dryers. *Some:* safes. **Leisure Activities:** exercise room. **Guest Services:** valet and coin laundry. **Business Services:** meeting rooms. **Cards:** AX, DC, DS, JC, MC, VI. **Special Amenities: free continental breakfast and free local telephone calls.**

SOME UNITS

COURTYARD BY MARRIOTT
Phone: 734/462-2000 **85**

All Year   1P: $59-$124

Location: I-275, exit 170, just e. 17200 N Laurel Park Dr 48152. Fax: 734/462-5907. **Facility:** 149 units. 137 one-bedroom standard units. 12 one-bedroom suites. 2-3 stories, interior corridors. *Bath:* combo or shower only. **Parking:** on-site. **Terms:** cancellation fee imposed, [BP], [CP] & [ECP] meal plans available. **Amenities:** high-speed Internet, voice mail, irons, hair dryers. **Pool(s):** heated indoor. **Leisure Activities:** whirlpool, exercise room. **Guest Services:** valet and coin laundry. **Business Services:** meeting rooms. **Cards:** AX, CB, DC, DS, JC, MC, VI.

SOME UNITS

EMBASSY SUITES HOTEL
Phone: (734)462-6000 **83**

All Year [BP]   1P: $89-$159   2P: $99-$169   XP: $10   F17

Location: I-275, exit 169B, just e, then 0.5 mi n. Located in Victor Corporate Park. 19525 Victor Pkwy 48152. Fax: 734/462-6003. **Facility:** 239 units. 236 one- and 3 two-bedroom suites, some with whirlpools. 5 stories, interior corridors. **Parking:** on-site. **Terms:** [AP] meal plan available. **Amenities:** video games, high-speed Internet (fee), dual phone lines, voice mail, irons, hair dryers. **Pool(s):** heated indoor. **Leisure Activities:** sauna, whirlpool, exercise room. **Guest Services:** gift shop, complimentary evening beverages, valet and coin laundry. **Business Services:** conference facilities. **Cards:** AX, CB, DC, DS, JC, MC, VI.

SOME UNITS

FEE

FAIRFIELD INN DETROIT/LIVONIA
Phone: (734)953-8888 **86**

4/29-10/3 [ECP]   1P: $79-$89   2P: $79-$89   XP: $10   F
4/1-4/28 & 10/4-3/31 [ECP] 1P: $69-$86   2P: $69-$86   XP: $10   F

Location: I-275, exit 170, just nw. 17350 Fox Dr 48152. Fax: 734/953-0732. **Facility:** 103 one-bedroom standard units, some with whirlpools. 4 stories, interior corridors. *Bath:* combo or shower only. **Parking:** on-site. **Amenities:** voice mail, irons, hair dryers. **Pool(s):** heated indoor. **Leisure Activities:** whirlpool, exercise room. **Guest Services:** valet and coin laundry. **Business Services:** meeting rooms. **Cards:** AX, CB, DC, DS, MC, VI. **Special Amenities: free continental breakfast and free local telephone calls.**

SOME UNITS

(See map p. 228)

HOLIDAY INN LIVONIA-WEST
Phone: (734)464-1300 [88]

AAA SAVE

Small-scale Hotel

All Year   1P: $99-$149   2P: $99-$149
Location: I-275, exit 170, just e. Located across from the Laurel Park Mall. 17123 Laurel Park Dr N 48152. Fax: 734/464-1596. **Facility:** 226 one-bedroom standard units, some with whirlpools. 3 stories, interior corridors. **Parking:** on-site. **Terms:** check-in 4 pm. **Amenities:** dual phone lines, voice mail, irons, hair dryers. **Dining:** 6:30 am-10 pm, Fri & Sat-11 pm, cocktails, nightclub. **Pool(s):** heated indoor. **Leisure Activities:** sauna, whirlpool, putting green, exercise room. **Guest Services:** coin laundry. **Business Services:** conference facilities. **Cards:** AX, DC, DS, MC, VI. **Special Amenities:** free newspaper and free room upgrade (subject to availability with advanced reservations). *(See color ad p 258)*

SOME UNITS

LIVONIA MARRIOTT
Phone: 734/462-3100 [90]

AAA SAVE

Small-scale Hotel

All Year   1P: $89-$159   2P: $89-$159
Location: I-275, exit 170, just w. Located in Laurel Park Mall. 17100 Laurel Park Dr N 48152. Fax: 734/462-2815. **Facility:** 224 units. 221 one-bedroom standard units. 3 one-bedroom suites ($250). 6 stories, interior corridors. **Parking:** on-site. **Terms:** check-in 4 pm. **Amenities:** high-speed Internet, voice mail, irons, hair dryers. **Dining:** Sweet Lorraine's Cafe & Bar, see separate listing. **Pool(s):** heated indoor. **Leisure Activities:** saunas, whirlpool, exercise room. **Guest Services:** gift shop, valet laundry. **Business Services:** conference facilities, business center. **Cards:** AX, CB, DC, DS, JC, MC, VI. **Special Amenities:** early check-in/late check-out and free newspaper.

SOME UNITS

FEE

RESIDENCE INN DETROIT-LIVONIA
Phone: 734/462-4201 [89]

SAVE

Small-scale Hotel

All Year [BP]   1P: $94-$124
Location: I-275, exit 170, just nw. 17250 Fox Dr 48152. Fax: 734/462-4203. **Facility:** 112 units. 56 one-bedroom standard units with efficiencies. 38 one- and 18 two-bedroom suites, some with efficiencies or kitchens. 4 stories, interior corridors. **Bath:** combo or shower only. **Parking:** on-site. **Terms:** check-in 4 pm, pets ($200 fee). **Amenities:** video games, dual phone lines, voice mail, irons, hair dryers. **Pool(s):** heated outdoor. **Leisure Activities:** whirlpool, exercise room, sports court. **Guest Services:** complimentary evening beverages: Mon-Thurs, valet and coin laundry. **Business Services:** meeting rooms. **Cards:** AX, CB, DC, DS, MC, VI.

SOME UNITS

TOWNEPLACE SUITES
Phone: (734)542-7400 [87]

SAVE

Small-scale Hotel

All Year   1P: $69-$89
Location: I-275, exit 170; just nw. 17450 Fox Dr 48152. Fax: 734/542-7401. **Facility:** Smoke free premises. 95 units. 69 one-bedroom standard units with kitchens. 4 one- and 22 two-bedroom suites ($69-$159) with kitchens. 3 stories, interior corridors. **Bath:** combo or shower only. **Parking:** on-site. **Terms:** cancellation fee imposed, weekly rates available. **Amenities:** dual phone lines, voice mail, irons, hair dryers. **Pool(s):** heated outdoor. **Leisure Activities:** exercise room. **Guest Services:** sundries, valet and coin laundry. **Business Services:** business center. **Cards:** AX, DC, DS, JC, MC, VI.

SOME UNITS

———— WHERE TO DINE ————

DEPALMAS RISTORANTE
Lunch: $6-$15   **Dinner: $10-$20**   **Phone: 734/261-2430** [80]

Italian

Location: Jct Plymouth and Merriman rds, just w. 31735 Plymouth Rd 48150. **Hours:** 11 am-11 pm, Sun 4 pm-9 pm. Closed: 1/1, 12/25. **Reservations:** suggested; weekends. **Features:** Such specialties as roasted veal Depalma and chicken Lamborghini are popular choices on a menu that centers on Italian preparations of seafood, ribs and steak. Live jazz ensembles perform many nights. The established restaurant is a local favorite. Casual dress; cocktails; entertainment. **Parking:** on-site. **Cards:** AX, DC, DS, MC, VI.

FAMILY BUGGY RESTAURANT
Lunch: $7-$9   **Dinner: $9-$15**   **Phone: 734/427-8360** [79]

AAA

American

Location: Jct I-96 and Middlebelt Rd, 1 mi s. 11502 Middlebelt Rd 48150. **Hours:** 11 am-9 pm, Fri & Sat-10 pm. Closed: 1/1, 11/27, 12/25. **Features:** Antique furnishings and decorations give you the feeling that you've slipped into yesteryear. The homey, family-oriented restaurant is a comfortable place in which to enjoy such reliable favorites as smothered chicken breast and pot roast. Casual dress. **Parking:** on-site. **Cards:** MC, VI.

SWEET LORRAINE'S CAFE & BAR
Lunch: $6-$10   **Dinner: $8-$12**   **Phone: 734/953-7480** [78]

American

Location: I-275, exit 170, just w; in Laurel Park Shopping Mall; in Livonia Marriott. 17100 N Laurel Park Dr 48152. **Hours:** 6:30 am-11 pm, Fri-midnight, Sat 7 am-midnight, Sun 7 am-11 pm. **Reservations:** suggested. **Features:** A step above the typical hotel restaurant, this bright and cheerful space serves an eclectic menu of continental standards such as steak and seafood as well as globally influenced items such as French pot pie or Spanish paella. Casual dress; cocktails. **Parking:** on-site. **Cards:** AX, CB, DC, DS, JC, MC, VI.

MADISON HEIGHTS pop. 31,101 (See map p. 228; index p. 231)

———— **WHERE TO STAY** ————

BEST WESTERN TROY-MADISON INN
Phone: (248)583-7000 **29**

🔺🔺🔺 [SAVE] All Year [ECP] 1P: $69-$109 2P: $69-$109 XP: $5 F17
🔻🔻 🔻🔻 **Location:** I-75, exit 65B, just w. 1331 W 14 Mile Rd 48071. Fax: 248/583-1455. **Facility:** 81 one-bedroom standard units, some with whirlpools. 2 stories, interior corridors. **Parking:** on-site. **Amenities:** safes, irons, hair dryers. **Pool(s):** small heated indoor. **Leisure Activities:** exercise room. *Fee:* game room. **Guest Services:**
Small-scale Hotel valet laundry. **Business Services:** meeting rooms, business center. **Cards:** AX, CB, DC, DS, JC, MC, VI. **Special Amenities:** free continental breakfast and free newspaper.

SOME UNITS

🆂 📶 🛎 📹 [DATA PORT] 🗄 📺 🖥 / ⊗ /

ECONO LODGE
Phone: (248)583-7700 **31**

[SAVE] 6/1-9/30 1P: $47-$50 2P: $47-$50 XP: $4 F16
🔻🔻 10/1-3/31 1P: $43-$50 2P: $43-$50 XP: $4 F16
Motel 4/1-5/31 1P: $43-$46 2P: $43-$46 XP: $4 F16
Location: I-75, exit 65B, just w, then just s. 32703 Stephenson Hwy 48071. Fax: 248/583-0516. **Facility:** 149 one-bedroom standard units, some with kitchens (no utensils) and/or whirlpools. 1 story, exterior corridors. **Parking:** on-site. **Terms:** weekly rates available, package plans. **Pool(s):** outdoor. **Cards:** AX, DC, DS, MC, VI.

SOME UNITS

🆂 📶 🛎 📹 / ⊗ 🗄 📺

FAIRFIELD INN BY MARRIOTT
Phone: (248)588-3388 **30**

[SAVE] All Year [ECP] 1P: $59-$99 2P: $59-$99
🔺🔺🔺 🔺🔺🔺 **Location:** I-75, exit 65B, just w, then just s. 32800 Stephenson Hwy 48071. Fax: 248/588-3388. **Facility:** 134 one-bedroom standard units. 3 stories, interior/exterior corridors. *Bath:* combo or shower only. **Parking:** on-site.
Small-scale Hotel MC, VI. **Amenities:** irons, hair dryers. **Pool(s):** heated outdoor. **Guest Services:** valet laundry. **Cards:** AX, DC, DS,

SOME UNITS

📶 📹 🛎 📹 [DATA PORT] / ⊗ /

HAMPTON INN
Phone: 248/585-8881 **34**

[SAVE] All Year [CP] 1P: $104-$109
🔻🔻🔻 **Location:** I-75, exit 65B, just w, then just s. 32420 Stephenson Hwy 48071. Fax: 248/585-9446. **Facility:** 124 one-bedroom standard units. 4 stories, interior corridors. **Parking:** on-site. **Amenities:** voice mail, irons, hair dryers. **Leisure Activities:** sauna, exercise room. **Guest Services:** valet laundry. **Business Services:**
Small-scale Hotel meeting rooms. **Cards:** AX, CB, DC, DS, JC, MC, VI. *(See color ad below)*

SOME UNITS

🆂 📹 📹 [DATA PORT] 🖥 / ⊗ /

RED ROOF INN
Phone: (248)583-4700 **33**

🔺🔺🔺 [SAVE] 5/25-11/1 1P: $52-$66 2P: $57-$71 XP: $5 F18
🔻🔻 🔻🔻 11/2-3/31 1P: $47-$64 2P: $52-$69 XP: $5 F18
Motel 4/1-5/24 1P: $46-$58 2P: $51-$63 XP: $5 F18
Location: I-75, exit 65A, just e, then just s. Located opposite from the shopping mall. 32511 Concord Dr 48071. Fax: 248/583-2982. **Facility:** 108 one-bedroom standard units. 2 stories, exterior corridors. *Bath:* combo or shower only. **Parking:** on-site. **Terms:** small pets only. **Amenities:** video games (fee), voice mail. **Cards:** AX, CB, DC, DS, MC, VI. **Special Amenities:** free local telephone calls and free newspaper.

SOME UNITS

🐾 📶 📹 📹 / ⊗ [DATA PORT] 🗄 📺 /
FEE   FEE

RESIDENCE INN BY MARRIOTT-MADISON HEIGHTS
Phone: (248)583-4322 **32**

[SAVE] All Year 1P: $125-$161
🔺🔺🔺 **Location:** I-75, exit 65B, just w, then just s. 32650 Stephenson Hwy 48071. Fax: 248/583-9092. **Facility:** 96 units. 72 one-bedroom standard units with kitchens. 24 one-bedroom suites with kitchens. 2 stories, exterior corridors. *Bath:* combo or shower only. **Parking:** on-site. **Terms:** cancellation fee imposed, [BP] meal plan available,
Condominium pets ($300 fee, $6 extra charge). **Amenities:** voice mail, irons, hair dryers. **Pool(s):** heated outdoor. **Leisure Activities:** whirlpool, exercise room, sports court. **Guest Services:** valet and coin laundry.
Cards: AX, CB, DC, DS, JC, MC, VI.

SOME UNITS

🆂 🐾 📶 📹 🛎 ⊗ 📹 [DATA PORT] 🗄 📺 🖥 / ⊗ /

(See map p. 228)

------ WHERE TO DINE ------

BIG FISH SEAFOOD BISTRO
▼▼▼
Seafood
Lunch: $6-$13   **Dinner:** $7-$24   **Phone:** 248/585-9533   39
Location: I-75, exit 65 (14 Mile Rd), just w to Stephenson Hwy. 1111 W 14 Mile Rd 48071. **Hours:** 11 am-10 pm, Fri & Sat-11 pm, Sun 3 pm-9 pm. Closed major holidays. **Features:** Hot and cold soups, varied appetizers and creative desserts complement such innovatively prepared seafood entrees as whitefish Oscar. The festive, nautical atmosphere is inviting to families. The wait staff provides attentive service from start to finish. Casual dress; cocktails. **Parking:** on-site. **Cards:** AX, DC, DS, MC, VI.

BOODLE'S RESTAURANT
▼▼▼
American
Lunch: $8-$13   **Dinner:** $9-$28   **Phone:** 248/399-5960   40
Location: I-75, exit 62, just e. 935 W 11 Mile Rd 48071. **Hours:** 11 am-11 pm, Fri-midnight, Sat 4 pm-midnight, Sun 10 am-10 pm. Closed major holidays. **Reservations:** suggested; weekends. **Features:** A wide selection of well-prepared entrees—from steak Diane to Alaskan crab legs to seafood pasta—is listed on the restaurant's menu. The dark-stained walls give the dining room a warm, comfortable feel. Dessert choices are tempting and tasty. Casual dress; cocktails; entertainment. **Parking:** on-site. **Cards:** AX, DC, DS, MC, VI.

MILFORD pop. 6,272

------ WHERE TO DINE ------

APPLETEASER
▼▼▼
American
Lunch: $10-$15   **Dinner:** $10-$15   **Phone:** 248/685-0989
Location: Downtown. 355 Main St 48381. **Hours:** 11 am-midnight, Sun 10:30 am-2:30 & 3-midnight. Closed major holidays. **Features:** In business for more than 20 years, this three story restaurant and bar offers something for every taste and whim. Burgers and pizza are offered beside grilled herb salmon and chocolate souffles. Dressy casual; cocktails. **Parking:** street. **Cards:** AX, DC, MC, VI.

FIVE LAKES GRILL
AAA
▼▼▼
Regional
American
Dinner: $14-$20   **Phone:** 248/684-7455
Location: At Main St and Commerce Rd. 424 N Main 48381. **Hours:** 4 pm-10 pm, Fri & Sat-11 pm. Closed major holidays; also Sun. **Reservations:** suggested. **Features:** Stylishly avant-garde and SoHo chic, the inviting dining room is deliberately stark. Imaginative creations include potato-crusted Lake Superior whitefish with lobster mousseline, pastaless Mediterranean vegetable lasagna and grilled portobello sandwich. Dressy casual; cocktails. **Parking:** on-site and street. **Cards:** AX, MC, VI.

MOUNT CLEMENS pop. 17,312

------ WHERE TO STAY ------

BEST WESTERN CONCORDE INN
SAVE
▼▼▼▼
Small-scale Hotel
Phone: (586)493-7300
All Year   1P: $79-$259   2P: $79-$259   XP: $10   F17
Location: I-94, exit 240B, 1 mi w, 0.5 mi s. 44315 Grotiot Ave 48036. **Fax:** 586/493-7330. **Facility:** 160 units. 141 one-bedroom standard units, some with kitchens and/or whirlpools. 19 one-bedroom suites ($119-$259) with whirlpools. 4 stories, interior corridors. *Bath:* combo or shower only. **Parking:** on-site. **Terms:** [ECP] meal plan available. **Amenities:** video games, dual phone lines, voice mail, irons, hair dryers. **Leisure Activities:** sauna, racquetball court. *Fee:* massage, game room. **Guest Services:** sundries, valet and coin laundry, area transportation. **Business Services:** conference facilities, business center. **Cards:** AX, CB, DC, DS, MC, VI.
SOME UNITS

------ WHERE TO DINE ------

PAUL'S RIVERHOUSE
▼▼▼
American
Lunch: $7-$13   **Dinner:** $9-$23   **Phone:** 586/465-5111
Location: I-94, exit 237, just w. 24240 N River Rd 48043. **Hours:** 11:30 am-11 pm, Fri & Sat 1 pm-1 am, Sun 1 pm-10 pm. Closed: 1/1, 12/25. **Reservations:** suggested; weekends. **Features:** Hearty portions of creative preparations of seafood, chicken and veal characterize the restaurant's menu. From the cozy lakefront patio, diners enjoy great views of the river and its resident wildlife. Black bean chili is among interesting soup choices. Casual dress; cocktails. **Parking:** on-site. **Cards:** AX, DC, DS, MC, VI.

NORTHVILLE pop. 6,459   (See map p. 228; index p. 233)

------ WHERE TO STAY ------

HAMPTON INN
SAVE
▼▼▼
Small-scale Hotel
Phone: (734)462-1119   80
All Year   1P: $69-$104   2P: $74-$109
Location: I-275, exit 167, just w, then just s. 20600 Haggerty Rd 48167. **Fax:** 734/462-6270. **Facility:** 125 one-bedroom standard units. 4 stories, interior corridors. **Parking:** on-site. **Terms:** [ECP] meal plan available, package plans. **Amenities:** voice mail, irons. **Pool(s):** heated outdoor. **Leisure Activities:** sauna, exercise room. **Guest Services:** valet laundry. **Business Services:** meeting rooms.
SOME UNITS

RAMADA LIMITED OF NOVI
▼▼▼
Motel
Phone: 248/349-7400   79
Property failed to provide current rates
Location: I-275, exit 167, just w, then 0.4 mi n. 21100 Haggerty Rd 48167. **Fax:** 248/349-7454. **Facility:** 125 one-bedroom standard units. 2 stories, interior/exterior corridors. **Parking:** on-site. **Amenities:** voice mail, safes (fee), irons, hair dryers. **Leisure Activities:** exercise room. **Guest Services:** valet and coin laundry. **Business Services:** meeting rooms. **Cards:** AX, CB, DC, DS, MC, VI.
SOME UNITS

(See map p. 228)

———— **WHERE TO DINE** ————

EMILY'S
▼▼▼▼
American

Dinner: $20-$30   **Phone:** 248/349-0505
Location: Just n of jct Main and Center sts; downtown. 505 N Center St 48167. **Hours:** 5:30 pm-10 pm. Closed major holidays; also Sun, Mon. **Reservations:** accepted. **Features:** Be prepared for an enjoyable evening at this attractive converted house, as the chef/owner is an advocate of slow-cooked food. Seasonal and fresh ingredients are used to create a Mediterranean menu that changes regularly. Dressy casual; cocktails. **Parking:** on-site. **Cards:** AX, DC, DS, MC, VI.
[&M] [X]

LITTLE ITALY RISTORANTE
▼▼▼
Italian

Lunch: $12-$15   **Dinner:** $19-$25   **Phone:** 248/348-0575
Location: Jct Main and Sutton sts, just w; downtown. 227 Hutton St 48167. **Hours:** 11:30 am-2:30 & 5-10 pm, Fri & Sat-11 pm, Sun 4 pm-9 pm. Closed major holidays. **Reservations:** suggested. **Features:** An upscale lounge just off the main dining room is perfect for meeting friends or relaxing before enjoying an extensive menu of Italian specialties including handmade pasta in this converted Victorian house, where every room is individually decorated and romantic nooks are available. Casual dress; cocktails. **Parking:** on-site. **Cards:** AX, DC, DS, MC, VI.
[Y] [X]

MACKINNON'S RESTAURANT
▼▼ ▼▼
Steak & Seafood

Lunch: $9-$12   **Dinner:** $19-$34   **Phone:** 248/348-1991
Location: Downtown. 126 E Main St 48167. **Hours:** 11:30 am-3 & 5-10 pm, Fri & Sat 5 pm-11 pm. Closed major holidays; also Sun. **Reservations:** suggested. **Features:** Innovative steak, chops, seafood and live lobster served in charming country inn ambience; all food is fresh and all sauces, entrees and desserts are house-made. Very popular are the blown-up duck and the chicken strudel. Dressy casual; cocktails. **Parking:** on-site. **Cards:** AX, DC, DS, MC, VI.
[&M] [Y] [X]

NOVI pop. 47,386   (See map p. 228; index p. 233)

———— **WHERE TO STAY** ————

COUNTRY INN & SUITES BY CARLSON
▼▼▼▼
Small-scale Hotel

All Year [ECP]   1P: $105   **Phone:** (248)596-9800   **75**
                                                      XP: $5   F16
Location: I-275, exit 167, just w, then 0.5 mi n. 21625 Haggerty Rd 48375. **Fax:** 248/596-9875. **Facility:** Smoke free premises. 100 units. 73 one-bedroom standard units, some with whirlpools. 27 one-bedroom suites ($115). 4 stories, interior corridors. *Bath:* combo or shower only. **Parking:** on-site. **Terms:** 7 day cancellation notice, weekly rates available, package plans, small pets only ($50 deposit). **Amenities:** high-speed Internet, voice mail, irons, hair dryers. **Pool(s):** heated indoor. **Leisure Activities:** whirlpool, exercise room. **Guest Services:** valet and coin laundry. **Business Services:** meeting rooms. **Cards:** AX, CB, DC, DS, JC, MC, VI. *(See color ad p 243)*
SOME UNITS
[ASK] [S/D] [🛏] [&M] [🚬] [⌐] [≈] [🏃] [DATA PORT] [💻] / [X] [📱] [🖥] /

COURTYARD BY MARRIOTT
[SAVE]
▼▼▼▼
Small-scale Hotel

All Year   1P: $119   2P: $129   **Phone:** (248)380-1234
Location: I-96, exit 162, just s, just e on Crescent Dr, then 0.4 mi s on Town Center Dr. 42700 11 Mile Rd 48375. **Fax:** 248/380-5699. **Facility:** 122 units. 118 one-bedroom standard units, some with whirlpools. 4 one-bedroom suites. 4 stories, interior corridors. *Bath:* combo or shower only. **Parking:** on-site. **Amenities:** high-speed Internet, dual phone lines, voice mail, irons, hair dryers. **Pool(s):** heated indoor. **Leisure Activities:** whirlpool, exercise room. **Guest Services:** valet and coin laundry. **Business Services:** meeting rooms, fax. **Cards:** AX, CB, DC, DS, JC, MC, VI.
SOME UNITS
[S/D] [🍴] [Y] [&M] [🚬] [⌐] [≈] [🏃] [DATA PORT] [💻] / [X] [📱] [🖥] /

DOUBLETREE HOTEL NOVI/DETROIT
[AAA] [SAVE]
▼▼▼▼
Small-scale Hotel

All Year   1P: $69-$170   2P: $79-$180   **Phone:** (248)348-5000
                                            XP: $10   F18
Location: I-96, exit 162, just n, then just w. 27000 Sheraton Dr 48377. **Fax:** 248/348-2315. **Facility:** 217 units. 209 one-bedroom standard units. 8 one-bedroom suites ($195-$375), some with whirlpools. 3 stories, interior corridors. **Parking:** on-site. **Amenities:** voice mail, irons, hair dryers. **Dining:** 6:30 am-10 pm, Fri & Sat-11 pm, cocktails. **Pool(s):** heated outdoor, heated indoor. **Leisure Activities:** sauna, whirlpool, exercise room. *Fee:* game room. **Guest Services:** gift shop, valet laundry, area transportation-within 5 mi. **Business Services:** meeting rooms, business center. **Cards:** AX, CB, DC, DS, MC, VI. **Special Amenities:** early check-in/late check-out and free newspaper.
SOME UNITS
[S/D] [🍴] [Y] [⌐] [≈] [X] [🏃] [DATA PORT] [💻] / [X] [📱] [🖥] /

HILTON NOVI
[SAVE]
▼▼▼
Large-scale Hotel

All Year   1P: $79-$199   2P: $79-$199   **Phone:** (248)349-4000   **76**
                                            XP: $10   F17
Location: I-275, exit 167, just w, then just n. 21111 Haggerty Rd 48375. **Fax:** 248/349-4066. **Facility:** 239 units. 236 one-bedroom standard units. 3 one-bedroom suites. 7 stories, interior corridors. **Parking:** on-site. **Terms:** cancellation fee imposed, small pets only ($150 deposit). **Amenities:** dual phone lines, voice mail, irons, hair dryers. **Pool(s):** heated indoor. **Leisure Activities:** sauna, whirlpool, exercise room. **Guest Services:** valet laundry, area transportation. **Business Services:** conference facilities. **Cards:** AX, CB, DC, DS, JC, MC, VI.
SOME UNITS
[S/D] [🛏] [🍴] [Y] [⌐] [≈] [X] [🏃] [DATA PORT] [💻] / [X] [VCR] [📱] [🖥] /

HOTEL BARONETTE
[AAA] [SAVE]
▼▼▼
Small-scale Hotel

All Year [BP]   1P: $135-$161   2P: $135-$161   **Phone:** (248)349-7800
                                                  XP: $10   F16
Location: I-96, exit 162, just n. Located in 12 Oaks Mall. 27790 Novi Rd 48377. **Fax:** 248/349-7467. **Facility:** 153 units. 145 one-bedroom standard units, some with kitchens. 8 one-bedroom suites ($209-$450), some with kitchens and/or whirlpools. 3 stories, interior corridors. **Parking:** on-site. **Terms:** check-in 4 pm. **Amenities:** video games (fee), high-speed Internet, voice mail, honor bars, irons, hair dryers. **Dining:** 5 pm-10 pm, Fri & Sat-11 pm, cocktails. **Pool(s):** heated indoor. **Leisure Activities:** sauna, whirlpool, putting green, exercise room. **Guest Services:** gift shop, complimentary evening beverages, valet and coin laundry. **Business Services:** conference facilities, business center. **Cards:** AX, CB, DC, DS, JC, MC, VI. **Special Amenities:** free continental breakfast and free newspaper.
SOME UNITS
[S/D] [🍴] [Y] [⌐] [≈] [X] [VCR] [🏃] [DATA PORT] [🖥] / [X] [📱] /

(See map p. 228)

TOWNEPLACE SUITES   Phone: (248)305-5533
SAVE
All Year   1P: $84   2P: $94
Small-scale Hotel
Location: I-96, exit 162, 1 mi s, then 0.5 mi e. 42600 11 Mile Rd 48375. Fax: 248/305-5566. **Facility:** 95 units. 54 one-bedroom standard units with kitchens. 4 one- and 37 two-bedroom suites with kitchens. 3 stories, interior corridors. **Parking:** on-site. **Terms:** age restrictions may apply, small pets only ($100 fee). **Amenities:** dual phone lines, voice mail, irons, hair dryers. **Pool(s):** small heated outdoor. **Leisure Activities:** exercise room. **Guest Services:** valet and coin laundry. **Business Services:** business center. **Cards:** AX, CB, DC, DS, JC, MC, VI.
SOME UNITS

WYNDHAM GARDEN HOTEL-NOVI   Phone: (248)344-8800
(AAA) SAVE
All Year   1P: $69-$121   2P: $69-$131   XP: $10   F18
Small-scale Hotel
Location: I-96, exit 162, just s, then 0.5 mi e. Located in Novi Town Center. 42100 Crescent Blvd 48375. Fax: 248/344-8535. **Facility:** 148 one-bedroom standard units. 2 stories (no elevator), interior corridors. **Parking:** on-site. **Terms:** cancellation fee imposed. **Amenities:** video games, high-speed Internet, voice mail, irons, hair dryers. **Dining:** 6:30 am-1 & 5-10 pm, Sat & Sun from 7 am, cocktails. **Pool(s):** heated indoor. **Leisure Activities:** sauna, whirlpool. **Guest Services:** valet laundry. **Business Services:** meeting rooms. **Cards:** AX, DC, DS, MC, VI.
SOME UNITS

——— WHERE TO DINE ———

NEW AH WOK   Lunch: $6-$10   Dinner: $8-$12   Phone: 248/349-9260   [71]
Chinese
Location: I-275 N, exit 1 (Grand River), just e, then just s on Grand River Ave, 2 mi w. 41563 W 10 Mile Rd 48375. **Hours:** 11 am-9:30 pm, Fri-11:30 pm, Sat 4 pm-11:30 pm, Sun noon-9:30 pm. Closed major holidays. **Reservations:** accepted. **Features:** For the adventuresome and others alike, New Ah Wok offers plenty of favorites but also serves up plenty of new and interesting choices such as Winter Melon Soup and Eight Treasures Taro Nest. Casual dress; cocktails. **Parking:** on-site. **Cards:** AX, DC, DS, MC, VI.

STEVE & ROCKY'S   Lunch: $9-$15   Dinner: $15-$25   Phone: 248/374-0688
American
Location: I-96, exit 162, just e. 3150 Grand River 48375. **Hours:** 11 am-10 pm, Fri & Sat-11 pm, Sun 1 pm-9 pm. Closed major holidays. **Features:** Vibrant contrasting colours and an eclectic decor set the tone for this restaurant known for its fresh fish and seafood. Emphasizing fresh food, the kitchen shows its creative side in both food presentation and creation. Daily specials such as the "Just Today" or "Just Tonight" highlight an ever-changing menu. Dressy casual; cocktails; entertainment. **Parking:** on-site. **Cards:** AX, DC, DS, MC, VI.

W F BIBIMBAB   Lunch: $6-$9   Dinner: $10-$18   Phone: 248/348-6800
Korean
Location: I-96, exit 162, 1.6 mi n, then just e; rear and inside Main St. Development Mall. 43155 Main St, Suite 300 48375. **Hours:** 11:30 am-10:30 pm, Fri & Sat-11 pm, Sun noon-10 pm. Closed major holidays. **Features:** Hidden in the back of the Main Street Complex, it's easy to overlook this bright and lively space. Specializing in Korean barbeque, where diners grill their own meat and seafood from barbeque tops set into most tables, the restaurant also offers sushi and it's namesake dish which has been described as "offering a different taste with every bite". Casual dress; cocktails. **Parking:** on-site. **Cards:** AX, DC, MC, VI.

PLYMOUTH pop. 9,022   (See map p. 228; index p. 234)

——— WHERE TO STAY ———

HILTON GARDEN INN - PLYMOUTH   Phone: (734)354-0001
SAVE
All Year   1P: $79-$149   2P: $89-$159   XP: $10   F17
Small-scale Hotel
Location: SR 14, exit 20, just n. 14600 Sheldon Rd 48170. Fax: 734/354-5121. **Facility:** 157 units. 155 one-bedroom standard units, some with whirlpools. 2 one-bedroom suites ($299-$399). 6 stories, interior corridors. *Bath:* combo or shower only. **Parking:** on-site. **Amenities:** video games (fee), dual phone lines, voice mail, irons, hair dryers. **Pool(s):** small heated indoor. **Leisure Activities:** whirlpool, exercise room. **Guest Services:** sundries, valet and coin laundry, area transportation. **Business Services:** meeting rooms, business center. **Cards:** AX, CB, DC, DS, JC, MC, VI.
SOME UNITS

QUALITY INN PLYMOUTH CLOCKTOWER   Phone: (734)455-8100   [96]
(AAA) SAVE
All Year   1P: $99-$129   2P: $109-$139   XP: $10   F17
Small-scale Hotel
Location: I-275, exit 28, just w, entry on Massey Dr. 40455 Ann Arbor Rd 48170. Fax: 734/455-5711. **Facility:** 123 one-bedroom standard units. 2 stories, interior corridors. **Parking:** on-site. **Terms:** [ECP] meal plan available. **Amenities:** voice mail, irons, hair dryers. **Pool(s):** outdoor. **Leisure Activities:** exercise room. **Guest Services:** valet laundry. **Business Services:** meeting rooms. **Cards:** AX, CB, DC, DS, JC, MC, VI. **Special Amenities:** early check-in/late check-out. *(See color ad p 226)*
SOME UNITS

RED ROOF INN-PLYMOUTH   Phone: (734)459-3300   [95]
(AAA) SAVE
All Year   1P: $49-$66   2P: $56-$73   XP: $7   F18
Motel
Location: I-275, exit 28, just e. 39700 Ann Arbor Rd 48170. Fax: 734/459-3072. **Facility:** 109 one-bedroom standard units. 2 stories, exterior corridors. *Bath:* combo or shower only. **Parking:** on-site. **Terms:** small pets only. **Amenities:** video games, voice mail. **Cards:** AX, CB, DC, DS, MC, VI. **Special Amenities:** free local telephone calls and free newspaper.
SOME UNITS

(See map p. 228)

———— WHERE TO DINE ————

CAFE BON HOMME   **Lunch:** $7-$13   **Dinner:** $29-$33   **Phone:** 734/453-6260
▼▼▼▼   **Location:** Between Main and Harvey sts; downtown. 844 Penniman Ave 48170. **Hours:** 11:30 am-3 & 5-9 pm,
Fri-10 pm, Sat noon-3 & 5-10 pm. Closed major holidays; also Sun. **Reservations:** suggested; dinner.
American   **Features:** In a quaint area of downtown, the small, romantic cafe has the feel of a European bistro.
Innovative French-American cuisine shows an unusual fusion of Asian influences in some preparations.
The wine list is well-rounded. Desserts are homemade. Dressy casual; cocktails. **Parking:** street. **Cards:** AX, DC, MC, VI.

⊠

COMPARI'S ON THE PARK   **Lunch:** $8-$10   **Dinner:** $12-$16   **Phone:** 734/416-0100
▼▼▼ ▼▼▼   **Location:** Downtown. 350 S Main St 48170. **Hours:** 11 am-10 pm, Thurs-11 pm, Fri & Sat-midnight, Sun 3
pm-9 pm. Closed major holidays. **Reservations:** accepted. **Features:** Exposed brick walls, murals and
Italian   large picture windows that overlook the city park give this upscale restaurant a comfortable feel. Focusing
on well prepared Italian specialities and pizza, this restaurant is popular with the local crowd. Casual dress;
cocktails. **Parking:** street. **Cards:** AX, MC, VI.

⊤ ⊠

PONTIAC pop. 66,337

———— WHERE TO STAY ————

COURTYARD BY MARRIOTT   **Phone:** (248)858-9595
[SAVE]   All Year   1P: $129-$169   2P: $129-$169   XP: $10   F21
Location: I-75, exit 75 (Square Lake Rd), w via Opdyke Rd. 3555 Centerpoint Pkwy 48341. **Fax:** 248/858-9696.
▼▼▼▼   **Facility:** 110 units. 106 one-bedroom standard units. 4 one-bedroom suites. 4 stories, interior corridors. *Bath:*
Small-scale Hotel   combo or shower only. **Parking:** on-site, winter plug-ins. **Amenities:** video games (fee), dual phone lines,
voice mail, irons, hair dryers. **Pool(s):** heated indoor. **Leisure Activities:** whirlpool, exercise room. **Guest
Services:** valet and coin laundry. **Business Services:** meeting rooms, business center. **Cards:** AX, CB, DC,
DS, MC, VI.
SOME UNITS
[S/D] [⊙] [❙¶] [⊤] [&] [🗇] [⊶] [✈] [DATA PORT] [▣] / [⊠] [❙] [🖼] /

DETROIT MARRIOTT PONTIAC AT CENTERPOINT   **Phone:** (248)253-9800
[AAA] [SAVE]   1/1-3/31   1P: $199-$235   2P: $199-$245   XP: $10   F18
4/1-12/31   1P: $189-$225   2P: $189-$235   XP: $10   F18
▼▼ ▼▼ ▼▼   **Location:** I-75, exit 75 (Square Lake Rd), just w via Opdyke Rd/Centerpoint. 3600 Centerpoint Pkwy 48341.
Fax: 248/253-9682. **Facility:** 290 units. 285 one-bedroom standard units. 5 one-bedroom suites ($425). 11
Large-scale Hotel   stories, interior corridors. *Bath:* combo or shower only. **Parking:** on-site and valet. **Terms:** cancellation fee
imposed. **Amenities:** dual phone lines, voice mail, safes, irons, hair dryers. *Fee:* video games, high-speed
Internet. *Some:* CD players. **Dining:** 6:30 am-11 pm, cocktails, wine only. **Pool(s):** heated outdoor, heated indoor. **Leisure Activities:** whirlpool, exercise room. *Fee:* massage. **Guest Services:** sundries, valet and coin laundry, area transportation (fee)-
within 5 mi. **Business Services:** conference facilities, business center. **Cards:** AX, CB, DC, DS, JC, MC, VI. **Special Amenities:**
free newspaper and free room upgrade (subject to availability with advanced reservations).
SOME UNITS
[S/D] [⊙] [❙¶] [⊤] [&] [⊶] [⊠] [✈] [DATA PORT] [❙] [🖼] / [⊠] /

RESIDENCE INN BY MARRIOTT DETROIT/PONTIAC   **Phone:** 248/858-8664
[SAVE]   All Year [BP]   1P: $159-$189   2P: $159-$189
Location: I-75, exit 75 (Square Lake Rd), w via Opdyke Rd. 3333 Centerpoint Pkwy 48341. **Fax:** 248/858-8665.
▼▼▼▼   **Facility:** 114 units. 47 one-bedroom standard units, some with efficiencies or kitchens. 43 one- and 24 two-
bedroom suites, some with efficiencies or kitchens. 3 stories, interior corridors. *Bath:* combo or shower only.
Small-scale Hotel   **Parking:** on-site. **Terms:** check-in 4 pm, pets ($50 deposit, $5 extra charge). **Amenities:** video games (fee),
dual phone lines, voice mail, irons, hair dryers. **Pool(s):** heated indoor. **Leisure Activities:** whirlpool, playground, exercise room, sports court. **Guest Services:** valet and coin laundry. **Business Services:** meeting rooms, business
center. **Cards:** AX, CB, DC, DS, MC, VI.
SOME UNITS
[🛏] [❙¶] [&] [🗇] [⊶] [⊠] [✈] [DATA PORT] [❙] [🖼] [▣] / [⊠] /

———— WHERE TO DINE ————

PARKWAY GRILLE   **Lunch:** $13-$25   **Dinner:** $13-$25   **Phone:** 248/648-6034
▼▼▼▼   **Location:** I-75, exit 75 (Square Lake Rd), just w via Opdyke Rd; in Detroit Marriott Pontiac at Centerpoint. 3600
Centerpoint Pkwy 48341. **Hours:** 6:30 am-10:30 pm. **Features:** Located inside the Detroit Marriott Pontiac,
American   this upscale and lively space is a definite step above the typical hotel restaurant. The gently trendy and
daring menu offers a "Napoleon" of tri colored tomatoes, rack of lamb with a mustard, mint and rosemary
crust, and sinful and creative desserts such as white-chocolate cherry bread pudding. Dressy casual; cocktails. **Parking:**
on-site and valet. **Cards:** AX, DC, DS, MC, VI.

[&M] [⊤] [⊠]

ROCHESTER pop. 10,467

———— WHERE TO DINE ————

FAMILY BUGGY RESTAURANT   **Lunch:** $5-$7   **Dinner:** $8-$13   **Phone:** 248/656-0850
[AAA]   **Location:** SR 59, 2.5 mi n on Rochester Rd; in South Hills Shopping Plaza. 870 S Rochester Rd 48307. **Hours:** 11
am-9 pm, Fri & Sat-10 pm. Closed: 1/1, 11/27, 12/25. **Features:** Located in the South Hills Shopping
▼▼ ▼▼   Plaza, the Family Buggy Restaurant is a popular local eatery 20th-century artifacts reminiscent of rural
America. Their menu is full of heartland American dishes that will please everyone in the family. Casual
American   dress. **Parking:** on-site. **Cards:** MC, VI.

⊠

SALSA'S MEXICAN CANTINA   **Lunch:** $5-$8   **Dinner:** $9-$14   **Phone:** 248/853-6800

Mexican

Location: 1 mi n of SR 59. 2601 S Rochester Rd 48307. **Hours:** 11 am-11 pm, Fri & Sat-midnight, Sun 11:30 am-10 pm. **Closed:** 11/27, 12/25. **Features:** Near the intersection of Rochester Road and Interstate 75, there is a lively Mexican restaurant called Salsa's Mexican Cantina. They serve traditional Mexican dishes like enchiladas, tacos and fajitas. Mexican beers, and tequilas are also available. You can expect quick, friendly service at the bar or in the dining room. Casual dress; cocktails. **Parking:** on-site. **Cards:** AX, DC, DS, MC, VI.

ROCHESTER HILLS pop. 68,825

——— WHERE TO STAY ———

BEST WESTERN CONCORDE INN   **Phone:** (248)299-1210

Small-scale Hotel

			XP: $10	F17
All Year	1P: $79-$129	2P: $79-$149		

Location: Jct Hall Rd (M-59) and Crooks Rd. 1919 Star-Batt Dr 48309. **Fax:** 248/852-4678. **Facility:** 124 units. 115 one-bedroom standard units, some with whirlpools. 9 one-bedroom suites ($99-$199) with whirlpools. 2 stories, interior corridors. **Parking:** on-site. **Terms:** [CP] & [ECP] meal plans available. **Amenities:** video games (fee), voice mail, irons, hair dryers. **Pool(s):** heated indoor. **Leisure Activities:** sauna, whirlpool. **Guest Services:** valet and coin laundry. **Business Services:** meeting rooms. **Cards:** AX, CB, DC, DS, MC, VI.

SOME UNITS

RED ROOF INN   **Phone:** (248)853-6400

Motel

5/4-10/11	1P: $58-$71	2P: $64-$77	XP: $6	F18
10/12-3/31	1P: $52-$71	2P: $58-$77	XP: $6	F18
4/1-5/3	1P: $51-$66	2P: $57-$72	XP: $6	F18

Location: Jct Hall Rd (M-59) and Crooks Rd. 2580 Crooks Rd 48309. **Fax:** 248/853-6391. **Facility:** 111 one-bedroom standard units. 2 stories, exterior corridors. *Bath:* combo or shower only. **Parking:** on-site. **Terms:** small pets only. **Amenities:** video games, voice mail. **Cards:** AX, CB, DC, DS, MC, VI. **Special Amenities: free local telephone calls and free newspaper.**

SOME UNITS

ROMEO pop. 3,721

——— WHERE TO STAY ———

THE BRABB HOUSE   **Phone:** (586)752-4726

Historic Bed & Breakfast

		XP: $10
All Year [ECP]	2P: $79-$99	

Location: Just s, then just w; downtown. 185 S Main St 48065. **Fax:** 586/752-5673. **Facility:** In the heart of a charming town, this grand Victorian home offers tastefully decorated rooms with private baths. Smoke free premises. 5 one-bedroom standard units. 2 stories (no elevator), interior corridors. *Bath:* shower only. **Parking:** on-site. **Terms:** check-in 4 pm, age restrictions may apply, 7 day cancellation notice-fee imposed, [CP] meal plan available. **Business Services:** meeting rooms. **Cards:** AX, MC, VI.

ROMULUS pop. 22,979   (See map p. 228; index p. 234)

——— WHERE TO STAY ———

BAYMONT INN & SUITES DETROIT-AIRPORT   **Phone:** (734)722-6000   **141**

Small-scale Hotel

All Year [ECP]	1P: $79-$89	2P: $79-$89

Location: I-94, exit 198 (Merriman Rd), just w. 9000 Wickham Rd 48174. **Fax:** 734/722-4737. **Facility:** 100 units. 98 one-bedroom standard units, some with kitchens. 2 one-bedroom suites. 3 stories, interior corridors. **Parking:** on-site. **Terms:** pets ($50 deposit). **Amenities:** video games, dual phone lines, voice mail, irons, hair dryers. **Guest Services:** valet and coin laundry. **Cards:** AX, CB, DC, DS, MC, VI. **Special Amenities: free continental breakfast and free newspaper.** *(See color ad p 241)*

SOME UNITS

BEST WESTERN GATEWAY INTERNATIONAL HOTEL   **Phone:** 734/728-2800   **132**

Small-scale Hotel

			XP: $7	F17
All Year [ECP]	1P: $79-$89	2P: $79-$89		

Location: I-94, exit 198 (Merriman Rd). 9191 Wickham 48174. **Fax:** 734/728-2260. **Facility:** 233 units. 220 one-bedroom standard units, some with whirlpools. 13 one-bedroom suites ($139-$179), some with whirlpools. 2 stories, interior corridors. **Parking:** on-site. **Terms:** 30 day cancellation notice, [AP], [BP] & [CP] meal plans available. **Amenities:** voice mail, irons, hair dryers. **Dining:** 6 am-1 & 5-11 pm; closed Sun, cocktails. **Pool(s):** heated outdoor, heated indoor. **Leisure Activities:** sauna, whirlpool, atrium recreation room, pool table, exercise room. *Fee:* game room. **Guest Services:** valet and coin laundry, tanning facility. **Business Services:** conference facilities, business center. **Cards:** AX, DS, MC, VI. **Special Amenities: free continental breakfast.**

SOME UNITS

CLARION BARCELO' HOTEL   **Phone:** (734)728-7900   **136**

Small-scale Hotel

All Year	1P: $59-$79

Location: I-94, exit 198 (Merriman Rd), just n. 8600 Merriman Rd 48174. **Fax:** 734/728-6518. **Facility:** 153 one-bedroom standard units. 2 stories, interior corridors. **Parking:** on-site. **Terms:** 19% service charge. **Amenities:** dual phone lines, voice mail, irons, hair dryers. **Dining:** 6:30 am-2 & 5-10 pm, Sat & Sun from 7 am, cocktails. **Pool(s):** outdoor. **Leisure Activities:** exercise room. **Guest Services:** valet laundry. **Business Services:** meeting rooms. **Cards:** AX, CB, DC, DS, JC, MC, VI.

SOME UNITS

(See map p. 228)

COMFORT INN METRO AIRPORT

(AAA) (SAVE)
WWW WW
Small-scale Hotel

Phone: (734)326-2100 — **143**

All Year [ECP]   1P: $65-$169   2P: $65-$169   XP: $5   F18
Location: I-94, exit 198 (Merriman Rd), 0.8 mi w. 31800 Wick Rd 48174-1916. Fax: 734/326-9020. **Facility:** 123 one-bedroom standard units, some with whirlpools. 3 stories, interior corridors. **Amenities:** video games (fee), voice mail, irons, hair dryers. **Dining:** 5 am-midnight. **Guest Services:** valet and coin laundry. **Business Services:** meeting rooms. **Cards:** AX, DC, DS, MC, VI. **Special Amenities:** free continental breakfast and free local telephone calls.

SOME UNITS

COURTYARD BY MARRIOTT-METRO AIRPORT

(AAA) (SAVE)
WWWW WW
Small-scale Hotel

Phone: (734)721-3200 — **135**

All Year   1P: $69-$119   2P: $69-$119
Location: I-94, exit 198 (Merriman Rd), just e. 30653 Flynn Dr 48174. Fax: 734/721-1304. **Facility:** 146 units. 134 one-bedroom standard units. 12 one-bedroom suites. 3 stories, interior corridors. *Bath:* combo or shower only. **Amenities:** voice mail, irons, hair dryers. **Dining:** 6-10:30 am, Sat & Sun 7 am-noon. **Pool(s):** heated indoor. **Leisure Activities:** whirlpool, exercise room. **Guest Services:** valet and coin laundry. **Business Services:** meeting rooms. **Cards:** AX, CB, DC, DS, JC, MC, VI. **Special Amenities:** early check-in/late check-out and free newspaper.

SOME UNITS

CROWNE PLAZA HOTEL AND RESORT DETROIT METRO AIRPORT

WW WWW WW
Large-scale Hotel

Phone: (734)729-2600 — **129**

All Year   1P: $109-$149
Location: I-94, exit 198 (Merriman Rd), just n. 8000 Merriman Rd 48174. Fax: 734/729-9414. **Facility:** 364 one-bedroom standard units. 11 stories, interior corridors. **Parking:** on-site. **Terms:** [AP] meal plan available, 18% service charge. **Amenities:** voice mail, irons, hair dryers. **Leisure Activities:** whirlpool, exercise room. *Fee:* game room. **Guest Services:** gift shop, valet laundry. **Business Services:** conference facilities, business center. **Cards:** AX, CB, DC, DS, JC, MC, VI.

SOME UNITS

DAYS INN

(AAA) (SAVE)
WWW WW
Small-scale Hotel

Phone: (734)946-4300 — **144**

All Year [CP]   1P: $69-$79   2P: $69-$79   XP: $10   F14
Location: I-94, exit 199 (Middlebelt Rd), just s. 9501 Middlebelt Rd 48174. Fax: 734/946-7787. **Facility:** 127 one-bedroom standard units, some with whirlpools. 3 stories, interior corridors. **Parking:** on-site. **Amenities:** voice mail, irons, hair dryers. **Dining:** 11 am-11 pm, cocktails. **Leisure Activities:** exercise room. **Business Services:** meeting rooms. **Cards:** AX, DC, DS, MC, VI. **Special Amenities:** free continental breakfast and free newspaper.

SOME UNITS

DETROIT AIRPORT MARRIOTT HOTEL

(SAVE)
WWWW WW
Small-scale Hotel

Phone: (734)941-9400 — **147**

All Year   1P: $159   2P: $159
Location: I-94, exit 198 (Merriman Rd). Detroit Metro Airport 48242. Fax: 734/941-2522. **Facility:** 160 one-bedroom standard units. 6 stories, interior corridors. *Bath:* combo or shower only. **Parking:** on-site (fee) and valet. **Terms:** check-in 4 pm, cancellation fee imposed, [CP] meal plan available, package plans, small pets only ($75 extra charge). **Amenities:** high-speed Internet (fee), voice mail, irons, hair dryers. **Leisure Activities:** exercise room. **Guest Services:** valet laundry. **Business Services:** meeting rooms, business center. **Cards:** AX, CB, DC, DS, JC, MC, VI.

SOME UNITS

DETROIT MARRIOTT ROMULUS AT METRO AIRPORT

(AAA) (SAVE)
WWWW WW
Small-scale Hotel

Phone: (734)729-7555 — **137**

All Year   1P: $79-$169   2P: $79-$169
Location: I-94, exit 198 (Merriman Rd). 30559 Flynn Dr 48174. Fax: 734/729-4888. **Facility:** 245 units. 244 one-bedroom standard units. 1 one-bedroom suite ($250-$400). 4 stories, interior corridors. **Parking:** on-site. **Terms:** [AP] meal plan available, package plans - weekends, 19% service charge, pets ($75 extra charge). **Amenities:** voice mail, irons, hair dryers. *Fee:* video games, high-speed Internet. **Dining:** 6 am-2 & 5-10 pm, cocktails. **Pool(s):** heated indoor. **Leisure Activities:** whirlpool, exercise room. **Guest Services:** gift shop, valet laundry, area transportation. **Business Services:** conference facilities, business center. **Cards:** AX, CB, DC, DS, JC, MC, VI. **Special Amenities:** early check-in/late check-out and free newspaper.

SOME UNITS

DOUBLETREE HOTEL DETROIT AIRPORT

(SAVE)
WWW WW
Small-scale Hotel

Phone: (734)467-8000 — **142**

All Year [ECP]   1P: $89-$149   2P: $89-$149   XP: $10   F17
Location: I-94, exit 198 (Merriman Rd). 31500 Wick Rd 48174. Fax: 734/721-8870. **Facility:** 263 units. 260 one-bedroom standard units. 3 one-bedroom suites. 4 stories, interior corridors. *Bath:* combo or shower only. **Parking:** on-site. **Terms:** cancellation fee imposed. **Amenities:** video games, dual phone lines, voice mail, irons, hair dryers. **Pool(s):** heated indoor/outdoor. **Leisure Activities:** sauna, whirlpool, exercise room. **Guest Services:** gift shop, valet laundry, area transportation. **Business Services:** conference facilities, business center. **Cards:** AX, CB, DC, DS, MC, VI.

SOME UNITS

EXTENDED STAY AMERICA

WW WW
Small-scale Hotel

Phone: (734)722-7780 — **138**

All Year   1P: $55   2P: $55
Location: I-94, exit 198 (Merriman Rd), 0.6 mi e. 30325 Flynn Dr 48174. Fax: 734/722-8028. **Facility:** 110 one-bedroom standard units with efficiencies. 3 stories, interior corridors. *Bath:* combo or shower only. **Parking:** on-site. **Terms:** cancellation fee imposed, weekly rates available. **Amenities:** dual phone lines, voice mail, hair dryers. **Guest Services:** coin laundry. **Cards:** AX, CB, DC, DS, MC, VI.

SOME UNITS

(See map p. 228)

FAIRFIELD INN BY MARRIOTT-METRO AIRPORT　　　　　　　　　　Phone: (734)728-2322　🆔134

All Year　　　　　　　1P: $84-$94　　　　　　　2P: $84-$94
Location: I-94, exit 198 (Merriman Rd). Located opposite Detroit Metro Airport. 31119 Flynn Dr 48174. Fax: 734/641-8726. **Facility:** 133 one-bedroom standard units. 3 stories, interior/exterior corridors. *Bath:* combo or shower only. **Parking:** on-site. **Amenities:** irons, hair dryers. **Pool(s):** heated outdoor. **Guest Serv-**
Small-scale Hotel **ices:** valet laundry. **Cards:** AX, DC, DS, MC, VI.

SOME UNITS

🅂Ⓓ 🔜 🍴 ♿Ⓜ 🐾 🌊 📷 📠 /✕/

FOUR POINTS BY SHERATON DETROIT METRO AIRPORT　　　　　　Phone: (734)729-9000　🆔140

All Year　　　　　　　1P: $89
Location: I-94, exit 198 (Merriman Rd). 8800 Wickham Rd 48174. Fax: 734/728-5580. **Facility:** 175 one-bedroom
Small-scale Hotel　standard units, some with whirlpools. 7 stories, interior corridors. **Parking:** on-site. **Terms:** [AP], [BP], [CP] & [ECP] meal plans available, 19% service charge, small pets only. **Amenities:** video games (fee), dual phone lines, voice mail, irons, hair dryers. **Pool(s):** small heated indoor. **Leisure Activities:** whirlpool, exercise room. **Guest Services:** valet laundry, area transportation. **Business Services:** meeting rooms, business center. **Cards:** AX, DC, DS, MC, VI.

SOME UNITS

Ⓐ$K 🅂Ⓓ 🔜 🐕 🍴 🍷 🐾 🌊 📷 📠 💻 /✕ 📞 📠/

HAMPTON INN-DETROIT METRO AIRPORT　　　　　　　　　　　Phone: (734)721-1100　🆔133

All Year [ECP]　　　　1P: $68　　　　　　　2P: $125　　　　　　XP: $10　F18
Location: I-94, exit 198 (Merriman Rd), just e. 30847 Flynn Dr 48174. Fax: 734/721-9915. **Facility:** 136 one-bedroom standard units. 3 stories, interior corridors. **Parking:** on-site. **Terms:** package plans - weekends. **Amenities:** high-speed Internet, dual phone lines, voice mail, irons, hair dryers. **Pool(s):** heated outdoor.
Small-scale Hotel **Leisure Activities:** exercise room. **Guest Services:** valet laundry. **Business Services:** meeting rooms. **Cards:** AX, DC, DS, MC, VI.

SOME UNITS

🅂Ⓓ 🔜 🍴 ♿Ⓜ 📷 🐾 📷 📠 /✕/

HILTON GARDEN INN-DETROIT METRO AIRPORT　　　　　　　Phone: (734)727-6000　🆔130

All Year　　　　　　1P: $69-$129　　　　2P: $79-$139　　　　XP: $10　F18
Location: I-94, exit 198 (Merriman Rd), 0.4 mi w. 31800 Smith Rd 48174. Fax: 734/727-6006. **Facility:** 165 one-bedroom standard units. 6 stories, interior corridors. *Bath:* combo or shower only. **Parking:** on-site. **Amenities:** video games (fee), high-speed Internet, dual phone lines, voice mail, irons, hair dryers. **Pool(s):**
Small-scale Hotel　heated indoor. **Leisure Activities:** whirlpool, exercise room. **Guest Services:** sundries, valet and coin laundry. **Business Services:** meeting rooms, business center. *(See ad below)*

SOME UNITS

🅂Ⓓ 🔜 🍴 ♿Ⓜ 🐾 🌊 📷 📠 📞 📷 💻 /✕/

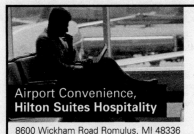

(See map p. 228)

HILTON SUITES-DETROIT METRO AIRPORT

SAVE

Small-scale Hotel

All Year   1P: $79-$189   2P: $89-$190   Phone: (734)728-9200   **139**   F18   XP: $10

Location: I-94, exit 198 (Merriman Rd), just n. 8600 Wickham Rd 48174. Fax: 734/728-9278. **Facility:** 151 one-bedroom suites. 3 stories, interior corridors. *Bath:* combo or shower only. **Parking:** on-site. **Terms:** cancellation fee imposed. **Amenities:** video library (fee), high-speed Internet, dual phone lines, voice mail, irons, hair dryers. **Leisure Activities:** whirlpool, exercise room. *Fee:* game room. **Guest Services:** complimentary evening beverages, valet and coin laundry, area transportation. **Business Services:** meeting rooms, business center. **Cards:** AX, CB, DC, DS, MC, VI. *(See ad p 267)*

SOME UNITS

HOWARD JOHNSON INN

AAA SAVE

Small-scale Hotel

All Year [CP]   1P: $69-$79   2P: $69-$79   Phone: (734)946-1400   **145**   F14   XP: $10

Location: I-94, exit 199 (Middlebelt Rd), just s. 9555 Middlebelt Rd 48174. Fax: 734/946-7480. **Facility:** 124 one-bedroom standard units, some with whirlpools. 3 stories, interior corridors. **Parking:** on-site. **Amenities:** voice mail, irons, hair dryers. **Leisure Activities:** exercise room. **Guest Services:** valet and coin laundry. **Business Services:** meeting rooms, fax. **Cards:** AX, DC, DS, MC, VI. **Special Amenities:** free continental breakfast and free newspaper.

SOME UNITS

PARK INN-DETROIT METRO AIRPORT

AAA SAVE

Small-scale Hotel

All Year [ECP]   1P: $80   2P: $80   Phone: (734)729-6300   **131**   F18   XP: $10

Location: I-94, exit 198 (Merriman Rd), just n. 8270 Wickham Rd 48174. Fax: 734/722-8740. **Facility:** 232 units. 226 one-bedroom standard units, some with whirlpools. 6 one-bedroom suites ($150-$250), some with whirlpools. 4 stories, interior corridors. *Bath:* combo or shower only. **Parking:** on-site. **Terms:** cancellation fee imposed, package plans. **Amenities:** dual phone lines, voice mail, safes, irons, hair dryers. **Dining:** 5 pm-1 am, cocktails. **Pool(s):** heated indoor. **Leisure Activities:** exercise room. *Fee:* game room. **Guest Services:** valet laundry. **Business Services:** meeting rooms. **Cards:** AX, CB, DC, DS, MC, VI. **Special Amenities:** free continental breakfast and free newspaper. *(See color ad p 463)*

SOME UNITS

QUALITY INN METRO AIRPORT

AAA SAVE

Motel

All Year [ECP]   1P: $59-$119   2P: $59-$119   Phone: (734)728-2430   **128**   F18   XP: $5

Location: I-94, exit 198 (Merriman Rd). 7600 Merriman Rd 48174. Fax: 734/728-3756. **Facility:** 140 one-bedroom standard units, some with whirlpools. 1 story, exterior corridors. **Parking:** on-site. **Terms:** weekly rates available, package plans. **Amenities:** video games, voice mail, irons, hair dryers. **Dining:** 11 am-1:30 & 4-midnight. **Leisure Activities:** exercise room. **Guest Services:** valet and coin laundry. **Business Services:** meeting rooms. **Cards:** AX, CB, DC, DS, MC, VI. **Special Amenities:** free continental breakfast and free local telephone calls.

SOME UNITS

SUPER 8 MOTEL-ROMULUS

Small-scale Hotel

All Year [CP]   1P: $59-$65   2P: $65-$71   Phone: (734)946-8808   **146**   F18   XP: $6

Location: I-94, exit 199 (Middlebelt Rd), just s. 9863 Middlebelt Rd 48174. Fax: 734/946-8808. **Facility:** 63 one-bedroom standard units, some with whirlpools. 3 stories, interior corridors. **Parking:** on-site. **Terms:** weekly rates available, package plans, small pets only. **Amenities:** safes. *Some:* hair dryers. **Cards:** AX, CB, DC, DS, MC, VI.

SOME UNITS

The following lodging was either not evaluated or did not meet AAA rating requirements but is listed for your information only.

WESTIN METROPOLITAN AIRPORT

fyi

Large-scale Hotel

All Year   1P: $109-$259   2P: $109-$259   Phone: 734/942-6500

Too new to rate, opening scheduled for December 2002. **Location:** I-94, exit 198 (Merriman Rd). 2501 Worldgateway Pl 48242. Fax: 734/942-6600. **Amenities:** 404 units, restaurant, coffeemakers, pool. **Terms:** cancellation fee imposed. 20% service charge. **Cards:** AX, CB, DC, DS, JC, MC, VI.

WHERE TO DINE

LEONARDO'S PIZZERIA & RISTORANTE

American

Lunch: $6-$10   Dinner: $6-$10   Phone: 734/326-2560   **95**

Location: I-94, exit 198 (Merriman Rd), just n. 7575 Merriman Rd 48174. **Hours:** 11 am-10 pm, Fri-midnight, Sat 4 pm-midnight, Sun 4 pm-10 pm. Closed major holidays. **Features:** Located near a number of the airport hotels, this family oriented restaurant specializes in home style Italian food such as fettucine alfredo, lasagna and pizzas. Casual dress; cocktails. **Parking:** on-site. **Cards:** AX, MC, VI.

MERRIMAN STREET GRILL

American

Lunch: $6-$10   Dinner: $6-$10   Phone: 734/595-6166   **96**

Location: I-94, exit 198 (Merriman Rd), just n. 7660 Merriman Rd 48174. **Hours:** 11 am-midnight, Sun 4 pm-10 pm. Closed major holidays. **Features:** Located a short distance from a number of the airport hotels, the Merriman Street Grill is a nice change from the deluge of fast food places and airport food. Casual dress; cocktails. **Parking:** on-site. **Cards:** AX, MC, VI.

ROSEVILLE pop. 48,129 (See map p. 228; index p. 231)

──────── **WHERE TO STAY** ────────

BAYMONT INN & SUITES DETROIT-ROSEVILLE
Phone: (586)296-6910 **24**
All Year [ECP] 1P: $69-$89 2P: $69-$89
Location: I-94, exit 232 (Little Mack Ave). 20675 13 Mile Rd 48066. Fax: 586/296-6073. **Facility:** 100 units. 99 one-bedroom standard units. 1 one-bedroom suite ($79-$99) with efficiency. 3 stories, interior corridors. **Parking:** on-site, winter plug-ins. **Terms:** 18 day cancellation notice, pets ($50 deposit). **Amenities:** video games, dual phone lines, voice mail, irons, hair dryers. **Guest Services:** valet and coin laundry. **Cards:** AX, CB, DC, DS, MC, VI. **Special Amenities: free continental breakfast and free newspaper.** *(See color ad p 241)*
Small-scale Hotel

SOME UNITS

COMFORT INN
Phone: 586/296-6700 **21**
Property failed to provide current rates
Location: I-94, exit 232 (Little Mack Ave), just s. 31960 Little Mack Ave 48066. Fax: 586/296-7412. **Facility:** 118 units. 104 one-bedroom standard units. 14 one-bedroom suites with kitchens. 3 stories, interior corridors. **Parking:** on-site, winter plug-ins. **Amenities:** voice mail, hair dryers. **Pool(s):** heated indoor. **Leisure Activities:** whirlpool. **Fee:** racquetball courts, massage, game room. **Guest Services:** valet and coin laundry. **Business Services:** meeting rooms. **Cards:** AX, CB, DC, DS, MC, VI.
Small-scale Hotel

SOME UNITS

EXTENDED STAYAMERICA
Phone: (586)294-0141 **26**
All Year 1P: $55 2P: $55
Location: I-94, exit 232 (Little Mack Ave), 0.3 mi n, then just w. 20200 13 Mile Rd 48066. Fax: 586/294-0141. **Facility:** 110 one-bedroom standard units with efficiencies. 3 stories, interior corridors. *Bath:* combo or shower only. **Parking:** on-site. **Terms:** cancellation fee imposed, weekly rates available. **Amenities:** dual phone lines, voice mail, hair dryers. **Guest Services:** coin laundry. **Cards:** AX, CB, DC, DS, MC, VI.
Small-scale Hotel

SOME UNITS

GEORGIAN INN
Phone: (586)294-0400 **23**
All Year [ECP] 1P: $70-$123 2P: $74-$123 XP: $5 F12
Location: I-94, exit 27 eastbound (Gratiot Ave) just w; exit 232 westbound (Little Mack Ave), on SR 3, then n of 13 Mile Rd. 31327 Gratiot Ave 48066. Fax: 586/294-1020. **Facility:** 111 units. 109 one-bedroom standard units, some with efficiencies and/or whirlpools. 2 one-bedroom suites with whirlpools. 2 stories, exterior corridors. **Parking:** on-site. **Amenities:** irons, hair dryers. **Dining:** 6 am-10 pm, Fri & Sat-11 pm, Sun from 7 am, cocktails. **Pool(s):** heated outdoor. **Leisure Activities:** exercise room. **Guest Services:** valet and coin laundry. **Business Services:** meeting rooms, PC, fax (fee). **Cards:** AX, CB, DC, DS, JC, MC. **Special Amenities: free continental breakfast and preferred room (subject to availability with advanced reservations).**
Motel

SOME UNITS

HOLIDAY INN EXPRESS & SUITES
Phone: (586)285-5800 **22**
All Year [ECP] 1P: $99-$109 2P: $99-$109 XP: $10 F19
Location: I-94, exit 232 (Little Mack Ave). 31900 Little Mack Ave 48066. Fax: 586/285-5811. **Facility:** 90 one-bedroom standard units, some with whirlpools. 3 stories, interior corridors. *Bath:* combo or shower only. **Parking:** on-site. **Terms:** cancellation fee imposed. **Amenities:** video games, dual phone lines, voice mail, irons, hair dryers. **Pool(s):** heated indoor. **Leisure Activities:** whirlpool, exercise room. **Guest Services:** valet and coin laundry. **Business Services:** meeting rooms, business center. **Cards:** AX, CB, DC, DS, JC, MC, VI.
Small-scale Hotel

SOME UNITS

MICROTEL INN & SUITES
Phone: (586)415-1000 **25**
All Year [CP] 1P: $50-$80 2P: $50-$80 XP: $10 F16
Location: I-94, exit 232 (Little Mack Ave), 0.3 mi n, just w. 20313 13 Mile Rd 48066. Fax: 586/415-1414. **Facility:** 98 one-bedroom standard units. 3 stories, interior corridors. *Bath:* combo or shower only. **Parking:** on-site. **Terms:** weekly rates available. **Amenities:** video games, voice mail. *Some:* irons, hair dryers. **Pool(s):** heated indoor. **Leisure Activities:** exercise room. **Guest Services:** complimentary laundry. **Business Services:** meeting rooms. **Cards:** AX, DC, DS, MC, VI.
Small-scale Hotel

SOME UNITS

──────── **WHERE TO DINE** ────────

MR. PAUL'S CHOPHOUSE
Lunch: $8-$15 Dinner: $10-$23 Phone: 586/777-7770 **36**
Location: I-94, exit 232 (Little Mack Ave), 0.3 mi n, 1.5 mi w on 13 Mile Rd, then 1 mi n. 29850 Groesbeck Hwy 48066. **Hours:** 11 am-11 pm, Sat from 4:30 pm. Closed major holidays; also Sun. **Reservations:** suggested. **Features:** Don't let the industrial corridor location fool you. Inside you will find wonderful tableside preparations of Chateau-Briand for two and Cherries Jubilee that make this restaurant perfect for special occasions. Dressy casual; cocktails. **Parking:** on-site.
American

PEARL CITY
Lunch: $6-$9 Dinner: $7-$10 Phone: 586/293-4640 **35**
Location: I-94, exit 232 (Little Mack Ave), just e. 20749 13 Mile Rd 48066. **Hours:** 11 am-10 pm, Fri & Sat-11 pm, Sun from noon. Closed: 7/4, 11/27. **Features:** Traditional preparations of chicken, beef and seafood show Cantonese, Mandarin, Szechuan and Hunan influences. The menu also lists a handful of American dishes. The large, open dining room is inviting to families. Service is attentive and cordial. Casual dress; cocktails.
Chinese
Parking: on-site. **Cards:** AX, DC, DS, MC, VI.

ROYAL OAK pop. 60,062   (See map p. 228; index p. 232)

―――――― WHERE TO STAY ――――――

TRAVELODGE
(AAA) SAVE
Motel

Phone: (248)549-1600   **37**
All Year [CP]   1P: $45-$56   2P: $56-$70   XP: $5   F16
Location: At jct 13 Mile Rd and Woodward Ave. 30776 Woodward Ave 48073. Fax: 248/549-2870. **Facility:** 78 one-bedroom standard units. 2 stories, exterior corridors. *Bath:* combo or shower only. **Parking:** on-site. **Terms:** weekly rates available. **Amenities:** hair dryers. **Cards:** AX, CB, DC, DS, MC, VI. **Special Amenities:** free continental breakfast and free newspaper.

SOME UNITS

―――――― WHERE TO DINE ――――――

D'AMATO'S NEIGHBORHOOD RESTAURANT   **Lunch:** $5-$9   **Dinner:** $10-$20   **Phone:** 248/584-7400   **44**
Italian
Location: At corner of S Washington Ave and Sherman Dr; downtown. 222 S Sherman Dr 48067. **Hours:** 11:30 am-2:30 & 5-10 pm, Fri & Sat-11 pm, Sun 4 pm-9 pm. Closed major holidays. **Reservations:** accepted; for 6 or more. **Features:** The friendly restaurant delivers large portions of simple favorites: light bites, salad, pizza, pasta, chicken, fish and sausage. The atmosphere is warm and inviting. Diners can watch cooking through a partial wall and enjoy delectable desserts. Casual dress; cocktails. **Parking:** street. **Cards:** AX, DC, DS, MC, VI.

LEPANTO   **Dinner:** $18-$25   **Phone:** 248/541-2228   **46**
Italian
Location: Jct Main and 4th sts, just w; downtown. 116 W 4th St 48067. **Hours:** 5:30 pm-10 pm, Fri & Sat-11 pm. Closed major holidays; also Sun & Mon. **Reservations:** accepted. **Features:** Soft background music and low level lighting foster a true sense of intimacy in this sophisticated and trendy dining room. House-made pastas like the tortul "candy wrapper" pasta show what levels fresh ingredients and creativity can achieve. Dressy casual; cocktails. **Parking:** street. **Cards:** AX, MC, VI.

MEMPHIS SMOKE   **Lunch:** $6-$9   **Dinner:** $7-$15   **Phone:** 248/543-4300   **43**
Regional American
Location: At the corner of 11 Mile Rd and Main St; downtown. 100 S Main 48073. **Hours:** 11 am-12:30 am, Fri & Sat-1:15 am, Sun noon-12:30 am. Closed major holidays. **Features:** Southern-style pork ribs, beef brisket, smoked turkey and meat slow-cooked over wood coals are examples of tasty, home-style dishes. The large, open dining room is loud, bustling and fun. Blues bands perform late in the evening most nights. Casual dress; cocktails; entertainment. **Parking:** on-site. **Cards:** AX, MC, VI.

PRONTO! 608   **Lunch:** $4-$8   **Dinner:** $4-$8   **Phone:** 248/544-7900   **48**
Deli/Subs
Sandwiches
Location: Jct Sixth and Main sts; center. 608 S Washington St 48067. **Hours:** 11 am-10 pm, Fri-midnight, Sat 9 am-midnight, Sun 9 am-2 pm. Closed major holidays. **Features:** Much of the produce that goes into the sandwiches and limited selection of entrees is specially grown for this fun and informal restaurant. While known for the enormous choices of sandwiches, the restaurant also offers a good selection of house-made desserts. Casual dress; cocktails. **Parking:** street. **Cards:** AX, MC, VI.

ROYAL OAK BREWERY   **Lunch:** $6-$10   **Dinner:** $8-$12   **Phone:** 248/544-1141   **45**
American
Location: Just e of jct Main and 4th sts; downtown. 215 E 4th St 48067. **Hours:** 11:30 am-10 pm, Fri & Sat-11 pm. Closed major holidays. **Features:** A dozen rotating microbrewed ales complement selections of lighter fare: soup, salad, sandwiches, appetizers, pasta dishes and gourmet pizza. Try the delicious, freshly baked pita bread. The cozy patio is a great place to unwind after a long day. Casual dress; cocktails. **Parking:** on-site (fee). **Cards:** AX, DC, DS, MC, VI.

WOOD-RUFF'S   **Dinner:** $14-$22   **Phone:** 248/586-1519   **47**
American
Location: Just w of jct of Main St; downtown. 212 W 6th St 48067. **Hours:** 5 pm-10 pm, Thurs-Sat to 11 pm, Sun 4 pm-9 pm. Closed major holidays; also Mon. **Reservations:** suggested. **Features:** This upscale supper club features live music performed just above and behind the Flamingo bar several nights a week. A unique and creative continental menu offers such dishes as grilled jumbo shrimp, marinated pork chops and seafood specials. Dressy casual; cocktails. **Parking:** valet and street. **Cards:** AX, CB, DC, DS, MC, VI.

SOUTHFIELD pop. 78,296   (See map p. 228; index p. 232)

―――――― WHERE TO STAY ――――――

COURTYARD BY MARRIOTT-SOUTHFIELD   **Phone:** (248)358-1222   **45**
SAVE
Small-scale Hotel

All Year [BP]   1P: $64-$169   2P: $64-$169
Location: Just se of jct Telegraph Rd and I-696, exit Lodge Frwy; or sw of Lasher St, exit Lodge Frwy. 27027 Northwestern Hwy 48034. Fax: 248/354-3820. **Facility:** 147 units. 133 one-bedroom standard units. 14 one-bedroom suites ($250). 2-3 stories, interior corridors. *Bath:* combo or shower only. **Parking:** on-site. **Terms:** cancellation fee imposed. **Amenities:** high-speed Internet (fee), dual phone lines, voice mail, irons, hair dryers. **Pool(s):** heated indoor. **Leisure Activities:** whirlpool, exercise room. **Guest Services:** valet and coin laundry. **Business Services:** meeting rooms. **Cards:** AX, CB, DC, DS, JC, MC, VI.

SOME UNITS

(See map p. 228)

EMBASSY SUITES DETROIT-SOUTHFIELD Phone: 248/350-2000 **41**

Property failed to provide current rates

Large-scale Hotel

Location: I-696, exit 8, 0.5 mi nw on SR 10. 28100 Franklin Rd 48034. **Fax:** 248/350-1185. **Facility:** 239 units. 237 one- and 2 two-bedroom suites, some with whirlpools. 9 stories, interior corridors. *Bath:* combo or shower only. **Parking:** on-site. **Terms:** small pets only. **Amenities:** voice mail, irons, hair dryers. *Fee:* video games, high-speed Internet. **Pool(s):** heated indoor. **Leisure Activities:** whirlpool, exercise room. *Fee:* game room. **Guest Services:** gift shop, complimentary evening beverages, valet and coin laundry, area transportation. **Business Services:** meeting rooms, business center. **Cards:** AX, CB, DC, DS, JC, MC, VI.

SOME UNITS

HAMPTON INN-SOUTHFIELD Phone: (248)356-5500 **44**

4/1-11/17	1P: $79-$109	2P: $104
1/16-3/31	1P: $89-$109	2P: $99
11/18-1/15	1P: $79-$89	2P: $99

Small-scale Hotel

Location: I-696, just n to 11 Mile Rd, then 0.5 mi e on Northwestern Service Dr. 27500 Northwestern Hwy 48034. **Fax:** 248/356-2083. **Facility:** 154 one-bedroom standard units. 2 stories, interior corridors. **Parking:** on-site. **Terms:** [ECP] meal plan available. **Amenities:** voice mail, irons, hair dryers. **Pool(s):** heated indoor. **Leisure Activities:** whirlpool, exercise room. **Guest Services:** valet and coin laundry. **Business Services:** meeting rooms. **Cards:** AX, CB, DC, DS, JC, MC, VI.

SOME UNITS

HILTON INN-SOUTHFIELD Phone: (248)357-1100 **43**

All Year	1P: $69-$159	2P: $69-$159	XP: $10 F17

Small-scale Hotel

Location: US 10 (Northwestern Hwy), just w on Beck Rd, then 0.3 mi s on Franklin Rd. 26000 American Dr 48034. **Fax:** 248/372-2323. **Facility:** 198 units. 196 one-bedroom standard units. 2 one-bedroom suites. 7 stories, interior corridors. **Parking:** on-site. **Terms:** [AP] meal plan available, pets ($50 deposit). **Amenities:** video games (fee), dual phone lines, voice mail, irons, hair dryers. **Pool(s):** heated indoor. **Leisure Activities:** sauna, whirlpool, exercise room. **Guest Services:** valet laundry, area transportation. **Business Services:** meeting rooms, business center. **Cards:** AX, DC, DS, MC, VI.

SOME UNITS

HOLIDAY INN-SOUTHFIELD Phone: (248)353-7700 **47**

All Year	1P: $94-$111	2P: $94-$111

Large-scale Hotel

Location: I-696, exit 10, just s on US 24. 26555 Telegraph Rd 48034. **Fax:** 248/353-8377. **Facility:** 415 one-bedroom standard units. 2-15 stories, interior corridors. *Bath:* combo or shower only. **Parking:** on-site. **Terms:** pets ($50 deposit, in smoking units). **Amenities:** voice mail, irons, hair dryers. **Pool(s):** heated indoor. **Leisure Activities:** whirlpool, exercise room. *Fee:* game room. **Guest Services:** gift shop, valet and coin laundry. **Business Services:** conference facilities. **Cards:** AX, DC, DS, MC, VI.

SOME UNITS

HOMESTEAD STUDIO SUITES HOTEL-DETROIT/SOUTHFIELD Phone: (248)213-4500 **40**

All Year	1P: $84-$94	2P: $94-$104 XP: $5 F17

Small-scale Hotel

Location: I-696, exit 9, just nw of jct US 24 (Telegraph Rd). 28500 Northwestern Hwy 48034. **Fax:** 248/213-4600. **Facility:** 134 one-bedroom standard units with efficiencies. 3 stories, interior corridors. *Bath:* combo or shower only. **Parking:** on-site. **Terms:** pets ($75 extra charge). **Amenities:** voice mail, irons. **Guest Services:** valet and coin laundry. **Cards:** AX, CB, DC, DS, JC, MC, VI.

SOME UNITS

RAMADA INN-SOUTHFIELD Phone: (248)552-7777 **50**

4/1-8/31	1P: $89-$109	2P: $89-$109	XP: $10 F18
9/1-3/31	1P: $79-$99	2P: $79-$99	XP: $10 F18

Small-scale Hotel

Location: US 10 and Southfield Rd, 0.3 mi e. 17017 W 9 Mile Rd 48075-4566. **Fax:** 248/552-7778. **Facility:** 216 units. 199 one-bedroom standard units, some with whirlpools. 17 one-bedroom suites ($158). 17 stories, interior corridors. **Parking:** on-site. **Terms:** [AP] meal plan available, 17% service charge. **Amenities:** video games (fee), voice mail. *Some:* hair dryers. **Pool(s):** heated outdoor. **Guest Services:** gift shop, valet laundry, area transportation. **Business Services:** conference facilities. **Cards:** AX, CB, DC, DS, MC, VI.

SOME UNITS

FEE FEE FEE

RAMADA LIMITED & SUITES Phone: (248)368-6130 **48**

All Year	1P: $79-$99	2P: $79-$99 XP: $6 F18

Small-scale Hotel

Location: I-696, exit 10, just s on US 24 (Telegraph Rd). 26111 Telegraph Rd 48034. **Fax:** 248/368-6143. **Facility:** 105 one-bedroom standard units, some with whirlpools. 3 stories, interior corridors. *Bath:* combo or shower only. **Parking:** on-site. **Terms:** weekly rates available, [ECP] meal plan available. **Amenities:** voice mail, irons, hair dryers. **Leisure Activities:** exercise room. **Guest Services:** valet laundry. **Business Services:** meeting rooms, fax. **Cards:** AX, CB, DC, DS, MC, VI.

SOME UNITS

RED ROOF INN-SOUTHFIELD Phone: (248)353-7200 **42**

4/27-8/30	1P: $59-$77	2P: $65-$83	XP: $6 F18
8/31-3/30	1P: $55-$74	2P: $61-$81	XP: $6 F18
4/1-4/26	1P: $55-$69	2P: $61-$75	XP: $6 F18

Motel

Location: I-696, exit 9, just nw of Telegraph Rd. 27660 Northwestern Hwy 48034. **Fax:** 248/353-1580. **Facility:** 114 one-bedroom standard units. 3 stories, exterior corridors. *Bath:* combo or shower only. **Parking:** on-site. **Terms:** small pets only. **Amenities:** video games, voice mail. **Guest Services:** valet laundry. **Business Services:** meeting rooms. **Cards:** AX, CB, DC, DS, MC, VI. **Special Amenities:** free local telephone calls and free newspaper.

SOME UNITS

FEE FEE

(See map p. 228)

SOUTHFIELD MARRIOTT HOTEL   Phone: (248)356-7400 46

SAVE
[diamond symbols]
Small-scale Hotel

All Year   1P: $89   2P: $189
Location: I-696, exit Lodge Frwy, just se of jct US 24 (Telegraph Rd); or sw of Lahser St exit of Lodge Frwy on North-western Service Rd. 27033 Northwestern Hwy 48034. **Fax:** 248/356-5501. **Facility:** 226 one-bedroom standard units. 6 stories, interior corridors. **Parking:** on-site. **Terms:** check-in 4 pm, [BP] meal plan available, package plans. **Amenities:** dual phone lines, voice mail, irons, hair dryers. *Fee:* video games, high-speed Internet. **Pool(s):** heated indoor. **Leisure Activities:** saunas, whirlpool, exercise room. **Guest Services:** gift shop, valet laundry. **Business Services:** meeting rooms, business center. **Cards:** AX, CB, DC, DS, JC, MC, VI.

SOME UNITS
[icons] / [icons] /

WESTIN HOTEL SOUTHFIELD-DETROIT   Phone: (248)827-4000 49

[diamond symbols]
Large-scale Hotel

All Year   1P: $99-$270   2P: $99-$270   XP: $10   F
Location: SR 10, exit Evergreen, 0.3 mi n on SR 10 (Northwestern Hwy). 1500 Town Center 48075. **Fax:** 248/827-4002. **Facility:** Well appointed rooms. Designated smoking area. 387 one-bedroom standard units, some with whirlpools. 12 stories, interior corridors. *Bath:* combo or shower only. **Parking:** on-site (fee) and valet. **Amenities:** dual phone lines, voice mail, irons, hair dryers. *Some:* high-speed Internet, safes. **Pool(s):** heated indoor. **Leisure Activities:** saunas, whirlpool, exercise room. **Guest Services:** gift shop, valet laundry, area transportation. **Business Services:** conference facilities, PC. **Cards:** AX, CB, DC, DS, JC, MC, VI.

SOME UNITS
[icons] / [icons] /
FEE FEE FEE

───────── *The following lodging was either not evaluated or did not* ─────────
meet AAA rating requirements but is listed for your information only.

SPRINGHILL SUITES BY MARRIOTT DETROIT/SOUTHFIELD
[fyi]   Under construction, scheduled to open June 2003. **Location:** I-94 E, exit M-39N (Southfield Frwy), to SR 10 N.
Small-scale Hotel   28555 Northwestern Hwy 48034. **Planned Amenities:** coffeemakers, microwaves, refrigerators, pool.

───────── **WHERE TO DINE** ─────────

BEVERLY HILLS GRILL   **Lunch:** $12-$20   **Dinner:** $12-$20   Phone: 248/642-2355 51

[diamond symbols]
American

Location: Just n of jct 13 Mile and Southfield rds. 31471 N Southfield Rd 48075. **Hours:** 7 am-11 pm, Fri-midnight, Sat 8 am-midnight, Sun 8:30 am-10 pm. Closed major holidays. **Reservations:** suggested. **Features:** Well known for their breakfast specials such as Banana Foster french toast and eggs benedict, this somewhat trendy diner also offers a California influenced lunch and dinner menu that has developed an ardent following, with specials such spicy rock shrimp on angel hair pasta. Casual dress; cocktails. **Parking:** on-site. **Cards:** AX, DC, MC, VI.

[icons]

C A MUER'S MERRIWETHER   **Lunch:** $7-$15   **Dinner:** $14-$30   Phone: 248/358-1310 55

[diamond symbols]
American

Location: I-696, exit US 24, 0.3 mi s. 25485 Telegraph Rd 48034. **Hours:** 11 am-10 pm, Sat from noon, Sun noon-9 pm. Closed major holidays. **Reservations:** suggested. **Features:** The surroundings are festive and upbeat in the English-style restaurant. Preparations of fowl, pork, beef and seafood are as eye-popping as they are palate-pleasing. Tantalizing desserts show the same artistic flair. Service is friendly and prompt. Casual dress; cocktails. **Parking:** valet. **Cards:** AX, DC, DS, MC, VI.

[icons]

IL POSTO RISTORONTE   **Lunch:** $12-$18   **Dinner:** $18-$28   Phone: 248/827-8070 53

[AAA diamonds]
[diamond symbols]
Italian

Location: I-696 W, exit 10, 0.6 mi w to SR 10 (Northwestern Hwy), then 1.1 mi n on SR 10/Northwestern Hwy. 29110 Franklin Rd 48034. **Hours:** 11:30 am-2:30 & 5:30-10 pm, Fri & Sat-10:30 pm. Closed major holidays; also Sun. **Reservations:** suggested; weekends. **Features:** An elegantly appointed restaurant that serves authentic regional Italian cuisine at its best. Highly recommended is the Carpaccio alla Mantovana and the desserts that are imported directly from Italy. Cocktails. **Parking:** street. **Cards:** AX, CB, DC, DS, MC, VI.

[icon]

JOE MUER'S GRILL   **Lunch:** $8-$15   **Dinner:** $19-$27   Phone: 248/644-5330 52

[diamond symbols]
Seafood

Location: Just s of jct Southfield Rd (M-39) and 13 Mile Rd. 30855 Southfield Rd 48076. **Hours:** 11 am-10 pm, Fri-11 pm, Sat 5 pm-11 pm. Closed major holidays; also Sun. **Reservations:** suggested; weekends. **Features:** Experience casual, delightful dining in a formal atmosphere. The menu highlights innovative preparations of steak, seafood and signature side dishes. Seasonal choices, such as soft shell crab, also are listed. The attentive staff shows great follow-up. Casual dress; cocktails. **Parking:** on-site. **Cards:** AX, CB, DC, DS, MC, VI.

[icons]

NEW SEOUL RESTAURANT   **Lunch:** $9-$20   **Dinner:** $9-$20   Phone: 248/827-1600 54

[diamond symbols]
Ethnic

Location: I-696, exit 9, jct US 24. 27566 Northwestern Hwy 48034. **Hours:** 11:30 am-10:30 pm, Sun noon-10 pm. Closed major holidays. **Reservations:** required. **Features:** A sushi bar and tempura choices are features that distinguish the restaurant, which delivers Korean and Japanese cuisine. Potted plants, natural lighting and attractive, solid-wood grill tables decorate the dining areas. Service is professional. Casual dress; cocktails. **Parking:** on-site. **Cards:** AX, DC, DS, MC, VI.

[icons]

SOUTHGATE pop. 30,136 (See map p. 228; index p. 235)

──── WHERE TO STAY ────

BAYMONT INN & SUITES DETROIT-SOUTHGATE

Phone: (734)374-3000 **151**

All Year [ECP] 1P: $64-$79 2P: $64-$79
Location: I-75, exit 37 (Northline Rd). 12888 Reeck Rd 48195. Fax: 734/374-3010. **Facility:** 100 units. 97 one-bedroom standard units. 3 one-bedroom suites ($74-$89), some with kitchens. 3 stories, interior corridors. **Parking:** on-site. **Terms:** small pets only. **Amenities:** video games, voice mail, irons, hair dryers. **Guest Services:** valet and coin laundry. **Business Services:** fax (fee). **Cards:** AX, CB, DC, DS, MC, VI. **Special Amenities: free continental breakfast and free newspaper.** (See color ad p 241)

AAA **SAVE**
Small-scale Hotel

SOME UNITS

COMFORT SUITES

Phone: (734)287-9200 **150**

All Year [ECP] 1P: $89-$179 2P: $99-$189 XP: $8 F18
Location: I-75, exit 37 (Northline Rd), just w. 18950 Northline Rd 48195. Fax: 734/287-8373. **Facility:** 78 one-bedroom standard units, some with whirlpools. 3 stories, interior corridors. *Bath:* combo or shower only. **Parking:** on-site. **Amenities:** dual phone lines, voice mail, irons, hair dryers. **Fee:** video games, high-speed Internet, safes. **Pool(s):** heated indoor. **Leisure Activities:** sauna, steamroom, exercise room. **Guest Services:** valet and coin laundry. **Business Services:** meeting rooms, business center. **Cards:** AX, CB, DC, DS, JC, MC, VI.

SAVE
Small-scale Hotel

SOME UNITS

CROSS COUNTRY INN

Phone: (734)287-8340 **153**

All Year 1P: $47-$56 2P: $56-$63 XP: $2 F17
Location: I-75, exit 37 (Northline Rd). 18777 Northline Rd 48195. Fax: 734/287-4380. **Facility:** 136 one-bedroom standard units. 2 stories, exterior corridors. *Bath:* combo or shower only. **Parking:** on-site. **Terms:** weekly rates available. **Amenities:** video games (fee), voice mail. **Pool(s):** heated indoor. **Business Services:** meeting rooms. **Cards:** AX, CB, DC, DS, MC, VI. **Special Amenities: free local telephone calls and preferred room (subject to availability with advanced reservations).** (See color ad p 236)

AAA **SAVE**
Motel

SOME UNITS

HOLIDAY INN SOUTHGATE HERITAGE CENTER

Phone: (734)283-4400 **152**

All Year 1P: $99 2P: $99
Location: I-75, exit 37 (Northline Rd). 17201 Northline Rd 48195. Fax: 734/283-6855. **Facility:** 160 units. 157 one-bedroom standard units. 3 one-bedroom suites ($165-$215) with whirlpools. 2 stories, interior corridors. *Bath:* combo or shower only. **Parking:** on-site. **Terms:** check-in 4 pm. **Amenities:** video games, dual phone lines, voice mail, irons, hair dryers. **Pool(s):** heated indoor. **Leisure Activities:** whirlpool, exercise room. **Guest Services:** valet and coin laundry, area transportation. **Business Services:** conference facilities. **Cards:** AX, CB, DC, DS, JC, MC, VI.

Small-scale Hotel

SOME UNITS

STERLING HEIGHTS pop. 124,471 (See map p. 228; index p. 230)

──── WHERE TO STAY ────

BEST WESTERN STERLING INN BANQUET & CONFERENCE CTR

Phone: (586)979-1400 **6**

All Year 1P: $109-$199 2P: $119-$209 XP: $25 F12
Location: I-696, exit 23, 4 mi n on SR 53, at jct 15 Mile Rd. 34911 Van Dyke Ave 48312. Fax: 586/979-7962. **Facility:** 245 units. 230 one-bedroom standard units, some with whirlpools. 15 one-bedroom suites ($199-$325) with whirlpools. 2-5 stories, interior/exterior corridors. *Bath:* combo or shower only. **Parking:** on-site. **Terms:** cancellation fee imposed. **Amenities:** video games, high-speed Internet, voice mail, safes, honor bars, irons, hair dryers. **Dining:** 6 am-11 pm, Fri-midnight, Sat 7 am-midnight, Sun 7 am-10 pm, cocktails, also, Loon River Cafe, see separate listing. **Leisure Activities:** saunas, whirlpools, waterslide, indoor water park, jogging, exercise room, basketball. **Fee:** game room. **Guest Services:** gift shop. **Business Services:** conference facilities, business center. **Cards:** AX, CB, DC, DS, MC, VI. (See ad below)

AAA **SAVE**
Small-scale Hotel

SOME UNITS

(See map p. 228)

TOWNEPLACE SUITES   Phone: 586/566-0900

SAVE
    5/1-3/31   1P: $99-$129
    4/1-4/30   1P: $89-$119

▼▼▼ ▼▼▼
Small-scale Hotel
Location: 1 mi e of jct M-53 (Van Dyke Ave) and M-59 (Hall Rd). Located across from Lakeside Mall. 14800 Lakeside Cir 48313. Fax: 586/566-8901. **Facility:** 95 units. 73 one-bedroom standard units with kitchens. 22 one-bedroom suites with kitchens. 3 stories, interior corridors. *Bath:* combo or shower only. **Parking:** on-site. **Terms:** age restrictions may apply, small pets only ($100 deposit, $5 extra charge). **Amenities:** dual phone lines, voice mail, irons, hair dryers. **Pool(s):** outdoor. **Leisure Activities:** exercise room. **Guest Services:** valet and coin laundry. **Cards:** AX, CB, DC, DS, JC, MC, VI.

SOME UNITS

─────── **WHERE TO DINE** ───────

LOON RIVER CAFE   **Lunch:** $6-$15   **Dinner:** $6-$15   **Phone:** 586/979-1420 ⑦
▼▼▼ ▼▼▼
    Location: I-696, exit 23, 4 mi n on SR 53, at jct 15 Mile Rd; in Best Western Sterling Inn Banquet & Conference Ctr.
American   34911 Van Dyke Ave 48312. **Hours:** 6 am-11 pm, Fri-midnight, Sat 7 am-midnight, Sun 7 am-10 pm. Closed major holidays. **Features:** The rustic 1930s hunting lodge is a quaint setting in which to enjoy specialties of local wild game and other creative dishes, such as lasagna soup and snake cakes. The master chef whips up all of the tantalizing desserts on the premises. Casual dress; cocktails. **Parking:** on-site. **Cards:** AX, DC, DS, MC, VI.
(See ad p 273)

TAYLOR pop. 65,868 (See map p. 228; index p. 234)

─────── **WHERE TO STAY** ───────

QUALITY INN & SUITES   Phone: (313)292-6730 **125**

SAVE
    All Year [ECP]   1P: $69-$89

▼▼▼ ▼▼▼
Small-scale Hotel
Location: I-94, exit 202B (Telegraph Rd), just s. 6778 S Telegraph Rd 48180. Fax: 313/292-5994. **Facility:** 78 units. 56 one-bedroom standard units, some with whirlpools. 22 one-bedroom suites ($129-$139), some with whirlpools. 3 stories, interior corridors. *Bath:* combo or shower only. **Parking:** on-site. **Terms:** package plans. **Amenities:** dual phone lines, voice mail, irons, hair dryers. *Fee:* high-speed Internet, safes. **Pool(s):** heated indoor. **Leisure Activities:** sauna, whirlpool, exercise room. **Guest Services:** valet and coin laundry. **Business Services:** meeting rooms. **Cards:** AX, CB, DC, DS, JC, MC, VI.

SOME UNITS

RED ROOF INN-TAYLOR   Phone: (734)374-1150

AAA **SAVE**
    6/9-11/23   1P: $58-$74   2P: $63-$79   XP: $5   F18
▼▼▼ ▼▼▼
    4/1-6/8   1P: $52-$69   2P: $57-$74   XP: $5   F18
Motel   11/24-3/31   1P: $52-$67   2P: $57-$72   XP: $5   F18
    Location: I-75, exit 36 (Eureka Rd). 21230 Eureka Rd 48180. Fax: 734/374-1159. **Facility:** 111 one-bedroom standard units. 2 stories, exterior corridors. *Bath:* combo or shower only. **Parking:** on-site. **Amenities:** video games, voice mail. **Cards:** AX, CB, DC, DS, MC, VI. **Special Amenities:** free local telephone calls and
free newspaper.

SOME UNITS

SUPER 8 MOTEL-TAYLOR   Phone: 734/283-8830
▼▼▼ ▼▼▼
    All Year   1P: $45-$65   2P: $55-$75   XP: $6   F17
    Location: I-75, exit 36 (Eureka Rd). 15101 Huron St 48180. Fax: 734/283-8830. **Facility:** 63 one-bedroom standard units, some with whirlpools. 3 stories, interior corridors. **Parking:** on-site. **Terms:** 14 day cancellation
Small-scale Hotel notice, weekly rates available, [CP] meal plan available. **Amenities:** safes. **Cards:** AX, CB, DC, DS, JC, MC, VI.

SOME UNITS

TRENTON pop. 19,584

─────── **WHERE TO DINE** ───────

EIGHTEEN '97 SMOKEHOUSE RESTAURANT Historic   **Lunch:** $7-$11   **Dinner:** $11-$22   **Phone:** 734/671-3772
▼▼▼ ▼▼▼
    Location: Just n of downtown. 2156 W Jefferson 48183. **Hours:** 11 am-10 pm, Fri & Sat-11 pm, Sun noon-9 pm. Closed major holidays. **Features:** In the older downtown area, the cozy, historical home is known for
Steak & Seafood its tempting selection of steak and seafood offerings, such as delicious pan-fried perch, as well as veal, lamb, pasta and chicken. The service is upbeat and casual, and the host sets the tone for a wonderful dining experience. Casual dress; cocktails. **Parking:** on-site. **Cards:** AX, DC, DS, MC, VI.

FRATELLO'S   **Lunch:** $8-$14   **Dinner:** $12-$23   **Phone:** 734/692-1730
▼▼▼ ▼▼▼
    Location: At jct of M-85 (Fort St) and Van Horn Rd. 4501 Fort St 48183. **Hours:** 11 am-10 pm, Fri & Sat-11 am, Sun noon-9 pm. Closed: 12/25. **Reservations:** suggested. **Features:** Specializing in steak and fresh
Italian seafood, with popular Italian items to choose from. Comfortable dining room with contemporary decor and warm, cozy foyer fireplace. Cheerful and friendly waitstaff. Casual dress; cocktails. **Parking:** on-site.
Cards: AX, DC, MC, VI.

SIBLEY GARDENS   **Lunch:** $8-$15   **Dinner:** $11-$22   **Phone:** 734/285-1707
▼▼▼ ▼▼▼
    Location: 1 mi n of downtown. 916 W Jefferson 48183. **Hours:** 11 am-midnight. Closed major holidays; also Sun. **Reservations:** accepted. **Features:** Just north of downtown Trenton, this local favorite serves up
Italian tradtional Italian fare such as veal piccata, fettuccine alfredo in a dark and romantic atmosphere. Casual dress; cocktails. **Parking:** on-site.

TROY pop. 72,900   (See map p. 228; index p. 231)

———— WHERE TO STAY ————

COURTYARD BY MARRIOTT
SAVE

Small-scale Hotel

Phone: 248/528-2800   **14**

All Year   1P: $69-$159   2P: $79-$169
Location: I-75, exit 67, 1 mi s on Stephenson Hwy, then just e. 1525 E Maple 48083. Fax: 248/528-0963. **Facility:** 147 units. 133 one-bedroom standard units. 14 one-bedroom suites ($149-$179). 3 stories, interior corridors. *Bath:* combo or shower only. **Parking:** on-site. **Terms:** package plans. **Amenities:** high-speed Internet, dual phone lines, voice mail, irons, hair dryers. **Pool(s):** heated indoor. **Leisure Activities:** whirlpool, exercise room. **Guest Services:** valet and coin laundry. **Business Services:** meeting rooms. **Cards:** AX, DC, DS, JC, MC, VI.

SOME UNITS

DRURY INN
AAA **SAVE**
Small-scale Hotel

Phone: (248)528-3330   **10**

1/1-3/31 [ECP]	1P: $109-$129	2P: $119-$139	XP: $10	F18
4/1-12/31 [ECP]	1P: $105-$125	2P: $115-$135	XP: $10	F18

Location: I-75, exit 69 (Big Beaver Rd), 0.3 mi e. 575 W Big Beaver Rd 48084. Fax: 248/528-3330. **Facility:** 152 one-bedroom standard units. 4 stories, interior corridors. **Parking:** on-site. **Terms:** small pets only. **Amenities:** irons, hair dryers. **Dining:** 11 am-midnight, cocktails. **Pool(s):** heated outdoor. **Leisure Activities:** exercise room. **Guest Services:** valet and coin laundry. **Cards:** AX, CB, DC, DS, MC, VI.
Special Amenities: free continental breakfast and free local telephone calls.

SOME UNITS

FEE

EMBASSY SUITES
AAA **SAVE**
Small-scale Hotel

Phone: (248)879-7500

All Year [BP]   1P: $229-$249   2P: $229-$249   XP: $20   F13
Location: I-75, exit 72 (Crooks Rd). 850 Tower Dr 48098. Fax: 248/879-9139. **Facility:** 251 units. 250 one- and 1 two-bedroom suites, some with whirlpools. 8 stories, interior corridors. **Parking:** on-site. **Terms:** cancellation fee imposed, 13% service charge. **Amenities:** dual phone lines, voice mail, irons, hair dryers. **Dining:** 6:30 am-2 & 5:30-10 pm, Sun 7 am-10 & 5:30-10 pm, cocktails. **Pool(s):** heated indoor. **Leisure Activities:** saunas, whirlpool, sun deck, exercise room. **Guest Services:** gift shop, valet and coin laundry. **Business Services:** conference facilities, business center. **Cards:** AX, CB, DC, MC, VI. *(See color ad below)*

SOME UNITS

FEE

HILTON NORTHFIELD
AAA **SAVE**
Small-scale Hotel

Phone: (248)879-2100

All Year   1P: $139   2P: $139   XP: $15   F18
Location: I-75, exit 72 (Crooks Rd). 5500 Crooks Rd 48098. Fax: 248/879-6054. **Facility:** 185 one-bedroom standard units. 3 stories, interior corridors. *Bath:* combo or shower only. **Parking:** on-site. **Terms:** cancellation fee imposed, 15% service charge. **Amenities:** dual phone lines, voice mail, irons, hair dryers. **Dining:** 6:30 am-2 & 5-10 pm, Fri & Sat-11 pm, cocktails. **Pool(s):** indoor. **Leisure Activities:** saunas, exercise equipment on pool deck. **Guest Services:** sundries, valet and coin laundry, area transportation-within 5 mi. **Business Services:** meeting rooms, business center. **Cards:** AX, CB, DC, DS, MC, VI.

SOME UNITS

HOLIDAY INN-TROY
Small-scale Hotel

Phone: (248)689-7500   **12**

All Year   1P: $69-$125   2P: $69-$125
Location: I-75, exit 67, 0.3 mi sw on Rochester Rd, just w. Located in a secluded area. 2537 Rochester Ct 48083. Fax: 248/689-9015. **Facility:** 150 units. 147 one-bedroom standard units, some with whirlpools. 3 one-bedroom suites with whirlpools. 4 stories, interior corridors. **Parking:** on-site. **Terms:** cancellation fee imposed, [BP] & [CP] meal plans available, 4% service charge. **Amenities:** video games, voice mail, irons, hair dryers. **Pool(s):** heated outdoor. **Leisure Activities:** exercise room. *Fee:* game room. **Guest Services:** valet and coin laundry. **Business Services:** meeting rooms. **Cards:** AX, CB, DC, DS, JC, MC, VI.

SOME UNITS

(See map p. 228)

RED ROOF INN-TROY
Phone: (248)689-4391 **13**

AAA SAVE

5/5-8/31	1P: $55-$63	2P: $61-$69	XP: $6	F18
4/1-5/4 & 9/1-3/31	1P: $49-$63	2P: $55-$69	XP: $6	F18

Motel

Location: I-75, exit 67, 0.3 mi sw. 2350 Rochester Ct 48083. Fax: 248/689-4397. **Facility:** 109 one-bedroom standard units. 2 stories, exterior corridors. **Parking:** on-site. **Terms:** small pets only. **Amenities:** voice mail. **Cards:** AX, CB, DC, DS, MC, VI. **Special Amenities:** free local telephone calls and free newspaper.

SOME UNITS

RESIDENCE INN BY MARRIOTT
Phone: (248)689-6856 **11**

SAVE

All Year [BP]   1P: $143-$169

Small-scale Hotel

Location: I-75, exit 69 (Big Beaver Rd), 0.5 mi e, then 0.5 mi s. 2600 Livernois Rd 48083. Fax: 248/689-3788. **Facility:** 152 units. 114 one- and 28 two-bedroom standard units with kitchens. 10 two-bedroom suites with kitchens. 2 stories, exterior corridors. **Parking:** on-site. **Terms:** small pets only ($75 deposit). **Amenities:** voice mail, irons, hair dryers. **Pool(s):** heated outdoor. **Leisure Activities:** whirlpool, exercise room, sports court. **Guest Services:** valet and coin laundry. **Business Services:** meeting rooms. **Cards:** AX, CB, DC, DS, JC, MC, VI.

SOME UNITS

TROY MARRIOTT
Phone: 248/680-9797 **9**

SAVE

All Year   1P: $209   2P: $229

Small-scale Hotel

Location: I-75, exit 69 (Big Beaver Rd). 200 W Big Beaver Rd 48084. Fax: 248/680-9774. **Facility:** 350 units. 346 one-bedroom standard units. 4 one-bedroom suites ($500). 17 stories, interior corridors. *Bath:* combo or shower only. **Parking:** on-site. **Terms:** cancellation fee imposed. **Amenities:** high-speed Internet, dual phone lines, voice mail, irons, hair dryers. **Pool(s):** heated indoor. **Leisure Activities:** sauna, whirlpool, steamroom, exercise room. **Guest Services:** gift shop, valet and coin laundry, area transportation. **Business Services:** conference facilities, business center. **Cards:** AX, DS, MC, VI.

SOME UNITS

FEE

——— WHERE TO DINE ———

ANITAS KITCHEN   **Lunch:** $6-$8   **Dinner:** $7-$10   **Phone:** 248/362-0680 **14**

Ethnic

Location: Just w of jct Livernois and W Maple Rd. 110 W Maple 48084. **Hours:** 6 am-9 pm, Fri & Sat-10 pm, Sun 7 am-9 pm. **Closed:** 12/25. **Features:** In this modest diner, adventurous palates will enjoy an exceptional variety of Lebanese and Vegetarian dishes as humus, hashweh and falafel. Casual dress. **Parking:** on-site. **Cards:** AX, DC, DS, MC, VI.

THE CAPITOL GRILLE   **Lunch:** $15-$20   **Dinner:** $20-$30   **Phone:** 248/649-5300 **10**

Steak & Seafood

Location: Somerset Collection-North; between Hudson's and Nordstrom. 2800 W Big Beaver Rd 48084. **Hours:** 11:30 am-3 & 5-10 pm, Fri & Sat-11 pm, Sun 3-8 pm. Closed major holidays. **Reservations:** accepted. **Features:** Everything from the presidential seal looming over the elegant dining room to the glass-fronted dry, aging lockers speaks volumes of this Washington-inspired steakhouse. Part of a national chain, this restaurant features outstanding cuts of aged beef and numerous seafood specials. Dressy casual; cocktails. **Parking:** on-site and valet. **Cards:** AX, DC, DS, MC, VI.

CHARLEY'S CRAB   **Lunch:** $7-$15   **Dinner:** $10-$33   **Phone:** 248/879-2060

Steak & Seafood

Location: I-75, exit 72 (Crooks Rd). 5498 Crooks Rd 48098. **Hours:** 11 am-10 pm, Fri-11 pm, Sat 5 pm-11 pm, Sun 11 am-2 & 4-9 pm. Closed major holidays. **Reservations:** suggested; weekends. **Features:** The comfortable restaurant is known for creative preparations of fresh seafood, such as tuna sashimi, crab-stuffed trout and the signature Charley's chowder. A good variety of wine is available. Service is attentive, friendly and fittingly inquisitive. Dressy casual; cocktails. **Parking:** valet. **Cards:** AX, DC, DS, MC, VI.

CHINESE KENO   **Lunch:** $4-$6   **Dinner:** $5-$9   **Phone:** 248/879-3232

Chinese

Location: I-75, exit 72 (Crooks Rd), 1.4 mi n; jct W South Blvd and Crooks Rd. 2081 W South Blvd 48098. **Hours:** 11 am-9:30 pm, Fri-10:30 pm, Sat noon-10:30 pm, Sun noon-9:30 pm. Closed major holidays. **Reservations:** accepted. **Features:** This attractively decorated restaurant features a wide range of Cantonese, Hong Kong and Szechuan cuisine on its menu. Casual dress. **Parking:** on-site. **Cards:** AX, DC, MC, VI.

MON JIN LAU   **Lunch:** $7-$12   **Dinner:** $12-$22   **Phone:** 248/689-2332 **12**

AAA

Chinese

Location: I-75, exit 67, 1 mi s on Stephenson Hwy. 1515 E Maple Rd 48083. **Hours:** 11 am-1 am, Fri-2 am, Sat 4 pm-2 am, Sun 3 pm-1 am. **Closed:** 11/27, 12/25. **Reservations:** suggested; weekends. **Features:** Food that is so original, that the term "Nu-Asian" was coined just to describe the endless influences that exert themselves in Mon Jin Lau's palate. Casual dress; cocktails. **Parking:** on-site. **Cards:** AX, DC, MC, VI.

PASTA TO GO   **Lunch:** $4-$7   **Dinner:** $9-$11   **Phone:** 248/828-3200

Italian

Location: Jct of Rochester and Square Lake rds; in Venus Plaza Shopping Center. 6026 Rochester Rd 48098. **Hours:** 9 am-9 pm, Sat from 11 am. Closed major holidays; also Sun. **Features:** Pasta to Go says it all; for a quick, but very tasty Italian meal, this popular lunch spot in Troy, serves traditional fare such as pizza, lasagna, and meatball subs that are prepared from scratch daily. Casual dress. **Parking:** on-site. **Cards:** AX, DS, MC, VI.

(See map p. 228)

P.F. CHANG'S CHINA BISTRO **Lunch:** $10-$15 **Dinner:** $10-$15 **Phone:** 248/816-8000 ⑪
Chinese **Location:** Somerset Collection-South. 2801 W Big Beaver Rd 48084. **Hours:** 11 am-11 pm, Fri & Sat-midnight, Sun 11 am-10 pm. **Reservations:** accepted. **Features:** Faux Ming Dynasty steeds flank the entrance to this elegant but casual restaurant which is part of a small chain of more than a dozen restaurants nationwide featuring creative Szechuan-style dishes. Dressy casual; cocktails. **Parking:** on-site and valet.
Cards: AX, DC, DS, MC, VI.

PRIYA **Lunch:** $8-$15 **Dinner:** $10-$20 **Phone:** 248/269-0100 ⑬
Ethnic **Location:** At northwest corner of Maple Rd (15 Mile Rd) and Livernois. 72 W Maple 48084. **Hours:** 11 am-2:30 & 5-10 pm, Fri-Sun 11 am-9 pm. Closed: 11/27, 12/25. **Reservations:** accepted. **Features:** Intriguing South Indian dishes are delightful in fragrance, appearance and taste. The menu lists seven kinds of dosas served with sambar and little bowls of tomato, coconut and mint sauces. The dining room is pretty, stylish and quietly serene. Casual dress; cocktails. **Parking:** on-site. **Cards:** AX, DS, MC, VI.

SHIELD'S OF TROY **Lunch:** $5-$10 **Dinner:** $5-$10 **Phone:** 248/637-3131 ⑮
Pizza **Location:** I-75, exit 69, 0.7 mi w on Big Beaver Rd, 1 mi s on Crooks Rd, then w. 1476 W Maple Rd 48084. **Hours:** 11 am-11 pm, Fri & Sat-midnight, Sun noon-10 pm. Closed major holidays. **Features:** Part of metro Detroit since 1937, the family-oriented restaurant specializes in mouthwatering deep-dish square pizza and specialty salads. Other notable menu items include pasta and barbecue pork ribs. Casual dress; cocktails.
Parking: on-site. **Cards:** AX, DC, DS, MC, VI.

UTICA pop. 4,577

—— **WHERE TO STAY** ——

AMERISUITES (DETROIT/UTICA) **Phone:** (586)803-0100

| | 4/1-9/4 [ECP] | 1P: $107-$117 | 2P: $107-$117 | XP: $10 | F17 |
| | 9/5-3/31 [ECP] | 1P: $99-$109 | 2P: $99-$109 | XP: $10 | F17 |

Small-scale Hotel **Location:** Jct Van Dyke Ave (M-53) and Hall Rd (M-59). 45400 Park Ave 48315. **Fax:** 586/803-0102. **Facility:** 124 one-bedroom standard units. 6 stories, interior corridors. *Bath:* combo or shower only. **Parking:** on-site. **Amenities:** video games (fee), voice mail, irons, hair dryers. *Some:* dual phone lines. **Pool(s):** heated indoor. **Leisure Activities:** exercise room. **Guest Services:** valet and coin laundry. **Business Services:** meeting rooms. **Cards:** AX, CB, DC, DS, JC, MC, VI.
SOME UNITS

BAYMONT INN & SUITES DETROIT-UTICA **Phone:** (586)731-4700

| | All Year [ECP] | 1P: $99-$119 | 2P: $99-$119 | | |

Small-scale Hotel **Location:** Jct of Van Dyke Ave (M-53) and Hall Rd (M-59). 45311 Park Ave 48315. **Fax:** 586/731-9870. **Facility:** 102 units. 98 one-bedroom standard units, some with whirlpools. 4 one-bedroom suites ($104-$139). 4 stories, interior corridors. *Bath:* combo or shower only. **Parking:** on-site. **Terms:** pets ($50 deposit). **Amenities:** video games (fee), voice mail, irons, hair dryers. **Pool(s):** heated indoor. **Leisure Activities:** whirlpool. **Guest Services:** valet and coin laundry. **Business Services:** meeting rooms. **Cards:** AX, CB, DC, DS, MC, VI.
Special Amenities: free continental breakfast and free newspaper. *(See color ad p 241)*
SOME UNITS

COMFORT INN **Phone:** (586)739-7111

| | All Year [ECP] | 1P: $89 | 2P: $99 | XP: $10 | F18 |

Small-scale Hotel **Location:** Jct Van Dyke Ave (M-53) and Hall Rd (M-59). 11401 Hall Rd 48317. **Fax:** 586/739-1041. **Facility:** 104 one-bedroom standard units, some with whirlpools. 3 stories, interior corridors. **Parking:** on-site. **Amenities:** video games (fee), hair dryers. *Some:* safes. **Guest Services:** valet and coin laundry. **Business Services:** meeting rooms, fax (fee). **Cards:** AX, CB, DC, DS, JC, MC, VI. **Special Amenities:** free continental breakfast and free local telephone calls.
SOME UNITS

COURTYARD BY MARRIOTT **Phone:** (586)997-6100

| | All Year | 1P: $109 | 2P: $109 | | |

Small-scale Hotel **Location:** Jct of Van Dyke Ave (M-53) and Hall Rd (M-59). 46000 Utica Park Blvd 48315. **Fax:** 586/997-9880. **Facility:** 90 units. 87 one-bedroom standard units, some with whirlpools. 3 one-bedroom suites ($129-$184), some with whirlpools. 3 stories, interior corridors. *Bath:* combo or shower only. **Parking:** on-site. **Amenities:** video games, voice mail, irons, hair dryers. **Pool(s):** heated indoor. **Leisure Activities:** whirlpool, exercise room. **Guest Services:** valet and coin laundry. **Business Services:** meeting rooms. **Cards:** AX, DC, DS, JC, MC, VI.
FEE SOME UNITS

STAYBRIDGE SUITES-UTICA **Phone:** (586)323-0101

| | All Year | 1P: $119-$189 | 2P: $119-$189 | | |

Small-scale Hotel **Location:** Jct Van Dyke Ave (M-53) and Hall Rd (M-59). 46155 Utica Park Blvd 48315. **Fax:** 586/323-0011. **Facility:** 108 units. 61 one-bedroom standard units with efficiencies. 30 one- and 17 two-bedroom suites with efficiencies. 3 stories, interior corridors. *Bath:* combo or shower only. **Parking:** on-site. **Terms:** cancellation fee imposed, [CP] meal plan available. **Amenities:** video library (fee). *Some:* dual phone lines, voice mail, irons, hair dryers. *Fee:* video games, high-speed Internet. **Pool(s):** heated indoor. **Leisure Activities:** whirlpool, exercise room. **Business Services:** meeting rooms, business center. **Cards:** AX, CB, DC, DS, JC, MC, VI.
SOME UNITS

——— WHERE TO DINE ———

FILIPPA'S WINE BARREL **Lunch:** $6-$12 **Dinner:** $10-$15 **Phone:** 586/254-1311

American

Location: At jct Mound Rd and M-59 (Hall Rd). 45125 Mound Rd 48317. **Hours:** 11 am-10 pm, Fri & Sat-11 pm, Sun noon-9 pm. Closed: 7/4, 12/25; also Super Bowl Sun. **Features:** The warm, vintage surroundings invite diners to unwind while enjoying a wide array of choices from fowl to beef. The cool, delicious gazpacho is an excellent contrast to the well-seasoned encrusted, stuffed salmon. Service is attentive and adaptable. Casual dress; cocktails. **Parking:** on-site. **Cards:** AX, DS, MC, VI.

RISTORANTE PICCIRILLI **Dinner:** $9-$21 **Phone:** 586/731-0610

Italian

Location: Jct Van Dyke Ave and 24 Mile Rd, just s. 52830 Van Dyke Rd 48316. **Hours:** 4:30 pm-10 pm, Sun 2 pm-8:30 pm. Closed major holidays; also Mon. **Reservations:** suggested; weekends. **Features:** The intimate dining room is a cozy setting in which to savor homemade Italian fare. Strolling musicians enhance the romantic ambience on Saturday evenings. In addition to a nice list of wines, the restaurant rolls out a tempting assortment of dessert. Casual dress; cocktails. **Parking:** on-site. **Cards:** AX, DC, MC, VI.

WALLED LAKE pop. 6,713

——— WHERE TO DINE ———

MICHIGAN STAR CLIPPER DINNER TRAIN **Lunch:** $39 **Dinner:** $70 **Phone:** 248/960-9440

American

Location: I-96, exit 159 (Wixom Rd), 1 mi n, then 4 mi e. 840 N Pontiac Trail 48390. **Hours:** Departure time 7 pm. Closed: 11/27, 12/24, 12/25; also Mon. **Reservations:** required. **Features:** Take a relaxing and memorable three-hour, linear ride through the woods, meadows and lake country in vintage 1950s dining cars. The prix fixe menu includes a choice of fish, poultry or beef entree. Formal attire; cocktails; entertainment. **Parking:** on-site. **Cards:** AX, DC, DS, MC, VI.

WALTZ

——— WHERE TO DINE ———

WALTZ INN Historic **Lunch:** $6-$10 **Dinner:** $8-$15 **Phone:** 734/654-9040

American

Location: I-275, exit 8, 0.5 mi w; in the village. 28080 Waltz Rd 48164. **Hours:** 11 am-9 pm, Fri & Sat-10 pm, Sun noon-8:30 pm. Closed major holidays; also Mon & Tues. **Features:** Built in 1900, the small country tavern is quaint and homey, with historical pictures decorating the walls. Reliable home-cooked food includes such choices as fish and chips, prime rib and porterhouse steak. Servers are personable and warm. Casual dress; cocktails. **Parking:** on-site. **Cards:** MC, VI.

WARREN pop. 138,247 (See map p. 228; index p. 232)

——— WHERE TO STAY ———

BAYMONT INN & SUITES DETROIT-WARREN TECH CENTER **Phone:** (586)574-0550 **57**

Small-scale Hotel

All Year [ECP] 1P: $74-$84 2P: $74-$84

Location: I-696, exit 23, 2 mi n, 12.5 mi n on SR 53. 30900 Van Dyke Rd 48093. **Fax:** 586/574-0750. **Facility:** 98 units. 95 one-bedroom standard units. 3 one-bedroom suites ($99-$109), some with kitchens. 3 stories, interior corridors. **Parking:** on-site. **Terms:** small pets only. **Amenities:** video games, voice mail, irons, hair dryers. **Guest Services:** valet and coin laundry. **Business Services:** meeting rooms. **Cards:** AX, CB, DC, DS, MC, VI. **Special Amenities:** free continental breakfast and free newspaper. *(See color ad p 241)*

SOME UNITS

CANDLEWOOD SUITES-DETROIT WARREN **Phone:** 586-978-1261 **54**

Small-scale Hotel

All Year 1P: $71-$107

Location: I-696, exit 23, 2.8 mi n. 7010 Convention Blvd 48092. **Fax:** 586/978-1701. **Facility:** 122 units. 98 one-bedroom standard units with efficiencies. 24 one-bedroom suites with efficiencies. 3 stories, interior corridors. *Bath:* combo or shower only. **Parking:** on-site. **Amenities:** video library, CD players, dual phone lines, voice mail, irons, hair dryers. **Guest Services:** complimentary laundry. **Cards:** AX, CB, DC, DS, JC, MC, VI.

SOME UNITS

COMFORT SUITES **Phone:** (586)427-7000 **62**

Small-scale Hotel

All Year 1P: $69-$259 2P: $74-$259 XP: $5 F18

Location: I-696, exit 20. 2020 Walter Ruether Service Dr 48091. **Fax:** 586/427-6000. **Facility:** 65 one-bedroom standard units, some with whirlpools. 2 stories, interior corridors. *Bath:* combo or shower only. **Parking:** on-site. **Terms:** [ECP] meal plan available. **Amenities:** dual phone lines, voice mail, irons, hair dryers. **Pool(s):** small heated indoor. **Guest Services:** valet laundry. **Business Services:** meeting rooms. **Cards:** AX, CB, DC, DS, JC, MC, VI. **Special Amenities:** free continental breakfast and free local telephone calls.

SOME UNITS

COURTYARD BY MARRIOTT-WARREN **Phone:** 586/751-5777 **58**

Small-scale Hotel

All Year 1P: $119 2P: $129

Location: I-696, exit 23, 1.6 mi n on SR 53. 30190 Van Dyke Ave 48093. **Fax:** 586/751-4463. **Facility:** 147 units. 133 one-bedroom standard units. 14 one-bedroom suites ($139-$149). 2-3 stories, interior corridors. *Bath:* combo or shower only. **Parking:** on-site. **Terms:** cancellation fee imposed, [ECP] meal plan available. **Amenities:** dual phone lines, voice mail, irons, hair dryers. **Pool(s):** small heated indoor. **Leisure Activities:** whirlpool, exercise room. **Guest Services:** valet and coin laundry. **Business Services:** meeting rooms. **Cards:** AX, CB, DC, DS, MC, VI.

SOME UNITS

(See map p. 228)

FAIRFIELD INN BY MARRIOTT

Motel
All Year [ECP]   1P: $59-$99   2P: $59-$99   **Phone:** (586)939-1700   55 F18
XP: $10
Location: I-696, exit 23, 2.8 mi n on Van Dyke Ave; between 13 Mile and 14 Mile rds. 7454 Convention Blvd 48092. **Fax:** 586/939-1700. **Facility:** 132 one-bedroom standard units. 3 stories, interior/exterior corridors. *Bath:* combo or shower only. **Parking:** on-site. **Amenities:** irons. **Pool(s):** heated outdoor. **Guest Services:** valet laundry. **Cards:** AX, CB, DC, DS, MC, VI.
SOME UNITS

FOUR POINTS BY SHERATON HOTEL & SUITES DETROIT NORTH
Small-scale Hotel
Phone: (586)573-7600   60 F17
All Year   1P: $109-$199   2P: $109-$199   XP: $10
Location: I-696, exit 23, 1.5 mi n, 13 mi n on SR 53. 30000 Van Dyke Ave 48093. **Fax:** 586/573-7356. **Facility:** 127 one-bedroom standard units, some with whirlpools. 6 stories, interior corridors. **Terms:** cancellation fee imposed, [AP] & [BP] meal plans available. **Amenities:** dual phone lines, voice mail, irons, hair dryers. **Pool(s):** heated indoor. **Leisure Activities:** whirlpool, exercise room. *Fee:* game room. **Guest Services:** valet laundry. **Business Services:** meeting rooms. **Cards:** AX, CB, DC, DS, MC, VI.
SOME UNITS   FEE FEE

HAMPTON INN-WARREN/STERLING HEIGHTS
Small-scale Hotel
Phone: (586)977-7270   53
All Year [ECP]   1P: $99   2P: $99
Location: I-696, exit 23, 2.8 mi n. 7447 Convention Blvd 48092. **Fax:** 586/977-3889. **Facility:** 124 units. 120 one-bedroom standard units, some with whirlpools. 4 one-bedroom suites ($149-$179), some with whirlpools. 3 stories, interior corridors. **Parking:** on-site. **Amenities:** voice mail, irons, hair dryers. **Guest Services:** valet laundry. **Business Services:** meeting rooms. **Cards:** AX, CB, DC, DS, MC, VI. **Special Amenities:** free continental breakfast and free newspaper.
SOME UNITS

HAWTHORN SUITES LTD
Small-scale Hotel
Phone: (586)264-8800   56
All Year   1P: $89-$189   2P: $89-$189
Location: I-696, exit 23, 1.8 mi n on SR 53. 7601 Chicago Rd 48092. **Fax:** 586/264-8184. **Facility:** 79 units. 45 one-bedroom standard units, some with whirlpools. 34 one-bedroom suites with efficiencies, some with whirlpools. 3 stories, interior corridors. *Bath:* combo or shower only. **Parking:** on-site. **Terms:** small pets only ($75 fee). **Amenities:** video games (fee), high-speed Internet, dual phone lines, voice mail, irons, hair dryers. *Some:* safes. **Pool(s):** heated indoor. **Leisure Activities:** exercise room. **Guest Services:** sundries, valet and coin laundry. **Business Services:** meeting rooms, business center. **Cards:** AX, CB, DC, DS, JC, MC, VI.
SOME UNITS

(See map p. 228)

HOLIDAY INN EXPRESS
Phone: (586)754-9700 **61**

▼▼▼ All Year   1P: $119-$139

Small-scale Hotel **Location:** I-696, exit 24 (Hoover Rd). 11500 11 Mile Rd 48089. Fax: 586/754-0376. **Facility:** 124 one-bedroom standard units, some with whirlpools. 2 stories, interior corridors. **Parking:** on-site. **Terms:** weekly rates available, [ECP] meal plan available. **Amenities:** video games, voice mail, irons, hair dryers. **Pool(s):** outdoor. **Leisure Activities:** exercise room. **Guest Services:** valet laundry. **Business Services:** meeting rooms. **Cards:** AX, CB, DC, DS, MC, VI.

SOME UNITS
(ASK) (SD) (↑↓) (⌂) (≈) (🐾) (DATA PORT) / (✕)

RED ROOF INN-WARREN
Phone: (586)573-4300 **63**

(AAA) (SAVE)   6/2-9/28   1P: $53-$73   2P: $57-$77   XP: $4   F18
              4/1-6/1 & 9/29-3/31 1P: $49-$69   2P: $53-$73   XP: $4   F18
▼▼ Motel **Location:** I-696, exit 20, just ne. 26300 Dequindre Rd 48091. Fax: 586/573-6157. **Facility:** 136 one-bedroom standard units. 2 stories, exterior corridors. *Bath:* combo or shower only. **Parking:** on-site. **Amenities:** video games, voice mail. **Cards:** AX, CB, DC, DS, MC, VI. **Special Amenities:** free local telephone calls and free newspaper.

SOME UNITS
(🐄) (↑↓) (⌂) (🐾) (DATA PORT) / (✕) (📶) (💻) /

RESIDENCE INN BY MARRIOTT
Phone: (586)558-8050 **59**

(AAA) (SAVE)   4/1-10/31   1P: $80-$116
              11/1-3/31   1P: $71-$107
▼▼▼ Small-scale Hotel **Location:** I-696, exit 23, 2 mi n on Van Dyke Ave. 30120 Civic Center Blvd 48093. Fax: 586/558-8214. **Facility:** 133 units. 115 one-bedroom standard units with efficiencies. 18 two-bedroom suites with efficiencies. 3 stories, interior/exterior corridors. *Bath:* combo or shower only. **Parking:** on-site. **Terms:** [BP] meal plan available, pets ($75 extra charge). **Amenities:** voice mail, irons, hair dryers. **Pool(s):** outdoor. **Leisure Activities:** whirlpool, activities court, exercise room, sports court. **Guest Services:** valet and coin laundry. **Business Services:** meeting rooms. **Cards:** AX, CB, DC, DS, JC, MC, VI. **Special Amenities:** free continental breakfast and free newspaper.

SOME UNITS
(SD) (🐄) (🚶) (⌂) (≈) (✕) (🐾) (DATA PORT) (📶) (💻) / (✕) (VCR)

------- **WHERE TO DINE** -------

ANDIAMO ITALIA RISTORANTE
Lunch: $9-$15   **Dinner:** $12-$24   Phone: 586/268-3200 **58**

▼▼▼ Italian **Location:** Jct Van Dyke Ave and 14 Mile Rd, just w. 7096 E 14 Mile Rd 48092. **Hours:** 11 am-11 pm, Sat 4 pm-midnight, Sun 4 pm-9 pm. Closed major holidays. **Reservations:** suggested. **Features:** Andiamo is an Italian ristorante that combines a sophisticated atmosphere and skilled use of traditional Mediterranean ingredients to produce unique creations that will satisfy your craving for Italian-style fare. Dressy casual; cocktails. **Parking:** on-site and valet. **Cards:** AX, MC, VI.

(🍽) (✕)

MICHELLE'S RESTAURANT & SWEETHEART BAKERY
Lunch: $6-$7   **Dinner:** $7-$10   Phone: 586/795-1665 **59**

▼▼ American **Location:** I-696, exit 23, 2.7 mi n. 31920 Van Dyke Ave 48093. **Hours:** 7 am-9 pm, Fri & Sat-10 pm. Closed major holidays. **Features:** Business executives sit side by side with moms and their toddlers in this popular local eatery. The menu may be basic and straightforward but having an attached bakery might complicate the decision process. Casual dress; cocktails. **Parking:** on-site. **Cards:** AX, DS, MC, VI.

(✕)

WATERFORD pop. 73,150

------- **WHERE TO STAY** -------

BEST WESTERN CONCORDE INN OF WATERFORD
Phone: (248)666-8555

(SAVE)   All Year   1P: $79-$129   2P: $79-$149   XP: $10   F17

▼▼▼ Small-scale Hotel **Location:** Jct M-59 (Highland Rd) and Airport Rd, 1 mi w. Located adjacent to shopping plaza. 7076 Highland Rd 48327. Fax: 248/666-8573. **Facility:** 111 units. 101 one-bedroom standard units, some with whirlpools. 10 one-bedroom suites ($99-$179) with whirlpools. 3 stories, interior corridors. *Bath:* combo or shower only. **Parking:** on-site. **Terms:** [CP] meal plan available. **Amenities:** video games (fee), dual phone lines, voice mail, irons, hair dryers. *Some:* honor bars. **Pool(s):** heated indoor, wading. **Leisure Activities:** sauna, exercise room. *Fee:* game room. **Guest Services:** valet and coin laundry, area transportation. **Business Services:** meeting rooms. **Cards:** AX, CB, DC, DS, JC, MC, VI.

SOME UNITS
(SD) (↑↓) (🚶) (⌂) (≈) (✕) (🐾) (DATA PORT) (💻) / (✕) (📶) (💻) /

HOLIDAY INN EXPRESS & SUITES
Phone: (248)674-3434

▼▼▼ All Year   1P: $79-$84   2P: $79-$84   XP: $10   F18

Small-scale Hotel **Location:** Jct M-59 (Highland Rd) and Pontiac Lake Rd. 4350 Pontiac Lake Rd 48328. Fax: 248/674-3446. **Facility:** Smoke free premises. 83 one-bedroom standard units, some with whirlpools. 3 stories, interior corridors. *Bath:* combo or shower only. **Parking:** on-site. **Terms:** cancellation fee imposed, [ECP] meal plan available. **Amenities:** video games (fee), high-speed Internet, dual phone lines, voice mail, irons, hair dryers. **Pool(s):** indoor. **Leisure Activities:** exercise room. *Fee:* game room. **Guest Services:** valet laundry. **Business Services:** meeting rooms, business center. **Cards:** AX, CB, DC, DS, MC.

SOME UNITS
(ASK) (SD) (↑↓) (🚶) (⌂) (≈) (🐾) (DATA PORT) (💻) / (✕) (📶) (💻) /

WEST BLOOMFIELD pop. 64,862 (See map p. 228; index p. 235)

——— WHERE TO DINE ———

THE LARK
Continental
Location: Just n of jct Maple and Farmington rds. 6430 Farmington Rd 48322. **Hours:** 6 pm-11 pm, Fri & Sat-midnight. Closed major holidays; also Sun & Mon. **Reservations:** required. **Features:** The dining room has the ambience of an intimate Portuguese country inn. The menu of classic European selections changes bimonthly, might include such selections as rack of lamb. The pre-appetizer and dessert carts are loaded with temptations. Formal attire; cocktails. **Parking:** on-site. **Cards:** AX, CB, DC, MC, VI.
Dinner: $55-$70
Phone: 248/661-4466 [32]

WIXOM pop. 13,263

——— WHERE TO STAY ———

BAYMONT INN & SUITES
(AAA) [SAVE]
Small-scale Hotel
All Year [CP] 1P: $94 2P: $94
Phone: (248)735-2781
XP: $7 F18
Location: I-96, exit 159, just n. Located in a business park. 48953 Alpha Dr 48393. Fax: 248/735-3905. **Facility:** 109 one-bedroom standard units, some with whirlpools. 4 stories, interior corridors. *Bath:* combo or shower only. **Parking:** on-site. **Terms:** small pets only. **Amenities:** video games, voice mail, irons, hair dryers. **Pool(s):** heated indoor. **Leisure Activities:** whirlpool, exercise room. **Guest Services:** valet and coin laundry, airport transportation (fee)-Detroit Metro Airport. **Business Services:** meeting rooms. **Cards:** AX, CB, DC, DS, JC, MC, VI. **Special Amenities: free continental breakfast and free newspaper.**
SOME UNITS

WOODHAVEN pop. 12,530 (See map p. 228; index p. 235)

——— WHERE TO STAY ———

BEST WESTERN WOODHAVEN INN
[SAVE]
Small-scale Hotel
All Year 1P: $72 2P: $76
Phone: (734)676-8000
XP: $5 F13
Location: I-75, exit 32 (West Rd). 21700 West Rd 48183. Fax: 734/676-7062. **Facility:** 126 one-bedroom standard units, some with whirlpools. 2 stories, interior corridors. **Parking:** on-site. **Terms:** 14 day cancellation notice. **Amenities:** video games, voice mail, safes, irons, hair dryers. **Pool(s):** heated indoor. **Leisure Activities:** sauna, exercise room. *Fee:* game room. **Guest Services:** valet laundry. **Business Services:** conference facilities, fax (fee). **Cards:** AX, CB, DC, DS, JC, MC, VI.
SOME UNITS

HOLIDAY INN EXPRESS & SUITES
Small-scale Hotel
All Year [ECP] 1P: $89
Phone: (734)362-0933
Location: I-75, exit 32 (West Rd), just w. 21500 West Rd 48183. Fax: 734/362-0937. **Facility:** 77 one-bedroom standard units, some with whirlpools. 3 stories, interior corridors. *Bath:* combo or shower only. **Parking:** on-site. **Terms:** check-in 4 pm. **Amenities:** video games (fee), dual phone lines, voice mail, irons, hair dryers. **Pool(s):** heated indoor. **Leisure Activities:** whirlpool, exercise room. **Guest Services:** valet and coin laundry. **Business Services:** meeting rooms, business center. **Cards:** AX, DC, DS, MC, VI.
SOME UNITS

This ends listings for the Detroit Vicinity.
The following page resumes the alphabetical listings of
cities in Michigan.

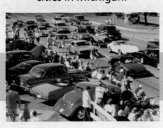

DE WITT pop. 4,702

―――― **WHERE TO STAY** ――――

SLEEP INN
[SAVE]
♦♦ ♦♦
Small-scale Hotel

Phone: (517)669-8823

All Year
Location: I-69, exit 87, 0.8 mi n on Old US 27. 1101 Commerce Park Dr 48820. Fax: 517/669-7816. **Facility:** 61 one-bedroom standard units. 2 stories, interior corridors. *Bath:* combo or shower only. **Parking:** on-site, winter plug-ins. **Terms:** [ECP] meal plan available. **Amenities:** video library (fee), safes, irons, hair dryers. **Pool(s):** outdoor. **Guest Services:** coin laundry. **Cards:** AX, CB, DC, DS, JC, MC, VI.

1P: $64-$104   2P: $74-$114   XP: $10   F

SOME UNITS

🅂🄳 🕪 ⬚ ⬚ ⬚ 📷 DATA PORT ▣ / ⊠ VCR 🔒 📷 /
FEE

DIXBORO

―――― **WHERE TO DINE** ――――

THE LORD FOX
♦♦ ♦♦
American

Historic   Lunch: $9-$16   Dinner: $16-$25   Phone: 734/662-1647
Location: US 23, exit 41 (Plymouth Rd), 2 mi e. 5400 Plymouth Rd 48105. **Hours:** 11:30 am-2 & 5-10 pm, Sat from 5 pm, Sun 3 pm-9 pm. Closed major holidays. **Reservations:** suggested. **Features:** Built in 1880, the rural family home is a sophisticated setting for classy dining. The menu blends classical preparations, such as beef Wellington and duck a l'orange, with innovative regional entrees, such as hazelnut whitefish and Amish chicken. Dressy casual; cocktails. **Parking:** on-site. **Cards:** AX, DC, MC, VI.

⊠

DOUGLAS pop. 1,214—*See also SAUGATUCK.*

―――― **WHERE TO STAY** ――――

AMERICINN OF SAUGATUCK/DOUGLAS
♦♦ ♦♦
Small-scale Hotel

Phone: (269)857-8581

7/1-9/30	1P: $129-$159	2P: $129-$159	XP: $10	F16
4/1-6/30	1P: $79-$129	2P: $89-$139	XP: $10	F16
10/1-10/31	1P: $119-$129	2P: $119-$129	XP: $10	F16
11/1-3/31	1P: $79-$109	2P: $79-$109	XP: $10	F16

Location: I-196, exit 36, 1 mi n. 2905 Blue Star Hwy 49406 (PO Box 2729). Fax: 269/857-3591. **Facility:** 46 units. 45 one-bedroom standard units. 1 one-bedroom suite ($169-$249). 2 stories (no elevator), interior corridors. *Bath:* combo or shower only. **Parking:** on-site. **Terms:** 7 day cancellation notice, [ECP] meal plan available, small pets only (in smoking units). **Amenities:** safes (fee), hair dryers. *Some:* irons. **Pool(s):** heated indoor. **Leisure Activities:** sauna, whirlpool. **Guest Services:** coin laundry. **Business Services:** meeting rooms. **Cards:** AX, CB, DC, DS, MC, VI.

SOME UNITS

(ASK) 🅂🄳 🐾 ⬚ ⬚ ⬚ 🗐 DATA PORT ▣ / ⊠ 🔒 📷

THE KIRBY HOUSE
(AAA) [SAVE]
♦♦ ♦♦
Bed & Breakfast

Phone: 269/857-2904

5/1-10/31   1P: $115-$175   2P: $115-$175   XP: $25
4/1-4/30 & 11/1-3/31   1P: $85-$145   2P: $85-$145   XP: $25
Location: Center. 294 W Center St 49406 (PO Box 1174, SAUGATUCK, 49453). Fax: 269/857-6156. **Facility:** Three rooms of this Victorian manor have fireplaces. Smoke free premises. 8 one-bedroom standard units. 3 stories (no elevator), interior corridors. *Bath:* some shared or private, combo or shower only. **Parking:** on-site, winter plug-ins. **Terms:** 2-3 night minimum stay - weekends, age restrictions may apply, 14 day cancellation notice-fee imposed, [BP] meal plan available, package plans. **Amenities:** irons. **Pool(s):** heated outdoor. **Leisure Activities:** whirlpool, bicycles, horseshoes. **Guest Services:** TV in common area. **Business Services:** meeting rooms. **Cards:** MC, VI. **Special Amenities:** free local telephone calls and free room upgrade (subject to availability with advanced reservations).

🕪 ⬚ ⊠ ⊠ 🐾 🛇

LAKE SHORE RESORT
♦♦ ♦♦
Motel

Phone: (269)857-7121

6/20-9/6 [ECP]   1P: $140-$180   2P: $140-$180   XP: $30
9/7-9/30 [CP]   1P: $90-$140   2P: $90-$140   XP: $20
5/16-6/19 & 10/1-10/19 [CP]   1P: $75-$110   2P: $75-$110   XP: $20
Location: From CR A2, 1 mi w on Wiley Rd, then 1 mi s. 2885 Lakeshore Dr 49406 (PO Box 121, SAUGATUCK, 49453). **Facility:** 30 one-bedroom standard units. 1 story, exterior corridors. **Parking:** on-site. **Terms:** open 5/16-10/19, 2-3 night minimum stay - weekends, 30 day cancellation notice-fee imposed, [ECP] meal plan available. **Pool(s):** heated outdoor. **Leisure Activities:** bicycles, hiking trails, volleyball. **Business Services:** meeting rooms. **Cards:** MC, VI.

SOME UNITS

⬚ ⊠ 🔒 / ⊠ /

ROSEMONT INN RESORT
♦♦ ♦♦
Bed & Breakfast

Phone: (269)857-2637

6/6-9/7 [BP]   1P: $215-$305   2P: $215-$305   XP: $15
9/8-11/16 [BP]   1P: $125-$255   2P: $125-$255   XP: $15
4/1-6/5 [BP]   1P: $125-$250   2P: $125-$250   XP: $15
11/17-3/31 [BP]   1P: $115-$230   2P: $115-$230   XP: $15
Location: From CR A2, 1 mi w on Center St, just n. 83 Lakeshore Dr 49453 (PO Box 857, 49406-0857). Fax: 269/857-3968. **Facility:** An English garden and cozy accommodations with fireplaces are featured at this historic house just across the road from Lake Michigan. Smoke free premises. 14 one-bedroom standard units, some with whirlpools. 2 stories (no elevator), interior corridors. *Bath:* combo or shower only. **Parking:** on-site. **Terms:** 2-3 night minimum stay - weekends, age restrictions may apply, 14 day cancellation notice-fee imposed. **Amenities:** hair dryers. **Pool(s):** heated outdoor. **Leisure Activities:** sauna, whirlpool, bicycles. **Guest Services:** complimentary evening beverages. **Business Services:** meeting rooms. **Cards:** AX, DS, MC, VI.

SHERWOOD FOREST BED & BREAKFAST

Phone: (269)857-1246

WWW

7/1-8/31 [BP]	1P: $115-$185	2P: $115-$185	XP: $10	F10
4/1-6/30 & 9/1-10/31 [BP]	1P: $105-$175	2P: $105-$175	XP: $10	F10
11/1-3/31 [BP]	1P: $95-$165	2P: $95-$165	XP: $10	F10

Bed & Breakfast   **Location:** CR A2, 1 mi w. Located in a residential setting. 938 Center St 49406 (PO Box 315, SAUGATUCK, 49453). **Fax:** 269/857-1996. **Facility:** The property is in the Victorian style. Smoke free premises. 6 units. 5 one-bedroom standard units, some with whirlpools. 1 cottage. 2 stories (no elevator), interior corridors. *Bath:* combo or shower only. **Parking:** on-site. **Terms:** 2 night minimum stay - weekends, age restrictions may apply, 10 day cancellation notice-fee imposed. **Amenities:** CD players, hair dryers. *Some:* irons. **Pool(s):** heated outdoor. **Leisure Activities:** bicycles. **Guest Services:** TV in common area. **Cards:** DC, DS, MC, VI.

SOME UNITS

DOWAGIAC pop. 6,147

——— WHERE TO STAY ———

AMERIHOST INN & SUITES-DOWAGIAC

Phone: (269)782-4270

AAA SAVE
WWW

All Year   1P: $69-$78   2P: $74-$88

Small-scale Hotel   **Location:** 0.4 mi s of jct US 51 and US 62. Located behind Parmide Shopping Plaza. 29291 Amerihost Dr 49047. **Fax:** 269/782-3219. **Facility:** 64 one-bedroom standard units, some with whirlpools. 2 stories (no elevator), interior corridors. *Bath:* combo or shower only. **Parking:** on-site. **Terms:** [ECP] meal plan available. **Amenities:** dual phone lines, voice mail, safes (fee), irons, hair dryers. **Pool(s):** heated indoor. **Leisure Activities:** exercise room. **Business Services:** meeting rooms. **Cards:** AX, DC, DS, MC, VI. **Special Amenities:** free continental breakfast and free newspaper.

SOME UNITS

DUNDEE pop. 3,522

——— WHERE TO STAY ———

AMERIHOST INN-DUNDEE

Phone: 734-529-5240

AAA SAVE
WWW

All Year [ECP]   1P: $74   2P: $78   XP: $5   F17

Small-scale Hotel   **Location:** US 23, exit 17, just w. 111 Waterstradt Commerce Dr 48131. Fax: 734/529-7435. **Facility:** 60 one-bedroom standard units, some with whirlpools. 2 stories, interior corridors. *Bath:* combo or shower only. **Parking:** on-site. **Amenities:** voice mail, safes (fee), irons, hair dryers. **Pool(s):** heated indoor/outdoor. **Leisure Activities:** whirlpool, exercise room. **Business Services:** meeting rooms. **Cards:** AX, DC, DS, MC, VI.

SOME UNITS

FEE   FEE

CARLTON LODGE

Phone: 734-529-5100

WWW

All Year [ECP]   1P: $79-$109   2P: $79-$109   XP: $8   F18

Small-scale Hotel   **Location:** Jct US 23 and SR 50. 100 White Tail Dr 48131. Fax: 734/529-5100. **Facility:** 77 units. 74 one-bedroom standard units, some with whirlpools. 3 one-bedroom suites, some with whirlpools. 2 stories, interior corridors. *Bath:* combo or shower only. **Parking:** on-site. **Amenities:** high-speed Internet, dual phone lines, voice mail, irons, hair dryers. *Some:* DVD players. **Pool(s):** heated indoor. **Leisure Activities:** exercise room. **Guest Services:** valet and coin laundry. **Cards:** AX, CB, DC, DS, JC, MC, VI.

SOME UNITS

COUNTRY INN & SUITES BY CARLSON (CABELA'S LOCATION)

Phone: (734)529-8822

WWW

6/1-8/31 [ECP]	1P: $79-$169	2P: $79-$169	XP: $10	F17
4/1-5/31 & 9/1-3/31 [ECP]	1P: $65-$99	2P: $65-$99	XP: $10	F17

Small-scale Hotel   **Location:** US 23, exit 17. 665 Tecumseh St 48131. Fax: 734/529-5975. **Facility:** 70 units. 60 one-bedroom standard units, some with whirlpools. 10 one-bedroom suites ($99-$179). 3 stories, interior corridors. *Bath:* combo or shower only. **Parking:** on-site. **Terms:** weekly rates available. **Amenities:** dual phone lines, voice mail, irons, hair dryers. **Pool(s):** heated indoor. **Leisure Activities:** whirlpool, exercise room. **Guest Services:** coin laundry. **Business Services:** meeting rooms. **Cards:** AX, CB, DC, DS, MC, VI. *(See color ad p 243)*

SOME UNITS

——— WHERE TO DINE ———

WILDERNESS SPORTS BAR & GRILLE

Lunch: $6-$10   **Dinner:** $6-$10   **Phone:** 734/529-7220

American   **Location:** US 23, exit 17, just w. 103 Cabela Blvd E 48131. **Hours:** 11 am-2 am. Closed major holidays. **Features:** A hunting and fishing themed restaurant, the menu offers a modest selection of regional seafood and traditional bar foods. Casual dress; cocktails. **Parking:** on-site. **Cards:** AX, DS, MC, VI.

EAGLE HARBOR

——— WHERE TO STAY ———

SHORELINE RESORT

Phone: (906)289-4441

AAA SAVE
WWW

6/15-10/15 & 1/1-3/31   1P: $66-$77   2P: $66-$77   XP: $4   F16

Motel   **Location:** On SR 26. Located along the water's edge of the harbor. 201 Front St, F #2015 49950 (HYC 1, Box 262). **Facility:** 8 one-bedroom standard units. 1 story, exterior corridors. *Bath:* shower only. **Parking:** on-site. **Terms:** open 6/15-10/15 & 1/1-3/31, cancellation fee imposed, weekly rates available, package plans, pets ($10 deposit). **Dining:** 8 am-8 pm. **Leisure Activities:** canoeing, paddleboats, kayaks. **Cards:** MC, VI. **Special Amenities:** early check-in/late check-out.

EAST GRAND RAPIDS pop. 10,764

——— WHERE TO DINE ———

ROSE'S

American

Lunch: $7-$12   Dinner: $8-$19   Phone: 616/458-1122
Location: 1.4 mi w of East Belt Line, then just nw. 550 Lakeside Dr 49506. **Hours:** 11 am-11 pm. **Features:** The noisy, bustling bistro and its breezy outdoor deck, overlook Reed's Lake. Pizzas cooked in a brick oven and homemade pasta dishes are at the center of a menu that features daily fish specials. Tiramisu and creme brulee are delicious dessert choices. Casual dress; cocktails. **Parking:** on-site. **Cards:** AX, DS, MC, VI.

EAST LANSING pop. 46,525—*See also LANSING.*

——— WHERE TO STAY ———

CANDLEWOOD SUITES   Phone: (517)351-8181
All Year   1P: $99-$119   2P: $99-$119
Location: Just e of I-496 and US 127, exit 11 (Jolly Rd). 3545 Forest Rd 48910. Fax: 517/351-8101. **Facility:** 128 units. 96 one-bedroom standard units with efficiencies. 32 one-bedroom suites with efficiencies. 3 stories, interior corridors. **Parking:** on-site. **Terms:** 2 night minimum stay - weekends, cancellation fee imposed.
Small-scale Hotel
Amenities: video library, CD players, high-speed Internet, dual phone lines, voice mail, irons, hair dryers. **Leisure Activities:** exercise room. **Guest Services:** sundries. **Cards:** AX, DC, DS, MC, VI.

SOME UNITS

EAST LANSING MARRIOTT AT UNIVERSITY PLACE   Phone: (517)337-4440
SAVE
All Year   1P: $189
Location: Just n of Grand River Ave; downtown. 300 M A C Ave 48823. Fax: 517/337-5001. **Facility:** 180 one-bedroom standard units. 7 stories, interior corridors. *Bath:* combo or shower only. **Parking:** on-site.
Large-scale Hotel
Terms: package plans. **Amenities:** voice mail, irons, hair dryers. **Pool(s):** heated indoor. **Leisure Activities:** sauna, whirlpool, exercise room. **Guest Services:** sundries, valet and coin laundry. **Business Services:** conference facilities, business center. **Cards:** AX, CB, DC, DS, JC, MC, VI.

SOME UNITS

HAMPTON INN   Phone: 517/324-2072
SAVE
All Year [ECP]   1P: $80-$89   2P: $85-$90
Location: US 127, exit Lake Lansing Rd, just e. 2500 Coolidge Rd 48823. Fax: 517/324-2073. **Facility:** 86 units. 84 one-bedroom standard units, some with whirlpools. 2 one-bedroom suites ($120-$140). 4 stories, interior corridors. *Bath:* combo or shower only. **Parking:** on-site. **Amenities:** video games (fee), dual phone lines, voice mail, irons, hair dryers. **Pool(s):** heated indoor. **Leisure Activities:** whirlpool, exercise room. **Guest Services:** valet laundry, area transportation. **Business Services:** meeting rooms. **Cards:** AX, CB, DC, DS, MC, VI.

SOME UNITS

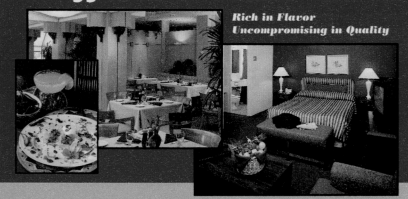

KELLOGG HOTEL AND CONFERENCE CENTER

Phone: (517)432-4000

(AAA) (SAVE)	1/1-3/31	1P: $99-$169	2P: $99-$169	XP: $10	D18
	4/1-12/31	1P: $94-$167	2P: $94-$167	XP: $10	D18

Location: I-496, exit 9 (Trowbridge), just e, then 0.5 mi n. Located on Michigan State University Campus. 55 S Harrison Rd 48824. Fax: 517/353-1872. **Facility:** 165 one-bedroom standard units. 7 stories, interior corridors. *Bath:*

Large-scale Hotel combo or shower only. **Parking:** on-site. **Terms:** cancellation fee imposed. **Amenities:** voice mail, irons, hair dryers. *Fee:* video games, high-speed Internet. **Dining:** 2 restaurants, 6:30 am-10 pm, cocktails, also, The State Room, see separate listing. **Leisure Activities:** exercise room. *Fee:* recreational priviliges at Michigan State University. **Guest Services:** gift shop, valet laundry, airport transportation-Capital City Airport, area transportation-within 5 mi. **Business Services:** conference facilities. **Cards:** AX, CB, DC, DS, MC, VI. **Special Amenities:** free local telephone calls and free room upgrade (subject to availability with advanced reservations). *(See color ad p 284)* SOME UNITS

RESIDENCE INN BY MARRIOTT

Phone: (517) 332-7711

(SAVE)	8/2-3/31 [ECP]	1P: $127-$137	2P: $145-$155
	6/2-8/1 [ECP]	1P: $125-$135	2P: $145-$150
	4/1-6/1 [ECP]	1P: $124-$134	2P: $145-$150

Location: US 127, exit Grand River Ave. 2.6 mi se on SR 43. 1600 E Grand River Ave 48823. Fax: 517/332-7711.

Small-scale Hotel **Facility:** 60 units. 44 one- and 16 two-bedroom standard units with kitchens. 2 stories, exterior corridors. **Parking:** on-site. **Terms:** pets ($25-$150 fee). **Amenities:** voice mail, irons, hair dryers. **Pool(s):** heated outdoor. **Leisure Activities:** whirlpool, exercise room, sports court. **Guest Services:** valet and coin laundry. **Cards:** AX, DC, DS, MC, VI. SOME UNITS

TOWNEPLACE SUITES

Phone: 517/203-1000

(SAVE) All Year 1P: $89 2P: $109

Location: I-96, exit 110 (Okemos Rd), 0.8 mi n, then 0.5 mi w, just n on Hagadorn Rd. 2855 Hannah Blvd 48823. Fax: 517/203-1234. **Facility:** Smoke free premises. 84 units. 63 one-bedroom standard units with kitchens.

Small-scale Hotel 21 two-bedroom suites with kitchens. 3 stories, interior corridors. *Bath:* combo or shower only. **Parking:** on-site. **Terms:** cancellation fee imposed, pets ($100 deposit, $5 extra charge). **Amenities:** video games (fee), dual phone lines, voice mail, irons, hair dryers. **Pool(s):** heated outdoor. **Leisure Activities:** exercise room. **Guest Services:** valet and coin laundry. **Business Services:** meeting rooms, business center. **Cards:** AX, CB, DC, DS, JC, MC, VI. SOME UNITS

———— WHERE TO DINE ————

ALL SEASONS BISTRO

Dinner: $16-$24 **Phone:** 517/336-9890

Location: US 127, exit Lake Lansing Rd, just e. 1500 W Lake Lansing Rd 48823. **Hours:** 5 pm-10 pm. Closed major holidays; also Sun & Mon. **Reservations:** suggested. **Features:** French influenced design has created a cozy and intimate dining room that speaks volumes with its seasonal menu. Traditional bistro

Regional French

inspired items such as pate du jour, coq au vin and cassoulet are featured along with classic dishes such as grilled tenderloin of beef. Dressy casual; cocktails. **Parking:** on-site. **Cards:** AX, DC, DS, MC, VI.

BEGGAR'S BANQUET

Lunch: $8-$21 **Dinner:** $8-$21 **Phone:** 517/351-4573

Location: Just n of Grand River Ave; center. 218 Abbott Rd 48823. **Hours:** 11 am-11:30 pm, Sat & Sun 10 am-midnight. Closed: 12/25. **Reservations:** suggested; weekends. **Features:** In business since the mid-1970s, the casual restaurant has two dining rooms: one classy and one rustic. Such dishes as baked

American

chili and chicken Kiev make up the traditional menu. Artwork created and donated by local students decorates the walls. Casual dress; cocktails. **Parking:** street. **Cards:** AX, DS, MC, VI.

EVERGREEN GRILL

Lunch: $8-$10 **Dinner:** $17-$24 **Phone:** 517/337-1200

Location: Just n of jct Grand River Ave; downtown. 327 Abbott 48823. **Hours:** 11 am-10 pm, Fri & Sat-midnight, Sun 9 am-10 pm. Closed major holidays. **Features:** Based in a converted post office, this attractive dining room features stark walls showcasing the works of local artists and plenty of green plants. A fairly creative

American

menu features regional ingredients such as Indiana Duck and Michigan Cherries used in conjunction with fresh imported seafoods and global seasonings. Dressy casual; cocktails. **Parking:** on-site and valet. **Cards:** AX, CB, DC, DS, MC, VI.

THE STATE ROOM

Lunch: $8-$12 **Dinner:** $12-$20 **Phone:** 517/452-5049

Location: I-496, exit 9 (Trowbridge), just e, then 0.5 mi n; in Kellogg Hotel and Conference Center. 55 S Harrison Rd 48824. **Hours:** 6:30 am-10 pm, Sun 10 am-2 pm. Closed major holidays. **Reservations:** accepted. **Features:** Located inside the Kellogg Hotel, this quietly upscale restaurant offers relaxed dining for all

American

three meals. Focusing on seasonal Michigan products, the menu is further supplemented by a visiting chef series which has brought some of the most exciting and innovative chefs to the restaurant. Dressy casual; cocktails. **Parking:** on-site (fee). **Cards:** AX, DC, DS, MC, VI.

TROPPO

Lunch: $6-$10 **Dinner:** $12-$20 **Phone:** 517/351-7768

Location: Just n of jct N Grand River and Mac aves; downtown. 213 Ann St E 48823. **Hours:** 11 am-2 am, Sun from noon. Closed major holidays. **Reservations:** accepted. **Features:** Half restaurant and half bar, this dark, eclectic upscale space offers a unique dining experience. Drawing from Pacific Rim influenes, the

American

contemporary menu offers such items as orange glazed salmon and sea bass Papillote, as well as interesting takes on steaks and pastas. Dressy casual; cocktails. **Parking:** street. **Cards:** AX, DC, DS, MC, VI.

EAST TAWAS pop. 2,951

———— WHERE TO STAY ————

BAMBI MOTEL
♦♦♦
Motel

			Phone: 989/362-4582	
6/1-10/31	1P: $54-$77	2P: $60-$77	XP: $5	F12
4/1-5/31 & 11/1-3/31	1P: $44-$58	2P: $49-$58	XP: $5	F12

Location: 0.5 mi n on US 23. Located in a commercial area. 1100 E Bay St 48730. **Facility:** 15 one-bedroom standard units. 1 story, exterior corridors. **Parking:** on-site. **Terms:** 2 night minimum stay - weekends in summer, cancellation fee imposed. **Cards:** DS, MC, VI.

SOME UNITS

/ ☒ 🖥 /
FEE

HOLIDAY INN-TAWAS BAY RESORT
♥♥♥♥
Large-scale Hotel

		Phone: (989)362-8601	
All Year	1P: $80-$179	XP: $8	F18

Location: On US 23 N. Located next to the state park marina. 300 E Bay St 48730. Fax: 989/362-5111. **Facility:** 103 one-bedroom standard units, some with whirlpools. 2 stories (no elevator), interior corridors. **Parking:** on-site. **Terms:** check-in 4 pm, 3 day cancellation notice, [AP] meal plan available, 18% service charge. **Amenities:** irons, hair dryers. **Pool(s):** heated indoor. **Leisure Activities:** sauna, whirlpool, rental paddleboats, boat dock, playground, exercise room, shuffleboard. *Fee:* game room. **Guest Services:** gift shop, coin laundry. **Business Services:** conference facilities, business center. **Cards:** AX, DS, MC, VI.

SOME UNITS

(ASK) (S₀) 🛏 🍴 🍸 🏊 ☒ 🎦 (DATA PORT) 🖥 / ☒ 🖥 /

ELK RAPIDS pop. 1,700

———— WHERE TO DINE ————

PEARL'S
♥♥ ♥♥
English

	Lunch: $4-$8	Dinner: $8-$20	Phone: 231-264-0530

Location: From US 31, 0.5 mi e of stop light. 617 Ames St 49629. **Hours:** 11 am-midnight, Sun-10 pm. Closed: 11/27, 12/24, 12/25. **Features:** Voodoo dolls, Mardi Gras beads, papier-mache doodads and the music all add to a taste of the Big Easy. On the menu is a variety of Cajun and Creole selections. Turn up the heat with gumbo ya ya or pasta jambalaya, or turn it back down with beef brisket or a muffuletta sandwich. Save room for one of the homemade desserts. Casual dress; cocktails. **Parking:** on-site. **Cards:** AX, MC, VI.

🍸 ☒

ELLSWORTH pop. 483

———— WHERE TO DINE ————

TAPAWINGO
♥♥♥♥
American

	Dinner: $29-$44	Phone: 231-588-7971

Location: Center. 9502 Lake St 49729. **Hours:** Open 4/1-11/8 & 12/4-3/31; 5:30 pm-9 pm. Closed: Mon & Tues 10/19-4/30. **Reservations:** required. **Features:** The changing menu revolves around the seasons, centering on creative modern American cooking in such entrees as rack of lamb and regional fish. The atmosphere is upbeat and jovial, making the restaurant a favorite for comfortable, relaxed dining. Dressy casual; cocktails. **Parking:** on-site. **Cards:** AX, MC, VI.

(🛢M) 🍸 ☒

ERIE

———— WHERE TO STAY ————

BEDFORD INN
(AAA) (SAVE)
♥♥ ♥♥
Motel

		Phone: (734)847-6768	
All Year	1P: $39	2P: $59	F12

Location: I-75, exit 210 (Alexis Rd exit in OH), 2 mi w, then 0.5 mi n on US 24. 6444 Telegraph Rd (US 24) 48133. Fax: 734/847-6768. **Facility:** 47 one-bedroom standard units, some with whirlpools. 1-2 stories (no elevator), interior corridors. **Parking:** on-site. **Terms:** 3 day cancellation notice-fee imposed, weekly rates available, [CP] meal plan available. **Amenities:** voice mail, irons, hair dryers. **Leisure Activities:** whirlpool, picnic area with grill. **Business Services:** fax (fee). **Cards:** AX, DC, DS, MC, VI.

SOME UNITS

🍴➕ (⚷) 🎦 (DATA PORT) 🖥 / ☒ (VCR) 🖥 🖼 /
FEE

ESCANABA pop. 13,140

———— WHERE TO STAY ————

BAY VIEW MOTEL
♥♥
Motel

			Phone: 906/786-2843	
6/1-9/15	1P: $47-$61	2P: $51-$61	XP: $5	F12
4/1-5/31	1P: $39-$51	2P: $41-$51	XP: $5	F12
9/16-3/31	1P: $37-$51	2P: $41-$51	XP: $5	F12

Location: 4.5 mi n on US 2/41 and SR 35. Located in a commercial area. 49829 (7110 Hwy 2, 41 & M-35, GLADSTONE, 49837). Fax: 906/786-8131. **Facility:** 22 one-bedroom standard units, some with whirlpools. 1-2 stories (no elevator), interior/exterior corridors. *Bath:* combo or shower only. **Parking:** on-site, winter plug-ins. **Terms:** 14 day cancellation notice. **Pool(s):** heated indoor. **Leisure Activities:** sauna, playground, basketball. **Cards:** AX, DS, MC, VI.

SOME UNITS

🍴➕ 🏊 ☒ 🎦 🖥 / ☒ 🖥 🖼 /

ECONO LODGE

Phone: (906)789-1066

AAA SAVE

6/1-9/30 [CP]	1P: $56-$69	2P: $61-$86	XP: $6	F18
10/1-3/31 [CP]	1P: $47-$57	2P: $52-$62	XP: $6	F18
4/1-5/31 [CP]	1P: $46-$56	2P: $51-$61	XP: $6	F18

Small-scale Hotel

Location: 0.5 mi n on US 2/41 and SR 35. Located next to the U.P. State Fairgrounds. 921 N Lincoln Rd 49829. Fax: 906/789-9202. **Facility:** 50 one-bedroom standard units. 2 stories (no elevator), interior corridors. **Parking:** on-site. **Terms:** 30 day cancellation notice. **Amenities:** hair dryers. **Leisure Activities:** sauna, whirlpool. **Business Services:** meeting rooms. **Cards:** AX, DC, DS, MC, VI. **Special Amenities:** free continental breakfast and free local telephone calls.

SOME UNITS

HIAWATHA MOTEL

Phone: (906)786-1341

AAA SAVE

5/1-9/30 [CP]	1P: $35-$40	2P: $50-$65	XP: $5	D16
4/1-4/30 & 10/1-3/31 [CP]	1P: $35-$40	2P: $45-$60	XP: $5	D16

Motel

Location: 0.5 mi w on US 2/41. Located in a commercial area. 2400 Ludington St 49829. Fax: 906/786-0828. **Facility:** 20 one-bedroom standard units, some with whirlpools. 1 story, exterior corridors. **Parking:** on-site. **Terms:** pets ($2 extra charge, in designated units). **Amenities:** video library (fee). **Cards:** AX, DS, MC, VI. **Special Amenities:** free continental breakfast and free local telephone calls.

SOME UNITS

FEE

TERRACE BAY INN BUDGET HOST

Phone: 906/786-7554

AAA SAVE

5/11-9/30	1P: $52-$58	2P: $63-$99	XP: $5	F16
4/1-5/10	1P: $36-$52	2P: $56-$69	XP: $5	F16
10/1-3/31	1P: $36-$50	2P: $50-$65	XP: $5	F16

Large-scale Hotel

Location: 4.6 mi n on US 2/41 and SR 35. Located in a quiet area. 7146 P Rd 49829 (PO Box 453). Fax: 906/786-7597. **Facility:** 71 one-bedroom standard units. 1-2 stories (no elevator), interior/exterior corridors. *Bath:* combo or shower only. **Parking:** on-site, winter plug-ins. **Dining:** 5 pm-9 pm; also 7-11 am 6/1-9/30, cocktails. **Pool(s):** heated indoor. **Leisure Activities:** sauna, whirlpool, boat ramp, fishing, snowmobiling. *Fee:* off-site golf privileges, game room. **Business Services:** meeting rooms. **Cards:** AX, DS, MC, VI. *(See color ad p 187)*

SOME UNITS

———— WHERE TO DINE ————

LOG CABIN SUPPER CLUB   **Lunch:** $5-$10   **Dinner:** $10-$20   **Phone:** 906/786-5621

Steak & Seafood

Location: 5.3 mi n on US 2. 7531 US 2 & 41 49837. **Hours:** 11 am-2 & 5-10 pm, Sun 4 pm-9 pm; close at 9 pm in winter. Closed: 7/4, 9/1, 12/25. **Features:** The charming log cabin is perched on a bluff overlooking the bay. Fresh fish, steak, pasta and ribs are representative of menu choices. The dessert tray entices with such eye-catching treats as chocolate decadence, cheesecake and key lime pie. Casual dress; cocktails. **Parking:** on-site. **Cards:** MC, VI.

THE STONEHOUSE   **Lunch:** $3-$9   **Dinner:** $6-$19   **Phone:** 906/786-5003

Steak & Seafood

Location: 0.3 mi n at jct US 2/41 and SR 35. 2223 Ludington St 49829. **Hours:** 10 am-2 & 5-9:30 pm, Fri & Sat 5 pm-10 pm. Closed major holidays; also Sun. **Features:** The cozy dining room is a casual, informal spot for enjoying thoughtful preparations of chicken, seafood and steak. The house specialty is succulent prime rib. Take time to check out the artwork and appreciate the attentive, efficient service. Casual dress; cocktails. **Parking:** on-site. **Cards:** AX, DC, DS, MC, VI.

FARMINGTON HILLS —See Detroit p. 255.

FENNVILLE pop. 1,459

———— WHERE TO STAY ————

THE KINGSLEY HOUSE   **Phone:** 269/561-6425

Bed & Breakfast

All Year [BP]   1P: $85-$200   2P: $85-$200

Location: I-196, exit 34, 5 mi e on SR 89. 626 W Main (M-89) 49408. Fax: 269/561-2593. **Facility:** This Victorian home was built in 1886 by the prominent Kingsley family; a Michigan historic site, it features a three-story turret. Smoke free premises. 8 one-bedroom standard units, some with whirlpools. 3 stories (no elevator), interior corridors. *Bath:* combo or shower only. **Parking:** on-site. **Terms:** check-in 4 pm, 2 night minimum stay - weekends 5/1-10/1, 10 day cancellation notice-fee imposed. **Amenities:** video library, hair dryers. *Some:* CD players. **Leisure Activities:** bicycles. **Cards:** AX, DS, MC, VI.

SOME UNITS

———— WHERE TO DINE ————

CRANE'S PIE PANTRY RESTAURANT   **Lunch:** $6-$10   **Dinner:** $8-$12   **Phone:** 269/561-2297

American

Location: I-196, exit 34 (M-89), 4 mi e. 6054 124th Ave (M-89) 49408. **Hours:** 9 am-7 pm, Sun from 11 am; 10 am-5 pm, Sun from 11 am, closed Mon 11/1-12/31; Sat & Sun only 11 am-5 pm 1/1-4/30. Closed major holidays. **Features:** Tucked at the back of the big "red barn," this popular restaurant serves freshly baked breads, seasonal fruit pies, fresh cider and hearty soups along with a section of hot or cold sandwiches. Casual dress. **Parking:** on-site. **Cards:** DS, MC, VI.

FENTON pop. 10,582

——— WHERE TO STAY ———

BEST WESTERN OF FENTON
AAA SAVE
◆◆◆◆◆
Motel

4/1-9/30	1P: $85-$150	2P: $85-$150	XP: $6	F12
10/1-3/31	1P: $73-$150	2P: $73-$150	XP: $6	F12

Phone: (810)750-1711

Location: US 23, exit 78 (Owen Rd). 3255 Owen Rd 48430. Fax: 810/750-9462. **Facility:** 82 units. 80 one-bedroom standard units, some with whirlpools. 2 one-bedroom suites, some with whirlpools. 2 stories, exterior corridors. **Parking:** on-site. **Terms:** cancellation fee imposed, [ECP] meal plan available. **Amenities:** video library, irons, hair dryers. **Pool(s):** heated indoor. **Guest Services:** coin laundry. **Business Services:** meeting rooms. **Cards:** AX, DC, DS, MC, VI. **Special Amenities:** free continental breakfast and free newspaper.

SOME UNITS
🅂🄳 🍴 🛟 📹 DATAPORT 🖨 💻 / ✕ 📼 📷 /
FEE

HOLIDAY INN EXPRESS HOTEL & SUITES
◆◆◆◆◆
Small-scale Hotel

5/16-9/15 [ECP]	1P: $90-$100	2P: $90-$100	XP: $10	F18
4/1-5/15 & 9/16-3/31 [ECP]	1P: $80-$100	2P: $80-$100	XP: $10	F18

Phone: (810)714-7171

Location: US 23, exit 78 (Owen Rd), just w, then 1 mi n. Located across from a shopping mall. 17800 Silver Pkwy 48430. Fax: 810/714-3402. **Facility:** 69 one-bedroom standard units, some with whirlpools. 2 stories, interior corridors. *Bath:* combo or shower only. **Parking:** on-site. **Terms:** small pets only. **Amenities:** dual phone lines, voice mail, irons, hair dryers. **Pool(s):** heated indoor. **Leisure Activities:** whirlpool, exercise room. **Guest Services:** valet and coin laundry. **Business Services:** meeting rooms. **Cards:** AX, CB, DC, DS, JC, MC, VI.

SOME UNITS
ASK 🅂🄳 🛏 🍴 🔊M ♿ 🛟 📹 DATAPORT 🖨 📷 💻 / ✕ /

——— WHERE TO DINE ———

THE FENTON HOTEL
AAA
◆◆ ◆◆
American

Lunch: $8-$12   **Dinner:** $10-$15   **Phone:** 810/750-9463
Location: US 23, exit 78 (Owen Rd), 1.1 mi e on Silver Lake Rd, just n. 302 N Leroy St 48430. **Hours:** 11:30 am-10 pm, Fri-11 pm, Sat 4 pm-11 pm. Closed major holidays; also Sun. **Reservations:** accepted. **Features:** Allegedly haunted by two ghosts, one of which occasionally orders a drink at the bar, the Fenton Hotel is a charming Victorian style restaurant with a hint of intrigue. Casual dress; cocktails. **Parking:** on-site.
🍽 ✕

FERNDALE —See Detroit p. 256.

FERRYSBURG pop. 3,040

——— WHERE TO DINE ———

ARBOREAL INN
◆◆ ◆◆
Steak & Seafood

Dinner: $15-$53   **Phone:** 616/842-3800
Location: 1 mi n from US 31, exit Van Wagoner Rd W, 0.3 mi n on 174th Ave. 18191 Old Grand Haven Rd 49456. **Hours:** 5 pm-10 pm. Closed major holidays; also Sun. **Reservations:** suggested; weekends. **Features:** Established in 1981, the cozy, moderately upscale restaurant is a favorite of the local crowd. There are several dining areas, including one with a warm, intimate fireplace. An extensive selection of wine accompanies choices on the diverse menu. Cocktails. **Parking:** on-site. **Cards:** AX, DS, MC, VI.
✕

FLAT ROCK —See Detroit p. 257.

FLINT pop. 124,943

——— WHERE TO STAY ———

AMERICINN FLINT
AAA SAVE
◆◆ ◆◆
Small-scale Hotel

All Year   1P: $79-$149   **Phone:** 810/233-9000
Location: US 23 and Hill Rd, exit 90; I-75 N, exit 475 to Hill Rd. 6075 Hill 23 Dr 48507 (2100 W Wackerly St, MIDLAND, 48640). Fax: 810/233-5286. **Facility:** 72 one-bedroom standard units, some with whirlpools. 3 stories, interior corridors. *Bath:* combo or shower only. **Parking:** on-site. **Terms:** [BP], [CP] & [ECP] meal plans available, small pets only. **Amenities:** voice mail, hair dryers. **Pool(s):** heated indoor. **Leisure Activities:** sauna, whirlpool. *Fee:* game room. **Business Services:** meeting rooms. **Cards:** AX, DC, DS, MC, VI. **Special Amenities:** free continental breakfast and free local telephone calls. *(See color ad p 201 & p 289)*

SOME UNITS
🅂🄳 🛏 🛟 ✕ 📹 DATAPORT 💻 / ✕ 🖨 📷

BAYMONT INN & SUITES-FLINT
AAA SAVE
◆◆ ◆◆
Small-scale Hotel

All Year [ECP]   1P: $50-$89   2P: $50-$89   XP: $10   F17
Phone: (810)732-2300
Location: I-75, exit 122, just w on Pierson Rd. 4160 Pier North Blvd 48504. Fax: 810/732-9777. **Facility:** 87 units. 84 one-bedroom standard units, some with kitchens and/or whirlpools. 3 one-bedroom suites ($99-$199). 4 stories, interior corridors. *Bath:* combo or shower only. **Parking:** on-site. **Terms:** weekly rates available, package plans, small pets only ($10 extra charge). **Amenities:** video games, voice mail, irons, hair dryers. **Guest Services:** valet and coin laundry. **Cards:** AX, CB, DC, DS, JC, MC, VI. **Special Amenities:** free continental breakfast and free newspaper.

SOME UNITS
🅂🄳 🛏 🍴 📹 DATAPORT 💻 / ✕ 🖨 📷

COMFORT INN

Small-scale Hotel

Phone: (810)232-4222
All Year [ECP]   1P: $69-$149   2P: $69-$149   XP: $10   F18
Location: I-75, exit 117B northbound; exit 117 southbound (Miller Rd). 2361 Austins Pkwy 48507. Fax: 810/232-9625.
Facility: 79 one-bedroom standard units, some with whirlpools. 2 stories, interior corridors. **Parking:** on-site.
Amenities: voice mail. *Some:* irons, hair dryers. **Pool(s):** heated indoor. **Leisure Activities:** whirlpool, exercise room. **Guest Services:** valet and coin laundry. **Business Services:** meeting rooms. **Cards:** AX, CB, DC, DS, JC, MC, VI.

SOME UNITS

COURTYARD BY MARRIOTT

Small-scale Hotel

Phone: (810)232-3500
All Year   1P: $69-$149   2P: $69-$149
Location: US 23, exit 90, just e on Hill Rd; adjacent to Holiday Inn. 5205 Gateway Center 48507. Fax: 810/232-7373.
Facility: 102 units. 99 one-bedroom standard units, some with whirlpools. 3 one-bedroom suites. 3 stories, interior corridors. *Bath:* combo or shower only. **Parking:** on-site. **Terms:** cancellation fee imposed, [BP] meal plan available, package plans. **Amenities:** dual phone lines, voice mail, irons, hair dryers. **Dining:** 6-10 am, Sat & Sun 7-11 am. **Pool(s):** small heated indoor. **Leisure Activities:** whirlpool, exercise room. **Guest Services:** valet and coin laundry. **Business Services:** meeting rooms, fax. **Cards:** AX, DC, DS, MC, VI.

SOME UNITS

HOLIDAY INN EXPRESS   Phone: (810)238-7744

(AAA) [SAVE] All Year [ECP]   2P: $69-$75

Small-scale Hotel

Location: I-475, exit 8A. 1150 Robert T Longway Blvd 48503. Fax: 810/233-7444. **Facility:** 124 one-bedroom standard units, some with whirlpools. 5 stories, interior corridors. **Parking:** on-site. **Terms:** [CP] meal plan available, small pets only ($25 extra charge). **Amenities:** dual phone lines, voice mail, safes, irons, hair dryers. **Guest Services:** valet and coin laundry, airport transportation-Bishop Airport, area transportation-within 5 mi. **Business Services:** meeting rooms. **Cards:** AX, CB, DC, DS, MC, VI.

SOME UNITS

[S₀] [✦] [🐾] [¶¶+] [⊘] [++] [*] [DATA PORT] [💻] / [✗] [VCR] [🔌] [📷] /

HOLIDAY INN GATEWAY CENTRE   Phone: (810)232-5300

(AAA) [SAVE] All Year   1P: $109-$149   2P: $109-$149

Small-scale Hotel

Location: US 23, exit 90, just e on Hill Rd; jct I-75 N and 475, 1 mi n, then 2 mi w on Hill Rd. 5353 Gateway Centre 48507. Fax: 810/232-9806. **Facility:** 171 one-bedroom standard units. 4 stories, interior corridors. *Bath:* combo or shower only. **Parking:** on-site. **Terms:** [BP] meal plan available. **Amenities:** video games (fee), dual phone lines, voice mail, irons, hair dryers. **Dining:** 6 am-10 pm, Fri-11 pm, Sat 7 am-11 pm, Sun from 7 am, cocktails. **Pool(s):** heated indoor. **Leisure Activities:** sauna, whirlpool, exercise room. *Fee:* game room. **Guest Services:** valet and coin laundry, area transportation. **Business Services:** conference facilities, business center. **Cards:** AX, CB, DC, DS, JC, MC, VI.

SOME UNITS

[S₀] [✦] [¶¶] [⊤] [⊘] [≈] [✗] [*] [DATA PORT] [💻] / [✗] [🔌] [📷] /

HOWARD JOHNSON LODGE   Phone: (810)733-5910

[◆]   5/1-9/30   1P: $50-$60   2P: $55-$65   XP: $5   F
      4/1-4/30   1P: $40-$50   2P: $45-$55   XP: $5   F
Motel 10/1-3/31   1P: $35-$45   2P: $40-$50   XP: $5   F

Location: I-75, exit 117 southbound; exit 117B northbound, just w. G-3277 Miller Rd 48507. Fax: 810/733-2713. **Facility:** 138 one-bedroom standard units, some with kitchens (no utensils) and/or whirlpools. 1 story, exterior corridors. **Parking:** on-site. **Terms:** weekly rates available, package plans, small pets only ($10 extra charge). **Amenities:** video library (fee). **Pool(s):** outdoor. **Guest Services:** coin laundry. **Cards:** AX, DS, MC, VI.

SOME UNITS

[ASK] [S₀] [🐾] [¶¶+] [≈] [*] [DATA PORT] [💻] / [✗] [VCR] [🔌] [📷] /
FEE

RAMADA INN & CONFERENCE CENTER   Phone: 810/732-0400

[▼▼▼] [▼▼▼] All Year [CP]   1P: $79-$99   2P: $79-$99   XP: $6   F18

Small-scale Hotel

Location: I-75, exit 122, just w. 4300 W Pierson Rd 48504. Fax: 810/732-2811. **Facility:** 190 one-bedroom standard units, some with whirlpools. 5 stories, interior corridors. **Parking:** on-site. **Terms:** check-in 4 pm, [ECP] meal plan available. **Amenities:** voice mail, safes, irons, hair dryers. **Pool(s):** heated indoor. **Leisure Activities:** whirlpool, exercise room. *Fee:* game room. **Guest Services:** valet and coin laundry. **Business Services:** conference facilities. **Cards:** AX, DC, DS, MC, VI. *(See color ad p 289)*

SOME UNITS

[ASK] [S₀] [✦] [¶¶] [≈] [✗] [*] [DATA PORT] [💻] / [✗] [🔌] [📷] /

RED ROOF INN-FLINT   Phone: (810)733-1660

(AAA) [SAVE] 5/24-9/7   1P: $46-$62   2P: $52-$68   XP: $6   F18
[▼▼▼] [▼▼▼] 4/1-5/23 & 9/8-3/31 1P: $39-$56   2P: $45-$62   XP: $6   F18

Motel

Location: I-75, exit 117B (Miller Rd), just w. G-3219 Miller Rd 48507. Fax: 810/733-6310. **Facility:** 107 one-bedroom standard units. 2 stories, exterior corridors. *Bath:* combo or shower only. **Parking:** on-site. **Terms:** small pets only. **Guest Services:** valet laundry. **Cards:** AX, CB, DC, DS, MC, VI. **Special Amenities:** free local telephone calls and free newspaper.

SOME UNITS

[🐾] [¶¶+] [♿] [⊘] [*] [DATA PORT] / [✗] [🔌] [📷] /

RESIDENCE INN   Phone: (810)424-7000

[SAVE]   All Year   1P: $103-$199   2P: $103-$199

[▼▼▼] [▼▼▼]

Small-scale Hotel

Location: US 23, exit 90 (Hill Rd), just e. 2202 W Hill Rd 48507. Fax: 810/424-9850. **Facility:** Smoke free premises. 87 units. 36 one-bedroom standard units, some with efficiencies or kitchens. 36 one- and 15 two-bedroom suites, some with efficiencies or kitchens. 3 stories, interior corridors. *Bath:* combo or shower only. **Parking:** on-site. **Terms:** [ECP] meal plan available, small pets only ($50 deposit, $10 extra charge). **Amenities:** dual phone lines, voice mail, irons, hair dryers. **Pool(s):** heated indoor. **Leisure Activities:** whirlpool, exercise room. **Guest Services:** valet and coin laundry. **Business Services:** meeting rooms. **Cards:** AX, DC, DS, MC, VI.

SOME UNITS

[S₀] [🐾] [⌂M] [♿] [≈] [*] [DATA PORT] [🔌] [📷] [💻] / [✗] /

SLEEP INN   Phone: (810)232-7777

[SAVE]   All Year [CP]   1P: $59-$89   2P: $59-$89   XP: $10   F18

[▼▼▼] [▼▼▼]

Small-scale Hotel

Location: I-75, exit 117B northbound; exit 117 southbound (Miller Rd). 2325 Austin Pkwy 48507. Fax: 810/232-9671. **Facility:** 60 one-bedroom standard units. 3 stories, interior corridors. *Bath:* combo or shower only. **Parking:** on-site. **Amenities:** voice mail, safes. *Some:* irons, hair dryers. **Pool(s):** heated indoor. **Leisure Activities:** whirlpool, exercise room. **Guest Services:** valet and coin laundry. **Business Services:** meeting rooms. **Cards:** AX, CB, DC, DS, JC, MC, VI.

SOME UNITS

[S₀] [¶¶+] [♿] [⊘] [≈] [*] [DATA PORT] / [✗] [💻] /

———— WHERE TO DINE ————

ITALIA GARDENS   **Lunch:** $8-$12   **Dinner:** $9-$16   Phone: 810/720-4112

[▼▼▼] [▼▼▼]

Italian

Location: Just w of jct I-75, exit 117 southbound; exit 117B northbound and Miller Rd. G-3273 Miller Rd 48507. **Hours:** 11 am-9 pm, Fri & Sat-10 pm, Sun noon-8 pm. Closed major holidays. **Features:** The small restaurant serves up many favorite entrees, such as spaghetti, ribs, manicotti and pizza. A modern Italian theme is evident in the casually upscale dining room, which is decorated with stone columns and candle-topped pedestal tables. Casual dress; beer & wine only. **Parking:** on-site. **Cards:** AX, DC, DS, MC, VI.

[✗]

MAKUCH RED ROOSTER
American
Lunch: $5-$6   **Dinner:** $18-$30   **Phone:** 810/742-9310
Location: 3.5 mi e at jct Davison Rd and Averill St; between Dort and Center rds. 3302 Davison Rd 48506. **Hours:** 11 am-9 pm, Sat from 5 pm. Closed major holidays; also Sun. **Reservations:** suggested; weekends. **Features:** The building may be small and unassuming, but the flavors are big and bold in innovative specialties prepared by the creative chef. Such dishes as the fruit, vegetable and salmon platter are colorful, fresh and tasty. Service is friendly and efficient. Casual dress; cocktails. **Parking:** on-site. **Cards:** MC, VI. ⊠

REDWOOD LODGE MESQUITE GRILL & BREW PUB
Steak & Seafood
Lunch: $9-$14   **Dinner:** $13-$38   **Phone:** 810/233-8000
Location: US 23, exit 90 (Hill Rd), just e on Hill Rd; jct I-75 N and 475, 1 mi n on I-475, 2 mi w on Hill Rd. 5304 Gateway Center Dr 48507. **Hours:** 11 am-midnight, Fri & Sat-1 am, Sun noon-10 pm. Closed: 1/1, 11/27, 12/25. **Features:** The warm hunting lodge theme of this micro-brewery sets the stage for a menu dedicated to mesquite grilled specialties including wild game, steak, seafood, and wood-fired pizza. Hand crafted beer and a relaxing cigar lounge add to your dining experience. Casual dress; cocktails. **Parking:** on-site. **Cards:** AX, DS, MC, VI. ♿Ⓜ 🍸 ⊠

SALVATORE SCALLOPINI
Italian
Lunch: $7-$8   **Dinner:** $9-$14   **Phone:** 810/732-1070
Location: I-75, exit 117 southbound; exit 117B northbound, just w. G-3227 Miller Rd 48507. **Hours:** 11 am-10 pm, Fri & Sat-11 pm, Sun noon-10 pm. Closed major holidays. **Features:** Popular and informal, the family-oriented restaurant delivers fresh and authentic entrees from a lengthy menu of traditional specialties. Seafood linguine is served piping hot with fresh mussels and squid. The wait staff is professional and friendly. Casual dress; cocktails. **Parking:** on-site. **Cards:** AX, DC, DS, MC, VI. ⊠

SHAP'S FAMILY RESTAURANT
American
Lunch: $4-$8   **Dinner:** $4-$8   **Phone:** 810/232-8677
Location: I-75, exit 90 (Hill Rd), 1 mi w. G-2520 W Hill Rd 48507. **Hours:** 24 hours. Closed major holidays. **Features:** You won't find anything fancy at this family-oriented dinner; what you will find is fast friendly service, good food and a smile on everyone's face. Casual dress. **Parking:** on-site. **Cards:** AX, DC, DS, MC, VI. ⊠

FOWLERVILLE pop. 2,972

——— **WHERE TO STAY** ———

BEST WESTERN FOWLERVILLE
Motel
Phone: 517/223-9165
Property failed to provide current rates
Location: I-96, exit 129, just n. 950 S Grand Ave 48836. **Fax:** 517/223-0497. **Facility:** 60 one-bedroom standard units. 2 stories (no elevator), exterior corridors. **Parking:** on-site. **Amenities:** voice mail, irons, hair dryers. **Pool(s):** heated indoor. **Guest Services:** coin laundry. **Business Services:** fax (fee). **Cards:** AX, CB, DC, DS, MC, VI.
SOME UNITS
🛏✦ 🏊 📹 🖥 🛗 📠 /⊠/

Hungry? Look for the

RED AAA Logo

*N*ext time you look through a AAA TourBook® guide in search of a place to dine, take note of the bright red AAA logo just under a select group of restaurant names! These Official Appointment restaurants place a high value on the business they receive from dedicated AAA travelers.

As a member, you already turn to TourBooks for quality travel information. Now look for restaurants that display the bright red AAA logo in their listing for dining experiences you'll long remember!

FRANKENMUTH pop. 4,838

—— WHERE TO STAY ——

BAVARIAN INN LODGE

Phone: 989/652-7200

[AAA] [SAVE]
♦♦♦♦

Resort
Large-scale Hotel

6/27-10/4	1P: $128-$173	2P: $133-$178
10/5-12/31	1P: $115-$173	2P: $120-$178
1/1-3/31	1P: $94-$173	2P: $99-$178
4/1-6/26	1P: $105-$170	2P: $110-$175

Location: Just e across covered bridge. 1 Covered Bridge Ln 48734. Fax: 989/652-6711. **Facility:** This riverfront lodge is on expansive grounds. 355 units. 344 one-bedroom standard units, some with whirlpools. 11 one-bedroom suites ($143-$265). 5 stories, interior corridors. *Bath:* combo or shower only. **Parking:** on-site, winter plug-ins. **Terms:** cancellation fee imposed. **Amenities:** dual phone lines, voice mail, irons, hair dryers. **Dining:** 2 restaurants, 7 am-11 pm; to midnight in season, cocktails, entertainment. **Pool(s):** 5 heated indoor. **Leisure Activities:** whirlpools, 4 tennis courts (2 lighted), exercise room, basketball. *Fee:* expanded family fun center includes 18-hole indoor mini-golf course, game room. **Guest Services:** gift shop, airport transportation (fee)-Maitland Bay Saginaw and Bishop airports, area transportation-within 0.3 mi. **Business Services:** conference facilities. **Cards:** AX, DS, MC, VI. *(See color ad below)*

SOME UNITS

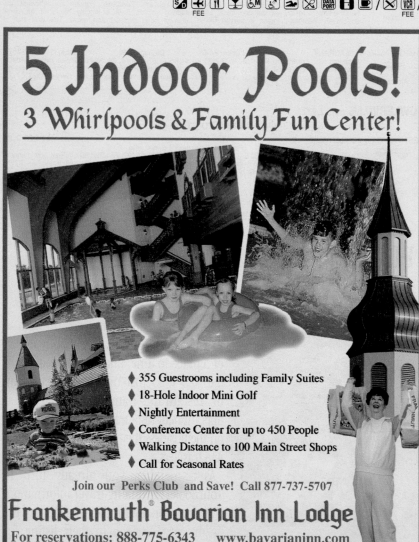

DRURY INN & SUITES

Phone: (989)652-2800

AAA SAVE

11/1-3/31 [ECP]	1P: $83-$121	2P: $93-$131	XP: $10	F18
4/1-10/31 [ECP]	1P: $80-$118	2P: $90-$128	XP: $10	F18

Small-scale Hotel

Location: On SR 83; center of downtown. 260 S Main St 48734. Fax: 989/652-2800. **Facility:** 78 one-bedroom standard units. 5 stories, interior corridors. *Bath:* combo or shower only. **Parking:** on-site, winter plug-ins. **Terms:** check-in 4 pm, small pets only. **Amenities:** irons, hair dryers. **Pool(s):** heated indoor. **Leisure Activities:** whirlpool. **Guest Services:** complimentary evening beverages: Mon-Thurs. **Business Services:** meeting rooms. **Cards:** AX, CB, DC, DS, MC, VI. **Special Amenities:** free continental breakfast and free local telephone calls.

SOME UNITS

FAIRFIELD INN

Phone: (989)652-5000

SAVE

7/1-12/31	1P: $79-$139	2P: $79-$139
4/1-6/30 & 1/1-3/31	1P: $59-$139	2P: $59-$139

Small-scale Hotel

Location: On SR 83; center of downtown. 430 S Main St 48734. Fax: 989/652-0327. **Facility:** 63 one-bedroom standard units, some with whirlpools. 3 stories, interior corridors. *Bath:* combo or shower only. **Parking:** on-site. **Terms:** [ECP] meal plan available. **Amenities:** irons, hair dryers. **Pool(s):** heated indoor. **Leisure Activities:** whirlpool, exercise room. **Guest Services:** valet laundry. **Cards:** AX, DC, DS, MC, VI.

SOME UNITS

FRANKENMUTH MOTEL

Phone: (989)652-6171

AAA SAVE

6/2-10/11	1P: $69-$89	2P: $79-$95
4/1-6/1 & 10/12-12/31	1P: $59-$69	2P: $59-$89
1/1-3/31	1P: $49-$69	2P: $59-$89

Motel

Location: E on SR 83. 1218 Weiss St 48734. Fax: 989/652-4538. **Facility:** 54 one-bedroom standard units. 1 story, exterior corridors. *Bath:* combo or shower only. **Parking:** on-site, winter plug-ins. **Terms:** weekly rates available. **Leisure Activities:** horseshoes. **Guest Services:** gift shop. **Cards:** AX, DS, MC, VI. **Special Amenities:** free local telephone calls and free room upgrade (subject to availability with advanced reservations). *(See ad below)*

SOME UNITS

SPRINGHILL SUITES BY MARRIOTT

Phone: (989)652-7500

SAVE

7/1-12/31	1P: $99-$139	2P: $99-$139
4/1-6/30	1P: $89-$129	2P: $89-$129
1/1-3/31	1P: $79-$129	2P: $79-$129

Small-scale Hotel

Location: On SR 83; center. 530 S Main St 48734 (430 S Main St). Fax: 989/652-3683. **Facility:** 64 one-bedroom standard units, some with whirlpools. 3 stories, interior corridors. *Bath:* combo or shower only. **Parking:** on-site. **Terms:** [ECP] meal plan available. **Amenities:** video games, dual phone lines, voice mail, irons, hair dryers. **Pool(s):** heated indoor. **Leisure Activities:** whirlpool, exercise room. *Fee:* game room. **Guest Services:** coin laundry. **Business Services:** meeting rooms. **Cards:** AX, DC, DS, JC, MC, VI.

SOME UNITS

ZEHNDER'S BAVARIAN HAUS

Phone: (989)652-0470

(AAA) (SAVE)

| | 7/1-10/31 | 1P: $69-$129 | 2P: $69-$129 |
| | 4/1-6/30 & 11/1-3/31 | 1P: $59-$119 | 2P: $59-$119 |

▼▼▼▼ **Location:** 0.5 mi s on SR 83. 1365 S Main St 48734 (PO Box 263). Fax: 989/652-9777. **Facility:** 137 units. 133 one-bedroom standard units. 4 one-bedroom suites ($129-$209) with whirlpools. 2 stories, interior/exterior corridors.

Small-scale Hotel **Parking:** on-site. **Terms:** check-in 4 pm, 1-2 night minimum stay - weekends, package plans. **Amenities:** irons, hair dryers. **Dining:** 7-10:30 am. **Pool(s):** heated outdoor, heated indoor. **Leisure Activities:** sauna, whirlpools, exercise room. *Fee:* golf-18 holes, game room. **Guest Services:** valet laundry. **Business Services:** meeting rooms. **Cards:** AX, DS, MC, VI. **Special Amenities:** early check-in/late check-out and free local telephone calls. *(See color ad below)*

SOME UNITS

[S/D] [†¶] [🏊] [✕] [🎮] [💻] / [✕] [DATA PORT] [☎]/ FEE

————— **WHERE TO DINE** —————

BAVARIAN INN RESTAURANT　　　　Lunch: $6-$9　　　　Dinner: $12-$20　　　　Phone: 989/652-9941
(AAA)
♦♦♦ ♦♦♦
German
Location: On SR 83. 713 S Main St 48734. **Hours:** 11 am-9:30 pm. **Reservations:** suggested. **Features:** A dozen German-themed dining rooms are decorated with hand-painted murals, steins and other Bavarian decor. The menu lists a good selection of American comfort foods—such as chicken, mashed potatoes and applesauce—as well as German entrees. Casual dress; cocktails. **Parking:** on-site. **Cards:** AX, DS, MC, VI. *(See color ad p 294)*　　　　　　　　　　　　　　　　　　　　　　　　　　　　　□Y□ □X□

ZEHNDER'S　　　　　　　　　　　Lunch: $6-$10　　　　Dinner: $14-$19　　　　Phone: 989/652-9925
(AAA)
♦♦♦ ♦♦♦
American
Location: On SR 83. 730 S Main St 48734. **Hours:** 11 am-9:30 pm. Closed: 12/24 for dinner. **Features:** One of America's largest family restaurants. This popular, well established restaurant has a very good selection of main dishes. Specializing in all-you-can-eat family-style chicken dinners. Zehnder's Marketplace and Z Chef's Cafe is open 8 am-9 pm daily. Casual dress; cocktails. **Parking:** on-site. **Cards:** DS, MC, VI.
(See color ad p 294)　　　　　　　　　　　　　　　　　　　　　　　　　　　　　　　　　　□Y□ □X□

————— *The following restaurants have not been evaluated by AAA* —————
but are listed for your information only.

FRANKEN ECK　　　　　　　　　　　　　　　　　　　　　　　　　　　　　Phone: 989/652-4586
[fyi]　　Not evaluated. **Location:** 100 S Main 48734. **Features:** Enjoy home-style German specialties at the pub-style eatery.

PEDALER'S EATERY　　　　　　　　　　　　　　　　　　　　　　　　　　Phone: 989/652-3070
[fyi]　　Not evaluated. **Location:** Center. 925 S Main St 48734. **Features:** Located in Frankenmuth River Place, serving a number of light meals, sandwiches, salads & pizza.

FREELAND pop. 5,147

————— **WHERE TO DINE** —————

RIVERSIDE FAMILY RESTAURANT　　　　Lunch: $2-$5　　　　Dinner: $5-$9　　　　Phone: 989/695-5563
♦♦♦
American
Location: 0.5 mi nw on SR 47. 8295 Midland Rd 48623. **Hours:** 6 am-9 pm. **Features:** Beside the Tittabawassee River, this casual restaurant offers up-close views of the water, woods and wildlife. Country-style decorations complement country-style cooking in such daily specials as meatloaf and pot roast. Save room for homemade pie. Casual dress. **Parking:** on-site. **Cards:** DS, MC, VI.　　　　　□X□

FREMONT pop. 4,224

————— **WHERE TO STAY** —————

THE HARRINGTON INN　　　　　　　　　　　　　　　　　　　　　　　Phone: (231)924-3083
♦♦♦ ♦♦♦
Small-scale Hotel
All Year　　　　　　　　　1P: $74-$139　　　　　　　　XP: $6　　　　　　　　F12
Location: 1 mi w on SR 82. 1117 W Main St 49412. Fax: 231/924-3772. **Facility:** 38 one-bedroom standard units, some with whirlpools. 1 story. interior corridors. **Parking:** on-site. **Terms:** [CP] meal plan available. **Amenities:** *Some:* hair dryers. **Pool(s):** heated outdoor. **Leisure Activities:** exercise room. **Guest Services:** valet laundry. **Business Services:** meeting rooms. **Cards:** AX, DS, MC, VI.
SOME UNITS
(ASK) (S□) (≈) (□) (DATA PORT) / (X) (□) /

GAYLORD pop. 3,681

————— **WHERE TO STAY** —————

BEST VALUE INN-ROYAL CREST MOTEL　　　　　　　　　　　　　　　Phone: (989)732-6451
(AAA) (SAVE)
♦♦♦ ♦♦♦
Small-scale Hotel
All Year [CP]　　　　　1P: $59-$99　　　　2P: $59-$99　　　　XP: $6　　　　　F17
Location: I-75, exit 279, 2.3 mi ne on I-75 business loop. Located in a quiet area. 803 S Otsego Ave 49735. Fax: 989/732-7634. **Facility:** 44 one-bedroom standard units. 2 stories (no elevator). interior corridors. **Parking:** on-site, winter plug-ins. **Terms:** 2 night minimum stay - 7/1-8/31, cancellation fee imposed. **Amenities:** irons, hair dryers. **Pool(s):** heated indoor. **Leisure Activities:** sauna, whirlpool, exercise room. **Fee:** game room. **Cards:** AX, CB, DC, DS, MC, VI. **Special Amenities:** free continental breakfast and free local telephone calls. *(See color ad below)*
SOME UNITS
(S□) (□) (□†) (≈) (X) (DATA PORT) (□) / (X) (□) (□) /

BEST WESTERN ALPINE LODGE

Phone: (989)732-2431

(AAA) [SAVE]

All Year   1P: $59-$99   2P: $69-$109   XP: $10   F16

Location: I-75, exit 282, 0.3 mi e on SR 32. Located in a commercial area. 833 W Main St 49735. Fax: 989/732-9640. **Facility:** 138 one-bedroom standard units. 2 stories (no elevator), interior/exterior corridors. **Parking:** on-site. **Terms:** 14 day cancellation notice-fee imposed, package plans, pets (in designated rooms).

Large-scale Hotel   **Amenities:** voice mail, safes (fee), irons, hair dryers. **Dining:** 7 am-10 pm, cocktails. **Pool(s):** heated indoor. **Leisure Activities:** sauna, whirlpool, snowmobiling, exercise room, indoor recreational area, pool table, shuffleboard. *Fee:* game room. **Guest Services:** coin laundry. **Business Services:** meeting rooms. **Cards:** AX, CB, DC, DS, MC, VI.

SOME UNITS

(icons) FEE FEE

DAYS INN

Phone: (989)732-2200

(AAA) [SAVE]

4/1-6/14 [ECP]   1P: $59-$82   2P: $69-$92   XP: $5   F17
6/15-3/31 [ECP]   1P: $57-$86   2P: $67-$89   XP: $5   F17

Location: I-75, exit 282, just w on SR 32. Located in commercial area. 1201 W Main St 49735 (PO Box 1370, 49734). Fax: 989/732-0300. **Facility:** 95 units. 94 one- and 1 two-bedroom standard units, some with whirlpools. 2

Small-scale Hotel   stories, interior corridors. **Parking:** on-site, winter plug-ins. **Terms:** package plans. **Amenities:** hair dryers. **Pool(s):** heated indoor. **Leisure Activities:** sauna, whirlpool, snowmobiling, exercise room. *Fee:* game room. **Guest Services:** coin laundry. **Business Services:** meeting rooms. **Cards:** AX, CB, DC, DS, MC, VI. **Special Amenities:** free continental breakfast and free local telephone calls. *(See color ad card insert)*

SOME UNITS

(icons)

DOWNTOWN MOTEL

Phone: (989)732-5010

(AAA) [SAVE]

All Year   1P: $36-$60   2P: $42-$70   XP: $4   F17

Location: I-75, exit 282, 0.5 mi e and 0.3 mi s on I-75 business route. Located in a commercial area. 208 S Otsego Ave

Motel   49735. **Facility:** 13 one-bedroom standard units. 2 stories (no elevator), exterior corridors. **Parking:** on-site. **Leisure Activities:** snowmobiling. **Special Amenities:** free continental breakfast and free local telephone calls.

SOME UNITS

(icons)

HAMPTON INN

Phone: 989/731-4000

(AAA) [SAVE]

All Year [ECP]   1P: $69-$149   2P: $69-$149

Location: I-75, exit 282, just w. Located in commercial area. 230 Dickerson Rd 49735. Fax: 989/731-4710. **Facility:** 83 one-bedroom standard units, some with whirlpools. 3 stories, interior corridors. *Bath:* combo or shower only. **Parking:** on-site. **Amenities:** dual phone lines, voice mail, irons, hair dryers. **Pool(s):** heated

Small-scale Hotel   indoor. **Leisure Activities:** whirlpool, snowmobiling, exercise room. *Fee:* game room. **Guest Services:** valet and coin laundry. **Business Services:** meeting rooms. **Cards:** AX, CB, DC, DS, MC, VI. **Special Amenities:** free continental breakfast and free local telephone calls.

SOME UNITS

(icons) FEE FEE

QUALITY INN

Phone: (989)732-7541

(AAA) [SAVE]

6/13-9/13   1P: $74-$139   2P: $84-$149   XP: $5   F18
4/1-6/12 & 9/14-3/31   1P: $59-$129   2P: $69-$139   XP: $5   F18

Location: I-75, exit 282, 0.3 mi e on SR 32. Located in a commercial area. 137 West St 49735. Fax: 989/732-0930. **Facility:** 117 one-bedroom standard units, some with whirlpools. 2 stories (no elevator), interior corridors.

Small-scale Hotel   **Parking:** on-site, winter plug-ins. **Terms:** 7 day cancellation notice-fee imposed, weekly rates available, [BP] meal plan available, package plans. **Amenities:** safes (fee), irons, hair dryers. **Dining:** 7 am-10 pm, cocktails. **Pool(s):** heated indoor. **Leisure Activities:** whirlpool, snowmobiling, exercise room. **Business Services:** meeting rooms. **Cards:** AX, DC, DS, JC, MC, VI. **Special Amenities:** free continental breakfast and free local telephone calls.

SOME UNITS

(icons) FEE

RED ROOF INN

Phone: (989)731-6331

(icons)

All Year   1P: $50   2P: $99   XP: $5   F18

Location: I-75, exit 282, just e on SR 32, then 0.4 mi s. Located in a commercial area. 510 S Wisconsin 49735.

Small-scale Hotel   Fax: 989/731-0190. **Facility:** 100 one-bedroom standard units. 2 stories (no elevator), interior corridors. *Bath:* combo or shower only. **Parking:** on-site. **Amenities:** video games, voice mail. **Pool(s):** heated indoor. **Leisure Activities:** snowmobiling. **Business Services:** meeting rooms.

SOME UNITS

(icons)

TIMBERLY MOTEL

Phone: 989/732-5166

(AAA) [SAVE]

All Year   1P: $38-$64   2P: $48-$88   XP: $6   F10

Location: I-75, exit 279, 2.5 mi n on I-75 business loop (Old US 27). Located in a commercial area. 881 S Otsego Ave 49735. Fax: 989/732-9189. **Facility:** 30 units. 28 one- and 2 two-bedroom standard units. 1-2 stories (no el-

Motel   evator), exterior corridors. **Parking:** on-site, winter plug-ins. **Terms:** 10 day cancellation notice-fee imposed, [ECP] meal plan available, pets ($6 extra charge, in smoking units). **Leisure Activities:** snowmobiling. **Cards:** AX, CB, DC, DS, MC, VI. **Special Amenities:** free continental breakfast and free local telephone calls.

SOME UNITS

(icons)

—— WHERE TO DINE ——

GOBBLERS FAMOUS TURKEY DINNER RESTAURANT   **Lunch:** $5-$7   **Dinner:** $7-$15   **Phone:** 989/732-9005
Location: I-75, exit 279 (Old US 27), 2 mi ne. 900 S Otsego 49735. Closed: 12/25-1/15. **Features:** Knickknacks and items from the past decorate the cozy dining room. The focus of the menu is on basic, wholesome food, such as turkey dinners, steak, ribs and seafood. Sandwiches, burgers and all-you-can-eat daily specials also are popular. Casual dress; cocktails. **Parking:** on-site. **Cards:** DS, MC, VI.

American

LA SENORITA   **Lunch:** $5-$7   **Dinner:** $7-$12   **Phone:** 989/732-1771
Location: I-75, exit 282, just e on SR 32. 737 W Main 49735. **Hours:** 11 am-10 pm, Fri & Sat-11 pm, Sun noon-10 pm; 11 am-11 pm, Fri & Sat-midnight 5/29-9/4. Closed: 4/20, 11/27, 12/25. **Features:** This family-friendly restaurant offers such traditional favorites as burritos, enchiladas and fajitas, as well as mesquite-grilled entrees served in a festive, lively atmosphere. Casual dress; cocktails. **Parking:** on-site.
Cards: AX, CB, DC, DS, MC, VI.

Mexican

SUGAR BOWL   **Lunch:** $3-$6   **Dinner:** $8-$19   **Phone:** 989/732-5524
Location: I-75, exit 282, 0.5 mi e on SR 32. 216 W Main St 49735. **Hours:** 7 am-11 pm, Sun-10 pm. Closed: 11/27, 12/25; also 3/28-4/9. **Features:** Established in 1919, the casual spot is one of Michigan's oldest family-owned restaurants. The menu includes Greek and American selections, with such popular choices as ribs, whitefish, perch and prime rib. Sink your teeth into homemade raspberry pie. Casual dress; cocktails. **Parking:** on-site. **Cards:** AX, DS, MC, VI.

American

GLADSTONE pop. 5,032

—— WHERE TO STAY ——

SHOREWOOD MOTEL   **Phone:** 906/428-9624

5/15-10/31	1P: $35-$40	2P: $46-$51	XP: $4 D12
4/1-5/14 & 11/1-3/31	1P: $25-$30	2P: $35-$45	XP: $4 D12

Location: US 41 N, exit Kipling; US 41 S, exit business district, 1 mi n. Located in a semi-residential area. 1226 N Lakeshore Dr 49837. **Facility:** 12 one-bedroom standard units. 1 story, exterior corridors. *Bath:* combo or shower only. **Parking:** on-site. **Terms:** 3 day cancellation notice. **Cards:** AX, DS, MC, VI.

Motel

SOME UNITS

GRAND BLANC

—— WHERE TO STAY ——

AMERIHOST INN-GRAND BLANC   **Phone:** (810)694-0000

All Year	1P: $69-$89	2P: $69-$89	XP: $6 F17

Location: I-75, exit 108 (Holly Rd). 9040 Holly Rd 48439. Fax: 810/694-0155. **Facility:** 60 one-bedroom standard units, some with whirlpools. 2 stories, interior corridors. *Bath:* combo or shower only. **Parking:** on-site. **Terms:** weekly rates available, [ECP] meal plan available. **Amenities:** dual phone lines, voice mail, safes (fee), irons, hair dryers. **Pool(s):** heated indoor. **Leisure Activities:** sauna, whirlpool, exercise room. **Guest Services:** valet laundry. **Business Services:** meeting rooms, fax. **Cards:** AX, CB, DC, DS, MC, VI.

Small-scale Hotel

SOME UNITS
FEE   FEE

WINGATE INN   **Phone:** (810)694-9900

All Year	1P: $95	2P: $95	XP: $10 F17

Location: I-475, exit 2, just e. 1359 Grand Pointe Ct 48439. Fax: 810/694-9902. **Facility:** 82 one-bedroom standard units, some with whirlpools. 3 stories, interior corridors. *Bath:* combo or shower only. **Parking:** on-site. **Terms:** cancellation fee imposed, [ECP] meal plan available. **Amenities:** video games, high-speed Internet, dual phone lines, voice mail, safes, irons, hair dryers. **Pool(s):** heated indoor. **Leisure Activities:** whirlpool, exercise room. **Guest Services:** valet and coin laundry, area transportation. **Business Services:** meeting rooms, business center. **Cards:** AX, CB, DC, DS, JC, MC, VI.

Small-scale Hotel

SOME UNITS

—— WHERE TO DINE ——

DA EDOARDO   **Lunch:** $6-$10   **Dinner:** $15-$25   **Phone:** 810/694-1300
Location: I-75, exit 108 (Holly Rd), 2 mi e. 8185 Holly Rd, Suite 7 48439. **Hours:** 11:30 am-10 pm, Fri-11 pm, Sat 2 pm-11 pm, Sun 2 pm-8 pm. Closed major holidays. **Reservations:** accepted. **Features:** With large picture windows overlooking a large reeded pond, it might be hard to remember that you are inside a tastefully upscale Italian restaurant rather than outside. Gnocchi with Bolognese sauce or chicken saltimbocca highlight a menu that features a wide selection of Italian favorites. Dressy casual; cocktails. **Parking:** on-site.
Cards: AX, DC, MC, VI.

Italian

KRUSE AND MUER   **Lunch:** $6-$10   **Dinner:** $8-$15   **Phone:** 810/603-2711
Location: I-75, exit 108 (Holly Rd), 2 mi e, just s; in Tile Grand Mall. 12793 S Saginaw 48439. **Hours:** 11 am-9 pm, Fri-10 pm, Sat noon-10 pm, Sun 12:30 pm-8:30 pm. Closed major holidays. **Reservations:** accepted. **Features:** A slightly upscale atmosphere sets the stage for a good variety of seafood specialities such as lobster and shrimp in saffron sauce or mahi mahi and other daily specials. Dressy casual; cocktails.
Parking: on-site. **Cards:** AX, DC, MC, VI.

American

GRAND HAVEN pop. 11,168

——— WHERE TO STAY ———

BEST WESTERN BEACON INN
Phone: (616)842-4720

SAVE

6/23-9/3	1P: $120	2P: $140	XP: $4 F12
5/1-6/22 & 9/4-3/31	1P: $90	2P: $110	XP: $4 F12
4/1-4/30	1P: $80	2P: $110	XP: $4 F12

Small-scale Hotel **Location:** 1.5 mi s on US 31. Located in a commercial area. 1525 S Beacon Blvd 49417. Fax: 616/847-7821. **Facility:** 107 one-bedroom standard units, some with whirlpools. 1-3 stories, interior/exterior corridors. *Bath:* combo or shower only. **Parking:** on-site. **Amenities:** voice mail, irons, hair dryers. **Pool(s):** heated indoor. **Leisure Activities:** whirlpool. **Guest Services:** valet laundry. **Business Services:** meeting rooms. **Cards:** AX, CB, DC, DS, MC, VI.

SOME UNITS

DAYS INN
Phone: (616)842-1999

SAVE

4/1-9/10 [CP]	1P: $85-$149	2P: $85-$149
9/11-3/31 [CP]	1P: $65-$99	2P: $65-$99

Small-scale Hotel **Location:** 1.5 mi s on US 31. Located in a commercial area. 1500 S Beacon Blvd 49417. Fax: 616/842-3892. **Facility:** 100 one-bedroom standard units. 2 stories (no elevator), interior corridors. **Parking:** on-site. **Terms:** check-in 4 pm. **Amenities:** voice mail, hair dryers. *Some:* irons. **Pool(s):** heated indoor. **Leisure Activities:** whirlpool. *Fee:* game room. **Guest Services:** valet and coin laundry. **Business Services:** meeting rooms. **Cards:** AX, CB, DC, DS, MC, VI./tq;rr *(See color ad card insert)*

SOME UNITS

HARBOR HOUSE INN
Phone: 616/846-0610

5/23-9/1 [ECP]	1P: $150-$190	2P: $150-$190 XP: $25
4/1-5/22 & 9/2-10/31 [ECP]	1P: $95-$170	2P: $95-$170 XP: $25
11/1-3/31 [ECP]	1P: $95-$155	2P: $95-$155 XP: $25

Bed & Breakfast **Location:** Corner of Harbor Dr and Clinton. 114 S Harbor Dr 49417. Fax: 616/846-0530. **Facility:** This attractive, modern Victorian style house is located across from the water, and is just steps from downtown stores. Smoke free premises. 17 units. 16 one-bedroom standard units, some with whirlpools. *Some:* whirlpools. 1 cottage ($145-$210) with whirlpool. 3 stories (no elevator), interior corridors. **Parking:** on-site. **Terms:** check-in 4 pm, 2 night minimum stay - weekends 5/26-9/30, age restrictions may apply, 7 day cancellation notice-fee imposed. **Amenities:** video library, voice mail. **Cards:** AX, MC, VI.

SOME UNITS

——— WHERE TO DINE ———

KIRBY GRILL
Lunch: $6-$11   **Dinner:** $8-$20   **Phone:** 616/846-3299

American **Location:** 0.7 mi w of US 31. 2 Washington St 49417. **Hours:** 11:30 am-10 pm, Fri & Sat-11 pm, Sun-9 pm. **Reservations:** accepted. **Features:** Old pictures and advertisements hang on the walls of the 1873 building, in the heart of downtown. Such specialties as white chili and fresh fish and lobster are favorites. Homemade cheesecakes, such as raspberry chocolate black bottom, are sinful. Casual dress; cocktails. **Parking:** street. **Cards:** AX, MC, VI.

THE STABLE INN
Lunch: $4-$6   **Dinner:** $10-$16   **Phone:** 616/846-8581

Steak & Seafood **Location:** 5 mi s on US 31. 11880 US 31 49417. **Hours:** 11 am-10 pm. Closed major holidays; also Sun. **Features:** Chicken Monterey, beer-battered shrimp and the 10-ounce ribeye are representative of menu selections. The decor is Western, with plenty of American Indian accents. The large, open dining room is inviting to families. Service is friendly and prompt. Casual dress; cocktails. **Parking:** on-site. **Cards:** DS, MC, VI.

GRAND MARAIS

——— WHERE TO STAY ———

ALVERSON MOTEL
Phone: 906/494-2681

Motel | All Year | 1P: $65 | 2P: $70 | XP: $5 F

Location: Just e of SR 77. Randolph Rd 49839 (PO Box 188). **Facility:** 15 one-bedroom standard units. 2 stories (no elevator), exterior corridors. **Parking:** on-site. **Terms:** 7 day cancellation notice. **Leisure Activities:** snowmobiling. **Cards:** MC, VI.

SOME UNITS

VOYAGEUR'S MOTEL
Phone: 906/494-2389

Motel | All Year | | 2P: $68 | XP: $20 F12

Location: 0.5 mi e of SR 77. Located in a quiet area. E Wilson St 49839 (PO Box 239). **Facility:** 10 one-bedroom standard units. 2 stories (no elevator), exterior corridors. **Parking:** on-site. **Terms:** cancellation fee imposed, small pets only. **Leisure Activities:** sauna, whirlpool, snowmobiling. **Cards:** DS, MC, VI.

SOME UNITS

——— WHERE TO DINE ———

The following restaurant has not been evaluated by AAA but is listed for your information only.

LAKE SUPERIOR BREWING COMPANY
Phone: 906/494-2337

[fyi] Not evaluated. **Location:** Lake Ave 49839. **Features:** Popular with families visiting the area, the downtown brew pub offers a number of American dishes and snacks.

GRAND RAPIDS pop. 197,800—

See also CASCADE, COMSTOCK PARK, GRANDVILLE, KENTWOOD, WALKER & WYOMING.

——— WHERE TO STAY ———

AMWAY GRAND PLAZA HOTEL

Phone: (616)774-2000

All Year   1P: $119-$189   2P: $119-$189   XP: $15   F18

Location: Pearl St at Monroe Ave; from US 131, exit Pearl St; center. 187 Monroe Ave NW 49502. Fax: 616/776-6489. **Facility:** The tower section of this service-oriented hotel features a number of rooms with views of the Grand River. 682 units. 650 one-bedroom standard units. 25 one- and 7 two-bedroom suites, some with whirlpools. 30 stories, interior corridors. *Bath:* combo or shower only. **Parking:** valet. **Terms:** cancellation fee imposed. **Amenities:** video games, voice mail, irons, hair dryers. *Some:* high-speed Internet, dual phone lines. **Dining:** 7 restaurants, 6:30 am-midnight, cocktails, also, The 1913 Room, Cygnus, see separate listing. **Pool(s):** heated indoor. **Leisure Activities:** saunas, whirlpool, 2 lighted tennis courts, racquetball courts, 1 squash court. *Fee:* tanning booth. **Guest Services:** gift shop, valet laundry, airport transportation (fee)-Gerald R Ford International Airport, area transportation. **Business Services:** conference facilities, business center. **Cards:** AX, DC, DS, MC, VI. *(See color ad below)*

Large-scale Hotel

COURTYARD BY MARRIOTT-DOWNTOWN

Phone: (616)242-6000

All Year   1P: $119-$129   2P: $124-$134

Location: Corner of Fulton St and Monroe Ave; center of downtown. 11 Monroe Ave NW 49503. Fax: 616/242-6605. **Facility:** 214 units. 209 one-bedroom standard units. 5 one-bedroom suites ($160-$185). 7 stories, interior corridors. *Bath:* combo or shower only. **Parking:** on-site. **Terms:** cancellation fee imposed. **Amenities:** dual phone lines, voice mail, irons, hair dryers. **Dining:** 6:30 am-10 & 11:30-2 pm, Sat & Sun 7 am-noon, cocktails. **Pool(s):** heated indoor. **Leisure Activities:** saunas, whirlpool, 2 lighted tennis courts, sports deck, exercise room, basketball. **Guest Services:** gift shop, valet and coin laundry. **Business Services:** meeting rooms. **Cards:** AX, CB, DC, DS, JC, MC, VI. **Special Amenities:** free newspaper.

Small-scale Hotel

SOME UNITS

DAYS INN-DOWNTOWN

Phone: 616/235-7611

All Year   1P: $73-$83   2P: $79-$89   XP: $7   F16

Location: US 131, exit Pearl St; downtown. 310 Pearl St NW 49504. Fax: 616/235-1995. **Facility:** 175 one-bedroom standard units. 8 stories, interior corridors. **Parking:** on-site. **Terms:** small pets only ($10 extra charge). **Amenities:** dual phone lines, voice mail, irons, hair dryers. **Pool(s):** heated indoor. **Leisure Activities:** whirlpool, limited exercise equipment. **Guest Services:** valet and coin laundry.
(See color ad card insert)

Large-scale Hotel

SOME UNITS

FAIRFIELD INN

Small-scale Hotel

All Year   1P: $60-$80   2P: $65-$85   **Phone:** (616)940-2700

Location: I-96, exit 43A (28th St SW), 1.5 mi w on SR 11, just n on E Paris, then just w. Located in an upscale office park. 3930 Stahl Dr SE 49546. Fax: 616/940-2700. **Facility:** 82 one-bedroom standard units. 3 stories, interior corridors. *Bath:* combo or shower only. **Parking:** on-site. **Terms:** [ECP] meal plan available. **Amenities:** voice mail, irons. **Pool(s):** heated indoor. **Leisure Activities:** whirlpool. **Guest Services:** valet laundry. **Cards:** AX, CB, DC, DS, MC, VI.

SOME UNITS

Best Western

the *Beauty* of the NORTH WOODS

Relax in the beauty of the north woods, at Kelly Inn and Suites of Holland. Enjoy all the amenities, including whirlpool and fireplace suites, fitness center, heated indoor pool, FREE continental breakfast and more.

Kelly Inn and Suites
2888 West Shore Drive
Holland, MI 49424
616-994-0400 • 800-528-1234
www.bestwestern.com/kellyinnandsuites
email: holland@kellyinns.com

COMFORT SUITES

Convenience *& Comfort*

Conveniently located 1/2 mile from RiverTown Crossings Mall, Comfort Suites offers 66 suites, including whirlpool or fireplace suites, with all the amenities. Enjoy our fitness center, heated indoor pool, FREE continental breakfast and more.

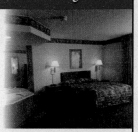

I-196 Exit 67, 44th Street,
4520 Kenowa Avenue SW
Grandville, MI 49418
616-667-0733 • 800-424-6423
www.choicehotels.com/hotel/mi169
email: grandville@kellyinns.com

Hampton Inn

1-616-956-9304
1-800-HAMPTON
Fax: 1-616-956-6617
www.brilyn.com

100% Satisfaction Guarantee

FREE • **Breakfast Bar**
 • **Local Calls**
 • **Kids Under 18 years**
• **Senior Discount**
• **Heated Outdoor Pool**
• **Non-Smoking Rooms**
• **In Room Movies**
• **TOUR BUSES WELCOME**

Exit #43A Off I-96, 4981 28th St. SE, Grand Rapids, Michigan 49512

Definitely **Quality Time**

4747 28th St., SE Grand Rapids, MI 49512
Mention AAA value rates to receive this discount
1-877-944-5866 or 1-800-HILTONS

Hilton
Grand Rapids Airport

$**89***

• Conveniently located 5 minutes from Gerald R. Ford Int'l. Airport • Complimentary airport shuttle service • Indoor pool, whirlpool, sauna, fitness room • In-room coffee makers and hair dryers
• Lodgenet On-command Movies and Nintendo
• Award winning restaurant and lounge, featuring live entertainment

It happens at the Hilton.

HOMEWOOD SUITES BY HILTON   **Phone:** 616/285-7100

Small-scale Hotel

All Year   1P: $84-$119   2P: $84-$119
Location: I-96, exit 43A (28th St SW), 1.5 mi w to E Paris Ave, then just n. Located in upscale office park. 3920 Stahl Dr SE 49546. Fax: 616/285-1505. **Facility:** 78 units. 71 one- and 7 two-bedroom suites with efficiencies. 3 stories, interior corridors. **Parking:** on-site. **Terms:** age restrictions may apply, [BP] meal plan available, pets ($80 extra charge). **Amenities:** voice mail, irons, hair dryers. **Pool(s):** heated indoor. **Leisure Activities:** whirlpool, exercise room. **Guest Services:** valet and coin laundry. **Business Services:** meeting rooms, business center. **Cards:** AX, DC, DS, MC, VI.

SOME UNITS

🔊📶 📶 📶 📶 📶 📶 📶 📶 📶 📶 /✕/

RADISSON HOTEL GRAND RAPIDS NORTH   **Phone:** (616)363-9001

(AAA) (SAVE)

Large-scale Hotel

All Year   1P: $89-$129
Location: US 131, exit 88, 1.8 mi n. 270 Ann St NW 49504. Fax: 616/363-0670. **Facility:** 164 one-bedroom standard units. 7 stories, interior corridors. **Parking:** on-site. **Amenities:** dual phone lines, voice mail, irons, hair dryers. **Dining:** 6:30 am-10 pm, Sat & Sun from 7 am, cocktails. **Pool(s):** heated indoor. **Leisure Activities:** sauna, whirlpool, exercise room. *Fee:* game room. **Guest Services:** valet and coin laundry. **Business Services:** meeting rooms. **Cards:** AX, CB, DC, DS, JC, MC, VI. *(See color ad p 241)*

SOME UNITS

📶 📶 📶 📶 📶 📶 📶 📶 /✕📶/

SPRINGHILL SUITES BY MARRIOTT   **Phone:** 616/785-1600
[fyi]   All Year   1P: $89-$139   2P: $99-$149
           Too new to rate, opening scheduled for October 2002. **Location:** I-96 and SR 37, exit Alpine Rd, just ne. Located
Small-scale Hotel in a commercial area. 250 N Center Dr 49544. Fax: 616/785-1601. **Amenities:** 76 units. **Cards:** AX, CB, DC, DS,
           MC, VI.

———— **WHERE TO DINE** ————

THE 1913 ROOM   **Lunch:** $9-$15   **Dinner:** $25-$38   **Phone:** 616/774-2000
(AAA)   **Location:** Pearl St at Monroe Ave; from US 131, exit Pearl St; center; in Amway Grand Plaza Hotel. 187 Monroe Ave
                        NW 49502. **Hours:** 11:30 am-2 & 5:30-10:30 pm, Fri & Sat from 5 pm. Closed: Sun.
                        Reservations: suggested. **Features:** Business professionals and couples frequent the elegant restaurant,
American   appointed in early 1900s decor. A number of exquisite dishes are offered, as are intriguing selections from
                        the chef's tasting menu. For dessert, savor the forbidden apple or rich Viennese chocolate cake. Dressy
                        casual; cocktails. **Parking:** on-site and valet. **Cards:** AX, CB, DC, DS, MC, VI. *(See color ad p 299)*

THE B.O.B. RESTAURANTS   **Lunch:** $5-$11   **Dinner:** $7-$30   **Phone:** 616/356-2000
                        Location: Across from Van Andel Arena; downtown. 20 Monroe Ave NW 49503. **Hours:** 11:30 am-11 pm, Sat from
                        4 pm. Closed: 1/1, 11/27, 12/25; also Sun. **Reservations:** accepted. **Features:** B.O.B. stands for "big old
American   building," in which several restaurants offering a cornucopia of food selections are housed. The location is
                        a hotbed for multifaceted entertainment. Casual dress; cocktails. **Parking:** street. **Cards:** AX, DS, MC, VI.

CHARLEY'S CRAB   **Lunch:** $7-$15   **Dinner:** $14-$25   **Phone:** 616/459-2500
                        Location: Jct US 131 and SR 45, exit 85. 63 Market St SW 49503. **Hours:** 11:30 am-10 pm, Fri-11 pm, Sat 4:30
                        pm-11 pm, Sun 10 am-2 & 4:30-9 pm. Closed major holidays. **Reservations:** suggested. **Features:** The
American   comfortable restaurant is known for creative preparations of fresh seafood, such as Maryland crab cakes
                        and Charley's bucket, which samples lobster, crab, mussels and clams. The eclectic decor includes items
from a mansion that was torn down. Casual dress; cocktails. **Parking:** on-site. **Cards:** AX, DC, DS, MC, VI.

CYGNUS   **Dinner:** $20-$30   **Phone:** 616/776-6425
(AAA)   **Location:** Pearl St at Monroe Ave; from US 131, exit Pearl St; center; in Amway Grand Plaza Hotel. Pearl St at
                        Monroe Ave 49502. **Hours:** 5:30 pm-10:30 pm, Sun 10:30 am-2 pm. Closed: Mon.
                        Reservations: suggested. **Features:** Enjoy great views from the 27th- and 28th-floor rooftop setting,
                        where you can dine and dance under the stars. Beautiful furnishings and fine tableware add to the
American   sophistication. Such specialties as Beefeater gin tomato soup are tasty and innovative. Semi-formal attire;
                        cocktails. **Parking:** on-site and valet. **Cards:** AX, CB, DC, DS, MC, VI. *(See color ad p 299)*

DUBA'S   **Lunch:** $8-$12   **Dinner:** $16-$23   **Phone:** 616/949-1011
                        Location: Jct I-96 and SR 37; E Beltline, exit 38. 420 E Beltline NE 49506. **Hours:** 11 am-10 pm, Fri & Sat-11
                        pm. Closed major holidays; also Sun. **Reservations:** suggested; weekends. **Features:** Since the late
American   1950s, the restaurant has been a local fixture for fine dining. Elegant table settings, with flowers and
                        candles, contribute to the sophistication. The menu centers on well-prepared prime rib and seafood, as
well as decadent desserts. Casual dress; cocktails. **Parking:** on-site. **Cards:** AX, MC, VI.

THE GREAT LAKES SHIPPING COMPANY   **Lunch:** $6-$8   **Dinner:** $10-$20   **Phone:** 616/949-9440
                        Location: At Breton Ave and Burton St; 3.8 mi e of US 131, exit 82A. 2455 Burton St SE 49546. **Hours:** 11:30 am-2
                        & 5-10 pm, Fri-11 pm, Sat from 5 pm. Closed major holidays; also Sun. **Reservations:** suggested;
Steak & Seafood   weekends. **Features:** Five fireplaces and nautical decorations give the restaurant a cozy, rustic flavor.
                        Menu specialties include prime rib, pan-fried walleye and filet tenderloin. Casual dress; cocktails. **Parking:**
on-site. **Cards:** AX, DS, MC, VI.

HUD'S ITALIAN EATERY   **Lunch:** $6-$9   **Dinner:** $7-$13   **Phone:** 616/942-5989
                        Location: I-96, exit 40, 0.5 mi e. 884 Forest Hill Ave SE 49546. **Hours:** 11 am-10 pm, Fri & Sat-11 pm; lunch
                        buffet 11 am-1 pm. **Features:** Brick-oven pizzas, homemade soup, salads and such pasta dishes as
Italian   five-cheese lasagna are among menu selections. The dining room is warm and intimate, and the
                        sports-themed bar is decorated with autographed memorabilia. Casual dress; cocktails. **Parking:** on-site.
Cards: AX, DC, DS, MC, VI.

SAN CHEZ, A TAPAS BISTRO   **Lunch:** $6-$12   **Dinner:** $6-$29   **Phone:** 616/774-8272
                        Location: Just e of Van Andel Arena; downtown. 38 W Fulton 49503. **Hours:** 11 am-10 pm, Fri-midnight, Sat
                        noon-midnight, Sun from 4 pm. Closed major holidays. **Features:** So many tapas, so little time. Guests
Spanish   can prepare their taste buds for an explosion of flavorful options in the lively, energetic bistro. The specialty
                        is tapas, available either hot or cold. Casual dress; cocktails. **Parking:** on-site (fee). **Cards:** AX, DC, DS,
MC, VI.

SAYFEE'S   **Lunch:** $5-$10   **Dinner:** $16-$29   **Phone:** 616/949-5750
                        Location: I-96, exit 43A, 2.5 mi w on SR 11, 0.3 mi n on SR 37, then 0.3 mi e; behind Eastbrook Shopping Mall. 3555
                        Lake Eastbrook Blvd 49546. **Hours:** 11 am-10 pm, Fri & Sat-11 pm. Closed: 12/25; also Sun.
American   **Reservations:** suggested. **Features:** A professional clientele frequents the elegant, upscale restaurant, a
                        local favorite for such entrees as steak Diane and Dover sole. Diners also may dance in the evenings from
Wednesday through Saturday. A large deck overlooks the sparkling water. Dressy casual; cocktails; entertainment. **Parking:**
on-site. **Cards:** AX, CB, DC, DS, MC, VI.

SCHNITZELBANK　　　**Lunch:** $5-$8　　　**Dinner:** $9-$18　　　**Phone:** 616/459-9527

AAA

▽▽▽ ▽▽▽

German

Location: Corner of Weathly SE and Jefferson Ave SE; downtown. 342 Jefferson Ave SE 49503. **Hours:** 11 am-8 pm, Fri-9 pm, Sat 4 pm-9 pm. Closed major holidays; also Sun. **Reservations:** suggested. **Features:** German music and mills painted in 1938 by the owner infuse the casual restaurant with Old World ambience. In addition to such specialties as schnitzels, red cabbage and potatoes, the menu lists American dishes. Save room for the wonderful apple strudel. Casual dress; cocktails. **Parking:** on-site. **Cards:** AX, DS, MC, VI.

The following restaurants have not been evaluated by AAA but are listed for your information only.

GIBSON'S　　　　　　　　　　　　　　　　　　　　　　　**Phone:** 616/774-8535

[fyi]　Not evaluated. **Location:** Just w of jct Fuller Ave and Lake Dr. 1033 Lake Dr SE 49506. **Features:** In the restored Wurzurg/Clark mansion, the restaurant treats guests to a fine-dining experience.

PIETRO'S RISTORANTE　　　　　　　　　　　　　　　　　**Phone:** 616/452-3228

[fyi]　Not evaluated. **Location:** Just n of SR 11, 1.5 mi w of SR 37. 2780 Birchcrest Dr 49506. **Features:** The restaurant is popular with families and couples looking for specialties such as veal Marsala and oven-baked pasta. The atmosphere is relaxed.

GRANDVILLE pop. 16,263—See also GRAND RAPIDS.

--- WHERE TO STAY ---

BEST WESTERN GRANDVILLAGE INN　　　　　　　　　**Phone:** 616/532-3222

SAVE

▽▽▽ ▽▽▽

Small-scale Hotel

All Year [CP]　　　1P: $79-$179　　　2P: $79-$179

Location: I-196, exit 69A. Located in a commercial area. 3425 Fairlane Ave 49418. Fax: 616/532-4959. **Facility:** 82 units. 75 one-bedroom standard units, some with whirlpools. 7 one-bedroom suites ($99-$199). 2 stories, interior corridors. **Terms:** weekly rates available, 10% service charge. **Parking:** on-site. **Amenities:** dual phone lines, voice mail, irons, hair dryers. **Pool(s):** heated indoor. **Leisure Activities:** whirlpool. Fee: game room. **Guest Services:** valet and coin laundry. **Business Services:** meeting rooms. **Cards:** AX, DC, DS, MC, VI.

SOME UNITS

COMFORT SUITES　　　　　　　　　　　　　　　　　**Phone:** (616)667-0733

AAA SAVE

▽▽▽ ▽▽▽

Small-scale Hotel

4/1-9/4 [ECP]　　　1P: $89-$139　　　2P: $89-$139
9/5-3/31 [ECP]　　　1P: $69-$129　　　2P: $69-$129

Location: I-196, exit 67, just sw. Located next to the Wal-Mart Shopping Center. 4520 Kenowa Ave SW 49418. Fax: 616/667-9375. **Facility:** 66 units. 64 one-bedroom standard units, some with whirlpools. 2 one-bedroom suites ($129-$159) with whirlpools. 3 stories, interior corridors. Bath: combo or shower only. **Parking:** on-site. **Amenities:** video games, voice mail, irons, hair dryers. **Pool(s):** heated indoor. **Leisure Activities:** whirlpool, exercise room. **Guest Services:** valet and coin laundry. **Business Services:** meeting rooms, business center. **Cards:** AX, CB, DC, DS, JC, MC, VI. **Special Amenities:** free continental breakfast and free local telephone calls. (See color ad p 301)

SOME UNITS

HOLIDAY INN EXPRESS　　　　　　　　　　　　　　　**Phone:** (616)532-0202

AAA SAVE

▽▽▽ ▽▽▽

Small-scale Hotel

4/1-9/1　　　　　1P: $89-$139
9/2-3/31　　　　1P: $89-$129

Location: I-196, exit 69A, just e to Fairlanes, then 0.4 mi s. Located in a semi-commercial area. 4651 36th St 49418. Fax: 616/257-3121. **Facility:** Smoke free premises. 78 units. 76 one-bedroom standard units, some with whirlpools. 2 one-bedroom suites. 3 stories, interior corridors. Bath: combo or shower only. **Parking:** on-site. **Terms:** [CP] meal plan available. **Amenities:** dual phone lines, voice mail, irons, hair dryers. **Pool(s):** heated indoor. **Leisure Activities:** whirlpool, sun deck, exercise room. **Guest Services:** valet and coin laundry. **Business Services:** meeting rooms. **Cards:** AX, DC, DS, MC, VI. **Special Amenities:** free continental breakfast and free local telephone calls.

SOME UNITS

LANDS INN SUITES　　　　　　　　　　　　　　　　**Phone:** (616)531-5263

▽▽▽ ▽▽▽

Small-scale Hotel

4/1-9/30 [ECP]　　　1P: $69-$79　　　2P: $69-$79
10/1-3/31 [ECP]　　　1P: $59-$69　　　2P: $59-$69

Location: I-196, exit 70, 0.5 mi e. 3825 28th St SW 49418. Fax: 616/531-5213. **Facility:** 89 units. 30 one- and 59 two-bedroom standard units, some with whirlpools. 3 stories, interior corridors. **Parking:** on-site. **Guest Services:** coin laundry. **Business Services:** meeting rooms. **Cards:** AX, DS, MC, VI.

SOME UNITS

RESIDENCE INN BY MARRIOTT GRAND RAPIDS WEST　　　**Phone:** 616/538-1100

SAVE

▽▽▽ ▽▽▽

Small-scale Hotel

All Year [ECP]　　　1P: $109-$149

Location: I-196, exit 67, 1.7 mi e. 3451 Rivertown Point Ct SW 49418. Fax: 616/538-6390. **Facility:** 90 units. 37 one-bedroom standard units, some with efficiencies or kitchens. 40 one- and 13 two-bedroom suites ($109-$149), some with efficiencies or kitchens. 3 stories, interior corridors. Bath: combo or shower only. **Parking:** on-site. **Terms:** cancellation fee imposed, [BP] meal plan available, pets ($125-$150 fee, $6 extra charge). **Amenities:** voice mail, irons, hair dryers. **Pool(s):** heated outdoor. **Leisure Activities:** whirlpool, exercise room, sports court, basketball, volleyball. **Guest Services:** valet and coin laundry. **Business Services:** meeting rooms. **Cards:** AX, CB, DC, DS, JC, MC, VI.

SOME UNITS

GRAYLING pop. 1,952

———— WHERE TO STAY ————

DAYS INN OF GRAYLING
`SAVE`
Small-scale Hotel
(See color ad card insert)

Phone: (989)344-0204

| | 6/1-9/20 [ECP] | 1P: $64-$85 | 2P: $69-$90 | XP: $5 | F17 |
| | 4/1-5/31 & 9/21-3/31 [ECP] | 1P: $54-$64 | 2P: $59-$69 | XP: $5 | F17 |

Location: I-75 business loop, 0.8 mi s. Located in a commercial area. 2556 I-75 Business Loop 49738. Fax: 989/344-9076. **Facility:** 65 one-bedroom standard units, some with whirlpools. 2 stories, interior corridors. **Parking:** on-site. **Amenities:** hair dryers. **Leisure Activities:** cross country skiing, snowmobiling. **Guest Services:** coin laundry. **Business Services:** meeting rooms. **Cards:** AX, CB, DC, DS, MC, VI.

SOME UNITS
`[S/D]` `[îl+]` `[▣]` `[🛏]` `/` `[✕]` `[DATA PORT]` `/`

HOLIDAY INN
`AAA` `SAVE`
Small-scale Hotel

Phone: (989)348-7611

	1/1-3/31	1P: $79-$120	2P: $79-$120	XP: $6	F19
	6/22-8/30	1P: $89-$119	2P: $89-$119	XP: $6	F19
	8/31-12/31	1P: $75-$104	2P: $75-$104	XP: $6	F19
	4/1-6/21	1P: $75-$95	2P: $75-$95	XP: $6	F19

Location: I-75 business loop, 0.8 mi s. 2650 S Business Loop 49738 (PO Box 473). Fax: 989/348-7984. **Facility:** 151 one-bedroom standard units, some with whirlpools. 2 stories (no elevator), interior/exterior corridors. *Bath:* combo or shower only. **Parking:** on-site. **Terms:** package plans. **Amenities:** voice mail, irons, hair dryers. **Dining:** 6 am-2 & 5-10 pm, cocktails, entertainment. **Pool(s):** heated indoor, wading. **Leisure Activities:** sauna, whirlpool, snowmobiling, ski shop, lighted cross country ski trails, domed recreation area, playground, exercise room, basketball, horseshoes, shuffleboard, volleyball, game room. *Fee:* ski equipment. **Business Services:** conference facilities. **Cards:** AX, CB, DC, DS, MC, VI. **Special Amenities:** early check-in/late check-out and free local telephone calls.

SOME UNITS
`[S/D]` `[🛏]` `[îl]` `[Y]` `[&M]` `[&]` `[🏊]` `[✕]` `[▣]` `[DATA PORT]` `[💻]` `/` `[✕]` `[VCR]` `[🛏]` `[▣]` `/`
FEE

NORTH COUNTRY LODGE
`AAA` `SAVE`
Motel

Phone: (989)348-8471

| | All Year | 1P: $54-$100 | 2P: $55-$170 | XP: $5 | F12 |

Location: 1 mi n. 617 N I-75 Business Loop 49738 (PO Box 290). Fax: 989/348-6114. **Facility:** 24 units. 23 one- and 1 two-bedroom standard units, some with efficiencies or kitchens. 1-2 stories (no elevator), exterior corridors. *Bath:* combo or shower only. **Parking:** on-site. **Terms:** pets (in designated units). **Amenities:** *Some:* hair dryers. **Leisure Activities:** snowmobiling, horseshoes. **Cards:** AX, CB, DC, MC, VI.

SOME UNITS
`[🛏]` `[💈]` `/` `[✕]` `[VCR]` `[🛏]` `[▣]` `/`

SUPER 8 MOTEL
`SAVE`
Small-scale Hotel

Phone: 989/348-8888

| | 5/23-9/1 | 1P: $60-$65 | 2P: $70-$75 | XP: $4 | F17 |
| | 4/1-5/22 & 9/2-3/31 | 1P: $48-$53 | 2P: $54-$59 | XP: $4 | F17 |

Location: I-75, exit 251. 5828 Nelson A Miles Pkwy 49738. Fax: 989/348-2030. **Facility:** 60 one-bedroom standard units, some with whirlpools. 2 stories (no elevator), interior corridors. **Parking:** on-site, winter plug-ins. **Terms:** [CP] meal plan available, pets ($50 deposit). **Pool(s):** heated indoor. **Leisure Activities:** whirlpool, snowmobiling, hiking trails. *Fee:* game room. **Guest Services:** coin laundry. **Cards:** AX, DC, DS, MC, VI.

SOME UNITS
`[ASK]` `[🛏]` `[💈]` `[🏊]` `[✕]` `[📺]` `[DATA PORT]` `/` `[✕]` `[🛏]` `/`

GREENBUSH

———— WHERE TO DINE ————

RED ROOSTER
`▼▼▼`
Italian

Lunch: $4-$6   Dinner: $8-$10   Phone: 989/739-7659

Location: On US 23, 1.8 mi s. 3228 S US 23 48738. **Hours:** 8 am-9 pm. **Features:** The dining room is homey and offers a view of Lake Huron. Selections of wholesome Italian cuisine are prepared with homemade pasta and sauces. Delicious cream pies melt in your mouth. Casual dress; cocktails. **Parking:** on-site. **Cards:** MC, VI.

`[✕]`

GREENVILLE pop. 7,935

———— WHERE TO DINE ————

HI-DELITE RESTAURANT
`AAA`
`▼▼▼`
American

Lunch: $5-$7   Dinner: $6-$12   Phone: 616/754-8249

Location: Just n on SR 91. 500 N Lafayette St 48838. **Hours:** 5:30 am-9 pm, Sun 8 am-2 pm. Closed major holidays. **Features:** The old-fashioned family restaurant is locally known for its hot beef plate and daily home-style specials. The warm, cozy dining room has an antique, country feel. Freshly baked breads, bread pudding and cream pies are mouthwatering treats. Casual dress. **Parking:** on-site. **Cards:** DS, MC, VI.

`[✕]`

GROSSE POINTE FARMS —See Detroit p. 257.

HANCOCK pop. 4,323

———— WHERE TO STAY ————

BEST WESTERN COPPER CROWN MOTEL
`SAVE`
`▼▼▼`
Small-scale Hotel

Phone: (906)482-6111

| | All Year | 1P: $55-$58 | 2P: $65-$68 | XP: $3 | F12 |

Location: On US 41 S; downtown. 235 Hancock Ave 49930. Fax: 906/482-0185. **Facility:** 46 one-bedroom standard units. 2 stories (no elevator), interior/exterior corridors. **Parking:** on-site, winter plug-ins. **Terms:** 7 day cancellation notice, [CP] meal plan available, small pets only (in limited units). **Amenities:** irons, hair dryers. **Pool(s):** heated indoor. **Leisure Activities:** saunas, whirlpool, snowmobiling. **Business Services:** meeting rooms. **Cards:** AX, DC, DS, MC, VI.

SOME UNITS
`[S/D]` `[🛏]` `[îl+]` `[🏊]` `[✕]` `[📺]` `[DATA PORT]` `[💻]` `/` `[✕]` `/`

RAMADA INN WATERFRONT

(AAA) (SAVE)

▽▽▽▽

Small-scale Hotel

Phone: (906)482-8400

7/1-10/31 & 12/12-3/31 [ECP]	1P: $80-$104	2P: $85-$109	XP: $5	F18
4/1-6/30 & 11/1-12/11 [ECP]	1P: $70-$94	2P: $75-$99	XP: $5	F18

Location: Off US 41, just nw of bridge. Located along the canal. 99 Navy St 49930. Fax: 906/482-8403. **Facility:** 51 one-bedroom standard units, some with whirlpools. 2 stories (no elevator), interior corridors. *Bath:* combo or shower only. **Parking:** on-site. **Amenities:** voice mail, irons, hair dryers. **Dining:** 11 am-10 pm, cocktails. **Pool(s):** heated indoor. **Leisure Activities:** sauna, whirlpool, snowmobiling. **Guest Services:** coin laundry. **Business Services:** meeting rooms. **Cards:** AX, DC, DS, MC, VI.

SOME UNITS

[icons]

HARBOR SPRINGS pop. 1,567

------- WHERE TO STAY -------

BEST WESTERN OF HARBOR SPRINGS

(AAA) (SAVE)

▽▽▽▽

Motel

Phone: (231)347-9050

All Year [CP]	1P: $68-$129	2P: $68-$129	XP: $10	F12

Location: 3 mi se on SR 119. Located in semi-rural area. 8514 M119 49740. Fax: 231/347-0837. **Facility:** 46 units. 42 one-bedroom standard units, some with whirlpools. 4 one-bedroom suites ($120-$210) with kitchens. 1 story, exterior corridors. **Parking:** on-site, winter plug-ins. **Terms:** 2-3 night minimum stay - seasonal, 3 day cancellation notice-fee imposed. **Amenities:** voice mail, irons, hair dryers. **Pool(s):** heated indoor. **Leisure Activities:** whirlpool, snowmobiling, playground. **Cards:** AX. **Special Amenities:** free continental breakfast. *(See color ad below)*

SOME UNITS

[icons]

------- WHERE TO DINE -------

THE NEW YORK RESTAURANT

▽▽▽▽

American

Dinner: $12-$24

Phone: 231/526-1904

Location: Just s of jct SR 119 and State St; center. 101 State St 49740. **Hours:** Open 5/1-3/31; 5 pm-10 pm. Closed: 11/27, 12/25. **Features:** Menu selections, such as Colorado lamb shank, Great Lakes whitefish, wolverine pork loin and petite filet of beef, are full in flavor and attractively presented. An antique bar and tin ceiling are charming characteristics of the 1904 building. Casual dress; cocktails. **Parking:** street.

Cards: AX, MC, VI.

[icon]

STAFFORD'S PIER RESTAURANT

▽▽▽▽

American

Lunch: $7-$15   **Dinner:** $18-$30

Phone: 231/526-6201

Location: Just s of jct SR 119 and State St; center. 102 Bay St 49740. **Hours:** 11:30 am-10 pm, Fri & Sat-11 pm. Closed: 12/25. **Reservations:** suggested. **Features:** Casual upscale dining overlooking marina; two favorites are the white fish and rack of lamb. Homemade style pie for dessert—don't forget the scoop of ice cream! Casual dress; cocktails. **Parking:** on-site. **Cards:** AX, DS, MC, VI.

[icons]

HARRISON (CLARE COUNTY)

———— WHERE TO STAY ————

THE CARRIAGE HOUSE INN
(AAA) [SAVE]
Bed & Breakfast

All Year [ECP]   1P: $60-$140   2P: $60-$140   XP: $15   F5
Phone: (989)539-1300
Location: 1 mi s from US 127, exit US 127 business route; 1.8 mi nw to Mostetler Rd/Grand Ave, then 0.3 mi nw. Located in a quiet area. 1515 Grant Ave 48625 (PO Box 757, HARRISON). Fax: 989/539-5661. **Facility:** On spacious grounds near Budd Lake, the inn offers rooms decorated with upscale antique furnishings. 10 one-bedroom standard units, some with whirlpools. 2 stories (no elevator), interior corridors. *Bath:* combo or shower only.
Parking: on-site, winter plug-ins. **Terms:** age restrictions may apply, [AP], [BP] & [CP] meal plans available, 15% service charge. **Amenities:** video library. **Leisure Activities:** sun deck, hiking trails. **Guest Services:** gift shop. **Business Services:** meeting rooms. **Cards:** AX, DS, MC, VI.

SOME UNITS
[S] [VCR] [▢] / [✕] [★] [🖥] /

SERENDIPITY BED & BREAKFAST INN
▼▼▼ ▼▼▼
Bed & Breakfast

All Year   1P: $75-$175   2P: $75-$175
Phone: 989/539-6602
Location: On SR 61, 2.2 mi w of US 127 business route. Located in a quiet area. 270 W M 61 48625 (PO Box 377, HARRISON). **Facility:** Smoke free premises. 4 one-bedroom standard units. 2 stories (no elevator), interior corridors. *Bath:* combo or shower only. **Parking:** on-site. **Terms:** age restrictions may apply, 7 day cancellation notice-fee imposed, [BP] & [ECP] meal plans available. **Amenities:** video library. **Leisure Activities:** whirlpool, cross country skiing, snowmobiling, hiking trails. **Cards:** AX, DS, MC, VI.

SOME UNITS
[ASK] [✕] [✕] [VCR] [☎] / [★] /

HART pop. 1,950

———— WHERE TO STAY ————

BUDGET HOST HART MOTEL
▼▼▼▼▼ ▼▼
Small-scale Hotel

7/1-9/5   1P: $69-$109   2P: $89-$119
4/1-6/30   1P: $59-$79   2P: $69-$89
9/6-3/31   1P: $39-$59   2P: $49-$69
Phone: (231)873-1855
Location: US 31, exit Mears/Hart, just e on US 31 business route. 4143 Polk Rd 49420. Fax: 231/873-1477. **Facility:** 20 one-bedroom standard units. 2 stories (no elevator), interior corridors. **Parking:** on-site. **Terms:** 7 day cancellation notice, small pets only ($20 deposit). **Cards:** DS, MC, VI. *(See color ad p 187)*

SOME UNITS
[ASK] [S] [🛏] [🐾] [DATA PORT] [▢] / [✕] /

COMFORT INN
(AAA) [SAVE]
▼▼▼ ▼▼▼
Small-scale Hotel

6/20-9/7   1P: $79-$165   2P: $89-$175   XP: $10   F18
5/30-6/19   1P: $69-$129   2P: $79-$139   XP: $10   F18
4/1-5/29 & 9/8-3/31   1P: $55-$99   2P: $65-$109   XP: $10   F18
Phone: (231)873-3456
Location: US 31, exit Mears/Hart, just e on US 31 business route. Located on a hill, back from the road. 2248 N Comfort Dr 49420. Fax: 231/873-2343. **Facility:** 61 one-bedroom standard units, some with whirlpools. 2 stories (no elevator), interior corridors. *Bath:* combo or shower only. **Parking:** on-site. **Terms:** [ECP] meal plan available, pets ($10 extra charge). **Amenities:** video library (fee). *Some:* irons, hair dryers. **Pool(s):** heated indoor. **Leisure Activities:** sauna, whirlpool, snowmobiling, tanning salon. *Fee:* bicycles. **Business Services:** meeting rooms. **Cards:** AX, DC, DS, JC, MC, VI. **Special Amenities:** free continental breakfast and free local telephone calls.

SOME UNITS
[S] [🛏] [🐾] [ᕤ] [▦] [✕] / [✕] [VCR] [DATA PORT] [🖥] /
FEE

HARTLAND

———— WHERE TO STAY ————

BEST WESTERN HARTLAND
(AAA) [SAVE]
▼▼▼ ▼▼▼
Motel

All Year   1P: $80-$125   2P: $88-$180   XP: $6   F12
Phone: (810)632-7177
Location: On SR 59, at jct US 23, exit 67. 10087 M-59 48353. Fax: 810/632-6480. **Facility:** 60 one-bedroom standard units. 2 stories, exterior corridors. **Parking:** on-site. **Terms:** check-in 4 pm, 7 day cancellation notice, [ECP] meal plan available. **Amenities:** irons, hair dryers. **Pool(s):** heated indoor. **Guest Services:** coin laundry. **Cards:** AX, MC, VI. **Special Amenities:** free continental breakfast and free newspaper.

SOME UNITS
[S] [▦] [ᕤ] [DATA PORT] [🖥] [▢] / [✕] [VCR] [🖥] /
FEE

HASTINGS pop. 7,095

———— WHERE TO STAY ————

PARKVIEW MOTEL
(AAA) [SAVE]
▼▼▼ ▼▼▼
Motel

All Year   1P: $47   2P: $54-$59   XP: $5   F10
Phone: 269/945-9511
Location: 0.3 mi n on SR 43. 429 N Broadway 49058. Fax: 269/945-4433. **Facility:** 18 units. 16 one- and 2 two-bedroom standard units. 2 stories, exterior corridors. **Parking:** on-site. **Terms:** cancellation fee imposed. **Cards:** AX, DS, MC, VI. **Special Amenities:** early check-in/late check-out and free local telephone calls.

SOME UNITS
[S] [ᕤ] [🖥] [▢] / [✕] /

HILLMAN pop. 685

―――― **WHERE TO STAY** ――――

THUNDER BAY GOLF RESORT

Phone: 989/742-4502

▼▼ ▼▼
Resort Motel

Property failed to provide current rates
Location: Just e on SR 32. 27800 M-32 E 49746. Fax: 989/742-3380. **Facility:** 34 units. 18 one-bedroom standard units with kitchens. 12 two- and 4 three-bedroom suites, some with kitchens and/or whirlpools. 2 stories (no elevator), exterior corridors. **Parking:** on-site. **Amenities:** irons, hair dryers. **Leisure Activities:** whirlpool, 2 tennis courts, cross country skiing, snowmobiling, ice skating, hiking trails. *Fee:* golf-18 holes. **Business Services:** meeting rooms. **Cards:** DS, MC, VI.

SOME UNITS

🍽 🍸 ✕ 🎬 [DATA PORT] 🔒 📦 ▣ / ✕ /

HILLSDALE pop. 8,233

―――― **WHERE TO STAY** ――――

DAYS INN HILLSDALE

Phone: 517/439-3297

SAVE

▼▼▼ ▼▼
Small-scale Hotel

All Year   1P: $74-$84   2P: $79-$89
Location: 2 mi n of town. 3241 Carleton Rd 49242. Fax: 517/439-1286. **Facility:** 41 units. 36 one-bedroom standard units, some with whirlpools. 5 one-bedroom suites ($84-$99). 2 stories (no elevator), interior corridors. **Parking:** on-site. **Terms:** [CP] & [ECP] meal plans available. **Amenities:** voice mail, irons, hair dryers. **Leisure Activities:** exercise room. **Guest Services:** valet laundry. **Cards:** AX, DC, DS, MC, VI.
(See color ad card insert)

SOME UNITS

[S🄳] 🍽 🌀 🎬 [DATA PORT] 🔒 📦 ▣ / ✕ /

HILLSDALE MOTEL

Phone: 517/437-3389
XP: $5

▼
Motel

All Year   1P: $35-$47   2P: $43-$53
Location: 2 mi s on SR 99; downtown. 1729 Hudson (M-99) Rd 49242. Fax: 517/437-3389. **Facility:** 25 one-bedroom standard units. 1 story, exterior corridors. **Parking:** on-site. **Amenities:** *Some:* hair dryers. **Cards:** AX, DC, DS, MC, VI.

SOME UNITS

🎬 🔒 / ✕ [DATA PORT]

HOLLAND pop. 35,048

―――― **WHERE TO STAY** ――――

BEST WESTERN KELLY INN & SUITES

Phone: (616)994-0400

(AAA) SAVE

▼▼▼ ▼▼
Small-scale Hotel

5/1-9/1 [ECP]   1P: $119-$159   2P: $119-$159
4/1-4/30 & 9/2-3/31 [ECP]   1P: $89-$129   2P: $89-$129
Location: US 31, exit Felch St E, just n. Located close to the mall. 2888 W Shore Dr 49424. Fax: 616/994-9955. **Facility:** Smoke free premises. 80 one-bedroom standard units, some with whirlpools. 3 stories, interior/exterior corridors. **Parking:** on-site. **Terms:** small pets only. **Amenities:** video games, voice mail, irons, hair dryers. **Pool(s):** heated indoor. **Leisure Activities:** whirlpool, exercise room. **Business Services:** valet and coin laundry. **Business Services:** meeting rooms, business center. **Cards:** AX, CB, DC, DS, JC, MC, VI. **Special Amenities:** early check-in/late check-out and free continental breakfast. *(See color ad p 301)*

SOME UNITS

[S🄳] 🐾 🍽 [&M] [🐕] 🌀 🏊 🎬 [DATA PORT] ▣ / 🔒 📦 /

BONNIE'S (THE) PARSONAGE 1908 B&B

Phone: (616)396-1316

▼▼▼ ▼▼
Historic Bed
& Breakfast
area.

All Year [BP]   1P: $85-$100   2P: $100-$130
Location: From US 31, 1 mi w on 24th St. Located in a quiet, residential area. 6 E 24th St and Central Ave 49423. **Facility:** Smoke free premises. 3 one-bedroom standard units. 2 stories (no elevator), interior corridors. *Bath:* shared or private, combo, shower or tub only. **Parking:** on-site. **Terms:** check-in 4 pm, 2 night minimum stay - weekends 7/1-8/31, age restrictions may apply, weekly rates available. **Guest Services:** TV in common

[ASK] ✕ 🅦 📞

COMFORT INN

Phone: (616)392-1000
XP: $8   F18

SAVE

▼▼▼ ▼▼
Small-scale Hotel

5/2-9/20 [ECP]   1P: $59-$159   2P: $59-$159
4/1-5/1 & 9/21-3/31 [ECP]   1P: $49-$69   2P: $49-$89
Location: Just w of US 31. Located in a commercial area. 422 E 32nd St 49423. Fax: 616/392-1421. **Facility:** 71 one-bedroom standard units, some with whirlpools. 2 stories (no elevator), interior corridors. **Parking:** on-site. **Terms:** check-in 4 pm, cancellation fee imposed, weekly rates available, package plans. **Amenities:** irons, hair dryers. **Pool(s):** heated outdoor. **Leisure Activities:** whirlpool. **Guest Services:** valet laundry. **Cards:** AX, CB, DC, DS, JC, MC, VI.

SOME UNITS

[S🄳] 🍽 🏊 🎬 [DATA PORT] 🔒 📦 / ✕ /

COUNTRY INN BY CARLSON

Phone: (616)396-6677

▼▼▼ ▼▼
Small-scale Hotel

7/2-9/30 [ECP]   1P: $89-$109   2P: $89-$109
4/1-7/1 & 10/1-3/31 [ECP]   1P: $79-$109   2P: $79-$109
Location: Jct US 31 N and James St, just e. Located at the Horizon Outlet Mall. 12260 James St 49424. Fax: 616/396-1197. **Facility:** 116 one-bedroom standard units, some with whirlpools. 2 stories (no elevator), interior corridors. **Parking:** on-site. **Terms:** cancellation fee imposed, [CP] meal plan available. **Amenities:** dual phone lines, voice mail, irons, hair dryers. **Pool(s):** heated indoor. **Guest Services:** valet laundry. **Business Services:** meeting rooms. **Cards:** AX, DC, DS, MC, VI. *(See color ad p 243)*

SOME UNITS

[ASK] [S🄳] 🍽 🏊 [⛲] 🎬 [DATA PORT] ▣ / ✕ [VCR] 🔒 /
             FEE   FEE

DUTCH COLONIAL INN

Phone: 616/396-3664

▼▼▼▼▼
Bed & Breakfast

All Year [BP] 1P: $100 2P: $160 XP: $20 F6
Location: US 31, 1 mi w on 24th St, then just n. 560 Central Ave 49423. Fax: 616/396-0461. **Facility:** Built in 1928, the inn is outfitted with classic decor from the 1930s and '40s. Smoke free premises. 4 one-bedroom standard units, some with whirlpools. 3 stories (no elevator), interior corridors. *Bath:* combo or shower only.
Parking: on-site. **Terms:** 10 day cancellation notice-fee imposed. **Amenities:** *Some:* CD players. **Business Services:** meeting rooms. **Cards:** AX, DS, MC, VI.

[⊗] [DATA PORT]

FAIRFIELD INN BY MARRIOTT

Phone: (616)786-9700

[SAVE]
▼▼▼▼▼
Small-scale Hotel

All Year 1P: $70-$90 2P: $75-$95
Location: Jct US 31 and Felch St. 2854 W Shore Dr 49424. Fax: 616/786-9700. **Facility:** 64 one-bedroom standard units. 3 stories, interior corridors. *Bath:* combo or shower only. **Parking:** on-site, winter plug-ins. **Terms:** [ECP] meal plan available. **Amenities:** irons. **Pool(s):** heated indoor. **Leisure Activities:** whirlpool.
Guest Services: valet laundry. **Cards:** AX, CB, DC, DS, MC, VI.

SOME UNITS
[S/D] [🍴] [🛗] [📶] [🏊] [📹] [DATA PORT] / [⊗] [🛄] [🖥] /

HAMPTON INN OF HOLLAND

Phone: (616)399-8500

[AAA] [SAVE]
▼▼▼▼▼
Small-scale Hotel

6/15-9/2 [ECP] 1P: $129-$179 2P: $139-$189
4/1-6/14 & 9/3-3/31 [ECP] 1P: $99-$139 2P: $109-$149
Location: Jct US 31 and Felch St. Located close to the mall. 12427 Felch St 49424. Fax: 616/399-9540. **Facility:** 178 one-bedroom standard units, some with whirlpools. 4 stories, interior corridors. *Bath:* combo or shower only. **Parking:** on-site. **Terms:** cancellation fee imposed. **Amenities:** dual phone lines, voice mail, irons, hair dryers. **Pool(s):** heated indoor. **Leisure Activities:** whirlpools, pool table, exercise room. *Fee:* game room.
Guest Services: valet and coin laundry. **Business Services:** meeting rooms. **Cards:** AX, DC, DS, MC, VI. **Special Amenities:** free continental breakfast and free local telephone calls.

SOME UNITS
[S/D] [🍸] [🛗M] [🛗] [🏊] [🍴⊗] [📹] [DATA PORT] [🖥] / [⊗] [🛄] [🖥] /

HAWORTH INN & CONFERENCE CENTER

Phone: (616)395-7200

▼▼▼▼▼
Small-scale Hotel

5/3-3/31 [ECP] 1P: $99-$159 2P: $99-$159
4/1-5/2 [ECP] 1P: $99 2P: $99
Location: Corner of 9th and College Ave; center. Located on Hope College Campus. 225 College Ave 49423. Fax: 616/395-7151. **Facility:** 50 one-bedroom standard units. 3 stories, interior corridors. *Bath:* combo or shower only. **Parking:** on-site. **Amenities:** irons, hair dryers. **Leisure Activities:** exercise room. **Guest Services:** gift shop, valet laundry. **Business Services:** conference facilities. **Cards:** AX, DS, MC, VI.

SOME UNITS
[ASK] [S/D] [➔] [🍴] [🛗] [DATA PORT] / [⊗] [🛄] /
FEE FEE

HOLIDAY INN & CONFERENCE CENTER

Phone: (616)394-0111

▼▼▼▼▼
Large-scale Hotel

6/2-9/6 1P: $129-$149
4/1-6/1 & 9/7-3/31 1P: $99-$109
Location: Just e of US 31. Located in a commercial area. 650 E 24th St 49423. Fax: 616/394-4832. **Facility:** 168 one-bedroom standard units. 4 stories, interior corridors. **Parking:** on-site. **Terms:** check-in 4 pm, [AP] meal plan available, 16% service charge. **Amenities:** video games, high-speed Internet, dual phone lines, voice mail, irons, hair dryers. **Pool(s):** heated indoor. **Leisure Activities:** sauna, whirlpool, exercise room. *Fee:* game room. **Guest Services:** valet and coin laundry, area transportation. **Business Services:** conference facilities, business center. **Cards:** AX, DC, DS, MC, VI.

SOME UNITS
[ASK] [S/D] [➔] [🍴] [🍸] [🏊] [🍴⊗] [📹] [DATA PORT] [🖥] / [⊗] [🛄] [🖥] /
FEE

HOLIDAY INN EXPRESS

Phone: (616)738-2800

[AAA] [SAVE]
▼▼▼▼▼
Small-scale Hotel

6/15-8/31 1P: $109-$225
5/2-6/14 1P: $99-$159
4/1-5/1 & 9/1-3/31 1P: $79-$149
Location: Jct US 31 and Felch St. Located in a commercial area. 12381 Felch St 49424. Fax: 616/738-3790. **Facility:** 118 one-bedroom standard units, some with whirlpools. 4 stories, interior corridors. *Bath:* combo or shower only. **Parking:** on-site. **Terms:** [ECP] meal plan available. **Amenities:** high-speed Internet, dual phone lines, voice mail, irons, hair dryers. **Pool(s):** heated indoor. **Leisure Activities:** sauna, whirlpool, lighted tennis court, exercise room. *Fee:* game room. **Guest Services:** valet and coin laundry. **Business Services:** meeting rooms, business center. **Cards:** AX, CB, DC, DS, MC, VI. **Special Amenities:** free continental breakfast and free local telephone calls.

SOME UNITS
[S/D] [🍴] [🛗M] [🛗] [🏊] [🍴⊗] [📹] [DATA PORT] [🛄] [🖥] [🖥] / [⊗] /

——— **WHERE TO DINE** ———

PIETROS ITALIAN RESTAURANT

Lunch: $4-$6 **Dinner: $9-$16** **Phone: 616/396-1000**

▼▼▼ ▼▼
Italian

Location: On I-196 business route, 1.3 mi w of US 31. 175 E 8th St 49423. **Hours:** 11:30 am-10 pm, Fri & Sat-11 pm. Closed: 11/27, 12/25. **Features:** The menu fuses Italian and Mediterranean cuisine in such dishes as fettuccine Michael—spinach and egg noodles with chicken and mushrooms in a cream sauce. Wood-fired pizza bubbles with flavor. If you're craving something sweet, try the tiramisu. Casual dress; cocktails.
Parking: on-site. **Cards:** AX, DS, MC, VI.

[⊗]

TILL MIDNIGHT

Lunch: $4-$8 **Dinner: $16-$23** **Phone: 616/392-6883**

▼▼▼▼
American

Location: Between 8th and 9th sts; downtown. 208 College Ave 49423. **Hours:** 11 am-2:30 & 5-10 pm, Fri & Sat-midnight. Closed major holidays; also Sun. **Reservations:** suggested. **Features:** Close to the college and downtown shopping areas, the small restaurant is often crowded. The use of fresh ingredients brings to life the flavors in the contemporary American-style cooking. Sidewalk dining is hard to come by when the weather's nice. Casual dress; cocktails. **Parking:** street. **Cards:** AX, DS, MC, VI.

[⊗]

--- *The following restaurants have not been evaluated by AAA* ---
but are listed for your information only.

CHINA INN
[fyi]
Phone: 616/786-9230
Not evaluated. **Location:** Located in the West Shore Shopping Center. 2863 West Shore Dr 49423. **Features:** The casual restaurant's menu incorporates Mandarin, Szechwan, Hunan and Cantonese dishes.

RIO GRAND STEAKHOUSE
[fyi]
Phone: 616/392-9900
Not evaluated. **Location:** US 31 and Felch St. 12420 Felch 49424. **Features:** Casual dining offering large cut, charbroiled, mesquite steak, barbecue ribs, rotisserie chicken and a variety of seafood entrees.

HONOR pop. 299

--- **WHERE TO STAY** ---

SUNNY WOODS RESORT
◆
Motel
Phone: 231/325-3952
Property failed to provide current rates
Location: 3 mi e on US 31. Located in rural area. 14065 Honor Hwy 49617 (14065 Honor Hwy, BEULAH). **Fax:** 231/325-2054. **Facility:** 14 units. 12 one-bedroom standard units, some with efficiencies. 2 cabins. 1 story, exterior corridors. **Bath:** combo, shower or tub only. **Parking:** on-site. **Terms:** small pets only ($25 deposit). **Amenities:** irons. **Leisure Activities:** fishing, snowmobiling, playground. **Guest Services:** coin laundry. **Cards:** AX, DS, MC, VI.

SOME UNITS
🐄 🍴 ✕ 📷 🛢 📷 📺 / ✕ 🎿 /

HOUGHTON pop. 7,010

--- **WHERE TO STAY** ---

BEST WESTERN-FRANKLIN SQUARE INN
AAA SAVE
◆◆◆
Large-scale Hotel
Phone: (906)487-1700

6/20-10/12 [BP]	1P: $99-$189	2P: $99-$189	XP: $8
10/13-3/31 [BP]	1P: $91-$179	2P: $91-$179	XP: $8
4/1-6/19 [BP]	1P: $89-$179	2P: $89-$179	XP: $8

Location: Center of downtown. 820 Shelden Ave 49931. **Fax:** 906/487-9432. **Facility:** 103 units. 98 one-bedroom standard units, some with whirlpools. 5 one-bedroom suites, some with whirlpools. 7 stories, interior corridors. **Parking:** on-site. **Terms:** pets ($9 extra charge). **Amenities:** voice mail, irons, hair dryers. **Dining:** 7 am-2 & 5-10 pm, Sun 5 pm-9 pm, cocktails. **Pool(s):** heated indoor. **Leisure Activities:** sauna, whirlpool, snowmobiling. **Guest Services:** valet laundry. **Business Services:** conference facilities. **Cards:** AX, DC, DS, MC, VI. **Special Amenities: preferred room (subject to availability with advanced reservations).**

SOME UNITS
🐄 📺 🍴 📡 🛢 ✕ 📷 📺 / ✕ [DATA PORT] 🛢 /

BEST WESTERN KING'S INN
SAVE
◆◆ ◆◆
Small-scale Hotel
Phone: (906)482-5000

6/22-10/25 [ECP]	1P: $79-$115	2P: $79-$115	XP: $6	F17
12/26-3/31 [ECP]	1P: $75-$111	2P: $75-$111	XP: $6	F17
4/1-6/21 & 10/26-12/25 [ECP]	1P: $67-$103	2P: $67-$103	XP: $6	F17

Location: On US 41; center of downtown. 215 Shelden Ave 49931. **Fax:** 906/482-9795. **Facility:** 69 one-bedroom standard units. 3 stories, interior corridors. **Parking:** on-site, winter plug-ins. **Terms:** cancellation fee imposed, pets ($6 extra charge). **Amenities:** irons, hair dryers. **Pool(s):** heated indoor. **Leisure Activities:** sauna, whirlpool, snowmobiling. **Business Services:** meeting rooms. **Cards:** AX, CB, DC, DS, MC, VI.

SOME UNITS
[S/D] 🐄 🍴 📡 ✕ 📷 [DATA PORT] 📺 / ✕ 🛢 🛢 /

BUDGET HOST INN
AAA SAVE
◆
Motel
Phone: (906)482-5351

6/27-9/6 [CP]	1P: $40-$70	2P: $46-$70	XP: $5	F11
9/7-10/11 [CP]	1P: $38-$65	2P: $43-$65	XP: $5	F11
4/1-6/26 & 10/12-3/31 [CP]	1P: $35-$60	2P: $40-$60	XP: $5	F11

Location: On US 41, 3.3 mi se. 46995 Hwy US 41 49931. **Facility:** 24 units. 22 one- and 2 two-bedroom standard units. 1-2 stories (no elevator), exterior corridors. **Bath:** combo or shower only. **Parking:** on-site. **Pool(s):** heated outdoor. **Leisure Activities:** snowmobiling, hiking trails, basketball. **Cards:** AX, DC, DS, MC, VI. **Special Amenities: free continental breakfast and free room upgrade (subject to availability with advanced reservations).** *(See color ad p 187)*

SOME UNITS
[S/D] 📡 ✕ [DATA PORT] / ✕ 🛢 🛢 /

CHARLESTON HOUSE HISTORIC INN
◆◆◆
Bed & Breakfast
Phone: (906)482-7790
All Year [ECP]   1P: $118-$168   2P: $118-$168   XP: $25   F5
Location: 0.3 mi se on US 41; downtown. 918 College Ave 49931. **Fax:** 906/482-7068. **Facility:** This inn is in a house dating from the turn of the 20th century. Smoke free premises. 4 one-bedroom standard units. 2 stories (no elevator), interior corridors. **Bath:** shower only. **Parking:** on-site. **Terms:** 14 day cancellation notice-fee imposed. **Amenities:** irons, hair dryers. **Business Services:** meeting rooms. **Cards:** AX, MC, VI.

✕ 📺

THE DOWNTOWNER MOTEL
AAA SAVE
◆
Motel
Phone: (906)482-4421
All Year   1P: $48-$68   2P: $48-$78   XP: $4
Location: On US 41; downtown. 110 Shelden Ave 49931. **Fax:** 906/482-3189. **Facility:** 27 units. 26 one- and 1 two-bedroom standard units. 2 stories (no elevator), exterior corridors. **Parking:** on-site, winter plug-ins. **Leisure Activities:** snowmobiling, access to riverwalk. **Cards:** AX, CB, DC, DS, MC, VI. **Special Amenities: early check-in/late check-out and free local telephone calls.**

SOME UNITS
🍴 📷 / ✕ /

SUPER 8 MOTEL
▼▼▼

Small-scale Hotel

Phone: (906)482-2240
All Year   1P: $65-$75   2P: $67-$77   XP: $3   F12
Location: 0.3 mi e, follow signs. Located in a quiet area on the canal. 1200 E Lakeshore Dr 49931. Fax: 906/482-0686.
Facility: 86 one-bedroom standard units, some with whirlpools. 2 stories (no elevator), interior corridors.
Bath: combo or shower only. **Parking:** on-site. **Terms:** [CP] meal plan available. **Amenities:** *Some:* dual
phone lines. **Pool(s):** heated indoor. **Leisure Activities:** sauna, whirlpool, boat dock, snowmobiling, hiking trails. **Guest Services:** coin laundry. **Business Services:** meeting rooms. **Cards:** AX, DC, DS, MC, VI.

SOME UNITS
ASK Ⓢ🄳 🖥 🏊 ✕ 🎥 / ✕ 🗄 🖨 /

—— WHERE TO DINE ——

MING GARDEN WOK & GRILL
▼▼▼

Chinese

Lunch: $4-$10   **Dinner:** $10-$24   **Phone:** 906/482-8000
Location: 1.5 mi sw on SR 26. 1301 Ridge Rd 49931. **Hours:** 11:30 am-9 pm, Fri & Sat-10 pm, Sun-8 pm.
Closed: 11/27, 12/25. **Reservations:** accepted. **Features:** On the outskirts of town, the modern Chinese
restaurant serves wok and grill dishes. Casual dress; cocktails. **Parking:** on-site. **Cards:** AX, DS, MC, VI.

🅺 ✕

---

*—— The following restaurants have not been evaluated by AAA ——
but are listed for your information only.*

AMBASSADOR
[fyi]

Phone: 906/482-5054
Not evaluated. **Location:** In the downtown area. 126 Sheldon Ave 49931. **Features:** The popular downtown
restaurant, with its antique bar and view of the canal, serves a number of snacks, salads and pizzas, as
well as daily pasta specials.

THE LIBRARY
[fyi]

Phone: 906/487-5882
Not evaluated. **Location:** In the downtown area. 62 N Isle Royale 49931. **Features:** Pizza, steak, seafood and
Mexican dishes—as well as on-site microbrews—are served.

UP-CLOSE, CASUAL, PERSONAL

HOUGHTON LAKE pop. 3,749

——— **WHERE TO STAY** ———

BEST WESTERN BEACHFRONT
Phone: 989/366-9126

	5/25-9/23 [ECP]	1P: $99-$129	2P: $99-$129	XP: $10	F18
	12/25-3/31 [ECP]	1P: $89-$119	2P: $89-$119	XP: $10	F18
	4/1-5/24 & 9/24-12/24 [ECP]	1P: $69-$89	2P: $69-$89	XP: $10	F18

Location: On SR 55, 4.5 mi e of US 27; 11.5 mi w of I-75. Located in a commercial area. 4990 W Houghton Lake Dr
Small-scale Hotel   48629. **Fax:** 989/366-1547. **Facility:** 60 one-bedroom standard units, some with whirlpools. 4 stories, interior
corridors. *Bath:* combo or shower only. **Parking:** on-site. **Amenities:** irons, hair dryers. **Pool(s):** heated indoor. **Leisure Activities:** whirlpool, boat dock, fishing, snowmobiling, exercise room. *Fee:* game room. **Guest Services:** coin
laundry. **Business Services:** meeting rooms. **Cards:** AX, CB, DC, DS, JC, MC, VI.

SOME UNITS
🆂🄳 🄺 🏊 ⊠ 🄳🄰🅃🄰🄿🄾🅁🅃 ▭ / ⊠ 🆅🄲🅁 /
FEE

HILLSIDE MOTEL
Phone: (989)366-5711

| | 5/15-9/15 | 1P: $56-$64 | 2P: $64-$74 | XP: $6 | F12 |
| | 4/1-5/14 & 9/16-3/31 | 1P: $52 | 2P: $64 | XP: $6 | F12 |

Motel   **Location:** On SR 55, 6 mi e of US 27; 10 mi w of I-75. Located next to Village Square Mall. 3419 W Houghton Lake Dr
48629. **Facility:** 12 one-bedroom standard units. 1 story, exterior corridors. **Parking:** on-site. **Terms:** 3 day
cancellation notice. **Leisure Activities:** snowmobiling. **Cards:** AX, DC, DS, MC, VI.

SOME UNITS
🄰🅂🄺 🆂🄳 🐾 🍽 🄱 / ⊠ /

HOLIDAY INN EXPRESS

6/13-8/16 [ECP]	1P: $69-$149	2P: $69-$149
4/1-6/12 & 8/17-3/31 [ECP]	1P: $59-$139	2P: $59-$139

XP: $6   F19
XP: $6   F19

Phone: (989)422-7829

Small-scale Hotel **Location:** Jct US 27 and SR 55, just e. Located in a commerical area. 200 Cloverleaf Ln 48629. Fax: 989/422-2625. **Facility:** 68 units. 66 one-bedroom standard units, some with whirlpools. 2 one-bedroom suites. 2 stories (no elevator), interior corridors. *Bath:* combo or shower only. **Parking:** on-site, winter plug-ins. **Amenities:** dual phone lines, voice mail, irons, hair dryers. **Pool(s):** heated indoor. **Leisure Services:** coin laundry. **Business Services:** meeting rooms. **Cards:** AX, DC, DS, MC, VI. *(See color ad p 312 & card insert)*

SOME UNITS

SUPER 8 MOTEL

5/23-9/1	1P: $69-$159	2P: $69-$164
4/1-5/22 & 9/2-3/31	1P: $49-$99	2P: $49-$99

XP: $5   F16
XP: $5   F16

Phone: 989/422-3119

Small-scale Hotel **Location:** Jct US 27 and SR 55. Located in a commercial area. 9580 W Lake City Rd 48629. Fax: 989/422-5561. **Facility:** 70 one-bedroom standard units, some with whirlpools. 2 stories (no elevator), interior corridors. **Parking:** on-site, winter plug-ins. **Terms:** [CP] meal plan available. **Pool(s):** heated indoor. **Leisure Activities:** sauna, whirlpool, snowmobiling, playground. **Guest Services:** coin laundry. **Cards:** AX, DS, MC, VI.

SOME UNITS

—— WHERE TO DINE ——

COYLES RESTAURANT   **Lunch:** $3-$5   **Dinner:** $6-$11   **Phone:** 989/422-3812

American   **Location:** Just n of jct SR 55. 9074 Old US 27 48629. **Hours:** 8 am-10 pm, Fri & Sat-11 pm; hours may vary seasonally. Closed: 12/25. **Features:** Pick and choose from the wide assortment of tempting options on the lunch and dinner buffets, or order from a menu that includes Alaskan king crab, frog legs and steak dinners. Meals are reasonably priced and please every member of the family. Casual dress; cocktails. **Parking:** on-site. **Cards:** DS, MC, VI.

HOWELL pop. 9,232

—— WHERE TO STAY ——

AMERIHOST INN & SUITES-HOWELL

All Year	1P: $66-$149	2P: $71-$149

XP: $5   F18

Phone: (517)546-0712

Small-scale Hotel **Location:** I-96, exit 133, just n on US 59 (Grand River Ave); then 0.5 mi e. 4120 Lambert Dr 48843. Fax: 517/546-0752. **Facility:** 75 one-bedroom standard units, some with whirlpools. 3 stories, interior corridors. *Bath:* combo or shower only. **Parking:** on-site. **Terms:** [ECP] meal plan available. **Amenities:** voice mail, safes (fee), irons, hair dryers. **Pool(s):** heated indoor. **Leisure Activities:** exercise room. **Cards:** AX, CB, DC, DS, JC, MC, VI. **Special Amenities:** free continental breakfast and free newspaper.

SOME UNITS

BEST WESTERN HOWELL

All Year	1P: $75-$99	2P: $125-$185

XP: $10   F10

Phone: 517/548-2900

Motel   **Location:** I-96, exit 137, just s on CR D19. Located in a semi-rural area. 1500 Pinckney Rd 48843. Fax: 517/548-2163. **Facility:** 60 one-bedroom standard units, some with whirlpools. 2 stories (no elevator), exterior corridors. **Parking:** on-site. **Terms:** 7 day cancellation notice, package plans - weekends, small pets only ($10 extra charge). **Amenities:** voice mail, irons, hair dryers. **Dining:** 6-11 am, Sun 7 am-noon. **Pool(s):** heated outdoor. **Guest Services:** coin laundry. **Business Services:** meeting rooms. **Cards:** AX, DC, DS, MC, VI. **Special Amenities:** early check-in/late check-out and free newspaper.

SOME UNITS

—— WHERE TO DINE ——

CHINESE DELIGHT   **Lunch:** $8-$12   **Dinner:** $8-$12   **Phone:** 517/545-9988

Chinese   **Location:** Downtown. 111 W Grand River 48843. **Hours:** 11 am-9:30 pm, Fri & Sat-10:30 pm, Sun noon-9:30 pm. Closed major holidays. **Features:** Rustic brick walls and hardwood floors give this space a bright and cheerful feeling. Locally popular, the Cantonese - American based menu offers a wide selection of traditional dishes. Casual dress. **Parking:** street. **Cards:** AX, DC, MC, VI.

HUDSONVILLE pop. 7,160

—— WHERE TO STAY ——

AMERIHOST INN-HUDSONVILLE

4/1-5/31	1P: $78-$81	2P: $84-$87
6/1-3/31	1P: $71-$74	2P: $76-$79

XP: $6   F16
XP: $6   F16

Phone: (616)662-4000

Small-scale Hotel **Location:** I-196, exit 62 (32nd Ave), just nw. Located in a quiet area. 3301 Highland Dr 49426. Fax: 616/662-5000. **Facility:** 61 one-bedroom standard units, some with whirlpools. 2 stories, interior corridors. *Bath:* combo or shower only. **Parking:** on-site. **Terms:** 3 day cancellation notice, [ECP] meal plan available. **Amenities:** safes (fee), irons, hair dryers. **Pool(s):** heated indoor. **Leisure Activities:** sauna, whirlpool, exercise room. **Guest Services:** valet laundry. **Business Services:** meeting rooms. **Cards:** AX, CB, DC, DS, JC, MC, VI. **Special Amenities:** free continental breakfast and free newspaper.

SOME UNITS

SUPER 8 MOTEL

AAA SAVE
Small-scale Hotel

Phone: 616/896-6710

All Year   1P: $54-$84   2P: $59-$89

Location: I-196, exit 62 (32nd Ave), just se. Located in a business park. 3005 Corporate Grove Dr 49426. **Fax:** 616/896-9958. **Facility:** 60 units. 54 one-bedroom standard units. 6 one-bedroom suites ($89-$139), some with whirlpools. 2 stories, interior corridors. *Bath:* combo or shower only. **Parking:** on-site, winter plug-ins. **Amenities:** *Some:* irons, hair dryers. **Pool(s):** heated indoor. **Leisure Activities:** sauna, whirlpool. **Guest Services:** coin laundry. **Cards:** AX, DS, MC, VI.

SOME UNITS

IMLAY CITY pop. 3,869

———— WHERE TO STAY ————

DAYS INN

AAA SAVE
Small-scale Hotel

Phone: (810)724-8005

4/1-10/31   1P: $69   2P: $79
11/1-3/31   1P: $59   2P: $69

Location: I-69, exit 168, 0.3 mi n. 6692 Newark Rd 48444. **Fax:** 810/724-0251. **Facility:** 60 one-bedroom standard units, some with whirlpools. 2 stories (no elevator), interior corridors. **Parking:** on-site. **Terms:** age restrictions may apply, weekly rates available, [ECP] meal plan available, pets ($50 deposit, $8 extra charge). **Amenities:** hair dryers. **Pool(s):** heated indoor. **Guest Services:** coin laundry. **Business Services:** meeting rooms. **Cards:** AX, DC, DS, MC, VI. **Special Amenities:** free continental breakfast and free local telephone lls.catq;rr *(See color ad card insert)*

SOME UNITS

SUPER 8 MOTEL-IMLAY CITY

Small-scale Hotel

Phone: (810)724-8700

All Year   1P: $35-$55   2P: $45-$65   XP: $6   F12

Location: I-69, exit 168, just n to Newark Rd, just e. 6951 Newark Rd 48444. **Fax:** 810/724-4013. **Facility:** 60 units. 59 one-bedroom standard units, some with whirlpools. 1 one-bedroom suite with efficiency (no utensils). 2 stories (no elevator), interior corridors. **Parking:** on-site. **Terms:** check-in 4 pm, [CP] meal plan available, small pets only ($50 deposit, $8 extra charge). **Amenities:** *Some:* hair dryers. **Leisure Activities:** whirlpool, playground. **Guest Services:** coin laundry. **Business Services:** meeting rooms, fax (fee). **Cards:** AX, DS, MC, VI.

SOME UNITS

———— WHERE TO DINE ————

LUCKY'S STEAKHOUSE

American

Lunch: $10-$14   **Dinner:** $10-$14   **Phone:** 810/724-4100

Location: I-69, exit 168, just n. 2000 S Cedar 48444. **Hours:** 11 am-10 pm, Fri & Sat-11 pm, Sun noon-9 pm. Closed major holidays. **Features:** Big portions are the trademark for this local family oriented favorite where service is quick and attentive. Casual dress; cocktails. **Parking:** on-site. **Cards:** AX, MC, VI.

INDIAN RIVER pop. 2,008

———— WHERE TO STAY ————

HOLIDAY INN EXPRESS

AAA SAVE
Small-scale Hotel

Phone: (231)238-3000

5/23-9/30 [ECP]   1P: $120-$150   2P: $120-$150   XP: $6   F19
11/21-3/31 [ECP]   1P: $80-$130   2P: $80-$130   XP: $6   F19
10/1-11/20 [ECP]   1P: $100-$120   2P: $100-$120   XP: $6   F19
4/1-5/22 [ECP]   1P: $80-$120   2P: $80-$120   XP: $6   F19

Location: I-75, exit 310, just e on SR 68. Located in a semi-rural area. 4375 Brudy Rd 49749 (PO Box 417). **Fax:** 231/238-8992. **Facility:** 50 one-bedroom standard units, some with whirlpools. 2 stories (no elevator), interior corridors. **Parking:** on-site, winter plug-ins. **Terms:** cancellation fee imposed. **Amenities:** irons, hair dryers. **Pool(s):** heated indoor. **Leisure Activities:** whirlpool, snowmobiling. *Fee:* game room. **Guest Services:** coin laundry. **Business Services:** meeting rooms. **Cards:** AX, CB, DC, DS, JC, MC, VI. **Special Amenities:** free local telephone calls and free newspaper. *(See color ad card insert)*

SOME UNITS

NOR GATE MOTEL

AAA SAVE
Motel

DS, MC, VI.

Phone: 231/238-7788

All Year   1P: $36-$46   2P: $40-$48   XP: $6   F4

Location: I-75, exit 310, 0.3 mi w, then 2 mi s on Old US 27. Located in a semi-rural area. 4846 S Straits Hwy 49749. **Facility:** 14 units. 6 one- and 6 two-bedroom standard units, some with efficiencies. 1 vacation home and 1 cabin ($48-$70). 1 story, exterior corridors. *Bath:* combo or shower only. **Parking:** on-site, winter plug-ins. **Terms:** 3 day cancellation notice-fee imposed, weekly rates available, small pets only (with prior approval). **Leisure Activities:** snowmobiling, picnic area, children's basketball, hiking trails, playground. **Cards:** AX, DS, MC, VI.

SOME UNITS

STAR GATE MOTEL

AAA SAVE
Motel

Phone: 231/238-7371

All Year   1P: $38-$48   XP: $6

Location: I-75, exit 310, 0.3 mi w, then 1.8 mi s on Old US 27. Located in a semi-rural area. 4646 S Straits Hwy 49749. **Facility:** 16 units. 11 one- and 3 two-bedroom standard units. 1 vacation home ($65-$85) and 1 cabin ($60-$75). 1 story, exterior corridors. *Bath:* combo or shower only. **Parking:** on-site, winter plug-ins. **Terms:** 3 day cancellation notice-fee imposed, weekly rates available, pets (with prior approval). **Leisure Activities:** snowmobiling, picnic area, hiking trails, playground, basketball, horseshoes. **Cards:** AX, DS, MC, VI. **Special Amenities:** free local telephone calls and preferred room (subject to availability with advanced reservations).

SOME UNITS

———— **WHERE TO DINE** ————

VIVIO'S NORTHWOOD INN
AAA
◇◇◇ (diamond)
American

Dinner: $8-$19 **Phone:** 231/238-9471
Location: I-75, exit 310, 0.3 mi w, then 1 mi s. 4531 S Straits Hwy 49749. **Hours:** 5 pm-11 pm. **Closed:** Mon-Wed 11/1-4/30. **Features:** The rustic log cabin is decorated with wall-mounted wildlife, including deer heads and a black bear cub. Shaded lamps throw adequate, yet modest, light. American and Italian cuisine, such as the specialty pizza, make up the restaurant's menu. Casual dress; cocktails. **Parking:** on-site.
Cards: MC, VI.

———— *The following restaurant has not been evaluated by AAA* ————
but is listed for your information only.

TGHE BROWN TROUT
[fyi]

Phone: 231/238-9441
Not evaluated. **Location:** 4653 S Straits Hwy 49749. **Features:** Just south of town, the restaurant serves steaks, fresh seafood and prime rib in an up-north atmosphere.

IONIA

———— **WHERE TO STAY** ————

SUPER 8 MOTEL
AAA [SAVE]
◇◇ ◇◇ (diamonds)
Small-scale Hotel

Phone: (616)527-2828
All Year [ECP] 1P: $49-$55 2P: $58-$64 XP: $7 F17
Location: I-96, exit 67 (SR 66). 7245 S State Rd 48846. **Fax:** 616/527-0729. **Facility:** 73 one-bedroom standard units, some with whirlpools. 2 stories (no elevator), interior corridors. **Parking:** on-site. **Terms:** small pets only. **Amenities:** *Some:* irons, hair dryers. **Business Services:** meeting rooms. **Cards:** AX, DC, DS, MC, VI.

SOME UNITS

IRON MOUNTAIN pop. 8,154

———— **WHERE TO STAY** ————

BEST WESTERN EXECUTIVES INN
◇◇ ◇◇ (diamonds)
Small-scale Hotel

Phone: 906/774-2040
Property failed to provide current rates
Location: 0.8 mi e on US 2. Located in a commercial area. 1518 S Stephenson Ave 49801. **Fax:** 906/774-0238. **Facility:** 57 one-bedroom standard units. 2 stories (no elevator), interior corridors. **Parking:** on-site. **Terms:** pets ($9 extra charge). **Pool(s):** heated indoor. **Guest Services:** valet laundry. **Business Services:** meeting rooms. **Cards:** AX, DC, DS, MC, VI.

SOME UNITS

BUDGET HOST INN
AAA [SAVE]
◇ (diamond)
Motel

Phone: (906)774-6797
All Year 1P: $39-$42 2P: $48-$54 XP: $5 D12
Location: 1.5 mi nw on US 2 and 141. Located in a commercial area. 1663 N Stephenson Ave 49801. **Fax:** 906/774-6910. **Facility:** 21 one-bedroom standard units, some with kitchens. 1 story, exterior corridors. **Parking:** on-site, winter plug-ins. **Terms:** cancellation fee imposed, [CP] meal plan available, small pets only ($5 extra charge, in designated units). **Leisure Activities:** snowmobiling. **Cards:** AX, DS, MC, VI. **Special Amenities:** free continental breakfast and free local telephone calls. *(See color ad p 187)*

SOME UNITS

COMFORT INN
AAA [SAVE]
◇◇ ◇◇ (diamonds)
Small-scale Hotel

Phone: (906)774-5505
All Year [ECP] 1P: $49-$66 2P: $56-$73 XP: $7 F18
Location: 1.3 mi nw on US 2. Located next to a bowling alley/lounge. 1555 N Stephenson Ave 49801 (PO Box 807). **Fax:** 906/774-2631. **Facility:** 48 one-bedroom standard units. 2 stories (no elevator), interior corridors. **Parking:** on-site, winter plug-ins. **Amenities:** high-speed Internet (fee), irons, hair dryers. **Leisure Activities:** whirlpool, snowmobiling. **Guest Services:** coin laundry. **Business Services:** meeting rooms. **Cards:** AX, CB, DC, DS, JC, MC, VI. **Special Amenities:** free continental breakfast and free local telephone calls.

SOME UNITS

DAYS INN
[SAVE]
◇◇ ◇◇ (diamonds)
Small-scale Hotel

Phone: (906)774-2181
All Year 1P: $50-$80 2P: $55-$85 XP: $5 F17
Location: 1.8 mi e on US 2. Located in a commercial area. W8176 S US 2 49801. **Fax:** 906/774-8252. **Facility:** 43 one-bedroom standard units, some with whirlpools. 1-2 stories (no elevator), interior/exterior corridors. **Parking:** on-site, winter plug-ins. **Terms:** 7 day cancellation notice, weekly rates available, [ECP] meal plan available, pets ($6 extra charge). **Amenities:** hair dryers. **Pool(s):** heated indoor. **Leisure Activities:** whirlpool, snowmobiling. **Guest Services:** valet laundry, area transportation (fee). **Business Services:** meeting rooms. **Cards:** AX, CB, DC, DS, MC, VI. /tq;rr *(See color ad card insert)*

SOME UNITS
FEE

GH GUESTHOUSE INN
◇ (diamond)
Small-scale Hotel

Phone: 906/774-6220
All Year 1P: $40-$65 2P: $45-$70
Location: 1 mi e on US 2. Located in a commercial area. 1609 S Stephenson Ave 49801. **Fax:** 906/776-1236. **Facility:** 63 one-bedroom standard units. 2 stories (no elevator), interior/exterior corridors. *Bath:* combo or shower only. **Parking:** on-site. **Terms:** pets (in designated units). **Amenities:** safes (fee). **Leisure Activities:** snowmobiling. *Fee:* game room. **Business Services:** meeting rooms. **Cards:** AX, DS, JC, MC, VI.

SOME UNITS

SUPER 8 MOTEL

Small-scale Hotel

All Year   1P: $59   2P: $59   **Phone:** (906)774-3400

Location: 2 mi nw on US 2 and 141. 2702 N Stephenson Ave 49801. **Fax:** 906/744-9903. **Facility:** 91 units. 82 one-bedroom standard units, some with whirlpools. 9 one-bedroom suites ($76-$106). 2 stories (no elevator), interior corridors. **Parking:** on-site, winter plug-ins. **Amenities:** *Some:* hair dryers. **Pool(s):** heated indoor. **Leisure Activities:** sauna, whirlpool, snowmobiling. *Fee:* game room. **Guest Services:** coin laundry. **Business Services:** meeting rooms. **Cards:** AX, DS, MC, VI.

SOME UNITS

(A$K) (S/D) (⇄) (✕) (✱) (DATA PORT) / (✕) (🔒) (📺) (💻) /

———— WHERE TO DINE ————

FONTANA'S SUPPER CLUB

Italian

MC, VI.

Dinner: $9-$23   **Phone:** 906/774-0044

Location: On US 2; center. 115 S Stephenson Ave 49801. **Hours:** 5 pm-10 pm, Mon-9 pm. Closed: 11/27, 12/25; also Sun. **Features:** Noted for charbroiled steaks and homemade Italian dishes, the restaurant is a favorite spot for casual, intimate dining. Attractive paintings and soft background music set a romantic tone in the casually upscale dining room. Casual dress; cocktails. **Parking:** on-site. **Cards:** AX, DC, DS,

(🍸) (✕)

IRON RIVER pop. 1,929

———— WHERE TO STAY ————

AMERICINN OF IRON RIVER

Small-scale Hotel

	1P	2P	XP	
12/20-3/31 [ECP]	1P: $79-$99	2P: $94-$100	XP: $5	F12
7/2-12/19 [ECP]	1P: $69-$74	2P: $79-$94	XP: $5	F12
4/1-7/1 [ECP]	1P: $54-$64	2P: $74-$94	XP: $5	F12

Phone: (906)265-9100

Location: On US 2; center of downtown. 40 E Adams St 49935 (PO Box 308). **Fax:** 906/265-4244. **Facility:** 66 units. 63 one-bedroom standard units, some with whirlpools. 3 one-bedroom suites ($90-$124), some with whirlpools. 3 stories, interior corridors. *Bath:* combo or shower only. **Parking:** on-site, winter plug-ins. **Terms:** 5 day cancellation notice, [CP] meal plan available, package plans. **Amenities:** hair dryers. **Pool(s):** heated indoor. **Leisure Activities:** sauna, whirlpool, snowmobiling, exercise room. **Guest Services:** coin laundry. **Business Services:** meeting rooms. **Cards:** AX, DC, DS, MC, VI.

SOME UNITS

(A$K) (🍴) (🔊) (⇄) (✕) (DATA PORT) (💻) / (✕) (🔒) (📺) /

IRONWOOD pop. 6,293

———— WHERE TO STAY ————

AMERICINN OF IRONWOOD

Small-scale Hotel

	1P	2P	XP	
12/5-3/31 [ECP]	1P: $82-$112	2P: $88-$118	XP: $6	F17
6/13-10/9 [ECP]	1P: $65-$92	2P: $71-$98	XP: $6	F17
4/1-6/12 & 10/10-12/4 [ECP]	1P: $58-$68	2P: $64-$74	XP: $6	F17

Phone: (906)932-7200

Location: 0.8 mi e on US 2. Located in a commercial area. 1117 E Cloverland Dr 49938. **Fax:** 906/932-7222. **Facility:** 49 one-bedroom standard units, some with whirlpools. 2 stories (no elevator), interior corridors. *Bath:* combo or shower only. **Parking:** on-site, winter plug-ins. **Amenities:** hair dryers. *Some:* irons. **Pool(s):** heated indoor. **Leisure Activities:** sauna, whirlpool, snowmobiling, limited exercise equipment. **Business Services:** meeting rooms. **Cards:** AX, DS, MC, VI. **Special Amenities:** free continental breakfast and free local telephone calls.

SOME UNITS

(S/D) (🍴) (🔊) (⇄) (✕) (✱) (DATA PORT) (💻) / (✕) (🔒) (📺) /

COMFORT INN

SAVE

Small-scale Hotel

All Year [ECP]   1P: $64-$200   2P: $70-$200   XP: $6   F18

Phone: (906)932-2224

Location: Jct US 2 and US 2 business route. Located in a commercial area. 210 E Cloverland Dr 49938. **Fax:** 906/932-9929. **Facility:** 63 one-bedroom standard units, some with whirlpools. 2 stories (no elevator), interior corridors. **Parking:** on-site, winter plug-ins. **Terms:** 8% service charge. **Amenities:** *Some:* hair dryers. **Pool(s):** heated indoor. **Leisure Activities:** whirlpool, snowmobiling. **Guest Services:** valet laundry. **Business Services:** meeting rooms. **Cards:** AX, DC, DS, MC, VI.

SOME UNITS

(🍴) (⇄) (✱) (DATA PORT) (💻) / (✕) (🔒) (📺) /

CRESTVIEW MOTEL

(AAA) SAVE

Motel

All Year   1P: $35-$65   2P: $45-$75   XP: $5   F10

Phone: (906)932-4845

Location: West edge. Located in a commercial area. US 2 49938. **Fax:** 906/932-3132. **Facility:** 12 one-bedroom standard units. 1 story, exterior corridors. **Parking:** on-site, winter plug-ins. **Terms:** cancellation fee imposed, pets ($5 extra charge). **Leisure Activities:** sauna, snowmobiling. **Guest Services:** coin laundry. **Cards:** AX, DS, MC, VI.

SOME UNITS

(S/D) (🐾) (🔒) (📺) / (✕) (📺) /
FEE

ROYAL MOTEL

(AAA) SAVE

Motel

newspaper.

	1P	2P	XP
12/1-3/31	1P: $31-$36	2P: $36-$41	XP: $5
4/1-11/30	1P: $31	2P: $36	XP: $5

Phone: (906)932-4230

Location: 1 mi w on US 2. Located in a commercial area. 715 W Cloverland Dr 49938. **Facility:** 16 one-bedroom standard units. 1 story, exterior corridors. **Parking:** on-site, winter plug-ins. **Terms:** 2 night minimum stay - weekends in winter, 7 day cancellation notice-fee imposed, small pets only (in smoking units). **Leisure Activities:** snowmobiling. **Cards:** DS, MC, VI. **Special Amenities:** free local telephone calls and free

SOME UNITS

(🐾) / (✕) /

SUPER 8 MOTEL

◆◆◆ Motel

All Year [ECP] 1P: $55-$75 2P: $65-$95 XP: $10 F12

Phone: 906/932-3395

Location: Jct US 2 and US 2 business route. Located in a commercial area. 160 E Cloverland Dr 49938. Fax: 906/932-2507. **Facility:** 42 one-bedroom standard units, some with whirlpools. 2 stories (no elevator), interior corridors. **Parking:** on-site, winter plug-ins. **Terms:** 30 day cancellation notice, weekly rates available, [CP] meal plan available, pets ($25 deposit, in designated units). **Amenities:** *Some:* irons, hair dryers. **Leisure Activities:** sauna, whirlpool, snowmobiling. **Cards:** AX, CB, DS, MC, VI.

SOME UNITS

(ASK) (S♦) (🛏) (📶) (✕) (☂) (DATA PORT) / (✕) (🔒) (📷) (💻) /

———— WHERE TO DINE ————

———— *The following restaurants have not been evaluated by AAA but are listed for your information only.* ————

DON & GG'S

fyi

Phone: 906/932-2312

Not evaluated. **Location:** 0.9 mi e on US 2. 1300 Cloverland Dr 49938. **Features:** This friendly neighborhood restaurant and bar is right off the main highway, and a great place to stop for their salads and nightly specials.

THE ELK & HOUND

fyi

Phone: 906/932-3742

Not evaluated. **Location:** Country Club Rd 49938. **Features:** You have to go east of town for this restaruant which has a number of lunch and dinner specials. Pizza available nightly.

TACCONELLI'S

fyi

Phone: 906/932-2101

Not evaluated. **Location:** 215 S Suffolk St 49938. **Features:** Located downtown this casual family restaurant has a number of mouth watering items on their menu from handcut steaks, to seafood, to a wide array of pasta.

ISHPEMING pop. 6,686

———— WHERE TO STAY ————

BEST WESTERN COUNTRY INN

(AAA) (SAVE)

◆◆◆ ◆◆

Small-scale Hotel

Phone: (906)485-6345

7/25-12/25	1P: $67-$77	2P: $72-$82	XP: $5 F18
12/26-1/30	1P: $74-$76	2P: $79-$81	XP: $5 F18
4/1-7/24 & 1/31-3/31	1P: $64-$74	2P: $69-$79	XP: $5 F18

Location: On US 41, just n of town. Located next to outdoor mall. 850 US 41 W 49849 (1035 Country Ln, # 281). Fax: 906/485-6348. **Facility:** 60 one-bedroom standard units, some with whirlpools. 2 stories (no elevator), interior corridors. **Parking:** on-site, winter plug-ins. **Terms:** small pets only (in smoking units). **Amenities:** irons, hair dryers. **Dining:** 6 am-10 pm, Fri & Sat-11 pm, cocktails. **Pool(s):** heated indoor. **Leisure Activities:** whirlpool, snowmobiling. *Fee:* game room. **Cards:** AX, CB, DC, DS, MC, VI. **Special Amenities:** early check-in/late check-out and free newspaper.

SOME UNITS

(S♦) (🐕) (📶) (Y) (🏊) (✕) (☂) (DATA PORT) (💻) / (✕) /

BEST WESTERN JASPER RIDGE INN

(AAA) (SAVE)

◆◆◆ ◆◆

Small-scale Hotel

Phone: (906)485-2378

12/26-1/30 [CP]	1P: $83-$85	2P: $88-$90	XP: $5 F18
7/25-12/25 & 1/31-3/31 [CP]	1P: $70-$85	2P: $75-$90	XP: $5 F18
4/1-7/24 [CP]	1P: $70-$78	2P: $75-$83	XP: $5 F18

Location: Off US 41, just n of town. Located behind an outdoor mall. 1000 River Pkwy 49849 (1035 Country Ln, # 316). Fax: 906/485-5176. **Facility:** 26 one-bedroom standard units, some with whirlpools. 2 stories (no elevator), interior corridors. **Parking:** on-site. **Amenities:** irons, hair dryers. *Some:* dual phone lines. **Leisure Activities:** snowmobiling. **Business Services:** meeting rooms. **Cards:** AX, CB, DC, DS, MC, VI. **Special Amenities:** free continental breakfast and free newspaper.

SOME UNITS

(S♦) (📶) (☂) (DATA PORT) (💻) / (✕) (🔒) (📷) /

ISLE ROYALE NATIONAL PARK

———— WHERE TO STAY ————

ROCK HARBOR LODGE

(AAA) (SAVE)

◆◆◆

Resort Motel

Phone: (906)337-4993

5/23-9/6 [AP] 1P: $127 2P: $203 XP: $68 D12

Location: Northeast end of island; accessible by boat only. Located in a quiet, secluded area. 49931 (PO Box 605, HOUGHTON). Fax: 906/337-4993. **Facility:** 80 one-bedroom standard units, some with efficiencies (no utensils). 2 stories, exterior corridors. *Bath:* combo or shower only. **Parking:** on-site. **Terms:** open 5/23-9/6, check-in 4 pm, 5 day cancellation notice. **Dining:** 2 restaurants, 7 am-8:30, noon-1:30 & 5:30-7:30 pm, wine/beer only. **Leisure Activities:** rental boats, rental canoes, marina, fishing, hiking trails. *Fee:* guides & boat tours of island. **Guest Services:** gift shop, coin laundry. **Business Services:** meeting rooms. **Cards:** AX, DS, MC, VI.

SOME UNITS

(📶) (✕) (🎣) (🛶) (☎) / (✕) (🔒) (💻) /

JACKSON pop. 36,316

———— WHERE TO STAY ————

BAYMONT INN-JACKSON

(AAA) (SAVE)

◆◆◆

Small-scale Hotel

Phone: (517)789-6000

All Year 1P: $59-$89 2P: $59-$89

Location: I-94, exit 138, just nw. 2035 Service Dr 49202. Fax: 517/782-6836. **Facility:** 67 one-bedroom standard units. 2 stories (no elevator), interior corridors. **Parking:** on-site. **Terms:** [ECP] meal plan available. **Amenities:** video games (fee), voice mail, irons, hair dryers. **Guest Services:** valet laundry. **Cards:** AX, DC, DS, MC, VI. **Special Amenities:** free continental breakfast and free newspaper.

SOME UNITS

(S♦) (📶) (♿M) (🔊) (📶) (☂) (DATA PORT) (💻) / (✕) (🔒) (📷) /

COMFORT INN & SUITES

SAVE

▼▼▼▼
Small-scale Hotel

Phone: (517)768-0088

All Year   1P: $74-$199   2P: $79-$199   XP: $5   F18
Location: I-94, exit 138, just n. 2435 Shirley Dr 49202. Fax: 517/768-4188. **Facility:** 70 one-bedroom standard units, some with whirlpools. 3 stories, interior corridors. *Bath:* combo or shower only. **Parking:** on-site. **Terms:** cancellation fee imposed, [ECP] meal plan available. **Amenities:** dual phone lines, voice mail, safes, irons, hair dryers. **Pool(s):** heated indoor. **Leisure Activities:** whirlpool, exercise room. **Guest Services:** valet and coin laundry. **Business Services:** meeting rooms. **Cards:** AX, CB, DC, DS, JC, MC, VI.

SOME UNITS
[icons] / ⊗ /

COUNTRY HEARTH INN

▼▼▼▼
Motel

Phone: (517)783-6404

All Year [ECP]   1P: $68   2P: $68
Location: I-94, exit 138, just sw. Located adjacent to shopping mall. 111 Boardman Rd 49202. Fax: 517/783-6529. **Facility:** 73 one-bedroom standard units. 2 stories (no elevator), exterior corridors. **Terms:** age restrictions may apply. **Guest Services:** valet laundry. **Cards:** AX, CB, DC, DS, JC, MC, VI.

SOME UNITS
[ASK] [icons] / ⊗ [icons] /
FEE

FAIRFIELD INN

SAVE

▼▼▼▼
Small-scale Hotel

Phone: (517)784-7877

All Year   1P: $60-$80   2P: $65-$85
Location: I-94, exit 138, just ne. 2395 Shirley Dr 49202. Fax: 517/784-7877. **Facility:** 57 one-bedroom standard units. 3 stories, interior corridors. **Parking:** on-site. **Terms:** [ECP] meal plan available. **Amenities:** irons. **Pool(s):** heated outdoor. **Leisure Activities:** whirlpool. **Guest Services:** valet laundry. **Cards:** AX, CB, DC, DS, MC, VI.

SOME UNITS
[icons] / ⊗ [icons] /

HAMPTON INN-JACKSON

SAVE

▼▼▼▼
Small-scale Hotel

Phone: (517)789-5151

All Year   1P: $65-$85   2P: $70-$90
Location: I-94, exit 138, just ne. 2225 Shirley Dr 49202. Fax: 517/789-8696. **Facility:** 64 one-bedroom standard units. 3 stories, interior corridors. *Bath:* combo or shower only. **Parking:** on-site. **Terms:** [ECP] meal plan available. **Amenities:** voice mail, irons, hair dryers. **Pool(s):** heated indoor. **Leisure Activities:** whirlpool. **Guest Services:** valet laundry. **Cards:** AX, CB, DC, DS, MC, VI.

SOME UNITS
[icons] / ⊗ [icons] /

HOLIDAY INN

▼▼▼▼
Small-scale Hotel

Phone: (517)783-2681

All Year   1P: $73-$89   2P: $73-$89
Location: I-94, exit 138, just nw. 2000 Holiday Inn Dr 49202. Fax: 517/783-5744. **Facility:** 184 one-bedroom standard units. 2 stories, interior/exterior corridors. *Bath:* combo or shower only. **Parking:** on-site. **Terms:** check-in 4 pm, age restrictions may apply, 8% service charge, pets ($15 extra charge). **Amenities:** dual phone lines, voice mail, irons, hair dryers. **Pool(s):** heated indoor. **Leisure Activities:** whirlpool, putting green, miniature golf, playground, exercise room. *Fee:* game room. **Guest Services:** valet and coin laundry. **Business Services:** meeting rooms. **Cards:** AX, CB, DC, DS, JC, MC, VI.

SOME UNITS
[ASK] [icons] / ⊗ [icons] /
FEE FEE

MOTEL 6 - 1088

▼▼
Motel

Phone: 517/789-7186

6/15-3/31   1P: $43-$53   2P: $49-$59   XP: $3   F17
4/1-6/14   1P: $41-$51   2P: $47-$57   XP: $3   F17
Location: I-94, exit 138, just se. 830 Royal Dr 49202. Fax: 517/789-7140. **Facility:** 95 one-bedroom standard units. 1 story, exterior corridors. **Parking:** on-site. **Terms:** small pets only. **Guest Services:** coin laundry. **Cards:** AX, CB, DC, DS, MC, VI.

SOME UNITS
[icons] / ⊗ /

------ **WHERE TO DINE** ------

DARYL'S DOWNTOWN

▼▼▼▼
American

Lunch: $8-$12   **Dinner:** $15-$20   **Phone:** 517/782-1895
Location: Downtown. 151 W Michigan 49201. **Hours:** 11 am-11 pm, Fri & Sat-midnight. Closed major holidays; also Sun & Mon. **Features:** A downtown storefront location, this large open space is warmed with the use of hardwood floors, soft wood accents, Tiffany lamps and a large fish tank near the kitchen. A good size menu of favorites from steak to seafood are well prepared and creatively presented. Dressy casual; cocktails. **Parking:** on-site and street. **Cards:** AX, MC, VI.

[icons]

FINLEY'S AMERICAN RESTAURANT

▼▼▼
American

Lunch: $6-$9   **Dinner:** $7-$15   **Phone:** 517/787-7440
Location: On I-94 business route; corner Michigan Ave and Brown St. 1602 W Michigan Ave 49201. **Hours:** 11 am-10 pm, Fri & Sat-11 pm. Closed: 12/24, 12/25. **Features:** Residing near Westwood Mall, this restaurant offers a wide variety of predictable menu items including char grilled steak, baby back ribs and seafood combinations. Casual dress; cocktails. **Parking:** on-site. **Cards:** AX, DC, DS, MC, VI.

[icons]

GILBERT'S STEAK HOUSE

▼▼▼▼
Steak & Seafood

Lunch: $7-$9   **Dinner:** $10-$18   **Phone:** 517/782-7135
Location: Jct I-94 and US 127, exit 138 N, 0.3 mi to Springport exit off US 127. 2323 Shirley Dr 49202. **Hours:** 11 am-10 pm, Fri & Sat-11 pm, Sun noon-7 pm. Closed major holidays. **Features:** Since 1946, this once quaint log cabin, serves a wide selection of steak and seafood items including USDA choice steaks, extra thick lamb chops, fried frog legs and stuffed flounder. The dining room boasts a collection of over 80 antique stained glass lamps and other memorabilia. Casual dress; cocktails. **Parking:** on-site. **Cards:** AX, DC, DS, MC, VI.

[icons]

KALAMAZOO pop. 77,145

──── WHERE TO STAY ────

BAYMONT INN & SUITES-KALAMAZOO
Phone: (269)372-7999

(AAA) [SAVE]

| | 6/1-8/31 & 9/1-11/30 | 1P: $60-$159 | 2P: $65-$165 | XP: $5 | F18 |
| | 4/1-5/31 & 12/1-3/31 | 1P: $60-$129 | 2P: $65-$135 | XP: $5 | F18 |

Location: US 131, exit 36B (Stadium Dr), just w. 2203 S 11th St 49009. Fax: 269/372-6095. **Facility:** 86 units. 83 one-bedroom standard units, some with whirlpools. 3 one-bedroom suites. 4 stories, interior corridors. **Parking:** on-site. **Terms:** weekly rates available, [ECP] meal plan available. **Amenities:** video games (fee), voice mail, irons, hair dryers. **Guest Services:** valet and coin laundry. **Cards:** AX, DC, DS, MC, VI.

Small-scale Hotel

Special Amenities: free continental breakfast and free newspaper.

SOME UNITS

BEST WESTERN HOSPITALITY INN
Phone: (269)381-1900

(AAA) [SAVE]

| | 4/1-11/15 | 1P: $60-$80 | 2P: $70-$100 |
| | 11/16-3/31 | 1P: $49-$79 | 2P: $59-$89 |

Location: I-94, exit 80, just nw. 3640 E Cork St 49001. Fax: 269/385-6136. **Facility:** 124 one-bedroom standard units, some with whirlpools. 3 stories, interior corridors. **Parking:** on-site. **Terms:** [ECP] meal plan available.

Small-scale Hotel

Amenities: video games (fee), irons, hair dryers. **Pool(s):** heated indoor. **Leisure Activities:** sauna, whirlpool, exercise room. **Guest Services:** valet and coin laundry. **Business Services:** meeting rooms.

Cards: AX, DC, DS, MC, VI. **Special Amenities:** early check-in/late check-out and free continental breakfast.

SOME UNITS

CLARION HOTEL
Phone: (269)385-3922

[SAVE]

| | 6/1-8/31 [BP] | 1P: $79-$89 | 2P: $87-$97 | XP: $8 | F17 |
| | 4/1-5/31 & 9/1-3/31 [BP] | 1P: $59-$79 | 2P: $67-$87 | XP: $8 | F17 |

Location: I-94, exit 80, just n. 3600 E Cork St 49001. Fax: 269/385-2747. **Facility:** 156 one-bedroom standard units, some with whirlpools. 6 stories, interior corridors. **Parking:** on-site. **Terms:** package plans, small pets only. **Amenities:** voice mail, irons, hair dryers. **Pool(s):** heated indoor. **Leisure Activities:** sauna, whirlpool, exercise room. *Fee:* game room. **Guest Services:** valet laundry. **Business Services:** conference facilities, business center. **Cards:** AX, DC, DS, MC, VI.

Small-scale Hotel

SOME UNITS

COMFORT INN
Phone: (269)381-7000

(AAA) [SAVE]

| | All Year | 1P: $60-$196 | 2P: $60-$196 |

Location: I-94, exit 80, 0.3 mi s. 3820 Sprinkle Rd 49001. Fax: 269/381-5334. **Facility:** 52 one-bedroom standard units, some with whirlpools. 3 stories, interior corridors. *Bath:* combo or shower only. **Parking:** on-site. **Terms:** weekly rates available. **Amenities:** dual phone lines, voice mail, irons, hair dryers. **Pool(s):** small heated indoor. **Guest Services:** valet laundry. **Business Services:** meeting rooms. **Cards:** AX, DC, DS, MC, VI.

Small-scale Hotel

SOME UNITS

COUNTRY INN & SUITES BY CARLSON
Phone: (269)382-2303

(AAA) [SAVE]

| | All Year [ECP] | 1P: $74-$89 | 2P: $74-$89 | XP: $10 | F18 |

Location: I-94, exit 78, just se. 1912 E Kilgore Rd 49002. Fax: 269/381-0032. **Facility:** 81 units. 46 one-bedroom standard units, some with whirlpools. 35 one-bedroom suites ($89-$129). 2 stories, interior corridors. *Bath:* combo or shower only. **Parking:** on-site. **Terms:** package plans. **Amenities:** voice mail, irons, hair dryers. **Pool(s):** heated indoor. **Leisure Activities:** whirlpool, exercise room. **Guest Services:** valet and coin laundry. **Business Services:** meeting rooms. **Cards:** AX, CB, DC, DS, MC, VI. **Special Amenities:** free continental breakfast and free newspaper. *(See color ad p 243)*

Small-scale Hotel

SOME UNITS

FAIRFIELD INN BY MARRIOTT
Phone: (269)344-8300

[SAVE]

| | All Year | 1P: $49-$99 | 2P: $49-$99 | XP: $10 | F18 |

Location: I-94, exit 80, just nw. 3800 E Cork St 49001. Fax: 269/344-8300. **Facility:** 133 one-bedroom standard units. 3 stories, interior/exterior corridors. *Bath:* combo or shower only. **Parking:** on-site. **Terms:** [ECP] meal plan available. **Amenities:** irons. **Pool(s):** heated outdoor. **Guest Services:** valet laundry. **Cards:** AX, DC, DS, MC, VI.

Small-scale Hotel

SOME UNITS

FAIRFIELD INN-WEST
Phone: 269/353-6400

[SAVE]

| | All Year | 1P: $79-$109 | 2P: $79-$109 |

Location: I-94, exit 72, just e. 6420 Cracker Barrel Dr 49009. Fax: 269/353-0680. **Facility:** 62 one-bedroom standard units, some with whirlpools. 3 stories, interior corridors. *Bath:* combo or shower only. **Parking:** on-site. **Amenities:** irons. **Pool(s):** heated indoor. **Leisure Activities:** whirlpool, exercise room. **Guest Services:** valet laundry. **Cards:** AX, DC, DS, MC, VI.

Small-scale Hotel

SOME UNITS

HALL HOUSE BED & BREAKFAST
Phone: (269)343-2500

| | All Year [ECP] | 1P: $79-$155 | 2P: $79-$155 | XP: $15 |

Location: US 131, exit 38A, 2.9 mi e on W Main St, then just s. 106 Thompson St 49006. Fax: 269/343-1374. **Facility:** Smoke free premises. 6 units. 4 one-bedroom standard units, some with whirlpools. 2 one-bedroom suites ($95-$155). 3 stories (no elevator), interior corridors. *Bath:* combo or shower only. **Parking:** on-site. **Terms:** check-in 4:30 pm, age restrictions may apply, 5 day cancellation notice-fee imposed, [BP] meal plan available. **Amenities:** video library. *Some:* CD players. **Cards:** AX, MC, VI.

Historic Bed & Breakfast

SOME UNITS

HAMPTON INN

SAVE

▼▼▼▼

Small-scale Hotel

Phone: (269)344-7774

All Year 1P: $70-$90 2P: $75-$95
Location: I-94, exit 78 westbound, just w; exit 76B eastbound, 0.6 mi n, then 1.5 mi e. 1550 E Kilgore Rd 49001. Fax: 269/344-9447. **Facility:** 64 one-bedroom standard units. 3 stories, interior corridors. *Bath:* combo or shower only. **Parking:** on-site. **Terms:** [ECP] meal plan available. **Amenities:** voice mail, irons. **Pool(s):** small heated indoor. **Leisure Activities:** whirlpool. **Guest Services:** valet laundry. **Cards:** AX, CB, DC, DS, MC, VI.

SOME UNITS

⟨S/D⟩ ⟨&M⟩ ⟨🖊⟩ ⟨📷⟩ ⟨🏊⟩ ⟨🍴⟩ ⟨DATA PORT⟩ ⟨💻⟩ / ⟨✕⟩ ⟨VCR⟩ ⟨🛏⟩ ⟨🖼⟩ /
   FEE FEE FEE

HAWTHORN SUITES

▼▼▼▼

Small-scale Hotel

Phone: (269)353-2547

All Year 1P: $119-$139 2P: $119-$139
Location: US 131, exit 36B (Stadium Dr), just w. 2575 S 11th St 49009. Fax: 269/353-2548. **Facility:** 64 one-bedroom standard units, some with whirlpools. 4 stories, interior corridors. *Bath:* combo or shower only. **Parking:** on-site. **Terms:** [BP] meal plan available. **Amenities:** video library (fee), high-speed Internet, dual phone lines, voice mail, irons, hair dryers. **Pool(s):** heated indoor. **Leisure Activities:** whirlpool, exercise room. **Guest Services:** sundries. **Business Services:** meeting rooms, business center. **Cards:** AX, DC, DS, MC, VI.

SOME UNITS

⟨ASK⟩ ⟨S/D⟩ ⟨🍴⟩ ⟨&M⟩ ⟨🏊⟩ ⟨VCR⟩ ⟨🍴⟩ ⟨DATA PORT⟩ ⟨🛏⟩ ⟨🖼⟩ ⟨💻⟩ / ⟨✕⟩ /

HOLIDAY INN EXPRESS HOTEL & SUITES

▼▼▼▼

Small-scale Hotel

Phone: (269)373-0770

6/1-8/31 [ECP] 1P: $99-$104 2P: $106-$111 XP: $7 F17
4/1-5/31 & 9/1-3/31 [ECP] 1P: $89-$94 2P: $96-$101 XP: $7 F17
Location: I-94, exit 80, just n. 3630 E Cork St 49001. Fax: 269/373-0773. **Facility:** 64 units. 49 one-bedroom standard units, some with efficiencies and/or whirlpools. 15 one-bedroom suites ($169), some with efficiencies. 3 stories, interior corridors. *Bath:* combo or shower only. **Parking:** on-site. **Terms:** package plans. **Amenities:** dual phone lines, voice mail, irons, hair dryers. **Pool(s):** heated indoor. **Leisure Activities:** exercise room. **Business Services:** meeting rooms, business center. **Cards:** AX, DC, DS, MC, VI.

SOME UNITS

⟨ASK⟩ ⟨S/D⟩ ⟨➕⟩ ⟨🍴⟩ ⟨&M⟩ ⟨🏊⟩ ⟨🍴⟩ ⟨DATA PORT⟩ ⟨💻⟩ / ⟨✕⟩ ⟨🛏⟩ ⟨🖼⟩ /

HOLIDAY INN-WEST

▼▼▼▼

Small-scale Hotel

Phone: (269)375-6000

All Year 1P: $119-$129 2P: $119-$129
Location: US 131, exit 36B (Stadium Dr), just w. 2747 S 11th St 49009. Fax: 269/375-1220. **Facility:** 186 one-bedroom standard units. 4 stories, interior corridors. *Bath:* combo or shower only. **Parking:** on-site. **Terms:** check-in 4 pm, cancellation fee imposed. **Amenities:** voice mail, irons, hair dryers. **Pool(s):** heated indoor. **Leisure Activities:** sauna, whirlpool, putting green, exercise room. *Fee:* basketball. **Guest Services:** valet and coin laundry, area transportation. **Business Services:** meeting rooms, fax. **Cards:** AX, DC, DS, MC, VI.

SOME UNITS

⟨ASK⟩ ⟨S/D⟩ ⟨➕⟩ ⟨🍴⟩ ⟨&M⟩ ⟨📷⟩ ⟨🏊⟩ ⟨✕⟩ ⟨🍴⟩ ⟨DATA PORT⟩ ⟨💻⟩ / ⟨✕⟩ ⟨VCR⟩ ⟨🛏⟩ /
   FEE FEE

KNIGHTS INN

ⒶⒶⒶ SAVE

▽▽▽

Motel

Phone: (269)381-5000

All Year 1P: $37-$70 2P: $40-$80 XP: $10 F12
Location: I-94, exit 76B, 3 mi n, w on Park Place, then just s. 1211 S Westnedge Ave 49008. Fax: 269/344-2061. **Facility:** 55 one-bedroom standard units. 2 stories, interior/exterior corridors. *Bath:* shower or tub only. **Parking:** on-site. **Terms:** weekly rates available, pets ($25 deposit). **Guest Services:** valet laundry. **Cards:** AX, CB, DC, DS, MC, VI. **Special Amenities:** free continental breakfast and free local telephone calls. *(See color ad below)*

⟨S/D⟩ ⟨🐾⟩ ⟨🍴⟩ / ⟨✕⟩ ⟨🛏⟩ ⟨🖼⟩ /

LEES INN & SUITES

▼▼▼▼

Small-scale Hotel

Phone: (269)382-6100

All Year 1P: $69-$149 XP: $10 F18
Location: I-94, exit 78, just s. 2615 Fairfield Rd 49002. Fax: 269/382-2136. **Facility:** 70 units. 63 one-bedroom standard units, some with whirlpools. 7 one-bedroom suites ($89-$109). 2 stories, interior corridors. **Terms:** on-site. **Terms:** weekly rates available, [BP] meal plan available, small pets only. **Amenities:** irons, hair dryers. **Pool(s):** heated indoor. **Leisure Activities:** whirlpool, exercise room. **Guest Services:** complimentary evening beverages: Mon-Thurs, valet and coin laundry. **Business Services:** meeting rooms, fax. **Cards:** AX, DC, DS, JC, MC, VI.

SOME UNITS

⟨ASK⟩ ⟨S/D⟩ ⟨➕⟩ ⟨🐾⟩ ⟨🍴⟩ ⟨&M⟩ ⟨🏊⟩ ⟨🍴⟩ ⟨💻⟩ / ⟨✕⟩ /

RADISSON PLAZA HOTEL

Phone: (269)343-3333

(AAA) (SAVE)

1/1-3/31	1P: $169	2P: $179	XP: $10	F16
4/1-12/31	1P: $159		XP: $10	F16

Large-scale Hotel

Location: At jct Michigan Ave and Rose St; downtown. Located in historic area. 100 W Michigan Ave 49007. Fax: 269/381-1560. **Facility:** The hotel, which is under renovation, is close to many shops and restaurants. 276 units. 265 one-bedroom standard units. 11 one-bedroom suites ($189-$400), some with kitchens and/or whirlpools. 9 stories, interior corridors. *Bath:* combo or shower only. **Parking:** on-site (fee) and valet. **Terms:** check-in 4 pm. **Amenities:** video games (fee), voice mail, irons, hair dryers. *Some:* CD players. **Dining:** 3 restaurants, 6:30 am-12:30 am, cocktails, also, Webster's, see separate listing, entertainment. **Pool(s):** heated indoor. **Leisure Activities:** saunas, whirlpool. **Guest Services:** gift shop, valet laundry, tanning facility. **Business Services:** conference facilities, business center. **Cards:** AX, DC, DS, JC, MC, VI. *(See ad below & color ad p 241)*

SOME UNITS / FEE FEE

RED ROOF INN-EAST

Phone: (269)382-6350

(AAA) (SAVE)

10/6-3/31	1P: $43-$63	2P: $49-$69	XP: $6	F18
5/24-10/5	1P: $51-$58	2P: $57-$64	XP: $6	F18
4/1-5/23	1P: $44-$51	2P: $50-$57	XP: $6	F18

Motel

Location: I-94, exit 80, just nw. 3701 E Cork St 49001. Fax: 269/382-6354. **Facility:** 79 one-bedroom standard units. 2 stories (no elevator), exterior corridors. *Bath:* combo or shower only. **Parking:** on-site. **Amenities:** video games, voice mail. **Cards:** AX, CB, DC, DS, MC, VI. **Special Amenities:** free local telephone calls and free newspaper.

SOME UNITS

RED ROOF INN-WEST

Phone: (269)375-7400

(AAA) (SAVE)

5/18-10/25	1P: $51-$68	2P: $56-$68	XP: $5	F18
10/26-3/31	1P: $48-$66	2P: $53-$66	XP: $5	F18
4/1-5/17	1P: $46-$66	2P: $51-$66	XP: $5	F18

Small-scale Hotel

Location: US 131, exit 36B (Stadium Dr), just nw. 5425 W Michigan Ave 49009. Fax: 269/375-7533. **Facility:** 108 one-bedroom standard units. 2 stories, exterior corridors. *Bath:* combo or shower only. **Parking:** on-site. **Terms:** small pets only. **Amenities:** video games, voice mail. **Cards:** AX, CB, DC, DS, MC, VI. **Special Amenities:** free local telephone calls and free newspaper.

SOME UNITS

May I Take Your Order Please?

When you look through a AAA TourBook® guide in search of a place to dine while traveling, **look for restaurants that advertise**. These establishments are committed to increasing their AAA patronage, and are willing to go the extra mile to capture your attention ... and your appetite!

STUART AVENUE INN BED AND BREAKFAST

Phone: (269)342-0230

All Year [BP]   1P: $75-$95   2P: $85-$105   XP: $10   F10

AAA SAVE

▽▽▽▽

Historic Bed
& Breakfast

Location: US 131, exit 38A, 3 mi e on W Main St. Located in a historic district. 229 Stuart Ave 49007. **Fax:** 269/385-3442. **Facility:** An English garden beautifies the grounds of these two elegant Victorian homes. Smoke free premises. 7 one-bedroom standard units. 3 stories (no elevator), interior corridors. **Parking:** on-site. **Terms:** 7 day cancellation notice-fee imposed, [ECP] meal plan available, no pets allowed (owner's dogs on premises). **Amenities:** *Some:* CD players. **Business Services:** meeting rooms. **Cards:** AX, CB, DC, DS, MC, VI.

SOME UNITS

[S⁄D] [✕] [☎] / [VCR] /

——— WHERE TO DINE ———

ARIE'S LONDON GRILL-SINGAPORE   **Lunch:** $6-$10   **Dinner:** $10-$20   **Phone:** 269/381-9212

▽▽▽

Provincial British

Location: Just e of Westnedge Ave; center of town. 214 E Michigan Ave 49007. **Hours:** 11 am-2 & 4-10 pm, Fri & Sat 4 pm-11 pm. Closed major holidays; also Sun. **Features:** The weekend Celtic music in this bistro makes for happy times, but the pleasantly presented dishes featuring curries and fresh seafood will delight you any day of the week. Casual dress; cocktails; entertainment. **Parking:** street. **Cards:** AX, DS, MC, VI.

[✕]

BLACK SWAN   **Dinner:** $13-$26   **Phone:** 269/375-2105

▽▽▽▽

American

Location: I-94, exit 75, 1.5 mi n on Oakland Dr, 1 mi w on Parkview Dr, then just s; in Parkview Hills Development. 3501 Greenleaf Blvd 49008. **Hours:** 11:30 am-3 & 5-9 pm, Fri & Sat-10 pm, Sun-7:30 pm. Closed major holidays. **Reservations:** suggested; weekends. **Features:** Nestled alongside Willow Lake and surrounded by a canopy of mature sycamore trees, this restaurant offers a park-like setting. The lake is viewed through paranomic floor to ceiling windows in the handsome and stylish main dining room. Picture perfect views of beautiful black and white swans gracefully swimming across the water delight patrons as they dine comfortably on classic Continental gourmet cuisine. Dressy casual; cocktails. **Parking:** on-site and valet. **Cards:** AX, DC, DS, MC, VI.

[&M] [Y] [✕]

BLUE DOLPHIN   **Lunch:** $5-$12   **Dinner:** $9-$15   **Phone:** 269/343-4993

▽▽

Greek

Location: From jct of Westnedge Ave or Park, just e on Cedar; town center. 502 S Burdick 49009. **Hours:** 7 am-11 pm, Sun 8 am-3 pm. Closed: 5/26, 9/1, 12/25. **Reservations:** accepted. **Features:** The downtown restaurant serves Greek dishes—such as moussaka, pastitsio and spanakopita—and American fare. Casual dress; cocktails. **Parking:** on-site. **Cards:** AX, DC, DS, MC, VI.

[Y] [✕]

BRAVO RESTAURANT & CAFE   **Lunch:** $10-$15   **Dinner:** $20-$25   **Phone:** 269/344-7700

▽▽▽▽

American

Location: I-94, exit 78, just s of freeway. 5402 Portage Rd 49002. **Hours:** 11:30 am-10 pm, Sat 5 pm-11 pm, Sun 11 am-2 & 4-9 pm. Closed major holidays. **Reservations:** suggested. **Features:** This delightful Italian/American eatery makes good use of its wood-burning ovens in preparing a cuisine that is at once, attractive, well prepared, and delicious. The atmosphere is casually chick and blends restrained traditional touches and attentive service in an entirely non-smoking environment. Casual dress; cocktails. **Parking:** on-site. **Cards:** AX, DS, MC, VI.

[&M] [Y] [✕]

CORK'N CLEAVER   **Lunch:** $6-$11   **Dinner:** $14-$28   **Phone:** 269/349-8758

▽▽▽▽

Steak & Seafood

Location: I-94, exit 80, just n, then just w. 3717 E Cork 49009. **Hours:** 11:30 am-2 & 5-10 pm, Fri-11 pm, Sat 5 pm-11 pm. Closed: 9/1, 11/27, 12/25; also Sun. **Reservations:** accepted. **Features:** An extensive salad bar complements a variety of steak and beef preparations and seafood dishes include lobster, shrimp and crab legs. Casual dress; cocktails. **Parking:** on-site. **Cards:** AX, DC, DS, MC, VI.

[Y] [✕]

COSMO'S CUCINA   **Lunch:** $5-$8   **Dinner:** $11-$16   **Phone:** 269/344-5666

▽▽▽▽

American

Location: From S Westnedge Ave, then just w; center. 804 W Vine 49007. **Hours:** 11 am-10 pm, Sat 8:30 am-1 & 5-10 pm, Sun 8:30 am-3 pm. Closed major holidays; also Mon. **Reservations:** accepted. **Features:** The casual eatery's often-changing menu may include such affordable dishes as cashew-crusted chicken. Casual dress; cocktails. **Parking:** street. **Cards:** DS, MC, VI.

[✕]

DISTRICT TWO ELEVEN   **Lunch:** $8-$12   **Dinner:** $20-$25   **Phone:** 269/226-9000

▽▽▽▽

American

Location: Jct Water and Edwards sts; downtown. 211 E Water St 49007. **Hours:** 11:30 am-2 & 5-10 pm, Fri-11 pm, Sat 5 pm-11 pm. Closed major holidays; also Sun. **Reservations:** suggested. **Features:** Located in the historic Globe building, this two-level restaurant features century old exposed brick walls, rustic wood pillars and warm hardwood floors, and floor-to-ceiling windows offer a great view of the city skyline. A wood fired grill in the small open kitchen focuses on such specialties such as shrimp and scallops, gnocchi and veggie pasta and New York strip steaks. Dressy casual; cocktails. **Parking:** on-site. **Cards:** AX, CB, DC, DS, MC, VI.

[&M] [Y] [✕]

FOOD DANCE CAFE   **Lunch:** $8-$10   **Dinner:** $10-$17   **Phone:** 269/382-1888

▽▽▽

American

Location: Just e of Westnedge Ave; town center. 161 E Michigan Ave 49007. **Hours:** 7 am-10 pm, Sun 8 am-3 pm. Closed major holidays; also Mon. **Reservations:** accepted. **Features:** You'll note this as a "food haven," from the herb garden at the entry to the 10-foot tall asparagus painted as a mural inside. Besides the eclectic interior, you'll enjoy interesting grilled and cold sandwich combinations such as white cheddar and tomatoes or smoked ham with horseradish and red onion. For dinner, choose from pasta dishes, entree salads or a fresh fish such as grilled, sesame ginger salmon. Casual dress; cocktails. **Parking:** on-site. **Cards:** DS, MC, VI.

[Y] [✕]

FRANCOIS' SEAFOOD & STEAKHOUSE   **Lunch:** $8-$15   **Dinner:** $15-$25   **Phone:** 269/381-4958

AAA

▽▽▽

Steak & Seafood

Location: Jct Michigan Ave and Portage Rd; downtown. 116 Portage Rd 49009. **Hours:** 11 am-11 pm, Sun 4 pm-10 pm. Closed major holidays. **Reservations:** accepted. **Features:** Featuring live music several nights a week, this Left Bank inspired restaurant offers an extensive menu ranging from grilled Salmon to classic and table side prepared dishes such as Steak Diane and drunken lobster. Dressy casual; cocktails. **Parking:** street. **Cards:** AX, CB, DC, DS, MC, VI.

[&M] [Y] [✕]

THE GREAT LAKES SHIPPING COMPANY **Dinner:** $13-$23 **Phone:** 269/375-3650

Steak & Seafood

Location: US 131, exit 36A, 0.3 mi e on Stadium Dr, 0.5 mi n on Drake Ave, then e. 4525 W KL Ave 49006. **Hours:** 5 pm-10 pm, Fri & Sat-11 pm. Closed major holidays. **Reservations:** accepted. **Features:** Serving a variety of fresh fish, slow roasted prime rib, choice aged steaks, and creatively prepared chicken and pasta, this nautically themed restaurant has something to suit everyone's taste. The large salad bar offers fresh items and lets you pick out how much you want of it. Dressy casual; cocktails. **Parking:** on-site. **Cards:** AX, DS, MC, VI.

OLDE PENINSULA BREW PUB & RESTAURANT **Lunch:** $6-$10 **Dinner:** $7-$14 **Phone:** 269/343-2739

American

Location: Just e of Westnedge Ave. 200 E Michigan Ave 49009. **Hours:** 11 am-10:30 pm, Sun noon-10 pm. Closed major holidays. **Features:** Pub foods, fresh seafood, great pasta and over two dozen beers as well as seasonal, hand-crafted beers are served in one of the city's oldest buildings. Casual dress; cocktails. **Parking:** street. **Cards:** AX, CB, DS, MC, VI.

RYKSE'S RESTAURANT & BAKERY **Lunch:** $6-$9 **Dinner:** $7-$12 **Phone:** 269/372-3838

American

Location: US 131, exit 36B (Stadium Dr), 0.5 mi w. 5924 Stadium Dr 49009. **Hours:** 6:30 am-9 pm. Closed major holidays; also Sun. **Features:** This family style restaurant offers home-style soup, a variety of vegetarian dishes, "crunchy" baked chicken and you may top it all off with a selection from the many fresh-baked goods, including giant cinnamon rolls. Casual dress. **Parking:** on-site. **Cards:** AX, DS, MC, VI.

WEBSTER'S **Dinner:** $17-$30 **Phone:** 269/343-4444

American

Location: At jct Michigan Ave and Rose St; downtown; in Radisson Plaza Hotel. 100 W Michigan Ave 49007. **Hours:** 5:30 pm-10 pm, Sat-11 pm. Closed major holidays; also Sun. **Reservations:** suggested. **Features:** The open display kitchen with its embossed copper front and Old World ambience set the stage for an exceptional dining experience. White tablecloths, monogrammed china, and subdued lighting combine to create a thoroughly gracious dining environment. Attentive, friendly service by the knowledgeable wait staff enhances the well prepared and beautifully presented continental cuisine. Dressy casual; cocktails. **Parking:** valet. **Cards:** AX, DC, DS, MC, VI.

KALKASKA pop. 2,226

—— WHERE TO STAY ——

ALL SEASONS RESORT **Phone:** (231)258-0000

Small-scale Hotel

	1P: $89-$159	2P: $99-$159	XP: $10	F13
6/16-9/15 & 12/16-3/31 [ECP]				
4/1-6/15 & 9/16-12/15 [ECP]	1P: $79-$119	2P: $89-$119	XP: $10	F13

Location: On US 131 and SR 72, 0.8 mi e. 760 S Cedar St 49646 (PO Box 1018). Fax: 231/258-7917. **Facility:** 61 one-bedroom standard units, some with whirlpools. 2 stories (no elevator), interior corridors. *Bath:* combo or shower only. **Parking:** on-site, winter plug-ins. **Terms:** 2 night minimum stay - seasonal weekends. **Pool(s):** heated indoor. **Leisure Activities:** whirlpool, snowmobiling, exercise room. **Business Services:** meeting rooms. **Cards:** AX, DC, DS, MC, VI.

SOME UNITS

KENTWOOD pop. 45,255—*See also GRAND RAPIDS.*

—— WHERE TO STAY ——

BEST WESTERN MIDWAY HOTEL **Phone:** (616)942-2550

Large-scale Hotel

| All Year [ECP] | 1P: $69-$89 | 2P: $79-$99 | XP: $10 | F18 |

Location: I-96, exit 43A, 1.5 mi w on SR 11. 4101 28th St SE 49512. Fax: 616/942-2446. **Facility:** 147 one-bedroom standard units, some with whirlpools. 3 stories, interior corridors. **Amenities:** voice mail, irons, hair dryers. **Dining:** The Hoffman House, see separate listing. **Pool(s):** heated indoor. **Leisure Activities:** saunas, whirlpool, indoor recreation area, exercise room. **Guest Services:** valet laundry, airport transportation-Gerald R Ford International Airport. **Business Services:** conference facilities. **Cards:** AX, CB, DC, DS, MC, VI. **Special Amenities:** free continental breakfast and preferred room (subject to availability with advanced reservations).

SOME UNITS

COMFORT INN **Phone:** (616)957-2080

Small-scale Hotel

| All Year | 1P: $65-$99 | 2P: $65-$99 |

Location: I-96, exit 43A, 1.5 mi w on SR 11. 4155 28th St SE 49512 (4155 28th St SE, GRAND RAPIDS). Fax: 616/957-9712. **Facility:** 107 one-bedroom standard units. 3 stories, interior corridors. *Bath:* combo or shower only. **Parking:** on-site. **Terms:** [ECP] meal plan available, small pets only. **Amenities:** dual phone lines, voice mail, safes, irons, hair dryers. **Leisure Activities:** exercise room. **Guest Services:** valet laundry. **Business Services:** meeting rooms. **Cards:** AX, CB, DC, DS, MC, VI.

SOME UNITS

COURTYARD BY MARRIOTT **Phone:** (616)954-0500

Small-scale Hotel

| All Year | 1P: $79-$149 | 2P: $89-$149 |

Location: I-96, exit 43A, 0.8 mi w on SR 11. Located in a commercial area. 4741 28th St SE 49512. Fax: 616/954-2299. **Facility:** 84 units. 81 one-bedroom standard units, some with whirlpools. 3 one-bedroom suites. 3 stories, interior corridors. *Bath:* combo or shower only. **Parking:** on-site. **Terms:** [BP] meal plan available. **Amenities:** voice mail, irons, hair dryers. **Pool(s):** heated indoor. **Leisure Activities:** whirlpool, exercise room. **Guest Services:** valet and coin laundry. **Business Services:** meeting rooms. **Cards:** AX, CB, DC, DS, JC, MC, VI.

SOME UNITS

HILTON GRAND RAPIDS AIRPORT

Phone: (616)957-0100

	5/1-10/31	1P: $179	2P: $179	XP: $10	F18
	4/1-4/30	1P: $169	2P: $169	XP: $10	F18
	11/1-3/31	1P: $159	2P: $159	XP: $10	F18

Location: I-96, exit 43A, 0.5 mi w on SR 11. Located in a commercial area. 4747 28th St SE 49512.
Large-scale Hotel **Fax:** 616/957-2977. **Facility:** 224 one-bedroom standard units. 4 stories, interior corridors. *Bath:* combo or shower only. **Parking:** on-site. **Terms:** 18% service charge. **Amenities:** video games, high-speed Internet, dual phone lines, voice mail, irons, hair dryers. **Dining:** 6:30 am-11 pm, Sat & Sun from 7 am, cocktails, entertainment. **Pool(s):** heated indoor. **Leisure Activities:** sauna, whirlpool, exercise room. **Guest Services:** valet laundry, airport transportation-Gerald R Ford International Airport, area transportation-within 2 mi. **Business Services:** conference facilities. **Cards:** AX, DC, DS, MC, VI. **Special Amenities:** free newspaper and free room upgrade (subject to availability with advanced reservations). *(See color ad p 301)*

SOME UNITS

QUALITY INN TERRACE CLUB

Phone: (616)956-8080

All Year [BP] 1P: $89-$129 2P: $89-$129
Location: I-96, exit 43A, 1 mi w on SR 11. Located next to Splash Water Theme Park. 4495 28th St SE 49512.
Fax: 616/956-0619. **Facility:** 126 units. 125 one-bedroom standard units, some with whirlpools. 1 two-bedroom suite with efficiency. 3 stories, interior corridors. **Parking:** on-site. **Terms:** package plans.
Small-scale Hotel **Amenities:** voice mail, irons, hair dryers. **Pool(s):** heated indoor. **Leisure Activities:** whirlpool. **Guest Services:** complimentary evening beverages, valet and coin laundry. **Business Services:** meeting rooms. **Cards:** AX, CB, DC, DS, MC, VI. *(See color ad p 302)*

SOME UNITS

RADISSON HOTEL GRAND RAPIDS EAST

Phone: (616)949-9222

All Year 1P: $139 2P: $139
Location: Jct SR 11 and E Beltline Ave (SR 37). 3333 28th St SE 49512. Fax: 616/949-3841. **Facility:** 195 one-bedroom standard units. 5 stories, interior corridors. *Bath:* combo or shower only. **Parking:** on-site.
Terms: check-in 4 pm. **Amenities:** dual phone lines, voice mail, irons, hair dryers. **Dining:** 6:30 am-2 & 5-10
Large-scale Hotel pm, Sat & Sun from 7 am, cocktails. **Pool(s):** heated indoor. **Leisure Activities:** sauna, whirlpool, indoor recreation area, exercise room. *Fee:* game room. **Guest Services:** valet and coin laundry, airport transportation-Gerald R Ford International Airport. **Business Services:** meeting rooms. **Cards:** AX, CB, DC, DS, JC, MC, VI. **Special Amenities:** free newspaper and free room upgrade (subject to availability with advanced reservations). *(See color ad p 241)*

SOME UNITS

FEE

RESIDENCE INN BY MARRIOTT EAST

Phone: (616)957-8111

All Year [BP] 1P: $79-$159
Location: Jct SR 11 and E Beltline Ave (SR 37). Located in a commercial area. 2701 E Beltline Ave 49546 (2701 E Beltline Ave, GRAND RAPIDS). Fax: 616/957-3699. **Facility:** 96 one-bedroom standard units with kitchens. 2 stories (no elevator), exterior corridors. **Parking:** on-site. **Terms:** pets ($125-$150 fee). **Amenities:** video games, voice mail, irons, hair dryers. **Pool(s):** heated outdoor. **Leisure Activities:** whirlpool, exercise room, sports court. **Guest Services:** complimentary evening beverages, valet and coin laundry. **Cards:** AX, DC, DS, MC, VI.

SOME UNITS

SLEEP INN

Phone: (616)975-9000

All Year [ECP] 1P: $79-$109 2P: $79-$109
Location: I-96, exit 43A, 1 mi w on SR 11, then just s on Acquest. Located in a commercial area. 4284 29th St 49512.
Fax: 616/954-6767. **Facility:** 80 one-bedroom standard units. 3 stories, interior corridors. *Bath:* combo or shower only. **Parking:** on-site. **Amenities:** *Some:* irons, hair dryers. **Pool(s):** heated indoor. **Leisure Activities:** whirlpool, exercise room. *Fee:* game room. **Guest Services:** valet and coin laundry. **Business Services:** meeting rooms. **Cards:** AX, CB, DC, DS, MC, VI. *(See color ad p 302)*

SOME UNITS

STAYBRIDGE SUITES BY HOLIDAY INN

Phone: (616)464-3200

| | 5/1-3/31 [ECP] | 1P: $99-$139 | 2P: $99-$139 |
| | 4/1-4/30 [ECP] | 1P: $94-$134 | 2P: $94-$134 |

Location: I-96, exit 43A, 2 mi w on SR 11, then just s. Located in a commercial area. 3000 Lake Eastbrook Blvd SE
Small-scale Hotel 49512. Fax: 616/464-3600. **Facility:** 94 units. 49 one-bedroom standard units with kitchens. 27 one- and 18 two-bedroom suites with kitchens. 3 stories, interior corridors. *Bath:* combo or shower only. **Parking:** on-site. **Terms:** pets ($75 fee). **Amenities:** video library (fee), high-speed Internet, dual phone lines, voice mail, irons, hair dryers. **Pool(s):** heated outdoor. **Leisure Activities:** whirlpool, exercise room. **Guest Services:** sundries, valet and coin laundry. **Business Services:** meeting rooms, business center. **Cards:** AX, CB, DC, DS, JC, MC, VI.

SOME UNITS

The following lodging was either not evaluated or did not meet AAA rating requirements but is listed for your information only.

HOLIDAY INN SELECT

Phone: 616/285-7601

Under construction, scheduled to open February 2003. **Location:** I-96, exit 43A, 2 mi w on SR 11, then just s. Located in a commercial area. 3031 Lake Eastbrook Blvd SE 49512. Fax: 616/285-7601.
Small-scale Hotel

WHERE TO DINE

THE HOFFMAN HOUSE   **Lunch:** $6-$8   **Dinner:** $12-$18   **Phone:** 616/949-3880
▼▼▼ ▼▼▼   **Location:** I-96, exit 43A, 1.5 mi w on SR 11; in Best Western Midway Hotel. 4101 28th St SE 49512. **Hours:** 6:30
American   am-2 & 5-10 pm, Sat from 7 am, Sun 7 am-2 & 5-9 pm. **Features:** The menu centers on traditional
offerings, such as prime rib, roasted turkey, lasagna and orange roughy. The Friday seafood buffet and
Saturday prime rib and pasta buffet are popular, as are such tempting desserts as apple cobbler and fudge
brownie. Casual dress; cocktails. **Parking:** on-site. **Cards:** AX, DC, DS, MC, VI.

SEOUL GARDEN   **Lunch:** $5-$6   **Dinner:** $8-$12   **Phone:** 616/956-1522
▼▼▼ ▼▼▼   **Location:** 0.3 mi n of SR 11, on SR 37. 2409 E Beltline SE 49546. **Hours:** 11 am-10 pm, Fri & Sat-11 pm.
Ethnic   Closed: 12/25; also Sun. **Features:** Mongolian beef and pepper steak are representative of Korean and
Chinese dishes on the extensive menu. The contemporary dining room is simple and elegant. Cocktails.
Parking: on-site. **Cards:** AX, DS, MC, VI.

The following restaurant has not been evaluated by AAA but is listed for your information only.

YEN CHING   **Phone:** 616/940-4111
[fyi]   Not evaluated. **Location:** 4605 28th St SE 49508. **Features:** Mandarin and Szechuan dishes are served in a
casual atmosphere.

LAKE CITY pop. 923

WHERE TO STAY

NORTHCREST MOTEL   **Phone:** 231/839-2075
(AAA) [SAVE]   All Year   1P: $51-$57   2P: $57-$64   XP: $5
▼▼▼   **Location:** 1 mi s on SR 55 and 66. 1341 S Lakeshore 49651 (PO Box M). **Facility:** 22 one-bedroom standard units.
Motel   1-2 stories (no elevator), exterior corridors. *Bath:* combo or shower only. **Parking:** on-site. **Terms:** small pets
only ($5 extra charge). **Pool(s):** heated indoor. **Leisure Activities:** whirlpool, snowmobiling. **Cards:** DS,
MC, VI. **Special Amenities: free local telephone calls and preferred room (subject to availability with
advanced reservations).**

LAKE ORION —*See Detroit p. 257.*

LAKESIDE

WHERE TO STAY

WHITE RABBIT INN   **Phone:** 269/469-4620
▼▼▼ ▼▼   4/1-12/1 & 12/26-3/31 [CP]   1P: $95-$160   2P: $95-$160   XP: $15
Bed & Breakfast   **Location:** I-94, exit 6, w on Union Pier, then 2 mi n. 14634 Red Arrow Hwy 49116 (PO Box 725, 49116-0725).
Fax: 269/469-5843. **Facility:** This couple-oriented inn has a romantic ambience. 8 units. 6 one-bedroom
standard units with whirlpools. 2 cabins ($185-$210) with whirlpools. 1 story, exterior corridors. **Parking:** on-
site. **Terms:** open 4/1-12/1 & 12/26-3/31, 2-3 night minimum stay - seasonal weekends, age restrictions may apply, 7 day cancellation notice, pets (with prior approval). **Amenities:** video library. **Cards:** AX, DC, MC, VI.
SOME UNITS

L'ANSE

WHERE TO STAY

L'ANSE MOTEL & SUITES   **Phone:** 906/524-7820
(AAA) [SAVE]   All Year   1P: $31   2P: $40   XP: $5   F5
▼▼   **Location:** Just s. (HCR 2, Box 506, 49946). Fax: 906/524-7247. **Facility:** 21 one-bedroom standard units. 1
Motel   story, exterior corridors. *Bath:* combo or shower only. **Parking:** on-site, winter plug-ins. **Leisure Activi-
ties:** snowmobiling. **Cards:** AX, CB, DC, DS, MC, VI. **Special Amenities: free local telephone calls and
preferred room (subject to availability with advanced reservations).**
SOME UNITS

LANSING pop. 119,128—*See also EAST LANSING.*

WHERE TO STAY

BEST WESTERN MIDWAY HOTEL   **Phone:** (517)627-8471
(AAA) [SAVE]   All Year   1P: $85-$125   2P: $85-$125   XP: $10   F18
▼▼▼ ▼▼   **Location:** I-96/SR 43, exit 93B, just e. 7711 W Saginaw Hwy 48917. Fax: 517/627-8597. **Facility:** 149 one-bedroom
Small-scale Hotel   standard units. 3 stories, interior corridors. **Parking:** on-site. **Terms:** age restrictions may apply, small pets
only ($15 extra charge). **Amenities:** voice mail, hair dryers. **Dining:** 6:30 am-2 & 5-10 pm, Fri & Sat-10:30
pm, Sun 8 am-2:30 & 4:30-8 pm, cocktails. **Pool(s):** heated indoor. **Leisure Activities:** sauna, whirlpool, exercise room. **Guest Services:** valet laundry. **Business Services:** meeting rooms. **Cards:** AX, DC, DS,
MC, VI. **Special Amenities: free continental breakfast and free room upgrade (subject to availability with advanced reservations).**
SOME UNITS

COUNTRY INN & SUITES BY CARLSON

Phone: (517)827-7000

(AAA) (SAVE)
▼▼▼▼

Small-scale Hotel

All Year   1P: $89-$129   2P: $89-$129
Location: I-496, exit 1 (Creyts Rd), just se. 6511 Centurion Dr 48917. Fax: 517/827-7001. **Facility:** Designated smoking area. 88 units. 83 one- and 5 two-bedroom standard units, some with whirlpools. 3 stories, interior corridors. *Bath:* combo or shower only. **Parking:** on-site. **Terms:** age restrictions may apply, cancellation fee imposed, [ECP] meal plan available. **Amenities:** voice mail, irons, hair dryers. **Pool(s):** heated indoor. **Leisure Activities:** whirlpool, exercise room. **Guest Services:** valet and coin laundry. **Business Services:** meeting rooms. **Cards:** AX, CB, DC, DS, MC, VI. *(See color ad p 243)*

SOME UNITS

[⑤🅳] [📞] [🍴] [🌊M] [🏊] [📹] [DATA PORT] [☕] / [✕] [🛏] [🖨] /

COURTYARD BY MARRIOTT

Phone: (517)482-0500

(AAA) (SAVE)
▼▼▼▼

Small-scale Hotel

All Year [BP]   1P: $79-$139   2P: $89-$149
Location: Jct 127 and Lake Lansing Rd. 2710 Lake Lansing Rd 48912. Fax: 517/482-0557. **Facility:** 129 one-bedroom standard units, some with whirlpools. 2 stories (no elevator), interior corridors. *Bath:* combo or shower only. **Parking:** on-site. **Terms:** cancellation fee imposed, $10 service charge. **Amenities:** video games (fee), dual phone lines, voice mail, irons, hair dryers. **Dining:** 6:30-9:30 am, Sat & Sun 7-10 am. **Pool(s):** heated indoor. **Leisure Activities:** whirlpool, exercise room. **Guest Services:** complimentary evening beverages, valet and coin laundry. **Business Services:** meeting rooms. **Cards:** AX, CB, DC, DS, JC, MC, VI. **Special Amenities:** early check-in/late check-out and free newspaper.

SOME UNITS

[⑤🅳] [🍴] [🌊M] [🏊] [📹] [DATA PORT] [☕] / [✕] [🛏] [🖨] /

FAIRFIELD INN BY MARRIOTT-WEST LANSING

Phone: (517)886-1066

(SAVE)
▼▼▼

Small-scale Hotel

All Year   1P: $60-$80   2P: $65-$85
Location: I-96/SR 43, exit 93B, 0.8 mi e on Saginaw Hwy. 810 Delta Commerce Dr 48917. Fax: 517/886-1066. **Facility:** 64 one-bedroom standard units. 3 stories, interior corridors. *Bath:* combo or shower only. **Parking:** on-site. **Terms:** [ECP] meal plan available. **Amenities:** irons. **Pool(s):** heated indoor. **Leisure Activities:** whirlpool. **Guest Services:** valet laundry. **Cards:** AX, CB, DC, DS, MC, VI.

SOME UNITS

[⑤🅳] [🍴] [🌊] [📹] [DATA PORT] / [✕] [🛏] [🖨] /

HAMPTON INN OF LANSING

Phone: (517)627-8381

(AAA) (SAVE)
▼▼▼

Small-scale Hotel

All Year   1P: $79-$89   2P: $89-$99   XP: $10   F18
Location: I-96/SR 43, exit 93B, just e on Saginaw Hwy. 525 N Canal Rd 48917. Fax: 517/627-5502. **Facility:** 107 one-bedroom standard units. 3 stories, interior corridors. **Parking:** on-site. **Terms:** small pets only ($100 deposit). **Amenities:** dual phone lines, voice mail, safes, irons, hair dryers. **Leisure Activities:** exercise room. **Guest Services:** valet laundry. **Business Services:** meeting rooms. **Cards:** AX, CB, DC, DS, MC, VI. **Special Amenities:** free continental breakfast and free local telephone calls.

SOME UNITS

[⑤🅳] [🐾] [🍴] [📶] [📹] [DATA PORT] [☕] / [✕] [🛏] [🖨] /

HOLIDAY INN LANSING WEST CONFERENCE CENTER

Phone: (517)627-3211

(AAA) (SAVE)
▼▼▼

Small-scale Hotel

All Year   1P: $89-$99   2P: $89-$99
Location: I-96/SR 43, exit 93B, just e. 7501 W Saginaw Hwy 48917. Fax: 517/627-5240. **Facility:** 244 one-bedroom standard units. 3 stories, interior corridors. **Parking:** on-site. **Terms:** check-in 4 pm, age restrictions may apply, cancellation fee imposed. **Amenities:** dual phone lines, voice mail, irons, hair dryers. **Dining:** 7:30 am-11 pm, Fri & Sat-1 am, cocktails. **Pool(s):** heated indoor. **Leisure Activities:** sauna, whirlpool, indoor recreation area, exercise room. **Guest Services:** valet laundry. **Business Services:** conference facilities, fax. **Cards:** AX, CB, DC, DS, MC, VI.

SOME UNITS

[⑤🅳] [🍴] [🍴] [🍷] [🏊] [✕] [📹] [DATA PORT] [☕] / [✕] [🛏] [🖨] /

HOLIDAY INN-SOUTH/CONVENTION CENTER

Phone: (517)694-8123

▼▼▼

Small-scale Hotel

All Year   1P: $134   2P: $154   XP: $10   F18
Location: I-96, exit 104 (Cedar St/Holt), just s. 6820 S Cedar St 48911. Fax: 517/699-3753. **Facility:** 300 one-bedroom standard units, some with whirlpools. 5 stories, interior corridors. *Bath:* combo or shower only. **Parking:** on-site. **Amenities:** video games (fee), dual phone lines, voice mail, irons, hair dryers. **Pool(s):** heated indoor. **Leisure Activities:** sauna, whirlpool, exercise room. **Guest Services:** valet and coin laundry. **Business Services:** conference facilities. **Cards:** AX, DC, DS, MC, VI.

SOME UNITS

[ASK] [⑤🅳] [✕] [🍴] [🍷] [🌊] [🏊] [✕] [📹] [DATA PORT] [🛏] [🖨] / [✕] /

LANSING'S QUALITY SUITES HOTEL

Phone: (517)886-0600

(AAA) (SAVE)
▼▼▼

Small-scale Hotel

MC, VI.

All Year   1P: $99   2P: $99
Location: I-96/SR 43, exit 93B, 0.8 mi e on Saginaw St. 901 Delta Commerce Dr 48917. Fax: 517/886-0103. **Facility:** 117 one-bedroom standard units. 4 stories, interior corridors. **Terms:** [BP] meal plan available, pets ($125 fee). **Amenities:** dual phone lines, voice mail, irons, hair dryers. **Leisure Activities:** sauna, whirlpool, exercise room. **Guest Services:** gift shop, complimentary evening beverages, valet laundry, area transportation-within 3 mi. **Business Services:** meeting rooms. **Cards:** AX, CB, DC, DS, JC,

SOME UNITS

[⑤🅳] [✕] [🐾] [✕] [📹] [DATA PORT] [🛏] [🖨] [☕] / [✕] /

QUALITY INN UNIVERSITY PLACE

Phone: (517)351-1440

(SAVE)
▼▼ ▼

Small-scale Hotel

All Year [BP]   1P: $69-$125   2P: $69-$125   XP: $10   F18
Location: On I-69 business route and SR 43, just e of US 127. 3121 E Grand River Ave 48912. Fax: 517/351-6220. **Facility:** 100 one-bedroom standard units, some with whirlpools. 3 stories, interior corridors. **Parking:** on-site. **Terms:** weekly rates available. **Amenities:** voice mail, safes, irons, hair dryers. **Pool(s):** heated indoor. **Leisure Activities:** whirlpool, exercise room. **Guest Services:** coin laundry. **Business Services:** meeting rooms. **Cards:** AX, DC, DS, MC, VI. *(See color ad p 327)*

SOME UNITS

[⑤🅳] [✕] [🍴] [🍷] [🏊] [📹] [DATA PORT] [☕] / [✕] [🛏] [🖨] /

We'll take 10%* off your stay. Sorry we can't do the same for your over-packed car.

CHOICE HOTELS
INTERNATIONAL®

800.228.1AAA
choicehotels.com

The Power of Being There. **Go**®

*AAA members can save 20% at many Clarion brand hotels.
©2003 Choice Hotels International, Inc.

10% OFF
AAA Discount
without reservations.

The Power of Being There. **Go**®

CHOICE HOTELS INTERNATIONAL®

Call us at 800.228.1AAA or visit us on the Web at choicehotels.com for more information and reservations.

*AAA members can save 20% at many Clarion brand hotels.
©2003 Choice Hotels International, Inc.

TourBookMark

Lodging Listing Symbols
Member Values
(see pg. 14)

AAA	Official Appointment
SAVE	Offers minimum 10% discount
SAVE	SYC&S chain partners
ASK	May offer discount
S$	Offers senior discount
fyi	Informational listing only

Member Services

✈	Airport transportation
🐕	Pets allowed
❢❢	Restaurant on premises
❢❢→	Restaurant off premises (walking distance)
24❢	24-hour room service
🍸	Cocktail lounge
🎠	Child care

Accessibility Features
(see pg. 18)

&M	Accessibility features
♿	Roll-in showers
👂	Hearing impaired

Leisure Activities

🎰	Full Service Casino
🏊	Pool
💪	Health Club on premises
💪→	Health Club off premises
✖	Recreational activities

In-Room Amenities

✖	Non-smoking rooms
🅰	No air conditioning
📺	No TV
📺	No Cable TV
VCR	VCR
🎬	Movies
DATA PORT	Data port/modem line
☎	No telephones
🧊	Refrigerator
📻	Microwave
☕	Coffee maker

Call property for detailed information about fees & restrictions relating to the lodging listing symbols.

Take the road less traveled or more traveled. We're on both.

RADISSON HOTEL LANSING
Phone: (517)482-0188

All Year   1P: $126-$146   2P: $126-$146
Location: Corner of Michigan and Grand Ave; center of downtown. 111 N Grand Ave 48933. Fax: 517/487-6646. **Facility:** 257 one-bedroom standard units, some with whirlpools. 11 stories, interior corridors. **Parking:** valet and street. **Terms:** check-in 4 pm, age restrictions may apply. **Amenities:** voice mail, irons, hair dryers.
Large-scale Hotel *Some:* dual phone lines. **Dining:** 6 am-11 pm, Sat & Sun from 7 am, cocktails. **Pool(s):** heated indoor. **Leisure Activities:** sauna, whirlpool, exercise room. **Guest Services:** gift shop, valet laundry, airport transportation-Capital City Airport. **Business Services:** conference facilities, business center. **Special Amenities:** free newspaper. *(See color ad p 241)*

SOME UNITS

RED ROOF INN-EAST
Phone: (517)332-2575

All Year   1P: $49-$73   2P: $55-$73   XP: $6   F18
Location: Just e of I-496 and US 127, exit 11 (Jolly Rd). 3615 Dunckel Rd 48910. Fax: 517/332-1459. **Facility:** 80 one-bedroom standard units. 2 stories, exterior corridors. **Parking:** on-site. **Terms:** small pets only.
Motel **Amenities:** video games (fee), voice mail. **Cards:** AX, CB, DC, DS, MC, VI. **Special Amenities:** free local telephone calls and free newspaper.

SOME UNITS

RED ROOF INN-WEST
Phone: (517)321-7246

4/1-11/1   1P: $49-$66   2P: $54-$66   XP: $5   F18
11/2-3/31   1P: $44-$59   2P: $49-$59   XP: $5   F18
Location: I-96, exit 93B (W Saginaw Hwy). 7412 W Saginaw Hwy 48917. Fax: 517/321-2831. **Facility:** 81 one-bedroom standard units. 2 stories, exterior corridors. **Parking:** on-site. **Terms:** age restrictions may apply,
Small-scale Hotel small pets only. **Amenities:** video games (fee), voice mail. **Cards:** AX, CB, DC, DS, MC, VI. **Special Amenities:** free local telephone calls and free newspaper.

SOME UNITS

RESIDENCE INN-LANSING WEST
Phone: 517/886-5030

All Year   1P: $109
Location: I-96/SR 43, exit 93B, 0.8 mi e on Saginaw Hwy. 922 Delta Commerce Dr 48917. Fax: 517/886-5030. **Facility:** 78 units. 66 one-bedroom standard units with efficiencies. 12 one-bedroom suites with kitchens. 3 stories, interior corridors. **Bath:** combo or shower only. **Parking:** on-site. **Terms:** age restrictions may apply,
Small-scale Hotel [BP] meal plan available, pets ($100 fee). **Amenities:** dual phone lines, voice mail, irons, hair dryers. **Pool(s):** heated indoor. **Leisure Activities:** whirlpool, exercise room, sports court. **Guest Services:** valet and coin laundry. **Business Services:** meeting rooms. **Cards:** AX, DC, DS, MC, VI.

SOME UNITS

SHERATON LANSING HOTEL

AAA SAVE All Year 1P: $89-$164 2P: $89-$164 XP: $12 Phone: (517)323-7100

F18

Small-scale Hotel **Location:** I-496, exit Creyts Rd, just n. Located in an office park. 925 S Creyts Rd 48917. Fax: 517/323-2180. **Facility:** 219 one-bedroom standard units. 5 stories, interior corridors. **Parking:** on-site. **Terms:** age restrictions may apply. **Amenities:** video games (fee), dual phone lines, voice mail, irons, hair dryers. **Dining:** 6:30 am-midnight, Sun from 7 am, cocktails. **Pool(s):** heated indoor. **Leisure Activities:** sauna, whirlpool, racquetball court, exercise room. **Guest Services:** gift shop, valet laundry, airport transportation-Capital City Airport, area transportation-within 10 mi. **Business Services:** conference facilities. **Cards:** AX, CB, DC, DS, JC, MC, VI. **Special Amenities:** free newspaper.

SOME UNITS

─────── **WHERE TO DINE** ───────

CARRABBA'S ITALIAN GRILLE Dinner: $8-$18 Phone: 517/323-8055

Italian **Location:** I-96/SR 43, exit 93B, 1 mi e. 6540 W Saginaw Hwy 48917. **Hours:** 4 pm-10 pm, Fri-11 pm, Sat 3 pm-11 pm, Sun 1 pm-9 pm. Closed major holidays. **Reservations:** accepted. **Features:** Tuscan influences run deep in this surprising cozy and intimate space. A large open kitchen allows diners to watch the Italian based dishes such as calamari, eggplant parmesan and pizza being prepared. Casual dress; cocktails. **Parking:** on-site. **Cards:** AX, DC, DS, MC, VI.

CLARA'S LANSING STATION Lunch: $6-$16 Dinner: $6-$16 Phone: 517/372-7120

American **Location:** Just e of Capitol Building Complex; downtown. 637 E Michigan Ave 48912. **Hours:** 11 am-11 pm, Fri & Sat-midnight, Sun 10 am-10 pm. Closed: 11/27, 12/25. **Reservations:** accepted. **Features:** Clara's is a railroad station built in 1905, that is now a restaurant with a long menu that has something to please everyone. Try the delicious chicken Hawaiian. The emphasis here is on fun, family dining, in a landmark location. Casual dress; cocktails. **Parking:** on-site. **Cards:** AX, DC, DS, MC, VI.

FINLEY'S AMERICAN RESTAURANT Lunch: $4-$8 Dinner: $6-$15 Phone: 517/323-4309

American **Location:** I-96, exit 93B (SR 43), 2 mi e. 5615 W Saginaw Hwy 48917. **Hours:** 11 am-10 pm, Fri & Sat-11 pm. Closed: 11/27, 12/25. **Features:** Everyone is welcome at the casual family restaurant. Baby back ribs and such succulent steak as top sirloin and New York strip are popular specialties on a menu that centers on good basic fare. The uniformed staff provides friendly, prompt service. Casual dress; cocktails. **Parking:** on-site. **Cards:** AX, DC, DS, MC, VI.

LAPEER pop. 9,072

─────── **WHERE TO STAY** ───────

BEST WESTERN LAPEER INN Phone: (810)667-9444

AAA SAVE All Year [ECP] 1P: $72-$75 2P: $72-$75 XP: $5 F12

Small-scale Hotel **Location:** I-69, exit 155, 2 mi n on SR 24. 770 West St 48446. Fax: 810/667-3744. **Facility:** 90 units. 74 one-bedroom standard units, some with whirlpools. 16 one-bedroom suites with whirlpools. 2 stories (no elevator), interior corridors. **Parking:** on-site. **Terms:** age restrictions may apply. **Amenities:** video library (fee), irons, hair dryers. *Some:* safes, honor bars. **Dining:** 11 am-10 pm, Fri & Sat-11 pm, Sun noon-9 pm, cocktails. **Pool(s):** heated outdoor, heated indoor. **Leisure Activities:** sauna, whirlpool, putting green, indoor recreation center, exercise room. *Fee:* game room. **Guest Services:** valet laundry. **Business Services:** meeting rooms. **Cards:** AX, CB, DC, DS, JC, MC, VI. **Special Amenities:** free continental breakfast and free newspaper.

SOME UNITS

FAIRFIELD INN LAPEER

Phone: 810/245-7700

(AAA) (SAVE)
◆◆◆◆

Small-scale Hotel

All Year [ECP]   1P: $75-$115   2P: $75-$115
Location: I-69, exit 155, 2 mi n on M-24, then e. 927 Demille Rd 48446. Fax: 810/245-7294. **Facility:** 72 one-bedroom standard units, some with whirlpools. 3 stories, interior corridors. *Bath:* combo or shower only. **Parking:** on-site. **Terms:** age restrictions may apply. **Amenities:** dual phone lines, irons. **Pool(s):** small heated indoor. **Leisure Activities:** whirlpool, exercise room. **Guest Services:** valet and coin laundry. **Business Services:** meeting rooms. **Cards:** AX, DC, DS, MC, VI. *(See ad p 328)*

SOME UNITS

————— WHERE TO DINE —————

E.G. NICK'S

◆◆ ◆◆

American

Lunch: $6-$9   **Dinner:** $10-$16   **Phone:** 810/664-6200
Location: 0.5 mi s on SR 24 and 21. 825 S Main St 48446. **Hours:** 11 am-10 pm, Fri & Sat-11 pm, Sun noon-9 pm. Closed: 11/27, 12/25. **Features:** Located in a bustling retail area near the interstate, this casual restaurant offers a menu of old favorites and innovative dishes including planked whitefish and their house specialty of basted ribs. Cocktails. **Parking:** on-site. **Cards:** AX, CB, MC, VI.

LELAND pop. 2,033

————— WHERE TO STAY —————

MANITOU MANOR BED & BREAKFAST

Phone: 231/256-7712

(AAA) (SAVE)
◆◆ ◆◆

Bed & Breakfast

6/1-11/1	1P: $140	2P: $140	XP: $15	F12
4/1-5/31 & 11/2-3/31	1P: $95	2P: $95	XP: $15	F12

Location: 0.8 mi s on SR 22 from jct SR 204. Located in a semi-rural area. 147 Manitou Tr W 49654 (PO Box 864). Fax: 231/256-7941. **Facility:** Smoke free premises. 5 one-bedroom standard units. 2 stories (no elevator), interior corridors. *Bath:* shared or private, combo or shower only. **Parking:** on-site. **Terms:** 7 day cancellation notice-fee imposed, [BP] meal plan available, no pets allowed (owner's pets on premises). **Leisure Activities:** horseshoes. **Guest Services:** TV in common area. **Cards:** DS, MC, VI. **Special Amenities: free local telephone calls and preferred room (subject to availability with advanced reservations).**

————— WHERE TO DINE —————

THE COVE

(AAA)
◆◆ ◆◆

American

Lunch: $5-$8   **Dinner:** $12-$19   **Phone:** 231/256-9834
Location: Just w of Main St. 111 River St 49654. **Hours:** Open 5/15-10/15; 11 am-9 pm, Fri & Sat-10 pm; to 10 pm 5/30-9/4. **Reservations:** suggested; in season. **Features:** Window tables and patio seating afford great views of Lake Michigan and the Manitou Islands. Seafood chowder and varied preparations of whitefish, such as macadamia nut whitefish, garlic Parmesan whitefish and campfire whitefish, are menu specialties. Casual dress; cocktails. **Parking:** street. **Cards:** AX, MC, VI.

LEWISTON pop. 990

————— WHERE TO STAY —————

GARLAND

Phone: (989)786-2211

(AAA) (SAVE)
◆◆◆◆ ◆◆◆◆

Resort
Small-scale Hotel

5/1-10/26 & 12/26-3/7   1P: $79-$249   2P: $129-$599
Location: 4.8 mi s. 4700 N Red Oak Rd 49756. Fax: 989/786-2254. **Facility:** Lodge, condo and villa units are available on this property's 3,500 wooded acres near a public airstrip; sleigh rides are offered in winter. 182 units. 56 one-bedroom standard units, some with whirlpools. 1 two-bedroom suite ($99-$259). 125 cottages ($199-$349), some with whirlpools. 1-3 stories, interior/exterior corridors. *Bath:* combo or shower only. **Parking:** on-site and valet, winter plug-ins. **Terms:** open 5/1-10/26 & 12/26-3/7, check-in 4 pm, 14 day cancellation notice, [AP] meal plan available. **Amenities:** voice mail. *Some:* irons, hair dryers. **Dining:** Herman's, see separate listing. **Pool(s):** heated outdoor, lap. **Leisure Activities:** sauna, whirlpools, 3 lighted tennis courts, cross country skiing, ice skating, rental snowmobiles, recreation programs in season, bicycle trails, hiking trails, exercise room, sports court, volleyball. *Fee:* fishing, golf-72 holes, golf instruction, bicycles. **Guest Services:** gift shop, valet laundry, airport transportation-Garland Airport. **Business Services:** conference facilities. **Cards:** AX, CB, DC, DS, JC, MC, VI. **Special Amenities: free room upgrade and preferred room (each subject to availability with advanced reservations).**

SOME UNITS

————— WHERE TO DINE —————

HERMAN'S

◆◆◆◆

American

Lunch: $7-$11   **Dinner:** $19-$33   **Phone:** 989/786-2211
Location: 4.8 mi s; in Garland. CR489 49756. **Hours:** Open 4/18-11/23 & 12/26-3/15; 5:30 am-11 pm; 6:30 am-10 pm in winter. **Reservations:** required. **Features:** Intimate dining. Enjoy the up-north atmosphere with view from a window seat. Regional Michigan cuisine. Entrees include such delicacies as fresh salmon, pheasant and venison. The steak, if you don't have it overcooked, will melt in your mouth. Dressy casual; cocktails; entertainment. **Parking:** on-site. **Cards:** AX, DC, DS, MC, VI.

LEXINGTON pop. 1,104

————— WHERE TO STAY —————

INN THE GARDEN BED & BREAKFAST

Phone: 810/359-8966

◆◆◆◆

Historic Bed
& Breakfast

All Year [BP]   2P: $85-$110   XP: $10   F5
Location: Center of town. 7156 Huron Ave 48450. Fax: 810/359-2119. **Facility:** Spacious grounds and a small greenhouse provide fresh herbs and produce for the breakfasts at this attractive Victorian style house. Smoke free premises. 4 units. 3 one-bedroom standard units. 1 two-bedroom suite. 3 stories (no elevator), interior corridors. *Bath:* combo or shower only. **Parking:** on-site. **Terms:** check-in 4 pm, 2 night minimum stay - in summer, 7 day cancellation notice, no pets allowed (owner's dog on premises). **Amenities:** video library.

SOME UNITS

LINCOLN PARK —*See Detroit p. 257.*

LINWOOD

—————— WHERE TO DINE ——————

LINWOOD CORNERS RESTAURANT   **Lunch:** $2-$4   **Dinner:** $6-$11   **Phone:** 989/697-5141
◈◈◈◈   **Location:** I-75, exit 173, 2.3 mi e on Linwood Rd, then 0.3 mi n on SR 13. 44 N Huron 48634. **Hours:** 5 am-8 pm.
American   Closed: 12/25; also 12/24 for dinner. **Features:** Home-style comfort foods, such as roast turkey, pork chops, steak and good old apple pie, make up the bulk of the family-oriented menu at the casual restaurant. Casual dress. **Parking:** on-site. **Cards:** DS, MC, VI.   ⊠

LIVONIA —*See Detroit p. 257.*

LUDINGTON pop. 8,357

—————— WHERE TO STAY ——————

DAYS INN OF LUDINGTON   **Phone:** 231/843-2233
◈◈◈   Property failed to provide current rates
     Location: On SR 10, 1 mi w of jct SR 31. Located next to a small amusement park. 5095 W US 10 49431.
Small-scale Hotel   Fax: 231/843-1945. **Facility:** 62 one-bedroom standard units, some with whirlpools. 3 stories (no elevator), interior/exterior corridors. **Parking:** on-site. **Terms:** small pets only ($7 extra charge). **Amenities:** hair dryers.
Guest Services: coin laundry. **Cards:** AX, DC, DS, MC, VI. *(See color ad card insert)*

SOME UNITS
🛏 📷 [DATA PORT] 💻 / ⊠ 📠 🖨 /

FOUR SEASONS MOTEL   **Phone:** (231)843-3448
(AAA) [SAVE]   7/4-8/31 [ECP]   1P: $85-$160   2P: $85-$160   XP: $20
◈◈◈◈   6/6-7/3 [ECP]   1P: $75-$140   2P: $75-$140   XP: $12
Motel   9/1-10/31 [ECP]   1P: $65-$110   2P: $65-$110   XP: $12
     5/1-6/5 [ECP]   1P: $65-$90   2P: $65-$110   XP: $12
     Location: 0.5 mi e. 717 E Ludington Ave 49431. Fax: 231/843-2635. **Facility:** Smoke free premises. 33 units. 30 one-bedroom standard units. 3 one-bedroom suites ($100-$170). 1 story, interior/exterior corridors. *Bath:* combo or shower only. **Parking:** on-site. **Terms:** open 5/1-10/31, 3 day cancellation notice-fee imposed. **Amenities:** *Some:* hair dryers. **Leisure Activities:** bicycles. *Fee:* off-site kayak excursions. **Business Services:** meeting rooms. **Cards:** AX, DS, MC, VI. **Special Amenities:** early check-in/late check-out and free continental breakfast. *(See color ad below)*

SOME UNITS
[S D] 🛏 ⊠ 📷 [DATA PORT] 💻 / [VCR] 📠 🖨 /
FEE   FEE   FEE   FEE

HOLIDAY INN EXPRESS   **Phone:** 231/845-7004
◈◈◈   All Year   1P: $72-$229   2P: $72-$229   XP: $10   F17
Small-scale Hotel   **Location:** 1.4 mi w of jct US 10 and 31. Located in a commercial area. 5323 W US 10 49431. Fax: 231/843-1677.
Facility: 102 units. 100 one-bedroom standard units, some with whirlpools. 1 one- and 1 two-bedroom suites with whirlpools. 2-3 stories, interior corridors. *Bath:* combo or shower only. **Parking:** on-site. **Terms:** [ECP] meal plan available, pets ($10 extra charge). **Amenities:** irons, hair dryers. *Some:* CD players. **Pool(s):** heated indoor. **Leisure Activities:** sauna, whirlpool, playground, exercise room, horseshoes, shuffleboard. *Fee:* game room. **Guest Services:** coin laundry. **Business Services:** meeting rooms. **Cards:** AX, CB, DC, DS, MC, VI. *(See color ad card insert)*

SOME UNITS
[A$K] 🛏 🍴 🐾 ⊠ 📷 [DATA PORT] 💻 / ⊠ [VCR] 📠 🖨 /

THE INN AT LUDINGTON

Phone: (231)845-7055

Bed & Breakfast

All Year [BP]   1P: $100-$110   2P: $100-$110   XP: $10   F10
Location: Just w of jct US 31 and 10. Located in a semi-residential area. 701 E Ludington Ave 49431. **Facility:** Smoke free premises. 6 one-bedroom standard units. 2 stories (no elevator), interior corridors. *Bath:* combo or shower only. **Parking:** on-site. **Terms:** 2-3 night minimum stay - weekends 5/1-9/30, 7 day cancellation notice-fee imposed, no pets allowed (owner's pet on premises). **Cards:** AX, DS, MC, VI. **Special Amenities:** free continental breakfast and free local telephone calls.

THE LAMPLIGHTER BED & BREAKFAST

Phone: (231)843-9792

Bed & Breakfast

4/1-10/31 & 12/1-3/31 [BP]   1P: $115-$155   2P: $115-$155
Location: 3 mi w of jct US 31 and 10 on US 10. Located in a semi-residential area. 602 E Ludington Ave 49431. Fax: 231/845-6070. **Facility:** This restored turn-of-the-20th-century Victorian home has an ambience of European-style elegance. Smoke free premises. 5 one-bedroom standard units, some with whirlpools. 2 stories (no elevator), interior corridors. *Bath:* shower only. **Parking:** on-site. **Terms:** open 4/1-10/31 & 12/1-3/31, check-in 4 pm, 2 night minimum stay - weekends, age restrictions may apply, 7 day cancellation notice, no pets allowed (owner's pet on premises). **Cards:** AX, CB, DC, DS, MC, VI. **Special Amenities:** free local telephone calls and preferred room (subject to availability with advanced reservations).

SNYDERS SHORELINE INN LLC

Phone: 231/845-1261

Small-scale Hotel

Property failed to provide current rates
Location: 0.3 mi w. 903 W Ludington Ave (PO Box 667). Fax: 231/843-4441. **Facility:** Smoke free premises. 44 one-bedroom standard units, some with whirlpools. 2 stories (no elevator), interior/exterior corridors. *Bath:* combo or shower only. **Parking:** on-site. **Terms:** open 5/3-10/19. **Amenities:** video library, voice mail. *Some:* hair dryers. **Pool(s):** heated outdoor. **Leisure Activities:** whirlpool. **Cards:** AX, MC, VI.

SOME UNITS

VIKING ARMS INN

Phone: (231)843-3441

Motel

6/13-8/31 [CP]   1P: $75-$120   2P: $75-$160   XP: $10
4/1-6/12 [CP]   1P: $59-$85   2P: $59-$100   XP: $10
9/1-10/31 [CP]   1P: $55-$90   2P: $55-$95   XP: $10
11/1-3/31 [CP]   1P: $45-$60   2P: $45-$60   XP: $10
Location: 0.8 mi e. Located in a semi-commercial area. 930 E Ludington Ave 49431. Fax: 231/845-7703. **Facility:** 45 one-bedroom standard units, some with whirlpools. 1 story, interior/exterior corridors. *Bath:* combo or shower only. **Parking:** on-site. **Terms:** age restrictions may apply, 7 day cancellation notice-fee imposed. **Amenities:** video library (fee), hair dryers. **Pool(s):** heated outdoor. **Leisure Activities:** whirlpool. **Business Services:** meeting rooms. **Cards:** MC, VI. **Special Amenities:** free continental breakfast and free local telephone calls. *(See color ad below)*

SOME UNITS

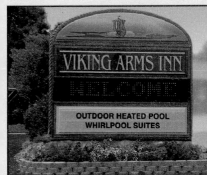
Get the Complete Picture.

When making travel plans online at **aaa.com**, look for lodgings and attractions with an online photo listing. The photographs and descriptive text not contained in standard listings allow you to "virtually" experience the property or attraction prior to making your reservations or buying your tickets. Properties with photo listings are easily located in the TourBook search section of AAA online. Simply begin your search by entering your trip criteria such as destination, and then look for the listings featuring the camera icon.

So, the next time you're making travel plans online at aaa.com, be sure to look at the photo listings prior to making your lodging decisions!

——— WHERE TO DINE ———

P M STEAMERS
▼▼ ▼▼
Steak & Seafood

Dinner: $9-$17   **Phone:** 231/843-9555
Location: Corner of Loomis and Lewis; center. 502 W Loomis 49431. **Hours:** Open 4/1-12/31; 5 pm-9 pm; 4 pm-10 pm 7/1-9/1. **Reservations:** suggested. **Features:** Across from the city marina, the casual waterfront restaurant is a comfortable place for family dining. The menu includes a good selection of steaks, seafood, pizza and burgers—as well as mouthwatering desserts. Sunday brunch is popular during summer. Casual dress; cocktails. **Parking:** on-site. **Cards:** AX, MC, VI.
▥ ☒

SCOTTY'S
ⒶⒶⒶ
▼▼ ▼▼
American

Lunch: $3-$7   **Dinner:** $9-$20   **Phone:** 231/843-4033
Location: 1.8 mi w of jct US 10 and 31. 5910 E Ludington Ave 49431. **Hours:** 11:30 am-2 & 5-9 pm, Fri & Sat-10 pm; 11:30 am-2 & 5-10 pm, Sun 9 am-1 pm 6/1-9/30. Closed major holidays. **Features:** Popular dishes include the roast prime rib of beef - the specialty of the house along with several seafood dishes such as their "renowned" lake perch or the seafood kabob. Booths available for more intimate dining. Casual dress; cocktails. **Parking:** on-site. **Cards:** AX, MC, VI.
▥ ☒

LUNA PIER pop. 1,483

——— WHERE TO STAY ———

SUPER 8 MOTEL-LUNA PIER
▼▼ ▼▼
Small-scale Hotel

			Phone: (734)848-8880	
4/1-9/30 [CP]	1P: $50-$70	2P: $54-$80	XP: $6	F12
10/1-3/31 [CP]	1P: $45-$50	2P: $50-$59	XP: $6	F12

Location: I-75, exit 6. 4163 Super 8 Dr 48157. **Fax:** 734/848-6146. **Facility:** 49 one-bedroom standard units, some with whirlpools. 3 stories, interior corridors. *Bath:* combo or shower only. **Parking:** on-site. **Amenities:** hair dryers. **Pool(s):** small heated indoor. **Business Services:** fax (fee). **Cards:** AX, CB, DC, DS, JC, MC, VI.

SOME UNITS
(ASK) (S🄳) (🍴) (🏊) (🐾) (DATA PORT) (🖥) / (☒) (🔒) (🖥) /

——— WHERE TO DINE ———

GANDERS FAMILY RESTAURANT
▼
American

Lunch: $6-$8   **Dinner:** $7-$13   **Phone:** 734/848-8913
Location: I-75, exit 6, just e. 4219 Luna Pier Rd 48157. **Hours:** 6 am-9 pm, Fri & Sat-10 pm. Closed: 12/25. **Features:** Fresh lake perch, hamburgers, chicken sandwiches and steaks are among home-style menu selections at this friendly restaurant. Pictures and ceramic figures of geese decorate the casual dining room. Diner-style service is friendly and efficient. Casual dress. **Parking:** on-site. **Cards:** AX, DS, MC, VI.
☒

MACKINAC ISLAND pop. 523   (See map p. 336; index p. 340)

——— WHERE TO STAY ———

GRAND HOTEL
ⒶⒶⒶ (SAVE)
▼▼ ▼▼ ▼▼
Classic Historic
Resort
Large-Scale
Hotel
(See ad p 333)

			Phone: (906)847-3331	63
6/13-9/1 [MAP]	1P: $325-$485	2P: $390-$550	XP: $99	F4
5/8-6/12 & 9/2-11/2 [MAP]	1P: $285-$445	2P: $350-$510	XP: $99	F4

Location: On Mackinac Island. Mackinac Island 49757. **Fax:** 906/847-3259. **Facility:** Those seeking a formal ambience will appreciate this historic 1887 hotel's strict after-six dress code. 385 units. 375 one-bedroom standard units. 6 two-bedroom suites. 6 stories, interior corridors. **Parking:** no self-parking. **Terms:** open 5/8-11/2, 10 day cancellation notice-fee imposed, 19% service charge. **Amenities:** video library (fee), safes, honor bars, irons, hair dryers. **Dining:** 2 restaurants, 7:30 am-9:30, noon-2 & 6:30-10 pm, cocktails, entertainment. **Pool(s):** heated outdoor. **Leisure Activities:** sauna, whirlpools, 4 tennis courts, recreation programs in season, jogging, exercise room, volleyball, game room. *Fee:* golf-18 holes, bicycles. **Guest Services:** gift shop, valet laundry. **Business Services:** conference facilities, business center. **Cards:** AX, DC, DS, MC, VI.

SOME UNITS
(🍴) (▥) (🏄) (📶) (🏊) (☒) (DATA PORT) / (☒) (🅺) (VCR) (🔒) (🖥) /

HARBOUR VIEW INN
ⒶⒶⒶ (SAVE)
▼▼ ▼▼ ▼▼
Small-scale Hotel

			Phone: (906)847-0101	65
5/23-8/23 [ECP]	1P: $145-$235	2P: $145-$235	XP: $20	
5/2-5/22 & 8/24-10/26 [ECP]	1P: $85-$235	2P: $85-$235	XP: $20	

Location: 4 blks e. Huron St 49757 (PO Box 1207). **Fax:** 906/847-3998. **Facility:** Smoke free premises. 65 units. 47 one-bedroom standard units, some with whirlpools. 18 one-bedroom suites ($165-$345). 4 stories (no elevator), interior corridors. *Bath:* combo or shower only. **Parking:** no self-parking. **Terms:** open 5/2-10/26, 2-3 night minimum stay - weekends, 10 day cancellation notice-fee imposed. **Leisure Activities:** whirlpool. **Business Services:** meeting rooms. **Cards:** AX, CB, DC, DS, MC, VI. **Special Amenities:** free continental breakfast and free local telephone calls. *(See ad p 333)*

SOME UNITS
(🅰️) (☒) (DATA PORT) / (🅺) (🔒) /

THE INN ON MACKINAC
▼▼ ▼▼
Bed & Breakfast

			Phone: (906)847-3360	64
5/7-10/4 [ECP]	1P: $104-$285	2P: $104-$285	XP: $15	F5

Location: 3 blks e. Main St 49757 (PO Box 476). **Fax:** 906/847-6110. **Facility:** Smoke free premises. 44 one-bedroom standard units. 3 stories, interior corridors. *Bath:* combo or shower only. **Parking:** no self-parking. **Terms:** open 5/7-10/4, 2 night minimum stay - weekends, 14 day cancellation notice-fee imposed, package plans, 6% service charge. **Amenities:** *Some:* hair dryers. **Cards:** MC, VI.

(ASK) (S🄳) (☒) (Ⓩ)

(See map p. 336)

THE ISLAND HOUSE

				Phone: (906)847-3347	62
6/7-9/1	1P: $150-$315		2P: $150-$315	XP: $20	D13
5/2-6/6 & 9/2-10/23	1P: $79-$255		2P: $79-$255	XP: $20	D13

Historic Small-scale Hotel

Location: 3 blks e. 1 Lake Shore Dr 49757 (PO Box 1410). **Fax:** 906/847-3819. **Facility:** 97 units. 94 one-bedroom standard units. 3 two-bedroom suites ($500-$600) with whirlpools. 4 stories, interior corridors. **Parking:** no self-parking. **Terms:** open 5/2-10/23, 3 day cancellation notice-fee imposed, [BP] & [MAP] meal plans available, 8% service charge. **Amenities:** voice mail, hair dryers. *Some:* safes, irons. **Dining:** 2 restaurants, 7:30 am-10:30 & 5:30-10 pm, cocktails, entertainment. **Pool(s):** heated indoor. **Leisure Activities:** sauna, whirlpool, recreation programs, playground. *Fee:* bicycles. **Business Services:** meeting rooms. **Cards:** AX, DS, MC, VI. **Special Amenities:** early check-in/late check-out and preferred room (subject to availability with advanced reservations). *(See color ad p 334)*

SOME UNITS

(See map p. 336)

LAKE VIEW HOTEL AND CONFERENCE CENTER

AAA SAVE

WWWW WWWW

Small-scale Hotel

6/6-8/23	1P: $179-$325	
5/9-6/5	1P: $150-$250	
8/24-10/19	1P: $140-$250	

Phone: (906)847-3384   67
XP: $25   F16
XP: $25   F16
XP: $25   F16

Location: Just w. 1 Huron St 49757 (PO Box 190). Fax: 906/847-6283. **Facility:** 85 one-bedroom standard units, some with whirlpools. 4 stories, interior corridors. **Parking:** no self-parking. **Terms:** open 5/9-10/19, 10 day cancellation notice-fee imposed, 8% service charge. **Dining:** 7:30 am-10 pm, cocktails. **Pool(s):** heated indoor. **Leisure Activities:** sauna, whirlpool. **Business Services:** conference facilities. **Cards:** DS, MC, VI.
(See color ad p 335)

SOME UNITS

🅢🄳 🍴 🍸 🚲 / ✕ 🐾 /

MURRAY HOTEL

WWW WW

Small-scale Hotel

5/7-10/11 [ECP]   1P: $94-$255   2P: $94-$255

Phone: (906)847-3360   66
XP: $15   F5

Location: Center. Located opposite Arnold Ferry Dock. Main St 49757 (PO Box 476). Fax: 906/847-6110. **Facility:** Smoke free premises. 69 one-bedroom standard units, some with whirlpools. 4 stories, interior corridors. *Bath:* combo or shower only. **Parking:** no self-parking. **Terms:** open 5/7-10/11, 2 night minimum stay - weekends, 14 day cancellation notice-fee imposed, package plans. **Leisure Activities:** whirlpool. **Cards:** MC, VI.

A$K 🅢🄳 🍴+ ✕ 🐾

Mackinaw City
Lodging & Dining

Miles   0   0.3

© AAA   1948-A   To Pellston   To Indian River   ©2002 NAVIGATION TECHNOLOGIES

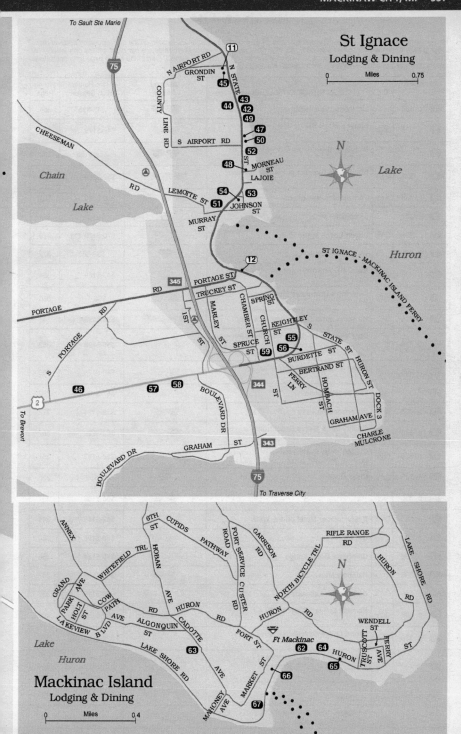

St Ignace
Lodging & Dining

Miles
0   0.75

To Sault Ste Marie

I-75

11

N AIRPORT RD

GRONDIN ST

N STATE

COUNTY LINE RD

45

43

44

42

49

47

50

S AIRPORT RD

52

48 ST

MORNEAU ST

LAJOIE

CHEESEMAN

Chain

Lake

RD

LEMOITE ST

54

51

53

JOHNSON ST

MURRAY ST

N

Lake

Huron

ST IGNACE - MACKINAC ISLAND FERRY

12

345

PORTAGE ST

RD

TRUCKEY ST

SPRING ST

PORTAGE

RD

1ST ST

MARLEY ST

CHAMBER ST

CHURCH ST

KEIGHTLEY ST

55

S STATE ST

HURON ST

S PORTAGE

SPRUCE ST

59

56

BURDETTE ST

DOCK 3

BERTRAND ST

FERRY LN

HOMBACH ST

GRAHAM AVE

46

57

58

BOULEVARD DR

344

S ST

CHARLE MULCRONE

I-2

To Brevort

BOULEVARD DR

GRAHAM ST

343

I-75

To Traverse City

Mackinac Island
Lodging & Dining

ANNEX

6TH ST

CUPIDS

FORT SERVICE ROAD

GARRISON RD

RIFLE RANGE RD

LAKE SHORE RD

WHITEFIELD TRL

HOBAN AVE

PATHWAY

CUSTER RD

NORTH BICYCLE TRL

HURON RD

GRAND AVE

PARK AVE

HOLT ST

COW PATH

HURON AVE

RD

N

WENDELL ST

LAKEVIEW BLVD

AVE

ALGONQUIN ST

CADOTTE AVE

FORT ST

HURON RD

RD

TRUSCOTT ST

FERRY AVE

1ST ST

HURON ST

Lake Huron

LAKE SHORE RD

63

Ft Mackinac

62

64

65

66

MAHONEY AVE

MARKET ST

67

Miles
0   0.4

Mackinaw City

This index helps you "spot" where approved accommodations and restaurants are located on the corresponding detailed maps. Lodging rate ranges are for comparison only and show the property's high season; rates are per night, unless only weekly (W) rates are available. Restaurant rate range is for dinner, unless only lunch (L) is served. Turn to the listing page for more detailed rate information and consult display ads for special promotions.

Spotter/Map Page Number	OA	MACKINAW CITY - Lodgings	Diamond Rating	Rate Range High Season	Listing Page
1 / p. 336		Lighthouse View Motel	◆◆	$45-$95	364
2 / p. 336	AAA	**Super 8 Motel Bridgeview** - see color ad p 351	◆◆	$49-$179 SAVE	369
3 / p. 336		Budget Host Mackinaw City - see color ad p 187	◆◆	$58-$158	354
4 / p. 336	AAA	**Holiday Inn Express at the Bridge** - see color ad card insert	◆◆◆	$52-$259 SAVE	363
5 / p. 336	AAA	**Parkside Inn-Bridgeside**	◆◆◆	$59-$199 SAVE	367
6 / p. 336		Lamplighter Motel	◆	$48-$92	364
7 / p. 336	AAA	**Econo Lodge at the Bridge**	◆◆	$70-$170 SAVE	360
8 / p. 336		Wa Wa Tam Motel	◆	$38-$62	372
9 / p. 336	AAA	**Motel 6-Downtown** - see color ad starting on p 362	◆	$47-$169 SAVE	364
10 / p. 336	AAA	**Downing's Downtown Motor Inn** - see color ad p 360	◆◆	$98 SAVE	360
11 / p. 336	AAA	**Baymont Inn & Suites-Mackinaw City**	◆◆◆	$99-$199 SAVE	341
12 / p. 336	AAA	**Best Western-Dockside Waterfront Inn** - see color ad starting on p 342, p 353, p 84, & card insert	◆◆◆	$58-$198 SAVE	352
13 / p. 336	AAA	**Super 8 Motel-Beachfront** - see color ad p 350 & p 84	◆◆	$48-$178 SAVE	369
14 / p. 336	AAA	**The Beach House**	◆	$57-$160 SAVE	352
15 / p. 336	AAA	**Waterfront Inn** - see color ad p 355	◆◆	$59-$124 SAVE	372
16 / p. 336	AAA	**Quality Inn & Suites Beachfront** - see color ad p 367	◆◆	$69-$229 SAVE	367
17 / p. 336	AAA	**Clarion Hotel Beachfront** - see color ad starting on p 346 & p 84	◆◆◆	$58-$198 SAVE	357
18 / p. 336	AAA	**Chief Motel**	◆	$49-$99 SAVE	355
19 / p. 336	AAA	**Clear Water Lakeshore Motel** - see color ad p 356	◆◆	$58-$138 SAVE	357
20 / p. 336	AAA	**Beachcomber Motel on the Water**	◆	$59-$145 SAVE	341
21 / p. 336	AAA	**Days Inn** - see color ad card insert & p 359	◆◆	$69-$198 SAVE	360
22 / p. 336	AAA	**Chippewa Motor Lodge** - see color ad p 355	◆◆	$59-$124 SAVE	356
23 / p. 336	AAA	**Rainbow Motel** - see color ad p 368	◆◆	$48-$139 SAVE	367
24 / p. 336	AAA	**Comfort Inn Lakeside** - see color ad p 358	◆◆◆	$58-$198 SAVE	357
25 / p. 336	AAA	**Ramada Limited Waterfront** - see color ad p 370	◆◆◆	$99-$189 SAVE	369
26 / p. 336	AAA	**Econo Lodge Bayview** - see color ad starting on p 348 & p 84	◆◆	$38-$168 SAVE	360
27 / p. 336	AAA	**Hamilton Inn Select-Beachfront** - see color ad starting on p 344, inside front cover, & p 84	◆◆◆	$38-$198 SAVE	361
28 / p. 336	AAA	**Hawthorn Inn & Suites** - see color ad starting on p 348 & p 84	◆◆◆	$58-$198 SAVE	363
29 / p. 336	AAA	**Hampton Inn of Mackinaw City** - see color ad starting on p 363	◆◆◆	$69-$183 SAVE	363

Spotter/Map Page Number	OA	**MACKINAW CITY** - Lodgings (continued)	Diamond Rating	Rate Range High Season	Listing Page
30 / p. 336	AAA	**Ramada Inn Conference Resort** - see color ad p 368	◊◊	$75 SAVE	368
31 / p. 336	AAA	**Capri Motel**	◊	$49-$89 SAVE	355
32 / p. 336	AAA	**Northpointe Inn** - see color ad p 366	◊◊◊	$99-$199 SAVE	366
33 / p. 336	AAA	**Grand View Resort-Beachfront** - see color ad p 361	◊◊	$56-$169 SAVE	360
34 / p. 336	AAA	**Travelodge-Bayview** - see color ad p 371	◊◊	$38-$168 SAVE	371
35 / p. 336	AAA	**Best Western Thunderbird Inn** - see color ad p 354	◊◊◊	$59-$139 SAVE	354
36 / p. 336	AAA	**Kings Inn**	◊	$39-$89 SAVE	364
37 / p. 336	AAA	**Anchor Inns** - see color ad p 341	◊◊	$52-$129 SAVE	341
38 / p. 336	AAA	**Budget Inns-Starlite**	◊	$37-$98 SAVE	354
39 / p. 336	AAA	**Best Western of Mackinaw City** - see color ad p 352	◊◊◊	$36-$180 SAVE	352
		MACKINAW CITY - Restaurants			
1 / p. 336	AAA	**Chippewa Room at Audie's**	◊◊	$11-$30	372
2 / p. 336	AAA	**Dixie's Saloon**	◊	$11-$18	373
3 / p. 336	AAA	**The Embers**	◊	$10-$15	373
4 / p. 336	AAA	**Mario's Ristorante**	◊	$9-$17	373
5 / p. 336	AAA	**Anna's Country Buffet** - see color ad p 372	◊	$7-$14	372
6 / p. 336	AAA	**Admiral's Table**	◊	$8-$20	372
7 / p. 336	AAA	**Lighthouse Restaurant**	◊◊	$11-$34	373
8 / p. 336	AAA	**Neath the Birches**	◊◊	$11-$34	373
		ST. IGNACE - Lodgings			
42 / p. 336	AAA	**Best Western-Kewadin Casino Lakefront Inn**	◊◊	$94-$104 SAVE	409
43 / p. 336		Bay View Motel	◊	$60-$76	409
44 / p. 336	AAA	**Days Inn St. Ignace** - see color ad card insert & p 415	◊◊	$69-$159 SAVE	415
45 / p. 336		Tradewinds Motel	◊	$50-$73	420
46 / p. 336	AAA	**Four Star Motel**	◊	$38-$46 SAVE	416
47 / p. 336	AAA	**K-Royale Motor Inn** - see color ad p 418	◊◊	$58-$150 SAVE	418
48 / p. 336	AAA	**Comfort Inn** - see color ad p 413	◊◊	$69-$198 SAVE	412
49 / p. 336	AAA	**Days Inn Lakefront & Suites** - see color ad card insert & p 415	◊◊◊	$79-$179 SAVE	414
50 / p. 336	AAA	**Quality Inn Lakefront** - see color ad p 419	◊◊	$94-$186 SAVE	419
51 / p. 336	AAA	**Budget Host Inn** - see color ad p 187, p 411	◊◊	$74-$156 SAVE	411
52 / p. 336		Holiday Inn Express Lakefront	◊◊◊	$114-$130	417
53 / p. 336	AAA	**Harbour Pointe Lakefront Lodging** - see color ad p 416	◊◊	$98-$179 SAVE	416
54 / p. 336	AAA	**Wayside Motel**	◊	$50-$75 SAVE	420
55 / p. 336	AAA	**Straits Breeze Motel** - see color ad p 419	◊◊	$69-$130 SAVE	420
56 / p. 336		Aurora Borealis Motor Inn - see ad p 410	◊◊	$49-$89	409
57 / p. 336		Super 8 of St. Ignace	◊◊	$88-$109	420

Spotter/Map Page Number	OA	ST. IGNACE - Lodgings (continued)	Diamond Rating	Rate Range High Season	Listing Page
58 / p. 336		Quality Inn St. Ignace	◆◆	$59-$139	419
59 / p. 336	AAA	**Rodeway Inn**	◆◆	$79-$185 SAVE	420
		ST. IGNACE - Restaurants			
11 / p. 336		North Bay Inn	◆	$8-$15	420
12 / p. 336	AAA	**The Galley Restaurant & Bar**	◆	$9-$16	420
		MACKINAC ISLAND - Lodgings			
62 / p. 336	AAA	**The Island House -** see color ad p 334	◆◆	$150-$315 SAVE	333
63 / p. 336	AAA	**Grand Hotel -** see ad p 333	◆◆◆◆	$325-$550 SAVE	332
64 / p. 336		The Inn on Mackinac	◆◆	$104-$285	332
65 / p. 336	AAA	**Harbour View Inn -** see ad p 333	◆◆◆	$145-$235 SAVE	332
66 / p. 336		Murray Hotel	◆◆	$94-$255	334
67 / p. 336	AAA	**Lake View Hotel and Conference Center -** see color ad p 335	◆◆◆	$179-$325 SAVE	334

MACKINAW CITY pop. 859   (See map p. 336; index p. 338)

─── **WHERE TO STAY** ───

ANCHOR INNS

AAA **SAVE**   Phone: (231)436-5553   **37**

6/25-8/17 [CP]	1P: $52-$119	2P: $59-$129	XP: $10	F10
5/1-6/24 & 8/18-10/30 [CP]	1P: $38-$78	2P: $38-$89	XP: $10	F10

Motel

Location: I-75, exit 338 southbound, 0.3 mi e; exit 337 northbound, just ne. 138 US 31 49701 (PO Box 812). Fax: 231/436-7440. **Facility:** 34 units. 32 one- and 2 two-bedroom standard units, some with whirlpools. 2 stories (no elevator), interior/exterior corridors. **Parking:** on-site. **Terms:** open 5/1-10/30, 3 day cancellation notice-fee imposed. **Amenities:** *Some:* hair dryers. **Pool(s):** heated indoor. **Leisure Activities:** snowmobiling, playground, spa. *Fee:* game room. **Cards:** DS, MC, VI. **Special Amenities:** free continental breakfast and free local telephone calls. *(See color ad below)*

SOME UNITS

BAYMONT INN & SUITES-MACKINAW CITY

AAA **SAVE**   Phone: (231)436-7737   **11**

6/20-8/23 [ECP]	1P: $99-$199	2P: $99-$199
5/2-6/19 & 8/24-10/26 [ECP]	1P: $69-$99	2P: $69-$99
4/1-5/1 [ECP]	1P: $59-$79	2P: $59-$79

Small-scale Hotel

Location: I-75, exit 338. 109 S Nicolet St 49701 (PO Box 860, MACKINAW). Fax: 231/436-5427. **Facility:** 80 one-bedroom standard units, some with whirlpools. 3 stories, interior corridors. *Bath:* combo or shower only. **Parking:** on-site. **Terms:** open 4/1-10/26, pets ($50 deposit, in smoking units). **Amenities:** video games, voice mail, irons, hair dryers. **Pool(s):** heated indoor. **Leisure Activities:** whirlpool, snowmobiling, exercise room. **Guest Services:** coin laundry. **Business Services:** meeting rooms. **Cards:** AX, DC, DS, MC, VI. **Special Amenities:** free continental breakfast and free newspaper.

SOME UNITS

BEACHCOMBER MOTEL ON THE WATER

AAA **SAVE**   Phone: 231/436-8451   **20**

6/22-8/18	1P: $59-$145	2P: $65-$145	XP: $5	F5
8/19-10/31	1P: $39-$45	2P: $45-$49	XP: $5	F5
5/1-6/21	1P: $32-$35	2P: $35-$39	XP: $5	F5

Motel

Location: 1 mi s on US 23. 1011 S Huron Dr 49701 (PO Box 159). **Facility:** 22 units. 21 one-bedroom standard units, some with whirlpools. 1 cottage ($79-$110). 1-2 stories (no elevator), exterior corridors. *Bath:* combo or shower only. **Parking:** on-site. **Terms:** open 5/1-10/31, 3 day cancellation notice, [CP] meal plan available, small pets only ($10 extra charge). **Amenities:** video library (fee). **Leisure Activities:** pool privileges. **Cards:** AX, DS, MC, VI. **Special Amenities:** free continental breakfast and free local telephone calls.

SOME UNITS

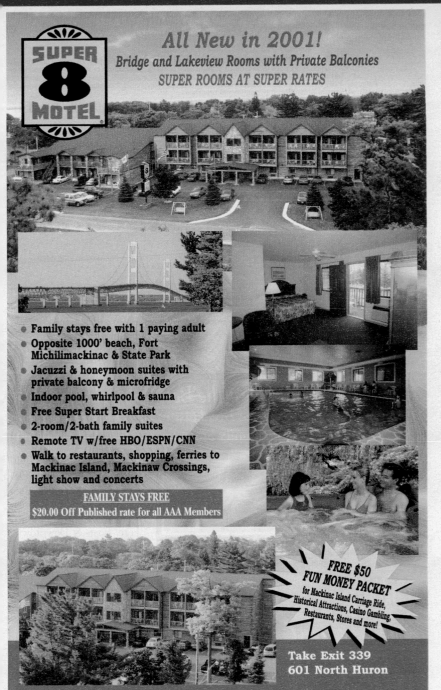

(See map p. 336)

THE BEACH HOUSE
Phone: (231)436-5353 **14**

AAA SAVE

7/1-8/23		2P: $57-$160	XP: $10 F
8/24-10/12		2P: $39-$115	
5/1-6/30		2P: $39-$115	XP: $10 F

Cottage

Location: 1.3 mi s. 11490 W US 23 St 49701 (PO Box 141). Fax: 231/436-4057. **Facility:** 28 units. 3 one-bedroom standard units. 25 cottages ($39-$160). 1 story, exterior corridors. *Bath:* combo or shower only. **Parking:** on-site. **Terms:** open 5/1-10/12, 14 day cancellation notice-fee imposed, [CP] meal plan available, small pets only ($10 extra charge). **Pool(s):** heated indoor. **Leisure Activities:** whirlpool, playground, basketball, horseshoes, volleyball. **Cards:** AX, DS, MC, VI. **Special Amenities:** free continental breakfast.

SOME UNITS

BEST WESTERN-DOCKSIDE WATERFRONT INN
Phone: (231)436-5001 **12**

AAA SAVE

6/27-8/16 [BP]	1P: $58-$198	2P: $58-$198	
4/1-6/26 & 8/17-11/1 [BP]	1P: $38-$148	2P: $38-$148	

Motel

Location: I-75, exit 338 northbound, just n to Central Ave, just e to Huron Ave, then just s; I-75, exit 338 southbound, 0.8 mi se; downtown. 505 S Huron 49701 (PO Box 722). Fax: 231/436-5933. **Facility:** 112 one-bedroom standard units, some with whirlpools. 4 stories, exterior corridors. **Parking:** on-site. **Terms:** open 4/1-11/1, 3 day cancellation notice-fee imposed, weekly rates available, package plans. **Amenities:** video library (fee), dual phone lines, voice mail, irons, hair dryers. **Pool(s):** heated indoor. **Leisure Activities:** whirlpool, waterslide, water trampoline. **Cards:** AX, CB, DC, DS, MC, VI. **Special Amenities: free continental breakfast and free room upgrade (subject to availability with advanced reservations).** *(See color ad starting on p 342, p 353, p 84 & card insert)*

SOME UNITS

FEE

BEST WESTERN OF MACKINAW CITY
Phone: (231)436-5544 **39**

AAA SAVE

8/15-10/19 [ECP]	1P: $36-$180	2P: $38-$180	
6/27-8/14 [ECP]	1P: $59-$169	2P: $59-$179	
4/18-6/26 [ECP]	1P: $36-$99	2P: $38-$99	

Motel

Location: I-75, exit 337 northbound, 0.5 mi n; exit 338 southbound, 0.5 mi s. 112 Old US 31 49701 (PO Box 777). Fax: 231/436-7180. **Facility:** 73 one-bedroom standard units, some with whirlpools. 2 stories (no elevator), exterior corridors. **Parking:** on-site. **Terms:** open 4/18-10/19, cancellation fee imposed, [CP] meal plan available. **Amenities:** irons, hair dryers. **Pool(s):** heated indoor. **Leisure Activities:** whirlpool. **Guest Services:** coin laundry. **Cards:** AX, CB, DC, DS, MC, VI. **Special Amenities: early check-in/late check-out and free continental breakfast.** *(See color ad below)*

SOME UNITS

(See map p. 336)

BEST WESTERN THUNDERBIRD INN   Phone: (231)436-5433   **35**

	6/26-8/23 [CP]	1P: $59-$129	2P: $69-$139	XP: $10	F17
	5/2-6/25 & 8/24-10/19 [CP]	1P: $39-$99	2P: $39-$99	XP: $5	F17

Motel   **Location:** I-75, exit 337 northbound, just ne; exit 338 southbound, 0.7 mi se. 146 Old US 31 49701 (PO Box 251). **Fax:** 231/436-7212. **Facility:** 50 one-bedroom standard units, some with whirlpools. 2 stories (no elevator), exterior corridors. **Parking:** on-site. **Terms:** open 5/2-10/19, 3 day cancellation notice. **Amenities:** irons, hair dryers. **Pool(s):** heated indoor. **Leisure Activities:** sauna, whirlpool, playground. **Guest Services:** coin laundry. **Cards:** AX, CB, DC, DS, MC, VI. **Special Amenities:** free continental breakfast and free room upgrade (subject to availability with advanced reservations). *(See color ad below)*

SOME UNITS

BUDGET HOST MACKINAW CITY   Phone: (231)436-5543   **3**

	6/20-8/23		2P: $58-$158	XP: $6	F12
	8/24-10/18		2P: $46-$128	XP: $10	F12
	5/3-6/19		2P: $42-$108	XP: $6	F12

Motel   **Location:** I-75, exit 339, just n of town. 517 N Huron Ave 49701. **Facility:** 23 one-bedroom standard units. 2 stories (no elevator), exterior corridors. **Parking:** on-site. **Terms:** open 5/3-10/18, 3 day cancellation notice-fee imposed. **Pool(s):** heated outdoor. **Leisure Activities:** playground. **Cards:** AX, DS, MC, VI. *(See color ad p 187)*

SOME UNITS

BUDGET INNS-STARLITE   Phone: (231)436-5959   **38**

	6/22-8/24 [CP]	1P: $37-$89	2P: $37-$98	XP: $10	F10
	4/25-6/21 [CP]	1P: $27-$69	2P: $27-$69	XP: $10	F10
	8/25-11/5 [CP]	1P: $28-$39	2P: $28-$59	XP: $10	F10

Motel   **Location:** I-75, exit 338 southbound, 0.3 mi e; I-75, exit 337 northbound, then just ne. 116 Old US 31 49701 (PO Box 758). **Fax:** 231/436-5244. **Facility:** 33 units. 30 one- and 3 two-bedroom standard units. 1 story, exterior corridors. **Parking:** on-site. **Terms:** open 4/25-11/5, 3 day cancellation notice-fee imposed, small pets only ($15 extra charge). **Pool(s):** heated outdoor. **Leisure Activities:** playground, spa, basketball. *Fee:* game room. **Cards:** AX, CB, DC, DS, MC, VI. **Special Amenities:** free continental breakfast and free local telephone calls.

SOME UNITS

See map p. 336)

APRI MOTEL

Motel

					Phone: (231)436-5498	**31**
6/23-9/8		1P: $49-$59		2P: $59-$89	XP: $5	F16
4/1-6/22 & 9/9-3/31		1P: $29-$39		2P: $39-$59	XP: $5	F16

Location: I-75, exit 338, just s. Located across from the information center. 801 S Nicolet St 49701. Fax: 231/436-7328. **Facility:** 27 one-bedroom standard units. 1 story, exterior corridors. **Parking:** on-site. **Terms:** cancellation fee imposed, small pets only ($10 extra charge). **Pool(s):** heated outdoor. **Leisure Activities:** snowmobiling, playground, horseshoes, volleyball. **Cards:** AX, DS, MC, VI. **Special Amenities:** free cal telephone calls.

SOME UNITS

HIEF MOTEL

Motel

					Phone: 231/436-7981	**18**
6/27-8/23		1P: $49-$99		2P: $56-$99	XP: $5	
5/23-6/26 & 8/24-9/27		1P: $32-$59		2P: $38-$65	XP: $5	

Location: 1 mi s. Located in a semi-rural area. 10470 US 23 49701 (PO Box 175). **Facility:** 16 one-bedroom standard units. 1 story, exterior corridors. *Bath:* combo or shower only. **Parking:** on-site. **Terms:** open 5/23-9/27, 3 day cancellation notice-fee imposed. **Pool(s):** heated outdoor. **Cards:** MC, VI. **Special Amenities:** free local telephone calls.

SOME UNITS

(See map p. 336)

CHIPPEWA MOTOR LODGE   Phone: 231/436-8661

6/22-8/16 [CP]	1P: $59-$124	2P: $64-$124
8/17-10/19 [CP]	1P: $32-$89	2P: $32-$89
5/2-6/21 [CP]	1P: $29-$89	2P: $29-$89

Motel

Location: 1 mi se on US 23. 929 S Huron St 49701 (PO Box 518). Fax: 231/436-8661. **Facility:** 39 units. 26 one bedroom standard units. 13 cabins ($59-$189). 1-3 stories (no elevator), exterior corridors. *Bath:* combo o shower only. **Parking:** on-site. **Terms:** open 5/2-10/19, 3 day cancellation notice. **Pool(s):** heated indoo **Leisure Activities:** whirlpool, playground, shuffleboard. **Fee:** game room. **Cards:** DS, MC, VI. **Special Amenities:** free conti nental breakfast and free local telephone calls. *(See color ad p 355)*

SOME UNITS

(See map p. 336)

CLARION HOTEL BEACHFRONT
Phone: (231)436-5539 **17**
△△△ SAVE 6/27-8/16 [BP] 1P: $58-$198 2P: $58-$198
4/1-6/26 & 8/17-11/1 [BP] 1P: $38-$148 2P: $38-$148
▽▽▽▽ **Location:** I-75, exit 337 northbound, 0.5 mi n to US 23, 0.3 mi e; exit 338 southbound, 0.8 mi se on US 23. 905 S Huron
Motel St 49701 (PO Box 508). Fax: 231/436-7107. **Facility:** 112 units. 85 one- and 27 two-bedroom standard units,
some with whirlpools. 2-4 stories, exterior corridors. **Parking:** on-site. **Terms:** open 4/1-11/1, 3 day cancellation notice-fee imposed, package plans. **Amenities:** video library (fee), dual phone lines, voice mail, irons,
hair dryers. **Pool(s):** heated indoor. **Leisure Activities:** whirlpool, playground. **Guest Services:** tanning facility. **Business Services:** meeting rooms. **Cards:** AX, CB, DC, DS, MC, VI. **Special Amenities:** free local telephone calls.
(See color ad starting on p 346 & p 84)

SOME UNITS
🅂🄳 🍽 ⬚ ⚓ 🎥 DATA PORT 🔌 💻 / ✕ VCR FEE 🖥 /

CLEAR WATER LAKESHORE MOTEL
Phone: (231)436-7800 **19**
△△△ SAVE 7/3-8/16 [CP] 1P: $58-$138 2P: $58-$138 XP: $10 F18
5/15-7/2 & 8/17-10/26 [CP] 1P: $38-$118 2P: $38-$118 XP: $10 F18
▽▽▽▽ **Location:** 1 mi s. 11380 W US 23 49701 (PO Box 327). Fax: 231/436-7880. **Facility:** 40 units. 38 one-bedroom
Motel standard units, some with whirlpools. 2 one-bedroom suites ($125-$240) with efficiencies, some with whirlpools. 2 stories (no elevator), interior/exterior corridors. **Parking:** on-site. **Terms:** open 5/15-10/26, 3 day
cancellation notice-fee imposed. **Amenities:** *Some:* irons. **Pool(s):** heated indoor. **Leisure Activities:** whirlpool, playground, basketball, horseshoes. **Cards:** AX, DS, MC, VI. **Special Amenities:** early check-in/late check-out and free
continental breakfast. *(See color ad p 356)*

SOME UNITS
🅂🄳 ⬚ ✕ 🎥 🔌 💻 / ✕ 🖥 /

COMFORT INN LAKESIDE
Phone: (231)436-5057 **24**
△△△ SAVE 6/27-8/26 [ECP] 1P: $58-$198 2P: $58-$198 XP: $10 F18
5/2-6/26 & 8/17-10/26 [ECP] 1P: $38-$148 2P: $38-$148 XP: $10 F18
▽▽▽▽ **Location:** I-75, exit 337 northbound, 0.5 mi n to US 23, 0.3 mi e, then just n; exit 338 southbound, 0.8 mi se on US 23,
Motel then just n. 611 S Huron St 49701 (PO Box 40). Fax: 231/436-7385. **Facility:** 60 one-bedroom standard units,
some with whirlpools. 3 stories (no elevator), exterior corridors. **Parking:** on-site. **Terms:** open 5/2-10/26, 3
day cancellation notice-fee imposed. **Amenities:** irons, hair dryers. **Pool(s):** heated indoor. **Leisure Activities:** whirlpool. **Cards:** AX, CB, DC, DS, MC, VI. **Special Amenities:** free continental breakfast. *(See color ad p 358)*

SOME UNITS
🅂🄳 🍽 ⬚ 🎥 DATA PORT 🔌 💻 / ✕

(See map p. 336)

DAYS INN

Phone: (231)436-5557 [21]

AAA SAVE	6/27-8/23	1P: $69-$198	2P: $69-$198	XP: $10	F17
	8/24-10/31	1P: $55-$178	2P: $55-$178	XP: $10	F17
Motel	4/1-6/26	1P: $49-$138	2P: $49-$138	XP: $10	F17

Location: I-75, exit 337 northbound, 0.5 mi n to US 23, 0.3 mi e; exit 338 southbound, 0.8 mi se on US 23. 825 S Huron St 49701 (PO Box 252). Fax: 231/436-5703. **Facility:** 84 one-bedroom standard units, some with whirlpools. 2 stories (no elevator), exterior corridors. **Parking:** on-site. **Terms:** open 4/1-10/31, 3 day cancellation notice-fee imposed, pets ($15 fee). **Amenities:** voice mail, hair dryers. **Dining:** 7 am-9 pm, cocktails. **Pool(s):** heated indoor. **Leisure Activities:** putting green, playground. **Guest Services:** coin laundry. **Business Services:** meeting rooms. **Cards:** AX, DC, MC, VI. **Special Amenities:** free local telephone calls and free room upgrade (subject to availability with advanced reservations).** (See color ad p 359 & card insert)

SOME UNITS

[icons] SD | [icons] / X VCR DATA/PORT FEE

DOWNING'S DOWNTOWN MOTOR INN

Phone: 231/436-5528 [10]

AAA SAVE	7/2-8/10	1P: $98	2P: $98	XP: $5	F17
	6/2-7/1	1P: $58	2P: $68	XP: $5	F17
Small-scale Hotel	4/1-6/1 & 8/11-3/31	1P: $48	2P: $68	XP: $5	F17

Location: Center. 202 E Central Ave 49701 (PO Box 747). Fax: 231/436-5346. **Facility:** 42 units. 36 one-bedroom standard units, some with whirlpools. 6 one-bedroom suites ($165) with whirlpools. 2 stories (no elevator), interior/exterior corridors. **Parking:** on-site. **Pool(s):** heated indoor. **Leisure Activities:** whirlpool, snowmobiling, exercise room. **Cards:** AX, MC, VI. (See color ad below)

SOME UNITS

[icons] / X

ECONO LODGE AT THE BRIDGE

Phone: (231)436-5026 [7]

AAA SAVE	6/15-9/1	1P: $70-$170	2P: $70-$170	XP: $8	F18
	4/1-6/14 & 9/2-3/31	1P: $45-$90	2P: $45-$90	XP: $8	F18
Motel				

Location: I-75, exit 339. 412 N Nicolet St 49701 (PO Box 69). Fax: 231/436-4172. **Facility:** 32 one-bedroom standard units. 1-2 stories (no elevator), exterior corridors. **Parking:** on-site. **Cards:** AX, DS, MC, VI. **Special Amenities:** free local telephone calls and preferred room (subject to availability with advanced reservations).

SOME UNITS

[icons] SD / X

ECONO LODGE BAYVIEW

Phone: (231)436-5777 [26]

AAA SAVE	6/27-8/16	1P: $38-$168	2P: $38-$168		
	4/1-6/26 & 8/17-11/1	1P: $38-$98	2P: $38-$98		
Motel				

Location: I-75, exit 337 northbound, 0.5 mi n to US 23, 0.3 mi e, then just n; exit 338 southbound, 0.8 mi se on US 23, then just n. 712 S Huron St 49701 (PO Box 282). Fax: 231/436-7023. **Facility:** 46 one-bedroom standard units, some with whirlpools. 1-2 stories (no elevator), exterior corridors. **Parking:** on-site. **Terms:** open 4/1-11/1, 3 day cancellation notice-fee imposed, weekly rates available, package plans. **Amenities:** video library (fee), dual phone lines, voice mail. **Pool(s):** heated indoor. **Leisure Activities:** sauna, whirlpool, playground. **Cards:** AX, CB, DC, DS, MC, VI. **Special Amenities:** free continental breakfast and free local telephone calls. (See color ad p 349 & p 84)

SOME UNITS

[icons] / X VCR FEE

GRAND VIEW RESORT-BEACHFRONT

Phone: (231)436-8100 [33]

AAA SAVE	6/28-8/18	1P: $56-$169	2P: $56-$169		
	5/16-6/27 & 8/19-10/19	1P: $36-$119	2P: $36-$119		
Motel				

Location: 1 mi s. 11384 W US 23 49701. Fax: 231/436-8200. **Facility:** 23 units. 22 one-bedroom standard units. 1 one-bedroom suite ($99-$499) with kitchen. 2 stories (no elevator), exterior corridors. **Parking:** on-site. **Terms:** open 5/16-10/19, 3 day cancellation notice-fee imposed, weekly rates available, [CP] meal plan available, package plans, pets ($10 extra charge, in designated units). **Amenities:** irons. **Pool(s):** heated outdoor. **Leisure Activities:** whirlpool, playground. *Fee:* jet ski. **Cards:** AX, CB, DC, DS, JC, MC, VI. **Special Amenities:** early check-in/late check-out and free local telephone calls. (See color ad p 361)

SOME UNITS

[icons] SD / X

(See map p. 336)

HAMILTON INN SELECT-BEACHFRONT

Phone: (231)436-5493 27

Small-scale Hotel

All Year [BP] 1P: $38-$198 2P: $38-$198

Location: I-75, exit 338 northbound, just n to Central Ave, just e to Huron Ave, then just s; exit 338 southbound, 0.8 mi se on US 23, then just n; downtown. 701 S Huron St 49701 (PO Box 831). Fax: 231/436-7869. **Facility:** 96 units. 83 one- and 13 two-bedroom standard units, some with whirlpools. 3 stories, interior corridors. **Parking:** on-site. **Terms:** 3 day cancellation notice-fee imposed, weekly rates available, package plans. **Amenities:** video library (fee), dual phone lines, irons, hair dryers. *Some:* video games (fee). **Pool(s):** heated indoor. **Leisure Activities:** whirlpool, snowmobiling, exercise room. *Fee:* two-person electric boats. **Guest Services:** coin laundry. *Fee:* tanning facility. **Business Services:** meeting rooms. **Cards:** AX, CB, DC, DS, MC, VI. **Special Amenities:** free continental breakfast and free local telephone calls. *(See color ad starting on p 344, inside front cover & p 84)*

SOME UNITS

(See map p. 336)

HAMPTON INN OF MACKINAW CITY

 (AAA) (SAVE)
▼▼▼▼

Phone: (231)436-7829　 29

	1P:	2P:
6/1-8/31 [ECP]	1P: $69-$179	2P: $74-$183
9/1-9/30 [ECP]	1P: $69-$139	2P: $74-$145
5/1-5/31 [ECP]	1P: $49-$129	2P: $54-$133
10/1-11/1 [ECP]	1P: $49-$76	2P: $53-$79

Small-scale Hotel **Location:** I-75, exit 337 northbound, 0.5 mi n to US 23, just e to Huron Ave, then just n; exit 338 southbound, 0.8 mi e on US 23. 726 S Huron Ave 49701 (PO Box 187). Fax: 231/436-9881. **Facility:** 62 one-bedroom standard units. 3 stories, interior corridors. *Bath:* combo or shower only. **Parking:** on-site. **Terms:** open 5/1-11/1, cancellation fee imposed. **Amenities:** voice mail, irons, hair dryers. **Pool(s):** heated indoor. **Cards:** AX, DC, DS, MC, VI. **Special Amenities:** free continental breakfast and free local telephone calls. *(See color ad starting below)*

SOME UNITS

🅢🄳 🍴 🕹 🏊 🐾 📠 DATA PORT 💻 / ✕ /

HAWTHORN INN & SUITES

(AAA) (SAVE)
▼▼▼▼

Phone: (231)436-5929　28

	1P:	2P:
6/27-8/16 [BP]	1P: $58-$198	2P: $58-$198
4/1-6/26 & 8/17-11/1 [BP]	1P: $38-$148	2P: $38-$148

Location: I-75, exit 337 northbound, 0.5 mi n to US 23, just e to Huron St, then just n; exit 338 southbound, 0.8 mi se on US 23, just n. 722 S Huron 49701 (PO Box 282). Fax: 231/436-8132. **Facility:** Smoke free premises. 40 units. **Small-scale Hotel** 13 one-bedroom standard units, some with whirlpools. 18 one- and 9 two-bedroom suites ($58-$248), some with whirlpools. 3 stories, interior/exterior corridors. *Bath:* combo or shower only. **Parking:** on-site. **Terms:** open 4/1-11/1, 3 day cancellation notice-fee imposed, package plans. **Amenities:** video library (fee), dual phone lines, voice mail, irons, hair dryers. **Leisure Activities:** pool privileges, recreational privileges. **Cards:** AX, CB, DC, DS, MC, VI. **Special Amenities:** free continental breakfast and free local telephone calls. *(See color ad p 349 & p 84)*

SOME UNITS

🅢🄳 🍴 🕹 ✕ VCR 🐾 DATA PORT 📟 💻 / 📠 /

HOLIDAY INN EXPRESS AT THE BRIDGE

(AAA) (SAVE)
▼▼▼▼

Phone: (231)436-7100　4

	1P:	2P:		
6/26-8/23 [ECP]	1P: $52-$259	2P: $52-$259	XP: $6	F17
4/1-6/25 & 8/24-3/31 [ECP]	1P: $42-$159	2P: $42-$159	XP: $6	F17

Location: I-75, exit 339; at bridge. 364 Louvingny 49701. Fax: 231/436-7070. **Facility:** 102 units. 95 one- and 2 two-bedroom standard units, some with whirlpools. 5 one-bedroom suites, some with whirlpools. 4 stories, **Small-scale Hotel** interior corridors. *Bath:* combo or shower only. **Parking:** on-site. **Terms:** check-in 4 pm, pets ($50 deposit, in designated units). **Amenities:** video library (fee), voice mail, irons, hair dryers. *Some:* dual phone lines. **Pool(s):** heated indoor. **Leisure Activities:** sauna, whirlpool, snowmobiling, sun deck, exercise room. *Fee:* game room. **Guest Services:** coin laundry. **Cards:** AX, CB, DC, DS, MC, VI. **Special Amenities:** free continental breakfast and free local telephone calls. *(See color ad p 362, p 365 & card insert)*

SOME UNITS

🅢🄳 🛏 🍴 ♿ 🏊 ✕ 🐾 DATA PORT 💻 / ✕ VCR 📟 📠 /
FEE

(See map p. 336)

KINGS INN

Phone: (231)436-5322 **36**

6/21-8/24 [CP]	1P: $39-$89	2P: $49-$89	XP: $10 F13
5/1-6/20 & 8/25-10/21 [CP]	1P: $29-$49	2P: $29-$49	XP: $10 F13

Location: I-75, exit 337 northbound, 0.5 mi n; exit 338 southbound, 0.5 mi s. 1020 S Nicolet St 49701 (PO Box 812). Fax: 231/436-5405. **Facility:** 25 one-bedroom standard units, some with whirlpools. 1-2 stories (no elevator), exterior corridors. **Parking:** on-site. **Terms:** open 5/1-10/21, 3 day cancellation notice, small pets only (in designated units). **Pool(s):** heated outdoor. **Leisure Activities:** playground, volleyball. **Cards:** MC, VI.
Special Amenities: free continental breakfast and free local telephone calls.

SOME UNITS

LAMPLIGHTER MOTEL

Phone: 231/436-5350 **6**

6/16-9/5	1P: $48-$92	2P: $48-$92	XP: $5 F
5/1-6/15 & 9/6-11/1	1P: $28-$55	2P: $28-$65	XP: $5 F

Location: I-75, exit 339, just n of town. Located in a quiet area. 303 Jamet St 49701 (PO Box 719). Fax: 231/436-7022. **Facility:** Smoke free premises. 10 units. 7 one- and 3 two-bedroom standard units, some with efficiencies. 1 story, exterior corridors. **Parking:** on-site. **Terms:** open 5/1-11/1. **Cards:** AX, DS, MC, VI.

SOME UNITS

LIGHTHOUSE VIEW MOTEL

Phone: (231)436-5304 **1**

6/27-8/16	1P: $45-$85	2P: $55-$95	XP: $10 F18
8/17-11/3	1P: $35-$55	2P: $45-$65	XP: $10 F18
4/25-6/26	1P: $25-$45	2P: $35-$55	XP: $10 F18

Location: I-75, exit 339. 699 N Huron St 49701 (PO Box 924). Fax: 231/436-5304. **Facility:** 24 one-bedroom standard units, some with whirlpools. 2 stories (no elevator), exterior corridors. **Parking:** on-site. **Terms:** open 4/25-11/3, 3 day cancellation notice, package plans. **Amenities:** hair dryers. **Pool(s):** heated indoor. **Leisure Activities:** whirlpool. **Cards:** AX, DC, DS, MC, VI.

SOME UNITS

MOTEL 6-DOWNTOWN

Phone: (231)436-8961 **9**

6/26-8/23	1P: $47-$169	2P: $47-$169	XP: $6 F17
5/1-6/25 & 8/24-10/31	1P: $37-$109	2P: $37-$109	XP: $6 F17

Location: I-75, exit 339; at bridge. 206 N Nicolet St 49701. Fax: 231/436-7317. **Facility:** 53 one-bedroom standard units, some with whirlpools. 2 stories (no elevator), interior/exterior corridors. **Parking:** on-site, winter plug-ins. **Terms:** open 5/1-10/31, pets ($50 deposit, in designated units). **Pool(s):** heated indoor. **Leisure Activities:** whirlpool, sun deck. **Cards:** AX, CB, DC, DS, MC, VI. **Special Amenities:** free local telephone calls and free room upgrade (subject to availability with advanced reservations). *(See color ad p 365)*

SOME UNITS
FEE

(See map p. 336)

NORTHPOINTE INN

AAA SAVE ▽▽▽▽

Small-scale Hotel

			Phone: (231)436-9812	**32**
6/27-8/31 [ECP]	1P: $99-$199	2P: $99-$199	XP: $10	F18
5/10-6/26 & 9/1-10/19 [ECP]	1P: $49-$129	2P: $49-$129	XP: $10	F18

Location: 1.1 mi s on US 23. 1027 S Huron St 49701. **Fax:** 231/436-4010. **Facility:** 98 units. 92 one-bedroom standard units, some with whirlpools. 6 one-bedroom suites, some with whirlpools. 3 stories, interior corridors. **Bath:** combo or shower only. **Parking:** on-site. **Terms:** open 5/10-10/19, cancellation fee imposed, package plans. **Pool(s):** heated indoor. **Leisure Activities:** whirlpool. **Business Services:** meeting rooms. **Cards:** AX, DS, MC, VI. **Special Amenities:** free continental breakfast and free local telephone calls.
(See color ad below)

SOME UNITS

⬛⬛⬛⬛⬛⬛ / ⬛⬛⬛ /

Mackinaw's Newest Beachfront Hotel

- 250' Private Sandy Beach
- Indoor Pool and Hot tub
- Spacious Beachfront Suites
- Jacuzzi Rooms and Suites
- 24 Hour Coffee Bar
- Casino Packages
- Complimentary Continental Breakfast
- Magnificent View of
  Mackinac Island and Mackinac Bridge
- Guest Laundry
- Kids Stay Free
- Extra Large Rooms
  with Refrigerators

For Reservations Call
(800) 576-2842 or
(231) 436-9812

Visit our website for seasonal specials
at www.northpointeinn.com

1027 S. Huron, Mackinaw City, MI 49701

(See map p. 336)

PARKSIDE INN-BRIDGESIDE

Phone: (231)436-8301 5

	6/26-9/1 [ECP]	1P: $59-$199	2P: $59-$199	XP: $10	F15
AAA SAVE	5/1-6/25 & 9/2-10/27 [ECP]	1P: $48-$158	2P: $48-$158	XP: $10	F15

Motel

Location: I-75, exit 39. Located opposite Fort Michilimackinac. 771 N Huron Ave 49701 (PO Box 788). Fax: 231/436-8301. **Facility:** 54 one-bedroom standard units, some with whirlpools. 1-3 stories, exterior corridors. **Parking:** on-site. **Terms:** open 5/1-10/27, 3 day cancellation notice. **Amenities:** video library (fee), hair dryers. **Pool(s):** heated indoor. **Leisure Activities:** whirlpool, exercise room. *Fee:* game room. **Guest Services:** coin laundry. **Business Services:** meeting rooms. **Cards:** AX, DS, MC, VI. **Special Amenities: free continental breakfast and free local telephone calls.**

SOME UNITS

QUALITY INN & SUITES BEACHFRONT

Phone: (231)436-5051 16

	6/27-8/31 [ECP]	1P: $69-$229	2P: $69-$229	XP: $10	F18
AAA SAVE	9/1-10/19 [ECP]	1P: $29-$135	2P: $29-$135	XP: $10	F18
	4/25-6/26 [ECP]	1P: $29-$129	2P: $31-$129	XP: $10	F18

Motel

Location: 1 mi se on US 23. 917 S Huron St 49701 (PO Box 519). Fax: 231/436-7221. **Facility:** 74 units. 63 one- and 3 two-bedroom standard units, some with whirlpools. 8 one-bedroom suites ($109-$279). 1-4 stories, exterior corridors. *Bath:* combo or shower only. **Parking:** on-site. **Terms:** open 4/25-10/19, cancellation fee imposed. **Amenities:** hair dryers. *Some:* irons. **Pool(s):** heated indoor. **Leisure Activities:** sauna, whirlpool, playground, volleyball. **Business Services:** meeting rooms. **Cards:** AX, CB, DC, DS, MC, VI. **Special Amenities: free continental breakfast and free local telephone calls.** *(See color ad below)*

SOME UNITS

RAINBOW MOTEL

Phone: 231/436-5518 23

	6/27-8/16	1P: $48-$139	2P: $54-$139	XP: $10
AAA SAVE	8/17-10/18	1P: $32-$98	2P: $34-$139	XP: $10
	5/2-6/26	1P: $32-$79	2P: $34-$98	XP: $10

Motel

Location: I-75, exit 337 northbound, 0.5 mi n to US 23, 0.3 mi e, then just n; exit 338 southbound, 0.8 mi se on US 23, then just n. 602 S Huron St 49701 (PO Box 546). Fax: 231/436-7006. **Facility:** 29 units. 27 one-bedroom standard units, some with whirlpools. 2 cottages, some with whirlpools. 1 story, exterior corridors. *Bath:* combo or shower only. **Parking:** on-site. **Terms:** open 5/2-10/18, 3 day cancellation notice. **Pool(s):** heated indoor. **Leisure Activities:** whirlpools, playground, basketball. **Cards:** AX, DS, MC, VI. **Special Amenities: free local telephone calls and preferred room (subject to availability with advanced reservations).** *(See color ad p 368)*

SOME UNITS

(See map p. 336)

RAMADA INN CONFERENCE RESORT   **Phone:** (231)436-5535 ⓪

♛♛♛ [SAVE]
8/1-9/1	1P: $75	2P: $75
7/6-7/31	1P: $69	2P: $69
5/1-7/5 & 9/2-10/25	1P: $59	2P: $59

♦♦ ♦♦

Large-scale Hotel

Location: I-75, exit 338. 450 S Nicolet 49701 (PO Box 57). Fax: 231/436-5849. **Facility:** 148 one-bedroom standard units, some with whirlpools. 3 stories, interior corridors. **Parking:** on-site, winter plug-ins. **Terms:** open 5/1-10/25, check-in 4 pm, [BP] meal plan available, $6 service charge, pets ($50 deposit, $10 extra charge). **Amenities:** voice mail, irons, hair dryers. *Some:* video games. **Dining:** 7 am-10 pm. **Pool(s):** heated indoor. **Leisure Activities:** sauna, whirlpool. *Fee:* game room. **Guest Services:** coin laundry. **Business Services:** meeting rooms. **Cards:** AX, DC, DS, MC, VI. **Special Amenities:** free continental breakfast and free local telephone calls. *(See color ad below)*

SOME UNITS

[$Ⓢ] [🛒] [🍽] [⑳] [🛳] [✖] [📷] [DATA PORT] [💻] / [✖] [🔓] [📺] /

(See map p. 336)

RAMADA LIMITED WATERFRONT

Phone: (231)436-5055 [25]

AAA SAVE	6/20-8/23 [ECP]	1P: $99-$189	2P: $99-$189	XP: $10	F18
▼▼▼▼	8/24-10/5 [ECP]	1P: $69-$159	2P: $69-$159	XP: $10	F18
	4/25-6/19 [ECP]	1P: $49-$139	2P: $49-$139	XP: $10	F18
	10/6-10/19 [ECP]	1P: $49-$119	2P: $49-$119	XP: $10	F18

Small-scale Hotel **Location:** I-75, exit 337 northbound, 0.5 mi n to US 23, just e to Huron St, then just n; exit 338 southbound, 0.8 mi se on US 23. 723 S Huron St 49701 (PO Box 547). Fax: 231/436-5921. **Facility:** 42 units. 40 one- and 2 two-bedroom standard units, some with whirlpools. 3 stories, interior corridors. **Parking:** on-site. **Terms:** open 4/25-10/19, cancellation fee imposed. **Amenities:** voice mail, irons, hair dryers. **Pool(s):** heated indoor. **Leisure Activities:** whirlpools. **Guest Services:** coin laundry. **Cards:** AX, CB, DC, DS, MC, VI. **Special Amenities:** free continental breakfast and free local telephone calls. *(See color ad p 370)*

SOME UNITS

SUPER 8 MOTEL-BEACHFRONT

Phone: (231)436-7111 [13]

AAA SAVE	6/27-8/16	1P: $48-$178	2P: $48-$178
▼▼▼ ▼▼	4/1-6/26 & 8/17-11/1	1P: $38-$128	2P: $38-$128

Motel **Location:** I-75, exit 337 northbound, 0.5 mi n to US 23, 0.3 mi e, then just n; exit 338 southbound, 0.8 mi se on US 23, then just n. 519 S Huron St 49701 (PO Box 566). Fax: 231/436-5011. **Facility:** 59 one-bedroom standard units, some with whirlpools. 2 stories (no elevator), exterior corridors. **Parking:** on-site. **Terms:** open 4/1-11/1, 3 day cancellation notice-fee imposed, weekly rates available, package plans. **Pool(s):** heated indoor. **Leisure Activities:** sauna, whirlpool, fishing. **Cards:** AX, CB, DC, DS, MC, VI. **Special Amenities:** early check-in/late check-out and free local telephone calls. *(See color ad p 350 & 84)*

SOME UNITS

SUPER 8 MOTEL BRIDGEVIEW

Phone: (231)436-5252 [2]

AAA SAVE	6/27-8/16 [ECP]	1P: $49-$179	2P: $49-$179
▼▼▼ ▼▼	8/17-11/1 [ECP]	1P: $38-$128	2P: $39-$128
	4/1-6/26 [ECP]	1P: $38-$128	2P: $38-$128

Small-scale Hotel **Location:** I-75, exit 339 northbound (Nicolet St), just n, then just e. 601 N Huron Ave 49701 (PO Box 98). Fax: 231/436-7004. **Facility:** 65 units. 61 one-bedroom standard units, some with whirlpools. 4 one-bedroom suites ($49-$228). 2-3 stories, interior/exterior corridors. **Parking:** on-site. **Terms:** open 4/1-11/1, 3 day cancellation notice-fee imposed, weekly rates available, package plans, pets ($50 deposit, in designated units). **Pool(s):** heated indoor. **Leisure Activities:** sauna, whirlpool, snowmobiling, exercise room. **Fee:** game room. **Guest Services:** coin laundry. **Cards:** AX, CB, DC, DS, MC, VI. **Special Amenities:** early check-in/late check-out and free local telephone calls. *(See color ad p 351)*

SOME UNITS

The One That Does It All

For years, people have turned to AAA for their emergency road service needs. But AAA is more than just towing. Access to AAA's travel services can give you the world. Its financial services can help you pay for it. And AAA insurance can give you the peace of mind to enjoy the ride. Plus, AAA gives you exclusive Show Your Card & Save® offers, bail bond benefits, and much more.

Discover the ways AAA can simplify your life. Call or stop by your nearest AAA office today to find out about the specific products and services they offer.

▼▼▼

WATERFRONT

On Lake Huron Overlooking Mackinac Island

2002
Gold Key Ramada

85° Heated Indoor Pool
with 2 Whirlpools

At The Mackinac Island Ferry Docks

ALL ROOMS INCLUDE:
- Private Balcony
- King and Queen Beds
- Big 32" TV, HBO
- Refrigerator, A/C
- Sofa or Rocking Chair
- Coffee Makers
- Dataports & Voicemail
- Complimentary Breakfast

ALSO AVAILABLE:
- In-Room Jacuzzis
- Honeymoon Suite
- Two Bedroom Suites
- Non-Smoking Rooms
- Interior Corridor with Elevator
- Private Sandy Beach
- Casino Packages

Rooftop Sundeck With Outdoor Whirlpool

Reservations: **1-888-852-4165** 8 am-11 pm Property Direct

or **1-800-2-RAMADA** Anytime

723 S. Huron, P.O. Box 547, Mackinaw City, MI 49701

(231) 436-5055   Fax:(231) 436-5921

*Visit Us On At These Web Sites: www.ramada.com or
www.mackinawcity.com (Under Accommodations)*

E-mail Inquiries Welcomed at ramadaltd@triton.net

Open: April 25-October 18, 2003

Sorry, No Pets On Premises • No Bicycles In Room

(See map p. 336)

TRAVELODGE-BAYVIEW

 Motel

5/15-8/17	1P: $38-$168
8/18-10/20	1P: $38-$98

Phone: (231)436-7900 **34**

Location: I-75, exit 337 northbound, 0.5 mi n to US 23, just e; exit 338 southbound, 0.7 mi se on US 23. 150 Old US 31 49701 (PO Box 298). Fax: 231/436-8200. **Facility:** 46 one-bedroom standard units, some with whirlpools. 2 stories (no elevator), exterior corridors. **Parking:** on-site. **Terms:** open 5/15-10/20, 3 day cancellation notice-fee imposed, [CP] meal plan available, package plans. **Amenities:** irons. **Pool(s):** heated outdoor, heated indoor. **Leisure Activities:** whirlpool, playground, basketball, volleyball. **Cards:** AX, CB, DC, DS, JC, MC, VI. **Special Amenities:** free local telephone calls and free newspaper. *(See color ad below)* SOME UNITS

(See map p. 336)

WATERFRONT INN
Phone: 231/436-5527 **15**

AAA SAVE

▼▼▼▼ ▼▼▼▼

Motel

6/22-8/16 [CP]	1P: $59-$124	2P: $64-$124	
8/17-10/19 [CP]	1P: $32-$89	2P: $32-$89	
5/2-6/21 [CP]	1P: $29-$89	2P: $29-$89	

Location: 1 mi s on US 23. 1009 S Huron Ave 49701 (PO Box 302). Fax: 231/436-5527. **Facility:** 69 units. 63 one- and 3 two-bedroom standard units. 3 cottages ($59-$189). 1-2 stories (no elevator), exterior corridors. *Bath:* combo or shower only. **Parking:** on-site. **Terms:** open 5/2-10/19, 3 day cancellation notice. **Pool(s):** heated indoor. **Leisure Activities:** whirlpool, playground, shuffleboard. *Fee:* game room. **Cards:** AX, DS, MC, VI. **Special Amenities:** free continental breakfast and free local telephone calls. *(See color ad p 355)*

SOME UNITS

🍴⊞ 🏊 ✕ 🎥 DATA PORT / ✕ 📶 🖥 /

WA WA TAM MOTEL
Phone: 231/436-8871 **8**

▼▼▼

Motel

6/21-9/3	1P: $38-$52	2P: $44-$62	XP: $6	F18
5/1-6/20 & 9/4-11/1	1P: $28-$36	2P: $38-$48	XP: $6	F18

Location: I-75, exit 339, just w. Located in a quiet area. 219 W Jamet St 49701 (PO Box 402). **Facility:** 11 one-bedroom standard units. 1 story, exterior corridors. *Bath:* combo or shower only. **Parking:** on-site. **Terms:** open 5/1-11/1, 3 day cancellation notice, [CP] meal plan available. **Cards:** DS, MC, VI.

SOME UNITS

ASK S/D 🍴⊞ 🖥 / ✕ /

——— **WHERE TO DINE** ———

ADMIRAL'S TABLE
Lunch: $5-$10   Dinner: $8-$20   Phone: 231/436-5687 **6**

AAA

▼▼▼▼

Steak & Seafood

Location: Opposite Mackinac Island Ferry Docks; center. 502 S Huron Ave 49701. **Hours:** Open 5/3-10/20; 7 am-9 pm, to 10 pm 7/1-9/2. **Features:** Visit the warm, friendly restaurant for such favorites as prime rib and Great Lakes whitefish. Servers in sport tops, shorts and sneakers pass through the restaurant, appointed in a nautical theme. The seasonal breakfast buffet is especially popular. Casual dress; cocktails. **Parking:** on-site. **Cards:** AX, DC, DS, MC, VI.

🍷 ✕

ANNA'S COUNTRY BUFFET
Lunch: $6-$9   Dinner: $7-$14   Phone: 231/436-5195 **5**

AAA

▼▼▼▼

American

Location: Just se; opposite ferry docks. 416 S Huron Ave 49701. **Hours:** Open 5/1-10/31; 7 am-9:30 pm. **Features:** Although the buffet is popular at breakfast, lunch and dinner, you're welcomed to order from a menu of traditional favorites. The laid-back dining room has a large gift shop in the back section. Casual dress; cocktails. **Parking:** on-site. **Cards:** AX, DC, DS, MC, VI. *(See color ad below)*

✕

CHIPPEWA ROOM AT AUDIE'S
Dinner: $11-$30   Phone: 231/436-5744 **1**

AAA

▼▼▼▼ ▼▼

American

Location: I-75, exit 339; at bridge. 314 Nicolet St 49701. **Hours:** 7:30 am-9 pm; hours vary seasonally. Closed: 11/27, 12/25. **Reservations:** suggested. **Features:** Native American artwork and knickknacks enhance the dining room where one can enjoy the leisurely atmosphere. Six tasty preparations of whitefish stand out on the varied menu and they have an array of dessert which includes many tempting choices. Casual dress; cocktails. **Parking:** on-site. **Cards:** MC, VI.

🍷 ✕

(See map p. 336)

DIXIE'S SALOON
American
Lunch: $6-$8   Dinner: $11-$18   Phone: 231/436-5449   ②
Location: Corner of Central and Huron sts; center. 401 E Central St 49701. **Hours:** 11 am-10 pm; noon-9 pm 9/4-5/27. Closed: 11/27, 12/25. **Features:** The impressive two-story restaurant—with its massive wood beams, attractive wood decor and warm atmosphere—welcomes all. Booths along the windows on the lower and upper levels provide a view of the water and ferry docks. Choice cuts of steak stand out amid a selection of American dishes and snacks. Casual dress; cocktails. **Parking:** street. **Cards:** AX, DS, MC, VI.

THE EMBERS
American
Lunch: $5-$7   Dinner: $10-$15   Phone: 231/436-5773   ③
Location: 0.5 mi s on US 23. 810 S Huron St 49701. **Hours:** Open 4/1-10/31; 7 am-10 pm; 8 am-9 pm 4/1-5/29. **Features:** The restaurant's specialty is its smorgasbord, a tempting array of such selections as roast beef, broasted chicken, Cajun whitefish, crab legs and shrimp stir-fry. A daily breakfast buffet also is available. Service is prompt and pleasant. Casual dress; cocktails. **Parking:** on-site. **Cards:** DS, MC, VI.

LIGHTHOUSE RESTAURANT
American
Dinner: $11-$34   Phone: 231/436-5191   ⑦
Location: I-75, exit 337 northbound, 0.5 mi n to US 23, 0.8 mi e, then just n; exit 338 southbound, 0.8 mi se on US 23, then just n. 618 S Huron St 49701. **Hours:** Open 4/1-11/15; 4 pm-10 pm; hours vary off season. **Features:** Tender prime rib, whitefish and all-you-can-eat crab legs are favorite selections at the comfortable restaurant, a hot spot with the tourist crowd. The copper-top bar, wall-mounted brass lamps and lighthouse-motif candles decorate the dining room. Casual dress; cocktails. **Parking:** on-site. **Cards:** AX, CB, DC, DS, MC, VI.

MARIO'S RISTORANTE
Italian
Dinner: $9-$17   Phone: 231/436-7818   ④
Location: Just s on US 23. 918 S Huron 49701. **Hours:** Open 5/10-10/20; 4 pm-9 pm; to 10 pm in summer. **Features:** Order the Italian sampler to taste a nice selection of manicotti, cannelloni and meat and cheese ravioli, or opt for a delicious pizza. During the summer, seating is nice on the breezy patio. Casual dress; cocktails. **Parking:** on-site. **Cards:** AX, DC, DS, MC, VI.

NEATH THE BIRCHES
Steak & Seafood
Dinner: $11-$34   Phone: 231/436-5401   ⑧
Location: I-75, exit 337 northbound, exit 338 (Cheboygan-Alpena) southbound, 1 mi s of blinker on Old US 31 (SR 108). M-108 49701. **Hours:** Open 5/1-10/22; 4 pm-9 pm, Fri & Sat-10 pm. **Features:** In a natural, wooded setting, the restaurant is frequently visited by wild turkeys, raccoons and deer that live nearby. Slow-roasted prime rib, which is served with homemade bread and the salad bar is a succulent choice. Service is warm and friendly. Casual dress; cocktails. **Parking:** on-site. **Cards:** AX, CB, DC, DS, MC, VI.

——— *The following restaurant has not been evaluated by AAA* ———
but is listed for your information only.

DARROW'S FAMILY RESTAURANT   Phone: 231/436-5514
[fyi] Not evaluated. **Location:** I-75, exit 339, just w. 1106 Louvigny St 49701. **Features:** Old-fashioned, home-style cooking includes such specialties as fresh whitefish, hamburgers and pie.

MADISON HEIGHTS —See Detroit p. 260.

MANCELONA pop. 1,408

——— **WHERE TO DINE** ———

WINDMILL FARMS
American
Lunch: $4-$7   Dinner: $8-$22   Phone: 231/587-5258
Location: 1.5 mi e on CR C38. 2927 CR 38 49659. **Hours:** Open 4/1-10/31 & 12/1-3/31; 11 am-9 pm, Fri & Sat-10 pm, Sun noon-8 pm; hours may vary off season. Closed: 1/1, 11/27, 12/24, 12/25; also Mon in winter. **Features:** The family-owned and operated restaurant, decorated with rustic accents, is locally known for its succulent, barbecue baby back ribs and a Sunday special of roast pork. Among wonderful, in-house dessert is the sinful hot fudge caramel cream puff. Casual dress; cocktails. **Parking:** on-site. **Cards:** DS, MC, VI.

MANCHESTER pop. 2,160

——— **WHERE TO DINE** ———

DAN'S RIVER GRILL
American
Lunch: $6-$10   Dinner: $10-$15   Phone: 734/428-9500
Location: Downtown. 223 E Main St 48158. **Hours:** 11 am-9 pm, Sat 4 pm-10 pm. Closed major holidays. **Features:** Housed in a former hardware store with exposed brick walls and oak paneling, the eatery featuers several large picture windows overlooking the town stream and former mill. A comedy club on the lower level is popular on weekends. Dressy casual; cocktails. **Parking:** street. **Cards:** AX, CB, DC, DS, MC, VI.

MANISTEE pop. 6,586

──── WHERE TO STAY ────

DAYS INN
SAVE
◆◆◆◆
Small-scale Hotel

6/27-8/31 [CP]	1P: $80-$150	2P: $80-$150	XP: $10 F16
5/23-6/26 [CP]	1P: $50-$130	2P: $50-$130	XP: $10 F16
4/1-5/22 & 9/1-3/31 [CP]	1P: $50-$100	2P: $50-$100	XP: $10 F16

Phone: (231)723-8385

Location: 1.3 mi s on US 31. Located in a commercial area. 1462 Manistee Hwy 49660. Fax: 231/723-2154. **Facility:** 94 one-bedroom standard units, some with whirlpools. 2 stories (no elevator), interior corridors. **Parking:** on-site, winter plug-ins. **Terms:** 2 night minimum stay - seasonal weekends, 3 day cancellation notice. **Amenities:** hair dryers. **Pool(s):** heated indoor. **Leisure Activities:** whirlpool, snowmobiling. *Fee:* game room. **Guest Services:** coin laundry. **Business Services:** meeting rooms. **Cards:** AX, DC, DS, MC, VI. *(See color ad card insert)*

SOME UNITS
🍽️ 🏊 ⊠ 🐕 🖥️ / ⊠ 🔌 📷 /

HILLSIDE MOTEL
ⒶⒶⒶ SAVE
◆◆◆
Motel

6/16-9/15	1P: $55-$125	2P: $55-$150
4/1-6/15	1P: $35-$75	2P: $35-$85
9/16-12/1	1P: $35-$75	2P: $35-$75

Phone: 231/723-2584

Location: 1.5 mi s. 1675 US 31 S 49660. Fax: 231/723-0578. **Facility:** 20 one-bedroom standard units. 1 story, exterior corridors. *Bath:* combo or shower only. **Parking:** on-site, winter plug-ins. **Terms:** open 4/1-12/1, cancellation fee imposed, small pets only ($8 extra charge, no cats). **Pool(s):** heated outdoor. **Leisure Activities:** whirlpool, playground. **Cards:** AX, DS, VI. **Special Amenities:** early check-in/late check-out and free local telephone calls.

SOME UNITS
🛏️ 🍽️ 🏊 🐕 🔌 📷 / ⊠ /

MANISTEE INN & MARINA
◆◆◆◆
Small-scale Hotel

6/7-9/8	1P: $90-$120	2P: $90-$120	XP: $10 F12
4/15-6/6 & 9/9-3/31	1P: $60-$75	2P: $60-$75	XP: $10 F12
4/1-4/14	1P: $54-$68	2P: $54-$68	XP: $10 F12

Phone: 231/723-4000

Location: US 31, just w; downtown. 378 River St 49660. Fax: 231/723-0007. **Facility:** 25 one-bedroom standard units, some with whirlpools. 2 stories, interior corridors. **Parking:** on-site. **Terms:** weekly rates available, [CP] meal plan available, package plans. **Amenities:** video library (fee), irons, hair dryers. **Leisure Activities:** boat dock. *Fee:* massage. **Guest Services:** coin laundry. **Business Services:** meeting rooms. **Cards:** AX, DC, DS, MC, VI.

SOME UNITS
ⒶⓈⓀ 🍽️ 📺 🔌 📷 / ⊠ 🔌 📷 /
FEE FEE

MICROTEL INN & SUITES
◆◆◆
Small-scale Hotel

All Year [CP]	1P: $59-$99	2P: $79-$99	XP: $7 F16

Phone: (231)398-0008

Location: Jct US 31 and SR 55, just n of town. Located at the outskirts of town. 226 Parkdale Ave 49660. Fax: 231/398-2770. **Facility:** 83 one-bedroom standard units. 3 stories, interior corridors. *Bath:* combo or shower only. **Parking:** on-site. **Terms:** 5 day cancellation notice. **Cards:** AX, CB, DC, DS, MC, VI.

SOME UNITS
ⒶⓈⓀ 📷 ♿ 🐕 🔌 / ⊠ 🔌 📷 📷 /

SUPER 8 MOTEL
◆◆◆
Small-scale Hotel

9/3-12/31 [CP]	1P: $66-$100	2P: $76-$110	XP: $5 F17
6/28-9/2 [CP]	1P: $65-$100	2P: $75-$110	XP: $5 F17
4/1-6/27 & 1/1-3/31 [CP]	1P: $50-$85	2P: $60-$95	XP: $5 F17

Phone: (231)398-8888

Location: 1 mi n on US 31. Located in a commercial area. 220 Arthur St 49660. Fax: 231/398-8888. **Facility:** 67 one-bedroom standard units, some with whirlpools. 2 stories (no elevator), interior corridors. *Bath:* combo or shower only. **Parking:** on-site. **Terms:** cancellation fee imposed. **Amenities:** *Some:* hair dryers. **Guest Services:** coin laundry. **Cards:** AX, DS, MC, VI.

SOME UNITS
ⒶⓈⓀ 📷 ♿ 🔌 / ⊠ 🔌 📷 /

──── *The following lodging was either not evaluated or did not* ────
meet AAA rating requirements but is listed for your information only.

LITTLE RIVER CASINO RESORT
[fyi]
Resort
Small-scale Hotel

All Year	1P: $99-$159	2P: $99-$159	XP: $10 F18

Phone: 231/723-1535

Too new to rate. **Location:** I-31, exit 22, just n. 2700 Orchard Hwy 49660 (PO Box 417). Fax: 231/398-2593. **Amenities:** 100 units, coffeemakers, microwaves, refrigerators, pool. **Terms:** cancellation fee imposed. **Cards:** AX, DC, DS, MC, VI.

──── WHERE TO DINE ────

FOUR FORTY WEST
◆◆
American
DS, MC, VI.

Lunch: $4-$7   **Dinner:** $10-$26   **Phone:** 231/723-7902

Location: Just w. 440 W River St 49660. **Hours:** 11 am-10 pm, Sun from 10 am; to 9 pm Sun-Thurs 1/1-5/30. **Features:** Overlooking the scenic Manistee River, the casual restaurant is open and airy, with lots of windows. Menu favorites include varied preparations of local seafood, as well as prime rib, barbecue ribs and Mike's club sandwich with tasty boneless chicken. Casual dress; cocktails. **Parking:** street. **Cards:** AX,

⊠

MANISTIQUE pop. 3,583

——— **WHERE TO STAY** ———

BEACHCOMBER MOTEL
Phone: (906)341-2567

6/1-9/4	1P: $58-$60	2P: $68-$84	XP: $5	D5
9/5-12/1	1P: $44-$52	2P: $52-$64	XP: $5	D5
4/1-5/31	1P: $42-$50	2P: $48-$60	XP: $5	D5
12/2-3/31	1P: $40-$46	2P: $46-$56	XP: $5	D5

Motel
Location: 1 mi e on US 2. Located in a semi-commercial area. 795 E Lakeshore Dr 49854 (3944 Brenlor Dr, HESPERIA, 49421). Fax: 906/341-2700. **Facility:** 19 one-bedroom standard units. 1 story, exterior corridors. **Parking:** on-site. **Terms:** cancellation fee imposed. **Business Services:** fax. **Cards:** DC, MC, VI. **Special Amenities:** early check-in/late check-out and preferred room (subject to availability with advanced reservations).

SOME UNITS

BEST WESTERN-THE BREAKERS MOTEL
Phone: (906)341-2410

5/30-8/23 [ECP]	1P: $79-$129	2P: $89-$129	XP: $10	F12
8/24-10/12 [ECP]	1P: $69-$119	2P: $69-$119	XP: $10	F12
4/1-5/29 & 10/13-3/31 [ECP]	1P: $59-$109	2P: $69-$109	XP: $10	F12

Motel
Location: 2 mi e on US 2. Located in a semi-commercial area. 1199 E Lakeshore US 2 Dr 49854 (PO Box 322). Fax: 906/341-2207. **Facility:** 40 one-bedroom standard units, some with whirlpools. 2 stories (no elevator), exterior corridors. **Parking:** on-site. **Terms:** pets ($10 extra charge, in designated units). **Amenities:** irons, hair dryers. **Pool(s):** heated indoor/outdoor. **Leisure Activities:** whirlpool. Fee: bicycles, game room. **Guest Services:** coin laundry. **Cards:** AX, CB, DC, DS, MC, VI.

SOME UNITS

COMFORT INN
Phone: (906)341-6981

6/14-10/26 [ECP]	1P: $99-$139	2P: $99-$139	XP: $10	F18
4/1-6/13 & 10/27-3/31 [ECP]	1P: $69-$99	2P: $69-$99	XP: $10	F18

Small-scale Hotel
Location: 0.5 mi e on US 2. Located in a semi-commercial area. 726 E Lakeshore Dr 49854. Fax: 906/341-6339. **Facility:** 57 one-bedroom standard units, some with whirlpools. 2 stories (no elevator), interior corridors. **Parking:** on-site. **Terms:** pets ($10 extra charge). **Amenities:** hair dryers. Some: irons. **Leisure Activities:** whirlpool, snowmobiling, exercise room. Fee: bicycles. **Guest Services:** coin laundry. **Business Services:** meeting rooms. **Cards:** AX, DS, MC, VI. **Special Amenities:** free continental breakfast and free local telephone calls.

SOME UNITS
FEE FEE

ECONO LODGE LAKESHORE
Phone: (906)341-6014

7/1-9/3 [ECP]	1P: $80-$110	2P: $80-$110	XP: $10	F
6/16-6/30 [ECP]	1P: $70-$110	2P: $70-$110	XP: $10	F
9/4-3/31 [ECP]	1P: $70-$100	2P: $70-$100	XP: $10	F
4/1-6/15 [ECP]	1P: $60-$100	2P: $60-$100	XP: $10	F

Motel
Location: 1.5 mi e on US 2. Located in a semi-commercial area. 1101 E Lakeshore Dr 49854 (PO Box 184). Fax: 906/341-2979. **Facility:** 32 one-bedroom standard units, some with whirlpools. 1 story, interior/exterior corridors. Bath: combo or shower only. **Parking:** on-site, winter plug-ins. **Amenities:** Some: irons. **Leisure Activities:** whirlpool, snowmobiling, exercise room. **Cards:** AX, DC, DS, MC, VI.

SOME UNITS

HOLIDAY INN EXPRESS
Phone: (906)341-3777

6/15-9/30 [ECP]	1P: $99	XP: $10	F19
4/1-6/14 & 10/1-3/31 [ECP]	1P: $69	XP: $10	F19

Small-scale Hotel
Location: 1.4 mi e on US 2. Located in a commercial area. 955 E Lakeshore Dr 49854. Fax: 906/341-7457. **Facility:** 55 one-bedroom standard units, some with whirlpools. 2 stories (no elevator), interior corridors. Bath: combo or shower only. **Parking:** on-site. **Amenities:** dual phone lines, voice mail, irons, hair dryers. **Leisure Activities:** snowmobiling. **Guest Services:** coin laundry. **Cards:** AX, CB, DC, DS, MC, VI. **Special Amenities:** free continental breakfast and free local telephone calls.

SOME UNITS
FEE

KEWADIN CASINO INN
Phone: 906/341-6911

All Year	1P: $50-$59	2P: $50-$59	XP: $10	F17

Small-scale Hotel
Location: 2.5 mi e on US 2. Located in a semi-commercial area. Lakeshore Dr 49854 (Rt 1, Box 1938). Fax: 906/341-6471. **Facility:** 40 one-bedroom standard units, some with whirlpools. 2 stories (no elevator), interior corridors. **Parking:** on-site. **Pool(s):** heated indoor. **Leisure Activities:** basketball. Fee: game room. **Guest Services:** coin laundry, area transportation-casino shuttle. **Special Amenities:** free continental breakfast and free local telephone calls.

SOME UNITS

MANISTIQUE MOTOR INN/BUDGET HOST
Phone: (906)341-2552

All Year	1P: $49-$60	2P: $55-$65	XP: $5	F12

Motel
Location: 3.5 mi e on US 2. Located in a semi-rural area. 49854 (Rt 1, Box 1505). Fax: 906/341-2552. **Facility:** 26 one-bedroom standard units, some with whirlpools. 1 story, exterior corridors. Bath: combo or shower only. **Parking:** on-site, winter plug-ins. **Terms:** cancellation fee imposed. **Pool(s):** heated outdoor. **Leisure Activities:** snowmobiling, playground. **Cards:** AX, CB, DC, DS, MC, VI. *(See color ad p 187)*

SOME UNITS

MAPLE CITY

──────── WHERE TO DINE ────────

LEELANAU COUNTRY INN
▼▼▼▼
American
Dinner: $16-$25 **Phone: 231/228-5060**
Location: 4.5 mi n on CR 667, then just w on SR 22. 149 E Harbor Hwy 49664. **Hours:** 5 pm-9 pm, Fri & Sat-9:30 pm; hours may vary in off season. Closed: Sun; Mon-Wed 11/1-6/14. **Reservations:** suggested. **Features:** Opposite Little Traverse Lake, the renovated 1891 inn is a comfortable spot for upscale casual dining. A combination of seafood, steaks, chicken and pasta makes up the menu. For dessert, try the chocolate mousse cake with raspberry-chocolate sauce. Casual dress; cocktails. **Parking:** on-site. **Cards:** MC, VI. [K] [X]

MAPLE VALLEY

──────── WHERE TO DINE ────────

MAPLE VALLEY RESTAURANT & LOUNGE
▼▼ ▼▼
American
Dinner: $8-$22 **Phone: 989/389-7005**
Location: I-75, exit 227 (SR 55), just w. 4995 E West Branch Rd 48656. **Hours:** 4 pm-9 pm, Fri & Sat-10 pm, Sun noon-8 pm. Closed: 11/27, 12/24, 12/25. **Features:** Inviting up-north type dining room with wood chainsaw carvings, deer antler chandeliers, and wildlife mounts and artwork. Although walleye, ribs and prime rib remain their specialties, they also have lighter fare and pasta dishes. Casual dress; cocktails.
Parking: on-site. **Cards:** DC, DS, MC, VI. [Y] [X]

MARENISCO

──────── WHERE TO DINE ────────

THE FISHERMAN RESORT RESTAURANT
▲▲▲
Steak & Seafood
Lunch: $4-$7 **Dinner: $8-$15** **Phone: 906/842-3366**
Location: 2 mi e on US 2, 10 mi n on SR 64; on Lake Gogebic. M-64 49947. **Hours:** 7 am-10 pm, Sun-8 pm. Closed: 11/27, 12/25; also 4/1-4/30. **Features:** Overlooking a scenic lake, the casual restaurant is a favorite spot for locals and tourists alike. Steak, ribs, chops, burgers and seafood are among familiar menu offerings. Turtle pie stands out on the dessert menu. Casual dress; cocktails. **Parking:** on-site.
Cards: MC, VI. [Y]

MARINE CITY pop. 4,652

──────── WHERE TO STAY ────────

THE HEATHER HOUSE **Phone: 810/765-3175**
▼▼▼▼
Historic Bed
& Breakfast

	1P	2P	XP	
6/1-10/31 [BP]	1P: $95-$150	2P: $115-$170	XP: $20	F6
2/13-3/31 [BP]	1P: $95-$150	2P: $105-$160	XP: $20	F6
4/1-5/31 & 11/1-12/15 [BP]	1P: $85-$140	2P: $105-$160	XP: $20	F6

Location: I-94, exit 248, 14 mi e on M-29. 409 N Main 48039. Fax: 810/765-5639. **Facility:** Overlooking the St. Clair River, this handsome Queen Anne house features two turrets and a large wraparound porch. Smoke free premises. 4 one-bedroom standard units, some with whirlpools. 3 stories (no elevator), interior corridors. *Bath:* combo or shower only. **Parking:** on-site. **Terms:** open 4/1-12/15 & 2/13-3/31, 7 day cancellation notice-fee imposed, no pets allowed (owner's cats on premises). **Amenities:** video library, irons, hair dryers. **Cards:** AX, DS, MC, VI. [↑] [X] [VCR] [☎] [▣]

MARQUETTE pop. 19,661

──────── WHERE TO STAY ────────

BIRCHMONT MOTEL **Phone: 906/228-7538**
(AAA) [SAVE]
▲▲▲
Motel
	1P	2P	
5/1-11/1	1P: $35-$54	2P: $45-$65	

Location: 4.3 mi s on US 41 and SR 28. Located in a semi-commercial area. 2090 US 41 S 49855. **Facility:** 29 one-bedroom standard units. 2 stories (no elevator), exterior corridors. **Parking:** on-site. **Terms:** open 5/1-11/1, weekly rates available, pets ($6 extra charge). **Pool(s):** heated outdoor. **Cards:** AX, DS, MC, VI. **Special Amenities:** early check-in/late check-out and free local telephone calls.

SOME UNITS
[S/D] [🐾] [↑] [⇌] [K] / [X] [☎] [🗄] [▣] /

BUDGET HOST-BRENTWOOD MOTOR INN **Phone: 906/228-7494**
(AAA) [SAVE]
▲▲▲ ▼▼
Motel
	1P	2P	
All Year [CP]	1P: $42-$48	2P: $45-$53	XP: $3

Location: 2.8 mi w on US 41 and SR 28. Located in a semi-commercial area. 2603 US 41 W 49855. **Facility:** 41 one-bedroom standard units. 2 stories (no elevator), exterior corridors. *Bath:* combo or shower only. **Parking:** on-site, winter plug-ins. **Terms:** weekly rates available. **Amenities:** *Some:* hair dryers. **Leisure Activities:** snowmobiling. **Cards:** MC, VI. **Special Amenities:** free continental breakfast.
(See color ad p 187)

SOME UNITS
[S/D] [↑] / [X] [DATA PORT] [🗄] [▣] /

CEDAR MOTOR INN **Phone: (906)228-2280**
▲▲▲ ▼▼
Small-scale Hotel
	1P	2P	
All Year	1P: $50-$65	2P: $60-$70	XP: $5 F5

Location: 2.8 mi w on US 41 and SR 28. Located in a semi-commercial area. 2523 US 41 W 49855. Fax: 906/228-2280. **Facility:** 44 one-bedroom standard units. 2 stories (no elevator), interior/exterior corridors. *Bath:* combo or shower only. **Parking:** on-site. **Pool(s):** heated indoor. **Leisure Activities:** sauna, whirlpool, snowmobiling. **Business Services:** meeting rooms. **Cards:** AX, DC, DS, MC, VI.

SOME UNITS
[↑] [⇌] [X] [🍽] [DATA PORT] [▣] / [X] [🗄] [▣] /

COMFORT SUITES

SAVE

Small-scale Hotel

			Phone: (906)228-0028
6/13-9/13 [CP]	1P: $99-$159	2P: $109-$159	XP: $10 F18
4/1-6/12 & 9/14-3/31 [CP]	1P: $89-$159	2P: $99-$159	XP: $10 F18

Location: 2.5 mi w on US 41 and SR 28. Located in a semi-commercial area. 2463 US 41 W 49855. Fax: 906/228-3893. **Facility:** 60 one-bedroom standard units, some with whirlpools. 3 stories, interior corridors. *Bath:* combo or shower only. **Parking:** on-site, winter plug-ins. **Amenities:** irons, hair dryers. **Pool(s):** heated indoor. **Leisure Activities:** sauna, whirlpool, snowmobiling, exercise room. **Guest Services:** gift shop, coin laundry. **Business Services:** meeting rooms. **Cards:** AX, CB, DC, DS, JC, MC, VI. *(See color ad below)*

SOME UNITS

DAYS INN

SAVE

Small-scale Hotel

			Phone: (906)225-1393
6/13-9/13 [CP]	1P: $69-$119	2P: $79-$129	XP: $10 F18
4/1-6/12 & 9/14-3/31 [CP]	1P: $59-$109	2P: $69-$119	XP: $10 F18

Location: 2.3 mi w on US 41 and SR 28. Located in a semi-commercial area. 2403 US 41 W 49855. Fax: 906/225-9845. **Facility:** 65 one-bedroom standard units. 2 stories, interior corridors. **Parking:** on-site, winter plug-ins. **Terms:** 7 day cancellation notice. **Amenities:** irons, hair dryers. **Pool(s):** heated indoor. **Leisure Activities:** sauna, whirlpools, snowmobiling. **Guest Services:** gift shop. **Business Services:** meeting rooms. **Cards:** AX, CB, DC, DS, JC, MC, VI. *(See color ad below & card insert)*

SOME UNITS

ECONO LODGE LAKESIDE

(AAA) SAVE

Small-scale Hotel

			Phone: (906)225-1305
All Year	1P: $59-$65	2P: $69-$75	XP: $8 F18

Location: 4 mi s on US 41 and SR 28. Located opposite Lake Superior. 2050 US 41 S 49855. Fax: 906/228-7342. **Facility:** 47 one-bedroom standard units. 1-2 stories (no elevator), interior/exterior corridors. **Parking:** on-site, winter plug-ins. **Terms:** cancellation fee imposed, [AP] meal plan available, package plans, 17% service charge, pets ($5 extra charge). **Amenities:** voice mail, hair dryers. **Dining:** 7 am-9 pm, cocktails. **Leisure Activities:** snowmobiling. **Business Services:** meeting rooms. **Cards:** AX, DS, MC, VI. **Special Amenities:** free continental breakfast and free local telephone calls. *(See color ad p 378)*

SOME UNITS

HOLIDAY INN

Large-scale Hotel

			Phone: (906)225-1351
All Year	1P: $104	2P: $109	XP: $5 F12

Location: 1.8 mi w on US 41 and SR 28. Located in a semi-commerical area. 1951 US 41 W 49855. Fax: 906/228-4329. **Facility:** 200 one-bedroom standard units. 5 stories, interior corridors. **Parking:** on-site. **Amenities:** irons, hair dryers. **Pool(s):** heated indoor. **Leisure Activities:** sauna, snowmobiling, exercise room. *Fee:* game room. **Guest Services:** valet and coin laundry. **Business Services:** meeting rooms. **Cards:** AX, CB, DC, DS, MC, VI.

SOME UNITS

IMPERIAL MOTEL

Motel

			Phone: (906)228-7430
All Year	1P: $45-$55	2P: $55-$75	XP: $5 F12

Location: 2.8 mi w on US 41 and SR 28. Located in a semi-commercial area. 2493 US 41 W 49855. Fax: 906/228-3883. **Facility:** 43 one-bedroom standard units. 2 stories (no elevator), exterior corridors. **Parking:** on-site, winter plug-ins. **Pool(s):** heated indoor. **Leisure Activities:** sauna, snowmobiling, basketball. **Business Services:** fax (fee). **Cards:** AX, DC, DS, MC, VI.

SOME UNITS

LANDMARK INN

(AAA) SAVE

Classic
Large-scale Hotel

			Phone: (906)228-2580
5/1-10/18	1P: $112-$192	2P: $112-$192	XP: $10
10/19-3/31	1P: $95-$179	2P: $95-$179	XP: $10

Location: Just n; center. 230 N Front St 49855. Fax: 906/228-5676. **Facility:** 60 units. 56 one-bedroom standard units, some with whirlpools. 4 one-bedroom suites. 6 stories, interior corridors. *Bath:* combo or shower only. **Parking:** on-site. **Terms:** cancellation fee imposed. **Amenities:** voice mail, hair dryers. **Dining:** 7-10 am, 11:30-2 & 5-9 pm, cocktails. **Leisure Activities:** sauna, whirlpools, exercise room. **Guest Services:** gift shop, valet laundry, airport transportation (fee)-Sawyer International Airport. **Business Services:** conference facilities. **Cards:** AX, DC, DS, MC, VI. **Special Amenities:** free room upgrade (subject to availability with advanced reservations).

SOME UNITS

FEE

RAMADA INN
Large-scale Hotel

Phone: (906)228-6000

All Year   1P: $104-$109   2P: $109-$114   XP: $5   F18

Location: 0.5 w on US 41 business route. 412 W Washington St 49855. Fax: 906/228-2963. **Facility:** 113 units. 107 one-bedroom standard units. 6 one-bedroom suites, some with whirlpools. 7 stories, interior corridors. **Parking:** on-site. **Amenities:** voice mail, irons, hair dryers. **Pool(s):** heated indoor. **Leisure Activities:** sauna, whirlpool. **Fee:** game room. **Guest Services:** valet and coin laundry. **Business Services:** meeting rooms. **Cards:** AX, DC, DS, MC, VI.

SOME UNITS
FEE FEE

SUPER 8 MOTEL
Small-scale Hotel

Phone: 906-228-8100

5/1-3/31   1P: $55   2P: $72   XP: $9   F12
4/1-4/30   1P: $51   2P: $69   XP: $9   F12

Location: 1 mi w on US 41 and SR 28. Located in a semi-commercial area. 1275 US 41 W 49855. Fax: 906/228-8100. **Facility:** 80 one-bedroom standard units. 2 stories (no elevator), interior corridors. **Parking:** on-site, winter plug-ins. **Terms:** [CP] meal plan available. **Pool(s):** heated indoor. **Leisure Activities:** sauna, whirlpool, snowmobiling. **Guest Services:** coin laundry. **Business Services:** meeting rooms. **Cards:** AX, DC, MC, VI.

SOME UNITS

TIROLER HOF INN
Motel

Phone: (906)226-7516

All Year   1P: $50   2P: $66   XP: $3   F12

Location: 1.8 mi se on US 41 and SR 28. 1880 US 41 S 49855. Fax: 906/226-0699. **Facility:** 44 one-bedroom standard units. 2 stories (no elevator), exterior corridors. **Terms:** cancellation fee imposed, [AP] meal plan available, small pets only. **Dining:** 7 am-2 & 4:30-9 pm, Fri & Sat 7 am-9 pm, Sun 7 am-3 pm, cocktails. **Leisure Activities:** sauna, snowmobiling, hiking trails. **Guest Services:** coin laundry. **Business Services:** meeting rooms. **Cards:** AX, DC, DS, MC, VI. **Special Amenities:** free local telephone calls.

SOME UNITS

TRAVELODGE
Small-scale Hotel

Phone: (906)249-1712

All Year [ECP]   1P: $61   2P: $66   XP: $5   F17

Location: Jct US 41 S and SR 28 E. Located in a semi-commercial area. 1010 M-28 E 49855. Fax: 906/249-9051. **Facility:** 39 one-bedroom standard units, some with whirlpools. 2 stories (no elevator), interior corridors. *Bath:* combo or shower only. **Parking:** on-site, winter plug-ins. **Terms:** pets ($5 extra charge, in designated units). **Amenities:** hair dryers. **Pool(s):** heated indoor. **Leisure Activities:** whirlpool, snowmobiling. **Business Services:** meeting rooms. **Special Amenities:** free continental breakfast and free newspaper.

SOME UNITS

─────── **WHERE TO DINE** ───────

GREAT HUNAN
Chinese

Lunch: $5-$7   **Dinner:** $8-$13   Phone: 906/226-8649

Location: 2.8 mi w on US 41 and SR 28. 2680 US 41 W 49855. **Hours:** 11:30 am-9 pm, Fri & Sat-10 pm, Sun noon-8:30 pm. Closed: 11/27. **Features:** If you like seafood, try the seafood combination dish, which blends crab, fresh fish and vegetables in a tasty sauce. Otherwise, you can't go wrong with the excellent selection and great value of traditional choices. Service is friendly and attentive. **Parking:** on-site. **Cards:** MC, VI.

NORTHWOODS SUPPER CLUB
American

Lunch: $5-$8   **Dinner:** $8-$28   Phone: 906/228-4343

Location: 3.5 mi w on US 41 and SR 28, 0.3 mi s at sign. 49855. **Hours:** 11 am-10 pm, Fri & Sat-11 pm, Sun 10 am-10 pm. Closed: 12/24-12/26; also Mon. **Features:** Beef is aged in the on-site meat shop, and desserts are prepared in the in-house bakery at the charming, log cabin restaurant. One of the dining rooms looks out at a lovely waterfall in the back. The grounds are appointed with fresh flowers. Cocktails. **Parking:** on-site. **Cards:** AX, DS, MC, VI.

STEER & STEIN
Steak House

Lunch: $4-$7   **Dinner:** $7-$14   Phone: 906/228-7011

Location: 3.5 mi w on US 41 and SR 28. US Hwy 41 W 49855. **Hours:** 11 am-2 & 4-9 pm, Fri & Sat-10 pm. Closed: 12/25. **Features:** Grill your own steak on an indoor barbecue pit, or enjoy selections of pasta, chicken and seafood. The decor of the cozy, romantic dining room shows a Southwestern flair. The Snickers and Bailey's Irish creme cheesecakes are decadent desserts. Cocktails. **Parking:** on-site. **Cards:** AX, MC, VI.

THE VIERLING RESTAURANT & MARQUETTE HARBOR BREWERY
American

Historic   **Lunch:** $4-$7   **Dinner:** $10-$15   Phone: 906/228-3533

Location: Corner Front and Main sts. 119 S Front St 49855. **Hours:** 11 am-10 pm. Closed major holidays; also Sun. **Features:** An antique bar, stained-glass windows and varied memorabilia decorate the casual 1883 saloon, which is restored to an Old World elegance. A good selection of microbrewed beers complements such dishes as Lake Superior whitefish, ribs and steak. Casual dress; cocktails. **Parking:** street. **Cards:** AX, DS, MC, VI.

─────── *The following restaurants have not been evaluated by AAA but are listed for your information only.* ───────

SWEET WATER CAFE
[fyi]

Phone: 906/226-7009

Not evaluated. **Location:** Just n. 517 N Third 49855. **Features:** Most of the cafe's great tasting food is made from scratch using natural, organic and locally raised food.

UPFRONT & COMPANY
[fyi]

Phone: 906/228-5200

Not evaluated. **Location:** 102 E Main St 49855. **Features:** On the downtown restaurant's menu are fresh fish, steak, pasta and pizza.

MARSHALL pop. 7,459

——— WHERE TO STAY ———

AMERIHOST INN-MARSHALL
AAA **(SAVE)**
WWWW
Small-scale Hotel

Phone: (269)789-7890
All Year   1P: $79-$119   2P: $79-$119   XP: $6   F18
Location: I-69, exit 36, just se. 204 Winston 49068. Fax: 269/789-7891. **Facility:** 61 one-bedroom standard units, some with whirlpools. 2 stories (no elevator), interior corridors. *Bath:* combo or shower only. **Parking:** on-site. **Amenities:** voice mail, safes (fee), irons, hair dryers. **Pool(s):** heated indoor. **Leisure Activities:** sauna, whirlpool, exercise room. **Guest Services:** valet laundry. **Business Services:** meeting rooms. **Cards:** AX, CB, DC, DS, JC, MC, VI.

SOME UNITS
[icons]

ARBOR INN OF HISTORIC MARSHALL
AAA **(SAVE)**
WWW
Motel

Phone: 269/781-7772
All Year [CP]   1P: $43-$54   2P: $48-$62   XP: $5   F13
Location: I-69, exit 36, just w. 15435 W Michigan Ave 49068. Fax: 269/781-2660. **Facility:** 48 one-bedroom standard units, some with kitchens. 1 story, exterior corridors. **Parking:** on-site, winter plug-ins. **Terms:** check-in 4 pm, pets ($5 extra charge, in limited units). **Pool(s):** outdoor. **Cards:** AX, DS, MC, VI. **Special Amenities:** free continental breakfast and free local telephone calls.

SOME UNITS
[icons]

HOLIDAY INN EXPRESS
WWW
Small-scale Hotel

Phone: 269/789-9301
All Year [ECP]   1P: $89-$109   2P: $89-$109   XP: $8   F18
Location: I-94, exit 110. 17252 Sam Hill Dr 49068. Fax: 269/789-9301. **Facility:** 66 units. 65 one-bedroom standard units, some with whirlpools. 1 one-bedroom suite with whirlpool. 3 stories, interior corridors. *Bath:* combo or shower only. **Parking:** on-site. **Amenities:** high-speed Internet (fee), dual phone lines, voice mail, irons, hair dryers. **Pool(s):** small heated indoor. **Leisure Activities:** exercise room. **Guest Services:** valet laundry. **Cards:** AX, CB, DC, DS, JC, MC, VI.

SOME UNITS
[icons]

THE NATIONAL HOUSE INN
WWW
Historic Bed & Breakfast

Phone: (269)781-7374
All Year   1P: $105   2P: $145   XP: $15   F7
Location: Fountain Circle; downtown. 102 S Parkview 49068. Fax: 269/781-4510. **Facility:** Closed 12/24 and 12/25. Restored 1835 inn. Smoke free premises. 15 units. 13 one-bedroom standard units. 2 one-bedroom suites. 2 stories, interior corridors. *Bath:* combo or shower only. **Parking:** on-site. **Terms:** 7 day cancellation notice-fee imposed, [BP] meal plan available. **Guest Services:** gift shop. **Cards:** AX, MC, VI.

[icons]

ROSE HILL INN B & B
WWW
Historic Bed & Breakfast

Phone: 269/789-1992
All Year   1P: $99-$140   2P: $99-$140
Location: Fountain Circle, just n to Mansion St, 0.7 mi w; downtown. 1110 Verona Rd 49068. Fax: 269/781-4723. **Facility:** An elegant 1860 Italianate-style mansion with a large front porch, the B&B is set on three acres of groomed grounds which include a tennis court. Smoke free premises. 6 one-bedroom standard units. 2 stories, interior corridors. *Bath:* combo or shower only. **Parking:** on-site. **Terms:** age restrictions may apply, 14 day cancellation notice-fee imposed, [BP] meal plan available, package plans, no pets allowed (owner's cat on premises). **Amenities:** hair dryers. **Pool(s):** outdoor. **Leisure Activities:** tennis court. **Cards:** AX, MC, VI.

[icons]

——— WHERE TO DINE ———

MALIA
WWW
Nouvelle Italian

Lunch: $9-$11   **Dinner:** $15-$20   **Phone:** 269/781-2171
Location: Just e of circle; downtown. 130 W Michigan 49068. **Hours:** 11:30 am-2 & 5:30-8 pm, Mon-2 pm, Fri & Sat-9 pm. Closed major holidays; also Sun. **Reservations:** accepted. **Features:** Located in a converted downtown storefront, the exposed brick walls and spotlighted artwork create a tendy but comfortable atmosphere to enjoy the homemade pastas and innovative sauces. Casual dress. **Parking:** on-site. **Cards:** AX, CB, DC, DS, MC, VI.

[icons]

SCHULER'S   Classic
AAA
WWW
American

Lunch: $9-$13   **Dinner:** $15-$26   **Phone:** 269/781-0600
Location: Just e of US 27 and circle, 1 mi s of I-94. 115 S Eagle St 49068. **Hours:** 11 am-9 pm, Fri & Sat-10 pm, Sun 10 am-9 pm. Closed: 12/25. **Reservations:** suggested. **Features:** Childhood memories of eating freshly baked bread and butter are evoked as you savor the flavor of the homemade bread at this almost 100-year-old establishment. The atmosphere whisks you away to the early 20th-century and allows you to experience lovingly created foods like your great grandmother might have prepared for the family table. Hearty portions of the many German inspired dishes will satisfy even the hungriest of diners, and desserts will tempt even the most strong willed of dieters. Casual dress; cocktails. **Parking:** on-site. **Cards:** AX, DC, DS, MC, VI.

MARYSVILLE pop. 9,684

——— WHERE TO STAY ———

DAYS INN OF PORT HURON-MARYSVILLE
AAA **(SAVE)**
WW
Motel

Phone: 810/364-8400
All Year   1P: $48-$58   2P: $60-$65   XP: $10   F12
Location: I-94, exit 266, 3 mi e on Business I-94. 70 Gratiot Blvd 48040. Fax: 810/364-8401. **Facility:** 26 one-bedroom standard units, some with whirlpools. 1 story, exterior corridors. **Parking:** on-site, winter plug-ins. **Terms:** cancellation fee imposed. **Amenities:** video library, hair dryers. **Pool(s):** heated outdoor. **Cards:** AX, DC, DS, JC, MC, VI. **Special Amenities:** free continental breakfast. *(See color ad card insert)*

SOME UNITS

FEE

SUPER 8 MOTEL PORT HURON/MARYSVILLE
All Year [CP]   1P: $59-$89   2P: $59-$89   XP: $5   Phone: (810)364-7500
(AAA) (SAVE)

Small-scale Hotel
Location: I-94, exit 266, 1 mi e, 0.3 mi s of Port Huron on I-94 business loop. Located in a secluded area. 1484 Gratiot Blvd 48040. Fax: 810/364-4423. **Facility:** 70 one-bedroom standard units, some with whirlpools. 2 stories, interior/exterior corridors. *Bath:* combo or shower only. **Parking:** on-site. **Amenities:** hair dryers. **Pool(s):** heated indoor. **Leisure Activities:** whirlpool, exercise room. *Fee:* game room. **Guest Services:** coin laundry. **Business Services:** meeting rooms. **Cards:** AX, DS, MC, VI. **Special Amenities:** free continental breakfast and free local telephone calls.

SOME UNITS

MEARS

──────── **WHERE TO STAY** ────────

DUNES WATERFRONT RESORT   Phone: 231/873-5500
6/27-8/23   1P: $120-$160   2P: $145-$195   XP: $10   F12
4/1-6/26 & 8/24-10/26   1P: $80-$140   2P: $100-$160   XP: $10   F12

Small-scale Hotel
Location: US 31, exit Hart/Mears, 7 mi w to Silver Lake, follow signs. Located next to the lake. 1180 N Shore Dr 49436. Fax: 231/873-7653. **Facility:** 72 one-bedroom standard units, some with whirlpools. 4 stories, interior corridors. *Bath:* combo or shower only. **Parking:** on-site. **Terms:** open 4/1-10/26, 2 night minimum stay - with Saturday stayover 6/27-8/16, 3 day cancellation notice. **Amenities:** video library (fee), irons, hair dryers. **Pool(s):** heated indoor. **Leisure Activities:** whirlpool, boat dock, exercise room. *Fee:* game room. **Guest Services:** coin laundry. **Business Services:** meeting rooms. **Cards:** DS, MC, VI. *(See color ad below)*

SOME UNITS
FEE

MENOMINEE pop. 9,131

──────── **WHERE TO STAY** ────────

AMERICINN OF MENOMINEE   Phone: 906/863-8699
All Year [ECP]   1P: $80-$120   2P: $80-$120   XP: $6   F17

Small-scale Hotel
Location: 0.8 mi n on US 41. Located in a commercial area. 2330 10th St 49858. Fax: 906/863-8190. **Facility:** 63 units. 59 one-bedroom standard units, some with whirlpools. 4 one-bedroom suites, some with whirlpools. 2 stories (no elevator), interior corridors. *Bath:* combo or shower only. **Parking:** on-site. **Amenities:** hair dryers. *Some:* irons. **Pool(s):** heated indoor. **Leisure Activities:** whirlpool, boat ramp, playground. **Guest Services:** coin laundry. **Business Services:** meeting rooms. **Cards:** AX, DC, DS, MC, VI.

SOME UNITS
FEE

ECONO LODGE ON THE BAY

AAA SAVE

4/1-9/30	1P: $75-$100	2P: $85-$100	XP: $5 F18
10/1-3/31	1P: $60-$100	2P: $70-$100	XP: $5 F18

Phone: (906)863-4431

Small-scale Hotel

Location: 1 mi n on US 41. Located in a commercial area. 2516 10th St 49858. Fax: 906/863-3069. **Facility:** 50 one-bedroom standard units. 2 stories (no elevator), interior corridors. **Parking:** on-site, winter plug-ins. **Terms:** cancellation fee imposed, small pets only. **Leisure Activities:** sauna, whirlpool. **Business Services:** meeting rooms. **Cards:** AX, DS, MC, VI. **Special Amenities:** free continental breakfast and free local telephone calls. *(See color ad p 381)*

SOME UNITS

———— WHERE TO DINE ————

THE LANDING

▼▼ ▼▼

American

cocktails.

Lunch: $4-$8   **Dinner:** $9-$18   **Phone:** 906/863-8034

Location: From US 41, just e on 10th Ave; in historic district. 450 1st St 49858. **Hours:** 11:30 am-2 & 5-9 pm, Fri & Sat 5 pm-10 pm. Closed major holidays. **Features:** Jack Daniels New York strip stands out on a menu of traditionally prepared steak and seafood choices. The nautically appointed dining room overlooks Green Bay. The atmosphere is lively and upbeat, as is the staff, which provides efficient service. Casual dress; cocktails. **Parking:** on-site. **Cards:** DS, MC, VI.

SCHLOEGEL'S

AAA

▼▼ ▼▼

American

Lunch: $5-$6   **Dinner:** $6-$9   **Phone:** 906/863-7888

Location: 1 mi n on US 41. 2720 10th St 49858. **Hours:** 6 am-8 pm, Sun from 7:30 am; to 9 pm in summer, Sun-8 pm. Closed: 11/27, 12/25. **Features:** Guests can enjoy panoramic views of Green Bay from the quiet dining room, attractively decorated with local art. The menu lists a wide selection of family-style foods. Homemade pies and fresh bread and "pasties" make mouths water. Service is friendly. Casual dress. **Parking:** on-site. **Cards:** MC, VI.

MIDLAND pop. 41,685

———— WHERE TO STAY ————

ASHMAN COURT MARRIOTT CONFERENCE HOTEL

AAA SAVE

▼▼▼ ▼▼

Large-scale Hotel

All Year	1P: $79-$159	2P: $79-$159

Phone: (989)839-0500

Location: Corner of Main and Ashman sts; downtown. 111 W Main St 48640. Fax: 989/837-6000. **Facility:** 121 units. 112 one-bedroom standard units. 9 one-bedroom suites ($99-$199) with whirlpools. 6 stories, interior corridors. *Bath:* combo or shower only. **Parking:** on-site. **Amenities:** dual phone lines, voice mail, irons, hair dryers. **Dining:** The Crossings, see separate listing. **Pool(s):** heated indoor. **Leisure Activities:** whirlpool, jogging, exercise room. *Fee:* in-line skates, bicycles, game room. **Guest Services:** sundries, valet laundry, airport transportation-Tri-City Airport. **Business Services:** conference facilities, business center. **Cards:** AX, CB, DC, DS, MC, VI. **Special Amenities:** free local telephone calls and free newspaper.

SOME UNITS

BEST WESTERN VALLEY PLAZA RESORT

SAVE

▼▼▼ ▼▼

Large-scale Hotel

All Year	1P: $69-$83	2P: $69-$83

Phone: (989)496-2700

Location: US 10, exit Midland/Bay City Rd. 5221 Bay City Rd 48642. Fax: 989/496-9233. **Facility:** 162 units. 160 one-bedroom standard units. 2 one-bedroom suites ($132-$182) with whirlpools. 2 stories, interior corridors. **Parking:** on-site. **Terms:** check-in 4 pm, package plans, small pets only. **Amenities:** voice mail, safes (fee), irons, hair dryers. **Pool(s):** heated indoor, wading. **Leisure Activities:** sauna, whirlpool, putting green, ice skating, basketball, horseshoes, volleyball. *Fee:* game room. **Guest Services:** valet laundry. **Business Services:** conference facilities. **Cards:** AX, CB, DC, DS, MC, VI.

SOME UNITS

FEE   FEE

FAIRVIEW INN

AAA SAVE

▼▼ ▼▼

Small-scale Hotel

All Year [ECP]	1P: $75-$99	2P: $79-$99

Phone: (989)631-0070

Location: Jct US 10 and Eastman Rd, just n. Located in a commercial area. 2200 W Wackerly St 48640. Fax: 989/631-1604. **Facility:** 90 units. 83 one-bedroom standard units. 7 one-bedroom suites. 2 stories (no elevator), interior corridors. **Parking:** on-site, winter plug-ins. **Terms:** pets ($25 deposit). **Amenities:** voice mail. *Some:* irons, hair dryers. **Pool(s):** heated indoor. **Leisure Activities:** whirlpool, exercise room. **Guest Services:** coin laundry, airport transportation-Tri-City Airport. **Business Services:** meeting rooms. **Cards:** AX, DC, DS, MC, VI. **Special Amenities:** free continental breakfast and free local telephone calls.

SOME UNITS

FEE

HAMPTON INN

AAA SAVE

▼▼▼ ▼▼

Small-scale Hotel

All Year	1P: $81-$149	2P: $81-$149

Phone: (989)837-4000

Location: US 10, exit Eastman Rd, just n. Located opposite Midland Mall. 6701 Eastman Ave 48642. Fax: 989/837-7241. **Facility:** 87 units. 78 one-bedroom standard units, some with whirlpools. 9 one-bedroom suites, some with whirlpools. 3 stories, interior corridors. *Bath:* combo or shower only. **Parking:** on-site. **Terms:** check-in 4 pm, [ECP] meal plan available. **Amenities:** video games, dual phone lines, voice mail, irons, hair dryers. **Pool(s):** heated indoor. **Leisure Activities:** whirlpool, exercise room. **Guest Services:** coin laundry, tanning facility. **Business Services:** meeting rooms. **Cards:** AX, CB, DC, DS, JC, MC, VI. **Special Amenities:** free continental breakfast and free local telephone calls. *(See color ad p 383)*

SOME UNITS

HOLIDAY INN

AAA SAVE

Large-scale Hotel

Phone: 989/631-4220

All Year   1P: $55-$199   2P: $55-$199   XP: $10   F18
Location: Jct US 10 and Eastman Rd. Located in a commercial area. 1500 W Wackerly St 48640. Fax: 989/631-3776. **Facility:** 235 units. 219 one-bedroom standard units, some with whirlpools. 16 one-bedroom suites ($109-$199) with whirlpools. 2 stories (no elevator), interior/exterior corridors. **Parking:** on-site, winter plug-ins. **Terms:** check-in 4 pm, 16% service charge, pets (in smoking units). **Amenities:** video games, voice mail, irons, hair dryers. *Some:* dual phone lines. **Dining:** 6 am-11 pm, Fri & Sat-midnight, cocktails. **Pool(s):** heated indoor. **Leisure Activities:** sauna, whirlpool, indoor recreation area, exercise room, basketball, volleyball. *Fee:* racquetball courts, game room. **Guest Services:** valet and coin laundry, airport transportation-Tri-City Airport. **Business Services:** conference facilities, business center. **Cards:** AX, CB, DC, DS, JC, MC, VI.

SOME UNITS

PLAZA SUITES HOTEL

Small-scale Hotel

Phone: (989)496-0100

All Year   1P: $89-$106   2P: $89-$106
Location: US 10, exit Midland/Bay City Rd. 5217 Bay City Rd 48642. Fax: 989/496-2353. **Facility:** 74 units. 66 one-bedroom standard units. 8 one-bedroom suites ($132-$182) with whirlpools. 2 stories (no elevator), interior corridors. **Parking:** on-site. **Terms:** check-in 4 pm, package plans, small pets only. **Amenities:** dual phone lines, voice mail, safes (fee), honor bars, irons, hair dryers. **Guest Services:** valet laundry. **Cards:** AX, CB, DC, DS, MC, VI.

SOME UNITS

SLEEP INN OF MIDLAND　　　　　　　　　　　　　　　　　　　　**Phone:** (989)837-1010

🏨🅂🅰🆅🅴　All Year [ECP]　　　　　　1P: $65-$85　　　　2P: $70-$110
▼▼▼▼　**Location:** Jct US 10 and Eastman Rd. Located in a commercial area. 2100 W Wackerly 48640. Fax: 989/837-2470.
Facility: 79 units. 77 one-bedroom standard units. 2 one-bedroom suites ($105-$140) with whirlpools. 3 stories, interior corridors. *Bath:* combo or shower only. **Parking:** on-site. **Amenities:** voice mail, irons, hair
Small-scale Hotel　dryers. **Pool(s):** heated indoor. **Leisure Activities:** sauna. **Guest Services:** coin laundry. **Business Services:** meeting rooms. **Cards:** AX, CB, DC, DS, MC, VI. **Special Amenities: free continental breakfast and
free local telephone calls.** *(See ad p 383)*

SOME UNITS
🆂🅳 🐾 🍴➜ 🔑M 🛋 🏊 📷 📠 💻 / ✕ 🆅🅲🆁 📶 📷 /

──────── **WHERE TO DINE** ────────

BAMBOO GARDEN　　　　　**Lunch:** $5-$8　　　**Dinner:** $9-$14　　　**Phone:** 989/832-7967
🅰🅰　**Location:** Jct US 10 and Eastman Rd, 1 mi s, then 0.5 mi w. 2600 N Saginaw Rd 48640. **Hours:** 11:30 am-2 &
▼▼ ▼▼　4-8:30 pm, Fri-9:30 pm, Sat 5 pm-9:30 pm, Sun noon-8 pm. Closed: 1/1, 11/27, 12/25.
Chinese　**Reservations:** suggested; weekends. **Features:** Szechuan and Shanghai cuisine are specialties on a
menu that lists entrees from many regions of China. The comfortable, intimate dining room is decorated
with attractive Oriental furnishings and appointments. Lunch buffet. Casual dress; cocktails. **Parking:**
on-site. **Cards:** DS, MC, VI.
✕

CHINA PALACE　　　　　**Lunch:** $4-$7　　　**Dinner:** $7-$17　　　**Phone:** 989/832-3177
▼▼ ▼▼　**Location:** Just n of US 10 business route. 1908 S Saginaw Rd 48640. **Hours:** 11 am-9:30 pm, Fri-10:30 pm, Sat
Chinese　noon-10:30 pm, Sun noon-8:30 pm. Closed major holidays. **Reservations:** suggested. **Features:** In
business since the mid-1980s, the restaurant has several dining areas, all of which are decorated in an
Oriental motif. Mongolian beef is among the delicious dishes of Mandarin, Szechuan, Hunan and Shanghai
cuisine. The atmosphere is family-friendly. Casual dress; cocktails. **Parking:** on-site. **Cards:** AX, DS, MC, VI.
✕

THE CROSSINGS　　　　　**Lunch:** $5-$10　　　**Dinner:** $13-$25　　　**Phone:** 989/837-6030
▼▼ ▼▼　**Location:** Corner of Main and Ashman sts; downtown; in Ashman Court Marriott Conference Hotel. 111 W Main St
American　48640. **Hours:** 6:30 am-2 & 5-10 pm, Sat & Sun from 7 am. **Features:** The restaurant is great for couples
or businesspeople who seek a relaxed setting in which to enjoy conversation. An extensive lunch buffet is
Cocktails. **Parking:** on-site. **Cards:** AX, CB, DC, DS, MC, VI.　popular on weekdays. The cozy summer terrace overlooks the picturesque waterfront. Service is friendly.
🍸 ✕

MILAN pop. 4,775

──────── **WHERE TO STAY** ────────

SLEEP INN & SUITES　　　　　　　　　　　　　　　　　　　　**Phone:** (734)439-1400
🏨🅂🅰🆅🅴　4/1-12/31　　　　　1P: $59-$159　　　2P: $59-$159　　　XP: $6　　　F18
　　　　　1/1-3/31　　　　　1P: $49-$119　　　2P: $49-$119　　　XP: $6　　　F18
▼▼▼▼ ▼▼▼▼　**Location:** I-23, exit 27, just w. 1230 Dexter St 48160. Fax: 734/439-4181. **Facility:** 63 one-bedroom standard
Small-scale Hotel　units, some with whirlpools. 3 stories, interior corridors. *Bath:* shower only. **Parking:** on-site. **Terms:** [CP]
meal plan available. **Amenities:** dual phone lines, voice mail, safes, hair dryers. **Pool(s):** heated indoor.
Leisure Activities: exercise room. **Guest Services:** valet and coin laundry. **Business Services:** meeting
rooms. **Cards:** AX, CB, DC, DS, JC, MC, VI. **Special Amenities: free continental breakfast and free local telephone calls.**

SOME UNITS
🆂🅳 🔑M 🛋 🏊 📷 📠 / ✕ 📶 📷 💻 /

MILFORD —See Detroit p. 261.

MIO pop. 2,016

──────── **WHERE TO STAY** ────────

HINCHMAN ACRES RESORT　　　　　　　　　　　　　　　　　　**Phone:** (989)826-3267
🏨🅂🅰🆅🅴　All Year　　　　　1P: $60-$100　　　2P: $70-$150　　　XP: $15
▼▼ ▼▼　**Location:** 0.5 mi n on SR 33 and 72. 702 N Morenci St 48647 (PO Box 220). Fax: 989/826-3267. **Facility:** 11 cot-
Cottage　tages. 1 story, exterior corridors. *Bath:* combo or shower only. **Parking:** on-site. **Terms:** 30 day cancellation
notice-fee imposed. **Amenities:** hair dryers. **Leisure Activities:** rental canoes, rental tubes & rafts, cross
country skiing, recreation programs, bike trails, indoor recreation area, hiking trails, playground, basketball,
horseshoes, shuffleboard, volleyball. *Fee:* fishing, ski equipment, snowshoes, game room. **Guest Services:**
coin laundry.
🆂🅳 ✕ 📷 📶 📷 💻

MIO MOTEL　　　　　　　　　　　　　　　　　　　　　　　　**Phone:** 989/826-3248
▼▼ ▼▼　All Year　　　　　1P: $50-$60　　　2P: $50-$70　　　XP: $10
Motel　**Location:** Just n on SR 33 and 72. 415 N Morenci St 48647. **Facility:** 25 one-bedroom standard units. 2 stories,
exterior corridors. *Bath:* combo or shower only. **Parking:** on-site, winter plug-ins. **Terms:** 3 day cancellation
notice. **Cards:** MC, VI.

SOME UNITS
🍴➜ 📷 📶 📷 / ✕ /

MONROE pop. 22,076

—— WHERE TO STAY ——

AMERIHOST INN-MONROE
AAA **SAVE**
Small-scale Hotel
Phone: (734)384-1600
All Year [ECP]   1P: $69-$99   2P: $69-$99   XP: $5   F17
Location: I-75, exit 11 (La Plaisance Rd), just w. Located opposite an outlet mall. 14774 La Plaisance Rd 48161. Fax: 734/384-1180. **Facility:** 63 one-bedroom standard units. 2 stories, interior corridors. *Bath:* combo or shower only. **Parking:** on-site. **Amenities:** voice mail, safes (fee), irons, hair dryers. **Pool(s):** heated indoor. **Leisure Activities:** sauna, whirlpool, exercise room. **Guest Services:** valet laundry. **Business Services:** meeting rooms. **Cards:** AX, CB, DC, DS, JC, MC, VI. **Special Amenities:** free continental breakfast and free newspaper.

SOME UNITS

COMFORT INN
AAA **SAVE**
Small-scale Hotel
Phone: (734)384-1500

9/1-12/31	1P: $79-$199	2P: $79-$199	XP: $10 F17
6/1-8/31	1P: $85-$185	2P: $85-$185	XP: $10 F17
4/1-5/31	1P: $79-$179	2P: $79-$179	XP: $10 F17
1/1-3/31	1P: $59-$159	2P: $59-$159	XP: $10 F17

Location: I-75, exit 11 (La Plaisance Rd), just w. Located opposite an outlet mall. 6500 Albain Rd 48161. Fax: 734/384-1515. **Facility:** 64 one-bedroom standard units, some with whirlpools. 3 stories, interior corridors. *Bath:* combo or shower only. **Parking:** on-site. **Terms:** [ECP] meal plan available, pets ($10 extra charge). **Amenities:** irons, hair dryers. **Pool(s):** heated indoor. **Leisure Activities:** whirlpool. **Guest Services:** valet laundry. **Business Services:** meeting rooms, business center. **Cards:** AX, DC, DS, MC, VI. **Special Amenities:** early check-in/late check-out and free continental breakfast.

SOME UNITS

CROSS COUNTRY INN
AAA **SAVE**
Motel
Phone: (734)289-2330
All Year   1P: $41-$48   2P: $45-$52   XP: $2   F17
Location: I-75, exit 15 (SR 50). 1900 Welcome Way 48162. Fax: 734/289-3683. **Facility:** 120 one-bedroom standard units. 2 stories, exterior corridors. *Bath:* combo or shower only. **Parking:** on-site. **Terms:** weekly rates available. **Amenities:** video games, voice mail. **Pool(s):** heated outdoor. **Business Services:** fax (fee). **Cards:** AX, CB, DC, DS, MC, VI. **Special Amenities:** free local telephone calls and preferred room (subject to availability with advanced reservations). *(See color ad p 236)*

SOME UNITS

HAMPTON INN
SAVE
Small-scale Hotel
Phone: (734)289-5700

4/1-5/31 & 10/1-3/31	1P: $69-$79	2P: $79-$89
6/1-9/30	1P: $79-$89	2P: $89

Location: I-75, exit 15 (SR 50), just e. 1565 N Dixie Hwy 48162. Fax: 734/289-3300. **Facility:** 74 one-bedroom standard units, some with whirlpools. 3 stories, interior corridors. *Bath:* combo or shower only. **Parking:** on-site. **Terms:** cancellation fee imposed, [ECP] meal plan available. **Amenities:** video games, dual phone lines, voice mail, irons, hair dryers. **Pool(s):** heated indoor. **Leisure Activities:** sauna, whirlpool, exercise room. **Guest Services:** valet and coin laundry. **Business Services:** meeting rooms, business center. **Cards:** AX, CB, DC, DS, JC, MC, VI.

SOME UNITS
FEE

HOLIDAY INN EXPRESS HOTEL & SUITES
Small-scale Hotel
Phone: (734)242-6000
All Year [ECP]   1P: $99   2P: $109
Location: I-75, exit 15 (SR 50). 1225 N Dixie Hwy 48162. Fax: 734/242-0555. **Facility:** 161 units. 158 one-bedroom standard units, some with whirlpools. 3 two-bedroom suites ($109-$119) with efficiencies. 4 stories, interior corridors. *Bath:* combo or shower only. **Parking:** on-site. **Terms:** cancellation fee imposed. **Amenities:** video games, dual phone lines, voice mail, irons, hair dryers. **Pool(s):** heated indoor. **Leisure Activities:** whirlpool, exercise room. **Fee:** game room. **Guest Services:** valet and coin laundry. **Business Services:** meeting rooms, business center. **Cards:** AX, DC, DS, MC, VI.

SOME UNITS

HOMETOWN INN
AAA **SAVE**
Motel
Phone: 734-289-1080
All Year [ECP]   1P: $27-$45   2P: $28-$49
Location: I-75, exit 15 (SR 50). 1885 Welcome Way 48162. Fax: 734/289-1673. **Facility:** 89 one-bedroom standard units, some with whirlpools. 1 story, exterior corridors. **Parking:** on-site. **Guest Services:** coin laundry. **Business Services:** meeting rooms. **Cards:** AX, DC, DS, MC, VI. **Special Amenities:** free continental breakfast and free local telephone calls.

SOME UNITS

LOTUS BED AND BREAKFAST, LC
Historic Bed & Breakfast
Phone: 734-735-1077
All Year [BP]   1P: $105   2P: $105
Location: I-75, exit 11 (La Plaisance Rd), 2.5 mi w to Scott St, just n to Fourth St, just w. 324 Washington St 48161. Fax: 734/735-1077. **Facility:** Smoke free premises. 4 units. 2 one-bedroom standard units. 2 one-bedroom suites. 3 stories (no elevator), interior corridors. **Parking:** on-site. **Terms:** check-in 4 pm, 3 day cancellation notice-fee imposed, no pets allowed (owner's cat on premises). **Guest Services:** complimentary laundry. **Cards:** AX, MC, VI.

SOME UNITS

—— WHERE TO DINE ——

ERNIE'S GATHERING PLACE
American
Lunch: $5-$8   Dinner: $10-$14   Phone: 734-242-2330
Location: Just n of W Dunbar Rd. 15425 S Dixie Hwy 48161. **Hours:** 7 am-10 pm, Fri-Sun to 11 pm. Closed major holidays. **Features:** Located in front of a bowling alley, this comfortable family restaurant serves pizzas, hamburgers and fish specials. The turtle soup is a popular choice, but leave room for homemade desserts. Casual dress; cocktails. **Parking:** on-site. **Cards:** AX, MC, VI.

JOE'S FRENCH-ITALIAN INN ▼▼ ▼▼ **Lunch:** $6-$12 **Dinner:** $10-$23 **Phone:** 734/289-2800
Location: I-75, exit 15 (SR 50), 2 mi e. 2896 N Dixie Hwy 48162. **Hours:** 11 am-9:30 pm, Fri-10:30 pm, Sat 4
pm-10:30 pm, Sun & Mon 4 pm-9:30 pm. Closed: 1/1, 12/25. **Reservations:** suggested. **Features:** Stained
glass and an attractive mural help to set an Italian theme in the quiet, casual restaurant. The menu of
American French and Italian specialties includes preparations of seafood, prime rib and veal—in addition to a lengthy
selection of pasta dishes. Casual dress; cocktails. **Parking:** on-site. **Cards:** AX, MC, VI. 🍽 ✕

QUATRO'S ▼▼ ▼▼ **Lunch:** $5-$7 **Dinner:** $8-$18 **Phone:** 734/242-6788
Location: Jct US 24 (Telegraph Rd) and Stewart Rd; adjacent to Meijer Shopping Center. 1295 Stewart Rd 48162.
Hours: 11 am-11 pm, Fri & Sat 4 pm-midnight, Sun 4 pm-10 pm. Closed: 1/1, 12/25.
American **Reservations:** suggested; weekends. **Features:** Prime rib, crab legs and seafood fettuccine stand out on
a menu of varied choices. Decor that reflects the style of a modern tavern gives the dining room a warm,
cozy feel. A popular restaurant with locals, the place delivers consistent friendly service. Casual dress; cocktails. **Parking:**
on-site. **Cards:** AX, MC, VI. 🍽 ✕

MOUNT CLEMENS —*See Detroit p. 261.*

MOUNT PLEASANT pop. 25,946

———— WHERE TO STAY ————

BAYMONT INN-MOUNT PLEASANT **Phone:** (989)775-5555
(AAA) (SAVE) 5/1-9/30 1P: $69-$129 2P: $69-$129 XP: $5 F18
▼▼ ▼▼ 4/1-4/30 & 10/1-3/31 1P: $59-$119 2P: $59-$119 XP: $5 F18
Location: On SR 20 E, 0.5 mi e of US 27. 5858 E Pickard St 48858. Fax: 989/775-5566. **Facility:** 102 one-bedroom
standard units, some with whirlpools. 3 stories, interior corridors. **Parking:** on-site, winter plug-ins.
Small-scale Hotel **Terms:** [ECP] meal plan available. **Amenities:** video games, voice mail, irons, hair dryers. **Pool(s):** heated
indoor. **Leisure Activities:** whirlpool. **Guest Services:** coin laundry. **Cards:** AX, DC, DS, MC, VI.
Special Amenities: free continental breakfast and free newspaper. SOME UNITS

BEST WESTERN INN **Phone:** (989)772-1101
(AAA) (SAVE) 4/1-12/31 [CP] 1P: $69-$99 2P: $69-$99
▼▼ ▼▼ 1/1-3/31 [CP] 1P: $59-$99 2P: $59-$99
Location: Jct US 27 and SR 20 E. 5770 E Pickard Ave 48858. Fax: 989/772-8986. **Facility:** 51 one-bedroom stan-
dard units. 1 story, interior corridors. **Parking:** on-site, winter plug-ins. **Amenities:** irons, hair dryers. **Pool(s):**
Small-scale Hotel heated indoor. **Leisure Activities:** sauna, whirlpool. **Cards:** AX, DC, DS, MC, VI. **Special Amenities:** free
continental breakfast and preferred room (subject to availability with advanced reservations).
SOME UNITS

COMFORT INN **Phone:** 989/772-4000
(AAA) (SAVE) All Year 1P: $89 2P: $129
▼▼ ▼▼ ▼▼ **Location:** 2 mi s on US 27 business route. 2424 S Mission St 48858. Fax: 989/773-6052. **Facility:** 138 units. 126
one-bedroom standard units, some with whirlpools. 12 one-bedroom suites ($129-$179) with whirlpools. 2
stories (no elevator), interior corridors. *Bath:* combo or shower only. **Parking:** on-site, winter plug-ins.
Small-scale Hotel **Terms:** check-in 4 pm, cancellation fee imposed, [ECP] meal plan available. **Amenities:** voice mail, irons,
hair dryers. **Pool(s):** heated indoor. **Leisure Activities:** exercise room. *Fee:* game room. **Guest Services:**
valet and coin laundry. **Business Services:** conference facilities. **Cards:** AX, DS, MC, VI. **Special Amenities:** free continental
breakfast and free local telephone calls. *(See color ad below)* SOME UNITS

FAIRFIELD INN BY MARRIOTT

Phone: (989)775-5000

AAA [SAVE]
◇◇◇◇◇

Small-scale Hotel

6/1-9/30	1P: $75-$99	2P: $75-$99
10/1-3/31	1P: $69-$94	2P: $69-$94
4/1-5/31	1P: $69-$89	2P: $69-$89

Location: 2 mi s on US 27 business route. 2525 S University Park Dr 48858. Fax: 989/773-1371. **Facility:** 74 one-bedroom standard units, some with whirlpools. 3 stories, interior corridors. *Bath:* combo or shower only. **Parking:** on-site. **Terms:** check-in 4 pm, [ECP] meal plan available. **Amenities:** irons, hair dryers. **Pool(s):** heated indoor. **Leisure Activities:** whirlpool, hiking trails. **Guest Services:** valet laundry. **Cards:** CB, DC, DS, MC, VI.
(See color ad p 386)

SOME UNITS
[🍴] [♿] [⟲] [👪] [📷] [DATA PORT] / [✕] [🛏] [🖥] /
FEE

GREEN SUITES

Phone: (989)772-1703

◇◇◇

Motel

All Year   1P: $65-$503   2P: $65-$503   XP: $10   F18

Location: Jct US 27 and SR 20, just e on SR 20, then just n. 1900 Summerton Rd 48858. Fax: 989/772-1721. **Facility:** 42 units. 22 one-bedroom standard units. 20 one-bedroom suites ($79-$505) with kitchens (utensil deposit required). 2 stories, exterior corridors. *Bath:* shower only. **Parking:** on-site. **Terms:** check-in 4 pm, 3 day cancellation notice, weekly rates available, package plans - seasonal. **Amenities:** voice mail, hair dryers. *Some:* irons. **Cards:** AX, CB, DC, DS, JC, MC, VI.

SOME UNITS
[ASK] [S/D] [🍴] [👪] [DATA PORT] [🖥] / [✕] [🛏] [🖥] /
FEE

HAMPTON INN

Phone: (989)772-5500

[SAVE]
◇◇◇◇

Small-scale Hotel

| 5/2-10/30 [ECP] | 1P: $76-$139 | 2P: $81-$139 |
| 4/1-5/1 & 10/31-3/31 [ECP] | 1P: $74-$139 | 2P: $79-$139 |

Location: Jct US 27 and SR 20, just w on SR 20. 5205 E Pickard Rd 48858. Fax: 989/772-7401. **Facility:** 89 one-bedroom standard units, some with whirlpools. 3 stories, interior corridors. *Bath:* combo or shower only. **Parking:** on-site, winter plug-ins. **Terms:** check-in 4 pm. **Amenities:** video games, voice mail, irons, hair dryers. **Pool(s):** heated indoor. **Leisure Activities:** whirlpool, exercise room. *Fee:* game room. **Guest Services:** valet and coin laundry. **Business Services:** meeting rooms, fax (fee). **Cards:** AX, CB, DC, DS, JC, MC, VI.
(See color ad below)

SOME UNITS
[S/D] [🍴] [♿] [⟲] [✕] [📷] [DATA PORT] [🖥] / [✕] [🛏] [🖥] /

HOLIDAY INN

Phone: (989)772-2905

◇◇◇

Resort
Small-scale Hotel

All Year   1P: $84-$154   2P: $84-$154   XP: $10   F16

Location: Jct US 27 and SR 20 E. 5665 E Pickard Ave 48858. Fax: 989/772-4952. **Facility:** Close to the casino. 184 one-bedroom standard units, some with whirlpools. 2-3 stories, interior/exterior corridors. *Bath:* combo or shower only. **Parking:** on-site, winter plug-ins. **Terms:** check-in 4 pm, 3 day cancellation notice-fee imposed, small pets only. **Amenities:** video games (fee), voice mail, irons, hair dryers. **Leisure Activities:** sauna, whirlpools, fishing, 2 lighted tennis courts, snowmobiling, playground. *Fee:* golf-36 holes, racquetball courts, massage, game room. **Guest Services:** gift shop, valet and coin laundry. *Fee:* tanning facility. **Business Services:** conference facilities. **Cards:** AX, DS, JC, MC, VI.

SOME UNITS
[ASK] [S/D] [🐾] [🍴] [🍸] [♿] [👪] [✕] [📷] [DATA PORT] [🖥] / [✕] [🛏] [🖥] /

MICROTEL INN

Phone: (989)772-7777

◇◇◇

Small-scale Hotel

All Year [CP]   1P: $56-$95   2P: $56-$95

Location: Jct US 27 and SR 20. 5500 E Pickard Rd 48858. Fax: 989/773-5144. **Facility:** 82 one-bedroom standard units. 3 stories, interior corridors. *Bath:* combo or shower only. **Parking:** on-site. **Cards:** AX, CB, DC, DS, MC, VI.

SOME UNITS
[ASK] [S/D] [🍴] [♿] [📷] [DATA PORT] / [✕] /

Where elegance meets excitement.

Exquisite accommodations. Exhilarating fun. From the AAA Four Diamond luxury hotel to the Midwest's largest gaming floor, you'll experience ultimate elegance. Call for special AAA rates and packages.

Four Diamond Award

An hour north of Lansing. Mt. Pleasant, Michigan www.soaringeaglecasino.com

1-888-7-EAGLE-7

Restrictions may apply.

SOARING EAGLE CASINO & RESORT

Phone: (989)775-7777

AAA [SAVE]

Resort
Large-scale Hotel

All Year   1P: $119-$219   2P: $119-$219   XP: $10   F6
Location: US 27, 1.5 mi e on SR 20, just s on Leaton Rd. 6800 Soaring Eagle Blvd 48858. **Fax:** 989/775-5686.
Facility: American Indian artwork adorns this resort, which offers casual and fine dining, recreational facilities, a casino and luxurious rooms. 512 units. 491 one-bedroom standard units, some with whirlpools. 21 one-bedroom suites ($299-$399) with whirlpools. 7 stories, interior corridors. *Bath:* combo or shower only.
Parking: on-site and valet. **Terms:** check-in 4 pm, 2-4 night minimum stay - weekends, 3 day cancellation notice, package plans. **Amenities:** video games (fee), voice mail, irons, hair dryers. *Some:* dual phone lines.
Dining: 4 restaurants, 7 am-10:30 pm, cocktails, also, The Water Lily, see separate listing, entertainment. **Pool(s):** heated indoor. **Leisure Activities:** whirlpools, steamrooms, recreation programs, playground, exercise room, spa. **Guest Services:** gift shop, valet laundry, airport transportation (fee)-Tri-City Airport, area transportation. **Business Services:** conference facilities.
Cards: AX, CB, DC, DS, JC, MC, VI. **Special Amenities:** free local telephone calls and free newspaper.
(See color ad p 388)

SOME UNITS

[SD] [✈] [❄] [24] [Y] [🍴] [👤] [≈] [✕] [🎬] [DATA PORT] [💻] / [✕] [🔒] [📺] /
FEE

SUPER 8 MOTEL

Phone: 989/773-8888

Small-scale Hotel

All Year [ECP]   1P: $49-$129   2P: $49-$129
Location: 1.8 mi s on US 27 business route. 2323 S Mission 48858. **Fax:** 989/772-5371. **Facility:** 142 one-bedroom standard units, some with whirlpools. 3 stories, interior corridors. *Bath:* combo or shower only. **Parking:** on-site, winter plug-ins. **Terms:** cancellation fee imposed. **Amenities:** video games (fee), hair dryers. **Guest Services:** coin laundry. **Cards:** AX, DC, DS, MC, VI.

SOME UNITS

[ASK] [SD] [❄] [👤] [✕] [🎬] [💻] / [✕] [🔒] [📺] /

------- **WHERE TO DINE** -------

EMBERS

Lunch: $6-$16   **Dinner:** $18-$29   **Phone:** 989/773-5007

American

Location: 1.3 mi s on US 27 business route. 1217 S Mission St 48858. **Hours:** 11:30 am-10 pm, Sat from 4 pm, Sun 10 am-8 pm. Closed major holidays; also 12/24. **Features:** A delicious, Chinese red sauce glazes the one-pound pork chop for which the restaurant is known. The intimate dining room sets the tone for a moderately upscale experience. A professional, friendly staff provides efficient service with good follow-up.
Casual dress; cocktails. **Parking:** on-site. **Cards:** AX, DC, DS, MC, VI.

[Y] [✕]

LA SENORITA

Lunch: $5-$7   **Dinner:** $7-$12   **Phone:** 989/772-1331

Mexican

Location: 2.8 mi s on US 27 business route. 1516 S Mission St 48858. **Hours:** 11 am-10 pm, Fri & Sat-11 pm; 11 am-midnight, Sun noon-10 pm 5/29-9/4. Closed: 4/20, 11/27, 12/24, 12/25. **Features:** Fun-type restaurant for either casual or family dining. The Mexican decor throughout is inviting. Mesquite grill items. Sizzling fajitas. Casual dress; cocktails. **Parking:** on-site. **Cards:** AX, DC, DS, MC, VI.

[Y] [✕]

THE WATER LILY

Dinner: $20-$30   **Phone:** 989/775-7777

American

Location: From US 27, 1.5 mi e on SR 20, just s on Leaton Rd; in Soaring Eagle Casino & Resort. 6800 Soaring Eagle Dr 48858. **Hours:** 7 am-10:30 & 5-10:30 pm. **Reservations:** suggested. **Features:** For a special occasion or night to remember, visit this casual, yet upscale, spot. Choose from a wide range of dishes—from American to seafood to wild game. Representative of the outstanding fare is the Western elk tenderloin with red onion marmalade, savory plum cornbread stuffing and lingonberry cognac glace. Wine recommendations are well-paired with each dish. Dressy casual; cocktails. **Parking:** on-site. **Cards:** AX, DS, MC, VI.

[👤M] [Y] [✕]

MUNISING pop. 2,539

------- **WHERE TO STAY** -------

ALGER FALLS MOTEL

Phone: (906)387-3536

AAA [SAVE]

Motel

6/27-8/31 & 12/1-3/31   1P: $48-$65   2P: $48-$65   XP: $4   F12
4/1-6/26 & 9/1-11/30   1P: $35-$48   2P: $35-$48   XP: $4   F12
Location: 2 mi e on SR 28 and 94. E9427 E SR M-28 49862. **Fax:** 906/387-5228. **Facility:** 17 units. 16 one- and 1 two-bedroom standard units, some with kitchens. 1 story, exterior corridors. **Parking:** on-site, winter plug-ins. **Terms:** small pets only. **Leisure Activities:** snowmobiling. *Fee:* game room. **Guest Services:** coin laundry. **Cards:** DS, MC, VI. **Special Amenities:** free local telephone calls.

SOME UNITS

[SD] [🐾] [🔒] [📺] / [✕] /

BEST WESTERN

Phone: (906)387-4864

AAA [SAVE]

Motel

12/2-3/31   1P: $89-$119   2P: $89-$129
6/16-9/6   1P: $79-$109   2P: $89-$109
4/1-6/15 & 9/7-12/1   1P: $69-$79   2P: $89-$99
Location: 3 mi e on SR 28. Located in a semi rural area. M-28 49862 (PO Box 30, WETMORE, 49895). **Fax:** 906/387-2038. **Facility:** 80 units. 68 one-bedroom standard units, some with whirlpools. 12 one-bedroom suites ($99-$139). 2 stories (no elevator), interior/exterior corridors. **Parking:** on-site, winter plug-ins. **Terms:** 3 day cancellation notice, [CP] meal plan available, small pets only. **Amenities:** irons, hair dryers. **Dining:** 7 am-10 pm; hours vary off season, cocktails. **Pool(s):** heated indoor. **Leisure Activities:** sauna, whirlpool, snowmobiling, playground. *Fee:* game room. **Guest Services:** gift shop, coin laundry. **Cards:** AX, CB, DC, DS, MC, VI.

SOME UNITS

[SD] [🐾] [❄] [Y] [≈] [✕] [🎬] [💻] / [✕] [🔒] [📺] /

COMFORT INN

Phone: 906/387-5292

[SAVE]

Small-scale Hotel

All Year   1P: $65-$110   2P: $75-$110   XP: $15
Location: 1.5 mi e on SR 28. Located in a semi-commercial area. M-28 E 49862 (PO Box 276). **Fax:** 906/387-3753. **Facility:** 61 one-bedroom standard units, some with whirlpools. 2 stories (no elevator), interior corridors. **Parking:** on-site, winter plug-ins. **Terms:** small pets only (in smoking units). **Amenities:** hair dryers. *Some:* irons. **Pool(s):** heated indoor. **Leisure Activities:** whirlpool, snowmobiling, exercise room. **Guest Services:** coin laundry. **Business Services:** meeting rooms. **Cards:** AX, CB, DC, DS, JC, MC, VI.

SOME UNITS

[🐾] [≈] [✕] [🎬] [DATA PORT] [💻] / [✕] /

DAYS INN

Small-scale Hotel

Phone: (906)387-2493

All Year   1P: $65-$110   2P: $75-$110   XP: $15   F16

Location: 0.5 mi e on SR 28. On M-28 49862. Fax: 906/387-5214. **Facility:** 66 units. 63 one-bedroom standard units. 3 one-bedroom suites ($135-$150), some with whirlpools. 2 stories (no elevator), interior corridors. **Parking:** on-site. **Terms:** pets (in smoking units). **Amenities:** hair dryers. **Pool(s):** heated indoor. **Leisure Activities:** sauna, whirlpool, snowmobiling. **Guest Services:** gift shop. **Cards:** AX, CB, DC, DS, JC MC, VI. *(See color ad card insert)*

SOME UNITS

SUNSET MOTEL

Motel

Phone: (906)387-4574

6/15-9/2 & 12/12-3/31   1P: $57-$64   2P: $57-$64   XP: $4
4/1-6/14 & 9/3-12/11   1P: $42-$49   2P: $42-$49   XP: $4

Location: 1 mi e on E Munising Ave (CR 58). Located in a quiet area. 1315 Bay St 49862 (PO Box 291). **Facility:** 17 units. 9 one- and 8 two-bedroom standard units. 1-2 stories (no elevator), exterior corridors. *Bath:* combo o shower only. **Parking:** on-site. **Terms:** weekly rates available, pets ($10 extra charge, 1 dog per unit, in smoking rooms only). **Leisure Activities:** boat dock, fishing, playground. **Cards:** DS, MC, VI.
Special Amenities: early check-in/late check-out.

SOME UNITS

SUPER 8 MOTEL-MUNISING

Small-scale Hotel

Phone: 906/387-2466

All Year [CP]   1P: $59-$95   2P: $79-$104   XP: $5   F12

Location: 2.5 mi e on SR 28. Located in a semi-commercial area. M-28 & Fed Hwy 13 49862 (PO Box 359, 49682). Fax: 906/387-2355. **Facility:** 43 one-bedroom standard units, some with whirlpools. 2 stories (no elevator), interior corridors. **Parking:** on-site, winter plug-ins. **Leisure Activities:** sauna, whirlpool, snowmobiling. **Cards:** DS, MC, VI.

SOME UNITS

TERRACE MOTEL

Motel

Phone: 906/387-2735

6/26-8/31 & 12/19-3/31   1P: $50   2P: $50-$55
4/1-6/25 & 9/1-12/18   1P: $40   2P: $40-$45

Location: 0.5 mi e, just off SR 28. Located in a residential area. 420 Prospect 49862. Fax: 906/387-2754. **Facility:** 18 units. 14 one- and 4 two-bedroom standard units. 1 story, exterior corridors. *Bath:* combo or shower only. **Parking:** on-site. **Terms:** pets ($3 extra charge). **Leisure Activities:** sauna, snowmobiling, recreation room. **Cards:** DS, MC, VI. **Special Amenities: early check-in/late check-out and preferred room (subject to availability with advanced reservations).**

SOME UNITS

——— WHERE TO DINE ———

DOGPATCH

American

Lunch: $4-$7   **Dinner:** $9-$14   Phone: 906/387-9948

Location: Just off SR 28; center. 820 E Superior St 49862. **Hours:** 7 am-9 pm. Closed: 12/25. **Features:** Established in 1966, the restaurant is a great place to take your kids for a relaxed meal. The menu lists country-style breakfasts, a great selection of sandwiches and charbroiled steaks. The popular seafood buffet with all the fixings is served nightly. Cocktails. **Parking:** on-site. **Cards:** MC, VI.

Look For Savings

When you pick up a AAA TourBook® guide, look for establishments that display a bright red AAA logo, SAVE icon, and Diamond rating in their listing. These Official Appointment establishments place a high value on the patronage they receive from AAA members. And, by offering members great room rates*, they are willing to go the extra mile to get your business.

So, when you turn to the AAA TourBook guide to make your travel plans, look for the establishments that will give you the special treatment you deserve.

* See TourBook Navigator section, page 14, for complete details.

MUSKEGON pop. 40,105

───── WHERE TO STAY ─────

COMFORT INN
[SAVE]

6/1-9/1	1P: $139-$199	2P: $144-$199	XP: $5 F18
4/1-5/31 & 9/2-3/31	1P: $79-$199	2P: $85-$199	XP: $5 F18

Small-scale Hotel **Location:** Jct US 31 and CR B-72, exit Sherman Blvd. Located next to shopping mall. 1675 E Sherman Blvd 49444. **Fax:** 231/739-2264. **Facility:** 117 one-bedroom standard units, some with efficiencies and/or whirlpools. 2 stories (no elevator), interior corridors. **Parking:** on-site. **Amenities:** voice mail, irons, hair dryers. *Fee:* video library, safes. **Pool(s):** heated outdoor, heated indoor. **Leisure Activities:** exercise room. *Fee:* game room. **Guest Services:** valet and coin laundry. **Business Services:** meeting rooms, business center. **Cards:** AX, DC, DS, MC, VI.

Phone: (231)739-9092

SOME UNITS
[icons] / [icons] / FEE

HOLIDAY INN-MUSKEGON HARBOR

6/1-8/31	1P: $129-$179	2P: $129-$179	XP: $10 F12
4/1-5/31	1P: $89-$139	2P: $89-$139	XP: $10 F12
9/1-3/31	1P: $99	2P: $99	XP: $10 F12

Large-scale Hotel **Location:** Center of downtown. 939 Third St 49440. **Fax:** 231/722-5118. **Facility:** 201 one-bedroom standard units, some with whirlpools. 8 stories, interior corridors. **Parking:** on-site. **Terms:** check-in 4 pm, cancellation fee imposed, [AP], [BP], [CP] & [ECP] meal plans available, 18% service charge. **Amenities:** video games, dual phone lines, voice mail, irons, hair dryers. **Pool(s):** heated indoor. **Leisure Activities:** sauna, whirlpool, steamroom, exercise room. **Guest Services:** valet laundry. **Business Services:** conference facilities. **Cards:** AX, CB, DC, DS, MC, VI.
(See ad below)

Phone: (231)722-0100

SOME UNITS
[icons] / [icons] / FEE

PORT CITY VICTORIAN INN
[AAA] [SAVE]

6/1-9/1 [BP]		2P: $100-$150	XP: $20 F12
4/1-5/31 & 9/2-3/31 [BP]		2P: $80-$125	XP: $20 F12

Bed & Breakfast **Location:** US 31, exit Laketon Ave, 3.7 mi w, 0.5 mi n. 1259 Lakeshore Dr 49441. **Fax:** 231/759-0205. **Facility:** Smoke free premises. 5 one-bedroom standard units, some with whirlpools. 2 stories, interior corridors. *Bath:* combo or shower only. **Parking:** on-site. **Terms:** check-in 4 pm, 7 day cancellation notice-fee imposed, weekly rates available, no pets allowed (owner's pet on premises). **Amenities:** hair dryers. *Some:* CD players, safes. **Leisure Activities:** horseshoes. **Business Services:** meeting rooms. **Cards:** AX, DC, DS, MC, VI. **Special Amenities:** free continental breakfast and free local telephone calls.

Phone: (231)759-0205

SOME UNITS
[icons] / [VCR]

───── WHERE TO DINE ─────

FINLEY'S AMERICAN RESTAURANT   Lunch: $5-$9   Dinner: $8-$16   Phone: 231/733-9928
American **Location:** 3 mi s, just w of US 31 business route. 3055 Henry St 49441. **Hours:** 11 am-10 pm, Fri & Sat-11 pm. **Closed:** 11/27, 12/25. **Features:** Casual family dining, steak, seafood, chicken and a favorite - baby back ribs. Casual dress; cocktails. **Parking:** on-site. **Cards:** AX, DC, DS, MC, VI.
[icon]

TONY'S RESTAURANT   Lunch: $5-$8   Dinner: $9-$18   Phone: 231/739-7196
Steak House **Location:** 2.8 mi s, just e of Henry St. 785 W Broadway 49441. **Hours:** 11 am-9 pm, Fri-11 pm, Sat 5 pm-11 pm. **Closed:** major holidays; also Sun. **Reservations:** suggested; weekends. **Features:** Family owned and operated since 1969. Greek themed dining room with picturesque lighted murals on the walls. Good selection of steak, chops, chicken and seafood as well as unique daily specials not often found in a steakhouse such as Hungarian Goulash on Mondays, or Souviaki (pork kebab) served on Thursdays. Casual dress; cocktails. **Parking:** on-site. **Cards:** AX, CB, DC, DS, MC, VI.
[icons]

NEWBERRY pop. 2,686

——— WHERE TO STAY ———

BEST WESTERN NEWBERRY
Phone: (906)293-4000
(AAA) (SAVE) All Year [CP]   1P: $53-$85   2P: $61-$93   XP: $8   F12
▼▼▼ **Location:** On SR 28, 1 mi e of SR 123. Located in a semi-rural area. 12956 M-28 49868 (Rt 1, Box 680).
Fax: 906/293-4005. **Facility:** 66 units. 64 one-bedroom standard units, some with whirlpools. 1 one- and 1
Small-scale Hotel two-bedroom suites ($108-$164). 2 stories, interior corridors. *Bath:* combo or shower only. **Parking:** on-site.
Amenities: safes (fee), irons, hair dryers. **Pool(s):** heated indoor. **Leisure Activities:** sauna, whirlpool,
snowmobiling. **Guest Services:** coin laundry. **Business Services:** meeting rooms. **Cards:** AX, DC, DS,
MC, VI. **Special Amenities:** free continental breakfast.

SOME UNITS

COMFORT INN TAHQUAMENON FALLS
Phone: (906)293-3218
(AAA) (SAVE) All Year   1P: $69-$89   2P: $89-$125   XP: $10   F18
▼▼▼ **Location:** Jct SR 28 and 123. Junction M-123 & M-28 49868 (13954 St Hwy M-28). Fax: 906/293-9375. **Facility:** 54
Small-scale Hotel one-bedroom standard units, some with whirlpools. 2 stories (no elevator), interior corridors. *Bath:* combo or
shower only. **Parking:** on-site. **Amenities:** hair dryers. *Some:* irons. **Leisure Activities:** sauna, whirlpool,
snowmobiling. *Fee:* game room. **Guest Services:** gift shop, coin laundry. **Business Services:** meeting
rooms. **Cards:** AX, CB, DC, DS, MC, VI. **Special Amenities:** free continental breakfast and free local
telephone calls.

SOME UNITS

——— WHERE TO DINE ———

TIMBER CHARLIE'S FOOD "N" SPIRITS
Lunch: $4-$7   **Dinner:** $9-$18   **Phone:** 906/293-3363
(AAA) **Location:** On SR 123, north side of town. 110 Newberry Ave 49868. **Hours:** 10:30 am-9 pm, to 10 pm in season,
▼▼ Sun from noon. Closed: 4/20, 11/27, 12/25; also 12/24 for dinner. **Features:** Baby back ribs, Italian and
Mexican fare and a tempting variety of sizzling steaks make up the restaurant's varied menu. Knotty pine
American walls and wildlife art contribute to the rustic atmosphere. Tourists and locals alike frequent the casual
eatery. Casual dress; cocktails. **Parking:** street. **Cards:** AX, DS, MC, VI.

NEW BUFFALO pop. 2,200

——— WHERE TO STAY ———

BEST WESTERN PLAZA HOTEL
Phone: (269)469-4193
(AAA) (SAVE) 7/1-9/3 [ECP]   1P: $129-$209
▼▼▼ 4/1-6/30 [ECP]   1P: $99-$149
9/4-3/31 [ECP]   1P: $89-$149
Small-scale Hotel **Location:** I-94, exit 1, just w. 18800 La Porte Rd 49117. Fax: 269/469-4211. **Facility:** 69 units. 61 one-bedroom standard units, some with whirlpools. 8 one-bedroom suites ($149-$229). 3 stories, interior corridors. *Bath:* combo or
shower only. **Parking:** on-site. **Terms:** 2 night minimum stay - some weekends in summer, cancellation fee imposed. **Amenities:** dual phone lines, voice mail, irons, hair dryers. **Pool(s):** heated indoor. **Leisure Activities:** whirlpool, exercise
room. **Guest Services:** valet and coin laundry. **Cards:** AX, DC, DS, MC, VI. **Special Amenities:** free continental breakfast and
free newspaper. *(See color ad below)*

SOME UNITS

GRAND BEACH MOTEL
Phone: (269)469-1555

Motel

5/15-10/15 [CP]   1P: $35-$55   2P: $45-$75
Location: I-94, exit 1, 1.2 mi w to US 12, 2.5 mi s. 19189 US 12 49117. **Facility:** 14 units. 13 one-bedroom standard units. 1 two-bedroom suite ($70-$90). 1 story, exterior corridors. *Bath:* combo or shower only. **Parking:** on-site. **Terms:** open 5/15-10/15, 2 night minimum stay - weekends, 3 day cancellation notice. **Pool(s):** heated outdoor. **Cards:** DC, MC, VI. **Special Amenities:** free continental breakfast and free local telephone calls.

SOME UNITS

HARBOR GRAND HOTEL
Phone: (269)469-7700

Small-scale Hotel

All Year   1P: $129-$349   2P: $129-$349   XP: $20   F11
Location: Just sw on SR 39; downtown. 111 Oselka Dr 49117 (111 W Water St). Fax: 269/469-7386. **Facility:** 55 units. 33 one-bedroom standard units, some with whirlpools. 22 one-bedroom suites ($149-$299). 4 stories, interior corridors. *Bath:* combo or shower only. **Parking:** on-site. **Terms:** check-in 4 pm, 2 night minimum stay - weekends, cancellation fee imposed, [ECP] meal plan available. **Amenities:** hair dryers. **Pool(s):** heated indoor. **Leisure Activities:** whirlpool, bicycles, exercise room. *Fee:* massage. **Business Services:** meeting rooms. **Cards:** AX, DS, MC, VI.
(See color ad below)

SOME UNITS

HOLIDAY INN EXPRESS HOTEL & SUITES
Phone: (269)469-3436

Small-scale Hotel

6/13-8/16 [ECP]   1P: $89-$189   2P: $89-$189   XP: $6   F19
4/1-6/12 & 8/17-3/31 [ECP]   1P: $79-$189   2P: $79-$189   XP: $6   F19
Location: I-94, exit 1, just w. 11500 Holiday Dr 49117. Fax: 269/469-8463. **Facility:** 80 one-bedroom standard units, some with whirlpools. 3 stories, interior corridors. *Bath:* combo or shower only. **Parking:** on-site, winter plug-ins. **Amenities:** dual phone lines, voice mail, irons, hair dryers. **Pool(s):** heated indoor. **Leisure Activities:** whirlpool. *Fee:* game room. **Guest Services:** valet and coin laundry. **Business Services:** meeting rooms. **Cards:** AX, DC, DS, MC, VI.
(See color ad card insert & below)

SOME UNITS

HANNAH'S RESTAURANT **Lunch: $7-$11** **Dinner: $9-$26** **Phone: 269/469-1440**
▼▼ ▼▼
American
Location: I-94, exit 1, 1 mi w. 115 S Whittaker 49117. **Hours:** 11:30 am-10 pm, Fri & Sat-11 pm. Closed: 12/25. **Reservations:** accepted. **Features:** The wide selection offered in this bustling restaurant includes their prime rib specialty dinner, many sandwiches, fresh sauteed seafood, pasta dishes and even some Southwestern style fajitas. The homemade desserts come in ample portions just made to share. Casual dress; cocktails. **Parking:** on-site. **Cards:** AX, DS, MC, VI.
[icons]

REDAMAK'S **Lunch: $4-$9** **Dinner: $5-$10** **Phone: 269/469-4522**
▼▼▼
American
Location: Just n of jct SR 39; town center. 616 E Buffalo St 49117. **Hours:** Open 4/1-11/15. **Features:** A local institution, this casual and informal restaurant is known for its hamburgers. Casual dress; cocktails. **Parking:** on-site.
[icons]

NILES pop. 12,204

———— WHERE TO STAY ————

HOLIDAY INN EXPRESS **Phone: (269)684-3900**
▼▼▼▼▼
Small-scale Hotel

8/16-11/16 [ECP]	1P: $199-$279	2P: $199-$279	XP: $10	F
7/11-8/15 [ECP]	1P: $84-$94	2P: $84-$94	XP: $10	F
4/1-7/10 [ECP]	1P: $79-$89	2P: $79-$89	XP: $10	F
11/17-3/31 [ECP]	1P: $74-$79	2P: $79-$84	XP: $10	F

Location: I-80/90, exit 77, n on SR 933 at stateline (SR 933 becomes M-51), 3.5 mi n. 1265 S 11th St (M-51) 49120. **Fax:** 269/684-2900. **Facility:** 51 units. 43 one-bedroom standard units, some with whirlpools. 8 one-bedroom suites ($99-$149). 3 stories, interior corridors. **Bath:** combo or shower only. **Parking:** on-site, winter plug-ins. **Amenities:** dual phone lines, voice mail, irons, hair dryers. **Pool(s):** heated indoor. **Leisure Activities:** exercise room. **Guest Services:** valet laundry. **Business Services:** business center. **Cards:** AX, DC, DS, MC, VI.

SOME UNITS
[icons]

NORTHVILLE —See Detroit p. 261.

NORTON SHORES pop. 22,527

———— WHERE TO STAY ————

AMERIHOST INN-MUSKEGON **Phone: (231)798-0220**
(AAA) [SAVE]
▼▼ ▼▼
Small-scale Hotel

4/1-9/7 [ECP]	1P: $109-$119	2P: $119-$129	XP: $6	F18
9/8-3/31 [ECP]	1P: $74-$84	2P: $79-$89	XP: $6	F18

Location: Just se of jct I-96 and US 31; I-96 (westbound), exit 1A, follow signs to race track; from US 31, exit Sternberg Rd, just e to Harvey Rd, 1 mi n. Located opposite the race track. 4677 Harvey Rd 49441. **Fax:** 231/798-0221. **Facility:** 61 one-bedroom standard units, some with whirlpools. 2 stories, interior corridors. **Bath:** combo or shower only. **Parking:** on-site. **Amenities:** voice mail, safes (fee), irons, hair dryers. **Pool(s):** heated indoor. **Leisure Activities:** sauna, whirlpool, exercise room. **Guest Services:** valet laundry. **Business Services:** meeting rooms. **Cards:** AX, DC, DS, MC, VI.

SOME UNITS
[icons]

HAMPTON INN OF MUSKEGON **Phone: (231)799-8333**
[SAVE]
▼▼ ▼▼
Small-scale Hotel

6/2-9/1	1P: $115
9/2-3/31	1P: $89
4/1-6/1	1P: $84

Location: Just se of jct I-96 and US 31; I-96 (westbound), exit 1A, follow signs to race track; from US 31, exit Sternberg Rd, just e to Harvey Rd, 0.4 mi n, then just w. 1401 E Ellis Rd 49441. **Fax:** 231/799-8334. **Facility:** 81 units. 80 one-bedroom standard units, some with whirlpools. 1 one-bedroom suite. 4 stories, interior corridors. **Bath:** combo or shower only. **Parking:** on-site. **Terms:** [CP] meal plan available. **Amenities:** video games, dual phone lines, voice mail, irons, hair dryers. **Pool(s):** heated indoor. **Leisure Activities:** whirlpool, exercise room. **Guest Services:** valet laundry. **Business Services:** meeting rooms. **Cards:** AX, DC, DS, MC, VI.

SOME UNITS
[icons] FEE FEE FEE

———— *The following lodging was either not evaluated or did not meet AAA rating requirements but is listed for your information only.* ————

BEL AIRE MOTEL **Phone: 231/733-2196**
[fyi]
Motel
Did not meet all AAA rating requirements for. **Location:** Jct Business US 31 and I-96; US 31, exit Business US 31 northbound, exit 1A Airline Rd; exit Airline Rd southbound, westbound I-96, exit Airline Rd. Located in a semi-commercial area. 4240 Airline Rd 49444 (4240 Airline Rd, MUSKEGON). Facilities, services, and decor characterize a basic property.

———— WHERE TO DINE ————

———— *The following restaurant has not been evaluated by AAA but is listed for your information only.* ————

SAM'S JOINT **Phone: 231/798-7155**
[fyi]
Not evaluated. **Location:** 6618 Grand Haven Rd 49441. **Features:** Memorabilia spills over from the lounge into the dining areas at this fun spot.

NORWAY

──── **WHERE TO STAY** ────

AMERICINN OF NORWAY
Phone: (906)563-7500

5/30-10/9 [ECP]   1P: $71-$81   2P: $76-$86   XP: $5   F12
4/1-5/29 & 10/10-3/31 [ECP]   1P: $69-$79   2P: $74-$84   XP: $5   F12

Small-scale Hotel   **Location:** 0.7 mi w. W 6002 US Hwy 2 49870. **Fax:** 906/563-5853. **Facility:** 45 units. 42 one-bedroom standard units, some with whirlpools. 3 one-bedroom suites ($89-$139), some with whirlpools. 2 stories (no elevator), interior corridors. *Bath:* combo or shower only. **Parking:** on-site. **Terms:** weekly rates available, pets (in smoking units). **Amenities:** *Some:* hair dryers. **Pool(s):** heated indoor. **Leisure Activities:** sauna, whirlpool, snowmobiling. **Guest Services:** coin laundry. **Business Services:** meeting rooms. **Cards:** AX, DC, DS, MC, VI.

SOME UNITS

NOVI —*See Detroit p. 262.*

OKEMOS

──── **WHERE TO STAY** ────

COMFORT INN-E. LANSING/OKEMOS
Phone: (517)349-8700

SAVE

All Year   1P: $85-$139   2P: $85-$139   XP: $10   F18

Small-scale Hotel   **Location:** I-96, exit 110, 0.3 mi n on Okemos Rd, just e. Located in University Commerce Park. 2209 University Park 48864. **Fax:** 517/349-5638. **Facility:** 159 units. 127 one-bedroom standard units, some with whirlpools. 32 one-bedroom suites with whirlpools. 2 stories (no elevator), interior corridors. **Parking:** on-site. **Terms:** [ECP] meal plan available. **Amenities:** voice mail, irons, hair dryers. *Fee:* video games, safes. **Pool(s):** heated indoor. **Leisure Activities:** saunas, whirlpool, exercise room. **Guest Services:** valet and coin laundry. **Business Services:** meeting rooms. **Cards:** AX, DC, DS, MC, VI.

SOME UNITS

FAIRFIELD INN BY MARRIOTT
Phone: 517/347-1000

SAVE

All Year   1P: $75-$89

Small-scale Hotel   **Location:** I-96, exit 110, 0.3 mi n on Okemos Rd, just w. Located in an office park. 2335 Woodlake Dr 48864. **Fax:** 517/347-5092. **Facility:** 78 one-bedroom standard units, some with whirlpools. 2 stories, interior corridors. *Bath:* combo or shower only. **Parking:** on-site. **Terms:** [ECP] meal plan available. **Amenities:** irons, hair dryers. **Pool(s):** heated indoor. **Leisure Activities:** whirlpool, exercise room. **Guest Services:** valet laundry. **Business Services:** meeting rooms. **Cards:** AX, CB, DC, DS, MC, VI.

SOME UNITS

HAMPTON INN & SUITES
Phone: (517)349-6100

SAVE

All Year   1P: $79-$179   2P: $79-$179

Small-scale Hotel   **Location:** I-96, exit 110, 0.5 mi n on Okemos Rd. 2200 Hampton Pl 48864. **Fax:** 517/349-0885. **Facility:** 100 units. 91 one-bedroom standard units, some with whirlpools. 9 one-bedroom suites ($114-$179), some with whirlpools. 3 stories, interior corridors. *Bath:* combo or shower only. **Parking:** on-site. **Terms:** [ECP] meal plan available. **Amenities:** dual phone lines, voice mail, irons, hair dryers. **Pool(s):** heated indoor. **Leisure Activities:** whirlpool, exercise room. *Fee:* game room. **Guest Services:** sundries, valet and coin laundry. **Business Services:** meeting rooms. **Cards:** AX, DC, DS, MC, VI. *(See color ad below)*

SOME UNITS

HOLIDAY INN EXPRESS- E. LANSING/OKEMOS **Phone:** (517)347-6690
▼▼▼ All Year 1P: $79-$109 2P: $79-$109 XP: $10 F18
Location: I-96, exit 110, 0.3 mi n on Okemos Rd, just e; in University Commerce Park. 2187 University Park Dr 48864.
Small-scale Hotel **Fax:** 517/347-8163. **Facility:** 90 one-bedroom standard units. 2 stories (no elevator), interior corridors. *Bath:* combo or shower only. **Parking:** on-site. **Terms:** age restrictions may apply, [CP] meal plan available.
Amenities: video games (fee), voice mail, irons, hair dryers. **Guest Services:** valet laundry. **Business Services:** meeting rooms. **Cards:** AX, DC, DS, MC, VI. *(See color ad card insert)*

SOME UNITS

(ASK) (S/D) (▮+) (▦) (DATA PORT) (🖥) / (✕) (🛢) (🖳) /

ONEKAMA pop. 647

─────── WHERE TO STAY ───────

ALPINE MOTOR LODGE-BUDGET HOST **Phone:** 231/889-4281
(AAA) (SAVE) 6/20-8/12 [CP] 1P: $80-$90 2P: $80-$90
9/9-3/31 [CP] 1P: $60-$70 2P: $60-$70
▼▼ ▼▼▼ 8/13-9/8 [CP] 1P: $70 2P: $70
4/1-6/19 [CP] 1P: $60-$70
Motel **Location:** Jct US 31 and 8 Mile Rd. 8127 US 31 49675 (PO Box 366). **Fax:** 231/889-3689. **Facility:** 25 one-bedroom standard units. 1 story, exterior corridors. **Parking:** on-site. **Pool(s):** heated outdoor. **Leisure Activities:** miniature golf, snowmobiling, horseshoes. **Cards:** DS, MC, VI. **Special Amenities:** free continental breakfast and free local telephone calls. *(See color ad p 187)*

SOME UNITS

(S/D) (🏊) (✕) (▦) (DATA PORT) (🛢) (🖥) / (✕) /

ONSTED pop. 813

─────── WHERE TO DINE ───────

GOLDEN NUGGET **Lunch:** $7-$11 **Dinner:** $9-$15 **Phone:** 517/467-2190
(AAA) **Location:** 0.3 mi e. 7305 US 12 49265. **Hours:** 5 pm-9:30 pm, Fri & Sat-11 pm, Sun noon-9 pm. Closed: 1/1, 11/27, 12/25; also Mon & Tues 9/1-3/31. **Features:** Turn-of-the-20th-century decor includes leaded-glass
▼▼ ▼▼ chandeliers, antique furnishings and Tiffany-style lamps. The menu samples a little of a lot of things—
American ranging from steak, pork chops and sandwiches to broiled fish, pizza and homemade cheesecake. Casual dress; cocktails. **Parking:** on-site. **Cards:** AX, DS, MC, VI.

(🍴) (✕)

ONTONAGON pop. 1,769

─────── WHERE TO STAY ───────

PETERSON'S CHALET COTTAGES **Phone:** 906/884-4230
(AAA) (SAVE) All Year 2P: $100-$150 XP: $15 D14
Location: 1.5 mi sw on SR 64. Located in a semi-rural area. 287 Lakeshore Rd 49953. **Fax:** 906/884-2965.
▼▼ ▼▼ **Facility:** 16 units. 2 vacation homes and 14 cottages, some with whirlpools. 1 story, exterior corridors. *Bath:*
Cottage combo or shower only. **Parking:** on-site, winter plug-ins. **Terms:** check-in 4 pm, 3-7 night minimum stay - seasonal & weekends, 60 day cancellation notice-fee imposed. **Leisure Activities:** canoeing, paddleboats, fishing, cross country skiing, snowmobiling, bicycles, playground, horseshoes, volleyball. *Fee:* kayaks, snowshoes. **Guest Services:** gift shop. **Cards:** AX, DS, MC, VI. **Special Amenities:** free local telephone calls.

SOME UNITS

(✕) (🎿) (▦) (🛢) (🖳) (🖥) / (✕) /

OSCODA pop. 992

─────── WHERE TO STAY ───────

AMERICINN OF OSCODA **Phone:** (989)739-1986
(AAA) (SAVE) 6/15-9/6 1P: $82-$122 2P: $82-$122 XP: $5 F18
9/7-12/31 1P: $72-$112 2P: $72-$112 XP: $5 F18
▼▼ ▼▼ ▼▼ 4/1-6/14 & 1/1-3/31 1P: $62-$102 2P: $62-$102 XP: $5 F18
Location: Just w of US 23, at Smith and 2nd sts. Located in a semi-residential area. 720 E Harbor St 48750.
Small-scale Hotel **Fax:** 989/739-1987. **Facility:** 47 units. 44 one-bedroom standard units, some with whirlpools. 3 one-bedroom suites ($122-$162), some with whirlpools. 2 stories (no elevator), interior corridors. *Bath:* combo or shower only. **Parking:** on-site. **Terms:** [ECP] meal plan available. **Amenities:** hair dryers. **Pool(s):** heated indoor. **Leisure Activities:** sauna, whirlpool, boat dock, fishing. **Guest Services:** coin laundry. **Business Services:** meeting rooms. **Cards:** AX, CB, DC, DS, MC, VI. **Special Amenities:** free continental breakfast and free local telephone calls.

SOME UNITS

(S/D) (▮+) (⅙M) (🄴) (🏊) (✕) (▦) (DATA PORT) (🖥) / (✕) (🛢) (🖳) /

REDWOOD MOTOR LODGE **Phone:** 989/739-2021
(AAA) (SAVE) 5/20-9/5 1P: $70-$109 2P: $70-$109 XP: $5 F5
4/1-5/19 & 9/6-3/31 1P: $50-$99 2P: $50-$99 XP: $5 F5
▼▼ ▼▼ **Location:** 2.5 mi s on US 23. Located on the main highway along the lake. 3111 US 23 48750. **Fax:** 989/739-1121.
Facility: 46 units. 37 one-bedroom standard units. 9 cottages ($110-$170), some with whirlpools. 1-2 stories
Small-scale Hotel (no elevator), interior/exterior corridors. *Bath:* combo or shower only. **Parking:** on-site, winter plug-ins.
Terms: check-in 4 pm, 2 night minimum stay - weekends 6/15-9/3, weekly rates available, package plans.
Pool(s): heated indoor. **Leisure Activities:** sauna, whirlpool, indoor recreational area, playground, horseshoes. *Fee:* game room. **Business Services:** meeting rooms. **Cards:** AX, DC, DS, MC, VI. **Special Amenities:** free local telephone calls and preferred room (subject to availability with advanced reservations).

SOME UNITS

(🍴) (🏊) (✕) (▦) / (✕) (🄴) (🛢) (🖳) (🖥) /

SUPER 8 MOTEL

Phone: 989-739-8822

6/8-9/7 [CP]	1P: $65-$119	2P: $65-$119	XP: $5	F12
9/8-3/31 [CP]	1P: $55-$109	2P: $55-$109	XP: $5	F12
4/1-6/7 [CP]	1P: $50-$80	2P: $50-$80	XP: $5	F12

Small-scale Hotel

Location: 1.5 mi s on US 23. Located along the lake. 4270 N US 23 48750. Fax: 989/739-0160. **Facility:** 76 one-bedroom standard units, some with whirlpools. 2 stories (no elevator), interior corridors. *Bath:* combo or shower only. **Parking:** on-site. **Terms:** 2-3 night minimum stay - some weekends. **Pool(s):** heated indoor. **Leisure Activities:** sauna, whirlpool, playground. *Fee:* game room. **Guest Services:** coin laundry. **Cards:** AX, DS, MC, VI.

SOME UNITS

——— WHERE TO DINE ———

WILTSE'S BREW PUB & FAMILY RESTAURANT   **Lunch:** $4-$6   **Dinner:** $7-$14   **Phone:** 989-739-2231

American

Location: On CR F-41, 1 mi nw of US 23. 5606 N F-41 48750. **Hours:** 7 am-9 pm, Fri & Sat-10 pm; 7 am-10 pm, Fri & Sat-11 pm, 5/30-9/6. Closed: 11/27, 12/25. **Features:** Craft brewed ale and lager brewed on premise. Good selection of main dishes, from specialties like Paul Bunyan's Mess Burger served with everything but the kitchen sink to the the sirloin tips which has been a popular dish for over 18 years. Casual dress; cocktails. **Parking:** on-site. **Cards:** MC, VI.

OWOSSO pop. 15,713

——— WHERE TO DINE ———

EDDIE O'FLYNN'S   **Lunch:** $4-$7   **Dinner:** $9-$12   **Phone:** 989-723-6741

American

Location: 1.8 mi w on SR 21. 2280 W M-21 48867. Closed major holidays. **Hours:** 11 am-10 pm, Fri-11 pm, Sat 4 pm-11 pm, Sun noon-8 pm. Closed major holidays. **Features:** Antique furnishings and knickknacks, including plenty of 1950s memorabilia, decorate the dining room. The broad menu lists ribs, steak, fish, burgers, salad, stir-fry and pitas, plus a variety of tempting desserts. Drop in for breakfast on the weekend. Casual dress; cocktails. **Parking:** on-site. **Cards:** AX, DS, MC, VI.

PARADISE pop. 4,191

——— WHERE TO STAY ———

BEST WESTERN LAKEFRONT INN & SUITES

Phone: (906)492-3770

4/1-6/20 & 9/6-3/31	1P: $100-$130	2P: $100-$130
6/21-9/5	1P: $148-$175	

Small-scale Hotel

Location: Just s on SR 123. Located on the shores of Whitefish Bay. 8112 N M 123 49768 (PO Box 55). Fax: 906/492-3771. **Facility:** 41 one-bedroom standard units. 3 stories, interior corridors. **Parking:** on-site, winter plug-ins. **Terms:** 3 day cancellation notice. **Amenities:** voice mail, irons, hair dryers. **Pool(s):** heated indoor. **Leisure Activities:** sauna, whirlpool, rental paddleboats, snowmobiling. **Guest Services:** coin laundry. **Business Services:** meeting rooms. **Cards:** AX, CB, DC, DS, MC, VI. *(See color ad below)*

SOME UNITS

PARADISE INN

Phone: 906/492-3940

All Year   1P: $45-$99   2P: $45-$99

Small-scale Hotel

Location: On SR 123; center. M 123 & Whitefish Point Rd 49768 (PO Box 134). Fax: 906/492-3943. **Facility:** 36 one-bedroom standard units, some with whirlpools. 2 stories (no elevator), interior corridors. **Parking:** on-site, winter plug-ins. **Terms:** cancellation fee imposed, [CP] meal plan available. **Amenities:** video library (fee). **Leisure Activities:** snowmobiling. **Guest Services:** coin laundry. **Business Services:** meeting rooms. **Cards:** AX, DS, MC, VI. **Special Amenities:** early check-in/late check-out and free local telephone calls.

SOME UNITS

FEE

PAW PAW pop. 3,363

———— WHERE TO STAY ————

QUALITY INN & SUITES

SAVE

▼▼▼▼
Small-scale Hotel

Phone: (269)655-0303

10/1-3/31	1P: $65-$100	2P: $75-$100	XP: $10 F18
5/24-9/30	1P: $70-$100	2P: $70-$100	XP: $10 F18
4/1-5/23	1P: $60-$100	2P: $70-$100	XP: $10 F18

Location: I-94, exit 60, just nw. 153 Ampey Rd 49079 (PO Box 228). Fax: 269/657-1015. **Facility:** 65 units. 52 one-bedroom standard units, some with whirlpools. 13 one-bedroom suites ($80-$140), some with efficiencies. 2 stories, interior corridors. *Bath:* combo or shower only. **Parking:** on-site. **Terms:** 2 night minimum stay - summer weekends, cancellation fee imposed, [ECP] meal plan available, package plans - seasonal, small pets only ($10 extra charge, in smoking units). **Amenities:** voice mail, irons, hair dryers. **Pool(s):** heated indoor. **Leisure Activities:** exercise room. **Guest Services:** coin laundry. **Business Services:** meeting rooms. **Cards:** AX, CB, DC, DS, JC, MC, VI.

SOME UNITS

[icons]

———— WHERE TO DINE ————

LA CANTINA

▼▼▼

Italian

Dinner: $14-$18

Phone: 269/657-7033

Location: Downtown. 139 W Michigan Ave 49079. **Hours:** Open 4/1-12/24 & 1/15-3/31; 5 pm-10 pm. Closed major holidays; also Mon. **Reservations:** accepted. **Features:** Raffini wrapped chianti bottles decorate the entry way to this comfortable restaurant which boasts large picture windows overlooking a serene brook and a menu that features a wide variety of traditional Italian dishes. Casual dress; cocktails. **Parking:** on-site. **Cards:** AX, DC, DS, MC, VI.

[icons]

PELLSTON pop. 600

———— WHERE TO STAY ————

HOLIDAY INN EXPRESS PELLSTON

▼▼▼▼
Small-scale Hotel

Phone: (231)539-7000

All Year [ECP]	1P: $59-$149	2P: $59-$149	XP: $6 F19

Location: 1.2 mi n. Located opposite the airport. 1600 US 31 N 49769. Fax: 231/539-7010. **Facility:** 52 one-bedroom standard units, some with whirlpools. 2 stories (no elevator), interior corridors. *Bath:* combo or shower only. **Parking:** on-site, winter plug-ins. **Amenities:** video library (fee), dual phone lines, voice mail, irons, hair dryers. **Pool(s):** heated indoor. **Leisure Activities:** whirlpool, snowmobiling, exercise room. *Fee:* game room. **Guest Services:** coin laundry. **Business Services:** meeting rooms. **Cards:** AX, DC, DS, MC, VI.
(See color ad card insert & p 364)

SOME UNITS

[icons] FEE FEE

———— WHERE TO DINE ————

DAM SITE INN

▼▼

American

Dinner: $11-$26

Phone: 231/539-8851

Location: 1.5 mi s of Pellston on US 31; near the Dam on the Maple River. US 31 49769. **Hours:** Open 4/15-10/24; 5 pm-9 pm, Sun 3 pm-8 pm; 5 pm-10 pm, Sun 3 pm-9 pm 7/1-8/31. Closed: Mon except 7/1-8/31. **Features:** Family-style preparations of chicken, steak and seafood are what the casual restaurant is all about. In business since 1953, the establishment offers views of the dam from many dining room windows. Service is friendly and efficient. Casual dress; cocktails. **Parking:** on-site. **Cards:** MC, VI.

[icons]

PETOSKEY pop. 6,080

———— WHERE TO STAY ————

APPLE TREE INN

🅰🅰🅰 **SAVE**

▼▼▼▼
Small-scale Hotel

Phone: 231/348-2900

6/13-8/31	1P: $110-$165	XP: $10 F16
9/1-10/31	1P: $84-$165	XP: $10 F16
11/1-3/31	1P: $69-$155	XP: $10 F16
4/1-6/12	1P: $65-$110	XP: $10 F16

Location: 1.1 mi s on US 131. 915 Spring St 49770. Fax: 231/348-9748. **Facility:** Smoke free premises. 37 one-bedroom standard units, some with whirlpools. 4 stories, interior corridors. **Parking:** on-site, winter plug-ins. **Terms:** [ECP] meal plan available, package plans - seasonal. **Amenities:** video library (fee). **Pool(s):** heated indoor. **Leisure Activities:** whirlpool. **Guest Services:** valet and coin laundry. **Cards:** AX, DC, MC, VI. **Special Amenities:** free continental breakfast and free local telephone calls. *(See color ad p 399)*

[icons]

BAYWINDS INN

🅰🅰🅰 **SAVE**

▼▼▼▼
Small-scale Hotel

Phone: 231/347-4193

6/1-10/25	1P: $75-$165	XP: $5 F17
10/26-3/31	1P: $55-$165	XP: $5 F17
4/1-5/31	1P: $55-$125	XP: $5 F17

Location: 1 mi s on US 131. Located in a commercial area. 909 Spring St 49770. Fax: 231/347-5927. **Facility:** 50 one-bedroom standard units, some with whirlpools. 2 stories, interior corridors. **Parking:** on-site, winter plug-ins. **Terms:** cancellation fee imposed, [ECP] meal plan available, package plans - seasonal. **Amenities:** hair dryers. *Some:* irons. **Pool(s):** heated indoor. **Leisure Activities:** whirlpool, playground, exercise room. **Cards:** AX, DS, MC, VI. **Special Amenities:** free continental breakfast and free room upgrade (subject to availability with advanced reservations). *(See color ad p 400)*

SOME UNITS

[icons]

BEST WESTERN INN OF PETOSKEY

Phone: (231)347-3925

AAA [SAVE]

5/23-9/1 [ECP]	1P: $80-$150	2P: $85-$150	XP: $5	F16
9/2-3/31 [ECP]	1P: $57-$150	2P: $62-$150	XP: $5	F16
4/1-5/22 [ECP]	1P: $57-$100	2P: $62-$105	XP: $5	F16

Motel

Location: 1.3 mi s on US 131. Located in a commercial area. 1300 Spring St 49770. Fax: 231/347-3341. **Facility:** 85 units. 83 one- and 2 two-bedroom standard units, some with whirlpools. 2 stories (no elevator), interior/exterior corridors. **Parking:** on-site. **Terms:** cancellation fee imposed. **Amenities:** irons, hair dryers. **Pool(s):** heated indoor. **Leisure Activities:** sauna, whirlpool, exercise room. *Fee:* game room. **Business Services:** meeting rooms. **Cards:** AX, DS, MC, VI. **Special Amenities:** free continental breakfast and free newspaper. *(See color ad p 401)*

SOME UNITS

ECONO LODGE

Phone: (231)348-3324

AAA [SAVE]

6/13-8/31	1P: $65-$95	2P: $70-$125	XP: $6	F18
12/12-3/31	1P: $50-$95	2P: $55-$125	XP: $6	F18
4/1-6/12 & 9/1-12/11	1P: $50-$80	2P: $55-$90	XP: $6	F18

Motel

Location: 2 mi s of US 31. Located next to a casino. 1858 US 131 S 49770. Fax: 231/348-3521. **Facility:** 59 one-bedroom standard units. 2 stories (no elevator), exterior corridors. **Parking:** on-site, winter plug-ins. **Terms:** [CP] meal plan available, package plans. **Pool(s):** heated indoor. **Leisure Activities:** whirlpool. **Cards:** AX, DC, DS, MC, VI. **Special Amenities:** free continental breakfast and free local telephone calls.

SOME UNITS

GREEN ROOF INN

◆◆ ◆◆◆ 6/13-8/16   1P: $49-$119   2P: $49-$119   XP: $6   F18

         4/1-6/12 & 8/17-3/31   1P: $39-$99   2P: $39-$99   XP: $6   F18

Motel   **Phone:** (231)348-3900

Location: 1.3 mi s. Located in a commercial area. 1420 US 131 S 49770. **Fax:** 231/348-8375. **Facility:** 138 one-bedroom standard units, some with whirlpools. 2 stories (no elevator), exterior corridors. **Parking:** on-site. **Terms:** pets ($10 extra charge). **Amenities:** *Some:* dual phone lines, irons. **Cards:** AX, DC, DS, MC, VI.

(See color ad p 401)

SOME UNITS

ASK ⓢⒹ 🛏️ 🕼 / ✕ 🖧 🔲 🖥️ /
                                 FEE   FEE

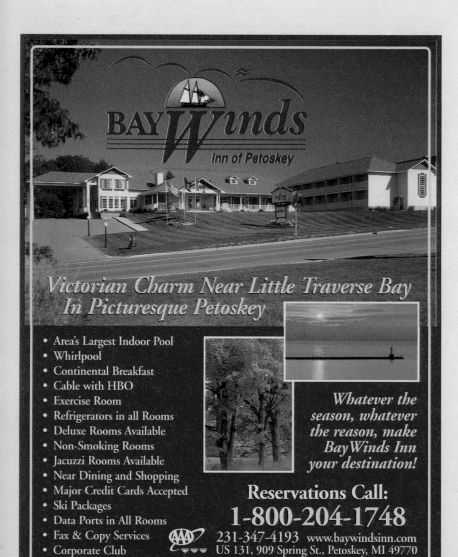

BAY Winds
Inn of Petoskey

Victorian Charm Near Little Traverse Bay In Picturesque Petoskey

- Area's Largest Indoor Pool
- Whirlpool
- Continental Breakfast
- Cable with HBO
- Exercise Room
- Refrigerators in all Rooms
- Deluxe Rooms Available
- Non-Smoking Rooms
- Jacuzzi Rooms Available
- Near Dining and Shopping
- Major Credit Cards Accepted
- Ski Packages
- Data Ports in All Rooms
- Fax & Copy Services
- Corporate Club

Whatever the season, whatever the reason, make BayWinds Inn your destination!

Reservations Call:
1-800-204-1748
231-347-4193   www.baywindsinn.com
US 131, 909 Spring St., Petoskey, MI 49770

HAMPTON INN & SUITES

Phone: 231/348-9555

[SAVE]

Small-scale Hotel

5/25-9/2 [ECP]	1P: $119-$139	2P: $124-$144	
9/3-10/19 [ECP]	1P: $89-$109	2P: $94-$114	
4/1-5/24 & 10/20-3/31 [ECP]	1P: $89	2P: $94	

Location: 1.2 mi s on US 131. Located in a commercial area. 920 Spring St 49770. Fax: 231/348-9666. **Facility:** 77 one-bedroom standard units, some with whirlpools. 4 stories, interior corridors. *Bath:* combo or shower only. **Parking:** on-site. **Terms:** check-in 4 pm. **Amenities:** video games, dual phone lines, voice mail, irons, hair dryers. **Pool(s):** heated indoor. **Leisure Activities:** whirlpool, exercise room. **Guest Services:** valet and coin laundry. **Business Services:** meeting rooms, business center. **Cards:** AX, DC, DS, MC, VI.

SOME UNITS

STAFFORD'S PERRY HOTEL

Phone: (231)347-4000

Small-scale Hotel

5/23-10/27	1P: $85-$240	2P: $85-$240	XP: $15 F14
12/27-3/31	1P: $85-$135	2P: $85-$135	XP: $15 F14
4/1-5/22 & 10/28-12/26	1P: $85-$115	2P: $85-$115	XP: $15 F14

Location: Center. Adjoins the Gas Light District. Bay & Lewis sts 49770. Fax: 231/347-0636. **Facility:** 80 one-bedroom standard units. 3 stories, interior corridors. *Bath:* combo or shower only. **Parking:** on-site. **Terms:** cancellation fee imposed, [AP], [BP] & [CP] meal plans available, package plans - seasonal. **Amenities:** *Some:* dual phone lines, voice mail. **Leisure Activities:** whirlpool. **Guest Services:** gift shop, valet laundry. **Business Services:** meeting rooms. **Cards:** AX, DS, MC, VI.

SOME UNITS

SUPER 8 MOTEL

Phone: 231/439-8000

Small-scale Hotel

All Year	1P: $69-$149	2P: $69-$149	XP: $6

Location: US 31, 1 mi w of jct US 131. Located in a semi-commercial area. 2645 Charlevoix Ave 49770. Fax: 231/439-8004. **Facility:** 56 one-bedroom standard units, some with efficiencies. 2 stories (no elevator), interior corridors. *Bath:* combo or shower only. **Parking:** on-site. **Terms:** 7 day cancellation notice, [CP] meal plan available. **Pool(s):** heated indoor. **Leisure Activities:** whirlpool. **Guest Services:** coin laundry. **Business Services:** meeting rooms. **Cards:** AX, DS, MC, VI.

SOME UNITS

VICTORIES HOTEL

Phone: 231/347-6041

Large-scale Hotel

7/2-3/31	1P: $79-$99	2P: $79-$99	XP: $20 F17
4/1-7/1	1P: $59-$99	2P: $59-$99	XP: $20 F17

Location: 1.5 mi s. Located in a commercial area. 1444 US 131 S 49770. Fax: 231/347-6041. **Facility:** 144 one-bedroom standard units. 5 stories, interior corridors. **Parking:** on-site, winter plug-ins. **Terms:** check-in 4 pm, 3 day cancellation notice, package plans - seasonal, 18% service charge. **Amenities:** video games, voice mail, irons, hair dryers. **Pool(s):** heated indoor. **Leisure Activities:** whirlpool, exercise room. *Fee:* game room. **Guest Services:** valet and coin laundry. **Business Services:** meeting rooms. **Cards:** AX, DS, MC, VI.

SOME UNITS

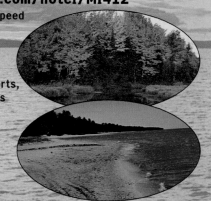

——— **WHERE TO DINE** ———

CITY PARK GRILL
♦♦♦
American
Dinner: $10-$15
Phone: 231/347-0101
Location: Center. 432 E Lake St 49770. **Hours:** 11:30 am-10 pm. **Features:** Ernest Hemingway is reputed to have spent a fair amount of time at the massive 100 year old mirrored cherry bar that dominates this casual restaurant. The honey-grilled pork chops marinated in jalapenos, soy sauce and Dijon mustard lead a continental menu that offers a wide range of choices. Casual dress; cocktails. **Parking:** street.
Cards: AX, DC, DS, MC, VI.

VILLA RISTORANTE ITALIANO
♦♦
Italian
Dinner: $18-$30
Phone: 231/347-1440
Location: On US 131, just s of jct US 31. 887 Spring St 49770. **Hours:** 4:30 pm-10:30 pm. Closed major holidays; also Sun. **Features:** Gnocchi and shrimp with gorgonzola represent traditional preparations of Italian cuisine. The homemade Italian ice cream is hard to top as a meal finisher. Casual dress; cocktails. **Parking:** on-site. **Cards:** AX, MC, VI.

PLAINWELL pop. 3,933

——— **WHERE TO STAY** ———

COMFORT INN
(AAA) (SAVE)
♦♦♦♦
Small-scale Hotel
Phone: 269/685-9891

	1P	2P	XP	
4/1-10/1	1P: $79-$180	2P: $99-$180	XP: $5	F18
10/2-3/31	1P: $79-$180	2P: $79-$180	XP: $5	F18

Location: US 131, exit 49A, just e. 622 Allegan St 49080. Fax: 269/685-9892. **Facility:** 65 units. 64 one-bedroom standard units, some with whirlpools. 1 one-bedroom suite ($150-$180) with whirlpool. 2 stories (no elevator), interior corridors. **Parking:** on-site. **Terms:** [ECP] meal plan available, pets ($10 extra charge). **Amenities:** dual phone lines, voice mail, irons, hair dryers. **Pool(s):** outdoor. **Business Services:** meeting rooms. **Cards:** AX, DC, DS, MC, VI. **Special Amenities:** free continental breakfast and free local telephone calls.

SOME UNITS
FEE

——— **WHERE TO DINE** ———

ARIE'S LONDON GRILL-BOMBAY
♦♦
Provincial British
Dinner: $10-$20
Phone: 269/685-1877
Location: US 131, exit 49A, 2 mi e; center of town. 127 E Bridge 49080. **Hours:** 5 pm-10 pm. Closed major holidays. **Features:** The quintessential British pub, this small, lively space is adorned with British and Colonial Indian memorabilia. A small menu reflects a mix of both British pub favorites and Indian curries. Casual dress; cocktails. **Parking:** street. **Cards:** AX, DS, MC, VI.

PLYMOUTH —*See Detroit p. 263.*

PONTIAC —*See Detroit p. 264.*

PORTAGE pop. 44,897

——— **WHERE TO DINE** ———

FINLEY'S AMERICAN RESTAURANT
♦♦
Steak House
Lunch: $5-$8
Dinner: $7-$18
Phone: 269/323-1104
Location: I-94, exit 78, 1 mi s. 6301 S Westnedge Ave 49081. **Hours:** 11 am-10 pm, Fri & Sat-11 pm. Closed: 11/27, 12/25. **Features:** Casual friendly service marks this family-oriented restaurant. They offer something for everyone as the menu covers everything from steak to seafood to sandwiches. Casual dress; cocktails. **Parking:** on-site. **Cards:** AX, DC, DS, MC, VI.

PORT AUSTIN pop. 737

——— **WHERE TO STAY** ———

THE GARFIELD INN
♦♦♦
Historic Bed & Breakfast
Phone: 989/738-5254
All Year [BP]   1P: $110-$130   2P: $110-$130   XP: $20
Location: Just s on M-53; downtown. 8544 Lake St 48647 (PO Box 366). Fax: 989/738-6384. **Facility:** Designated smoking area. 6 one-bedroom standard units. 3 stories (no elevator), interior corridors. *Bath:* some shared or private, combo or shower only. **Parking:** on-site. **Terms:** 14 day cancellation notice-fee imposed. **Dining:** restaurant, see separate listing. **Cards:** AX, DS, MC, VI.

LAKE STREET MANOR BED & BREAKFAST
♦♦♦
Historic Bed & Breakfast
Phone: 989/738-7720
5/1-10/28 [ECP]   2P: $55-$75
Location: Just s of downtown on M-53. 8569 Lake St (M-53) 48467. **Facility:** 5 one-bedroom standard units. 2 stories (no elevator), interior/exterior corridors. *Bath:* some shared or private, combo or shower only. **Parking:** on-site. **Terms:** open 5/1-10/28, 2 night minimum stay - weekends 5/30-9/4, cancellation fee imposed, no pets allowed (owner's dog on premises). **Amenities:** video library. **Leisure Activities:** whirlpool, bicycles.
Cards: DC, MC, VI.

LAKE VISTA MOTEL & COTTAGES RESORT

Phone: (989)738-8612

(AAA) (SAVE)

| 6/11-9/20 | 1P: $90 | 2P: $165 | XP: $20 |
| 4/10-6/10 & 9/21-11/30 | 1P: $54 | 2P: $150 | XP: $10 |

Motel

Location: On M-25 (Spring St), 0.5 mi w of town. 168 W Spring St 48467 (PO Box 429). Fax: 989/738-8612. **Facility:** 17 units. 10 one-bedroom standard units. 7 two-bedroom suites ($150-$850) with kitchens (no utensils). 1-2 stories (no elevator), exterior corridors. *Bath:* combo or shower only. **Parking:** on-site. **Terms:** open 4/10-11/30, 2 night minimum stay - weekends in motel, 7 day cancellation notice-fee imposed. **Pool(s):** heated outdoor. **Leisure Activities:** fishing, barbecue grills, sandbox, swing set, horseshoes. *Fee:* live bait & tackle. **Guest Services:** gift shop, coin laundry. **Cards:** AX, DC, MC, VI. **Special Amenities:** preferred room (subject to availability with advanced reservations).

SOME UNITS

—— WHERE TO DINE ——

THE FARM RESTAURANT

Dinner: $16-$24   **Phone:** 989/874-5700

Regional American

Location: SR 53 (Van Dyke Rd), 2 mi w. 699 Port Crescent Rd 48467. **Hours:** Open 5/13-11/1; 5 pm-10 pm, Sun noon-8 pm; weekends only 9/1-11/1. Closed major holidays; also Mon. **Reservations:** accepted. **Features:** Located 8 miles from Port Austin, this converted farmhouse serves as a training kitchen for Livonia's Schoolcraft Culinary Program and uses locally grown ingredients to create innovative dishes. Casual dress; cocktails. **Parking:** on-site. **Cards:** MC, VI.

THE GARFIELD INN   Historic

Lunch: $6-$9   **Dinner:** $17-$25   **Phone:** 989/738-5254

American

Location: Just s on M-53; downtown; in The Garfield Inn. 8544 Lake St 48467. **Hours:** Open 4/1-12/31 & 2/14-3/31; 11:30 am-2 & 5-8 pm, Sun 9 am-2 pm; noon-3 & 5-9 pm, Fri & Sat-10 pm 4/2-8/31. Closed: 11/27, 12/25. **Reservations:** suggested; weekends. **Features:** Near the beautiful sandy shores of Lake Huron, the 1930s Victorian Inn is a sophisticated spot for intimate, formal dining. The restaurant garners praise for its innovative preparations. During the summer, request garden seating for a relaxed experience. Casual dress; cocktails. **Parking:** on-site. **Cards:** AX, DS, MC, VI.

PORT HURON pop. 32,338

—— WHERE TO STAY ——

AMERIHOST INN-PORT HURON

Phone: (810)364-8000

(AAA) (SAVE)

All Year [ECP]   1P: $64-$99   2P: $69-$109   XP: $5   F17

Small-scale Hotel

Location: I-94, exit 269, just w. Located opposite an outlet mall. 1611 Range Rd 48074. Fax: 810/364-8844. **Facility:** 60 one-bedroom standard units, some with whirlpools. 2 stories, interior corridors. *Bath:* combo or shower only. **Parking:** on-site. **Terms:** 14 day cancellation notice, weekly rates available. **Amenities:** dual phone lines, voice mail, safes (fee), irons, hair dryers. **Pool(s):** heated indoor. **Leisure Activities:** sauna, whirlpool, exercise room. **Guest Services:** valet laundry. **Business Services:** meeting rooms. **Cards:** AX, DC, DS, MC, VI. **Special Amenities:** free continental breakfast and free newspaper.

SOME UNITS

COMFORT INN

Phone: (810)982-5500

(SAVE)

All Year [ECP]   1P: $69-$139   2P: $69-$139   XP: $10   F18

Small-scale Hotel

Location: I-94, exit 274 (Water St). 1700 Yeager St 48060. Fax: 810/982-7199. **Facility:** 80 one-bedroom standard units, some with whirlpools. 2 stories, interior corridors. **Parking:** on-site. **Amenities:** hair dryers. *Some:* irons. **Pool(s):** heated indoor. **Leisure Activities:** whirlpool, exercise room. *Fee:* game room. **Guest Services:** valet and coin laundry. **Business Services:** meeting rooms. **Cards:** AX, CB, DC, DS, JC, MC, VI.

SOME UNITS

FAIRFIELD INN BY MARRIOTT

Phone: (810)982-8500

(SAVE)

| 5/30-8/30 [ECP] | 1P: $59-$99 | 2P: $59-$99 |
| 4/1-5/29 & 8/31-3/31 [ECP] | 1P: $54-$84 | 2P: $54-$84 |

Small-scale Hotel

Location: I-94, exit 274 (Water St). 1635 Yeager St 48060. Fax: 810/982-4114. **Facility:** 63 one-bedroom standard units, some with whirlpools. 3 stories, interior corridors. *Bath:* combo or shower only. **Parking:** on-site. **Terms:** [CP] meal plan available. **Amenities:** irons, hair dryers. **Pool(s):** small heated indoor. **Leisure Activities:** whirlpool, exercise room. **Guest Services:** valet laundry. **Cards:** AX, DC, DS, MC, VI.

SOME UNITS

FEE FEE

HAMPTON INN

Phone: (810)966-9000

(AAA) (SAVE)

| 4/1-10/31 | 1P: $65-$75 | 2P: $69-$79 | XP: $5 | F18 |
| 11/1-3/31 | 1P: $59-$69 | 2P: $65-$75 | | |

Small-scale Hotel

Location: I-94, exit 274 (Water St). 1655 Yeager St 48060. Fax: 810/966-9010. **Facility:** 71 one-bedroom standard units, some with whirlpools. 3 stories, interior corridors. *Bath:* combo or shower only. **Parking:** on-site. **Terms:** [ECP] meal plan available. **Amenities:** dual phone lines, voice mail, irons, hair dryers. **Pool(s):** heated indoor. **Leisure Activities:** whirlpool, exercise room. **Guest Services:** valet laundry. **Business Services:** meeting rooms. **Cards:** AX, DC, DS, MC, VI. **Special Amenities:** free continental breakfast and free local telephone calls.

SOME UNITS

HOLIDAY INN EXPRESS HOTEL & SUITES

Phone: (810)987-5999

All Year   1P: $84-$119   2P: $84-$119

Small-scale Hotel

Location: Business loop I-69 and 94 E, then e. 1720 Hancock St 48060. Fax: 810/987-5954. **Facility:** 96 units. 93 one-bedroom standard units, some with whirlpools. 3 one-bedroom suites ($89-$199) with whirlpools. 4 stories, interior corridors. *Bath:* combo or shower only. **Parking:** on-site. **Terms:** [ECP] meal plan available. **Amenities:** irons, hair dryers. **Pool(s):** heated indoor. **Leisure Activities:** whirlpool, exercise room. *Fee:* game room. **Guest Services:** valet and coin laundry. **Business Services:** meeting rooms, business center. **Cards:** AX, CB, DC, DS, JC, MC, VI. *(See color ad card insert)*

SOME UNITS

RAMADA LIMITED   Phone: (810)987-1600

▼▼▼ ▼▼▼   All Year [CP]   2P: $59-$119
           Location: I-94, exit 274 (Water St), just n. 2282 Water St 48060. Fax: 810/987-5479. Facility: 63 one-bedroom
Small-scale Hotel standard units, some with whirlpools. 3 stories, interior corridors. Bath: combo or shower only. Parking: on-
site. Terms: cancellation fee imposed. Amenities: dual phone lines, voice mail, irons, hair dryers. Pool(s):
heated indoor. Leisure Activities: exercise room. Guest Services: valet and coin laundry. Business Services: meeting rooms.
Cards: AX, DC, DS, MC, VI.

SOME UNITS

(A$K) (S/D) (†l+) (🛢) (🏊) (🎥) (DATA PORT) (🖥) / (✕) (VCR) (🔌) (🖨) /
                                                              FEE

THOMAS EDISON INN   Phone: (810)984-8000

◆▼◆ ▼◆▼   12/26-3/31   1P: $100-$140   XP: $10
           4/1-12/23   1P: $89-$124   XP: $10
Small-scale Hotel Location: 1.5 mi n, just e on Thomas Edison Pkwy, off Pine Grove Ave. 500 Thomas Edison Pkwy 48060.
Fax: n10/984-3230. Facility: 149 units. 145 one-bedroom standard units, some with whirlpools. 4 one-
bedroom suites ($165-$475) with whirlpools. 3 stories, interior/exterior corridors. Parking: on-site, winter plug-ins. Terms: open
4/1-12/23 & 12/26-3/31, cancellation fee imposed, [AP] meal plan available, package plans, 18% service charge.
Amenities: voice mail, irons, hair dryers. Pool(s): heated indoor. Leisure Activities: sauna, whirlpool, exercise room. Guest
Services: gift shop, valet laundry, area transportation. Business Services: conference facilities. Cards: AX, DC, DS, MC, VI.

SOME UNITS

(A$K) (S/D) (🔌) (†l) (🏊) (✕) (🎥) (DATA PORT) (🖥) / (✕) /

──────── **WHERE TO DINE** ────────

BISTRO 1882   Lunch: $11-$14   Dinner: $16-$25   Phone: 810/966-6900

▼▼▼ ▼▼▼   Location: 2333 Gratiot Ave 48060. Hours: 11 am-3 & 5:30-8:30 pm. Closed major holidays.
American   Reservations: suggested. Features: Tucked away almost under the Blue Water Bridge, this small and
intimate dining room offers a modest but creative menu in a classy dining room warmed with exposed brick
walls and upscale lighting. Dressy casual; cocktails. Parking: on-site. Cards: AX, DC, DS, MC, VI.
                                                                                          (✕)

FOGCUTTER   Lunch: $8-$10   Dinner: $12-$22   Phone: 810/987-3300

▼▼ ▼▼   Location: On top of Peoples Bank Bldg; downtown. 511 Fort St 48060. Hours: 11 am-9 pm, Fri & Sat-10 pm,
American   Sun noon-7 pm. Closed: 1/1, 9/1, 12/25. Reservations: suggested. Features: Perched atop a downtown
office complex, this casual seafood restaurant offers a bounty of seafood items including lake perch,
whitefish, and frog legs. Casual dress; cocktails. Parking: on-site. Cards: AX, DC, DS, MC, VI.
                                                                          (&M) (🍸) (✕)

QUAY STREET BREWING COMPANY   Lunch: $6-$12   Dinner: $6-$12   Phone: 810/982-4100

▼▼ ▼▼   Location: Adjacent to drawbridge; downtown. 330 Quay St 48060. Hours: 11:30 am-9 pm, Fri & Sat-10 pm, Sun
noon-8 pm. Closed major holidays. Features: Situated on the riverfront, this microbrewery not only offers a
American   variety of hand crafted brews but also features selections from other Michigan microbreweries. As well as
offering traditional bar foods, the menu offers a few surprises such as house version of Louisiana's famous
muffuletta and grilled lamb burgers. Casual dress; cocktails. Parking: street. Cards: AX, DC, DS, MC, VI.
                                                                                    (&M) (✕)

PORTLAND pop. 3,798

──────── **WHERE TO STAY** ────────

BEST WESTERN AMERICAN HERITAGE INN   Phone: (517)647-2200

(AAA) [SAVE]   All Year   1P: $69-$79   2P: $79-$89   XP: $6   F18
           Location: I-96, exit 77, just n. 1681 Grand River Ave 48875. Fax: 517/647-2250. Facility: 48 one-bedroom stan-
▼▼▼ ▼▼▼   dard units, some with whirlpools. 2 stories (no elevator), interior corridors. Bath: combo or shower only.
Parking: on-site. Terms: small pets only. Amenities: video library (fee), irons, hair dryers. Pool(s): heated
Small-scale Hotel indoor. Leisure Activities: whirlpool, exercise room. Fee: game room. Guest Services: coin laundry. Business Services: meeting rooms. Cards: AX, CB, DC, DS, MC, VI. Special Amenities: early check-in/late
check-out and free continental breakfast.

SOME UNITS

(S/D) (🐾) (🔌) (🏊) (✕) (🎥) (DATA PORT) (🖥) / (✕) (VCR) (🔌) (🖨) /
                                                              FEE

PORT SANILAC pop. 658

──────── **WHERE TO STAY** ────────

THE RAYMOND HOUSE AND INN   Phone: 810/622-8800

(AAA) [SAVE]   5/1-10/31 [BP]   1P: $95-$110   2P: $95-$110   XP: $15
           4/1-4/30 & 11/1-3/31 [BP]   1P: $65-$85   2P: $65-$85   XP: $15
▼▼▼ ▼▼▼   Location: On M-25. 111 S Ridge St 48469 (PO Box 439). Fax: 810/622-8485. Facility: The property is in a sleepy
Historic Bed harbor village a short walk from the waterfront. Smoke free premises. 7 one-bedroom standard units. 3 sto-
& Breakfast   ries (no elevator), interior corridors. Bath: some shared or private, shower only. Parking: on-site. Terms: no
pets allowed (owner's dogs on premises). Amenities: video library. Some: irons, hair dryers. Guest Serv-
ices: gift shop. Cards: AX, DS, MC, VI. Special Amenities: free local telephone calls.

(S/D) (†l+) (✕) (VCR)

PRUDENVILLE pop. 1,737

——— WHERE TO STAY ———

SHEA'S LAKE FRONT LODGE   **Phone:** (989)366-5910

AAA SAVE

| | 5/23-9/2 & 12/24-3/31 [CP] | 1P: $57 | 2P: $61 | XP: $5 | D18 |
| | 4/1-5/22 & 9/3-12/23 [CP] | 1P: $40 | 2P: $44 | XP: $5 | D18 |

Location: I-75, exit 227, 8 mi w on SR 55. Located in a semi-residential area. 125 12th St 48651 (PO Box 357). **Facility:** 39 units. 34 one-bedroom standard units. 5 cottages. 2 stories (no elevator), interior/exterior corri-

Classic Small-scale Hotel

dors. *Bath:* combo or shower only. **Parking:** on-site. **Terms:** 10 day cancellation notice, weekly rates avail-able, small pets only. **Leisure Activities:** rental boats, rental paddleboats, boat dock, fishing, snowmobiling, badminton, barbecue pits, playground, basketball, horseshoes, shuffleboard, volleyball. *Fee:* game room.
Cards: AX, DS, MC, VI. **Special Amenities:** free continental breakfast. *(See ad p 312)*

SOME UNITS

🛏️ ⊠ 🅺 ☎ / 🅗 🖥️ 🖵 /

SWISS INN ON THE LAKE   **Phone:** (989)366-7881

AAA SAVE

	7/1-9/30	1P: $50-$60	2P: $50-$85
	4/1-6/30	1P: $45-$55	2P: $50-$65
	10/1-3/31	1P: $45-$55	2P: $50-$60

Motel

Location: On SR 55, 0.3 mi e of jct SR 18. Located in a commercial area. 472 W Houghton Lake Dr 48651 (PO Box 204). Fax: 989/366-1064. **Facility:** 11 one-bedroom standard units. 1 story, exterior corridors. *Bath:* shower only. **Parking:** on-site, winter plug-ins. **Terms:** 5 day cancellation notice, weekly rates available.
Amenities: video library (fee). **Leisure Activities:** rental boats, rental paddleboats, boat dock, fishing, snowmobiling, horse-shoes, shuffleboard, volleyball. **Cards:** AX, DC, MC, VI.

SOME UNITS

🅢 ⊞ ⊠ 🅺 ☎ 🅗 / 🆅🅲🆁 /
FEE

——— WHERE TO DINE ———

BRASS LANTERN   **Dinner:** $11-$20   **Phone:** 989/366-8312

Location: Just e on SR 18 and 55. 729 Houghton Lake Dr 48651. **Hours:** 4 pm-9 pm, Fri & Sat-10 pm; to 10

American

pm, Sun noon-9 pm 5/23-9/4. Closed: 4/20, 11/27, 12/25. **Features:** Barbecue ribs, New York strip and roasted salmon stand out on a diverse menu of beef, seafood, chicken and pasta dishes. The warm, inviting dining room has the ambience of a rustic cabin, with a log interior, fireplace and brass wall
sculptures. Casual dress; cocktails. **Parking:** on-site. **Cards:** DS, MC, VI.

🍸 ⊠

ROCHESTER —See Detroit p. 264.

ROCHESTER HILLS —See Detroit p. 265.

ROGERS CITY pop. 3,322

——— WHERE TO STAY ———

DRIFTWOOD MOTEL   **Phone:** 989/734-4777

| | 5/23-11/3 | 1P: $70-$90 | 2P: $80-$100 | XP: $5 | F16 |
| | 4/1-5/22 & 11/4-3/31 | 1P: $50-$70 | 2P: $65-$95 | XP: $5 | F16 |

Motel

Location: 1 mi nw on US 23 business route. 540 W Third St 49779. **Facility:** 44 one-bedroom standard units. 2 stories, exterior corridors. **Parking:** on-site, winter plug-ins. **Amenities:** hair dryers. **Pool(s):** heated indoor.
Leisure Activities: whirlpool, snowmobiling. **Cards:** AX, DC, DS, MC, VI.

SOME UNITS

⊞ 🏊 🎥 🖵 / ⊠ /

——— WHERE TO DINE ———

WATERS EDGE   **Lunch:** $4-$6   **Dinner:** $9-$19   **Phone:** 989/734-4747

Location: Adjacent to Driftwood Motel. 530 W Third St 49779. **Hours:** 11 am-9:30 pm; Sat 4 pm-9 pm off

American

season. Closed: 1/1, 12/25. **Reservations:** suggested. **Features:** The restaurant delivers such well-prepared food as whitefish, prime rib, chicken and pasta. The nautically themed dining room, affords views of Lake Huron. For dessert, try the Kentucky Derby pie. Casual dress; cocktails. **Parking:** on-site.
Cards: AX, DC, DS, MC, VI.

🍸 ⊠

ROMEO —See Detroit p. 265.

ROMULUS —See Detroit p. 265.

ROSEVILLE —See Detroit p. 269.

ROTHBURY pop. 416

——— WHERE TO DINE ———

——— *The following restaurant has not been evaluated by AAA* ———
but is listed for your information only.

SUNDANCE SALOON & STEAKHOUSE   **Phone:** 231/894-4444

fyi   Not evaluated. **Location:** Located at the Double JJ Resort. Water Rd 49452. **Features:** The casual restaurant overlooks the golf course of an adult-exclusive resort.

ROYAL OAK —*See Detroit p. 270.*

SAGINAW pop. 61,799

─────── **WHERE TO STAY** ───────

BEST WESTERN - SAGINAW

SAVE
Large-scale Hotel
Phone: (989)755-0461
All Year [ECP]　　　　1P: $59-$109　　2P: $69-$109　　XP: $8　　F17
Location: I-75, exit 149B (SR 46). 1408 S Outer Dr 48601. Fax: 989/755-0600. **Facility:** 158 one-bedroom standard units. 4 stories, interior corridors. **Parking:** on-site. **Terms:** 7 day cancellation notice. **Amenities:** video games, irons, hair dryers. **Pool(s):** heated indoor. **Leisure Activities:** sauna, whirlpool, racquetball court, exercise room. *Fee:* game room. **Guest Services:** valet and coin laundry. **Business Services:** meeting rooms. **Cards:** AX, CB, DC, DS, JC, MC, VI.
SOME UNITS

COMFORT SUITES
SAVE
Small-scale Hotel
Phone: (989)797-8000
All Year　　　　1P: $65-$85　　2P: $70-$90
Location: I-675, exit 6, 0.6 mi w on Tittabawassee Rd. Located in a commercial area. 5180 Fashion Square Blvd 48603. Fax: 989/797-8000. **Facility:** 66 one-bedroom standard units. 3 stories, interior corridors. *Bath:* combo or shower only. **Parking:** on-site. **Terms:** [ECP] meal plan available. **Amenities:** irons. *Some:* hair dryers. **Pool(s):** heated indoor. **Leisure Activities:** whirlpool. **Guest Services:** valet laundry. **Business Services:** meeting rooms. **Cards:** AX, CB, DC, DS, MC, VI.
SOME UNITS

FAIRFIELD INN
SAVE
Small-scale Hotel
Phone: (989)797-6100
All Year　　　　1P: $60-$80　　2P: $65-$85
Location: I-675, exit 6, 0.5 mi w on Tittabawassee Rd. Located in a commercial area. 5200 Fashion Square Blvd 48603. Fax: 989/797-6100. **Facility:** 76 one-bedroom standard units. 3 stories, interior corridors. *Bath:* combo or shower only. **Parking:** on-site, winter plug-ins. **Terms:** [ECP] meal plan available. **Amenities:** voice mail, irons. **Pool(s):** heated indoor. **Leisure Activities:** whirlpool. **Guest Services:** valet laundry. **Business Services:** meeting rooms. **Cards:** AX, CB, DC, DS, MC, VI.
SOME UNITS

FOUR POINTS BY SHERATON SAGINAW
Large-scale Hotel
Phone: (989)790-5050
All Year　　　　1P: $79　　2P: $79　　XP: $10　　F17
Location: I-675, exit 6, just w on Tittabawassee Rd. Located in a commercial area. 4960 Towne Centre Rd 48604. Fax: 989/790-1466. **Facility:** 156 one-bedroom standard units. 6 stories, interior corridors. **Parking:** on-site. **Amenities:** video games, high-speed Internet, dual phone lines, voice mail, irons, hair dryers. *Some:* fax. **Pool(s):** heated indoor/outdoor. **Leisure Activities:** sauna, whirlpool, exercise room. **Guest Services:** gift shop, valet laundry. **Business Services:** conference facilities. **Cards:** AX, CB, DC, DS, MC, VI.
SOME UNITS

HAMPTON INN
SAVE
Small-scale Hotel
Phone: (989)792-7666
All Year [ECP]　　　　1P: $59-$80　　2P: $59-$80
Location: Jct I-675 and Tittabawassee Rd. Located in a commercial area. 2222 Tittabawassee Rd 48604. Fax: 989/792-3213. **Facility:** 120 one-bedroom standard units. 2 stories (no elevator), interior corridors. **Parking:** on-site, winter plug-ins. **Amenities:** video games, voice mail, irons. **Pool(s):** heated outdoor. **Guest Services:** valet laundry. **Business Services:** meeting rooms. **Cards:** AX, CB, DC, DS, MC, VI.
(See color ad below)
SOME UNITS

MONTAGUE INN
Country Inn
Phone: 989/752-3939
All Year　　　　1P: $70-$175　　2P: $70-$175
Location: 1.5 mi s. Located in a residential area opposite a park. 1581 S Washington Ave 48601. Fax: 989/752-3159. **Facility:** This elegantly restored Georgian mansion is on manicured grounds overlooking Lake Linton and Ojibway Island. Smoke free premises. 17 units. 15 one-bedroom standard units. 2 one-bedroom suites, some with whirlpools. 2-3 stories, interior corridors. *Bath:* combo or shower only. **Parking:** on-site. **Terms:** cancellation fee imposed, [CP] meal plan available. **Guest Services:** valet laundry. **Business Services:** meeting rooms. **Cards:** AX, DS, MC, VI.

PLAZA HOTEL AND CONVENTION CENTER
All Year   1P: $89   2P: $89   **Phone:** (989)753-6608
◆◆◆ ◆◆◆ **Location:** I-675, exit 2, just s. Located opposite the Saginaw County Event Center. 400 Johnson St 48607.
Large-scale Hotel Fax: 989/753-2387. **Facility:** 177 one-bedroom standard units. 8 stories, interior corridors. *Bath:* combo or shower only. **Parking:** on-site. **Amenities:** video games, voice mail, irons, hair dryers. **Pool(s):** heated indoor. **Leisure Activities:** whirlpool, exercise room. **Guest Services:** valet laundry. **Business Services:** conference facilities.
Cards: AX, CB, DC, DS, JC, MC, VI.
SOME UNITS
(ASK) (S_D) (✈) (¶) (Y) (🖑) (🏊) (DATA PORT) (💻) / (✕) (🔒) /

RED ROOF INN
◆◆◆ (SAVE)   5/27-10/18   1P: $39-$56   2P: $46-$63   XP: $7   F18
10/19-3/31   1P: $38-$45   2P: $38-$45
◆◆◆ ◆◆◆   4/1-5/26   1P: $37-$44   2P: $37-$44   **Phone:** (989)754-8414
Motel **Location:** I-75, exit 149B (SR 46). Located in commercial area. 966 S Outer Dr 48601. Fax: 989/754-8926.
Facility: 79 one-bedroom standard units. 2 stories (no elevator), exterior corridors. **Parking:** on-site.
Terms: small pets only. **Amenities:** video games, voice mail. **Cards:** AX, CB, DC, DS, MC, VI.
Special Amenities: free local telephone calls and free newspaper.
SOME UNITS
(🛏) (¶+) (📽) / (✕) (DATA PORT) (🔒) (📺) /

──────── **WHERE TO DINE** ────────

FORBIDDEN CITY RESTAURANT   **Lunch:** $4-$6   **Dinner:** $7-$14   **Phone:** 989-799-9340
◆◆◆ **Location:** SR 58, 2 mi n on SR 84; in Town Campus Mall. 4024 Bay Rd 48603. **Hours:** 11 am-9:30 pm, Fri & Sat-10 pm, Sun noon-8:30 pm. Closed major holidays; also 9/4 for lunch & 12/24 for dinner.
◆◆◆ ◆◆◆ **Reservations:** suggested; weekends. **Features:** A local fixture since 1973, this comfortable restaurant is decorated with red tablecloths, wood accents and Oriental artwork. The focus is on Mandarin-style food,
Chinese such as almond chicken and Mongolian beef. Try the crab cheese appetizers or the vegetable bean curd soup. Service is professional and friendly. Casual dress; cocktails. **Parking:** on-site. **Cards:** AX, MC, VI.
(✕)

HUNAN RESTAURANT   **Lunch:** $5-$6   **Dinner:** $7-$18   **Phone:** 989-792-0303
◆◆◆ ◆◆◆ **Location:** SR 58, 2.5 mi n on SR 84; opposite Fashion Square Mall. 3109 Bay Plaza 48604. **Hours:** 11:15 am-9:30 pm, Fri & Sat-10 pm, Sun noon-9 pm. Closed major holidays. **Features:** Hunan, Szechuan and Mandarin
Chinese dishes, such as beef with broccoli and sweet and sour pork, are served in plentiful portions. The quiet dining rooms are decorated with classy, Oriental appointments. Servers are friendly and adept at follow-up.
Casual dress; cocktails. **Parking:** on-site. **Cards:** AX, DC, DS, MC, VI.
(✕)

KINGS HOUSE CHINESE RESTAURANT　　　**Lunch:** $3-$5　　　**Dinner:** $4-$5　　　**Phone:** 989/790-1072
♦♦♦　**Location:** SR 58, 1.5 mi n of SR 84. 3649 Bay Rd 48603. **Hours:** 11 am-9 pm. Closed major holidays; also Sun
Chinese　6/1-8/31. **Features:** Delicious soup and tasty, Cantonese-style chow mein are popular selections at the
unpretentious family restaurant. Lots of plants and pictures of the Great Wall enhance the warm, bright
MC, VI.　dining room. The menu also lists several American choices. Casual dress. **Parking:** on-site. **Cards:** DS,
MC, VI.　🃏 ✕

SULLIVAN'S WEST　　　**Lunch:** $5-$8　　　**Dinner:** $7-$15　　　**Phone:** 989/799-1940
♦♦♦　**Location:** 5 mi w on SR 46. 5235 Gratiot Rd 48603. **Hours:** 7 am-9 pm. Closed: 11/27, 12/25.
American　**Features:** Serving the area since 1946, the restaurant delivers home-cooked daily specials, as well as
such dishes as seafood, Swiss steak and chicken. Soups and sandwiches are favorite lighter fare. Wood
DS, MC, VI.　and brass accents lend to the contemporary feel. Casual dress; cocktails. **Parking:** on-site. **Cards:** AX,
DS, MC, VI.　✕

TONY'S　　　**Lunch:** $4-$6　　　**Dinner:** $6-$9　　　**Phone:** 989/249-8669
♦♦♦　**Location:** I-675, exit 6, 0.7 mi w on Tittabawassee Rd, then just s. 4880 Fashion Square Blvd 48603. **Hours:** 7
American　am-10 pm, Thurs-Sat to 11 pm. Closed major holidays. **Features:** The restaurant is well known in the area
for its steak sandwiches and WOP salad, as well as huge portions for breakfast, lunch and dinner. Save
room for one of the tempting desserts. Casual dress. **Parking:** on-site. **Cards:** MC, VI.　✕

ST. CLAIR pop. 5,802

───── **WHERE TO STAY** ─────

ST. CLAIR INN　　　　　　　　　　　　　　　　　**Phone:** 810/329-2222
(AAA) [SAVE]　All Year　　　　2P: $85-$145　　　XP: $10　　　F18
♦♦♦♦　**Location:** 1.3 mi n on SR 29. 500 N Riverside Ave 48079. Fax: 810/329-7664. **Facility:** 78 units. 74 one-bedroom
Historic　standard units, some with whirlpools. 4 one-bedroom suites ($240). 2 stories (no elevator), interior corridors.
Small-scale Hotel　*Bath:* combo or shower only. **Parking:** on-site. **Terms:** 3 day cancellation notice, [AP], [BP] & [CP] meal plans
available, package plans. **Amenities:** *Some:* hair dryers. **Dining:** 7 am-9 pm, Fri & Sat-10 pm, Sun 8 am-9
pm, cocktails. **Leisure Activities:** boat dock, fishing. **Guest Services:** valet laundry. **Business Services:**
conference facilities. **Cards:** AX, MC, VI.

SOME UNITS
🍴 ⛷ [DATA PORT] 💻 / ✕ [VCR] 📷 /
FEE

───── **WHERE TO DINE** ─────

RIVER CRAB　　　**Lunch:** $6-$14　　　**Dinner:** $14-$30　　　**Phone:** 810/329-2261
(AAA)　**Location:** Adjacent to River Crab Blue Water Inn. 1337 N River Rd 48079. **Hours:** 11:30 am-9 pm, Fri &
♦♦♦♦　Sat-10:30 pm, Sun from 10 am. Closed: 1/1, 12/25. **Reservations:** suggested; weekends.
Seafood　**Features:** Overlooking the St. Clair River, the restaurant is warm and romantic—a perfect spot for couples.
The menu lists a lengthy selection of daily fish specials, such as salmon in a flavorful mustard sauce.
Casual dress; cocktails. **Parking:** on-site. **Cards:** AX, DC, DS, MC, VI.　🍸 ✕

ST. IGNACE pop. 2,678　(See map p. 336; index p. 339)

───── **WHERE TO STAY** ─────

AURORA BOREALIS MOTOR INN　　　　　　　**Phone:** 906/643-7488　　56
♦♦ ♦♦　6/26-8/23　　1P: $49-$89　　2P: $49-$89　　XP: $6
　　　8/24-11/16　1P: $39-$79　　2P: $39-$79　　XP: $5
Motel　4/1-6/25　　1P: $39-$69　　2P: $39-$69　　XP: $5
Location: 1 mi e of bridge tollgate on I-75 business route and US 2. 635 W US 2 49781. **Facility:** 56 one-bedroom
standard units. 2 stories (no elevator), exterior corridors. **Parking:** on-site. **Terms:** open 4/1-11/16. **Cards:** DS, MC, VI.
(See ad p 410)

SOME UNITS
[S/D] [🍴] / ✕ /

BAY VIEW MOTEL　　　　　　　　　　　　　**Phone:** 906/643-9444　　43
♦♦　6/16-9/7　　1P: $60　　　2P: $76　　　XP: $5　　D12
　　4/20-6/15　　1P: $32-$42　　2P: $36-$48　　XP: $5　　D12
Motel　9/8-10/31　　1P: $32-$42　　2P: $36　　　XP: $5　　D12
Location: 3 mi n of bridge tollgate on I-75 business route. Located on the lake. 1133 N State St 49781. **Facility:** 23
one-bedroom standard units. 1-2 stories (no elevator), exterior corridors. *Bath:* combo or shower only. **Parking:** on-site.
Terms: open 4/20-10/31, cancellation fee imposed, pets ($5 extra charge). **Cards:** DC, MC, VI.

SOME UNITS
[🐾] [🍴] [🎬] [Z] / ✕ /

BEST WESTERN-KEWADIN CASINO LAKEFRONT INN　　**Phone:** (906)643-8411　　42
(AAA) [SAVE]　6/16-10/15　1P: $94-$104　2P: $94-$104　XP: $10　F16
　　　10/16-3/31　1P: $74-$84　　2P: $74-$84　　XP: $10　F16
♦♦ ♦♦　4/1-6/15　　1P: $74-$84　　2P: $84　　　XP: $10　F16
Motel　**Location:** 3 mi n of bridge tollgate on I-75 business route. 1131 N State St 49781. Fax: 906/643-8924. **Facility:** 85
one-bedroom standard units, some with whirlpools. 2 stories, interior/exterior corridors. **Parking:** on-site.
Terms: cancellation fee imposed, [CP] meal plan available. **Amenities:** irons, hair dryers. **Pool(s):** heated
indoor. **Leisure Activities:** whirlpool, snowmobiling, indoor recreation area, playground. **Guest Services:** coin laundry. **Business Services:** meeting rooms. **Cards:** AX, DC, DS, MC, VI. **Special Amenities:** early check-in/late check-out and free continental breakfast.

SOME UNITS
[S/D] [🍴] [🏊] ✕ [🐾] [DATA PORT] 💻 / ✕ 📷 /

(See map p. 336)

BUDGET HOST INN

Small-scale Hotel

6/26-8/16 [BP]	1P: $74-$156	2P: $74-$156	XP: $6
4/1-6/25 & 8/17-3/31 [BP]	1P: $58-$135	2P: $58-$135	XP: $6

Phone: 906/643-9666 **51**

Location: 1.8 mi n of bridge tollgate on I-75 business route. Located in a semi-commercial area. 700 N State St 49781. Fax: 906/643-9126. **Facility:** 58 units. 45 one-bedroom standard units, some with whirlpools. 3 one- and 10 two-bedroom suites ($96-$156), some with whirlpools. 2 stories, interior/exterior corridors. **Parking:** on-site, winter plug-ins. **Terms:** cancellation fee imposed, pets ($20 deposit). **Amenities:** *Some:* hair dryers. **Pool(s):** heated indoor. **Leisure Activities:** whirlpool, snowmobiling, playground. *Fee:* game room. **Guest Services:** coin laundry. **Business Services:** meeting rooms. **Cards:** AX, CB, DC, DS, MC, VI. **Special Amenities:** early check-in/late check-out and free local telephone calls. *(See color ad p 187 & below)*

SOME UNITS

(See map p. 336)

COMFORT INN

6/27-8/23	1P: $69-$198	2P: $69-$198	XP: $10	F18
8/24-10/15	1P: $55-$178	2P: $55-$178	XP: $10	F18
4/1-6/26 & 10/16-3/31	1P: $49-$138	2P: $49-$138	XP: $10	F18

Phone: (906)643-7733 48

Small-scale Hotel **Location:** 2 mi n of bridge tollgate on I-75 business route. Located on the lake. 927 N State St 49781. **Fax:** 906/643-6420. **Facility:** 100 units. 97 one-bedroom standard units, some with whirlpools. 3 one-bedroom suites. 4 stories, interior corridors. **Parking:** on-site. **Terms:** cancellation fee imposed, [CP] meal plan available, package plans. **Amenities:** hair dryers. *Some:* irons. **Pool(s):** heated indoor. **Leisure Activities:** whirlpool, snowmobiling, playground. *Fee:* game room. **Cards:** AX, CB, DC, DS, MC, VI. **Special Amenities:** free continental breakfast and free local telephone calls. *(See color ad p 413)*

SOME UNITS

(See map p. 336)

DAYS INN LAKEFRONT & SUITES — Phone: 906/643-8008 — **49**

(AAA) (SAVE)	6/26-8/23 [ECP]	1P: $79-$179	2P: $79-$179	XP: $6	D12
	8/24-10/11 [ECP]	1P: $59-$129	2P: $59-$129	XP: $6	D12
▽▽▽▽	4/1-6/25 [ECP]	1P: $59-$109	2P: $59-$109	XP: $6	D12
	10/12-3/31 [ECP]	1P: $49-$109	2P: $49-$109	XP: $6	D12

Small-scale Hotel **Location:** 2.8 mi n of bridge tollgate on I-75 business route. Located on the lake. 1067 N State St 49781. Fax: 906/643-9400. **Facility:** 105 units. 93 one- and 1 two-bedroom standard units, some with whirlpools. 11 one-bedroom suites ($89-$229), some with whirlpools. 2-3 stories, interior corridors. **Parking:** on-site. **Terms:** package plans. **Amenities:** irons, hair dryers. **Pool(s):** heated indoor. **Leisure Activities:** sauna, whirlpools, exercise room, volleyball. *Fee:* game room. **Guest Services:** coin laundry. **Cards:** AX, CB, DC, DS, MC, VI. **Special Amenities:** free continental breakfast and free newspaper. *(See color ad below & card insert)*

SOME UNITS

(See map p. 336)

DAYS INN ST. IGNACE
Phone: 906/643-7777 [44]

6/26-8/23 [ECP]	1P: $69-$159	2P: $69-$159	XP: $6	F12
8/24-10/11 [ECP]	1P: $49-$109	2P: $49-$109	XP: $6	F12
4/25-6/25 [ECP]	1P: $49-$99	2P: $49-$99	XP: $6	F12
10/12-10/26 [ECP]	1P: $49-$89	2P: $49-$89	XP: $6	F12

Motel **Location:** 2.8 mi n of bridge tollgate on I-75 business route. Located opposite the lake. 1074 N State St 49781. Fax: 906/643-9400. **Facility:** 74 one-bedroom standard units, some with whirlpools. 2 stories (no elevator), exterior corridors. **Parking:** on-site. **Terms:** open 4/25-10/26, package plans. **Amenities:** irons, hair dryers. **Pool(s):** heated indoor. **Leisure Activities:** whirlpool. *Fee:* game room. **Guest Services:** coin laundry. **Special Amenities:** free continental breakfast and free local telephone calls. *(See color ad below & card insert)*

SOME UNITS

(See map p. 336)

FOUR STAR MOTEL   Phone: 906/643-9360   46

6/21-9/8	2P: $38-$46	XP: $4
5/19-6/20 & 9/9-10/5	2P: $36-$40	XP: $4

Motel

Location: 2 mi w on US 2. Located in a semi-commercial area. 1064 US 2 W 49781. **Facility:** 20 units. 19 one- and 1 two-bedroom standard units. 1-2 stories (no elevator), exterior corridors. *Bath:* combo or shower only. **Parking:** on-site. **Terms:** open 5/19-10/5, 3 day cancellation notice. **Leisure Activities:** playground. **Cards:** AX, MC, VI.

HARBOUR POINTE LAKEFRONT LODGING   Phone: (906)643-6000   53

7/4-8/16 [ECP]	1P: $98-$179	2P: $98-$179
8/17-10/25 [ECP]	1P: $59-$159	2P: $59-$159
4/18-7/3 [ECP]	1P: $59-$139	2P: $59-$139

Small-scale Hotel

Location: 2 mi n of bridge tollgate on I-75 business route. 797 N State St 49781. Fax: 906/643-6946. **Facility:** 150 units. 140 one- and 10 two-bedroom standard units, some with whirlpools. 3 stories, interior/exterior corridors. **Parking:** on-site. **Terms:** open 4/18-10/25, cancellation fee imposed, package plans. **Amenities:** video library (fee), irons. **Pool(s):** heated outdoor, heated indoor. **Leisure Activities:** whirlpools, playground. *Fee:* game room. **Guest Services:** coin laundry. **Cards:** AX, DC, DS, MC, VI. **Special Amenities:** free continental breakfast and free local telephone calls. *(See color ad starting below)*

SOME UNITS

(See map p. 336)

HOLIDAY INN EXPRESS LAKEFRONT

Small-scale Hotel

	1P: $114-$129	2P: $114-$130	Phone: 906/643-0200	**52**
6/21-8/29			XP: $6	F16
8/30-12/31		2P: $80-$100	XP: $6	F16
4/1-6/20 & 1/1-3/31		2P: $60-$100	XP: $6	F16

Location: 2.3 mi n of bridge tollgate on I-75 business route. 965 N State St 49781. Fax: 906/643-0133. **Facility:** 85 one-bedroom standard units, some with whirlpools. 4 stories, interior corridors. *Bath:* combo or shower only. **Parking:** on-site. **Terms:** 3 day cancellation notice-fee imposed, [CP] & [ECP] meal plans available. **Amenities:** irons, hair dryers. **Pool(s):** heated indoor. **Leisure Activities:** whirlpool, snowmobiling. **Guest Services:** coin laundry. **Cards:** AX, DC, DS, MC, VI.

SOME UNITS

[ASK] [SD] [T+] [&] [🏊] [▶] [DATA PORT] / [X] /

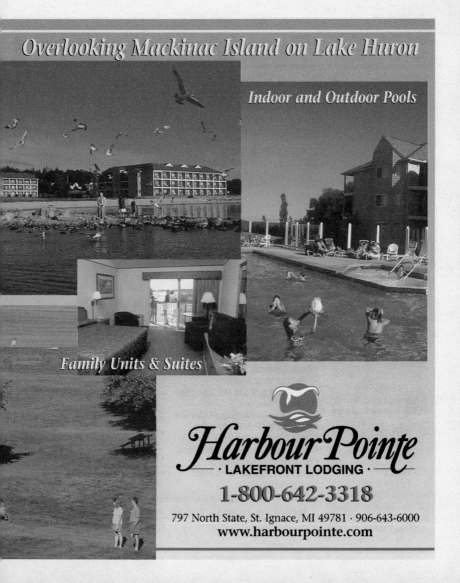

Overlooking Mackinac Island on Lake Huron

Indoor and Outdoor Pools

Family Units & Suites

Harbour Pointe
· LAKEFRONT LODGING ·

1-800-642-3318

797 North State, St. Ignace, MI 49781 · 906-643-6000

www.harbourpointe.com

(See map p. 336)

K-ROYALE MOTOR INN

AAA SAVE

Motel

				Phone: (906)643-7737	**47**
7/3-8/20 [CP]	1P: $58-$150	2P: $65-$150	XP: $5		F18
4/5-7/2 & 8/21-10/30 [CP]	1P: $42-$125	2P: $42-$125	XP: $5		F18

Location: 2.3 mi n of bridge toligate on I-75 business route. Located on the lake. 1037 N State St 49781. **Fax:** 906/643-8556. **Facility:** 95 units. 93 one- and 2 two-bedroom standard units. 3 stories (no elevator), exterior corridors. **Parking:** on-site. **Terms:** open 4/5-10/30, package plans. **Amenities:** *Some:* hair dryers. **Pool(s):** heated indoor. **Leisure Activities:** whirlpool, playground, volleyball. *Fee:* game room. **Guest Services:** gift shop, coin laundry. **Business Services:** meeting rooms. **Cards:** DC, MC, VI. *(See color ad below)*

SOME UNITS

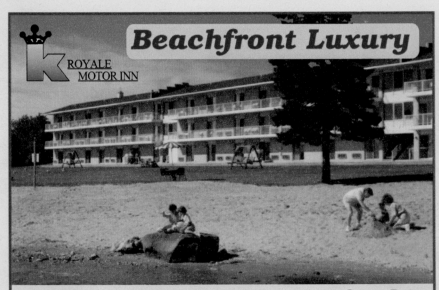

(See map p. 336)

QUALITY INN LAKEFRONT

			Phone: 906/643-7581	50
6/21-9/7	1P: $94-$180	2P: $104-$186	XP: $6	F16
4/7-6/20 & 9/8-10/31	1P: $44-$108	2P: $48-$116	XP: $6	F16

Motel

Location: 2.3 mi n of bridge tollgate, on I-75 business route. 1021 N State St 49781. Fax: 906/643-8573. **Facility:** 66 one-bedroom standard units, some with whirlpools. 3 stories, exterior corridors. **Parking:** on-site. **Terms:** open 4/7-10/31, 3 day cancellation notice-fee imposed, [CP] meal plan available. **Pool(s):** heated indoor. **Leisure Activities:** whirlpool, playground. **Cards:** AX, CB, DS, MC, VI. *(See color ad below)*

SOME UNITS

QUALITY INN ST. IGNACE

SAVE

Small-scale Hotel

			Phone: (906)643-9700	58
All Year [BP]	1P: $59-$129	2P: $69-$139	XP: $10	F17

Location: Jct I-75 and US 2 W. Located in a semi-commercial area. 913 Boulevard Dr 49781. Fax: 906/643-6762. **Facility:** 57 one-bedroom standard units, some with whirlpools. 2 stories (no elevator), interior corridors. **Parking:** on-site, winter plug-ins. **Terms:** weekly rates available, package plans - seasonally, pets ($10 extra charge). **Amenities:** irons, hair dryers. **Pool(s):** heated indoor. **Leisure Activities:** sauna, whirlpool, exercise room, basketball. *Fee:* snowmobiling, bicycles, game room. **Guest Services:** gift shop, coin laundry. **Business Services:** meeting rooms. **Cards:** AX, DS, MC, VI.

SOME UNITS

(See map p. 336)

RODEWAY INN

Phone: (906)643-8511 ②

AAA SAVE	6/16-9/6	1P: $79-$185	2P: $79-$185	XP: $8	F17
	4/1-6/15	1P: $49-$125	2P: $49-$125	XP: $6	F17
▼▼▼ ▼▼	9/7-3/31	1P: $49-$125	2P: $49-$125	XP: $8	F17

Location: At jct I-75 business route and US 2, just e. Located in a commercial area. 750 W US 2 49781.
Small-scale Hotel Fax: 906/643-6358. **Facility:** 42 one-bedroom standard units, some with whirlpools. 1-2 stories, interior/exterior corridors. **Parking:** on-site, winter plug-ins. **Terms:** cancellation fee imposed. **Amenities:** *Some:* hair dryers. **Pool(s):** heated indoor. **Leisure Activities:** whirlpool, snowmobiling. **Cards:** AX, CB, DC, DS, JC, MC, VI. **Special Amenities:** free continental breakfast and free local telephone calls.

SOME UNITS

🗕 🍽 🚦 🎥 🖨 / ✖ 🔓 📱 🖥 /

STRAITS BREEZE MOTEL

Phone: (906)643-9688 ④

AAA SAVE	6/26-8/25 [CP]	1P: $69-$130	2P: $69-$130	XP: $6	F17
	4/1-6/25 & 8/26-3/31 [CP]	1P: $49-$89	2P: $49-$99	XP: $6	F17

Location: Just e and on I-75 business route and US 2. 680 US 2 W 49781. Fax: 906/643-6320. **Facility:** 77 units. 70 Motel one- and 7 two-bedroom standard units, some with whirlpools. 1-2 stories (no elevator), interior/exterior corridors. **Parking:** on-site. **Pool(s):** heated indoor. **Leisure Activities:** whirlpool, snowmobiling, playground, shuffleboard. *Fee:* game room. **Business Services:** meeting rooms. **Cards:** AX, CB, DC, DS, MC, VI. **Special Amenities:** free continental breakfast and free local telephone calls. *(See color ad p 419)*

SOME UNITS

🗕 🍽 🚦 ✖ 🎥 🖥 / ✖ 🖨 /

SUPER 8 OF ST. IGNACE

Phone: 906/643-7616 ⑧

▼▼▼ ▼▼	6/26-8/31	1P: $88-$99	2P: $99-$109	XP: $5	F5
	4/1-6/25 & 9/1-3/31	1P: $58-$78	2P: $62-$88	XP: $5	F5

Small-scale Hotel **Location:** I-75, exit 344B, 0.5 mi w. Located in a commercial area. 923 W US 2 49781. Fax: 906/643-9286. **Facility:** 61 one-bedroom standard units, some with whirlpools. 3 stories, interior corridors. *Bath:* combo or shower only. **Parking:** on-site. **Terms:** [CP] meal plan available. **Amenities:** *Some:* hair dryers. **Pool(s):** heated indoor. **Leisure Activities:** whirlpool, snowmobiling. **Guest Services:** coin laundry. **Cards:** AX, DC, DS, MC, VI.

SOME UNITS

ASK 🗕 🍽 🚦 🎥 🖨 / ✖ 🖨 /

TRADEWINDS MOTEL

Phone: 906/643-9388 ⑵

▼	6/21-9/8	1P: $50-$65	2P: $59-$73	XP: $5	D
	4/1-6/20 & 9/9-10/28	1P: $35-$45	2P: $39-$49	XP: $5	D

Motel **Location:** 3 mi n of bridge tollgate on I-75 business route. Located in a semi-commercial area. 1190 N State St 49781. Fax: 906/643-9388. **Facility:** 25 one-bedroom standard units. 1 story, exterior corridors. *Bath:* shower only. **Parking:** on-site. **Terms:** open 4/1-10/28, weekly rates available. **Pool(s):** heated outdoor. **Leisure Activities:** playground.

SOME UNITS

🍽 🚦 🎥 🖥 🖨 / ✖ /

WAYSIDE MOTEL

Phone: (906)643-8944 ⑴

AAA SAVE	6/16-8/31	1P: $50-$75	2P: $50-$75	XP: $5	F12
▼▼	4/1-6/15 & 9/1-3/31	1P: $35-$50	2P: $35-$50	XP: $5	F12

Motel **Location:** 2 mi n of bridge toll gate on I-75 business route. Located in a semi-commercial area. 751 N State St 49781. Fax: 906/643-0207. **Facility:** 19 one-bedroom standard units. 1 story, exterior corridors. *Bath:* combo or shower only. **Parking:** on-site. **Terms:** small pets only ($5 extra charge). **Leisure Activities:** snowmobiling, basketball. **Cards:** DS, MC, VI. **Special Amenities:** free local telephone calls and preferred room (subject to availability with advanced reservations).

SOME UNITS

🗕 🚧 🎥 🖨 / ✖ /

───── WHERE TO DINE ─────

THE GALLEY RESTAURANT & BAR

Lunch: $5-$7   **Dinner:** $9-$16   **Phone:** 906/643-7960 ⑪

AAA ▼▼ **Location:** Center. 241 N State St 49781. **Hours:** Open 5/1-10/15; 7 am-10 pm. **Features:** On the shores of Lake Huron, the restaurant features photographs of freighters, lighthouses and ships as well as wildlife prints of ducks and loons. Great Lakes whitefish, trout and juicy roast prime rib are well-prepared and flavorful. Casual dress; cocktails. **Parking:** on-site. **Cards:** DS, MC, VI.

Steak & Seafood

🕳 ✖

NORTH BAY INN

Lunch: $4-$6   **Dinner:** $8-$15   **Phone:** 906/643-8304 ⑩

▼▼ **Location:** 3 mi n of bridge tollgate on I-75 business route. 1192 N State St 49781. **Hours:** Open 5/1-10/30; 7 am-9 American pm; to 10 pm 6/16-9/2. **Features:** Plants, flowers and paintings and photographs by local artists enhance the warm, comfortable feel of the dining room, a popular spot for family dining. Charbroiled steaks, whitefish, pasta and ribs are representative of menu options. Service is friendly. Casual dress; cocktails. **Parking:** on-site. **Cards:** MC, VI.

✖

ST. JOSEPH pop. 8,789

———— WHERE TO STAY ————

THE BOULEVARD INN & BISTRO
                 Phone: (269)983-6600
All Year   1P: $145-$225   2P: $145-$225   XP: $15   F18
Location: I-94, exit 23, 5 mi n on Red Arrow Highway, just w on Broad St, then just s; downtown. 521 Lake Blvd 49085.
Fax: 269/983-0520. **Facility:** 82 one-bedroom suites, some with whirlpools. 7 stories, interior corridors.
Parking: on-site. **Terms:** check-in 4 pm. **Amenities:** dual phone lines, voice mail, irons, hair dryers.
Small-scale Hotel **Dining:** 6:30 am-10 pm, cocktails. **Leisure Activities:** exercise room. **Guest Services:** valet laundry. **Business Services:** meeting rooms, business center. **Cards:** AX, DC, DS, MC, VI. **Special Amenities:** free local
telephone calls.

SOME UNITS

[🍽] [📷] [DATA PORT] [🔒] [💻] / [✕] [VCR] / FEE

CLARION HOTEL
                 Phone: (269)983-7341
6/21-9/10   1P: $94-$144   XP: $10   F18
4/1-6/20 & 9/11-3/31 1P: $79-$99   XP: $10   F18
Location: I-94 E, exit 27, 5 mi nw to Main St; I-94 W, exit 33, 4.8 mi w on Business I-94, then nw to Main St. 100 Main
St 49085. Fax: 269/983-0650. **Facility:** 149 one-bedroom standard units, some with whirlpools. 7 stories, in-
Small-scale Hotel terior corridors. *Bath:* combo or shower only. **Parking:** on-site. **Terms:** [ECP] meal plan available.
Amenities: irons, hair dryers. **Pool(s):** heated indoor. **Leisure Activities:** sauna, whirlpool, exercise room.
Fee: game room. **Business Services:** meeting rooms, business center. *(See color ad below)*

SOME UNITS

[S/D] [Y] [🛎] [🏊] [✕] [📷] [DATA PORT] [💻] / [✕] [VCR] [🔒] /

HOLIDAY INN EXPRESS HOTEL & SUITES
         Phone: (269)982-0004
5/1-10/31   1P: $92-$249   2P: $92-$249
4/1-4/30 & 11/1-3/31 1P: $92-$199   2P: $92-$199
Location: I-94, exit 23, 3.5 mi n. 3019 Lake Shore Dr 49085. Fax: 269/982-0023. **Facility:** 64 units. 61 one-
Small-scale Hotel bedroom standard units, some with whirlpools. 3 one-bedroom suites ($135-$249), some with whirlpools. 3
stories, interior corridors. *Bath:* combo or shower only. **Parking:** on-site. **Terms:** cancellation fee imposed, [ECP] meal plan available. **Amenities:** dual phone lines, voice mail, irons, hair dryers. **Pool(s):** heated indoor. **Leisure Activities:** whirlpool, exercise
room. **Guest Services:** complimentary laundry. **Business Services:** meeting rooms, business center. **Cards:** AX, CB, DC, DS,
JC, MC, VI. *(See color ad card insert)*

SOME UNITS

[ASK] [S/D] [🍽] [🛎] [🏊] [📷] [DATA PORT] [💻] / [✕] [VCR] [🔒] [📺] /

WHERE TO DINE

CLEMENTINE'S TOO
American
Lunch: $9-$14   **Dinner:** $9-$20   **Phone:** 269/983-0990
Location: I-94, exit 27 (SR 63), 2.6 mi n to Napier Ave, 0.3 mi e to Langley Ave, 1 mi n. 1235 Broad St 49085. **Hours:** 11 am-10 pm, Fri & Sat-11 pm, Sun noon-11 pm. Closed major holidays. **Features:** This is a relaxed family restaurant located next to the marina and a short walk from downtown. The menu features a lot of salads and lighter entrees with the house specialty being a hot apple dumpling dessert. Casual dress; cocktails. **Parking:** on-site. **Cards:** AX, DS, MC, VI.

MANSION GRILLE BY THE LAKE
American
Lunch: $6-$9   **Dinner:** $11-$25   **Phone:** 269/982-1500
Location: I-94, exit 23, 3.5 mi n. 3029 Lake Shore Dr 49085. **Hours:** 11 am-2 & 5-10 pm, Sat & Sun from 5 pm. Closed major holidays; also 12/24 & Mon. **Reservations:** suggested. **Features:** In a renovated 1892 mansion, the restaurant overlooks Lake Michigan. Dining is relaxed in the dining rooms and on the lovely front porch. The menu delivers large portions of such dishes as shrimp rangoon and broiled lobster with garlic mashed potatoes. Cocktails. **Parking:** on-site. **Cards:** AX, DS, MC, VI.

SCHU'S GRILL & BAR
American
Lunch: $4-$10   **Dinner:** $7-$15   **Phone:** 269/983-7248
Location: Between Pleasant and Ship sts; downtown. 501 Pleasant St 49085. **Hours:** 11 am-10 pm, Fri & Sat-11 pm, Sun noon-9 pm. Closed: 12/25. **Reservations:** accepted. **Features:** Rustic appointments give the casual dining room the ambience of a warm, friendly lodge. Traditional comfort foods, ranging from burgers and steaks to pasta and overstuffed sandwiches, please all members of the family. The local crowd flocks to this place. Casual dress; cocktails. **Parking:** street. **Cards:** AX, DS, MC, VI.

ST. LOUIS pop. 4,494

WHERE TO DINE

THE COUNTRY INN
American
Lunch: $5-$7   **Dinner:** $9-$14   **Phone:** 989/681-2213
Location: On SR 46, 1 mi e of US 127. 1875 W Monroe 48880. **Hours:** 11 am-8:30 pm, Sun-4 pm. Closed major holidays; also Mon. **Reservations:** accepted. **Features:** Country knickknacks decorate the homey dining room, an inviting spot in which families can relax. Sandwiches on fresh baked bread, homemade soup and such entrees as deep-fried cod are well-prepared and wholesome. Service is friendly and prompt. Casual dress. **Parking:** on-site. **Cards:** DS, MC, VI.

SANDUSKY pop. 2,745

WHERE TO STAY

WEST PARK INN
Small-scale Hotel
All Year [BP]   1P: $52-$62   2P: $57-$67   **Phone:** (810)648-4300   XP: $5
Location: In town on SR 46. 440 W Sanilac 48471. Fax: 810/648-4300. **Facility:** 29 one-bedroom standard units, some with whirlpools. 1-2 stories (no elevator), interior/exterior corridors. *Bath:* combo or shower only. **Parking:** on-site, winter plug-ins. **Amenities:** hair dryers. *Some:* irons. **Leisure Activities:** whirlpool, exercise room. **Guest Services:** valet laundry. **Business Services:** meeting rooms. **Cards:** AX, CB, DC, DS, MC, VI.
SOME UNITS

SAUGATUCK pop. 1,065—See also DOUGLAS.

WHERE TO STAY

CAPTAIN'S QUARTERS
Motel
Phone: (269)857-2525
6/2-9/10   1P: $69   2P: $185
4/20-6/1 & 9/11-10/25   1P: $59   2P: $185
Location: I-196, exit 41, 2 mi s; exit 36, 2 mi n. 3242 Blue Star Hwy (A-2) 49453. **Facility:** 16 one-bedroom standard units. 1 story, exterior corridors. *Bath:* combo or shower only. **Parking:** on-site. **Terms:** open 4/20-10/25, 2-3 night minimum stay - weekends, 7 day cancellation notice-fee imposed. **Amenities:** hair dryers. **Cards:** DS, MC, VI.
SOME UNITS

HOLIDAY INN EXPRESS
Small-scale Hotel
Phone: (269)857-7178
4/1-11/30   1P: $89-$189   2P: $89-$189   XP: $5   F
12/1-3/31   1P: $79-$129   2P: $79-$129   XP: $5   F
Location: I-196, exit 41, 1.3 mi sw on CR A2. 3457 Blue Star Hwy 49453. Fax: 269/857-7169. **Facility:** 52 one-bedroom standard units, some with whirlpools. 2 stories (no elevator), interior corridors. **Parking:** on-site. **Terms:** 2 night minimum stay - summer weekends, cancellation fee imposed, [CP] meal plan available. **Amenities:** irons, hair dryers. **Pool(s):** heated indoor. **Leisure Activities:** whirlpool, exercise room. **Guest Services:** coin laundry. **Business Services:** meeting rooms. **Cards:** AX, DC, DS, MC, VI. **Special Amenities:** free continental breakfast and free local telephone calls.
SOME UNITS

SAUGATUCK'S VICTORIAN INN
Bed & Breakfast
Phone: (269)857-3325
5/1-10/31   1P: $120-$220   2P: $120-$220
4/1-4/30 & 11/1-3/31   1P: $95-$175   2P: $95-$175
Location: Center of downtown. 447 Butler St 49453. Fax: 269/857-6043. **Facility:** Built in 1905 as the residence of the Koenig Hardware store owners, the inn includes an art gallery on the premises. Smoke free premises. 7 one-bedroom standard units, some with whirlpools. 2 stories (no elevator), interior corridors. *Bath:* combo or shower only. **Parking:** on-site. **Terms:** 2-3 night minimum stay - weekends in season, 7 day cancellation notice, [BP] meal plan available, no pets allowed (owner's pet on premises). **Amenities:** hair dryers. **Cards:** AX, DS, MC, VI. **Special Amenities:** free local telephone calls.

THE TIMBERLINE

AAA SAVE

Motel

	4/1-9/15 [CP]	1P: $95-$140	2P: $105-$160	XP: $10	F5
	9/16-10/31	1P: $55-$105	2P: $65-$115	XP: $10	F5
	11/1-3/31	1P: $50-$85	2P: $60-$95	XP: $10	F5

Phone: (269)857-2147

Location: I-196, between exits 36 and 41, on CR A2. Located in a quiet, country setting. 3353 Blue Star Hwy 49453 (PO Box 666). Fax: 269/857-2147. **Facility:** 28 units. 27 one-bedroom standard units, some with whirlpools. 1 one-bedroom suite ($160-$190) with kitchen. 1 story, exterior corridors. *Bath:* combo or shower only. **Parking:** on-site, winter plug-ins. **Terms:** 2-3 night minimum stay - weekends in season, 7 day cancellation notice-fee imposed. **Pool(s):** heated outdoor. **Leisure Activities:** whirlpool, picnic area, playground, horseshoes, volleyball. **Cards:** MC, VI.

SOME UNITS

[icons] / FEE

SAULT STE. MARIE pop. 16,542

──────── WHERE TO STAY ────────

BEST WESTERN SAULT STE MARIE

AAA SAVE

Small-scale Hotel

| | 6/14-10/12 [ECP] | 1P: $69-$149 | 2P: $69-$149 | XP: $6 | F18 |
| | 4/1-6/13 & 10/13-3/31 [ECP] | 1P: $49-$149 | 2P: $49-$149 | XP: $6 | F18 |

Phone: (906)632-2170

Location: I-75, exit 392, 0.3 mi ne. Located in a commercial area. 4281 I-75 Business Loop 49783. Fax: 906/632-7877. **Facility:** 108 units. 105 one-bedroom standard units, some with whirlpools. 3 one-bedroom suites ($89-$149) with efficiencies and whirlpools. 2 stories, interior/exterior corridors. *Bath:* combo or shower only. **Parking:** on-site. **Terms:** cancellation fee imposed, weekly rates available, package plans, pets ($15 fee, in designated units). **Amenities:** video library (fee), irons, hair dryers. **Pool(s):** heated indoor. **Leisure Activities:** sauna, snowmobiling. *Fee:* game room. **Guest Services:** coin laundry. **Business Services:** meeting rooms. **Cards:** AX, CB, DC, DS, MC, VI. **Special Amenities:** free continental breakfast and free room upgrade (subject to availability with advanced reservations).** *(See color ad below)*

SOME UNITS

[icons] FEE / [icons] FEE

BUDGET HOST CRESTVIEW INN

AAA SAVE

Motel

| | 6/15-10/15 [CP] | 1P: $49-$59 | 2P: $59-$79 | XP: $5 | F12 |
| | 4/1-6/14 & 10/16-3/31 [CP] | 1P: $39-$49 | 2P: $49-$69 | XP: $5 | F12 |

Phone: (906)635-5213

Location: I-75, exit 392, 2.8 mi ne on I-75 business loop. Located in a semi-commercial area. 1200 Ashmun St 49783. Fax: 906/635-9672. **Facility:** 43 one-bedroom standard units. 1 story, exterior corridors. *Bath:* combo or shower only. **Parking:** on-site, winter plug-ins. **Terms:** package plans, pets (in smoking units). **Cards:** AX, DS, MC, VI. **Special Amenities:** free continental breakfast and free local telephone calls.

(See color ad p 187 & below)

SOME UNITS

[icons] /

COMFORT INN

AAA SAVE

◆◆◆◆◆

Small-scale Hotel

			Phone: (906)635-1118
All Year	1P: $59-$299	2P: $59-$299	XP: $5 F18

Location: I-75, exit 392, at business spur. Located in front of Cascade Crossing Strip Mall. 4404 I-75 Business Spur 49783. Fax: 906/635-1119. **Facility:** 86 one-bedroom standard units, some with whirlpools. 2 stories, interior corridors. *Bath:* combo or shower only. **Parking:** on-site. **Terms:** weekly rates available. **Amenities:** safes (fee), hair dryers. *Some:* irons. **Pool(s):** heated indoor. **Leisure Activities:** whirlpool, snowmobiling, exercise room. **Guest Services:** coin laundry. **Cards:** AX, CB, DC, DS, JC, MC, VI. **Special Amenities:** free room upgrade and preferred room (each subject to availability with advanced reservations). *(See color ad below)*

SOME UNITS

DAYS INN

AAA SAVE

◆◆◆ ◆◆◆

Small-scale Hotel

			Phone: (906)635-5200
5/16-10/15 [ECP]	1P: $71-$80	2P: $71-$80	XP: $10 F
4/1-5/15 & 10/16-3/31 [ECP]	1P: $53-$62	2P: $53-$62	XP: $10 F

Location: I-75, exit 392, 0.8 mi ne on I-75 business loop. Located in a commercial area. 3651 I-75 Business Spur 49783. Fax: 906/635-9750. **Facility:** 84 one-bedroom standard units, some with whirlpools. 2 stories, interior corridors. **Parking:** on-site. **Amenities:** safes (fee), hair dryers. *Some:* irons. **Pool(s):** heated indoor. **Leisure Activities:** whirlpool, snowmobiling, limited exercise equipment. *Fee:* game room. **Guest Services:** coin laundry. **Cards:** AX, CB, DC, DS, MC, VI. **Special Amenities:** free continental breakfast and free local telephon calls.e/tq;rr *(See color ad card insert)*

SOME UNITS

DORAL MOTEL

AAA SAVE

◆◆◆

Motel

			Phone: (906)632-6621
6/16-10/30	1P: $62-$69	2P: $66-$72	XP: $5 F14
4/20-6/15	1P: $46-$52	2P: $48-$58	XP: $4 F14

Location: On I-75 business loop, just e of town. Located opposite Locks Boat Tour. 518 E Portage Ave 49783. Fax: 906/635-1089. **Parking:** on-site. **Terms:** open 4/20-10/30, weekly rates available, package plans. **Pool(s):** heated outdoor. **Leisure Activities:** sauna, whirlpool. *Fee:* game room. **Cards:** DS, MC, VI. **Special Amenities:** early check-in/late check-out and free local telephone calls.

SOME UNITS

HOLIDAY INN EXPRESS

Phone: (906)632-3999

AAA SAVE

6/16-10/16 [ECP]	1P: $69-$109	2P: $69-$109	XP: $10	F18
4/1-6/15 & 10/17-3/31 [ECP]	1P: $59-$89	2P: $59-$89	XP: $10	F18

Small-scale Hotel

Location: I-75, exit 394. Located close to the university. 1171 Riverview Way 49783. Fax: 906/632-9633. **Facility:** 97 one-bedroom standard units, some with whirlpools. 5 stories, interior corridors. *Bath:* combo or shower only. **Parking:** on-site, winter plug-ins. **Terms:** check-in 4 pm. **Amenities:** irons, hair dryers. **Pool(s):** heated indoor. **Leisure Activities:** whirlpool, exercise room. *Fee:* game room. **Guest Services:** valet and coin laundry. **Business Services:** meeting rooms. **Cards:** AX, CB, DC, DS, JC, MC, VI. **Special Amenities:** free continental breakfast and free local telephone calls. *(See color ad card insert)*

SOME UNITS

LA FRANCE TERRACE MOTEL

Phone: (906)632-7823

AAA SAVE

6/20-9/7	1P: $49-$59	2P: $49-$69	XP: $5	F12
9/8-10/26	1P: $42-$52	2P: $42-$62	XP: $5	F12
5/1-6/19	1P: $39-$49	2P: $42-$59	XP: $5	F12

Motel

Location: I-75, exit 392. 2.3 mi ne on I-75 business loop. Located in a commercial area. 1608 Ashmun St 49783. **Facility:** 30 units. 20 one- and 10 two-bedroom standard units. 1 story, exterior corridors. **Parking:** on-site. **Terms:** open 5/1-10/26. **Pool(s):** heated outdoor. **Leisure Activities:** playground. **Cards:** AX, DS, MC, VI. **Special Amenities:** free continental breakfast and free local telephone calls.

SOME UNITS

LAWSON MOTEL

Phone: 906/632-3322

AAA SAVE

7/1-9/10	1P: $48-$56	2P: $52-$62	XP: $5	F8
9/11-10/14	1P: $36-$48	2P: $42-$48	XP: $5	F8
4/1-6/30	1P: $36-$46	2P: $42-$48	XP: $5	F8
10/15-3/31	1P: $34-$42	2P: $38-$48	XP: $5	F8

Motel

Location: I-75, exit 392. 2 mi ne on I-75 business loop. Located in a commercial area. 2049 Ashmun St 49783. Fax: 906/632-4234. **Facility:** 16 one-bedroom standard units. 2 stories (no elevator), exterior corridors. **Parking:** on-site. **Leisure Activities:** playground. **Guest Services:** airport transportation-Chippewa County Airport. **Cards:** AX, DS, MC, VI. **Special Amenities:** early check-in/late check-out and free local telephone calls. *(See color ad below)*

SOME UNITS

MID-CITY MOTEL

Phone: (906)632-6832

AAA SAVE

6/15-10/15	1P: $48-$54	2P: $54-$58	XP: $5	D12
4/1-6/14 & 10/16-3/31	1P: $36-$48	2P: $46-$52	XP: $4	D12

Motel

Location: Just e of town, on I-75 business loop. 304 E Portage Ave 49783. **Facility:** 26 one-bedroom standard units. 2 stories (no elevator), exterior corridors. *Bath:* combo or shower only. **Parking:** on-site, winter plug-ins. **Terms:** small pets only. **Cards:** AX, DS, JC, MC, VI. **Special Amenities:** free local telephone calls and preferred room (subject to availability with advanced reservations).

SOME UNITS

One Perfect Gift

Give the gift of security, service, and savings — buy someone you care about a AAA gift membership. AAA memberships provide your loved ones more than emergency road service.

AAA members also have access to travel services, insurance, financial services, exclusive Show Your Card & Save® discounts, bail bond services, and more.

Give them more than a gift. Give them AAA. And let them discover how AAA can simplify their lives. Call or stop by your nearest AAA office today. And make AAA the one for you.

RAMADA PLAZA HOTEL OJIBWAY

Phone: (906)632-4100

(AAA) (SAVE)

◆◆◆ ◆◆

Classic
Large-scale Hotel

5/16-10/15	1P: $90-$155	2P: $90-$155	XP: $10	F18
4/1-5/15 & 10/16-3/31	1P: $72-$115	2P: $72-$115	XP: $10	F18

Location: Just w of I-75 business loop; center of downtown. 240 W Portage Ave 49783. Fax: 906/632-6050. **Facility:** 71 units. 65 one-bedroom standard units. 6 one-bedroom suites ($150-$250) with whirlpools. 6 stories, interior corridors. **Parking:** on-site, winter plug-ins. **Terms:** cancellation fee imposed, [BP] meal plan available. **Amenities:** voice mail, irons, hair dryers. **Dining:** Freighters, see separate listing. **Pool(s):** heated indoor. **Leisure Activities:** sauna, whirlpool, exercise room. **Guest Services:** valet and coin laundry, area transportation. **Business Services:** meeting rooms, business center. **Special Amenities:** early check-in/late check-out and free newspaper. *(See color ad p 426)*

SOME UNITS

ROYAL MOTEL

Phone: (906)632-6323

◆◆◆

Motel

5/15-10/15	1P: $38-$46	2P: $46-$54	XP: $6	F13

Location: I-75, exit 392, 2 mi ne on I-75 business loop. Located in a commercial area. 1707 Ashmun St 49783. **Facility:** 20 one-bedroom standard units. 1 story, exterior corridors. *Bath:* combo or shower only. **Parking:** on-site. **Terms:** open 5/15-10/15, weekly rates available, [CP] meal plan available, small pets only. **Leisure Activities:** playground, basketball. **Cards:** DC, MC, VI.

SOME UNITS

SKYLINE MOTEL

Phone: (906)632-3393

◆◆◆

Motel

5/1-10/31 [CP]	1P: $38-$48	2P: $48-$68

Location: I-75, exit 392, 1.5 mi ne. Located in a commercial area. 2601 I-75 Business Loop 49783. **Facility:** 24 one-bedroom standard units. 2 stories (no elevator), exterior corridors. **Parking:** on-site, winter plug-ins. **Terms:** open 5/1-10/31, cancellation fee imposed, weekly rates available. **Leisure Activities:** snowmobiling. **Cards:** AX, DS, MC, VI.

SOME UNITS

SUNSET MOTEL

Phone: 906/632-3906

(AAA) (SAVE)

◆◆◆

Motel

6/1-10/15	1P: $42-$46	2P: $45-$49	XP: $4

Location: I-75, exit 386, 0.3 mi e to jct SR 28 and CR H-63. Located in a rural area. 8929 S Mackinaw Tr 49783. **Facility:** 15 one-bedroom standard units. 1 story, exterior corridors. *Bath:* combo or shower only. **Parking:** on-site. **Terms:** open 6/1-10/15. **Leisure Activities:** playground, basketball. **Cards:** DS, MC, VI. **Special Amenities:** free local telephone calls.

SOME UNITS

SUPER 8 MOTEL

Phone: (906)632-8882

◆◆◆ ◆◆

Small-scale Hotel

6/20-9/30 [CP]	1P: $61-$71	2P: $65-$75	XP: $5	F17
4/25-6/19 [CP]	1P: $52-$62	2P: $58-$68	XP: $5	F17
10/1-3/31 [CP]	1P: $45-$55	2P: $55-$65	XP: $5	F17
4/1-4/24 [CP]	1P: $44-$54	2P: $54-$64	XP: $5	F17

Location: I-75, exit 392, 0.5 mi ne. Located in a commercial area. 3826 I-75 Business Loop 49783. Fax: 906/632-3766. **Facility:** 61 one-bedroom standard units, some with whirlpools. 2 stories (no elevator), interior corridors. **Parking:** on-site. **Terms:** pets ($50 deposit). **Leisure Activities:** snowmobiling. **Guest Services:** coin laundry. **Cards:** AX, CB, DC, DS, MC, VI.

SOME UNITS

———— **WHERE TO DINE** ————

ABNER'S

◆◆◆

American

Lunch: $4-$6   Dinner: $8-$19   Phone: 906/632-4221

Location: I-75, exit 392, 1.3 mi ne on I-75 business loop. 3783 I-75 Business Spur 49783. **Hours:** 8 am-midnight, Sun-10 pm. Closed: 11/27, 12/25. **Reservations:** accepted. **Features:** The "backwoods buffet", available for breakfast, lunch and dinner, lays out a nice variety of home-style dishes made from scratch. Fireplaces, hardwood floors and country antiques contribute to the warm, homey ambience. Service is friendly. Casual dress; cocktails. **Parking:** on-site. **Cards:** AX, DC, MC, VI.

THE ANTLER'S

◆◆◆

American

Lunch: $5-$8   Dinner: $9-$19   Phone: 906/632-3571

Location: 8 blks e at end of I-75 business spur. 804 E Portage Ave 49783. **Hours:** 11am-10 pm, closing times vary in winter. Closed: 4/20, 11/27, 12/24, 12/25. **Features:** More than 200 mounted animals and a bell-and-whistle sound display lend to the casual ambience of the large, noisy restaurant. A tasty homemade barbecue sauce wakes up the flavor in slow-cooked baby back ribs. Service is friendly and efficient. Casual dress; cocktails. **Parking:** on-site. **Cards:** MC, VI.

CUP OF THE DAY

◆◆◆

American

Lunch: $4-$8   Dinner: $4-$8   Phone: 906/635-7272

Location: Center. 406 Ashmun St 49783. **Hours:** 7 am-8 pm. Closed: 1/1, 11/27, 12/25. **Features:** As you might guess from the name, the restaurant specializes in coffee drinks. The menu centers on lighter fare—salad, sandwiches and delicious dessert. A wide variety of juice is available at the raw juice bar. Casual dress. **Parking:** street. **Cards:** DS, MC, VI.

FREIGHTERS

◆◆◆ ◆◆

American

Lunch: $7-$10   Dinner: $15-$25   Phone: 906/632-4211

Location: Just w of I-75 business loop; center of downtown; in Ramada Plaza Hotel Ojibway. 240 W Portage 49783. **Hours:** 7 am-9 pm. **Features:** Overlooking the Soo Locks and a little park below, the intimate restaurant is a comfortable spot for casual upscale dining. The specials are always a treat, especially the succulent prime rib offered on Sunday nights. Cocktails. **Parking:** on-site. **Cards:** AX, CB, DC, MC, VI.

(See color ad p 426)

LA SENORITA
△△ (diamond symbol)

Mexican

Lunch: $4-$7   **Dinner:** $8-$13   **Phone:** 906/632-1114
Location: Jct I-75 and I-75 business spur, exit 392. 4478 I-75 Business Spur 49783. **Hours:** 11 am-10 pm, Fri & Sat-11 pm, Sun noon-10 pm. Closed major holidays. **Reservations:** accepted. **Features:** This family friendly restaurant offers such traditional favorites as burritos, enchiladas and fajitas, as well as mesquite-grilled entrees served in a festive, lively atmosphere. Vibrant Mexican decorations brighten the dining room. Casual dress; cocktails. **Parking:** on-site. **Cards:** AX, DC, DS, MC, VI.

STUDEBAKERS
(AAA) △△

American

Lunch: $4-$8   **Dinner:** $9-$20   **Phone:** 906/632-4262
Location: I-75, exit 392, 0.8 mi ne on I-75 business spur. 3583 I-75 Business Spur 49783. **Hours:** 7 am-9 pm, Fri & Sat-10 pm; 7 am-10 pm 6/1-10/15. Closed: 11/27, 12/25. **Reservations:** accepted. **Features:** An interesting collection of old Studebaker pictures—as well as parts and other period collectibles—decorates the restaurant, which is likely to stir feelings of nostalgia. The specialty is whitefish, which is served pan-fried, broiled or deep-fried. Casual dress; cocktails. **Parking:** on-site. **Cards:** AX, MC, VI.

The following restaurant has not been evaluated by AAA but is listed for your information only.

GREAT WALL
[fyi]

    Phone: 906/635-1188
Not evaluated. **Location:** 3440 I-75 Business Spur 49783. **Features:** The buffet and carry-out menus feature Hunan, Szechuan and Cantonese dishes.

SAWYER

--- **WHERE TO STAY** ---

SUPER 8 MOTEL
(AAA) [SAVE]
△△ △△

Small-scale Hotel

    Phone: (269)426-8300

5/1-9/30 [CP]	1P: $59-$89	2P: $64-$104
4/1-4/30 & 10/1-3/31 [CP]	1P: $55-$85	2P: $60-$90

Location: I-94, exit 12, just e. 12850 Super Dr 49125. Fax: 269/426-6500. **Facility:** 61 one-bedroom standard units, some with whirlpools. 3 stories, interior corridors. *Bath:* combo or shower only. **Parking:** on-site. **Terms:** 5 day cancellation notice, weekly rates available, package plans. **Amenities:** voice mail. *Some:* hair dryers. **Pool(s):** heated indoor. **Business Services:** meeting rooms. **Cards:** AX, DC, DS, MC, VI.

SOME UNITS

--- **WHERE TO DINE** ---

HORSEFEATHERS RESTAURANT & MARKET   **Lunch:** $8-$15   **Dinner:** $12-$18   **Phone:** 269/426-3237
△△ △△

American

Location: I-94, exit 12, 0.3 mi w on Sawyer Rd, then just n. 12857 Three Oaks Rd 49125. **Hours:** 11:30 am-10 pm, Fri-11 pm, Sat 9 am-11 pm, Sun 9 am-10 pm. Closed major holidays. **Features:** Contemporary American cuisine such as hearty soups, harbor chicken marsala and barbecued ribs are all prominently featured in this attractive and whimsical roadside diner. Casual dress; cocktails. **Parking:** on-site. **Cards:** MC, VI.

SHELBYVILLE

--- **WHERE TO DINE** ---

BAY POINTE RESTAURANT   Historic   **Lunch:** $7-$10   **Dinner:** $17-$24   **Phone:** 269/672-5202
△△ △△

American

Location: US 131, exit 59 (Shelbyville), 4 mi e on 124th to dead end, then 2 mi s. 11456 Marsh Rd 49344. **Hours:** 11:30 am-3 & 5-10 pm, Sat from 5 pm, Sun 10:30 am-1:30 pm; Fri & Sat 5 pm-10 pm 1/1-1/3. Closed: 12/25; also Mon. **Features:** The 1902 Dutch Colonial house affords beautiful views of the adjacent lake. Specialties of whitefish, Yankee Springs pork loin and roasted duck stand out on the varied menu. Desserts change often. The dining room is casual, with a slightly elegant flair. Semi-formal attire; cocktails. **Parking:** on-site. **Cards:** AX, DS, MC, VI.

SILVER CITY

——— WHERE TO STAY ———

AMERICINN OF THE PORCUPINE MOUNTAINS

Phone: (906)885-5311

<AAA> (SAVE)
♦♦♦ ♦♦♦

Large-scale Hotel

6/15-10/14 & 12/15-3/31 [CP]	1P: $87-$115	2P: $87-$115	XP: $6
4/1-6/14 & 10/15-12/14 [CP]	1P: $77-$105	2P: $77-$105	XP: $6

Location: On SR 107, 0.3 mi w of SR 64. 120 Lincoln Ave (120 Lincoln Ave, ONTONAGON, 49953). Fax: 906/885-5847. **Facility:** 70 units. 64 one-bedroom standard units, some with whirlpools. 6 one-bedroom suites. 3 stories, interior corridors. **Parking:** on-site, winter plug-ins. **Terms:** pets ($10 extra charge, no cats). **Amenities:** irons, hair dryers. **Dining:** 4:30 pm-9 pm, cocktails. **Pool(s):** heated indoor. **Leisure Activities:** sauna, whirlpool, fishing, snowmobiling. **Guest Services:** gift shop. **Business Services:** meeting rooms. **Cards:** AX, DC, DS, MC, VI. **Special Amenities:** free continental breakfast and free local telephone calls. *(See color ad below)*

SOME UNITS

(S⊘D) ☐ ☐ ⊞ ⬜ ➔ ⊠ ⛷ DATA/PORT ⬜ / ⊠ ⊟ /

MOUNTAIN VIEW LODGES

Phone: 906/885-5256

♦♦♦ ♦♦♦

Cottage

4/1-10/16	1P: $119-$124	2P: $119-$124	XP: $11	D17
10/17-12/24	1P: $124	2P: $124	XP: $11	D17
12/25-3/31	1P: $104-$119	2P: $104-$119	XP: $11	D17

Location: Jct SR 107 and 64, 0.8 mi w on SR 107. 237 M-107 49953 (237 M-107, ONTONAGON). Fax: 906/885-5947. **Facility:** 11 cottages. 1 story, exterior corridors. **Parking:** on-site. **Terms:** check-in 4 pm, 2 night minimum stay, 14 day cancellation notice-fee imposed, pets (in designated units). **Leisure Activities:** snowmobiling. **Cards:** AX, DC, MC, VI.

SOME UNITS

☐ Ⓐ VCR DATA/PORT ⬛ ⬜ ⬜ / ⊠ /

TOMLINSON'S RAINBOW LODGING

Phone: (906)885-5348

<AAA> (SAVE)
♦♦♦ ♦♦♦

Motel

6/15-10/31 & 12/20-3/31	1P: $58-$75	2P: $69-$75	XP: $5 F12
4/1-6/14 & 11/1-12/19	1P: $49-$59	2P: $59-$65	XP: $5 F12

Location: SR 64, just e of jct SR 107. 2900 M-64 49953 (2900 M-64, ONTONAGON). Fax: 906/885-5272. **Facility:** 17 units. 12 one-bedroom standard units, some with kitchens. 2 one-, 1 two- and 1 three-bedroom suites ($83-$95), some with efficiencies, kitchens and/or whirlpools. 1 vacation home ($150). 1 story, exterior corridors. *Bath:* combo or shower only. **Parking:** on-site, winter plug-ins. **Terms:** 30 day cancellation notice, weekly rates available, [ECP] meal plan available, small pets only ($5 fee, $50 deposit, no cats). **Leisure Activities:** sauna, whirlpool, paddleboats, snowmobiling, screen-house gazebo on Lake Superior, playground. *Fee:* miniature golf, bicycles. **Guest Services:** coin laundry, tanning facility. **Cards:** AX, DS, MC, VI.

SOME UNITS

(S⊘D) ☐ ⊞↦ ⊠ DATA/PORT ⬛ ⬜ ⬜ / ⊠ /

SOUTHFIELD —See Detroit p. 270.

SOUTHGATE —See Detroit p. 273.

SOUTH HAVEN pop. 5,021

———— WHERE TO STAY ————

CARRIAGE HOUSE AT THE HARBOR BED & BREAKFAST
Phone: 269/639-2161

(AAA) (SAVE)

▽▼▽▼▽▼▽

Bed & Breakfast

4/1-11/1 [BP]	1P: $145-$240	2P: $145-$240
11/2-3/31 [BP]	1P: $120-$195	2P: $120-$195

Location: 1.2 mi n of downtown on Dyckman Ave, just s on North Shore Dr. Located in a residential area. 118 Woodman St 49090. Fax: 269/639-2308. **Facility:** Just a block from Lake Michigan, this B&B is decorated with antiques and offers rooms with gas fireplaces or views of the harbor. Smoke free premises. 11 one-bedroom standard units, some with whirlpools. 3 stories (no elevator), interior corridors. *Bath:* combo or shower only. **Parking:** on-site. **Terms:** 2 night minimum stay - weekends, age restrictions may apply, 10 day cancellation notice. **Amenities:** video library, hair dryers. **Business Services:** meeting rooms. **Cards:** AX, DS, MC, VI.

S🄳 ✕ VCR ☎

GUESTHOUSE INTERNATIONAL LIGHTHOUSE INN
Phone: (269)639-9900

▽▼▽▼▽▼▽

Small-scale Hotel

6/27-9/2 [ECP]	1P: $95-$135	2P: $95-$135	XP: $5	F18
5/23-6/26 [ECP]	1P: $80-$99	2P: $80-$99	XP: $5	F18
9/3-3/31 [ECP]	1P: $79-$89	2P: $79-$89	XP: $5	F18
4/1-5/22 [ECP]	1P: $65-$79	2P: $65-$79	XP: $5	F18

Location: I-196, exit 20, just e. 1555 Phoenix St 49090. Fax: 269/639-9900. **Facility:** 91 units. 90 one-bedroom standard units, some with whirlpools. 1 one-bedroom suite ($110-$250) with whirlpool. 3 stories, interior corridors. *Bath:* combo or shower only. **Parking:** on-site, winter plug-ins. **Terms:** check-in 4 pm, 3 day cancellation notice-fee imposed, weekly rates available. **Amenities:** irons, hair dryers. *Some:* DVD players. **Pool(s):** heated indoor. **Leisure Activities:** whirlpool, exercise room. **Business Services:** meeting rooms. **Cards:** AX, DC, DS, MC, VI.

SOME UNITS
A$K S🄳 🍴+ ⌖M ⌖ 🏊 📷 DATAPORT 🖥 📠 🖥 / ✕ VCR /

HAMPTON INN
Phone: (269)639-8550

(SAVE)

▽▼▽▼▽▼▽

Small-scale Hotel

6/1-9/7 [ECP]	1P: $109-$149	2P: $109-$149
9/8-12/31 [ECP]	1P: $89-$109	2P: $89-$109
4/1-5/31 [ECP]	1P: $89-$99	2P: $89-$99
1/1-3/31 [ECP]	1P: $79-$99	2P: $79-$99

Location: I-196, exit 20, just e. 04299 Cecilia Dr 49090. Fax: 269/639-8555. **Facility:** 62 units. 60 one-bedroom standard units, some with whirlpools. 2 one-bedroom suites ($109-$179) with whirlpools. 3 stories, interior corridors. *Bath:* combo or shower only. **Parking:** on-site. **Amenities:** dual phone lines, voice mail, irons, hair dryers. **Pool(s):** heated indoor. **Leisure Activities:** whirlpool, exercise room. **Guest Services:** coin laundry. **Business Services:** meeting rooms. **Cards:** AX, CB, DC, DS, JC, MC, VI.

SOME UNITS
S🄳 🍴+ 🏊 DATAPORT 🖥 / ✕ 🖥 🖥 /

HOLIDAY INN EXPRESS HOTEL & SUITES
Phone: (269)637-8800

▽▼▽▼▽▼

Small-scale Hotel

7/1-9/5	1P: $99-$199	2P: $99-$199	XP: $10	F18
4/1-6/30	1P: $69-$179	2P: $69-$179	XP: $10	F18
9/6-10/31	1P: $89-$159	2P: $89-$159	XP: $10	F18
11/1-3/31	1P: $69-$139	2P: $69-$139	XP: $10	F18

Location: I-196, exit 20, just e. 1741 Phoenix Rd 49090. Fax: 269/637-8810. **Facility:** 62 units. 61 one-bedroom standard units, some with whirlpools. 1 one-bedroom suite with whirlpool. 3 stories, interior corridors. *Bath:* combo or shower only. **Parking:** on-site. **Terms:** cancellation fee imposed. **Amenities:** dual phone lines, voice mail, irons, hair dryers. **Pool(s):** heated indoor. **Leisure Activities:** exercise room. **Guest Services:** valet laundry. **Business Services:** meeting rooms. **Cards:** AX, CB, DC, DS, MC, VI.

SOME UNITS
A$K S🄳 🏊 📷 DATAPORT 🖥 / ✕ 🖥 🖥 /

INN AT THE PARK BED & BREAKFAST
Phone: 269/639-1776

▽▼▽▼▽▼

Bed & Breakfast

7/1-9/5 [BP]	1P: $140-$235	2P: $140-$235
9/6-10/31 [BP]	1P: $110-$205	2P: $110-$205
4/1-6/30 [BP]	1P: $80-$205	2P: $80-$205
11/1-3/31 [BP]	1P: $80-$175	2P: $80-$175

Location: I-196, exit 20, 0.9 mi w on Phoenix St, just n on Broadway, then just w; across the bridge. 233 Dyckman Ave 49090. Fax: 269/639-2409. **Facility:** Stained glass and sun-filled common areas add to the appeal of this Victorian-style home resembling a country inn. Smoke free premises. 9 one-bedroom standard units, some with whirlpools. 2 stories (no elevator), interior corridors. *Bath:* combo or shower only. **Parking:** on-site. **Terms:** 2-3 night minimum stay - weekends, age restrictions may apply, 14 day cancellation notice. **Amenities:** video library. **Business Services:** meeting rooms. **Cards:** AX, MC, VI.

🍴+ ✕ VCR ☎

OLD HARBOR INN
Phone: (269)637-8480

(AAA) (SAVE)

▽▼▽▼▽▼▽

Small-scale Hotel

6/1-9/1 [CP]	1P: $119-$299	2P: $119-$299	XP: $10	F18
9/2-10/31 [CP]	1P: $79-$299	2P: $79-$299	XP: $10	F18
4/1-5/31 [CP]	1P: $79-$239	2P: $79-$239	XP: $10	F18
11/1-3/31 [CP]	1P: $79-$199	2P: $79-$199	XP: $10	F18

Location: I-196, exit 20, 1 mi w on Phoenix St, just n on Center St. Located in a commercial area. 515 Williams St 49090. Fax: 269/637-9496. **Facility:** 44 units. 43 one-bedroom standard units, some with whirlpools. 1 two-bedroom suite. 3 stories, interior/exterior corridors. **Parking:** on-site. **Amenities:** irons. *Some:* hair dryers. **Dining:** 5 pm-10 pm, cocktails. **Pool(s):** small heated indoor. **Leisure Activities:** whirlpool. **Guest Services:** coin laundry. **Business Services:** meeting rooms. **Cards:** AX, CB, DC, DS, JC, MC, VI. **Special Amenities:** free local telephone calls and free newspaper.

SOME UNITS
S🄳 🍴 Y 🏊 🖥 🖥 🖥 / ✕ 🖥 /

SAND CASTLE INN

Phone: 269/639-1110

Bed & Breakfast

4/1-8/31 [BP]	1P: $110-$225	2P: $110-$225	XP: $20
9/1-10/31 [BP]	1P: $110-$210	2P: $110-$210	XP: $20
11/1-3/31 [BP]	1P: $110-$175	2P: $110-$175	XP: $20

Location: I-196, exit 20, 0.9 mi n on Broadway, then just w; across the bridge. 203 Dyckman Ave 49090. Fax: 269/637-1050. **Facility:** The inn offers a retreat-like ambience and is within walking distance of the river, the lake and downtown. Smoke free premises. 9 one-bedroom standard units. 3 stories (no elevator), interior/exterior corridors. *Bath:* shower only. **Parking:** on-site. **Terms:** 2 night minimum stay - weekends, age restrictions may apply, 10 day cancellation notice-fee imposed, weekly rates available. **Amenities:** video library, hair dryers. **Cards:** AX, DS, MC, VI.

THE SEYMOUR HOUSE BED & BREAKFAST

Phone: 269/227-3918

Historic Bed & Breakfast

All Year	1P: $110-$140	2P: $110-$140

Location: I-196, exit 26, 1 mi w, 3 mi n. Located in a quiet, rural area. 1248 Blue Star Hwy 49090. Fax: 269/227-3010. **Facility:** Built in 1862, this countryside B&B is on 11 acres of old apple orchard and offers a relaxed, country-house ambience. Smoke free premises. 7 units. 5 one-bedroom standard units, some with whirlpools. 2 cabins ($125-$145). 2 stories (no elevator), interior/exterior corridors. *Bath:* combo or shower only. **Parking:** on-site. **Terms:** check-in 4 pm, age restrictions may apply, 14 day cancellation notice-fee imposed, [BP] meal plan available. **Amenities:** video library. **Leisure Activities:** canoeing, paddleboats, fishing, cross country skiing. **Business Services:** fax. **Cards:** DC, MC, VI.

THE VICTORIA RESORT B&B

Phone: 269/637-6414

Bed & Breakfast

5/23-10/31 [ECP]	1P: $85-$175	2P: $85-$175	XP: $20
4/1-5/22 & 11/1-3/31 [ECP]	1P: $60-$145	2P: $60-$145	XP: $10

Location: I-196, exit 20, 0.9 mi w on Broadway to Dyckman Ave, just w to Park St, 0.4 mi n, then just e. 241 Oak St 49090. Fax: 269/637-6127. **Facility:** Designated smoking area. 14 units. 7 one-bedroom standard units, some with whirlpools. 2 one-bedroom suites with whirlpools. 5 cottages ($1120-$1225), some with whirlpools. 1-2 stories (no elevator), interior/exterior corridors. **Parking:** on-site. **Terms:** 2 night minimum stay - weekends, 7 day cancellation notice-fee imposed, package plans - in winter, no pets allowed (owner's pets on premises). **Amenities:** video library, hair dryers. **Pool(s):** outdoor. **Leisure Activities:** tennis court, bicycles, playground, basketball, shuffleboard. **Cards:** MC, VI.

——— WHERE TO DINE ———

CLEMENTINE'S

American

Lunch: $9-$14 **Dinner: $9-$20** **Phone: 269/637-4755**

Location: I-196, exit 20, 2.5 mi w. 500 Phoenix St 49090. **Hours:** 11 am-11 pm, Fri & Sat-midnight, Sun noon-11 pm. Closed major holidays. **Features:** This is a relaxed, family restaurant located right downtown. The menu features alot of salad and lighter entrees with the house specialty being a hot apple dumpling dessert. Casual dress; cocktails. **Parking:** street. **Cards:** AX, DS, MC, VI.

HAWKSHEAD

American

Lunch: $8-$14 **Dinner: $17-$30** **Phone: 269/639-2146**

Location: I-196, exit 22, just e on N Shore Dr, 2.5 mi n on 71st St/103rd Ave, then 0.4 mi e. 6959 105th Ave 49090. **Hours:** 11 am-9:30 pm. Closed major holidays. **Reservations:** accepted. **Features:** Located in a converted Tudor house, this relaxing space with large floor to ceiling windows allows a good view of the golf course and landscaped gardens. A creative touch is evident on this continental menu that not only offers steaks and duck but also seafood such as shrimp and locally caught whitefish. Dressy casual; cocktails. **Parking:** on-site. **Cards:** MC, VI.

MAGNOLIA GRILLE

American

Lunch: $7-$12 **Dinner: $17-$23** **Phone: 269/637-8435**

Location: I-196, exit 20, 1 mi w on Phoenix St, just n on Center St; in Old Harbor Village. 515 Williams St #10 49090. **Hours:** Open 4/1-9/12; 11 am-2 & 5-10 pm, Fri & Sat-11 pm, Sun 11 am-3 & 4-9 pm. **Reservations:** suggested; weekends. **Features:** Docked at Nichols Landing on the Black River, the floating riverboat restaurant has many windows that look out at natural settings. Blackened prime rib, Bloody Mary linguine and piquant seafood jambalaya are representative of tasty menu offerings. Casual dress; cocktails. **Parking:** on-site. **Cards:** AX, CB, DC, DS, MC, VI.

PHOENIX STREET CAFE

Deli/Subs Sandwiches

Lunch: $5-$7 **Phone: 269/637-3600**

Location: I-196, exit 20. 524 Phoenix St 49090. **Hours:** 7 am-3 pm. Closed major holidays. **Features:** Resort posters adorn the walls of this cheerful downtown restaurant, specializing in house made soups and an extensive sandwich menu. Casual dress. **Parking:** on-site and street. **Cards:** AX, MC, VI.

THE THREE PELICANS

American

Lunch: $7-$13 **Dinner: $16-$24** **Phone: 269/637-5123**

Location: I-196, exit 22, 0.9 mi w on Phoenix St, just n on Dyckman Ave, then just s. 38 North Shore Dr 49090. **Hours:** Open 4/25-10/25; 11:30 am-10 pm, Fri & Sat-11 pm, Sun-9 pm; hours and days vary, call to verify. **Reservations:** suggested. **Features:** The atmosphere is nautical inside the cozy restaurant, a favorite spot for boaters and beachgoers. Ribs stand out on a menu of traditional surf and turf choices. Opt for seating on the outdoor deck to watch boats pass by on the peaceful Black River. Casual dress; cocktails. **Parking:** on-site. **Cards:** AX, DC, DS, MC, VI.

SPRING LAKE pop. 2,514

————— WHERE TO STAY —————

HOLIDAY INN GRAND HAVEN-SPRING LAKE
▼▼▼∿∿∿

	7/1-9/2	1P: $139-$199	XP: $20	F18
	5/22-6/30	1P: $129-$159	XP: $20	F18
	4/1-5/21 & 9/3-3/31	1P: $119-$139	XP: $20	F18

Phone: (616)846-1000

Large-scale Hotel   **Location:** On SR 104, just e of US 131. Located on the river. 940 W Savidge St 49456. Fax: 616/846-0462.
Facility: 120 one-bedroom standard units, some with whirlpools. 4 stories, interior corridors. *Bath:* combo or shower only.
Parking: on-site. **Terms:** check-in 4 pm, 2 night minimum stay - 5/1-8/31, package plans, pets ($25 extra charge, dogs only).
Amenities: dual phone lines, voice mail, irons, hair dryers. **Pool(s):** heated outdoor, heated indoor. **Leisure Activities:** whirlpool, recreation programs, bicycles, exercise room, horseshoes, volleyball. *Fee:* charter fishing. **Guest Services:** valet and coin laundry. **Business Services:** meeting rooms. **Cards:** AX, CB, DC, DS, JC, MC, VI.

SOME UNITS

(ASK) (S/D) 🛏 (¶¶) (Y) (➰) (✕) (🐾) (DATA PORT) (💻) / (✕) ▢ / FEE

STERLING pop. 533

————— WHERE TO DINE —————

IVA'S CHICKEN DINNERS   **Lunch:** $5-$7   **Dinner:** $8-$14   **Phone:** 989/654-3552
◉◉◉   **Location:** I-75, exit 195, 1.8 mi e on Sterling Rd/State, 0.3 mi s on Saginaw St, follow signs. 201 Chestnut St 48659.
∿∿∿   **Hours:** 11:30 am-8:30 pm. Closed: Tues 11/16-1/14, also Mon-Wed 1/15-5/15. **Features:** Family owned
since 1938, the restaurant—in a late-19th-century house—features family- and plate-style chicken, steak,
chops and seafood. Pictures around the laid-back dining room are of a religious nature. Servers are
American   friendly and efficient. Casual dress; cocktails. **Parking:** on-site. **Cards:** MC, VI.   (✕)

STERLING HEIGHTS —See Detroit p. 273.

STEVENSVILLE pop. 1,191

————— WHERE TO STAY —————

BAYMONT INN & SUITES-ST. JOSEPH (STEVENSVILLE)   **Phone:** (269)428-9111
◉◉◉ (SAVE)   All Year [CP]   1P: $59-$79
∿▼∿▼∿   **Location:** I-94, exit 23, just w. 2601 W Marquette Woods Rd 49127. Fax: 269/428-6774. **Facility:** 100 units. 98
one-bedroom standard units. 2 one-bedroom suites, some with kitchens. 3 stories, interior corridors. *Bath:*
combo or shower only. **Parking:** on-site. **Terms:** pets ($50 deposit). **Amenities:** video games (fee), voice
Small-scale Hotel   mail, irons, hair dryers. **Guest Services:** valet and coin laundry. **Business Services:** meeting rooms.
Cards: AX, CB, DC, DS, MC, VI. **Special Amenities:** free continental breakfast and free newspaper.

SOME UNITS

(S/D) 🛏 (¶¶+) (&M) (✎) (➰) (🐾) (🎥) (DATA PORT) (💻) / (✕) ▢ (🖥) /

HAMPTON INN   **Phone:** (269)429-2700
(SAVE)   All Year   1P: $69-$75
∿▼∿▼∿   **Location:** I-94, exit 23, just se. 5050 Red Arrow Hwy 49127. Fax: 269/429-5552. **Facility:** 75 one-bedroom standard units, some with whirlpools. 3 stories, interior corridors. *Bath:* combo or shower only. **Parking:** on-site.
Small-scale Hotel   **Terms:** [CP] meal plan available. **Amenities:** video games, voice mail, irons, hair dryers. **Pool(s):** heated indoor. **Guest Services:** valet laundry. **Business Services:** meeting rooms, fax (fee). **Cards:** AX, DC, DS,
MC, VI.

SOME UNITS

(S/D) 🛏 (¶¶+) (&M) (✎) (➰) (➰) (🐾) (🎥) (DATA PORT) (💻) / (✕) ▢ / FEE

PARK INN INTERNATIONAL   **Phone:** (269)429-3218
◉◉◉ (SAVE)

| | 5/24-9/1 [BP] | 1P: $79-$154 | 2P: $79-$154 | XP: $10 | F19 |
| | 4/1-5/23 & 9/2-3/31 [BP] | 1P: $64-$129 | 2P: $64-$129 | XP: $10 | F19 |

∿▼∿▼∿   **Location:** I-94, exit 23, 0.5 mi n. 4290 Red Arrow Hwy 49127. Fax: 269/429-8882. **Facility:** 90 units. 85 one-bedroom standard units, some with efficiencies and/or whirlpools. 5 one-bedroom suites ($109-$154), some
Small-scale Hotel   with efficiencies and/or whirlpools. 2 stories, interior/exterior corridors. *Bath:* combo or shower only. **Parking:**
on-site. **Amenities:** high-speed Internet, voice mail, irons, hair dryers. **Dining:** 6 am-9 pm, Fri & Sat-10 pm,
Sun 7:30 am-2 pm, cocktails. **Pool(s):** small heated outdoor, heated indoor. **Leisure Activities:** whirlpool, bocci, exercise room,
basketball, horseshoes, shuffleboard, volleyball. **Guest Services:** valet and coin laundry. **Business Services:** meeting rooms.
Cards: AX, CB, DC, DS, JC, MC, VI. *(See color ad p. 463)*

SOME UNITS

(S/D) 🛏 (¶¶) (✎) (➰) (✕) (🎥) (DATA PORT) (💻) / (✕) ▢ (🖥) / FEE FEE

—————— *The following lodging was either not evaluated or did not* ——————
meet AAA rating requirements but is listed for your information only.

CHALET ON THE LAKE   **Phone:** 269/465-6365
(fyi)   Did not meet all AAA rating requirements for locking devices in some guest rooms at time of last evaluation
on 01/16/2002. **Location:** I-94, exit 23, just w, then 0.8 mi n. 5340 Notre Dame Ave 49127. Facilities, services, and
Cottage   decor characterize a basic property.

——— WHERE TO DINE ———

GRANDE MERE INN
Steak & Seafood
Dinner: $11-$23
Phone: 269/429-3591
Location: I-94, exit 23, 1.5 mi s. 5800 Red Arrow Hwy 49127. **Hours:** 4:30 pm-9:30 pm, Fri & Sat-10 pm. Closed major holidays; also Sun & Mon. **Reservations:** suggested. **Features:** The popular restaurant is a local favorite for fresh seafood specialties, including blue gill and lake perch, as well as succulent ribs. Views of Lake Michigan are certain to enhance your experience. Try to save room for dessert; it won't disappoint. Casual dress; cocktails. **Parking:** on-site. **Cards:** AX, DC, DS, MC, VI.

SCHULER'S
American
Lunch: $8-$11 **Dinner:** $10-$24 **Phone:** 269/429-3273
Location: I-94, exit 23, just sw. 5000 Red Arrow Hwy 49127. **Hours:** 11 am-10 pm, Fri-11 pm, Sat noon-11 pm, Sun noon-9 pm. Closed: 1/1, 12/25. **Reservations:** accepted. **Features:** Cozy and trendy define the atmosphere in the casual dining room, which is inviting to all members of the family. Attractive artwork hangs on cream-painted barn-siding walls. Representative of menu choices are pork medallions in a sweet sauce. Casual dress; cocktails. **Parking:** on-site. **Cards:** AX, DC, DS, MC, VI.

STURGIS pop. 11,285

——— WHERE TO STAY ———

GREEN BRIAR MOTOR INN
Motel
Phone: (269)651-2361

	1P	2P	XP	
5/1-10/31	1P: $38	2P: $48-$55	XP: $5	F10
4/1-4/30 & 11/1-3/31	1P: $28	2P: $32	XP: $5	F10

Location: I-90, exit 121, 0.4 mi n. 71381 S Centerville Rd (SR 66) 49091. **Fax:** 269/651-1701. **Facility:** 19 one-bedroom standard units. 1 story, exterior corridors. **Parking:** on-site. **Terms:** weekly rates available, small pets only ($5 extra charge). **Pool(s):** outdoor. **Cards:** AX, DS, MC, VI. **Special Amenities:** early check-in/late check-out and free local telephone calls.

SOME UNITS

HAMPTON INN
Small-scale Hotel
Phone: (269)651-4210

	1P	2P	
All Year	1P: $79-$114	2P: $79-$114	

Location: I-90, exit 121, 0.4 mi n. 71451 S Centerville Rd (SR 66) 49091. **Fax:** 269/651-7085. **Facility:** 60 one-bedroom standard units. 3 stories, interior corridors. **Bath:** combo or shower only. **Parking:** on-site. **Terms:** [CP] meal plan available. **Amenities:** voice mail, irons. **Pool(s):** heated indoor. **Leisure Activities:** whirlpool. **Business Services:** fax. **Cards:** AX, CB, DC, DS, JC, MC, VI. **Special Amenities:** free continental breakfast and free local telephone calls.

SOME UNITS

SUTTONS BAY pop. 589

——— WHERE TO STAY ———

RED LION MOTOR LODGE
Motel
Phone: 231/271-6694

	1P	2P	XP	
6/2-9/2	1P: $89-$105	2P: $89-$145	XP: $10	F18
4/1-6/1 & 9/3-10/30	1P: $65-$95	2P: $75-$125	XP: $10	F18
10/31-3/31	1P: $55-$75	2P: $65-$95	XP: $10	F18

Location: 5 mi s on SR 22. Located opposite the bay on main highway. 4290 S West Bay Shore Rd 49682. **Fax:** 231/271-5227. **Facility:** Smoke free premises. 16 units. 14 one- and 2 two-bedroom standard units, some with efficiencies. 1 story, exterior corridors. **Bath:** combo or shower only. **Parking:** on-site, winter plug-ins. **Terms:** pets ($10 extra charge). **Cards:** AX, DS, MC, VI.

SOME UNITS

TRAVERSE BAY CASINO RESORTS THE LODGE
[fyi]
Motel
Did not meet all AAA rating requirements for property operations at time of last evaluation on 09/10/2002.
Location: 4 mi n on SR 22. 2579 NW Bayshore Dr 49682. Facilities, services, and decor characterize a basic property. **(See color ad p. 103)**
Phone: 231/271-6330

———— **WHERE TO DINE** ————

CAFE BLISS
▼▼▼ ▼▼
Seafood
Lunch: $7-$12 **Dinner:** $14-$27 **Phone: 231/271-5000**
Location: On SR 22; center. 420 St. Joseph's Ave 49682. **Hours:** 5 pm-10 pm; Sat & Sun from 10 am 5/28-9/3; Thurs-Sat 5 pm-10 pm 9/20-10/21. Closed: Mon. **Reservations:** suggested. **Features:** Although this restaurant is specializing in seafood, they are well known for their vegetarian and ethnic cuisine. They use natural, fresh, healthful ingredients. A small number of their house specialties are sold in jars, and make a nice gift. Casual dress; cocktails. **Parking:** street. **Cards:** AX, CB, DC, DS, MC, VI.
[⊠]

BOONE'S PRIME TIME PUB
[fyi]
Not evaluated. **Location:** Center. 102 St. Joseph Ave 49682. **Features:** Specialties here include steak, shrimp, fish, chicken, soup and sandwiches.
Phone: 231/271-6688

TAWAS CITY pop. 2,005

———— **WHERE TO STAY** ————

DALE MOTEL
(AAA) [SAVE]
▼▼▼
Motel
Phone: 989/362-6153

5/1-10/31	1P: $49-$72	2P: $50-$82	XP: $6	F5
4/1-4/30 & 11/1-3/31	1P: $35-$58	2P: $40-$68	XP: $6	F5

Location: 1.6 mi s on US 23. 1086 US 23 S 48763. Fax: 989/362-6154. **Facility:** 16 one-bedroom standard units. 1 story, exterior corridors. **Parking:** on-site, winter plug-ins. **Terms:** 2-3 night minimum stay - weekends, 3 day cancellation notice-fee imposed. **Cards:** AX, DS, MC, VI.
SOME UNITS
[📷] [🛗] [▯] / [⊠] /

DAYS INN-TAWAS CITY
(AAA) [SAVE]
▼▼▼ ▼▼▼
Small-scale Hotel
Phone: (989)362-0088

All Year [CP]	1P: $70-$150	2P: $70-$150	XP: $6 F18

Location: 1.5 mi s on US 23. 1020 W Lake St 48763. Fax: 989/362-0088. **Facility:** 41 one-bedroom standard units, some with whirlpools. 2 stories (no elevator), interior corridors. **Parking:** on-site. **Terms:** check-in 4 pm, 3 day cancellation notice. **Amenities:** irons, hair dryers. **Pool(s):** heated indoor. **Leisure Activities:** whirlpool. **Guest Services:** coin laundry. **Business Services:** meeting rooms. **Cards:** AX, DC, DS, MC, VI. **Special Amenities:** free continental breakfast and free local telephone calls.

(See color ad card insert)
SOME UNITS
[S/D] [🏊] [📷] [DATA PORT] [🛗] [🖥] [▯] / [⊠] /

TAWAS MOTEL-RESORT
(AAA) [SAVE]
▼▼▼
Motel
Phone: (989)362-3822

5/21-10/1 [CP]	1P: $45-$70	2P: $50-$80
4/1-5/20 & 10/2-3/31 [CP]	1P: $35-$50	2P: $40-$60

Location: 1.8 mi s on US 23. 1124 US 23 S 48764 (PO Box 248). Fax: 989/362-3822. **Facility:** 21 one-bedroom standard units, some with whirlpools. 1 story, exterior corridors. **Bath:** combo or shower only. **Parking:** on-site, winter plug-ins. **Terms:** 3 day cancellation notice, pets (with prior approval). **Pool(s):** heated outdoor. **Leisure Activities:** sauna, whirlpool, playground, basketball, horseshoes, shuffleboard. **Fee:** game room. **Cards:** AX, DS, MC, VI. **Special Amenities:** free local telephone calls and preferred room (subject to availability with advanced reservations).
SOME UNITS
[S/D] [🛏] [🏊] [⊠] [📷] [🛗] / [⊠] [DATA PORT] [🖥] [▯]

TAYLOR —See Detroit p. 274.

TECUMSEH pop. 8,574

———— **WHERE TO STAY** ————

TECUMSEH INN MOTEL
▼▼▼
Motel
Phone: (517)423-7401

All Year	1P: $50-$150

Location: On SR 50, 1.5 mi w of city. 1445 W Chicago Blvd 49286. Fax: 517/423-3324. **Facility:** 61 one-bedroom standard units. 2 stories (no elevator), interior corridors. **Parking:** on-site. **Terms:** small pets only ($25 deposit). **Dining:** Fox's Pizza Den, see separate listing. **Guest Services:** complimentary evening beverages, valet laundry. **Cards:** AX, DC, MC, VI.
SOME UNITS
[ASK] [S/D] [🛏] [🍴] [Y] [📷] [DATA PORT] [🖥] / [⊠] [VCR] [🛗] [🖥]

--------- WHERE TO DINE ---------

EVANS STREET STATION   Lunch: $8-$12   Dinner: $12-$15   Phone: 517/424-5555
▼▼▼ ▼▼   **Location:** Just s of SR 50; 15 mi w of US 23, exit 17 (Dundee); downtown. 110 S Evans St 49286. **Hours:** 11 am-9
                      pm, Fri-10 pm, Sat 4:30 pm-10 pm, Sun noon-8 pm. Closed major holidays. **Reservations:** accepted.
American   **Features:** Ansel Adams prints adorn the walls of this upscale yet comfortable family owned restaurant.
                      Global influences run rampant through the creative menu, which features a wide range of seafood, pasta
and steaks. Dressy casual; cocktails. **Parking:** on-site. **Cards:** AX, DS, MC, VI.
                                                                                            [M] [Y] [X]

FOX'S PIZZA DEN   Dinner: $6-$10   Phone: 517/423-7000
▼▼▼   **Location:** On SR 50, 1.5 mi w of city; in Tecumseh Inn Motel. 1441 W Chicago Blvd 49286. **Hours:** 4:30 pm-9 pm.
                      Closed major holidays; also Mon. **Features:** This family-style pizzeria delivers a wide assortment of
Pizza   gourmet pizza, stromboli, hoagies and sandwiches. The owner's hobby is airplanes, which is appropriately
                      reflected in the many aviation pictures that adorn the walls. Casual dress; beer & wine only. **Parking:**
on-site. **Cards:** AX, MC, VI.
                                                                                                         [X]

THOMPSONVILLE pop. 457

--------- WHERE TO STAY ---------

CRYSTAL MOUNTAIN   Phone: (231)378-2000
[AAA] [SAVE]   All Year   1P: $89-$279   2P: $89-$279   XP: $20
▼▼▼ ▼▼   **Location:** On SR 115, 2 mi w. 12500 Crystal Mountain Dr 49683. Fax: 231/378-4594. **Facility:** This scenic year-
                      round resort on Michigan's Lower Peninsula features golf as well as downhill and cross-country skiing. 222
Resort   units. 83 one-bedroom standard units, some with efficiencies and/or whirlpools. 51 one- and 29 two-bedroom
Small-scale Hotel   suites ($99-$359), some with kitchens and/or whirlpools. 59 cottages, some with whirlpools. 1-3 stories (no
                      elevator), interior/exterior corridors. *Bath:* combo or shower only. **Parking:** on-site. **Terms:** check-in 6 pm, 14
                      day cancellation notice, weekly rates available, package plans. **Amenities:** irons, hair dryers. *Some:* voice
mail. **Dining:** 2 restaurants, 11 am-10 pm, Fri & Sat-11 pm, also, The Wildflower Restaurant, see separate listing. **Pool(s):**
heated outdoor, heated indoor. **Leisure Activities:** whirlpool, cross country skiing, snowmobiling, ice skating, recreation programs, hiking trails, exercise room. *Fee:* golf-36 holes, golf equipment, golf instruction, practice center, family golf clinic & junior
golf privileges, 2 tennis courts, downhill skiing, bicycles. **Guest Services:** gift shop, coin laundry, airport transportation (fee)-
Cherry Capital Airport. **Business Services:** conference facilities, business center. **Cards:** AX, DC, DS, MC, VI.
                                                                                            SOME UNITS
                   [✈] [¶] [Y] [♿] [🐾] [≋] [X] [VCR] [⌖] [▯] [▭] [▱] / [X] [DATA PORT] /
                   FEE

--------- WHERE TO DINE ---------

THE WILDFLOWER RESTAURANT   Lunch: $6-$10   Dinner: $9-$25   Phone: 231/378-2000
▼▼▼ ▼▼   **Location:** On SR 115, 2 mi w; in Crystal Mountain. 12500 Crystal Mountain Dr 49683. **Hours:** 7-11 am, 11:30-2 &
                      5-10 pm; hours vary off season. **Reservations:** suggested. **Features:** Relax and enjoy a casual dining
American   experience in the comfortable restaurant. A good selection of menu items includes chicken and pasta
                      dishes, as well as tasty seafood and savory steak, which is cooked to your liking. Service is friendly and
prompt. Cocktails. **Parking:** on-site. **Cards:** AX, DC, DS, MC, VI.
                                                                                                       [Y] [X]

THREE RIVERS pop. 7,328

--------- WHERE TO STAY ---------

HOLIDAY INN EXPRESS HOTEL & SUITES   Phone: (269)278-7766
▼▼▼   All Year [CP]   1P: $89-$128   2P: $89-$128   XP: $10   F12
                      Location: 2 mi sw on US 131 and SR 60. 1207 W Broadway 49093. Fax: 269/278-7722. **Facility:** 56 one-bedroom
Small-scale Hotel   standard units, some with whirlpools. 2 stories, interior corridors. *Bath:* combo or shower only. **Parking:** on-
                      site. **Amenities:** voice mail, irons, hair dryers. *Some:* dual phone lines. **Pool(s):** heated indoor. **Leisure Ac-
tivities:** whirlpool, exercise room. **Guest Services:** valet and coin laundry. **Business Services:** meeting rooms. **Cards:** AX, CB,
DC, DS, JC, MC, VI.
                                                                                            SOME UNITS
                   [ASK] [S▫] [M] [♿] [🕭] [≋] [⌖] [DATA PORT] / [X] [▯] [▭] [▱] /

THREE RIVERS INN   Phone: (269)273-9521
▼▼▼   All Year [CP]   1P: $43-$63   2P: $53-$73   XP: $10   F12
                      Location: 2 mi sw on US 131 and SR 60. 1200 W Broadway 49093-9362. Fax: 269/278-7205. **Facility:** 100 one-
Small-scale Hotel   bedroom standard units. 2 stories, interior corridors. **Parking:** on-site. **Terms:** weekly rates available, pets
                      ($10 extra charge). **Pool(s):** heated indoor. **Leisure Activities:** whirlpool. *Fee:* game room. **Guest Services:**
coin laundry. **Business Services:** meeting rooms. **Cards:** AX, DC, DS, MC, VI.
                                                                                            SOME UNITS
                   [🐾] [¶] [≋] [⌖] [DATA PORT] / [X] [▯] /

--------- The following lodging was either not evaluated or did not
      meet AAA rating requirements but is listed for your information only. ---------

BEST VALUE INN EXTENDED STAY   Phone: 269/278-7766
[fyi]   All Year   1P: $59-$79   2P: $59-$79   XP: $10   F12
                      Too new to rate, opening scheduled for December 2002. **Location:** 2 mi sw on US 131 and SR 60. 1211 W
Small-scale Hotel   Broadway 49093. Fax: 269/278-7722. **Amenities:** 44 units, coffeemakers, microwaves, refrigerators.
                      Cards: AX, CB, DC, DS, JC, MC, VI.

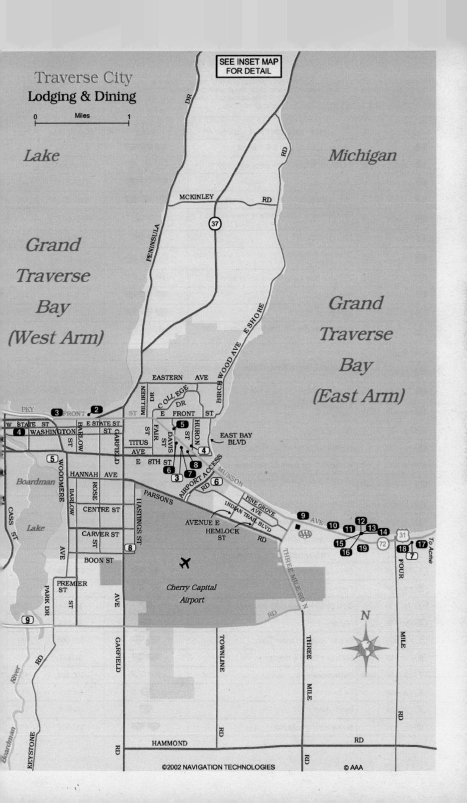

Traverse City

This index helps you "spot" where approved accommodations and restaurants are located on the corresponding detailed maps. Lodging rate ranges are for comparison only and show the property's high season; rates are per night, unless only weekly (W) rates are available. Restaurant rate range is for dinner, unless only lunch (L) is served. Turn to the listing page for more detailed rate information and consult display ads for special promotions.

Spotter/Map Page Number	OA	**TRAVERSE CITY** - Lodgings	Diamond Rating	Rate Range High Season	Listing Page
❶ / p. 436		Chateau Chantal Bed & Breakfast	◈◈◈	$125-$150	441
❷ / p. 436	AAA	**Bayshore Resort** - see color ad p 440	◈◈◈	$155-$220 SAVE	440
❸ / p. 436		Holiday Inn	◈◈◈	$158-$161	445
❹ / p. 436		Park Place Hotel - see color ad p 448	◈◈◈	$189-$199	448
❺ / p. 436	AAA	**Best Western Four Seasons** - see color ad p 441	◈◈	$99-$154 SAVE	441
❻ / p. 436		Pine Crest Motel	◈◈	$70-$145	448
❼ / p. 436	AAA	**Days Inn & Suites** - see color ad card insert & p 442	◈◈◈	$99-$159 SAVE	444
❽ / p. 436	AAA	**Traverse Bay Lodge** - see color ad p 450	◈◈◈	$139-$229 SAVE	451
❾ / p. 436		Hampton Inn	◈◈◈	$139-$169	445
❿ / p. 436		Park Shore Resort	◈◈◈	$159-$289	448
⓫ / p. 436	AAA	**Cherry Tree Inn On The Beach** - see color ad p 443	◈◈◈	$129-$189 SAVE	442
⓬ / p. 436	AAA	**Driftwood Resort** - see color ad p 444	◈	$105-$155 SAVE	444
⓭ / p. 436	AAA	**The Grand Beach Resort Hotel** - see color ad p 446	◈◈◈	$160-$400 SAVE	445
⓮ / p. 436	AAA	**Motel 6 - 4065**	◈◈	$80-$140 SAVE	445
⓯ / p. 436	AAA	**AmericInn of Traverse City** - see color ad p 440, p 216	◈◈	$86-$178 SAVE	439
⓰ / p. 436	AAA	**Quality Inn**	◈◈	$39-$169 SAVE	449
⓱ / p. 436		Pointes North Inn - see color ad p 449	◈◈◈	$125-$275	448
⓲ / p. 436	AAA	**Waterfront Inn Resort** - see color ad p 450	◈◈	$74-$183 SAVE	451
⓳ / p. 436	AAA	**Sugar Beach Resort Hotel** - see color ad p 446	◈◈◈	$160-$450 SAVE	449
⓴ / p. 436		Courtyard By Marriott - see ad p 441	◈◈◈	$109-$155	444
㉑ / p. 436	AAA	**Baymont Inn & Suites-Traverse City**	◈◈◈	$60-$160 SAVE	440
㉒ / p. 436		Fairfield Inn by Marriott	◈◈◈	$109-$129	444
		TRAVERSE CITY - Restaurants			
① / p. 436		Bower's Harbor Inn	◈◈	$18-$28	451
② / p. 436		Freshwater Lodge	◈◈	$11-$18	451
③ / p. 436		Cottage Cafe - see color ad p 442	◈	$8-$14	451
④ / p. 436		Mabel's	◈	$9-$15	452
⑤ / p. 436		Grand Traverse Dinner Train	◈◈	$62-$65	451
⑥ / p. 436		Schelde's Grille & Spirits	◈◈	$8-$17	452
⑦ / p. 436	AAA	**Reflections** - see color ad p 450	◈◈	$10-$25	452
⑧ / p. 436		La Senorita	◈	$8-$12	451
⑨ / p. 436		Panda North	◈	$8-$14	452
⑩ / p. 436		Boone's Long Lake Inn	◈◈	$12-$22	451

TRAVERSE CITY pop. 14,532 (See map p. 436; index p. 438)

─── WHERE TO STAY ───

AMERICINN OF TRAVERSE CITY

Phone: (231)938-0288 **15**

(AAA) (SAVE)
▽▽ ▽▽

	1P	2P
5/31-8/31	1P: $86-$178	2P: $86-$178
4/1-5/30	1P: $56-$105	2P: $66-$115
9/1-12/31	1P: $55-$102	2P: $65-$102
1/1-3/31	1P: $56-$92	2P: $56-$92

Small-scale Hotel **Location:** 4.4 mi e on US 31. Located in a commercial area. 1614 US 31 N 49686. Fax: 231/938-0262. **Facility:** 48 units. 45 one-bedroom standard units, some with whirlpools. 3 one-bedroom suites, some with whirlpools. 2 stories, interior corridors. *Bath:* combo or shower only. **Parking:** on-site. **Terms:** [ECP] meal plan available. **Pool(s):** heated indoor. **Leisure Activities:** sauna, whirlpool. **Guest Services:** coin laundry. **Business Services:** meeting rooms. **Cards:** AX, DC, DS, MC, VI. **Special Amenities:** free continental breakfast and free local telephone calls. *(See color ad p 440 & p 216)*

SOME UNITS

BAYMONT INN & SUITES-TRAVERSE CITY
Phone: (231)933-4454 **21**
AAA SAVE
All Year [ECP]   1P: $60-$160   XP: $5   F18
▼▼▼▼
Location: 3.5 mi s on SR 37. 2326 N US 31 S 49684. Fax: 231/933-5212. **Facility:** 121 one-bedroom standard units, some with whirlpools. 3 stories, interior corridors. *Bath:* combo or shower only. **Parking:** on-site, winter plug-ins. **Amenities:** dual phone lines, voice mail, irons, hair dryers. *Fee:* video games, high-speed Internet.
Small-scale Hotel **Pool(s):** heated indoor. **Leisure Activities:** whirlpool, playground, exercise room. **Guest Services:** valet and coin laundry. **Business Services:** meeting rooms. **Cards:** AX, DC, DS, MC, VI. **Special Amenities:** free continental breakfast and free newspaper.

SOME UNITS

BAYSHORE RESORT
Phone: (231)935-4400 **2**
AAA SAVE
6/15-8/31 [ECP]   1P: $155-$220   2P: $155-$220   XP: $10   F12
9/1-10/18 [ECP]   1P: $95-$210   2P: $95-$210   XP: $10   F12
▼▼▼▼
4/1-6/14 [ECP]   1P: $90-$190   2P: $90-$190   XP: $10   F12
10/19-3/31 [ECP]   1P: $75-$160   2P: $85-$160   XP: $10   F12
Small-scale Hotel **Location:** 0.8 mi e on US 31. Located along the bay. 833 E Front St 49686. Fax: 231/935-0262. **Facility:** Smoke free premises. 120 units. 112 one-bedroom standard units, some with whirlpools. 8 one-bedroom suites ($195-$325) with whirlpools. 3 stories, interior corridors. **Parking:** on-site. **Terms:** check-in 4 pm, 2 night minimum stay - seasonal, with Saturday stayover. **Amenities:** high-speed Internet, irons, hair dryers. **Pool(s):** heated indoor. **Leisure Activities:** whirlpool, exercise room. *Fee:* game room. **Guest Services:** coin laundry. **Business Services:** meeting rooms. **Cards:** AX, DC, DS, VI. **Special Amenities:** free continental breakfast and free local telephone calls. *(See color ad below)*

SOME UNITS

(See map p. 436)

BEST WESTERN FOUR SEASONS   Phone: (231)946-8424 **5**

AAA SAVE ▼▼ ▼▼▼ Motel

7/4-9/1 [CP]	1P: $99-$154	2P: $99-$154	XP: $7	F17
9/2-11/1 [CP]	1P: $59-$109	2P: $59-$109	XP: $7	F17
4/1-7/3 [CP]	1P: $49-$94	2P: $49-$94	XP: $7	F17
11/2-3/31 [CP]	1P: $44-$84	2P: $44-$84	XP: $7	F17

Location: 2 mi e on US 31. Located in a semi-commercial area on 5 acres. 305 Munson Ave 49686. Fax: 231/946-1971. **Facility:** 111 units. 106 one-bedroom standard units, some with whirlpools. 5 one-bedroom suites with whirlpools, some with efficiencies. 1-2 stories (no elevator), interior/exterior corridors. **Parking:** on-site, winter plug-ins. **Terms:** 2 night minimum stay - weekends & seasonal, cancellation fee imposed, package plans, pets ($7 fee, in designated units). **Amenities:** video library (fee), irons, hair dryers. **Pool(s):** heated outdoor, heated indoor. **Leisure Activities:** whirlpool. *Fee:* game room. **Cards:** AX, CB, DC, DS, JC, MC, VI. **Special Amenities:** free continental breakfast and preferred room (subject to availability with advanced reservations). *(See color ad below)*

SOME UNITS

🅂🄳 ▮ ⦙†⦙ 🛥 🖳 💻 / ✕ 🆅🅲🆁 ▯ 📷 /

CHATEAU CHANTAL BED & BREAKFAST   Phone: 231/223-4110 **1**

▼▼▲▲▼▼ Bed & Breakfast

1/1-3/31 [BP]	1P: $125	2P: $150	XP: $25	F3
4/1-12/31 [BP]	1P: $135-$165	2P: $135	XP: $25	F3

Location: 12 mi n on SR 37. Located in a rural area. 15900 Rue de Vin 49686. Fax: 231/223-4110. **Facility:** Evening wine tastings are offered at this elegant property set on a high ridge with sweeping views of the vineyards and bay. Smoke free premises. 3 one-bedroom standard units. 2 stories (no elevator), interior corridors. *Bath:* combo or shower only. **Parking:** on-site. **Terms:** 2 night minimum stay - weekends, 7 day cancellation notice-fee imposed. **Amenities:** irons. **Cards:** AX, CB, DC, DS, JC, MC, VI.

✕

(See map p. 436)

CHERRY TREE INN ON THE BEACH

AAA SAVE

			Phone: 231/938-8888	**11**
	6/20-8/23 [ECP]	2P: $129-$189	XP: $7	D17
	8/24-10/18 [ECP]	2P: $83-$135	XP: $7	D17
	4/1-6/19 [ECP]	2P: $69-$92	XP: $7	D17
	10/19-3/31 [ECP]	2P: $69-$89	XP: $7	D17

Small-scale Hotel **Location:** 5.7 mi e on US 31. Located on the main road along the bay. 2345 US 31 N 49686. Fax: 231/938-3333. **Facility:** Smoke free premises. 64 units. 51 one-bedroom standard units, some with whirlpools. 13 one-bedroom suites, some with whirlpools. 5 stories, interior corridors. *Bath:* combo or shower only. **Parking:** on-site. **Terms:** 2 night minimum stay - weekends, cancellation fee imposed. **Amenities:** video games, CD players, voice mail, irons, hair dryers. **Pool(s):** heated indoor. **Leisure Activities:** whirlpool, exercise room. *Fee:* jet boat, jet skis, game room. **Guest Services:** coin laundry. **Business Services:** meeting rooms. **Cards:** AX, DC, DS, MC, VI. **Special Amenities:** free continental breakfast and free newspaper. *(See color ad p 443)*

SOME UNITS

Now…a new level of luxury and service on the bay in Traverse City!

Cherry Tree Inn
ON THE BEACH

- Quiet, spacious beachside rooms and suites offer all king and queen size beds, plus all the comforts and conveniences to satisfy the needs of both our leisure and corporate guests.
- Fifth floor Grand Suites offer whirlpool spas, fireplaces and breathtaking views of Grand Traverse Bay.
- Watercraft rentals and snacks are available at *Gilhooley's Beach Shack*.
- Spectacular sunrises and sunsets, sugar sand beach, indoor pool and spa, continental breakfast, conference facilities and close proximity to all the Grand Traverse area has to offer—just the beginning of the many reasons you will want to return to *Cherry Tree Inn*, again and again.

Smoke Free Property

"The Hunt For a Great Room Ends Here!"

800-439-3093   (231) 938-8888
Fax (231) 938-3333 • www.cherrytreeinn.com
2345 US 31 North, Traverse City, MI 49686
For information: cti@cherrytreeinn.com   Sorry, no pets or bicycles in rooms.

(See map p. 436)

COURTYARD BY MARRIOTT　　　　　　　　　　　　　　　　　**Phone:** (231)929-1800　⑳

SAVE

6/1-9/3	1P: $109-$155	2P: $109-$155
9/4-3/31	1P: $72-$99	2P: $72-$99
5/1-5/31	1P: $79-$94	2P: $79-$94
4/1-4/30	1P: $69-$89	2P: $69-$89

Small-scale Hotel **Location:** 3.2 mi s on US 31, then just w. Located in a commercial area. 3615 W South Airport Rd 49684. Fax: 231/929-1808. **Facility:** 83 units. 80 one-bedroom standard units, some with whirlpools. 3 one-bedroom suites with whirlpools. 3 stories, interior corridors. *Bath:* combo or shower only. **Parking:** on-site. **Terms:** cancellation fee imposed. **Amenities:** video games, dual phone lines, voice mail, irons, hair dryers. **Pool(s):** heated indoor. **Leisure Activities:** whirlpool, exercise room. **Guest Services:** valet and coin laundry. **Business Services:** meeting rooms. **Cards:** AX, CB, DC, DS, JC, MC, VI. *(See ad p 441)*

SOME UNITS

DAYS INN & SUITES　　　　　　　　　　　　　　　　　　**Phone:** (231)941-0208　❼

(AAA) SAVE

6/6-8/18 [ECP]	1P: $99-$159	2P: $99-$159	XP: $10　F17
4/1-6/5 & 8/19-10/20 [ECP]	1P: $69-$139	2P: $69-$139	XP: $10　F17
10/21-3/31 [ECP]	1P: $59-$139	2P: $59-$139	XP: $10　F17

Small-scale Hotel **Location:** 2 mi e on US 31. 420 Munson Ave 49686. Fax: 231/941-7521. **Facility:** 182 units. 132 one-bedroom standard units, some with whirlpools. 50 one-bedroom suites ($79-$229), some with whirlpools. 2 stories, interior corridors. **Parking:** on-site, winter plug-ins. **Amenities:** video games, voice mail, safes (fee), hair dryers. *Some:* irons. **Pool(s):** heated indoor. **Leisure Activities:** whirlpool, picnic area with grills, playground, exercise room. **Guest Services:** coin laundry, airport transportation-Traverse City Airport. **Business Services:** meeting rooms. **Cards:** AX, CB, DC, DS, JC, MC, VI. **Special Amenities:** free continental breakfast and free newspaper. *(See color ad p 442 & card insert)*

SOME UNITS

DRIFTWOOD RESORT　　　　　　　　　　　　　　　　　**Phone:** 231/938-1600　⑫

(AAA) SAVE

6/20-9/7	1P: $105-$155	2P: $105-$155	XP: $5
5/23-6/19	1P: $60-$95	2P: $60-$95	XP: $5
9/8-10/31	1P: $45-$95	2P: $45-$95	XP: $5
4/1-5/22	1P: $45-$75	2P: $45-$75	XP: $5

Motel **Location:** 4.5 mi e. Located along the bay. 1861 US 31 N 49686. Fax: 231/938-2178. **Facility:** 39 units. 38 one- and 1 two-bedroom standard units, some with kitchens and/or whirlpools. 2 stories (no elevator), interior/exterior corridors. **Parking:** on-site. **Terms:** open 4/1-10/31, 2-3 night minimum stay - weekends & seasonal, 7 day cancellation notice. **Pool(s):** heated indoor. **Leisure Activities:** whirlpool. **Fee:** game room. **Cards:** DS, MC, VI. *(See color ad below)*

SOME UNITS

FAIRFIELD INN BY MARRIOTT　　　　　　　　　　　　　**Phone:** (231)922-7900　㉒

SAVE

7/4-8/23	2P: $109-$129
8/24-10/12	2P: $79-$95
4/1-7/3	2P: $62-$89
10/13-3/31	2P: $62-$69

Small-scale Hotel **Location:** 3.6 mi s on SR 37. Located in a quiet area. 3701 N Country Dr 49684. Fax: 231/946-8845. **Facility:** 85 one-bedroom standard units, some with whirlpools. 3 stories, interior corridors. *Bath:* combo or shower only. **Parking:** on-site. **Terms:** weekly rates available, [ECP] meal plan available. **Amenities:** irons, hair dryers. **Pool(s):** heated indoor. **Leisure Activities:** whirlpool, snowmobiling, exercise room. **Guest Services:** valet and coin laundry. **Cards:** AX, DC, DS, MC, VI.

SOME UNITS

(See map p. 436)

THE GRAND BEACH RESORT HOTEL

Phone: 231/938-4455 ⓭

6/27-8/31 [ECP]		2P: $160-$400	XP: $10	F16
4/1-6/26 [ECP]	1P: $59-$269	2P: $59-$269	XP: $10	F16
9/1-10/31 [ECP]		2P: $89-$249	XP: $10	F16
11/1-3/31 [ECP]		2P: $59-$199	XP: $10	F16

Small-scale Hotel **Location:** 4.5 mi e. Located on the main road along the bay. 1683 US 31 N 49686. Fax: 231/938-4435. **Facility:** 97 units. 96 one-bedroom standard units, some with whirlpools. 1 three-bedroom suite with kitchen and whirlpool. 3 stories, interior corridors. **Parking:** on-site. **Terms:** cancellation fee imposed, package plans. **Amenities:** video library (fee), irons, hair dryers. **Pool(s):** heated indoor. **Leisure Activities:** whirlpool, exercise room. *Fee:* paddleboats, jet boats, waverunners, game room. **Guest Services:** coin laundry. **Business Services:** meeting rooms. **Cards:** AX, CB, DC, DS, MC, VI. *(See color ad starting on p 446)*

SOME UNITS

HAMPTON INN

Phone: (231)946-8900 ⑨

7/1-8/31 [ECP]	1P: $139-$159	2P: $149-$169
4/1-6/30 [ECP]	1P: $69-$139	2P: $79-$159
9/1-10/24 [ECP]	1P: $95-$119	2P: $99-$139
10/25-3/31 [ECP]	1P: $75-$95	2P: $85-$119

Small-scale Hotel **Location:** 4.3 mi e on US 31 and SR 72. Located opposite the state park beach area. 1000 US 31 N 49686. Fax: 231/946-2817. **Facility:** 127 one-bedroom standard units. 4 stories, interior corridors. **Parking:** on-site. **Terms:** check-in 4 pm, package plans. **Amenities:** video games, voice mail, irons, hair dryers. **Pool(s):** heated indoor. **Leisure Activities:** whirlpool. **Guest Services:** valet laundry. **Business Services:** meeting rooms. **Cards:** AX, DC, DS, MC, VI.

SOME UNITS

FEE   FEE

HOLIDAY INN

Phone: (231)947-3700 ③

6/15-9/2	1P: $158-$161	2P: $158-$161	XP: $8	F18
9/3-3/31	1P: $121-$134	2P: $121-$134	XP: $8	F18
5/20-6/14	1P: $107-$125	2P: $107-$125	XP: $8	F18
4/1-5/19	1P: $98-$116	2P: $98-$116	XP: $8	F18

Large-scale Hotel **Location:** 0.5 mi e on US 31. Located along the bay. 615 E Front St 49686. Fax: 231/947-0361. **Facility:** 179 one-bedroom standard units, some with whirlpools. 4 stories, interior corridors. **Parking:** on-site. **Terms:** check-in 4 pm, package plans - seasonal & weekends, 18% service charge, pets ($10 extra charge). **Amenities:** voice mail, irons, hair dryers. **Pool(s):** heated indoor. **Leisure Activities:** sauna, whirlpool, boat dock, fishing, exercise room. *Fee:* sailboats, charter fishing. **Guest Services:** gift shop, valet and coin laundry. **Business Services:** conference facilities. **Cards:** AX, CB, DC, DS, MC, VI.

SOME UNITS

FEE

MOTEL 6 - 4065

Phone: 231/938-3002 ⓮

6/13-8/31	1P: $80-$120	2P: $90-$140	XP: $10	F17
4/1-6/12 & 9/1-3/31	1P: $35-$85	2P: $45-$95	XP: $6	F17

Small-scale Hotel **Location:** 4.3 mi e. Located in a commercial area. 1582 US 31 N 49686. Fax: 231/938-3179. **Facility:** 45 one-bedroom standard units. 2 stories, interior corridors. **Parking:** on-site. **Terms:** pets ($6 extra charge, in designated units). **Pool(s):** heated indoor. **Leisure Activities:** whirlpool. **Guest Services:** coin laundry. **Cards:** AX, CB, DC, DS, MC, VI. **Special Amenities:** free local telephone calls.

SOME UNITS

(See map p. 436)

PARK PLACE HOTEL

Large-scale Hotel

	6/1-9/2	1P: $189-$199	2P: $189-$199	XP: $10	F17
	9/3-3/31	1P: $129-$139	2P: $129-$139	XP: $10	F17
	4/1-5/31	1P: $119-$129	2P: $119-$129	XP: $10	F17

Phone: (231)946-5000 — [4]

Location: Corner of E State and Park sts; center. 300 E State St 49684. Fax: 231/946-2772. **Facility:** 140 units. 137 one-bedroom standard units. 3 one-bedroom suites. 4-10 stories, interior corridors. **Parking:** on-site, winter plug-ins. **Terms:** check-in 4 pm. **Amenities:** video games, high-speed Internet, voice mail, irons, hair dryers. **Pool(s):** heated indoor. **Leisure Activities:** sauna, whirlpool, exercise room. **Guest Services:** gift shop, valet laundry. **Business Services:** conference facilities. **Cards:** AX, DC, DS, MC, VI. *(See color ad below)*

SOME UNITS

PARK SHORE RESORT

Small-scale Hotel

| | 7/1-9/1 | 1P: $159-$289 | 2P: $159-$289 | XP: $10 | F18 |
| | 4/1-6/30 & 9/2-3/31 | 1P: $59-$209 | 2P: $59-$209 | XP: $10 | F18 |

Phone: (231)947-3800 — [10]

Location: On US 31, 3.2 mi e. Located on the main road along the bay. 1401 US 31 N 49686. Fax: 231/947-9900. **Facility:** 80 units. 74 one-bedroom standard units, some with whirlpools. 6 one-bedroom suites ($119-$309), some with efficiencies and/or whirlpools. 4 stories, interior corridors. *Bath:* combo or shower only. **Parking:** on-site. **Terms:** check-in 4 pm, 2 night minimum stay - weekends, cancellation fee imposed, [CP] & [ECP] meal plans available. **Amenities:** voice mail, safes (fee), irons, hair dryers. *Some:* dual phone lines. **Pool(s):** heated indoor. **Leisure Activities:** whirlpool, exercise room. *Fee:* paddleboats, sailboats, game room. **Guest Services:** coin laundry. **Business Services:** meeting rooms. **Cards:** AX, DC, DS, MC, VI.

SOME UNITS

PINE CREST MOTEL

Motel

	7/1-8/31	1P: $70-$135	2P: $80-$145	XP: $10
	9/1-10/31	1P: $55-$95	2P: $65-$105	XP: $10
	11/1-3/31	1P: $40-$65	2P: $50-$105	XP: $10
	4/1-6/30	1P: $55-$95	2P: $65-$95	XP: $10

Phone: 231/947-8900 — [6]

Location: 2 mi e on US 31. Located in a commercial area. 360 Munson Ave 49686. Fax: 231/947-8900. **Facility:** 35 one-bedroom standard units, some with whirlpools. 2 stories (no elevator), exterior corridors. **Parking:** on-site, winter plug-ins. **Terms:** [CP] meal plan available. **Amenities:** video library (fee), irons. *Some:* hair dryers. **Pool(s):** heated outdoor, small heated indoor. **Leisure Activities:** whirlpool. **Cards:** AX, CB, DC, DS, JC, MC, VI.

SOME UNITS

POINTES NORTH INN

Condominium

	6/16-9/1	1P: $125-$275	2P: $125-$275
	9/2-10/31	1P: $100-$185	2P: $100-$185
	4/1-6/15	1P: $70-$185	2P: $70-$185
	11/1-3/31	1P: $70-$160	2P: $70-$160

Phone: (231)938-9191 — [17]

Location: 5 mi e. Located along the bay. 2211 US 31 N 49686. Fax: 231/938-0070. **Facility:** 51 units. 50 one-bedroom standard units with whirlpools. 1 one-bedroom suite with kitchen and whirlpool. 3 stories, exterior corridors. **Parking:** on-site. **Terms:** 2 night minimum stay - weekends in summer, cancellation fee imposed, [CP] meal plan available. **Amenities:** irons, hair dryers. **Pool(s):** heated outdoor. **Leisure Activities:** volleyball. **Cards:** AX, MC, VI. *(See color ad p 449)*

SOME UNITS

(See map p. 436)

QUALITY INN

All Year   1P: $39-$169   2P: $39-$169   XP: $10   **Phone:** (231)929-4423   **16**   F

Small-scale Hotel   **Location:** 3.3 mi e. Located on the main road along bay. 1492 US 31 N 49686. Fax: 231/929-7842. **Facility:** 96 units. 94 one-bedroom standard units, some with whirlpools. 2 one-bedroom suites. 2-3 stories, interior/exterior corridors. *Bath:* combo or shower only. **Parking:** on-site, winter plug-ins. **Terms:** check-in 4 pm, cancellation fee imposed, weekly rates available, [CP] meal plan available, pets ($10 fee, in designated rooms). **Amenities:** video games, safes (fee), irons, hair dryers. **Pool(s):** heated indoor. **Leisure Activities:** whirlpool. **Guest Services:** valet laundry. **Cards:** AX, CB, DC, DS, JC, MC, VI. **Special Amenities: free continental breakfast and free local telephone calls.**

SOME UNITS

SUGAR BEACH RESORT HOTEL

6/27-8/31 [ECP]	1P: $160-$450	2P: $160-$450	XP: $10	F16
4/1-6/26 [ECP]	1P: $59-$269	2P: $59-$269	XP: $10	F16
9/1-10/31 [ECP]	1P: $89-$249	2P: $89-$249	XP: $10	F16
11/1-3/31 [ECP]	1P: $59-$199	2P: $59-$199	XP: $10	F16

Phone: 231/938-0100   **19**

Small-scale Hotel   **Location:** 4.8 mi e. Located on the main road along the bay. 1773 US 31 N 49686. Fax: 231/938-0200. **Facility:** 96 one-bedroom standard units, some with whirlpools. 3 stories, interior corridors. *Bath:* combo or shower only. **Parking:** on-site, winter plug-ins. **Terms:** cancellation fee imposed, package plans. **Amenities:** video library (fee), irons, hair dryers. **Pool(s):** heated indoor. **Leisure Activities:** whirlpool, exercise room. *Fee:* paddleboats, jet boats, wave runners, game room. **Guest Services:** coin laundry. **Business Services:** meeting rooms. **Cards:** AX, CB, DC, DS, MC, VI.

(See color ad p 446)

SOME UNITS

(See map p. 436)

TRAVERSE BAY LODGE   Phone: (231)947-5436   [8]

AAA SAVE	6/27-9/8 [ECP]	1P: $139-$229	2P: $139-$229	XP: $10	F18
	5/24-6/26 [ECP]	1P: $99-$169	2P: $99-$169	XP: $10	F18
	9/9-3/31 [ECP]	1P: $89-$149	2P: $89-$149	XP: $10	F18
	4/1-5/23 [ECP]	1P: $69-$129	2P: $69-$129	XP: $10	F18

Small-scale Hotel **Location:** 2.3 mi e on US 31. 460 Munson Ave 49686. **Fax:** 231/947-0859. **Facility:** 61 units. 60 one-bedroom standard units, some with whirlpools. 1 one-bedroom suite with kitchen. 2 stories, interior corridors. *Bath:* combo or shower only. **Parking:** on-site. **Terms:** check-in 4 pm, 7 day cancellation notice-fee imposed. **Amenities:** hair dryers. **Pool(s):** heated indoor. **Leisure Activities:** whirlpool, exercise room. *Fee:* game room. **Business Services:** meeting rooms. **Cards:** AX, CB, DC, DS, MC, VI. **Special Amenities:** free continental breakfast and free local telephone calls.
(See color ad p 450)

SOME UNITS

🆘 🛇 🎬 ⛵ ✗ 🐾 DATA PORT 🖥 / ✗ VCR 🖥 📷 /

WATERFRONT INN RESORT   Phone: (231)938-1100   [18]

AAA SAVE	5/23-8/31 [CP]	1P: $74-$178	2P: $79-$183	XP: $10	F17
	9/1-10/25 [CP]	1P: $74-$106	2P: $79-$111	XP: $10	F17
	4/1-5/22 & 10/26-3/31 [CP]	1P: $64-$106	2P: $69-$111	XP: $10	F17

Small-scale Hotel **Location:** 4.8 mi e. 2061 US 31 N 49686. **Fax:** 231/938-9711. **Facility:** 127 one-bedroom standard units, some with efficiencies and/or whirlpools. 4 stories, interior corridors. **Parking:** on-site. **Terms:** check-in 4 pm, package plans - seasonal. **Amenities:** voice mail. **Dining:** Reflections, see separate listing. **Pool(s):** heated indoor. **Leisure Activities:** saunas, whirlpool, exercise room. *Fee:* game room. **Guest Services:** airport transportation-Cherry Capital Airport. **Business Services:** conference facilities. **Cards:** AX, DC, DS, MC, VI. **Special Amenities:** free continental breakfast and free newspaper. *(See color ad p 450)*

SOME UNITS

🏸 🍴 🍸 ⛵ ✗ 🐾 DATA PORT 🖥 🖥 /✗/

─────── *The following lodging was either not evaluated or did not* ───────
meet AAA rating requirements but is listed for your information only.

GREAT WOLF LODGE-TRAVERSE CITY, MI   Phone: 231-941-3600

[fyi]   All Year   1P: $229-$404   2P: $229-$404   XP: $15
Cabin   Too new to rate, opening scheduled for March 2003. **Location:** I-31 S, in Garfield Township, just s. 3575 N US Hwy 31 S 49684. **Fax:** 231/941-3700. **Amenities:** 281 units, coffeemakers, microwaves, refrigerators, pool. **Terms:** 3 day cancellation notice-fee imposed. **Cards:** AX, CB, DC, DS, MC, VI. *(See color ad p 445)*

─────── WHERE TO DINE ───────

BOONE'S LONG LAKE INN   **Dinner:** $12-$22   **Phone:** 231/946-3991   [10]

            Location: 5.5 mi sw, 1.3 mi s on US 31, 4 mi sw on Silver Lake Rd, 1.5 mi w off Secor Rd. 7208 Secor Rd 49684. **Hours:** 4 pm-10 pm, Sat-11 pm, Sun noon-10 pm. Closed: 11/27, 12/25; also for dinner 12/24.
Steak & Seafood **Features:** Casual dining. The 18-ounce New York strip steak is still the "house specialty", but you may want to try one of the nightly specials or the fresh seafood which is worth the wait to get seated when they are busy. Casual dress; cocktails. **Parking:** on-site. **Cards:** AX, MC, VI.
✗

BOWER'S HARBOR INN   Historic   **Dinner:** $18-$28   **Phone:** 231/223-4222   [1]

            Location: 0.8 mi n on SR 37, 8.8 mi nw. 13512 Peninsula Dr 49686. **Hours:** 5 pm-10 pm, Fri & Sat-11 pm; 5 pm-9 pm, Fri & Sat-10 pm 11/1-4/15. Closed: 11/27, 12/25; also 12/24 for dinner.
American   **Reservations:** suggested. **Features:** Casually upscale dining in a restored home on west Bay. The cuisine is unique, with dishes such as the Fish in a Bag, an "Inn Tradition" served with shrimp, king crab, scallops and orange roughy, and Horseradish crusted New York strip, the Harbor Duck to the Frenched Rack of Spring Lamb. The Bowery - located in back, is also a fun place to eat. Casual dress; cocktails. **Parking:** on-site. **Cards:** AX, DS, MC, VI.
✗

COTTAGE CAFE   **Lunch:** $5-$8   **Dinner:** $8-$14   **Phone:** 231/947-9261   [3]

            Location: 2 mi ne on US 31. 420 Munson Ave 49684. **Hours:** 7 am-10 pm. Closed: 12/25. **Features:** The family-style restaurant delivers such familiar fare as pot pies, beef stew, shepherd's pie and local whitefish.
American   Antiques, knickknacks and pictures decorate the dining room, which resembles a cozy cottage. Service is courteous and efficient. Casual dress. **Parking:** on-site. **Cards:** AX, DS, MC, VI. *(See color ad p 442)*
🍸 ✗

FRESHWATER LODGE   **Lunch:** $5-$13   **Dinner:** $11-$18   **Phone:** 231/932-4694   [2]

            Location: On SR 22, just n of SR 72. 13890 S West Bayshore Dr 49684. **Hours:** 11 am-11 pm, Fri & Sat-midnight, Sun 10 am-10 pm. Closed: 11/27, 12/25. **Features:** Opposite the bay, the restaurant nurtures a warm, up-north atmosphere, in part due to its high stone fireplaces and hunting and fishing memorabilia.
American   Hand-cut lodge steak is marinated in a sweet and savory sauce then flame-broiled to the patron's liking. Casual dress; cocktails. **Parking:** on-site. **Cards:** AX, DS, MC, VI.
🍸 ✗

GRAND TRAVERSE DINNER TRAIN **Lunch:** $47-$50 **Dinner:** $62-$65   **Phone:** 231/933-3768   [5]

            Location: Historic station on Boardman Lake; center. 642 Railroad Pl 49686. **Hours:** train departs noon & 6:30 pm; schedules vary with season. **Reservations:** required. **Features:** Get a taste of nostalgia on the
American   charming tour of the scenic Grand Traverse Bay area. All tables are next to windows on the comfortable Pullman-style dining coaches. The monthly changing menu highlights a limited selection of gourmet cuisine. Casual dress; cocktails. **Parking:** on-site. **Cards:** DS, MC, VI.
✗

LA SENORITA   **Lunch:** $5-$10   **Dinner:** $8-$12   **Phone:** 231/947-8820   [8]

            Location: 1.3 mi s of jct US 31, SR 37 and 72 (Old Mission Peninsula). 1245 S Garfield 49685. **Hours:** 11 am-10 pm, Fri & Sat-11 pm; to 11 pm, Fri & Sat-midnight, Sun noon-10 pm 5/29-9/4. Closed: 4/20, 11/27, 12/25.
Mexican   **Features:** Casual dining. Warm atmosphere with Mexican knickknacks throughout. Good variety of reasonably priced Mexican dishes, snacks and salad. Mesquite cooked items. Smoking permitted in the lounge only (on Sundays). Casual dress; cocktails. **Parking:** on-site. **Cards:** AX, DS, MC, VI.
🍸 ✗

(See map p. 436)

MABEL'S
American

Lunch: $5-$9   Dinner: $9-$15   Phone: 231/947-0252   ④
Location: 2.4 mi e on US 31. 457 Munson Ave 49686. **Hours:** 7 am-11 pm. Closed: 11/27, 12/25. **Features:** The popular family restaurant has a number of reasonably priced menu items and vegetarian choices, as well as lighter fare and children's dishes. The award-winning Traverse City cherry pie is worth savoring. Casual dress. **Parking:** on-site. **Cards:** AX, DS, MC, VI.

PANDA NORTH
Chinese

Lunch: $4-$8   Dinner: $8-$14   Phone: 231/929-9722   ⑨
Location: 3.5 mi s on US 31 and SR 37, 2 mi e. 2038 S Airport Rd 49684. **Hours:** 11 am-9:30 pm, Fri & Sat-10:30 pm. Closed: 11/27. **Reservations:** suggested; weekends. **Features:** On the river at Logans Landing, the restaurant lays out a tempting, all-you-can-eat lunch and dinner buffet. Such selections as soups and egg rolls complement entrees of sweet and sour chicken, lomein and beef with broccoli. Servers are pleasant and prompt. Casual dress. **Parking:** on-site. **Cards:** AX, MC, VI.

REFLECTIONS
American

Lunch: $8-$10   Dinner: $10-$25   Phone: 231/938-2321   ⑦
Location: 4.8 mi e; in Waterfront Inn Resort. 2061 US 31 N 49686. **Hours:** 7 am-2:30 & 5-9:30 pm, Sun 8 am-2 & 5-9:30 pm. Closed: 11/27, 12/25; also 12/24 for dinner. **Reservations:** suggested. **Features:** Rooftop dining room overlooking the bay. Noted for their fresh fish dishes and juicy steaks. Try the "Smoked Whitefish Pate" as an appetizer and the "Old Mission Salad" - but be careful - they're filling, and the main dishes are hearty. Casual dress; cocktails. **Parking:** on-site. **Cards:** AX, DC, DS, MC, VI.
(See color ad p 450)

SCHELDE'S GRILLE & SPIRITS
American

Lunch: $5-$7   Dinner: $8-$17   Phone: 231/946-0981   ⑥
Location: 2.8 mi ne on US 31 and SR 72. 714 Munson Ave 49684. **Hours:** 11 am-10 pm, Fri-11 pm, Sat & Sun 8 am-10 pm. Closed: 11/27, 12/25; also 12/24 for dinner. **Features:** Casual dining. Featured items include chicken, steak and seafood. The baked crab and artichoke dip appetizer is a great way to start your meal. The prime rib and the St. Louis Style BBQ ribs are favorites. For a sandwich try their "famous" Reuben. Casual dress; cocktails. **Parking:** on-site. **Cards:** AX, DS, MC, VI.

WINDOWS
Continental

Dinner: $21-$38   Phone: 231/941-0100
Location: Jct SR 72 and 22, 6.5 mi n on SR 22. 7677 W Bay Shore Dr 49684. **Hours:** Open 4/1-2/15; 5 pm-9 pm, Fri & Sat-10 pm. Closed: 11/27, 12/25; also Sun & Mon 11/1-5/6. **Reservations:** required. **Features:** Located on the banks of West Grand Traverse Bay, this restaurant offers up-scale dining, featuring American cuisine that draws on French and Cajun influences. They also have an extensive, award winning wine list. Dressy casual; cocktails. **Parking:** on-site. **Cards:** AX, DC, DS, MC, VI.

───── *The following restaurants have not been evaluated by AAA* ─────
but are listed for your information only.

APACHE TROUT GRILL   Phone: 231/947-7079
[fyi]   Not evaluated. **Location:** 2 mi n on SR 22; jct SR 22 and 72. 13671 SW Bayshore Dr 49684. **Features:** On the bay, the restaurant affords good views of the water from inside and on the seasonal patio. Specialties include seafood and steaks, as well as a number of mixed-grill items.

AUNTIE PASTA'S ITALIAN CAFE   Phone: 231/941-8147
[fyi]   Not evaluated. **Location:** On the river at Logans Landing. 2030 S Airport Rd 49684. **Features:** Freshly-baked breads and desserts accompany pasta, veal and Italian dishes.

DILL'S OLDE TOWNE SALOON   Phone: 231/947-7534
[fyi]   Not evaluated. **Location:** 423 S Union St 49686. **Features:** A favorite local restaurant noted for a variety of dishes, especially the chicken and pasta selections.

DON'S DRIVE INN   Phone: 231/938-1860
[fyi]   Not evaluated. **Location:** 2030 US 31 N 49686. **Features:** This 1950s diner still has the great burgers and shakes being served in the atmosphere of that era.

GORDIE HOWE'S TAVERN & EATERY   Phone: 231/929-4693
[fyi]   Not evaluated. **Location:** 851 S Garfield 49686. **Features:** This family restaurant is filled with hockey memorabilia, and serves BBQ ribs, prime rib, burgers, salads and pizza.

MODE'S BUM STEER   Phone: 231/947-9832
[fyi]   Not evaluated. **Location:** 125 E Front St 49686. **Features:** This small, loud, smoky tavern is one of the best places in town for steaks and prime rib. Children under 8 not allowed after 5 pm.

NORTH PEAK BREWING COMPANY   Phone: 231/941-7325
[fyi]   Not evaluated. **Location:** 400 W Front St 49686. **Features:** Located downtown, beers brewed on location, serving wood-fired pizza, snacks and steaks.

OMELETTE SHOPPE AND BAKERY   Phone: 231/946-0590
[fyi]   Not evaluated. **Location:** 1209 E Front 49686. **Features:** One of two locations in town, noted for their award winning breakfast and lunch.

SLEDER'S FAMILY TAVERN   Phone: 231/947-9213
[fyi]   Not evaluated. **Location:** 717 Randolph 49684. **Features:** Established in 1882, the tavern features an array of hearty American favorites.

TRENTON —*See Detroit p. 274.*

TROUT LAKE

──────── **WHERE TO STAY** ────────

TONY LONDON'S MOTEL
Phone: (906)569-3276
▼▼ ▼▼▼▼

	7/1-9/3	1P: $72-$90	2P: $90-$105	XP: $6	F12
	12/19-3/24	1P: $76-$82	2P: $84-$94	XP: $6	F12
Motel	9/4-10/18	1P: $52-$56	2P: $70-$74	XP: $6	F12
	5/16-6/30	1P: $52-$56	2P: $64-$74	XP: $6	F12

Location: 1.3 mi s on SR 123. Located in a quiet area. 22321 S Hwy 123 49793 (PO Box 127). **Facility:** 41 one-bedroom standard units, some with whirlpools. 2 stories (no elevator), exterior corridors. **Parking:** on-site. **Terms:** open 5/16-10/18 & 12/19-3/24, cancellation fee imposed. **Pool(s):** heated indoor. **Leisure Activities:** sauna, whirlpool, snowmobiling, playground, shuffleboard. *Fee:* game room. **Cards:** AX, DC, DS, MC, VI.

SOME UNITS
🅂🄳 🍴 🏊 ✕ 🎦 /✕/

TROY —*See Detroit p. 275.*

UNION PIER

──────── **WHERE TO STAY** ────────

GARDEN GROVE BED & BREAKFAST
Phone: (269)469-6346
▼▼▼▼
    All Year [BP]   2P: $90-$200
Bed & Breakfast **Location:** I-94, exit 6, just w. Located in a residential area. 9549 Union Pier Rd 49129. Fax: 269/469-3419. **Facility:** Brightly painted, well-appointed rooms enhance this 1925 cottage-style home whose large terraces overlook wooded gardens. Designated smoking area. 4 one-bedroom standard units, some with whirlpools. 2 stories (no elevator), interior corridors. **Parking:** on-site. **Terms:** check-in 4 pm, 2 night minimum stay - weekends, 10 day cancellation notice-fee imposed, weekly rates available, package plans - midweek. **Amenities:** video library. *Some:* CD players. **Leisure Activities:** whirlpool, bicycles. **Cards:** AX, DS, MC, VI.

SOME UNITS
(ASK) 🅂🄳 ✕ (VCR) /🖥/

RIVERS EDGE BED & BREAKFAST
Phone: 269/469-6860
▼▼ ▼▼▼▼

4/1-10/31 [BP]	2P: $99-$240	XP: $25
11/1-3/31 [BP]	2P: $90-$216	XP: $25

Bed & Breakfast **Location:** I-94, exit 6, just w to Community Hall Rd, 1 mi s. Located in a quiet area. 9902 Community Hall Rd 49129. Fax: 269/469-9138. **Facility:** On 30 acres of orchards and woodlands, the B&B is well suited for outdoor enthusiasts; each guest room has rocking chairs and a gas fireplace. Designated smoking area. 8 units. 5 one-bedroom standard units with whirlpools. 3 one-bedroom suites with whirlpools. 2 stories (no elevator), interior/exterior corridors. **Parking:** on-site. **Terms:** check-in 4 pm, 2 night minimum stay - weekends, age restrictions may apply, 7 day cancellation notice-fee imposed, no pets allowed (owner's dog on premises). **Amenities:** video library. *Some:* CD players. **Leisure Activities:** canoeing, fishing, cross country skiing, bicycles. **Business Services:** meeting rooms. **Cards:** AX, DS, MC, VI.

SOME UNITS
✕ ✕ (VCR) /☎ 🖥 📠/

──────── *The following lodgings were either not evaluated or did not* ────────
meet AAA rating requirements but are listed for your information only.

PINE GARTH COTTAGES
Phone: 269/469-1642
[fyi]   Did not meet all AAA rating requirements for locking devices in some guest rooms at time of last evaluation
    on 01/16/2002. **Location:** I-94, exit 6, 2 mi w, then 0.4 mi n. 15790 Lakeshore Rd 49129 (PO Box 347). Facilities, serv-
Cottage ices, and decor characterize a mid-range property.

PINE GARTH INN
Phone: 269/469-1642
[fyi]   Did not meet all AAA rating requirements for locking devices in some guest rooms at time of last evaluation
    on 01/16/2002. **Location:** I-94, exit 6, 2 mi w, then 0.4 mi n. 15790 Lakeshore Rd 49129 (PO Box 347). Facilities, serv-
Bed & Breakfast ices, and decor characterize a mid-range property.

SWEETHAVEN RESORT
Phone: 269/469-0332
[fyi]   Did not meet all AAA rating requirements for locking devices in some guest rooms at time of last evaluation
    on 01/16/2002. **Location:** I-94, exit 6, just w. Located in rural area. 9517 Union Pier Rd 49129. Facilities, services, and
Cabin decor characterize a mid-range property.

──────── **WHERE TO DINE** ────────

MILLER'S COUNTRY HOUSE   **Lunch:** $7-$9   **Dinner:** $18-$26   **Phone:** 269/469-5950

    Location: I-94, exit 6, 1 mi w on Union Pier Rd, 0.3 mi s. 16409 Red Arrow Hwy 49129. **Hours:** 5 pm-11 pm, Sat &
▼▼ ▼▼   Sun from noon. Closed: 11/27, 12/24, 12/25; also Tues 9/2-5/30. **Features:** A comfy roadside
American establishment featuring a large, airy dining room that looks out over gardens and a small pond. New Zealand rack of lamb and American selections make up the varied menu. Casual dress; cocktails. **Parking:** on-site. **Cards:** AX, CB, DC, DS, MC, VI.

🅱M 🍽 ✕

UPPER PENINSULA

To help you more easily locate accommodations in the Upper Peninsula region of Michigan, please see the map on page 455. You can find accommodation listings under the alphabetical header for each city whose name appears on the map in red type.

UTICA —See Detroit p. 277.

WALKER pop. 21,842—See also GRAND RAPIDS.

──────── WHERE TO STAY ────────

AMERIHOST INN-GRAND RAPIDS NORTH
Phone: (616)791-8500

AAA SAVE

All Year   1P: $71-$75   2P: $75-$79   XP: $6   F17
Location: I-96, exit 28 (Walker Ave), just s. Located in a commercial area. 2171 Holton Ct 49544. Fax: 616/791-8630. **Facility:** 60 one-bedroom standard units, some with whirlpools. 2 stories, interior corridors. *Bath:* combo or shower only. **Parking:** on-site. **Terms:** [ECP] meal plan available. **Amenities:** voice mail, safes (fee), irons, hair dryers. **Pool(s):** heated indoor. **Leisure Activities:** sauna, whirlpool, exercise room. **Guest Services:** valet laundry. **Business Services:** meeting rooms. **Cards:** AX, CB, DC, DS, JC, MC, VI. **Special Amenities:** free continental breakfast and free newspaper.

Small-scale Hotel

SOME UNITS

BAYMONT INN & SUITES GRAND RAPIDS-WALKER
Phone: (616)735-9595

AAA SAVE

All Year [ECP]   1P: $79-$120   2P: $89-$140   XP: $10   F18
Location: I-96, exit 28 (Walker Ave), just s. Located in a commercial area. 2151 Holton Ct NW 49544. Fax: 616/735-9600. **Facility:** 89 one-bedroom standard units, some with whirlpools. 4 stories, interior corridors. *Bath:* combo or shower only. **Parking:** on-site. **Terms:** 1-3 night minimum stay, weekly rates available, package plans. **Amenities:** video games, voice mail, irons, hair dryers. **Pool(s):** heated indoor. **Leisure Activities:** whirlpool, exercise room. **Guest Services:** valet and coin laundry. **Business Services:** meeting rooms. **Cards:** AX, CB, DC, DS, MC, VI. **Special Amenities:** free continental breakfast and free newspaper.

Small-scale Hotel

SOME UNITS

HAMPTON INN- GRAND RAPIDS NORTH
Phone: (616)647-1000

SAVE

All Year [ECP]   1P: $85   2P: $89
Location: I-96 and SR 37, exit Alpine Rd, just ne. Located in a commercial area. 500 Center Dr 49544 (500 Center Dr, GRAND RAPIDS). Fax: 616/647-1001. **Facility:** 84 units. 81 one-bedroom standard units, some with whirlpools. 3 one-bedroom suites ($109-$139). 4 stories, interior corridors. *Bath:* combo or shower only. **Parking:** on-site, winter plug-ins. **Terms:** cancellation fee imposed. **Amenities:** video games, dual phone lines, voice mail, irons, hair dryers. **Pool(s):** heated indoor. **Leisure Activities:** whirlpool, exercise room. **Guest Services:** valet laundry. **Business Services:** meeting rooms. **Cards:** AX, CB, DC, DS, MC, VI.

Small-scale Hotel

SOME UNITS

HOLIDAY INN EXPRESS HOTEL & SUITES
Phone: (616)647-4100

All Year [ECP]   1P: $69-$99   2P: $69-$99
Location: I-96 and SR 37, exit Alpine Rd, just ne. Located in a commercial area. 358 RiverRidge Dr 49544. Fax: 616/647-4101. **Facility:** 94 one-bedroom standard units, some with whirlpools. 3 stories, interior corridors. *Bath:* combo or shower only. **Parking:** on-site. **Amenities:** video games, high-speed Internet, dual phone lines, voice mail, irons, hair dryers. **Pool(s):** heated indoor. **Leisure Activities:** whirlpool, exercise room. *Fee:* game room. **Guest Services:** valet and coin laundry. **Business Services:** meeting rooms, business center. **Cards:** AX, DC, DS, JC, MC, VI.

Small-scale Hotel

SOME UNITS

WALLED LAKE —See Detroit p. 278.

WALTZ —See Detroit p. 278.

WARREN —See Detroit p. 278.

WATERFORD —See Detroit p. 280.

Upper Peninsula

AAA recommended lodgings and restaurants are listed ONLY under places shown in Red Type on this map.

Miles

0   46

WATERSMEET

———— WHERE TO STAY ————

AMERICINN OF WATERSMEET-LAC VIEUX DESERT   **Phone:** (906)358-4949
▼▼▼▼   All Year   1P: $60   2P: $140   XP: $10   F17
           Location: 1.8 mi n of US 2. N5384 US Hwy 45 49969 (PO Box 99). Fax: 906/358-4950. **Facility:** 129 units. 124
Large-scale Hotel   one-bedroom standard units, some with whirlpools. 5 one-bedroom suites, some with whirlpools. 2 stories,
           interior corridors. *Bath:* combo or shower only. **Parking:** on-site, winter plug-ins. **Terms:** check-in 4 pm, [CP]
meal plan available, package plans, pets ($100 deposit, in smoking units). **Amenities:** voice mail. **Pool(s):** heated indoor.
Leisure Activities: sauna, whirlpool, snowmobiling, exercise room. *Fee:* golf-9 holes, game room. **Guest Services:** gift shop,
coin laundry. **Business Services:** meeting rooms. **Cards:** AX, DS, MC, VI.

SOME UNITS

🎱 ASK 🅂🄳 🐾 🍽 🛅 ➲ ⊠ 📷 💻 /⊠ 🖥 🛢 🖼 /

WEST BLOOMFIELD —See Detroit p. 281.

WEST BRANCH pop. 1,926

———— WHERE TO STAY ————

LA HACIENDA MOTEL   **Phone:** 989/345-2345
▼   Property failed to provide current rates
           Location: I-75, exit 215, 1.5 mi e on I-75 business loop. 969 W Houghton Ave 48661. **Facility:** 13 one-bedroom stan-
Motel   dard units. 1 story, exterior corridors. *Bath:* combo or shower only. **Parking:** on-site, winter plug-ins. **Leisure**
Activities: snowmobiling. **Cards:** AX, DS, MC, VI.

SOME UNITS

🐑 🛗 /⊠ 🛢 🖼 /

QUALITY INN-FOWARDS CONFERENCE CENTER

Phone: (989)345-3503

AAA SAVE

Small-scale Hotel

All Year · 1P: $65-$95 · 2P: $71-$99 · XP: $6 · F
Location: I-75, exit 212 (Cook Rd). 2980 Cook Rd 48661 (PO Box 369). Fax: 989/345-4194. **Facility:** 80 one-bedroom standard units, some with whirlpools. 2 stories, interior corridors. *Bath:* combo or shower only. **Parking:** on-site, winter plug-ins. **Amenities:** video library (fee), irons, hair dryers. *Some:* dual phone lines. **Dining:** 6 am-11 pm, cocktails. **Pool(s):** heated indoor. **Leisure Activities:** whirlpool. *Fee:* game room. **Guest Services:** gift shop, valet laundry. **Business Services:** conference facilities. **Cards:** AX, CB, DC, DS, JC, MC, VI. **Special Amenities:** early check-in/late check-out and free local telephone calls. *(See color ad p 456)*

SOME UNITS

SUPER 8 MOTEL

Phone: (989)345-8488

AAA SAVE

Small-scale Hotel

All Year [CP] · 1P: $59-$89 · 2P: $65-$95 · XP: $6
Location: I-75, exit 212 (Cook Rd). 2596 Austin's Way 48661 (PO Box 338). Fax: 989/345-8497. **Facility:** 77 one-bedroom standard units, some with whirlpools. 2 stories (no elevator), interior corridors. *Bath:* combo or shower only. **Parking:** on-site, winter plug-ins. **Terms:** small pets only. **Amenities:** video library (fee). **Pool(s):** heated indoor. **Leisure Activities:** whirlpool. *Fee:* game room. **Guest Services:** coin laundry. **Cards:** AX, CB, DC, DS, JC, MC, VI. **Special Amenities:** free continental breakfast and free local telephone calls. *(See ad p 456)*

SOME UNITS

------- WHERE TO DINE -------

------- *The following restaurant has not been evaluated by AAA* -------
but is listed for your information only.

COYLES

Phone: 989/343-9440

fyi

Not evaluated. **Location:** I-75, exit 215, 1 mi e on SR 55. 3444 M-55 48661. **Features:** Patrons can pick and choose from the wide assortment of tempting options on the lunch and dinner buffets or order from a menu of reasonably priced items.

WHITE CLOUD pop. 1,420

------- WHERE TO STAY -------

THE SHACK

Phone: 231/924-6683

Resort
Small-scale Hotel

All Year [BP] · 2P: $60-$190
Location: From blinker; 5.5 mi w to Jugville. 2263 W 14th St 49349. Fax: 231/924-5065. **Facility:** Smoke free premises. 44 units. 42 one- and 2 two-bedroom standard units, some with whirlpools. 1-2 stories (no elevator), interior/exterior corridors. *Bath:* combo or shower only. **Parking:** on-site. **Terms:** 20 day cancellation notice-fee imposed. **Amenities:** voice mail, hair dryers. *Some:* irons. **Leisure Activities:** paddleboats, fishing, cross country skiing, horseshoes, shuffleboard, volleyball. *Fee:* game room. **Business Services:** meeting rooms. **Cards:** DS, MC, VI.

SOME UNITS

WHITEHALL pop. 2,884

------- WHERE TO STAY -------

LAKE LAND MOTEL

Phone: (231)894-5644

AAA SAVE

Motel

6/8-9/1	1P: $65-$75	2P: $70-$75	XP: $5
4/1-6/7	1P: $40-$50	2P: $45-$55	XP: $5
9/2-10/31	1P: $40-$45	2P: $45-$55	XP: $5
11/1-3/31	1P: $35-$40	2P: $40-$45	XP: $5

Location: On US 31 business route, 0.8 mi w of US 31. Located in a commercial area. 1002 E Colby St 49461. **Facility:** 12 one-bedroom standard units. 1 story, exterior corridors. **Parking:** on-site. **Terms:** small pets only ($5 extra charge). **Cards:** AX, DS, MC, VI. **Special Amenities:** early check-in/late check-out and free local telephone calls.

SOME UNITS

RAMADA INN

Phone: (231)893-3030

AAA SAVE

Small-scale Hotel

All Year · 1P: $100-$144 · 2P: $100-$144 · XP: $5 · F17
Location: US 31, exit Whitehall/Montague, just e. 2865 Colby Rd 49461. Fax: 231/893-0030. **Facility:** 66 one-bedroom standard units, some with whirlpools. 2 stories (no elevator), interior corridors. **Parking:** on-site. **Terms:** [ECP] meal plan available. **Amenities:** video library (fee), dual phone lines, voice mail, irons, hair dryers. **Pool(s):** heated indoor. **Leisure Activities:** sauna, exercise room. *Fee:* game room. **Guest Services:** coin laundry. **Business Services:** meeting rooms. **Cards:** AX, CB, DC, DS, MC, VI.

SOME UNITS

------- WHERE TO DINE -------

PINHEAD'S GUTTERS & GRUB

Lunch: $5-$10 · Dinner: $5-$12 · Phone: 231/894-4103

American

Location: Just w of center. 115 South Lake 49461. **Hours:** 4 pm-10 pm, Fri-11 pm, Sat 11 am-11 pm, Sun noon-9 pm. Closed: 1/1, 11/27, 12/25. **Features:** The friendly restaurant is a cozy place in which to enjoy such choices as wood-fired pizza and half-pound burgers while bowling a few frames. The loud and lively atmosphere attracts boaters and vacationers during summer and families during winter. Casual dress; cocktails. **Parking:** on-site. **Cards:** AX, DS, MC, VI.

WHITMORE LAKE pop. 6,574

────── **WHERE TO STAY** ──────

BEST WESTERN WHITMORE LAKE
AAA SAVE
WWWW
Motel

All Year   1P: $75   2P: $75   XP: $6   F12

Phone: (734)449-2058

Location: US 23, exit 53. 9897 Main St 48189. Fax: 734/449-8635. **Facility:** 61 units. 59 one-bedroom standard units. 1 one- and 1 two-bedroom suites ($95-$150), some with kitchens and/or whirlpools. 2 stories, exterior corridors. **Parking:** on-site, winter plug-ins. **Terms:** [CP] meal plan available, pets ($25 extra charge, in limited units). **Amenities:** irons, hair dryers. **Pool(s):** heated indoor. **Leisure Activities:** sauna. **Guest Services:** coin laundry. **Business Services:** meeting rooms, fax (fee). **Cards:** AX, DC, DS, MC, VI. **Special Amenities:** free continental breakfast and free newspaper.

SOME UNITS

🆂 🐕 🍽️ 🏊 🎿 🖧 📠 📺 / ✕ /

WILLIAMSTON pop. 3,441

────── **WHERE TO STAY** ──────

ACORN MOTEL
AAA SAVE
W
Motel

All Year   1P: $52   2P: $59   XP: $4   F17

Phone: (517)655-6793

Location: I-96, exit 117, 1.5 mi n, 0.7 mi e on SR 43. 2346 E Grand River Ave 48895 (PO Box 327). Fax: 517/655-4309. **Facility:** 8 one-bedroom standard units. 1 story, exterior corridors. **Terms:** 3 day cancellation notice-fee imposed. **Cards:** MC, VI. **Special Amenities:** free local telephone calls.

SOME UNITS

🆂 🖧 📠 📺 / ✕ /

TOPLIFF'S TARA BED & BREAKFAST
WWW
Bed & Breakfast

All Year   1P: $65-$115   2P: $75-$125   XP: $15

Phone: 517/655-8860

Location: I-96, exit 117, just s, 3.5 mi w. 251 Noble Rd 48895. Fax: 847/556-0241. **Facility:** Built in 1905, this rural farmhouse is in a serene, natural setting; it has been restored and is furnished with period antiques. Smoke free premises. 5 one-bedroom standard units, some with whirlpools. 3 stories (no elevator), interior corridors. *Bath:* some shared or private, combo or shower only. **Parking:** on-site. **Terms:** check-in 4 pm, 10 day cancellation notice-fee imposed, [BP] meal plan available, no pets allowed (owner's pet on premises). **Amenities:** hair dryers. **Pool(s):** outdoor. **Guest Services:** gift shop. **Cards:** DC, JC, VI.

SOME UNITS

🏊 ✕ 🕿 / 📺 /

────── **WHERE TO DINE** ──────

RED CEDAR GRILL
WW
American

Dinner: $10-$15

Phone: 517/655-3766

Location: I-96, exit 117, 1.5 mi n; downtown. 150 E Grand River Ave 48895. **Hours:** 11 am-10 pm, Fri & Sat-11 pm, Sun noon-9 pm. Closed major holidays. **Reservations:** accepted. **Features:** An eclectic mixture of art and mirrors adorns the walls of this casual, open concept restaurant. A large and varied menu features a number of creatively prepared dishes and makes for interesting reading in its own right. Casual dress; cocktails. **Parking:** on-site. **Cards:** AX, DC, DS, MC, VI.

♿ 🍸 ✕

WIXOM —*See Detroit p. 281.*

WOODHAVEN —*See Detroit p. 281.*

WYMAN

——— **WHERE TO DINE** ———

MAXFIELD'S
▽▽ ▽▽
American

Lunch: $6-$8   **Dinner:** $12-$20   **Phone:** 989/427-5630
Location: 3 mi n of SR 46 and blinker light in Edmore. 11228 Wyman Rd 49310. **Hours:** 11 am-9 pm, Fri & Sat-10 pm, Sun noon-5 pm. Closed: 12/24, 12/25; also Mon. **Features:** An area institution since 1959, the family-oriented restaurant is decorated with paintings and tapestries created by the owner's mother. More than 100 homemade items line the tempting salad bar—the cornerstone of guests' dining experience.
Casual dress; cocktails. **Parking:** on-site. **Cards:** AX, DS, MC, VI.

WYOMING pop. 69,368—*See also GRAND RAPIDS.*

——— **WHERE TO STAY** ———

HAMPTON INN GRAND RAPIDS SOUTH
[SAVE]
▽▽▽▽
Small-scale Hotel

Phone: (616)261-5500
All Year [ECP]   1P: $89-$129   2P: $89-$129
Location: US 131 and 54th St, exit 78. Located in a commercial area. 755 54th St SW 49509. Fax: 616/261-9120. **Facility:** 139 one-bedroom standard units, some with whirlpools. 4 stories, interior corridors. *Bath:* combo or shower only. **Parking:** on-site. **Terms:** check-in 4 pm. **Amenities:** voice mail, irons, hair dryers. **Pool(s):** heated indoor. **Leisure Activities:** whirlpool, exercise room. *Fee:* game room. **Guest Services:** valet and coin laundry. **Business Services:** meeting rooms. **Cards:** AX, DC, DS, MC, VI.

SOME UNITS
FEE

HOWARD JOHNSON PLAZA HOTEL
AAA [SAVE]
▽▽▽▽
Large-scale Hotel

Phone: (616)241-6444
All Year   1P: $59   2P: $109   XP: $10   F12
Location: On SR 11, 0.3 mi e of jct US 131, exit 28th St. Located in a commercial area. 255 28th St SW 49548. Fax: 616/241-1807. **Facility:** 155 one-bedroom standard units. 5 stories, interior corridors. **Parking:** on-site. **Terms:** check-in 4 pm, 3 day cancellation notice-fee imposed, 13% service charge. **Amenities:** irons, hair dryers. **Dining:** 6:30 am-9 pm, Fri & Sat-10 pm, Sun 7 am-8 pm, cocktails. **Pool(s):** heated outdoor, heated indoor. **Leisure Activities:** sauna, whirlpool, putting green, exercise room, shuffleboard. *Fee:* pool tables, game room. **Guest Services:** valet and coin laundry. **Business Services:** meeting rooms. **Cards:** AX, CB, DC, DS, JC, MC, VI.
Special Amenities: early check-in/late check-out and free newspaper.

SOME UNITS

RAMADA LIMITED
▽▽▽ ▽▽▽
Small-scale Hotel

Phone: (616)452-1461
4/1-9/1 [ECP]   1P: $62-$79   2P: $69-$79   XP: $7   F18
9/2-3/31 [ECP]   1P: $59-$69   2P: $65-$69   XP: $7   F18
Location: On SR 11, 0.4 mi e of US 131. Located in a commercial area. 65 28th St SW 49548. Fax: 616/452-5115. **Facility:** 54 one-bedroom standard units, some with whirlpools. 2 stories (no elevator), interior/exterior corridors. **Parking:** on-site. **Amenities:** voice mail. *Some:* irons, hair dryers. **Pool(s):** small heated indoor. **Leisure Activities:** exercise room. **Cards:** AX, CB, DC, DS, MC, VI.

SOME UNITS

SUPER 8 MOTEL
▽▽
Motel

Phone: (616)530-8588
All Year   1P: $47-$59   2P: $59-$64   XP: $5   F12
Location: US 131, exit 79. Located in a commercial area. 727 44th St SW 49509. Fax: 616/530-8588. **Facility:** 62 one-bedroom standard units. 3 stories (no elevator), interior corridors. **Parking:** on-site, winter plug-ins. **Terms:** 3 day cancellation notice, weekly rates available, small pets only ($10 fee). **Amenities:** safes (fee).
Cards: AX, DC, MC, VI.

SOME UNITS

YALE pop. 2,063

——— **WHERE TO STAY** ———

THE ROUSH HOUSE BED & BREAKFAST
▽▽▽ ▽▽▽
Bed & Breakfast

Phone: (810)387-2810
All Year [BP]   1P: $75   2P: $75
Location: Center. 103 E Mechanic St 48097. **Facility:** This Victorian house dating back to 1905, is tastefully appointed with assorted antiques, polished woodwork and stained glass windows. Open Thursday through Sunday only. Smoke free premises. 4 one-bedroom standard units. 2 stories (no elevator), interior corridors. *Bath:* some shared, combo or shower only. **Parking:** on-site. **Terms:** check-in 4 pm, age restrictions may apply, cancellation fee imposed, weekly rates available, package plans, no pets allowed (owner's pets on premises). **Amenities:** *Some:* hair dryers. **Leisure Activities:** whirlpool. **Guest Services:** TV in common area. **Cards:** DS, MC, VI.

YPSILANTI pop. 22,362

——— WHERE TO STAY ———

PARISH HOUSE INN
▼▼ ▼▼

Historic Bed
& Breakfast

Phone: (734)480-4800

All Year   1P: $89-$99   2P: $99-$165   XP: $20   F5
Location: I-94, exit 183, 0.5 mi n. Located in the historic district. 103 S Huron St 48197. **Fax:** 734/480-7472. **Facility:** Smoke free premises. 8 units. 7 one-bedroom standard units. 1 one-bedroom suite. 3 stories (no elevator), interior corridors. *Bath:* combo or shower only. **Parking:** on-site. **Terms:** check-in 4 pm, 7 day cancellation notice, [BP] meal plan available. **Amenities:** video library, voice mail. **Business Services:** meeting rooms. **Cards:** AX, DS, MC, VI.

SOME UNITS
[YI◆] [✕] [DATA PORT] / [VCR] /

YPSILANTI MARRIOTT AT EAGLE CREST
ⒶⒶⒶ [SAVE]
▼▼ ▼▼ ▼▼

Resort
Large-scale Hotel

Phone: (734)487-2000

All Year   1P: $79-$169   2P: $79-$169   XP: $10   F
Location: I-94, exit 183, just se. 1275 S Huron St 48197. **Fax:** 734/487-0773. **Facility:** Bordering a river and the rolling terrain of a golf course, this big-city hotel is in a country-club setting. 236 one-bedroom standard units. 8 stories, interior corridors. **Parking:** on-site, winter plug-ins. **Amenities:** dual phone lines, voice mail, irons, hair dryers. **Dining:** 6:30 am-2 & 5-11 pm, cocktails. **Pool(s):** heated indoor. **Leisure Activities:** sauna, whirlpool, steamroom, boat dock, fishing, cross country skiing, exercise room, volleyball. *Fee:* golf-18 holes, driving range, game room. **Guest Services:** gift shop, valet laundry. **Business Services:** conference facilities, business center. **Cards:** AX, CB, DC, DS, JC, MC, VI. **Special Amenities:** free newspaper. *(See color ad p 194)*

SOME UNITS
[YI] [Y] [&M] [🎧] [🏊] [✕] [📽] [DATA PORT] [💻] / [✕] [🛏] /

——— WHERE TO DINE ———

HAAB'S
ⒶⒶⒶ
▼▼ ▼▼
American

Lunch: $6-$11   **Dinner:** $9-$19   **Phone:** 734-483-8200
Location: Downtown. 18 W Michigan Ave 48197. **Hours:** 11 am-9 pm, Fri & Sat-10 pm. **Closed:** 12/25. **Reservations:** suggested; weekends. **Features:** A local landmark since 1934, the longtime favorite is known for its rustic-looking dining room and traditional menu of delicious, well-prepared beef and seafood. Casual dress; cocktails. **Parking:** on-site. **Cards:** AX, DC, DS, MC, VI.

[✕]

Wisconsin

ABBOTSFORD pop. 1,956

────── **WHERE TO STAY** ──────

SLEEP INN
SAVE

Small-scale Hotel

MC, VI.

All Year [ECP]   1P: $49-$79   2P: $53-$79   XP: $5   F18
Location: SR 29, exit 132 (SR 13), just se. 300 E Elderberry Rd 54455 (PO Box 590). Fax: 715/223-0508.
Facility: 60 one-bedroom standard units, some with whirlpools. 3 stories, interior corridors. *Bath:* combo or
shower only. **Parking:** on-site, winter plug-ins. **Terms:** check-in 4 pm, pets ($15 extra charge, in designated
units). **Amenities:** voice mail. *Some:* irons, hair dryers. **Pool(s):** small heated indoor. **Leisure Activities:** exercise room. *Fee:* game room. **Business Services:** meeting rooms, fax (fee). **Cards:** AX, CB, DC, DS, JC,

Phone: (715)223-3337

SOME UNITS

────── **WHERE TO DINE** ──────

ABBY CAFE

American

Lunch: $4-$8   **Dinner:** $4-$8   Phone: 715/223-3943
Location: On Business Rt 29; downtown. 206 E Spruce 54405. **Hours:** 6 am-10 pm. Closed: 11/27, 12/25.
Features: Simple, made-from-scratch entrees and homemade desserts are the draw at the popular diner.
The country decor is representative of the surrounding farming community. Casual dress. **Parking:** on-site.
Cards: MC, VI.

ALGOMA pop. 3,357

────── **WHERE TO STAY** ──────

ALGOMA BEACH MOTEL & CONDOS
AAA **SAVE**

Small-scale Hotel

Phone: 920/487-2828
5/24-3/31   1P: $79-$259   2P: $79-$259   XP: $15   F15
4/1-5/23   1P: $59-$199   2P: $59-$199   XP: $15   F15
Location: From jct SR 22 and 72; 2 mi n on SR 22. Located in a semi-commercial area. 1500 Lake St 54201.
Fax: 920/487-2844. **Facility:** 32 units. 28 one-bedroom standard units, some with efficiencies and/or whirlpools. 4 vacation homes ($199-$259). 1-2 stories (no elevator), interior/exterior corridors. *Bath:* combo or
shower only. **Parking:** on-site. **Terms:** 3 day cancellation notice, [CP] meal plan available, package plans,
pets ($15 extra charge, in smoking units). **Amenities:** voice mail. *Some:* irons, hair dryers. **Leisure Activities:** fishing, beach-
side picnic tables & grills. **Cards:** AX, CB, DC, DS, MC, VI. **Special Amenities:** free continental breakfast and free local telephone calls.

SOME UNITS

SCENIC SHORE INN

Motel

Phone: 920/487-3214
6/20-8/31   1P: $49   2P: $59   XP: $8   F15
4/1-6/19 & 9/1-10/31   1P: $40   2P: $49   XP: $8   F15
11/1-3/31   1P: $36   2P: $44   XP: $8   F15
Location: Jct SR 54, 0.8 mi s on SR 42. Located in a semi-commercial area. 2221 Lake St 54201. **Facility:** 13 one-
bedroom standard units. 2 stories (no elevator), exterior corridors. **Parking:** on-site, winter plug-ins. **Terms:** 3 day cancellation
notice, weekly rates available, small pets only (in smoking units). **Leisure Activities:** Fee: charter fishing. **Cards:** AX, DS,
MC, VI.

SOME UNITS

ANTIGO pop. 8,560

────── **WHERE TO STAY** ──────

SLEEP INN
SAVE

Small-scale Hotel

Phone: (715)623-0506
All Year [CP]   1P: $49-$71   2P: $53-$76   XP: $6   F18
Location: On US 45 N, 0.3 mi n of jct SR 64 E. 525 Memory Ln 54409. Fax: 715/623-0602. **Facility:** 45 one-
bedroom standard units. 2 stories, interior corridors. *Bath:* combo or shower only. **Parking:** on-site.
Amenities: voice mail, irons, hair dryers. **Pool(s):** small heated indoor. **Leisure Activities:** whirlpool. **Busi-
ness Services:** fax (fee). **Cards:** AX, DC, DS, JC, MC, VI.

SOME UNITS

SUPER 8 MOTEL-ANTIGO

Small-scale Hotel

MC, VI.

Phone: (715)623-4188
All Year [CP]   1P: $51-$99   2P: $55-$99   XP: $5   F12
Location: On US 45 at jct SR 64 E. 535 Century Ave 54409. Fax: 715/623-5787. **Facility:** 52 one-bedroom stan-
dard units, some with whirlpools. 2 stories (no elevator), interior corridors. *Bath:* combo or shower only.
Parking: on-site, winter plug-ins. **Terms:** pets ($15 extra charge, in smoking units). **Amenities:** safes (fee).
Pool(s): heated indoor. **Leisure Activities:** whirlpool. **Business Services:** meeting rooms, fax (fee). **Cards:** AX, CB, DC, DS,

SOME UNITS

APPLETON pop. 70,087

────── **WHERE TO STAY** ──────

APPLETON WINGATE INN
AAA **SAVE**

Small-scale Hotel

calls and free newspaper.

Phone: (920)993-1200
All Year [ECP]   1P: $59-$130   XP: $10   F18
Location: US 41, exit 137 (SR 125), just nw. 300 Mall Dr 54913. Fax: 920/993-9090. **Facility:** 80 one-bedroom
standard units. 3 stories, interior corridors. *Bath:* combo or shower only. **Parking:** on-site, winter plug-ins.
Amenities: high-speed Internet, dual phone lines, voice mail, irons, hair dryers. **Pool(s):** small heated indoor.
Leisure Activities: whirlpool, exercise room. **Guest Services:** valet laundry. **Business Services:** meeting
rooms, business center. **Cards:** AX, CB, DC, DS, JC, MC, VI. **Special Amenities:** free local telephone

SOME UNITS

BEST WESTERN MIDWAY HOTEL
Phone: (920)731-4141

(AAA) (SAVE)
◇◇◇ ◇◇◇
Small-scale Hotel

All Year [CP]   1P: $89-$109   2P: $89-$109   XP: $10   F18
Location: US 41, exit 137 (SR 125), 0.5 mi e. 3033 W College Ave 54914. Fax: 920/731-6343. **Facility:** 105 one-bedroom standard units, some with whirlpools. 2 stories (no elevator), interior corridors. **Parking:** on-site, winter plug-ins. **Terms:** pets ($10 extra charge). **Amenities:** voice mail, irons, hair dryers. **Dining:** 6:30 am-10 pm, Sat & Sun from 11 am, cocktails. **Pool(s):** heated indoor. **Leisure Activities:** sauna, whirlpool, domed recreation area, exercise room. **Guest Services:** valet laundry, area transportation-within 4 mi. **Business Services:** meeting rooms, fax (fee). **Cards:** AX, DC, DS, MC, VI. **Special Amenities:** free continental breakfast and free newspaper.

SOME UNITS

🆂ᴅ ✈ 🐾 🍴 🍽 🏋 ⛵ ✕ 🎥 [DATA PORT] 🖥 / ✕ [VCR] 🖴 🖵 /

BUDGETEL INN APPLETON
Phone: (920)734-6070

(AAA) (SAVE)
◇◇◇ ◇◇◇
Motel

All Year [ECP]   1P: $59-$79   2P: $59-$79
Location: US 41, exit 137 (SR 125), just e. 3920 W College Ave 54914. Fax: 920/734-0460. **Facility:** 83 one-bedroom standard units. 2 stories (no elevator), interior/exterior corridors. *Bath:* combo or shower only. **Parking:** on-site, winter plug-ins. **Terms:** small pets only (in designated units). **Amenities:** video games (fee), voice mail, irons, hair dryers. **Pool(s):** heated outdoor. **Leisure Activities:** 2 tennis courts, volleyball. **Guest Services:** valet and coin laundry. **Business Services:** meeting rooms, fax (fee). **Cards:** AX, CB, DC, DS, MC, VI. **Special Amenities:** free continental breakfast and free newspaper. *(See color ad below)*

SOME UNITS

🆂ᴅ ✈ 🐾 🍴 ⛵ 🎥 [DATA PORT] 🖥 / ✕ 🖴 🖵 /

COMFORT SUITES COMFORT DOME

Phone: (920)730-3800

(AAA) (SAVE)

All Year [ECP]   1P: $90-$126   2P: $100-$136   XP: $10   F18

Small-scale Hotel

Location: US 41, exit 138 (Wisconsin Ave), just e. 3809 W Wisconsin Ave 54914. Fax: 920/730-9558. **Facility:** 130 one-bedroom standard units, some with kitchens and/or whirlpools. 2 stories (no elevator), interior corridors. **Parking:** on-site, winter plug-ins. **Amenities:** voice mail, irons, hair dryers. *Fee:* video games, safes. **Pool(s):** heated indoor. **Leisure Activities:** sauna, whirlpool, seasonal patio and gazebo, exercise room. *Fee:* game room. **Guest Services:** complimentary evening beverages, valet and coin laundry, area transportation. **Business Services:** meeting rooms, fax (fee). **Cards:** AX, CB, DC, DS, JC, MC, VI. **Special Amenities:** free continental breakfast. *(See color ad p 587)*

SOME UNITS

$\boxed{S_D}$ $\boxed{\leftarrow}$ $\boxed{}$ $\boxed{}$ $\boxed{\approx}$ $\boxed{\times}$ $\boxed{}$ $\boxed{{}^{DATA}_{PORT}}$ $\boxed{}$ $\boxed{}$ $\boxed{}$ / $\boxed{\times}$ $\boxed{VCR}$ /
FEE

COUNTRY INN & SUITES BY CARLSON

Phone: (920)830-3240

(AAA) (SAVE)

All Year   1P: $69-$99   2P: $69-$99   XP: $10   F18

Small-scale Hotel

Location: US 41, exit 137 (W SR 125), just nw. 355 Fox River Dr 54913. Fax: 920/830-9868. **Facility:** 106 units. 97 one-bedroom standard units, some with whirlpools. 9 one-bedroom suites ($99-$199), some with whirlpools. 3 stories, interior corridors. *Bath:* combo or shower only. **Parking:** on-site, winter plug-ins. **Terms:** [ECP] meal plan available, small pets only. **Amenities:** video games (fee), voice mail, irons, hair dryers. **Pool(s):** heated indoor. **Leisure Activities:** whirlpool, limited exercise equipment. **Guest Services:** valet and coin laundry, area transportation-mall. **Business Services:** meeting rooms, fax (fee). **Cards:** AX, DC, DS, MC, VI. **Special Amenities:** free continental breakfast and free newspaper. *(See color ad starting on p 556 & below)*

SOME UNITS

$\boxed{S_D}$ $\boxed{\leftarrow}$ $\boxed{}$ $\boxed{\uparrow\uparrow}$ $\boxed{\&}$ $\boxed{\approx}$ $\boxed{}$ $\boxed{{}^{DATA}_{PORT}}$ $\boxed{}$ / $\boxed{\times}$ $\boxed{}$ $\boxed{}$ /

EXEL INN OF APPLETON

Phone: (920)733-5551

(AAA) (SAVE)

Motel

6/1-8/31 [CP]   1P: $36-$52   2P: $42-$59   XP: $6   F18
4/1-5/31 & 9/1-3/31 [CP]   1P: $36-$48   2P: $42-$54   XP: $6   F18

Location: US 41, exit 137 (SR 125), just e. 210 Westhill Blvd 54914. Fax: 920/733-7199. **Facility:** 104 one-bedroom standard units, some with whirlpools. 2 stories (no elevator), interior corridors. **Parking:** on-site. **Terms:** small pets only (in smoking units). **Amenities:** irons. *Some:* hair dryers. **Leisure Activities:** limited exercise equipment. **Guest Services:** coin laundry. **Business Services:** fax (fee). **Cards:** AX, CB, DC, DS, MC, VI. **Special Amenities:** early check-in/late check-out and free continental breakfast. *(See color ad below)*

SOME UNITS

$\boxed{S_D}$ $\boxed{}$ $\boxed{\uparrow\uparrow}$ $\boxed{}$ $\boxed{{}^{DATA}_{PORT}}$ $\boxed{}$ / $\boxed{\times}$ $\boxed{}$ $\boxed{}$ /
FEE FEE

FAIRFIELD INN BY MARRIOTT

Phone: (920)954-0202

[SAVE]

5/1-10/31 [CP]	1P: $65-$78	2P: $71-$84	XP: $6 F18
4/1-4/30 & 11/1-3/31 [CP]	1P: $60-$74	2P: $66-$80	XP: $6 F18

Small-scale Hotel

Location: US 41, exit 137 (W SR 125), just nw. 132 Mall Dr 54913. Fax: 920/954-0202. **Facility:** 63 one-bedroom standard units. 3 stories, interior corridors. **Parking:** on-site, winter plug-ins. **Amenities:** irons, hair dryers. **Pool(s):** small heated indoor. **Leisure Activities:** whirlpool. **Guest Services:** valet laundry. **Business Services:** fax (fee). **Cards:** AX, DC, DS, MC, VI.

SOME UNITS

🅂🄳 🕄➕ 🅿 ⛵ ⊞ 🎦 [DATA PORT] / ⊠ 🅱 🖼 /

HAMPTON INN APPLETON

Phone: (920)954-9211

[SAVE]

1/1-3/31 [ECP]	1P: $85-$150	2P: $95-$150	
4/1-12/31 [ECP]	1P: $83-$150	2P: $93-$150	

Small-scale Hotel

Location: US 41, exit 137 (W SR 125), just nw. 350 Fox River Dr 54913. Fax: 920/954-6514. **Facility:** 123 one-bedroom standard units. 4 stories, interior corridors. *Bath:* combo or shower only. **Parking:** on-site. **Terms:** 14 day cancellation notice-fee imposed, package plans - seasonal & weekends. **Amenities:** video games (fee), voice mail, irons, hair dryers. **Pool(s):** small heated indoor. **Leisure Activities:** whirlpool, limited exercise equipment. **Guest Services:** valet laundry, area transportation. **Business Services:** meeting rooms, fax (fee). **Cards:** AX, CB, DC, DS, MC, VI.

SOME UNITS

🅂🄳 ➕ 🕄➕ 🅰 🅿 ⛵ 🎦 [DATA PORT] ⊟ / ⊠ 🅱 🖼 /
FEE FEE

MICROTEL INN & SUITES

Phone: (920)997-3121

[AAA] [SAVE]

All Year [CP]	1P: $47-$82 XP: $5 F17

Small-scale Hotel

Location: US 41, exit 137 (W SR 125), just nw. 321 Metro Dr 54913. Fax: 920/997-3321. **Facility:** 79 one-bedroom standard units. 3 stories, interior corridors. *Bath:* combo or shower only. **Parking:** on-site, winter plug-ins. **Terms:** weekly rates available, pets ($10 deposit, in smoking units). **Leisure Activities:** whirlpool, limited exercise equipment. **Guest Services:** valet laundry. **Business Services:** meeting rooms, fax (fee). **Cards:** AX, DC, DS, MC, VI.

SOME UNITS

🛏 🕄➕ 🅰 🎦 [DATA PORT] / ⊠ 🅱 🖼 ⊟ /

RADISSON PAPER VALLEY HOTEL

Phone: (920)733-8000

All Year   1P: $89-$179   2P: $89-$179   XP: $10   F17

Location: 3 mi e of US 41, exit 137 (SR 125); downtown. 333 W College Ave 54911. Fax: 920/733-9220. **Facility:** 390 one-bedroom standard units, some with whirlpools. 7 stories, interior corridors. *Bath:* combo or shower only. **Parking:** on-site (fee) and street. **Terms:** cancellation fee imposed. **Amenities:** video games (fee), voice mail, irons, hair dryers. **Dining:** 2 restaurants, 6 am-11 pm, Sat & Sun from 6:30 am, cocktails, also, Vince Lombardi's Steakhouse, see separate listing. **Pool(s):** heated indoor. **Leisure Activities:** sauna, whirlpool, miniature golf, exercise room. **Guest Services:** gift shop, valet laundry. **Business Services:** conference facilities, business center. **Cards:** AX, CB, DC, DS, JC, MC, VI. *(See color ad p 466 & p 562)*

Large-scale Hotel

SOME UNITS

RESIDENCE INN BY MARRIOTT

Phone: (920)954-0570

All Year [BP]   1P: $90-$105   2P: $90-$105

Location: US 41, exit 137 (W SR 125), just nw on Mall Dr. 310 Metro Dr 54913. Fax: 920/954-0570. **Facility:** 66 units. 18 one-bedroom standard units with efficiencies. 36 one- and 12 two-bedroom suites ($90-$105), some with efficiencies or kitchens. 3 stories, interior corridors. **Parking:** on-site, winter plug-ins. **Terms:** [MAP] meal plan available, pets ($25 fee, $10 extra charge). **Amenities:** dual phone lines, voice mail, irons, hair dryers. **Pool(s):** small heated indoor. **Leisure Activities:** whirlpool, exercise room, sports court. **Guest Services:** complimentary evening beverages: Mon-Thurs, valet and coin laundry. **Business Services:** meeting rooms, fax (fee). **Cards:** AX, CB, DC, DS, JC, MC, VI.

Small-scale Hotel

SOME UNITS

SUPER 8 MOTEL

Phone: (920)731-0880

6/1-8/31 [CP]   1P: $55-$70   2P: $55-$75
4/1-5/31 & 9/1-3/31 [CP]   1P: $53-$57   2P: $53-$57

Location: US 41, exit 137 (SR 125), just e. 3624 W College Ave 54914. Fax: 920/731-0880. **Facility:** 81 one-bedroom standard units. 2 stories (no elevator), interior corridors. **Parking:** on-site, winter plug-ins. **Terms:** weekly rates available. **Amenities:** video games (fee). **Leisure Activities:** limited exercise equipment. **Guest Services:** coin laundry. **Business Services:** fax (fee). **Cards:** AX, CB, DC, DS, MC, VI.

Motel

SOME UNITS

FEE   FEE

WOODFIELD SUITES APPLETON

Phone: (920)734-7777

All Year [ECP]   1P: $109-$139   2P: $109-$139

Location: US 41, exit 137 (SR 125), just e. 3730 W College Ave 54914. Fax: 920/734-0049. **Facility:** 98 units. 23 one-bedroom standard units. 75 one-bedroom suites, some with efficiencies and/or whirlpools. 2 stories, interior corridors. **Parking:** on-site, winter plug-ins. **Terms:** pets ($50 deposit, $10 extra charge). **Amenities:** video games (fee), voice mail, irons, hair dryers. **Pool(s):** heated indoor. **Leisure Activities:** sauna, whirlpool, steamroom, indoor children's play area, exercise room. **Guest Services:** complimentary evening beverages, valet and coin laundry. **Business Services:** meeting rooms, fax (fee). **Cards:** AX, CB, DC, DS, MC, VI. **Special Amenities:** free continental breakfast and free newspaper. *(See color ad p 466)*

Small-scale Hotel

SOME UNITS

──── WHERE TO DINE ────

FOX RIVER BREWING COMPANY & RESTAURANT

Lunch: $7-$10   Dinner: $7-$18   Phone: 920/991-0000

Location: US 41, exit 138 (Wisconsin Ave), just sw; in Fox River Mall. 4301 W Wisconsin Ave 54915. **Hours:** 11 am-10 pm, Fri & Sat-11 pm. Closed: 4/20, 11/27, 12/25. **Reservations:** accepted. **Features:** Gourmet pizza and Cap'n Crunch chicken are prepared in the wood-stone oven of the open display kitchen. Beers are created in the second-story brewery loft, and burgers, sandwiches and pasta complete the menu. Seating is available in the dining room or on the seasonal patio. Casual dress; cocktails. **Parking:** on-site. **Cards:** AX, MC, VI.

American

MONGO'S

Lunch: $6   Dinner: $13   Phone: 920/730-8304

Location: Just n of College Ave, via Richmond; center. 231 W Franklin 54911. **Hours:** 11 am-2 & 5-9:30 pm, Sat from 5 pm. Closed major holidays; also Sun. **Reservations:** suggested; Sun-Fri. **Features:** Diners can create stir-fry combinations from fresh ingredients and watch capable cooks prepare them at the unusual, downtown restaurant. The atmosphere is accented by ethnic background music, dim lighting and draped tapestries. Casual dress; cocktails. **Parking:** on-site. **Cards:** AX, DC, MC, VI.

Mongolian

THE SEASONS

Lunch: $7-$11   Dinner: $16-$27   Phone: 920/993-9860

Location: US 41, exit 137 (SR 125), then just sw; in Nicolet Square. 213 S Nicolet Rd 54914. **Hours:** 11:30 am-2:30 & 5:30-9:30 pm, Sat from 5:30 pm, Sun 3 pm-8 pm. Closed major holidays. **Reservations:** suggested. **Features:** Fresh ingredients and attractive entree presentations make this American bistro popular with both business and leisure guests. Complemented by an extensive wine list, the menu, which changes seasonally, always features fresh fish. Delicious desserts are made in-house. Patio dining is offered in season, and smoking is permitted only in the lounge. Dressy casual; cocktails. **Parking:** on-site. **Cards:** AX, MC, VI.

American

TRIM B'S

Lunch: $4-$19   Dinner: $4-$19   Phone: 920/734-9204

Location: Just s of College Ave at jct Lawrence St; downtown. 201 S Walnut St 54911. **Hours:** 11 am-10 pm, Fri-11 pm, Sat 4 pm-10 pm, Sun 4 pm-9 pm. **Reservations:** accepted; except Fri. **Features:** Seafood dinners—including fresh perch, planked Lake Superior whitefish, shrimp and pike—are popular at the established, centrally located restaurant. A nautical theme characterizes the dining room. Other tempting choices are Wisconsin cheddar cheese soup and chef specials. Steaks and chicken and pasta dishes round out the menu. Casual dress; cocktails. **Parking:** on-site. **Cards:** AX, DS, MC, VI.

American

VICTORIA'S **Lunch:** $5-$12 **Dinner:** $7-$16 **Phone:** 920/730-9595

Italian

Location: At jct Walnut St, 2.7 mi e of US 41, exit 137; downtown. 503 W College Ave 54911. **Hours:** 11 am-10 pm, Sun & Mon-9 pm. Closed: 4/20, 11/27, 12/25; also 12/24 after 4 pm. **Features:** Huge servings of fresh, flavorful food are the norm at the centrally located eatery. Among the numerous menu selections are Sicilian and Italian specialties, salads, seafood, made-to-order gourmet pizzas and create-your-own pasta dishes with a variety of sauces and meats. Casual dress; cocktails. **Parking:** street. **Cards:** AX, DC, DS, MC, VI.

VINCE LOMBARDI'S STEAKHOUSE **Dinner:** $12-$25 **Phone:** 920/380-9390

Steak & Seafood

Location: 3 mi e of US 41, exit 137 (SR 125); downtown; in Radisson Paper Valley Hotel. 333 W College Ave 54911. **Hours:** 5 pm-10 pm, Fri & Sat-10:30 pm. Closed: 12/24 for dinner. **Reservations:** suggested. **Features:** Vince Lombardi's Steakhouse is a shrine to the former Green Bay Packer coach. The restaurant abounds with memorabilia of both a personal nature and equipment and photographs depicting his many football exploits. The restaurant appeals to those hungry for some of the finest steak in this area and those looking for a glimpse into the life of the legend and the man. The atmosphere is decidedly upscale but with a casual ambience. Dressy casual; cocktails. **Parking:** on-site (fee). **Cards:** AX, CB, DC, DS, MC, VI.

WISCONSIN MACHINE SHED RESTAURANT **Lunch:** $4-$9 **Dinner:** $7-$20 **Phone:** 920/830-2326

American

Location: US 41, exit 137 (SR 125), just nw. 220 N Fox River Dr 54913. **Hours:** 6 am-10 pm, Sun 7 am-9 pm. Closed: 1/1, 11/27, 12/25. **Features:** Very hearty portions of farm style cooking, specializing in pork and beef. Foods are made from scratch. The restaurant is dedicated to the American farmer and uses real dairy products and locally produced meats. Friendly servers in overalls. Well-stocked gift shop. Casual dress; cocktails. **Parking:** on-site. **Cards:** AX, CB, DC, DS, MC, VI.

ARBOR VITAE

———— WHERE TO DINE ————

MARTY'S PLACE NORTH **Dinner:** $8-$30 **Phone:** 715-356-4335

American

Location: 5.8 mi n on US 51 from jct SR 47. 2721 US 51 N 54568. **Hours:** 4:30 pm-10 pm. Closed: 11/27, 12/24, 12/25; also week of Easter. **Reservations:** accepted. **Features:** A warm, "up-north" ambience pervades the cozy dining room, which is decorated with log walls, stone accents and wildlife prints. The restaurant is known locally for specialty dinners of stuffed orange roughy, veal Oscar, roast duck and Oriental steak. Casual dress; cocktails. **Parking:** on-site. **Cards:** AX, DS, MC, VI.

ARCADIA pop. 2,402

———— WHERE TO STAY ————

RKD MOTEL **Phone:** (608)323-3338

Motel

			XP: $12	F12
All Year	1P: $40	2P: $48-$50		

Location: On SR 95, 0.6 mi w of jct SR 93. 915 E Main St 54612. **Fax:** 608/323-7416. **Facility:** 27 one-bedroom standard units. 1 story, exterior corridors. *Bath:* combo or shower only. **Parking:** on-site, winter plug-ins. **Terms:** pets ($5 extra charge). **Business Services:** fax. **Cards:** AX, DC, MC, VI.

SOME UNITS

ASHLAND pop. 8,620

———— WHERE TO STAY ————

AMERICINN OF ASHLAND **Phone:** (715)682-9950

Small-scale Hotel

6/20-10/10 [ECP]	1P: $81-$116	2P: $87-$122	XP: $6	F17
1/1-3/31 [ECP]	1P: $72-$92	2P: $78-$98	XP: $6	F17
4/1-6/19 [ECP]	1P: $76-$89	2P: $82-$95	XP: $6	F17
10/11-12/31 [ECP]	1P: $72-$83	2P: $78-$89	XP: $6	F17

Location: On US 2, 2.1 mi e of jct SR 13 S. 3009 Lakeshore Dr E 54806. **Fax:** 715/682-9964. **Facility:** 64 units. 62 one-bedroom standard units, some with whirlpools. 2 one-bedroom suites ($94-$155). 2 stories, interior corridors. *Bath:* combo or shower only. **Parking:** on-site, winter plug-ins. **Terms:** cancellation fee imposed, pets ($6 fee, $20 deposit). **Amenities:** hair dryers. *Some:* irons. **Pool(s):** heated indoor. **Leisure Activities:** sauna, whirlpool, pool table, kiddie corner with movies, exercise room. **Guest Services:** coin laundry. **Business Services:** meeting rooms, business center. **Cards:** AX, DS, MC, VI. **Special Amenities:** free continental breakfast and free local telephone calls.

SOME UNITS

ANDERSON'S CHEQUAMEGON MOTEL **Phone:** (715)682-4658

Motel

6/15-10/18	1P: $47-$61	2P: $55-$75	XP: $6	F12
4/1-6/14 & 10/19-3/31	1P: $32-$55	2P: $39-$60	XP: $6	F12

Location: 1.8 mi w on US 2. 2200 W Lakeshore Dr 54806. **Fax:** 715/685-9887. **Facility:** 18 one-bedroom standard units. 1 story, exterior corridors. **Parking:** on-site, winter plug-ins. **Amenities:** *Some:* hair dryers. **Leisure Activities:** snowmobile & waterfront trail. **Cards:** AX, CB, DC, DS, MC, VI. **Special Amenities:** free continental breakfast and free local telephone calls.

SOME UNITS

BEST WESTERN HOLIDAY HOUSE **Phone:** (715)682-5235

Small-scale Hotel

5/30-10/12	1P: $89-$119	2P: $94-$124	XP: $5	F12
10/13-3/31	1P: $54-$99	2P: $59-$104	XP: $5	F12
4/1-5/29	1P: $59-$79	2P: $64-$84	XP: $5	F12

Location: 2.5 mi w. 30600 US Hwy 2 54806. **Fax:** 715/682-4730. **Facility:** 65 units. 64 one-bedroom standard units. 1 one-bedroom suite. 2 stories, interior/exterior corridors. *Bath:* combo or shower only. **Parking:** on-site, winter plug-ins. **Terms:** [CP] meal plan available. **Amenities:** irons, hair dryers. **Dining:** 5 pm-10 pm, Sun from 10 am; Sunday brunch, cocktails. **Pool(s):** heated indoor. **Leisure Activities:** whirlpool, fishing. *Fee:* game room. **Business Services:** administrative services (fee). **Cards:** AX, DC, DS, MC, VI.

SOME UNITS

SUPER 8 MOTEL

				Phone: (715)682-9377
▿▿▿ ▿▿▿	9/26-10/11	1P: $110-$136	2P: $110-$136	XP: $6	F12
	5/23-9/25	1P: $70-$116	2P: $80-$126	XP: $6	F12
Motel	4/1-5/22 & 10/12-3/31	1P: $50-$72	2P: $54-$78	XP: $6	F12

Location: On US 2 at jct 16th Ave. 1610 W Lakeshore Dr 54806. Fax: 715/682-9377. **Facility:** 70 one-bedroom standard units. 2 stories, interior corridors. *Bath:* combo or shower only. **Parking:** on-site, winter plug-ins. **Terms:** cancellation fee imposed, [CP] meal plan available, small pets only ($50 deposit, $10 extra charge). **Amenities:** *Some:* hair dryers. **Pool(s):** small heated indoor. **Leisure Activities:** whirlpool. **Guest Services:** coin laundry. **Business Services:** meeting rooms, fax (fee). **Cards:** AX, DC, DS, MC, VI.

SOME UNITS

(ASK) (S/D) (🐾) (&M) (👤) (🅿) (🔾) (🎥) (DATA PORT) / (✕) (🛏) (🍽) (💻) /

—————— WHERE TO DINE ——————

THE BREAKWATER CAFE

| | **Lunch:** $4-$6 | **Dinner:** $6-$10 | **Phone:** 715/682-8388 |

▿▿   **Location:** US 2, 1.2 mi e of jct SR 13 S. 1808 Lake Shore Dr E 54806. **Hours:** 5 am-10 pm. Closed: 12/25.
American   **Features:** The casual, family-friendly restaurant delivers an all-day menu of breakfast choices, plus sandwiches, soups, salads and burgers. The views of Lake Superior are beautiful. Delicious homemade baked goods include caramel rolls and doughnuts. Casual dress. **Parking:** on-site. **Cards:** MC, VI.   (✕)

ZEIS'S PLATTER RESTAURANT

| | **Lunch:** $5-$8 | **Dinner:** $10-$25 | **Phone:** 715/682-2626 |

▿▿ ▿▿   **Location:** 2 mi w on US 2, follow signs for Prentice Park, just s. 315 Turner Rd 54806. **Hours:** 11:30 am-2 & 4:30-9:30 pm, Fri & Sat-10 pm, Sun 9 am-2 & 4:30-9:30 pm. Closed: 1/1, 7/4, 12/25.
American   **Reservations:** suggested. **Features:** A charmingly restored turn-of-the-20th-century home welcomes diners. Country Victorian decor sets the stage. Regional cuisine shows interest both for a contemporary, unusual contrast of flavors and a respect for tradition. Squash bisque is drizzled with maple syrup, roasted duck is accompanied with perfumes of citrus and cranberries, and planked fish—fish filet backed on a maple board—echoes of Lake Superior old times and methods. Casual dress; cocktails. **Parking:** on-site. **Cards:** DS, MC, VI.   (🍸) (✕)

BAILEYS HARBOR —*See Door County p. 481.*

BALDWIN pop. 2,667

—————— WHERE TO STAY ——————

AMERICINN OF BALDWIN

				Phone: 715/684-5888
▿▿▿▿	All Year	1P: $72-$124	2P: $81-$130	XP: $6	F18

Location: I-94, exit 19 (US 63), just ne. 500 Baldwin Plaza Dr 54002. Fax: 715/684-5890. **Facility:** 65 units. 59
Small-scale Hotel   one-bedroom standard units, some with whirlpools. 6 one-bedroom suites, some with whirlpools. 2 stories, interior corridors. *Bath:* combo or shower only. **Parking:** on-site, winter plug-ins. **Terms:** weekly rates available, [CP] meal plan available. **Amenities:** hair dryers. **Pool(s):** heated indoor. **Leisure Activities:** whirlpool. *Fee:* game room. **Guest Services:** coin laundry. **Business Services:** meeting rooms, administrative services (fee). **Cards:** AX, DC, DS, MC, VI.

SOME UNITS

(ASK) (S/D) (&) (🔾) (🎥) (DATA PORT) (💻) / (✕) (🛏) (🍽) /

SUPER 8 MOTEL

				Phone: (715)684-2700
▿▿ ▿▿	4/1-10/31 [CP]	1P: $69-$78	2P: $69-$78	
	11/1-3/31 [CP]	1P: $66-$73	2P: $66-$73	
Motel				

Location: I-94, exit 19 (US 63), just se. 2110 10th Ave 54002. Fax: 715/684-2750. **Facility:** 61 one-bedroom standard units, some with whirlpools. 2 stories, interior corridors. *Bath:* combo or shower only. **Parking:** on-site, winter plug-ins. **Terms:** check-in 4 pm, weekly rates available, pets (with prior approval). **Pool(s):** small heated indoor. **Leisure Activities:** whirlpool. *Fee:* game room. **Guest Services:** coin laundry. **Business Services:** meeting rooms, administrative services (fee). **Cards:** AX, CB, DC, DS, MC, VI.

SOME UNITS

(ASK) (S/D) (🐾) (🍽+) (&) (🔾) (🎥) / (✕) (DATA PORT) (🛏) (🍽) /

BARABOO pop. 10,711

—————— WHERE TO STAY ——————

BEST WESTERN BARABOO INN

				Phone: (608)356-1100
(AAA) (SAVE)	6/20-8/31 [ECP]	1P: $84-$124	2P: $89-$129	XP: $7
	5/16-6/19 & 9/1-3/31 [ECP]	1P: $84-$114	2P: $89-$119	XP: $7
▿▿▿ ▿▿▿	4/1-5/15 [ECP]	1P: $74-$94	2P: $79-$99	XP: $7

Location: On US 12, 0.3 mi n of SR 33. 725 W Pine 53913. Fax: 608/356-4585. **Facility:** 84 units. 83 one-
Small-scale Hotel   bedroom standard units. 1 one-bedroom suite ($109-$149) with whirlpool. 3 stories, interior corridors. *Bath:* combo or shower only. **Parking:** on-site. **Terms:** 2-4 night minimum stay - seasonal, cancellation fee imposed. **Amenities:** irons, hair dryers. *Some:* dual phone lines. **Dining:** 4 pm-10 pm, cocktails. **Pool(s):** heated indoor. **Leisure Activities:** whirlpool, exercise room. **Guest Services:** gift shop, valet and coin laundry. **Business Services:** meeting rooms. **Cards:** AX, CB, DC, DS, MC, VI. **Special Amenities:** free continental breakfast.

SOME UNITS

(S/D) (🍽) (🍸) (&) (🅿) (🔾) (🎥) (DATA PORT) (💻) / (✕) (🛏) (🍽) /

HO-CHUNK CASINO & HOTEL

				Phone: (608)356-6210
▿▿▿▿	5/16-9/30	1P: $130-$150	2P: $130-$150	XP: $10	F12
	4/1-5/15 & 10/1-3/31	1P: $69-$89	2P: $69-$89	XP: $10	F12

Location: I-90/94, exit 92, 2.6 mi e on US 12. S 3214 Hwy 12 53913. Fax: 608/355-1501. **Facility:** 315 units. 313
Large-scale Hotel   one-bedroom standard units, some with whirlpools. 2 one-bedroom suites ($89-$270) with whirlpools. 4 stories, interior corridors. *Bath:* combo or shower only. **Parking:** on-site and valet. **Terms:** check-in 4 pm. **Amenities:** dual phone lines, voice mail, safes, hair dryers. *Some:* irons. **Leisure Activities:** exercise room. *Fee:* game room. **Guest Services:** gift shop, coin laundry. **Business Services:** conference facilities, fax (fee). **Cards:** AX, DS, MC, VI.

SOME UNITS

(ASK) (S/D) (🍽) (🍸) (🔾) (&) (DATA PORT) (🛏) (🍽) (💻) / (✕) /

PARK PLAZA BARABOO

Phone: (608)356-6422

(AAA) (SAVE)
▽▽▽

7/5-8/17 [ECP]	1P: $99-$164	2P: $99-$164	XP: $10	F18
8/18-12/24 [ECP]	1P: $79-$144	2P: $79-$144	XP: $10	F18
4/1-7/4 [ECP]	1P: $74-$144	2P: $74-$144	XP: $10	F18
12/25-3/31 [ECP]	1P: $81-$130	2P: $81-$130	XP: $10	F18

Small-scale Hotel **Location:** On US 12, 0.3 mi n of SR 33. 626 W Pine St 53913. Fax: 608/356-0520. **Facility:** 84 units. 72 one-bedroom standard units, some with whirlpools. 8 one- and 4 two-bedroom suites ($109-$164), some with whirlpools. 5 stories, interior corridors. **Parking:** on-site. **Terms:** cancellation fee imposed, small pets only (1st floor). **Amenities:** dual phone lines, voice mail, irons, hair dryers. **Dining:** 7 am-10 pm, cocktails. **Pool(s):** heated indoor. **Leisure Activities:** whirlpool, steamroom, exercise room. **Guest Services:** valet and coin laundry. **Business Services:** meeting rooms. **Cards:** AX, DC, MC, VI. **Special Amenities:** free local telephone calls and free newspaper. *(See color ad p 463)*

SOME UNITS

PINEHAVEN BED & BREAKFAST

Phone: (608)356-3489

(AAA) (SAVE)
▽▽▽

5/1-11/1 [BP]	2P: $99-$145	XP: $15
4/1-4/30 & 11/2-2/28 [BP]	2P: $79-$125	XP: $15

Bed & Breakfast **Location:** SR 33, 4.8 mi e from jct US 12. Located in a quiet, rural area. E13083 Hwy 33 53913. Fax: 608/356-0818. **Facility:** The outstanding feature of this B&B is its scenic location amid rolling hills, a farm pond and mature conifers; a gazebo offers panoramic views. 5 units. 4 one-bedroom standard units. 1 two-bedroom suite with kitchen and whirlpool. 2 stories (no elevator), interior/exterior corridors. **Parking:** on-site. **Terms:** open 4/1-2/28, 2 night minimum stay - seasonal weekends, age restrictions may apply, 7 day cancellation notice-fee imposed. **Amenities:** *Some:* hair dryers. **Leisure Activities:** boating, paddleboats, fishing, hiking trails. **Cards:** MC, VI. **Special Amenities:** free local telephone calls.

SOME UNITS

------ **WHERE TO DINE** ------

LOG CABIN FAMILY RESTAURANT AND BAKERY

Lunch: $4-$7　　**Dinner: $6-$13**　　**Phone: 608/356-8034**

▽▽
American

Location: 2.5 mi e on SR 33 from jct US 12. 1215 8th St 53913. **Hours:** 6 am-10 pm. Closed: 4/20, 11/27, 12/25; also 12/24 for dinner. **Features:** This restaurant is made of log construction and is popular with locals and visitors alike. The food tastes great and many of the items are homemade. Breakfast is served all day. Casual dress. **Parking:** on-site. **Cards:** DS, MC, VI.

BARRON pop. 3,284

------ **WHERE TO STAY** ------

BARRON MOTEL & RV CAMPGROUND

Phone: 715/637-3154

▽▽
Motel

All Year	1P: $40-$51	2P: $51-$61	XP: $6	F16

Location: On US 8, 1 mi e of jct SR 25 N. 1521 E Division Ave 54812. Fax: 715/637-9254. **Facility:** 11 one-bedroom standard units. 1 story, exterior corridors. **Parking:** on-site, winter plug-ins. **Amenities:** hair dryers. **Business Services:** administrative services (fee). **Cards:** AX, DS, MC, VI.

SOME UNITS

BAYFIELD pop. 611

------ **WHERE TO STAY** ------

BAYFIELD ON THE LAKE

Phone: 715/779-3621

▽▽▽
Condominium

6/15-10/16	1P: $180-$220	2P: $180-$220	XP: $20	F5
4/1-6/14 & 10/17-3/31	1P: $120-$150	2P: $120-$150	XP: $20	F5

Location: Just s of SR 13; on lakefront. 10 S 1st St 54814 (PO Box 70). Fax: 715/779-3181. **Facility:** 7 units. 1 one-, 3 two- and 3 three-bedroom suites with kitchens, some with whirlpools. 3 stories, interior corridors. **Parking:** on-site, winter plug-ins. **Terms:** check-in 4 pm, 2 night minimum stay - weekends, 10 day cancellation notice-fee imposed, weekly rates available. **Amenities:** irons, hair dryers. *Some:* CD players. **Guest Services:** complimentary laundry. **Cards:** MC, VI.

SOME UNITS

COOPER HILL HOUSE

Phone: 715/779-5060

▽▽▽
Historic Bed
& Breakfast

5/16-10/31 [ECP]	1P: $86-$106	2P: $89-$109
4/1-5/15 & 11/1-3/31 [ECP]	1P: $79	2P: $79

Location: On SR 13. 33 S 6th St 54814 (PO Box 1288). Fax: 715/779-3999. **Facility:** Smoke free premises. 4 one-bedroom standard units. 2 stories, interior corridors. *Bath:* combo or shower only. **Parking:** on-site. **Terms:** 2 night minimum stay - weekends, age restrictions may apply, 7 day cancellation notice. **Cards:** MC, VI.

OLD RITTENHOUSE INN

Phone: 715/779-5111

▽▽▽
Historic
Country Inn

4/1-6/13 & 10/14-3/31	1P: $99-$299	XP: $20
6/14-10/13	1P: $99-$249	XP: $20

Location: Just w on SR 13. 301 Rittenhouse Ave 54814 (PO Box 584). Fax: 715/779-5887. **Facility:** Two late-1800s Victorian mansions decorated with antiques make up this stately hillside inn; most rooms have fireplaces and some have bay views. Smoke free premises. 19 units. 15 one-bedroom standard units, some with whirlpools. 4 one-bedroom suites, some with whirlpools. 3 stories, interior corridors. *Bath:* combo or shower only. **Parking:** on-site, winter plug-ins. **Terms:** check-in 3:30 pm, [CP] meal plan available. **Amenities:** *Some:* CD players, hair dryers. **Dining:** dining room, see separate listing. **Guest Services:** valet laundry, area transportation. **Business Services:** meeting rooms, administrative services. **Cards:** MC, VI.

SOME UNITS

WHERE TO DINE

OLD RITTENHOUSE INN   **Lunch:** $10-$15   **Dinner:** $45   **Phone:** 715/779-5111

Continental

Location: Just w on SR 13; in Old Rittenhouse Inn. 301 Rittenhouse Ave 54814. **Hours:** 7:30 am-9:30 & 5-9:30 pm, hours may vary off season; also 11 am-2:30 pm 5/15-10/15. **Reservations:** suggested. **Features:** A charming, Victorian-styled restaurant in a restored 1890 mansion, this restaurant offers incredible atmosphere for diners who seek romance and fine dining. The decor is classic and elegant, yet not intimidating in the least. The waitstaff is thoroughly knowledgeable about the constantly changing menu. The various courses of the prix fixe menu do not disappoint the palatte. Everything is fresh, well prepared and a joy to eat. Cocktails. **Parking:** on-site. **Cards:** MC, VI.

BAYSIDE —*See Milwaukee p. 566.*

BEAVER DAM pop. 15,169

WHERE TO STAY

AMERICINN LODGE & SUITES   **Phone:** (920)356-9000

Small-scale Hotel

5/24-3/31 [ECP]	1P: $75-$120	2P: $75-$120	XP: $6	F12
4/1-5/23 [ECP]	1P: $72-$116	2P: $72-$116	XP: $6	F12

Location: US 151, exit 134 (CR B/Industrial Dr). 325 Seippel Blvd 53916 (PO Box 718). **Fax:** 920/356-9094. **Facility:** 64 units. 63 one-bedroom standard units, some with whirlpools. 1 one-bedroom suite with whirlpool. 3 stories, interior corridors. *Bath:* combo or shower only. **Parking:** on-site, winter plug-ins. **Terms:** pets ($10 extra charge, in designated units). **Amenities:** dual phone lines, hair dryers. *Some:* irons. **Pool(s):** small heated indoor. **Leisure Activities:** whirlpool, limited exercise equipment. **Guest Services:** valet and coin laundry. **Business Services:** meeting rooms, fax (fee). **Cards:** AX, CB, DC, DS, MC, VI. **Special Amenities:** free continental breakfast and free local telephone calls.

SOME UNITS

SUPER 8 MOTEL   **Phone:** 920/887-8880

Motel

All Year [CP]	1P: $48-$77	2P: $53-$77	XP: $5	D12

Location: US 151, exit 132 (SR 33), just w. 711 Park Ave 53916 (PO Box 778). **Fax:** 920/887-8880. **Facility:** 50 one-bedroom standard units. 3 stories (no elevator), interior corridors. **Parking:** on-site, winter plug-ins. **Terms:** pets ($50 deposit). **Guest Services:** valet and coin laundry. **Business Services:** fax. **Cards:** AX, CB, DC, DS, MC, VI.

SOME UNITS

WHERE TO DINE

BENVENUTO'S ITALIAN GRILL   **Lunch:** $6-$8   **Dinner:** $7-$15   **Phone:** 920/887-7994

Italian

Location: US 151, exit 132 (SR 33), just sw. 831 Park Ave 53916. **Hours:** 11 am-10:30 pm, Fri & Sat-11 pm, Sun-10 pm. **Closed:** 11/27, 12/24, 12/25. **Reservations:** accepted. **Features:** The casual eatery's menu comprises Italian and American fare, including gourmet calzones, pasta, ribs, wood-fired pizzas, meatball sandwiches, steaks, mushroom and mozzarella burgers, walleye pike and popcorn shrimp. Casual dress; cocktails. **Parking:** on-site. **Cards:** AX, DS, MC, VI.

THE NILE CLUB   **Dinner:** $7-$23   **Phone:** 920/885-6611

American

Location: US 151, exit 132 (SR 33), 4.2 mi e. W 6711 Hwy 33 53916. **Hours:** 5 pm-10 pm, Sun 10 am-2 & 4-9 pm. **Closed:** 12/25; also Mon. **Features:** The distinctive pyramid-shaped building stands out in a landscape of Wisconsin farms. The Egyptian decor and relaxing background music enhance the restaurant's appeal. Supper club fare includes broiled or pan-fried seafood, steak and fowl. Casual dress; cocktails. **Parking:** on-site. **Cards:** AX, MC, VI.

BELOIT pop. 35,775

WHERE TO STAY

COMFORT INN OF BELOIT   **Phone:** (608)362-2666

Small-scale Hotel

4/1-9/30	1P: $59-$69	2P: $69-$79	XP: $5	F14
10/1-3/31	1P: $54-$64	2P: $64-$74	XP: $5	F14

Location: I-90, exit 185A, just w, at jct I-43 and SR 81. 2786 Milwaukee Rd 53511. **Fax:** 608/362-2666. **Facility:** 56 one-bedroom standard units. 2 stories, interior corridors. **Parking:** on-site, winter plug-ins. **Terms:** 15 day cancellation notice-fee imposed, pets ($10 extra charge). **Amenities:** hair dryers. **Pool(s):** small heated indoor. **Leisure Activities:** whirlpool. **Guest Services:** valet laundry. **Cards:** AX, DC, DS, MC, VI. **Special Amenities:** free continental breakfast and free local telephone calls.

SOME UNITS

HOLIDAY INN EXPRESS   **Phone:** (608)365-6000

Small-scale Hotel

All Year	1P: $79	2P: $119	XP: $6	F19

Location: I-90, exit 185A, just w, at jct I-43 and SR 81. 2790 Milwaukee Rd 53511. **Fax:** 608/365-1974. **Facility:** 73 one-bedroom standard units, some with whirlpools. 2 stories, interior corridors. **Parking:** on-site, winter plug-ins. **Terms:** [ECP] meal plan available. **Amenities:** dual phone lines, voice mail, irons, hair dryers. **Pool(s):** heated indoor. **Leisure Activities:** whirlpool, exercise room. **Guest Services:** valet and coin laundry. **Business Services:** meeting rooms, fax (fee). **Cards:** AX, CB, DC, DS, JC, MC, VI. **Special Amenities:** free continental breakfast and free local telephone calls.

SOME UNITS

SUPER 8 MOTEL

Small-scale Hotel

All Year [CP]

1P: $51-$61   2P: $56-$66

Phone: (608)365-8680
XP: $5   F12

Location: I-90, exit 185A, just w, at jct I-43 and SR 81. 3002 Milwaukee Rd 53511. **Fax:** 608/365-2411. **Facility:** 64 one-bedroom standard units. 2 stories, interior corridors. **Parking:** on-site, winter plug-ins. **Terms:** pets ($10 extra charge, dogs only). **Amenities:** safes (fee). **Guest Services:** coin laundry. **Cards:** AX, CB, DC, DS, MC, VI.

SOME UNITS

(ASK) (S✦) (🛏) (†l†) (🏃M) (🐾) (DATA PORT) / (✕) (🔒) (📷) /

────── WHERE TO DINE ──────

BUTTERFLY CLUB

American

Dinner: $9-$16

Phone: 608/362-8577

Location: I-90, exit 185B, 1.5 mi e on I-43, exit 2, then 0.5 mi e. 5246 E CR X 53511. **Hours:** 5 pm-9:30 pm, Fri & Sat-10 pm, Sun noon-8 pm. **Closed:** 1/1, 12/24, 12/25; also Mon. **Reservations:** suggested. **Features:** Picturesque rural setting with deck dining in season. Fish fry on Wednesday and Friday. Established in 1924. Offering USDA prime Angus steak, poultry and seafood. Cinnamon rolls accompany all meals. Dressy casual; cocktails. **Parking:** on-site. **Cards:** AX, DC, DS, MC, VI.

(Y) (✕)

GUN CLUB

American

Dinner: $16-$23

Phone: 608/362-9900

Location: I-90, exit 185A, 2 mi w, then 0.5 mi s. 1122 E Colley Rd 53511. **Hours:** 5 pm-9 pm, Sun 4 pm-9 pm. Closed major holidays; also Mon. **Reservations:** suggested. **Features:** In operation since 1938, the restaurant is known for its hearty steaks and chops. Casual dress; cocktails. **Parking:** on-site. **Cards:** AX, MC, VI.

(🏃M) (Y) (✕)

BERLIN pop. 5,305

────── WHERE TO STAY ──────

BEST WESTERN COUNTRYSIDE

(SAVE)

Motel

All Year [ECP]

1P: $64-$84   2P: $69-$89

Phone: (920)361-4411

Location: On SR 49, at jct CR F. 227 Ripon Rd 54923. **Fax:** 920/361-1125. **Facility:** 20 one-bedroom standard units. 2 stories (no elevator), interior corridors. **Parking:** on-site, winter plug-ins. **Terms:** package plans, pets (small dogs only). **Amenities:** irons, hair dryers. **Leisure Activities:** whirlpool, exercise room. **Guest Services:** valet laundry. **Business Services:** fax (fee). **Cards:** AX, DC, DS, MC, VI.

SOME UNITS

(S✦) (🛏) (DATA PORT) (📠) / (✕) (🔒) (📷) /

BLACK RIVER FALLS pop. 3,618

────── WHERE TO STAY ──────

BEST WESTERN-ARROWHEAD LODGE & SUITES

(AAA) (SAVE)

Small-scale Hotel

5/1-10/15	1P: $61-$90	2P: $61-$90	XP: $6	F18
10/16-3/31	1P: $57-$90	2P: $57-$90	XP: $6	F18
4/1-4/30	1P: $57-$75	2P: $57-$75	XP: $6	F18

Phone: (715)284-9471

Location: I-94, exit 116, at jct SR 54. 600 Oasis Rd 54615. **Fax:** 715/284-9664. **Facility:** 143 units. 114 one-bedroom standard units, some with whirlpools. 29 one-bedroom suites ($87-$189), some with whirlpools. 2-3 stories, interior corridors. *Bath:* combo or shower only. **Parking:** on-site, winter plug-ins. **Terms:** [ECP] meal plan available, small pets only. **Amenities:** voice mail, irons, hair dryers. *Some:* dual phone lines. **Dining:** 6:30 am-2 & 5-10 pm, cocktails. **Pool(s):** heated indoor. **Leisure Activities:** whirlpool, rental paddleboats, ice skating, access to ATV snowmobile trails, hiking trails, jogging. **Guest Services:** coin laundry. **Business Services:** meeting rooms, administrative services (fee). **Cards:** AX, CB, DC, DS, MC, VI. **Special Amenities:** free continental breakfast and free room upgrade (subject to availability with advanced reservations). *(See color ad p 473)*

SOME UNITS

(S✦) (🛏) (†l†) (Y) (🏊) (🌀) (⛵) (✕) (🐾) (DATA PORT) (📠) / (✕) (VCR) (🔒) (📷) /

DAYS INN   Phone: (715)284-4333

AAA SAVE   5/23-9/30 & 12/16-3/31   1P: $69-$89   2P: $81-$89   XP: $6   F18
           4/1-5/22 & 10/1-12/15   1P: $60-$79   2P: $69-$89   XP: $6   F18
WWW WWW   **Location:** I-94, exit 116, just w. 919 Hwy 54 E 54615. **Fax:** 715/284-9068. **Facility:** 84 one-bedroom standard
           units, some with whirlpools. 2 stories, interior corridors. *Bath:* combo or shower only. **Parking:** on-site, winter
Small-scale Hotel plug-ins. **Terms:** small pets only (in smoking units). **Amenities:** irons, hair dryers. **Pool(s):** heated indoor.
           Leisure Activities: sauna, whirlpool. *Fee:* game room. **Guest Services:** coin laundry. **Business Services:**
meeting rooms, administrative services (fee). **Cards:** AX, CB, DC, DS, MC, VI. **Special Amenities:** free continental breakfast
and free local telephone calls. *(See color ad below)*

SOME UNITS

FEE   FEE

HOLIDAY INN EXPRESS HOTEL & SUITES   Phone: (715)284-0888

AAA SAVE   5/23-9/1 [ECP]   1P: $74-$124   2P: $74-$124   XP: $6   F19
           4/1-5/22 & 9/2-3/31 [ECP]   1P: $74-$104   2P: $74-$104   XP: $6   F19
WWWWW WWW **Location:** I-94, exit 116. W10170 Hwy 54 E 54615. **Fax:** 715/284-9789. **Facility:** 75 one-bedroom standard units,
           some with whirlpools. 2 stories (no elevator), interior corridors. *Bath:* combo or shower only. **Parking:** on-site,
Small-scale Hotel winter plug-ins. **Amenities:** irons, hair dryers. **Pool(s):** heated indoor, wading. **Leisure Activities:** whirlpool,
           exercise room. **Guest Services:** valet and coin laundry. **Business Services:** meeting rooms, fax (fee).
Cards: AX, CB, DC, DS, JC, MC, VI. **Special Amenities:** free continental breakfast and free local telephone calls.

SOME UNITS

———— WHERE TO DINE ————

THE RUSTIC MILL SUPPER CLUB
American
cocktails.

Dinner: $7-$22   **Phone:** 715/284-4913
Location: 2.3 mi s. Hwy 54 54615. **Hours:** 5 pm-10 pm. Closed: 11/27, 12/25; also Tues.
Reservations: suggested. **Features:** Cozy setting in a feed and flour mill built in 1866. Vaulted ceiling, knotty pine walls and fireplace enhance the ambience. Some tables have a nice view of a small river and waterfall. Specializes in prime rib and seafood. Homemade soup. Smoking in lounge only. Casual dress; **Parking:** on-site. **Cards:** MC, VI.

BOSCOBEL pop. 3,047

———— WHERE TO STAY ————

SAND'S MOTEL
Motel
ins.

	1P	2P	XP	
4/1-12/31	1P: $44-$52	2P: $51-$62	XP: $7	F18
1/1-3/31	1P: $41-$48	2P: $48-$59	XP: $7	F18

Phone: 608-375-4167

Location: 0.5 mi nw on US 61. Truck parking on premises. Hwy 61 N 53805 (300 Elm St). **Facility:** 32 one-bedroom standard units. 1 story, interior/exterior corridors. *Bath:* combo or shower only. **Parking:** on-site, winter plug-ins. **Terms:** small pets only. **Amenities:** *Some:* hair dryers. **Cards:** AX, DS, MC, VI.

SOME UNITS

SUPER 8 MOTEL
Small-scale Hotel
winter plug-ins.

	1P	2P	XP	
6/1-10/31	1P: $61-$71	2P: $66-$86	XP: $5	F12
4/1-5/31 & 11/1-3/31	1P: $56-$66	2P: $61-$76	XP: $5	F12

Phone: 608-375-8000

Location: Just s on US 61. 1700 Elm St 53805. Fax: 608/375-9199. **Facility:** 40 one-bedroom standard units, some with whirlpools. 2 stories (no elevator), interior corridors. *Bath:* combo or shower only. **Parking:** on-site, **Terms:** 2 night minimum stay - weekends in summer, [CP] meal plan available. **Amenities:** video library (fee). **Pool(s):** heated indoor. **Leisure Activities:** sauna, whirlpool, limited exercise equipment. **Guest Services:** tanning facility. **Business Services:** meeting rooms. **Cards:** AX, DC, DS, MC, VI.

SOME UNITS

BOULDER JUNCTION

———— WHERE TO STAY ————

BOULDER JUNCTION MOTOR LODGE
Motel

	1P	2P	XP	
All Year	1P: $59-$92	2P: $62-$95	XP: $10	F6

Phone: 715/385-2825

Location: Just w on CR K. Located in a semi-commercial area. 10432 Main St 54512 (PO Box 294). **Facility:** 20 one-bedroom standard units, some with whirlpools. 1 story, interior corridors. **Parking:** on-site, winter plug-ins. **Terms:** 3 day cancellation notice. **Leisure Activities:** whirlpool, snowmobiling. **Cards:** DS, MC, VI.

SOME UNITS

WHITE BIRCH VILLAGE
Resort
Vacation Home

	2P	XP	
7/5-8/15 Wkly	2P: $831-$1317	XP: $172	F14
8/16-8/29 Wkly	2P: $723-$1145	XP: $150	F14
5/17-7/4 Wkly	2P: $650-$1145	XP: $136	F14
8/30-10/12 Wkly	2P: $650-$1031	XP: $136	F14

Phone: 715/385-2182

Location: On CR K, 8 mi se. Located in a remote wooded area. 8764 Hwy K 54512 (PO Box 284). Fax: 715/385-2537. **Facility:** Fireplaces, park-like grounds and a lakefront setting distinguish these one- to four-bedroom vacation homes. 13 vacation homes ($1575-$2000), some with whirlpools. 1-2 stories (no elevator), exterior corridors. *Bath:* combo or shower only. **Parking:** on-site. **Terms:** open 5/17-10/12, check-out 9 am, 7 night minimum stay - 6/1-9/30, 21 day cancellation notice-fee imposed. **Amenities:** video library. **Leisure Activities:** rental boats, canoeing, paddleboats, boat dock, fishing, playground, basketball, horseshoes, shuffleboard, volleyball. *Fee:* game room. **Guest Services:** coin laundry.

SOME UNITS

———— WHERE TO DINE ————

THE GUIDE'S INN
American

Dinner: $9-$23   **Phone:** 715/385-2233
Location: Just s on CR M and K. Hwy M 54512. **Hours:** 5 pm-10 pm. Closed: 4/20, 11/27, 12/24, 12/25. **Features:** This restaurant offers Continental cuisine prepared by a chef certified by the American Culinary Association. Fresh ingredients, complimentary fresh French bread and appetizer tray, and a wide menu variety are the hallmarks. Cocktails. **Parking:** on-site. **Cards:** MC, VI.

BOWLER pop. 343

———— WHERE TO STAY ————

KONKAPOT LODGE
Small-scale Hotel

	1P	2P	
All Year [ECP]	1P: $83-$130	2P: $83-$130	F5

Phone: 715/787-4747

Location: 4.7 mi e on CR A. W12635 CR A 54416. Fax: 715/787-4749. **Facility:** 28 one-bedroom standard units, some with whirlpools. 2 stories (no elevator), interior corridors. **Parking:** on-site. **Terms:** 3 day cancellation notice. **Amenities:** hair dryers. **Guest Services:** gift shop. **Business Services:** meeting rooms, fax (fee). **Cards:** AX, DC, DS, MC, VI.

SOME UNITS

BROOKFIELD —See Milwaukee p. 566.

BROWN DEER —See Milwaukee p. 568.

BURLINGTON pop. 9,936

──────── WHERE TO STAY ────────

AMERICINN LODGE & SUITES
Phone: (262)534-2125
All Year [ECP]   1P: $79-$149   2P: $87-$149   XP: $6   F18
Location: 3 mi n on SR 36 and 83, at jct CR W. 205 S Browns Lake Rd 53105. Fax: 262/534-5221. **Facility:** 50 units. 43 one-bedroom standard units, some with whirlpools. 7 one-bedroom suites ($109-$149) with efficiencies.
Small-scale Hotel   2 stories (no elevator), interior corridors. **Bath:** combo or shower only. **Parking:** on-site. **Terms:** 2 night minimum stay - 5/26-9/1. **Amenities:** hair dryers. **Some:** irons. **Pool(s):** small heated indoor. **Leisure Activities:** whirlpool. **Guest Services:** coin laundry. **Business Services:** meeting rooms. **Cards:** AX, CB, DC, DS, JC, MC, VI.

SOME UNITS

ASK SD 🛏 & 🏊 📶 🐃 🎦 DATA PORT 🖥 / ✕ 🛏 📷 /

RAINBOW MOTEL
Phone: (262)763-2491
4/1-9/14   1P: $49-$59   2P: $59-$88   XP: $8   F12
9/15-3/31   1P: $47-$55   2P: $55-$80   XP: $8   F12
Location: 0.5 mi ne on SR 36 and 83. 733 Milwaukee Ave 53105. Fax: 262/763-2431. **Facility:** 46 one-bedroom standard units. 2 stories, exterior corridors. **Parking:** on-site, winter plug-ins. **Terms:** 1-3 night minimum stay
Small-scale Hotel   - weekends, cancellation fee imposed. **Amenities:** dual phone lines. **Pool(s):** heated outdoor. **Leisure Activities:** shuffleboard, volleyball. **Guest Services:** valet laundry. **Cards:** AX, DC, MC, VI. **Special Amenities:** early check-in/late check-out and free local telephone calls.

SOME UNITS

SD 🛏 🐃 🎦 DATA PORT 🛏 🖥 / ✕ /

──────── WHERE TO DINE ────────

THE COTTONPICKER   Lunch: $4-$10   Dinner: $12-$25   Phone: 262/534-5151
Location: 3 mi n on SR 36 and 83; at jct CR W. 210 S Browns Lake Rd 53105. **Hours:** 11:30 am-10 pm, Fri & Sat-10:30 pm, Sun 10 am-9 pm. **Closed:** 11/27, 12/25; also 12/24 for dinner. **Reservations:** suggested.
American   **Features:** Window tables in the country-themed dining room overlook a pretty courtyard landscape and soothing pond. The menu comprises such well-prepared entrees as prime rib, steak Oscar and roast duck. Don't pass up the sinful chocolate mocha cheesecake. Casual dress; cocktails. **Parking:** on-site. **Cards:** AX, MC, VI.

🍽 ✕

CABLE

──────── WHERE TO STAY ────────

CONNORS BED & BREAKFAST
Phone: (715)798-3661
5/15-10/15 & 12/26-3/15 [BP]   1P: $85-$105   2P: $85-$105   XP: $15   F5
Location: 1.7 mi n on US 63, then 0.3 mi e on Birch Ln. Located in a quiet, rural area. RR 1, Box 255 54821.
Bed & Breakfast   Fax: 715/798-3663. **Facility:** On 77 acres, this rural B&B offers access to many outdoor activities; accommodations include a cabin that is 110 years old. Smoke free premises. 4 units. 3 one-bedroom standard units, some with whirlpools. 1 one-bedroom suite with efficiency (no utensils). 2 stories, interior corridors. **Parking:** on-site. **Terms:** open 5/15-10/15 & 12/26-3/15, 7 day cancellation notice-fee imposed, weekly rates available. **Amenities:** **Some:** hair dryers. **Leisure Activities:** cross country skiing, hiking trails. **Guest Services:** gift shop. **Business Services:** PC, fax (fee). **Cards:** AX, MC, VI.

SOME UNITS

✕ 🛏 🖥 / 🎦 📺 VCR 🎞 📷 /

LAKEWOODS RESORT
Phone: 715/794-2561
All Year   1P: $35-$500   2P: $50-$500   XP: $15   F18
Location: 8 mi e on CR M. 21540 CH M 54821. Fax: 715/794-2553. **Facility:** Spacious tree-covered grounds surround these lodge-, cottage- and apartment-style units, some of which offer lake views. 92 units. 84 one-bedroom standard units, some with whirlpools. 8 one-bedroom suites, some with kitchens and/or whirlpools.
Resort   1-3 stories, interior/exterior corridors. **Parking:** on-site, winter plug-ins. **Terms:** 30 day cancellation notice-fee
Small-scale Hotel   imposed, [AP] meal plan available, package plans, pets ($50 fee, in designated units). **Amenities:** video library (fee), dual phone lines, voice mail, irons, hair dryers. **Some:** CD players. **Dining:** 7 am-3:30 & 5-10 pm, cocktails. **Pool(s):** heated outdoor, heated indoor. **Leisure Activities:** sauna, whirlpool, rental boats, rental canoes, rental paddleboats, fishing, 2 tennis courts, cross country skiing, ice skating, tobogganing, recreation programs, hiking trails, jogging, playground, volleyball. **Fee:** sailboats, kayaks, pontoons, golf-18 holes, snowmobiling, ski equipment, bicycles. **Guest Services:** gift shop, coin laundry, area transportation (fee). **Business Services:** meeting rooms, business center. **Cards:** AX, DC, DS, MC, VI. **Special Amenities:** free local telephone calls and free room upgrade (subject to availability with advanced reservations).** *(See ad p 504)*

SOME UNITS

🏄 🐎 🍴 🍽 & 🏊 🐃 ✕ 🎦 DATA PORT 🖥 / ✕ VCR 🛏 📷 /
FEE

CADOTT pop. 1,345

──────── WHERE TO STAY ────────

COUNTRYSIDE MOTEL
Phone: 715/289-4000
All Year   1P: $38-$80   2P: $45-$80   XP: $7   F10
Location: SR 29, exit 91 (SR 27), just s. Located in a rural setting. 545 Lavorata Rd 54727. Fax: 715/289-4572.
Motel   **Facility:** 18 one-bedroom standard units, some with whirlpools. 1 story, interior corridors. **Parking:** on-site, winter plug-ins. **Leisure Activities:** playground. **Business Services:** fax (fee). **Cards:** AX, DC, DS, MC, VI.

SOME UNITS

🛏 🛏 🎦 DATA PORT / ✕ /

CALEDONIA

—————— WHERE TO DINE ——————

SEBASTIANS
▽▼▽▼▽
American

Dinner: $14-$24   **Phone:** 212/681-5465

Location: On SR 32 at jct Five Mile Rd. 6025 Douglas Ave 53402. **Hours:** 5 pm-9 pm, Fri & Sat-10 pm. Closed major holidays; also Sun & Mon. **Reservations:** suggested. **Features:** The family-owned and operated restaurant offers fine country dining in a casual atmosphere. Fresh fish, choice meats, distinctive sauces and homemade desserts are notable. Great care is given to the presentation of all courses. Dressy casual; cocktails. **Parking:** on-site. **Cards:** AX, DS, MC, VI.

CAMBRIDGE pop. 1,101

—————— WHERE TO DINE ——————

CAMBRIDGE COUNTRY INN & PUB
▽▼▽
American

Lunch: $5-$15   **Dinner:** $5-$15   **Phone:** 608/423-3275

Location: On US 12; center. 206 W Main St 53523. **Hours:** 10:30 am-8 pm, Fri & Sat-9 pm, Sat 9 am-9 pm, Sun 9 am-8 pm. **Closed:** 11/27, 12/24, 12/25. **Reservations:** accepted. **Features:** Enjoy hearty, home-style cooking in a country setting. The menu lists daily specials, as well as charbroiled steak, salad, specialty sandwiches and pasta. Noteworthy are the wonderful soups, chili and pot pie. For dessert, splurge on fudge cheesecake. Casual dress; cocktails. **Parking:** on-site. **Cards:** MC, VI.

CARDINAL RIDGE SUPPER CLUB
▽▼▽▼ ▽▼▽▼
American

Dinner: $10-$22   **Phone:** 608/423-3956

Location: 2.5 mi ne on US 18. W 9298 Hwy 18 53523. **Hours:** 5 pm-9 pm, Fri & Sat-10 pm. **Closed:** 12/24, 12/25; also Mon. **Reservations:** suggested. **Features:** Mature oak trees and neatly tended gardens envelop the rural, cozy restaurant, operated as the same supper club since 1951. Specialty dishes are Wiener schnitzel, barbecue pork ribs and veal Neptune. Simple desserts are made in-house. Dressy casual; cocktails. **Parking:** on-site. **Cards:** DS, MC, VI.

CAMERON pop. 1,546

—————— WHERE TO STAY ——————

VIKING MOTEL
▽▼▽
Motel

All Year   1P: $50-$60   2P: $55-$65   XP: $6

Location: On US 8 and CR SS. 201 S 1st St 54822 (PO Box 264). **Facility:** 20 one-bedroom standard units. 1 story, exterior corridors. **Parking:** on-site, winter plug-ins. **Terms:** small pets only (with prior approval). **Cards:** DS, MC, VI.

SOME UNITS

CAMP DOUGLAS pop. 592

—————— WHERE TO STAY ——————

K & K MOTEL
▽▼▽
Motel

4/1-9/30	1P: $55-$65	2P: $65-$75	XP: $5 F12
10/1-3/31	1P: $50-$65	2P: $65-$70	XP: $5 F12

Phone: 608/427-3100

Location: I-90/94, exit 55, just s. 219 Hwy 12 & 16 54618. Fax: 608/427-3824. **Facility:** 14 one-bedroom standard units. 1 story, exterior corridors. *Bath:* combo or shower only. **Parking:** on-site, winter plug-ins. **Terms:** small pets only ($5-$10 fee). **Amenities:** video library. **Guest Services:** coin laundry. *Fee:* tanning facility. **Business Services:** administrative services. **Cards:** AX, DC, DS, MC, VI.

SOME UNITS

—————— WHERE TO DINE ——————

TARGET BLUFF SUPPER CLUB
▽▼▽▼ ▽▼▽▼
German

Lunch: $5-$16   **Dinner:** $5-$16   **Phone:** 608/427-6542

Location: I-90/94, exit 55, just s. 208 SR 12 & 16 54618. **Hours:** 11 am-10 pm. **Closed:** 11/27, 12/25; also 12/24 for dinner. **Reservations:** accepted. **Features:** Unique hand-painted murals of castles and countryside adorn the walls of this Bavarian-themed restaurant. The menu consists of Old World German specialties as well as traditional American favorites. A few seafood dishes are also offered. Casual dress; cocktails. **Parking:** on-site. **Cards:** AX, DC, DS, MC, VI.

CARTER

—————— WHERE TO STAY ——————

INDIAN SPRINGS LODGE AND CONFERENCE CENTER
(AAA) (SAVE)
▽▼▽▼▽▼
Small-scale Hotel

5/30-9/11 & 1/1-3/31 [BP]		2P: $75-$85	XP: $15 F17
4/1-5/29 & 9/12-12/31 [BP]		2P: $65-$75	XP: $15 F17

Phone: (715)473-6300

Location: Just n. Located next to a casino. SR 32 54566 (PO Box 249, WABENO). Fax: 715/473-5908. **Facility:** 99 units. 97 one-bedroom standard units, some with whirlpools. 2 one-bedroom suites ($70-$150). 2 stories, interior corridors. *Bath:* combo or shower only. **Parking:** on-site, winter plug-ins. **Terms:** check-in 4 pm, 2 night minimum stay - weekends, package plans, 15% service charge. **Amenities:** hair dryers. **Dining:** 7 am-9 pm, Fri & Sat-10 pm, cocktails. **Pool(s):** heated indoor. **Leisure Activities:** whirlpool. *Fee:* game room. **Guest Services:** gift shop, coin laundry. **Business Services:** meeting rooms. **Cards:** AX, DS, MC, VI. **Special Amenities:** free local telephone calls and preferred room (subject to availability with advanced reservations).

SOME UNITS
FEE

CASHTON pop. 1,005

———— WHERE TO STAY ————

AGES PAST COUNTRY HOUSE
[AAA] [SAVE]
▽▽▽▽
Bed & Breakfast

Phone: 608/654-5950

All Year   2P: $95-$130   XP: $15

Location: Just e of center. 1223 Front St 54619. Fax: 608/654-5709. **Facility:** Chandeliers from Belgium and antique furnishings dating to 1600 are featured in this 1898 Victorian home, which was formerly a Catholic rectory. Smoke free premises. 4 one-bedroom standard units. 2 stories (no elevator), interior corridors. **Parking:** on-site, winter plug-ins. **Terms:** check-in 4 pm, age restrictions may apply, 10 day cancellation notice. **Amenities:** CD players, irons, hair dryers. **Dining:** Back Door Cafe', see separate listing. **Guest Services:** gift shop, complimentary laundry. **Cards:** AX, DS, MC, VI. **Special Amenities: early check-in/late check-out and free local telephone calls.**

[ⁿ] [⊗] [VCR] [⋇] [DATA PORT]

———— WHERE TO DINE ————

BACK DOOR CAFE'
▽▽▽▽
American

Lunch: $8-$15   Dinner: $15-$25   Phone: 608/654-5950

Location: Just e of center; in Ages Past Country House. 1223 Front St 54619. **Hours:** 11 am-2 & 6-9 pm. Closed major holidays; also Sun & Mon. **Reservations:** required. **Features:** Each night the dining room of the Ages Past Country House is transformed into a European cafe for guests' relaxation and dining pleasure. A one-time table seating keeps patrons from feeling pressured or hurried. Among delicacies are duck in fig sauce, lamb chops and beef Wellington. The wine list offers a good selection, and servers are happy to help with pairings and suggestions. Dressy casual; cocktails. **Parking:** on-site. **Cards:** AX, DS, MC, VI.

[⊗]

CEDARBURG —See Milwaukee p. 568.

CHIPPEWA FALLS pop. 12,925

———— WHERE TO STAY ————

AMERICINN MOTEL & SUITES
▽▽▽▽▽
Small-scale Hotel

Phone: (715)723-5711

6/1-8/31 [ECP]   1P: $74-$149   2P: $74-$149   XP: $6   F17
4/1-5/31 & 9/1-3/31 [ECP]   1P: $69-$139   2P: $69-$139   XP: $6   F17

Location: 2 mi s on SR 124, access via CR J. 11 W South Ave 54729. Fax: 715/723-5254. **Facility:** 62 units. 61 one-bedroom standard units, some with whirlpools. 1 one-bedroom suite with whirlpool. 2 stories, interior corridors. **Bath:** combo or shower only. **Parking:** on-site, winter plug-ins. **Terms:** small pets only (in designated units). **Amenities:** irons, hair dryers. **Pool(s):** heated indoor. **Leisure Activities:** whirlpool. **Business Services:** fax (fee). **Cards:** AX, DC, DS, MC, VI.

[ASK] [S⊘] [🐾] [⅃] [🔇] [⇌] [💪] [⋇] [DATA PORT] [▥] / [⊗] [VCR] [📶] [🖼] /
SOME UNITS
FEE

COUNTRY INN BY CARLSON
▽▽▽▽
Small-scale Hotel

Phone: (715)720-1414

All Year   1P: $80-$120   2P: $88-$130   F

Location: Jct SR 124 and CR J. 1021 W Park Ave 54729. Fax: 715/720-1122. **Facility:** 62 one-bedroom standard units, some with whirlpools. 2 stories (no elevator), interior corridors. **Bath:** combo or shower only. **Parking:** on-site, winter plug-ins. **Terms:** [ECP] meal plan available. **Amenities:** voice mail, irons, hair dryers. **Pool(s):** small heated indoor. **Leisure Activities:** whirlpool. **Guest Services:** valet and coin laundry. **Business Services:** fax (fee). **Cards:** AX, DC, DS, MC, VI. **(See color ad starting on p 556.)**

[ASK] [S⊘] [ⁿ⅃] [🔇] [⇌] [💪] [⋇] [DATA PORT] [▥] / [⊗] [🖼] /
SOME UNITS

PARK INN
[AAA] [SAVE]
▽▽ ▽▽
Small-scale Hotel

Phone: (715)723-2281

All Year [BP]   1P: $79   2P: $89   XP: $10   F18

Location: Jct SR 124 and CR J. 1009 W Park Ave 54729. Fax: 715/723-2283. **Facility:** 67 one-bedroom standard units, some with kitchens and/or whirlpools. 1 story, interior/exterior corridors. **Parking:** on-site, winter plug-ins. **Terms:** small pets only ($10 extra charge). **Amenities:** high-speed Internet, irons, hair dryers. **Dining:** 6:30 am-10 pm, cocktails. **Pool(s):** heated indoor. **Leisure Activities:** whirlpool. **Guest Services:** valet laundry, airport transportation-Chippewa Valley Regional Airport. **Business Services:** meeting rooms, fax (fee). **Cards:** AX, DC, DS, MC, VI. **Special Amenities: free continental breakfast and free local telephone calls.**
(See color ad at p. 463)

[S⊘] [⊹] [🐾] [ⁿ] [Y] [⇌] [💪] [⋇] [DATA PORT] [▥] / [⊗] [📶] [🖼] /
SOME UNITS

———— WHERE TO DINE ————

THE FILL INN STATION
▽▽
American

Lunch: $5-$12   Dinner: $5-$12   Phone: 715/723-6551

Location: Corner of Bay and Columbia St; downtown. 104 W Columbia St 54729. **Hours:** 11 am-10 pm. Closed major holidays; also Sun. **Reservations:** accepted. **Features:** This converted gas station features original brick pillars and a monkey wrench on the door. The menu consists of hand-made pizza, sandwhiches and salad, prepared to order beef and buffalo burgers and a few Mexican dishes. Casual dress; cocktails. **Parking:** on-site. **Cards:** AX, DC, DS, MC, VI.

[Y] [⊗]

COLUMBUS pop. 4,479

———— WHERE TO STAY ————

THE COLUMBUS SUPER 8
▽▽▽▽
Small-scale Hotel

Phone: (920)623-8800

All Year [CP]   1P: $54-$72   2P: $59-$77   XP: $5   F12

Location: US 151, exit 118 (SR 16/60), just ne. 219 Industrial Dr 53925. Fax: 920/623-3304. **Facility:** 50 one-bedroom standard units, some with whirlpools. 3 stories, interior corridors. **Parking:** on-site, winter plug-ins. **Amenities:** hair dryers. Some: dual phone lines. **Pool(s):** heated indoor. **Leisure Activities:** whirlpool. **Guest Services:** coin laundry. **Business Services:** meeting rooms. **Cards:** AX, CB, DC, DS, MC, VI.

[ASK] [S⊘] [🔇] [⇌] [⋇] [DATA PORT] / [⊗] [📶] [🖼] /
SOME UNITS

COUDERAY pop. 96

——— WHERE TO DINE ———

THE HIDEOUT
AAA
▼▼▼
American

Lunch: $6-$17   **Dinner:** $10-$25   **Phone:** 715/945-2746
Location: 6 mi n on CR CC. 12101 W County Road CC 54828. **Hours:** Open 5/13-12/31; call for hours. Closed: 12/25. **Reservations:** suggested. **Features:** At the 500-acre former estate of Al Capone, the restaurant is a quiet, relaxed spot that's popular with tourists. The menu includes some Italian specialties, as well as seafood, steak & chops. After dining, enjoy a guided tour. Casual dress; cocktails. **Parking:** on-site. **Cards:** MC, VI.

CRANDON pop. 1,961

——— WHERE TO STAY ———

FOUR SEASONS MOTEL
▼
Motel

Phone: 715/478-3377
All Year   2P: $38-$45   XP: $5   F10
Location: 0.5 mi w on US 8. Located in a commercial area. 304 W Glen 54520 (PO Box 37). Fax: 715/478-3785. **Facility:** 20 one-bedroom standard units. 1 story, interior/exterior corridors. **Parking:** on-site, winter plug-ins. **Terms:** cancellation fee imposed. **Leisure Activities:** snowmobiling. **Business Services:** meeting rooms. **Cards:** DS, MC, VI.

SOME UNITS

CRIVITZ pop. 998

——— WHERE TO STAY ———

SHAFFER PARK RESORT
▼▼▼ ▼▼▼
Motel

Phone: 715/854-2186

	1P	2P	XP	
5/23-9/1	1P: $67-$72	2P: $67-$72	XP: $15	F3
9/2-11/30	1P: $60-$66	2P: $60-$66	XP: $15	F3
4/1-5/22 & 12/1-3/31	1P: $54-$66	2P: $54-$66	XP: $15	F3

Location: 5 mi w on CR W. Located in a rural area. N 7217 Shaffer Rd 54114. **Facility:** 28 units. 27 one-bedroom standard units with efficiencies. 1 cottage ($95-$145). 1 story, exterior corridors. *Bath:* shower only. **Parking:** on-site. **Terms:** 1-3 night minimum stay - seasonal, 14 day cancellation notice, weekly rates available, pets ($5 extra charge, dogs only). **Leisure Activities:** boating, rental paddleboats, boat dock, fishing, tennis court, cross country skiing, snowmobiling, playground, horseshoes, volleyball. **Cards:** MC, VI.

CUMBERLAND pop. 2,280

——— WHERE TO DINE ———

5 O'CLOCK CLUB
▼▼▼ ▼▼▼
American

Dinner: $10-$20   **Phone:** 715/822-2924
Location: 3.5 mi n on US 63 from jct SR 48, then 0.4 mi e. 2639 7th St 54829. **Hours:** 5 pm-10 pm; limited hours in winter. Closed: 4/20, 11/27, 12/25; also 3/1-3/31. **Reservations:** suggested. **Features:** This is a unique restaurant that offers a wide variety of flavorful foods in a rural and picturesque setting on a lakeshore. The dining room sports a fun nautical theme. The menu offerings range from fresh seafood and steak to pasta and Chinese. A nice selection of homemade desserts are presented tableside on a tray. Casual dress; cocktails. **Parking:** on-site. **Cards:** DS, MC, VI.

DE FOREST pop. 7,368

——— WHERE TO STAY ———

HOLIDAY INN EXPRESS
▼▼▼ ▼▼▼
Small-scale Hotel

Phone: (608)846-8686

	1P	2P
5/29-9/1 [ECP]	1P: $69-$129	2P: $69-$129
4/1-5/28 & 9/2-3/31 [ECP]	1P: $69-$99	2P: $69-$99

Location: I-90/94, exit 126 (CR V), just e. 7184 Morrisonville Rd 53532. Fax: 608/846-8687. **Facility:** 72 one-bedroom standard units, some with whirlpools. 3 stories, interior corridors. *Bath:* combo or shower only. **Parking:** on-site, winter plug-ins. **Terms:** 7 day cancellation notice, pets ($20 deposit). **Amenities:** irons, hair dryers. **Pool(s):** small heated indoor. **Leisure Activities:** whirlpool. **Guest Services:** valet and coin laundry. **Business Services:** meeting rooms. **Cards:** AX, DC, DS, MC, VI.

SOME UNITS

——— WHERE TO DINE ———

TONY'S
▼▼▼ ▼▼▼
Italian

Lunch: $4-$7   **Dinner:** $6-$15   **Phone:** 608/846-2755
Location: I-90/94, exit 126, 0.5 mi e. 637 W North St 53532. **Hours:** 4 pm-8:30 pm, Thurs 11 am-3 & 4-8:40 pm, Fri 11 am-2 & 4-9:30 pm, Sat 4 pm-9 pm, Sun 3 pm-8 pm. Closed major holidays; also Mon. **Reservations:** accepted. **Features:** Stuffed, gourmet white and traditional-style pizzas are prepared at the casual restaurant. Casual dress; cocktails. **Parking:** on-site. **Cards:** AX, DC, DS, MC, VI.

DELAFIELD —*See Milwaukee p. 569.*

DELAVAN pop. 7,956

———— WHERE TO STAY ————

LAKE LAWN RESORT
Phone: (262)728-7950

5/21-9/20	1P: $169-$249	2P: $169-$249	XP: $20	F17
4/1-5/20 & 9/21-10/31	1P: $99-$179	2P: $99-$179	XP: $20	F17
11/1-3/31	1P: $99-$159	2P: $99-$159	XP: $20	F17

Resort
Large-scale Hotel

Location: I-43, exit 21 (SR 50), 1 mi e. 2400 E Geneva St 53115. Fax: 262/728-2347. **Facility:** Water views enhance many guest rooms at this lakefront resort set on spacious, tree-covered grounds. 284 one-bedroom standard units. 8 one- and 2 three-bedroom suites ($199-$439), some with kitchens. 2 stories, interior/exterior corridors. **Bath:** combo or shower only. **Parking:** on-site. **Terms:** check-in 4 pm, 2 night minimum stay - weekends, 5 day cancellation notice, package plans. **Amenities:** video games (fee), voice mail, irons. *Some:* hair dryers. **Dining:** 2 restaurants, 7 am-10 pm, cocktails. **Pool(s):** outdoor, heated indoor. **Leisure Activities:** sauna, whirlpool, rental boats, fishing, 3 lighted tennis courts, ice skating, recreation programs, walking trail, playground. *Fee:* sailboats, marina, waterskiing, cruise boat, jet ski, pontoon, golf-18 holes, miniature golf, driving range, cross country skiing, carriage rides, horse drawn sleds in winter, petting zoo, lighted runway, bicycles, horseback riding, massage. **Guest Services:** gift shop, valet laundry, area transportation-dog track. **Business Services:** conference facilities, business center. **Cards:** AX, DC, DS, MC, VI.

SOME UNITS

SUPER 8 MOTEL-DELAVAN
Phone: (262)728-1700

All Year [CP]   1P: $58-$199   2P: $65-$199

Small-scale Hotel

Location: I-43, exit 21 (SR 50), just w. 518 Borg Rd 53115. Fax: 262/728-1700. **Facility:** 69 one-bedroom standard units. 2 stories (no elevator), interior corridors. **Parking:** on-site, winter plug-ins. **Amenities:** video library (fee). **Guest Services:** coin laundry. **Business Services:** meeting rooms. **Cards:** AX, CB, DC, DS, JC, MC, VI. **Special Amenities:** free continental breakfast and free local telephone calls.

SOME UNITS

FEE

———— WHERE TO DINE ————

MILLIE'S RESTAURANT & SHOPPING VILLAGE
Lunch: $5-$15   Phone: 262/728-2434

American

Location: 3.5 mi s on Second St (becomes CR O); at jct South Shore Dr. N 2484 CR O 53115. **Hours:** 8 am-4 pm. Closed: 11/27, 12/25; also Mon-Fri 1/1-2/28, Mon 3/1-6/30 & 9/2-12/31. **Features:** On beautiful landscaped grounds with English gardens, the charming restaurant comprises five dining rooms decorated with antiques. The menu outlines Pennsylvania Dutch-style dinners, as well as sandwiches and salads. The various flavored pancakes are a hit among breakfast dishes that are served all day. Casual dress; cocktails. **Parking:** on-site.

DE PERE pop. 20,559

———— WHERE TO STAY ————

KRESS INN
Phone: (920)403-5100

All Year   1P: $79-$139   2P: $79-$139

Small-scale Hotel

Location: US 41, exit 163 (Main St), then just s on 3rd St. Located next to Norbert College. 300 Grant St 54115. Fax: 920/403-5198. **Facility:** 46 units. 44 one-bedroom standard units, some with whirlpools. 2 one-bedroom suites ($99-$189) with kitchens (no utensils). 3 stories, interior corridors. **Bath:** shower only. **Parking:** on-site. **Terms:** cancellation fee imposed. **Amenities:** high-speed Internet, dual phone lines, voice mail, irons, hair dryers. **Guest Services:** valet laundry. **Business Services:** meeting rooms. **Cards:** AX, DC, DS, MC, VI.

SOME UNITS

FEE

SLEEP INN & SUITES GREEN BAY/DEPERE
Phone: (920)338-8800

All Year [ECP]	1P: $59-$89	2P: $59-$89	XP: $10	F18

Small-scale Hotel

Location: US 41, exit 161. 1600 Lawrence Dr 54115. Fax: 920/338-8881. **Facility:** 76 one-bedroom standard units, some with whirlpools. 3 stories, interior corridors. **Bath:** combo or shower only. **Parking:** on-site. **Terms:** pets (no cats). **Amenities:** dual phone lines, voice mail, safes (fee), irons, hair dryers. **Pool(s):** heated indoor. **Leisure Activities:** whirlpool, exercise room. **Guest Services:** coin laundry. **Business Services:** meeting rooms, business center. **Cards:** AX, DC, DS, JC, MC, VI.

SOME UNITS

———— WHERE TO DINE ————

A'S RESTAURANT & MUSIC CAFE
Lunch: $5-$8   Dinner: $9-$15   Phone: 920/336-2277

American

Location: On east side of bridge; center. 112 N Broadway 54115. **Hours:** 11:30 am-2 & 4-10 pm. Closed major holidays; also Sun & Mon. **Reservations:** accepted. **Features:** Greek shrimp, tenderloin Sicilia and chicken saltimboca are among flavorful selections on a menu of charbroiled seafood, chicken and beef selections. Musicians perform several nights a week. The dining room has the cozy feel of a French cafe. Casual dress; cocktails. **Parking:** on-site. **Cards:** AX, DC, MC, VI.

BLACK & TAN GRILLE
Dinner: $13-$22   Phone: 920/336-4430

American

Location: US 41, exit 163 (Main Ave), 1 mi e. 101 Fort Howard Ave 54115. **Hours:** 5 pm-9 pm, Fri & Sat-10 pm, Sun-8 pm. Closed: 4/20, 11/27, 12/25. **Reservations:** accepted; Sun-Fri. **Features:** The contemporary restaurant serves traditional dishes with a twist and prides itself on offering cuisine different from what is common in the area. The menu changes seasonally, and Fridays and Saturdays always feature something special. Dressy casual; cocktails. **Parking:** street. **Cards:** AX, MC, VI.

DODGEVILLE pop. 4,220

─────── **WHERE TO STAY** ───────

BEST WESTERN QUIET HOUSE & SUITES
Phone: 608/935-7739

🔺🔺🔺 [SAVE]

	5/16-10/31 [ECP]	1P: $89-$108	2P: $99-$118	XP: $10	F12
	11/1-3/31 [ECP]	1P: $69	2P: $79	XP: $10	F12
	4/1-5/15 [ECP]	1P: $69	2P: $69	XP: $10	F12

Small-scale Hotel
Location: On US 18, just e of jct SR 23. 1130 N Johns St 53533. Fax: 608/935-7724. **Facility:** 39 units. 35 one-bedroom standard units, some with whirlpools. 4 one-bedroom suites, some with whirlpools. 2 stories (no elevator), interior corridors. *Bath:* combo or shower only. **Parking:** on-site, winter plug-ins. **Terms:** package plans - seasonal, pets ($15 extra charge, in designated units). **Amenities:** irons, hair dryers. **Pool(s):** heated indoor/outdoor. **Leisure Activities:** whirlpool, limited exercise equipment. **Business Services:** meeting rooms, fax. **Cards:** AX, CB, DC, DS, MC, VI. **Special Amenities:** free continental breakfast and free newspaper. *(See ad p 555)*

SOME UNITS

HOUSE ON THE ROCK INN
Phone: 608/935-3711

🔺🔺🔺

All Year [CP]   1P: $89-$149   2P: $89-$149

Small-scale Hotel
Location: On SR 23, 1 mi n of jct SR 23. 3591 SR 23 53533. Fax: 608/935-1691. **Facility:** 113 units. 97 one-bedroom standard units, some with whirlpools. 16 one-bedroom suites. 4 stories, interior corridors. *Bath:* combo or shower only. **Parking:** on-site. **Terms:** cancellation fee imposed. **Amenities:** video games (fee), voice mail, hair dryers. **Pool(s):** heated outdoor, heated indoor, wading. **Leisure Activities:** whirlpool, exercise room. *Fee:* game room. **Guest Services:** gift shop, coin laundry. **Business Services:** meeting rooms. **Cards:** AX, DS, MC, VI.

SOME UNITS

NEW CONCORD INN
Phone: 608/935-3770

🔺🔺

	5/23-10/31 [ECP]	1P: $89-$149	2P: $89-$149	XP: $6	F13
	4/1-5/22 [ECP]	1P: $59-$79	2P: $59-$79	XP: $5	F13
	11/1-3/31 [ECP]	1P: $59-$79	2P: $59-$79	XP: $6	F13

Small-scale Hotel
Location: On SR 23, 2 mi n of jct US 18. 3637 Hwy 23 N 53533. Fax: 608/935-9605. **Facility:** 63 units. 59 one-bedroom standard units, some with whirlpools. 4 one-bedroom suites. 3 stories, interior corridors. **Parking:** on-site, winter plug-ins. **Terms:** cancellation fee imposed. **Amenities:** *Some:* irons. **Pool(s):** heated indoor. **Leisure Activities:** whirlpool. *Fee:* game room. **Cards:** AX, DC, DS, MC, VI.

SOME UNITS

FEE

PINE RIDGE MOTEL
Phone: 608/935-3386

🔺🔺🔺 [SAVE]

| | 4/1-10/26 | 1P: $39-$49 | 2P: $45-$59 | XP: $3 | |
| | 10/27-3/31 | 1P: $25-$35 | 2P: $30-$45 | XP: $3 | |

Motel
Location: On CR YZ, 0.5 mi e of jct SR 23. 405 County Rd YZ 53533. **Facility:** 22 one-bedroom standard units. 1 story, exterior corridors. *Bath:* combo or shower only. **Parking:** on-site, winter plug-ins. **Terms:** cancellation fee imposed, small pets only ($5 fee). **Cards:** AX, DS, MC, VI.

SOME UNITS

SUPER 8 MOTEL OF DODGEVILLE
Phone: (608)935-3888

🔺🔺 🔺🔺

	5/11-9/3 [CP]	1P: $55-$75	2P: $85-$95	XP: $5	F12
	9/4-10/31 [CP]	1P: $60-$70	2P: $70-$85	XP: $5	F12
	4/1-5/10 & 11/1-3/31 [CP]	1P: $50-$60	2P: $60-$70	XP: $5	F12

Small-scale Hotel
Location: Just n of US 18. 1308 Johns St 53533. Fax: 608/935-3888. **Facility:** 43 one-bedroom standard units, some with whirlpools. 2 stories (no elevator), interior corridors. **Parking:** on-site, winter plug-ins. **Terms:** 7 day cancellation notice, pets ($50 deposit). **Business Services:** meeting rooms. **Cards:** AX, CB, DC, DS, JC, MC, VI.

SOME UNITS

FEE

─────── **WHERE TO DINE** ───────

THYM'S RESTAURANT
Dinner: $8-$20   Phone: 608/935-3344

🔺🔺

American
Location: On SR 23, 1.5 mi n of jct US 18. 3625 State Hwy 23 N 53533. **Hours:** 5 pm-9 pm. Closed: 12/25. **Reservations:** accepted. **Features:** The family-owned restaurant prepares nightly specials, as well as steaks, seafood and chicken. Friendly service and a relaxed atmosphere make this place enjoyable for a hearty meal. Cocktails. **Parking:** on-site. **Cards:** AX, DS, MC, VI.

DOOR COUNTY

BAILEYS HARBOR

———— **WHERE TO STAY** ————

GARDEN INN/MOTEL

Phone: 920/839-2617

⧫ [SAVE]

Motel

| | 6/20-8/31 & 9/19-10/31 | 1P: $75 | 2P: $75 | XP: $10 |
| | 5/1-6/19 & 9/1-9/18 | 1P: $65 | 2P: $65 | XP: $10 |

Location: Just w of SR 57; between Bluff Rd and Howard St. Located in a quiet area. 8076 Guy St 54202 (Box 51). **Facility:** Smoke free premises. 6 one-bedroom standard units. 1 story, exterior corridors. **Parking:** on-site. **Terms:** open 5/1-10/31, 2 night minimum stay - weekends, 7 day cancellation notice. **Cards:** DS, MC, VI. **Special Amenities:** free local telephone calls and free newspaper.

SOME UNITS

GORDON LODGE

Phone: 920/839-2331

⧫ [SAVE]

Resort
Small-scale Hotel

| | 6/20-10/19 [BP] | 1P: $117-$246 | 2P: $117-$246 | XP: $29 |
| | 5/23-6/19 | 1P: $100-$203 | 2P: $100-$203 | XP: $12 |

Location: 0.8 mi n on SR 57, 6.5 mi ne on CR Q. Located in a secluded, quiet area. 1420 Pine Dr 54202 (PO Box 189). Fax: 920/839-2450. **Facility:** Fronting on the North Bay of Lake Michigan, the property features cottages and lodge units, several with fireplaces. 40 units. 20 one-bedroom standard units. 20 cottages. 1 story, interior/exterior corridors. *Bath:* combo or shower only. **Parking:** on-site. **Terms:** open 5/23-10/19, check-in 3:30 pm, 18 day cancellation notice. **Dining:** 7:30 am-10 & 5:30-8:30 pm, cocktails. **Pool(s):** heated outdoor. **Leisure Activities:** whirlpool, boating, rental paddleboats, fishing, putting green, 2 lighted tennis courts, badminton, fitness trail, ping pong, basketball, shuffleboard. *Fee:* bicycles. **Business Services:** meeting rooms. **Cards:** AX, DS, MC, VI. *(See color ad below)*

SOME UNITS

———— WHERE TO DINE ————

THE COMMON HOUSE

Dinner: $10-$29

Phone: 920/839-2708

American

Location: At south end of village, on SR 57. 8041 Hwy 57 54202. **Hours:** Open 5/1-10/31; 5:30 pm-10 pm. **Reservations:** suggested. **Features:** The converted 1890 hardware store delivers an eclectic menu of creatively prepared and thoughtfully presented dishes, such as mouthwatering pork tenderloin, duckling, rack of lamb and poached salmon. An extensive selection of wine complements the food. Casual dress; cocktails. **Parking:** street. **Cards:** DS, MC, VI.

EGG HARBOR pop. 250

———— WHERE TO STAY ————

THE ASHBROOKE

Phone: 920/868-3113

Small-scale Hotel

All Year   1P: $89-$185   2P: $99-$195   XP: $25

Location: Just n on SR 42. 7942 Egg Harbor Rd 54209. **Fax:** 920/868-9684. **Facility:** Smoke free premises. 36 units. 28 one-bedroom standard units, some with whirlpools. 8 one-bedroom suites with whirlpools. 2 stories (no elevator), interior corridors. **Parking:** on-site. **Terms:** age restrictions may apply, 14 day cancellation notice-fee imposed, package plans. **Amenities:** video library, irons, hair dryers. **Pool(s):** heated indoor. **Leisure Activities:** sauna, whirlpool, exercise room. **Cards:** AX, DC, MC, VI.

BAY POINT INN

Phone: (920)868-3297

Condominium

All Year   1P: $195-$239   2P: $195-$239   XP: $20   F6

Location: Just n on SR 42. 7933 Hwy 42 54209. **Fax:** 920/868-2876. **Facility:** Smoke free premises. 10 one-bedroom suites with efficiencies, some with whirlpools. 2 stories (no elevator), exterior corridors. **Parking:** on-site, winter plug-ins. **Terms:** 3 night minimum stay - 6/1-10/31, 14 day cancellation notice, weekly rates available, [ECP] meal plan available. **Amenities:** video library, CD players, dual phone lines, voice mail, irons, hair dryers. **Pool(s):** heated outdoor. **Leisure Activities:** whirlpool. **Business Services:** meeting rooms. **Cards:** AX, CB, DC, DS, MC, VI.

LANDMARK RESORT

Phone: (920)868-3205

Resort Condominium

10/18-3/31   1P: $80-$205
6/27-10/17   1P: $129-$148
5/30-6/26   1P: $82-$128
4/1-5/29   1P: $67-$89

Location: 1 mi sw on CR G and Hillside Tr; 1 mi nw of SR 42 from jct Hillside Tr. Located in a rural area. 7643 Hillside Rd 54209. **Fax:** 920/868-2569. **Facility:** Views of the bay enhance some of this resort's one- and two-bedroom condo units. 293 units. 151 one-, 134 two- and 8 three-bedroom suites with kitchens. 2-3 stories, interior corridors. **Parking:** on-site, winter plug-ins. **Terms:** 14 day cancellation notice-fee imposed. **Amenities:** video library (fee), voice mail, irons, hair dryers. **Dining:** 6:30 am-2 & 5-9:30 pm; hours vary off season, cocktails. **Pool(s):** 3 heated outdoor, heated indoor. **Leisure Activities:** whirlpools, steamrooms, adjacent to 27-hole golf course, 5 tennis courts (3 lighted), cross country skiing, snowmobiling, ice skating, recreation programs, exercise room, basketball, horseshoes, shuffleboard, volleyball. *Fee:* game room. **Guest Services:** gift shop, coin laundry. **Business Services:** conference facilities. **Cards:** AX, DC, DS, MC, VI.

LULL-ABI MOTEL

Phone: 920/868-3135

Motel

6/28-10/31   1P: $79-$99   2P: $79-$99   XP: $15
5/15-6/27   1P: $68-$89   2P: $68-$89   XP: $15
4/20-5/14   1P: $56-$75   2P: $56-$75   XP: $15

Location: Just n on SR 42. 7928 SR 42 54209 (PO Box 527). **Facility:** 23 units. 18 one-bedroom standard units. 5 one-bedroom suites ($75-$160). 2 stories (no elevator), exterior corridors. *Bath:* combo or shower only. **Parking:** on-site. **Terms:** open 4/20-10/31, 14 day cancellation notice-fee imposed. **Amenities:** hair dryers. **Leisure Activities:** whirlpool, bicycles. **Cards:** AX, DS, MC, VI.

SOME UNITS

THE SHALLOWS   Phone: 920/868-3458

(AAA) (SAVE)

♦♦♦♦♦

Resort Motel

	6/20-8/23 [CP]	1P: $100-$350	2P: $100-$350	XP: $20	D18
	5/23-6/19 & 8/24-10/31 [CP]	1P: $80-$250	2P: $80-$250	XP: $20	D18
	5/1-5/22 [CP]	1P: $65-$210	2P: $65-$210	XP: $20	D18

Location: 2.5 mi s on CR G. Located in a quiet area. 7353 Horse Shoe Bay Rd, Hwy G 54209 (PO Box 20). **Fax:** 920/868-2327. **Facility:** Most of the accommodations at this wooded resort offer water views; some units have fireplaces. 34 units. 16 one-bedroom standard units, some with efficiencies. 8 one- and 4 two-bedroom suites with efficiencies. 3 vacation homes and 3 cottages. 1-2 stories (no elevator), exterior corridors. *Bath:* combo or shower only. **Parking:** on-site. **Terms:** open 5/1-10/31, 30 day cancellation notice-fee imposed. **Amenities:** *Some:* CD players, hair dryers. **Pool(s):** heated outdoor. **Leisure Activities:** whirlpool, boating, canoeing, fishing, tennis court, lakeside evening campfires, bicycles, playground, basketball. **Cards:** AX, DS, MC, VI. **Special Amenities:** free continental breakfast. *(See color ad p 482)*

SOME UNITS

🏊 ⊠ 🅿 📠 / ⊠ 🅰 VCR ☎ 🖥 /

──────── **WHERE TO DINE** ────────

TRIO RESTAURANT   Phone: 920/868-2090

♦♦♦ ♦♦♦

Italian

Location: On SR 42 at jct CR E. 4655 County Rd E 54209. **Hours:** Open 5/10-10/25; 5 pm-9 pm, Fri & Sat-9:30 pm. **Features:** The monthly changing menu samples a good variety of well-prepared French and Italian country "peasant" foods, all served in hearty portions. The atmosphere has the flavor and energy of an upbeat bistro. Casual dress; beer & wine only. **Parking:** on-site. **Cards:** AX, DC, DS, MC, VI.   ⊠

VILLAGE CAFE   **Lunch:** $6-$8   Phone: 920/868-3342

◆

American

Location: On SR 42, just n of jct CR E. 7918 Egg Harbor Rd 54209. **Hours:** Open 5/1-10/3; 7 am-2 pm; hours may vary in winter. **Features:** Known for homemade delights, the restaurant specializes in lighter fare. Gourmet omelets and fresh fruit are popular selections from the breakfast menu. For lunch, diners favor specialty salad, burgers and sandwiches. Fish boils Tuesday and Thursday-Saturday 5 pm and 6:30 pm seatings. Patio dining is nice in season. Casual dress; beer & wine only. **Parking:** on-site. **Cards:** DS, MC, VI.   ⊠

ELLISON BAY

──────── **WHERE TO STAY** ────────

GRAND VIEW MOTEL   Phone: 920/854-5150

(AAA) (SAVE)

♦♦♦ ♦

Motel

	6/20-10/26 [CP]	1P: $85-$141	2P: $85-$141	XP: $8	D14
	6/6-6/19 [CP]	1P: $75-$110	2P: $75-$110	XP: $8	D14
	5/16-6/5 [CP]	1P: $68-$110	2P: $68-$110	XP: $8	D14
	5/9-5/15 [CP]	1P: $61-$110	2P: $61-$110	XP: $8	D14

Location: 0.6 mi s on SR 42. Located in a quiet area. 11885 Hwy 42 54210 (PO Box 135). **Fax:** 920/854-7538. **Facility:** Smoke free premises. 28 one-bedroom standard units, some with whirlpools. 2 stories (no elevator), exterior corridors. **Parking:** on-site. **Terms:** open 5/9-10/26, 2 night minimum stay, 14 day cancellation notice-fee imposed. **Amenities:** *Some:* irons, hair dryers. **Leisure Activities:** bicycles, hiking trails, jogging, basketball. **Guest Services:** gift shop, valet laundry. **Cards:** AX, DS, MC, VI. **Special Amenities:** free continental breakfast and free local telephone calls. *(See ad below)*

SOME UNITS

⊠ ⊠ 🅿 / DATA PORT /

PARKSIDE INN   Phone: (920)854-9050

(AAA) (SAVE)

♦♦♦ ♦♦♦

Motel

	8/22-9/19	1P: $82-$95	2P: $82-$95	XP: $7
	9/20-3/31	1P: $72-$95	2P: $72-$95	XP: $7
	6/21-8/21	1P: $95	2P: $95	XP: $7
	4/1-6/20	1P: $65-$72	2P: $65-$72	XP: $7

Location: 0.3 mi s on SR 42. Located across from the park. 11946 Hwy 42 54210. **Fax:** 920/854-9050. **Facility:** Smoke free premises. 15 one-bedroom standard units. 2 stories (no elevator), exterior corridors. *Bath:* combo or shower only. **Parking:** on-site. **Terms:** 7 day cancellation notice-fee imposed. **Cards:** DS, MC, VI. **Special Amenities:** free continental breakfast. *(See ad below)*

⊠ 🅿 📠

WAGON TRAIL RESORT, RESTAURANT & CONFERENCE CENTER

Phone: 920-854-2385

(AAA) (SAVE)

6/30-10/31	1P: $119-$189	2P: $119-$189	XP: $10	F17
5/1-6/29 & 11/1-11/10	1P: $99-$169	2P: $99-$169	XP: $10	F17

▽▽▽▽

Resort
Large-scale Hotel

Location: 3.5 mi se on Mink River Rd; 6 mi ne of Sister Bay on CR ZZ. Located in a rural area, opposite the bay. 1041 County Road ZZ 54210. Fax: 920/854-5278. **Facility:** The property features lodge and vacation homes within a natural setting on Rowley's Bay. 114 units. 73 one-bedroom standard units, some with whirlpools. 3 two- and 4 three-bedroom suites ($189-$269) with efficiencies. 27 vacation homes ($129-$329) and 7 cabins, some with whirlpools. 1-3 stories, interior/exterior corridors. **Bath:** combo or shower only. **Parking:** on-site, winter plug-ins. **Terms:** open 5/1-11/10, check-in 4 pm, 2-7 night minimum stay - seasonal, 10 day cancellation notice-fee imposed. **Amenities:** Some: irons, hair dryers. **Dining:** Grandma's Swedish Restaurant & Bakery, see separate listing. **Pool(s):** heated indoor. **Leisure Activities:** sauna, whirlpool, rental boats, rental paddleboats, fishing, tennis court, cross country skiing, snowmobiling, playground, exercise room, basketball, volleyball. Fee: marina, bicycles, game room. **Guest Services:** gift shop, coin laundry. **Business Services:** conference facilities. **Cards:** DS, MC, VI.

SOME UNITS

🔊 🍴 🎇 🖋 🏊 ✕ / ✕ 🐾 🖥 🖸 🖵 /

─── WHERE TO DINE ───

GRANDMA'S SWEDISH RESTAURANT & BAKERY

Lunch: $5-$9   **Dinner:** $10-$17   **Phone:** 920-854-2385

▽▽ ▽▽

American

Location: 3.5 mi se on Mink River Rd; 6 mi ne of Sister Bay on CR ZZ; in Wagon Trail Resort, Restaurant & Conference Center. 1041 Hwy ZZ 54210. **Hours:** 7:30 am-2 & 5-8 pm; winter hours vary. **Features:** Overlooking a picturesque lake, the Swedish country dining room is a quaint spot for home-cooking and tempting bakery treats. Especially popular is the fish boil and Swedish smorgasbord, available three nights a week, June through October. Casual dress; beer & wine only. **Parking:** on-site. **Cards:** DS, MC, VI.

✕

MINK RIVER BASIN SUPPER CLUB

Dinner: $15-$34   **Phone:** 920-854-2250

(AAA)

▽▽ ▽▽

American

Location: On SR 42; center. 12010 Hwy 42 54210. **Hours:** 5 pm-9:30 pm, Sat & Sun-10 pm; winter hours vary. Closed: 11/27, 12/25. **Reservations:** accepted. **Features:** The menu samples a wide variety of home-style selections, ranging from fresh fish, pasta and duck to prime rib and baby back ribs. Premium wine created from Door County fruit include some nonalcoholic selections. The dessert bar is especially popular. Casual dress; cocktails. **Parking:** on-site. **Cards:** AX, DC, DS, MC, VI.

🍴

T. ASHWELL'S

Dinner: $20-$32   **Phone:** 920-854-4306

▽▽▽▽

American

Parking: on-site. **Cards:** MC, VI.

Location: From jct SR 42, just e. 11976 Mink River Rd 54212. **Hours:** Open 5/1-2/29; 5 pm-10 pm. Closed: Tues. **Reservations:** suggested. **Features:** The contemporary restaurant serves traditional dishes with a twist and prides itself on offering cuisine different from what is common in the area. The menu changes seasonally, and Fridays and Saturdays always feature something special. Dressy casual; cocktails.

🍴 ✕

THE VIKING GRILL

Lunch: $5-$11   **Dinner:** $9-$16   **Phone:** 920-854-2998

▽▽

American

Cards: AX, DS, MC, VI.

Location: Center. 12029 Hwy 42 54210. **Hours:** 6 am-8 pm; to 9 pm 6/15-10/15. Closed: 4/20, 11/27, 12/25; also 3/1-3/31. **Features:** Nightly fish boils draw hungry crowds to the family-oriented restaurant from late May through mid-October. Tourists enjoy experiencing the event, which is a big part of area culture. Other choices center on familiar fare, such as broasted chicken. Casual dress; cocktails. **Parking:** on-site.

🍴 ✕

EPHRAIM pop. 353

─── WHERE TO STAY ───

EPHRAIM GUEST HOUSE

Phone: 920-854-2319

▽▽▽▽

Condominium

8/18-10/31	2P: $95-$165	XP: $12	F7
6/14-8/17	2P: $150-$160	XP: $12	F7
11/1-3/31	2P: $80-$160	XP: $12	F7
4/1-6/13	2P: $80-$105	XP: $12	F7

Location: Just n of Village Hall, then just e. Located in a quiet area. 3042 Cedar St 54211 (PO Box 349). **Facility:** Smoke free premises. 14 units. 7 one- and 6 two- and 1 three-bedroom suites ($95-$225) with kitchens, some with whirlpools. 2 stories (no elevator), interior/exterior corridors. **Parking:** on-site. **Terms:** 2 night minimum stay, 21 day cancellation notice-fee imposed. **Amenities:** video library, irons, hair dryers. **Leisure Activities:** whirlpool. **Guest Services:** coin laundry. **Cards:** AX, DS, MC, VI.

(ASK) 🔊 🍴 ✕ (VCR) 🖸 🖵 🖵

TROLLHAUGEN LODGE, SUITE, MOTEL & LOG CABIN

Phone: (920)854-2713

(AAA) (SAVE)

▽▽ ▽▽

Motel

4/25-11/1 [CP]   1P: $49-$92   2P: $49-$92   XP: $10   D9

Location: 0.6 mi n of Village Hall. 10176 Rt 42 54211 (PO Box 142). **Facility:** Smoke free premises. 14 units. 13 one-bedroom standard units. 1 cabin ($109-$149). 1-2 stories (no elevator), interior/exterior corridors. **Bath:** shower only. **Parking:** on-site. **Terms:** open 4/25-11/1, 7 day cancellation notice-fee imposed, weekly rates available. **Amenities:** Some: hair dryers. **Leisure Activities:** whirlpool. **Cards:** DS, MC, VI. **Special Amenities:** free continental breakfast and free local telephone calls. (See ad p 481)

SOME UNITS

🔊 ✕ 🎦 🖸 🖵 / (VCR) 🖵 /

FISH CREEK

———— WHERE TO STAY ————

HOMESTEAD SUITES

Phone: 920/868-3748

		XP	
7/20-8/23 [ECP]	2P: $139-$189	XP: $10	F16
6/8-7/19 [ECP]	2P: $99-$189	XP: $10	F16
8/24-3/31 [ECP]	2P: $94-$159	XP: $10	F16
4/1-6/7 [ECP]	2P: $79-$149	XP: $10	F16

Small-scale Hotel

Location: 0.3 mi n on SR 42. Located next to Peninsula State Park. 4006 Main St 54212 (PO Box 730). Fax: 920/868-2874. **Facility:** Smoke free premises. 64 units. 48 one-bedroom standard units, some with whirlpools. 16 two-bedroom suites ($129-$189) with kitchens and whirlpools. 2 stories (no elevator), interior/exterior corridors. **Parking:** on-site. **Terms:** 2-3 night minimum stay - weekends & seasonal, 21 day cancellation notice. **Amenities:** video library. *Some:* irons. **Pool(s):** 2 heated outdoor, heated indoor. **Leisure Activities:** sauna, whirlpools, exercise room, basketball. *Fee:* game room. **Guest Services:** coin laundry. **Business Services:** meeting rooms. **Cards:** DS, MC, VI.

JULIE'S PARK CAFE & MOTEL

Phone: 920/868-2999

			XP	
6/28-8/15	1P: $77-$84	2P: $77-$84	XP: $10	
8/16-10/20	1P: $67-$84	2P: $67-$84	XP: $10	
4/11-6/27	1P: $54-$77	2P: $54-$77	XP: $10	
10/21-11/1	1P: $41-$56	2P: $41-$56	XP: $10	

Motel

Location: 0.3 mi n on SR 42. Located at the entrance to Peninsula State Park. 4020 Hwy 42 54212 (PO Box 548). Fax: 920/854-7722. **Facility:** Smoke free premises. 13 units. 12 one- and 1 two-bedroom standard units. 1 story, exterior corridors. *Bath:* combo or shower only. **Parking:** on-site. **Terms:** open 4/11-11/1, 2 night minimum stay - weekends, 10 day cancellation notice, weekly rates available, small pets only ($15 extra charge, in designated units). **Cards:** DS, MC, VI.

SOME UNITS / FEE

SETTLEMENT COURTYARD INN

Phone: 920/868-3524

			XP	
7/3-10/25 [CP]	1P: $114-$129	2P: $119-$134	XP: $12	F3
5/16-7/2 [CP]	1P: $79-$94	2P: $84-$99	XP: $12	F3
10/26-3/31	1P: $67-$82	2P: $72-$87	XP: $12	F3
4/1-5/15	1P: $67-$77	2P: $72-$82	XP: $12	F3

Small-scale Hotel

Location: 1 mi s on SR 42. Located in a rural area. 9126 Hwy 42 54212 (PO Box 729). Fax: 920/868-3048. **Facility:** 33 units. 29 one- and 1 two-bedroom standard units, some with whirlpools. 1 one- and 2 two-bedroom suites ($150-$250) with whirlpools. 2 stories (no elevator), interior corridors. **Parking:** on-site, winter plug-ins. **Terms:** 2-3 night minimum stay - weekends in season, 10 day cancellation notice, weekly rates available, package plans - weekdays. **Amenities:** *Some:* irons. **Leisure Activities:** cross country skiing, hiking trails, horseshoes. **Cards:** AX, DS, MC, VI.

SOME UNITS / FEE

THE WHITE GULL INN

Phone: (920)868-3517

All Year   2P: $128-$188

Historic Country Inn

Location: Just w of SR 42; center. 4225 Main St 54212 (PO Box 160). Fax: 920/868-2367. **Facility:** This country inn built in 1896 has nicely appointed rooms, most with gas fireplaces; phone for seasonal closures. Smoke free premises. 17 units. 10 one-bedroom standard units, some with whirlpools. 3 one-bedroom suites ($188-$265), some with whirlpools. 4 cottages ($200-$350). 1-2 stories (no elevator), interior/exterior corridors. *Bath:* combo or shower only. **Parking:** on-site. **Terms:** 2 night minimum stay - weekends, 14 day cancellation notice, weekly rates available, [BP] meal plan available, package plans - in winter, 15% service charge. **Amenities:** video library, CD players, hair dryers. *Some:* voice mail. **Dining:** dining room, see separate listing. **Business Services:** PC. **Cards:** AX, CB, DC, DS, MC, VI.

SOME UNITS /

———— WHERE TO DINE ————

THE COOKERY

Lunch: $5-$9   **Dinner:** $9-$13   **Phone: 920/868-3634**

American

Location: On SR 42; center. 4135 Hwy 42 54212. **Hours:** Open 4/1-10/31; 7 am-9 pm; open some weekends off season. Closed: 11/27; also 11/30-12/25. **Features:** Flavorful foods cooked from scratch include the specialty creamy whitefish chowder. Desserts, cinnamon rolls and other baked goods are made on the premises. The dining room has a cozy, country-style ambience. Service is upbeat and friendly. Casual dress; beer & wine only. **Parking:** street. **Cards:** MC, VI.

ENGLISH INN

Dinner: $18-$50   **Phone: 920/868-3076**

Continental

Location: 2 mi n on SR 42. 3713 Hwy 42 54212. **Hours:** Open 5/3-10/27; 5:30 pm-9:30 pm, Sat-10 pm. **Features:** Three attractive dining areas are decorated in an English theme with lots of wood and beautiful stained glass. Baked grouper and prime rib stand out on a menu of veal, pasta, ribs, beef, lamb and seafood. Delicious desserts are made on the premises. Casual dress; cocktails; entertainment. **Parking:** on-site. **Cards:** DC, MC, VI.

WHITE GULL INN

Country Inn   **Lunch:** $7-$10   **Dinner:** $17-$21   **Phone: 920/868-3517**

American

Location: Just w of SR 42; center; in The White Gull Inn. 4225 Main St 54212. **Hours:** 7:30 am-2:30 & 5-8 pm. Closed: 11/27, 12/25. **Reservations:** suggested; for dinner. **Features:** Enjoy traditional fish boils at dinner or hearty breakfasts of cherry-stuffed French toast. The 1896 country inn is appointed with period antiques. Such dishes as crabmeat and wild rice salad are delicious and satisfying. Servers are pleasant. Casual dress; beer & wine only. **Parking:** street. **Cards:** AX, DC, DS, MC, VI.

GILLS ROCK

─────── WHERE TO STAY ───────

HARBOR HOUSE INN
Phone: 920/854-5196

◆◆◆ ◆◆◆	6/13-10/19 [ECP]	1P: $69-$185	2P: $69-$185	XP: $20	D18
	5/27-6/12 & 10/20-10/31 [ECP]	1P: $59-$175	2P: $59-$175	XP: $20	D18
Bed & Breakfast	4/24-5/26 [ECP]	1P: $49-$165	2P: $49-$165	XP: $20	D18

Location: On SR 42; center. Located across from Weburg's Wharf. 12666 SR 42 54210. **Facility:** Smoke free premises. 14 units. 12 one-bedroom standard units, some with whirlpools. 2 cottages ($129-$139). 1-2 stories (no elevator), interior/exterior corridors. *Bath:* combo or shower only. **Parking:** on-site. **Terms:** open 4/24-10/31, 21 day cancellation notice-fee imposed, weekly rates available, pets ($20 extra charge). **Leisure Activities:** sauna, whirlpool. *Fee:* bicycles. **Cards:** AX, MC, VI.

SOME UNITS

MAPLE GROVE MOTEL
Phone: (920)854-2587

◆◆◆	5/1-11/1	1P: $55-$65	2P: $60-$75	XP: $10	F4
Motel					

Location: 0.3 mi e on SR 42, 1.5 mi w of car ferry. Located in a rural area. 809 SR 42 54210. Fax: 920/854-7817. **Facility:** 6 units. 4 one- and 2 two-bedroom standard units. 1 story, exterior corridors. *Bath:* shower only. **Parking:** on-site. **Terms:** open 5/1-11/1, 2-3 night minimum stay - weekends, 15 day cancellation notice-fee imposed, pets ($5 extra charge). **Cards:** MC, VI.

SOME UNITS

THE SHORELINE RESORT
Phone: 920/854-2606

◆◆◆ ◆◆◆	6/13-10/20	1P: $84-$124	2P: $89-$129	XP: $10	
Motel	4/25-6/12 & 10/21-10/29	1P: $69-$104	2P: $74-$109	XP: $10	

Location: On SR 42; center. Located on the bay. 12747 Hwy 42 54210 (12747 Hwy 42, ELLISON BAY). Fax: 920/854-5971. **Facility:** Smoke free premises. 14 one-bedroom standard units. 2 stories (no elevator), exterior corridors. **Parking:** on-site. **Terms:** open 4/25-10/29, 2-3 night minimum stay - weekends, 14 day cancellation notice. **Leisure Activities:** fishing. *Fee:* marina, scuba diving, charter fishing. **Guest Services:** gift shop. **Cards:** DS, MC, VI.

SISTER BAY pop. 886

─────── WHERE TO STAY ───────

BIRCHWOOD LODGE
Phone: (920)854-7195

△△△ SAVE	7/12-8/18	1P: $159-$219	2P: $159-$219	XP: $10	F18
	8/19-10/19	1P: $109-$205	2P: $109-$205	XP: $10	F18
◆◆◆ ◆◆◆	4/1-7/11	1P: $80-$179	2P: $80-$179	XP: $10	F18
Small-scale Hotel	10/20-3/31	1P: $80-$170	2P: $80-$170	XP: $10	F18

Location: Jct SR 42 and 57, just se. Located in a semi-rural area. 337 Hwy 57 54234 (PO Box 646). Fax: 920/854-6316. **Facility:** Smoke free premises. 46 units. 39 one-bedroom standard units with whirlpools. 6 one- and 1 two-bedroom suites with kitchens, some with whirlpools. 3 stories, interior corridors. *Bath:* combo or shower only. **Parking:** on-site. **Terms:** 14 day cancellation notice-fee imposed, $15 service charge. **Amenities:** video library (fee), hair dryers. **Pool(s):** heated outdoor, heated indoor. **Leisure Activities:** sauna, whirlpool, tennis court, snowmobiling, exercise room. *Fee:* game room. **Guest Services:** coin laundry. **Business Services:** meeting rooms. **Cards:** AX, CB, DC, DS, MC, VI. **Special Amenities:** early check-in/late check-out and preferred room (subject to availability with advanced reservations).** *(See color ad below)*

THE COUNTRY HOUSE RESORT

Phone: 920/854-4551

AAA [SAVE]
▼▼▼

Resort Motel

6/20-10/19 [ECP]	1P: $113-$182	2P: $113-$182	XP: $22
10/20-3/31 [CP]	1P: $91-$153	2P: $91-$153	XP: $22
5/2-6/19 [ECP]	1P: $91-$153	2P: $91-$153	XP: $22
4/1-5/1 [CP]	1P: $70-$130	2P: $70-$130	XP: $22

Location: 0.5 mi s on SR 42, just w. Located in a quiet, secluded area. 715 N Highland Rd 54234. Fax: 920/854-9809. **Facility:** The resort, on 16 wooded acres, offers a parklike setting, and many rooms feature balconies overlooking the water. 46 units. 37 one-bedroom standard units, some with efficiencies. 4 one- and 5 two-bedroom suites ($137-$320) with whirlpools, some with kitchens. 2 stories (no elevator), exterior corridors. **Parking:** on-site, winter plug-ins. **Terms:** 3 night minimum stay, age restrictions may apply, 14 day cancellation notice-fee imposed, package plans. **Amenities:** voice mail, irons, hair dryers. **Pool(s):** heated outdoor. **Leisure Activities:** whirlpool, boating, fishing, tennis court, bicycles, hiking trails, horseshoes, shuffleboard, volleyball. **Business Services:** meeting rooms. **Cards:** AX, CB, DC, DS, MC, VI. **Special Amenities: free continental breakfast and free local telephone calls.** *(See color ad below)*

SOME UNITS
🏊 ✕ [VCR] [DATA PORT] 🛗 🖥 / ✕ 🖼 /

HELM'S FOUR SEASON'S MOTEL

Phone: (920)854-2356

▼▼ ▼▼

Small-scale Hotel

6/13-10/19	1P: $95-$230	2P: $107-$230	XP: $15	D
5/2-6/12	1P: $74-$170	2P: $86-$170	XP: $15	D
10/20-3/31	1P: $75-$160	2P: $91-$160	XP: $15	D
4/1-5/1	1P: $70-$130	2P: $78-$150	XP: $10	D

Location: Just w of SR 42; center of downtown. Located next to Village Park. 414 Mill Rd 54234 (PO Box 255). Fax: 920/854-1836. **Facility:** 41 units. 36 one- and 5 two-bedroom standard units, some with efficiencies. 1-2 stories (no elevator), interior/exterior corridors. **Parking:** on-site, winter plug-ins. **Terms:** 2 night minimum stay - 6/14-10/20, 14 day cancellation notice-fee imposed, weekly rates available, [ECP] meal plan available. **Amenities:** video library (fee). **Pool(s):** heated indoor. **Leisure Activities:** whirlpool, rental canoes, boat dock, fishing. **Guest Services:** coin laundry. **Business Services:** meeting rooms, fax. **Cards:** MC, VI.

SOME UNITS
[🍴+] 🏊 ✕ 🛗 / ✕ [VCR] 🖼 🖥
FEE

PHEASANT PARK RESORT

Phone: (920)854-7287

▼▼▼

Condominium

6/27-8/23	1P: $175-$259	2P: $175-$259	XP: $12	F6
8/24-3/31	1P: $88-$259	2P: $88-$259	XP: $12	F6
5/16-6/26	1P: $105-$208	2P: $105-$208	XP: $12	F6
4/1-5/15	1P: $88-$162	2P: $88-$162	XP: $12	F6

Location: Just e on Mill Rd, then just n. Located in a semi-rural area. 130 Park Ln 54234 (PO Box 230). Fax: 920/854-4195. **Facility:** Smoke free premises. 58 units. 43 one- and 15 two-bedroom suites with kitchens and whirlpools. 3 stories, interior corridors. **Parking:** on-site, winter plug-ins. **Amenities:** video library (fee), irons, hair dryers. **Pool(s):** heated outdoor, heated indoor. **Leisure Activities:** sauna, whirlpool, 2 tennis courts, snowmobiling, ice skating, playground, exercise room, basketball. *Fee:* bicycles, game room. **Guest Services:** coin laundry. **Business Services:** meeting rooms.

[A$K] [$⌃] 🛅 [👤] 🏊 ✕ ✕ [VCR] 🎦 [DATA PORT] 🛗 🖼 🖥

VOYAGER INN

Phone: 920/854-4242

▼▼ ▼▼

Motel

5/23-10/20	1P: $66-$90	2P: $66-$90	XP: $7
5/2-5/22 & 10/21-11/3	1P: $55-$65	2P: $55-$65	XP: $7

Location: Jct SR 42, 0.5 mi se. Located in a quiet area. 232 SR 57 54234. Fax: 920/854-2670. **Facility:** 29 one-bedroom standard units. 2 stories (no elevator), interior/exterior corridors. **Parking:** on-site. **Terms:** open 5/2-11/3, 14 day cancellation notice-fee imposed, package plans - seasonal. **Pool(s):** heated outdoor. **Leisure Activities:** sauna, whirlpool, horseshoes. **Cards:** DC, MC, VI.

SOME UNITS
🏊 ✕ 🎦 🛗 / ✕ /

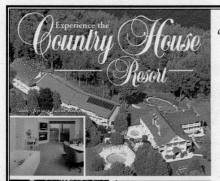

——— WHERE TO DINE ———

SISTER BAY CAFE　　　　**Lunch:** $3-$13　　　**Dinner:** $9-$15　　　**Phone:** 920/854-2429

American

Location: On SR 42; downtown. 611 N Bayshore Dr 54234. **Hours:** Open 4/1-10/31; 8 am-3:30 & 5-8:30 pm; hours vary seasonally. **Features:** The restaurant delivers Norwegian specialties, such as lapskaus, meatballs and salmon. Entrees are attractively presented. The dining room is appointed with well-coordinated Scandinavian decor, including watercolors and flags. Casual dress; beer & wine only.
Parking: on-site. **Cards:** MC, VI.　　　　　　　　　　　　　　　　　　　　　　　　　X

STURGEON BAY pop. 9,437

——— WHERE TO STAY ———

AMERICINN MOTEL & SUITES　　　　　　　　　　　　　　　　　**Phone:** (920)743-5898

Small-scale Hotel

7/1-10/31	1P: $99-$155	2P: $109-$165	XP: $10	F12
5/1-6/30	1P: $79-$145	2P: $89-$155	XP: $10	F12
11/1-3/31	1P: $59-$145	2P: $69-$155	XP: $10	F12
4/1-4/30	1P: $59-$139	2P: $69-$149	XP: $10	F12

Location: On SR 42, 0.5 mi s of jct CR C/S. Located in a commercial area. 622 S Ashland Ave 54235. Fax: 920/743-6899. **Facility:** 46 units. 43 one-bedroom standard units, some with whirlpools. 3 one-bedroom suites, some with whirlpools. 2 stories, interior corridors. *Bath:* combo or shower only. **Parking:** on-site, winter plug-ins. **Terms:** 2 night minimum stay - weekends 7/1-10/31, [ECP] meal plan available. **Amenities:** irons, hair dryers. **Pool(s):** heated indoor. **Leisure Activities:** sauna, whirlpool. **Guest Services:** coin laundry. **Business Services:** meeting rooms. **Cards:** AX, DC, DS, MC, VI.

SOME UNITS

(A$K) (S/D) (t|+) (□) (□) (≈) (※) (DATA PORT) (目) (□) (□) / X /

BEST WESTERN MARITIME INN　　　　　　　　　　　　　　　**Phone:** (920)743-7231

Small-scale Hotel

7/4-10/31 [CP]	1P: $85-$105	2P: $95-$115	XP: $7	F12
5/9-7/3 [CP]	1P: $70-$100	2P: $78-$105	XP: $7	F12
4/1-5/8 & 11/1-3/31 [CP]	1P: $55-$80	2P: $61-$90	XP: $7	F12

Location: 1 mi n on Business Rt SR 42/57. Located in a commercial area. 1001 N 14th Ave 54235. Fax: 920/743-9341. **Facility:** 90 one-bedroom standard units, some with whirlpools. 2 stories (no elevator), interior corridors. **Parking:** on-site, winter plug-ins. **Terms:** 7 day cancellation notice, package plans - 11/1-4/30. **Amenities:** irons, hair dryers. **Pool(s):** heated indoor. **Leisure Activities:** whirlpool. *Fee:* game room. **Cards:** AX, CB, DC, DS, MC, VI. **Special Amenities:** early check-in/late check-out and free continental breakfast.

SOME UNITS

(S/D) (t|+) (≈) (DATA PORT) (□) / X (目) (□) /

CHERRY HILLS LODGE & GOLF RESORT　　　　　　　　　　**Phone:** (920)743-4222

Small-scale Hotel

4/1-6/30	1P: $89-$197	2P: $89-$197	XP: $15
1/31-3/14	1P: $89-$129	2P: $89-$129	XP: $15
9/2-11/1	1P: $89-$115	2P: $89-$115	XP: $15
7/1-9/1	1P: $115	2P: $115	XP: $15

Location: 5 mi n on SR 42, 1.5 mi w on CR P. Located in a rural area. 5905 Dunn Rd 54235. Fax: 920/743-4222. **Facility:** Smoke free premises. 31 one-bedroom standard units, some with whirlpools. 2 stories, interior corridors. **Parking:** on-site. **Terms:** open 4/1-11/1 & 1/31-3/14, 14 day cancellation notice-fee imposed, package plans. **Amenities:** hair dryers. **Dining:** The Restaurant at Cherry Hills, see separate listing. **Pool(s):** heated outdoor. **Leisure Activities:** whirlpool, hiking trails. *Fee:* golf-18 holes, driving range. **Business Services:** meeting rooms. **Cards:** AX, DS, MC, VI.
(See color ad below)

(¶|) (Y) (≈) (X) (X) (※) (目)

LEATHEM SMITH LODGE & MARINA

	Phone: (920)743-5555

(AAA) (SAVE)

6/29-9/1 [ECP]	1P: $105-$210	2P: $105-$210	XP: $15	F9
9/2-10/18 [ECP]	1P: $99-$210	2P: $99-$210	XP: $15	F9
4/1-6/28 [ECP]	1P: $72-$175	2P: $72-$175	XP: $15	F9
10/19-3/31 [ECP]	1P: $64-$149	2P: $64-$149	XP: $15	F9

Resort
Small-scale Hotel

Location: SR 42/57, exit Utah St, 0.5 mi n of Bay View Bridge, then just w. 1640 Memorial Dr 54235. **Fax:** 920/743-5355. **Facility:** Across from the marina, the lodge features a variety of room types, and its suites have gas fireplaces. 63 units. 51 one-bedroom standard units, some with whirlpools. 12 one-bedroom suites ($103-$210) with whirlpools. 2 stories (no elevator), interior corridors. **Parking:** on-site, winter plug-ins. **Terms:** 3 day cancellation notice, 18% service charge. **Amenities:** video library (fee). *Some:* irons. **Dining:** 11:30 am-1:30 & 5:30-9 pm; hours may vary seasonally, cocktails. **Pool(s):** heated outdoor. **Leisure Activities:** excursion boat, 2 tennis courts. *Fee:* marina, golf-9 holes. **Guest Services:** gift shop. **Business Services:** meeting rooms. **Cards:** AX, DS, MC, VI. **Special Amenities:** free continental breakfast and free local telephone calls. *(See color ad p 489)*

SOME UNITS

SCOFIELD HOUSE BED & BREAKFAST

	Phone: 920/743-7727

(AAA) (SAVE)

All Year	1P: $112-$220	2P: $112-$220	XP: $20

Bed & Breakfast

Location: Center. Located in a residential area. 908 Michigan St 54235-0761. **Fax:** 920/743-7727. **Facility:** This elegantly restored 1902 Victorian home has stained-glass windows and many original furnishings; some rooms feature gas fireplaces and whirlpools. Smoke free premises. 6 one-bedroom standard units, some with whirlpools. 3 stories (no elevator), interior corridors. *Bath:* combo or shower only. **Parking:** on-site. **Terms:** 2 night minimum stay - weekends 5/1-11/15, age restrictions may apply, 14 day cancellation notice-fee imposed, [BP] meal plan available. **Amenities:** video library. *Some:* CD players. **Cards:** MC, VI. **Special Amenities:** free local telephone calls. *(See color ad p 489)*

SOME UNITS

SUPER 8 MOTEL

	Phone: 920/743-9211

7/3-11/3 [CP]	1P: $84-$94	2P: $91-$101	XP: $7	F12
4/1-7/2 [CP]	1P: $63-$73	2P: $70-$80	XP: $7	F12
11/4-3/31 [CP]	1P: $44-$54	2P: $54-$64	XP: $7	F12

Small-scale Hotel

Location: 1 mi s on Business Rt SR 42/57. Located in a commercial area. 409 Green Bay Rd 54235. **Fax:** 920/743-4143. **Facility:** 63 one-bedroom standard units, some with whirlpools. 2 stories (no elevator), interior corridors. **Parking:** on-site, winter plug-ins. **Terms:** 7 day cancellation notice, pets ($20 deposit). **Amenities:** *Some:* hair dryers. **Pool(s):** heated indoor. **Leisure Activities:** whirlpool. **Cards:** AX, DC, MC, VI.

SOME UNITS

WHITE LACE INN

	Phone: 920/743-1105

(AAA) (SAVE)

5/22-10/25 [BP]	1P: $134-$249	2P: $134-$249	XP: $15
4/1-5/21 & 10/26-3/31 [BP]	1P: $69-$224	2P: $69-$224	XP: $15

Bed & Breakfast

Location: Center. Located in a residential area. 16 N 5th Ave 54235. **Fax:** 920/743-8180. **Facility:** Close to downtown, this B&B has tastefully decorated rooms in four historic homes; breakfast is served in the main house. Smoke free premises. 18 one-bedroom standard units, some with whirlpools. 2 stories (no elevator), interior corridors. *Bath:* combo or shower only. **Parking:** on-site. **Terms:** 2-3 night minimum stay - weekends, age restrictions may apply, 21 day cancellation notice-fee imposed. **Amenities:** video library, irons. *Some:* CD players. **Guest Services:** gift shop. **Cards:** AX, CB, DC, DS, MC, VI. **Special Amenities:** free local telephone calls and free newspaper. *(See color ad p 489)*

SOME UNITS

──────── **WHERE TO DINE** ────────

THE NAUTICAL INN

Lunch: $5-$15	**Dinner:** $5-$15	**Phone:** 920/743-3399

American

Location: Center. 234 Kentucky St 54235. **Hours:** 11 am-2 & 5:30-9 pm, Fri & Sat-10 pm. **Features:** This restaurant has a history of serving tasty food since 1886. The menu is varied and features fresh seafood, fajitas, sandwiches and salad, and steak. The cheesecurd appetizer and apple cheesecake dessert are popular. Casual dress; cocktails. **Parking:** on-site. **Cards:** AX, MC, VI.

THE RESTAURANT AT CHERRY HILLS

Lunch: $4-$6	**Dinner:** $9-$18	**Phone:** 920/743-4222

American

Location: 5 mi n on SR 42, 1.5 mi w on CR P; in Cherry Hills Lodge & Golf Resort. 5905 Dunn Rd 54235. **Hours:** Open 5/25-10/15; 8 am-1:30 & 5:30-8 pm. Closed: 12/25; also Mon for dinner. **Reservations:** accepted. **Features:** The restaurant specializes in made-to-order continental cuisine, fresh seafood and beef, including delicious whitefish and prime rib. The dining room and breezy outdoor deck look out over the golf course and countryside. Stop by for the great Sunday breakfast buffet and brunch. Casual dress; cocktails. **Parking:** on-site. **Cards:** AX, DC, DS, MC, VI.

The previous listings were for Door County.
This page resumes the alphabetical listings of cities in Wisconsin.

EAGLE RIVER pop. 1,443

———— WHERE TO STAY ————

BEST WESTERN DERBY INN   **Phone: (715)479-1600**

6/27-8/16 & 12/26-3/31 [ECP]	1P: $80-$170	2P: $80-$170	XP: $6 F12
8/17-12/25 [ECP]	1P: $70-$170	2P: $70-$170	XP: $6 F12
4/1-6/26 [ECP]	1P: $69-$80	2P: $69-$80	XP: $6 F12

SAVE

Small-scale Hotel **Location:** 1 mi n. 1800 Hwy 45 N 54521 (PO Box 2470). Fax: 715/479-1143. **Facility:** 47 one-bedroom standard units, some with whirlpools. 2 stories (no elevator), interior corridors. *Bath:* combo or shower only. **Parking:** on-site, winter plug-ins. **Terms:** 3 day cancellation notice, small pets only (in smoking units). **Amenities:** irons, hair dryers. **Pool(s):** heated indoor. **Leisure Activities:** sauna, whirlpool, snowmobiling. *Fee:* game room. **Guest Services:** coin laundry. **Business Services:** meeting rooms. **Cards:** AX, DC, DS, MC, VI.

SOME UNITS

CHANTICLEER INN   **Phone: (715)479-4486**

7/1-9/1 & 12/25-3/31	1P: $119-$160	2P: $119-$160	XP: $12 F
4/1-6/30 & 9/2-12/24	1P: $59-$160	2P: $79-$160	XP: $12 F

Resort
Large-scale Hotel **Location:** 2 mi e on SR 70, 0.5 mi n. Located in a rural wooded area. 1458 E Dollar Lake Rd 54521. Fax: 715/479-0004. **Facility:** Condos, motel units and one- to three-bedroom villas are offered at this resort on a chain of lakes. 55 units. 29 one-bedroom standard units, some with efficiencies and/or whirlpools. 10 two- and 8 three-bedroom suites with kitchens. 8 cottages, some with whirlpools. 1-3 stories (no elevator), exterior corridors. **Parking:** on-site, winter plug-ins. **Terms:** 2-3 night minimum stay - weekends, cancellation fee imposed, weekly rates available. **Amenities:** *Some:* hair dryers. **Dining:** 5:30 pm-8:30 pm, Sat & Sun 8 am-10 & 5:30-8:30 pm; to 9:30 pm 6/16-9/14; closed Tues 9/5-6/17, cocktails. **Leisure Activities:** rental boats, rental canoes, boat dock, fishing, cross country skiing, snowmobiling, hiking trails, jogging, playground, basketball, volleyball. *Fee:* pontoon boat, 2 tennis courts (1 lighted), game room. **Guest Services:** gift shop, coin laundry. **Business Services:** meeting rooms. **Cards:** AX, DC, DS, MC, VI.

SOME UNITS

DAYS INN   **Phone: (715)479-5151**

7/1-9/15	1P: $75-$92	2P: $80-$97	XP: $6 F18
9/16-3/31	1P: $71-$92	2P: $76-$97	XP: $6 F18
4/1-6/30	1P: $71-$81	2P: $76-$86	XP: $6 F18

Small-scale Hotel **Location:** 0.5 mi n on US 45. Located in a commercial area. 844 Railroad St N 54521. Fax: 715/479-8259. **Facility:** 93 one-bedroom standard units, some with whirlpools. 2 stories (no elevator), interior corridors. *Bath:* combo or shower only. **Parking:** on-site, winter plug-ins. **Terms:** small pets only (in smoking units). **Amenities:** irons, hair dryers. **Pool(s):** heated indoor. **Leisure Activities:** sauna, whirlpool, snowmobiling. *Fee:* game room. **Guest Services:** coin laundry. **Business Services:** meeting rooms. **Cards:** AX, CB, DC, DS, MC, VI. **Special Amenities:** free continental breakfast and free local telephone calls.

SOME UNITS

TRAVELER'S INN MOTEL   **Phone: (715)479-4403**

6/1-3/31	1P: $40-$75	2P: $45-$75	
4/1-5/31	1P: $36-$60	2P: $45-$60	XP: $5 F12

Motel **Location:** Center of downtown. 309 Wall St 54521 (PO Box 1175). Fax: 715/479-4404. **Facility:** 27 one-bedroom standard units, some with efficiencies (utensils extra charge) and/or whirlpools. 2 stories (no elevator), interior/exterior corridors. *Bath:* combo or shower only. **Parking:** on-site, winter plug-ins. **Terms:** [CP] meal plan available, pets (with prior approval, in smoking units). **Leisure Activities:** snowmobiling. **Cards:** AX, DS, MC, VI.

SOME UNITS

———— WHERE TO DINE ————

THE LOGGING CAMP RESTAURANT & STILL   **Dinner: $10-$21**   **Phone: 715/479-9208**

American **Location:** 3 mi n on US 45, 0.3 mi e; on the grounds of Pine-Aire Resort Campground. 4443 Chain-O-Lakes Rd 54521. **Hours:** Open 5/1-10/20; 5 pm-9 pm; to 10 pm 6/1-8/25; also Fri-Sun 8-11 am 6/1-8/25; hours vary off season. Closed: Wed. **Features:** Delightful entrees, many local ingredients, delicious hearth breads and homemade dessert. Known for pan fried Blue Gill, Veal Chardonnay and Pork Filet Normandy. Salad prepared tableside. Mexican dishes Sunday-Tuesday. Glassed, climate-controlled wine room. Casual dress; cocktails. **Parking:** on-site. **Cards:** AX, DC, MC, VI.

EAST TROY pop. 3,564

———— WHERE TO STAY ————

COUNTRY INN & SUITES   **Phone: (262)642-2100**

All Year [ECP]	1P: $74-$129	2P: $90-$135	XP: $6 F17

Small-scale Hotel **Location:** I-43, exit 36, at jct SR 120. 2921 O'Leary Ln 53120. Fax: 414/642-9811. **Facility:** 51 units. 36 one-bedroom standard units, some with whirlpools. 15 one-bedroom suites ($84-$199). 2 stories (no elevator), interior corridors. *Bath:* combo or shower only. **Parking:** on-site, winter plug-ins. **Terms:** weekly rates available, package plans. **Amenities:** dual phone lines, voice mail, irons, hair dryers. **Pool(s):** small heated indoor. **Leisure Activities:** whirlpool. **Guest Services:** valet and coin laundry. **Business Services:** meeting rooms, fax. **Cards:** AX, DC, DS, MC, VI. **Special Amenities:** free continental breakfast and free newspaper.
(See color ad starting on p 556)

SOME UNITS

FEE

EAU CLAIRE pop. 61,704

———— WHERE TO STAY ————

AMERICINN MOTEL & SUITES
Small-scale Hotel
Phone: (715)874-4900
All Year — 1P: $81-$138 — 2P: $81-$138 — XP: $6 — F17
Location: I-94, exit 59, at jct US 12. 6200 Texaco Dr 54703. Fax: 715/874-4901. **Facility:** 50 units. 45 one-bedroom standard units, some with whirlpools. 5 one-bedroom suites ($121-$138), some with whirlpools. 2 stories, interior corridors. *Bath:* combo or shower only. **Parking:** on-site, winter plug-ins. **Terms:** cancellation fee imposed, pets ($25 deposit). **Amenities:** hair dryers. **Pool(s):** heated indoor. **Leisure Activities:** sauna, whirlpool. **Guest Services:** coin laundry. **Business Services:** meeting rooms, fax (fee). **Cards:** AX, DC, DS, MC, VI.

SOME UNITS

ANTLERS MOTEL
Motel
Phone: (715)834-5313
All Year [CP] — 1P: $42-$50 — 2P: $52-$62 — XP: $5 — F12
Location: Jct US 12 and 53. 2245 S Hastings Way 54701. Fax: 715/839-7582. **Facility:** 33 one-bedroom standard units. 1-2 stories, exterior corridors. **Parking:** on-site, winter plug-ins. **Leisure Activities:** playground. **Business Services:** fax (fee). **Cards:** AX, DS, MC, VI. **Special Amenities:** free continental breakfast and free local telephone calls.

SOME UNITS

BEST WESTERN WHITE HOUSE INN
Small-scale Hotel
Phone: (715)832-8356
All Year [CP] — 1P: $63-$80 — 2P: $63-$80 — XP: $5 — F13
Location: On US 53, 1.3 mi n of jct US 12. 1828 S Hastings Way 54701. Fax: 715/836-9686. **Facility:** 66 one-bedroom standard units, some with whirlpools. 2 stories, interior corridors. **Parking:** on-site, winter plug-ins. **Terms:** cancellation fee imposed. **Amenities:** irons, hair dryers. **Pool(s):** heated indoor. **Leisure Activities:** sauna, whirlpool. *Fee:* game room. **Guest Services:** valet laundry. **Business Services:** meeting rooms, fax (fee). **Cards:** AX, DC, DS, MC, VI.

SOME UNITS
VCR FEE

COMFORT INN
Small-scale Hotel
Phone: 715/833-9798
Property failed to provide current rates
Location: I-94, exit 65, 1.3 mi n on SR 37, just s of jct US 12. 3117 Craig Rd 54701. Fax: 715/833-9798. **Facility:** 56 one-bedroom standard units. 2 stories, interior corridors. **Parking:** on-site, winter plug-ins. **Terms:** pets ($10 extra charge). **Amenities:** *Some:* irons, hair dryers. **Pool(s):** small heated indoor. **Leisure Activities:** whirlpool. **Business Services:** fax (fee). **Cards:** AX, CB, DC, DS, MC, VI.

SOME UNITS

COUNTRY INN & SUITES BY CARLSON
Small-scale Hotel
Phone: (715)832-7289
All Year — 1P: $80-$110 — 2P: $85-$115 — XP: $8 — F
Location: I-94, exit 70, 0.8 mi n on US 53, then just ne on CR AA (Golf Rd). 3614 Gateway Dr 54701. Fax: 715/832-7289. **Facility:** 58 one-bedroom standard units. 3 stories, interior corridors. *Bath:* combo or shower only. **Parking:** on-site, winter plug-ins. **Terms:** [CP] meal plan available, pets ($20 deposit, in smoking units). **Amenities:** irons, hair dryers. **Pool(s):** small heated indoor. **Leisure Activities:** whirlpool. **Guest Services:** valet laundry. **Business Services:** fax (fee). **Cards:** AX, DC, DS, MC, VI. **Special Amenities:** free continental breakfast and free newspaper. *(See color ad starting on p 556)*

SOME UNITS

DAYS INN-WEST
Small-scale Hotel
Phone: (715)874-5550
All Year [CP] — 1P: $55-$95 — 2P: $63-$100 — XP: $8 — F17
Location: I-94, exit 59, at jct US 12. 6319 Truax Ln 54703. Fax: 715/874-6101. **Facility:** 71 one-bedroom standard units, some with whirlpools. 2 stories, interior corridors. *Bath:* combo or shower only. **Parking:** on-site, winter plug-ins. **Terms:** pets ($25 deposit, in smoking units). **Amenities:** hair dryers. *Some:* irons. **Pool(s):** small heated indoor. **Leisure Activities:** whirlpool, exercise room. **Guest Services:** coin laundry. **Business Services:** fax (fee). **Cards:** AX, DC, DS, JC, MC, VI.

SOME UNITS

ECONO LODGE
Motel
Phone: (715)833-8818
6/1-9/30 — 1P: $50-$55 — 2P: $65 — XP: $10 — F17
4/1-5/31 & 10/1-3/31 — 1P: $40 — 2P: $50 — XP: $5 — F17
Location: I-94, exit 68, just n on SR 93, just w on Golf Rd, then just s. 4608 Royal Dr 54701. Fax: 715/833-8970. **Facility:** 36 one-bedroom standard units, some with whirlpools. 1 story, interior corridors. **Parking:** on-site, winter plug-ins. **Terms:** cancellation fee imposed, weekly rates available, [CP] meal plan available, pets (dogs only, with prior approval). **Business Services:** fax (fee). **Cards:** AX, CB, DC, DS, JC, MC, VI.

SOME UNITS

EXEL INN OF EAU CLAIRE
Motel
Phone: (715)834-3193
6/1-10/31 [CP] — 1P: $35-$62 — 2P: $41-$65 — XP: $6 — F18
4/1-5/31 & 11/1-3/31 [CP] — 1P: $35-$49 — 2P: $41-$53 — XP: $6 — F18
Location: I-94, exit 65, 1.3 mi n on SR 37, just w of jct US 12. 2305 Craig Rd 54701. Fax: 715/839-9905. **Facility:** 100 units. 99 one-bedroom standard units, some with whirlpools. 1 one-bedroom suite ($75-$105) with kitchen (no utensils). 2 stories, interior corridors. **Parking:** on-site, winter plug-ins. **Terms:** small pets only. **Amenities:** irons, hair dryers. **Leisure Activities:** limited exercise equipment, game room. **Guest Services:** coin laundry. **Business Services:** fax (fee). **Cards:** AX, CB, DC, DS, MC, VI. **Special Amenities:** early check-in/late check-out and free continental breakfast. *(See color ad p 465)*

SOME UNITS
FEE FEE

HAMPTON INN

SAVE

▼▼▼ ▼▼▼

Small-scale Hotel

All Year | 1P: $79 | 2P: $139 | **Phone:** (715)833-0003
XP: $10 | F18

Location: I-94, exit 65, 1.3 mi n on SR 37, just s of jct US 12. 2622 Craig Rd 54701. **Fax:** 715/833-0915. **Facility:** 106 one-bedroom standard units. 3 stories, interior corridors. **Parking:** on-site. **Terms:** package plans. **Amenities:** video games (fee), voice mail, irons, hair dryers. **Pool(s):** small heated indoor. **Leisure Activities:** whirlpool, limited exercise equipment. **Guest Services:** valet laundry. **Business Services:** meeting rooms, fax (fee). **Cards:** AX, CB, DC, DS, MC, VI.

SOME UNITS

🅂🄳 🍽⁺ 📷 🐾 🎦 [DATA PORT] 🖥 / ⊠ 🖬 / FEE

HEARTLAND INN

▼▼ ▼▼▼

Small-scale Hotel

All Year [ECP] | 1P: $70-$80 | 2P: $70-$80 | **Phone:** (715)839-7100
XP: $5 | F16

Location: I-94, exit 70, 0.8 mi n on US 53, just w on Golf Rd, then just s. 4075 Commonwealth Ave 54701. **Fax:** 715/839-7050. **Facility:** 86 one-bedroom standard units. 2 stories, interior corridors. **Parking:** on-site, winter plug-ins. **Terms:** pets (in designated rooms). **Amenities:** *Some:* hair dryers. **Pool(s):** small heated indoor. **Leisure Activities:** sauna. **Guest Services:** valet and coin laundry. **Business Services:** meeting rooms, fax. **Cards:** AX, DC, DS, MC, VI. *(See color ad below)*

SOME UNITS

ⒶⓈⓀ 🅂🄳 🐾 🍽⁺ 📷 ♨ 🎦 🖥 / ⊠ [DATA PORT] 🖬 🖬 / FEE

HOLIDAY INN CAMPUS AREA

▼▼▼ ▼▼▼

Small-scale Hotel

All Year | 1P: $62-$139 | **Phone:** (715)835-2211

Location: I-94, exit 65, 1.3 mi n on SR 37, just w of jct US 12. 2703 Craig Rd 54701. **Fax:** 715/835-1249. **Facility:** 137 one-bedroom standard units, some with whirlpools. 2 stories, interior corridors. **Parking:** on-site. **Terms:** weekly rates available, [AP] meal plan available, 15% service charge, pets ($15 extra charge, in smoking units). **Amenities:** irons, hair dryers. **Leisure Activities:** whirlpool, limited exercise equipment. *Fee:* game room. **Guest Services:** valet and coin laundry. **Business Services:** meeting rooms, fax (fee). **Cards:** AX, DC, DS, MC, VI.

SOME UNITS

ⒶⓈⓀ 🅂🄳 🐾 🍽 🍸 🏊 ⊠ 🎦 [DATA PORT] 🖥 / ⊠ 🖬 🖬 /

MAPLE MANOR MOTEL

ⒶⒶⒶ **SAVE**

▼▼▼

Motel

All Year | 1P: $35-$40 | 2P: $35-$45 | **Phone:** 715/834-2618
XP: $5

Location: I-94, exit 65, 3 mi n on US 53, exit US 12 (Clairemont Ave), just se, follow signs for Storrs Ave. 2507 S Hastings Way 54701. **Fax:** 715/834-1148. **Facility:** 34 one-bedroom standard units. 1 story, exterior corridors. **Parking:** on-site, winter plug-ins. **Terms:** small pets only. **Dining:** 6:30 am-1:30 & 5-9 pm, Sun-11:30 am, cocktails. **Guest Services:** valet laundry. **Business Services:** fax (fee). **Cards:** AX, DC, DS, MC, VI. **Special Amenities:** free continental breakfast and free local telephone calls.

SOME UNITS

🐾 🍽 🍸 🎦 / ⊠ 🖬 🖬 🖥 /

OTTER CREEK INN

▼▼▼ ▼▼▼

Bed & Breakfast

All Year [BP] | 1P: $60-$150 | 2P: $90-$180 | **Phone:** 715/832-2945

Location: 0.5 mi e of jct US 53, on north side of US 12. 2536 Hillcrest Pkwy 54720. **Fax:** 715/832-4607. **Facility:** On a hillside along Otter Creek, this English Tudor is decorated in a country-Victorian theme and features some rooms with gas fireplaces. Smoke free premises. 6 one-bedroom standard units with whirlpools. 3 stories (no elevator), interior corridors. **Parking:** on-site. **Terms:** check-in 4 pm, age restrictions may apply, 8 day cancellation notice. **Amenities:** video library. **Pool(s):** heated outdoor. **Business Services:** fax (fee). **Cards:** AX, CB, DC, DS, MC, VI.

SOME UNITS

🏊 ⊠ [VCR] 🖥 / 🖬 /

PARK INN & SUITES INTERNATIONAL

ⒶⒶⒶ **SAVE**

▼▼▼ ▼▼▼

Small-scale Hotel

All Year | 1P: $94-$144 | 2P: $94-$144 | **Phone:** (715)838-9989
XP: $10 | F16

Location: I-94, exit 65, just n. 3340 Mondovi Rd 54701. **Fax:** 715/832-2542. **Facility:** 85 units. 45 one-bedroom standard units, some with whirlpools. 40 one-bedroom suites, some with whirlpools. 3 stories, interior corridors. **Parking:** on-site. **Terms:** [ECP] meal plan available, small pets only ($10 extra charge). **Amenities:** voice mail, irons, hair dryers. **Pool(s):** small heated indoor. **Leisure Activities:** whirlpool, limited exercise equipment, game room. **Guest Services:** valet and coin laundry. **Business Services:** meeting rooms, fax. **Cards:** AX, DC, DS, MC, VI. **Special Amenities:** free continental breakfast and free local telephone calls. *(See color ad p. 463)*

SOME UNITS

🅂🄳 🐾 ♿ 🏊 ⊠ 🎦 [DATA PORT] 🖥 / ⊠ 🖬 🖬 /

RAMADA INN & CONFERENCE CENTER
Phone: (715)834-3181

(AAA) [SAVE]

[WWW] (rating symbols)

Small-scale Hotel

All Year   1P: $69   2P: $109
Location: I-94, exit 65, 1.3 mi n on SR 37, just w of jct US 12. 1202 W Clairemont Ave 54701. **Fax:** 715/834-1630. **Facility:** 233 units. 228 one-bedroom standard units, some with whirlpools. 5 one-bedroom suites ($129-$199) with whirlpools. 2-5 stories, interior corridors. *Bath:* combo or shower only. **Parking:** on-site, winter plug-ins. **Terms:** 30 day cancellation notice, weekly rates available, [ECP] meal plan available, package plans, 17% service charge, small pets only ($15 fee). **Amenities:** video games (fee), voice mail, irons, hair dryers. *Some:* dual phone lines. **Dining:** 6:30 am-2 & 5:30-9 pm, Fri & Sat-10 pm, Sun-2 pm, cocktails. **Pool(s):** heated indoor, wading. **Leisure Activities:** whirlpool, exercise room. *Fee:* game room. **Guest Services:** gift shop, valet and coin laundry. **Business Services:** conference facilities, business center. **Cards:** AX, CB, DC, DS, JC, MC, VI. **Special Amenities:** free continental breakfast and free newspaper.

SOME UNITS

(icon row) / [VCR] FEE

———— WHERE TO DINE ————

FANNY HILL DINNER THEATRE AND DINING ROOM
Dinner: $12-$30   Phone: 715-836-8184

(rating symbols)

American

Location: Jct US 12 and SR 37, 1 mi nw on US 12, 0.3 mi w on Menomonie St, 0.5 mi s on Ferry St, then 1.5 mi w; in Fanny Hill Victorian Inn. 3919 Crescent Ave 54703. **Hours:** 5 pm-9 pm, Fri & Sat-10 pm, Sun 10 am-2 & 5-9 pm. Closed: Mon & Tues. **Reservations:** suggested. **Features:** A quaint Victorian charm infuses the dining room, which is decorated with enchanting seasonal accents. Many windows afford panoramic river valley views. Grilled pork tenderloin stands out on a menu of creative entrees. Servers exude charm and hospitality. Dressy casual; cocktails. **Parking:** on-site. **Cards:** AX, CB, DC, DS, MC, VI.

MONA LISA'S RESTAURANT
Dinner: $7-$24   Phone: 715/839-8969

(rating symbols)

Italian

Location: At Fifth Ave; downtown. 428 Water St 54703. **Hours:** 4 pm-11 pm, Fri & Sat-midnight. Closed major holidays; also Sun & Mon. **Features:** In historic downtown, the trendy restaurant prepares creative and contemporary Italian cuisine, which contrasts with the decor: wood floors and lofty high ceilings from a century ago. Local markets and friends' gardens provide inspiration for the weekly menu. Fish, pasta and meat dishes are interpreted with gaiety and flair. Guests can order from an extensive list of martinis or choose from among a good variety of wines by the glass. Casual dress; cocktails. **Parking:** street. **Cards:** AX, MC, VI.

NORTHWOODS PUB & GRILL
Lunch: $6-$18   Dinner: $6-$18   Phone: 715/552-0510

(rating symbols)

American

Location: I-94, exit 70 (US 53), just nw at end of Oakwood Mall. 3560 Oakwood Mall Dr 54701. **Hours:** 11 am-10 pm, Fri & Sat-11 pm, Sun 10 am-8 pm. Closed major holidays. **Features:** Bustling with activity and the happy laughter of friends out for a good time, the local pub proudly features homemade beers and sodas. The thematic decor incorporates canoes, wood beams and artifacts reminiscent of Alaska. The menu suggests culinary explorations of elk, deer and buffalo steaks, while trout, walleye and salmon complete the Nordic feast. Well-known American fare is also featured. Casual dress; cocktails. **Parking:** on-site. **Cards:** AX, DS, MC, VI.

PEKING GARDEN
Lunch: $4-$6   Dinner: $6-$10   Phone: 715/835-3229

(rating symbol)

Chinese

Location: I-94, exit 68, 1.2 mi w on SR 93, just w on Mall Dr; in Hamilton Square Shopping Center. 2823 E Hamilton Sq 54701. **Hours:** 11 am-9:30 pm, Fri & Sat-10:30 pm. Closed major holidays; also Sun. **Reservations:** accepted. **Features:** Smaller restaurant with simple decor and good food. Traditional selection of egg foo young, chow mein, beef, pork, chicken dishes and chef's suggestions. Daily buffet from 11 am-2 pm. Good value for the dollar. Casual dress; beer only. **Parking:** on-site.

RANDY'S FAMILY RESTAURANT
Lunch: $5-$10   Dinner: $5-$10   Phone: 715/839-8449

(rating symbol)

American

Location: I-94, exit 65, 1.3 mi n on SR 37, just s of jct US 12. 1132 W MacArthur 54701. **Hours:** 6 am-10 pm, Fri & Sat-11 pm. Closed: 4/20, 11/27, 12/25; also Sun. **Reservations:** accepted. **Features:** Family-operated for more than 40 years, the nice, casual restaurant serves generous portions of tasty comfort foods, including an extensive selection of tempting fresh pies. Each meal, including the tasty daily specials, is accompanied by a complimentary cup of warm, homemade vanilla pudding. Breakfast is served all day. Casual dress. **Parking:** on-site. **Cards:** MC, VI.

SWEETWATERS RESTAURANT & BAR
Lunch: $6-$8   Dinner: $8-$22   Phone: 715/834-5777

(rating symbols)

American

Location: Just w of jct US 12 and SR 37. 1104 W Clairemont Ave 54701. **Hours:** 11 am-9 pm, Fri-10 pm, Sat 4 pm-10 pm. Closed: 12/25. **Reservations:** suggested. **Features:** Nice variety of seafood, steak and pasta is attractively presented. Outdoor seasonal dining. Casual environment, seating conducive to small groups, families and couples. Casual dress; cocktails. **Parking:** on-site. **Cards:** AX, DC, DS, MC, VI.

WOO'S PAGODA
Lunch: $5-$8   Dinner: $6-$12   Phone: 715/832-6431

(rating symbols)

Chinese

Location: 0.7 mi n of jct US 12 and 53. 1700 S Hastings Way 54701. **Hours:** 11 am-11 pm, Sat from 4:30 pm. Closed: 1/1, 11/27, 12/24, 12/25. **Reservations:** accepted. **Features:** The varied menu blends several cooking styles: Cantonese, Mandarin, Hunan and Szechuan. Beef and scallions is in a flavorful mixture of garlic, wine and soy sauce. Taiwanese lamps are among Oriental appointments that decorate the quiet dining room. Casual dress; cocktails. **Parking:** on-site. **Cards:** DS, MC, VI.

Great Lakes. Great Rates!

Days Inn offers year-round savings throughout the state of Michigan. So come ski the slopes, roam the Locks, bask on one of our beautiful beaches or hit the casinos. Days Inn awaits with a clean comfortable room, friendly service and affordable Michigan Money Saver Rates.* Reserve your room today!

DAYS INN

There you go.®

For reservations, call
1-800-DAYS-INN®
www.daysinntravelplanner.com

PARTICIPATING DAYS INNS LOCATIONS

Alma
989-463-6131
Alpena 💼
989-356-6118
Battle Creek
269-979-3561
Cadillac 💼
231-775-4414
Cheboygan
231-627-3126
Detroit - Canton
734-721-5200
Frankenmuth 💼
Bridgeport
989-777-1611
Gaylord
989-732-2200
Grand Haven
616-842-1999
Grand Rapids - Airport
616-949-8400
Grand Rapids 💼
Downtown
616-235-7611
Grayling
989-344-0204
Hillsdale
517-439-3297

Imlay City
810-724-8005
Iron Mountain
906-774-2181
Ludington
231-843-2233
Mackinaw
231-436-5557
Manistee
231-723-8385
Marquette
906-225-1393
Munising
906-387-2493
Port Huron
810-364-8400
Sault Ste. Marie
906-635-5200
St. Ignace
906-643-7777
St. Ignace-Lakefront
906-643-8008
Tawas City
989-362-0088
Traverse City 💼
231-941-0208

DAYS INN
There you go.®

For reservations, call
1-800-DAYS-INN®
(1-800-329-7466)
For driving directions visit
www.daysinntravelplanner.com

 Days Business Place hotels include a large work desk, data port, refrigerator, microwave, coffeemaker, full-size ironing board and iron and an in-room snack pack for every night you stay.

EDGERTON pop. 4,933

―――――― WHERE TO STAY ――――――

COMFORT INN
SAVE
▼▼▼▼▼
Small-scale Hotel

Phone: 608/884-2118
All Year   1P: $58-$150   2P: $64-$150   XP: $8   F18
Location: I-90, exit 163, just e. 11102 Goede 53534. Fax: 608/884-4490. **Facility:** 50 one-bedroom standard units, some with whirlpools. 2 stories, interior corridors. *Bath:* combo or shower only. **Parking:** on-site. **Terms:** [ECP] meal plan available, pets ($10 deposit). **Amenities:** *Some:* irons, hair dryers. **Pool(s):** small heated indoor. **Leisure Activities:** whirlpool. *Fee:* game room. **Guest Services:** valet and coin laundry. **Cards:** AX, DC, DS, MC, VI.

SOME UNITS

EGG HARBOR —See Door County p. 482.

ELKHART LAKE pop. 1,021

―――――― WHERE TO STAY ――――――

THE OSTHOFF RESORT
▲▲▲ **SAVE**
▼▼▼ ▼▼▼
Resort
Condominium

Phone: (920)876-3366
5/23-10/16   2P: $195-$475
10/17-3/31   2P: $160-$350
4/1-5/22   2P: $155-$325
Location: 0.5 mi w of SR 67 via CR A/J, then 0.4 mi nw. Located in a rural area. 101 Osthoff Ave 53020. Fax: 920/876-3228. **Facility:** All accommodations at this rural, family-oriented resort are contemporary in style and offer balconies and gas fireplaces; some have lake views. Designated smoking area. 145 units. 123 one-, 20 two- and 2 three-bedroom suites with efficiencies, some with whirlpools. 4 stories, interior corridors. *Bath:* combo or shower only. **Parking:** on-site and valet. **Terms:** 3 night minimum stay - weekends 7/1-8/31, 3 day cancellation notice-fee imposed. **Amenities:** voice mail, irons, hair dryers. *Fee:* video library, high-speed Internet. **Dining:** 7 am-9 pm, Fri & Sat-10 pm, cocktails. **Pool(s):** 2 heated outdoor, heated indoor. **Leisure Activities:** saunas, whirlpools, rental boats, rental canoes, rental paddleboats, fishing, 2 tennis courts, recreation programs, bocci, exercise room, basketball, volleyball. *Fee:* sailboats, waterskiing, bicycles, game room. **Guest Services:** gift shop, valet and coin laundry, area transportation (fee). **Business Services:** conference facilities, administrative services (fee), PC. **Cards:** AX, DC, DS, MC, VI. *(See color ad p 553)*

ELKHORN pop. 7,305

―――――― WHERE TO STAY ――――――

AMERICINN
▼▼▼ ▼▼▼
Small-scale Hotel

Phone: (262)723-7799
5/16-9/30 [CP]   1P: $78-$150   2P: $78-$150   XP: $6   F14
10/1-3/31 [CP]   1P: $70-$150   2P: $70-$150   XP: $6   F14
4/1-5/15 [CP]   1P: $68-$150   2P: $68-$150   XP: $6   F14
Location: I-43, exit 25, just s. 210 E Commerce Ct 53121. Fax: 262/723-5623. **Facility:** 58 units. 49 one-bedroom standard units, some with whirlpools. 8 one- and 1 two-bedroom suites ($110-$150), some with efficiencies or kitchens. 2 stories, interior corridors. *Bath:* combo or shower only. **Parking:** on-site, winter plug-ins. **Terms:** cancellation fee imposed. **Amenities:** dual phone lines. *Some:* irons, hair dryers. **Pool(s):** small heated indoor. **Leisure Activities:** sauna, whirlpool. **Guest Services:** coin laundry. **Business Services:** meeting rooms. **Cards:** AX, DC, DS, MC, VI.

SOME UNITS

ELLISON BAY —See Door County p. 483.

ELM GROVE —See Milwaukee p. 570.

EPHRAIM —See Door County p. 484.

FENNIMORE pop. 2,387

―――――― WHERE TO STAY ――――――

FENMORE HILLS MOTEL
▲▲▲ **SAVE**
▼
Small-scale Hotel

Phone: (608)822-3281
4/1-11/30   1P: $56-$61   2P: $65-$70   XP: $6   F14
12/1-3/31   1P: $53-$58   2P: $62-$67   XP: $6   F14
Location: 2.4 mi w. 5814 Hwy 18 W 53809. **Facility:** 24 one-bedroom standard units, some with whirlpools. 2 stories, interior corridors. **Parking:** on-site, winter plug-ins. **Terms:** weekly rates available, package plans, small pets only. **Guest Services:** coin laundry. **Business Services:** meeting rooms. **Cards:** DS, MC, VI. **Special Amenities:** early check-in/late check-out and free local telephone calls.

SOME UNITS

FIFIELD

―――――― WHERE TO DINE ――――――

NORTHWOODS SUPPER CLUB
▼
American
Casual dress; cocktails.

Dinner: $10-$20   **Phone:** 715/762-4447
Location: Jct SR 13 and 70. N14066 S Flameau Ave 54524. **Hours:** 4:30 pm-9 pm, Sun 4 pm-8 pm. Closed: 12/24, 12/25; also Mon. **Reservations:** suggested. **Features:** Generous portions of traditional favorites, such as succulent prime rib, are what the family-oriented restaurant is all about. The Saturday prime rib buffet and Friday night fish fry are popular offerings, as are the wholesome and flavorful homemade soups. **Parking:** on-site. **Cards:** AX, CB, DC, DS, MC, VI.

FISH CREEK —*See Door County p. 485.*

FITCHBURG

———— **WHERE TO STAY** ————

QUALITY INN & SUITES
(AAA) [SAVE]

| | | | **Phone:** (608)274-7200 |
| All Year | 1P: $79-$159 | 2P: $79-$159 | XP: $10   F18 |

Location: US 12/18, exit 260 (Fish Hatchery/CR D), then 1.5 mi s at jct CR PD. 2969 Cahill Main 53711. Fax: 608/274-7720. **Facility:** 75 units. 50 one-bedroom standard units. 25 one-bedroom suites, some with whirlpools. 4 stories, interior corridors. *Bath:* combo or shower only. **Parking:** on-site. **Terms:** 2-4 night Small-scale Hotel minimum stay - seasonal, cancellation fee imposed, [BP] meal plan available, pets ($25 fee). **Amenities:** high-speed Internet, dual phone lines, voice mail, irons, hair dryers. **Pool(s):** small heated indoor. **Leisure Activities:** whirlpool, exercise room. *Fee:* game room. **Guest Services:** gift shop, complimentary evening beverages, valet and coin laundry, area transportation. **Business Services:** meeting rooms, business center. **Cards:** AX, DC, DS, MC, VI. **Special Amenities:** free local telephone calls and free newspaper. *(See color ad p 528)*

SOME UNITS

FOND DU LAC pop. 42,203

———— **WHERE TO STAY** ————

BAYMONT INN & SUITES-FOND DU LAC
(AAA) [SAVE]

			Phone: (920)921-4000
9/1-3/31	1P: $82-$125	2P: $82-$125	XP: $10 F17
4/1-8/31	1P: $72-$125	2P: $72-$125	XP: $10 F17

Location: Sw of jct US 41 and 151. 77 Holiday Ln 54937. Fax: 920/921-4472. **Facility:** 79 one-bedroom standard units, some with whirlpools. 2 stories, interior corridors. **Parking:** on-site, winter plug-ins. **Terms:** pets ($5 Small-scale Hotel extra charge). **Amenities:** dual phone lines, voice mail, safes (fee), irons, hair dryers. **Pool(s):** small heated indoor. **Leisure Activities:** whirlpool, limited exercise equipment. *Fee:* game room. **Guest Services:** complimentary evening beverages: Sun-Thurs, valet and coin laundry. **Business Services:** meeting rooms. **Cards:** AX, DC, DS, MC, VI. **Special Amenities:** free continental breakfast and free newspaper. *(See color ad below)*

SOME UNITS

ECONO LODGE OF FOND DU LAC
[SAVE]

			Phone: (920)923-2020
6/1-8/31 [CP]	1P: $59-$69	2P: $69-$79	XP: $5 F18
4/1-5/31 & 9/1-3/31 [CP]	1P: $54-$64	2P: $64-$74	XP: $5 F18

Location: On SR 23, 0.3 mi e jct of US 41. 649 W Johnson 54935. Fax: 920/929-9352. **Facility:** 48 one-bedroom Small-scale Hotel standard units. 2 stories, interior corridors. *Bath:* combo or shower only. **Parking:** on-site, winter plug-ins. **Pool(s):** small heated indoor. **Leisure Activities:** whirlpool. **Guest Services:** valet laundry. **Cards:** AX, CB, DC, DS, MC, VI.

SOME UNITS

FEE

HOLIDAY INN
(AAA) [SAVE]

			Phone: (920)923-1440
6/1-8/31 [ECP]	1P: $109-$179	2P: $119-$189	XP: $10 F18
1/1-3/31 [ECP]	1P: $99-$119	2P: $109-$130	XP: $10 F18
4/1-5/31 & 9/1-12/31 [ECP]	1P: $89-$110	2P: $99-$120	XP: $10 F18

Location: On US 151, just sw of jct US 41. 625 W Rolling Meadows Dr 54937. Fax: 920/923-1366. **Facility:** 139 Small-scale Hotel one-bedroom standard units. 2 stories, interior corridors. *Bath:* combo or shower only. **Parking:** on-site, winter plug-ins. **Terms:** 3 day cancellation notice, pets ($100 deposit). **Amenities:** voice mail, irons, hair dryers. **Dining:** 6:30 am-10 pm, Sat from 7 am, Sun 7 am-2 pm, cocktails. **Pool(s):** heated indoor. **Leisure Activities:** sauna, whirlpool, indoor recreational area, exercise room, shuffleboard. **Guest Services:** complimentary evening beverages: Sun-Thurs, coin laundry, area transportation. **Business Services:** meeting rooms. **Cards:** AX, CB, DC, DS, JC, MC, VI. **Special Amenities:** early check-in/late check-out and free newspaper. *(See color ad below)*

SOME UNITS

MICROTEL INN & SUITES

AAA SAVE

WWW

Small-scale Hotel

Phone: (920)929-4000

All Year   1P: $43-$48   2P: $48-$63   XP: $5   F18

Location: Jct US 41 and 151. 920 S Military Rd 54935. Fax: 920/929-4001. **Facility:** 79 one-bedroom standard units. 3 stories, interior corridors. **Bath:** combo or shower only. **Parking:** on-site. **Terms:** cancellation fee imposed, [CP] meal plan available, pets ($10 extra charge). **Leisure Activities:** whirlpool, limited exercise equipment. **Guest Services:** valet laundry. **Business Services:** meeting rooms. **Cards:** AX, DC, DS, MC, VI. **Special Amenities:** free continental breakfast and free local telephone calls.

SOME UNITS

🛎️ 🐕 ♿ 🎦 📠 / ✕ VCR 🔌 📺 📱 /
FEE

RAMADA PLAZA HOTEL

WWW WWW

Historic
Large-scale Hotel

Phone: (920)923-3000

5/1-8/31   1P: $119   2P: $129   XP: $10   F18
4/1-4/30 & 9/1-3/31   1P: $79   2P: $89   XP: $10   F18

Location: Downtown. 1 N Main St 54935. Fax: 920/923-2561. **Facility:** 132 units. 125 one-bedroom standard units. 7 one-bedroom suites ($99-$249), some with whirlpools. 8 stories, interior corridors. **Parking:** on-site. **Terms:** package plans - seasonal, pets ($10 extra charge). **Amenities:** voice mail, irons, hair dryers. **Pool(s):** heated indoor. **Leisure Activities:** sauna, whirlpool. **Guest Services:** valet laundry. **Business Services:** conference facilities, administrative services (fee). **Cards:** AX, DC, DS, MC, VI.

SOME UNITS

ASK 🛎️ 🐕 🍽️ 📺 🏊 ✝️ 🎦 📠 📱 / ✕ 🔌 📺 /

SUPER 8 MOTEL

WWW WWW

Small-scale Hotel

Phone: 920/922-1088

4/1-9/30   1P: $51-$56   2P: $56-$61   XP: $5   F13
10/1-3/31   1P: $50   2P: $55   XP: $5   F13

Location: US 41, exit SR 23, just n on east frontage road (CR VV). 391 N Pioneer Rd 54935. Fax: 920/922-1088. **Facility:** 48 one-bedroom standard units. 2 stories, interior corridors. **Parking:** on-site, winter plug-ins. **Terms:** 30 day cancellation notice-fee imposed, [CP] meal plan available, pets ($10 fee). **Amenities:** safes (fee), hair dryers. **Guest Services:** coin laundry. **Business Services:** meeting rooms. **Cards:** AX, DC, DS, MC, VI.

SOME UNITS

ASK 🛎️ 🐕 🍽️ 🌀 🎦 / ✕ 🔌 📺 /

The following lodging was either not evaluated or did not meet AAA rating requirements but is listed for your information only.

COUNTRY INN & SUITES BY CARLSON

[fyi]

Small-scale Hotel

Phone: 920/924-8800

4/1-9/30   1P: $89-$159
10/1-3/31   1P: $79-$159

Too new to rate, opening scheduled for November 2002. **Location:** I-41, exit 96B. 121 Merwin Way 54937. Fax: 920/322-9166. **Amenities:** 65 units, coffeemakers, pool. **Terms:** cancellation fee imposed. **Cards:** AX, DC, DS, MC, VI.

--- **WHERE TO DINE** ---

ROLLING MEADOWS FAMILY RESTAURANT   **Lunch:** $6-$14   **Dinner:** $6-$14   **Phone:** 920/922-9140

WWW WWW

American

Location: Just nw of jct US 41 and 151. 947 S Rolling Meadows Dr 54937. **Hours:** 6 am-9 pm. Closed: 11/27. **Reservations:** accepted. **Features:** The menu covers a broad territory, with an extensive selection of sandwiches, salad and soup; all-day breakfast choices, and steak, seafood and Italian entrees. Desserts are homemade. The Friday night fish fry and weekend prime rib specials are popular. Casual dress; cocktails. **Parking:** on-site. **Cards:** AX, DC, DS, MC, VI.   ✕

SCHREINER'S RESTAURANT   **Lunch:** $4-$12   **Dinner:** $4-$12   **Phone:** 920/922-0590

WWW WWW

American

Location: Jct US 41 and SR 23. 168 N Pioneer Rd 54935. **Hours:** 6:30 am-8:30 pm. Closed: 4/20, 11/27, 12/25. **Features:** This popular restaurant has been serving up homestyle meals of comfort foods since 1938. There is an inhouse bakery that produces fresh desserts daily. Breakfast is served all day. Tours of the kitchen are available upon request. Casual dress; cocktails. **Parking:** on-site. **Cards:** AX, DC, DS, MC, VI.   ✕

FONTANA pop. 1,600

--- **WHERE TO STAY** ---

FONTANA VILLAGE INN

WWW WWW

Motel

Phone: 262/275-6700

5/23-9/2   1P: $98-$128   2P: $98-$128   XP: $10   F12
4/1-5/22 & 9/3-11/2   1P: $68-$88   2P: $68-$88   XP: $10   F12
11/3-3/31   1P: $48-$68   2P: $48-$68   XP: $10   F12

Location: On SR 67. 100 Dewey Ave 53125. Fax: 262/275-8004. **Facility:** 22 one-bedroom standard units, some with whirlpools. 2 stories (no elevator), exterior corridors. **Parking:** on-site, winter plug-ins. **Terms:** 3 day cancellation notice-fee imposed, [CP] meal plan available. **Amenities:** voice mail, hair dryers. **Guest Services:** coin laundry. **Cards:** AX, MC, VI.

SOME UNITS

ASK 📠 📱 / ✕ /

FORT ATKINSON pop. 11,621

--- **WHERE TO STAY** ---

BEST WESTERN COURTYARD INN

AAA SAVE

WWW WWW

Small-scale Hotel

Phone: (920)563-6444

All Year [ECP]   1P: $63-$99   2P: $63-$99   XP: $10   F12

Location: 2 mi s on SR 26 business route. 1225 Janesville Ave 53538. Fax: 920/563-9510. **Facility:** 58 units. 56 one-bedroom standard units, some with whirlpools. 2 one-bedroom suites ($85-$125). 2 stories, interior corridors. **Parking:** on-site, winter plug-ins. **Terms:** weekly rates available, package plans - 1/1-3/31. **Amenities:** safes (fee), irons, hair dryers. **Pool(s):** small heated indoor. **Leisure Activities:** whirlpool, gazebo, exercise room. **Guest Services:** gift shop, valet and coin laundry. **Business Services:** meeting rooms. **Cards:** AX, DC, DS, MC, VI. **Special Amenities:** free continental breakfast and free newspaper.

SOME UNITS

🛎️ 🌀 🏊 ✕ 🎦 📠 🔌 📺 📱 / ✕ VCR /
FEE

HOLIDAY INN EXPRESS HOTEL & SUITES
Phone: (920)563-3600
▼▼▼▼▼ All Year   1P: $62-$98
Location: Jct SR 26 bypass and US 12. 1680 Madison Ave 53538. **Fax:** 920/563-3030. **Facility:** 78 one-bedroom standard units, some with whirlpools. 3 stories, interior corridors. *Bath:* combo or shower only. **Parking:** on-site. **Terms:** [ECP] meal plan available. **Amenities:** dual phone lines, voice mail, irons, hair dryers. **Pool(s):** heated indoor. **Leisure Activities:** whirlpool, limited exercise equipment. *Fee:* game room. **Guest Services:** valet and coin laundry. **Business Services:** meeting rooms, fax (fee). **Cards:** AX, CB, DC, DS, JC, MC, VI.
Small-scale Hotel

SOME UNITS

(ASK) (S/D) (&M) (&) (⌐) (⌐) (X) (⌐) (DATA PORT) (⌐) / (X) (⌐) (⌐)

——— **WHERE TO DINE** ———

THE ORIGINAL STOCKADE RESTAURANT & PUB   **Lunch:** $6-$14   **Dinner:** $6-$14   **Phone:** 920/568-9498
▼▼▼▼ **Location:** On US 12; just e of jct SR 26. 855 Lexington Blvd 53538. **Hours:** 11 am-9 pm, Fri & Sat 8 am-11 pm, Sun 8 am-9 pm. **Reservations:** accepted. **Features:** The distinctive log fort restaurant is decorated with historical pictures of the area. Among features that cater to children are crayons on the tables and an activity room. Offerings range from sandwiches, burgers and salads to steaks, pork and "Wisconsin-Mex.". Casual dress; cocktails. **Parking:** on-site. **Cards:** AX, DC, DS, MC, VI.
American

(Y) (X)

SALAMONE'S   **Dinner:** $5-$10   **Phone:** 920/563-9213
▼▼ ▼▼ **Location:** On US 12; just nw of downtown. 1245 Madison Ave 53538. **Hours:** 4 pm-11 pm. Closed major holidays; also Tues. **Features:** Delicious deep-dish and thin-crust pizzas are made from fresh ingredients at the family-owned restaurant. Some traditional dishes, including pasta and sausage with marinara sauce, are also listed on the dinner menu. Italian background music and beautiful murals add to the ambience. A brew pub is adjacent. Casual dress; cocktails. **Parking:** on-site. **Cards:** MC, VI.
Pizza

(Y) (X)

GENESEE DEPOT —See Milwaukee p. 570.

GERMANTOWN —See Milwaukee p. 571.

GILLS ROCK —See Door County p. 486.

GLENDALE —See Milwaukee p. 572.

GRAFTON —See Milwaukee p. 573.

GREEN BAY pop. 102,313

——— **WHERE TO STAY** ———

AIRPORT SETTLE INN
Phone: (920)499-1900
▼▼▼▼ All Year [CP]   1P: $67-$125   2P: $72-$125
Location: US 41, exit 165, 1 mi w on SR 172, just s on CR (EB). Located in a commercial area. 2620 S Packerland Dr 54313. **Fax:** 920/499-1973. **Facility:** 115 one-bedroom standard units, some with whirlpools. 2 stories, interior corridors. *Bath:* combo or shower only. **Parking:** on-site, winter plug-ins. **Amenities:** irons, hair dryers. **Pool(s):** small heated indoor. **Leisure Activities:** whirlpool, exercise room. *Fee:* game room. **Guest Services:** valet laundry, area transportation. **Business Services:** meeting rooms. **Cards:** AX, CB, DC, DS, MC, VI.
Small-scale Hotel

SOME UNITS

(ASK) (S/D) (✈) (Y↑) (&) (⌐) (X) (⌐) (DATA PORT) / (X) (⌐) (⌐)

AMERICINN
Phone: (920)434-9790
(AAA) (SAVE)
All Year [ECP]   1P: $60-$109   2P: $65-$109   XP: $5   F12
Location: US 41, exit 170, 0.3 mi w. Located in a commercial area. 2032 Velp Ave 54303. **Fax:** 920/434-8790.
▼▼▼▼ **Facility:** 82 units. 73 one-bedroom standard units, some with whirlpools. 9 one-bedroom suites ($90-$140), some with whirlpools. 3 stories, interior corridors. *Bath:* combo or shower only. **Parking:** on-site, winter plug-ins. **Terms:** pets ($10 extra charge). **Amenities:** hair dryers. **Pool(s):** heated indoor. **Leisure Activities:** whirlpool, exercise room. **Guest Services:** coin laundry. **Business Services:** meeting rooms.
Small-scale Hotel
Cards: AX, DC, DS, MC, VI. **Special Amenities:** free continental breakfast and free local telephone calls.

SOME UNITS

(S/D) (🛏) (Y↑) (&M) (&) (⌐) (X) (DATA PORT) (⌐) / (X) (VCR) (⌐)

AMERIHOST INN-GREEN BAY
Phone: (920)406-8200
(AAA) (SAVE)
5/12-12/31   1P: $69-$225   2P: $79-$225   XP: $10   F17
4/1-5/11 & 1/1-3/31   1P: $69-$129   2P: $79-$155   XP: $10   F17
▼▼ ▼▼ **Location:** I-43, exit 183 (Mason St). Located in an office park. 2911 Voyager Dr 54311. **Fax:** 920/406-8130.
Facility: 60 one-bedroom standard units, some with whirlpools. 2 stories (no elevator), interior corridors.
Small-scale Hotel *Bath:* combo or shower only. **Parking:** on-site. **Terms:** [ECP] meal plan available. **Amenities:** voice mail, safes (fee), irons, hair dryers. **Pool(s):** heated indoor. **Leisure Activities:** sauna, whirlpool, exercise room. **Guest Services:** valet laundry. **Business Services:** meeting rooms. **Cards:** AX, DC, DS, MC, VI. **Special Amenities:** free continental breakfast and free local telephone calls.

SOME UNITS

(S/D) (Y↑) (&M) (&) (⌐) (⌐) (X) (⌐) (DATA PORT) (⌐) / (X) (⌐) (⌐)
FEE FEE

THE ASTOR HOUSE

Phone: (920)432-3585

(AAA) (SAVE)

Historic Bed & Breakfast

All Year [CP]　　　　　　　1P: $95-$110　　　　2P: $130-$169

Location: On SR 57, just s of jct SR 54. Located in a semi-residential area. 637 S Monroe Ave 54301. Fax: 920/436-3145. **Facility:** This restored 1888 home, close to downtown and Lambeau Field, has such modern amenities as gas fireplaces and in-room whirlpools. Smoke free premises. 5 one-bedroom standard units, some with whirlpools. 3 stories (no elevator), interior corridors. *Bath:* combo or shower only. **Parking:** on-site. **Terms:** check-in 4 pm, 30 day cancellation notice-fee imposed. **Amenities:** video library, CD players, irons, hair dryers. *Some:* high-speed Internet. **Cards:** AX, DS, MC, VI.

[S/D] [X] [VCR]

BAYMONT INN-GREEN BAY

Phone: (920)494-7887

(AAA) (SAVE)

Small-scale Hotel

All Year　　　　　　　　1P: $59-$99　　　　2P: $67-$109　　　XP: $8　　　F18

Location: US 41, exit 164 (Oneida St), just e. Located in a commercial area. 2840 S Oneida St 54304. Fax: 920/494-3370. **Facility:** 78 one-bedroom standard units. 2 stories (no elevator), interior corridors. **Parking:** on-site, winter plug-ins. **Terms:** [ECP] meal plan available, small pets only. **Amenities:** video games, voice mail, irons, hair dryers. **Guest Services:** valet laundry. **Cards:** AX, DC, DS, MC, VI.
Special Amenities: free continental breakfast and free newspaper.

SOME UNITS

[S/D] [🛏] [11+] [🛁+] [🐾] [▶] [DATA PORT] [💻] / [X] [VCR] [📶] /
FEE

BAY MOTEL

Phone: 920/494-3441

(AAA) (SAVE)

Motel

All Year　　　　　　　　1P: $38-$49　　　　2P: $44-$62　　　XP: $6　　　F18

Location: US 41, exit 167 (Lombardi Ave), 0.4 mi e to Marlee, then 0.6 mi n. 1301 S Military Ave 54304. Fax: 920/494-8260. **Facility:** 53 one-bedroom standard units. 1 story, exterior corridors. *Bath:* combo or shower only. **Parking:** on-site, winter plug-ins. **Terms:** pets ($5 extra charge). **Dining:** Bay Motel Restaurant, see separate listing. **Business Services:** meeting rooms, fax (fee). **Cards:** AX, DS, MC, VI.
Special Amenities: free local telephone calls and free newspaper.

SOME UNITS

[🛏] [11] [▶] [DATA PORT] / [X] /

BEST WESTERN SUITES

Phone: (920)494-8790

(AAA) (SAVE)

Small-scale Hotel

All Year [ECP]　　　　　　1P: $72-$129　　　2P: $82-$139　　　XP: $10　　　F17

Location: US 41, exit 164 (Oneida St), just e to Ramada Way, then just n. Located in a commercial area. 2815 Ramada Way 54304. Fax: 920/494-8749. **Facility:** 79 one-bedroom standard units, some with whirlpools. 2 stories (no elevator), interior corridors. *Bath:* combo or shower only. **Parking:** on-site, winter plug-ins. **Terms:** weekly rates available, package plans - seasonal. **Amenities:** irons, hair dryers. **Pool(s):** heated indoor. **Leisure Activities:** whirlpool. *Fee:* game room. **Guest Services:** valet laundry. **Cards:** AX, CB, DC, DS, JC, MC, VI.
Special Amenities: free continental breakfast and free newspaper.

SOME UNITS

[S/D] [11+] [👤M] [👨‍🦽] [🏊] [▶] [DATA PORT] [💻] / [X] /

BEST WESTERN WASHINGTON ST INN & CONFERENCE CENTER

Phone: (920)437-8771

(AAA) (SAVE)

Small-scale Hotel

All Year [ECP]　　　　　　1P: $69-$109　　　2P: $79-$119　　　XP: $10　　　F18

Location: On east side of Fox River, just s of Walnut St (SR 29); center of downtown. 321 S Washington St 54301-4214. Fax: 920/437-3839. **Facility:** 130 one-bedroom standard units. 2 stories (no elevator), interior corridors. **Parking:** on-site, winter plug-ins. **Amenities:** voice mail, irons, hair dryers. **Pool(s):** heated indoor, wading. **Leisure Activities:** saunas, whirlpool, putting green. *Fee:* game room. **Guest Services:** valet laundry, airport transportation-A. Straubel International Airport. **Business Services:** meeting rooms. **Cards:** AX, DC, DS, MC, VI.

SOME UNITS

[S/D] [✈] [🚗] [🏊] [X] [▶] [DATA PORT] [💻] / [X] [VCR] [📶] /
FEE　　FEE

COMFORT INN

Phone: (920)498-2060

(SAVE)

Small-scale Hotel

9/21-3/31 [ECP]　　　　　1P: $60-$136　　　2P: $66-$136　　　XP: $6　　　F17
6/2-9/20 [ECP]　　　　　 1P: $70-$116　　　2P: $76-$116　　　XP: $6　　　F17
4/1-6/1 [ECP]　　　　　　1P: $60-$80　　　 2P: $66-$86　　　 XP: $6　　　F17

Location: US 41, exit 164 (Oneida St), just e. Located in a commercial area. 2841 Ramada Way 54304. Fax: 920/498-2060. **Facility:** 60 one-bedroom standard units. 2 stories (no elevator), interior corridors. **Parking:** on-site, winter plug-ins. **Terms:** weekly rates available. **Amenities:** *Some:* irons, hair dryers. **Pool(s):** heated indoor. **Leisure Activities:** whirlpool. **Guest Services:** valet laundry. **Cards:** AX, CB, DC, DS, JC, MC, VI.

SOME UNITS

[S/D] [11+] [🚗] [🏊] [▶] [DATA PORT] / [X] [📶] [💻] /

COUNTRY INN & SUITES BY CARLSON

Phone: (920)336-6600

(AAA) (SAVE)

Small-scale Hotel

All Year [ECP]　　　　　　1P: $68-$150　　　2P: $78-$150　　　XP: $10　　　F18

Location: US 41, exit 164 (Oneida St), just nw. Located next to a bowling alley. 2945 Allied St 54301. Fax: 920/336-6618. **Facility:** 75 one-bedroom standard units, some with whirlpools. 2 stories, interior corridors. *Bath:* combo or shower only. **Parking:** on-site, winter plug-ins. **Amenities:** voice mail, irons, hair dryers. *Some:* dual phone lines. **Pool(s):** heated indoor. **Leisure Activities:** whirlpool, exercise room. *Fee:* game room. **Guest Services:** coin laundry. **Cards:** AX, DC, DS, MC, VI. **Special Amenities: free continental breakfast and free newspaper.** *(See color ad starting on p 556)*

SOME UNITS

[S/D] [11+] [👤] [🏊] [X] [▶] [DATA PORT] [💻] / [X] [VCR] [📶] /
FEE

DAYS INN-LAMBEAU FIELD

Phone: 920/498-8088

(AAA) (SAVE)

	7/4-8/30 [CP]	1P: $79-$105	2P: $78-$105	XP: $5	F18
	4/1-7/3 [CP]	1P: $59-$79	2P: $59-$79	XP: $5	F18
	8/31-12/31 [CP]	1P: $52-$76	2P: $52-$76	XP: $5	F18
	1/1-3/31 [CP]	1P: $49-$69	2P: $49-$69	XP: $5	F18

Small-scale Hotel **Location:** US 41, exit 167 (Lombardi Ave), 1.4 mi e, just s. 1978 Holmgren Way 54304. **Fax:** 920/498-8492. **Facility:** 77 one-bedroom standard units. 2 stories (no elevator), interior corridors. **Parking:** on-site, winter plug-ins. **Terms:** pets ($10 extra charge, in smoking units). **Amenities:** hair dryers. **Pool(s):** heated indoor. **Leisure Activities:** whirlpool. **Cards:** AX, CB, DC, DS, JC, MC, VI. **Special Amenities:** free continental breakfast and free newspaper. *(See color ad below)*

SOME UNITS

🛏 🍴 🕸 🏊 🎥 📠 💻 / ⊠ 🔌 📠

EXEL INN OF GREEN BAY

Phone: (920)499-3599

(AAA) (SAVE)

| | 6/1-8/31 [CP] | 1P: $45-$57 | 2P: $51-$63 | XP: $6 | F18 |
| | 4/1-5/31 & 9/1-3/31 [CP] | 1P: $40-$52 | 2P: $46-$58 | XP: $6 | F18 |

Location: US 41, exit 164 (Oneida St), just e. Located in a commercial area. 2870 Ramada Way 54304. **Fax:** 920/498-4055. **Facility:** 104 one-bedroom standard units, some with whirlpools. 2 stories (no elevator), Small-scale Hotel interior corridors. **Parking:** on-site. **Terms:** small pets only (in smoking units). **Amenities:** irons, hair dryers. **Leisure Activities:** exercise room. **Guest Services:** valet and coin laundry. **Cards:** AX, CB, DC, DS, MC, VI. **Special Amenities:** early check-in/late check-out and free continental breakfast. *(See color ad p 465)*

SOME UNITS

Ⓢ🄳 🛏 🍴 🎥 📠 💻 / ⊠ 🔌 📠
FEE FEE

EXTENDED STAY AIRPORT

Phone: 920/499-3600

| | All Year | 1P: $38-$75 | 2P: $40-$80 | XP: $5 | F17 |

Location: US 41, exit 165, 1 mi w on SR 172, just s. Located in a commercial area. 1639 Commanche Ave 54313. Small-scale Hotel **Fax:** 920/965-6520. **Facility:** 76 one-bedroom standard units with efficiencies. 2 stories, interior corridors. *Bath:* combo or shower only. **Parking:** on-site, winter plug-ins. **Terms:** weekly rates available. **Amenities:** dual phone lines, voice mail, irons. **Guest Services:** valet and coin laundry. **Business Services:** meeting rooms. **Cards:** AX, CB, DC, DS, MC, VI.

SOME UNITS

🅺 🍴 🖥 🕸 🏖 🎥 📠 🔌 📠 💻 / ⊠

HAMPTON INN GREEN BAY

Phone: (920)498-9200

(SAVE)

| | All Year [ECP] | 1P: $59-$139 | 2P: $59-$139 | XP: $10 | F18 |

Location: US 41, exit 164 (Oneida St), just e. Located in a commercial area. 2840 Ramada Way 54304. **Fax:** 920/498-3376. **Facility:** 115 one-bedroom standard units. 4 stories, interior corridors. **Parking:** on-site. **Amenities:** video games, voice mail, irons, hair dryers. **Pool(s):** heated indoor. **Leisure Activities:** whirlpool. Small-scale Hotel exercise room. **Guest Services:** valet laundry. **Business Services:** meeting rooms. **Cards:** AX, CB, DC, DS, JC, MC, VI.

SOME UNITS

Ⓢ🄳 🍴 🕸 🏊 🎥 📠 💻 / ⊠ 🔌 📠 /
FEE FEE

HILTON GARDEN INN

Phone: (920)405-0400

(SAVE)

| | All Year | 1P: $70-$150 | 2P: $70-$150 | XP: $10 | F18 |

Location: US 41, exit 167 (Lombardi Ave), 1.6 mi e. 1015 Lombardi Ave 54304. **Fax:** 920/405-0512. **Facility:** 125 one-bedroom standard units, some with whirlpools. 5 stories, interior corridors. *Bath:* combo or shower only. **Parking:** on-site. **Terms:** [BP], [CP] & [ECP] meal plans available. **Amenities:** video games, high-speed Internet, dual phone lines, voice mail, irons, hair dryers. **Pool(s):** heated indoor. **Leisure Activities:** whirlpool, Small-scale Hotel exercise room. **Business Services:** meeting rooms, business center. **Cards:** AX, CB, DC, DS, JC, MC, VI.

SOME UNITS

Ⓢ🄳 🅺 🍴 🖥M 🖥 🏊 🎥 📠 🔌 📠 💻 / ⊠ /

HOLIDAY INN-AIRPORT

Phone: 920/499-5121

| | 4/1-9/30 | 1P: $86 | 2P: $86 | XP: $10 | F18 |
| | 10/1-3/31 | 1P: $76 | 2P: $76 | XP: $10 | F18 |

Large-scale Hotel **Location:** SR 172, exit SR 32 (Ashland Ave), just se on US 41 business route. 2580 S Ashland Ave 54304. **Fax:** 920/499-6777. **Facility:** 146 one-bedroom standard units. 2 stories (no elevator), interior/exterior corridors. *Bath:* combo or shower only. **Parking:** on-site. **Terms:** [AP] meal plan available. **Amenities:** voice mail, irons, hair dryers. **Pool(s):** heated indoor. **Leisure Activities:** whirlpool. *Fee:* game room. **Guest Services:** valet and coin laundry. **Business Services:** conference facilities. **Cards:** AX, DC, DS, MC, VI.

SOME UNITS

🄰🅂🄺 Ⓢ🄳 🅺 🍴 🍸 🖥M 🖥 🕸 🏊 🎥 📠 💻 / ⊠ 🔌 📠 /

HOLIDAY INN CITY CENTRE
Phone: (920)437-5900
WWW All Year 1P: $89 2P: $89 XP: $10 F18
Location: Downtown. Located opposite Port Plaza Mall. 200 Main St 54301. Fax: 920/437-1199. **Facility:** 146 one-bedroom standard units. 7 stories, interior corridors. *Bath:* combo or shower only. **Parking:** on-site. **Terms:** pets ($25 deposit). **Amenities:** video games, voice mail, irons, hair dryers. **Pool(s):** heated indoor. **Leisure Activities:** sauna, exercise room. *Fee:* marina. **Guest Services:** valet and coin laundry. **Business Services:** meeting rooms, business center. **Cards:** AX, CB, DC, DS, JC, MC, VI.
Large-scale Hotel

SOME UNITS

MICROTEL INN & SUITES
Phone: (920)338-9000
(AAA) [SAVE] All Year [CP] 1P: $49-$115 2P: $59-$115 XP: $10 F18
WWW WWW **Location:** US 41, exit 164 (Oneida St), just sw. Located in a commercial area. 3031 Allied St 54304. Fax: 920/338-9100. **Facility:** 68 one-bedroom standard units, some with whirlpools. 3 stories, interior corridors. **Parking:** on-site, winter plug-ins. **Terms:** 10 day cancellation notice-fee imposed. **Amenities:** *Some:* irons. **Pool(s):** heated indoor. **Leisure Activities:** whirlpool. **Guest Services:** coin laundry. **Cards:** AX, DC, DS, MC, VI. **Special Amenities: free continental breakfast and free local telephone calls.**
Small-scale Hotel

SOME UNITS
FEE

RADISSON HOTEL & CONFERENCE CENTER
Phone: (920)494-7300
(AAA) [SAVE] 1/1-3/31 1P: $149-$169 2P: $159-$179 XP: $10 F17
WWW 4/1-12/31 1P: $139-$159 2P: $149-$169 XP: $10 F17
Location: US 41, exit 165, 2 mi w on SR 172. Connected to a casino. 2040 Airport Dr 54313. Fax: 920/494-9599. **Facility:** 414 units. 375 one-bedroom standard units. 39 one-bedroom suites ($169-$399), some with whirlpools. 3-6 stories, interior corridors. *Bath:* combo or shower only. **Parking:** on-site. **Terms:** 14 day cancellation notice-fee imposed, weekly rates available. **Amenities:** video games, dual phone lines, voice mail, irons, hair dryers. *Some:* high-speed Internet. **Dining:** 3 restaurants, 6 am-11 pm, cocktails. **Pool(s):** heated indoor, lap. **Leisure Activities:** sauna, whirlpool, exercise room. **Guest Services:** gift shop, valet laundry, airport transportation-Austin Straubel International Airport, area transportation-within 5 mi. **Business Services:** conference facilities, business center. **Cards:** AX, CB, DC, DS, JC, MC, VI. *(See ad below & color ad p 562)*
Large-scale Hotel

SOME UNITS
FEE FEE

RAMADA PLAZA GREEN BAY
Phone: (920)499-0631
(AAA) [SAVE] All Year [BP] 1P: $78-$114 2P: $88-$124 XP: $10 F18
WWW WWW **Location:** US 41, exit 164 (Oneida St), just e to Ramada Way, 0.3 mi n. Located in a commercial area. 2750 Ramada Way 54304. Fax: 920/499-5476. **Facility:** 148 one-bedroom standard units, some with whirlpools. 5 stories, interior corridors. *Bath:* combo or shower only. **Parking:** on-site. **Terms:** 30 day cancellation notice-fee imposed, 15% service charge, pets ($15 extra charge). **Amenities:** voice mail, safes (fee), irons, hair dryers. **Dining:** 6 am-10 pm, cocktails. **Pool(s):** heated indoor, wading. **Leisure Activities:** sauna, whirlpool, waterslide, indoor water park, exercise room. **Guest Services:** valet laundry, airport transportation-A Straubel Airport. **Business Services:** meeting rooms, business center. **Cards:** AX, CB, DC, DS, JC, MC, VI. **Special Amenities: free local telephone calls and free newspaper.**
Large-scale Hotel

SOME UNITS
FEE

RESIDENCE INN BY MARRIOTT
Phone: (920)435-2222
[SAVE] All Year 1P: $139-$179 XP: $10 F18
WWW **Location:** SR 172, exit Riverside Dr, 1.1 mi n on SR 57, then just e. Located in a semi-commercial area. 335 W St Joseph St 54301. Fax: 920/435-4068. **Facility:** 96 units. 72 one- and 24 two-bedroom standard units with kitchens. 2 stories (no elevator), exterior corridors. **Parking:** on-site. **Terms:** [BP] meal plan available, pets ($150 fee, $5 extra charge). **Amenities:** voice mail, irons, hair dryers. **Pool(s):** heated outdoor. **Leisure Activities:** whirlpool, sports court, basketball, volleyball. **Guest Services:** complimentary evening beverages: Mon-Thurs, valet and coin laundry. **Business Services:** meeting rooms, fax (fee). **Cards:** AX, CB, DC, DS, MC, VI.
Small-scale Hotel

SOME UNITS

SUPER 8 MOTEL
Phone: (920)494-2042

AAA SAVE

Small-scale Hotel

| 6/15-9/27 | 1P: $55-$64 | 2P: $62-$70 |
| 4/1-6/14 & 9/28-3/31 | 1P: $53-$62 | 2P: $60-$68 |

Location: US 41, exit 164 (Oneida St), just e. Located in a commercial area. 2868 S Oneida St 54304. Fax: 920/494-6959. **Facility:** 84 one-bedroom standard units. 2 stories (no elevator), interior corridors. **Parking:** on-site, winter plug-ins. **Terms:** 14 day cancellation notice, [CP] meal plan available, pets ($25 deposit). **Amenities:** voice mail. **Leisure Activities:** sauna, whirlpool. **Guest Services:** valet and coin laundry, airport transportation-Austin Straubel International Airport. **Business Services:** meeting rooms. **Cards:** AX, CB, DC, DS, MC, VI. **Special Amenities:** free continental breakfast and free local telephone calls.

SOME UNITS

WINGATE INN AIRPORT
Phone: 920/617-2000

AAA SAVE

Small-scale Hotel

| All Year [ECP] | 1P: $85 | 2P: $95 | XP: $10 | F18 |

Location: US 41, exit 165, 2 mi w on SR 172. Located opposite a casino. 2065 Airport Dr 54313. Fax: 920/617-2001. **Facility:** 80 units. 76 one-bedroom standard units. 4 one-bedroom suites ($149-$189) with whirlpools. 3 stories, interior corridors. *Bath:* combo or shower only. **Parking:** on-site. **Terms:** package plans. **Amenities:** video games, high-speed Internet, dual phone lines, voice mail, safes, irons, hair dryers. **Leisure Activities:** whirlpool, exercise room. **Guest Services:** sundries, valet and coin laundry, airport transportation-A Straubel International Airport. **Business Services:** meeting rooms, business center. **Cards:** AX, DC, DS, MC, VI. **Special Amenities:** free continental breakfast and free local telephone calls.

SOME UNITS

——— WHERE TO DINE ———

BAY MOTEL RESTAURANT
Lunch: $5-$9   Dinner: $5-$9   Phone: 920/494-3441

American

Location: US 41, exit 167 (Lombardi Ave), 0.4 mi e to Marlee, then 0.6 mi n; in Bay Motel. 1301 S Military Ave 54304. **Hours:** 6 am-8 pm. Closed: 11/27, 12/25; also 12/24 & 1/1 for dinner. **Features:** The casual restaurant is popular for its menu of reasonably priced food and friendly service. Breakfast is served all day, and the menu includes salads, deluxe burgers and sandwiches, as well as standard fare. Casual dress. **Parking:** on-site. **Cards:** AX, DC, DS, MC, VI.

BISTRO JOHN PAUL
Dinner: $17-$22   Phone: 920/432-2897

AAA

American

Location: 2 mi e of downtown on US 141/SR 29. 1244 Main St 54302. **Hours:** 5 pm-9 pm. Closed major holidays; also Sun & Mon. **Reservations:** required. **Features:** Mouthwatering, made-to-order French American cuisine shows eye-catching presentation and thoughtful preparation. The decor of the late 19th-century restaurant, originally a hardware store, is country French. The tempting menu changes weekly. Dressy casual; cocktails. **Parking:** on-site. **Cards:** AX, DC, DS, MC, VI.

EVES SUPPER CLUB
Lunch: $5-$12   Dinner: $10-$50   Phone: 920/435-1571

American

Location: 1 mi n on SR 57 from jct SR 172. 2020 Riverside Dr 54301. **Hours:** 11 am-2 & 5-closing, Sat from 5 pm. Closed major holidays; also Sun. **Reservations:** suggested; weekdays. **Features:** Overlooking the Fox River, the casual restaurant affords great fourth-floor views. Steak and seafood specialties include tenderloin, ribeye and walnut-crusted baked salmon. For dessert, try one of the cheesecakes. Service is friendly and efficient. Casual dress; cocktails. **Parking:** on-site. **Cards:** AX, DC, DS, MC, VI.

LORELIE
Lunch: $4-$7   Dinner: $7-$15   Phone: 920/432-5921

German

Location: 1.8 mi n from jct SR 172. 1412 S Webster Ave 54301. **Hours:** 11:30 am-1:30 & 5-9:30 pm, Fri-10 pm, Sat 5 pm-10 pm. Closed major holidays; also Sun. **Reservations:** accepted. **Features:** A limited selection of German dishes—plus well-seasoned steak—are listed on the family-operated restaurant's menu. The place is filled with locals, who enjoy catching up with their friends at other tables. The service is friendly and efficient. Casual dress; cocktails. **Parking:** on-site. **Cards:** MC, VI.

TITLETOWN BREWING COMPANY
Lunch: $6-$9   Dinner: $6-$15   Phone: 920/437-2337

American

Location: On SR 29 at west end of Fox River Bridge, just w of downtown. 200 Dousman St 54303. **Hours:** 11 am-11 pm, Fri & Sat-midnight. Closed: 11/27, 12/25. **Features:** The microbrewery serves hand-crafted ales and root beer as well as delicious dishes and tempting specials. An 85-foot clock tower, hardwood floors and historical artwork decorate the restored 1899 train depot. Casual dress; cocktails. **Parking:** on-site. **Cards:** AX, DC, DS, MC, VI.

THE WELLINGTON RESTAURANT
Lunch: $8-$10   Dinner: $16-$28   Phone: 920/499-2000

American

Location: US 41, exit 164 (Oneida St), 0.5 mi ne, then 0.5 mi w. 1060 Hansen Rd 54304. **Hours:** 11:30 am-2 & 5-9 pm, Sat from 5 pm. Closed major holidays; also Sun. **Reservations:** suggested. **Features:** On the edge of town, the restaurant is known as a great place for steak. Also on the menu is a selection of fresh seafood, pork and poultry. The relaxing ambience is highlighted by an English motif, soft background music and large windows overlooking the lawn. Dressy casual; cocktails. **Parking:** on-site. **Cards:** AX, DC, MC, VI.

——— The following restaurant has not been evaluated by AAA ——— but is listed for your information only.

LOS BANDITOS
Phone: 920/494-4505

fyi

Not evaluated. Location: US 41, exit Mason St, just w. 2335 W Mason St 54303. **Features:** Located just west of highway US 41, this eatery is well-known for their Mexican dishes.

GREENFIELD —See Milwaukee p. 573.

GREEN LAKE pop. 1,100

———— WHERE TO STAY ————

BAY VIEW MOTEL & RESORT   **Phone:** 920/294-6504

	5/1-10/31	1P: $88-$98	2P: $88-$98	XP: $10	D12
	11/1-3/31	1P: $42-$50	2P: $42-$50	XP: $10	D12
Motel	4/1-4/30	1P: $40-$48	2P: $40-$48	XP: $10	D12

Location: 0.3 mi se. 439 Lake St 54941. Fax: 920/294-0888. **Facility:** 17 one-bedroom standard units, some with efficiencies. 1 story, exterior corridors. *Bath:* combo or shower only. **Parking:** on-site, winter plug-ins. **Leisure Activities:** rental boats, boat dock, fishing. **Business Services:** fax.

SOME UNITS

LAKESIDE MOTEL   **Phone:** 920/294-3318

	4/1-10/31	1P: $80-$90	2P: $80-$90	XP: $15	F10
Motel	11/1-3/31	1P: $60-$65	2P: $60-$65	

Location: Just w of downtown on Business SR 23. 488 South St 54941. Fax: 920/294-0687. **Facility:** Designated smoking area. 15 one-bedroom standard units. 1 story, interior/exterior corridors. *Bath:* combo or shower only. **Parking:** on-site, winter plug-ins. **Terms:** 2 night minimum stay - seasonal, 12 day cancellation notice. **Amenities:** *Some:* hair dryers. **Business Services:** fax. **Cards:** MC, VI.

SOME UNITS

———— WHERE TO DINE ————

NORTON'S MARINE DINING ROOM   **Lunch:** $6-$14   **Dinner:** $20-$36   **Phone:** 920/294-6577

Steak & Seafood

Location: 0.7 mi w on Business SR 23. 380 S Lawson Dr 54941. **Hours:** 11 am-3 & 5-10 pm; hours may vary off season. Closed: 12/25; also 12/24 for dinner. **Features:** Nautical theme, overlooking Green Lake. Patio seating for lunch. Boat docking available. Supper club type fare featuring yellow fin tuna chops and roast duck. Homemade soup, rolls and dessert. Friday night fish fry of fresh lake perch in season. Casual dress; cocktails. **Parking:** on-site. **Cards:** AX, MC, VI.

HARTFORD —See Milwaukee p. 574.

HAYWARD pop. 2,129

———— WHERE TO STAY ————

AMERICINN OF HAYWARD   **Phone:** (715)634-2700

	6/8-10/11 [ECP]	1P: $66-$119	2P: $87-$125	XP: $6	F17
	1/1-3/31 [ECP]	1P: $66-$96	2P: $72-$102	XP: $6	F17
	4/1-6/7 & 10/12-12/31 [ECP]	1P: $66-$76	2P: $72-$82	XP: $6	F17

Small-scale Hotel **Location:** On US 63, just n of jct SR 77. 15601 US Hwy 63 54843. Fax: 715/634-3958. **Facility:** 42 units. 39 one-bedroom standard units, some with whirlpools. 3 one-bedroom suites ($81-$145). 2 stories, interior corridors. *Bath:* combo or shower only. **Parking:** on-site, winter plug-ins. **Terms:** cancellation fee imposed, pets ($6 extra charge, in smoking units). **Amenities:** video library, hair dryers. *Some:* irons. **Pool(s):** small heated indoor. **Leisure Activities:** sauna, whirlpool. *Fee:* pool table. **Guest Services:** valet laundry. **Business Services:** meeting rooms, PC, fax (fee). **Cards:** AX, DS, MC, VI. **Special Amenities:** free continental breakfast and free local telephone calls.

SOME UNITS

FEE

BEST WESTERN NORTHERN PINE INN   **Phone:** (715)634-4959

	5/16-10/15 & 12/16-3/31	1P: $79	2P: $79	XP: $5
	4/1-5/15 & 10/16-12/15	1P: $59	2P: $59	XP: $5

Small-scale Hotel **Location:** 1.7 mi s on SR 27 S from jct US 63. 9966 N Hwy 27 54843. Fax: 715/634-8999. **Facility:** 39 units. 38 one-bedroom standard units, some with whirlpools. 1 one-bedroom suite ($79-$109) with whirlpool. 1-2 stories, interior/exterior corridors. *Bath:* combo or shower only. **Parking:** on-site, winter plug-ins. **Terms:** 3 day cancellation notice, [CP] meal plan available, pets ($5 extra charge). **Amenities:** irons, hair dryers. **Pool(s):** small heated indoor. **Leisure Activities:** sauna, whirlpool. *Fee:* game room. **Business Services:** fax. **Cards:** AX, CB, DC, DS, MC, VI. **Special Amenities:** free continental breakfast.

SOME UNITS

CEDAR INN MOTEL   **Phone:** 715/634-5332

	6/15-3/31 [CP]	1P: $61	2P: $76	XP: $15	F12
Motel	4/1-6/14 [CP]	1P: $51	2P: $66	XP: $15	F12

Location: On SR 77, just e of jct US 63. 15659 SR 77 54843. Fax: 715/634-1343. **Facility:** 23 one-bedroom standard units, some with whirlpools. 1 story, interior corridors. **Parking:** on-site, winter plug-ins. **Leisure Activities:** sauna, whirlpool, limited exercise equipment. **Business Services:** fax (fee). **Cards:** AX, DS, MC, VI.

SOME UNITS

COMFORT SUITES

Phone: (715)634-0700

AAA SAVE
Motel

All Year [CP] 1P: $69-$164 2P: $69-$164 XP: $10 F18
Location: On CR B, 0.5 mi s of jct SR 27. 15586 CR B 54843. Fax: 715/634-0800. **Facility:** 60 one-bedroom standard units, some with whirlpools. 2 stories, interior corridors. *Bath:* combo or shower only. **Parking:** on-site, winter plug-ins. **Terms:** pets ($10 fee, $25 deposit). **Amenities:** irons, hair dryers. **Pool(s):** heated indoor. **Leisure Activities:** sauna, whirlpool, rental paddleboats, boat dock, fishing, sun deck, cross country skiing, snowmobiling, exercise room. *Fee:* game room. **Guest Services:** coin laundry. **Business Services:** meeting rooms, administrative services (fee). **Cards:** AX, CB, DC, DS, JC, MC, VI. **Special Amenities:** free continental breakfast and free local telephone calls. *(See color ad below)*

SOME UNITS

COUNTRY INN & SUITES BY CARLSON

Phone: 715/634-4100

Small-scale Hotel

4/1-5/11 & 10/13-3/31 [ECP] 1P: $83-$133 2P: $83-$133 XP: $6 F18
5/12-10/12 [ECP] 1P: $73-$118 2P: $73-$118 XP: $6 F18
Location: On SR 27 S, 0.7 mi s of jct US 63. 10290 Hwy 27 S 54843 (PO Box 1010). Fax: 715/634-2403. **Facility:** 66 units. 58 one-bedroom standard units, some with whirlpools. 8 one-bedroom suites with whirlpools. 2 stories, interior corridors. **Parking:** on-site, winter plug-ins. **Amenities:** voice mail, irons, hair dryers. **Pool(s):** small heated indoor. **Leisure Activities:** whirlpool. *Fee:* game room. **Business Services:** meeting rooms, administrative services (fee). **Cards:** AX, DC, DS, MC, VI. *(See color ad starting on p 556)*

SOME UNITS

EDELWEISS MOTEL
Phone: 715/634-4679

[AAA] [SAVE]

♦♦ ♦♦

Motel

6/16-3/31 [CP]	1P: $49-$59	2P: $55-$65	XP: $5	F15
4/1-6/15 [CP]	1P: $39-$49	2P: $49-$59	XP: $5	F15

Location: 1.8 mi s on SR 27 from jct US 63. Hwy 27 S & Park Rd (16081 W Park Rd). **Facility:** 8 one-bedroom standard units. 1 story, exterior corridors. **Parking:** on-site, winter plug-ins. **Cards:** AX, DS, MC, VI.

[S/D] [X] [▥] [🖥]

GRAND PINES RESORTS
Phone: 715/462-3564

♦♦ ♦♦ ♦♦

Vacation Home

6/1-9/30	2P: $200-$315
4/1-5/31 & 10/1-3/31	2P: $175-$200

Location: 8.5 mi e on CR B. 12355 W Richardson Bay Rd 54843. Fax: 715/462-9754. **Facility:** 20 units. 10 one-bedroom standard units. 10 cabins ($1458-$2100). 1-2 stories (no elevator), exterior corridors. **Parking:** on-site. **Terms:** check-out 8 am, 2 night minimum stay - weekends, cancellation fee imposed, weekly rates available. **Amenities:** video library (fee). **Dining:** The Original Famous Dave's, see separate listing. **Leisure Activities:** rental boats, fishing. **Guest Services:** gift shop. **Business Services:** fax. **Cards:** AX, DS, MC, VI.

SOME UNITS

[S/D] [▥] [🖥] [🖥] [🖥] / [VCR] [DATA PORT] [📷] /

LUMBERMAN'S MANSION INN
Phone: 715/634-3012

♦♦ ♦♦ ♦♦

Historic Bed & Breakfast

All Year [BP]	1P: $95-$100	2P: $95-$100	XP: $16 F3

Location: Just w of US 63; corner of 4th St and Kansas Ave. 15844 E 4th St 54843 (PO Box 554). Fax: 715/634-5724. **Facility:** Whirlpools are featured in every guest room of this 1887 Queen Anne Victorian, which is within walking distance of downtown. Smoke free premises. 5 units. 3 one-bedroom standard units with whirlpools. 2 one-bedroom suites ($95-$100) with whirlpools. 2 stories (no elevator), interior corridors. **Parking:** on-site. **Terms:** 7 day cancellation notice. **Amenities:** video library. **Guest Services:** complimentary evening beverages. **Business Services:** meeting rooms, administrative services (fee). **Cards:** MC, VI.

[X] [▥] [VCR] [☎]

ROSS' TEAL LAKE LODGE AND TEAL WING GOLF CLUB
Phone: (715)462-3631

[AAA] [SAVE]

♦♦ ♦♦ ♦♦ ♦♦

Historic Resort
Small-scale Hotel

6/21-8/20	1P: $196-$343	2P: $221-$368	XP: $25	D18
5/25-6/20 & 8/21-10/15	1P: $154-$275	2P: $189-$300	XP: $25	D18
4/1-5/24	1P: $105-$155	2P: $130-$180	XP: $25	D18

Location: On SR 77, 20 mi ne of jct SR 77. Located in Chequamegon-Nicolet National Forest. 12425 N Ross Rd 54843. **Facility:** 23 units. 3 one-bedroom standard units. 8 one-, 6 two- and 6 three-bedroom suites, some with kitchens. 1 story, exterior corridors. **Parking:** on-site, winter plug-ins. **Terms:** open 4/1-10/15, 21 day cancellation notice-fee imposed, weekly rates available, [BP], [CP] & [MAP] meal plans available, package plans, 15% service charge, pets ($5 extra charge). **Amenities:** video library. **Dining:** 7:30 am-11, noon-4 & 6-8 pm, cocktails. **Pool(s):** heated outdoor. **Leisure Activities:** sauna, rental boats, rental canoes, rental sailboats, boat dock, fishing, fishing instruction & guide service, hydro bikes, pontoon boats, driving range, tennis court, cross country skiing, bicycles, hiking trails, jogging, horseshoes, shuffleboard. **Fee:** golf-18 holes. **Guest Services:** coin laundry. **Business Services:** meeting rooms. **Cards:** MC, VI. **Special Amenities:** early check-in/late check-out and free local telephone calls.

SOME UNITS

[🐾] [▥] [▼] [🏊] [X] [▥] [☎] [🖥] [🖥] / [VCR] / FEE

SUPER 8 MOTEL
Phone: (715)634-2646

♦♦ ♦♦

Motel

5/17-10/20	1P: $55-$86	2P: $65-$96	XP: $7	F12
10/21-3/31	1P: $52-$86	2P: $60-$90	XP: $7	F12
4/1-5/16	1P: $50-$86	2P: $58-$90	XP: $7	F12

Location: On SR 27, 0.3 mi s of jct US 63. 10444 N SR 27 54843. Fax: 715/634-6482. **Facility:** 46 one-bedroom standard units, some with whirlpools. 1-2 stories, interior/exterior corridors. **Parking:** on-site, winter plug-ins. **Terms:** 3 day cancellation notice. **Pool(s):** small heated indoor. **Leisure Activities:** whirlpool. **Business Services:** administrative services (fee). **Cards:** AX, DC, DS, MC, VI.

SOME UNITS

[S/D] [🐾] [▥+] [🏊] / [X] [DATA PORT]

WHERE TO DINE

CHIPPEWA INN
Dinner: $11-$22   **Phone:** 715/462-3648

[AAA]

♦♦ ♦♦

German

Location: On CR B, at jct CR A, 15 mi e. 9702 N CR B 54843. **Hours:** 5 pm-10 pm; hours vary seasonally. Closed: Tues. **Reservations:** suggested. **Features:** Set on a quiet, secluded location on the Chequamegon National Forest scenic drive, the restaurant delivers a mixture of American dishes and German specialties. Famous for their relish tray featuring assorted salad, vegetables and cheese spread. Casual dress; cocktails. **Parking:** on-site. **Cards:** MC, VI.

[▼] [X]

CLUB 77
Dinner: $12-$30   **Phone:** 715/462-3712

[AAA]

♦♦ ♦♦

American

Location: On SR 77, 8 mi e. 10494 N Airport Rd 54843. **Hours:** 5 pm-9 pm. Closed: Mon-Wed 10/1-6/1. **Reservations:** suggested. **Features:** Located just outside of town, this well-known area restaurant features excellent food in a casual and non-pretentious manner. Unlike most restaurants, all diners receive a tray of crudites, a cheese fondue and diced bread for dipping. Very popular with locals and out-of-towners, this is a good choice for a hearty meal. Casual dress; cocktails. **Parking:** on-site. **Cards:** MC, VI.

[▼] [X]

MAXIMILIAN INN
Dinner: $14-$22   **Phone:** 715/865-2080

♦♦ ♦♦

American

Location: On SR 27, 0.6 mi s of jct SR 70 W. 15866 W State Rd 27/70 54871. **Hours:** 5 pm-10 pm. Closed: Sun-Wed 11/1-5/15. **Reservations:** suggested; on weekends. **Features:** The varied menu dabbles in both German and American cuisine, with such tempting offerings as fresh fish, barbecue ribs, steaks, seafood and schnitzels. An alpine theme prevails in the casual dining room. Delicious desserts are made from scratch. Cocktails. **Parking:** on-site. **Cards:** DS, MC, VI.

[▼] [X]

THE ORIGINAL FAMOUS DAVE'S   **Lunch:** $7-$19   **Dinner:** $7-$19   **Phone:** 715/462-3352
Location: 8.5 mi e on CR B; in Grand Pines Resorts. 12355 W Richardson Bay Rd 54843. **Hours:** 11 am-10 pm,
Sun from 8 am. **Closed:** 11/27, 12/24, 12/25. **Reservations:** suggested; summer. **Features:** The
Barbecue   Southern-style barbecue shack, tucked amid the towering pines on Big Round Lake, is known for its
flavorful, Texas-style beef brisket, Georgian-chopped pork, country roast chicken and pit barbecue ribs.
During the summer, outdoor seating is a favorite. Casual dress; cocktails. **Parking:** on-site. **Cards:** AX, CB, DC, DS, MC, VI.

HAZELHURST

———— **WHERE TO DINE** ————

JACOBI'S OF HAZELHURST   **Dinner:** $15-$25   **Phone:** 715/356-5591
Location: 0.3 mi s on US 51, 0.3 mi w on Oneida St. 9820 Cedar Falls Rd 54531. **Hours:** 5 pm-9 pm, Sat-10 pm.
Closed: Mon; Sun-Wed 10/15-5/1. **Features:** This intimate restaurant is easily recognized by its pastel
Continental   house-like exterior with beautiful seasonal flower landscaping. A complimentary appetizer is served. Soup,
bread and dessert are all made in-house. Try the signature garlic-stuffed beef filet. Casual dress; cocktails.
Parking: on-site. **Cards:** MC, VI.

HEWITT

———— **WHERE TO DINE** ————

VILLAGE HEARTH   **Dinner:** $10-$25   **Phone:** 715/384-8755
Location: On CR T, 4 mi e of Marshfield, 1.3 mi n of US 10. 11040 Main St 54441. **Hours:** 5 pm-10 pm. Closed
major holidays; also Sun, week of July 4. **Reservations:** accepted. **Features:** The romantic atmosphere is
American   enhanced by a cozy fireplace and upscale dining rooms decorated with a Victorian flair. Rack of lamb
marinated with Dijon mustard marinate and coconut shrimp with orange marmalade sauce are
representative gourmet offerings. Dressy casual; cocktails. **Parking:** on-site. **Cards:** AX, DS, MC, VI.

HUBERTUS

———— **WHERE TO DINE** ————

THE FOX & HOUNDS   **Dinner:** $14-$25   **Phone:** 262/628-1111
Location: 6 mi w on SR 167 from jct US 45, 1 mi s at sign. 1298 Friess Lake Rd 53033. **Hours:** 4 pm-10 pm.
Closed: 1/1, 12/24, 12/25; also Sun & Mon. **Reservations:** suggested. **Features:** Roast goose, chicken
American   cordon bleu and sauerbraten with spaetzle and red cabbage are among dishes on the varied menu. Once
a hunt club, the 1845 log cabin was converted to a restaurant in 1933. Stone fireplaces burn during the
chilly winter months. Casual dress; cocktails. **Parking:** on-site and valet. **Cards:** AX, DC, DS, MC, VI.

HUDSON pop. 8,775

———— **WHERE TO STAY** ————

SUPER 8 MOTEL OF HUDSON   **Phone:** (715)386-8800

5/23-8/31 [ECP]	1P: $69-$84	2P: $79-$104	
4/1-5/22 & 9/1-3/31 [ECP]	1P: $57-$84	2P: $72-$104	

Location: I-94, exit 2 (CR F), 1 mi w on south frontage road (Crestview Dr). 808 Dominion Dr 54016.
Fax: 715/386-3805. **Facility:** 56 one-bedroom standard units, some with whirlpools. 2 stories, interior corri-
Motel   dors. **Parking:** on-site, winter plug-ins. **Terms:** small pets only ($50 deposit). **Amenities:** hair dryers.
Pool(s): heated indoor. **Leisure Activities:** whirlpool. **Guest Services:** coin laundry. **Business Services:**
meeting rooms, fax. **Cards:** AX, CB, DC, DS, MC, VI. **Special Amenities:** free continental breakfast and free local telephone
calls.

SOME UNITS

———— *The following lodging was either not evaluated or did not* ————
meet AAA rating requirements but is listed for your information only.

HOLIDAY INN EXPRESS   **Phone:** 715/386-6200
[fyi]   Not evaluated. **Location:** I-94, exit 2 (CR F), 0.3 mi s. 1200 Gateway Blvd 54016 (PO Box 719). Facilities, services,
and decor characterize a mid-range property.

———— **WHERE TO DINE** ————

BARKER'S   **Lunch:** $8-$16   **Dinner:** $8-$16   **Phone:** 715/386-4123
Location: Downtown. 413 2nd St 54016. **Hours:** 11 am-11 pm. Closed: 11/27. **Reservations:** accepted.
Features: The casual pub offers 16 beers on tap to complement made-to-order sandwiches. Casual dress;
American   cocktails. **Parking:** street. **Cards:** MC, VI.

SAN PEDRO CAFE   **Lunch:** $8-$15   **Dinner:** $8-$15   **Phone:** 715/386-4003
Location: Downtown. 426 2nd St 54016. **Hours:** 10:30 am-10 pm, Fri & Sat 8 am-11 pm, Sun 8 am-10 pm.
Closed: 1/1, 11/27, 12/25. **Features:** Fresh, flavorful ingredients are staples at the trendy restaurant.
Caribbean   Tropical salsa, Caribbean and jerk spices and a variety of peppers add zing to homemade recipes.
Wood-fired pizzas and seafood preparations are popular. Casual dress; cocktails. **Parking:** street.
Cards: MC, VI.

HURLEY pop. 1,818

—— WHERE TO STAY ——

DAYS INN OF HURLEY
Phone: (715)561-3500

AAA SAVE
| | 12/1-3/31 | 1P: $69-$79 | 2P: $75-$85 | XP: $6 | F18 |
| | 4/1-11/30 | 1P: $63-$73 | 2P: $69-$83 | XP: $6 | F18 |

Small-scale Hotel
Location: S of jct US 2 and 51. 850 10th Ave N 54534. Fax: 715/561-3236. **Facility:** 70 one-bedroom standard units, some with whirlpools. 2 stories (no elevator), interior corridors. **Parking:** on-site, winter plug-ins. **Terms:** [CP] meal plan available, small pets only (in smoking units). **Amenities:** video library (fee), hair dryers. **Pool(s):** heated indoor. **Leisure Activities:** sauna, whirlpool, snowmobiling, ATV trails. *Fee:* game room. **Guest Services:** coin laundry. **Cards:** AX, CB, DC, DS, MC, VI. **Special Amenities:** free continental breakfast and free local telephone calls.

SOME UNITS

—— WHERE TO DINE ——

KIMBALL INN
Dinner: $8-$14
Phone: 715/561-4095

American
Location: 3.7 mi w on US 2. 6622 US 2 54534. **Hours:** 4 pm-11 pm. Closed: 4/20, 11/27, 12/25; also Mon. **Reservations:** accepted. **Features:** The friendly owner is often found in the dining room discussing the food or what's happening in the area. The menu lists a good selection of classic dinners, as well as a number of Italian dishes. Casual dress; cocktails. **Parking:** on-site. **Cards:** AX, MC, VI.

———— *The following restaurants have not been evaluated by AAA* ————
but are listed for your information only.

EL MONTERREY CAFE
Phone: 715/561-4777

fyi
Not evaluated. **Location:** 208 Silver St 54534. **Features:** If you're looking for authentic Mexican food, this is the place to go in town.

FONTECCHIO'S BELL CHALET
Phone: 715/561-3753

fyi
Not evaluated. **Location:** 109 5th Ave S 54534. **Features:** Located in town, this restaurant has been serving Italian food for over 70 years. Also serving a number of American dishes, light meals, salads & pizza.

PETRUSHA'S
Phone: 715/561-9888

fyi
Not evaluated. **Location:** Rt 1, US 51 54534. **Features:** Go south of town, and you'll find this well-established family restaurant.

IRON RIDGE pop. 998

—— WHERE TO STAY ——

IRON RIDGE INN MOTEL
Phone: 920/387-4090

| | All Year [CP] | 1P: $49-$65 | 2P: $55-$85 | XP: $3 |

Small-scale Hotel
Location: On CR S; center. 129 S Main St 53035. Fax: 920/387-4090. **Facility:** 20 one-bedroom standard units, some with kitchens (no utensils) and/or whirlpools. 2 stories (no elevator), interior corridors. **Parking:** on-site, winter plug-ins. **Pool(s):** small heated indoor. **Leisure Activities:** whirlpool. **Guest Services:** valet laundry. **Business Services:** fax (fee). **Cards:** AX, MC, VI.

SOME UNITS

IRON RIVER

—— WHERE TO STAY ——

IRON RIVER TROUT HAUS
Phone: (715)372-4219

| | All Year [BP] | 2P: $60-$75 | XP: $10 |

Bed & Breakfast
Location: 0.3 mi n on Lea St from jct US 2 and CR A S, then just w. Located in a quiet area. 7420 Drummond St 54847 (PO Box 662). Fax: 715/372-5511. **Facility:** Smoke free premises. 4 one-bedroom standard units. 2 stories (no elevator), interior corridors. *Bath:* some shared or private, shower only. **Parking:** on-site. **Terms:** 2 night minimum stay - weekends, age restrictions may apply, cancellation fee imposed. **Leisure Activities:** Fee: fishing. **Guest Services:** TV in common area. **Cards:** MC, VI.

JACKSON —See Milwaukee p. 574.

JANESVILLE pop. 59,498

—— WHERE TO STAY ——

BAYMONT INN & SUITES-JANESVILLE
Phone: (608)758-4545

| | All Year | 1P: $60-$75 | 2P: $60-$75 |

AAA SAVE
Small-scale Hotel
Location: I-90, exit 175B (SR 11), just ne. 616 Midland Rd 53546. Fax: 608/758-4594. **Facility:** 107 one-bedroom standard units, some with whirlpools. 4 stories, interior corridors. *Bath:* combo or shower only. **Parking:** on-site, winter plug-ins. **Terms:** weekly rates available, [ECP] meal plan available, pets ($15 extra charge). **Amenities:** video games (fee), voice mail, irons, hair dryers. **Pool(s):** small heated indoor. **Leisure Activities:** whirlpool. **Guest Services:** valet and coin laundry. **Business Services:** meeting rooms. **Cards:** AX, DC, DS, MC, VI. **Special Amenities:** free continental breakfast and free newspaper.

SOME UNITS

BEST WESTERN JANESVILLE

Phone: (608)756-4511

(AAA) [SAVE]

△▽△▽

Small-scale Hotel

All Year   1P: $64-$149   2P: $64-$149   XP: $10   F18
Location: I-90, exit 171A (SR 26), just e. 3900 Milton Ave 53546. Fax: 608/756-0025. **Facility:** 105 one-bedroom standard units. 2-3 stories, interior corridors. **Parking:** on-site, winter plug-ins. **Terms:** cancellation fee imposed, [ECP] meal plan available, small pets only ($10 fee). **Amenities:** voice mail, irons, hair dryers. **Dining:** 11 am-10 pm, Sat & Sun from 7 am, cocktails. **Pool(s):** heated indoor. **Leisure Activities:** whirlpool, domed recreation area, exercise room. **Guest Services:** valet laundry, area transportation. **Business Services:** meeting rooms. **Cards:** AX, CB, DC, DS, MC, VI. **Special Amenities:** free continental breakfast and free newspaper.
(See color ad below)

SOME UNITS

[S🄳] [✈] [📶] [🍴] [Y] [🏊] [⊠] [🎥] [DATA PORT] [💻] [/] [⊠] [🔌] [📷] [/]

HAMPTON INN-JANESVILLE

Phone: (608)754-4900

[SAVE]

△▽△▽

Small-scale Hotel

All Year   1P: $74
Location: I-90, exit 171A (SR 26), just ne. 2400 Fulton St 53546. Fax: 608/754-4980. **Facility:** 99 one-bedroom standard units, some with whirlpools. 3 stories, interior corridors. *Bath:* combo or shower only. **Parking:** on-site, winter plug-ins. **Terms:** [ECP] meal plan available. **Amenities:** video games (fee), voice mail, irons, hair dryers. **Pool(s):** small heated indoor. **Leisure Activities:** whirlpool. **Guest Services:** valet laundry. **Business Services:** meeting rooms. **Cards:** AX, DC, DS, MC, VI.

SOME UNITS

[S🄳] [🍴] [♿] [🐾] [🏊] [➕] [🎥] [DATA PORT] [💻] [/] [⊠] [🔌] [📷] [/]

HOLIDAY INN EXPRESS & JANESVILLE CONFERENCE CENTER

Phone: (608)756-3100

(AAA) [SAVE]

△▽△▽

Small-scale Hotel

All Year [ECP]   1P: $73   2P: $73   XP: $8   F18
Location: I-90, exit 171C (US 14), just e. 3100 Wellington Pl 53546. Fax: 608/756-3111. **Facility:** 142 units. 137 one-bedroom standard units, some with whirlpools. 5 one-bedroom suites. 5 stories, interior corridors. *Bath:* combo or shower only. **Parking:** on-site. **Amenities:** voice mail, irons, hair dryers. **Pool(s):** heated indoor. **Leisure Activities:** whirlpool, exercise room. *Fee:* game room. **Guest Services:** valet and coin laundry, area transportation. **Business Services:** meeting rooms. **Cards:** AX, CB, DC, DS, JC, MC, VI. **Special Amenities:** free continental breakfast and free local telephone calls.

SOME UNITS

[S🄳] [✈] [🍴] [♿M] [♿] [🐾] [🏊] [⊠] [🎥] [DATA PORT] [💻] [/] [⊠] [🔌] [📷] [/]

MICROTEL INN

Phone: (608)752-3121

(AAA) [SAVE]

△▽△▽

Small-scale Hotel

All Year   1P: $44-$69   2P: $44-$69   XP: $5   F16
Location: I-90, exit 171C (US 14), just se. 3121 Wellington Pl 53546. Fax: 608/752-3321. **Facility:** 61 one-bedroom standard units. 2 stories (no elevator), interior corridors. *Bath:* combo or shower only. **Parking:** on-site. **Terms:** [CP] meal plan available, pets ($10 extra charge). **Guest Services:** valet laundry. **Business Services:** meeting rooms, fax (fee). **Cards:** AX, CB, DC, DS, JC, MC, VI. **Special Amenities:** free continental breakfast and free local telephone calls.

SOME UNITS

[🛏] [🍴] [♿M] [♿] [🐾] [🎥] [DATA PORT] [💻] [/] [⊠] [🔌] [📷] [/]

RAMADA INN

(AAA) (SAVE)
◆◆◆◆

Small-scale Hotel

Phone: (608)756-2341

All Year [CP]   1P: $58-$63   2P: $67-$72   XP: $10   F17
Location: I-90, exit 171A (SR 26), just sw. 3431 Milton Ave 53545. Fax: 608/756-4183. **Facility:** 189 units. 188 one-bedroom standard units, some with whirlpools. 1 one-bedroom suite ($75-$210) with whirlpool. 2 stories, interior corridors. **Parking:** on-site, winter plug-ins. **Terms:** weekly rates available. **Amenities:** video games (fee), voice mail, irons, hair dryers. *Some:* CD players. **Dining:** 6 am-2 & 5-10 pm, Sun 10 am-2 & 5-9 pm, cocktails. **Pool(s):** small heated indoor. **Leisure Activities:** sauna, whirlpool, putting green, exercise room. **Guest Services:** valet and coin laundry, area transportation. **Business Services:** meeting rooms. **Cards:** AX, CB, DC, DS, JC, MC, VI. **Special Amenities:** early check-in/late check-out and free room upgrade (subject to availability with advanced reservations).

SOME UNITS

[⑤ᴰ] [❧] [ᵀ] [✦] [✕] [✦] [ᴰᴬᵀᴬ ᴾᴼᴿᵀ] [☐] / [✕] [ⱽᶜᴿ] [☐] [☐] /

SELECT INN

(AAA) (SAVE)
◆◆◆

Small-scale Hotel

Phone: (608)754-0251

All Year [CP]   1P: $35-$45   2P: $42-$52   XP: $5   F16
Location: I-90, exit 171A (SR 26), just sw. 3520 Milton Ave 53545. Fax: 608/754-0251. **Facility:** 62 units. 61 one-bedroom standard units. 1 one-bedroom suite. 2 stories, interior corridors. *Bath:* combo or shower only. **Parking:** on-site. **Terms:** weekly rates available, small pets only ($25 deposit). **Amenities:** safes (fee). *Some:* hair dryers. **Guest Services:** coin laundry. **Business Services:** fax (fee). **Cards:** AX, CB, DC, DS, JC, MC, VI. **Special Amenities:** free continental breakfast. *(See color ad p 508)*

SOME UNITS

[⑤ᴰ] [❧] [❧] [⚁] [✦] / [✕] [ᴰᴬᵀᴬ ᴾᴼᴿᵀ] [☐] [☐] /

──── WHERE TO DINE ────

PEKING CHINESE RESTAURANT
◆◆◆
Chinese

Lunch: $4-$6   **Dinner:** $7-$14   Phone: 608/752-9177

Location: On SR 26, 0.4 mi s from jct US 14. 2632 Milton Ave 53545. **Hours:** 11:30 am-2 & 4-10 pm. Closed major holidays; also Sun. **Reservations:** accepted. **Features:** Ornate Oriental appointments, such as hanging lamps and sconces, decorate the cozy dining room. Northern Mandarin and Szechwan specialties, as well as chef specials of Szechuan squid and Peking duck, are served in large portions. The luncheon menu offers an exceptionally good value. Family dinners are available in the evening. Casual dress; cocktails. **Parking:** on-site. **Cards:** DS, MC, VI.

[✕]

ROHERTY'S
◆◆◆
Irish

Lunch: $5-$10   **Dinner:** $6-$12   Phone: 608/752-2393

Location: On SR 26, 0.6 mi s from jct US 14. 2121 Milton Ave 53545. **Hours:** 11 am-9 pm, Fri & Sat-10 pm. Closed major holidays. **Reservations:** accepted. **Features:** Family-owned and operated since 1903, the restaurant is known for Irish dishes and such American standbys as salads, sandwiches, chicken, steak and seafood. Only USDA choice, corn-fed beef is served. Fish fry, a Wisconsin tradition, is available daily. Servers are friendly and prompt. Smoking is allowed only in the lounge. Casual dress; cocktails. **Parking:** on-site. **Cards:** AX, DS, MC, VI.

[ᵀ] [✕]

JEFFERSON pop. 7,338

──── WHERE TO STAY ────

RODEWAY INN
(SAVE)
◆◆◆◆
Motel

Phone: 920/674-4404

4/25-10/4 [CP]	1P: $64-$185	2P: $64-$185	XP: $6 F17
4/1-4/24 [CP]	1P: $55-$130	2P: $55-$130	XP: $6 F17
10/5-3/31 [CP]	1P: $55-$120	2P: $55-$120	XP: $6 F17

Location: On SR 26, 1.2 mi s of jct US 18. 1456 S Ryan Ave 53549. Fax: 920/674-9034. **Facility:** 42 one-bedroom standard units, some with whirlpools. 2 stories, interior corridors. *Bath:* combo or shower only. **Parking:** on-site, winter plug-ins. **Terms:** cancellation fee imposed, pets ($10 extra charge). **Amenities:** *Some:* irons, hair dryers. **Pool(s):** small heated indoor. **Leisure Activities:** whirlpool, limited exercise equipment. **Guest Services:** coin laundry. **Business Services:** meeting rooms, fax (fee). **Cards:** AX, CB, DC, DS, JC, MC, VI.

SOME UNITS

[⑤ᴰ] [❧] [❧] [⚁ᴹ] [⚁] [⚲] [✦] [✦] [ᴰᴬᵀᴬ ᴾᴼᴿᵀ] / [✕] [☐] [☐] [☐] /

JOHNSON CREEK pop. 1,581

──── WHERE TO STAY ────

DAYS INN-JOHNSON CREEK
(AAA) (SAVE)
◆◆◆ ◆◆◆

Small-scale Hotel

Phone: (920)699-8000

All Year   1P: $64-$82   2P: $72-$94   XP: $5   F12
Location: I-94, exit 267 (SR 26), just ne. W4545 Linmar Ln 53038 (PO Box 69). Fax: 920/699-8000. **Facility:** 45 units. 44 one-bedroom standard units, some with whirlpools. 1 one-bedroom suite ($99-$175) with whirlpool. 2 stories (no elevator), interior corridors. *Bath:* combo or shower only. **Parking:** on-site, winter plug-ins. **Terms:** [CP] meal plan available, pets ($5 extra charge, $50 deposit). **Amenities:** hair dryers. *Some:* irons. **Pool(s):** small heated indoor. **Leisure Activities:** whirlpool, exercise room. *Fee:* game room. **Guest Services:** coin laundry. **Business Services:** meeting rooms, fax (fee). **Cards:** AX, DC, DS, MC, VI. **Special Amenities:** free continental breakfast and free local telephone calls.

SOME UNITS

[⑤ᴰ] [❧] [❧] [⚁] [⚲] [✕] [✦] [ᴰᴬᵀᴬ ᴾᴼᴿᵀ] / [✕] [☐] [☐] [☐] /

KAUKAUNA pop. 12,983

──── WHERE TO STAY ────

SETTLE INN
◆◆◆
Small-scale Hotel

Phone: (920)766-0088

6/1-9/30 [ECP]	1P: $65-$80	2P: $70-$85	XP: $5 F18
4/1-5/31 [ECP]	1P: $57-$79	2P: $64-$84	XP: $5 F18
10/1-12/31 [ECP]	1P: $55-$70	2P: $60-$75	XP: $5 F18
1/1-3/31 [ECP]	1P: $50-$70	2P: $55-$75	XP: $5 F18

Location: US 41, exit 148, just e. Located in a commercial area. 1201 Maloney Rd 54130. Fax: 920/766-9428. **Facility:** 46 one-bedroom standard units, some with whirlpools. 2 stories (no elevator), interior corridors. **Parking:** on-site. **Terms:** pets ($3 extra charge). **Pool(s):** heated indoor. **Leisure Activities:** whirlpool. **Guest Services:** coin laundry. **Cards:** AX, DS, MC, VI.

SOME UNITS

[ASK] [⑤ᴰ] [❧] [⚲] [✦] [ᴰᴬᵀᴬ ᴾᴼᴿᵀ] / [✕] [☐] [☐] /

KENOSHA pop. 90,352

—————— **WHERE TO STAY** ——————

BEST WESTERN EXECUTIVE INN

AAA **SAVE**
◆◆◆◆

Phone: (262)857-7699

5/23-8/30 [ECP]	1P: $82-$91	2P: $82-$91
1/1-3/31 [ECP]	1P: $74-$84	2P: $74-$84
8/31-12/31 [ECP]	1P: $72-$82	2P: $72-$82
4/1-5/22 [ECP]	1P: $71-$81	2P: $71-$81

Small-scale Hotel **Location:** I-94, exit 344 (SR 50), just nw. 7220 122nd Ave 53142. Fax: 262/857-2698. **Facility:** 116 units. 112 one-bedroom standard units. 4 one-bedroom suites ($158-$203), some with whirlpools. 4 stories, interior corridors. **Parking:** on-site. **Terms:** package plans. **Amenities:** video games (fee), voice mail, irons, hair dryers. **Pool(s):** small heated indoor. **Leisure Activities:** whirlpool. *Fee:* game room. **Guest Services:** valet laundry. **Business Services:** meeting rooms. **Cards:** AX, CB, DC, DS, MC, VI. **Special Amenities: free continental breakfast and free newspaper.**

SOME UNITS

COUNTRY INN & SUITES BY CARLSON

AAA **SAVE**
◆◆◆◆

Phone: (262)857-3680

6/1-8/31	1P: $80-$120	2P: $87-$127	XP: $7	F18
4/1-5/31 & 9/1-3/31	1P: $75-$110	2P: $82-$117	XP: $7	F18

Small-scale Hotel **Location:** I-94, exit 344 (SR 50), just nw. 7011 122nd Ave 53142. Fax: 262/857-3670. **Facility:** 89 units. 62 one-bedroom standard units, some with whirlpools. 27 one-bedroom suites. 3 stories, interior corridors. *Bath:* combo or shower only. **Parking:** on-site, winter plug-ins. **Terms:** [ECP] meal plan available. **Amenities:** voice mail, irons, hair dryers. **Pool(s):** heated indoor. **Leisure Activities:** whirlpool, exercise room. *Fee:* game room. **Guest Services:** valet and coin laundry. **Business Services:** meeting rooms, fax (fee). **Cards:** AX, CB, DC, DS, MC, VI. **Special Amenities: free continental breakfast and free newspaper.** *(See color ad starting on p 556 & below)*

SOME UNITS

HOLIDAY INN EXPRESS-HARBORSIDE

◆◆◆

Phone: (262)658-3281

6/27-8/24 [ECP]	1P: $129-$145	2P: $139-$155	XP: $10	F19
4/1-6/26 & 8/25-11/30 [ECP]	1P: $119-$135	2P: $129-$145	XP: $10	F19
12/1-3/31 [ECP]	1P: $109-$125	2P: $119-$135	XP: $10	F19

Small-scale Hotel **Location:** Just ne of jct SR 32 and 158; downtown. 5125 6th Ave 53140. Fax: 262/658-3420. **Facility:** 111 one-bedroom standard units. 5 stories, interior corridors. **Parking:** on-site. **Terms:** 2 night minimum stay - weekends 5/26-10/31, cancellation fee imposed, small pets only ($25 fee). **Amenities:** voice mail, irons, hair dryers. **Pool(s):** wading. **Leisure Activities:** whirlpool. *Fee:* game room. **Guest Services:** complimentary evening beverages: Mon-Fri, valet laundry. **Business Services:** conference facilities, administrative services (fee). **Cards:** AX, CB, DC, DS, JC, MC, VI.

SOME UNITS

FEE FEE

QUALITY SUITES

AAA **SAVE**
◆◆◆◆

Phone: (262)857-3450

5/23-8/30 [BP]	1P: $91-$109	2P: $91-$109
4/1-5/22 & 8/31-3/31 [BP]	1P: $81-$90	2P: $81-$90

Small-scale Hotel **Location:** I-94, exit 344 (SR 50), just nw. 7206 122nd Ave 53142. Fax: 262/857-2378. **Facility:** 72 units. 2 one-bedroom standard units. 70 one-bedroom suites ($158-$225), some with whirlpools. 3 stories, interior corridors. *Bath:* combo or shower only. **Parking:** on-site. **Terms:** package plans. **Amenities:** dual phone lines, voice mail, irons, hair dryers. *Fee:* video library, video games. **Pool(s):** small heated indoor. **Leisure Activities:** whirlpool, limited exercise equipment. *Fee:* game room. **Guest Services:** valet and coin laundry. **Business Services:** meeting rooms, business center. **Cards:** AX, CB, DC, DS, MC, VI. **Special Amenities: free local telephone calls and free newspaper.**

SOME UNITS

———— **WHERE TO DINE** ————

BOAT HOUSE PUB & EATERY   **Lunch:** $8-$22   **Dinner:** $8-$22   **Phone:** 262-654-9922
▼▼▼ ▼▼▼   **Location:** Just ne of jct SR 32 and 158; downtown. 4917 7th Ave 53140. **Hours:** 11 am-10 pm, Sat & Sun from 8
American   am. Closed: 4/20, 12/25. **Reservations:** accepted. **Features:** The nautical-themed restaurant affords great
views of Lake Michigan, particularly from the seasonal outdoor seating. Although the menu focus is on
seafood, other offerings include sandwiches, barbecue chicken and ribs, weekly specials and such
homemade soups as fresh clam chowder. Courtesy customer docking is available. Casual dress; cocktails. **Parking:** on-site.
Cards: AX, DC, DS, MC, VI.
[icons]

MANGIA   **Lunch:** $8-$15   **Dinner:** $13-$26   **Phone:** 262-652-4285
▼▼▼ ▼▼▼   **Location:** On SR 32 N, 0.4 mi n of jct SR 50. 5717 Sheridan Rd 53140. **Hours:** 11:30 am-2 & 5-9 pm, Fri-10 pm,
Italian   Sat 5 pm-10 pm, Sun 4 pm-9 pm. Closed major holidays. **Reservations:** suggested. **Features:** Among
outstanding offerings are fresh seafood, wonderful pasta and daily specials. Aromas of rosemary, garlic
and a hint of smoke from the wood-burning oven waft through the air. Representative of delectable
in-house desserts are tiramisu and creme brulee. Dressy casual; cocktails. **Parking:** on-site (fee). **Cards:** AX, DS, MC, VI.
[icon]

TASTE OF WISCONSIN   **Lunch:** $6-$12   **Dinner:** $6-$12   **Phone:** 262-857-9110
▼▼▼ ▼▼   **Location:** I-94, exit 344 (SR 50), 0.3 mi w. 7515 125th Ave 53142. **Hours:** 9 am-9 pm. Closed: 12/25; also 12/24
American   for dinner. **Reservations:** accepted. **Features:** Wisconsin's German heritage is reflected in the restaurant's
food. Entrees made from fresh ingredients include bratwurst, sausage and split roast chicken. The
on-premises bakery provides bread and tempting desserts. Not surprisingly, cheese and a selection of local
microbrews are popular, too. Casual dress; cocktails. **Parking:** on-site. **Cards:** AX, DS, MC, VI.
[icons]

KEWAUNEE pop. 2,806

———— **WHERE TO STAY** ————

THE HISTORIC KARSTEN INN   **Phone:** (920)388-3800

5/24-10/31	1P: $79-$149	2P: $79-$149	XP: $10	F12
11/1-3/31	1P: $69-$99	2P: $69-$99	XP: $10	F12
4/1-5/23	1P: $59-$99	2P: $59-$99	XP: $10	F12

Small-scale Hotel   **Location:** Center. 122 Ellis St 54216. Fax: 920/388-3808. **Facility:** 23 one-bedroom standard units, some with
whirlpools. 3 stories (no elevator), interior corridors. *Bath:* combo or tub only. **Parking:** on-site. **Terms:** 3 day cancellation notice,
[ECP] & [MAP] meal plans available, package plans, small pets only ($25 fee). **Amenities:** voice mail, irons, hair dryers. **Business Services:** meeting rooms. **Cards:** AX, DC, DS, MC, VI.
SOME UNITS
[icons] (ASK) (SD) [icons]

KIMBERLY pop. 6,146

———— **WHERE TO STAY** ————

AMERIHOST INN-KIMBERLY   **Phone:** 920-788-4400
(AAA) (SAVE)   All Year [ECP]   1P: $59-$175   2P: $69-$200   XP: $10   F17
▼▼ ▼▼▼ ▼▼   **Location:** US 41, exit 145 (SR 441), 2.7 mi s to CR CE, then 0.4 mi e. Located in a commercial area. 761 Truman St
Small-scale Hotel   54136. Fax: 920/788-4466. **Facility:** 63 one-bedroom standard units, some with whirlpools. 2 stories (no elevator), interior corridors. *Bath:* combo or shower only. **Parking:** on-site. **Amenities:** voice mail, safes (fee),
irons, hair dryers. **Pool(s):** heated indoor. **Leisure Activities:** sauna, whirlpool, exercise room. **Guest Services:** valet laundry. **Business Services:** meeting rooms. **Cards:** AX, DC, DS, MC, VI. **Special Amenities:**
free continental breakfast and free local telephone calls.
SOME UNITS
[icons]

HILTON GARDEN INN   **Phone:** (920)730-1900
(AAA) (SAVE)   11/1-3/31   1P: $79-$129   2P: $79-$129   XP: $10   F18
     4/1-10/31   1P: $79-$119   2P: $79-$119   XP: $10   F18
▼▼ ▼▼▼ ▼▼   **Location:** US 41, exit 145 (SR 441), 2.7 mi s to CR CE, then 0.4 mi e. Located in a commercial area. 720 Eisenhower
Small-scale Hotel   Dr 54136. Fax: 920/734-7565. **Facility:** 125 one-bedroom standard units, some with whirlpools. 5 stories, interior corridors. *Bath:* combo or shower only. **Parking:** on-site. **Amenities:** video games, high-speed Internet,
dual phone lines, voice mail, irons, hair dryers. **Dining:** 6:30 am-10 & 5-9 pm, Sat & Sun 7-11 am, cocktails.
Pool(s): heated indoor. **Leisure Activities:** whirlpool, exercise room. **Guest Services:** valet and coin laundry. **Business Services:** meeting rooms, business center. **Cards:** AX, CB, DC, DS, MC, VI. **Special Amenities: free continental breakfast.**
SOME UNITS
[icons]

KOHLER pop. 1,926

──── WHERE TO STAY ────

THE AMERICAN CLUB
Phone: (920)457-8000

AAA SAVE

5/1-10/31	1P: $239-$269	2P: $269-$299	XP: $15 F16
4/1-4/30 & 11/1-3/31	1P: $139-$179	2P: $169-$209	XP: $15 F16

Classic Historic Resort
Large-Scale Hotel

Location: I-43, exit 126, 0.5 mi w on SR 23, 1 mi s on CR Y and Highland Dr. Highland Dr 53044. Fax: 920/457-0299. **Facility:** Built in 1918 to house workers for the Kohler Company, this grand resort offers extensive grounds and year-round recreational activities. 237 units. 216 one-bedroom standard units with whirlpools. 21 one-bedroom suites ($299-$1015) with whirlpools. 3 stories, interior corridors. **Parking:** on-site and valet. **Terms:** check-in 4 pm, 7 day cancellation notice-fee imposed, package plans, no pets allowed (kennels available). **Amenities:** CD players, dual phone lines, voice mail, safes, honor bars, irons, hair dryers. *Fee:* video games, high-speed Internet. **Dining:** 4 restaurants, 6:30 am-11 pm, cocktails, also, The Immigrant Restaurant & Winery, The Wisconsin Room, Blackwolf Run, see separate listing. **Pool(s):** 2 heated indoor, small heated indoor. **Leisure Activities:** saunas, whirlpools, steamrooms, rental canoes, rental paddleboats, fishing, ice skating, tobogganing, recreation programs, carriage rides, hiking trails, jogging, spa. *Fee:* charter fishing, golf-72 holes, 16 tennis courts (8 indoor, 16 lighted), cross country skiing, snowmobiling, bicycles, horseback riding. **Guest Services:** gift shop, valet laundry, airport transportation (fee)-Sheboygan County Municipal Airport, area transportation-within village. **Business Services:** conference facilities, business center. **Cards:** AX, CB, DC, DS, MC, VI. **Special Amenities: free newspaper and free room upgrade (subject to availability with advanced reservations).** *(See color ad p 553)*

SOME UNITS

[icons] / [icons] FEE

INN ON WOODLAKE
Phone: (920)452-7800

AAA SAVE

5/1-10/31	1P: $152-$167	2P: $172-$187	
11/1-3/31	1P: $92-$102	2P: $112-$122	
4/1-4/30	1P: $89-$99	2P: $109-$119	XP: $10 F16

Small-scale Hotel

Location: I-43, exit 126, 0.5 mi w on SR 23, 0.5 mi s on CR Y and Highland Dr; in Woodlake Shopping Center. 705 Woodlake Rd 53044. Fax: 920/452-6288. **Facility:** 121 one-bedroom standard units, some with whirlpools. 3 stories, interior corridors. *Bath:* combo or shower only. **Parking:** on-site. **Terms:** check-in 4 pm, 7 day cancellation notice-fee imposed, [ECP] meal plan available, package plans, no pets allowed (kennels available). **Amenities:** video games (fee), dual phone lines, voice mail, irons, hair dryers. **Dining:** 8 restaurants, 6 am-11 pm. **Pool(s):** 2 heated indoor. **Leisure Activities:** saunas, whirlpools, rental boats, rental canoes, rental paddleboats, fishing, ice skating, tobogganing, recreation programs, hiking trails, jogging, spa. *Fee:* charter fishing, golf-72 holes, 16 tennis courts (8 indoor, 16 lighted), cross country skiing, snowmobiling, bicycles, horseback riding. **Guest Services:** valet and coin laundry, area transportation-health club. **Business Services:** meeting rooms, fax (fee). **Cards:** AX, CB, DC, DS, MC, VI. **Special Amenities: free continental breakfast and free newspaper.** *(See color ad p 561)*

SOME UNITS

[icons] FEE / [icons] FEE /

──── WHERE TO DINE ────

BLACKWOLF RUN
Lunch: $7-$15 **Dinner:** $17-$30 **Phone:** 920/457-4446

American

Location: I-43, exit 126, 0.5 mi w on SR 23, 1 mi s on CR Y and Highland Dr; in Blackwolf Run Golf Course Club House; at The American Club. 1111 W Riverside Dr 53044. **Hours:** 11 am-10 pm; from 6 am 5/1-10/31; 11 am-3 & 6-10 pm 11/1-4/30. Closed: 12/25; also Sun, Mon 11/1-4/30. **Reservations:** suggested. **Features:** In the clubhouse of the Blackwolf Run PGA Championship Golf Course, the impressive Canadian log cabin structure overlooks the Sheboygan River and golf course. The seasonally changing menu features hearty portions of foods from the heartland. Specialties include Angus beef, wild game, fish, seafood and free-range chicken. Casual dress; cocktails. **Parking:** on-site. **Cards:** AX, DC, DS, MC, VI.

[icons]

CUCINA
Lunch: $7-$15 **Dinner:** $14-$20 **Phone:** 920/452-3888

Italian

Location: I-43, exit 126, 0.5 mi w on SR 23, 0.5 mi s on CR Y and Highland Dr; in Woodlake Shopping Center. 725 E Woodlake Rd 53044. **Hours:** 11 am-9 pm, Fri & Sat-10 pm. Closed: 1/1, 11/27, 12/25. **Reservations:** suggested. **Features:** Delicious pasta, veal, seafood and gourmet pizza are among the traditional dishes available at this bistro. Fresh ingredients, ample use of garlic, eye-catching dessert presentations and professional service complete the dining experience. Window tables and the seasonal terrace overlook Wood Lake. Casual dress; cocktails. **Parking:** on-site. **Cards:** AX, DC, DS, MC, VI.

[icons]

THE IMMIGRANT RESTAURANT & WINERY
Dinner: $25-$40 **Phone:** 920/457-8888

Regional American

Location: I-43, exit 126, 0.5 mi w on SR 23, 1 mi s on CR Y and Highland Dr; in The American Club. Highland Dr 53044. **Hours:** 6 pm-10 pm. Closed: Sun & Mon 11/1-4/30. **Reservations:** suggested. **Features:** What once housed a bowling alley and laundry for immigrant workers now celebrates the heritage of people who helped grow Kohler Co. into a multinational corporation. The menu is contemporary, and adventurous offerings incorporate international influences. Service is formal and detailed while remaining refreshingly unpretentious. For a special treat, consider the seven-course degustation menu paired with specially selected wines. Semi-formal attire; cocktails. **Parking:** on-site and valet. **Cards:** AX, CB, DC, DS, JC, MC, VI.

[icons]

THE WISCONSIN ROOM
Dinner: $19-$30 **Phone:** 920/457-8888

Regional American

Location: I-43, exit 126, 0.5 mi w on SR 23, 1 mi s on CR Y and Highland Dr; in The American Club. Highland Dr 53044. **Hours:** 6:30 am-11 & 6-9 pm, Sat 6:30 am-11:30 & 6-10 pm, Sun 10 am-2 & 6-9 pm. **Reservations:** suggested. **Features:** The main dining room features a menu of Wisconsin and regional specialties that incorporate products from the upper Midwest. The wine list is all American. Dressy casual; cocktails. **Parking:** on-site and valet. **Cards:** AX, CB, DC, DS, JC, MC, VI.

[icons]

LA CROSSE pop. 51,818

--- WHERE TO STAY ---

BEST WESTERN-MIDWAY HOTEL
Phone: (608)781-7000

All Year 1P: $55-$75 2P: $65-$129 XP: $10 F18

Location: I-90, exit 3, 1 mi s on US 53. 1835 Rose St 54603. Fax: 608/781-3195. **Facility:** 121 one-bedroom standard units, some with whirlpools. 2 stories (no elevator), interior corridors. **Parking:** on-site, winter plug-ins. **Terms:** package plans - seasonal. **Amenities:** video library (fee), dual phone lines, voice mail, irons, hair dryers. **Dining:** 6:30 am-10 pm, Sat & Sun from 7 am, cocktails, entertainment. **Pool(s):** heated indoor. **Leisure Activities:** sauna, whirlpool, boat dock, miniature golf, domed recreation area, exercise room, volleyball. **Guest Services:** valet laundry, area transportation-Amtrak station. **Business Services:** meeting rooms. **Cards:** AX, CB, DC, DS, JC, MC, VI. *(See color ad below)*

SOME UNITS

BROOKSTONE INN
Phone: (608)781-1400

4/1-10/31 [CP] 1P: $49-$80 2P: $55-$85
11/1-3/31 [CP] 1P: $44-$75 2P: $49-$80

Location: I-90, exit 3, 1 mi s on US 53. 1830 Rose St 54603. Fax: 608/781-3948. **Facility:** 84 units. 82 one-bedroom standard units, some with whirlpools. 2 one-bedroom suites ($80-$140). 3 stories, interior corridors. **Parking:** on-site. **Terms:** cancellation fee imposed. **Amenities:** irons, hair dryers. **Leisure Activities:** whirlpool, limited exercise equipment. **Fee:** game room. **Guest Services:** valet laundry. **Business Services:** meeting rooms, fax (fee). **Cards:** AX, CB, DC, DS, MC, VI. **Special Amenities:** free continental breakfast and free local telephone calls. *(See color ad below)*

SOME UNITS

CHATEAU LA CROSSE
Phone: 608-796-1090

AAA SAVE

Historic Country Inn

All Year [BP]   1P: $100-$175   2P: $125-$200   XP: $50
Location: On SR 16 at jct with US 53; downtown; at east end of Mississippi River Bridge. 410 Cass St 54601. Fax: 608/796-0700. **Facility:** This 1854 stone house, known as the Mons Anderson House, features decoratively painted ceilings, ornate wood floors and several antique fireplaces. Smoke free premises. 6 units. 5 one-bedroom standard units, some with whirlpools. 1 two-bedroom suite ($100-$300) with kitchen. 4 stories (no elevator), interior/exterior corridors. *Bath:* combo or shower only. **Parking:** on-site. **Terms:** check-in 4 pm, 2 night minimum stay - 9/25-10/20, age restrictions may apply, 7 day cancellation notice-fee imposed, no pets allowed (owner's pet on premises). **Amenities:** video library, hair dryers. **Dining:** dinner by reservation only. **Guest Services:** gift shop, complimentary laundry, area transportation-train and bus depots. **Business Services:** fax. **Cards:** AX, DC, DS, MC, VI. **Special Amenities: free local telephone calls and preferred room (subject to availability with advanced reservations).**

DAYS INN HOTEL & CONFERENCE CENTER
Phone: (608)783-1000

AAA SAVE

Small-scale Hotel

5/1-10/31   1P: $55-$89   2P: $55-$89   XP: $5   F17
4/1-4/30 & 11/1-3/31 1P: $45-$75   2P: $45-$75   XP: $5   F17
Location: I-90, exit 2, just sw; on French Island. 101 Sky Harbour Dr 54603. Fax: 608/783-2948. **Facility:** 148 units. 144 one-bedroom standard units. 4 one-bedroom suites ($99-$169) with whirlpools. 2 stories (no elevator), interior corridors. **Parking:** on-site. **Terms:** [AP] meal plan available, pets ($10 extra charge). **Amenities:** voice mail, hair dryers. *Some:* irons. **Dining:** 6:30 am-1 & 5-9 pm, Sat-10 pm, Sun 6:30 am-9 pm, cocktails. **Pool(s):** heated indoor. **Leisure Activities:** whirlpool, limited exercise equipment. **Guest Services:** valet laundry. **Business Services:** meeting rooms, fax (fee). **Cards:** AX, DC, DS, MC, VI. **Special Amenities: free local telephone calls and free newspaper.**

EXEL INN OF LA CROSSE
Phone: (608)781-0400

AAA SAVE

Small-scale Hotel

6/1-10/31 [CP]   1P: $39-$51   2P: $45-$65   XP: $6   F18
4/1-5/31 & 11/1-3/31 [CP] 1P: $37-$49 2P: $43-$55   XP: $6   F18
Location: I-90, exit 3, 0.8 mi s on US 53. 2150 Rose St 54603. Fax: 608/781-1216. **Facility:** 101 one-bedroom standard units, some with whirlpools. 2 stories (no elevator), interior corridors. **Parking:** on-site. **Terms:** small pets only (in smoking units). **Amenities:** irons. **Leisure Activities:** limited exercise equipment. **Guest Services:** coin laundry. **Business Services:** fax (fee). **Cards:** AX, CB, DC, DS, MC, VI. **Special Amenities: early check-in/late check-out and free continental breakfast.** *(See color ad p 465)*

GUEST HOUSE MOTEL
Phone: (608)784-8840

AAA SAVE

Small-scale Hotel

All Year   1P: $48-$55   2P: $55-$65   XP: $7   F12
Location: 0.5 mi s on US 14, 61 and SR 33. 810 S 4th St 54601. Fax: 608/782-5598. **Facility:** 39 one-bedroom standard units. 2 stories (no elevator), interior corridors. *Bath:* combo or shower only. **Parking:** on-site, winter plug-ins. **Terms:** small pets only ($10 deposit). **Amenities:** voice mail. **Dining:** 7-11 am, Sun 7:30-11:30 am. **Pool(s):** small heated outdoor. **Business Services:** fax (fee). **Cards:** AX, DC, DS, MC, VI.

HAMPTON INN
Phone: (608)781-5100

SAVE

Small-scale Hotel

6/1-10/31 [ECP]   1P: $69-$119   2P: $69-$129
4/1-5/31 [ECP]   1P: $59-$79   2P: $69-$89
11/1-3/31 [ECP]   1P: $49-$79   2P: $59-$89
Location: I-90, exit 3, 0.9 mi s on US 53. 2110 Rose St 54603. Fax: 608/781-3574. **Facility:** 101 one-bedroom standard units. 2 stories (no elevator), interior corridors. **Parking:** on-site. **Terms:** 7 day cancellation notice. **Amenities:** video games (fee), high-speed Internet, voice mail, irons, hair dryers. **Pool(s):** small heated indoor. **Leisure Activities:** whirlpool, limited exercise equipment. **Guest Services:** valet laundry. **Business Services:** meeting rooms, fax (fee). **Cards:** AX, CB, DC, DS, MC, VI.

HOLIDAY INN HOTEL & SUITES

Phone: (608)784-4444

AAA SAVE

6/1-8/31	1P: $119-$129	2P: $119-$129	XP: $10	F17
4/1-5/31 & 9/1-3/31	1P: $109-$119	2P: $109-$119	XP: $10	F17

Location: Downtown. 200 Pearl St 54601. Fax: 608/784-4480. **Facility:** 114 one-bedroom standard units, some with whirlpools. 5 stories, interior corridors. *Bath:* combo or shower only. **Parking:** on-site. **Terms:** check-in 4 pm. **Amenities:** voice mail, irons, hair dryers. *Fee:* video games, high-speed Internet. *Some:* dual phone lines. **Dining:** 6:30 am-10 pm, Sat & Sun from 7 am, cocktails. **Pool(s):** small heated indoor. **Leisure Activities:** whirlpool. **Guest Services:** valet and coin laundry. **Business Services:** meeting rooms, fax (fee). **Cards:** AX, CB, DC, DS, JC, MC, VI. **Special Amenities:** free local telephone calls and free newspaper. *(See color ad p 514)*

Small-scale Hotel

SOME UNITS

THE RADISSON HOTEL LA CROSSE

Phone: (608)784-6680

AAA SAVE

All Year | 1P: $129-$169 | 2P: $139-$179

Location: Just w of US 53; downtown. 200 Harborview Plaza 54601. Fax: 608/784-6694. **Facility:** 169 one-bedroom standard units, some with whirlpools. 8 stories, interior corridors. **Parking:** on-site. **Terms:** small pets only. **Amenities:** dual phone lines, voice mail, irons, hair dryers. **Dining:** 2 restaurants, 6:30 am-11 pm, Fri & Sat from 7 am, cocktails. **Pool(s):** heated indoor. **Leisure Activities:** whirlpool, exercise room. *Fee:* game room. **Guest Services:** gift shop, valet laundry. **Business Services:** conference facilities. **Cards:** AX, CB, DC, DS, JC, MC, VI. **Special Amenities:** free newspaper. *(See color ad p 563 & p 562)*

Large-scale Hotel

SOME UNITS
FEE

SUPER 8 OF LA CROSSE

Phone: (608)781-8880

All Year | 1P: $69-$180 | 2P: $84-$180

Location: I-90, exit 3, 1.2 mi s on US 53. 1625 Rose St 54603. Fax: 608/781-4366. **Facility:** 82 one-bedroom standard units, some with whirlpools. 2 stories (no elevator), interior corridors. **Parking:** on-site. **Amenities:** hair dryers. **Pool(s):** heated indoor. **Leisure Activities:** whirlpool, exercise room. **Guest Services:** coin laundry. **Business Services:** fax. **Cards:** AX, CB, DC, DS, MC, VI.

Small-scale Hotel

SOME UNITS

--------- WHERE TO DINE ---------

DOC POWELL'S

| | Lunch: $6-$16 | Dinner: $6-$16 | **Phone:** 608/785-7026 |

Location: Just w of US 53; downtown. 200 Main St 54601. **Hours:** 11 am-10 pm. Closed: 7/4, 12/25; also Sun. **Reservations:** accepted. **Features:** Named after a local historic figure, the restaurant is known for its microbrews, diverse menu and homemade bread pudding. Creativity is exhibited in the recipes and food presentations. Casual dress; cocktails. **Parking:** street. **Cards:** AX, DC, DS, MC, VI.

American

EDWARDO'S PIZZA WAGON

| | Dinner: $8-$14 | **Phone:** 608/783-8282 |

Location: I-90, exit 3, 0.5 mi s. 1930 Rose St 54601. **Hours:** 4 pm-11 pm. Closed major holidays. **Reservations:** accepted. **Features:** Family-owned and operated since 1955, the restaurant prepares pizzas in a wood-fired oven. Natural ingredients, custom dough and fresh vegetables make the pizza a standout. An extensive beer selection is offered. Casual dress; cocktails. **Cards:** AX, MC, VI.

American

THE FREIGHT HOUSE RESTAURANT Historic

| | Dinner: $9-$30 | **Phone:** 608/784-6211 |

AAA

Location: Just w of US 53; downtown. 107 Vine 54601. **Hours:** 5:30 pm-10 pm, Fri & Sat 5 pm-10:30 pm, Sun 5 pm-9:30 pm. Closed: 4/20, 11/27, 12/24, 12/25. **Reservations:** suggested. **Features:** The former railroad freight house, built in the late 1800s, features timbers, three fireplaces and historic pictures. Menu offerings include teriyaki preparations of chicken and steak. Prime rib and Alaskan crab legs are complemented by many wines. Casual dress; cocktails. **Parking:** on-site. **Cards:** AX, DC, DS, MC, VI.

American

MR D'S

| | Lunch: $5-$7 | Dinner: $5-$7 | **Phone:** 608/784-6737 |

Location: 0.4 mi e of US 53; at jct West Ave and State St; downtown. 1146 State St 54601. **Hours:** 6 am-3 pm, Fri & Sat-7:30 pm. Closed major holidays. **Features:** A local fixture since 1967, the neighborhood cafe delivers lighter fare: creative sandwiches, hearty soup and mouthwatering baked goods, especially its signature fritters. Friendly servers in street clothes show menu familiarity and good follow-up. Casual dress; wine only. **Parking:** on-site. **Cards:** AX, DS, MC, VI.

American

PICASSO'S CAFE

| | Lunch: $6-$9 | Dinner: $6-$17 | **Phone:** 608/784-4485 |

Location: I-90, exit 3, 3.2 mi s on US 53; in Sampson Gallery. 600 N Third St 54601. **Hours:** 7 am-9 pm, Fri-10 pm, Sat 8 am-10 pm, Sun 8 am-3 pm. Closed: 7/4, 11/27, 12/25. **Reservations:** accepted. **Features:** Voodoo fettuccine, blackened chicken pita, seafood sparkler and the very veggie sandwich are examples of unusual selections on the restaurant's diverse menu. Lots of windows and fun artwork give this cafe a California feel. Desserts are homemade. Casual dress; cocktails. **Parking:** on-site. **Cards:** AX, DS, MC, VI.

American

PIGGY'S RESTAURANT

| | Dinner: $9-$28 | **Phone:** 608/784-4877 |

Location: Just w of US 53; downtown. 328 S Front St 54601. **Hours:** 5 pm-10 pm, Sun 4 pm-9 pm. Closed: 11/27, 12/25; also 5/27, 12/24 for dinner. **Reservations:** suggested. **Features:** Hickory-smoked, American-cut pork chops, baby back ribs, prime steak and seafood are specialties at this restaurant on the Mississippi River. The comprehensive wine list is lengthier than the menu. The antique wood bar is a focal point of the dining room. Casual dress; cocktails. **Parking:** on-site. **Cards:** AX, CB, DC, DS, MC, VI.

American

LADYSMITH pop. 3,932

─────── **WHERE TO STAY** ───────

AMERICINN MOTEL　　　　　　　　　　　　　　　　　　　　　**Phone:** 715/532-6650
　　　　　　　　　　　Property failed to provide current rates
▽▽▽▽　**Location:** On SR 27, 0.5 mi s of US 8. 800 W College Ave 54848. Fax: 715/532-6987. **Facility:** 38 one-bedroom
Small-scale Hotel　standard units. 2 stories, interior corridors. *Bath:* combo or shower only. **Parking:** on-site, winter plug-ins.
　　　　　　　　Pool(s): small heated indoor. **Leisure Activities:** sauna, whirlpool. **Business Services:** meeting rooms, fax.
Cards: AX, DC, DS, MC, VI.

SOME UNITS
🅗 🏊 🎥 🖭 🖦 / 🗙 📼 🔌 🖼 /

─────── *The following lodging was either not evaluated or did not* ───────
meet AAA rating requirements but is listed for your information only.

AMERICINN LODGE AND SUITES　　　　　　　　　　　　　　**Phone:** 715/532-7811
[fyi]　　　　　　Property failed to provide current rates
　　　　Too new to rate. **Location:** On Hwy 27, 0.5 mi s. 700 W 9th St S 54848. Fax: 715/532-7397. **Amenities:** 42 units,
Motel　coffeemakers, microwaves, refrigerators, pool. **Cards:** AX, CB, DC, DS, MC, VI.

LAKE GENEVA pop. 7,148

─────── **WHERE TO STAY** ───────

BELLA VISTA SUITES HOTEL　　　　　　　　　　　　　　　**Phone:** 262/248-2100
▽▽▽▽　6/13-9/1 [ECP]　　　　1P: $249-$599
　　　　9/2-3/31 [ECP]　　　　1P: $128-$569
Condominium　4/1-6/12 [ECP]　　　1P: $119-$559
Location: Just s of SR 50. Located across from Lake Geneva. 335 Wrigley Dr 53147. Fax: 262/248-2144.
Facility: Smoke free premises. 39 units. 33 one- and 6 two-bedroom suites with whirlpools, some with kitchens. 4 stories, interior corridors. *Bath:* combo or shower only. **Parking:** on-site. **Terms:** 3 day cancellation notice-fee imposed. **Amenities:** video library, dual phone lines, voice mail, irons, hair dryers. *Some:* DVD players, CD players. **Pool(s):** heated indoor. **Leisure Activities:** whirlpool, exercise room. *Fee:* boat dock, massage. **Business Services:** meeting rooms.

🍽 🏋M 🅗 🏊 🗙 🗙 📼 🔌 🖼 🖦

BUDGET HOST DIPLOMAT MOTEL　　　　　　　　　　　　**Phone:** (262)248-1809
(AAA) [SAVE]　5/30-9/14　　　1P: $68-$81　　2P: $78-$91　　XP: $10　　F12
　　　　　4/1-5/29　　　1P: $48-$71　　2P: $58-$81　　XP: $10　　F12
▽▽▽ ▽▽▽　9/15-3/31　　　1P: $48-$61　　2P: $58-$71　　XP: $10　　F12
Motel　**Location:** On CR H, 1 mi s of jct SR 50. 1060 Wells St 53147. Fax: 262/248-7215. **Facility:** 23 one-bedroom standard units. 2 stories, exterior corridors. **Parking:** on-site, winter plug-ins. **Terms:** 7 day cancellation notice.
　　　　Pool(s): heated outdoor. **Cards:** AX, DS, MC, VI. **Special Amenities:** early check-in/late check-out and
free local telephone calls. *(See color ad p 464)*

SOME UNITS
🆂🅳 🏊 🎥 🔌 / 🗙 🖼 /

THE COVE OF LAKE GENEVA
▼▼▼▼
Condominium

Phone: 262/249-9460
Property failed to provide current rates
Location: Just s of SR 50. Located across from Lake Geneva. 111 Center St 53147. Fax: 262/249-1532. **Facility:** 211 units. 149 one-bedroom standard units with efficiencies and whirlpools. 59 one- and 3 two-bedroom suites with kitchens and whirlpools. 4 stories, interior corridors. *Bath:* combo or shower only. **Parking:** on-site.
Amenities: video library (fee), voice mail, irons, hair dryers. *Some:* CD players. **Pool(s):** 2 heated outdoor, heated indoor.
Leisure Activities: sauna, whirlpools, lighted tennis court, exercise room, basketball. *Fee:* game room. **Guest Services:** gift shop, coin laundry, area transportation (fee). **Business Services:** conference facilities. **Cards:** AX, DC, DS, MC, VI.

SOME UNITS

GENERAL BOYD'S BED & BREAKFAST
ⒶⒶⒶ SAVE
▼▼▼▼
Bed & Breakfast

Phone: (262)248-3543
All Year [BP]   1P: $95-$140   2P: $95-$140   XP: $25
Location: Jct CR BB and SR 120, 2.7 mi s of downtown. W2915 County Trunk BB 53147. Fax: 262/248-3362.
Facility: An 1843 Colonial Revival farmhouse on five acres of landscaped grounds, this spacious B&B is accented with a large collection of antiques. Smoke free premises. 4 one-bedroom standard units. 2 stories, interior corridors. *Bath:* combo or shower only. **Parking:** on-site. **Terms:** age restrictions may apply, 10 day cancellation notice-fee imposed. **Amenities:** hair dryers. *Some:* CD players. **Leisure Activities:** croquet, horseshoes. **Business Services:** fax. **Cards:** AX, DS, MC, VI.

SOME UNITS

GRAND GENEVA RESORT & SPA
ⒶⒶⒶ SAVE
▼▼▼▼ ▼▼▼▼
Resort
Large-scale Hotel

Phone: (262)248-8811
5/18-10/11   1P: $269-$339   2P: $269-$339   XP: $10   F18
4/1-5/17 & 10/12-3/31   1P: $159-$199   2P: $159-$199   XP: $10   F18
Location: On SR 50, just e of jct US 12. Located in a quiet area. 7036 Grand Geneva Way 53147 (PO Box 130).
Fax: 262/249-4763. **Facility:** This sprawling spa resort features Frank Lloyd Wright-inspired architecture and has multiple golf courses on its 1,300 acres of rolling countryside. 355 units. 352 one-bedroom standard units, some with whirlpools. 3 one-bedroom suites with whirlpools. 2 stories, interior corridors. **Parking:** on-site and valet. **Terms:** check-in 4 pm, 3 day cancellation notice-fee imposed. **Amenities:** video games (fee), voice mail, irons, hair dryers. *Some:* CD players. **Dining:** 3 restaurants, 6:30 am-11 pm, Fri & Sat-midnight, cocktails, also, Ristorante Brissago, see separate listing, entertainment. **Pool(s):** heated outdoor, 2 heated indoor, wading. **Leisure Activities:** saunas, whirlpools, steamrooms, rental paddleboats, access to nearby Moose Mountain indoor/outdoor water park, recreation programs, 3845 ft lighted airport runway, hiking trails, playground, spa, volleyball. *Fee:* golf-36 holes, 6 tennis courts (2 indoor, 6 lighted), downhill & cross country skiing, ice skating, bicycles, horseback riding. **Guest Services:** gift shop, valet laundry, area transportation within 5 mi. *Fee:* beauty salon. **Business Services:** conference facilities, business center. **Cards:** AX, CB, DC, DS, MC, VI. **Special Amenities:** early check-in/late check-out and free newspaper.
(See color ad p 516)

SOME UNITS

━━━━━ **WHERE TO DINE** ━━━━━

RISTORANTE BRISSAGO
▼▼▼▼
Northern
Italian

Dinner: $10-$30   Phone: 262/248-8811
Location: On SR 50, just e of jct US 12; in Grand Geneva Resort & Spa. 7036 Grand Geneva Way 53147. **Hours:** 5 pm-10 pm. Closed: Mon. **Reservations:** suggested. **Features:** Careful attention is paid to the preparation of traditional pastas, wood-roasted pizza and veal dishes in this dining room overlooking the Wisconsin countryside. Service is professional and attentive. The imported Milano sorbets are wonderful. Dressy casual; cocktails. **Parking:** on-site and valet. **Cards:** AX, DC, DS, MC, VI. *(See color ad p 516)*

SCUTTLEBUTTS
▼▼▼▼
American

Lunch: $6-$13   Dinner: $7-$16   Phone: 262/248-1111
Location: Just s of SR 50; lakeside. 831 Wrigley 53147. **Hours:** 7 am-9 pm, Fri & Sat-10 pm; hours may vary in winter. **Features:** The casual restaurant features a selection of flavorful gourmet burgers, sandwiches and salads, as well as a handful of Swedish specialties. Large windows in the dining room look out over Lake Geneva. Key lime pie and specialty ice cream desserts are wonderful. Casual dress; cocktails. **Parking:** street. **Cards:** MC, VI.

LAKE MILLS pop. 4,843

━━━━━ **WHERE TO DINE** ━━━━━

PINE KNOLL SUPPER CLUB
▼▼▼
American

Lunch: $4-$8   Dinner: $10-$20   Phone: 920/648-2303
Location: I-94, exit 259, 3 mi n. N7755 Hwy 89 53551. **Hours:** 4:30 pm-9 pm, Fri 11 am-2 & 4:30-9:30 pm, Sun 10 am-8 pm. Closed: 1/1, 7/4, 12/24, 12/25; also Mon. **Reservations:** suggested. **Features:** Supper club fare highlights such selections as breaded or broiled seafood, hand-cut steaks and succulent ribs. Rolling farmland characterizes the rural setting. Dining rooms blend contemporary and Early American influences. Sunday brunch is popular. Casual dress; cocktails. **Parking:** on-site. **Cards:** CB, DC, DS, MC, VI.

LANCASTER pop. 4,070

━━━━━ **WHERE TO STAY** ━━━━━

BEST WESTERN WELCOME INN
SAVE
▼▼▼
Small-scale Hotel

Phone: (608)723-4162
4/1-10/31 [CP]   1P: $58-$68   2P: $66-$76   XP: $7   F12
11/1-3/31 [CP]   1P: $56-$68   2P: $64-$76   XP: $7   F12
Location: Just w of downtown square. 420 W Maple St 53813. Fax: 608/723-4843. **Facility:** 22 one-bedroom standard units. 2 stories (no elevator), interior corridors. **Parking:** on-site. **Amenities:** irons, hair dryers. **Guest Services:** coin laundry. **Cards:** AX, CB, DC, DS, MC, VI.

SOME UNITS

MAPLE HARRIS GUEST HOUSE
▼▼▼▼
Bed & Breakfast

Phone: 608/723-4717
All Year [BP]   1P: $59   2P: $79   XP: $20   F6
Location: Just w of downtown square. Located in a residential area. 445 W Maple St 53813. **Facility:** Smoke free premises. 6 one-bedroom standard units. 2 stories (no elevator), interior/exterior corridors. *Bath:* some shared or private, combo or shower only. **Parking:** street. **Terms:** check-in 4 pm, 7 day cancellation notice. **Amenities:** *Some:* irons. **Guest Services:** TV in common area. **Cards:** DS, MC, VI.

SOME UNITS

LAND O'LAKES

──── WHERE TO STAY ────

SUNRISE LODGE
    Phone: (715)547-3684

▼▼▼▼ All Year   1P: $68-$94   2P: $72-$188   XP: $10   D17

Cottage   **Location:** 2 mi s on US 45, 2.8 mi e on CR E, then 1 mi n. Located in a rural wooded area. 5894 W Shore Dr 54540. Fax: 715/547-6110. **Facility:** 24 units. 5 vacation homes and 19 cottages. 1-2 stories (no elevator), exterior corridors. *Bath:* combo or shower only. **Parking:** on-site, winter plug-ins. **Terms:** 21 day cancellation notice-fee imposed, weekly rates available, [AP], [BP] & [MAP] meal plans available, package plans. **Amenities:** video library, hair dryers. **Leisure Activities:** rental boats, rental canoes, boat dock, fishing, miniature golf, tennis court, cross country skiing, snowmobiling, recreation programs in season, bicycles, playground, basketball, horseshoes, shuffleboard, volleyball. *Fee:* game room. **Guest Services:** gift shop. **Business Services:** meeting rooms. **Cards:** DS, MC, VI.

SOME UNITS

(ASK) ✈ 🐾 🍽 ✕ VCR 🕿 🖪 🖳 🖵 / 🅇 /

LA POINTE

──── WHERE TO STAY ────

MADELINE ISLAND MOTEL
    Phone: 715/747-3000

(AAA) (SAVE)   7/2-9/1 [ECP]   1P: $90   2P: $95   XP: $10   F18

▼▼   4/1-7/1 & 9/2-12/1 [ECP]   1P: $65-$75   2P: $70-$80   XP: $10   F18

Motel   **Location:** Just e of ferry boat landing. 261 Colonel Woods Ave 54850 (PO Box 51). Fax: 715/747-3003. **Facility:** 11 one-bedroom standard units. 2 stories, exterior corridors. *Bath:* combo or shower only. **Parking:** on-site. **Terms:** open 4/1-12/1, 3 day cancellation notice-fee imposed. **Leisure Activities:** rental canoes, badminton, board games, hiking trails, horseshoes, volleyball. *Fee:* miniature golf, bicycles. **Guest Services:** airport transportation-La Pointe Airport, area transportation-marina. **Cards:** DS, MC, VI.

SOME UNITS

✈ 🕽 ✕ 🕿 🖪 🖳 / ✕ /

LODI pop. 2,882

──── WHERE TO STAY ────

VICTORIAN TREASURE INN
    Phone: (608)592-5199

(AAA) (SAVE)   All Year   2P: $119-$209

▼▼▼ ▼▼▼   **Location:** Just w of jct SR 60 and 113. 115 Prairie St 53555. **Facility:** Leaded, stained-glass windows, hardwood floors and decoratively trimmed pocket doors accent these two 19th-century Victorian

Bed & Breakfast   homes. Smoke free premises. 7 units. 2 one-bedroom standard units, some with whirlpools. 5 one-bedroom suites with whirlpools. 2 stories (no elevator), interior/exterior corridors. **Parking:** on-site. **Terms:** 2 night minimum stay - weekends, age restrictions may apply, 14 day cancellation notice-fee imposed, [BP] meal plan available, package plans. **Amenities:** CD players, irons, hair dryers. **Leisure Activities:** Fee: massage. **Guest Services:** gift shop. **Cards:** DS, MC, VI. **Special Amenities:** early check-in/late check-out and free local telephone calls.

SOME UNITS

🕽 ✕ / 🝢 VCR 🖪 🖳 🖵 /

LOMIRA pop. 2,233

──── WHERE TO STAY ────

AMERIHOST INN & SUITES
    Phone: 920/269-7477

(AAA) (SAVE)   All Year [ECP]   1P: $71   2P: $76   XP: $6   F18

▼▼▼▼   **Location:** US 41, exit 85 (SR 67), just nw. 645 E Ave 53048. Fax: 920/269-7738. **Facility:** 60 one-bedroom standard units, some with whirlpools. 2 stories (no elevator), interior corridors. *Bath:* combo or shower only.

Small-scale Hotel   **Parking:** on-site. **Amenities:** voice mail, safes (fee), irons, hair dryers. **Pool(s):** small heated indoor. **Leisure Activities:** whirlpool, seasonal patio, limited exercise equipment. **Business Services:** meeting rooms, fax (fee). **Cards:** AX, DC, DS, JC, MC, VI. **Special Amenities:** free continental breakfast and free newspaper.

SOME UNITS

🆂 🕽 🛁 🏊 ✕ 👤 DATA PORT 🖳 / ✕ 🖪 🖵 /

LUCK pop. 1,210

──── WHERE TO STAY ────

LUCK COUNTRY INN
    Phone: 715/472-2000

(AAA) (SAVE)   All Year   1P: $60-$94   2P: $60-$94   XP: $9

▼▼ ▼▼   **Location:** Jct SR 35 and 48. 10 Robertson Rd 54853 (PO Box 179). Fax: 715/472-2171. **Facility:** 38 units. 37 one-bedroom standard units. 1 one-bedroom suite ($83-$176) with kitchen. 2 stories, interior corridors. *Bath:*

Small-scale Hotel   combo or shower only. **Parking:** on-site, winter plug-ins. **Terms:** cancellation fee imposed, package plans - seasonal, weekends. **Dining:** 6 am-9 pm, Sun-Thurs to 8 pm in winter, wine/beer only. **Pool(s):** small heated indoor. **Leisure Activities:** sauna, whirlpool. **Guest Services:** gift shop. **Business Services:** meeting rooms, administrative services (fee). **Cards:** AX, CB, DC, DS, MC, VI. **Special Amenities:** early check-in/late check-out and free local telephone calls.

SOME UNITS

🆂 🐾 🍽 🏊 👤 / ✕ VCR 🖪 🖳 🖵 /

Madison
Lodging & Dining

© AAA

©2002 NAVIGATION TECHNOLOGIES

1947-A

Madison and Vicinity

This index helps you "spot" where approved accommodations and restaurants are located on the corresponding detailed maps. Lodging rate ranges are for comparison only and show the property's high season; rates are per night, unless only weekly (W) rates are available. Restaurant rate range is for dinner, unless only lunch (L) is served. Turn to the listing page for more detailed rate information and consult display ads for special promotions.

Spotter/Map Page Number	OA	**MADISON** - Lodgings	Diamond Rating	Rate Range High Season	Listing Page
1 / p. 519	AAA	**Woodfield Suites-Madison -** see color ad p 530	▽▽ ▽▽ ▽▽	$89-$129 SAVE	530
2 / p. 519		Fairfield Inn By Marriott	▽▽ ▽▽	Failed to provide	525
3 / p. 519		GrandStay Residential Suites	▽▽ ▽▽ ▽▽	$89-$139	525
4 / p. 519	AAA	**Staybridge Suites**	▽▽ ▽▽ ▽▽	$109-$149 SAVE	529
5 / p. 519		Hampton Inn-East	▽▽ ▽▽ ▽▽	$79-$99	525
6 / p. 519	AAA	**Red Roof Inn-Madison**	▽▽ ▽▽	$44-$74 SAVE	528
7 / p. 519	AAA	**Select Inn -** see color ad p 508	▽▽	$45-$70 SAVE	529
8 / p. 519		Residence Inn	▽▽ ▽▽ ▽▽	$86-$149	528
9 / p. 519		Comfort Inn Madison	▽▽ ▽▽ ▽▽	$69-$159	523
10 / p. 519	AAA	**Econo Lodge of Madison**	▽▽ ▽▽	$55-$79	525
11 / p. 519	AAA	**Best Western East Towne Suites**	▽▽ ▽▽ ▽▽	$62-$97 SAVE	522
12 / p. 519	AAA	**Crowne Plaza Hotel and Resort -** see color ad p 524	▽▽ ▽▽ ▽▽	$149-$199 SAVE	523
13 / p. 519	AAA	**Microtel Inn & Suites**	▽▽ ▽▽	$43-$150 SAVE	528
14 / p. 519	AAA	**Exel Inn of Madison -** see color ad p 465	▽▽ ▽▽	$42-$72 SAVE	525
15 / p. 519	AAA	**Holiday Inn Madison East -** see color ad p 524	▽▽ ▽▽ ▽▽	$119-$139 SAVE	527
16 / p. 519	AAA	**Comfort Suites -** see color ad p 523	▽▽ ▽▽ ▽▽	$108-$118 SAVE	523
17 / p. 519	AAA	**Holiday Inn Hotel & Suites -** see color ad p 526	▽▽ ▽▽ ▽▽	$129-$319 SAVE	526
18 / p. 519	AAA	**Mansion Hill Inn**	▽▽ ▽▽ ▽▽ ▽▽	$130-$340 SAVE	527
19 / p. 519	AAA	**Baymont Inn & Suites-Madison West -** see color ad p 523	▽▽ ▽▽ ▽▽	$59-$119 SAVE	522
20 / p. 519		The Madison Concourse Hotel & Governor's Club	▽▽ ▽▽ ▽▽	$107-$169	527
21 / p. 519		Canterbury Inn	▽▽ ▽▽ ▽▽	$88-$375	522
22 / p. 519	AAA	**Best Western Inn On The Park**	▽▽ ▽▽	$89-$179 SAVE	522
23 / p. 519		Hilton Madison Monona Terrace	▽▽ ▽▽ ▽▽	$115-$219	526
24 / p. 519	AAA	**Best Western InnTowner & the Highland Club**	▽▽ ▽▽ ▽▽	$89-$172 SAVE	522
26 / p. 519	AAA	**Howard Johnson Plaza Hotel -** see color ad p 560	▽▽ ▽▽ ▽▽	$79-$200 SAVE	527
27 / p. 519		University Heights Bed & Breakfast	▽▽ ▽▽ ▽▽	Failed to provide	530
28 / p. 519		Residence Inn By Marriott-Madison West	▽▽ ▽▽ ▽▽	$129-$169	528
29 / p. 519		Hampton Inn West	▽▽ ▽▽ ▽▽	$74-$99	526

Spotter/Map Page Number	OA	MADISON - Lodgings (continued)	Diamond Rating	Rate Range High Season	Listing Page
30 / p. 519	AAA	**Radisson Inn Madison** - see color ad p 562	▽▽▽	$89-$139 SAVE	528
31 / p. 519		Best Western West Towne Suites	▽▽	$49-$109	522
32 / p. 519	AAA	**Days Inn-Madison**	▽▽	$65-$95 SAVE	524
33 / p. 519	AAA	**Holiday Inn Express-Madison**	▽▽▽	$79-$109 SAVE	526
34 / p. 519		Sheraton Madison Hotel	▽▽▽	$119-$139	529
35 / p. 519	AAA	**Wingate Inn**	▽▽▽	$89-$99 SAVE	530
36 / p. 519	AAA	**Clarion Suites Central** - see color ad p 523	▽▽▽	$79-$229 SAVE	522
37 / p. 519		Super 8 Motel	▽▽	$49-$99	530
		MADISON - Restaurants			
1 / p. 519		The Mariner's Inn	▽▽	$14-$40	531
2 / p. 519	AAA	**Imperial Garden-East**	▽▽	$8-$13	531
3 / p. 519		Prime Quarter Steak House	▽	$15	532
4 / p. 519		Ella's Kosher Style Deli & Ice Cream Parlor	▽	$7-$8	531
5 / p. 519		Bellini	▽▽	$14-$22	531
6 / p. 519		The Blue Marlin	▽▽▽	$22-$30	531
7 / p. 519		L'Etoile	▽▽▽	$23-$36	531
8 / p. 519	AAA	**Nadia's Restaurant**	▽▽▽	$17-$26	531
9 / p. 519	AAA	**Cafe Continental**	▽▽	$7-$28	531
10 / p. 519		Smoky's Club	▽▽	$10-$25	532
11 / p. 519		White Horse Inn	▽▽	$12-$23	532
12 / p. 519		Johnny Delmonico's	▽▽▽	$9-$27	531
13 / p. 519		The Opera House	▽▽▽	$18-$37	532
		MONONA - Lodgings			
40 / p. 519	AAA	**AmericInn of Madison South/Monona**	▽▽▽	$80-$119 SAVE	582
41 / p. 519	AAA	**Country Inn & Suites By Carlson** - see color ad starting on p 556	▽▽▽	$84-$150 SAVE	582
		MIDDLETON - Lodgings			
44 / p. 519		Fairfield Inn Madison West/Middleton	▽▽▽	$69-$99	538
45 / p. 519	AAA	**Marriott Madison West** - see ad p 527	▽▽▽	$119 SAVE	538
		MIDDLETON - Restaurants			
16 / p. 519		Louisianne's Etc	▽▽▽	$12-$30	538
17 / p. 519	AAA	**Imperial Garden West**	▽▽▽	$7-$14	538

MADISON pop. 208,054 (See map p. 519; index p. 520)

———— WHERE TO STAY ————

BAYMONT INN & SUITES-MADISON WEST

(AAA) (SAVE)
◊◊◊
Small-scale Hotel

Phone: (608)831-7711 [19]
F18

All Year 1P: $59-$109 2P: $69-$119 XP: $10
Location: US 12 and 14, exit 253 (Old Sauk Rd), just nw. 8102 Excelsior Dr 53717. Fax: 608/831-1942. **Facility:** 129 one-bedroom standard units, some with kitchens and/or whirlpools. 2 stories, interior corridors. *Bath:* combo or shower only. **Parking:** on-site, winter plug-ins. **Terms:** 7 day cancellation notice, [ECP] meal plan available. **Amenities:** video games, voice mail, irons, hair dryers. **Pool(s):** heated indoor. **Leisure Activities:** sauna, whirlpool, exercise room. **Guest Services:** complimentary evening beverages, valet and coin laundry, area transportation-University Hospital. **Business Services:** meeting rooms. **Cards:** AX, DC, DS, MC, VI. **Special Amenities:** free continental breakfast and free newspaper. *(See color ad p 523)*

SOME UNITS
[icons] FEE

BEST WESTERN EAST TOWNE SUITES

(AAA) (SAVE)
◊◊◊
Small-scale Hotel

Phone: (608)244-2020 [11]
F14

All Year [BP] 1P: $62-$89 2P: $70-$97 XP: $8
Location: I-90/94, exit 135A, just sw on US 151. 4801 Annamark Dr 53704. Fax: 608/244-3434. **Facility:** 123 units. 119 one-bedroom standard units, some with whirlpools. 4 one-bedroom suites. 4 stories, interior corridors. **Parking:** on-site. **Terms:** package plans, pets ($20 deposit). **Amenities:** irons, hair dryers. **Pool(s):** small heated indoor. **Leisure Activities:** whirlpool, limited exercise equipment. **Guest Services:** valet laundry. **Business Services:** meeting rooms. **Cards:** AX, CB, DC, DS, MC, VI. **Special Amenities:** free newspaper.

SOME UNITS
[icons] FEE

BEST WESTERN INN ON THE PARK

(AAA) (SAVE)
◊◊◊
Small-scale Hotel

Phone: (608)257-8811 [22]

4/1-11/22 & 2/20-3/31 1P: $89-$179 2P: $89-$179 XP: $10 F18
11/23-2/19 1P: $69-$99 2P: $69-$99 XP: $10 F18
Location: Downtown. Located opposite the Wisconsin State Capitol. 22 S Carroll 53703. Fax: 608/257-5995. **Facility:** 213 units. 177 one-bedroom standard units. 36 one-bedroom suites. 9 stories, interior corridors. **Parking:** valet. **Terms:** 3 day cancellation notice. **Amenities:** high-speed Internet, dual phone lines, voice mail, irons, hair dryers. **Dining:** 7 am-2 & 5-9 pm, cocktails. **Pool(s):** heated indoor. **Leisure Activities:** sauna, whirlpool, limited exercise equipment. **Guest Services:** gift shop, valet laundry, area transportation-University of Wisconsin. **Business Services:** meeting rooms. **Cards:** AX, CB, DC, DS, MC, VI. **Special Amenities:** free newspaper and free room upgrade (subject to availability with advanced reservations).

SOME UNITS
[icons]

BEST WESTERN INNTOWNER & THE HIGHLAND CLUB

(AAA) (SAVE)
◊◊◊
Small-scale Hotel

Phone: (608)233-8778 [24]
F12

All Year 1P: $89-$165 2P: $96-$172 XP: $5
Location: 2.3 mi nw. 2424 University Ave 53726. Fax: 608/233-1325. **Facility:** 176 units. 171 one-bedroom standard units. 5 one-bedroom suites ($155-$275), some with whirlpools. 4 stories, interior corridors. *Bath:* combo or shower only. **Parking:** on-site. **Amenities:** video games (fee), voice mail, irons, hair dryers. *Some:* CD players, high-speed Internet. **Dining:** 6:30 am-2 & 5-10 pm, cocktails. **Pool(s):** small heated indoor. **Leisure Activities:** whirlpool, exercise room. *Fee:* game room. **Guest Services:** valet laundry, area transportation-within 2 mi. **Business Services:** meeting rooms, fax (fee). **Cards:** AX, CB, DC, DS, MC, VI. **Special Amenities:** free newspaper and free room upgrade (subject to availability with advanced reservations).

SOME UNITS
[icons]

BEST WESTERN WEST TOWNE SUITES

(SAVE)
◊◊◊
Small-scale Hotel

Phone: (608)833-4200 [31]
F14

All Year [BP] 1P: $49-$109 2P: $49-$109 XP: $10
Location: US 12 and 14, exit 255 (Gammon Rd), just e on Odana Rd, then just sw. 650 Grand Canyon Dr 53719. Fax: 608/833-5614. **Facility:** 101 units. 76 one-bedroom standard units, some with efficiencies and/or whirlpools. 25 one-bedroom suites ($59-$129), some with efficiencies. 2 stories, interior corridors. **Parking:** on-site, winter plug-ins. **Terms:** weekly rates available, pets ($25 deposit, with prior approval). **Amenities:** safes (fee), irons, hair dryers. **Leisure Activities:** limited exercise equipment. **Guest Services:** valet and coin laundry. **Business Services:** meeting rooms. **Cards:** AX, CB, DC, DS, MC, VI.

SOME UNITS
[icons]

CANTERBURY INN

◊◊◊
Bed & Breakfast

Phone: 608-258-8899 [21]

All Year [ECP] 1P: $88-$355 2P: $104-$375 XP: $30
Location: Just w of State St; downtown. Located above a book store. 315 W Gorham St 53703. Fax: 608/283-2541. **Facility:** This well-appointed B&B features hand-painted murals and guest rooms themed after characters from classic literature. Smoke free premises. 6 one-bedroom standard units, some with whirlpools. 2 stories, interior corridors. **Parking:** valet. **Terms:** check-in 4 pm, 14 day cancellation notice-fee imposed, package plans. **Amenities:** CD players, voice mail, irons, hair dryers. **Guest Services:** valet laundry. **Cards:** AX, DC, DS, MC, VI.

SOME UNITS
[icons]

CLARION SUITES CENTRAL

(AAA) (SAVE)
◊◊◊
Small-scale Hotel

Phone: (608)284-1234 [36]
F19

All Year [BP] 1P: $79-$229 2P: $79-$229 XP: $5
Location: US 12 and 18, exit 262 (Rimrock Rd), just nw. Located next to Alliant Energy Center. 2110 Rimrock Rd 53713. Fax: 608/284-9401. **Facility:** 140 units. 98 one-bedroom standard units. 42 one-bedroom suites with efficiencies. 8 stories, interior corridors. *Bath:* combo or shower only. **Parking:** on-site. **Terms:** pets ($25 extra charge). **Amenities:** video games (fee), voice mail, irons, hair dryers. **Pool(s):** heated indoor. **Leisure Activities:** exercise room. **Guest Services:** complimentary evening beverages: Mon-Thurs, valet and coin laundry, area transportation-downtown Madison. **Business Services:** meeting rooms. **Cards:** AX, DC, DS, MC, VI. **Special Amenities:** free continental breakfast and free newspaper. *(See color ad p 523)*

SOME UNITS
[icons]

(See map p. 519)

COMFORT INN MADISON
Phone: (608)244-6265 **9**
All Year   1P: $69-$149   2P: $79-$159   XP: $10   F18

Location: I-90/94, exit 135A, just w on US 151. 4822 E Washington Ave 53704. Fax: 608/244-1293. Facility: 152 units. 150 one-bedroom standard units, some with whirlpools. 2 one-bedroom suites with whirlpools. 2-6 stories, interior corridors. Bath: combo or shower only. Parking: on-site. Amenities: video games (fee), voice mail, irons, hair dryers. Pool(s): small heated indoor. Leisure Activities: whirlpool, exercise room. Guest Services: valet and coin laundry, area transportation. Business Services: conference facilities. Cards: AX, CB, DC, DS, JC, MC, VI.

Small-scale Hotel

SOME UNITS

COMFORT SUITES
Phone: (608)836-3033 **16**
4/1-10/15 & 2/16-3/31 [ECP]   1P: $108   2P: $118   XP: $10   F18
10/16-2/15 [ECP]   1P: $105   2P: $115   XP: $10   F18
Location: US 12 and 14, exit 252 (Greenway Blvd), just sw. 1253 John Q Hammons Dr 53717. Fax: 608/836-0949. Facility: 95 one-bedroom standard units, some with whirlpools. 3 stories, interior corridors. Bath: combo or shower only. Parking: on-site. Amenities: voice mail, safes (fee), irons, hair dryers. Pool(s): heated indoor. Leisure Activities: whirlpool, exercise room. Fee: game room. Guest Services: complimentary evening beverages: Mon-Sat, valet and coin laundry, area transportation-University Hospital. Business Services: meeting rooms. Cards: AX, DC, DS, MC, VI. Special Amenities: free continental breakfast and free newspaper. (See color ad below)

Small-scale Hotel

SOME UNITS

CROWNE PLAZA HOTEL AND RESORT
Phone: 608/244-4703 **12**
All Year   1P: $149-$189   2P: $159-$199   XP: $10   F17
Location: I-90/94, exit 135A, 0.4 mi w on US 151. 4402 E Washington Ave 53704. Fax: 608/244-7829. Facility: 226 one-bedroom standard units, some with whirlpools. 6 stories, interior corridors. Parking: on-site. Terms: check-in 4 pm, cancellation fee imposed. Amenities: voice mail, irons, hair dryers. Fee: video games, high-speed Internet. Some: fax. Dining: 6 am-11 pm, cocktails. Pool(s): heated indoor. Leisure Activities: whirlpool, limited exercise equipment. Guest Services: gift shop, valet and coin laundry. Business Services: conference facilities, business center. Cards: AX, CB, DC, DS, JC, MC, VI. Special Amenities: early check-in/late check-out and free room upgrade (subject to availability with advanced reservations). (See color ad p 524)

Large-scale Hotel

SOME UNITS

(See map p. 519)

DAYS INN-MADISON

AAA SAVE

Small-scale Hotel

All Year [ECP]   1P: $65-$95   2P: $65-$95   XP: $8   F17

Phone: (608)223-1800   32

Location: US 12 and 18, exit 266 (US 51), just ne. 4402 E Broadway Service Rd 53716. Fax: 608/223-1374. **Facility:** 68 one-bedroom standard units, some with whirlpools. 3 stories, interior corridors. *Bath:* combo or shower only. **Parking:** on-site, winter plug-ins. **Terms:** pets ($50 deposit). **Amenities:** irons, hair dryers. **Pool(s):** small heated indoor. **Leisure Activities:** whirlpool, exercise room. **Business Services:** meeting rooms. **Cards:** AX, CB, DC, DS, JC, MC, VI. **Special Amenities: free continental breakfast and free newspaper.**

SOME UNITS

Make some serious splash time.

• 1 Mile from I-90/94 and minutes from downtown • 5 Minutes from Dane County Airport-complimentary shuttle • Just 45 miles from Wisconsin Dells Water Parks • Restaurant & Lounge • Hair dryers and coffee makers in each room • In-room movies, Nintendo, HBO, CNN, ESPN & Weather Channel • Largest indoor pool in Madison and whirlpool, video game fun center, exercise room

Holiday Inn®

MADISON EAST
3841 E. Washington Ave. Madison,WI 53704
www.holiday-inn.com/madison-east
Mention AAA Value Rates to receive above discount.
For reservations and information call:

1-608-244-2481 or 1-866-791-3349

*Includes full hot breakfast buffet for up to 2 adults per room. Kids stay and eat free.

*Rate valid 4/1/02-3/31/03. Single or double occupancy, per night, plus tax. Black out dates may apply. Subject to availability. 24 hour cancellation required.

AAA Value Rate
$69*
Full HOT Breakfast Buffet included

Relax, it's our turn to work.

• 1/2 mile from I-90/94 exit 135A
• 5 Minutes from Dane County Airport
• Across from the East Towne Mall
• Just 45 miles to Wisconsin Dells Water Parks
• Rooms include coffee makers, voicemail, weekday USA Today newspaper
• Wayport hi-speed internet
• Indoor pool, whirlpool, workout area
• In-room movies, Nintendo, HBO, CNN, ESPN & Weather Channel
• Restaurant and lounge
• Kids stay and eat free

AAA Value Rate
$89
4402 E. Washington Ave. • Madison, WI 53704
www.crowneplaza.com/madison-etown
Mention AAA Value Rates to receive above discount.
For reservations and information call:
1-608-244-4703 or 1-800-404-7630
Rate valid 4/1/02-3/31/03. Single or double occupancy, per night, plus tax. Black out dates may apply. Subject to availability. 24 hour cancellation notice, please.

CROWNE PLAZA
HOTELS · RESORTS

MADISON

(See map p. 519)

ECONO LODGE OF MADISON

Phone: (608)241-4171 **10**

AAA SAVE ◆◆◆◆ **Small-scale Hotel**

All Year [CP]   1P: $55-$75   2P: $59-$79   XP: $4   F19
Location: I-90/94, exit 135A, just w on US 151. 4726 E Washington Ave 53704. Fax: 608/241-1715. **Facility:** 98 one-bedroom standard units. 2 stories, interior corridors. *Bath:* combo or shower only. **Parking:** on-site, winter plug-ins. **Terms:** weekly rates available, pets ($5 extra charge, in designated units). **Amenities:** safes (fee). *Some:* video games, fax, hair dryers. **Guest Services:** coin laundry. **Business Services:** meeting rooms. **Cards:** AX, CB, DC, DS, JC, MC, VI. **Special Amenities:** free continental breakfast.

SOME UNITS
🛎 🕑 🍴 🚫 🛏 🐾 / ✕ 🆅🅲🆁 🖨 🛜 🖥 🖵 /
FEE

EXEL INN OF MADISON

Phone: (608)241-3861 **14**

AAA SAVE ◆◆◆◆ **Small-scale Hotel**

6/1-10/31 [CP]   1P: $42-$69   2P: $48-$72   XP: $6   F18
4/1-5/31 & 11/1-3/31 [CP]   1P: $40-$52   2P: $46-$58   XP: $6   F18
Location: I-90/94, exit 135A, 0.5 mi w on US 151. 4202 E Towne Blvd 53704. Fax: 608/241-9752. **Facility:** 100 one-bedroom standard units, some with whirlpools. 2 stories, interior corridors. **Parking:** on-site. **Terms:** small pets only. **Amenities:** irons, hair dryers. **Business Services:** fax (fee). **Cards:** AX, CB, DC, DS, MC, VI. **Special Amenities:** early check-in/late check-out and free continental breakfast. *(See color ad p 465)*

SOME UNITS
🛎 🕑 🍴 🎥 🖨 🖵 / ✕ 🖨 🛜 /
FEE FEE

FAIRFIELD INN BY MARRIOTT

Phone: 608/249-5300 **2**

◆◆◆ **Motel**

Property failed to provide current rates
Location: I-90/94, exit 135A, just sw on US 151. 4765 Hayes Rd 53704. Fax: 608/240-9335. **Facility:** 135 one-bedroom standard units. 3 stories, interior/exterior corridors. *Bath:* combo or shower only. **Amenities:** irons, winter plug-ins. **Pool(s):** small heated outdoor. **Guest Services:** valet laundry. **Cards:** AX, CB, DC, DS, JC, MC, VI.

SOME UNITS
🚫 🎨 🏊 🎥 🖨 / ✕ /

GRANDSTAY RESIDENTIAL SUITES

Phone: (608)241-2500 **3**

◆◆◆◆ **Small-scale Hotel**

All Year   1P: $89-$139   2P: $89-$139
Location: US 51, exit 98A, just e, then 0.5 mi s. 5317 High Crossing Blvd 53718. Fax: 608/241-0900. **Facility:** 53 units. 8 one-bedroom standard units with kitchens. 41 one- and 4 two-bedroom suites with kitchens. 3 stories, interior corridors. *Bath:* combo or shower only. **Parking:** on-site. **Amenities:** video games (fee), high-speed Internet, voice mail, irons. **Pool(s):** small heated indoor. **Leisure Activities:** whirlpool, exercise room. **Guest Services:** valet and coin laundry. **Business Services:** meeting rooms. **Cards:** AX, DC, DS, MC, VI.

SOME UNITS
🅰🆂🅺 🛎 🕑 🅼 🚫 🏊 🎥 🖨 🖨 🛜 🖥 🖵 / ✕ /

HAMPTON INN-EAST

Phone: (608)244-9400 **5**

SAVE ◆◆◆ **Small-scale Hotel**

All Year [ECP]   1P: $79-$99   2P: $79-$99
Location: I-90/94, exit 135A, just w on US 151. 4820 Hayes Rd 53704. Fax: 608/244-7177. **Facility:** 116 one-bedroom standard units. 4 stories, interior corridors. *Bath:* combo or shower only. **Parking:** on-site, winter plug-ins. **Amenities:** video games (fee), voice mail, irons, hair dryers. **Pool(s):** small heated indoor. **Leisure Activities:** whirlpool, limited exercise equipment. **Guest Services:** valet laundry. **Business Services:** meeting rooms. **Cards:** AX, CB, DC, DS, MC, VI.

SOME UNITS
🛎 🍴 🅼 🚫 🎨 🏊 🎥 🖨 🖵 / ✕ 🖨 🛜 /
FEE FEE

(See map p. 519)

HAMPTON INN WEST

SAVE
▽▼△▽▼△
Small-scale Hotel

Phone: (608)833-3511 🆕29 F17

All Year — 1P: $74-$89 — 2P: $84-$99 — XP: $10

Location: US 12 and 14, exit 255 (Gammon Rd), just n, then 0.5 mi e on Odana Rd. 516 Grand Canyon Dr 53719. Fax: 608/833-7140. **Facility:** 122 one-bedroom standard units. 5 stories, interior corridors. *Bath:* combo or shower only. **Parking:** on-site. **Terms:** [ECP] meal plan available. **Amenities:** video games (fee), dual phone lines, voice mail, irons, hair dryers. **Pool(s):** small heated indoor. **Leisure Activities:** whirlpool, limited exercise equipment. **Guest Services:** valet laundry. **Business Services:** meeting rooms. **Cards:** AX, DC, DS, MC, VI.

SOME UNITS

🛎️ 📶 🍽️ 🔥M ⛵ 🎿 🎥 [DATA PORT] 🖥️ / ✖️ 📶 🖥️ /
　　　　　　　　　　　　　　　　　　　　　FEE　FEE

HILTON MADISON MONONA TERRACE

SAVE
▽▼△▽▼△
Large-scale Hotel

Phone: (608)255-5100 🆕23 F18

All Year — 1P: $115-$209 — 2P: $125-$219 — XP: $10

Location: 2 blks e of Capitol Square; downtown. 9 E Wilson St 53703. Fax: 608/251-4550. **Facility:** 240 units. 237 one-bedroom standard units. 3 one-bedroom suites with whirlpools. 13 stories, interior corridors. *Bath:* combo or shower only. **Parking:** on-site (fee) and valet. **Terms:** 3 day cancellation notice-fee imposed, 13% service charge. **Amenities:** video games (fee), dual phone lines, voice mail, irons, hair dryers. **Pool(s):** small heated indoor. **Leisure Activities:** whirlpool, exercise room. **Guest Services:** gift shop, valet laundry. **Business Services:** meeting rooms, administrative services (fee). **Cards:** AX, CB, DC, DS, MC, VI.

SOME UNITS

🛎️ ⛵ 🍽️ 24 ⎕ 🔥 🎧 🎿 🎥 [DATA PORT] 🖥️ / ✖️ 📶 /
　　　　　　　　　　　　　　　　　　　　　FEE

HOLIDAY INN EXPRESS-MADISON

AAA SAVE
▽▼△▽▼△
Small-scale Hotel

Phone: (608)255-7400 🆕33

6/1-8/31 [ECP] — 1P: $79-$109 — 2P: $85-$109 — XP: $6 — F18
4/1-5/31 & 9/1-3/31 [ECP] — 1P: $79-$99 — 2P: $85-$99 — XP: $6 — F18

Location: US 12 and 18, exit 263 (John Nolen Dr), just ne. 722 John Nolen Dr 53713. Fax: 608/255-3152. **Facility:** 92 one-bedroom standard units, some with whirlpools. 4 stories, interior corridors. *Bath:* combo or shower only. **Parking:** on-site. **Terms:** small pets only (in smoking units). **Amenities:** irons, hair dryers. **Pool(s):** small heated indoor. **Leisure Activities:** whirlpool, limited exercise equipment. **Guest Services:** complimentary evening beverages, valet laundry. **Business Services:** business center. **Cards:** AX, CB, DC, DS, MC, VI. **Special Amenities:** free continental breakfast and free local telephone calls.

SOME UNITS

🛎️ 🐾 🍽️ ⛵ 🎧 🎿 🎥 [DATA PORT] 🖥️ / ✖️ 📶 🖥️ /

HOLIDAY INN HOTEL & SUITES

AAA SAVE
▽▼△▽▼△
Small-scale Hotel

Phone: (608)826-0500 🆕17

4/1-10/31 — 1P: $129-$299 — 2P: $139-$319 — XP: $10 — F12
11/1-3/31 — 1P: $99-$259 — 2P: $109-$269 — XP: $10 — F12

Location: US 12 and 14, exit 253 (Old Sank Rd), 0.5 mi nw. 1109 Fourier Dr 53717. Fax: 608/826-0550. **Facility:** 158 units. 157 one-bedroom standard units, some with whirlpools. 1 one-bedroom suite ($159-$299). 4 stories, interior corridors. *Bath:* combo or shower only. **Parking:** on-site. **Terms:** 2-3 night minimum stay - seasonal, [AP] meal plan available, package plans. **Amenities:** dual phone lines, voice mail, irons, hair dryers. *Fee:* video games, high-speed Internet, safes. *Some:* CD players. **Dining:** 6:30 am-10 pm, cocktails. **Pool(s):** heated indoor, wading. **Leisure Activities:** whirlpool, waterslide, exercise room. *Fee:* game room. **Guest Services:** gift shop, complimentary evening beverages, valet and coin laundry, area transportation. **Business Services:** meeting rooms, business center. **Cards:** AX, CB, DC, DS, JC, MC, VI. **Special Amenities:** early check-in/late check-out and free room upgrade (subject to availability with advanced reservations). *(See color ad below)*

SOME UNITS

🛎️ ⛵ 🍽️ ⎕ 🔥M 🎧 🎿 ✖️ 🎥 [DATA PORT] 📶 🖥️ 🖥️ / ✖️ VCR /

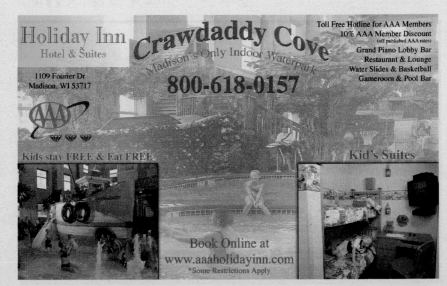

(See map p. 519)

HOLIDAY INN MADISON EAST

Small-scale Hotel

Phone: 608/244-2481 **15** F17

All Year   1P: $119-$129   2P: $129-$139   XP: $10

Location: I-90/94, exit 135A, 1 mi w on US 151. 3841 E Washington Ave 53704. Fax: 608/244-0383. **Facility:** 197 one-bedroom standard units. 2 stories, interior corridors. *Bath:* combo or shower only. **Parking:** on-site. **Terms:** cancellation fee imposed, small pets only (in designated units). **Amenities:** video games (fee), voice mail, irons, hair dryers. **Dining:** 6:30 am-2 & 5-10 pm, cocktails. **Pool(s):** heated indoor. **Leisure Activities:** whirlpool, limited exercise equipment. *Fee:* game room. **Guest Services:** valet laundry. **Business Services:** meeting rooms. **Cards:** AX, CB, DC, DS, JC, MC, VI. **Special Amenities:** early check-in/late check-out and free room upgrade (subject to availability with advanced reservations). *(See color ad p 524)*

SOME UNITS

HOWARD JOHNSON PLAZA HOTEL

Small-scale Hotel

Phone: (608)251-5511 **26**

All Year   1P: $79-$200   2P: $79-$200   XP: $10   F18

Location: 0.5 mi sw of Capitol Square. Located adjacent to University of Wisconsin Campus. 525 W Johnson St 53703. Fax: 608/251-4824. **Facility:** 163 units. 159 one-bedroom standard units. 4 one-bedroom suites ($150-$225). 7 stories, interior corridors. *Bath:* combo or shower only. **Parking:** on-site. **Terms:** check-in 4 pm. **Amenities:** video games (fee), voice mail, irons, hair dryers. **Dining:** 6 am-1:30 & 5-10 pm, cocktails. **Pool(s):** heated indoor. **Leisure Activities:** whirlpool, exercise room. **Guest Services:** valet laundry, area transportation-campus area. **Business Services:** meeting rooms, fax (fee). **Cards:** AX, CB, DC, DS, JC, MC, VI. **Special Amenities:** early check-in/late check-out and free newspaper. *(See color ad p 560)*

SOME UNITS

FEE

THE MADISON CONCOURSE HOTEL & GOVERNOR'S CLUB

Large-scale Hotel

Phone: (608)257-6000 **20** F16

All Year   1P: $107-$159   2P: $117-$169   XP: $10

Location: Just n of Capitol Square. 1 W Dayton St 53703. Fax: 608/257-5280. **Facility:** 356 one-bedroom standard units, some with whirlpools. 13 stories, interior corridors. *Bath:* combo or shower only. **Parking:** on-site and valet. **Terms:** cancellation fee imposed. **Amenities:** video games (fee), voice mail, irons, hair dryers. *Some:* CD players, dual phone lines. **Pool(s):** small heated indoor. **Leisure Activities:** whirlpool, steamroom, exercise room. *Fee:* massage, game room. **Guest Services:** gift shop, valet laundry, area transportation, tanning facility, beauty salon. **Business Services:** conference facilities, business center. **Cards:** AX, CB, DC, DS, JC, MC, VI.

SOME UNITS

ASK

FEE   FEE

MANSION HILL INN

Historic Bed
& Breakfast

Phone: (608)255-3999 **18**

All Year   1P: $130-$320   2P: $150-$340   XP: $20

Location: Just n of Capitol Square. 424 N Pinckney St 53703. Fax: 608/255-2217. **Facility:** This 1858 stone mansion, which is furnished with antiques, features some rooms with four-poster beds. Smoke free premises. 11 units. 10 one-bedroom standard units, some with whirlpools. 1 one-bedroom suite with whirlpool. 3 stories (no elevator), interior corridors. *Bath:* combo or shower only. **Parking:** valet. **Terms:** check-in 4 pm, age restrictions may apply, cancellation fee imposed, [CP] meal plan available. **Amenities:** honor bars, irons, hair dryers. **Guest Services:** complimentary evening beverages, valet laundry. **Cards:** AX, MC, VI. **Special Amenities:** free continental breakfast and free newspaper.

(See map p. 519)

MICROTEL INN & SUITES
Phone: (608)242-9000 **13**
(AAA) [SAVE] All Year [CP] 1P: $43-$150 2P: $48-$150 XP: $5 F16
♦♦♦ **Location:** I-90/94, exit 135A, just s, then 0.5 mi e. 2139 E Springs Dr 53704. Fax: 608/242-8700. **Facility:** 100 one-bedroom standard units, some with whirlpools. 3 stories, interior corridors. **Parking:** on-site, winter plug-ins. **Terms:** pets ($10 extra charge). **Amenities:** Some: irons. **Cards:** AX, CB, DC, DS, MC, VI.
Small-scale Hotel **Special Amenities:** free local telephone calls and free newspaper.

SOME UNITS
[S/D] [icons] / [X] [icons] /

RADISSON INN MADISON
Phone: (608)833-0100 **30**
(AAA) [SAVE] All Year [CP] 1P: $89-$139 2P: $89-$139 XP: $10 F
♦♦♦ **Location:** US 12 and 14, exit 255 (Gammon Rd), 0.5 mi e on Odana. Located in a commercial area. 517 Grand Canyon Dr 53719. Fax: 608/833-6543. **Facility:** 153 units. 147 one-bedroom standard units. 6 one-bedroom suites ($159-$179), some with whirlpools. 2 stories, interior corridors. **Parking:** on-site. **Terms:** 17% service charge.
Small-scale Hotel **Amenities:** voice mail, irons, hair dryers. **Dining:** 6:30 am-2 & 5-10 pm, cocktails. **Pool(s):** heated indoor. **Leisure Activities:** whirlpool, exercise room. **Guest Services:** valet laundry. **Business Services:** meeting rooms, business center. **Cards:** AX, CB, DC, DS, MC, VI. **Special Amenities:** free local telephone calls and free newspaper.** (See color ad p 562)

SOME UNITS
[S/D] [icons] / [X] [VCR] [icons] /
FEE FEE

RED ROOF INN-MADISON
Phone: (608)241-1787 **6**
(AAA) [SAVE] 6/14-8/16 1P: $44-$69 2P: $49-$74 XP: $5 F18
♦♦ 4/1-6/13 & 8/17-3/31 1P: $39-$44 2P: $44-$49 XP: $5 F18
Motel **Location:** I-90/94, exit 135A, just sw on US 151. 4830 Hayes Rd 53704. Fax: 608/241-7034. **Facility:** 108 one-bedroom standard units. 2 stories, exterior corridors. Bath: combo or shower only. **Parking:** on-site. **Terms:** small pets only. **Amenities:** video games (fee), voice mail. **Cards:** AX, CB, DC, DS, MC, VI. **Special Amenities:** free local telephone calls and free newspaper.

SOME UNITS
[icons] / [X] /

RESIDENCE INN
Phone: (608)244-5047 **8**
[SAVE] All Year 1P: $86-$149
♦♦♦ **Location:** I-90/94, exit 135A, just sw on US 151. 4862 Hayes Rd 53704. Fax: 608/244-5047. **Facility:** 66 units. 54 one- and 12 two-bedroom suites with kitchens. 3 stories, interior corridors. Bath: combo or shower only.
Condominium **Parking:** on-site. **Terms:** cancellation fee imposed, [BP] meal plan available, pets ($25-$100 extra charge). **Amenities:** voice mail, irons, hair dryers. **Pool(s):** small heated indoor. **Leisure Activities:** whirlpool, exercise room, sports court. **Guest Services:** valet and coin laundry. **Business Services:** meeting rooms. **Cards:** AX, DC, DS, MC, VI.

SOME UNITS
[S/D] [icons] / [X] /

RESIDENCE INN BY MARRIOTT-MADISON WEST
Phone: (608)833-8333 **28**
[SAVE] 6/1-3/31 [BP] 1P: $129-$169
♦♦♦ 4/1-5/31 [BP] 1P: $119-$169
Location: US 12 and 14, exit 254 (Mineral Point Rd), 0.4 mi e, then just s. 501 D'Onofrio Dr 53719. Fax: 608/833-2693.
Condominium **Facility:** 80 one-bedroom standard units with kitchens. 2 stories, exterior corridors. **Parking:** on-site, winter plug-ins. **Terms:** cancellation fee imposed, pets ($150 fee, $5 extra charge). **Amenities:** voice mail, irons, hair dryers. **Pool(s):** heated outdoor. **Leisure Activities:** whirlpool, exercise room, sports court. **Guest Services:** valet and coin laundry. **Business Services:** meeting rooms. **Cards:** AX, CB, DC, DS, MC, VI.

SOME UNITS
[S/D] [icons] / [X] [VCR]
FEE

(See map p. 519)

SELECT INN

(AAA) (SAVE)

Phone: (608)249-1815 **7**

| | 6/1-9/30 [CP] | 1P: $45-$70 | 2P: $55-$70 | XP: $5 | F16 |
| | 4/1-5/31 & 10/1-3/31 [CP] | 1P: $39-$49 | 2P: $46-$65 | XP: $5 | F16 |

Small-scale Hotel

Location: I-90/94, exit 135A, just sw on US 151. 4845 Hayes Rd 53704. Fax: 608/249-1815. **Facility:** 97 units. 96 one-bedroom standard units, some with kitchens. 1 one-bedroom suite with kitchen. 3 stories (no elevator), interior corridors. *Bath:* combo or shower only. **Parking:** on-site. **Terms:** weekly rates available, small pets only ($25 deposit, $5 extra charge). **Amenities:** safes. *Some:* hair dryers. **Leisure Activities:** whirlpool. **Business Services:** meeting rooms. **Cards:** AX, CB, DC, DS, JC, MC, VI. **Special Amenities:** free continental breakfast.

(See color ad p 508)

SOME UNITS

🔊 🛏️ 🍴 📶 📷 / ✕ 📠 🖥️ 📷 💻 /

SHERATON MADISON HOTEL
▽▽△▽▽

Phone: (608)251-2300 **34**

| | 5/12-11/15 | 1P: $119-$139 | 2P: $119-$139 | |
| | 11/16-3/31 | 1P: $109-$129 | 2P: $109-$129 | |

Large-scale Hotel

Location: US 12 and 18, exit 263 (John Nolen Dr), just n. 706 John Nolen Dr 53713. Fax: 608/251-1189. **Facility:** 237 units. 235 one-bedroom standard units. 2 one-bedroom suites. 8 stories, interior corridors. **Parking:** on-site. **Terms:** 2-5 night minimum stay - seasonal, cancellation fee imposed, [AP] meal plan available, package plans - seasonal. **Amenities:** video games (fee), dual phone lines, voice mail, irons, hair dryers. *Some:* fax. **Pool(s):** heated indoor. **Leisure Activities:** sauna, whirlpool, exercise room. *Fee:* game room. **Guest Services:** gift shop, valet laundry, area transportation. **Business Services:** conference facilities, business center. **Cards:** AX, CB, DC, DS, JC, MC, VI.

SOME UNITS

(ASK) 🔊 ✈️ 🍴 🍷 📶 🏊 ✕ 📷 💻 / ✕ 📠 /

STAYBRIDGE SUITES
(AAA) (SAVE)
▽▽▽△

Phone: (608)241-2300 **4**

| | All Year [BP] | 1P: $109-$149 | 2P: $109-$149 | |

Small-scale Hotel

Location: US 151, exit 98A, just e, then 0.5 mi s on High Crossing Blvd. 3301 City View Dr 53718. Fax: 608/241-8845. **Facility:** 90 units. 47 one-bedroom standard units with kitchens. 34 one- and 9 two-bedroom suites with kitchens. 3 stories, interior corridors. *Bath:* combo or shower only. **Parking:** on-site. **Terms:** cancellation fee imposed, package plans, pets ($75 fee). **Amenities:** dual phone lines, voice mail, irons, hair dryers. *Fee:* video library, high-speed Internet. **Pool(s):** small heated indoor. **Leisure Activities:** whirlpool, patio with gas grill, library, exercise room. **Guest Services:** sundries, complimentary evening beverages: Tues-Thurs, area transportation. **Business Services:** meeting rooms, business center. **Cards:** AX, CB, DC, DS, MC, VI. **Special Amenities:** free continental breakfast and free local telephone calls.

SOME UNITS

✈️ 🛏️ 📶 🏊 ✕ (VCR) 📷 📠 🖥️ 📷 💻 / ✕ /

LOOK FOR
THE RED

*N*ext time you pore over a AAA TourBook® guide in search of a lodging establishment, take note of the vibrant red AAA logo, (SAVE) icon, and Diamond rating just under a select group of property names! These Official Appointment properties place a high value on the business they receive from dedicated AAA travelers and offer members great room rates*.

* See TourBook Navigator section, page 14, for complete details.

(See map p. 519)

SUPER 8 MOTEL

Phone: (608)258-8882 **37**

▼▼▼▼ *Small-scale Hotel*

All Year [ECP] 1P: $49-$99 2P: $49-$99
Location: US 12 and 18, exit 260B (CR D), just w on north frontage road. 1602 W Beltline Hwy 53713. Fax: 608/258-9575. **Facility:** 88 units. 87 one-bedroom standard units. 1 one-bedroom suite with whirlpool. 3 stories, interior corridors. *Bath:* combo or shower only. **Parking:** on-site, winter plug-ins. **Terms:** check-in 4 pm, pets ($10 fee, in 2nd floor smoking units). **Amenities:** irons. **Pool(s):** heated indoor. **Leisure Activities:** whirlpool, limited exercise equipment. **Guest Services:** coin laundry. **Business Services:** business center. **Cards:** AX, CB, DC, DS, JC, MC, VI.

SOME UNITS
(ASK) (S/D) (🐾) (T|↓) (🎮) (🔒) (🏊) (🎥) (DATA PORT) / (✕) (🗄) (🖥) /

UNIVERSITY HEIGHTS BED & BREAKFAST

Phone: 608/233-3340 **27**

▼▼▼▼ *Bed & Breakfast*

Property failed to provide current rates
Location: 2 mi w. 1812 Van Hise Ave 53705. Fax: 608/233-3255. **Facility:** Built in 1923, this B&B is close to the university and features finely crafted, solid oak woodwork throughout. Smoke free premises. 4 units. 3 one-bedroom standard units, some with whirlpools. 1 one-bedroom suite with whirlpool. 2 stories, interior corridors. *Bath:* combo or shower only. **Parking:** on-site, winter plug-ins. **Terms:** age restrictions may apply. **Amenities:** irons, hair dryers. *Some:* CD players. **Guest Services:** complimentary laundry, area transportation. **Business Services:** PC, fax. **Cards:** AX, DS, MC, VI.

(✕) (W)

WINGATE INN

Phone: (608)224-1500 **35**

(AAA) (SAVE) ▼▼▼▼ *Small-scale Hotel*

5/22-10/6 [ECP] 1P: $89-$99 2P: $89-$99 XP: $10 F18
4/1-5/21 & 10/7-3/31 [ECP] 1P: $79-$99 2P: $79-$99 XP: $10 F18
Location: I-90, exit 142B, just e on US 12/18, then w on south frontage road. 3510 Mill Pond Rd 53718. Fax: 608/224-0586. **Facility:** 100 one-bedroom standard units, some with whirlpools. 4 stories, interior corridors. *Bath:* combo or shower only. **Parking:** on-site. **Terms:** 7 day cancellation notice, package plans, pets ($50 deposit, $15 extra charge). **Amenities:** video games (fee), high-speed Internet, dual phone lines, voice mail, safes, irons, hair dryers. **Pool(s):** heated indoor. **Leisure Activities:** whirlpool, exercise room. **Guest Services:** valet laundry. **Business Services:** meeting rooms, business center. **Cards:** AX, CB, DC, DS, JC, MC, VI. **Special Amenities:** free continental breakfast and free local telephone calls.

SOME UNITS
(S/D) (🐾) (🔒) (🏊) (🎥) (DATA PORT) (🗄) (🖥) / (✕) (VCR) (🖥) /
FEE

WOODFIELD SUITES-MADISON

Phone: (608)245-0123 **1**

(AAA) (SAVE) ▼▼▼▼ *Small-scale Hotel*

All Year [ECP] 1P: $89-$129 2P: $89-$129
Location: US 151, exit 98B (American Pkwy), just sw. 5217 E Terrace Dr 53718. Fax: 608/245-1644. **Facility:** 120 units. 60 one-bedroom standard units. 60 one-bedroom suites ($119-$149), some with efficiencies and/or whirlpools. 4 stories, interior corridors. *Bath:* combo or shower only. **Parking:** on-site. **Terms:** pets ($10 deposit). **Amenities:** video games (fee), dual phone lines, voice mail, irons, hair dryers. **Pool(s):** heated indoor. **Leisure Activities:** whirlpool, limited exercise equipment. **Guest Services:** complimentary evening beverages, valet and coin laundry, area transportation. **Business Services:** meeting rooms. **Cards:** AX, CB, DC, DS, MC, VI. **Special Amenities:** free continental breakfast and free newspaper. *(See color ad below)*

SOME UNITS
(S/D) (🔧) (🐾) (🔒M) (🔒) (🔒) (🏊) (🎥) (DATA PORT) (🗄) (🖥) (🖥) / (✕) (VCR) /

(See map p. 519)

─── *The following lodging was either not evaluated or did not* ───
meet AAA rating requirements but is listed for your information only.

COURTYARD BY MARRIOTT-MADISON EAST   Phone: 608/661-8100
[fyi]   6/1-3/31   1P: $79-$179   2P: $79-$179
             4/1-5/31   1P: $69-$169   2P: $69-$169
Small-scale Hotel Too new to rate, opening scheduled for February 2003. **Location:** I-90/94, exit 135C (High Crossing Blvd). 2502
             Crossroads Dr 53718. **Fax:** 608/661-8101. **Amenities:** 127 units, coffeemakers, pool. **Cards:** AX, CB, DC, DS,
MC, VI.

─────── **WHERE TO DINE** ───────

BELLINI   Dinner: $14-$22   Phone: 608/250-0097   5
▼▼▼   **Location:** Just e of Capitol Square; downtown. 401 E Washington Ave 53703. **Hours:** 5 pm-9 pm, Fri & Sat-10
           pm. Closed major holidays; also Sun. **Reservations:** suggested. **Features:** Creative Italian-American
Italian   dishes are served in the beautifully restored landmark church, which features original stained-glass
           windows and woodwork. The menu includes mouthwatering pastas and pizzas, as well as the delicious
dessert specialty: cheesecake wrap. Casual dress; cocktails. **Parking:** street. **Cards:** AX, CB, DS, MC, VI.

THE BLUE MARLIN   Lunch: $8-$10   Dinner: $22-$30   Phone: 608/255-2255   6
▼▼▼   **Location:** Just n of Capitol Square. 101 N Hamilton St 53703. **Hours:** 11:30 am-2:30 & 5:30-10 pm. Closed: 7/4,
           12/25; also Mon. **Reservations:** suggested. **Features:** Grilled seafood dishes center on fresh tuna,
Seafood   swordfish, salmon and live Maine lobster. Dressy casual; cocktails. **Parking:** on-site (fee) and street.
           Cards: AX, DC, DS, MC, VI.

CAFE CONTINENTAL   Lunch: $7-$9   Dinner: $7-$28   Phone: 608/251-4880   9
ⒶⒶⒶ   **Location:** Just e of Capitol Square; downtown. 108 King St 53703. **Hours:** 11 am-10 pm, Sat from 10 am, Sun
▼▼▼   from 9 am. Closed: 11/27, 12/24, 12/25. **Reservations:** suggested. **Features:** A zinc bar is the centerpiece
           of the trendy Parisian-themed dining room, marked by hanging lamps, high ceilings and soft lighting. The
Italian   menu centers on creatively prepared pasta, gourmet pizza and Continental cuisine. In-house desserts are
           rich. Casual dress; cocktails. **Parking:** street. **Cards:** AX, MC, VI.

ELLA'S KOSHER STYLE DELI & ICE CREAM PARLOR   Lunch: $3-$8   Dinner: $7-$8   Phone: 608/241-5291   4
▼   **Location:** Just e of exit 135A, 3 mi w on US 151. 2902 E Washington Ave 53704. **Hours:** 10 am-11 pm, Fri &
           Sat-midnight; to 10 pm, Fri & Sat-11 pm in winter. Closed: 11/27, 12/25. **Features:** The extensive menu
Ethnic   primarily centers on kosher sandwiches and salad. Antique and motorized toys, which decorate the
           charming restaurant, please adults and children alike. Noteworthy on the dessert menu is the delicious,
old-fashioned frozen custard. Casual dress. **Parking:** on-site. **Cards:** MC, VI.

IMPERIAL GARDEN-EAST   Lunch: $6-$8   Dinner: $8-$13   Phone: 608/249-0466   2
ⒶⒶⒶ   **Location:** I-90/94, exit 135A, 0.5 mi w on US 151. 4214 E Washington Ave 53704. **Hours:** 11:30 am-2 & 4-9:30
▼▼▼   pm, Fri-10:30 pm, Sat 11:30 am-10:30 pm, Sun 11:30 am-9 pm. Closed: 11/27, 12/24, 12/25.
           Reservations: suggested; weekends. **Features:** Traditional specialties—such as cashew chicken,
Chinese   Mongolian beef and the happy family platter are filling and flavorful. Also featured is a sushi bar. An
           attractive tiger carving is among beautiful Asian appointments in the moderately upscale dining room.
           Lighting is subtle. Dressy casual; cocktails. **Parking:** on-site. **Cards:** AX, DS, MC, VI.

JOHNNY DELMONICO'S   Dinner: $9-$27   Phone: 608/257-8325   12
▼▼▼   **Location:** Corner of Doty St; downtown. 130 S Pinckney St 53703. **Hours:** 5 pm-9 pm, Fri & Sat-10 pm. Closed:
           1/1, 12/25. **Reservations:** suggested. **Features:** Near the State Capitol, the stylish and trendy dining room
Steak & Seafood specializes in premium aged steaks, fresh fish and seafood. Menu options include oysters on the half shell,
           free-range chicken, French-style pork chops, roasted lamb shank and sirloin burgers. Seating is
comfortable, and the service is refined. Casual dress; cocktails. **Parking:** on-site. **Cards:** AX, MC, VI.

L'ETOILE   Dinner: $23-$36   Phone: 608/251-0500   7
▼▼▼   **Location:** On Capitol Square; downtown. 25 N Pinckney St 53703. **Hours:** 6 pm-8:45 pm, Fri 5:30 pm-9:45 pm,
           Sat 5 pm-9:45 pm. Closed major holidays; also Sun. **Reservations:** suggested. **Features:** Located right on
Regional American Capitol Square in the heart of Madison, this restaurant is known for using locally grown, fresh ingredients.
           The chef and proprietor takes pride in selecting Wisconsin grown vegetables, seasonings, dairy products
and meats for the seasonally changing menu. Great attention is given to food presentation. There is a team approach to
service. Dressy casual; cocktails. **Parking:** street. **Cards:** DC, DS, MC, VI.

THE MARINER'S INN   Dinner: $14-$40   Phone: 608/246-3120   1
▼▼▼   **Location:** 6 mi n on SR 113, just w on CR M, then left on Westport Rd 0.3 mi, follow signs. 5339 Lighthouse Bay Dr
           53704. **Hours:** 5 pm-9:30 pm, Fri & Sat 4:30 pm-10 pm, Sun 4:30 pm-9 pm. Closed major holidays; also
Steak & Seafood 12/24 & Super Bowl Sun. **Reservations:** accepted. **Features:** Located on the north shore of Lake
           Mendota, the restaurant offers a straight forward seafood menu along with a few beef selections. You can
enjoy a view of a picturesque marina and the lake from most tables. Casual dress; cocktails. **Parking:** on-site. **Cards:** MC, VI.

NADIA'S RESTAURANT   Dinner: $17-$26   Phone: 608/257-1740   8
ⒶⒶⒶ   **Location:** 0.4 mi w of Capitol Square. 508 State 53703. **Hours:** 5 pm-11 pm, Sun-10 pm. Closed: 7/4, 12/25.
▼▼▼   **Reservations:** suggested. **Features:** In the bustling State Street area, the restaurant offers such traditional
           French Provencal cuisine as roasted lamb and chicken amaretto. Dressy casual; cocktails. **Parking:** street.
French   **Cards:** AX, DS, MC, VI.

(See map p. 519)

THE OPERA HOUSE
▼▼▼▼
American
Lunch: $9-$10   Dinner: $18-$37   Phone: 608/284-8466   ⑬
Location: South side of Capitol Square; downtown. 117 Martin Luther King Jr Blvd 53703. **Hours:** 11 am-2:30 & 5-9:30 pm, Sat-10 pm. Closed major holidays; also Sun. **Reservations:** suggested. **Features:** A marble bar is the centerpiece of the sophisticated, contemporary dining room, decorated with oversized art. The seasonally changing menu capitalizes on fresh ingredients produced locally. Enjoy homemade desserts and many by-the-glass wine choices. Dressy casual; cocktails. **Parking:** street. **Cards:** AX, DS, MC, VI.   🐍Ⓜ Ⓨ ☒

PRIME QUARTER STEAK HOUSE
▼
Steak House
Dinner: $15   Phone: 608/244-3520   ③
Location: On US 151, just w of jct US 51. 3520 E Washington Ave 53704. **Hours:** 5 pm-10 pm, Sat from 4 pm, Sun 4 pm-9 pm. Closed major holidays. **Reservations:** suggested. **Features:** Choose from a fine selection of USDA Choice steak, tuna or salmon. Enjoy a beverage and socialize as you grill-your-own steak on an open charcoal pit. All entrees are the same price and include all-you-can-eat baked potatoes, Texas toast and salad bar. Casual dress; cocktails. **Parking:** on-site. **Cards:** AX, DS, MC, VI.   Ⓨ ☒

QUIVEY'S GROVE STONE HOUSE, STABLE GRILL   Historic   Dinner: $12-$23   Phone: 608/273-4900
▼▼▼ ▼▼▼
American
Location: US 18 and 151, exit PD, just w, then 0.6 mi s. 6261 Nesbitt Rd 53719. **Hours:** 5 pm-9 pm, Fri & Sat-10 pm. Closed major holidays; also Sun. **Reservations:** suggested. **Features:** The converted 1855 rural mansion and rustic stable are appointed with period furnishings. The menu includes such dishes as baked trout, roast duck, roast pork and the chicken/mushroom-filled popover. The five-acre estate is in the historic district. Casual dress; cocktails. **Parking:** on-site. **Cards:** AX, DS, MC, VI.   Ⓨ ☒

SMOKY'S CLUB
▼▼▼ ▼▼
Steak House
Dinner: $10-$25   Phone: 608/233-2120   ⑩
Location: On University Ave, 0.5 mi e of jct Midvale Blvd. 3005 University Ave 53705. **Hours:** 5 pm-10 pm. Closed major holidays; also Sun & Tues. **Reservations:** accepted. **Features:** The popular, established restaurant attracts much of its clientele from the university. Complementary bread baskets and relishes on ice, along with homemade soups and succulent, sizzling steaks served with fries or hash browns, satisfy the heartiest appetites. Smoking is allowed only in the lounge. Casual dress; cocktails. **Parking:** on-site.   Ⓨ ☒

WHITE HORSE INN
▼▼▼ ▼▼
American
Dinner: $12-$23   Phone: 608/255-9933   ⑪
Location: Just off Capitol Square; next to Civic Center. 202 N Henry 53703. **Hours:** 5 pm-10 pm, Fri & Sat-11 pm, Sun 10 am-2 & 5-9 pm. **Reservations:** suggested. **Features:** A good selection of wine complements such dishes as grilled stuffed pork tenderloin, White Horse shrimp and scallops and Caesar planked Atlantic salmon. The dining room has the ambience of an American bistro—quiet, upscale and dignified. Casual dress; cocktails. **Parking:** on-site. **Cards:** AX, DC, MC, VI.   Ⓨ ☒

MANITOWISH WATERS

──── WHERE TO DINE ────

BLUE BAYOU INN
△△△
▼▼▼ ▼▼▼
Regional
American
Dinner: $15-$25   Phone: 715/543-2537
Location: At Spider Lake Bridge, 3 mi s of CR W on US 51. 288 US Hwy 51 54545. **Hours:** Open 5/1-10/31; 5 pm-9 pm. Closed: Sun. **Reservations:** accepted. **Features:** The lakefront restaurant delivers authentic Louisiana Cajun-Creole cuisine, with such choices as seafood gumbo, jambalaya and shrimp Creole with steamed rice and vegetables. A nice selection of beer and wine is available. Servers are knowledgeable. Smoking in lounge only. Casual dress; cocktails. **Parking:** on-site. **Cards:** DS, MC, VI.   Ⓨ ☒

MICHAEL'S
▼
American
Lunch: $4-$7   Phone: 715/543-2550
Location: 5 mi s on US 51. 397 S US 51 54545. **Hours:** 7 am-4 pm; to 9:30 pm in summer. Closed: 11/27, 12/24, 12/25. **Features:** Homemade baked goods, flavorful soup and hearty chili are tasty, basically prepared favorites at the quaint country cafe. Breakfast selections are served well into the afternoon. During the summer, the soda fountain brings in a good crowd. Casual dress. **Parking:** on-site. **Cards:** AX, DS, MC, VI.   ☒

MANITOWOC pop. 34,053

------ WHERE TO STAY ------

AMERICINN　　　　　　　　　　　　　　　　　　　　　　　　　　　　　　**Phone:** 920/684-3344
▽▽▽▽　　　　　　　　　　Property failed to provide current rates
　　　　　　　Location: I-43, exit 149, just sw. Located in a semi-commercial area. 5020 Hecker Rd 54220. Fax: 920/686-9106.
Small-scale Hotel　**Facility:** 65 units. 58 one-bedroom standard units, some with whirlpools. 7 one-bedroom suites, some with
　　　　　　　whirlpools. 2 stories (no elevator), interior corridors. *Bath:* combo or shower only. **Parking:** on-site.
Amenities: dual phone lines, hair dryers. **Pool(s):** heated indoor. **Leisure Activities:** whirlpool. *Fee:* game room. **Guest Services:** coin laundry. **Business Services:** meeting rooms. **Cards:** AX, DS, MC, VI.

SOME UNITS
[icons]

COMFORT INN　　　　　　　　　　　　　　　　　　　　　　　　　　　**Phone:** (920)683-0220
[SAVE]　　6/1-8/31 [ECP]　　　　1P: $99　　　　2P: $109　　　　XP: $10　　　F18
　　　　　9/1-3/31 [ECP]　　　　1P: $54-$89　　2P: $64-$99　　　XP: $10　　　F18
▽▽▽ ▽▽▽　4/1-5/31 [ECP]　　　　1P: $49-$89　　2P: $59-$99　　　XP: $10　　　F18
Small-scale Hotel　**Location:** I-43, exit 149, just e. Located in a commercial area. 2200 S 44th St 54220. Fax: 920/683-0220. **Facility:** 47
　　　　　　one-bedroom standard units. 2 stories (no elevator), interior corridors. **Parking:** on-site, winter plug-ins.
　　　　　　Amenities: *Some:* irons, hair dryers. **Leisure Activities:** exercise room. **Guest Services:** valet laundry.
Cards: AX, DC, DS, JC, MC, VI.

SOME UNITS
[icons]

HOLIDAY INN　　　　　　　　　　　　　　　　　　　　　　　　　　　**Phone:** (920)682-6000
▽▽▽▽　6/2-10/31　　　　　　1P: $99　　　　2P: $104
　　　　4/1-6/1 & 11/1-3/31　　1P: $85　　　　2P: $85
Large-scale Hotel　**Location:** I-43, exit 149, just e. Located in a commercial area. 4601 Calumet Ave 54220. Fax: 920/682-6140.
　　　　　　Facility: 203 units. 197 one-bedroom standard units. 6 one-bedroom suites ($135-$160). 3 stories, interior
corridors. *Bath:* combo or shower only. **Parking:** on-site. **Terms:** cancellation fee imposed, pets ($150 deposit). **Amenities:** video
games, dual phone lines, voice mail, irons, hair dryers. **Pool(s):** heated indoor. **Leisure Activities:** sauna, whirlpool, playground,
exercise room. *Fee:* game room. **Guest Services:** gift shop, valet laundry. **Business Services:** conference facilities, business
center. **Cards:** AX, CB, DC, DS, JC, MC, VI.

SOME UNITS
[icons]
FEE FEE

INN ON MARITIME BAY　　　　　　　　　　　　　　　　　　　　　**Phone:** (920)682-7000
(AAA) [SAVE]　6/1-8/31　　　　　　1P: $99-$109　　2P: $109-$119　　XP: $10　　　F17
▽▽▽ ▽▽▽　4/1-5/31 & 9/1-3/31　　1P: $79-$89　　2P: $89-$99　　　XP: $10　　　F17
　　　　　　Location: I-43, exit 152, 4.2 mi e on SR 42 N, then 1 mi s. Located on the waters edge. 101 Maritime Dr 54220.
Large-scale Hotel　Fax: 920/682-7013. **Facility:** 107 one-bedroom standard units. 3 stories, interior corridors. **Parking:** on-site.
　　　　　　Terms: check-in 4 pm, cancellation fee imposed, [AP] meal plan available, package plans, 16% service
　　　　　　charge, pets ($25 extra charge). **Amenities:** *Some:* irons, hair dryers. **Dining:** 6 am-9 pm, Fri-10 pm, Sat 7
am-10 pm, Sun 7 am-9 pm, cocktails. **Pool(s):** heated indoor. **Leisure Activities:** sauna, whirlpool. *Fee:* game room. **Guest
Services:** valet laundry, area transportation-car ferry. **Business Services:** conference facilities. **Cards:** AX, CB, DC, DS, MC, VI.
Special Amenities: free local telephone calls. *(See ad below)*

SOME UNITS
[icons]
FEE

WHERE TO DINE

FOUR SEASONS

American

| | **Lunch:** $4-$9 | **Dinner:** $4-$9 | **Phone:** 920/683-1444 |

Location: I-43, exit 149, 0.9 mi e. 3950 Calumet Ave 54220. **Hours:** 5:30 am-11 pm. **Features:** The casual restaurant features an extensive menu of simple recipes and offers a coffee-shop ambience that is comfortable for families and popular with the locals. Breakfast is served all day. Dessert and bread are made on the premises. Casual dress; wine only. **Parking:** on-site. **Cards:** MC, VI. ⊠

The following restaurant has not been evaluated by AAA but is listed for your information only.

LUIGI'S

[fyi]

Phone: 920/684-4200

Not evaluated. **Location:** I-43, exit 149, 1 mi w. 6124 Calumet Ave (Hwy 151) 54220. **Features:** This eatery is well-known for its traditional, pan and Chicago style pizza.

MARINETTE pop. 11,749

WHERE TO STAY

BEST WESTERN RIVERFRONT INN

(AAA) (SAVE)

▽▽ ▽▽

Large-scale Hotel

Phone: (715)732-1000

6/1-10/31	1P: $79-$89	2P: $79-$89	XP: $10 F
4/1-5/31 & 11/1-3/31	1P: $69-$79	2P: $69-$79	XP: $10 F

Location: Just w of US 41; center. 1821 Riverside Ave 54143. Fax: 715/732-0800. **Facility:** 120 one-bedroom standard units, some with whirlpools. 6 stories, interior corridors. **Parking:** on-site. **Terms:** $15 service charge. **Amenities:** video games, voice mail, irons, hair dryers. **Dining:** 6 am-10 pm, cocktails. **Pool(s):** heated indoor. **Leisure Activities:** whirlpool, limited exercise equipment. **Guest Services:** valet and coin laundry. **Business Services:** conference facilities. **Cards:** AX, CB, DC, DS, JC, MC, VI. **Special Amenities:** free newspaper.

SOME UNITS

[icons]

COMFORT INN OF MARINETTE

(AAA) (SAVE)

▽▽ ▽▽

Small-scale Hotel

Phone: 715/732-2321

5/1-10/31	1P: $48-$57	2P: $54-$63	XP: $6 F18
4/1-4/30 & 11/1-3/31	1P: $41-$50	2P: $47-$56	XP: $6 F18

Location: 2 mi s on US 41. Located in a commercial area. 2180 Roosevelt Rd 54143. Fax: 715/732-3663. **Facility:** 48 one-bedroom standard units, some with whirlpools. 2 stories (no elevator), interior corridors. *Bath:* combo or shower only. **Parking:** on-site, winter plug-ins. **Terms:** [ECP] meal plan available. **Amenities:** hair dryers. *Some:* irons. **Leisure Activities:** whirlpool, exercise room. **Business Services:** meeting rooms. **Cards:** AX, DC, DS, MC, VI. **Special Amenities:** free continental breakfast and free local telephone calls.

SOME UNITS

[icons] FEE

WHERE TO DINE

MEMORIES RESTAURANT

▽▽

American

| | **Lunch:** $3-$6 | **Dinner:** $3-$6 | **Phone:** 715/735-3348 |

Location: 0.5 mi s of US 41; downtown. 1378 Main St 54143. **Hours:** 5:30 am-7 pm, Sun from 6:30 am. Closed: 12/25. **Features:** Step back into the 1950s at this casual downtown restaurant known for its homestyle sandwiches and chargrilled burgers. Soup, chili, bread and old-fashioned dessert are made in-house. Breakfast is served all day. Casual dress. **Parking:** on-site. **Cards:** MC, VI. ⊠

MARSHFIELD pop. 18,800

WHERE TO STAY

AMERIHOST INN AND SUITES-MARSHFIELD

(AAA) (SAVE)

▽▽ ▽▽

Small-scale Hotel

Phone: (715)384-5240

All Year [ECP]	1P: $65-$79	2P: $71-$85	XP: $6 F17

Location: On SR 97, 1.2 mi n of SR 13. 2107 N Central Ave 54449. Fax: 715/384-4812. **Facility:** 60 one-bedroom standard units, some with whirlpools. 2 stories, interior corridors. *Bath:* combo or shower only. **Parking:** on-site. **Amenities:** voice mail, safes (fee), irons, hair dryers. **Pool(s):** heated indoor. **Leisure Activities:** whirlpool, exercise room. **Guest Services:** valet laundry. **Business Services:** meeting rooms, fax (fee). **Cards:** AX, DC, DS, MC, VI. **Special Amenities:** free continental breakfast and free local telephone calls.

SOME UNITS

[icons]

COMFORT INN

(SAVE)

▽▽ ▽▽

Small-scale Hotel

Phone: 715/387-8691

All Year	1P: $59-$77	2P: $59-$77	XP: $5 F18

Location: On SR 97, 0.6 mi n of jct SR 13. 114 E Upham St 54449. Fax: 715/387-3001. **Facility:** 46 one-bedroom standard units, some with whirlpools. 2 stories (no elevator), interior corridors. **Parking:** on-site, winter plug-ins. **Terms:** [CP] meal plan available. **Amenities:** video library (fee), irons, hair dryers. **Pool(s):** heated indoor. **Leisure Activities:** whirlpool. **Business Services:** fax (fee). **Cards:** AX, DC, DS, MC, VI.

SOME UNITS

[icons] FEE

PARK MOTEL

(AAA) (SAVE)

▽▽

Motel

Phone: (715)387-1741

All Year	1P: $35-$39	2P: $42-$46	XP: $5 F12

Location: 1 mi s on SR 13. Located next to Wildwood Park and Zoo. 1806 Roddis Ave 54449. Fax: 715/387-0290. **Facility:** 20 one-bedroom standard units. 1 story, exterior corridors. *Bath:* combo or shower only. **Parking:** on-site, winter plug-ins. **Terms:** 3 day cancellation notice-fee imposed. **Business Services:** fax (fee). **Cards:** AX, DC, MC, VI. **Special Amenities:** free local telephone calls.

SOME UNITS

[icons]

SUPER 8

Phone: 715/387-2233

Small-scale Hotel

All Year [CP]   1P: $59-$76   2P: $63-$80   XP: $5   F17
Location: On SR 97, 0.8 mi n of jct SR 13. 1651 N Central Ave 54449. Fax: 715/384-8366. **Facility:** 104 one-bedroom standard units, some with whirlpools. 2 stories (no elevator), interior corridors. **Parking:** on-site, winter plug-ins. **Amenities:** hair dryers. **Pool(s):** heated indoor. **Leisure Activities:** whirlpool. *Fee:* game room. **Business Services:** meeting rooms, fax (fee). **Cards:** AX, DC, DS, MC, VI.

SOME UNITS
FEE

──────── **WHERE TO DINE** ────────

ROYAL TOKYO

Japanese

Lunch: $7-$12   Dinner: $15-$23   Phone: 715/486-8868
Location: Just e of Central Ave; adjacent railroad tracks; downtown. 112 E 1st St 54449. **Hours:** 11:30 am-2:30 & 4:30-9:30 pm. Closed: 11/27, 12/25. **Reservations:** accepted. **Features:** Skilled teppanyaki chefs put on quite a show as they prepare your food before your eyes on heated steel grills. Visitors tend to socialize at the large tables in this professionally restored train depot. Miso soup, a variety of sushis and entrees of beef, seafood & chicken highlight the menu. Dressy casual; cocktails. **Parking:** on-site. **Cards:** AX, DC, MC, VI.

MAUSTON pop. 3,740

──────── **WHERE TO STAY** ────────

BEST WESTERN PARK OASIS INN

Phone: (608)847-6255

Small-scale Hotel

5/1-9/30   1P: $85-$150   2P: $90-$155   XP: $5   F17
10/1-3/31   1P: $75-$125   2P: $80-$130   XP: $5   F17
4/1-4/30   1P: $70-$120   2P: $75-$125   XP: $5   F17
Location: I-90/94, exit 69, just se. W5641 Hwy 82 E 53948. Fax: 608/847-7311. **Facility:** 53 units. 51 one-bedroom standard units, some with whirlpools. 2 one-bedroom suites, some with kitchens. 3 stories, interior corridors. **Parking:** on-site, winter plug-ins. **Amenities:** irons, hair dryers. **Dining:** 5 am-10 pm, cocktails. **Pool(s):** small heated outdoor, small heated indoor. **Leisure Activities:** sauna, whirlpool, horseshoes. *Fee:* miniature golf. **Guest Services:** gift shop, valet and coin laundry. **Business Services:** meeting rooms, administrative services (fee). **Cards:** AX, CB, DC, DS, MC, VI. **Special Amenities:** free newspaper.

SOME UNITS

COUNTRY INN BY CARLSON

Phone: (608)847-5959

Small-scale Hotel

5/25-9/30 [ECP]   1P: $79-$87   2P: $87-$95   XP: $8   F18
4/1-5/24 & 10/1-3/31 [ECP]   1P: $66-$74   2P: $67-$74   XP: $8   F18
Location: I-90/94, exit 69, just ne. 1001 SR 82 53948. Fax: 608/847-4160. **Facility:** 62 one-bedroom standard units, some with whirlpools. 2 stories, interior corridors. **Parking:** on-site, winter plug-ins. **Terms:** small pets only ($5 extra charge). **Amenities:** irons, hair dryers. **Pool(s):** small heated indoor. **Leisure Activities:** whirlpool. *Fee:* game room. **Guest Services:** coin laundry. **Business Services:** meeting rooms, administrative services (fee). **Cards:** AX, DC, DS, MC, VI. **Special Amenities:** free continental breakfast and free newspaper.
(See color ad starting on p 556)

SOME UNITS

SUPER 8 MOTEL

Phone: (608)847-2300

Motel

6/1-9/15 [CP]   1P: $69-$74   2P: $92-$97   XP: $5   F18
9/16-3/31 [CP]   1P: $61-$85   2P: $66-$89   XP: $5   F18
4/1-5/31 [CP]   1P: $59-$83   2P: $64-$87   XP: $5   F18
Location: I-90/94, exit 69, just ne. 1001A Hwy 82 E 53948. Fax: 608/847-6769. **Facility:** 49 units. 47 one-bedroom standard units. 2 one-bedroom suites ($148-$190) with whirlpools. 2 stories, interior corridors. **Parking:** on-site, winter plug-ins. **Terms:** 7 day cancellation notice, pets ($5 extra charge). **Amenities:** dual phone lines, hair dryers. **Pool(s):** small heated indoor. **Leisure Activities:** whirlpool. **Guest Services:** coin laundry. **Business Services:** administrative services (fee). **Cards:** AX, CB, DC, DS, MC, VI.

SOME UNITS

MAYVILLE pop. 4,902

──────── **WHERE TO STAY** ────────

THE MAYVILLE INN

Phone: 920/387-1234

Small-scale Hotel

All Year   1P: $57-$93   2P: $57-$93   XP: $8   F12
Location: 1.3 mi w on SR 28. 701 S Mountin Dr 53050 (PO Box 86). Fax: 920/387-1234. **Facility:** 29 one-bedroom standard units, some with whirlpools. 2 stories, interior corridors. **Parking:** on-site, winter plug-ins. **Leisure Activities:** whirlpool. **Guest Services:** valet laundry. **Business Services:** meeting rooms. **Cards:** AX, DS, MC, VI.

SOME UNITS

MAZOMANIE pop. 1,485

──────── **WHERE TO DINE** ────────

THE OLD FEED MILL

American

Lunch: $5-$7   Dinner: $11-$21   Phone: 608/795-4909
Location: 0.3 mi n of US 14. 114 Cramer St 53560. **Hours:** 11 am-2 & 4:30-8 pm, Fri & Sat-9 pm, Sun 10 am-2:30 & 4:30-8 pm; open 1 hour later daily 5/27-9/2. Closed: 12/25; also Mon. **Reservations:** accepted. **Features:** Country cooking is dished up at a wonderfully restored 1857 flour feed mill furnished with antiques. Each day, the restaurant grinds its own flour for use in breads and pastries. Pot roast and pot pie are mouthwatering choices, as is scrumptious bread pudding from the dessert menu. Casual dress; cocktails. **Parking:** on-site.
Cards: AX, DS, MC, VI.

MEDFORD pop. 4,350

──────── **WHERE TO STAY** ────────

AMERICINN OF MEDFORD
▼▼ ▼▼▼▼
Small-scale Hotel
All Year   1P: $69-$82   2P: $75-$88   XP: $6   Phone: 715/748-2330   F12
Location: On SR 13, 0.5 mi s of jct SR 64. 435 S 8th St 54451. Fax: 715/748-5543. **Facility:** 38 units. 37 one-bedroom standard units. 1 one-bedroom suite ($88-$103). 2 stories (no elevator), interior corridors. *Bath:* combo or shower only. **Parking:** on-site. **Terms:** [ECP] meal plan available. **Pool(s):** small heated indoor. **Leisure Activities:** sauna, whirlpool. **Guest Services:** valet laundry. **Business Services:** meeting rooms. **Cards:** AX, DS, MC, VI.

SOME UNITS

MALIBU INN MOTEL
▼▼ ▼▼
Motel
All Year   1P: $59   2P: $68   XP: $8   Phone: 715/748-3995   F9
Location: On SR 13, 0.6 mi n of jct SR 64. 854 N 8th St 54451. Fax: 715/748-3995. **Facility:** 26 units. 24 one-bedroom standard units. 2 one-bedroom suites ($83-$105). 1 story, interior corridors. **Parking:** on-site, winter plug-ins. **Pool(s):** small heated indoor. **Leisure Activities:** sauna, whirlpool. **Business Services:** fax (fee). **Cards:** AX, DS, MC, VI.

SOME UNITS

──────── **WHERE TO DINE** ────────

MEDFORD CAFE
▼▼
American
Lunch: $5-$8   **Dinner:** $5-$8   Phone: 715/748-2233
Location: On SR 13, 0.5 mi s of jct SR 64. 403 S 8th St 54451. **Hours:** 6 am-9 pm. Closed: 11/27, 12/25. **Reservations:** accepted. **Features:** This restaurant features a homey and contemporary decor that is in a country and patriotic theme. The menu consists of a traditional selection of sandwiches and burgers, as well as a variety of country dinners. Casual dress. **Parking:** on-site. **Cards:** AX, DS, MC, VI.

MENOMONIE pop. 14,937

──────── WHERE TO STAY ────────

AMERIHOST INN & SUITES MENOMONIE
Phone: (715)233-1500
(AAA) (SAVE)
▽▽▽▽ All Year [CP] 1P: $69 2P: $69
Small-scale Hotel **Location:** I-94, exit 45 (CR B), just sw. 1721 Plaza Dr NE 54751. Fax: 715/233-6198. **Facility:** 62 one-bedroom standard units, some with whirlpools. 3 stories, interior corridors. *Bath:* combo or shower only. **Parking:** on-site. **Amenities:** high-speed Internet, dual phone lines, voice mail, safes, irons, hair dryers. **Pool(s):** heated indoor. **Leisure Activities:** whirlpool, limited exercise equipment. **Guest Services:** valet and coin laundry. **Business Services:** meeting rooms, fax. **Cards:** AX, DC, DS, MC, VI.

SOME UNITS

COUNTRY INN & SUITES
Phone: (715)235-5664
▽▽▽▽ All Year 1P: $71-$131 2P: $71-$131 F18
Small-scale Hotel **Location:** I-94, exit 41 (SR 25), just se. 320 Oak Ave 54751. Fax: 715/233-3241. **Facility:** 68 units. 57 one-bedroom standard units, some with whirlpools. 11 one-bedroom suites ($89-$149). 3 stories, interior corridors. *Bath:* combo or shower only. **Parking:** on-site, winter plug-ins. **Terms:** [ECP] meal plan available, pets ($25 fee). **Amenities:** high-speed Internet, dual phone lines, voice mail, irons, hair dryers. **Pool(s):** small heated indoor. **Leisure Activities:** exercise room. **Guest Services:** coin laundry. **Business Services:** meeting rooms, administrative services (fee). **Cards:** AX, DC, DS, MC, VI. *(See color ad starting on p 556)*

SOME UNITS

MENOMONIE MOTEL 6
Phone: 715/235-6901
▽▽ All Year 1P: $38-$52 2P: $44-$58 XP: $3 F17
Motel **Location:** I-94, exit 41 (SR 25), just se. 2100 Stout St 54751 (603 Grandview Hts). Fax: 715/235-8664. **Facility:** 63 one-bedroom standard units. 3 stories, interior corridors. *Bath:* combo or shower only. **Parking:** on-site. **Terms:** weekly rates available. **Amenities:** high-speed Internet (fee). **Guest Services:** coin laundry. **Business Services:** administrative services (fee). **Cards:** AX, DC, DS, MC, VI.

SOME UNITS

SUPER 8 MOTEL-MENOMONIE
Phone: (715)235-8889
▽▽ All Year [CP] 1P: $49-$69 2P: $54-$79 XP: $5 F12
Motel **Location:** I-94, exit 41 (SR 25), just s. 1622 N Broadway 54751. Fax: 715/235-9127. **Facility:** 81 one-bedroom standard units. 3 stories, interior corridors. **Parking:** on-site, winter plug-ins. **Terms:** pets ($15 fee). **Amenities:** safes (fee). **Pool(s):** heated indoor. **Leisure Activities:** whirlpool. **Guest Services:** coin laundry. **Business Services:** meeting rooms, administrative services (fee). **Cards:** AX, CB, DC, DS, MC, VI.

SOME UNITS
FEE FEE

MEQUON —*See Milwaukee p. 574.*

MERRILL pop. 10,146

──────── WHERE TO STAY ────────

PINE RIDGE INN
Phone: (715)536-9526
(AAA) (SAVE)
▽▽▽▽
	6/16-9/29	1P: $40-$52	2P: $49-$64	XP: $5	F12
	9/30-12/31	1P: $40-$50	2P: $49-$62	XP: $5	F12
	1/1-3/31	1P: $40-$50	2P: $49-$55	XP: $5	F12
	4/1-6/15	1P: $40-$50	2P: $49-$54	XP: $5	F12
Motel **Location:** I-39, exit 208, just w. 200 S Pine Ridge 54452. Fax: 715/536-4520. **Facility:** 40 one-bedroom standard units, some with kitchens. 2 stories (no elevator), interior corridors. **Parking:** on-site, winter plug-ins. **Terms:** [CP] meal plan available, pets ($5 extra charge, with prior approval). **Business Services:** fax (fee). **Cards:** AX, DC, MC, VI. **Special Amenities:** free local telephone calls and free room upgrade (subject to availability with advanced reservations).

SOME UNITS
FEE

SUPER 8 MOTEL
Phone: (715)536-6880
(AAA) (SAVE)
▽▽▽▽
	6/16-9/28	1P: $60-$118	2P: $67-$125	XP: $7	F13
	9/29-3/31	1P: $65-$108	2P: $72-$115	XP: $7	F13
	4/1-6/15	1P: $55-$80	2P: $62-$87	XP: $7	F13
Small-scale Hotel **Location:** I-39, exit 208, 0.5 mi w on SR 64. 3209 E Main St 54452. Fax: 715/539-2602. **Facility:** 57 units. 56 one-bedroom standard units, some with whirlpools. 1 one-bedroom suite ($75-$125). 2 stories (no elevator), interior corridors. *Bath:* combo or shower only. **Parking:** on-site, winter plug-ins. **Terms:** 3 day cancellation notice, [ECP] meal plan available, pets ($5 fee). **Amenities:** *Some:* irons, hair dryers. **Pool(s):** small heated indoor. **Leisure Activities:** sauna, whirlpool. *Fee:* game room. **Guest Services:** valet and coin laundry. **Business Services:** meeting rooms, fax. **Cards:** AX, CB, DC, DS, MC, VI. **Special Amenities:** free continental breakfast and free newspaper.

SOME UNITS

──────── *The following lodging was either not evaluated or did not* ────────
meet AAA rating requirements but is listed for your information only.

AMERICINN LODGE & SUITES OF MERRILL   **Phone:** 715/536-7979
[fyi]   5/30-9/2 [ECP]   1P: $79-$139   2P: $79-$139   XP: $5   F12
                 9/3-3/31 [ECP]   1P: $69-$139   2P: $69-$139   XP: $5   F12
Small-scale Hotel 4/1-5/29 [ECP]   1P: $69-$119   2P: $69-$119   XP: $5   F12
Too new to rate. **Location:** Hwy 51, exit 208, 0.5 mi w on SR 64. 3300 E Main St 54452. Fax: 715/536-7975.
Amenities: 45 units, coffeemakers, microwaves, refrigerators, pool. **Cards:** AX, CB, DC, DS, MC, VI.

MIDDLETON pop. 15,770 (See map p. 519; index p. 521)

──────── WHERE TO STAY ────────

FAIRFIELD INN MADISON WEST/MIDDLETON   **Phone:** 608/831-1400   **44**
SAVE   6/16-10/31   1P: $69-$99   2P: $74-$99   XP: $5   F18
                 11/1-3/31   1P: $59-$64   2P: $59-$64
                 4/1-6/15   1P: $59-$64   2P: $59-$64
                 Location: US 12 and 14, exit 252 (Greenway Blvd), then just w. 8212 Greenway Blvd 53562. Fax: 608/831-1435.
Small-scale Hotel **Facility:** 104 one-bedroom standard units. 3 stories, interior corridors. *Bath:* combo or shower only. **Parking:**
on-site, winter plug-ins. **Terms:** [ECP] meal plan available. **Amenities:** video games (fee), dual phone lines,
irons, hair dryers. **Pool(s):** small heated indoor. **Leisure Activities:** whirlpool. **Guest Services:** valet laundry. **Business Services:** meeting rooms. **Cards:** AX, CB, DC, DS, MC, VI.

SOME UNITS
⊞ 🄫 🕎 🛄 📺 📠 🖥 / ⊠ 🛗 🖨 /

MARRIOTT MADISON WEST   **Phone:** 608/831-2000   **45**
AAA **SAVE** All Year   1P: $119   2P: $119   XP: $15
                 Location: US 12 and 14, exit 252 (Greenway Blvd), then just w. 1313 John Q Hammons Dr 53562. Fax: 608/831-2040.
                 Facility: 292 units. 256 one-bedroom standard units. 36 one-bedroom suites, some with whirlpools. 10 sto-
                 ries, interior corridors. **Parking:** on-site. **Terms:** check-in 4 pm. **Amenities:** high-speed Internet (fee), dual
Small-scale Hotel phone lines, voice mail, irons, hair dryers. **Dining:** 6 am-9 pm, cocktails. **Pool(s):** heated indoor. **Leisure
                 Activities:** sauna, whirlpool, sun deck, exercise room. **Guest Services:** gift shop, valet and coin laundry.
area transportation. **Business Services:** conference facilities, business center. **Cards:** AX, CB, DC, DS, MC, VI.
(See ad p 527)

SOME UNITS
✈ 🛏 🍴 🍽 🕎 🛄 🖃 📺 📠 🖥 / ⊠ VCR 🛗 🖨 /
                                                                           FEE

──────── *The following lodging was either not evaluated or did not* ────────
meet AAA rating requirements but is listed for your information only.

STAYBRIDGE SUITES BY HOLIDAY INN   **Phone:** 608/664-5888
[fyi]   All Year [BP]   1P: $119-$159   2P: $119-$159
                 Too new to rate, opening scheduled for January 2003. **Location:** US 12 and 14, exit University Ave, just nw. 7790
Small-scale Hotel Elmwood Ave 53562. Fax: 608/664-5877. **Amenities:** 91 units, pets, coffeemakers, microwaves, refrigerators,
                 pool. **Terms:** cancellation fee imposed. **Cards:** AX, CB, DC, DS, MC, VI.

──────── WHERE TO DINE ────────

IMPERIAL GARDEN WEST   **Lunch:** $5-$9   **Dinner:** $7-$14   **Phone:** 608/238-6445   **17**
AAA   **Location:** US 12 and 14, exit 251, 1.7 mi e on University Ave. 2039 Allen Blvd 53562. **Hours:** 11:30 am-2 & 4-9:30
                 pm, Fri-10:30 pm, Sat 4 pm-10:30 pm, Sun 4 pm-9 pm. Closed: 7/4, 11/27, 12/24, 12/25.
                 Reservations: accepted. **Features:** This restaurant has a large menu selection of traditional pork, beef,
                 chicken, lamb, duck and seafood dishes. There are also some vegetarian entrees including rice and
Chinese   noodles. This restaurant is well-established and locally popular. Dressy casual; cocktails. **Parking:** on-site.
                 Cards: AX, DC, DS, MC, VI.
                                                                                                    🍽 ⊠

LOUISIANNE'S ETC   **Dinner:** $12-$30   **Phone:** 608/831-1929   **16**
                 Location: Se of jct US 12 and University Ave, via Parmenter. 7464 Hubbard Ave 53562. **Hours:** 5 pm-10 pm,
                 Mon-9 pm. Closed major holidays; also Sun. **Reservations:** suggested. **Features:** The piquant Creole
American   flavors of New Orleans infuse colorfully presented dishes of seafood, beef and chicken. Original stone
                 walls and soft lighting give the dining room an almost cavernous feel. The sounds of live jazz resonate off
the walls. Casual dress; cocktails. **Parking:** street. **Cards:** AX, DS, MC, VI.
                                                                                                    🍽 ⊠

MORELS   **Dinner:** $15-$25   **Phone:** 608/836-7151
                 Location: 4.1 mi sw on Airport Rd from jct US 12. 4635 Chalet St 53562. **Hours:** 5 pm-9 pm, Fri & Sat-9:30 pm,
                 Sun 4:30 pm-9 pm. Closed: Mon. **Reservations:** suggested. **Features:** The chef's creative, seasonally
American   changing menu takes advantage of the freshest vegetables, fruits and locally produced meats, including
                 pheasant, elk and duckling. A good variety of fresh fish entrees, as well as USDA prime beef, pork and
some chicken selections, satisfy those looking for something more tame. Desserts are made in house. Wildlife artwork adorns
the walls of the rural dining room. Casual dress; cocktails. **Parking:** on-site. **Cards:** AX, MC, VI.
                                                                                                    🍽 ⊠

Look for the Signs Along the Way

When selecting a place to dine while traveling, look for Official Appointment restaurants that display the AAA Approved sign. It's the only sign you need to be assured of an enjoyable dining experience.

As a member, you already know the AAA sign indicates quality establishments. So, when you don't have advance dining reservations, look for the AAA Approved sign along the way, for a meal you'll long remember!

Destination Milwaukee
pop. 596,974

Milwaukee City Hall
Built in 1895, city hall boasts a 350-foot bell tower that can be seen for miles. (See listing page 153)

Milwaukee is naturally a great spot for water sports: Not only is the city right on Lake Michigan, it's also divided in half by the Milwaukee River.

Those who would rather stay dry can hit the mall, cheer on the area's sports teams and attend a performance by the opera or ballet.

Skylight Opera Theater, Milwaukee.
Colorful costumes play a major role in the productions held at this theater. (See mention page 158)

Places included in this AAA Destination City:

Indian Summer Fest, Milwaukee.
American Indian tribes showcase their culture with elaborate costumes and demonstrations. (See mention page 159)

Dining, Milwaukee.
Catch a cool breeze and a hot bite at one of the many restaurants lining the Milwaukee River.

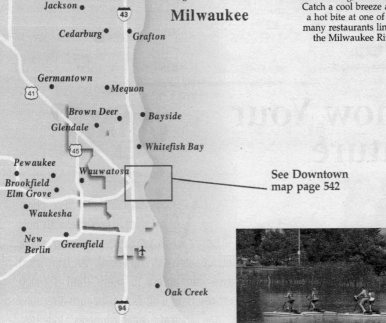

West Bend

Port Washington

Jackson

Milwaukee

43

Cedarburg

Grafton

Germantown

41

Mequon

Brown Deer

Bayside

Glendale

45

Whitefish Bay

Pewaukee

Wauwatosa

See Downtown map page 542

Brookfield
Elm Grove

Waukesha

New Berlin

Greenfield

Oak Creek

94

Veterans Park, Milwaukee.
Paddling on hydrobikes is the perfect way to get around on one of the more than 15,000 inland lakes Wisconsin has to offer. (See mention page 157)

Downtown Milwaukee Lodging & Dining

© 2002 NAVIGATION TECHNOLOGIES   1944-A

Know Your Future

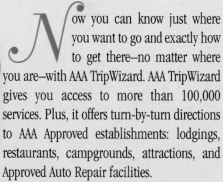

Downtown Milwaukee

This index helps you "spot" where approved accommodations and restaurants are located on the corresponding detailed maps. Lodging rate ranges are for comparison only and show the property's high season; rates are per night, unless only weekly (W) rates are available. Restaurant rate range is for dinner, unless only lunch (L) is served. Turn to the listing page for more detailed rate information and consult display ads for special promotions.

Spotter/Map Page Number	OA	DOWNTOWN MILWAUKEE - Lodgings	Diamond Rating	Rate Range High Season	Listing Page
1 / p. 542	AAA	**Park East Hotel**	▽▽▽	$114 SAVE	549
2 / p. 542	AAA	**Wyndham Milwaukee Center** - see color ad p 550	▽▽▽	$119-$125 SAVE	550
3 / p. 542	AAA	**Hyatt Regency Milwaukee** - see color ad p 549	▽▽▽	$99-$175 SAVE	549
4 / p. 542		Hotel Metro-Milwaukee	▽▽▽	$189-$269	548
5 / p. 542	AAA	**The Pfister Hotel**	▽▽▽▽	$244-$264 SAVE	550
6 / p. 542	AAA	**Best Western Inn Towne** - see color ad p 548	▽▽▽	$89-$159 SAVE	548
7 / p. 542	AAA	**Howard Johnson Inn & Suites** - see color ad p 560, p 549	▽▽▽	$89-$199 SAVE	548
8 / p. 542	AAA	**Hilton Milwaukee City Center**	▽▽▽	$99-$219 SAVE	548
9 / p. 542	AAA	**Holiday Inn Milwaukee City Centre**	▽▽▽	$89-$139 SAVE	548
10 / p. 542		Residence Inn-Downtown Milwaukee	▽▽▽	$129-$199	550
11 / p. 542		Ramada Inn City Centre	▽▽	$99-$108	550
		DOWNTOWN MILWAUKEE - Restaurants			
1 / p. 542		Sanford Restaurant	▽▽▽▽	$45-$75	551
2 / p. 542		Third Street Pier	▽▽▽	$20-$47	552
3 / p. 542	AAA	**Mader's German Restaurant**	▽▽	$18-$24	551
4 / p. 542		Polaris	▽▽▽	$17-$35	551
5 / p. 542		Boulevard Inn	▽▽▽	$18-$45	551
6 / p. 542		Watts Tea Shop	▽▽	$6-$12(L)	552
7 / p. 542		Karl Ratzsch's Restaurant	▽▽	$15-$28	551
8 / p. 542		Ed Debevic's	▽▽	$6-$8	551
9 / p. 542	AAA	**Celia**	▽▽▽▽	$16-$28	551
10 / p. 542		Piece's Of Eight	▽▽	$16-$25	551
11 / p. 542		Coquette Cafe	▽▽	$8-$17	551

©2002 NAVIGATION TECHNOLOGIES

© AAA

To Sheboygan

Lake Michigan

SEE DOWNTOWN
MAP FOR DETAIL

Milwaukee
Lodging & Dining

0 ____ Miles ____ 3.19

1943-A

To Chicago

✈ Airport Accommodations

Spotter/Map Page Number	OA	GENERAL MITCHELL INTERNATIONAL	Diamond Rating	Rate Range High Season	Listing Page
⑪ / p. 544	(AAA)	Clarion Hotel Airport, 0.5 mi w of terminal	◈◈◈	$89-$109 SAVE	554
⑬ / p. 544	(AAA)	Country Inns & Suites By Carlson, 2.3 mi s of terminal	◈◈◈	$80-$117 SAVE	554
⑯ / p. 544	(AAA)	Econo Lodge Airport, 2.9 mi s of terminal	◈◈	$39-$199 SAVE	555
⑨ / p. 544	(AAA)	Four Points by Sheraton Milwaukee Airport, 0.5 mi w of terminal	◈◈◈	$79-$109 SAVE	555
⑭ / p. 544	(AAA)	Hampton Inn-Milwaukee Airport, 2.7 mi s of terminal	◈◈◈	$79-$129 SAVE	558
⑦ / p. 544	(AAA)	Holiday Inn Hotel and Suites, 1.3 mi w of terminal	◈◈◈	$105-$135 SAVE	559
⑥ / p. 544		Hospitality Inn, 3.5 mi nw of terminal	◈◈◈	$80-$300	560
⑧ / p. 544	(AAA)	Howard Johnson Milwaukee Airport Inn, 2.8 mi nw from terminal	◈◈	$59-$159 SAVE	560
⑫ / p. 544	(AAA)	Manchester Suites Airport, 0.5 mi w of terminal	◈◈◈	$79-$109 SAVE	561
⑰ / p. 544	(AAA)	Radisson Hotel Milwaukee Airport, 2.8 mi s of terminal	◈◈◈	$79-$159 SAVE	562
⑩ / p. 544	(AAA)	Super 8 Motel-Milwaukee Airport, 0.5 mi w of terminal	◈◈	$71-$249 SAVE	563
⑱ / p. 544	(AAA)	Comfort Suites, 2.9 mi s of terminal	◈◈◈	$99-$159 SAVE	575
⑮ / p. 544	(AAA)	Exel Inn of Milwaukee South, 2.8 mi s of terminal	◈◈	$47-$69 SAVE	575

Milwaukee and Vicinity

This index helps you "spot" where approved accommodations and restaurants are located on the corresponding detailed maps. Lodging rate ranges are for comparison only and show the property's high season; rates are per night, unless only weekly (W) rates are available. Restaurant rate range is for dinner, unless only lunch (L) is served. Turn to the listing page for more detailed rate information and consult display ads for special promotions.

Spotter/Map Page Number	OA	MILWAUKEE - Lodgings	Diamond Rating	Rate Range High Season	Listing Page
❶ / p. 544	(AAA)	Hilton Garden Inn Milwaukee Park Place	◈◈◈	$59-$179 SAVE	559
❷ / p. 544		Hampton Inn-Milwaukee NW	◈◈◈	$49-$119	559
❸ / p. 544	(AAA)	Manchester Suites NW	◈◈◈	$79-$109 SAVE	561
❹ / p. 544	(AAA)	Baymont Inn & Suites-Milwaukee NW - see color ad p 552	◈◈	$69-$89 SAVE	552
❺ / p. 544	(AAA)	Best Western Woodsview Inn	◈◈	$79-$87 SAVE	553
❻ / p. 544		Hospitality Inn	◈◈◈	$80-$300	560
❼ / p. 544	(AAA)	Holiday Inn Hotel and Suites - see color ad p 559	◈◈◈	$105-$135 SAVE	559
❽ / p. 544	(AAA)	Howard Johnson Milwaukee Airport Inn - see color ad p 560, p 560	◈◈	$59-$159 SAVE	560
❾ / p. 544	(AAA)	Four Points by Sheraton Milwaukee Airport	◈◈◈	$79-$109 SAVE	555
❿ / p. 544	(AAA)	Super 8 Motel-Milwaukee Airport	◈◈	$71-$249 SAVE	563
⑪ / p. 544	(AAA)	Clarion Hotel Airport	◈◈◈	$89-$109 SAVE	554
⑫ / p. 544	(AAA)	Manchester Suites Airport	◈◈◈	$79-$109 SAVE	561
⑬ / p. 544	(AAA)	Country Inns & Suites By Carlson - see color ad starting on p 556	◈◈◈	$80-$117 SAVE	554
⑭ / p. 544	(AAA)	Hampton Inn-Milwaukee Airport - see color ad p 558	◈◈◈	$79-$129 SAVE	558

Spotter/Map Page Number	OA	MILWAUKEE - Lodgings (continued)	Diamond Rating	Rate Range High Season	Listing Page
16 / p. 544	AAA	**Econo Lodge Airport**	◆◆	$39-$199 SAVE	555
17 / p. 544	AAA	**Radisson Hotel Milwaukee Airport -** see color ad p 562, p 562	◆◆◆	$79-$159 SAVE	562
		MILWAUKEE - Restaurants			
1 / p. 544		Yen Ching Restaurant	◆◆	$8-$13	565
2 / p. 544		West Bank Cafe	◆	$5-$17	565
3 / p. 544		Bartolotta's Lake Park Bistro	◆◆◆	$10-$35	565
4 / p. 544		Au Bon Appetit Restaurant & Catering	◆◆	$8-$14	565
5 / p. 544		Saz's State House	◆◆	$7-$22	565
6 / p. 544		Heinemann's Restaurant	◆◆	$5-$7	565
7 / p. 544		Old Town Serbian Gourmet House	◆◆	$12-$18	565
8 / p. 544		Paul's Omega Family Restaurant	◆	$8-$17	565
9 / p. 544		The Packing House	◆◆	$10-$23	565
		OAK CREEK - Lodgings			
15 / p. 544	AAA	**Exel Inn of Milwaukee South -** see color ad p 555	◆◆	$47-$69 SAVE	575
18 / p. 544	AAA	**Comfort Suites -** see color ad p 558	◆◆◆	$99-$159 SAVE	575
19 / p. 544	AAA	**Red Roof Inn-Milwaukee**	◆	$46-$69 SAVE	576
61 / p. 544		MainStay Suites Oak Creek	◆◆◆	$80-$160	575
62 / p. 544	AAA	**Baymont Inn & Suites Milwaukee-Airport -** see color ad p 552	◆◆	$69-$89 SAVE	575
		MEQUON - Lodgings			
22 / p. 544		The Chalet Motel of Mequon	◆◆	$69-$149	574
23 / p. 544	AAA	**Best Western Quiet House & Suites -** see ad p 555	◆◆◆	$95-$133 SAVE	574
		MEQUON - Restaurants			
15 / p. 544		The Centennial	◆◆	$5-$13	574
16 / p. 544		Heinemann's Restaurant	◆	$5-$9	574
		BROWN DEER - Lodgings			
26 / p. 544		Holiday Inn Express	◆◆◆	$79-$115	568
27 / p. 544		Courtyard by Marriott Milwaukee North Brown Deer	◆◆◆	$109-$129	568
		GLENDALE - Lodgings			
30 / p. 544		Residence Inn by Marriott	◆◆◆	$109-$299	573
31 / p. 544	AAA	**Manchester East Hotel & Suites -** see color ad p 561	◆◆◆	$112-$126 SAVE	573
32 / p. 544	AAA	**Exel Inn of Milwaukee Northeast -** see color ad p 555	◆◆	$55-$81 SAVE	572
33 / p. 544	AAA	**Woodfield Suites Milwaukee-Glendale -** see color ad p 572	◆◆◆	$129-$189 SAVE	573
34 / p. 544	AAA	**Baymont Inn and Suites -** see color ad p 552	◆◆◆	$59-$94 SAVE	572
35 / p. 544	AAA	**Hilton Milwaukee River -** see color ad p 559	◆◆◆	$101-$157 SAVE	572
		GLENDALE - Restaurants			
22 / p. 544		The Bavarian Inn	◆	$9-$18	573
23 / p. 544		Anchorage Restaurant	◆◆◆	$16-$24	573

Spotter/Map Page Number	OA	BROOKFIELD - Lodgings	Diamond Rating	Rate Range High Season	Listing Page
38 / p. 544		TownePlace Suites by Marriott	▽▽▽	$69-$109	567
39 / p. 544		Courtyard by Marriott/Brookfield	▽▽▽	$90-$120	566
40 / p. 544	AAA	Sheraton Milwaukee Brookfield - see color ad p 563	▽▽▽	$89-$119 SAVE	567
41 / p. 544	AAA	Best Western Midway Hotel-Brookfield	▽▽▽	$80-$134 SAVE	566
42 / p. 544		Embassy Suites Hotel-Milwaukee West	▽▽▽	$89-$1000	566
43 / p. 544	AAA	Country Inn & Suites Milwaukee West - see color ad starting on p 556	▽▽▽	$99-$129 SAVE	566
		WAUWATOSA - Lodgings			
46 / p. 544	AAA	Radisson Hotel Milwaukee West - see color ad p 562	▽▽▽	$149-$159 SAVE	579
47 / p. 544	AAA	Holiday Inn Express-Mayfair - see color ad p 558	▽▽▽	$104-$159 SAVE	579
48 / p. 544	AAA	Exel Inn of Milwaukee West - see color ad p 555	▽▽	$50-$84 SAVE	579
		WAUWATOSA - Restaurants			
30 / p. 544	AAA	Heinemann's Restaurant	▽▽	$5-$8	579
31 / p. 544		RJ's an American Bar & Grille	▽▽	$15-$25	579
32 / p. 544		Ristorante Bartolotta	▽▽▽	$16-$29	579
33 / p. 544		Eddie Martini's	▽▽▽	$18-$34	579
		ELM GROVE - Lodgings			
51 / p. 544	AAA	Sleepy Hollow Motel - see color ad p 564	▽	$47-$75 SAVE	570
		ELM GROVE - Restaurant			
36 / p. 544		Elm Grove Inn	▽▽▽	$18-$25	570
		NEW BERLIN - Lodgings			
54 / p. 544	AAA	Holiday Inn Express Hotel and Suites-New Berlin	▽▽▽	$99 SAVE	575
55 / p. 544	AAA	Baymont Inn & Suites Milwaukee-New Berlin - see color ad p 552	▽▽▽	$89-$109 SAVE	575
		NEW BERLIN - Restaurant			
39 / p. 544		Timber Creek Grille	▽▽▽	$15-$28	575
		GREENFIELD - Lodgings			
58 / p. 544		Golden Key Motel	▽	$45-$75	573
		GERMANTOWN - Restaurant			
12 / p. 544		Jerry's Old Town	▽▽	$14-$26	572
		BAYSIDE - Restaurant			
19 / p. 544		Pandl's in Bayside	▽▽▽	$12-$30	566
		WHITEFISH BAY - Restaurants			
26 / p. 544		Heinemann's Restaurant	▽▽	$5-$8	580
27 / p. 544		Jack Pandl's Whitefish Bay Inn	▽▽	$17-$24	580

DOWNTOWN MILWAUKEE (See map p. 542; index p. 543)

------ **WHERE TO STAY** ------

BEST WESTERN INN TOWNE
Phone: (414)224-8400 **6**

(AAA) [SAVE]

6/1-9/30	1P: $89-$149	2P: $99-$159	XP: $10	F17
10/1-3/31	1P: $74-$89	2P: $84-$99	XP: $10	F17
4/1-5/31	1P: $72-$82	2P: $82-$92	XP: $10	F17

Small-scale Hotel **Location:** Corner of Wisconsin Ave and N Old World 3rd St. 710 N Old World 3rd St 53203. Fax: 414/224-8696. **Facility:** 97 one-bedroom standard units. 12 stories, interior corridors. *Bath:* combo or shower only. **Parking:** on-site (fee). **Terms:** cancellation fee imposed, package plans - seasonal, 15% service charge, small pets only. **Amenities:** *Some:* dual phone lines, voice mail, irons, hair dryers. **Dining:** 7 am-10 pm. **Leisure Activities:** exercise room. **Guest Services:** valet laundry. **Business Services:** meeting rooms, PC, fax. **Cards:** AX, CB, DC, DS, JC, MC, VI. **Special Amenities:** free continental breakfast and free newspaper. *(See color ad below)*

SOME UNITS

HILTON MILWAUKEE CITY CENTER
Phone: 414-271-7250 **8**

(AAA) [SAVE]

| All Year | 1P: $99-$219 | 2P: $99-$219 | XP: $20 | F18 |

Large-scale Hotel **Location:** Corner of W Wisconsin Ave and 5th St. 509 W Wisconsin Ave 53203. Fax: 414/271-1039. **Facility:** 730 units. 706 one-bedroom standard units. 11 one- and 13 two-bedroom suites, some with whirlpools. 24 stories, interior corridors. *Bath:* combo or shower only. **Parking:** on-site (fee). **Terms:** cancellation fee imposed. **Amenities:** video games (fee), dual phone lines, voice mail, irons, hair dryers. *Some:* CD players. **Dining:** 3 restaurants; 6:30 am-midnight, cocktails. **Leisure Activities:** indoor water park with hydro therapy spa, kiddie pool, exercise room. *Fee:* game room. **Guest Services:** gift shop, valet laundry. **Business Services:** conference facilities, business center. **Cards:** AX, CB, DC, DS, JC, MC, VI. **Special Amenities:** early check-in/late check-out and free newspaper.

SOME UNITS

HOLIDAY INN MILWAUKEE CITY CENTRE
Phone: (414)273-2950 **9**

(AAA) [SAVE]

| All Year | 1P: $89-$139 | 2P: $89-$139 | XP: $10 | F18 |

Large-scale Hotel **Location:** Corner of W Wisconsin Ave and 6th St. 611 W Wisconsin Ave 53203. Fax: 414/273-7662. **Facility:** 247 units. 246 one-bedroom standard units. 1 one-bedroom suite. 10 stories, interior corridors. **Parking:** on-site (fee) and valet. **Terms:** cancellation fee imposed. **Amenities:** video games (fee), dual phone lines, voice mail, irons, hair dryers. **Dining:** 6 am-2 & 5-10 pm, cocktails. **Pool(s):** heated outdoor. **Leisure Activities:** exercise room. **Guest Services:** valet laundry. **Business Services:** conference facilities, business center. **Cards:** AX, CB, DC, DS, JC, MC, VI. **Special Amenities:** free newspaper and free room upgrade (subject to availability with advanced reservations).

SOME UNITS

HOTEL METRO-MILWAUKEE
Phone: (414)272-1937 **4**

| 5/23-9/6 | 1P: $189-$269 | 2P: $189-$269 | XP: $25 | F18 |
| 4/1-5/22 & 9/7-3/31 | 1P: $159-$229 | 2P: $159-$229 | XP: $25 | F18 |

Small-scale Hotel **Location:** Corner of Mason and Milwaukee sts. 411 E Mason St 53202. Fax: 414/223-1158. **Facility:** 65 units. 16 one-bedroom standard units. 47 one- and 2 two-bedroom suites, some with whirlpools. 6 stories, interior corridors. *Bath:* combo or shower only. **Parking:** on-site (fee) and valet. **Terms:** cancellation fee imposed. **Amenities:** video library (fee), CD players, dual phone lines, voice mail, safes, honor bars, irons, hair dryers. **Leisure Activities:** bicycles. **Guest Services:** valet laundry. **Business Services:** meeting rooms, fax. **Cards:** AX, CB, DC, DS, JC, MC, VI.

SOME UNITS

HOWARD JOHNSON INN & SUITES
Phone: 414-271-4656 **7**

(AAA) [SAVE]

| 6/1-8/31 [CP] | 1P: $89-$199 | 2P: $89-$199 | XP: $10 | F18 |
| 4/1-5/31 & 9/1-3/31 [CP] | 1P: $79-$189 | 2P: $79-$189 | XP: $10 | F18 |

Small-scale Hotel **Location:** I-794, exit 10, 0.3 mi n on Plankinton, just w. 176 W Wisconsin Ave 53203. Fax: 414/329-4656. **Facility:** 142 one-bedroom standard units, some with whirlpools. 10 stories, interior corridors. **Parking:** on-site (fee). **Terms:** check-in 4 pm. **Amenities:** dual phone lines, voice mail, irons, hair dryers. *Some:* safes (fee). **Leisure Activities:** exercise room. **Guest Services:** sundries, valet and coin laundry. **Business Services:** meeting rooms, fax (fee). **Cards:** AX, DC, DS, MC, VI. **Special Amenities:** free continental breakfast and free newspaper. *(See color ad p 560 & p 549)*

SOME UNITS

(See map p. 542)

HYATT REGENCY MILWAUKEE

Phone: (414)276-1234

All Year   1P: $99-$175   2P: $99-$175   XP: $25   F18

Location: At N 3rd St. Walkway to Midwest Express Center and Grand Ave Mall. 333 W Kilbourn Ave 53203. Fax: 414/276-6338. **Facility:** 484 units. 465 one-bedroom standard units. 19 one-bedroom suites. 18 stories, interior corridors. *Bath:* combo or shower only. **Parking:** on-site (fee). **Terms:** cancellation fee imposed. **Amenities:** voice mail, irons, hair dryers. *Some:* CD players, dual phone lines, fax, safes. **Dining:** 2 restaurants, 7 am-midnight, cocktails, also, Polaris, see separate listing. **Leisure Activities:** exercise room. **Guest Services:** gift shop, valet laundry. **Business Services:** conference facilities, business center. **Cards:** AX, CB, DC, DS, JC, MC, VI. *(See color ad below)*

Large-scale Hotel

SOME UNITS
FEE FEE FEE

PARK EAST HOTEL

Phone: (414)276-8800

5/2-10/1   1P: $114   2P: $114   XP: $10   D17
10/2-3/31   1P: $94   2P: $94   XP: $10   D17
4/1-5/1   1P: $89   2P: $89   XP: $10   D17

Location: Between Marshall and Astor sts. 916 E State St 53202. Fax: 414/765-1919. **Facility:** 159 units. 155 one-bedroom standard units, some with whirlpools. 4 one-bedroom suites, some with kitchens. 5 stories, interior corridors. *Bath:* combo or shower only. **Parking:** on-site. **Terms:** cancellation fee imposed, [CP] meal plan available. **Amenities:** video games (fee), voice mail, irons, hair dryers. **Dining:** 6:30-9:30 am, 11:30-2 & 5-10 pm, Sun 7-10 am, cocktails. **Leisure Activities:** exercise room. **Guest Services:** valet and coin laundry, area transportation-downtown. **Business Services:** meeting rooms, business center. **Cards:** AX, CB, DC, DS, JC, MC, VI. **Special Amenities:** free continental breakfast and free newspaper.

Small-scale Hotel

SOME UNITS
FEE FEE

(See map p. 542)

THE PFISTER HOTEL
(AAA) [SAVE]   **Phone: (414)273-8222** [5]
All Year   1P: $244   2P: $264   XP: $20   F18
🔻🔻🔻🔻 🔻🔻
Location: Corner of E Wisconsin Ave and Mason St. 424 E Wisconsin Ave 53202. Fax: 414/273-5025. **Facility:** Built in 1893 by Milwaukee industrialist Guido Pfister, this landmark hotel is now home to an impressive collection of Victorian art. 307 units. 236 one-bedroom standard units. 63 one- and 8 two-bedroom suites ($294-$1050),
Large-scale Hotel   some with whirlpools. 8-23 stories, interior corridors. **Parking:** on-site (fee) and valet. **Terms:** cancellation fee imposed, package plans. **Amenities:** video games (fee), voice mail, safes, honor bars, irons, hair dryers.
Dining: 3 restaurants, 6 am-10 pm, cocktails, also, Celia, see separate listing, entertainment. **Pool(s):** heated indoor. **Leisure Activities:** exercise room. *Fee:* massage. **Guest Services:** gift shop, valet laundry. **Business Services:** conference facilities, PC. **Cards:** AX, DC, DS, MC, VI. **Special Amenities:** early check-in/late check-out and free newspaper.
SOME UNITS
[S🄳] [🍽] [24🛎] [▼] [🔥M] [🗔] [🏊] [🎥] [DATA PORT] / [✕] [VCR]

RAMADA INN CITY CENTRE   **Phone: (414)272-8410** [11]
🔻🔻🔻 🔻🔻🔻   6/27-9/8   1P: $99   2P: $108   XP: $10   F18
                5/1-6/26   1P: $88   2P: $97   XP: $10   F18
Small-scale Hotel 9/9-3/31   1P: $83   2P: $92   XP: $10   F18
                4/1-4/30   1P: $79   2P: $88   XP: $10   F18
Location: I-794, exit 10, just w. 633 W Michigan St 53203. Fax: 414/272-4651. **Facility:** 155 one-bedroom standard units. 7 stories, interior corridors. **Parking:** on-site. **Amenities:** voice mail, irons, hair dryers. **Pool(s):** heated outdoor. **Leisure Activities:** limited exercise equipment. **Guest Services:** valet laundry. **Business Services:** meeting rooms, fax (fee). **Cards:** AX, CB, DC, DS, JC, MC, VI.
SOME UNITS
[A$K] [S🄳] [🕁] [🍽] [▼] [🗔] [🏊] [🎥] [DATA PORT] [🖥] / [✕] [🛢] /
      FEE

RESIDENCE INN-DOWNTOWN MILWAUKEE   **Phone: (414)224-7890** [10]
[SAVE]   6/1-8/31 [ECP]   1P: $129-$199
              4/1-5/31 & 9/1-3/31 [ECP]   1P: $99-$124
🔻🔻🔻🔻   **Location:** I-794, exit 1D, just n, at jct Wisconsin Ave. Located on the Riverwalk. 648 N Plankinton Ave 53203.
              Fax: 414/224-7923. **Facility:** 131 units. 84 one-bedroom standard units with kitchens. 36 one- and 11 two-
Small-scale Hotel bedroom suites with kitchens. 8 stories, interior corridors. *Bath:* combo or shower only. **Parking:** on-site (fee).
              Terms: cancellation fee imposed. **Amenities:** dual phone lines, voice mail, irons, hair dryers. **Leisure Ac-
tivities:** exercise room. **Guest Services:** complimentary evening beverages: Mon-Thurs, valet laundry. **Business Services:** meeting rooms, fax (fee). **Cards:** AX, CB, DC, DS, JC, MC, VI.
SOME UNITS
[S🄳] [🔥M] [&] [🎥] [DATA PORT] [🛢] [🖥] / [✕] /

WYNDHAM MILWAUKEE CENTER   **Phone: (414)276-8686** [2]
(AAA) [SAVE]   All Year   1P: $119-$125   2P: $119-$125   XP: $10   F18
🔻🔻🔻🔻   **Location:** At Water St. 139 E Kilbourn Ave 53202. Fax: 414/276-8007. **Facility:** 220 one-bedroom standard units.
              10 stories, interior corridors. *Bath:* combo or shower only. **Parking:** on-site (fee). **Terms:** cancellation fee im-
              posed. **Amenities:** high-speed Internet, dual phone lines, voice mail, irons, hair dryers. *Fee:* video games,
Large-scale Hotel safes. **Dining:** 6:30 am-11 pm, cocktails. **Leisure Activities:** saunas, whirlpool, steamrooms, sun deck, ex-
              ercise room. **Guest Services:** gift shop, valet laundry. **Business Services:** conference facilities, fax.
Cards: AX, CB, DC, DS, JC, MC, VI. **Special Amenities:** free newspaper and preferred room (subject to availability with advanced reservations). *(See color ad below)*
SOME UNITS
[S🄳] [🍽] [▼] [&] [🗔] [✕] [🎥] [DATA PORT] [🖥] / [✕] [VCR] [🛢] [🖥] /
                                                                  FEE

(See map p. 542)

———— WHERE TO DINE ————

BOULEVARD INN   Historic   **Lunch:** $8-$14   **Dinner:** $18-$45   **Phone:** 414/765-1166   ⑤
Location: I-794, exit 1E, 0.4 mi n on Van Buren, just e; in Cudahy Tower Building. 925 E Wells St 53202. **Hours:** 11:30 am-9:30 pm, Fri & Sat-10 pm, Sun-9 pm. **Closed:** 5/26, 7/4, 9/1; also 12/24.
Continental   **Reservations:** suggested. **Features:** The restaurant has been family owned since 1946, the bustling restaurant serves such dishes as schnitzel, honey duck, sauerbraten and nightly fish specials. Overlooking Lake Michigan, the romantic dining room has a friendly, European ambience. Service is efficient. Dressy casual; cocktails. **Parking:** valet and street. **Cards:** AX, DC, DS, MC, VI.

CELIA   **Lunch:** $10-$15   **Dinner:** $16-$28   **Phone:** 414/390-3832   ⑨
Location: Corner of E Wisconsin Ave and Mason St; in The Pfister Hotel. 424 E Wisconsin Ave 53202. **Hours:** 11:30 am-2 & 5-10 pm, Sat from 5 pm. **Closed:** Sun. **Reservations:** suggested. **Features:** Bright, elegant, sumptuous and contemporary are the words that best describe this newest addition to Milwaukee's fine dining scene. The atmosphere is upscale casual with a very relaxed yet luxurious feel, and the service staff is attentive and friendly. The ever changing menu features food and stylings from a global marketplace, while balancing creativity and eye appeal with a Midwestern sensibility for value. Rounding out the experience is an award winning wine list to suit all tastes. Dressy casual; cocktails. **Parking:** valet. **Cards:** AX, CB, DC, DS, JC, MC, VI.

COQUETTE CAFE   **Dinner:** $8-$17   **Phone:** 414/291-2655   ⑪
Location: Just s of St Paul St in Historic Third Ward; center. 316 N Milwaukee St 53202. **Hours:** 11 am-10 pm, Fri-11 pm, Sat 5 pm-11 pm. Closed major holidays; also Sun. **Reservations:** suggested. **Features:** In a historic building, the lively French-style cafe offers a menu of fine bistro cuisine. Among choices are mussels, cassoulet, pork chops, roast chicken and thin-crust, French-style pizzas. Casual dress; cocktails. **Parking:** on-site and street. **Cards:** AX, CB, DC, MC, VI.

ED DEBEVIC'S   **Lunch:** $6-$8   **Dinner:** $6-$8   **Phone:** 414/226-2200   ⑧
Location: N Jefferson and E Well St; downtown. 780 N Jefferson St 53202. **Hours:** 11 am-9 pm, Fri & Sat-10 pm. Closed major holidays. **Features:** The '50s-style diner serves comfort foods, such as burgers, chili cheese fries and homemade malts, and a heap of good atmosphere. Servers are tart and curt to patrons in a joking and light-hearted manner, adding to an entertaining and unusual dining experience. Casual dress; cocktails. **Parking:** on-site (fee). **Cards:** AX, DC, DS, MC, VI.

KARL RATZSCH'S RESTAURANT   Historic   **Dinner:** $15-$28   **Phone:** 414/276-2720   ⑦
Location: Jct E Mason and N Milwaukee sts. 320 E Mason St 53202. **Hours:** 4:30 pm-9:30 pm, Sat-10 pm. Closed major holidays; also Sun. **Reservations:** suggested. **Features:** This German themed restaurant offers a charming Old World atmosphere and has been family-owned and operated since 1904. Menu selections are homemade. The kassler rippchen is a wonderful dinner choice consisting of pork chops, sauerkraut and potato dumplings. The potato soup makes for a great start to your dining experience with a tasty blend of seasonings and large chunks of potato in a creamy base. Casual dress; cocktails. **Parking:** on-site. **Cards:** AX, DC, DS, MC, VI.

MADER'S GERMAN RESTAURANT   Historic   **Lunch:** $8-$11   **Dinner:** $18-$24   **Phone:** 414/271-3377   ③
Location: Jct W State and N 3rd sts. 1037 N Old World 3rd St 53203. **Hours:** 11:30 am-9 pm, Fri & Sat-10 pm, Sun from 10:30 am. **Closed:** 12/24 for dinner. **Reservations:** suggested. **Features:** This family-owned and operated restaurant has been a local favorite since 1902. All meals are prepared in German tradition with a Continental flair. The setting is that of Germany with the many medieval pieces of weaponry, steins, wood carvings and glassware throughout. Noted for their unique dishes of oxtail soup, sauerbraten and homemade apple or cherry strudel. For the beer lover, there are over 200 imported and domestic beers. Also, a wine list boasting over 100 vintage wines. Casual dress; cocktails. **Parking:** on-site. **Cards:** AX, DC, DS, MC, VI.

PIECE'S OF EIGHT   **Lunch:** $7-$14   **Dinner:** $16-$25   **Phone:** 414/271-0597   ⑩
Location: I-794, exit Van Buren St, then e on Michigan St to lakeside. 550 N Harbor Dr 53202. **Hours:** 11 am-3 & 4:30-10 pm, Fri & Sat-11 pm, Sun 9 am-2 & 4-10 pm. **Reservations:** suggested. **Features:** On the historic downtown cargo pier, the restaurant affords excellent views of Lake Michigan and Milwaukee's skyline. On the menu are traditional preparations of chicken, beef, freshwater and saltwater fish and pasta. Servers are knowledgeable. Casual dress; cocktails. **Parking:** on-site. **Cards:** AX, DC, DS, MC, VI.

POLARIS   **Lunch:** $8-$13   **Dinner:** $17-$35   **Phone:** 414/276-1234   ④
Location: At N 3rd St; downtown; in Hyatt Regency Milwaukee. 333 W Kilbourn Ave 53203. **Hours:** 5 pm-10:30 pm, Sun also 10 am-2:30 pm. **Reservations:** suggested. **Features:** Diners can appreciate beautiful views of the city skyline from many perspectives at the top-floor revolving restaurant. Dressy casual; cocktails. **Parking:** on-site (fee). **Cards:** AX, CB, DC, DS, JC, MC, VI.

SANFORD RESTAURANT   **Dinner:** $45-$75   **Phone:** 414/276-9608   ①
Location: Southeast corner of N Jackson and Pleasant sts. 1547 N Jackson St 53202. **Hours:** 5:30 pm-9 pm, Fri-10 pm, Sat 5 pm-10 pm. Closed major holidays; also Sun. **Reservations:** suggested. **Features:** In a small residential building, the cozy, intimate dining room is home to a wonderful adventure. The competent, smartly attired wait staff employs a seamless team approach to service, making guests feel special and at ease. The ever-changing menu offers three-, four-, five- and seven-course options. Cuisine is as varied as the market and often includes game dishes. Presentations are creative and eye-appealing, and everything is prepared to order. Dressy casual; cocktails. **Parking:** valet and street. **Cards:** AX, DC, DS, MC, VI.

(See map p. 542)

THIRD STREET PIER   **Dinner: $20-$47**   **Phone:** 414/272-0330   ②
▼▼▼▼ **Location:** Just s of jct Juneau Ave; in Riverfront Plaza Building. 1110 N Old World Third St 53203. **Hours:** 5 pm-10
Steak & Seafood pm, Sun 4 pm-9 pm. Closed major holidays; also 12/24. **Reservations:** suggested. **Features:** On the
Milwaukee River, the restaurant benefits from a wonderful location. Diners can watch boats cruising the
river while enjoying dinner in an elegant setting. In addition to steak and seafood specialties, weekly
specials are offered. Start off with hearty seafood chowder followed by tender filet mignon. Finish the meal with a slice of
apple strudel. Live jazz adds to the ambience Friday and Saturday. Dressy casual; cocktails. **Parking:** valet. **Cards:** AX, DC,
DS, MC, VI.

🍽 ✖

WATTS TEA SHOP   Historic   **Lunch: $6-$12**   **Phone:** 414/291-5120   ⑥
▼▼▼ **Location:** E Mason and N Jefferson sts. 761 N Jefferson St 53202. **Hours:** 9 am-4 pm. Closed major holidays;
also Sun. **Reservations:** suggested. **Features:** This family-owned and operated restaurant is a local
American favorite. It was established in 1926 and is located on the second floor of the George Watts & Son
Incorporated building. It is known for its homemade bread, soup, salad, sandwiches and dessert. Afternoon
tea is from 2:30-4 pm daily. Casual dress. **Parking:** valet. **Cards:** AX, DS, MC, VI.

✖

MILWAUKEE pop. 596,974   (See map p. 544; index p. 545)

─────── WHERE TO STAY ───────

BAYMONT INN & SUITES-MILWAUKEE NW   **Phone:** (414)535-1300   ④
AAA SAVE   All Year [ECP]   1P: $69-$89   2P: $69-$89
▼▼▼▼ **Location:** US 45, exit 46 (Silver Spring Rd), just se. 5442 N Lovers Lane Rd 53225. Fax: 414/535-1724. **Facility:** 123
units. 119 one-bedroom standard units. 4 one-bedroom suites ($89-$109). 3 stories, interior corridors.
Parking: on-site. **Terms:** small pets only ($50 deposit). **Amenities:** video games (fee), voice mail, irons, hair
Small-scale Hotel dryers. **Leisure Activities:** limited exercise equipment. **Guest Services:** valet and coin laundry. **Business
Services:** meeting rooms, fax (fee). **Cards:** AX, CB, DC, DS, MC, VI. **Special Amenities:** free continental
breakfast and free newspaper. *(See color ad below)*   SOME UNITS

S🄳 🛏 🍴 ⟲ 📷 DATA PORT 💻 / ✖ 🔋 🖥 /

BEST WESTERN WOODSVIEW INN

5/23-3/31 [CP]	1P: $79	2P: $87	XP: $8
4/1-5/22 [CP]	1P: $77	2P: $85	XP: $8

Phone: (414)671-6400 **5**

F18
F18

Small-scale Hotel

Location: I-94, exit 308B, 0.5 mi s on Miller Pkwy, just w on SR 59. Located adjacent to Veterans Hospital. 5501 W National Ave 53214. Fax: 414/671-1029. **Facility:** 62 one-bedroom standard units, some with kitchens and/or whirlpools. 3 stories, interior corridors. *Bath:* combo or shower only. **Parking:** on-site. **Amenities:** voice mail, safes (fee), irons, hair dryers. *Some:* dual phone lines. **Dining:** 11 am-11 pm; closed Sun. **Pool(s):** heated indoor. **Leisure Activities:** whirlpool, game room. **Guest Services:** valet laundry. **Business Services:** meeting rooms, fax. **Cards:** AX, CB, DC, DS, MC, VI. **Special Amenities:** free continental breakfast and free newspaper.

The Osthoff Resort's all-suite accommodations, four seasons of recreation, fine cuisine, breathtaking beachfront scenery, and Old World charm combine with all the services and amenities one would expect from a AAA Four Diamond property.

145 spacious suites up to 2,300 sq. ft., indoor and outdoor pools, whirlpools, saunas, fitness centers, tennis courts, basketball court, adjacent golf course, Pleasures™ acitivity program for adults and children.

THE OSTHOFF
RESORT

101 Osthoff Avenue, Elkhart Lake, Wisconsin 53020-0151
For reservations and further information,
call 800.876.3399 or visit www.osthoff.com

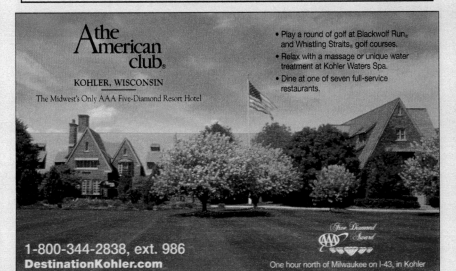

A the American club.

KOHLER, WISCONSIN

The Midwest's Only AAA Five-Diamond Resort Hotel

• Play a round of golf at Blackwolf Run₀ and Whistling Straits₀ golf courses.
• Relax with a massage or unique water treatment at Kohler Waters Spa.
• Dine at one of seven full-service restaurants.

1-800-344-2838, ext. 986
DestinationKohler.com

One hour north of Milwaukee on I-43, in Kohler

CLARION HOTEL AIRPORT

(AAA) [SAVE]
▽▽▽▽
Small-scale Hotel

Phone: (414)481-2400 ⓫

9/2-3/31 [CP]	1P: $89-$99	2P: $104-$109	XP: $10 F18
4/1-8/25 [CP]	1P: $84-$94	2P: $94-$99	XP: $10 F18

Location: I-94, exit 318 (Airport), 1.1 mi e at jct SR 38. 5311 S Howell Ave 53207. Fax: 414/481-4471. **Facility:** 180 units. 156 one-bedroom standard units. 23 one- and 1 two-bedroom suites, some with whirlpools. 3 stories, interior corridors. *Bath:* combo or shower only. **Parking:** on-site. **Terms:** open 4/1-8/25 & 9/2-3/31. **Amenities:** video games (fee), dual phone lines, voice mail, irons, hair dryers. **Dining:** 6:30 am-10 pm, Sun 9 am-9 pm, cocktails. **Pool(s):** heated indoor. **Leisure Activities:** limited exercise equipment. **Guest Services:** valet and coin laundry. **Business Services:** conference facilities, business center. **Cards:** AX, CB, DC, DS, JC, MC, VI. **Special Amenities:** free continental breakfast and free local telephone calls.

SOME UNITS

COUNTRY INNS & SUITES BY CARLSON

(AAA) [SAVE]
▽▽▽▽
Small-scale Hotel

Phone: (414)762-6018 ⓭

All Year	1P: $80-$110	2P: $87-$117	XP: $7 F18

Location: I-94, exit 319, just e on College Ave (CR ZZ). 6200 S 13th St 53221. Fax: 414/762-8806. **Facility:** 81 units. 53 one-bedroom standard units, some with whirlpools. 28 one-bedroom suites ($90-$150). 3 stories, interior corridors. *Bath:* combo or shower only. **Parking:** on-site. **Terms:** [ECP] meal plan available. **Amenities:** dual phone lines, voice mail, irons, hair dryers. **Pool(s):** small heated indoor. **Leisure Activities:** whirlpool, exercise room. *Fee:* game room. **Guest Services:** valet and coin laundry. **Business Services:** meeting rooms, fax (fee). **Cards:** AX, CB, DC, DS, MC, VI. **Special Amenities:** free continental breakfast and free newspaper.
(See color ad starting on p 556)

SOME UNITS

(See map p. 544)

ECONO LODGE AIRPORT

Motel

Phone: (414)764-2510   **16**

All Year [CP]   1P: $39-$199   2P: $49-$199   XP: $5   F17
Location: I-94, exit 319, just e on College Ave (CR ZZ), then just s. 6541 S 13th St 53221. Fax: 414/764-2510.
Facility: 106 one-bedroom standard units. 2 stories, interior corridors. *Bath:* shower only. **Parking:** on-site, winter plug-ins. **Amenities:** video library (fee). **Business Services:** fax (fee). **Cards:** AX, CB, DC, DS, JC, MC, VI. **Special Amenities:** free continental breakfast and free local telephone calls.

SOME UNITS

FOUR POINTS BY SHERATON MILWAUKEE AIRPORT

Large-scale Hotel

Phone: (414)481-8000   **9**

All Year   1P: $79-$99   2P: $89-$109   XP: $10   F17
Location: I-94, exit 318 (Airport), 1.1 mi e to Howell/SR 38, 0.7 mi n. 4747 S Howell Ave 53207. Fax: 414/481-8065.
Facility: 508 units. 504 one-bedroom standard units, some with whirlpools. 4 one-bedroom suites ($200). 6 stories, interior corridors. *Bath:* combo or shower only. **Parking:** on-site. **Amenities:** video games (fee), voice mail, irons, hair dryers. *Some:* dual phone lines. **Dining:** 2 restaurants, 6 am-2 am, cocktails, nightclub. **Pool(s):** heated outdoor, small heated indoor. **Leisure Activities:** exercise room. **Guest Services:** gift shop, valet and coin laundry. **Business Services:** conference facilities, business center. **Cards:** AX, CB, DC, DS, JC, MC, VI. **Special Amenities:** free newspaper.

SOME UNITS

Wisconsin
Appleton
Chippewa Falls
East Troy
Eau Claire

Germantown
Green Bay
Hayward
Kenosha
Madison

Mauston
Menomonie
Milwaukee-Airport
Milwaukee-West

10% MEMBER DISCOUNT OFF PUBLISHED RATES. Refer to property listings for more information.

Country Hospitality.

Wherever your

travels take you,

a cozy lobby fireplace,

comfortable guest rooms

and a friendly staff

are always

waiting for you.

Platteville
Port Washington
River Falls
Shawano
Sparta

Stevens Point
Turtle lake
Waunakee
Wausau
West Bend

COUNTRY
INNS & SUITES
BY CARLSON

A Cozy Stay At A
Comfortable Price

800-456-4000
www.countryinns.com

(See map p. 544)

HAMPTON INN-MILWAUKEE AIRPORT Phone: (414)762-4240

All Year [ECP] 1P: $79-$129 2P: $89-$129

Location: I-94, exit 319, just e on College Ave (CR ZZ). 1200 W College Ave 53221. Fax: 414/762-9810. **Facility:** 105 one-bedroom standard units. 3 stories, interior corridors. *Bath:* combo or shower only. **Parking:** on-site. **Amenities:** video games (fee), dual phone lines, voice mail, irons, hair dryers. **Pool(s):** small heated indoor. **Leisure Activities:** whirlpool, limited exercise equipment. **Guest Services:** valet laundry. **Business Services:** meeting rooms, fax. **Cards:** AX, CB, DC, DS, MC, VI. **Special Amenities:** free continental breakfast and free local telephone calls. *(See color ad below)*

Small-scale Hotel

SOME UNITS

(See map p. 544)

HAMPTON INN-MILWAUKEE NW

Small-scale Hotel

Phone: (414)466-8881 [2]
All Year 1P: $49-$119 XP: $10 F17
Location: US 45, exit 46 (Silver Spring Dr), just ne. 5601 N Lovers Lane Rd 53225. Fax: 414/466-3840. **Facility:** 108 one-bedroom standard units. 4 stories, interior corridors. *Bath:* combo or shower only. **Parking:** on-site. **Terms:** [ECP] meal plan available. **Amenities:** video games (fee), voice mail, irons, hair dryers. **Pool(s):** small heated indoor. **Leisure Activities:** whirlpool, limited exercise equipment. **Guest Services:** valet laundry. **Business Services:** meeting rooms, fax (fee). **Cards:** AX, DC, DS, MC, VI.

SOME UNITS

FEE FEE

HILTON GARDEN INN MILWAUKEE PARK PLACE

Small-scale Hotel

Phone: (414)359-9823 [1]
All Year 1P: $59-$159 2P: $59-$179 XP: $20 F17
Location: US 45, exit 43B (Good Hope Rd), just e, then 0.5 mi n at jct SR 100 and 145 (107th St). 11600 W Park Pl 53224. Fax: 414/359-9824. **Facility:** 126 units. 124 one-bedroom standard units. 2 one-bedroom suites ($99-$229). 3 stories, interior corridors. *Bath:* combo or shower only. **Parking:** on-site. **Terms:** cancellation fee imposed. **Amenities:** video games (fee), high-speed Internet, dual phone lines, voice mail, irons, hair dryers. **Dining:** 6 am-2 & 5-10 pm, Sat & Sun 7 am-noon & 5-10 pm, cocktails. **Pool(s):** heated indoor. **Leisure Activities:** sauna, whirlpool, sun deck, exercise room, game room. **Guest Services:** valet and coin laundry. **Business Services:** conference facilities, business center. **Cards:** AX, CB, DC, DS, MC, VI. **Special Amenities:** free newspaper.

SOME UNITS

HOLIDAY INN HOTEL AND SUITES

Small-scale Hotel

Phone: (414)482-4444 [7]
All Year 1P: $105-$135
Location: I-94, exit 317, 1.3 mi e. 545 W Layton Ave 53207. Fax: 414/482-1111. **Facility:** 130 units. 118 one-bedroom standard units, some with kitchens and/or whirlpools. 12 one-bedroom suites with kitchens. 3 stories, interior corridors. *Bath:* combo or shower only. **Parking:** on-site. **Terms:** package plans. **Amenities:** video games (fee), dual phone lines, voice mail, irons, hair dryers. **Dining:** 6 am-10 & 4-11 pm, cocktails. **Pool(s):** heated indoor. **Leisure Activities:** whirlpool, sun deck with grill, limited exercise equipment. **Guest Services:** gift shop, valet and coin laundry. **Business Services:** meeting rooms, business center. **Cards:** AX, CB, DC, DS, JC, MC, VI. **Special Amenities:** free newspaper. *(See color ad below)*

SOME UNITS

(See map p. 544)

HOSPITALITY INN
Phone: 414/282-8800 [6]

6/2-9/1 [ECP]   1P: $80-$200   2P: $90-$300
4/1-6/1 & 9/2-3/31 [ECP]   1P: $60-$80   2P: $70-$90

Small-scale Hotel   **Location:** I-894, exit 9 (SR 241), just n. 4400 S 27th St 53221. Fax: 414/282-7713. **Facility:** 192 units. 121 one-bedroom standard units, some with whirlpools. 71 one-bedroom suites, some with whirlpools. 3-5 stories, interior/exterior corridors. *Bath:* combo or shower only. **Parking:** on-site. **Terms:** weekly rates available, [BP] & [MAP] meal plans available. **Amenities:** voice mail, irons, hair dryers. *Some:* dual phone lines. **Pool(s):** 2 small heated indoor. **Leisure Activities:** sauna, whirlpool, limited exercise equipment. *Fee:* game room. **Guest Services:** valet and coin laundry. **Business Services:** meeting rooms, fax (fee). **Cards:** AX, DC, DS, MC, VI.

SOME UNITS

HOWARD JOHNSON MILWAUKEE AIRPORT INN
Phone: (414)282-7000 [8]

(AAA) (SAVE)   All Year   1P: $59-$129   2P: $69-$159   XP: $10   F17

Location: I-94, exit 317. 1716 W Layton Ave 53221. Fax: 414/282-1552. **Facility:** 96 one-bedroom standard units, some with whirlpools. 2 stories (no elevator), interior corridors. **Parking:** on-site. **Terms:** package plans.

Small-scale Hotel   **Amenities:** *Some:* irons, hair dryers. **Dining:** 5:30 am-10 pm, Fri & Sat-11 pm, Sun-9 pm, cocktails. **Pool(s):** heated outdoor. **Guest Services:** coin laundry. **Business Services:** meeting rooms, fax. **Cards:** AX, DS, MC, VI. **Special Amenities:** free local telephone calls and free newspaper. *(See color ads below)*

SOME UNITS

(See map p. 544)

MANCHESTER SUITES AIRPORT
Phone: (414)744-3600 [12]
(AAA) [SAVE] All Year [BP] 1P: $79-$109 2P: $79-$109 XP: $10 F14
▼▼▼▼ Location: I-94, exit 318 (Airport), 1.1 mi e, just n on Howell Ave/SR 38, then just w. 200 W Grange Ave 53207.
Small-scale Hotel Fax: 414/744-4188. **Facility:** 100 one-bedroom standard units. 4 stories, interior corridors. **Parking:** on-site.
Amenities: voice mail, irons, hair dryers. **Guest Services:** valet laundry. **Business Services:** meeting
rooms, business center. **Cards:** AX, CB, DC, DS, MC, VI. **Special Amenities:** free continental breakfast
and free local telephone calls.

SOME UNITS
[S/D] [🔌] [🛋] [📶] [🛁] [🎬] [🖥] [🖨] [💻] / [✕] [DATA PORT] /

MANCHESTER SUITES NW
Phone: (414)462-3500 [3]
(AAA) [SAVE] All Year [BP] 1P: $79-$109 2P: $79-$109 XP: $10 F14
▼▼▼▼ Location: US 45, exit 46 (Silver Spring Dr), just w. 11777 W Silver Spring Dr 53225. Fax: 414/462-8166. **Facility:** 123
Small-scale Hotel one-bedroom standard units. 4 stories, interior corridors. **Parking:** on-site. **Amenities:** voice mail, irons, hair
dryers. *Some:* dual phone lines. **Leisure Activities:** exercise room. **Guest Services:** valet laundry. **Busi-**
ness Services: meeting rooms, fax. **Cards:** AX, CB, DC, DS, MC, VI. **Special Amenities:** free continental
breakfast and free local telephone calls.

SOME UNITS
[S/D] [🛋] [♿M] [📶] [🎬] [DATA PORT] [🖥] [🖨] [💻] / [✕] /

(See map p. 544)

RADISSON HOTEL MILWAUKEE AIRPORT
Phone: (414)764-1500 **17**
F17

(AAA) (SAVE)
All Year 1P: $79-$149 2P: $89-$159 XP: $10

Small-scale Hotel

Location: I-94, exit 319, just e on College Ave (CR ZZ). 6331 S 13th St 53221. Fax: 414/764-6531. **Facility:** 159 one-bedroom standard units. 3 stories, interior corridors. *Bath:* combo or shower only. **Parking:** on-site, winter plug-ins. **Terms:** 18% service charge. **Amenities:** video games (fee), dual phone lines, voice mail, irons, hair dryers. **Dining:** 6:30 am-2 & 5-10 pm, cocktails. **Pool(s):** heated indoor. **Leisure Activities:** sun deck, exercise room. *Fee:* game room. **Guest Services:** valet and coin laundry, area transportation-upon availability. **Business Services:** conference facilities, PC, fax. **Cards:** AX, CB, DC, DS, JC, MC, VI. *(See color ads below.)*

SOME UNITS

(See map p. 544)

SUPER 8 MOTEL-MILWAUKEE AIRPORT   Phone: (414)481-8488

Motel

All Year   1P: $71-$249   2P: $78-$249
Location: I-94, exit 318 (Airport), 1.1 mi e, then just n on SR 38. 5253 S Howell Ave 53207. Fax: 414/481-8086.
Facility: 116 one-bedroom standard units. 3 stories, interior corridors. **Parking:** on-site, winter plug-ins.
Terms: [CP] meal plan available. **Leisure Activities:** whirlpool. **Guest Services:** coin laundry. **Business Services:** meeting rooms, fax (fee). **Cards:** AX, CB, DC, DS, JC, MC, VI. **Special Amenities:** free continental breakfast and free local telephone calls.
SOME UNITS

—— WHERE TO DINE ——

AU BON APPETIT RESTAURANT & CATERING   **Dinner:** $8-$14   **Phone:** 414/278-1233   ④
Lebanese   **Location:** Just e of jct Van Buren Ave, at jct Humboldt Ave. 1016 E Brady St 53202. **Hours:** 5 pm-9 pm, Fri & Sat-10 pm. Closed major holidays; also Sun & Mon. **Reservations:** suggested. **Features:** This family-owned and operated restaurant offers Mediterranean food with a Lebanese and French flair prepared by the owner/chef. It is a small, intimate restaurant with cozy seating and gracious owners who welcome you immediately upon entering with a friendly hello and a warm bon appetit as you begin to eat. The Royal couscous with chicken is a wonderful entree of choice with a variety of herbs and spices making for a tasty dinner treat. Basque chicken is a specialty of the house. Casual dress; beer & wine only. **Parking:** street. **Cards:** MC, VI.   ✕

BARTOLOTTA'S LAKE PARK BISTRO   **Lunch:** $8-$15   **Dinner:** $10-$35   **Phone:** 414/962-6300   ③
French   **Location:** I-43, exit 74 (Locust St), 2 mi e to Lake Dr, then just s; in Lake Park. 3133 E Newberry Blvd 53211. **Hours:** 11:30 am-2 & 5:30-9 pm, Fri-10 pm, Sat 5 pm-10 pm, Sun 10:30 am-2 & 5-8 pm. Closed major holidays. **Reservations:** suggested. **Features:** A fabulous view of Lake Michigan is offered as you dine at this elegant restaurant in Lake Park. The exterior setting is striking and a welcomed site. The interior is stylishly decorated and gives one a bistro feel. Menu offerings are varied and capture the essence of French cooking with wonderful herbs and sauces. Specialties include the grilled Atlantic salmon, filet medallions a'poivre and the praline parfait is a fabulous dessert choice with the creative presentation and wonderful flavor. Dressy casual; cocktails. **Parking:** on-site. **Cards:** AX, DC, DS, MC, VI.   ✗ ✕

HEINEMANN'S RESTAURANT   **Lunch:** $4-$7   **Dinner:** $5-$7   **Phone:** 414/258-6800   ⑥
American   **Location:** Just s of jct US 18 (W Bluemound Rd). 317 N 76th St 53213. **Hours:** 7 am-8 pm, Sun-2:30 pm. Closed major holidays; also 12/24 for dinner. **Features:** A local favorite established in 1923, this restaurant is known for its made-from-scratch menu items. Only natural ingredients are used in the homemade bread, sauces and soup. There are no preservatives, which is something of which they pride themselves. The setting is country cozy and the service staff is friendly and welcoming. Casual dress; beer & wine only. **Parking:** on-site. **Cards:** MC, VI.   ✕

OLD TOWN SERBIAN GOURMET HOUSE   **Lunch:** $5-$9   **Dinner:** $12-$18   **Phone:** 414/672-0206   ⑦
Ethnic   **Location:** I-94, exit 312B (W Lincoln Ave), just w. 522 W Lincoln Ave 53207. **Hours:** 11:30 am-2:30 & 5-10 pm. Closed: 5/26, 7/4, 9/1; also Mon. **Reservations:** suggested. **Features:** Flavorful foods and unusual recipes are the draw at the family-operated restaurant, a fixture for more than 30 years. Old World decor and ethnic background music set the mood. Among selections of Serbian/European cuisine are preparations of chicken, beef, lamb, fish and veal. Locals favor such hearty, made-from-scratch entrees as moussaka, goulash and Burak beef. Casual dress; cocktails. **Parking:** on-site. **Cards:** AX, DC, DS, MC, VI.   ✗ ✕

THE PACKING HOUSE   **Lunch:** $6-$10   **Dinner:** $10-$23   **Phone:** 414/483-5054   ⑨
Steak & Seafood   **Location:** 0.5 mi e of SR 38/Howell Ave. 900 E Layton Ave 53207. **Hours:** 11:30 am-2 & 5-10 pm, Fri 11:30 am-2 & 4-11 pm, Sat 5-11 pm, Sun 10 am-1:30 & 4-9 pm. Closed: 12/24 for dinner. **Reservations:** suggested. **Features:** Choose from a variety of cuts and preparations, including garlic-stuffed fillet, beef Wellington and filet Oscar. Seafood—such as Canadian walleye and king crab legs—also is offered. Rounding out the menu are a few vegetarian dishes, prime rib, chops, ribs and poultry. Dressy casual; cocktails. **Parking:** on-site. **Cards:** AX, DC, DS, MC, VI.   ✗ ✕

PAUL'S OMEGA FAMILY RESTAURANT   **Lunch:** $6-$13   **Dinner:** $8-$17   **Phone:** 414/645-6595   ⑧
Greek   **Location:** I-894, exit 9, 0.9 mi n SR 241. 3473 S 27th St 53215. **Hours:** 24 hours. **Features:** The lengthy menu dabbles in many varieties of food, ranging from barbecue and seafood dishes to traditional Italian and Greek cuisine. Oh, and breakfast items are served all day. Plates are piled high with tasty offerings. Baked goods are homemade. Casual dress; cocktails. **Parking:** on-site. **Cards:** DS, MC, VI.   ✕

SAZ'S STATE HOUSE   **Lunch:** $7-$14   **Dinner:** $7-$22   **Phone:** 414/453-2410   ⑤
American   **Location:** Jct of Hawley Rd overpass. 5539 W State St 53208. **Hours:** 11 am-9:30 pm, Fri & Sat-11 pm, Sun & Mon-9 pm, Sunday brunch 10:30 am-2 pm. Closed: 12/25; also 12/24 for dinner. **Reservations:** accepted. **Features:** The popular, bustling restaurant has been serving tasty food since 1976. Fall-off-the-bone pork and beef barbecue with Saz's own award-winning sauces are the big draw. The recipe for delicious cottage fries has been perfected over many years. Casual dress; cocktails. **Parking:** on-site. **Cards:** AX, DS, MC, VI.   ✗ ✕

WEST BANK CAFE   **Dinner:** $5-$17   **Phone:** 414/562-5555   ②
Vietnamese   **Location:** Jct N Fratney St. 732 E Burleigh St 53212. **Hours:** 5:30 pm-9:30 pm, Fri & Sat-10 pm. Closed major holidays. **Features:** In a residential neighborhood, the restaurant is simple and unpretentious. The menu is anything but ordinary, with thick curries that are slightly sweet and catfish cooked in a Vietnamese clay pot. Vegetarian and European entrees also are offered. Casual dress; cocktails. **Parking:** on-site. **Cards:** AX, DC, DS, MC, VI.   ✕

YEN CHING RESTAURANT   **Lunch:** $5-$6   **Dinner:** $8-$13   **Phone:** 414/353-6677   ①
Chinese   **Location:** Just w of SR 181 (76th St). 7630 W Good Hope Rd 53223. **Hours:** 11:30 am-2 & 4:30-9:30 pm, Fri-10 pm, Sat 4:30 pm-10 pm, Sun 11:30 am-2:30 & 4:30-9 pm. Closed: 7/4, 11/27. **Features:** Sweet and sour pork and almond chicken are among examples of Mandarin cuisine on the restaurant's extensive menu. The decor is Oriental, with carved, red-stained wood throughout. Servers exhibit strong knowledge of the menu and preparation style. Casual dress; cocktails. **Parking:** on-site. **Cards:** AX, DS, MC, VI.   ✕

The Milwaukee Vicinity

BAYSIDE pop. 4,518   (See map p. 544; index p. 547)

——— WHERE TO DINE ———

PANDL'S IN BAYSIDE   **Lunch:** $6-$15   **Dinner:** $12-$30   **Phone:** 414/352-7300   (19)
▼▼◆◇▼   **Location:** I-43, exit 82A, 1.1 mi e on SR 100/32 (Brown Deer Rd) at jct Lake Dr. 8825 N Lake Dr 53217.
American   **Hours:** 11:30 am-10 pm, Fri & Sat-11 pm, Sun 10 am-2 & 4:30-9 pm. Closed: 7/4, 12/24, 12/25.
Reservations: suggested. **Features:** The casual restaurant has the atmosphere of a country club. Many
windows in the open dining room afford views of a seasonally changing wooded landscape. Fresh fish is
the house specialty, but flavorful preparations of steak and lamb also line the varied menu. Dressy casual; cocktails. **Parking:**
on-site. **Cards:** AX, DC, DS, MC, VI.
🍽 ✕

BROOKFIELD pop. 38,649   (See map p. 544; index p. 547)

——— WHERE TO STAY ———

BAYMONT INN & SUITES MILWAUKEE-BROOKFIELD   **Phone:** (262)782-9100
(AAA) [SAVE]   5/30-8/31 [ECP]   1P: $84-$104   2P: $84-$104
          4/1-5/29 & 9/1-3/31 [ECP]   1P: $74-$94   2P: $74-$94
▼▼◆◇▼   **Location:** I-94, exit 297, just e on US 18. 20391 W Bluemound Rd 53045. Fax: 262/782-8560. **Facility:** 97 units. 94
one-bedroom standard units. 3 one-bedroom suites ($109-$154). 3 stories, interior corridors. **Parking:** on-
Small-scale Hotel site, winter plug-ins. **Terms:** small pets only. **Amenities:** voice mail, irons, hair dryers. **Fee:** video games,
high-speed Internet. **Leisure Activities:** exercise room. **Guest Services:** valet and coin laundry. **Business
Services:** meeting rooms. **Cards:** AX, CB, DC, DS, MC, VI. **Special Amenities: free continental breakfast and free news-
paper.** (See color ad p 552)
SOME UNITS
[S/D] 🐾 🍴 ⊘ ⊘ 📷 [DATA PORT] ▣ / ✕ 🛢 🖥 /

BEST WESTERN MIDWAY HOTEL-BROOKFIELD   **Phone:** (262)786-9540   (41)
(AAA) [SAVE]   6/1-8/31   1P: $80-$134   2P: $80-$134
          4/1-5/31 & 9/1-3/31   1P: $80-$98   2P: $80-$98
▼▼◆◇▼   **Location:** I-94, exit 301A, just s. 1005 S Moorland Rd 53005. Fax: 262/786-4561. **Facility:** 125 units. 108 one-
bedroom standard units. 17 one-bedroom suites. 6 stories, interior corridors. **Parking:** on-site.
Small-scale Hotel **Amenities:** video library (fee), voice mail, irons, hair dryers. **Some:** high-speed Internet, fax, honor bars.
Dining: 6:30 am-9 pm; Sunday brunch, cocktails. **Pool(s):** heated indoor. **Leisure Activities:** sauna, whirl-
pool, domed recreation area, limited exercise equipment. **Fee:** game room. **Guest Services:** valet laundry, area transportation-
within 10 mi. **Business Services:** meeting rooms, fax (fee). **Cards:** AX, DC, DS, MC, VI. **Special Amenities: free room
upgrade (subject to availability with advanced reservations).**
SOME UNITS
[S/D] ✈ 🍴 🍽 ⊘ 🏊 ✕ [VCR] 📷 [DATA PORT] ▣ / ✕ 🛢 /

COUNTRY INN & SUITES MILWAUKEE WEST   **Phone:** (262)782-1400   (43)
(AAA) [SAVE]   5/27-8/28 [ECP]   1P: $99-$129   2P: $99-$129   XP: $10   F19
          4/1-5/26 & 8/29-10/31 [ECP]   1P: $89-$119   2P: $89-$119   XP: $10   F19
▼▼◆◇▼   11/1-3/31 [ECP]   1P: $79-$109   2P: $79-$109   XP: $10   F19
          Location: I-94, exit 301A, just se. 1250 S Moorland Rd 53005. Fax: 262/782-1408. **Facility:** 150 one-bedroom
Large-scale Hotel standard units, some with whirlpools. 3 stories, interior corridors. **Bath:** combo or shower only. **Parking:** on-
site. **Amenities:** dual phone lines, voice mail, irons, hair dryers. **Pool(s):** small heated indoor. **Dining:** 2 restaurants, 11 am-midnight, cock-
tails. **Pool(s):** small heated indoor. **Leisure Activities:** whirlpool, exercise room. **Fee:** game room. **Guest Services:** valet and
coin laundry. **Business Services:** conference facilities, business center. **Cards:** AX, CB, DC, DS, JC, MC, VI.
Special Amenities: free continental breakfast and free newspaper. (See color ad starting on p 556)
SOME UNITS
[S/D] ✈ 🍴 🍽 ⊘ 🏊 ✕ 📷 [DATA PORT] ▣ / ✕ 🛢 🖥 /

COURTYARD BY MARRIOTT/BROOKFIELD   **Phone:** (262)821-1800   (39)
[SAVE]   7/6-9/1   1P: $90-$120   2P: $90-$120
          5/10-7/5   1P: $70-$110   2P: $70-$110
▼▼◆◇▼   4/1-5/9 & 9/2-3/31   1P: $50-$90   2P: $50-$90
Small-scale Hotel   **Location:** I-94, exit 297 eastbound, 2.2 mi e on US 18; exit 301B westbound, 1.5 mi n on Moorland, then 0.3 mi w on
US 18. 16865 W Bluemound Rd 53005. Fax: 262/821-1548. **Facility:** 147 units. 138 one-bedroom standard
units. 9 one-bedroom suites ($90-$130). 3 stories, interior corridors. **Bath:** combo or shower only. **Parking:**
on-site. **Terms:** [BP] meal plan available. **Amenities:** voice mail, irons, hair dryers. **Pool(s):** small heated indoor. **Leisure Ac-
tivities:** whirlpool, exercise room. **Guest Services:** valet and coin laundry. **Business Services:** meeting rooms. **Cards:** AX, CB,
DC, DS, JC, MC, VI.
SOME UNITS
[S/D] 🍴 🍽 [&M] ⊘ 🏊 📷 [DATA PORT] ▣ / ✕ 🛢 🖥 /

EMBASSY SUITES HOTEL-MILWAUKEE WEST   **Phone:** (262)782-2900   (42)
[SAVE]   All Year [BP]   1P: $89-$1000   2P: $99-$1000   XP: $20   F18
          Location: I-94, exit 301 (A and B), just s. 1200 S Moorland Rd 53008-1463 (PO Box 1463). Fax: 262/796-9159.
▼▼◆◇▼   **Facility:** 203 units. 199 one- and 4 two-bedroom suites, some with whirlpools. 5 stories, interior corridors.
Small-scale Hotel **Parking:** on-site. **Terms:** check-in 4 pm, 10 day cancellation notice. **Amenities:** video games (fee), irons,
hair dryers. **Pool(s):** heated indoor. **Leisure Activities:** sauna, whirlpool, steamroom, exercise room. **Guest
Services:** gift shop, complimentary evening beverages, valet and coin laundry, area transportation. **Busi-
ness Services:** conference facilities, business center. **Cards:** AX, DC, DS, MC, VI.
SOME UNITS
[S/D] ✈ 🍴 🍽 [&M] 🏊 ✕ 📷 🛢 🖥 ▣ / ✕ [VCR]

(See map p. 544)

HAMPTON INN-BROOKFIELD

Phone: 262/796-1500

SAVE

All Year [CP]   1P: $69-$149   2P: $69-$149

Small-scale Hotel

Location: I-94, exit 297, just e on US 18. 575 N Barker 53045. **Fax:** 262/796-0977. **Facility:** 120 one-bedroom standard units. 4 stories, interior corridors. *Bath:* combo or shower only. **Parking:** on-site. **Amenities:** video games (fee), dual phone lines, voice mail, irons, hair dryers. **Pool(s):** small heated indoor. **Leisure Activities:** whirlpool, exercise room. **Guest Services:** valet laundry. **Business Services:** meeting rooms.

SOME UNITS

HOMESTEAD STUDIO SUITES HOTEL-MILWAUKEE/BROOKFIELD

Phone: (262)782-9300

6/27-8/16	1P: $95-$105	2P: $105-$115	XP: $5	F17
4/1-6/26 & 8/17-3/31	1P: $75-$85	2P: $85-$95	XP: $5	F17

Small-scale Hotel

Location: I-94, exit 297, 1.1 mi e on US 18, just e. 325 N Brookfield Rd 53045. **Fax:** 262/782-9451. **Facility:** 137 one-bedroom standard units with efficiencies. 3 stories, interior corridors. *Bath:* combo or shower only. **Parking:** on-site. **Terms:** pets ($75 fee). **Amenities:** voice mail, irons. **Guest Services:** sundries, valet and coin laundry. **Business Services:** meeting rooms. **Cards:** AX, CB, DC, DS, JC, MC, VI.

SOME UNITS

FEE

SHERATON MILWAUKEE BROOKFIELD

Phone: (262)786-1100

AAA **SAVE**

5/1-9/30	1P: $89-$109	2P: $99-$119	XP: $10	F18
4/1-4/30 & 10/1-3/31	1P: $79-$89	2P: $89-$99	XP: $10	F18

Large-scale Hotel

Location: I-94, exit 301B, just n. 375 S Moorland Rd 53005. **Fax:** 262/786-5210. **Facility:** 389 units. 382 one-bedroom standard units. 7 one-bedroom suites. 6 stories, interior corridors. *Bath:* combo or shower only. **Parking:** on-site. **Terms:** [AP], [BP] & [CP] meal plans available. **Amenities:** dual phone lines, voice mail, irons, hair dryers. *Some:* fax. **Dining:** 6:30 am-10 pm, Sat & Sun from 7 am, cocktails. **Pool(s):** heated outdoor, heated indoor. **Leisure Activities:** sauna, whirlpool, exercise room. **Guest Services:** gift shop, valet and coin laundry. **Business Services:** conference facilities, business center. **Cards:** AX, CB, DC, DS, JC, MC, VI. **Special Amenities:** early check-in/late check-out and free newspaper. *(See color ad p 563)*

SOME UNITS

TOWNEPLACE SUITES BY MARRIOTT

Phone: (262)784-8450

SAVE

5/27-8/18	1P: $69-$109	2P: $69-$109	
8/19-10/31	1P: $59-$94	2P: $59-$94	
4/1-5/26 & 11/1-3/31	1P: $59-$79	2P: $59-$79	

Small-scale Hotel

Location: I-94, exit 297 eastbound, 2.1 mi e on US 18; exit 301B westbound, 1.5 mi n on Moorland, then 0.4 mi w on US 18. 600 N Calhoun Rd 53005. **Fax:** 262/784-8503. **Facility:** 112 units. 92 one-bedroom standard units with kitchens. 20 two-bedroom suites with kitchens. 2-3 stories, interior corridors. *Bath:* combo or shower only. **Parking:** on-site. **Terms:** 13% service charge, pets ($25-$75 fee). **Amenities:** dual phone lines, voice mail, irons, hair dryers. **Pool(s):** small heated outdoor. **Leisure Activities:** exercise room. **Guest Services:** valet and coin laundry. **Cards:** AX, DC, DS, MC, VI.

SOME UNITS

WYNDHAM GARDEN HOTEL-BROOKFIELD

Phone: (262)792-1212

AAA **SAVE**

All Year   1P: $69-$105   2P: $69-$115   XP: $10   F18

Small-scale Hotel

Location: I-94, exit 297, 1.5 mi e on US 18. 18155 W Bluemound Rd 53045. **Fax:** 262/792-1201. **Facility:** 178 units. 169 one-bedroom standard units. 9 one-bedroom suites ($155-$179). 3 stories, interior corridors. *Bath:* combo or shower only. **Parking:** on-site. **Terms:** cancellation fee imposed. **Amenities:** voice mail, irons, hair dryers. *Fee:* video games, high-speed Internet. *Some:* CD players. **Dining:** 6:30 am-10 pm, cocktails. **Pool(s):** small heated indoor. **Leisure Activities:** whirlpool, complete locker room facilities, exercise room. **Guest Services:** valet laundry, airport transportation-within 5 mi, area transportation. **Business Services:** meeting rooms. **Cards:** AX, DC, DS, MC, VI.

SOME UNITS

—— WHERE TO DINE ——

HEINEMANN'S RESTAURANT

Lunch: $4-$8   **Dinner:** $4-$8   **Phone:** 262/792-1500

AAA

American

Location: I-94, exit 297, 1.5 mi e on US 18. 18000-A W Bluemound Rd 53045. **Hours:** 7 am-8 pm, Fri-9 pm, Sun from 7:30 am. Closed major holidays. **Reservations:** accepted. **Features:** The established, family-oriented restaurant delivers fresh, flavorful items, such as soups, sandwiches and salads. All courses are made from scratch without additives or preservatives. Noteworthy are the aromatic baked goods and tantalizing desserts. Casual dress; beer & wine only. **Parking:** on-site. **Cards:** MC, VI.

JAKE'S RESTAURANT

Dinner: $18-$27   **Phone:** 262/781-7995

American

Location: Just n off SR 190, 1.7 mi e of jct SR 164. 21445 Gumina Rd 53072. **Hours:** 5 pm-9 pm, Fri-10 pm, Sat 4:30 pm-10 pm, Sun 4:30 pm-8 pm. Closed major holidays; also 12/24 & Super Bowl Sun. **Reservations:** accepted; except Saturday. **Features:** On a small hilltop in a rural area, the restaurant has been a local favorite since the 1970s. Although the exterior and interior design is rustic in appearance, tables are set in an intimate style and a large fireplace central to the dining room offers a romantic charm. The menu is varied with poultry, steak, pork chops, prime rib and seafood choices, as well as a few seasonal selections. Casual dress; cocktails. **Parking:** on-site. **Cards:** AX, CB, DC, MC, VI.

(See map p. 544)

TASTE OF INDIA
▼▼ ▼▼▼
Indian

Lunch: $7   Dinner: $9-$15   Phone: 262/796-8200

Location: I-94, exit 297, 1.6 mi e on US 18; in Brookmound Plaza. **Hours:** 11:30 am 3 & 5-10 pm, Fri & Sat-10:30 pm. **Reservations:** accepted. **Features:** This clean, bright and open restaurant is located at the back of a small strip mall kitty-corner to the Wyndham Garden Hotel. It features a small buffet lunch service and an expanded a la carte menu at dinner with a sampling of vegetarian, meat and seafood dishes. There is an excellent selection of Indian breads available as well. Casual dress; beer & wine only. **Parking:** on-site. **Cards:** AX, DC, DS, MC, VI.

⊠

——— *The following restaurant has not been evaluated by AAA* ———
but is listed for your information only.

KOPP'S FROZEN CUSTARD   Phone: 262/789-1359

[fyi]   Not evaluated. **Location:** I-94, exit 297, 1.1 mi e on US 18. 18880 W Bluemound Rd 53045. **Features:** Don't leave Milwaukee without trying frozen custard. Kopp's is just one of many outlets offering this dairy treat. Watch for street sign postings of daily flavors in addition to chocolate and vanilla.

BROWN DEER pop. 12,170   (See map p. 544; index p. 546)

——— **WHERE TO STAY** ———

COURTYARD BY MARRIOTT MILWAUKEE NORTH BROWN DEER   Phone: (414)355-7500   [27]
[SAVE]
▼▼▼▼▼
Small-scale Hotel

| | 4/1-10/1 | 1P: $109-$119 | 2P: $119-$129 |
| | 10/2-3/31 | 1P: $99-$109 | 2P: $109-$119 |

Location: On SR 100, 0.7 mi w of jct SR 57. 5200 W Brown Deer Rd 53223. Fax: 414/355-8900. **Facility:** 122 units. 118 one-bedroom standard units, some with whirlpools. 4 one-bedroom suites ($139-$169). 4 stories, interior corridors. **Parking:** on-site. **Terms:** cancellation fee imposed. **Amenities:** video games (fee), dual phone lines, voice mail, irons, hair dryers. **Pool(s):** small heated indoor. **Leisure Activities:** whirlpool, exercise room. **Guest Services:** valet and coin laundry. **Business Services:** meeting rooms. **Cards:** AX, CB, DC, DS, JC, MC, VI.

SOME UNITS

[S🄳] [🍴] [ᴪM] [🛏] [🖉] [🛋] [🐾] [🖳] [DATA PORT] [🖳] / [⊠] [🔒] [🖨] /

HOLIDAY INN EXPRESS   Phone: (414)355-1300   [26]
▼▼▼▼▼
Small-scale Hotel

All Year [ECP]   1P: $79-$115   XP: $8   F18

Location: Just nw of jct SR 100 and 57. 4443 W Schroeder Dr 53223. Fax: 414/355-7368. **Facility:** 78 units. 77 one-bedroom standard units, some with whirlpools. 1 one-bedroom suite ($115-$225) with whirlpool. 3 stories, interior corridors. **Bath:** combo or shower only. **Parking:** on-site, winter plug-ins. **Amenities:** high-speed Internet, dual phone lines, voice mail, irons, hair dryers. **Some:** fax. **Pool(s):** small heated indoor. **Leisure Activities:** whirlpool, exercise room. **Guest Services:** valet laundry. **Business Services:** meeting rooms, business center. **Cards:** AX, CB, DC, DS, JC, MC, VI.

SOME UNITS

[ASK] [S🄳] [🍴+] [ᴪM] [🛏] [🖉] [🐾] [🖳] [DATA PORT] [🖳] / [⊠] [🔒] [🖨] /

CEDARBURG pop. 10,908

——— **WHERE TO STAY** ———

THE WASHINGTON HOUSE INN   Phone: (262)375-3550
▼▼▼▼▼
Historic Bed
& Breakfast

All Year   2P: $89-$219   XP: $20   D

Location: Downtown. W62, N573 Washington Ave 53012. Fax: 262/375-9422. **Facility:** The inn, furnished with period antiques, collectibles and reproductions, offers some fireplace rooms. 34 one-bedroom standard units, some with whirlpools. 3 stories (no elevator), interior corridors. **Parking:** on-site. **Terms:** [ECP] meal plan available. **Amenities:** video library (fee), hair dryers. **Leisure Activities:** sauna. **Guest Services:** complimentary evening beverages. **Business Services:** meeting rooms. **Cards:** AX, CB, DC, MC, VI.

SOME UNITS

[ASK] [S🄳] [🍴+] [🛁+] [VCR] [🐾] [DATA PORT] / [⊠] [🖳] /

——— **WHERE TO DINE** ———

CREAM & CREPE CAFE Historic   Lunch: $4-$9   Dinner: $4-$9   Phone: 262/377-0900
▼▼ ▼▼
American

Location: At Cedar Creek Settlement; downtown. N70 W6340 Bridge Rd 53012. **Hours:** 10 am-8 pm, Sun 11 am-5 pm, Mon 10 am-5 pm. Closed major holidays. **Reservations:** accepted. **Features:** Soups, sandwiches, entrees and dessert crepes are served in a rustic old mill. Casual dress; beer & wine only. **Parking:** on-site. **Cards:** AX, DS, MC, VI.

⊠

KLUG'S CREEKSIDE INN   Lunch: $7-$11   Dinner: $8-$18   Phone: 262/377-0660
▼▼ ▼▼
American

Location: Downtown. N58 W6194 Columbia Rd 53012. **Hours:** 11 am-2 & 4-9 pm, Fri & Sat-9:30 pm, Sun 10 am-2 & 4-8 pm. Closed major holidays; also Mon. **Reservations:** suggested. **Features:** Antiques and local art decorate the owner-operated restaurant. The menu blends American favorites, such as prime rib and barbecue ribs, with German entrees. The strawberry Schaum torte is particularly tasty. Service is friendly and attentive. Casual dress; cocktails. **Parking:** on-site. **Cards:** AX, CB, DC, MC, VI.

[Ⓨ] [⊠]

DELAFIELD pop. 6,472

———— WHERE TO STAY ————

BAYMONT INN & SUITES MILWAUKEE-DELAFIELD
Phone: (262)646-8500

(AAA) (SAVE)

Small-scale Hotel

| 5/31-8/30 [ECP] | 1P: $89-$159 | 2P: $89-$159 |
| 4/1-5/30 & 8/31-3/31 [ECP] | 1P: $59-$104 | 2P: $59-$104 |

Location: I-94, exit 287, just s on SR 83, then just e. 2801 Hillside Dr 53018. **Fax:** 262/646-7660. **Facility:** 96 units. 93 one-bedroom standard units. 3 one-bedroom suites ($89-$159). 3 stories, interior corridors. *Bath:* combo or shower only. **Parking:** on-site, winter plug-ins. **Terms:** small pets only (in smoking units). **Amenities:** video games (fee), voice mail, irons, hair dryers. *Some:* dual phone lines. **Pool(s):** small heated indoor. **Leisure Activities:** whirlpool, exercise room. **Guest Services:** valet and coin laundry. **Business Services:** meeting rooms. **Cards:** AX, CB, DC, DS, MC, VI. **Special Amenities:** free continental breakfast and free newspaper.
(See color ad p 552)

SOME UNITS

HOLIDAY INN EXPRESS
Phone: 262/646-7077

(AAA) (SAVE)

Small-scale Hotel

| All Year [ECP] | 1P: $89-$129 | 2P: $89-$129 |

Location: I-94, exit 287, just n, then just e. 3030 Golf Rd 53018. **Fax:** 262/646-7088. **Facility:** 84 one-bedroom standard units. 3 stories, interior corridors. *Bath:* combo or shower only. **Parking:** on-site, winter plug-ins. **Amenities:** video games (fee), irons, hair dryers. **Pool(s):** heated indoor. **Leisure Activities:** whirlpool. *Fee:* game room. **Guest Services:** valet laundry. **Business Services:** meeting rooms. **Cards:** AX, DC, DS, MC, VI. **Special Amenities:** free continental breakfast and free local telephone calls.
(See color ad below)

SOME UNITS

FEE

———— WHERE TO DINE ————

FISHBONE'S

Cajun

Dinner: $9-$22 **Phone:** 262/646-4696

Location: I-94, exit 287, just n, then just w. 1704 Milwaukee St 53018. **Hours:** 4 pm-11 pm, Fri & Sat 3 pm-midnight, Sat 4 pm-10 pm. **Closed:** 11/27; also Mon. **Features:** This is the place to be for ragin' Cajun in a great atmosphere of upbeat, bright colors and artwork. Menu options include tempting jambalaya, Cajun pasta dishes and desserts such as bourbon pecan pie. Diners may have to remind themselves they're along the banks of Lake Nagawicka in Wisconsin and not on Bourbon Street in Louisiana. Casual dress; cocktails. **Parking:** on-site. **Cards:** AX, MC, VI.

SAXE'S CASUAL FINE DINING

American

Lunch: $5-$9 **Dinner:** $9-$19 **Phone:** 262/968-4600

Location: I-94, exit 287, 2.7 mi s on SR 83, then 0.4 mi w on US 18. W 325 S 1767 Mickle Rd 53018. **Hours:** 11 am-10 pm, Sun from 9:30 am. **Closed:** 1/1, 7/4, 12/25; also Mon. **Features:** Baked ribs coated in barbecue sauce as well as fresh fish specials are among traditional American menu selections. Art deco lighting and attractive art decorate the Southwestern dining room. The menu of tempting desserts changes frequently. Casual dress; cocktails. **Parking:** on-site. **Cards:** AX, DC, DS, MC, VI.

SEVEN SEAS ON NAGAWICKA LAKE

Steak & Seafood

Dinner: $14-$25 **Phone:** 262/367-3903

Location: I-94, exit 287, 1.2 mi n on SR 83, 0.7 mi w. 1807 Nagawicka Rd 53029. **Hours:** 5 pm-10 pm, Sun 10:30 am-2 & 4-9 pm. **Closed** major holidays; also Tues 10/15-4/30. **Reservations:** accepted; except Fri. **Features:** Relax in the lovely, lakefront setting to enjoy creative preparations of seafood, beef and poultry. Such entrees as roast goose with cherry compote or broiled Atlantic salmon with dill-hollandaise sauce are complemented by an extensive list of wines. Dressy casual; cocktails. **Parking:** on-site. **Cards:** AX, DC, DS, MC, VI.

WATERSTREET BREWERY LAKE COUNTRY

American

Lunch: $6-$16 **Dinner:** $10-$24 **Phone:** 262/646-7878

Location: I-94, exit 287, just nw. 3191 Golf Rd 53018. **Hours:** 11 am-11 pm, Fri & Sat-midnight. **Closed:** 11/27, 12/25. **Reservations:** accepted. **Features:** Served here are a variety of salads, sandwiches, pasta and some seafood and steak preparations. Try homemade pot pie or daily soup specials. Several beers, including seasonal specialties, are brewed on the premises. The dining room reflects a Western flair. Casual dress; cocktails. **Parking:** on-site. **Cards:** AX, DS, MC, VI.

ELM GROVE pop. 6,249 (See map p. 544; index p. 547)

------- WHERE TO STAY -------

SLEEPY HOLLOW MOTEL
Phone: (262)782-8333   51

(AAA) [SAVE]

	6/1-8/31	1P: $47-$75	2P: $56-$75
	9/1-3/31	1P: $48	2P: $50-$60
	4/1-5/31	1P: $47	2P: $50-$60

Motel

Location: I-94, exit 304, just n on SR 100, 1 mi w on US 18. 12600 W Bluemound Rd 53122. Fax: 262/782-8304. **Facility:** 31 units. 28 one- and 3 two-bedroom standard units. 1 story, exterior corridors. *Bath:* combo or shower only. **Parking:** on-site, winter plug-ins. **Terms:** [CP] meal plan available. **Pool(s):** outdoor. **Leisure Activities:** playground, volleyball. **Cards:** AX, DS, MC, VI. **Special Amenities:** free continental breakfast and free local telephone calls. Affiliated with Best Value Inn Brand Membership. *(See color ad p 564)*

SOME UNITS
[S/D] [icons] [DATA PORT] / [X] [icon] /
FEE

------- WHERE TO DINE -------

ELM GROVE INN
Lunch: $9-$14   **Dinner:** $18-$25   **Phone:** 262/782-7090   36

Continental

Location: Center. 13275 Watertown Plank Rd 53122. **Hours:** 11:30 am-2 & 5-9:30 pm, Sat from 5 pm. Closed major holidays; also Sun. **Reservations:** suggested. **Features:** Once a stagecoach stop, the mid-19th-century inn now operates as a casually upscale restaurant that is popular with businesspeople at lunch and those looking for a special night out at dinner. Service is attentive and knowledgeable. Among decadent desserts are assorted souffles and cognac. Dressy casual; cocktails. **Parking:** on-site. **Cards:** AX, DS, MC, VI.

[icon] [X]

GENESEE DEPOT

------- WHERE TO DINE -------

THE UNION HOUSE Historic
Dinner: $16-$30   **Phone:** 262/968-4281

American

Location: On SR 83; downtown. S42 W31320 Hwy 83 53127. **Hours:** 4:30 pm-9 pm, Fri & Sat-10 pm. Closed major holidays; also Sun & Mon. **Reservations:** suggested. **Features:** In a quaint and historic inn, the restaurant offers a specialty of beef Wellington, as well as fresh fish, poultry and creative preparations of game. The Friday fish fry is as much an event as it is a dinner. Servers show good menu knowledge. Casual dress; cocktails. **Parking:** on-site. **Cards:** AX, CB, DC, DS, MC, VI.

[icon] [X]

GERMANTOWN pop. 13,700 (See map p. 544; index p. 547)

──── WHERE TO STAY ────

AMERICINN LODGE & SUITES OF GERMANTOWN
Phone: (262)502-9750

All Year [ECP]   1P: $74-$78   2P: $74-$78   XP: $6   F13

Small-scale Hotel

Location: US 41 and 45, exit Lannon/Mequon rds, then just e on SR 167 to Maple Rd. W190 N10862 Commerce Cir 53022. Fax: 262/502-9751. **Facility:** 47 units. 43 one-bedroom standard units, some with whirlpools. 4 one-bedroom suites ($99-$139), some with whirlpools. 2 stories, interior corridors. *Bath:* combo or shower only. **Parking:** on-site. **Amenities:** irons, hair dryers. **Pool(s):** small heated indoor. **Leisure Activities:** whirlpool. **Guest Services:** coin laundry. **Business Services:** meeting rooms. **Cards:** AX, DC, DS, MC, VI.

SOME UNITS

COUNTRY INN & SUITES BY CARLSON
Phone: (262)251-7700

All Year [ECP]   1P: $80-$92   2P: $80-$92   XP: $6   F18

Small-scale Hotel

Location: US 41 and 45, exit Lannon/Mequon rds, then just e on SR 167. W188 N11020 Maple Rd 53022. Fax: 262/251-7919. **Facility:** 62 one-bedroom standard units, some with whirlpools. 2 stories, interior corridors. *Bath:* combo or shower only. **Parking:** on-site. **Amenities:** irons, hair dryers. *Some:* high-speed Internet. **Pool(s):** heated indoor. **Leisure Activities:** whirlpool, limited exercise equipment. **Guest Services:** gift shop, valet and coin laundry. **Business Services:** meeting rooms. **Cards:** AX, DC, DS, MC, VI. **Special Amenities:** free continental breakfast and free newspaper. *(See color ad starting on p 556)*

SOME UNITS

HOLIDAY INN EXPRESS MILWAUKEE NW-GERMANTOWN
Phone: (262)255-1100

All Year [ECP]   1P: $69-$109

Small-scale Hotel

Location: US 41 and 45, exit CR Q (County Line Rd), then just w. W 177 N9675 Riversbend Ln 53022. Fax: 262/255-1086. **Facility:** 74 one-bedroom standard units. 2 stories, interior corridors. *Bath:* combo or shower only. **Parking:** on-site. **Amenities:** video games (fee), irons, hair dryers. **Pool(s):** heated indoor. **Leisure Activities:** whirlpool, limited exercise equipment. *Fee:* game room. **Guest Services:** valet laundry. **Business Services:** meeting rooms. **Cards:** AX, CB, DC, DS, JC, MC, VI. **Special Amenities:** free continental breakfast and free local telephone calls. *(See color ad below)*

SOME UNITS

SUPER 8 MOTEL-GERMANTOWN/MILWAUKEE
Phone: (262)255-0880

6/1-9/30 [ECP]   1P: $69-$79   2P: $79-$89
10/1-3/31 [ECP]   1P: $59-$69   2P: $65-$79
4/1-5/31 [ECP]   1P: $59-$69   2P: $65-$79

Small-scale Hotel

Location: US 41 and 45, exit CR Q (County Line Rd), then just w. N96 W17490 County Line Rd 53022. Fax: 262/255-7741. **Facility:** 100 one-bedroom standard units. 2 stories (no elevator), interior corridors. *Bath:* combo or shower only. **Parking:** on-site. **Terms:** pets ($50 deposit). **Amenities:** *Some:* irons. **Pool(s):** small heated indoor. **Leisure Activities:** whirlpool. *Fee:* game room. **Guest Services:** coin laundry. **Cards:** AX, DC, DS, MC, VI. *(See ad p 564)*

SOME UNITS

(See map p. 544)

────── WHERE TO DINE ──────

JERRY'S OLD TOWN   **Dinner:** $14-$26   **Phone:** 262/251-4455   ⑫
♦♦♦ ♦♦♦
Barbecue
Location: 0.4 mi n on SR 145 from jct SR 167, just nw on Fond Du Lac Ave, then just w. N 116 W 15841 Main St 53022. **Hours:** 4 pm-10 pm, Fri & Sat-10:30 pm, Sun-9 pm. Closed major holidays. **Reservations:** suggested. **Features:** Patrons go hog wild over the delicious homemade food and eclectic swine decor of the laid-back restaurant, which was founded in 1878. Servings of such dishes as tender barbecue ribs, corn-fed steer steak, blackened seafood and Cajun chicken satisfy all appetites. The huge "pig slop" ice cream dessert is worth a squeal for delight. Casual dress; cocktails. **Parking:** on-site. **Cards:** AX, MC, VI.   🍸 ✕

GLENDALE pop. 13,367   (See map p. 544; index p. 546)

────── WHERE TO STAY ──────

BAYMONT INN AND SUITES   **Phone:** (414)964-8484   ㉞
⒜⒜⒜ SAVE
♦♦♦♦
Small-scale Hotel
All Year [ECP]   1P: $59-$94   2P: $59-$94
Location: I-43, exit 78A (Silver Spring Dr), just s. 5110 N Port Washington Rd 53217. **Fax:** 414/964-2110. **Facility:** 103 one-bedroom standard units, some with kitchens. 3 stories, interior corridors. **Parking:** on-site, winter plug-ins. **Terms:** pets ($50 deposit). **Amenities:** video games (fee), voice mail, irons, hair dryers. **Business Services:** fax (fee). **Cards:** AX, DC, DS, MC, VI. *(See color ad p 552)*

SOME UNITS
🅂🄳 🐾 🛎 📠 🖥 / ✕ 🎆 📺 /

EXEL INN OF MILWAUKEE NORTHEAST   **Phone:** (414)961-7272   ㉜
⒜⒜⒜ SAVE
♦♦♦
Small-scale Hotel
6/1-9/30 [CP]   1P: $55-$75   2P: $61-$81   XP: $6   F18
4/1-5/31 & 10/1-3/31 [CP]   1P: $50-$66   2P: $56-$72   XP: $6   F18
Location: I-43, exit 78A (Silver Spring Dr). 5485 N Port Washington Rd 53217. **Fax:** 414/961-1721. **Facility:** 124 one-bedroom standard units, some with whirlpools. 3 stories, interior corridors. **Parking:** on-site, winter plug-ins. **Terms:** small pets only. **Amenities:** irons, hair dryers. **Leisure Activities:** exercise room. **Guest Services:** coin laundry. **Cards:** AX, CB, DC, DS, MC, VI. **Special Amenities:** early check-in/late check-out and free continental breakfast. *(See color ad p 555)*

SOME UNITS
🅂🄳 🐾 🛎 📠 🖥 / ✕ 🎆 📺 /
FEE FEE

HILTON MILWAUKEE RIVER   **Phone:** (414)962-6040   ㉟
⒜⒜⒜ SAVE
♦♦♦♦
Large-scale Hotel
All Year [ECP]   1P: $101-$142   2P: $101-$157   XP: $15   F18
Location: I-43, exit 77A northbound, just e on Hampton Ave; exit 78A southbound, just e on Silver Springs Dr, then just s. 4700 N Port Washington Rd 53212. **Fax:** 414/962-6166. **Facility:** 163 one-bedroom standard units. 5 stories, interior corridors. *Bath:* combo or shower only. **Parking:** on-site. **Amenities:** dual phone lines, voice mail, irons, hair dryers. **Dining:** Anchorage Restaurant, see separate listing. **Pool(s):** small heated indoor. **Leisure Activities:** exercise room. **Guest Services:** valet laundry. **Business Services:** meeting rooms. **Cards:** AX, CB, DC, DS, JC, MC, VI. **Special Amenities:** free continental breakfast and free room upgrade (subject to availability with advanced reservations). *(See color ad p 559)*

SOME UNITS
🅂🄳 🍴 🍸 ⛴ 🏊 🎆 📠 🖥 / ✕ 🎆 /

(See map p. 544)

MANCHESTER EAST HOTEL & SUITES

[AAA] [SAVE]

Phone: (414)351-6960 **31**

5/11-9/17	1P: $112-$119	2P: $112-$126	XP: $10
4/1-5/10 & 9/18-3/31	1P: $95	2P: $95	XP: $10

F17

Small-scale Hotel

Location: I-43, exit 80 (Good Hope Rd), just e. 7065 N Port Washington Rd 53217. **Fax:** 414/351-5194. **Facility:** 133 units. 125 one-bedroom standard units, some with whirlpools. 8 one-bedroom suites ($106-$170). 3 stories, 3 stories, interior corridors. **Parking:** on-site. **Terms:** [BP] meal plan available. **Amenities:** voice mail, irons, hair dryers. **Dining:** 6:30-9:30 am, 11:30-2 & 5-8:30 pm, Fri-9:30 pm, Sat 7:30-10:30 am, 11:30-2 & 5-9:30 pm, Sun 7:30-10:30 am, cocktails. **Pool(s):** heated indoor. **Leisure Activities:** sauna, whirlpool, atrium recreation area, exercise room. **Guest Services:** valet laundry, airport transportation-Milwaukee County Airport. **Business Services:** conference facilities. **Cards:** AX, CB, DC, DS, MC, VI. **Special Amenities:** free continental breakfast and free local telephone calls.
(See color ad p 561)

SOME UNITS

🔊 ⊞ ❤️ ⛑ 🍽 🍸 🗄 🏊 ☒ 🎦 [DATA PORT] 🛏 🖥 💻 / ☒ [VCR] /

RESIDENCE INN BY MARRIOTT

[SAVE]

Phone: (414)352-0070 **30**

6/1-9/30 [BP]	1P: $109-$299	
4/1-5/31 & 10/1-3/31 [BP]	1P: $99-$199	

Condominium

Location: I-43, exit 80 (Good Hope Rd), just e. 7275 N Port Washington Rd 53217. **Fax:** 414/352-3743. **Facility:** 96 units. 90 one-bedroom standard units with kitchens. 6 one-bedroom suites with kitchens. 2 stories, exterior corridors. *Bath:* combo or shower only. **Parking:** on-site. **Terms:** check-in 4 pm, cancellation fee imposed, pets ($175 fee, $6 extra charge). **Amenities:** voice mail, irons, hair dryers. **Pool(s):** heated outdoor. **Leisure Activities:** whirlpool, limited exercise equipment, sports court. **Guest Services:** valet and coin laundry, area transportation. **Business Services:** meeting rooms. **Cards:** AX, DC, DS, JC, MC, VI.

SOME UNITS

🔊 ⊞ ❤️ ⛑ 🗄 🏊 ☒ 🎦 [DATA PORT] 🛏 🖥 💻 / ☒ /

WOODFIELD SUITES MILWAUKEE-GLENDALE

[AAA] [SAVE]

Phone: (414)962-6767 **33**

All Year [ECP]	1P: $129-$189	2P: $129-$189

Small-scale Hotel

Location: I-43, exit 78A (Silver Spring Dr), just se. 5423 N Port Washington Rd 53217. **Fax:** 414/962-8811. **Facility:** 109 units. 30 one-bedroom standard units. 79 one-bedroom suites ($164-$199), some with efficiencies and/or whirlpools. 4 stories, interior corridors. *Bath:* combo or shower only. **Parking:** on-site. **Terms:** pets ($50 deposit). **Amenities:** video games (fee), voice mail, irons, hair dryers. **Pool(s):** heated indoor. **Leisure Activities:** whirlpool, exercise room. *Fee:* game room. **Guest Services:** complimentary evening beverages, valet and coin laundry. **Business Services:** meeting rooms. **Cards:** AX, CB, DC, DS, MC, VI. **Special Amenities:** free continental breakfast and free newspaper. *(See color ad p 572)*

SOME UNITS

🔊 ❤️ ⛑ 🗄M 🗄 🗄 🏊 ☒ [VCR] 🎦 [DATA PORT] 🛏 🖥 💻 / ☒ /

——— WHERE TO DINE ———

ANCHORAGE RESTAURANT

Seafood

Lunch: $8-$16   **Dinner:** $16-$24   **Phone:** 414/962-4710 **23**

Location: I-43, exit 77A northbound, just e on Hampton Ave; exit 78A southbound, just e on Silver Springs Dr, then just s; in Hilton Milwaukee River. 4700 N Port Washington Rd 53212. **Hours:** 6:30 am-2:30 & 4:30-10 pm, Sat 7 am-2:30 & 4:30-10 pm, Sun 7 am-1 & 4:30-10 pm. Closed: 1/1, 11/27, 12/25. **Reservations:** suggested. **Features:** Great Lakes fresh fish and seafood from the Gulf of Mexico and the Pacific and Atlantic Oceans is offered along with traditional flavorful soups and sauces. Try red snapper soup for some "zing." Tables overlook the Milwaukee River. Casual dress; cocktails. **Parking:** on-site. **Cards:** AX, DC, DS, JC, MC, VI.

🍸 ☒

THE BAVARIAN INN

German

Lunch: $7   **Dinner:** $9-$18   **Phone:** 414/964-0300 **22**

Location: Just s of Silver Spring Dr, just w of Port Washington Rd. 700 W Lexington Blvd 53217. **Hours:** 11:30 am-2 & 5-9 pm, Fri-10 pm, Sat 5 pm-9 pm, Sun 10:30 am-2 pm. Closed: 12/24, 12/25; also Mon. **Reservations:** accepted. **Features:** Ethnic decor and a festive atmosphere add to the charm of the relaxed restaurant, a favorite for great German food. Menu choices include bratwurst, potato pancakes, pork chops, spaetzle and potato salad. The daily luncheon buffet and Sunday brunch are popular. Guests can enjoy the traditional Friday fish fry while soaking up live entertainment. Casual dress; cocktails. **Parking:** on-site. **Cards:** AX, DC, DS, MC, VI.

🍸 ☒

GRAFTON pop. 10,312

——— WHERE TO STAY ———

BAYMONT INN & SUITES-GRAFTON

[AAA] [SAVE]

Phone: (262)387-1180 **F18**

All Year [ECP]	1P: $74-$125	2P: $74-$125	XP: $8

Small-scale Hotel

Location: I-43, exit 92 (SR 60), just w, then just s. 1415 Port Washington Rd 53024. **Fax:** 262/387-1168. **Facility:** 67 units. 64 one-bedroom standard units, some with whirlpools. 3 one-bedroom suites. 4 stories, interior corridors. *Bath:* combo or shower only. **Parking:** on-site, winter plug-ins. **Amenities:** video games (fee), dual phone lines, voice mail, irons, hair dryers. **Pool(s):** heated indoor. **Leisure Activities:** limited exercise equipment. **Guest Services:** coin laundry. **Business Services:** meeting rooms. **Cards:** AX, CB, DC, DS, MC, VI. **Special Amenities:** free continental breakfast and free newspaper.

SOME UNITS

🔊 ⛑ 🏊 🎦 [DATA PORT] 💻 / ☒ 🛏 🖥 /

GREENFIELD pop. 35,476 (See map p. 544; index p. 547)

——— WHERE TO STAY ———

GOLDEN KEY MOTEL

Motel

Phone: 414/543-5300 **58**

6/1-8/31	1P: $45-$55	2P: $50-$75	XP: $5
4/1-5/31	1P: $42-$55	2P: $45-$65	XP: $5
9/1-3/31	1P: $40-$45	2P: $45-$55	XP: $5

Location: I-894, exit 3, 0.5 mi w on Beloit Rd (CR T), just n on SR 100. 3600 S 108th St 53228. **Fax:** 414/543-5300. **Facility:** 23 one-bedroom standard units. 2 stories, interior/exterior corridors. **Parking:** on-site. **Terms:** weekly rates available. **Amenities:** voice mail, hair dryers. **Pool(s):** small heated outdoor. **Business Services:** fax (fee). **Cards:** AX, CB, DS, MC, VI.

SOME UNITS

[ASK] 🔊 ⛑ 🏊 🎦 [DATA PORT] 🛏 / ☒ [VCR] /

HARTFORD pop. 10,905

―――― **WHERE TO STAY** ――――

AMERICINN MOTEL & SUITES   **Phone:** 262/673-2200

▼▼▼   All Year   1P: $65-$134   2P: $65-$134   XP: $6   F12

Small-scale Hotel   **Location:** On SR 60, 1 mi e of center. 1527 E Sumner St 53027. Fax: 262/673-4741. **Facility:** 46 units. 43 one-bedroom standard units, some with whirlpools. 3 one-bedroom suites ($94-$124), some with whirlpools. 2 stories (no elevator), interior corridors. *Bath:* combo or shower only. **Parking:** on-site, winter plug-ins. **Pool(s):** heated indoor. **Leisure Activities:** whirlpool. **Guest Services:** coin laundry. **Business Services:** meeting rooms, fax (fee). **Cards:** AX, DC, DS, MC, VI.

SOME UNITS

(ASK) (S/D) (🛏✦) (👤M) (🔆) (🕊) (🏊) (🐾) (DATA PORT) (📺) (✕) (🛗) (📠) /

SUPER 8 MOTEL-HARTFORD   **Phone:** 262/673-7431

▼▼   All Year   1P: $45-$65   2P: $55-$85   XP: $5   F12

Small-scale Hotel   **Location:** On SR 60, 1.1 mi e of center. 1539 E Sumner St 53027. Fax: 262/673-3080. **Facility:** 32 one-bedroom standard units, some with whirlpools. 2 stories (no elevator), interior corridors. **Parking:** on-site, winter plug-ins. **Terms:** 7 day cancellation notice, pets ($10 extra charge). **Leisure Activities:** whirlpool. **Business Services:** meeting rooms. **Cards:** AX, DC, MC, VI.

SOME UNITS

(ASK) (S/D) (🛏) (🛏✦) (🕊) (✕) (🛗) (📠) /

JACKSON pop. 4,938

―――― **WHERE TO STAY** ――――

HAWTHORN INN AND SUITES OF JACKSON   **Phone:** (262)677-1133

▼▼▼   All Year [BP]   1P: $72-$105   2P: $72-$105   F17

Small-scale Hotel   **Location:** Ne of jct US 45 and SR 60. W227 N16890 Tillie Lake Ct 53037. Fax: 262/677-1144. **Facility:** 54 units. 50 one-bedroom standard units, some with whirlpools. 4 one-bedroom suites. 2 stories (no elevator), interior corridors. *Bath:* combo or shower only. **Parking:** on-site. **Terms:** package plans - seasonal, pets ($50 deposit). **Amenities:** high-speed Internet, dual phone lines, voice mail, irons, hair dryers. **Pool(s):** heated indoor/outdoor. **Leisure Activities:** whirlpool. *Fee:* game room. **Guest Services:** sundries, valet and coin laundry. **Business Services:** meeting rooms. **Cards:** AX, DS, MC, VI.

SOME UNITS

(ASK) (S/D) (🛏) (🛏✦) (🔆) (🐾) (🕊) (DATA PORT) (🛗) (📠) (📺) / (✕) (VCR)

MEQUON pop. 21,823   (See map p. 544; index p. 546)

―――― **WHERE TO STAY** ――――

BEST WESTERN QUIET HOUSE & SUITES   **Phone:** 262/241-3677   🅱🅱

(AAA) (SAVE)   5/16-12/31 [ECP]   1P: $95-$123   2P: $105-$133   XP: $10   F12

▼▼▼   4/1-5/15 & 1/1-3/31 [ECP]   1P: $95-$113   2P: $105-$123   XP: $10   F12

Small-scale Hotel   **Location:** I-43, exit 85, just w on SR 167, then 1 mi s on CR W. 10330 N Port Washington Rd 53092. Fax: 262/241-3707. **Facility:** 55 units. 52 one-bedroom standard units, some with whirlpools. 3 one-bedroom suites. 2 stories (no elevator), interior corridors. **Parking:** on-site. **Terms:** package plans - seasonal, pets ($15 extra charge). **Amenities:** voice mail, irons, hair dryers. **Pool(s):** heated indoor/outdoor. **Leisure Activities:** whirlpool, exercise room. **Guest Services:** valet laundry. **Cards:** AX, CB, DC, DS, MC, VI. **Special Amenities:** free continental breakfast and free newspaper. *(See ad p 555)*

SOME UNITS

(S/D) (🛏) (🛏✦) (👤M) (🔆) (🕊) (🏊) (🐾) (🕊) (DATA PORT) (🛗) (📠) (📺) / (✕) /

THE CHALET MOTEL OF MEQUON   **Phone:** (262)241-4510   🅱🅱

▼▼ ▼▼   6/27-8/16   1P: $69-$139   2P: $79-$149   XP: $10   F17

   4/1-6/26 & 8/17-3/31   1P: $55-$110   2P: $65-$120   XP: $10   F17

Small-scale Hotel   **Location:** I-43, exit 85, just w on SR 167, then 1 mi s on CR W. 10401 N Port Washington Rd 53092. Fax: 262/241-5542. **Facility:** 53 one-bedroom standard units. 2 stories (no elevator), exterior corridors. *Bath:* combo or shower only. **Parking:** on-site. **Terms:** 2-3 night minimum stay - seasonal weekends, cancellation fee imposed, weekly rates available, pets ($10 extra charge, in smoking units). **Amenities:** voice mail. *Some:* irons, hair dryers. **Guest Services:** complimentary laundry. **Cards:** AX, DC, DS, MC, VI.

SOME UNITS

(ASK) (S/D) (🛏) (🍴) (🍸) (👤✦) (🕊) (DATA PORT) (🛗) (📺) / (✕) (VCR) (📠) /

―――― **WHERE TO DINE** ――――

THE CENTENNIAL   **Lunch:** $5-$7   **Dinner:** $5-$13   **Phone:** 262/241-4353   15

▼▼   **Location:** I-43, exit 85, just w on SR 167, then 1 mi s on CR W. 10352 N Port Washington Rd 53092. **Hours:** 11:30 am-10 pm, Fri & Sat-10:30 pm. Closed: 12/31 for dinner. **Features:** This restaurant prides itself on its food, American   and it shows. Flashes of creativity are evident in the extensive variety of sandwiches, homemade soups and entrees made with quality ingredients. A 100-year-old decorative wood bar is the centerpiece of the dining room, which has the atmosphere of a casual pub. Casual dress; cocktails. **Parking:** on-site. **Cards:** MC, VI. (🍸) (✕)

HEINEMANN'S RESTAURANT   **Lunch:** $5-$9   **Dinner:** $5-$9   **Phone:** 414/352-2244   16

▼▼   **Location:** I-43, exit 82A, just e. 333 W Brown Deer Rd 53217. **Hours:** 7 am-8 pm, Sun from 7:30 am. Closed major holidays; also 12/24 for dinner. **Features:** The well-established, family-oriented restaurant delivers American   fresh, flavorful items, such as soup, sandwiches and salad, made from scratch without additives or preservatives. Highly noteworthy are the aromatic baked goods and tantalizing desserts. Casual dress; beer & wine only. **Parking:** on-site. **Cards:** MC, VI. (✕)

Free Breakfast Bar

- **Clean Comfortable Rooms**
- **Indoor Pool & Spa** (at most locations)
- **Free Local Phone Calls**
- **Data Port Access**
- **In-room Hair Dryers, Iron & Ironing Boards**
- **Priority Club® Worldwide Program - Free Airline Miles**

Holiday Inn EXPRESS®

Stay Smart®

Stay Smart®
& SAVE UP TO
20% OFF
PUBLISHED ROOM RATES

Valid only at participating Michigan Holiday Inn Express® Hotels. Present coupon at check-in only. Not valid with any other discounts.

Stay Smart®
& SAVE UP TO
20% OFF
PUBLISHED ROOM RATES

Valid only at participating Michigan Holiday Inn Express® Hotels. Present coupon at check-in only. Not valid with any other discounts.

Stay Smart®
& SAVE UP TO
20% OFF
PUBLISHED ROOM RATES

Valid only at participating Michigan Holiday Inn Express® Hotels. Present coupon at check-in only. Not valid with any other discounts.

Stay Smart®
& SAVE UP TO
20% OFF
PUBLISHED ROOM RATES

Valid only at participating Michigan Holiday Inn Express® Hotels. Present coupon at check-in only. Not valid with any other discounts.

Holiday Inn Express® Hotels are conveniently located throughout Michigan. Check AAA listings within this book or call 1-800-HOLIDAY to make your reservations.

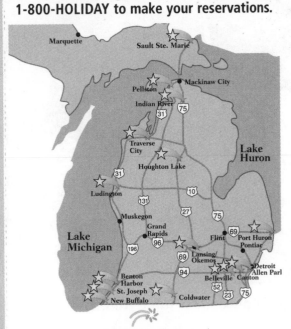

Holiday Inn EXPRESS®

Allen Park •
3600 Enterprise Dr.
800-DIAL INN

Belleville •
46194 N. I-94 Service Drive
734-857-6200

Benton Harbor
2276 Pipestone Rd.
269-927-4599

Coldwater
630 E. Chicago St.
517-279-0900

Canton •
3950 S. Lotz Road
734-721-5500

Houghton Lake
200 Cloverleaf Lane
989-422-STAY (7829)

Indian River
4375 Brudy Rd.
888-255-3365

Lansing / Okemos
2187 University Park Dr.
517-347-6690

Ludington
5323 West US 10
231-845-7004

New Buffalo •
11500 Holiday Dr.
269-469-1400

Pellston
1600 US 31 N
231-539-7000

Port Huron •
1720 Hancock St.
810-987-5999

Sault Ste. Marie
1171 Riverview Way
800-632-7879

St. Joseph •
3019 Lake Shore Dr.
269-982-0004

Traverse City •
3536 Mt. Hope Rd.
231-938-2600

• Denotes Holiday Inn Express® Hotel & Suites location

Stay Smart®

NEW BERLIN pop. 38,220   (See map p. 544; index p. 547)

———— WHERE TO STAY ————

BAYMONT INN & SUITES MILWAUKEE-NEW BERLIN   **Phone:** (262)717-0900   55

(AAA) (SAVE)
▽▽▽▽
Small-scale Hotel

All Year [ECP]   1P: $89-$109   2P: $89-$109
Location: I-43, exit 57 (Moorland Rd), just se. 15300 W Rock Ridge Rd 53151. **Fax:** 262/717-0905. **Facility:** 88 one-bedroom standard units, some with whirlpools. 4 stories, interior corridors. **Bath:** combo or shower only. **Parking:** on-site. **Terms:** check-in 4 pm. **Amenities:** video games (fee), voice mail, irons, hair dryers. **Pool(s):** small heated indoor. **Leisure Activities:** whirlpool, exercise room. **Guest Services:** valet and coin laundry. **Business Services:** meeting rooms. **Cards:** AX, CB, DC, DS, MC, VI. **Special Amenities:** free continental breakfast and free newspaper. (See color ad p 552)

SOME UNITS

HOLIDAY INN EXPRESS HOTEL AND SUITES-NEW BERLIN   **Phone:** (262)787-0700   54

(AAA) (SAVE)
▽▽▽▽
Small-scale Hotel

All Year   1P: $99   2P: $99   XP: $8   F17
Location: I-43, exit 57 (Moorland Rd), just ne. 15451 W Beloit Rd 53151. **Fax:** 262/787-0738. **Facility:** 101 one-bedroom standard units. 4 stories, interior corridors. **Bath:** combo or shower only. **Parking:** on-site. **Amenities:** video games (fee), dual phone lines, voice mail, irons, hair dryers. **Pool(s):** heated indoor. **Leisure Activities:** whirlpool, exercise room. **Guest Services:** valet and coin laundry. **Business Services:** meeting rooms. **Cards:** AX, DC, DS, MC, VI. **Special Amenities:** free continental breakfast and free local telephone calls.

SOME UNITS

———— WHERE TO DINE ————

TIMBER CREEK GRILLE   **Lunch:** $8-$15   **Dinner:** $15-$28   **Phone:** 262/432-3000   39
▽▽▽
Wild Game

Location: I-94, exit 301A, 0.5 mi s on Moorland Rd, then just e. 15375 W Greenfield Ave 53151. **Hours:** 11 am-10 pm, Fri & Sat-11 pm. Closed: 1/1, 12/25; also Sun. **Reservations:** suggested. **Features:** Pheasant Wellington, venison schnitzel, seared elk medallions, bison steak, fresh fish and Wisconsin prairie wild rice are among fresh items served at the distinctive restaurant. Entrees are attractively presented, and the dining room sports a northwoods theme. Smoking is allowed only in the lounge. Dressy casual; cocktails. **Parking:** on-site. **Cards:** AX, DC, DS, MC, VI.

OAK CREEK pop. 28,456   (See map p. 544; index p. 546)

———— WHERE TO STAY ————

BAYMONT INN & SUITES MILWAUKEE-AIRPORT   **Phone:** (414)762-2266   62

(AAA) (SAVE)
▽▽▽▽
Small-scale Hotel

All Year [ECP]   1P: $69-$89   2P: $69-$89
Location: I-94, exit 320, just se on Rawson Ave (CR BB). 7141 S 13th St 53154. **Fax:** 414/762-0513. **Facility:** 98 units. 96 one-bedroom standard units. 2 one-bedroom suites ($79-$139). 3 stories, interior corridors. **Parking:** on-site, winter plug-ins. **Terms:** small pets only. **Amenities:** video games (fee), voice mail, irons, hair dryers. **Leisure Activities:** exercise room. **Guest Services:** valet and coin laundry. **Cards:** AX, CB, DC, DS, MC, VI. **Special Amenities:** free continental breakfast and free newspaper. (See color ad p 552)

SOME UNITS

COMFORT SUITES   **Phone:** (414)570-1111   18

(AAA) (SAVE)
▽▽▽▽
Small-scale Hotel

All Year   1P: $99-$149   2P: $109-$159
Location: I-94, exit 319, just e on College Ave (CR 22), then just s. 6362 S 13th St 53154. **Fax:** 414/570-3333. **Facility:** 138 units. 136 one-bedroom standard units, some with whirlpools. 2 two-bedroom suites with whirlpools. 3 stories, interior corridors. **Bath:** combo or shower only. **Parking:** on-site. **Terms:** [ECP] meal plan available. **Amenities:** dual phone lines, voice mail, irons, hair dryers. **Fee:** video games, safes. **Pool(s):** heated indoor. **Leisure Activities:** whirlpool, children's pool, limited exercise equipment. **Fee:** game room. **Guest Services:** complimentary evening beverages: Mon-Thurs, valet and coin laundry, area transportation. **Business Services:** meeting rooms. **Cards:** AX, CB, DC, DS, JC, MC, VI. **Special Amenities:** free continental breakfast and free room upgrade (subject to availability with advanced reservations). (See color ad p 558)

SOME UNITS

EXEL INN OF MILWAUKEE SOUTH   **Phone:** (414)764-1776   15

(AAA) (SAVE)
▽▽▽
Small-scale Hotel

6/1-9/30 [CP]   1P: $47-$69   2P: $47-$69   XP: $6   F18
4/1-5/31 & 10/1-3/31 [CP]   1P: $35-$47   2P: $41-$53   XP: $6   F18
Location: I-94, exit 319, just e on College Ave (CR 22). 1201 W College Ave 53154. **Fax:** 414/762-8009. **Facility:** 109 one-bedroom standard units, some with whirlpools. 2 stories (no elevator), interior corridors. **Parking:** on-site. **Terms:** small pets only (in smoking units). **Amenities:** irons. **Leisure Activities:** exercise room. **Guest Services:** coin laundry. **Cards:** AX, CB, DC, DS, MC, VI. **Special Amenities:** early check-in/late check-out and free continental breakfast. (See color ad p 555)

SOME UNITS
FEE FEE

MAINSTAY SUITES OAK CREEK   **Phone:** (414)571-8800   61
▽▽▽▽
Small-scale Hotel

All Year [ECP]   1P: $80-$160   2P: $80-$160   XP: $10   F
Location: I-94, exit 319, just e on College Ave (CR 22). 1001 W College Ave 53154. **Fax:** 414/571-8820. **Facility:** 76 units. 37 one-bedroom standard units with efficiencies. 37 one- and 2 two-bedroom suites with efficiencies. 3 stories, interior corridors. **Bath:** combo or shower only. **Parking:** on-site. **Terms:** cancellation fee imposed, weekly rates available, pets ($15 extra charge). **Amenities:** dual phone lines, voice mail, irons, hair dryers. **Leisure Activities:** limited exercise equipment. **Guest Services:** valet and coin laundry. **Business Services:** business center. **Cards:** AX, CB, DC, DS, JC, MC, VI.

SOME UNITS

(See map p. 544)

RED ROOF INN-MILWAUKEE

Phone: (414)764-3500　[19]

[AAA] [SAVE]

5/25-8/30	1P: $46-$64	2P: $51-$69	XP: $5	F18
8/31-9/27	1P: $39-$53	2P: $44-$58	XP: $5	F18
4/1-5/24	1P: $35-$52	2P: $40-$57	XP: $5	F18
9/28-3/31	1P: $35-$48	2P: $40-$53	XP: $5	F18

Motel

Location: I-94, exit 319, just e on College Ave (CR 22). 6360 S 13th St 53154. Fax: 414/764-5138. **Facility:** 108 one-bedroom standard units. 2 stories, exterior corridors. **Parking:** on-site. **Terms:** small pets only. **Amenities:** video games (fee), voice mail. **Business Services:** fax (fee). **Cards:** AX, CB, DC, DS, MC, VI. **Special Amenities:** free local telephone calls and free newspaper.

SOME UNITS
[icons] FEE　FEE

OKAUCHEE

──────── WHERE TO DINE ────────

GOLDEN MAST INN

Dinner: $19-$30　　　**Phone:** 262/567-7047

German

Location: SR 16, exit 178 (Sawyer), 1 mi n, follow signs. W349 N5293 Lacy's Ln 53069. **Hours:** 5 pm-10 pm, Sun 11 am-2 & 4-9 pm. Closed: Mon. **Reservations:** accepted. **Features:** From entering this grand Bavarian-style restaurant with high ceilings and liberal use of wood, rock and glass, to the last bite of apple strudel; you'll experience authentic German cuisine and a setting to match. The menu offers seafood and steak, but the key elements are the veal dumpling soup, Wiener Schnitzel, beef rouladen, kassler ripchen, and other German touches. Plus, the view of Okauchee Lake from the dining room is delightful. Dressy casual; cocktails. **Parking:** on-site. **Cards:** AX, MC, VI.

PEWAUKEE pop. 11,783

──────── WHERE TO STAY ────────

COMFORT SUITES

Phone: (262)506-2000

[SAVE]

All Year [ECP]	1P: $89-$149	2P: $99-$159	XP: $10　F18

Small-scale Hotel

Location: I-94, exit 294 (CR J), just nw. N14 W24121 Tower Pl 53072 (PO Box 430). Fax: 262/523-5848. **Facility:** 94 units. 84 one-bedroom standard units, some with whirlpools. 10 one-bedroom suites ($169-$199), some with efficiencies (no utensils) and/or whirlpools. 3 stories, interior corridors. **Bath:** combo or shower only. **Parking:** on-site, winter plug-ins. **Terms:** check-in 4 pm, cancellation fee imposed. **Amenities:** video games (fee), voice mail, irons, hair dryers. **Some:** dual phone lines. **Pool(s):** heated indoor. **Leisure Activities:** whirlpool, exercise room. **Guest Services:** gift shop, valet and coin laundry. **Business Services:** meeting rooms. **Cards:** AX, CB, DC, DS, MC, VI.

SOME UNITS
[icons]

THE RADISSON HOTEL PEWAUKEE

Phone: (262)506-6300

All Year	1P: $99-$129	2P: $99-$129

Small-scale Hotel

Location: I-94, exit 294 (CR J), just nw. N 14 W 24140 Tower Pl 53072. Fax: 262/523-1299. **Facility:** 119 units. 112 one-bedroom standard units, some with whirlpools. 5 one- and 2 two-bedroom suites ($129-$499), some with kitchens and/or whirlpools. 3 stories, interior corridors. **Bath:** combo or shower only. **Parking:** on-site. **Amenities:** video games (fee), dual phone lines, voice mail, irons, hair dryers. **Some:** CD players, safes. **Dining:** Thunder Bay Grille, see separate listing. **Pool(s):** heated indoor. **Leisure Activities:** whirlpool, exercise room. **Guest Services:** gift shop, valet laundry. **Business Services:** conference facilities, business center. **Cards:** AX, CB, DC, DS, MC, VI. *(See color ad p 562)*

SOME UNITS
[icons]

──────── WHERE TO DINE ────────

THUNDER BAY GRILLE

Lunch: $6-$10　　　**Dinner:** $7-$15　　　**Phone:** 262/523-4244

American

Location: I-94, exit 294 (CR J), just nw; in The Radisson Hotel Pewaukee. N 14W 24130 Tower Pl 53072. **Hours:** 11 am-10 pm, Fri & Sat-11 pm, Sun 10 am-9 pm. Closed major holidays. **Features:** Log chairs, antlers on the walls and canoes in the rafters contribute to the folksy northwoods atmosphere at this casual restaurant. The large variety of foods includes homemade soup, hand-cut steaks, fresh fish, pasta, slow-roasted prime rib and hardwood-smoked ribs. Casual dress; cocktails. **Parking:** on-site. **Cards:** AX, DC, DS, MC, VI.

WISCONSIN MACHINE SHED RESTAURANT

Lunch: $6-$11　　　**Dinner:** $8-$20　　　**Phone:** 262/523-1322

American

Location: I-94, exit 294 (CR J), just nw. N14 W24145 Tower Pl 53072. **Hours:** 6 am-10 pm, Sun 7 am-9 pm. Closed: 1/1, 11/27, 12/25. **Reservations:** accepted. **Features:** Antiques and farm implements decorate the decidedly rustic dining room. Tried-and-true comfort foods—such as pot roast, ham and roast pork—please every member of the family. The Friday night fish fry draws a hungry crowd. Servers in overalls are friendly and prompt. Casual dress; cocktails. **Parking:** on-site. **Cards:** AX, DC, DS, MC, VI.

PORT WASHINGTON pop. 10,467

—— WHERE TO STAY ——

BEST WESTERN HARBORSIDE

			Phone: (262)284-9461	
5/23-8/31	1P: $105-$169	2P: $105-$169	XP: $10	F12
9/1-10/25	1P: $89-$159	2P: $89-$159	XP: $10	F12
10/26-3/31	1P: $84-$139	2P: $84-$139	XP: $10	F12
4/1-5/22	1P: $84-$129	2P: $84-$129	XP: $10	F12

Small-scale Hotel **Location:** On SR 43, waterfront of Lake Michigan; downtown. 135 E Grand Ave 53074. Fax: 262/284-3169. **Facility:** 96 units. 92 one-bedroom standard units, some with whirlpools. 4 one-bedroom suites ($129-$169) with whirlpools. 5 stories, interior corridors. **Parking:** on-site, winter plug-ins. **Terms:** 3 day cancellation notice, [BP] meal plan available, package plans - 10/1-5/20, pets (in smoking units). **Amenities:** video games (fee), voice mail, irons, hair dryers. *Some:* dual phone lines. **Dining:** 6:30-9:30 am, Sat & Sun-10:30 am; closed Mon. **Pool(s):** heated indoor. **Leisure Activities:** sauna, whirlpool, fishing, limited exercise equipment. *Fee:* game room. **Guest Services:** valet and coin laundry. **Business Services:** meeting rooms. **Cards:** AX, CB, DC, DS, MC, VI. **Special Amenities:** free newspaper. *(See color ad below)*

SOME UNITS

COUNTRY INN & SUITES BY CARLSON

			Phone: (262)284-2100	
All Year	1P: $74-$89	2P: $74-$89	XP: $6	F18

Small-scale Hotel **Location:** I-43, exit 100 (SR 32 S), just ne. 350 E Seven Hills Rd 53074. Fax: 262/284-6740. **Facility:** 85 units. 58 one-bedroom standard units, some with whirlpools. 27 one-bedroom suites ($99-$179), some with whirlpools. 3 stories, interior corridors. *Bath:* combo or shower only. **Parking:** on-site. **Terms:** [CP] meal plan available. **Amenities:** high-speed Internet, dual phone lines, voice mail, irons, hair dryers. **Pool(s):** small heated indoor. **Leisure Activities:** whirlpool, exercise room. *Fee:* game room. **Guest Services:** complimentary evening beverages: Sun-Thurs, coin laundry. **Business Services:** conference facilities, administrative services (fee). **Cards:** AX, DC, DS, MC, VI. **Special Amenities:** free continental breakfast and free newspaper. *(See color ad starting on p 556)*

SOME UNITS

—— WHERE TO DINE ——

BEANIES

Mexican

	Lunch: $5-$11	Dinner: $5-$11	Phone: 262/284-7200

Location: On SR 32; downtown. 102 E Grand Ave 53074. **Hours:** 11 am-9 pm, Fri & Sat-10 pm, Sun noon-8 pm. Closed: 4/20, 12/24, 12/25. **Features:** Just off the waterfront, the tiny restaurant hits the spot for those seeking tasty food at a reasonable price. In addition to Mexican favorites, subs and burgers make up the menu. Complimentary chips and salsa accompany every meal. Casual dress; beer & wine only. **Parking:** on-site. **Cards:** MC, VI.

SMITH BROS 'FISH SHANTY' RESTAURANT

Seafood

	Lunch: $5-$13	Dinner: $5-$18	Phone: 262/284-5592

Location: I-43, exit 96, 2 mi e on SR 33, 1.5 mi e on SR 32 at waterfront. 100 N Franklin St 53074. **Hours:** 11 am-10 pm, Fri & Sat-11 pm; 11 am-9 pm, Fri & Sat-10 pm 9/2-5/27. Closed: 11/27, 12/25; also 12/24 for dinner. **Reservations:** suggested. **Features:** Enjoy a nice view of the harbor from the relaxed dining room. A menu of mostly American fare shows a heavy concentration on seafood, particularly Great Lakes fish. The summer patio is comfortable and breezy. Servers are knowledgeable and efficient. Casual dress; cocktails. **Parking:** on-site. **Cards:** AX, DC, DS, MC, VI.

WAUKESHA pop. 64,825

──────── WHERE TO STAY ────────

BEST WESTERN WAUKESHA GRAND

AAA SAVE

▽▽▽▽

Small-scale Hotel

Phone: (262)524-9300

6/1-9/30 [ECP]	1P: $69-$89	2P: $75-$95	XP: $6	F18
4/1-5/31 & 10/1-3/31 [ECP]	1P: $69-$79	2P: $75-$85	XP: $6	F18

Location: I-94, exit 293, just s on CR T. 2840 N Grandview Blvd 53072. **Fax:** 262/524-9305. **Facility:** 97 one-bedroom standard units, some with whirlpools. 3 stories, interior corridors. *Bath:* combo or shower only. **Parking:** on-site. **Terms:** small pets only. **Amenities:** irons, hair dryers. **Pool(s):** small heated indoor. **Leisure Activities:** whirlpool, exercise room. **Guest Services:** coin laundry. **Business Services:** business center. **Cards:** AX, CB, DC, DS, MC, VI. **Special Amenities:** early check-in/late check-out and free continental breakfast.

SOME UNITS

[icons] FEE FEE

RAMADA LIMITED

AAA SAVE

▽▽▽ ▽▽▽

Small-scale Hotel

Phone: (262)547-7770

All Year [ECP]	1P: $50-$145	2P: $55-$145	XP: $6	F18

Location: I-94, exit 297, 1 mi w on US 18. 2111 E Moreland Blvd 53186. **Fax:** 262/547-0688. **Facility:** 92 one-bedroom standard units, some with whirlpools. 2 stories (no elevator), interior corridors. **Parking:** on-site winter plug-ins. **Terms:** cancellation fee imposed, pets ($10 extra charge). **Amenities:** voice mail, irons, hair dryers. **Pool(s):** small heated indoor. **Leisure Activities:** sauna, whirlpool, limited exercise equipment. **Guest Services:** valet and coin laundry. **Business Services:** meeting rooms. **Cards:** AX, CB, DC, DS, MC, VI. **Special Amenities:** early check-in/late check-out and free room upgrade (subject to availability with advanced reservations). *(See color ad below)*

SOME UNITS

[icons] FEE

SELECT INN

AAA SAVE

▽▽▽ ▽▽▽

Small-scale Hotel

Phone: (262)786-6015

6/1-9/30 [ECP]	1P: $55-$70	2P: $60-$75	XP: $5	F16
4/1-5/31 & 10/1-3/31 [ECP]	1P: $44-$54	2P: $49-$59	XP: $5	F16

Location: I-94, exit 297, just w on CR JJ (Bluemound Rd). 2510 Plaza Ct 53186. **Fax:** 262/786-5784. **Facility:** 99 one-bedroom standard units. 3 stories (no elevator), interior corridors. *Bath:* combo or shower only. **Parking:** on-site. **Terms:** weekly rates available, small pets only ($25 deposit, $5 extra charge). **Amenities:** safes (fee). *Some:* hair dryers. **Guest Services:** coin laundry. **Business Services:** meeting rooms. **Cards:** AX, CB, DC, DS, JC, MC, VI. **Special Amenities:** free continental breakfast. *(See color ad p 508)*

SOME UNITS

[icons]

──────── WHERE TO DINE ────────

WEISSGERBER'S GASTHAUS

▽▽▽▽

German

Lunch: $8-$12   **Dinner:** $17-$25   **Phone:** 262/544-4460

Location: I-94, exit 293, just s on CR T. 2720 N Grandview Blvd 53188. **Hours:** 11:30 am-2 & 5-10 pm, Sat from 5 pm, Sun 4 pm-9 pm. **Closed:** 12/24, 12/25. **Reservations:** suggested. **Features:** Enjoy an authentic Bavarian experience complete with Old World decor, servers in ethnic period uniforms and genuine cuisine. The menu features a special Bavarian bean soup, sausage lover's selections and a few American favorites. The tortes and pies are made in-house. Dressy casual; cocktails. **Parking:** on-site. **Cards:** AX, DC, DS, MC, VI.

[icons]

WAUWATOSA pop. 47,271 (See map p. 544; index p. 547)

———— WHERE TO STAY ————

EXEL INN OF MILWAUKEE WEST
Phone: (414)257-0140 **48**

AAA SAVE	6/1-8/31 [CP]	1P: $50-$79	2P: $56-$84	XP: $6	F18
	4/1-5/31 & 9/1-3/31 [CP]	1P: $47-$59	2P: $53-$65	XP: $6	F18

Location: I-94, exit 304B, just n on SR 100. 115 N Mayfair Rd 53226. **Fax:** 414/475-7875. **Facility:** 122 one-bedroom standard units, some with whirlpools. 2 stories (no elevator), interior corridors. **Parking:** on-site.
Small-scale Hotel **Terms:** small pets only (in smoking units). **Amenities:** irons, hair dryers. **Leisure Activities:** limited exercise equipment. **Guest Services:** coin laundry. **Cards:** AX, CB, DC, DS, MC, VI. **Special Amenities: early check-in/late check-out and free continental breakfast.** *(See color ad p 555)*

SOME UNITS

HOLIDAY INN EXPRESS-MAYFAIR
Phone: 414/778-0333 **47**

AAA SAVE	6/16-8/31 [CP]	1P: $104-$159	2P: $104-$159
	4/1-6/15 & 9/1-3/31 [CP]	1P: $99-$149	2P: $99-$149

Location: US 45, exit 42A, just n on SR 100, then just w. 11111 W North Ave 53226. **Fax:** 414/778-0331. **Facility:** 122 units. 114 one-bedroom standard units, some with whirlpools. 8 one-bedroom suites ($129-$159). 3 stories,
Small-scale Hotel interior corridors. *Bath:* combo or shower only. **Parking:** on-site. **Amenities:** voice mail, irons, hair dryers. **Guest Services:** valet laundry. **Business Services:** meeting rooms. **Cards:** AX, CB, DC, DS, JC, MC. **Special Amenities: free continental breakfast and free local telephone calls.** *(See color ad p 558)*

SOME UNITS

RADISSON HOTEL MILWAUKEE WEST
Phone: (414)257-3400 **46**

AAA SAVE	6/1-8/31	1P: $149-$159	2P: $149-$159
	4/1-5/31 & 9/1-3/31	1P: $144-$154	2P: $144-$154

Location: US 45, exit 42A, just n on SR 100 at jct North Ave. Located across from shopping center. 2303 N Mayfair Rd 53226. **Fax:** 414/257-0900. **Facility:** 151 units. 149 one-bedroom standard units. 2 one-bedroom suites. 8
Small-scale Hotel stories, interior corridors. *Bath:* combo or shower only. **Parking:** on-site. **Terms:** cancellation fee imposed. **Amenities:** voice mail, irons, hair dryers. **Dining:** RJ's an American Bar & Grille, see separate listing. **Pool(s):** heated indoor. **Leisure Activities:** sauna, exercise room. **Guest Services:** valet laundry, area transportation-within 5 mi. **Business Services:** conference facilities. **Cards:** AX, CB, DC, DS, JC, MC, VI. **Special Amenities: early check-in/late check-out and free newspaper.** *(See color ad p 562)*

SOME UNITS

———— WHERE TO DINE ————

EDDIE MARTINI'S
Lunch: $9-$17 **Dinner:** $18-$34 **Phone:** 414/771-6680 **33**

Traditional American

Location: US 45, exit 40, 0.7 mi e. 8612 W Watertown Plank Rd 53226. **Hours:** 11:30 am-2 & 5-10 pm, Fri-11 pm, Sat 5 pm-11 pm, Sun 4 pm-8 pm. Closed major holidays. **Reservations:** suggested. **Features:** The casually elegant 1940s-style supper club is locally known for excellent food and professional service. Steak, chops and seafood are prepared with high-quality ingredients. Signature items include the ocean martini appetizer and bread pudding dessert. Dressy casual; cocktails. **Parking:** on-site. **Cards:** AX, DC, DS, MC, VI.

HEINEMANN'S RESTAURANT
Lunch: $5-$8 **Dinner:** $5-$8 **Phone:** 414/774-5200 **30**

American

Location: US 45, exit 42A, just e, then 0.5 mi n on SR 100. 2717 N Mayfair Rd 53226. **Hours:** 7 am-8 pm, Fri-9 pm, Sun 7:30 am-8 pm. Closed major holidays. **Features:** The well-established, family-oriented restaurant delivers fresh, flavorful items, such as soup, sandwiches and salad, made from scratch without additives or preservatives. Highly noteworthy are the aromatic baked goods and tantalizing desserts. Casual dress. **Parking:** on-site. **Cards:** MC, VI.

RISTORANTE BARTOLOTTA
Dinner: $16-$29 **Phone:** 414/771-7910 **32**

Northern Italian

Location: Just w of jct Wauwatosa Ave; downtown. 7616 W State St 53213. **Hours:** 5:30 pm-9:30 pm, Fri & Sat 5 pm-10 pm, Sun 5 pm-8 pm. Closed major holidays. **Reservations:** suggested. **Features:** The bustling trattoria captures the essence of rustic, peasant-style cooking. Roasted chicken and veal are cooked in a large, wood-burning oven. Duck, lamb and fresh seafood are included in other creative offerings, as well as varied pasta dishes. Service is upscale and attentive. The strictly Italian wine list remains true to its roots. In season, a few outdoor tables are available. Dressy casual; cocktails. **Parking:** valet and street. **Cards:** AX, CB, DC, DS, MC, VI.

RJ'S AN AMERICAN BAR & GRILLE
Lunch: $8-$14 **Dinner:** $15-$25 **Phone:** 414/257-3400 **31**

American

Location: US 45, exit 42A, just n on SR 100 at jct North Ave; in Radisson Hotel Milwaukee West. 2303 N Mayfair Rd 53226. **Hours:** 6 am-2 & 5-10 pm, Sat & Sun from 7 am. **Reservations:** suggested. **Features:** Convenient to the Mayfair Shopping Mall, the contemporary hotel restaurant has an Art Deco motif. The menu offers salads, sandwiches and a variety of fresh catches prepared to order. The patio is open seasonally. Dressy casual; cocktails. **Parking:** on-site. **Cards:** AX, CB, DC, DS, JC, MC, VI.

WEST BEND pop. 28,152

──────── **WHERE TO STAY** ────────

COUNTRY INN & SUITES BY CARLSON
Phone: (262)334-9400

5/1-9/30	1P: $85-$155	2P: $91-$161	XP: $6　F18
4/1-4/30 & 10/1-3/31	1P: $83-$145	2P: $89-$151	XP: $6　F18

Small-scale Hotel **Location:** US 45, exit Paradise Rd, just se. 2000 Gateway Ct 53095. Fax: 262/334-9504. **Facility:** 58 units. 46 one-bedroom standard units, some with whirlpools. 12 one-bedroom suites, some with whirlpools. 3 stories, interior corridors. **Parking:** on-site, winter plug-ins. **Terms:** cancellation fee imposed, [CP] meal plan available. **Amenities:** voice mail, irons, hair dryers. **Pool(s):** small heated indoor. **Leisure Activities:** whirlpool. **Guest Services:** valet laundry. **Business Services:** meeting rooms, fax (fee). **Cards:** AX, DC, DS, MC, VI. *(See color ad starting on p 556)*

SOME UNITS

(ASK) (S⁄) (¶↑) (⅄M) (🅪) (➾) (➕) (⅀) (DATA PORT) (▨) / (⊠) (📶) (🖵) /

──────── **WHERE TO DINE** ────────

OMICRON FAMILY RESTAURANT　　**Lunch:** $6-$11　　**Dinner:** $6-$11　　**Phone:** 262/335-0777

Location: US 45, exit Paradise Rd, 0.4 mi e, 0.3 mi n. 1505 S Main St 53095. **Hours:** 6 am-10 pm, Fri & Sat-11 pm. Closed: 12/24, 12/25. **Features:** Reasonably priced selections of primarily comfort foods mingle with an array of all-day breakfast items and some Greek fare on the diverse menu. The atmosphere is family-friendly and unpretentious. Several beers and wines are listed. Casual dress; beer & wine only.
American
Parking: on-site. **Cards:** MC, VI.

(⊠)

WHITEFISH BAY pop. 14,163　(See map p. 544; index p. 547)

──────── **WHERE TO DINE** ────────

HEINEMANN'S RESTAURANT　　**Lunch:** $5-$8　　**Dinner:** $5-$8　　**Phone:** 414/964-6060　(26)

Location: I-43, exit 78, 0.5 mi e. 412 E Silver Spring Dr 53217. **Hours:** 7 am-8 pm, Sat-4 pm, Sun 7:30 am-3 pm. Closed major holidays. **Features:** A local favorite since 1960, this restaurant is known for its made-from-scratch menu items. Only natural ingredients are used in the homemade bread, sauces and soup and there are no preservatives. The setting is cozy and the service staff is friendly and welcoming.
American
Casual dress; beer & wine only. **Parking:** street. **Cards:** MC, VI.

(⊠)

JACK PANDL'S WHITEFISH BAY INN　　**Lunch:** $7-$13　　**Dinner:** $17-$24　　**Phone:** 414/964-3800　(27)

Location: On SR 32, 0.6 mi s of jct Silver Spring Dr. 1319 E Henry Clay St 53217. **Hours:** 11:30 am-2:30 & 5-9 pm, Fri & Sat-10 pm, Sun 10:30 am-2:30 & 4-8 pm. Closed major holidays. **Reservations:** suggested. **Features:** This designated county landmark has been operated by the same family since 1915. Fresh de-boned whitefish is the house specialty, but the German pancakes are also notable. Dressy casual;
American
cocktails. **Parking:** on-site. **Cards:** AX, DC, DS, MC, VI.

(Y) (⊠)

This ends listings for the Milwaukee Vicinity.
The following page resumes the alphabetical listings of
cities in Wisconsin.

MINERAL POINT pop. 2,617

──── WHERE TO STAY ────

COMFORT INN
SAVE
▽▽▽▽
Small-scale Hotel

5/23-10/23 [ECP]	1P: $70-$150	2P: $75-$150	XP: $8	F18
4/1-5/22 & 10/24-3/31 [ECP]	1P: $50-$150	2P: $50-$150	XP: $8	F18

Phone: (608)987-4747

Location: On US 151, 0.6 mi n of jct SR 23 and 39. 1345 Business Park Rd 53565. **Fax:** 608/987-4545. **Facility:** 50 one-bedroom standard units, some with whirlpools. 2 stories (no elevator), interior corridors. *Bath:* combo or shower only. **Parking:** on-site, winter plug-ins. **Terms:** cancellation fee imposed, pets ($25 deposit). **Amenities:** *Some:* irons, hair dryers. **Pool(s):** heated indoor. **Leisure Activities:** whirlpool. **Guest Services:** coin laundry. **Business Services:** meeting rooms. **Cards:** AX, DC, DS, JC, MC, VI.

SOME UNITS

REDWOOD MOTEL
▽
Motel

4/1-11/30 [CP]	1P: $47-$57	2P: $47-$57	XP: $5	F12
12/1-3/31 [CP]	1P: $32	2P: $32	XP: $5	F12

Phone: (608)987-2317

Location: On US 151, just n of jct SR 23 and 39. 625 Dodge St 53565. **Fax:** 608/987-2317. **Facility:** 26 one-bedroom standard units. 2 stories (no elevator), interior corridors. **Parking:** on-site, winter plug-ins. **Terms:** small pets only ($10 fee). **Cards:** DS, MC, VI.

SOME UNITS

──── WHERE TO DINE ────

BREWERY CREEK
▽▽▽▽
American

Lunch: $7-$9   **Dinner:** $8-$15   **Phone:** 608/987-3298

Location: Downtown. 23 Commerce St 53565. **Hours:** 11:30 am-8 pm 6/1-10/31; Thurs-Sat only 11/1-5/31. **Features:** With its walls of limestone, original oak ceiling joists and pine plank flooring, the quaint establishment exudes English charm. In fact, many furnishings were imported from England pubs. The menu combines staple pub items, such as burgers, with pastas, steaks and daily chef's specials. Patrons can sip a tasty microbrew or a homemade root beer. Casual dress; beer & wine only. **Parking:** street. **Cards:** AX, DS, MC, VI.

MINOCQUA

──── WHERE TO STAY ────

AMERICINN OF MINOCQUA
AAA **SAVE**
▽▽▽▽
Small-scale Hotel

6/8-10/11 [ECP]	1P: $102-$139	2P: $108-$145	XP: $6	F17
1/1-3/31 [ECP]	1P: $70-$116	2P: $76-$122	XP: $6	F17
4/1-6/7 [ECP]	1P: $67-$99	2P: $73-$105	XP: $6	F17
10/12-12/31 [ECP]	1P: $66-$76	2P: $72-$82	XP: $6	F17

Phone: (715)356-3730

Location: On US 51; center. 700 Hwy 51 54548 (PO Box 115). **Fax:** 715/356-6958. **Facility:** 66 units. 60 one-bedroom standard units, some with whirlpools. 6 one-bedroom suites ($86-$153) with whirlpools. 2 stories (no elevator), interior corridors. *Bath:* combo or shower only. **Parking:** on-site, winter plug-ins. **Terms:** cancellation fee imposed, pets ($50 deposit). **Amenities:** hair dryers. *Some:* irons. **Pool(s):** heated indoor. **Leisure Activities:** sauna, whirlpool. **Guest Services:** coin laundry. **Business Services:** meeting rooms. **Cards:** AX, DS, MC, VI. **Special Amenities:** free continental breakfast and free local telephone calls.

SOME UNITS

COMFORT INN-MINOCQUA
SAVE
▽▽▽▽
Small-scale Hotel

All Year [ECP]   1P: $59-$135   2P: $59-$135   XP: $6   F17

Phone: (715)358-2588

Location: On US 51 at jct SR 70 w. Located in a commercial area. 8729 Hwy 51 N 54548 (PO Box 1004). **Fax:** 715/356-1402. **Facility:** 51 one-bedroom standard units, some with whirlpools. 2 stories (no elevator), interior corridors. **Parking:** on-site, winter plug-ins. **Terms:** pets ($10 extra charge, in smoking units). **Amenities:** safes (fee), irons, hair dryers. **Pool(s):** small heated indoor. **Leisure Activities:** whirlpool. **Business Services:** meeting rooms. **Cards:** AX, CB, DC, DS, MC, VI.

SOME UNITS

LAKEVIEW MOTOR LODGE
AAA **SAVE**
▽▽▽▽
Motel

6/8-8/31 [ECP]	1P: $86-$116	2P: $86-$116	XP: $8	F12
10/12-3/31 [ECP]	1P: $41-$116	2P: $41-$116	XP: $8	F12
9/1-10/11 [ECP]	1P: $68-$93	2P: $68-$93	XP: $8	F12
4/1-6/7 [ECP]	1P: $41-$93	2P: $41-$93	XP: $8	F12

Phone: (715)356-5208

Location: North end of US 51 bridge; downtown. 311 E Park Ave 54548 (PO Box 575). **Fax:** 715/356-1412. **Facility:** 41 one-bedroom standard units, some with whirlpools. 2 stories (no elevator), interior/exterior corridors. *Bath:* combo or shower only. **Parking:** on-site, winter plug-ins. **Terms:** cancellation fee imposed, pets ($8 extra charge). **Amenities:** hair dryers. **Leisure Activities:** sauna, whirlpool, boat dock, fishing, playground. **Cards:** AX, DC, DS, MC, VI. **Special Amenities:** free continental breakfast and free local telephone calls.

SOME UNITS

THE POINTE WATERFRONT RESORT HOTEL
AAA **SAVE**
▽▽▽▽
Condominium

6/27-9/1	1P: $99-$159	2P: $99-$159	XP: $10	F12
12/26-3/31	1P: $69-$119	2P: $69-$119	XP: $10	F12
9/2-12/25	1P: $69-$109	2P: $69-$109	XP: $10	F12
4/1-6/26	1P: $69-$99	2P: $69-$99	XP: $10	F12

Phone: 715/356-4431

Location: On US 51, just s of downtown. 8269 S Hwy 51 54548 (PO Box 880). **Fax:** 715/356-7821. **Facility:** Smoke free premises. 69 units. 12 one-bedroom standard units with efficiencies, some with whirlpools. 48 one- and 9 two-bedroom suites with kitchens, some with whirlpools. 3 stories (no elevator), interior/exterior corridors. **Parking:** on-site, winter plug-ins. **Terms:** check-in 4 pm, 2-3 night minimum stay - weekends, 7 day cancellation notice-fee imposed, [CP] meal plan available. **Amenities:** video library (fee), irons, hair dryers. **Pool(s):** heated indoor. **Leisure Activities:** sauna, whirlpool, boat dock, fishing, snowmobiling, gas grill, picnic areas, playground, exercise room, basketball. *Fee:* game room. **Guest Services:** gift shop, coin laundry. **Business Services:** meeting rooms. **Cards:** AX, MC, VI.

SOME UNITS
FEE

SUPER 8 MOTEL

Phone: 715/356-9541

AAA SAVE

Motel

| 6/15-9/14 | 1P: $70-$80 | 2P: $80-$90 | XP: $10 | F12 |
| 4/1-6/14 & 9/15-3/31 | 1P: $55-$65 | 2P: $65-$75 | XP: $10 | F12 |

Location: On US 51 at jct SR 70 W. Located in a commercial area. 8730 Hwy 51 N 54548 (PO Box 325). **Fax:** 715/358-2152. **Facility:** 34 one-bedroom standard units, some with whirlpools. 1 story, interior/exterior corridors. **Parking:** on-site, winter plug-ins. **Terms:** pets (in designated units). **Cards:** AX, CB, DC, DS, MC, VI. **Special Amenities:** free local telephone calls.

SOME UNITS

🅂🄳 🐾 🕻📶 📺 DATA PORT / ✕ VCR FEE 🔌 🛏 💻 /

THE WATERS OF MINOCQUA

Phone: (715)358-4000

Large-scale Hotel

6/13-8/31	1P: $135-$199	2P: $135-$199
9/1-3/31	1P: $110-$185	2P: $110-$185
4/1-6/12	1P: $105-$155	2P: $105-$155

Location: 1 mi s on US 51. 8116 S Hwy 51 54548 (PO Box 1053). **Fax:** 715/358-4010. **Facility:** 106 units. 100 one-bedroom standard units, some with whirlpools. 6 one-bedroom suites ($210-$385). 3 stories, interior corridors. *Bath:* combo or shower only. **Parking:** on-site, winter plug-ins. **Terms:** [AP] meal plan available, package plans, 10% service charge. **Amenities:** high-speed Internet, dual phone lines, voice mail, hair dryers. **Pool(s):** heated indoor, heated indoor/outdoor, wading. **Leisure Activities:** whirlpool, cross country skiing, snowmobiling, exercise room. *Fee:* game room. **Guest Services:** gift shop, coin laundry. **Business Services:** meeting rooms. **Cards:** AX, CB, DC, DS, MC, VI.

ASK 🅂🄳 🕻 🍴 🍸 🄶M 🔌 🏊 🗡 ✕ 📶 DATA PORT 🔌 🛏 💻

——— **WHERE TO DINE** ———

LITTLE SWISS VILLAGE

Lunch: $3-$8 **Phone:** 715/356-3675

American

Location: 3 mi s on US 51, 2.5 mi w. 7650 Blue Lake Rd 54548. **Hours:** Open 5/9-10/5; 8 am-3 pm; hours vary off season. Closed: Mon-Thurs 9/2-10/2. **Reservations:** accepted. **Features:** Windowside tables in the quaint dining room overlook a whimsical chipmunk village called Chesterville, in addition to the beautifully landscaped grounds and nearby lake. Tasty choices include Swiss and German pancakes, waffles and omelets. Casual dress. **Parking:** on-site. **Cards:** DS, MC, VI.

🄺 ✕

MAMA'S SUPPER CLUB

Dinner: $6-$17 **Phone:** 715/356-5070

Italian

Location: 3 mi w of Minocqua. 10486 Hwy 70 54548. **Hours:** 5 pm-10 pm. Closed: 11/27, 12/24, 12/25; also 3/30. **Reservations:** accepted. **Features:** Overlooking a small lake, the dining room is charming and casual. The menu centers on traditional Italian preparations, such as Sicilian veal and a wide variety of pasta. You'll also find American dishes, including a succulent tenderloin steak. Casual dress; cocktails. **Parking:** on-site. **Cards:** AX, CB, DC, DS, MC, VI.

🍸 ✕

NORWOOD PINES SUPPER CLUB

Dinner: $10-$25 **Phone:** 715/356-3666

American

Location: On SR 70, 2 mi w of jct US 51. 10171 Hwy 70 W 54548. **Hours:** 5 pm-10 pm. Closed: 12/24, 12/25; also Sun. **Reservations:** accepted. **Features:** This restaurant offers an authentic Northwoods Supper Club experience complete with a traditional menu, friendly service and warm decor. Supper clubs are a tradition in rural Wisconsin. As you enter the restaurant, the scent of the pine trees permeates the air. Casual dress; cocktails. **Parking:** on-site. **Cards:** CB, DC, DS, MC, VI.

🍸 ✕

——— *The following restaurant has not been evaluated by AAA* ———
but is listed for your information only.

MINOCQUA BREWING COMPANY

Phone: 715/358-3040

fyi

Not evaluated. **Location:** 238 Lake Shore Dr 54548. **Features:** Located on the water's edge in the downtown area, this restaurant is in a restored 1927 lodge building.

MONONA pop. 8,018 (See map p. 519; index p. 521)

——— **WHERE TO STAY** ———

AMERICINN OF MADISON SOUTH/MONONA

Phone: (608)222-8601 **40**

AAA SAVE

Small-scale Hotel

| All Year [ECP] | 1P: $80-$110 | 2P: $85-$119 | XP: $5 | F12 |

Location: US 12/18, exit 265 (Monona Dr), just nw. 101 W Broadway 53716-3901. **Fax:** 608/222-4070. **Facility:** 62 units. 59 one-bedroom standard units, some with whirlpools. 3 one-bedroom suites ($109-$179), some with whirlpools. 3 stories, interior/exterior corridors. *Bath:* combo or shower only. **Parking:** on-site, winter plug-ins. **Terms:** pets ($5 fee). **Amenities:** dual phone lines, voice mail, hair dryers. *Some:* CD players. **Pool(s):** heated indoor. **Leisure Activities:** sauna, whirlpool, game room. **Guest Services:** valet and coin laundry. **Business Services:** meeting rooms, fax. **Cards:** AX, DC, DS, MC, VI. **Special Amenities:** free continental breakfast and free newspaper.

SOME UNITS

🅂🄳 🐾 🕻📶 🔌 🏊 ✕ 📶 DATA PORT 🔌 🛏 💻 / ✕

COUNTRY INN & SUITES BY CARLSON

Phone: (608)221-0055 **41**

AAA SAVE

Small-scale Hotel

| All Year | 1P: $84-$150 | | XP: $6 | F18 |

Location: US 12 and 18, exit 265 (Monona Dr), just nw. 400 River Pl 53716. **Fax:** 608/221-9809. **Facility:** 87 units. 68 one-bedroom standard units, some with whirlpools. 19 one-bedroom suites ($100-$150). 3 stories, interior corridors. *Bath:* combo or shower only. **Parking:** on-site. **Terms:** [ECP] meal plan available. **Amenities:** voice mail, irons, hair dryers. **Pool(s):** small heated indoor. **Leisure Activities:** whirlpool, exercise room. **Guest Services:** valet and coin laundry. **Business Services:** meeting rooms. **Cards:** AX, DC, DS, MC, VI. **Special Amenities:** free continental breakfast and free newspaper. *(See color ad starting on p 556)*

SOME UNITS

🅂🄳 🕻📶 🔌 🏊 📶 DATA PORT 💻 / ✕ 🔌 🛏 /

MONROE pop. 10,843

―――― WHERE TO STAY ――――

AMERICINN OF MONROE
Phone: (608)328-3444
5/1-9/30 [ECP]   1P: $69-$114   2P: $77-$121   XP: $8   F12
4/1-4/30 & 10/1-3/31 [ECP]   1P: $64-$109   2P: $72-$117   XP: $8   F12
Small-scale Hotel   **Location:** On SR 69 S, 0.4 mi s from jct SR 81/11. 424 4th Ave 53566. **Facility:** 54 one-bedroom standard units, some with whirlpools. 2 stories (no elevator), interior corridors. *Bath:* combo or shower only. **Parking:** on-site, winter plug-ins. **Terms:** 5 day cancellation notice. **Amenities:** hair dryers. **Pool(s):** small heated indoor. **Leisure Activities:** whirlpool. *Fee:* game room. **Guest Services:** coin laundry. **Business Services:** meeting rooms. **Cards:** AX, DS, MC, VI.
SOME UNITS
(ASK) (S/D) (TI+) (&M) (&) (🏊) (📷) (DATA PORT) (📺) / (✕) (📦) (📷) /

GASTHAUS MOTEL
Phone: (608)328-8395
Motel   All Year   1P: $35-$43   2P: $41-$51   XP: $5   F12
Location: 1.5 mi s on SR 69. 685 30th St (808 30th St). Fax: 608/328-8383. **Facility:** 18 one-bedroom standard units. 1 story, exterior corridors. **Parking:** on-site, winter plug-ins. **Amenities:** video library (fee), voice mail. **Leisure Activities:** Fee: bicycles. **Cards:** AX, DS, MC, VI. **Special Amenities:** early check-in/late check-out and free room upgrade (subject to availability with advanced reservations).
SOME UNITS
(S/D) (DATA PORT) / (✕) (VCR) (📦) /
FEE FEE

SUPER 8 MOTEL
Phone: 608-325-1500
Small-scale Hotel   All Year [CP]   1P: $47-$62   2P: $53-$72   XP: $5   F12
Location: On SR 69 S, 0.5 mi s from jct SR 81/11. 500 6th St 53566. Fax: 608/325-1500. **Facility:** 42 one-bedroom standard units, some with whirlpools. 2 stories (no elevator), interior corridors. **Parking:** on-site, winter plug-ins. **Amenities:** video library (fee). *Some:* high-speed Internet. **Leisure Activities:** whirlpool. **Cards:** AX, CB, DC, DS, MC, VI.
SOME UNITS
(ASK) (S/D) (TI+) (🐾) (📷) (DATA PORT) / (✕) (VCR) (📦) (📷) /
FEE

―――― WHERE TO DINE ――――

PEPPERCORN CAFE   **Lunch:** $6-$8   **Dinner:** $9-$17   Phone: 608/329-2233
Continental   **Location:** Just s of jct SR 69 N/18th Ave N 53566. **Hours:** 11:30 am-1:30 & 5-9 pm, Fri & Sat-10 pm. Closed major holidays; also Sun & Mon. **Reservations:** suggested. **Features:** All entrees—including barbecue ribs, daily fresh fish specials and the signature peppercorn steak—are made to order in the lively restaurant. Beverages include fine cocktails, locally brewed beers and Italian sodas. Desserts are a real treat. Try white chocolate mousse with Godiva chocolate sauce or raisin bread pudding with caramel. Casual dress; cocktails. **Parking:** on-site. **Cards:** AX, DC, DS, MC, VI.
(&M) (Y) (✕)

MONTELLO pop. 1,397

―――― WHERE TO DINE ――――

TIMBERS SUPPER CLUB   **Dinner:** $8-$18   Phone: 920/293-4589
American   **Location:** 8 mi n on SR 22; between Wautoma and Montello, 2.7 mi n of jct CR J. SR 22 54960. **Hours:** Open 4/1-12/31 & 2/15-3/31; 4:30 pm-10 pm. Closed: 11/27, 12/24, 12/25; also Tues & Wed. **Reservations:** accepted. **Features:** Prime rib and barbecue ribs are served daily in the popular, family-owned and operated restaurant. The modest dining room is in a tree grove in the beautiful Wisconsin countryside. Daily specials, homemade soups, broiled or fried seafood, some pork and poultry entrees and lighter selections complete the menu. Casual dress; cocktails. **Parking:** on-site.
(Y) (✕)

MOSINEE pop. 4,063

―――― WHERE TO STAY ――――

AMERIHOST INN-MOSINEE
Phone: (715)693-9000
Small-scale Hotel   All Year [ECP]   1P: $67-$73   2P: $78-$83   XP: $6   F18
Location: I-39, exit 179 (SR 153), just sw. 400 Orbiting Dr 54455. Fax: 715/693-9006. **Facility:** 53 one-bedroom standard units, some with whirlpools. 2 stories (no elevator), interior corridors. *Bath:* combo or shower only. **Parking:** on-site, winter plug-ins. **Terms:** 15 day cancellation notice. **Amenities:** safes (fee), irons, hair dryers. **Pool(s):** heated indoor. **Leisure Activities:** whirlpool, limited exercise equipment. **Guest Services:** valet laundry. **Business Services:** meeting rooms, fax (fee). **Cards:** AX, CB, DC, DS, JC, MC, VI. **Special Amenities:** free continental breakfast and free newspaper.
SOME UNITS
(S/D) (✈) (TI+) (🐾) (🍽) (🏊) (📷) (DATA PORT) (📺) / (✕) (📦) (📷) /

COMFORT INN
Phone: 715-355-4449
Small-scale Hotel   All Year [ECP]   1P: $59-$79   2P: $59-$79   XP: $6   F17
Location: I-39, exit 185 (US Business 51), just se. 1510 County Hwy XX 54455. Fax: 715/359-0603. **Facility:** 60 one-bedroom standard units, some with whirlpools. 2 stories (no elevator), interior corridors. **Parking:** on-site, winter plug-ins. **Amenities:** irons, hair dryers. **Pool(s):** heated indoor. **Leisure Activities:** whirlpool. **Guest Services:** valet laundry. **Business Services:** meeting rooms, fax (fee). **Cards:** AX, CB, DC, DS, JC, MC, VI.
SOME UNITS
(S/D) (TI+) (🐾) (🏊) (♿) (📷) (DATA PORT) (📺) / (✕) (📦) (📷) /

RODEWAY INN

SAVE

Small-scale Hotel

Phone: 715/355-3030

All Year [ECP]   1P: $55-$75   2P: $55-$75   XP: $6   F17
Location: I-39, exit 185 (US Business 51), just se. 904 Industrial Park Ave 54455. Fax: 715/355-4770. **Facility:** 39 one-bedroom standard units, some with whirlpools. 2 stories (no elevator), interior corridors. **Parking:** on-site. **Amenities:** video library (fee). **Pool(s):** small heated indoor. **Leisure Activities:** whirlpool, limited exercise equipment. **Guest Services:** valet laundry. **Business Services:** meeting rooms, fax (fee). **Cards:** AX, CB, DC, DS, JC, MC, VI.

SOME UNITS
FEE

STONEY CREEK INN

Small-scale Hotel

Phone: (715)355-6858

All Year   1P: $72   2P: $175   XP: $10   F17
Location: I-39, exit 185 (US Business 51), just e. 1100 Imperial Ave 54455. Fax: 715/355-0913. **Facility:** 107 one-bedroom standard units, some with whirlpools. 3 stories, interior corridors. **Bath:** combo or shower only. **Parking:** on-site, winter plug-ins. **Terms:** [ECP] meal plan available. **Amenities:** voice mail, hair dryers. *Some:* irons. **Pool(s):** heated indoor. **Leisure Activities:** sauna, whirlpool, snowmobiling, exercise room. *Fee:* game room. **Guest Services:** gift shop, valet and coin laundry, area transportation. **Business Services:** conference facilities, fax (fee). **Cards:** AX, CB, DC, DS, MC, VI.

SOME UNITS
FEE

NEENAH pop. 24,507

--------- WHERE TO STAY ---------

DAYS INN OF FOX CITIES

AAA **SAVE**

Motel

Phone: (920)720-9020

All Year   1P: $49-$85   2P: $56-$85   XP: $5   F12
Location: US 41, exit 131 (Winneconne Rd), just e, then just n. 495 S Greenbay Rd 54956. Fax: 920/720-9020. **Facility:** 51 one-bedroom standard units, some with whirlpools. 2 stories, interior corridors. **Parking:** on-site, winter plug-ins. **Terms:** cancellation fee imposed, [CP] meal plan available. **Amenities:** hair dryers. **Pool(s):** small heated indoor. **Leisure Activities:** whirlpool. **Business Services:** fax (fee). **Cards:** AX, DC, DS, MC, VI. **Special Amenities:** free continental breakfast.

SOME UNITS

PARK PLAZA VALLEY INN

Small-scale Hotel

Phone: (920)725-8441

1/1-3/31   1P: $89-$123   2P: $89-$123   XP: $10   F18
4/1-12/31   1P: $89-$119   2P: $89-$119   XP: $10   F18
Location: US 41, exit 132 (Main), then 2 mi e; downtown. 123 E Wisconsin Ave 54956 (PO Box 795, 54957-0795). Fax: 920/725-4387. **Facility:** 107 one-bedroom standard units. 7 stories, interior corridors. **Parking:** on-site. **Terms:** [CP] meal plan available, package plans - weekends. **Amenities:** video games (fee), voice mail, irons, hair dryers. **Pool(s):** heated indoor. **Leisure Activities:** whirlpool, exercise room. **Guest Services:** valet laundry. **Business Services:** conference facilities, fax (fee). **Cards:** AX, CB, DC, DS, MC, VI. *(See color ad p. 463)*

SOME UNITS
FEE

--------- WHERE TO DINE ---------

CALIBAN'S

American

Phone: 920/725-0573

Lunch: $6-$15   Dinner: $7-$17
Location: At corner of Church St; downtown. 134 W Wisconsin Ave 54956. **Hours:** 11 am-2 & 4:30-9:30 pm, Fri & Sat-10:30 pm. Closed major holidays; also Sun. **Reservations:** accepted. **Features:** Hardwood floors and a high, pressed-tin ceiling distinguish the city's oldest building. The menu lays out a nice selection of homemade sandwiches and soups, as well as thin-crust pizzas and build-your-own fettuccine choices. An extensive selection of beers is offered. Casual dress; cocktails. **Parking:** street. **Cards:** DS, MC, VI.

NEW BERLIN —See Milwaukee p. 575.

NEW LISBON pop. 1,436

--------- WHERE TO STAY ---------

EDGE O' THE WOOD MOTEL

AAA **SAVE**

Motel

Phone: (608)562-3705

All Year   1P: $45-$65   2P: $60-$65   XP: $5   F5
Location: I-90/94, exit 61 (SR 80), just e. W 7396 Frontage Rd 53950. Fax: 608/562-3912. **Facility:** 21 one-bedroom standard units. 1 story, exterior corridors. **Parking:** on-site, winter plug-ins. **Terms:** small pets only. **Pool(s):** heated outdoor. **Leisure Activities:** picnic area with grill, playground, basketball. **Guest Services:** coin laundry. **Business Services:** administrative services (fee). **Cards:** DS, MC, VI. **Special Amenities:** free local telephone calls.

SOME UNITS

TRAVELODGE OF NEW LISBON

AAA **SAVE**

Small-scale Hotel

Phone: (608)562-5141

5/25-3/31 [CP]   1P: $55-$90   2P: $65-$110   XP: $8   F16
4/1-5/24 [CP]   1P: $48-$90   2P: $58-$100   XP: $8   F16
Location: I-90/94, exit 61 (SR 80), just ne. 1700 E Bridge St 53950. Fax: 608/562-6205. **Facility:** 61 one-bedroom standard units, some with whirlpools. 3 stories, interior corridors. **Bath:** combo or shower only. **Parking:** on-site, winter plug-ins. **Terms:** 3 day cancellation notice, pets ($50 deposit). **Amenities:** video library, voice mail, safes (fee), hair dryers. *Some:* dual phone lines. **Pool(s):** small heated indoor. **Leisure Activities:** whirlpool. *Fee:* game room. **Business Services:** meeting rooms, administrative services (fee). **Cards:** AX, CB, DS, JC, MC, VI. **Special Amenities:** free continental breakfast.

SOME UNITS

NEW LONDON pop. 7,085

──────── WHERE TO STAY ────────

AMERICINN LODGE & SUITES OF NEW LONDON
Phone: (920)982-5700

(AAA) (SAVE)

Small-scale Hotel

All Year [ECP]   1P: $59-$89   2P: $69-$99   XP: $8   F12
Location: US 45, exit Hwy 54, just n. 1404 N Shawano St 54961. Fax: 920/982-5769. **Facility:** 49 units. 43 one-bedroom standard units, some with whirlpools. 6 one-bedroom suites ($109-$164), some with kitchens and/or whirlpools. 2 stories, interior corridors. *Bath:* combo or shower only. **Parking:** on-site, winter plug-ins. **Terms:** small pets only ($10 extra charge). **Amenities:** irons, hair dryers. *Some:* high-speed Internet. **Pool(s):** heated indoor. **Leisure Activities:** whirlpool, exercise room. **Guest Services:** coin laundry. **Business Services:** meeting rooms. **Cards:** AX, DC, MC, VI. **Special Amenities:** free continental breakfast and free local telephone calls.

SOME UNITS

NEW RICHMOND pop. 6,310

──────── WHERE TO STAY ────────

AMERICINN MOTEL
Phone: 715/246-3993

Small-scale Hotel

All Year [CP]   1P: $79-$99   2P: $79-$103   XP: $6   F12
Location: Just s on SR 65. 1020 S Knowles Ave 54017. Fax: 715/246-3207. **Facility:** 45 one-bedroom standard units, some with whirlpools. 2 stories, interior corridors. *Bath:* combo or shower only. **Parking:** on-site, winter plug-ins. **Terms:** pets ($25 deposit). **Amenities:** irons, hair dryers. **Pool(s):** heated indoor. **Leisure Activities:** sauna, whirlpool. **Business Services:** administrative services (fee). **Cards:** AX, CB, DC, DS, MC, VI.

SOME UNITS

SUPER 8 MOTEL
Phone: (715)246-7829

Motel

All Year [ECP]   1P: $45-$71   2P: $50-$76   XP: $8   F12
Location: Just s on SR 65. 1561 Dorset Ln 54017. Fax: 715/246-9754. **Facility:** 34 units. 33 one-bedroom standard units, some with whirlpools. 1 one-bedroom suite. 2 stories, interior corridors. **Parking:** on-site, winter plug-ins. **Terms:** pets ($15 extra charge). **Amenities:** dual phone lines. **Business Services:** administrative services. **Cards:** AX, CB, DC, DS, MC, VI.

SOME UNITS

OAK CREEK —See Milwaukee p. 575.

OKAUCHEE —See Milwaukee p. 576.

ONALASKA pop. 14,839

──────── WHERE TO STAY ────────

BAYMONT INN & SUITES LACROSSE-ONALASKA
Phone: (608)783-7191

(AAA) (SAVE)

Small-scale Hotel

All Year   1P: $74-$184   2P: $74-$184
Location: I-90, exit 5, just ne. 3300 Kinney Coulee Rd N 54650. Fax: 608/783-1557. **Facility:** 67 one-bedroom standard units, some with whirlpools. 3 stories, interior corridors. *Bath:* combo or shower only. **Parking:** on-site, winter plug-ins. **Terms:** pets ($5 fee). **Amenities:** video games (fee), voice mail, irons, hair dryers. *Some:* dual phone lines. **Pool(s):** heated indoor. **Leisure Activities:** whirlpool, exercise room. **Guest Services:** valet and coin laundry. **Business Services:** meeting rooms. **Cards:** AX, DC, DS, MC, VI. **Special Amenities:** free continental breakfast and free newspaper.

SOME UNITS

COMFORT INN
Phone: (608)781-7500

(SAVE)

Small-scale Hotel

6/1-10/31 [ECP]	1P: $69-$129	2P: $74-$134	XP: $5 F18
11/1-3/31 [ECP]	1P: $64-$89	2P: $69-$94	XP: $5 F18
4/1-5/31 [ECP]	1P: $59-$89	2P: $64-$94	XP: $5 F18

Location: I-90, exit 4, just e on SR 157, then e on CR SS. 1223 Crossing Meadows Dr 54650. Fax: 608/781-7500. **Facility:** 69 one-bedroom standard units. 2 stories, interior corridors. **Parking:** on-site, winter plug-ins. **Amenities:** irons, hair dryers. **Pool(s):** small heated indoor. **Leisure Activities:** whirlpool. **Guest Services:** valet laundry. **Business Services:** meeting rooms. **Cards:** AX, CB, DC, DS, JC, MC, VI.

SOME UNITS

HAMPTON INN OF ONALASKA
Phone: (608)779-5000

(SAVE)

Small-scale Hotel

5/11-10/31	1P: $79-$129	2P: $89-$139	XP: $10 F17
4/1-5/10 & 11/1-3/31	1P: $69-$89	2P: $79-$99	XP: $10 F17

Location: I-90, exit 5, 0.4 mi e on SR 16, just w on CR OS, then just s on Market Dr. 308 Hampton Ct 54650. Fax: 608/779-9199. **Facility:** 107 one-bedroom standard units, some with whirlpools. 3 stories, interior corridors. *Bath:* combo or shower only. **Parking:** on-site. **Terms:** [CP] meal plan available. **Amenities:** video games (fee), CD players, voice mail, irons, hair dryers. **Pool(s):** heated indoor. **Leisure Activities:** whirlpool, limited exercise equipment. **Guest Services:** valet and coin laundry. **Business Services:** meeting rooms, fax (fee).

SOME UNITS

HOLIDAY INN EXPRESS

Phone: (608)783-6555

▼▼▼▼

Small-scale Hotel

All Year [ECP]   1P: $79-$109   2P: $79-$109

Location: I-90, exit 5, 1 mi e on SR 16. 9409 Hwy 16 54650. **Fax:** 608/783-6554. **Facility:** 75 one-bedroom standard units, some with whirlpools. 3 stories, interior corridors. *Bath:* combo or shower only. **Parking:** on-site, winter plug-ins. **Terms:** cancellation fee imposed. **Amenities:** irons, hair dryers. **Pool(s):** heated indoor. **Leisure Activities:** whirlpool, exercise room. **Guest Services:** valet and coin laundry. **Business Services:** meeting rooms. **Cards:** AX, DC, DS, MC, VI.

SOME UNITS

(ASK) [S/D] [🛏] [🍴] [🛋] [🏊] [🐾] [📶] [DATA PORT] [📺] / [✕] [🛗] [🖨] /

MICROTEL INN

Phone: (608)783-0833

▼▼ ▼▼   (AAA) (SAVE)

Small-scale Hotel

6/1-10/31 [CP]	1P: $47-$52	2P: $52-$57	XP: $5	F16
4/1-5/31 [CP]	1P: $40-$45	2P: $45-$50	XP: $5	F16
11/1-3/31 [CP]	1P: $38-$43	2P: $43-$48	XP: $5	F16

Location: I-90, exit 5, just ne. 3240 N Kinney Coulee Rd 54650. **Fax:** 608/783-0988. **Facility:** 63 one-bedroom standard units. 3 stories, interior corridors. *Bath:* combo or shower only. **Parking:** on-site. **Terms:** cancellation fee imposed, pets ($5 extra charge). **Guest Services:** valet laundry. **Cards:** AX, DC, DS, MC, VI. **Special Amenities:** free continental breakfast and free local telephone calls.

SOME UNITS

[S/D] [🛏] [🛋] [📶] [DATA PORT] / [✕] [🛗]

FEE

--- **WHERE TO DINE** ---

SEVEN BRIDGES RESTAURANT

Dinner: $8-$29   **Phone:** 608/783-6103

▼▼ ▼▼

Steak & Seafood

Location: I-90, exit 3, 2 mi n on SR 35. 910 2nd Ave N 54650. **Hours:** 5 pm-9 pm, Fri & Sat-10 pm. Closed major holidays. **Reservations:** accepted. **Features:** This restaurant offers nice views of the Black River and Lake Onalaska, especially at sunset. The walls are adorned with wildlife prints, and pictures of the local history. Casual dress; cocktails. **Parking:** on-site. **Cards:** AX, CB, DC, DS, MC, VI.

[🍽] [✕]

TRADITIONS RESTAURANT

Dinner: $18-$25   **Phone:** 608/783-0200

(AAA)

▼▼▼▼

American

Location: I-90, exit 3, 1 mi n on SR 35. 201 Main St 54650. **Hours:** 5:30 pm-10 pm. Closed: Sun & Mon. **Reservations:** suggested. **Features:** In historic downtown, the upscale, fine-dining restaurant is in a restored bank and lets patrons dine in the vault for a more intimate experience. The palate-tempting, monthly changing menu reflects the tastes of the season. Dressy casual; cocktails. **Parking:** on-site. **Cards:** AX, DS, MC, VI.

[✕]

OSCEOLA pop. 2,421

--- **WHERE TO STAY** ---

RIVER VALLEY INN

Phone: (715)294-4060

(AAA) (SAVE)

▼▼ ▼▼

Motel

All Year [ECP]   1P: $66-$110   2P: $66-$110   XP: $16   F16

Location: Just n on SR 35. 1030 Cascade St 54020 (PO Box 726). **Fax:** 715/294-4038. **Facility:** 32 units. 29 one-bedroom standard units, some with whirlpools. 3 one-bedroom suites ($91-$110). 2 stories, interior corridors. **Parking:** on-site, winter plug-ins. **Terms:** pets ($5 extra charge). **Amenities:** *Some:* irons. **Pool(s):** small heated indoor. **Leisure Activities:** whirlpool. *Fee:* video games in pool area, books and board games. **Guest Services:** valet and coin laundry. **Business Services:** meeting rooms, fax. **Cards:** AX, DC, DS, MC, VI. **Special Amenities:** free continental breakfast and free local telephone calls.

SOME UNITS

[S/D] [🛏] [🍴] [🐾] [📶] [DATA PORT] / [✕] [VCR] [🛗] [🖨] [📺] /

FEE

OSHKOSH pop. 62,916

--- **WHERE TO STAY** ---

AMERICINN OF OSHKOSH

Phone: (920)232-0300

▼▼▼▼

Small-scale Hotel

5/31-10/1 [ECP]	1P: $65-$102	2P: $65-$102	XP: $6	F15
4/1-5/30 & 10/2-3/31 [ECP]	1P: $59-$97	2P: $59-$97	XP: $6	F15

Location: US 41, exit 116, 0.5 mi s on SR 44. 1495 W South Park Ave 54902. **Fax:** 920/232-0669. **Facility:** 66 one-bedroom standard units, some with whirlpools. 2 stories (no elevator), interior corridors. *Bath:* combo or shower only. **Parking:** on-site, winter plug-ins. **Amenities:** hair dryers. **Pool(s):** heated indoor. **Leisure Activities:** whirlpool. **Guest Services:** valet and coin laundry. **Business Services:** meeting rooms, fax (fee). **Cards:** AX, DC, DS, MC, VI.

SOME UNITS

(ASK) [S/D] [🍴] [🛋] [🐾] [📶] [📺] [DATA PORT] [📺] / [✕] [VCR] [🛗] [🖨] /

BAYMONT INN OSHKOSH

Phone: (920)233-4190

(AAA) (SAVE)

▼▼ ▼▼

Small-scale Hotel

All Year [ECP]   1P: $64-$74   2P: $64-$74

Location: US 41, exit 119, at jct SR 21. 1950 Omro Rd 54902. **Fax:** 920/233-8197. **Facility:** 97 one-bedroom standard units. 2 stories (no elevator), interior corridors. **Parking:** on-site, winter plug-ins. **Terms:** small pets only. **Amenities:** video games (fee), voice mail, irons, hair dryers. **Guest Services:** valet laundry. **Business Services:** meeting rooms, fax (fee). **Cards:** AX, CB, DC, DS, MC, VI. **Special Amenities:** free continental breakfast and free newspaper. *(See color ad p 587)*

SOME UNITS

[S/D] [🛏] [🍴] [🎮] [📶] [📺] / [✕] [DATA PORT]

FAIRFIELD INN BY MARRIOTT

Phone: (920)233-8504

(SAVE)

▼▼ ▼▼

Small-scale Hotel

All Year [ECP]   1P: $50-$100   2P: $50-$100

Location: US 41, exit 117 (9th Ave), 0.8 mi s on east frontage road. 1800 S Koeller Rd 54902. **Fax:** 920/233-8504. **Facility:** 57 one-bedroom standard units. 3 stories, interior corridors. **Parking:** on-site, winter plug-ins. **Amenities:** irons, hair dryers. **Pool(s):** small heated indoor. **Leisure Activities:** whirlpool. **Guest Services:** valet laundry. **Business Services:** fax. **Cards:** AX, DC, DS, MC, VI.

SOME UNITS

[S/D] [🍴] [🎮] [🐾] [📶] [📺] [DATA PORT] / [✕] [DATA PORT] /

FEE

HAWTHORN INN & SUITES

All Year [BP]   1P: $89   2P: $249
Phone: (920)303-1133   XP: $10   F16

▼▼▼▼▼

Small-scale Hotel

Location: US 41, exit 116 (SR 44), just w, then just s. 3105 S Washburn St 54904. Fax: 920/303-2103. **Facility:** 77 units. 68 one-bedroom standard units, some with whirlpools. 9 one-bedroom suites ($199-$449) with efficiencies. 3 stories, interior corridors. *Bath:* combo or shower only. **Parking:** on-site, winter plug-ins. **Terms:** pets ($50 deposit). **Amenities:** high-speed Internet (fee), dual phone lines, voice mail, irons, hair dryers. **Pool(s):** heated indoor, wading. **Leisure Activities:** whirlpool, exercise room. **Guest Services:** sundries, valet and coin laundry. **Cards:** AX, DC, DS, MC, VI.

SOME UNITS

HILTON GARDEN INN OSHKOSH

AAA SAVE

▼▼▼▼▼

Small-scale Hotel

All Year   1P: $69-$199   2P: $79-$299
Phone: (920)966-1300   XP: $10   F18

Location: US 41, exit 116 (SR 44), 0.5 mi e. Located next to the airport. 1355 W 20th Ave 54902. Fax: 920/966-1305. **Facility:** 126 units. 124 one-bedroom standard units. 2 one-bedroom suites ($129-$399) with whirlpools. 3 stories, interior corridors. *Bath:* combo or shower only. **Parking:** on-site, winter plug-ins. **Terms:** [BP] & [MAP] meal plans available, package plans. **Amenities:** video games (fee), dual phone lines, voice mail, irons, hair dryers. *Some:* DVD players. **Dining:** 6:30 am-10 & 5-9 pm, Sat & Sun 7 am-11 & 5-9 pm. **Pool(s):** heated indoor. **Leisure Activities:** whirlpool, exercise room. *Fee:* game room. **Guest Services:** sundries, valet and coin laundry, area transportation-within 10 mi. **Business Services:** conference facilities, business center. **Cards:** AX, CB, DC, DS, JC, MC, VI. **Special Amenities:** free newspaper and free room upgrade (subject to availability with advanced reservations).

SOME UNITS

HOLIDAY INN EXPRESS HOTEL & SUITES

Phone: (920)303-1300

AAA **SAVE**

Small-scale Hotel

All Year [CP] 1P: $99 2P: $109

Location: US 41, exit 119, 0.4 mi sw from jct SR 21. 2251 Westowne Ave 54904. Fax: 920/303-9330. **Facility:** 68 units. 66 one-bedroom standard units, some with whirlpools. 2 two-bedroom suites ($125) with whirlpools. 3 stories, interior corridors. *Bath:* combo or shower only. **Parking:** on-site. **Amenities:** voice mail, irons, hair dryers. **Pool(s):** heated indoor. **Leisure Activities:** whirlpool, exercise room. *Fee:* game room. **Guest Services:** complimentary evening beverages: Mon-Thurs, valet and coin laundry, area transportation. **Business Services:** meeting rooms, fax (fee). **Cards:** AX, CB, DC, DS, JC, MC, VI. **Special Amenities:** free continental breakfast and free local telephone calls. *(See color ad p 587)*

SOME UNITS

PARK PLAZA HOTEL & CONVENTION CENTER

Phone: (920)231-5000

AAA **SAVE**

Small-scale Hotel

4/1-7/28 1P: $99-$129 2P: $99-$129 XP: $10 F18
8/6-3/31 1P: $89-$129 2P: $89-$129 XP: $10 F18

Location: On shore of Fox River; downtown. 1 N Main St 54901. Fax: 920/231-6706. **Facility:** 179 one-bedroom standard units. 8 stories, interior corridors. **Parking:** on-site. **Terms:** open 4/1-7/28 & 8/6-3/31, cancellation fee imposed. **Amenities:** voice mail, irons, hair dryers. **Dining:** 6:30 am-2 & 5-10 pm, cocktails. **Pool(s):** heated indoor. **Leisure Activities:** whirlpool, boat dock, limited exercise equipment. *Fee:* game room. **Guest Services:** valet laundry. **Business Services:** conference facilities, business center. **Cards:** AX, CB, DC, DS, MC, VI. **Special Amenities:** free local telephone calls and free newspaper. *(See color ad p. 463)*

SOME UNITS

------- WHERE TO DINE -------

FRATELLO'S RESTAURANT & FOX RIVER BREWING COMPANY **Lunch:** $7-$12 **Dinner:** $7-$17 **Phone:** 920/232-2337

American

Location: US 41, exit 119 (Omro Rd), 1 mi e on SR 21. 1501 Arboretum Dr 54901. **Hours:** 11 am-10 pm, Fri & Sat-11 pm, Sun-9 pm. **Reservations:** accepted. **Features:** Nine microbrews are crafted on the premises of this restaurant on the Fox River. Seasonal boat docking and patio dining are available. Menu selections include gourmet pizza, pasta, burgers and a few steak and seafood entrees. Casual dress; cocktails. **Parking:** on-site. **Cards:** AX, MC, VI.

FRIAR TUCK'S

Lunch: $6-$8 **Dinner:** $6-$8 **Phone:** 920/231-9555

American

Location: US 41, exit 116, 0.4 mi e on SR 44. 1651 W South Park Ave 54903. **Hours:** 11 am-10 pm, Fri & Sat-11 pm. Closed: 1/1, 12/25. **Features:** "Ye hearty" sandwiches are prepared on a choice of many fresh breads baked in house. Daily homemade soup also are popular. All appetizers are prepared in the deep "friar." Servers are dressed in brown monks' garb. Casual dress; cocktails. **Parking:** on-site. **Cards:** AX, MC, VI.

LARA'S TORTILLA FLATS

Lunch: $4-$8 **Dinner:** $6-$14 **Phone:** 920/233-4440

Northern Mexican

Location: Center. 715 N Main St 54901. **Hours:** 11 am-10 pm. Closed major holidays; also Sun. **Reservations:** accepted. **Features:** Delicious food is made from scratch with fresh ingredients and served with complimentary chips and a choice of salsa. Notable are the daily specials and traditional desserts, such as cookies and caramel, cinnamon chips and ice cream flower. The service staff is attentive. Casual dress; cocktails. **Parking:** on-site. **Cards:** AX, DC, DS, MC, VI.

OSSEO pop. 1,669

------- WHERE TO STAY -------

SUPER 8 MOTEL

Phone: 715/597-5000

Motel

All Year 1P: $61-$120 2P: $66-$125 XP: $5 F12

Location: I-94, exit 88 (US 10), just se. 50663 Oak Grove Rd 54758. Fax: 715/597-5555. **Facility:** 53 units. 50 one- and 3 two-bedroom standard units, some with whirlpools. *Bath:* combo or shower only. **Parking:** on-site, winter plug-ins. **Terms:** check-in 4 pm. **Pool(s):** heated indoor. **Leisure Activities:** sauna, whirlpool. **Guest Services:** coin laundry. **Business Services:** meeting rooms, administrative services (fee). **Cards:** AX, CB, DC, DS, JC, MC, VI.

SOME UNITS

------- WHERE TO DINE -------

THE NORSKE NOOK

Lunch: $3-$11 **Dinner:** $3-$11 **Phone:** 715/597-3069

Norwegian

Location: I-94, exit 88 (US 10), 0.8 mi w. 207 W 7th St 54758. **Hours:** 5:30 am-10 pm, Sun from 8 am. **Features:** This quaint yet renown restaurant serves homemade Norwegian dishes in addition to sandwiches and breakfast. On-premise bakery produces fresh bread and an excellent selection of pies. Menus change seasonally and includes lefse specialties. Two locations downtown. Casual dress. **Parking:** street. **Cards:** DS, MC, VI.

PARK FALLS pop. 2,793

------- WHERE TO STAY -------

SUPER 8 MOTEL PARK FALLS

Phone: (715)762-3383

Motel

5/21-10/10 1P: $50-$70 2P: $58-$75 XP: $6 F12
10/11-3/31 1P: $48-$60 2P: $55-$75 XP: $6 F12
4/1-5/20 1P: $47-$60 2P: $54-$70 XP: $6 F12

Location: Just s on SR 13. 1212 Hwy 13 S 54552. Fax: 715/762-2256. **Facility:** 30 one-bedroom standard units. 2 stories (no elevator), interior corridors. **Parking:** on-site, winter plug-ins. **Leisure Activities:** whirlpool, snowmobiling. **Cards:** AX, DC, DS, MC, VI.

SOME UNITS

PEPIN pop. 878

------- **WHERE TO STAY** -------

LAKE PEPIN INN

Motel

Phone: 715/442-5400

All Year   1P: $50-$55   2P: $60-$65
Location: On SR 35; center. 311 3rd St 54759 (PO Box 301). **Facility:** 7 one-bedroom standard units, some with whirlpools. 1 story, exterior corridors. **Parking:** on-site, winter plug-ins. **Terms:** check-in 4 pm, 3 day cancellation notice-fee imposed. **Guest Services:** gift shop. **Cards:** DS, MC, VI.

------- **WHERE TO DINE** -------

HARBOR VIEW CAFE   **Lunch:** $10-$20   **Dinner:** $10-$20   **Phone:** 715/442-3893
American
Parking: street.
Location: Just w of SR 35 on Lake Pepin; center. 100 1st St 54759. **Hours:** Open 4/1-11/15 & 3/15-3/31; 11 am-2:30 & 5-9 pm, Mon-8 pm, Sun noon-7:30 pm. Closed: 4/20; also Mon-Wed. **Features:** Creative cuisine made with fresh ingredients and a garlic influence make this restaurant unique in the area. The ambience is highlighted by the historic feel and location on the Mississippi River. Casual dress; cocktails.

PEWAUKEE —*See Milwaukee p. 576.*

PHILLIPS pop. 1,675

------- **WHERE TO STAY** -------

SUPER 8 MOTEL

Small-scale Hotel

Phone: (715)339-2898
XP: $5   F12

All Year [CP]   1P: $45-$65   2P: $50-$70
Location: 0.6 mi s on SR 13. Located in a semi-rural area. 726 S Lake Ave 54555. Fax: 715/339-2887. **Facility:** 32 one-bedroom standard units. 2 stories (no elevator), interior corridors. **Parking:** on-site, winter plug-ins. **Terms:** pets (in smoking units). **Leisure Activities:** whirlpool, snowmobiling. **Cards:** AX, DC, DS, MC, VI.

SOME UNITS

------- **WHERE TO DINE** -------

BONNIE'S DINER   **Lunch:** $3-$6   **Dinner:** $3-$6   **Phone:** 715/339-3404
American
Location: On SR 13; downtown. 126 S Lake Ave 54555. **Hours:** 5:30 am-10 pm. Closed: 1/1, 11/27, 12/25. **Features:** The simple, coffee shop-type restaurant is known for its tasty homemade food. Service is friendly, as are the locals who frequent the diner. Breakfast is served all day. Try one of the great pies. Casual dress. **Parking:** on-site.

PLATTEVILLE pop. 9,989

------- **WHERE TO STAY** -------

COUNTRY INN BY CARLSON   **Phone:** (608)348-7373
Small-scale Hotel
(See color ad starting on p 556)
All Year [CP]   1P: $59-$94   2P: $64-$99   XP: $6   F18
Location: Jct US 151 and SR 80/81. 630 S Water St 53818. Fax: 608/348-4600. **Facility:** 49 units. 48 one-bedroom standard units, some with whirlpools. 1 one-bedroom suite with whirlpool. 2 stories (no elevator), interior corridors. **Parking:** on-site. **Amenities:** irons, hair dryers. **Pool(s):** small heated indoor. **Leisure Activities:** whirlpool. **Guest Services:** valet and coin laundry. **Business Services:** meeting rooms. **Cards:** AX, DC, DS, MC, VI.

SOME UNITS

MOUND VIEW INN   **Phone:** (608)348-9518
Small-scale Hotel
4/1-10/31   1P: $45-$60   2P: $55-$70   XP: $5   F10
11/1-3/31   1P: $40-$50   2P: $50-$65   XP: $5   F10
Location: On US 151, 2 mi n of jct SR 80/81 E Hwy 151 53818. Fax: 608/348-7207. **Facility:** 32 one-bedroom standard units, some with whirlpools. 2 stories, interior corridors. **Parking:** on-site, winter plug-ins. **Terms:** 3 day cancellation notice, [CP] meal plan available, pets ($20 deposit). **Leisure Activities:** whirlpool, limited exercise equipment. *Fee:* miniature golf. **Guest Services:** valet laundry. **Cards:** AX, DS, MC, VI.

SOME UNITS

SUPER 8 MOTEL   **Phone:** (608)348-8800
Small-scale Hotel
All Year   1P: $47-$69   2P: $58-$90   XP: $6   F12
Location: Jct US 151 and SR 80. 100 Hwy 80/81 S 53818 (PO Box 413). Fax: 608/348-7233. **Facility:** 72 one-bedroom standard units, some with whirlpools. 2 stories, interior corridors. **Parking:** on-site, winter plug-ins. **Terms:** [ECP] meal plan available, pets ($10 fee). **Amenities:** *Some:* irons, hair dryers. **Leisure Activities:** whirlpool, steamroom, gazebo. **Guest Services:** valet and coin laundry. **Cards:** AX, DC, DS, MC, VI. **Special Amenities:** free continental breakfast and free local telephone calls.

SOME UNITS

──── WHERE TO DINE ────

ARTHUR HOUSE

American

Dinner: $8-$16
Phone: 608/348-7899
Location: North on SR 80 to Arthur, WI; located on left side of SR 80 in Arthur. 9315 Hwy. 80 N 53590. **Hours:** 4:30 pm-9 pm, Fri & Sat-10 pm, Sun 10 am-2 pm. Closed: 12/24, 12/25; also Mon & Tues. **Reservations:** suggested. **Features:** The family-owned restaurant features nightly specials and a children's menu. Prime rib, roast duckling, pond-raised catfish and roast pork loin are among menu options. Nationally known comedy acts provide weekend entertainment. Casual dress; cocktails. **Parking:** on-site. **Cards:** MC, VI.

THE TIMBERS RESTAURANT AND LOUNGE
American

Lunch: $6-$9   **Dinner:** $9-$20   **Phone:** 608/348-2406
Location: On US 151 at jct of SR 80/81. 670 Ellen St 53818. **Hours:** 11 am-1:30 & 5-9 pm, Sun 10:30 am-2 pm. Closed: 12/24, 12/25. **Reservations:** suggested. **Features:** This restaurant is known for its unique organ/grand piano shows that occur two times nightly. The dining rooms are airy and flowing, and perimeter windows look into the surrounding trees. The lunch menu is casual, while the dinner menu features such entrees as fresh fish, beef, veal, pork and a few vegetarian and pasta dishes. Dressy casual; cocktails. **Parking:** on-site. **Cards:** DS, MC, VI.

PLEASANT PRAIRIE pop. 16,136

──── WHERE TO STAY ────

BAYMONT INN KENOSHA-PLEASANT PRAIRIE
Small-scale Hotel

Phone: (262)857-7911
All Year [ECP]   1P: $64-$79   2P: $64-$79
Location: I-94, exit 344 (SR 50), just e. 7540 118th Ave 53158. Fax: 262/857-2370. **Facility:** 92 one-bedroom standard units. 2 stories, interior corridors. **Parking:** on-site, winter plug-ins. **Terms:** small pets only (in smoking units). **Amenities:** video games (fee), voice mail, irons, hair dryers. **Guest Services:** valet laundry. **Cards:** AX, CB, DC, DS, MC, VI. **Special Amenities:** free continental breakfast and free newspaper.
(See color ad below)

SOME UNITS

HAWTHORN SUITES LTD HOTEL
Small-scale Hotel

Phone: (262)942-6000
All Year   1P: $99-$149   2P: $99-$149
Location: I-94, exit 344 (SR 50), 0.3 mi s. 7887 94th Ave 53158. Fax: 262/942-6100. **Facility:** 81 one-bedroom standard units, some with efficiencies. 3 stories, interior corridors. *Bath:* combo or shower only. **Parking:** on-site. **Terms:** 2 night minimum stay - weekends 7/1-8/31, [BP] meal plan available, pets ($50-$100 fee). **Amenities:** video library (fee), dual phone lines, voice mail, irons, hair dryers. **Pool(s):** heated indoor. **Leisure Activities:** whirlpool, limited exercise equipment. **Guest Services:** complimentary evening beverages: Mon-Thurs, valet and coin laundry. **Business Services:** meeting rooms, administrative services (fee). **Cards:** AX, CB, DC, DS, MC, VI. **Special Amenities:** free continental breakfast and free local telephone calls.

SOME UNITS

RADISSON HOTEL & CONFERENCE CENTER KENOSHA
Large-scale Hotel

Phone: (262)857-3377
6/1-8/31   2P: $119   XP: $10
4/1-5/31 & 9/1-3/31   2P: $109   XP: $10
Location: I-94, exit 347 (SR 165), just s on east frontage road. 11800 108th St 53158. Fax: 262/857-3383. **Facility:** 120 units. 102 one-bedroom standard units, some with whirlpools. 18 one-bedroom suites. 6 stories, interior corridors. *Bath:* combo or shower only. **Parking:** on-site. **Amenities:** video games (fee), dual phone lines, voice mail, irons, hair dryers. **Pool(s):** small heated indoor. **Leisure Activities:** whirlpool, exercise room. **Guest Services:** valet laundry, area transportation. **Business Services:** conference facilities, PC. **Cards:** AX, DC, DS, MC, VI. *(See color ad p 562)*

SOME UNITS

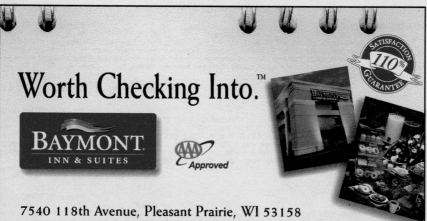

PLOVER pop. 10,520

——— WHERE TO STAY ———

AMERICINN-PLOVER/STEVENS POINT
Phone: (715)342-1244
(AAA) [SAVE]   All Year   1P: $65   2P: $100   XP: $5   F12
▼▼▼▼   **Location:** I-39, exit 153 (CR B), just w. 1501 American Dr 54467. **Fax:** 715/342-1325. **Facility:** 65 one-bedroom
standard units, some with whirlpools. 2 stories (no elevator), interior corridors. *Bath:* combo or shower only.
Small-scale Hotel   **Parking:** on-site, winter plug-ins. **Terms:** [ECP] meal plan available. **Amenities:** voice mail, hair dryers.
Some: irons. **Pool(s):** heated indoor. **Leisure Activities:** sauna, whirlpool, exercise room. **Business Services:** meeting rooms, fax (fee). **Cards:** AX, DC, MC, VI. **Special Amenities:** free continental breakfast and
free local telephone calls.

SOME UNITS

[SD] [&] [≈] [✕] [⚑] [DATA PORT] [▣] / [✕] [🛏] [▤] /

——— WHERE TO DINE ———

SKY CLUB   **Dinner:** $9-$23   **Phone:** 715/341-4000
▼▼▼ ▼▼   **Location:** On US 51 business route. 2202 Post Rd 54467. **Hours:** 4 pm-10 pm, Fri & Sat-10:30 pm, Sun 10
am-10 pm. Closed: 12/24; also Mon. **Reservations:** accepted. **Features:** This well-established restaurant
American   has been an area fixture since 1961. The restaurant is known for home-style cooking, and guests don't
leave hungry! An extensive salad bar is set up at all times. Bread, soup, salad dressings and cheesecakes
are made in-house. USDA choice steaks are served sizzling, and there's a good selection of fresh seafood. Casual dress;
cocktails. **Parking:** on-site. **Cards:** AX, DC, DS, MC, VI.

[Y] [✕]

PORTAGE pop. 9,728

——— WHERE TO STAY ———

BEST WESTERN RESORT & CONFERENCE CENTER
Phone: (608)742-2200
(AAA) [SAVE]   All Year   1P: $58-$95   2P: $58-$95   XP: $6   F12
▼▼▼▼   **Location:** I-39, exit 92, just s, then 0.5 mi w. 2701 S CR CX 53901. **Fax:** 608/742-2200. **Facility:** 100 units. 95 one-
bedroom standard units, some with whirlpools. 5 one-bedroom suites ($75-$195) with whirlpools. 5 stories,
interior corridors. **Parking:** on-site. **Terms:** [CP] meal plan available. **Amenities:** irons, hair dryers. **Pool(s):**
Small-scale Hotel   small heated indoor. **Leisure Activities:** sauna, whirlpool, limited exercise equipment. *Fee:* game room.
Guest Services: coin laundry. **Business Services:** meeting rooms. **Cards:** AX, DC, DS, MC, VI.
Special Amenities: free continental breakfast.

SOME UNITS

[SD] [¶↑] [Y] [≈] [✕] [⚑] [DATA PORT] [▣] / [✕] [🛏] [▤] /

BREESE WAY BED AND BREAKFAST
Phone: (608)742-5281
▼▼▼   All Year [BP]   1P: $70-$80   2P: $70-$80   XP: $10   D18
Location: I-39, exit 92, 2.2 mi s. 816 MacFarlane Rd 53901. **Facility:** Said to have been built by Wisconsin's first
Bed & Breakfast   secretary of state, this 1880 Italianate Victorian home offers well-appointed rooms. Smoke free premises. 4
one-bedroom standard units. 2 stories (no elevator), interior corridors. *Bath:* combo or shower only. **Parking:**
on-site. **Terms:** check-in 4 pm, age restrictions may apply, 5 day cancellation notice. **Amenities:** video library, hair dryers. **Guest
Services:** complimentary evening beverages, valet laundry.

SOME UNITS

[✕] [☎] / [W] [VCR]

COMFORT SUITES
Phone: (608)745-4717
[SAVE]   All Year [ECP]   1P: $69-$159   2P: $69-$159   XP: $8   F18
▼▼▼   **Location:** I-90/94, exit 108A (SR 78). N5780 Kinney Rd 53901. **Fax:** 608/745-1231. **Facility:** 83 units. 72 one-
bedroom standard units, some with whirlpools. 11 one-bedroom suites, some with whirlpools. 3 stories, inte-
Small-scale Hotel   rior corridors. *Bath:* combo or shower only. **Parking:** on-site. **Terms:** check-in 4 pm. **Amenities:** dual phone
lines. **Pool(s):** heated indoor. **Leisure Activities:** whirlpools, limited exercise equipment. *Fee:* game room.
Guest Services: coin laundry. **Business Services:** meeting rooms. **Cards:** AX, DC, DS, MC, VI.

SOME UNITS

[SD] [¶↑] [&M] [&] [≈] [✕] [⚑] [DATA PORT] [🛏] [▤] / [✕]

SUPER 8 MOTEL-PORTAGE
Phone: (608)742-8330
▼▼   All Year [CP]   1P: $49-$69   2P: $49-$69   XP: $5   F12
Location: I-39, exit 92, just s. 3000 New Pinery 53901. **Fax:** 608/745-0167. **Facility:** 61 one-bedroom standard
Small-scale Hotel   units. 2 stories (no elevator), interior corridors. **Parking:** on-site, winter plug-ins. **Terms:** pets ($10 fee).
Amenities: safes (fee). **Guest Services:** coin laundry. **Business Services:** meeting rooms. **Cards:** AX, CB,
DC, DS, MC, VI.

SOME UNITS

[ASK] [SD] [🛏] [¶↑] [⊘] [⚑] / [✕] [DATA PORT] /

——— WHERE TO DINE ———

BLANKENHAUS   **Dinner:** $7-$17   **Phone:** 608/742-7555
▼▼▼   **Location:** 1 mi se on US 51. 1223 E Wisconsin 53901. **Hours:** 4 pm-10 pm, Sun from 10:30 am. Closed: 1/1,
11/27, 12/25; also 12/24 for dinner & Mon. **Reservations:** suggested. **Features:** Well-coordinated Bavarian
American   decor distinguishes the big, mom-and-pop-type restaurant, a local favorite for traditional surf and turf fare.
Steak and barbecue ribs, in addition to the Friday fish fry, are popular choices. Service is friendly and
attentive. Casual dress; cocktails. **Parking:** on-site. **Cards:** AX, DS, MC, VI.

[Y] [✕]

PORT WASHINGTON —See Milwaukee p. 577.

PRAIRIE DU CHIEN pop. 6,018

——— WHERE TO STAY ———

AMERICINN LODGE & SUITES
Phone: 608/326-7878

| | 6/1-10/31 | 1P: $104-$159 | 2P: $104-$159 | XP: $6 | F12 |
| | 4/1-5/31 & 11/1-3/31 | 1P: $94-$149 | 2P: $94-$149 | XP: $6 | F12 |

Small-scale Hotel **Location:** On US 18 W, at east end of Mississippi River Bridge. 130 S Main St 53821. Fax: 608/326-7879. **Facility:** 44 units. 40 one-bedroom standard units, some with whirlpools. 4 one-bedroom suites, some with whirlpools. 2 stories, interior corridors. *Bath:* combo or shower only. **Parking:** on-site. **Amenities:** video library, dual phone lines, irons, hair dryers. **Pool(s):** small heated indoor. **Leisure Activities:** whirlpool, limited exercise equipment. **Guest Services:** coin laundry. **Business Services:** meeting rooms. **Cards:** AX, DC, DS, MC, VI.

SOME UNITS

🍴➕ 🛁M 🎣 🐾 📠 💻 / ✕ 📼 🛗 🖥 /

BEST WESTERN QUIET HOUSE & SUITES
Phone: 608/326-4777

| | 5/16-10/31 [ECP] | 1P: $89-$119 | 2P: $99-$129 | XP: $10 | F12 |
| | 4/1-5/15 & 11/1-3/31 [ECP] | 1P: $89-$99 | 2P: $99-$109 | XP: $10 | F12 |

Small-scale Hotel **Location:** On US 18, 1.9 mi e of jct SR 27 N. US 18 and SR 35 53821. Fax: 608/326-4787. **Facility:** 42 units. 40 one-bedroom standard units, some with whirlpools. 2 one-bedroom suites, some with whirlpools. 2 stories, interior/exterior corridors. **Parking:** on-site, winter plug-ins. **Terms:** package plans - seasonal, pets ($15 extra charge). **Amenities:** irons, hair dryers. **Pool(s):** small heated indoor. **Leisure Activities:** whirlpool, limited exercise equipment. **Business Services:** meeting rooms. **Cards:** AX, CB, DC, DS, MC, VI. **Special Amenities:** free continental breakfast and free newspaper. *(See ad p 555)*

SOME UNITS

🆂🅳 ➕ 🐾 🍴➕ 🐾 🎿 📠 🛗 🖥 💻 / ✕

BRIDGEPORT INN
Phone: (608)326-6082

| | 4/1-10/31 | 1P: $81-$121 | 2P: $89-$126 | XP: $8 | F13 |
| | 11/1-3/31 | 1P: $79-$120 | 2P: $87-$125 | XP: $8 | F13 |

Small-scale Hotel **Location:** On US 18, 2.2 mi e of jct SR 27 N. Hwy 18, 35 & 60 S 53821 (PO Box 436). Fax: 608/326-2800. **Facility:** 50 one-bedroom standard units, some with whirlpools. 2 stories, interior corridors. **Parking:** on-site, winter plug-ins. **Terms:** [CP] meal plan available, package plans, pets ($15 extra charge). **Amenities:** hair dryers. **Pool(s):** small heated indoor. **Leisure Activities:** whirlpool, limited exercise equipment. **Guest Services:** valet laundry. **Business Services:** meeting rooms, fax. **Cards:** AX, DS, MC, VI. **Special Amenities:** free continental breakfast and free local telephone calls.

SOME UNITS

🆂🅳 🐾 🍴➕ 🐾 🎿 📠 🛗 / ✕ 🖥 /

BRISBOIS MOTOR INN
Phone: (608)326-8404

| | All Year [CP] | 1P: $49-$82 | 2P: $54-$92 | XP: $7 | F17 |

Location: On SR 35 N, 0.5 mi n of jct US 18/SR 35 S and 27 N. 533 N Marquette Rd 53821 (PO Box 37).

Motel Fax: 608/326-0001. **Facility:** 46 units. 45 one-bedroom standard units. 1 one-bedroom suite with kitchen. 2 stories, interior/exterior corridors. *Bath:* combo or shower only. **Parking:** on-site, winter plug-ins. **Terms:** weekly rates available, pets ($7 extra charge). **Amenities:** *Some:* hair dryers. **Pool(s):** small heated outdoor. **Leisure Activities:** playground. **Business Services:** meeting rooms. **Cards:** AX, DC, DS, MC, VI. **Special Amenities:** free continental breakfast and free local telephone calls. *(See color ad below)*

SOME UNITS

🆂🅳 🐾 🍴➕ 🐾 🎿 📠 💻 / ✕ 🛗 🖥 /

DELTA MOTEL
AAA SAVE

Motel

			Phone: (608)326-4951	
5/15-11/1	1P: $35-$45	2P: $43-$79	XP: $5	F12
4/1-5/14 & 11/2-3/31	1P: $35-$41	2P: $43-$69		

Location: On US 18, 1.6 mi e of jct SR 27 N. 1733 1/2 S Marquette Rd 53821. Fax: 608/326-4988. **Facility:** 16 one-bedroom standard units. 1 story, exterior corridors. **Parking:** on-site, winter plug-ins. **Terms:** 2 night minimum stay - some weekends, [CP] meal plan available. **Guest Services:** area transportation-Riverboat Casino. **Cards:** DS, MC, VI. **Special Amenities:** free continental breakfast and free local telephone calls.

HOLIDAY MOTEL

Motel

			Phone: 608/326-2448	
5/26-11/1	1P: $35-$55	2P: $45-$125	XP: $5	F18
4/1-5/25 & 11/2-3/31	1P: $25-$45	2P: $30-$110	XP: $5	F18

Location: On US 18, 1 mi e of jct SR 27 N. 1010 S Marquette Rd 53821. Fax: 608/326-8958. **Facility:** 18 one-bedroom standard units, some with whirlpools. 2 stories, exterior corridors. *Bath:* combo or shower only. **Parking:** on-site, winter plug-ins. **Terms:** cancellation fee imposed, [CP] meal plan available. **Amenities:** *Some:* hair dryers. **Cards:** AX, CB, DC, DS, JC, MC, VI.

SOME UNITS

SUPER 8 MOTEL
AAA SAVE

Small-scale Hotel

			Phone: 608/326-8777	
5/16-10/31	1P: $65-$83	2P: $69-$87	XP: $10	F12
4/1-5/15 & 11/1-3/31	1P: $65-$73	2P: $69-$77	XP: $10	F12

Location: On US 18, 1.9 mi e of jct SR 27 N. 1930 S Marquette Rd 53821. Fax: 608/326-2935. **Facility:** 30 one-bedroom standard units. 2 stories, interior/exterior corridors. **Parking:** on-site, winter plug-ins. **Terms:** small pets only ($15 extra charge). **Cards:** AX, CB, DC, DS, MC, VI. **Special Amenities:** free local telephone calls.

SOME UNITS

WINDSOR PLACE INN
AAA SAVE

Small-scale Hotel

			Phone: 608/326-7799	
5/16-10/31	1P: $79-$109	2P: $89-$119	XP: $10	F12
4/1-5/15 & 11/1-3/31	1P: $79-$89	2P: $89-$99	XP: $10	F12

Location: On US 18, 1.9 mi e of jct SR 27 N. 1936 S Marquette Rd 53821. Fax: 608/326-1010. **Facility:** Smoke free premises. 34 one-bedroom standard units. 2 stories, interior corridors. **Parking:** on-site, winter plug-ins. **Terms:** package plans. **Pool(s):** small heated indoor. **Leisure Activities:** whirlpool, limited exercise equipment. **Business Services:** fax. **Cards:** AX, CB, DC, DS, MC, VI. **Special Amenities:** free local telephone calls and free newspaper.

SOME UNITS

WHERE TO DINE

FORT MULLIGAN'S GRILL PUB   **Lunch:** $4-$7   **Dinner:** $8-$15   **Phone:** 608/326-0639

American

Location: Just n of US 18 W; downtown. 214 W Blackhawk 53821. **Hours:** 11 am-9 pm. Closed: 4/20, 11/27, 12/24, 12/25. **Reservations:** accepted. **Features:** Homemade appetizers, sandwiches, salads, pasta, steaks, seafood and fajitas are served at the downtown eatery. Cocktails. **Parking:** on-site. **Cards:** MC, VI.

PRAIRIE DU SAC pop. 3,231

WHERE TO DINE

BLUE SPOON CREAMERY CAFE   **Lunch:** $7-$10   **Dinner:** $7-$10   **Phone:** 608/643-0837

American

Location: Downtown. 550 Water St 53578. **Hours:** 6 am-8 pm, Sat from 7 am. Closed major holidays; also Sun. **Features:** The cozy cafe is adorned with granite tables, wood floors and lots of country charm. Guests can enjoy wonderful homemade soups and delicious sandwiches made from carved-to-order delicatessen meats and freshly baked breads. For a sweet treat, indulge in smooth, freshly churned custard or homemade cheesecake. Seasonal dining on the patio lends to panoramic views overlooking the Wisconsin River. Casual dress; beer & wine only. **Parking:** on-site. **Cards:** AX, MC, VI.

PRESCOTT pop. 3,764

WHERE TO DINE

STEAMBOAT INN   **Dinner:** $13-$19   **Phone:** 651/480-8222

American

Location: On US 10 at east end of St. Croix River Bridge; downtown. 307 Lake St N 54021. **Hours:** 4:30 pm-9 pm, Sun from 10 am. Closed: 12/24, 12/25; also Mon & Tues during off season. **Reservations:** accepted. **Features:** The well-established restaurant sits on the shore of the St. Croix River at the Minnesota border. Large windows in the dining room and the seasonal outdoor seating area offer close-up views. A dock caters to those who arrive by boat. The menu has a selection of surf and turf specialties, along with the traditional Wisconsin Friday night fish fry and Saturday night prime rib. Casual dress; cocktails. **Parking:** on-site. **Cards:** AX, DC, DS, MC, VI.

PRESQUE ISLE

WHERE TO DINE

The following restaurant has not been evaluated by AAA but is listed for your information only.

THE OUTPOST CAFE   **Phone:** 715/686-2193

fyi

Not evaluated. **Location:** Center. 8279 Main St 54557. **Features:** Located in town, this family restaurant with it's northwoods decor has a number of tables with a view of the countryside.

RACINE pop. 81,855

———— WHERE TO STAY ————

COMFORT INN RACINE
Phone: (262)886-6055

AAA SAVE

Small-scale Hotel

All Year [ECP]   1P: $59-$199   2P: $69-$199   XP: $6   F17
Location: I-94, exit 333, 4.1 mi e on SR 20. 1154 Prairie Dr 53406. Fax: 262/886-6117. **Facility:** 80 one-bedroom standard units. 2 stories, interior corridors. **Parking:** on-site, winter plug-ins. **Amenities:** voice mail, irons, hair dryers. **Leisure Activities:** whirlpool, limited exercise equipment. **Guest Services:** valet and coin laundry. **Business Services:** meeting rooms. **Cards:** AX, CB, DC, DS, JC, MC, VI. **Special Amenities:** free continental breakfast and free local telephone calls.

SOME UNITS

FAIRFIELD INN BY MARRIOTT
Phone: (262)886-5000

SAVE

Small-scale Hotel

All Year   1P: $60-$80   2P: $65-$85
Location: I-94, exit 333, 4.5 mi e on SR 20. 6421 Washington Ave 53406. Fax: 262/886-5000. **Facility:** 63 one-bedroom standard units. 3 stories, interior corridors. **Parking:** on-site, winter plug-ins. **Terms:** [ECP] meal plan available. **Amenities:** irons. **Pool(s):** small heated indoor. **Leisure Activities:** whirlpool. **Guest Services:** valet laundry. **Cards:** AX, CB, DC, DS, MC, VI.

SOME UNITS

KNIGHTS INN
Phone: (262)886-6667

Motel

6/1-9/5 [CP]   1P: $49-$119   2P: $59-$149   XP: $4   F16
4/1-5/31 & 9/6-3/31 [CP]   1P: $39-$49   2P: $49-$59   XP: $4   F16
Location: I-94, exit 333, 4 mi e on SR 20. 1149 Oakes Rd 53406. Fax: 262/886-6667. **Facility:** 106 one-bedroom standard units, some with whirlpools. 1 story, exterior corridors. **Parking:** on-site, winter plug-ins. **Guest Services:** valet and coin laundry. **Business Services:** meeting rooms, fax (fee). **Cards:** AX, DC, DS, MC, VI.

SOME UNITS

MICROTEL INN & SUITES
Phone: (262)554-8855

AAA SAVE

Small-scale Hotel

6/1-8/31 [CP]   1P: $57-$62   2P: $67-$82   XP: $5   F18
4/1-5/31 & 9/1-3/31 [CP]   1P: $54-$59   2P: $64-$79   XP: $5   F18
Location: On SR 11, 0.5 mi e of jct SR 31. 5419 Durand Ave 53406. Fax: 262/554-5005. **Facility:** 79 one-bedroom standard units. 2 stories, interior corridors. *Bath:* combo or shower only. **Parking:** on-site, winter plug-ins. **Terms:** pets ($10 extra charge). **Leisure Activities:** whirlpool, limited exercise equipment. **Guest Services:** valet laundry. **Business Services:** meeting rooms, fax (fee). **Cards:** AX, DC, DS, MC, VI. **Special Amenities:** free continental breakfast and free local telephone calls.

SOME UNITS

RACINE MARRIOTT HOTEL
Phone: (262)886-6100

SAVE

Large-scale Hotel

All Year   1P: $150   2P: $150
Location: I-94, exit 333, 4 mi e on SR 20. 7111 Washington Ave 53406. Fax: 262/886-1048. **Facility:** 222 one-bedroom standard units. 5 stories, interior corridors. **Parking:** on-site. **Terms:** small pets only. **Amenities:** voice mail, irons, hair dryers. **Pool(s):** heated indoor. **Leisure Activities:** whirlpool, limited exercise equipment. **Guest Services:** valet laundry. **Business Services:** meeting rooms, business center. **Cards:** AX, DC, DS, MC, VI.

SOME UNITS

RADISSON INN HARBOUR WALK
Phone: (262)632-7777

Small-scale Hotel

5/24-10/31   1P: $139-$239   2P: $149-$249   XP: $10   F17
4/1-5/23 & 11/1-3/31   1P: $129-$229   2P: $139-$239   XP: $10   F17
Location: Just e of Lake Ave; center. 223 Gaslight Cir 53403. Fax: 262/632-7334. **Facility:** 121 units. 117 one-bedroom standard units, some with kitchens and/or whirlpools. 4 one-bedroom suites with kitchens. 3 stories, interior corridors. *Bath:* combo or shower only. **Parking:** on-site (fee). **Amenities:** dual phone lines, voice mail, irons, hair dryers. **Pool(s):** small heated indoor. **Leisure Activities:** whirlpool, limited exercise equipment. **Guest Services:** valet and coin laundry, area transportation. **Business Services:** meeting rooms, business center. **Cards:** AX, CB, DC, DS, JC, MC, VI.
(See color ad p 562)

SOME UNITS

SUPER 8-RACINE
Phone: 262/884-0486

Small-scale Hotel

6/1-8/31   1P: $55   2P: $60   XP: $5   F12
4/1-5/31 & 9/1-10/31   1P: $50   2P: $55   XP: $5   F12
11/1-3/31   1P: $45   2P: $50   XP: $5   F12
Location: I-94, exit 333, 4 mi e on SR 20. 7141 Kinzie Ave 53406. Fax: 262/884-0486. **Facility:** 61 one-bedroom standard units. 3 stories, interior corridors. *Bath:* combo or shower only. **Parking:** on-site, winter plug-ins. **Terms:** [ECP] meal plan available, pets ($5 extra charge, in smoking units). **Guest Services:** valet laundry. **Cards:** AX, DC, DS, MC, VI.

SOME UNITS

———— WHERE TO DINE ————

CORNER HOUSE
Dinner: $9-$24   Phone: 262/637-1295

American

Location: On SR 20, 0.3 mi w of jct SR 32. 1521 Washington Ave 53403. **Hours:** 5 pm-10 pm, Fri & Sat-11 pm, Sun 4 pm-9 pm. Closed: 7/4, 9/1; also 12/24 & Super Bowl Sun. **Reservations:** suggested; weekends. **Features:** Specializing in succulent prime rib servings from petit to large, the restaurant has been owned and operated by the same family since 1945. The Friday night fish fry is popular. Most meals are geared toward hearty appetites, but an extensive lighter fare menu is also available. A complete list of foreign and domestic wines is offered. Casual dress; cocktails. **Parking:** on-site. **Cards:** AX, CB, DC, DS, MC, VI.

HE SUMMIT
◈◈
American

Lunch: $6-$10   Dinner: $9-$18   Phone: 262/886-9866

Location: I-94, exit 333, 4.4 mi e on SR 20. 6825 Washington Ave 53406. **Hours:** 11:30 am-2 & 5-8 pm, Fri 11:30 am-2 & 4:30-10 pm, Sat 5 pm-10 pm, Sun 10 am-1:30 & 4-8 pm. Closed: 7/4; also 12/24 for dinner. **Reservations:** suggested. **Features:** The casual restaurant is a local favorite for traditionally prepared seafood, pasta, steak, chicken and veal. Daily specials and homemade desserts don't disappoint. Stop by n Friday night for the all-you-can-eat fish fry. Dressy casual; cocktails. **Parking:** on-site. **Cards:** AX, CB, DC, DS, MC, VI.

REEDSBURG pop. 7,827

—— WHERE TO STAY ——

KING SUPER 8
◈◈ ◈◈
Small-scale Hotel

Phone: 608/524-2888

6/27-9/2 [CP]	1P: $70-$80	2P: $75-$95	XP: $5	F12
5/23-6/26 [CP]	1P: $60-$70	2P: $65-$85	XP: $5	F12
4/1-5/22 & 9/3-3/31 [CP]	1P: $50-$55	2P: $55-$70	XP: $5	F12

Location: 0.8 mi e on SR 23 and 33. 1470 E Main St 53959 (PO Box 350). Fax: 608/524-9658. **Facility:** 50 one-edroom standard units, some with whirlpools. 3 stories (no elevator), interior corridors. **Parking:** on-site, winter plug-ins. **ool(s):** small heated indoor. **Leisure Activities:** whirlpool. **Guest Services:** tanning facility. **Business Services:** fax (fee). **ards:** AX, CB, DC, DS, MC, VI.

SOME UNITS

OYAGEUR INN & CONFERENCE CENTER
(AAA) SAVE
◈◈ ◈◈
mall-scale Hotel

Phone: (608)524-6431

7/1-8/31	1P: $67-$97	2P: $67-$97	XP: $8	F16
4/1-6/30 & 9/1-3/31	1P: $49-$54	2P: $54-$74	XP: $8	F16

Location: 1 mi ne on CR H. 200 Viking Dr 53959 (PO Box 608). Fax: 608/524-0036. **Facility:** 72 one-bedroom standard units, some with whirlpools. 3 stories, interior corridors. **Parking:** on-site, winter plug-ins. **Terms:** cancellation fee imposed, package plans - seasonal. **Amenities:** Some: hair dryers. **Dining:** Marty's Steakhouse, see separate listing. **Pool(s):** heated indoor. **Leisure Activities:** saunas, whirlpool, exercise oom. Fee: game room. **Guest Services:** gift shop, complimentary evening beverages. **Business Services:** meeting rooms. **ards:** AX, DC, DS, MC, VI.

SOME UNITS

—— WHERE TO DINE ——

ARTY'S STEAKHOUSE
◈◈
American

Lunch: $4-$6   Dinner: $6-$20   Phone: 608/524-6431

Location: 1 mi ne on CR H; in Voyageur Inn & Conference Center. 200 Viking Dr 53959. **Hours:** 6:30 am-2 & 5-9 pm, Fri-10 pm, Sat 7 am-11:30 & 5-9 pm, Sun 7 am-2 & 5-9 pm. **Reservations:** accepted. **Features:** Soft music plays in the background in the relaxing dining room. The Friday night seafood buffet is popular, as are the weekly luncheon buffets which offer the guest a good value. Casual dress; cocktails. **Parking:** n-site. **Cards:** AX, DC, DS, MC, VI.

RHINELANDER pop. 7,735

———— WHERE TO STAY ————

AMERICINN

Phone: (715)369-9600

▼▼▼▼

Small-scale Hotel

6/1-9/30 [ECP]	1P: $75-$80	2P: $75-$80	XP: $8	F12
10/1-3/31 [ECP]	1P: $70-$75	2P: $70-$75	XP: $8	F12
4/1-5/31 [ECP]	1P: $65-$70	2P: $65-$70	XP: $8	F12

Location: On Business Rt US 8, 0.3 mi e of jct SR 47. Located in a commercial area. 648 W Kemp St 54501 **Fax:** 715/369-9613. **Facility:** 52 units. 51 one-bedroom standard units, some with whirlpools. 1 one-bedroom suite ($90-$100) with whirlpool. 2 stories, interior corridors. *Bath:* combo or shower only. **Parking:** on-site, winter plug-ins. **Terms:** pets (in smoking units). **Amenities:** irons. *Some:* hair dryers. **Pool(s):** heated indoor. **Leisure Activities:** sauna, whirlpool, putting green, snowmobiling, exercise room. **Guest Services:** coin laundry. **Business Services:** meeting rooms. **Cards:** AX, CB, DC, DS, MC, VI.

SOME UNITS

(ASK) (S/D) (free breakfast) (hairdryer) (restaurant) (pool) (microwave) (data port) / (no smoking) (refrigerator) (microwave)

CLARIDGE MOTOR INN, BEST WESTERN

Phone: (715)362-7100

(AAA) (SAVE)

▼▼▼ ▼▼▼

Large-scale Hotel

6/1-3/31	1P: $69-$120	2P: $79-$130	XP: $5	F17
4/1-5/31	1P: $64-$109	2P: $69-$120	XP: $5	F17

Location: On SR 17; center. 70 N Stevens St 54501. **Fax:** 715/362-3883. **Facility:** 80 units. 77 one-bedroom standard units. 3 one-bedroom suites with kitchens. 4 stories, interior corridors. **Parking:** on-site, winter plug-ins **Terms:** pets ($10 fee, $25 deposit, in designated units). **Amenities:** irons, hair dryers. **Dining:** 6:30 am-2 & 5-10 pm, Sat from 7 am, Sun 7 am-1:30 pm, cocktails. **Pool(s):** heated indoor. **Leisure Activities:** whirlpool, pool table, indoor recreational area, exercise room. *Fee:* game room. **Guest Services:** valet and coin laundry. **Business Services:** meeting rooms. **Cards:** AX, CB, DC, DS, MC, VI. **Special Amenities:** early check-in/late check-out.

SOME UNITS

(S/D) (free breakfast) (hairdryer) (restaurant) (cocktails) (pool) (microwave) (data port) / (no smoking) (VCR) (refrigerator) (microwave) /

FEE

COMFORT INN

Phone: (715)369-1100

(SAVE)

▼▼▼▼

Small-scale Hotel

MC, VI.

All Year	1P: $61-$92	2P: $65-$98	XP: $6	F18

Location: On Business Rt US 8, 2.6 mi e of jct SR 47. Located in a commercial area. 1490 Lincoln St 54501. **Fax:** 715/369-1123. **Facility:** 51 one-bedroom standard units, some with whirlpools. 2 stories (no elevator), interior corridors. **Parking:** on-site, winter plug-ins. **Terms:** cancellation fee imposed, [CP] meal plan available, pets ($25 deposit). **Amenities:** *Some:* irons, hair dryers. **Pool(s):** heated indoor. **Leisure Activities:** sauna, whirlpool, snowmobiling. **Business Services:** meeting rooms. **Cards:** AX, DC, DS, JC,

SOME UNITS

(S/D) (hairdryer) (pool) (restaurant) (microwave) (data port) / (no smoking) (VCR) (refrigerator) (microwave) (microwave)

HOLIDAY ACRES RESORT

Phone: (715)369-1500

(AAA) (SAVE)

▼▼ ▼▼

Resort

Large-scale Hotel

6/1-8/31	2P: $94-$269	XP: $12	F12
9/1-12/26	2P: $89-$249	XP: $12	F12
4/1-5/31 & 12/27-3/31	2P: $69-$199	XP: $12	F12

Location: 4.5 mi e on US Business Rt 8, 2.3 mi n on W Lake George Rd. Located in a rural area. 4060 S Shore Dr 54501 (PO Box 460). **Fax:** 715/369-3665. **Facility:** 58 units. 30 one-bedroom standard units, some with whirlpools. 2 vacation homes ($350-$595) and 26 cottages ($589). 1-2 stories (no elevator), interior/exterior corridors. *Bath:* combo or shower only. **Parking:** on-site, winter plug-ins. **Terms:** check-in 4 pm, 2 night minimum stay - weekends in winter & seasonal, 15 day cancellation notice-fee imposed, weekly rates available, package plans, pets ($9 extra charge). **Amenities:** *Some:* voice mail, hair dryers. **Dining:** Three Coins Dining Room, see separate listing. **Pool(s):** heated indoor. **Leisure Activities:** sauna, rental boats, rental canoes, windsurfing, boat dock, fishing, putting green, 2 tennis courts (1 lighted), cross country skiing, snowmobiling, snowshoes, cross country ski equipment, hay rides, hiking trails, playground, basketball, horseshoes, shuffleboard, volleyball. *Fee:* sailboats, waterskiing, pontoon boats, bicycles, horseback riding, game room. **Guest Services:** gift shop. **Business Services:** meeting rooms. **Cards:** AX, CB, DC, DS, MC, VI. *(See ad below)*

SOME UNITS

(S/D) (free breakfast) (hairdryer) (restaurant) (cocktails) (pool) (microwave) (data port) / (no smoking) (sports) (VCR) (data port) (phone) (refrigerator) (microwave) /

FEE

HOLIDAY INN EXPRESS

Phone: (715)369-3600

AAA SAVE

Small-scale Hotel

7/22-10/11 & 12/25-3/31 [CP] 1P: $70-$110 2P: $70-$110 XP: $10 F19
4/1-7/21 & 10/12-12/24 [CP] 1P: $65-$80 2P: $65-$80 XP: $10 F19
Location: On Business Rt US 8, just e of jct SR 47. Located in a commercial area. 668 W Kemp St 54501 (PO Box 675). **Fax:** 715/369-3601. **Facility:** 100 one-bedroom standard units, some with whirlpools. 2 stories (no elevator), interior corridors. *Bath:* combo or shower only. **Parking:** on-site, winter plug-ins. **Terms:** cancellation fee imposed, pets ($25 fee, in smoking units). **Amenities:** voice mail, irons, hair dryers. **Pool(s):** heated indoor. **Leisure Activities:** sauna, whirlpool, snowmobiling, exercise room. *Fee:* game room. **Guest Services:** valet and coin laundry. **Business Services:** meeting rooms, business center. **Cards:** AX, DS, MC, VI.

SOME UNITS

———— WHERE TO DINE ————

AL-GEN DINNER CLUB

Dinner: $6-$16

Phone: 715/362-2230

Steak House

Location: 2.4 mi e on Business Rt US 8, just n. 3428 Faust Lake Rd 54501. **Hours:** 5 pm-10 pm. Closed: 12/24, 12/25; also Mon. **Reservations:** suggested; Sat. **Features:** Constructed in 1932 using straightened hayrack wires, this log restaurant has a warm interior highlighted with rock fireplaces and wildlife prints. Barbecue ribs and walleye fillets are popular. Casual dress; cocktails. **Parking:** on-site. **Cards:** AX, DS, MC, VI.

THE RHINELANDER CAFE

Lunch: $4-$10 **Dinner:** $6-$25 **Phone:** 715/362-2918

AAA

American

Location: Just w of SR 17; center. 33 N Brown 54501. **Hours:** 7 am-11 pm. Closed: 11/27, 12/25; also 12/24 for dinner. **Reservations:** suggested. **Features:** The downtown restaurant and supper club has been owned and operated by same family since 1911. Often packed, the establishment delivers friendly service, a warm atmosphere and good, sometimes creative, food, including a number of Greek specialties. Casual dress; cocktails. **Parking:** on-site. **Cards:** AX, DC, DS, MC, VI.

THREE COINS DINING ROOM

Dinner: $8-$18

Phone: 715/369-1500

Steak & Seafood

Location: 4.5 mi e on US Business Rt 8, 2.3 mi n on W Lake George Rd; in Holiday Acres Resort. 4060 S Shore Dr 54501. **Hours:** Open 5/1-3/15; 5 pm-9:30 pm, Sun 8:30 am-1 & 5-9:30 pm; hours vary off season. **Reservations:** accepted. **Features:** Soothing music plays in the background of the attractive rustic dining room, which boasts high ceilings and wood accents. Windows overlook landscaped grounds where wildlife roam. Broiled walleye is excellent. Fresh bread is served in a clay flowerpot. Casual dress; cocktails. **Parking:** on-site. **Cards:** AX, CB, DC, DS, MC, VI.

WOLFF'S LOG CABIN

Lunch: $6-$16 **Dinner:** $6-$16 **Phone:** 715/362-2686

American

Location: On Business Rt US 8, just e of jct SR 47. 721 W Kemp 54501. **Hours:** 6:30 am-9:30 pm. Closed: 11/27, 12/25. **Features:** A wide selection of reasonably priced items makes up the menu at the modern restaurant. Casual dress; cocktails. **Parking:** on-site. **Cards:** AX, DS, MC, VI.

RICE LAKE pop. 8,320

———— WHERE TO STAY ————

AMERICINN MOTEL

Phone: 715/234-9060

Small-scale Hotel

All Year 1P: $59-$109 2P: $65-$115 XP: $6 F13
Location: US 53, exit 140, 0.7 mi e on CR 0. 2906 Pioneer Ave S 54868. **Fax:** 715/736-9060. **Facility:** 43 units. 42 one-bedroom standard units, some with whirlpools. 1 one-bedroom suite with whirlpool. 2 stories, interior corridors. *Bath:* combo or shower only. **Parking:** on-site, winter plug-ins. **Terms:** [ECP] meal plan available. **Amenities:** hair dryers. *Some:* irons. **Pool(s):** small heated indoor. **Leisure Activities:** whirlpool. *Fee:* game room. **Guest Services:** valet and coin laundry. **Business Services:** meeting rooms, fax (fee). **Cards:** AX, DC, DS, MC, VI.

SOME UNITS

CURRIER'S LAKEVIEW RESORT MOTEL

Phone: 715/234-7474

AAA SAVE

Motel

5/17-10/13 [CP] 1P: $52-$87 2P: $62-$97 XP: $6 F
4/1-5/16 & 10/14-3/31 [CP] 1P: $42-$66 2P: $49-$76 XP: $6 F
Location: Jct CR 0, 1.5 mi n on CR SS, 1 mi e, then n on CR C (Sawyer St). 2010 E Sawyer St 54868 (2010-21 1/4 St). **Fax:** 715/736-1501. **Facility:** 19 units. 18 one-bedroom standard units, some with kitchens. 1 two-bedroom suite ($110-$149) with kitchen. 2 stories, interior/exterior corridors. *Bath:* combo or shower only. **Parking:** on-site, winter plug-ins. **Terms:** 2 night minimum stay - weekends in summer, 7 day cancellation notice-fee imposed, weekly rates available. **Leisure Activities:** rental boats, canoeing, paddleboats, boat dock, fishing, recreation programs, playground. *Fee:* pontoon boats, small boat launch. **Guest Services:** gift shop. **Business Services:** fax (fee). **Cards:** AX, DS, MC, VI. **Special Amenities:** free continental breakfast and free local telephone calls.

SOME UNITS

FEE

MICROTEL INN & SUITES

Phone: 715/736-2010

Motel

All Year 1P: $50-$75 XP: $6 F16
Location: US 53, exit 140 (CR 0), just ne. 2771 Decker Dr 54868. **Fax:** 715/736-2012. **Facility:** 57 one-bedroom standard units. 3 stories, interior corridors. *Bath:* combo or shower only. **Parking:** on-site, winter plug-ins. **Terms:** [CP] meal plan available, pets ($10 fee). **Amenities:** high-speed Internet (fee), voice mail. **Leisure Activities:** limited exercise equipment. **Business Services:** meeting rooms, fax (fee). **Cards:** AX, DC, DS, MC, VI.

SOME UNITS

———— WHERE TO DINE ————

LEHMAN'S SUPPER CLUB　　　　**Lunch:** $3-$11　　　**Dinner:** $5-$23　　　**Phone:** 715/234-2428
🔺🔺🔺　　　**Location:** Just s on CR SS from jct CR 0. 2911 S Main St 54868. **Hours:** 11 am-10 pm, Fri & Sat-10:30 pm,
▽▽ ▽▽　　Sun-9:30 pm. Closed: 11/27, 12/25; also Mon. **Reservations:** suggested; weekends. **Features:** Located on
American　　the southeast side of town, this restaurant features a large dining room and an ample sized lounge.
　　　　　　Emphasizing steak, seafood, chicken and barbecue ribs at dinner, the food is well prepared and fresh.
　　　　　　Casual dress; cocktails. **Parking:** on-site. **Cards:** AX, CB, DC, DS, MC, VI.　　　　　　🔲Ⓜ 🍸 🗙

NORSKE NOOK　　　　　　　　**Lunch:** $6-$8　　　**Dinner:** $6-$8　　　**Phone:** 715/234-1733
◆◆◆　　　**Location:** US 53, exit 140, 0.7 mi e on CR 0. 2900 Pioneer Ave 54868. **Hours:** 5:30 am-8 pm, Fri & Sat-10 pm,
　　　　　Sun 8 am-8 pm; to 10 pm in summer. Closed major holidays. **Features:** Norwegian specialties,
Norwegian　sandwiches, breakfast dishes and freshly baked breads and pies are the attraction at the relaxed
　　　　　　restaurant. Casual dress. **Parking:** on-site. **Cards:** DS, MC, VI.　　　　　　　　　　🗙

RICHLAND CENTER pop. 5,114

———— WHERE TO STAY ————

SUPER 8 MOTEL-RICHLAND CENTER　　　　　　　　　　　**Phone:** (608)647-8988
🔺🔺🔺　　All Year [CP]　　　　1P: $60-$75　　　2P: $65-$80　　　XP: $5　　　F12
　　　　　Location: 0.9 mi e on US 14. 100 Foundry Dr 53581. Fax: 608/647-8988. **Facility:** 45 units. 43 one-bedroom stan-
Small-scale Hotel　dard units, some with whirlpools. 2 one-bedroom suites ($100-$130) with whirlpools. 2 stories, interior corri-
　　　　　dors. **Parking:** on-site. **Terms:** small pets only ($50 deposit). **Pool(s):** small heated indoor. **Leisure**
Activities: whirlpool, exercise room. *Fee:* game room. **Business Services:** meeting rooms. **Cards:** AX, CB, DC, DS, JC,
MC, VI.
　　　　　　　　　　　　　　　　　　　　　　　　　　　　　　　　　SOME UNITS
　　　　　Ⓐ🆂🅺 🆂⊘ 🐾 🐬 🗙 🎦 [DATA PORT] / 🗙 [VCR] 🔲 📷 💻 /

WHITE HOUSE TRAVELODGE　　　　　　　　　　　　**Phone:** (608)647-8869
🔺🔺 🔺🔺　1/1-3/31 [CP]　　　1P: $63-$83　　　2P: $68-$83　　　XP: $5　　　F17
　　　　　4/1-12/31 [CP]　　　1P: $63-$78　　　2P: $68-$83　　　XP: $5　　　F17
·Small-scale Hotel　**Location:** 0.5 mi e on US 14. 1450 Veterans Dr 53581. Fax: 608/647-7154. **Facility:** 43 units. 40 one-bedroom
standard units, some with whirlpools. 3 one-bedroom suites ($87-$295), some with whirlpools. 2 stories, interior corridors. *Bath:* combo or shower only. **Parking:** on-site, winter plug-ins. **Terms:** 2 night minimum stay - seasonal.
Amenities: voice mail, irons, hair dryers. *Some:* video games, safes. **Dining:** White House Supper Club, see separate listing.
Pool(s): heated indoor. **Leisure Activities:** sauna, whirlpool, exercise room. **Guest Services:** valet and coin laundry, beauty
salon. **Business Services:** conference facilities. **Cards:** AX, DS, MC, VI.
　　　　　　　　　　　　　　　　　　　　　　　　　　　　　SOME UNITS
　　　　　Ⓐ🆂🅺 🆂⊘ ✈ 🍴 ♿ 🐬 🗙 [VCR] 🎦 [DATA PORT] 🔲 📷 💻 / 🗙 /
　　　　　　　　　　　　FEE

———— WHERE TO DINE ————

WHITE HOUSE SUPPER CLUB　　　　**Lunch:** $5-$8　　　**Dinner:** $6-$23　　　**Phone:** 608/647-8869
▽▽ ▽▽　　**Location:** 0.5 mi e on US 14; in White House Travelodge. 1450 Veterans Dr 53581. **Hours:** 11 am-2 & 5-9 pm, Fri
　　　　　4:30 pm-9:30 pm, Sat 5 pm-9:30 pm, Sun 8:30 am-1 & 4:30-9 pm. Closed major holidays.
Steak & Seafood　**Reservations:** accepted. **Features:** This traditional Wisconsin supper club features steak, seafood and
　　　　　sandwiches. Lunchtime features a daily "no wait" special. There is a drive-thru for those who want
take-out. Casual dress; cocktails. **Parking:** on-site. **Cards:** AX, DS, MC, VI.　　　　　　🍸 🗙

RIPON pop. 6,828

———— WHERE TO STAY ————

AMERICINN OF RIPON　　　　　　　　　　　　　　**Phone:** (920)748-7578
🔺🔺 🔺🔺　5/1-8/3　　　　　　1P: $78-$118　　　2P: $86-$126　　　XP: $8　　　F12
　　　　　4/1-4/30 & 8/4-3/31　1P: $68-$115　　　2P: $76-$123　　　XP: $8　　　F12
Small-scale Hotel　**Location:** 1.8 mi w on SR 23. 1219 W Fond du Lac St 54971. Fax: 920/748-7897. **Facility:** 43 units. 42 one-
bedroom standard units, some with whirlpools. 1 one-bedroom suite with whirlpool. 2 stories (no elevator),
interior corridors. *Bath:* combo or shower only. **Parking:** on-site, winter plug-ins. **Terms:** [ECP] meal plan available.
Amenities: irons. *Some:* hair dryers. **Pool(s):** small heated indoor. **Leisure Activities:** sauna, whirlpool. **Guest Services:** valet
laundry. **Business Services:** meeting rooms, fax. **Cards:** AX, CB, DC, DS, MC, VI.
　　　　　　　　　　　　　　　　　　　　　　　　　　　SOME UNITS
　　　　　♿ 🐬 🎦 [DATA PORT] 🔲 💻 / 🗙 [VCR] 📷 /
　　　　　　　　　　　　　　　　　FEE

RIVER FALLS pop. 12,560

———— WHERE TO STAY ————

COUNTRY INN BY CARLSON　　　　　　　　　　　　**Phone:** (715)425-9500
🔺🔺🔺　　7/2-8/21 [ECP]　　　1P: $99-$169　　　2P: $99-$169　　　XP: $6　　　F18
　　　　　4/1-7/1 & 8/22-9/30 [ECP]　1P: $79-$149　　　2P: $79-$149　　　XP: $6　　　F18
　　　　　10/1-3/31 [ECP]　　　1P: $75-$129　　　2P: $75-$129　　　XP: $6　　　F18
Small-scale Hotel　**Location:** Just n of jct SR 65 and 35. 1525 Commerce Ct 54022. Fax: 715/425-9200. **Facility:** 46 one-bedroom
standard units, some with whirlpools. 2 stories, interior corridors. **Parking:** on-site. **Amenities:** voice mail, irons, hair dryers.
Pool(s): small heated indoor. **Leisure Activities:** whirlpool. **Guest Services:** coin laundry. **Business Services:** meeting rooms,
administrative services (fee). **Cards:** AX, DC, DS, MC, VI. *(See color ad starting on p 556)*
　　　　　　　　　　　　　　　　　　　　　　　　　　SOME UNITS
　　　　　Ⓐ🆂🅺 🆂⊘ ♿Ⓜ 🐕 🐬 🔓 🎦 [DATA PORT] 💻 / 🗙 🔲 📷 /

SUPER 8 MOTEL

▼▼ ▼▼
Motel

Phone: (715)425-8388

All Year   1P: $72-$112   2P: $82-$122

Location: On SR 65, 0.5 mi w jct SR 35. 1207 St. Croix St 54022. Fax: 715/425-7103. **Facility:** 48 one-bedroom standard units, some with whirlpools. 2 stories, interior corridors. **Parking:** on-site, winter plug-ins. **Terms:** [ECP] meal plan available. **Amenities:** irons, hair dryers. **Pool(s):** small heated indoor. **Leisure Activities:** whirlpool. **Guest Services:** coin laundry. **Business Services:** meeting rooms, administrative services (fee). **Cards:** AX, DC, DS, MC, VI.

SOME UNITS

(ASK) [S/D] [🐾] [➰] [♿] [📹] [DATA PORT] [💻] / [✕] [VCR] [🔒] [📼] /

ROME pop. 1,700

—— WHERE TO STAY ——

SHERMALOT MOTEL

▼▼ ▼▼
Motel

Phone: 715-325-2626

4/1-12/1   1P: $70-$75   2P: $70-$75

Location: 1.5 mi s on SR 13. 1148 W Queens Way 54457. Fax: 715/325-2627. **Facility:** 23 one-bedroom standard units, some with whirlpools. 2 stories (no elevator), exterior corridors. **Parking:** on-site. **Terms:** open 4/1-12/1, 2 night minimum stay - weekends, 30 day cancellation notice. **Leisure Activities:** boat ramp, fishing.
Cards: DS, MC, VI.

SOME UNITS

[🍴] [🔒] [💻] / [✕] /

ST. CROIX FALLS pop. 2,033

—— WHERE TO STAY ——

HOLIDAY INN EXPRESS HOTEL & SUITES

(AAA) [SAVE]
▼▼ ▼▼ ▼
Small-scale Hotel

Phone: (715)483-5775

5/24-10/31 [ECP]	1P: $85-$175	2P: $85-$175	XP: $10 F18
4/1-5/23 & 11/1-3/31 [ECP]	1P: $65-$145	2P: $65-$145	XP: $10 F18

Location: On US 8, 1.3 mi e of jct SR 35 S. 2190 E US Hwy 8 54024 (PO Box 888). Fax: 715/483-5316. **Facility:** 80 one-bedroom standard units, some with whirlpools. 4 stories, interior corridors. *Bath:* combo or shower only. **Parking:** on-site, winter plug-ins. **Terms:** package plans, small pets only ($50 deposit, $15 extra charge). **Amenities:** video games (fee), dual phone lines, voice mail, irons, hair dryers. **Dining:** 6:30 am-10 pm. **Pool(s):** heated indoor. **Leisure Activities:** whirlpool, exercise room. *Fee:* game room. **Guest Services:** gift shop. **Business Services:** meeting rooms, fax (fee). **Cards:** AX, CB, DC, DS, JC, MC, VI. **Special Amenities:** free continental breakfast and free local telephone calls.

SOME UNITS

[S/D] [🐾] [🍴] [&] [➰] [✕] [📹] [DATA PORT] / [✕] [🔒] [📼] [💻] /

—— WHERE TO DINE ——

DALLES HOUSE RESTAURANT

▼▼ ▼▼
American

Lunch: $5-$11   **Dinner:** $10-$20   **Phone:** 715/483-3246

Location: Just s of jct US 8 and SR 35. 720 Vincent St 54024. **Hours:** 11 am-9 pm, Fri & Sat-10 pm, Sun 7:30 am-9 pm. Closed: 12/25; also Mon. **Reservations:** suggested; Fri & Sat. **Features:** The emphasis is on burgers and sandwiches at lunch, and steak and seafood at dinner. The informal dining room surrounds an outdoor courtyard with a fountain, waterfall and abundant amount of plants and flowers. Service is friendly and efficient. Casual dress; cocktails. **Parking:** on-site. **Cards:** AX, DC, DS, MC, VI.

[🍽] [✕]

ST. GERMAIN

—— WHERE TO STAY ——

NORTH WOODS REST MOTEL

▼▼
Motel

Phone: 715/479-8770

All Year   1P: $40   2P: $50   XP: $5   F5

Location: 0.8 mi e on SR 70. Located in a semi-commercial area. 8083 Hwy 70 E 54558. **Facility:** 10 one-bedroom standard units. 1 story, exterior corridors. *Bath:* combo or shower only. **Parking:** on-site, winter plug-ins. **Terms:** 3 day cancellation notice-fee imposed, small pets only ($5 fee). **Leisure Activities:** snowmobiling.
Cards: DC, MC, VI.

SOME UNITS

[🐾] [🍴] [📹] [💻] / [🔒] /

—— WHERE TO DINE ——

GOLDEN PINES

(AAA)
▼▼ ▼▼ ▼
American

Dinner: $8-$19   **Phone:** 715/479-7178

Location: 1 mi e on SR 70. 8000 Hwy 70 E 54558. **Hours:** 4 pm-10 pm; winter hours may vary. Closed major holidays. **Reservations:** suggested. **Features:** In a massive log building with open beams, this charming restaurant is warm and inviting. The menu, with most dishes freshly prepared, include prime rib, roast duck, Wiener schnitzel, chops and seafood. Dessert selections include varieties of pies. Casual dress; cocktails. **Parking:** on-site. **Cards:** AX, DS, MC, VI.

[🍽]

WHITETAIL INN

▼▼ ▼▼
American

Lunch: $5-$8   **Dinner:** $9-$26   **Phone:** 715/542-2541

Location: 1.5 mi w on SR 70. 9038 Hwy 70 W 54558. **Hours:** 11 am-3 & 4:30-10 pm, Sun-9 pm in summer; hours vary off season. Closed: Mon 10/3-5/15, and week after Thanksgiving. **Features:** This restaurant is easily identifiable by its unique hand-crafted log architecture. Massive 200-year-old logs cut from neighboring Phels, Wisconsin are accented by antler chandeliers, a massive two-way stone fireplace and world-class whitetail deer mounts. Casual dress; cocktails. **Parking:** on-site. **Cards:** MC, VI.

[🍽] [✕]

SAUK CITY pop. 3,109

──── WHERE TO STAY ────

CEDARBERRY INN
AAA SAVE
▽▽▽
Small-scale Hotel
Phone: (608)643-6625
All Year   1P: $56-$104   2P: $62-$110   XP: $6   F17
Location: On US 12, 0.5 mi w. 855 Phillips Blvd 53583 (PO Box 634). Fax: 608/643-6459. **Facility:** 44 units. 42 one-bedroom standard units, some with whirlpools. 2 one-bedroom suites ($120-$131). 2 stories, interior corridors. **Parking:** on-site, winter plug-ins. **Amenities:** voice mail, hair dryers. **Pool(s):** heated indoor. **Leisure Activities:** sauna, whirlpool. **Guest Services:** sundries, coin laundry. **Business Services:** meeting rooms. **Cards:** AX, DC, DS, MC, VI.

SOME UNITS
Ⓢ🔻 ➡ 📷 📠 / ☒ 🛗 🖥 /

SCHOFIELD pop. 2,117

──── WHERE TO STAY ────

COUNTRY INN & SUITES BY CARLSON
▽▽▽
Small-scale Hotel
Phone: (715)359-1881
All Year   1P: $78-$80   2P: $88-$98   XP: $10   F18
Location: On Business US 51, 1 mi n of jct SR 29. 1520 Metro Dr 54476. Fax: 715/359-8420. **Facility:** 50 units. 39 one-bedroom standard units. 10 one- and 1 two-bedroom suites, some with kitchens. 2 stories, interior corridors. *Bath:* combo or shower only. **Parking:** on-site, winter plug-ins. **Terms:** [ECP] meal plan available. **Amenities:** dual phone lines, voice mail, irons, hair dryers. **Pool(s):** heated indoor. **Leisure Activities:** whirlpool, limited exercise equipment. **Guest Services:** valet and coin laundry. **Business Services:** meeting rooms. **Cards:** AX, CB, DC, DS, MC, VI. *(See color ad starting on p 556)*

SOME UNITS
🛗➕ � 🚬 ➡ 📷 📠 🖥 / ☒ 🛗 🖥 /

SHAWANO pop. 8,298

──── WHERE TO STAY ────

BEST WESTERN VILLAGE HAUS
AAA SAVE
▽▽ ▽▽
Small-scale Hotel
Phone: (715)526-9595
6/1-9/5 [BP]   1P: $70-$101   2P: $70-$101   XP: $7   F13
4/1-5/31 & 9/6-3/31 [BP]   1P: $60-$101   2P: $60-$101   XP: $7   F13
Location: 2 mi e on SR Business 29, just n on CR HHH. Located in a semi-commercial area. 201 N Airport Dr 54166. Fax: 715/526-9826. **Facility:** 89 one-bedroom standard units. 2 stories (no elevator), interior corridors. *Bath:* combo or shower only. **Parking:** on-site, winter plug-ins. **Amenities:** irons, hair dryers. **Dining:** 6 am-9 pm, Fri & Sat-10 pm, Sun 7 am-9 pm, cocktails. **Pool(s):** heated indoor. **Leisure Activities:** Fee: game room. **Guest Services:** valet laundry. **Business Services:** meeting rooms. **Cards:** AX, DC, DS, JC, MC, VI. **Special Amenities:** free continental breakfast and free newspaper.

SOME UNITS
Ⓢ🔻 🍴 🍷 🚬 ➡ 📷 📠 🖥 / ☒ 📹 🛗 🖥 /
FEE

COUNTRY INN & SUITES BY CARLSON
AAA SAVE
▽▽▽
Small-scale Hotel
Phone: (715)526-2044
6/2-10/1 [ECP]   1P: $75-$85   2P: $80-$90   XP: $6   F18
4/1-6/1 & 10/2-3/31 [ECP]   1P: $65-$75   2P: $70-$80   XP: $6   F18
Location: 2 mi e on SR Business 29 at jct CR HHH. Located in a semi-commercial area. 104 Airport Rd 54166. Fax: 715/524-3886. **Facility:** 38 units. 34 one-bedroom standard units, some with whirlpools. 4 one-bedroom suites, some with whirlpools. 2 stories (no elevator), interior corridors. **Parking:** on-site. **Terms:** cancellation fee imposed. **Amenities:** voice mail, irons, hair dryers. **Pool(s):** heated indoor. **Leisure Activities:** whirlpool, exercise room. **Guest Services:** coin laundry. **Business Services:** meeting rooms. **Cards:** AX, CB, DC, DS, MC, VI. **Special Amenities:** free continental breakfast and free newspaper. *(See color ad starting on p 556)*

SOME UNITS
Ⓢ🔻 🍴 ➡ 📷 📠 🛗 🖥 🖥 / ☒

SUPER 8 MOTEL-SHAWANO
▽▽ ▽▽
Small-scale Hotel
Phone: (715)526-6688
All Year [CP]   1P: $49-$65   2P: $49-$65   XP: $5   F12
Location: 1.2 mi e on SR Business 29. Located in a commercial area. 211 Waukechon St 54166. Fax: 715/526-6290. **Facility:** 55 one-bedroom standard units, some with whirlpools. 2 stories (no elevator), interior corridors. **Parking:** on-site, winter plug-ins. **Terms:** pets (with prior approval). **Amenities:** video library (fee). **Leisure Activities:** sauna, whirlpool. **Guest Services:** coin laundry. **Business Services:** meeting rooms. **Cards:** AX, CB, DC, DS, MC, VI.

SOME UNITS
ASK Ⓢ🔻 🐾 🍴 📷 🚬 📠 / ☒ 📹 🛗 🖥 🖥 /
FEE

──── WHERE TO DINE ────

ANELLO'S TORCH LITE
▽▽
American
Dinner: $7-$25   **Phone:** 715/526-5680
Location: 1.8 mi e on SR 29 business route. 1276 E Green Bay St 54166. **Hours:** 4 pm-10 pm, Fri & Sat-11 pm. Closed: 11/27; also 12/24. **Reservations:** accepted. **Features:** This well-established restaurant offers and extensive menu selection of both American and Italian dishes. There are traditional steak, chicken, seafood and barbecue ribs. House specialities include delicious lasagna, manicotti and beef-roll sausage. Casual dress; cocktails. **Parking:** on-site. **Cards:** AX, DS, MC, VI.

🍷 ☒

BLACK FOREST
▽▽ ▽▽
German
Lunch: $6-$12   **Dinner:** $10-$23   **Phone:** 715/526-5151
Location: Just e on SR 29 business route; center. 401 E Green Bay St 54166. **Hours:** 11 am-2 & 4-9 pm, Fri-10 pm, Sat 4 pm-10 pm. Closed: 12/25. **Reservations:** accepted. **Features:** The restaurant serves German specialities and American dishes in a comfortable, smoke-free dining room. Casual dress; cocktails. **Parking:** on-site. **Cards:** DS, MC, VI.

🍷 ☒

SHEBOYGAN pop. 50,792

―――― WHERE TO STAY ――――

AMERICINN OF SHEBOYGAN
Phone: (920)208-8130

6/2-10/1 [ECP]	1P: $99-$199	2P: $99-$199	XP: $9	F18
10/2-3/31 [ECP]	1P: $84-$184	2P: $84-$184	XP: $9	F18
5/2-6/1 [ECP]	1P: $89-$179	2P: $89-$179	XP: $9	F18
4/1-5/1 [ECP]	1P: $79-$179	2P: $79-$179	XP: $9	F18

Small-scale Hotel **Location:** I-43, exit 123, just e. 3664 S Taylor Dr 53081. Fax: 920/208-8138. **Facility:** 61 one-bedroom standard units, some with whirlpools. 3 stories, interior corridors. *Bath:* combo or shower only. **Parking:** on-site, winter plug-ins. **Terms:** package plans - off season, pets ($7 fee, $50 deposit). **Amenities:** hair dryers. **Pool(s):** heated indoor. **Leisure Activities:** whirlpool. **Guest Services:** valet and coin laundry. **Business Services:** meeting rooms. **Cards:** AX, CB, DC, DS, MC, VI. **Special Amenities: free continental breakfast and free local telephone calls.**

SOME UNITS

BAYMONT INN SHEBOYGAN
Phone: (920)457-2321

All Year [ECP]   1P: $74-$94   2P: $74-$94

Location: I-43, exit 126, 1 mi e on SR 23. 2932 Kohler Memorial Dr 53081. Fax: 920/457-0827. **Facility:** 96 units. 95 one-bedroom standard units. 1 one-bedroom suite with kitchen. 2 stories, interior corridors. *Bath:* combo or shower only. **Parking:** on-site, winter plug-ins. **Terms:** small pets only (in designated units). **Small-scale Hotel** **Amenities:** video games (fee), voice mail, irons, hair dryers. **Business Services:** fax (fee). **Cards:** AX, CB, DC, DS, MC, VI. **Special Amenities: free continental breakfast and free newspaper.**

(See color ad below)

SOME UNITS

COMFORT INN-SHEBOYGAN
Phone: (920)457-7724

5/16-3/31 [ECP]	1P: $79-$129	2P: $89-$139	XP: $5	F17
4/1-5/15 [ECP]	1P: $49-$99	2P: $59-$109	XP: $5	F17

Location: I-43, exit 128, 0.3 mi e on Business Rt 42. 4332 N 40th St 53083. Fax: 920/457-2597. **Facility:** 59 one-bedroom standard units, some with whirlpools. 2 stories, interior corridors. **Parking:** on-site, winter plug-ins. **Small-scale Hotel** **Terms:** pets ($25 fee). **Amenities:** safes (fee), hair dryers. *Some:* irons. **Pool(s):** small heated indoor. **Leisure Activities:** whirlpool. **Guest Services:** valet laundry. **Business Services:** meeting rooms. **Cards:** AX, CB, DC, DS, MC, VI.

SOME UNITS

HARBOR WINDS HOTEL
Phone: (920)452-9000

All Year   1P: $79-$150   2P: $79-$150

Location: On riverfront boardwalk, s of downtown. 905 S 8th St 53081. Fax: 920/452-0093. **Facility:** 28 one-bedroom standard units. 2 stories, interior corridors. *Bath:* combo or shower only. **Parking:** on-site. **Small-scale Hotel** **Terms:** [ECP] meal plan available. **Amenities:** dual phone lines, voice mail, irons, hair dryers. **Guest Services:** valet laundry. **Business Services:** business center. **Cards:** AX, DC, DS, MC, VI.

SOME UNITS

HOLIDAY INN EXPRESS

Phone: (920)451-8700

▼▼▼▼

6/1-9/1 [ECP]	1P: $92-$250	2P: $92-$250	XP: $8	F18
4/1-5/31 & 9/2-3/31 [ECP]	1P: $89-$150	2P: $89-$150	XP: $8	F18

Small-scale Hotel
Location: I-43, exit 123, just se. 3823 Germaine Ave 53081. Fax: 920/451-8700. **Facility:** 63 units. 61 one-bedroom standard units, some with whirlpools. 2 one-bedroom suites, some with whirlpools. 2 stories, interior corridors. *Bath:* combo or shower only. **Parking:** on-site, winter plug-ins. **Amenities:** dual phone lines, voice mail, irons, hair dryers. **Pool(s):** small heated indoor. **Leisure Activities:** limited exercise equipment. **Business Services:** meeting rooms. **Cards:** AX, DC, DS, MC, VI.

SOME UNITS

ⒶⓈⓀ Ⓢ🄳 🛏➔ 🅿 😩 🖥 🖵 / ✕ 🎦 🖼 /

SUPER 8 MOTEL

Phone: (920)458-8080

▼

All Year [CP]   1P: $52-$62   2P: $57-$67   XP: $5   F12

Small-scale Hotel
Location: I-43, exit 126, just ne. 3402 Wilgus Rd 53081. Fax: 920/458-8013. **Facility:** 60 one-bedroom standard units. 2 stories, interior corridors. **Parking:** on-site, winter plug-ins. **Terms:** small pets only ($10 extra charge, dogs only). **Amenities:** safes (fee). **Guest Services:** coin laundry. **Business Services:** meeting rooms. **Cards:** AX, CB, DC, DS, MC, VI.

SOME UNITS

ⒶⓈⓀ Ⓢ🄳 🐕 🍽➔ 🖥 🖵 / ✕ 🄳🄰🅃🄰 🎦 🖼 /

———— WHERE TO DINE ————

CITY STREETS-RIVERSIDE

Lunch: $6-$10   **Dinner:** $9-$20   **Phone:** 920/457-9050

▼▼ ▼▼
American
Location: E of 8th on Virginia; in Riverfront District. 712 Riverfront Dr 53081. **Hours:** 11 am-2 & 5-9 pm, Fri & Sat 5 pm-10 pm. Closed: 1/1, 12/24, 12/25; also Sun. **Reservations:** suggested; weekends. **Features:** Within walking distance of Lake Michigan and lakeshore specialty shops, the restaurant is popular for its fresh seafood. The area's nautical theme is maintained in the dining room decor. Good choices include locally caught broiled whitefish and salmon. Steaks, grilled pork loin and other American dishes are also offered. Casual dress; cocktails. **Parking:** on-site. **Cards:** AX, DC, MC, VI.

🍽 ✕

RUPP'S LODGE DOWNTOWN

Lunch: $6-$8   **Dinner:** $9-$22   **Phone:** 920/459-8155

▼
American
Location: Downtown. 925 N 8th St 53081. **Hours:** 11 am-2 & 4-9 pm, Fri-10 pm, Sat & Sun 4 pm-10 pm. Closed: 7/4, 11/27, 12/25. **Reservations:** accepted. **Features:** The family-owned restaurant delivers basic American fare—steaks, sandwiches and specials—with some selections of local fresh fish. The large salad bar is included with meals. Tables are nicely spaced throughout the supper club-style dining room. Casual dress; cocktails. **Parking:** street. **Cards:** AX, DC, DS, MC, VI.

🍽 ✕

TRATTORIA STEFANO

Dinner: $12-$29   **Phone:** 920/452-8455

▼▼
Italian
Location: Downtown. 522 S 8th St 53081. **Hours:** 5 pm-9 pm, Fri & Sat-10 pm. Closed major holidays; also Sun. **Reservations:** suggested. **Features:** The informal and lively restaurant, with simple wood tables and a trendy decor, complements its fine Italian dishes with good selection of Italian wines. Casual dress; cocktails. **Parking:** on-site. **Cards:** AX, DC, JC, MC, VI.

🍽 ✕

SHEBOYGAN FALLS pop. 6,772

———— WHERE TO STAY ————

ROCHESTER INN

Phone: 920/467-3123

ⒶⒶⒶ [SAVE]
▼▼▼▼
Historic Bed
& Breakfast

All Year   2P: $99-$169   F10

Location: Just e of downtown via CR PP. 504 Water St 53085. Fax: 920/467-9729. **Facility:** This 1848 Greek Revival B&B features two-level suites, four-poster beds, wet bars and large, jetted tubs. Smoke free premises. 6 units. 1 one-bedroom standard unit with whirlpool. 5 one-bedroom suites ($129-$169), some with whirlpools. 3 stories (no elevator), interior corridors. **Parking:** on-site. **Terms:** 2 night minimum stay - weekends 6/1-10/1, age restrictions may apply, 14 day cancellation notice-fee imposed, [BP] & [CP] meal plans available. **Amenities:** irons, hair dryers. *Some:* honor bars. **Guest Services:** valet laundry. **Cards:** AX, MC, VI.
Special Amenities: early check-in/late check-out and free continental breakfast.

SOME UNITS

🍽➔ 💪 ✕ 🎦 🄳🄰🅃🄰 / 🖼 🖵 /

SIREN pop. 988

———— WHERE TO STAY ————

BEST WESTERN NORTHWOODS LODGE

Phone: (715)349-7800

ⒶⒶⒶ [SAVE]
▼▼▼
Small-scale Hotel

All Year [ECP]   1P: $79-$300   2P: $79-$300   XP: $10   F17

Location: On SR 35 at jct SR 70 W and CR B E. 23986 SR 35 S 54872 (PO Box 49). Fax: 715/349-7855. **Facility:** 38 one-bedroom standard units. 2 stories, interior corridors. *Bath:* combo or shower only. **Parking:** on-site, winter plug-ins. **Amenities:** irons, hair dryers. **Pool(s):** heated indoor. **Leisure Activities:** sauna, whirlpool, board games. **Guest Services:** gift shop, coin laundry. **Business Services:** meeting rooms, administrative services (fee). **Cards:** AX, CB, DC, DS, MC, VI. **Special Amenities:** free continental breakfast.

SOME UNITS

Ⓢ🄳 🍽➔ ♿M 🅿 😩 ✕ 🎦 🄳🄰🅃🄰 🖵 / ✕ 🖼 🖼 /

THE LODGE AT CROOKED LAKE

Phone: (715)349-2500

▼▼▼▼

6/1-10/31 [ECP]	1P: $79-$109	2P: $79-$109	XP: $10	F18
11/1-3/31 [ECP]	1P: $69-$99	2P: $69-$99	XP: $10	F18
4/1-5/31 [ECP]	1P: $59-$89	2P: $59-$89	XP: $10	F18

Small-scale Hotel
Location: On SR 35, 0.5 mi n of jct SR 70. 24271 SR 35 N 54872 (PO Box 606). Fax: 715/349-2554. **Facility:** 60 one-bedroom standard units, some with whirlpools. 2 stories, interior corridors. *Bath:* combo or shower only. **Parking:** on-site, winter plug-ins. **Terms:** 2 night minimum stay - seasonal weekends, small pets only ($50 deposit, $10 extra charge). **Amenities:** voice mail. *Some:* CD players. **Pool(s):** small heated indoor. **Leisure Activities:** sauna, whirlpool, fishing, golf-18 holes, cross country skiing, snowmobiling, bicycles, hiking trails, limited exercise equipment. **Guest Services:** gift shop, valet laundry, area transportation. **Business Services:** conference facilities, PC, fax (fee). **Cards:** AX, CB, DS, MC, VI.

SOME UNITS

ⒶⓈⓀ Ⓢ🄳 ♿ 🐕 🍽 🍽 😩 ✕ 🎦 🄳🄰🅃🄰 🖵 / ✕ 🎦 🖼 🖼 /

PINE WOOD MOTEL

Phone: 715/349-5225

(AAA) (SAVE)
♦
Motel

All Year   1P: $32-$43   2P: $49-$60   XP: $5   D18
Location: On SR 35, 0.3 mi s of jct SR 70 W and CR B E. 23862 Hwy 35 S 54872. **Fax:** 715/349-8196. **Facility:** 14 one-bedroom standard units. 1 story, exterior corridors. *Bath:* combo or shower only. **Parking:** on-site, winter plug-ins. **Terms:** cancellation fee imposed, package plans, small pets only ($25 deposit, $5 fee). **Cards:** MC, VI.

SOME UNITS
[S/D] [🐾] [📷] [DATA PORT] [📠] [🖨] / [✕] /

SISTER BAY —*See Door County p. 486.*

SPARTA pop. 8,648

———— **WHERE TO STAY** ————

BEST NIGHTS INN

Phone: (608)269-3066

(AAA) (SAVE)
♦
Motel

All Year [CP]   1P: $33-$54   2P: $42-$69   XP: $5   F12
Location: I-90, exit 25 (SR 27), 0.5 mi s. 303 W Wisconsin St 54656. **Fax:** 608/269-3175. **Facility:** 28 one-bedroom standard units, some with whirlpools. 1 story, exterior corridors. **Parking:** on-site, winter plug-ins. **Terms:** weekly rates available, pets (with prior approval). **Amenities:** *Some:* hair dryers. **Pool(s):** small heated outdoor. **Leisure Activities:** playground. **Cards:** AX, DS, MC, VI. **Special Amenities:** free continental breakfast and free local telephone calls.

SOME UNITS
[S/D] [🐾] [🍴] [🛟] [📷] [DATA PORT] [📠] [🖨] / [✕] [VCR] [🖥] /

COUNTRY INN BY CARLSON

Phone: (608)269-3110

(AAA) (SAVE)
♦♦♦
Small-scale Hotel

6/1-3/31 [CP]   1P: $72-$110   2P: $80-$130   XP: $8   F17
4/1-5/31 [CP]   1P: $67-$105   2P: $75-$125   XP: $8   F17
Location: I-90, exit 25 (SR 27), just n. 737 Avon Rd 54656. **Fax:** 608/269-6726. **Facility:** 61 one-bedroom standard units. 2 stories (no elevator), interior corridors. **Parking:** on-site, winter plug-ins. **Terms:** small pets only ($5 extra charge). **Amenities:** irons, hair dryers. **Pool(s):** small heated indoor. **Leisure Activities:** whirlpool. **Guest Services:** gift shop, coin laundry. **Cards:** AX, CB, DC, DS, MC, VI. **Special Amenities:** free continental breakfast and free newspaper. *(See color ad starting on p 556)*

SOME UNITS
[S/D] [🐾] [🍴] [Y] [&M] [🛟] [📷] [DATA PORT] [🖥] / [✕] [📠] [🖨] /

SUPER 8 SPARTA

Phone: (608)269-8489

♦♦
Small-scale Hotel

4/1-9/30   1P: $60-$170   2P: $60-$180   XP: $5   F18
10/1-3/31   1P: $65   2P: $70-$80   XP: $5   F18
Location: I-90, exit 25 (SR 27), just n. 716 Avon Rd 54656. **Fax:** 608/269-8449. **Facility:** 49 one-bedroom standard units. 2 stories (no elevator), interior corridors. **Parking:** on-site, winter plug-ins. **Terms:** [CP] meal plan available, small pets only ($5 extra charge). **Amenities:** hair dryers. **Pool(s):** small heated indoor. **Leisure Activities:** whirlpool. **Guest Services:** coin laundry. **Cards:** AX, DC, DS, MC, VI.

SOME UNITS
[ASK] [S/D] [🐾] [🍴] [🛟] [📷] [DATA PORT] [🖥] / [✕] [VCR] [📠] [🖨] /

SPOONER pop. 2,653

———— **WHERE TO STAY** ————

BEST WESTERN-AMERICAN HERITAGE INN OF SPOONER

Phone: 715/635-9770

(AAA) (SAVE)
♦♦♦
Small-scale Hotel

5/25-9/3   1P: $72-$92   2P: $84-$99   XP: $6   F18
4/1-5/24 & 9/4-3/31   1P: $69-$80   2P: $79-$89   XP: $6   F18
Location: On SR 70 at jct US 63, 1 mi w of US 53. 101 Maple St 54801. **Fax:** 715/635-9774. **Facility:** 45 units. 44 one-bedroom standard units. 1 one-bedroom suite with whirlpool. 2 stories, interior corridors. **Parking:** on-site. **Terms:** small pets only (in smoking units). **Amenities:** irons, hair dryers. **Pool(s):** small heated indoor. **Leisure Activities:** sauna, whirlpool, snowmobiling, bicycles, hiking trails. *Fee:* game room. **Business Services:** meeting rooms, administrative services (fee). **Cards:** AX, CB, DC, DS, MC, VI. **Special Amenities:** early check-in/late check-out and free continental breakfast.

SOME UNITS
[🐾] [🍴] [🛟] [✕] [📷] [DATA PORT] [🖥] / [✕] /

COUNTRY HOUSE MOTEL & RV PARK

Phone: 715/635-8721

(AAA) (SAVE)
♦♦
Motel

6/15-9/15   1P: $50-$93   2P: $60-$119   XP: $6   F12
4/1-6/14 & 9/16-3/31   1P: $50-$82   2P: $60-$89   XP: $6   F12
Location: On US 63, 0.5 mi s of jct US 63. 717 S River St (US 63) 54801-9692. **Facility:** 23 one-bedroom standard units. 1-2 stories, interior/exterior corridors. *Bath:* combo or shower only. **Parking:** on-site, winter plug-ins. **Terms:** 2 night minimum stay - weekends, package plans, pets ($4-$5 extra charge, with prior approval). **Amenities:** video library. **Pool(s):** small heated indoor. **Leisure Activities:** whirlpool. *Fee:* video games. **Business Services:** meeting rooms, administrative services (fee), PC. **Cards:** DS, MC, VI. **Special Amenities:** free local telephone calls and preferred room (subject to availability with advanced reservations).

SOME UNITS
[🐾] [🍴] [Y] [&M] [🛟] [✏] [🛟] [DATA PORT] [🖥] / [✕] [VCR] [📠] /
FEE

———— **WHERE TO DINE** ————

The following restaurant has not been evaluated by AAA but is listed for your information only.

FOXXY'S

Phone: 715/635-2399

[fyi]

Not evaluated. Location: Elm St 54801. **Features:** The popular restaurant serves Italian specialties, seafood, salads and Chicago steakhouse grill selections.

SPRING GREEN pop. 1,444

------ WHERE TO STAY ------

HILL STREET
▼▼▼ ▼▼▼
Bed & Breakfast

Phone: 608/588-7751

All Year   1P: $80-$90   2P: $80-$90   XP: $20
Location: Just nw of downtown. 353 W Hill St 53588. **Facility:** Smoke free premises. 7 one-bedroom standard units. 2 stories (no elevator), interior corridors. *Bath:* some shared or private, combo or shower only. **Parking:** on-site. **Terms:** check-in 4 pm, 2 night minimum stay - weekends, age restrictions may apply, 14 day cancellation notice-fee imposed, [BP] meal plan available, no pets allowed (owner's cats on premises). **Guest Services:** TV in common area. **Cards:** MC, VI.

⊠ 𝒲 𝒵

THE HOUSE ON THE ROCK RESORT
▼▼▼ ◆◆ ▼▼
Resort
Small-scale Hotel

Phone: 608/588-7000

4/1-1/5   1P: $95-$205
Location: 2.5 mi s on SR 23, 0.8 mi e on CR C. 400 Springs Dr 53588. Fax: 608/588-2269. **Facility:** All units at this picturesque resort near the Wisconsin River have views of a golf course and surrounding wooded hills. 80 one-bedroom suites with whirlpools. 4 stories, interior corridors. *Bath:* combo or shower only. **Parking:** on-site. **Terms:** open 4/1-1/5, cancellation fee imposed. **Amenities:** dual phone lines, voice mail, hair dryers. **Pool(s):** heated outdoor, 2 heated indoor. **Leisure Activities:** saunas, whirlpool, steamrooms, 2 lighted tennis courts, racquetball court, hiking trails, jogging, exercise room, volleyball. *Fee:* golf-27 holes. **Guest Services:** gift shop. **Business Services:** conference facilities. **Cards:** AX, DS, MC, VI.

SOME UNITS

🍴 ▼ 👶 ⇆ ⊠ 💪 (DATA PORT) 🔌 📠 ▭ /⊠/

ROUND BARN LODGE
AAA SAVE
▼▼ ▼▼
Small-scale Hotel

Phone: 608/588-2568

5/1-10/31   1P: $80-$100   2P: $80-$100   XP: $5   F6
4/1-4/30   1P: $45-$85   2P: $55-$85   XP: $5   F6
11/1-3/31   1P: $45-$85   2P: $45-$85   XP: $5   F6
Location: On US 14, just w of jct SR 23 N. Hwy 14 53588 (PO Box 297). Fax: 608/588-2100. **Facility:** 44 one-bedroom standard units, some with whirlpools. 2 stories (no elevator), interior corridors. **Parking:** on-site, winter plug-ins. **Terms:** [AP] meal plan available. **Dining:** dining room, see separate listing. **Pool(s):** outdoor, heated indoor. **Leisure Activities:** sauna, whirlpool. **Business Services:** meeting rooms. **Cards:** AX, DS, MC, VI.

SOME UNITS

🍴 ⇆ 💪 /⊠ 🔌 📠 ▭

SPRING VALLEY INN
AAA SAVE
▼▼ ▼▼
Small-scale Hotel

Phone: 608/588-7828

4/1-10/31   1P: $75-$110   2P: $75-$110   XP: $5   F12
11/1-3/31   1P: $50-$90   2P: $50-$90   XP: $5   F12
Location: 3 mi e on US 14 at jct CR C. 6279 Cty Hwy C 53588. Fax: 608/588-2821. **Facility:** 35 one-bedroom standard units. 1 story, interior corridors. **Parking:** on-site. **Dining:** 11 am-9 pm, cocktails. **Pool(s):** heated indoor. **Leisure Activities:** sauna, whirlpool, steamroom, water aerobics, sun deck, cross country skiing, snowmobiling, outdoor patio with fire pit, hiking trails, exercise room. *Fee:* massage, game room. **Guest Services:** gift shop. **Business Services:** meeting rooms. **Cards:** DS, MC, VI. **Special Amenities:** free continental breakfast and free newspaper.

SOME UNITS

(S/D) 🍴 ▼ ⇆ ⊠ 💪 (DATA PORT) /⊠/

USONIAN INN
▼▼
Motel

Phone: 608/588-2323

6/5-9/1 [CP]   1P: $55-$75   2P: $55-$75   XP: $5   F18
9/2-10/31 [CP]   1P: $44-$75   2P: $49-$75   XP: $5   F18
5/1-6/4 [CP]   1P: $44-$59   2P: $49-$59   XP: $5   F18
Location: On US 14 at jct SR 23 S. E 5116 Hwy 14 53588 (PO Box 777). **Facility:** Smoke free premises. 11 one-bedroom standard units. 1 story, exterior corridors. *Bath:* shower only. **Parking:** on-site. **Terms:** open 5/1-10/31. **Cards:** DS, MC, VI.

SOME UNITS

⊠ /🔌 📠 ▭/

------ WHERE TO DINE ------

THE POST HOUSE-DUTCH KITCHEN
▼▼ ▼▼
American

Lunch: $5-$8   **Dinner:** $9-$17   **Phone: 608/588-2595**
Location: Downtown. 127 E Jefferson 53588. **Hours:** 11 am-9 pm, Fri & Sat-10 pm, Sun 9 am-8 pm. Closed major holidays; also Mon 11/1-5/1. **Reservations:** suggested. **Features:** Originally constructed in 1857, this centrally located restaurant is known for its home-style comfort foods. The restaurant houses a unique lounge and garden area designed in the Frank Lloyd Wright tradition. Casual dress; cocktails. **Parking:** street. **Cards:** MC, VI.

▼ ⊠

THE ROUND BARN
AAA
▼▼ ▼▼
American

Lunch: $4-$7   **Dinner:** $10-$17   **Phone: 608/588-2568**
Location: On US 14, just w of jct SR 23 N; in Round Barn Lodge. US 14 53588. **Hours:** 7 am-2 & 5-9 pm. Closed: Mon & Tues 12/1-3/31. **Reservations:** accepted. **Features:** Once home to 40 cattle, the skillfully converted 1914 round barn now is a cozy place in which diners can sample steak, barbecue ribs, chicken and seafood specialties. The family-oriented restaurant offers several children's selections, as well as a few vegetarian dishes. Casual dress; cocktails. **Parking:** on-site. **Cards:** AX, DC, DS, MC, VI.

▼ ⊠

SPRING GREEN GENERAL STORE
▼▼
American

Lunch: $4-$9   **Phone: 608/588-7070**
Location: Just w of SR 23. 137 S Albany St 53588. **Hours:** 9 am-6 pm, Sat from 8 am, Sun 8 am-4 pm. Closed major holidays. **Features:** The trendy cafe prepares weekend breakfasts and an extensive selection of vegetarian offerings from scratch. Beer only. **Parking:** street. **Cards:** AX, DS, MC, VI.

⊠

STANLEY pop. 1,898

―――― WHERE TO STAY ――――

SUPER 8 MOTEL
Phone: 715/644-3332
▼▼ ▼▼
All Year [CP]   1P: $49-$74   2P: $54-$79   XP: $5   F13
Small-scale Hotel
Location: SR 29, exit 101 (CR H), just n. 555 S Broadway 54768 (PO Box 85). Fax: 715/644-2120. **Facility:** 36 one-bedroom standard units, some with whirlpools. 2 stories, interior corridors. **Parking:** on-site, winter plug-ins. **Leisure Activities:** whirlpool. **Business Services:** meeting rooms. **Cards:** AX, CB, DC, DS, MC, VI.

SOME UNITS
ASK SD YI+ DATA PORT ⌷ / ✕ VCR 🛢 📶 /

STEVENS POINT pop. 24,551

―――― WHERE TO STAY ――――

A VICTORIAN SWAN ON WATER
Phone: (715)345-0595
▼▼ ▼▼
All Year   1P: $70-$145   2P: $70-$145   XP: $20
Bed & Breakfast
Location: On US 10, 0.7 mi w from jct US 51 business route, then 0.4 mi s. 1716 Water St 54481. Fax: 715/345-0569. **Facility:** Smoke free premises. 4 one-bedroom standard units, some with whirlpools. 2 stories (no elevator), interior corridors. *Bath:* combo or shower only. **Parking:** on-site. **Terms:** age restrictions may apply, 8 day cancellation notice-fee imposed, [BP] meal plan available. **Amenities:** hair dryers. **Business Services:** fax (fee). **Cards:** DS, MC, VI.

✕ 🎿 🕿

BAYMONT INN & SUITES STEVENS POINT
Phone: (715)344-1900
🆔 SAVE
▼▼ ▼▼
All Year [ECP]   1P: $54-$74   2P: $54-$74
Small-scale Hotel
Location: I-39, exit 158B (US 10), just w. 4917 Main St 54481. Fax: 715/344-1254. **Facility:** 75 units. 73 one-bedroom standard units. 2 one-bedroom suites ($64-$94). 3 stories, interior corridors. **Parking:** on-site, winter plug-ins. **Terms:** small pets only ($50 deposit). **Amenities:** video games (fee), voice mail, irons, hair dryers. **Pool(s):** small heated indoor. **Leisure Activities:** whirlpool. **Guest Services:** coin laundry. **Business Services:** fax (fee). **Cards:** AX, CB, DC, DS, MC, VI. **Special Amenities:** free continental breakfast and free newspaper.** *(See color ad below)*

SOME UNITS
SD 🐾 YI+ 🍳 ⇌ 🎥 DATA PORT ⌷ / ✕ 🛢 📶 /

COMFORT SUITES STEVENS POINT
Phone: (715)341-6000
SAVE
▼▼▼▼▼
All Year   1P: $72-$149   2P: $72-$149
Small-scale Hotel
Location: I-39, exit 161 (US 51 business route), 0.6 mi s. 300 Division St N 54481. Fax: 715/341-8908. **Facility:** 105 one-bedroom standard units, some with whirlpools. 3 stories, interior corridors. **Parking:** on-site, winter plug-ins. **Terms:** [ECP] meal plan available. **Amenities:** video games (fee), dual phone lines, irons, hair dryers. **Pool(s):** heated indoor. **Leisure Activities:** whirlpool, limited exercise equipment. **Guest Services:** valet and coin laundry. **Business Services:** meeting rooms, fax (fee). **Cards:** AX, CB, DC, DS, MC, VI.

SOME UNITS
SD YI+ ⇌ 🎥 DATA PORT 🛢 ⌷ / ✕ 📶 /

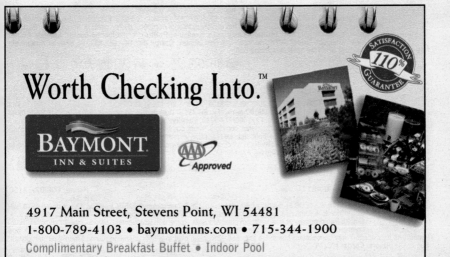

COUNTRY INN & SUITES BY CARLSON
Phone: (715)345-7000

AAA SAVE

| | 6/1-8/31 [ECP] | 1P: $64-$89 | 2P: $64-$89 |
| | 4/1-5/31 & 9/1-3/31 [ECP] | 1P: $64-$74 | 2P: $64-$74 |

Location: I-39, exit 161 (US 51 business route), 0.6 mi s. 301 Division St N 54481. Fax: 715/345-7008. **Facility:** 75 units. 56 one-bedroom standard units, some with whirlpools. 19 one-bedroom suites ($79-$109). 3 stories, Small-scale Hotel interior corridors. *Bath:* combo or shower only. **Parking:** on-site, winter plug-ins. **Terms:** pets ($25 extra small heated indoor. charge, in designated units). **Amenities:** voice mail, irons, hair dryers. *Some:* dual phone lines. **Pool(s):** small heated indoor. **Leisure Activities:** whirlpool, exercise room. **Guest Services:** coin laundry. **Business Services:** fax (fee). **Cards:** AX, DC, DS, MC, VI. **Special Amenities:** free continental breakfast and free newspaper. *(See color ad starting on p 556)*

SOME UNITS

FAIRFIELD INN BY MARRIOTT
Phone: (715)342-9300

SAVE

	6/1-8/31 [CP]	1P: $65	2P: $65
	9/1-9/30 [CP]	1P: $60	2P: $60
	4/1-5/31 [CP]	1P: $55	2P: $55
	10/1-3/31 [CP]	1P: $50	2P: $50

Small-scale Hotel **Location:** I-39, exit 158 (US 10), at jct US 51. 5317 Hwy 10 E 54481. Fax: 715/342-9300. **Facility:** 62 one-bedroom standard units. 3 stories, interior corridors. *Bath:* combo or shower only. **Parking:** on-site, winter plug-ins. **Terms:** 2-3 night minimum stay - summer weekends. **Amenities:** high-speed Internet, irons, hair dryers. **Pool(s):** small heated indoor. **Leisure Activities:** whirlpool. **Guest Services:** valet laundry. **Business Services:** fax (fee). **Cards:** AX, CB, DC, DS, JC, MC, VI.

SOME UNITS

POINT MOTEL
Phone: (715)344-8312

AAA SAVE

| | 5/1-8/31 | 1P: $35-$40 | 2P: $42-$48 | XP: $4 | F13 |
| | 4/1-4/30 & 9/1-3/31 | 1P: $33-$35 | 2P: $38-$42 | XP: $4 | F13 |

Location: 0.6 mi n on US 51 business route. 209 Division St 54481. Fax: 715/344-8313. **Facility:** 44 one-bedroom standard units. 1-2 stories (no elevator), exterior corridors. *Bath:* combo or shower only. **Parking:** on-site, Motel winter plug-ins. **Terms:** weekly rates available, [CP] meal plan available, small pets only ($5 extra charge). **Amenities:** *Some:* DVD players (fee). **Business Services:** meeting rooms, fax (fee). **Cards:** AX, DS, MC, VI. **Special Amenities:** free continental breakfast and free local telephone calls.

SOME UNITS

── WHERE TO DINE ──

THE RESTAURANT
Dinner: $14-$25   **Phone:** 715/346-6010

American

Location: I-39, exit 161 (US 51 business route), just se; in Sentry Headquarters. 1800 N Point Dr 54481. **Hours:** 5 pm-9 pm, Fri & Sat-10 pm. Closed major holidays; also Sun. **Reservations:** suggested. **Features:** The dining room has large windows that overlook a "northwoods" backyard with a wildlife feeding station. The chef makes use of organic and local ingredients, and is happy to accommodate dietary requests. The menu changes seasonally, and the entrees are nicely presented. Scrumptious desserts are prepared in-house. Lunch is served in the more casual Pagliace Taverna from 11 am Mon-Fri. Dressy casual; cocktails. **Parking:** on-site. **Cards:** AX, MC, VI.

STOUGHTON pop. 12,354

── WHERE TO STAY ──

CHOSE FAMILY INN
Phone: (608)873-0330

AAA SAVE

| | 5/1-10/31 [CP] | 1P: $66-$72 | 2P: $72-$78 | XP: $5 | F14 |
| | 4/1-4/30 & 11/1-3/31 [CP] | 1P: $55-$65 | 2P: $59-$69 | XP: $5 | F14 |

Location: On US 51 business route, just w of jct SR 138 S. 1124 W Main St 53589. Fax: 608/873-8904. **Facility:** 53 one-bedroom standard units. 2 stories (no elevator), interior corridors. *Bath:* combo or shower only. **Parking:** Small-scale Hotel on-site, winter plug-ins. **Terms:** weekly rates available. **Pool(s):** small heated indoor. **Leisure Activities:** whirlpool. **Guest Services:** valet and coin laundry. **Cards:** AX, DC, DS, MC, VI. **Special Amenities:** free continental breakfast and free local telephone calls.

SOME UNITS

COMFORT INN
Phone: (608)877-9000

SAVE

| | 6/1-10/31 [ECP] | 1P: $72-$149 | 2P: $75-$149 | XP: $8 | F18 |
| | 4/1-5/31 & 11/1-3/31 [ECP] | 1P: $72-$139 | 2P: $75-$139 | XP: $8 | F18 |

Location: On US 51 business route, 0.7 mi nw of jct SR 138 S. Truck parking on premises. 660 Nygaard St 53589 (6641 N Kennedy Rd, MILTON, 53563). Fax: 608/877-9799. **Facility:** 50 one-bedroom standard units, some with whirl-Small-scale Hotel pools. 2 stories (no elevator), interior corridors. *Bath:* combo or shower only. **Parking:** on-site, winter plug-ins. **Terms:** cancellation fee imposed, weekly rates available. **Amenities:** hair dryers. *Some:* dual phone lines, irons. **Pool(s):** heated indoor. **Leisure Activities:** whirlpool, limited exercise equipment. **Guest Services:** valet and coin laundry. **Business Services:** meeting rooms. **Cards:** AX, CB, DC, DS, MC, VI.

SOME UNITS

NAESET-ROE BED & BREAKFAST
Phone: 608/877-4150

| | All Year | 1P: $65-$160 | 2P: $75-$160 | XP: $25 |

Location: Just n of US 51 business route; downtown. 126 E Washington St 53589. **Facility:** The restored 1878 Ital-Historic Bed ianate home is furnished with period pieces; guest rooms are well appointed and some feature whirlpools. & Breakfast Smoke free premises. 4 one-bedroom standard units, some with whirlpools. 2 stories, interior corridors. *Bath:* combo or tub only. **Parking:** on-site. **Terms:** check-in 4 pm, 2 night minimum stay - weekends 7/1-10/31, age restrictions may apply, 7 day cancellation notice-fee imposed, [BP] meal plan available, package plans. **Amenities:** hair dryers. *Some:* CD players. **Cards:** MC, VI.

SOME UNITS

STURGEON BAY —See Door County p. 488.

STURTEVANT pop. 5,287

——— WHERE TO STAY ———

BEST WESTERN GRANDVIEW INN
Phone: (262)886-0385

(AAA) (SAVE)

| | 6/1-8/31 [ECP] | 1P: $64-$99 | 2P: $69-$104 | XP: $10 | F18 |
| | 4/1-5/31 & 9/1-3/31 [ECP] | 1P: $44-$79 | 2P: $49-$84 | XP: $10 | F18 |

Small-scale Hotel

Location: I-94, exit 333 (SR 20), just s on west frontage road. 910 S Sylvania Ave 53177. Fax: 262/886-4310. **Facility:** 50 one-bedroom standard units, some with whirlpools. 2 stories (no elevator), interior corridors. **Parking:** on-site. **Amenities:** irons, hair dryers. **Pool(s):** small heated indoor. **Leisure Activities:** whirlpool. *Fee:* game room. **Business Services:** meeting rooms, fax. **Cards:** AX, CB, DC, DS, JC, MC, VI. **Special Amenities:** free continental breakfast.

SOME UNITS

HOLIDAY INN EXPRESS-RACINE
Phone: (262)884-0200

(AAA) (SAVE)

| | 6/1-8/31 [ECP] | 1P: $72-$99 | 2P: $72-$99 | XP: $6 | F18 |
| | 4/1-5/31 & 9/1-3/31 [ECP] | 1P: $69-$79 | 2P: $69-$79 | XP: $6 | F18 |

Small-scale Hotel

Location: I-94, exit 333 (SR 20), just se. 13339 Hospitality Ct 53177. Fax: 262/884-0701. **Facility:** 107 one-bedroom standard units, some with whirlpools. 3 stories, interior corridors. *Bath:* combo or shower only. **Parking:** on-site. **Terms:** small pets only (in smoking units). **Amenities:** irons, hair dryers. **Pool(s):** small heated indoor. **Leisure Activities:** whirlpool, limited exercise equipment. **Guest Services:** valet and coin laundry. **Business Services:** meeting rooms, business center. **Cards:** AX, CB, DC, DS, MC, VI. **Special Amenities:** free continental breakfast and free local telephone calls.

SOME UNITS

RAMADA LIMITED OF RACINE
Phone: (262)884-6840

| | 6/1-9/3 [ECP] | 1P: $69 | 2P: $79 | XP: $5 | F18 |
| | 4/1-5/31 & 9/4-3/31 [CP] | 1P: $49 | 2P: $59 | XP: $5 | F18 |

Small-scale Hotel

Location: I-94, exit 333 (SR 20), just se. 13340 Hospitality Ct 53177. Fax: 262/884-6847. **Facility:** 48 one-bedroom standard units, some with whirlpools. 2 stories, interior corridors. **Parking:** on-site, winter plug-ins. **Amenities:** video library (fee), voice mail, irons, hair dryers. **Pool(s):** small heated indoor. **Leisure Activities:** limited exercise equipment. **Guest Services:** valet and coin laundry. **Business Services:** meeting rooms. **Cards:** AX, CB, DC, DS, JC, MC, VI.

SOME UNITS

FEE

SUN PRAIRIE pop. 20,369

——— WHERE TO STAY ———

AMERIHOST INN-SUN PRAIRIE
Phone: (608)834-9889

(AAA) (SAVE)

| | 6/1-10/31 [ECP] | 1P: $64-$89 | 2P: $69-$94 | XP: $5 | F12 |
| | 4/1-5/31 & 11/1-3/31 [ECP] | 1P: $59-$69 | 2P: $69-$84 | XP: $5 | F12 |

Small-scale Hotel

Location: US 151, exit 103 (CR N), just n. 105 Business Park Dr 53590. Fax: 608/834-9779. **Facility:** 62 one-bedroom standard units, some with whirlpools. 2 stories, interior corridors. *Bath:* combo or shower only. **Parking:** on-site, winter plug-ins. **Terms:** cancellation fee imposed. **Amenities:** voice mail, safes (fee), irons, hair dryers. **Pool(s):** heated indoor. **Leisure Activities:** whirlpool, exercise room. **Guest Services:** valet laundry. **Business Services:** meeting rooms. **Cards:** AX, CB, DC, DS, JC, MC, VI. **Special Amenities:** free continental breakfast and free newspaper.

SOME UNITS

MCGOVERN'S MOTEL & SUITES
Phone: 608/837-7321

(AAA) (SAVE)

| | All Year | 1P: $46-$82 | 2P: $57-$82 | XP: $4 | D18 |

Motel

Location: On US 151, exit 101, 1.2 mi ne. 820 W Main St 53590. Fax: 608/825-3800. **Facility:** 54 one-bedroom standard units, some with efficiencies. 2 stories, exterior corridors. *Bath:* combo or shower only. **Parking:** on-site, winter plug-ins. **Terms:** weekly rates available, [CP] meal plan available, small pets only ($5 extra charge). **Dining:** 11 am-10 pm, cocktails. **Guest Services:** complimentary laundry. **Business Services:** meeting rooms, fax (fee). **Cards:** AX, DS, MC, VI. **Special Amenities:** early check-in/late check-out and free continental breakfast.

SOME UNITS

SUPERIOR pop. 27,368

——— WHERE TO STAY ———

BARKERS ISLAND INN
Phone: (715)392-7152

(AAA) (SAVE)

| | All Year | 1P: $65-$200 | 2P: $65-$200 | XP: $5 | F18 |

Small-scale Hotel

Location: Just ne of US 2/53; on Barkers Island. Located adjacent to the marina. 300 Marina Dr 54880. Fax: 715/392-1180. **Facility:** 110 units. 108 one-bedroom standard units, some with whirlpools. 2 one-bedroom suites with whirlpools. 2 stories, interior corridors. **Parking:** on-site. **Terms:** pets ($50 deposit, $10 extra charge). **Amenities:** voice mail. *Some:* hair dryers. **Dining:** 6:30 am-9 pm, Fri & Sat-10 pm, Sun-8:30 pm; hours may vary seasonally. **Pool(s):** heated indoor. **Leisure Activities:** sauna, whirlpool. *Fee:* game room. **Guest Services:** valet and coin laundry. **Business Services:** conference facilities, fax (fee). **Cards:** AX, CB, DC, DS, MC, VI. *(See color ad p 608)*

SOME UNITS

BEST WESTERN BAY WALK INN   **Phone:** (715)392-7600

	5/16-9/30 [ECP]	1P: $65-$115	2P: $69-$119	XP: $4	F16
	10/1-3/31 [ECP]	1P: $55-$95	2P: $59-$99	XP: $4	F16
	4/1-5/15 [ECP]	1P: $51-$85	2P: $55-$89	XP: $4	F16

Motel

Location: Just e of US 2 on Belknap. 1405 Susquehanna Ave 54880. Fax: 715/392-7680. **Facility:** 50 one-bedroom standard units, some with whirlpools. 2 stories, interior corridors. **Parking:** on-site, winter plug-ins. **Terms:** small pets only. **Amenities:** video library (fee), irons, hair dryers. **Pool(s):** heated indoor. **Leisure Activities:** sauna, whirlpool. *Fee:* game room. **Guest Services:** valet and coin laundry. **Business Services:** meeting rooms, fax (fee). **Cards:** AX, CB, DC, DS, JC, MC, VI.

SOME UNITS

BEST WESTERN BRIDGEVIEW MOTOR INN   **Phone:** (715)392-8174

	6/13-10/18 [ECP]	1P: $69-$125	2P: $69-$125	XP: $5	F18
	5/23-6/12 [ECP]	1P: $49-$110	2P: $49-$110	XP: $5	F18
	4/1-5/22 & 10/19-3/31 [ECP]	1P: $49-$99	2P: $49-$99	XP: $5	F18

Small-scale Hotel

Location: 0.8 mi n at south end of Blatnik Bridge. 415 Hammond Ave 54880. Fax: 715/392-8487. **Facility:** 96 units. 85 one-bedroom standard units. 11 one-bedroom suites, some with whirlpools. 2 stories, interior corridors. **Parking:** on-site, winter plug-ins. **Terms:** small pets only. **Amenities:** video games (fee), irons, hair dryers. **Pool(s):** heated indoor. **Leisure Activities:** sauna, whirlpool. *Fee:* game room. **Guest Services:** complimentary evening beverages: Mon-Thurs, coin laundry. **Business Services:** meeting rooms. **Cards:** AX, CB, DC, DS, JC, MC, VI. **Special Amenities:** free continental breakfast and free local telephone calls. *(See ad below)*

SOME UNITS

HOLIDAY INN EXPRESS   **Phone:** (715)392-3444
▽▽▽▽   6/20-9/7 [ECP]   1P: $89-$179   2P: $89-$179   XP: $10   F18
              4/1-6/19 & 9/8-3/31 [ECP]   1P: $79-$159   2P: $79-$159   XP: $10   F18
Small-scale Hotel **Location:** Just n of jct US 2 W and 53 N. 303 2nd Ave E 54880. Fax: 715/395-7911. **Facility:** 84 one-bedroom
standard units, some with whirlpools. 3 stories, interior corridors. *Bath:* combo or shower only. **Parking:** on-
site, winter plug-ins. **Amenities:** high-speed Internet, dual phone lines, voice mail, irons, hair dryers. **Pool(s):** small heated indoor. **Leisure Activities:** whirlpool, limited exercise equipment. **Guest Services:** valet and coin laundry. **Business Services:**
meeting rooms, business center. **Cards:** AX, DC, DS, MC, VI. *(See color ad p 608)*

SOME UNITS

(ASK) (S🄳) (🛏📞) (🔥M) (🛗) (🍽) (🎥) (DATA PORT) (💻) / (✕) (🔒) (🖥) (📺) /

STOCKADE MOTEL   **Phone:** 715/398-3585
▽▽▽   All Year   1P: $25-$55   2P: $35-$75   XP: $5   F16
Motel   **Location:** On US 2/53, 2.8 mi se. 1610 E 2nd St 54880. **Facility:** 17 one-bedroom standard units. 1 story, exterior
corridors. *Bath:* combo or shower only. **Parking:** on-site, winter plug-ins. **Terms:** 7 day cancellation notice-fee
imposed, small pets only ($10 deposit). **Cards:** MC, VI.

SOME UNITS

(🐾) (💻) / (✕) /

SUPER 8 MOTEL OF SUPERIOR   **Phone:** (715)398-7686
▽▽▽   6/21-9/13 [ECP]   1P: $66-$96   2P: $66-$96   XP: $5   F12
              5/30-6/20 [ECP]   1P: $58-$86   2P: $58-$86   XP: $5   F12
Motel   9/14-3/31 [ECP]   1P: $53-$76   2P: $53-$76   XP: $5   F12
              4/1-5/29 [ECP]   1P: $51-$76   2P: $51-$76   XP: $5   F12
Location: E on US 2/53. 4901 E 2nd St 54880. Fax: 715/398-7339. **Facility:** 40 one-bedroom standard units. 2 stories, interior cor-
ridors. **Parking:** on-site, winter plug-ins. **Cards:** AX, CB, DC, DS, MC, VI.

SOME UNITS

(ASK) (S🄳) (🛏📞) (🎥) (DATA PORT) / (✕) (🔒) (🖥) (💻) /

SUPERIOR INN   **Phone:** (715)394-7706
(AAA) (SAVE)   6/17-10/21   1P: $65-$105   2P: $69-$120   XP: $4   F18
              4/1-6/16   1P: $55-$90   2P: $69-$95   XP: $4   F18
▽▽ ▽▽   10/22-3/31   1P: $39-$85   2P: $49-$85   XP: $4   F18
Small-scale Hotel **Location:** 0.8 mi n at south end of Blatnik Bridge. 525 Hammond Ave 54880. Fax: 715/394-7708. **Facility:** 69 units.
68 one-bedroom standard units. 1 one-bedroom suite ($100-$160) with whirlpool. 2 stories, interior corridors.
Parking: on-site, winter plug-ins. **Amenities:** voice mail, hair dryers. **Pool(s):** small heated indoor. **Leisure**
Activities: sauna, whirlpool. **Business Services:** fax (fee). **Cards:** AX, DS, MC, VI.

SOME UNITS

(S🄳) (🐾) (🛏📞) (🏊) (🎥) (DATA PORT) / (✕) (🔒) (🖥) (💻) /

——— WHERE TO DINE ———

THE SHACK SMOKEHOUSE & GRILLE   **Lunch:** $7-$19   **Dinner:** $7-$19   **Phone:** 715/392-9836
▽▽ ▽▽   **Location:** 1.5 mi w. 3301 Belknap St 54880. **Hours:** 11 am-9 pm, Sun-8 pm. Closed: 12/25.
              Reservations: accepted. **Features:** Steak, seafood, chicken, prime rib and the house specialty
American   smokehouse barbecue ribs—in addition to lunch choices of lighter fare—make up a diverse menu at the
              established restaurant. Service is friendly and unpretentious, and portion sizes are ample. Casual dress;
cocktails. **Parking:** on-site. **Cards:** DC, DS, MC, VI.

(🍸) (✕)

THE TOWN CRIER RESTAURANT   **Lunch:** $3-$10   **Dinner:** $3-$10   **Phone:** 715/398-7521
▽   **Location:** 6 mi se on US 2/53. 4927 E 2nd St 54880. **Hours:** 6 am-11 pm. Closed: 12/25. **Features:** An
              informal, family-oriented restaurant, the Town Crier serves simple meals without any fuss or pretense.
American   Menu items are well-prepared and service is quick. Breakfast is served all day long. **Parking:** on-site.
              Cards: AX, DC, DS, MC, VI.

(✕)

THORP pop. 1,536

——— WHERE TO STAY ———

AMERICINN LODGE & SUITES   **Phone:** 715/669-5959
(AAA) (SAVE)   All Year   1P: $49-$160   2P: $59-$180
▽▽ ▽▽   **Location:** US 29, exit 108 (SR 73), just nw. 203 1/2 W Hill St 54771. Fax: 715/669-5907. **Facility:** 42 one-bedroom
              standard units, some with whirlpools. 2 stories (no elevator), interior corridors. *Bath:* combo or shower only.
              Parking: on-site. **Terms:** weekly rates available, [ECP] meal plan available, pets ($10 fee). **Amenities:** hair
Small-scale Hotel dryers. *Some:* irons. **Pool(s):** heated indoor. **Leisure Activities:** sauna, whirlpool. **Guest Services:** coin
              laundry. **Business Services:** meeting rooms, fax (fee). **Cards:** AX, DS, MC, VI. **Special Amenities:** free
continental breakfast and free local telephone calls.

SOME UNITS

(🐾) (🛏📞) (🛗) (🎥) (DATA PORT) (💻) / (✕) (VCR FEE) (🔒) (🖥) /

TOMAH pop. 8,419

——— WHERE TO STAY ———

COMFORT INN-TOMAH   **Phone:** (608)372-6600
(SAVE)   6/1-9/30 [ECP]   1P: $64-$124   2P: $69-$129   XP: $5   F18
              10/1-3/31 [ECP]   1P: $54-$124   2P: $59-$129   XP: $5   F18
▽▽ ▽▽   4/1-5/31 [ECP]   1P: $54-$74   2P: $59-$79   XP: $5   F18
              Location: I-94, exit 143 (SR 21), just w. 305 Wittig Rd 54660. Fax: 608/372-6600. **Facility:** 52 one-bedroom stan-
Small-scale Hotel dard units. 2 stories (no elevator), interior corridors. **Parking:** on-site, winter plug-ins. **Terms:** pets (in
              smoking units). **Amenities:** *Some:* irons, hair dryers. **Pool(s):** small heated indoor. **Leisure Activities:** whirl-
pool. **Business Services:** fax (fee). **Cards:** AX, CB, DC, DS, JC, MC, VI.

SOME UNITS

(S🄳) (🐾) (🛏📞) (🍽) (🏊) (🎥) (DATA PORT) / (✕) (🔒) (🖥) (💻) /

CRANBERRY COUNTRY LODGE

ğŸ'ğŸ' 6/1-8/31 .... 1P: $99-$169 .... 2P: $99-$169

4/1-5/31 & 9/1-3/31 ... 1P: $59-$159 .... 2P: $59-$159

Phone: (608)374-2801

Small-scale Hotel **Location:** I-94, exit 143 (SR 21), just w. 319 Wittig Rd 54660. **Fax:** 608/374-2805. **Facility:** 93 units. 54 one-bedroom standard units, some with whirlpools. 39 one-bedroom suites, some with whirlpools. 2 stories, interior corridors. **Parking:** on-site, winter plug-ins. **Terms:** package plans - seasonal, weekends. **Amenities:** video games (fee), voice mail, irons, hair dryers. **Pool(s):** wading. **Leisure Activities:** whirlpool, waterslide, exercise room. **Guest Services:** gift shop, coin laundry. **Cards:** AX, CB, DC, DS, MC, VI.

SOME UNITS

(ASK) (S⊘) (¶†) (✕) (♥) (DATA PORT) (🖬) (🖾) (🖳) / (✕) (VCR) /

ECONO LODGE

SAVE   5/16-11/1 [ECP] .... 1P: $60-$82 ..... 2P: $65-$150 .... XP: $5 ...... F18

11/2-3/31 [ECP] .... 1P: $43-$76 ..... 2P: $48-$139 .... XP: $5 ...... F18

ğŸ'ğŸ' 4/1-5/15 [ECP] .... 1P: $42-$75 ..... 2P: $47-$138 .... XP: $5 ...... F18

Phone: (608)372-9100

Small-scale Hotel **Location:** I-94, exit 143 (SR 21), just w. 2005 N Superior Ave 54660 (PO Box 169). **Fax:** 608/372-6003. **Facility:** 77 one-bedroom standard units, some with whirlpools. 2 stories (no elevator), interior/exterior corridors. **Parking:** on-site, winter plug-ins. **Amenities:** video library (fee). *Some:* hair dryers. **Pool(s):** small heated indoor. **Leisure Activities:** whirlpool. **Guest Services:** coin laundry. **Business Services:** fax (fee). **Cards:** AX, CB, DC, DS, JC, MC, VI.

SOME UNITS

(S⊘) (🛏) (¶†) (◿) (🛶) (♥) (DATA PORT) / (✕) (🖬) (🖾) (🖳) /

HOLIDAY INN

ğŸ'ğŸ'ğŸ' 5/23-9/30 .... 2P: $86-$88

4/1-5/22 & 10/1-3/31 .... 2P: $77-$79

Phone: 608/372-3211

Small-scale Hotel **Location:** I-94, exit 143 (SR 21), just e. 1017 E McCoy Blvd 54660 (PO Box 845). **Fax:** 608/372-3243. **Facility:** 100 one-bedroom standard units. 2 stories, interior corridors. **Parking:** on-site, winter plug-ins. **Amenities:** video games (fee), dual phone lines, voice mail, irons, hair dryers. **Pool(s):** heated indoor. **Leisure Activities:** sauna, whirlpool, exercise room. **Guest Services:** valet and coin laundry. **Business Services:** meeting rooms, fax (fee). **Cards:** AX, CB, DC, DS, JC, MC.

SOME UNITS

(🛏) (¶†) (Y) (🛶) (✕) (♥) (DATA PORT) (🖳) / (✕) (🖬) (🖾) /

LARK INN

AAA SAVE

◆◆◆ ◆◆◆
Motel

4/1-10/31 [ECP]	1P: $55-$79	2P: $61-$85	XP: $6	D12
11/1-3/31 [ECP]	1P: $49-$66	2P: $55-$72	XP: $6	D12

Phone: (608)372-5981

Location: I-94, exit 143 (SR 21), 1.5 mi s on US 12; I-90, exit 41, 2 mi n on US 12. 229 N Superior Ave 54660. **Fax:** 608/372-3009. **Facility:** 25 units. 22 one-bedroom standard units. 2 one- and 1 two-bedroom suites ($89-$119) with kitchens. 2 stories, interior/exterior corridors. *Bath:* combo or shower only. **Parking:** on-site, winter plug-ins. **Terms:** weekly rates available, package plans, pets ($6 extra charge). **Amenities:** dual phone lines, voice mail. *Fee:* video library, high-speed Internet. *Some:* irons, hair dryers. **Leisure Activities:** gazebo. **Guest Services:** coin laundry. **Business Services:** meeting rooms. **Cards:** AX, CB, DC, DS, MC, VI. **Special Amenities:** free continental breakfast and free room upgrade (subject to availability with advanced reservations). *(See color ad p 610)*

SOME UNITS

[S] [D] [🐾] [🍴] [VCR] [DATA PORT] [🖥] [📷] / [✕] [🖨] /

SUPER 8 MOTEL-TOMAH

◆◆◆ ◆◆◆
Small-scale Hotel

All Year [CP]	1P: $49-$90	2P: $49-$90	XP: $5	F12

Phone: (608)372-3901

Location: I-94, exit 143 (SR 21), just e. 1008 E McCoy Blvd 54660. **Fax:** 608/372-5792. **Facility:** 65 one-bedroom standard units, some with whirlpools. 2 stories, interior corridors. *Bath:* combo or shower only. **Parking:** on-site, winter plug-ins. **Terms:** pets ($10 deposit). **Guest Services:** coin laundry. **Business Services:** meeting rooms. **Cards:** AX, CB, DC, DS, MC, VI.

SOME UNITS

[ASK] [S] [D] [🐾] [🍴] [♿] [📷] [DATA PORT] / [✕] [🖨] [🖥] [📷] /

WHERE TO DINE

BURNSTAD'S EUROPEAN CAFE

AAA

◆◆◆ ◆◆◆
American

Lunch: $5-$7　　**Dinner:** $8-$14　　**Phone:** 608/372-4040

Location: I-90, exit 43 (SR 21), 1 mi n on US 12 and 16; in Burnstad's European Village. 701 E Clifton St 54660. **Hours:** 8 am-9 pm, Sun-8 pm. Closed: 1/1, 11/27, 12/25; also 12/24 for dinner. **Reservations:** accepted. **Features:** This casual restaurant is adjacent to a quaint gift shop. The menu offers steak, seafood, pork and chicken dishes such as Canadian walleye, Rosemary pork loin and cranberry bog chicken. Light appetite menu and some Italian entrees are available. The bread and desserts are made from scratch in-house. Casual dress; cocktails. **Parking:** on-site. **Cards:** AX, DC, DS, MC, VI.

[Y] [✕]

TOMAHAWK pop. 3,770

WHERE TO STAY

BEST WESTERN LAKE AIRE MOTEL

SAVE

◆◆ ◆◆
Motel

4/1-9/30 & 1/1-3/15 [CP]	1P: $64-$150	2P: $64-$150	XP: $10	F12
10/1-12/31 & 3/16-3/31 [CP]	1P: $60-$135	2P: $60-$135	XP: $10	F12

Phone: (715)453-5189

Location: 0.6 mi n of jct US 8. Located on Lake Nokomis. N 11925 Business Hwy 51 54487. **Fax:** 715/453-1428. **Facility:** 25 units. 24 one-bedroom standard units, some with efficiencies and/or whirlpools. 1 cottage. 2 stories (no elevator), exterior corridors. **Parking:** on-site, winter plug-ins. **Terms:** 2 night minimum stay - weekends. **Amenities:** irons, hair dryers. **Leisure Activities:** boat dock, fishing, horseshoes, volleyball. **Business Services:** fax (fee). **Cards:** AX, CB, DC, DS, MC, VI.

SOME UNITS

[S] [D] [✕] [📷] [DATA PORT] [🖥] [📷] [🖨] / [✕] /

SUPER 8 MOTEL-TOMAHAWK

◆◆◆◆ ◆◆◆◆
Small-scale Hotel

5/25-9/30 [ECP]	1P: $66-$85	2P: $73-$85	XP: $6	F17
4/1-5/24 [ECP]	1P: $63-$82	2P: $71-$82	XP: $6	F17
10/1-3/31 [ECP]	1P: $62-$82	2P: $69-$81	XP: $6	F17

Phone: 715/453-5210

Location: On US 51 business route, 0.6 mi n of downtown. 108 W Mohawk Dr 54487. **Fax:** 715/453-9700. **Facility:** 56 units. 54 one-bedroom standard units, some with whirlpools. 2 one-bedroom suites. 3 stories, interior corridors. *Bath:* combo or shower only. **Parking:** on-site, winter plug-ins. **Terms:** weekly rates available, pets ($25 deposit). **Amenities:** hair dryers. **Pool(s):** heated indoor. **Leisure Activities:** sauna, whirlpool. **Guest Services:** coin laundry. **Business Services:** meeting rooms, fax (fee). **Cards:** AX, CB, DS, MC, VI.

SOME UNITS

[ASK] [S] [D] [🐾] [🍴] [♿] [🏊] [📷] [DATA PORT] / [🖥] [📷] /

TREMPEALEAU pop. 1,319

WHERE TO STAY

PLEASANT KNOLL MOTEL

AAA SAVE

◆◆◆ ◆◆◆
Motel

All Year	2P: $55-$80	XP: $5	F12

Phone: 608/534-6615

Location: Center. 11451 Main St 54661. **Facility:** 16 one-bedroom standard units, some with kitchens (no utensils). 1-2 stories, exterior corridors. *Bath:* combo or shower only. **Parking:** on-site. **Terms:** 2 night minimum stay - weekends in summer. **Amenities:** dual phone lines. *Some:* hair dryers. **Leisure Activities:** whirlpool. **Guest Services:** area transportation-marina. **Cards:** AX, DS, MC, VI. **Special Amenities:** free local telephone calls and preferred room (subject to availability with advanced reservations).

SOME UNITS

[📷] [DATA PORT] [🖥] / [✕] [🖨] [📷] /

TURTLE LAKE pop. 1,065

WHERE TO STAY

COUNTRY INN & SUITES BY CARLSON

◆◆◆ ◆◆◆
Small-scale Hotel

5/24-3/31 [CP]	1P: $74-$105	2P: $74-$105	XP: $5	F18
4/1-5/23 [CP]	1P: $63-$88	2P: $63-$88	XP: $5	F18

Phone: (715)986-2070

Location: On US 8, 0.4 mi e of jct US 63 S. 636 Hwy 8 & 63 54889. **Fax:** 715/986-2824. **Facility:** 46 one-bedroom standard units. 2 stories, interior corridors. *Bath:* combo or shower only. **Parking:** on-site, winter plug-ins. **Amenities:** voice mail, irons, hair dryers. **Pool(s):** small heated indoor. **Leisure Activities:** whirlpool. **Guest Services:** coin laundry. **Business Services:** meeting rooms, fax (fee). **Cards:** AX, DC, DS, MC, VI. *(See color ad starting on p 556)*

SOME UNITS

[ASK] [S] [D] [♿] [🏊] [📷] [DATA PORT] [🖥] / [✕] [🖨] [📷] /

ST. CROIX CASINO HOTEL
        Phone: 715/986-4000

5/1-8/31 [ECP]	1P: $55-$67	2P: $61-$73	XP: $4	F12
4/1-4/30 & 9/1-3/31 [ECP]	1P: $50-$62	2P: $55-$67	XP: $4	F12

Small-scale Hotel
Location: On US 8, 0.4 mi e jct US 63 S. 631 Hwy 8 54889 (777 Hwy 8/63). **Fax:** 715/986-4040. **Facility:** 162 units. 154 one-bedroom standard units. 8 one-bedroom suites ($95-$150) with whirlpools. 3 stories, interior corridors. *Bath:* combo or shower only. **Parking:** on-site. **Terms:** package plans, $25 service charge. **Amenities:** video games, hair dryers. **Pool(s):** heated indoor. **Leisure Activities:** sauna, whirlpool, limited exercise equipment. **Guest Services:** area transportation. **Business Services:** meeting rooms, fax (fee). **Cards:** AX, DS, MC, VI.

SOME UNITS

TWO RIVERS pop. 12,639

——— WHERE TO STAY ———

LIGHTHOUSE INN ON THE LAKE
        Phone: (920)793-4524

6/1-10/31	1P: $84-$99	2P: $94-$109	XP: $10	F17
11/1-3/31	1P: $74-$89	2P: $84-$99	XP: $10	F17
4/1-5/31	1P: $70-$85	2P: $80-$95	XP: $10	F17

Small-scale Hotel
Location: 0.3 mi s on SR 42. Located on the shore of Lake Michigan. 1515 Memorial Dr 54241. **Fax:** 920/793-4524. **Facility:** 67 one-bedroom standard units. 2 stories (no elevator), interior corridors. **Parking:** on-site, winter plug-ins. *Some:* hair dryers. **Dining:** Waters Edge Restaurant, see separate listing. **Pool(s):** heated indoor. **Leisure Activities:** sauna, whirlpool, fishing, exercise room. **Guest Services:** coin laundry. **Business Services:** conference facilities. **Cards:** AX, DC, DS, MC, VI.

SOME UNITS
FEE

RED FOREST BED & BREAKFAST
        Phone: (920)793-1794

All Year [BP]	1P: $92	2P: $97	XP: $15

Bed & Breakfast
Location: Just n of SR 42 on Washington St. Located in a residential area. 1421 25th St 54241. **Fax:** 920/793-3056. **Facility:** This shingle-style 1907 home close to downtown and historical attractions features stained glass, a country dining room and heirloom antiques. Smoke free premises. 4 one-bedroom standard units. 2 stories (no elevator), interior corridors. *Bath:* combo or shower only. **Parking:** on-site. **Terms:** age restrictions may apply, 7 day cancellation notice-fee imposed, weekly rates available. **Amenities:** CD players. **Cards:** DS, MC, VI.

SOME UNITS

——— WHERE TO DINE ———

WATERS EDGE RESTAURANT
  Lunch: $5-$10   **Dinner:** $8-$22   **Phone:** 920/793-4524

American
Location: 0.3 mi s on SR 42; in Lighthouse Inn on the Lake. 1515 Memorial Dr 54241. **Hours:** 6:30 am-10 pm; to 9 pm off season, Sun from 7:30 am. **Reservations:** accepted. **Features:** The views of Lake Michigan are wonderful from this casual restaurant with a nautical theme. The well-seasoned staff is familiar to regular guests. Bread and soup are made daily in-house. Casual dress; cocktails. **Parking:** on-site. **Cards:** AX, CB, DC, MC, VI.

VERONA pop. 7,052

——— WHERE TO STAY ———

SUPER 8 MOTEL-MADISON/VERONA
        Phone: (608)848-7829

6/1-10/31	1P: $58-$99	2P: $64-$105	XP: $6	F18
4/1-5/31 & 11/1-3/31	1P: $54-$95	2P: $60-$101	XP: $6	F18

Small-scale Hotel
Location: US 18 and 151, exit 94 southbound; exit 89 northbound, just n. 131 Horizon Dr 53593. **Fax:** 608/848-7833. **Facility:** 43 units. 42 one-bedroom standard units, some with whirlpools. 1 one-bedroom suite. 2 stories, interior corridors. **Parking:** on-site, winter plug-ins. **Terms:** [CP] meal plan available, small pets only ($10 fee). **Amenities:** voice mail, safes. *Some:* hair dryers. **Pool(s):** small heated indoor. **Leisure Activities:** whirlpool, exercise room. **Business Services:** meeting rooms. **Cards:** AX, DC, DS, MC, VI.

SOME UNITS

VIROQUA pop. 4,335

——— WHERE TO STAY ———

HICKORY HILL MOTEL
        Phone: (608)637-3104

4/1-11/25	1P: $40-$55	2P: $45-$70	XP: $5	F10
11/26-3/31	1P: $30-$45	2P: $35-$50	XP: $3	F10

Motel
Location: 1.8 mi se on SR 14, 27 and 82. Located in a rural area. US 14 S 3955 54665 (PO Box 126). **Fax:** 608/637-8792. **Facility:** 25 one-bedroom standard units, some with efficiencies (no utensils). 1 story, exterior corridors. *Bath:* combo or shower only. **Parking:** on-site, winter plug-ins. **Terms:** weekly rates available, [ECP] meal plan available. **Amenities:** hair dryers. **Pool(s):** small heated outdoor. **Business Services:** fax. **Cards:** AX, DC, DS, MC, VI.

SOME UNITS

VIROQUA SUPER 8
        Phone: 608/637-3100

All Year	1P: $55-$150	XP: $5	F12

Small-scale Hotel
Location: 1 mi n of center on SR 14, 16 and 27. 1325 N Main St 54665. **Fax:** 608/637-7026. **Facility:** 50 units. 49 one-bedroom standard units, some with whirlpools. 1 two-bedroom suite. 2 stories, interior corridors. *Bath:* combo or shower only. **Parking:** on-site, winter plug-ins. **Terms:** check-in 4 pm. **Pool(s):** small heated indoor. **Leisure Activities:** whirlpool. **Guest Services:** coin laundry. **Business Services:** meeting rooms. **Cards:** AX, CB, DC, MC, VI.

SOME UNITS

WASHBURN pop. 2,280

─────── **WHERE TO DINE** ───────

STEAK PIT
AAA
◈◈◈
Steak & Seafood

Dinner: $8-$19   **Phone:** 715/373-5492
Location: Just e of SR 13. 125 Harborview Dr 54891. **Hours:** 5 pm-10 pm, Sun 4 pm-9 pm. Closed: 11/27, 12/24, 12/25. **Reservations:** suggested. **Features:** Set alongside Lake Superior with views of the marina. This restaurant is an older style steakhouse that offers a good variety of meat and freshwater fish. Service is unpretentious and friendly and the food is well-prepared. Cocktails. **Parking:** on-site. **Cards:** MC, VI.

&M Y X

WATERFORD pop. 4,048

─────── **WHERE TO STAY** ───────

─────── *The following lodging was either not evaluated or did not* ───────
meet AAA rating requirements but is listed for your information only.

BAYMONT INNS & SUITES-WATERFORD   **Phone:** 262/534-4100
[fyi]   All Year   1P: $74-$140   2P: $74-$140   XP: $10   F17
Small-scale Hotel   Too new to rate, opening scheduled for October 2002. **Location:** On SR 36, 1 mi s of jct SR 164. 750 Fox Ln 53185. Fax: 262/534-4101. **Amenities:** 52 units. **Cards:** AX, DC, DS, MC, VI.

WATERTOWN pop. 21,598

─────── **WHERE TO STAY** ───────

HOLIDAY INN EXPRESS   **Phone:** (920)262-1910
◈◈◈   6/1-8/31 [ECP]   1P: $72-$89
          9/1-10/31 [ECP]   1P: $72-$85
Small-scale Hotel   4/1-5/31 & 11/1-3/31 [ECP]   1P: $72-$82
Location: On SR 26, 1.5 mi s of jct SR 19. 101 Aviation Way 53094 (PO Box 481). Fax: 920/262-0557. **Facility:** 79 one-bedroom standard units, some with whirlpools. 2 stories (no elevator), interior corridors. *Bath:* combo or shower only. **Parking:** on-site, winter plug-ins. **Terms:** pets ($50 deposit). **Amenities:** voice mail, irons, hair dryers. *Some:* dual phone lines. **Pool(s):** small heated indoor. **Leisure Activities:** sauna, whirlpool, exercise room. **Guest Services:** valet and coin laundry. **Business Services:** meeting rooms, fax (fee). **Cards:** AX, CB, DC, DS, JC, MC, VI.

SOME UNITS

ASK SÒ 🐾 ⊤†⊦ 🚳 ➤ ✕ 🎦 DATA PORT / ✕ 🍴 ▤ ▥ /

SUPER 8 MOTEL   **Phone:** (920)261-1188
◈◈◈   All Year   1P: $63-$78   2P: $68-$83   XP: $5   F12
Small-scale Hotel   **Location:** On SR 26, 1.5 mi s of jct SR 19. 1730 S Church St 53094 (PO Box 503). Fax: 920/261-1188. **Facility:** 45 units. 44 one-bedroom standard units, some with whirlpools. 1 one-bedroom suite with whirlpool. 2 stories (no elevator), interior corridors. *Bath:* combo or shower only. **Parking:** on-site, winter plug-ins. **Terms:** [CP] meal plan available, pets ($50 deposit). **Pool(s):** small heated indoor. **Leisure Activities:** whirlpool. *Fee:* game room. **Business Services:** meeting rooms, fax. **Cards:** AX, CB, DC, DS, JC, MC, VI.

SOME UNITS

ASK SÒ 🐾 ⊤†⊦ ➤ 🎦 DATA PORT / ✕ 🍴 ▤ ▥ /

─────── **WHERE TO DINE** ───────

THE UPPER KRUST   **Lunch:** $5-$7   **Dinner:** $5-$7   **Phone:** 920/206-9202
◈◈◈   **Location:** Just se of jct SR 26 and 19. 210 S Water St 53094. **Hours:** 10 am-7 pm, Fri-8 pm, Sat 11 am-6 pm,
American   Sun 11 am-4 pm. Closed major holidays. **Reservations:** accepted. **Features:** In The Market in the Old Mill District, the popular restaurant has charming country decor. Homemade pies are the big draw, but don't overlook the scrumptious soups, salads and sandwiches made daily from fresh ingredients. Casual dress.
Parking: on-site. **Cards:** AX, DS, MC, VI.

X

WAUKESHA *—See Milwaukee p. 578.*

WAUNAKEE pop. 8,995

─────── **WHERE TO STAY** ───────

COUNTRY INN & SUITES BY CARLSON   **Phone:** (608)849-6900
AAA [SAVE]   All Year   1P: $71-$81   2P: $78-$88   XP: $8   F18
◈◈◈   **Location:** 0.8 mi e on SR 19 and 113. 904 E Main St 53597. Fax: 608/849-5994. **Facility:** 38 units. 37 one-
Small-scale Hotel   bedroom standard units, some with whirlpools. 1 one-bedroom suite ($94-$199) with whirlpool. 2 stories (no elevator), interior corridors. **Parking:** on-site, winter plug-ins. **Terms:** cancellation fee imposed, [ECP] meal plan available. **Amenities:** voice mail, irons, hair dryers. **Pool(s):** small heated indoor. **Leisure Activities:** whirlpool. **Guest Services:** coin laundry. **Business Services:** meeting rooms. **Cards:** AX, DC, DS, MC, VI. **Special Amenities:** free continental breakfast and free newspaper. *(See color ad starting on p 556)*

SOME UNITS

SÒ ⊤†⊦ ➤ DATA PORT ▥ / ✕ 🍴 ▤ /

WAUPACA pop. 5,676

------ WHERE TO STAY ------

BAYMONT INN & SUITES-WAUPACA

Phone: (715)258-9212

| (AAA) (SAVE) | 5/16-9/27 [ECP] | 1P: $82-$119 | 2P: $129 | XP: $10 | F17 |
| ▼▼▼▼ | 4/1-5/15 & 9/28-3/31 [ECP] | 1P: $75-$99 | 2P: $109 | XP: $10 | F17 |

Location: At jct US 10 and SR 54. 110 Grand Seasons Dr 54981 (PO Box 529). Fax: 715/258-0475. **Facility:** 88
units. 84 one-bedroom standard units, some with whirlpools. 4 one-bedroom suites ($109-$229) with whirl-
Small-scale Hotel pools. 3 stories, interior corridors. *Bath:* combo or shower only. **Parking:** on-site, winter plug-ins.
Terms: package plans - seasonal, small pets only ($50 deposit). **Amenities:** video games (fee), voice mail,
safes, irons, hair dryers. *Some:* dual phone lines. **Pool(s):** heated indoor. **Leisure Activities:** sauna, whirlpool. *Fee:* massage,
game room. **Guest Services:** complimentary evening beverages, valet and coin laundry. **Business Services:** meeting rooms,
fax (fee). **Cards:** AX, CB, DC, DS, MC, VI. **Special Amenities: free continental breakfast and free newspaper.**

SOME UNITS

[icons]

WAUPUN pop. 10,718

------ WHERE TO STAY ------

INN TOWN MOTEL

Phone: (920)324-4211

| ▼▼▼ | All Year | 1P: $38-$42 | 2P: $48-$52 | XP: $5 | F10 |

Motel **Location:** US 151, exit 146 (SR 49), 1.3 mi w. 27 S State St 53963. **Facility:** 16 one-bedroom standard units, some
with kitchens. 1 story, exterior corridors. **Parking:** on-site, winter plug-ins. **Terms:** small pets only ($6 extra
charge, in designated units). **Cards:** AX, DS, MC, VI.

SOME UNITS

[icons]

WAUSAU pop. 38,426

------ WHERE TO STAY ------

BAYMONT INN-WAUSAU

Phone: (715)842-0421

| (AAA) (SAVE) | All Year [ECP] | 1P: $59-$79 | 2P: $59-$79 |

▼▼ ▼▼ **Location:** I-39, exit 192, just e. 1910 Stewart Ave 54401. Fax: 715/845-5096. **Facility:** 95 one-bedroom standard
units. 2 stories (no elevator), interior corridors. **Parking:** on-site, winter plug-ins. **Terms:** small pets only.
Amenities: video games (fee), voice mail, irons, hair dryers. **Pool(s):** small heated indoor. **Leisure Activi-**
Small-scale Hotel **ties:** whirlpool. **Guest Services:** valet laundry. **Business Services:** fax (fee). **Cards:** AX, CB, DC, DS,
MC, VI. **Special Amenities: free continental breakfast and free newspaper.** *(See color ad below)*

SOME UNITS

[icons]

COURTYARD BY MARRIOTT

Phone: (715)849-2124

(SAVE) All Year 1P: $80-$110

▼▼▼ **Location:** I-39, exit 191 (Sherman St), just se. 1000 S 22nd Ave 54401. Fax: 715/849-2227. **Facility:** 84 units. 81
one-bedroom standard units, some with whirlpools. 3 one-bedroom suites ($89-$169). 3 stories, interior cor-
Small-scale Hotel ridors. *Bath:* combo or shower only. **Parking:** on-site, winter plug-ins. **Terms:** 7 day cancellation notice,
weekly rates available. **Amenities:** video games (fee), dual phone lines, voice mail, irons, hair dryers.
Pool(s): small heated indoor. **Leisure Activities:** whirlpool, exercise room. **Guest Services:** valet and coin
laundry. **Business Services:** meeting rooms, fax (fee). **Cards:** AX, DC, DS, JC, MC, VI.

SOME UNITS

[icons]

DAYS INN-WAUSAU

Phone: 715/355-5501

All Year   1P: $54-$130   2P: $59-$130   XP: $5   D12

Location: I-39, exit 188, just e. 4700 Rib Mountain Dr 54401. **Fax:** 715/355-0710. **Facility:** 50 one-bedroom standard units, some with whirlpools. 2 stories (no elevator), interior corridors. **Parking:** on-site, winter plug-ins. **Terms:** [CP] meal plan available, pets ($10 fee). **Amenities:** video library, high-speed Internet, dual phone lines, voice mail, safes (fee), hair dryers. *Some:* DVD players, irons. **Pool(s):** small heated indoor. **Leisure Activities:** whirlpool. *Fee:* game room. **Guest Services:** valet laundry. **Business Services:** meeting rooms, business center. **Cards:** AX, CB, DC, DS, JC, MC, VI. **Special Amenities:** free continental breakfast and free local telephone calls.

Small-scale Hotel

SOME UNITS

EXEL INN OF WAUSAU

Phone: (715)842-0641

6/1-8/31 [CP]   1P: $39-$60   2P: $45-$63   XP: $6   F18
4/1-5/31 & 9/1-3/31 [CP]   1P: $39-$51   2P: $45-$57   XP: $6   F18

Location: I-39, exit 192, just e. 116 S 17th Ave 54401. **Fax:** 715/848-1356. **Facility:** 122 one-bedroom standard units, some with efficiencies and/or whirlpools. 2 stories (no elevator), interior corridors. **Parking:** on-site, winter plug-ins. **Terms:** small pets only. **Amenities:** irons, hair dryers. **Leisure Activities:** exercise room. **Guest Services:** valet and coin laundry. **Business Services:** fax (fee). **Cards:** AX, CB, DC, DS, MC, VI. **Special Amenities:** early check-in/late check-out and free continental breakfast. *(See color ad p 465)*

Motel

SOME UNITS

HAMPTON INN

Phone: (715)848-9700

10/18-3/31   1P: $69-$79   2P: $79-$84
5/23-10/17   1P: $64-$79   2P: $79-$84
4/1-5/22   1P: $64-$79   2P: $74-$79

Location: I-39, exit 191 (Sherman St), just n on east frontage road. 615 S 24th Ave 54401. **Fax:** 715/848-7299. **Facility:** 89 one-bedroom standard units, some with whirlpools. 3 stories, interior corridors. *Bath:* combo or shower only. **Parking:** on-site. **Terms:** weekly rates available, [CP] meal plan available. **Amenities:** dual phone lines, voice mail, irons. *Some:* DVD players. **Pool(s):** small heated indoor. **Leisure Activities:** whirlpool, limited exercise equipment. **Guest Services:** valet and coin laundry. **Business Services:** meeting rooms, business center. **Cards:** AX, DC, DS, MC, VI. **Special Amenities:** free continental breakfast and free local telephone calls.

Small-scale Hotel

SOME UNITS

PLAZA HOTEL & SUITES

Phone: (715)845-4341

All Year [CP]   1P: $70-$100   2P: $70-$100   XP: $10   F18

Location: I-39, exit 193, just e. 201 N 17th Ave 54401. **Fax:** 715/845-4990. **Facility:** 230 units. 219 one-bedroom standard units, some with whirlpools. 11 one-bedroom suites ($129-$199) with whirlpools. 6 stories, interior corridors. **Parking:** on-site, winter plug-ins. **Terms:** weekly rates available, [AP], [BP], [ECP] & [MAP] meal plans available, pets ($25 extra charge). **Amenities:** video games (fee), dual phone lines, voice mail, irons, hair dryers. **Pool(s):** heated indoor, wading. **Leisure Activities:** saunas, whirlpools, exercise room. *Fee:* game room. **Guest Services:** gift shop, valet and coin laundry. **Business Services:** conference facilities, fax (fee). **Cards:** AX, CB, DC, DS, JC, MC, VI.

Small-scale Hotel

SOME UNITS

RIB MOUNTAIN INN

Phone: 715/848-2802

All Year [BP]   1P: $69   2P: $69   XP: $10   F12

Location: I-39, exit 190 (CR NN), 1 mi w. 2900 Rib Mountain Way 54401. **Fax:** 715/848-1908. **Facility:** 24 units. 18 one-bedroom standard units, some with kitchens and/or whirlpools. 4 two- and 2 three-bedroom suites ($249-$269) with kitchens, some with whirlpools. 2-3 stories, interior/exterior corridors. **Parking:** on-site. **Terms:** 2 night minimum stay - winter, cancellation fee imposed, pets ($10 extra charge). **Amenities:** video library, voice mail, irons, hair dryers. **Leisure Activities:** sauna, whirlpool, downhill & cross country skiing, snowmobiling, bicycles, hiking trails. **Guest Services:** coin laundry. **Business Services:** fax. **Cards:** AX, CB, DC, DS, MC, VI.

Small-scale Hotel

ROSENBERRY INN

Phone: 715/842-5733

All Year [BP]   1P: $55-$160   2P: $70-$160   XP: $15

Location: Just n on SR 52, then just w. 511 Franklin 54403. **Fax:** 715/843-5659. **Facility:** Smoke free premises. 8 one-bedroom standard units, some with whirlpools. 2 stories (no elevator), interior/exterior corridors. *Bath:* combo or shower only. **Parking:** on-site. **Terms:** 10 day cancellation notice. **Amenities:** video library. **Business Services:** fax. **Cards:** MC, VI.

Historic Bed & Breakfast

SOME UNITS

SUPER 8 MOTEL

Phone: (715)848-2888

All Year   1P: $51-$64   2P: $58-$69

Location: I-39, exit 192, just e. 2006 Stewart Ave W 54401. **Fax:** 715/842-9578. **Facility:** 88 one-bedroom standard units. 2 stories (no elevator), interior corridors. *Bath:* combo or shower only. **Parking:** on-site, winter plug-ins. **Terms:** weekly rates available, [CP] meal plan available, small pets only ($5 extra charge). **Pool(s):** small heated indoor. **Leisure Activities:** whirlpool. **Business Services:** fax. **Cards:** AX, DC, DS, MC, VI. **Special Amenities:** free continental breakfast and free local telephone calls.

Small-scale Hotel

SOME UNITS

WHERE TO DINE

CARMELO'S

Phone: 715/845-5570

Dinner: $9-$17

Location: I-39, exit 190, 0.9 mi w. 3607 N Mountain Rd 54401. **Hours:** 5 pm-10 pm, Sun & Mon-9 pm. Closed major holidays. **Reservations:** accepted. **Features:** Convenient to a ski area and golf course, the lively restaurant offers food that is homemade and tasty. Servers are friendly and reliable. Casual dress; cocktails. **Parking:** on-site. **Cards:** AX, DS, MC, VI.

Italian

HEREFORD & HOPS
▼▼ ▼▼
American

Lunch: $6-$16   **Dinner:** $6-$16   **Phone:** 715/849-3700
Location: I-39, exit 191 (US 51), just se. 2305 Sherman St 54401. **Hours:** 11 am-10 pm, Sun-9 pm.
Reservations: accepted. **Features:** Diners can grill their own steak, create their own pizza or build their own sandwich while enjoying specialty beers that are brewed on the premises. The friendly staff helps guests become pros at the grills. Casual dress; cocktails. **Parking:** on-site. **Cards:** AX, DC, DS, MC, VI.

MICHAEL'S
▼▼ ▼▼
American
DS, MC, VI.

Dinner: $10-$20   **Phone:** 715/842-9856
Location: I-39, exit 190 (CR NN), 0.5 mi se. 2901 Rib Mountain Dr 54401. **Hours:** 5 pm-10 pm. Closed major holidays; also Sun. **Reservations:** accepted. **Features:** Fresh seafood, veal specialties and gourmet pizza highlight the menu. Friday night fish fry is popular. The chef is happy to accommodate special requests. Desserts are presented tableside on a tray. Casual dress; cocktails. **Parking:** on-site. **Cards:** AX, CB, DC,

MINO'S CUCINA ITALIANA
▼▼ ▼▼
Italian

Dinner: $11-$18   **Phone:** 715/675-5939
Location: On CR W, 1.3 mi n of jct SR 52 E, on east side of Wisconsin River. 900 Golf Club Rd 54401. **Hours:** 5 pm-10 pm. Closed major holidays; also Sun. **Reservations:** accepted. **Features:** Patrons can choose from classic dishes or the chef's creations. Seafood, pasta and pizza are popular. The tiramisu, which is made in house, is delicious. Casual dress; cocktails. **Parking:** on-site.

PS 2510 RESTAURANT
▼▼ ▼▼
American

Lunch: $5-$7   **Dinner:** $6-$20   **Phone:** 715/845-2510
Location: I-39, exit 192, 0.3 mi w. 2510 Stewart Ave 54401. **Hours:** 11 am-10 pm, Sun-9 pm. Closed: 11/27, 12/25. **Features:** This well-established restaurant is locally popular. The menu is vast and varied, and there is a deli and bakery attached. While reservations are not accepted, call-ahead seating is available. Casual dress; cocktails. **Parking:** on-site. **Cards:** AX, DC, DS, MC, VI.

WAUTOMA pop. 1,998

——— WHERE TO STAY ———

AMERICINN
▼▼ ▼▼
Small-scale Hotel

				Phone: (920)787-5050	
10/1-3/31	1P: $52-$83	2P: $58-$77	XP: $6	F12
4/1-9/30	1P: $58-$77	2P: $64-$70	XP: $6	F12

Location: 1.2 mi e on SR 21/73. W7696 SR 21/73 54982 (PO Box 644). **Fax:** 920/787-5911. **Facility:** 50 units. 34 one-bedroom standard units. 16 one-bedroom suites, some with efficiencies (no utensils) and/or whirlpools. 2 stories (no elevator), interior corridors. **Bath:** combo or shower only. **Parking:** on-site. **Terms:** pets ($25 deposit). **Amenities:** hair dryers. **Pool(s):** heated indoor. **Leisure Activities:** whirlpool. **Guest Services:** coin laundry. **Fee:** tanning facility. **Business Services:** meeting rooms.

SOME UNITS

SUPER 8 MOTEL-WAUTOMA
▼▼ ▼▼
Small-scale Hotel

				Phone: 920/787-4811	
4/1-9/27	1P: $58	2P: $63	XP: $6	F12
9/28-3/31	1P: $52	2P: $57	XP: $6	F12

Location: 1.5 mi e on SR 21 and 73. W7607 State Rd 21 and 73 54982 (PO Box 578). **Fax:** 920/787-4305. **Facility:** 51 units. 50 one-bedroom standard units. 1 one-bedroom suite. 2 stories (no elevator), interior corridors. **Parking:** on-site, winter plug-ins. **Terms:** pets ($25 deposit). **Pool(s):** heated indoor. **Leisure Activities:** sauna, whirlpool. **Guest Services:** coin laundry. **Business Services:** meeting rooms.

SOME UNITS

WAUWATOSA —See Milwaukee p. 579.

WEST BEND —See Milwaukee p. 580.

WESTBY pop. 2,045

——— WHERE TO DINE ———

OLD TOWNE INN
AAA
▼▼ ▼▼
American

Dinner: $7-$15   **Phone:** 608/634-3991
Location: 0.5 mi s on US 14. 101 E Old Town Rd 54667. **Hours:** 5 pm-9 pm, Fri & Sat-10 pm. Closed major holidays; also 12/24 & Mon. **Reservations:** suggested. **Features:** Enjoy casual, quiet dining in the contemporary country restaurant. Steak and seafood make up the bulk of a menu of tried-and-true favorites. Succulent prime rib is the special on Wednesday and on weekends. Sample Mexican fare on Tuesdays. Casual dress; cocktails. **Parking:** on-site. **Cards:** MC, VI.

WESTFIELD pop. 1,217

——— WHERE TO STAY ———

WESTFIELD PIONEER MOTOR INN
▼▼ ▼▼
Small-scale Hotel

				Phone: 608/296-2135	
4/1-9/30 [CP]	1P: $40-$88	2P: $45-$92	XP: $5	F12
10/1-3/31 [CP]	1P: $40-$83	2P: $45-$88	XP: $5	F12

Location: I-39, exit 113 (CR J and E), just nw. 242 N Pioneer Rd 53964 (PO Box 97). **Fax:** 608/296-3933. **Facility:** 30 one-bedroom standard units, some with whirlpools. 2 stories, interior corridors. **Parking:** on-site, winter plug-ins. **Terms:** [CP] meal plan available. **Amenities:** hair dryers. **Some:** dual phone lines. **Business Services:** meeting rooms. **Cards:** AX, DS, MC, VI.

SOME UNITS

FEE

WEST SALEM pop. 4,540

——— WHERE TO STAY ———

AMERICINN
▽▽▽▽
Small-scale Hotel

All Year   1P: $79-$139   2P: $87-$147
Phone: (608)786-3340
XP: $6   F16
Location: I-90, exit 12, just sw on CR C. 125 Buol Rd 54669. Fax: 608/786-3340. **Facility:** 50 units. 48 one-bedroom standard units, some with whirlpools. 2 one-bedroom suites with whirlpools. 2 stories, interior corridors. **Bath:** combo or shower only. **Parking:** on-site, winter plug-ins. **Terms:** [ECP] meal plan available. **Pool(s):** heated indoor. **Leisure Activities:** sauna, whirlpool. **Guest Services:** valet and coin laundry. **Business Services:** meeting rooms. **Cards:** AX, CB, DC, DS, MC, VI.

SOME UNITS
(ASK) (SD) (⌂) (♿) (⚓) (DATA PORT) (▭) / (✕) (🍴) (🖥) /

WHITEFISH BAY —See Milwaukee p. 580.

WHITEWATER pop. 13,437

——— WHERE TO STAY ———

AMERIHOST INN & SUITES
▽▽▽ ◆
Small-scale Hotel

All Year   1P: $74   2P: $79
Phone: (262)472-9400
XP: $10   F17
Location: On US 12, 0.5 mi w of jct SR 59 W. 1355 W Main St 53190. Fax: 262/472-9404. **Facility:** 61 one-bedroom standard units, some with whirlpools. 2 stories (no elevator), interior corridors. **Bath:** combo or shower only. **Parking:** on-site. **Terms:** package plans, pets ($10 fee, $10 deposit). **Amenities:** voice mail, safes (fee), irons, hair dryers. **Pool(s):** small heated indoor. **Leisure Activities:** sauna, whirlpool, exercise room. **Guest Services:** valet laundry. **Business Services:** meeting rooms. **Cards:** AX, CB, DC, DS, MC, VI.

SOME UNITS
(ASK) (SD) (⌂) (🍴) (♿M) (♿) (☎) (⚓) (✕) (🎥) (DATA PORT) (▭) / (✕) (🍴) (🖥) /

SUPER 8 MOTEL
▽▽ ▽▽
Small-scale Hotel

4/1-10/31 [CP]   1P: $53   2P: $59
11/1-3/31 [CP]   1P: $49   2P: $55
Phone: 262/473-8818
XP: $5   F12
XP: $5   F12
Location: On US 12, just e of jct SR 59 E. 917 E Milwaukee St 53190. Fax: 262/473-0688. **Facility:** 50 one-bedroom standard units, some with whirlpools. 2 stories, interior corridors. **Parking:** on-site, winter plug-ins. **Terms:** 2-3 night minimum stay - seasonal, cancellation fee imposed, weekly rates available, pets ($10 deposit). **Amenities:** safes (fee), hair dryers. **Leisure Activities:** whirlpool. **Business Services:** meeting rooms. **Cards:** AX, CB, DC, DS, MC, VI.

SOME UNITS
(ASK) (SD) (⌂) (🍴) (♿M) (🎥) (DATA PORT) / (✕) (VCR) (🖥) /
FEE

——— WHERE TO DINE ———

RANDY'S FUN HUNTERS BREWERY & RESTAURANT   **Lunch:** $6-$10   **Dinner:** $11-$18   **Phone:** 262/473-8000
▽▽▽
American
Location: On US 12, just e of jct SR 59 E. 841 E Milwaukee St 53190. **Hours:** 11 am-10 pm, Fri-10:30 pm, Sun 10:30 am-9 pm. Closed: 11/27, 12/25; also Mon & 12/24 for dinner. **Reservations:** suggested; except Fri. **Features:** Visitors can watch the brewing operation from the bar area of this laid-back restaurant. On the varied menu are such entrees as barbecue baby back ribs, sandwiches, burgers and salads. Tasty beverages include microbrewed beers and homemade root beer and cream soda. Historic area photographs adorn the walls. Casual dress; cocktails. **Parking:** on-site. **Cards:** DS, MC, VI.

(🍸) (✕)

WILSON

——— WHERE TO DINE ———

GINA'S PIES ARE SQUARE   **Lunch:** $4-$6   **Dinner:** $4-$6   **Phone:** 608/435-6541
▽▽
American
Location: SR 71, just s. 400 Main St 54670. **Hours:** 10 am-7 pm, Fri & Sat-8 pm; Sun-Thurs 10 am-3 pm 11/1-3/31. Closed major holidays. **Features:** Nestled along the Elroy-Sparta bike trail, the restaurant is legendary among bikers for its delicious square pies. Using a variety of wonderful, seasonal fruits, Gina bakes about 30 pies a day to keep up with demand. The menu also features tasty homemade sandwiches and pizzas that are so tempting it's almost hard to save room for dessert. Casual dress; beer & wine only. **Parking:** street. **Cards:** AX, DS, MC, VI.

(✕)

WINDSOR pop. 2,533

——— WHERE TO STAY ———

DAYS INN
(AAA) (SAVE)
▽▽▽▽
Small-scale Hotel

6/1-10/4   1P: $62-$82   2P: $67-$87
4/1-5/31   1P: $53-$73   2P: $56-$76
10/5-12/31   1P: $50-$60   2P: $56-$66
1/1-3/31   1P: $49-$59   2P: $55-$65
Phone: 608/846-7473
XP: $6   F17
XP: $6   F17
XP: $6   F17
XP: $6   F17
Location: I-90/94, exit 131 (SR 19). 6311 Rostad Circle 53598. Fax: 608/846-7473. **Facility:** 54 units. 53 one-bedroom standard units, some with whirlpools. 1 one-bedroom suite ($96-$120). 3 stories, interior corridors. **Bath:** combo or shower only. **Parking:** on-site, winter plug-ins. **Terms:** [CP] & [ECP] meal plans available, pets ($50 deposit). **Amenities:** voice mail, hair dryers. Some: irons. **Pool(s):** small heated indoor. **Leisure Activities:** sauna, whirlpool, exercise room. **Guest Services:** coin laundry. **Business Services:** meeting rooms, fax. **Cards:** AX, CB, DC, DS, JC, MC, VI. **Special Amenities:** free continental breakfast and free local telephone calls. (See color ad p 525)

SOME UNITS
(SD) (⌂) (🍴) (♿) (⚓) (✕) (🎥) (DATA PORT) / (✕) (🖥) (▭) /

SUPER 8 MOTEL-WINDSOR/NORTH MADISON
All Year   1P: $50-$60   2P: $54-$78   XP: $4   **Phone:** (608)846-3971   F
Location: I-90/94, exit 131 (SR 19). 4506 Lake Circle 53598. Fax: 608/846-9061. **Facility:** 55 one-bedroom standard units. 2 stories (no elevator), interior corridors. **Parking:** on-site, winter plug-ins. **Terms:** weekly rates available, small pets only ($10 extra charge, $20 deposit). **Amenities:** Some: irons, hair dryers. **Guest Services:** coin laundry. **Cards:** AX, DC, MC, VI.

Small-scale Hotel

SOME UNITS

WISCONSIN DELLS pop. 2,418

———— WHERE TO STAY ————

ALAKAI HOTEL & SUITES
			Phone: (608)253-3803
6/20-9/1	1P: $98-$125	2P: $110-$145	XP: $10
5/23-6/19	1P: $68-$88	2P: $78-$98	XP: $10
4/1-5/22 & 9/2-3/31	1P: $58-$78	2P: $68-$88	XP: $10

Small-scale Hotel **Facility:** 87 units. 83 one-bedroom standard units. 4 one-bedroom suites ($128-$198). 3 stories, interior corridors. **Parking:** on-site. **Terms:** 2 night minimum stay - 7/1-8/31 weekends, 3 day cancellation notice-fee imposed. **Amenities:** Some: hair dryers. **Pool(s):** small heated outdoor, heated indoor, wading. **Leisure Activities:** sauna, whirlpool. Fee: game room. **Guest Services:** coin laundry. **Cards:** AX, DC, MC, VI. **Special Amenities:** free newspaper and preferred room (subject to availability with advanced reservations).

SOME UNITS

BAKER'S SUNSET BAY RESORT
			Phone: 608/254-8406
7/3-9/1	1P: $122-$225	2P: $122-$225	
6/13-7/2	1P: $82-$170	2P: $82-$170	
4/1-6/12 & 9/2-3/31	1P: $54-$130	2P: $54-$130	

Location: I-90/94, exit 92 (US 12), 0.5 mi w, right on E Adams St, right on Canyon Rd, then 0.8 mi on left. 921 Canyon Small-scale Hotel Rd 53965. Fax: 608/253-2062. **Facility:** 70 units. 47 one-bedroom standard units, some with efficiencies. 19 one- and 4 two-bedroom suites, some with efficiencies, kitchens and/or whirlpools. 1-3 stories. interior/exterior corridors. Bath: combo or shower only. **Parking:** on-site. **Terms:** 1-3 night minimum stay - seasonal, 14 day cancellation notice-fee imposed, weekly rates available, package plans, pets (with prior approval, off season). **Pool(s):** heated outdoor, small heated indoor, wading. **Leisure Activities:** whirlpool, boating, fishing, pontoon rentals, bonfires, yard games, charcoal grills, playground, horseshoes, volleyball. Fee: rowboats. **Guest Services:** coin laundry. Fee: tanning facility. **Business Services:** meeting rooms. **Cards:** DS, MC, VI. **Special Amenities:** early check-in/late check-out and free local telephone calls.

SOME UNITS

BEST WESTERN AMBASSADOR INN AND SUITES
All Year   1P: $68-$278   2P: $68-$278   **Phone:** 608/254-4477
Location: I-90/94, exit 87 (SR 13), just e. 610 Frontage Rd S 53965. Fax: 608/253-6662. **Facility:** 181 units. 167 one-bedroom standard units, some with whirlpools. 12 one- and 2 two-bedroom suites, some with kitchens. 3 stories, interior corridors. **Parking:** on-site, winter plug-ins. **Terms:** check-in 4 pm, 3 day cancellation Small-scale Hotel notice-fee imposed. **Amenities:** irons, hair dryers. **Pool(s):** heated outdoor, heated indoor, wading. **Leisure Activities:** sauna, whirlpools, playground. Fee: game room. **Guest Services:** gift shop, coin laundry. **Business Services:** meeting rooms. **Cards:** AX, DC, DS, MC, VI. (See color ad p 620)

SOME UNITS
FEE

BLACK HAWK MOTEL

Phone: 608/254-7770

6/27-8/23	1P: $55-$135	2P: $55-$135	XP: $5
5/23-6/26	1P: $45-$120	2P: $45-$120	XP: $5
4/1-5/22 & 8/24-10/26	1P: $35-$95	2P: $35-$95	XP: $5

Motel

Location: I-90/94, exit 87, 2 mi e on SR 13, 16 and 23. 720 Race St 53965 (PO Box 15A). Fax: 608/253-7333. **Facility:** 75 units. 68 one- and 7 two-bedroom standard units, some with kitchens and/or whirlpools. 1-2 stories (no elevator), exterior corridors. **Parking:** on-site. **Terms:** open 4/1-10/26, 3 day cancellation notice-fee imposed, small pets only ($5 deposit). **Amenities:** *Some:* hair dryers. **Pool(s):** heated outdoor, heated indoor, wading. **Leisure Activities:** saunas, whirlpools, waterslide, playground. *Fee:* game room. **Guest Services:** coin laundry, area transportation-bus/train depot. **Cards:** AX, CB, DC, DS, MC, VI. **Special Amenities:** early check-in/late check-out and preferred room (subject to availability with advanced reservations). *(See color ad p 620)*

BRIDGE VIEW MOTEL

Phone: (608)254-6114

	1P	2P	XP
6/21-8/24	1P: $55-$75	2P: $69-$99	XP: $10
8/25-9/21	1P: $45-$65	2P: $69-$89	XP: $10
5/1-6/20	1P: $35-$45	2P: $49-$69	XP: $10
9/22-10/31	1P: $35-$45	2P: $49-$60	XP: $10

Motel

Location: Just n of SR 13 (Broadway); center. 1020 River Rd 53965. Fax: 608/254-6114. **Facility:** 17 one-bedroom standard units, some with efficiencies. 2 stories, exterior corridors. *Bath:* combo or shower only. **Parking:** on-site. **Terms:** open 5/1-10/31, 2 night minimum stay - weekends, 3 day cancellation notice-fee imposed, pets ($10 extra charge, with prior approval). **Amenities:** hair dryers. **Pool(s):** heated outdoor. **Leisure Activities:** waterslide, playground. **Cards:** DS, MC, VI.

SOME UNITS

[A$K] [icons] / [X][icon][icon] / FEE

CHIPPEWA MOTEL

Phone: 608/253-3982

	1P	2P	XP
6/21-9/7	1P: $75-$210	2P: $78-$230	XP: $7
4/1-6/20 & 9/8-3/31	1P: $35-$165	2P: $38-$170	XP: $7

(AAA) [SAVE]

Motel

Location: 0.5 mi e on SR 13. 1114 E Broadway 53965. Fax: 608/254-2577. **Facility:** 50 units. 42 one-bedroom standard units, some with whirlpools. 8 one-bedroom suites ($75-$230). 2 stories, interior/exterior corridors. **Parking:** on-site. **Terms:** 3 day cancellation notice-fee imposed. **Pool(s):** heated outdoor, heated indoor, wading. **Leisure Activities:** sauna, whirlpool. **Guest Services:** coin laundry, area transportation-bus/train depot. **Cards:** AX, DC, DS, MC, VI. **Special Amenities:** free local telephone calls.

SOME UNITS

[S][D] [icons] / [X][icon][icon] /

CHULA VISTA THEME RESORT

Phone: 608/254-8366

	2P	XP
6/27-8/31	2P: $149-$309	XP: $8
4/1-6/26 & 9/1-11/1	2P: $119-$309	XP: $8
11/2-3/31	2P: $89-$229	XP: $8

(AAA) [SAVE]

Resort
Large-scale Hotel

Location: 3 mi n. 4031 N River Rd 53965 (PO Box 30). Fax: 608/254-7653. **Facility:** On the Upper Dells of the Wisconsin River, this family-oriented resort offers several restaurants, a 350-foot waterslide and a variety of unit types. 291 units. 263 one-bedroom standard units, some with whirlpools. 28 one-bedroom suites. 2-7 stories, interior/exterior corridors. *Bath:* combo or shower only. **Parking:** on-site. **Terms:** check-in 4 pm, 2 night minimum stay - with Saturday stayover 6/1-8/31, 3 day cancellation notice-fee imposed. **Amenities:** video games (fee), voice mail. *Some:* high-speed Internet, irons, hair dryers. **Dining:** 4 restaurants, 7 am-10 pm, cocktails. **Pool(s):** heated outdoor, heated indoor. **Leisure Activities:** sauna, whirlpools, waterslide, childrens' activity pool, recreation programs, badminton, bonfires, hayrides, entertainment, hiking trails, playground, basketball, horseshoes, volleyball. *Fee:* miniature golf, game room. **Guest Services:** gift shop, coin laundry. **Business Services:** meeting rooms, business center. **Cards:** AX, CB, DC, DS, MC, VI. **Special Amenities:** free newspaper. *(See color ad below)*

SOME UNITS

[S][D] [icons] / [X][VCR] /

COMFORT INN

Small-scale Hotel

5/23-8/31 [ECP]   1P: $70-$160   2P: $70-$160   Phone: (608)253-3711
4/1-5/22 & 9/1-3/31 [ECP]   1P: $50-$130   2P: $50-$130   XP: $10   F18
                                                                          XP: $10   F18
Location: I-90/94, exit 87 (SR 13), just e. 703 N Frontage Rd 53965 (PO Box 330). Fax: 608/254-2164. **Facility:** 75 one-bedroom standard units, some with whirlpools. 3 stories, interior corridors. *Bath:* combo or shower only. **Parking:** on-site, winter plug-ins. **Terms:** check-in 4 pm, 2 night minimum stay - weekends. **Amenities:** hair dryers. *Some:* irons. **Pool(s):** small heated indoor. **Leisure Activities:** whirlpool, sun deck in season. **Cards:** AX, CB, DC, DS, JC, MC, VI. **Special Amenities:** free continental breakfast and free local telephone calls. *(See color ad below)*

SOME UNITS

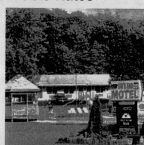

DAY'S END MOTEL

Phone: 608-254-8171

6/20-9/1	1P: $55-$114	2P: $55-$114	XP: $6
5/23-6/19	1P: $41-$88	2P: $41-$88	XP: $6
4/1-5/22 & 9/2-3/31	1P: $34-$76	2P: $34-$76	XP: $6

Motel

Location: I-90/94, exit 85 (US 12), 0.8 mi nw. N 604 Hwy 12-16 53965. **Facility:** 28 units. 27 one-bedroom standard units, some with whirlpools. 1 one-bedroom suite ($98-$172) with whirlpool. 1 story, exterior corridors. *Bath:* combo or shower only. **Parking:** on-site, winter plug-ins. **Terms:** 3 day cancellation notice-fee imposed, pets ($7 extra charge, with prior approval). **Pool(s):** heated outdoor. **Leisure Activities:** waterslide, miniature golf, playground. **Cards:** AX, DC, DS, MC, VI. **Special Amenities:** early check-in/late check-out and preferred room (subject to availability with advanced reservations). Affiliated with Best Value Inn Brand Membership. *(See ad p 622)*

SOME UNITS

THE GABLES MOTEL

Phone: 608/253-3831

6/21-8/18	1P: $69-$99	2P: $69-$99	XP: $5
8/19-9/22	1P: $45-$69	2P: $45-$69	XP: $5
4/1-6/20	1P: $35-$69	2P: $35-$69	XP: $5
9/23-3/31	1P: $35-$45	2P: $35-$50	XP: $5

Motel

Location: Just n of Broadway, US 16, SR 13 and 23; downtown. 822 Oak St 53965. **Facility:** 30 one-bedroom standard units. 2 stories, exterior corridors. **Parking:** on-site, winter plug-ins. **Pool(s):** heated outdoor. **Special Amenities:** free local telephone calls. *(See color ad below)*

SOME UNITS

Stop! Savings Ahead

When you see the red SAVE icon next to lodging listings in this book, you know these establishments offer great room rates to AAA members!

So, as you're turning the pages, remember to stop when you see SAVE. **It's your guarantee of savings.**

GREAT WOLF LODGE

AAA **SAVE**

Large-scale Hotel

All Year   1P: $159-$369   **Phone:** (608)253-2222

Location: I-90/94, exit 92 (US 12). 1400 Great Wolf Dr 53965 (PO Box 50). Fax: 608/253-2224. **Facility:** Designated smoking area. 309 units. 296 one-bedroom standard units, some with whirlpools. 13 one-bedroom suites. 3-4 stories, interior corridors. *Bath:* combo or shower only. **Parking:** on-site. **Terms:** check-in 4 pm, cancellation fee imposed, package plans. **Amenities:** voice mail, hair dryers. *Fee:* video games, high-speed Internet. **Dining:** 2 restaurants, 7 am-11 pm, cocktails. **Pool(s):** heated outdoor, heated indoor, wading. **Leisure Activities:** whirlpools, waterslide, extensive indoor/outdoor water park facilities with lazy river, exercise room, spa. *Fee:* game room. **Guest Services:** gift shop, coin laundry, area transportation-train depot. **Business Services:** conference facilities. **Cards:** AX, DC, DS, MC, VI. **Special Amenities:** free local telephone calls. *(See color ad below)*

HOWARD JOHNSON HOTEL AND ANTIQUA BAY WATERPARK

Phone: (608)254-8306

6/13-9/1	1P: $77-$169	2P: $77-$169	XP: $8 F18
9/2-3/31	1P: $77-$149	2P: $77-$149	XP: $8 F18
4/1-6/12	1P: $77-$119	2P: $77-$119	XP: $8 F18

Small-scale Hotel

Location: I-90/94, exit 87 (SR 13), just e. 655 Frontage Rd 53965 (PO Box 236). **Fax:** 608/253-2829. **Facility:** 229 one-bedroom standard units. 2 stories, interior corridors. **Parking:** on-site, winter plug-ins. **Terms:** check-in 4 pm, cancellation fee imposed, pets ($10 extra charge). **Amenities:** voice mail, irons, hair dryers. **Dining:** 7 am-10 pm, cocktails. **Pool(s):** 3 heated outdoor, 2 heated indoor, wading. **Leisure Activities:** sauna, whirlpools, waterslide, domed recreation area, exercise room. *Fee:* game room. **Guest Services:** gift shop, valet and coin laundry. **Business Services:** meeting rooms. **Cards:** AX, CB, DC, DS, JC, MC, VI. **Special Amenities:** preferred room (subject to availability with advanced reservations). *(See color ad below & p 560)*

SOME UNITS

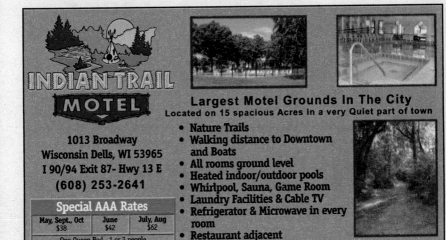

INDIAN TRAIL MOTEL

Phone: 608/253-2641

6/22-9/2	1P: $45-$150	2P: $45-$150	XP: $10 F12
5/23-6/21	1P: $35-$100	2P: $40-$100	XP: $10 F12
5/1-5/22	1P: $35-$90	2P: $40-$90	XP: $10 F12
9/3-10/20	1P: $35-$90	2P: $35-$90	XP: $10 F12

Motel

Location: 0.5 mi e on SR 13, 16 and 23. 1013 Broadway 53965. Fax: 608/253-3521. **Facility:** 46 one-bedroom standard units, some with whirlpools. 1 story, exterior corridors. *Bath:* combo or shower only. **Parking:** on-site. **Terms:** open 5/1-10/20, 3 day cancellation notice-fee imposed. **Pool(s):** heated outdoor, heated indoor. **Leisure Activities:** sauna, whirlpool, recreation programs, playground. *Fee:* game room. **Guest Services:** coin laundry. **Cards:** AX, DS, MC, VI. **Special Amenities:** early check-in/late check-out and free local telephone calls. *(See color ad p 625)*

SOME UNITS

KALAHARI

Phone: 608/254-5466

All Year	1P: $109-$279	2P: $109-$279	XP: $15 F

Resort
Large-scale Hotel

Location: I-90/94, exit 92 (US 12). 1305 Kalahari Dr 53965 (PO Box 590). Fax: 608/254-4460. **Facility:** This African-themed resort offers expansive indoor and outdoor water-park facilities with waterslides, a wave pool and several food-court outlets. 378 units. 251 one-bedroom standard units, some with whirlpools. 15 one- and 112 two-bedroom suites ($159-$849), some with whirlpools. 4 stories, interior corridors. *Bath:* combo or shower only. **Parking:** on-site. **Terms:** check-in 4 pm, 3 day cancellation notice-fee imposed. **Amenities:** voice mail, irons, hair dryers. *Some:* DVD players, CD players, safes. **Pool(s):** 3 heated outdoor, 4 heated indoor, 4 wading. **Leisure Activities:** whirlpools, waterslide, recreation programs, playground, exercise room, spa, basketball, horseshoes, volleyball. *Fee:* game room. **Guest Services:** gift shop, coin laundry, area transportation. **Business Services:** conference facilities, business center. **Cards:** AX, DS, MC, VI.

SOME UNITS

LUNA INN & SUITES

Phone: (608)253-2661

6/15-9/2	1P: $69-$98	2P: $69-$118	XP: $10 F12
5/24-6/14	1P: $59-$88	2P: $59-$98	XP: $10 F12
4/25-5/23 & 9/3-10/31	1P: $39-$59	2P: $45-$69	XP: $10 F12

Motel

Location: I-90/94, exit 92, 2.8 mi n on US 12. 1111 Wisconsin Dells Pkwy 53965. Fax: 608/253-2661. **Facility:** 72 units. 67 one-bedroom standard units, some with whirlpools. 5 one-bedroom suites ($89-$198). 2 stories, interior/exterior corridors. **Parking:** on-site. **Terms:** open 4/25-10/31, 2-3 night minimum stay - seasonal & weekends, 3 day cancellation notice-fee imposed. **Amenities:** hair dryers. **Pool(s):** heated outdoor, heated indoor. **Leisure Activities:** whirlpool, waterslide, playground. *Fee:* game room. **Guest Services:** coin laundry. **Business Services:** fax (fee). **Special Amenities:** free local telephone calls.

SOME UNITS

RAINTREE RESORT

Phone: (608)253-4386

7/1-8/31	1P: $100-$125	2P: $125-$160	XP: $10 F10
9/1-3/31	1P: $85-$100	2P: $100-$135	
4/1-6/30	1P: $85-$100	2P: $100-$135	XP: $10 F10

Large-scale Hotel

Location: I-90/94, exit 89 (SR 23), 0.5 mi e, then 1.5 mi n on US 12. 1435 Wisconsin Dells Pkwy 53965. Fax: 608/254-4647. **Facility:** 158 units. 142 one-bedroom standard units, some with whirlpools. 16 one-bedroom suites ($155-$275). 3-4 stories, interior corridors. *Bath:* combo or shower only. **Parking:** on-site. **Terms:** check-in 3:30 pm, cancellation fee imposed. **Amenities:** video games (fee), voice mail, irons, hair dryers. **Dining:** 8 am-10 pm, from 3 pm off season, cocktails. **Pool(s):** small heated indoor, heated indoor/outdoor, 2 wading. **Leisure Activities:** whirlpools, waterslide, recreation programs, small indoor/outdoor water park with multiple children activity areas, exercise room. *Fee:* game room. **Guest Services:** gift shop, coin laundry. **Business Services:** meeting rooms, fax (fee). **Cards:** AX, DC, DS, MC, VI. *(See color ad p 619)*

SOME UNITS

RAMADA LIMITED

AAA SAVE

Phone: 608/254-2218

	1P:	2P:	XP:	
7/7-11/1 [ECP]	1P: $99-$178	2P: $99-$178	XP: $10	F17
5/24-7/6 [ECP]	1P: $79-$160	2P: $79-$160	XP: $10	F17
4/1-5/23 [ECP]	1P: $79-$150	2P: $79-$150	XP: $10	F17
11/2-3/31 [ECP]	1P: $59-$150	2P: $59-$150	XP: $10	F17

Small-scale Hotel **Location:** I-90/94, exit 92 (US 12), 0.3 mi n. 1073 Wisconsin Dells Pkwy 53965 (PO Box 118). Fax: 608/254-2696. **Facility:** 73 units. 71 one-bedroom standard units. 2 one-bedroom suites ($150-$221) with whirlpools. 2 stories, interior corridors. **Parking:** on-site, winter plug-ins. **Terms:** check-in 4 pm, 2 night minimum stay - weekends 5/1-9/1, 3 day cancellation notice-fee imposed. **Amenities:** dual phone lines, voice mail, irons, hair dryers. **Pool(s):** small heated indoor. **Leisure Activities:** sauna, whirlpool. *Fee:* game room. **Guest Services:** coin laundry. *Fee:* tanning facility. **Business Services:** meeting rooms. **Cards:** AX, DC, DS, MC, VI. **Special Amenities:** free continental breakfast and free room upgrade (subject to availability with advanced reservations).

SOME UNITS

RODEWAY INN

AAA SAVE

Phone: 608/254-6492

	1P:	2P:	XP:	
5/17-9/9	1P: $89-$99	2P: $89-$99	XP: $6	F18
9/10-3/31	1P: $55-$89	2P: $55-$89	XP: $6	F18
4/1-5/16	1P: $55-$69	2P: $55-$69	XP: $6	F18

Small-scale Hotel **Location:** I-90/94, exit 89 (SR 23 N), 0.4 mi e. 350 W Munroe Ave 53965. Fax: 608/254-4542. **Facility:** 62 one-bedroom standard units, some with whirlpools. 2 stories, interior corridors. *Bath:* combo or shower only. **Parking:** on-site, winter plug-ins. **Terms:** 2 night minimum stay - seasonal weekends, weekly rates available, [CP] meal plan available, pets ($10 extra charge). **Amenities:** *Some:* irons, hair dryers. **Pool(s):** small heated indoor. **Leisure Activities:** whirlpool. **Guest Services:** coin laundry. **Business Services:** meeting rooms. **Cards:** AX, DC, DS, MC, VI. **Special Amenities:** free continental breakfast and free local telephone calls.

SOME UNITS

SKYLINE HOTEL & SUITES

Phone: (608)253-4841

	1P:	2P:	XP:	
All Year [CP]	1P: $44-$129	2P: $44-$129	XP: $5	F16

Small-scale Hotel **Location:** I-90/94, exit 92, 3.2 mi n on US 12. 1970 Wisconsin Dells Pkwy 53965. Fax: 608/254-6009. **Facility:** 87 units. 85 one-bedroom standard units, some with whirlpools. Some suites, some with whirlpools. 3 stories, interior/exterior corridors. **Parking:** on-site, winter plug-ins. **Terms:** 2 night minimum stay - seasonal weekends, cancellation fee imposed. **Pool(s):** heated outdoor, 2 heated indoor, 2 wading. **Leisure Activities:** saunas, whirlpools, waterslide, playground. *Fee:* game room. **Guest Services:** coin laundry, area transportation. *Fee:* tanning facility. **Business Services:** meeting rooms. **Cards:** AX, DS, MC, VI.

SOME UNITS

SUPER 8 MOTEL

Phone: 608/254-6464

	1P:	2P:	XP:	
7/4-9/1	1P: $73-$142	2P: $83-$142	XP: $6	
5/24-7/3	1P: $66-$127	2P: $76-$127	XP: $6	
9/2-3/31	1P: $55-$112	2P: $61-$112	XP: $6	
4/1-5/23	1P: $50-$107	2P: $56-$107	XP: $6	

Small-scale Hotel **Location:** I-90/94, exit 87 (SR 13), just e. 800 Co Hwy H 53965 (PO Box 467). Fax: 608/254-2692. **Facility:** 125 one-bedroom standard units. 3 stories, interior corridors. **Parking:** on-site, winter plug-ins. **Terms:** $1 service charge. **Amenities:** safes (fee), hair dryers. **Pool(s):** small heated indoor. **Leisure Activities:** sauna, whirlpool. *Fee:* game room. **Guest Services:** coin laundry. **Cards:** AX, DC, DS, MC, VI.

SOME UNITS

WINTERGREEN RESORT & CONFERENCE CENTER

AAA SAVE

Phone: 608/254-2285

	1P:	2P:	XP:	
7/14-8/18	1P: $179-$229	2P: $179-$229	XP: $8	F18
8/19-3/31	1P: $149-$205	2P: $149-$205	XP: $8	F18
6/8-7/13	1P: $119-$205	2P: $119-$205	XP: $8	F18
4/1-6/7	1P: $95-$119	2P: $95-$119	XP: $8	F18

Small-scale Hotel **Location:** I-90/94, exit 92 (US 12), just n. Located next to casino. 60 Gasser Rd 53965 (PO Box 296). Fax: 608/253-6235. **Facility:** 109 units. 99 one-bedroom standard units. 9 one- and 1 two-bedroom suites ($149-$369), some with whirlpools. 3 stories, interior corridors. *Bath:* combo or shower only. **Parking:** on-site. **Terms:** check-in 4 pm, 2-3 night minimum stay - seasonal, 3 day cancellation notice-fee imposed. **Amenities:** high-speed Internet, voice mail, hair dryers. **Dining:** 8 am-9 pm, Sun-Thurs to 7 pm in winter, cocktails. **Pool(s):** outdoor, heated indoor, 3 wading. **Leisure Activities:** sauna, whirlpools, waterslide, mini water park with pools, waterfalls, children's recreation area, playground, exercise room. *Fee:* game room. **Guest Services:** gift shop, coin laundry. **Business Services:** meeting rooms. **Cards:** AX, DS, MC, VI. **Special Amenities:** early check-in/late check-out and free room upgrade (subject to availability with advanced reservations). *(See color ad p 618)*

SOME UNITS

The following lodging was either not evaluated or did not meet AAA rating requirements but is listed for your information only.

ALOHA BEACH RESORT & SUITES

[fyi]

Phone: 608/253-4741

Did not meet all AAA rating requirements for property operations at time of last evaluation on 06/11/2002. **Location:** 0.8 mi e on CR A from jct US 12 and SR 23. 1370 E Hiawatha Dr 53965. Facilities, services, and decor characterize a basic property.

Small-scale Hotel

WHERE TO DINE

THE CHEESE FACTORY RESTAURANT

Vegetarian

Lunch: $5-$9   **Dinner:** $10-$13   **Phone:** 608/253-6065

Location: I-90/94, exit 92, 1.3 mi n on US 12. 521 Wisconsin Dells Pkwy S 53965. **Hours:** 9 am-9 pm. Closed: 11/27, 12/25; also Tues, Mon-Wed in winter. **Features:** Fresh, flavorful ingredients, unusual international recipes and pleasant service are staples at the restored cheese factory. An authentic soda fountain, jukebox and waiters in bow ties add to the nostalgic mood. Homemade desserts are wonderful. Casual dress. **Parking:** on-site. **Cards:** AX, DS, MC, VI.

THE DEL-BAR

▼▼▼▼

American

Dinner: $17-$38 **Phone:** 608/253-1861
Location: I-90/94, exit 92, 2.5 mi n on US 12 and SR 23. 800 Wisconsin Dells Pkwy 53940. **Hours:** 4:30 pm-9:30 pm, Fri & Sat-10 pm. **Closed:** 11/27, 12/24, 12/25. **Reservations:** suggested. **Features:** Owned and operated by same family since 1943. Excellent aged steak and fresh seafood. Also featuring Wisconsin duck. Terrace dining in season. Warm atmosphere with soft lighting and soothing player piano background music. Dressy casual; cocktails. **Parking:** on-site. **Cards:** AX, CB, DC, DS, MC, VI.

🍸 ✕

FAMILY CHEF RESTAURANT

AAA
▼▼▼

American

Lunch: $4-$12 **Dinner:** $4-$12 **Phone:** 608/254-7969
Location: 0.5 mi e of downtown on SR 16/13/23. 1101 Broadway 53965. **Hours:** Open 4/1-11/6 & 1/15-3/31; 7 am-9 pm; to 10 pm 7/1-8/31. **Features:** This notably clean and well-established restaurant caters to families with its extensive menu selection and casual atmosphere. Comfort foods abound, and fresh strawberry pie is the prize of the day. Casual dress; beer only. **Parking:** on-site. **Cards:** DS, MC, VI.

✕

FAMOUS DAVE'S

▼▼▼ ▼▼

Barbecue

Lunch: $5-$7 **Dinner:** $7-$18 **Phone:** 608/253-6683
Location: Downtown. 435 Broadway 53965. **Hours:** 11 am-8 pm; to 10 pm 6/1-9/1. **Closed:** 11/27, 12/25. **Features:** The casual restaurant's claim to fame is its award winning barbecue. Pork sandwiches, rib platters, burgers, chicken, salads and traditional side dishes are available for dining in or taking out. The lunch menu offers an exceptional value, with large portions at good prices. Casual dress; beer & wine only.
Parking: street. **Cards:** AX, DC, DS, MC, VI.

✕

PEDRO'S MEXICAN RESTAURANTE

▼▼▼ ▼▼

Mexican

Lunch: $5-$8 **Dinner:** $5-$17 **Phone:** 608/253-7233
Location: Just w of downtown on SR 23, 16 and 13. 951 Stand Rock Rd 53965. **Hours:** 11 am-9:30 pm, Fri & Sat-10:30 pm; 11 am-11 pm 5/20-9/20. **Closed:** 12/24, 12/25. **Reservations:** accepted. **Features:** Sizzling fajitas are a big hit at this restaurant, which delivers favorites from burritos and tacos to enchiladas and nachos. Complimentary fresh chips and salsa accompany all meals. Stucco walls, tile flooring and colorful decorations add to the South of the Border atmosphere. Casual dress; cocktails. **Parking:** on-site. **Cards:** AX, DS, MC, VI.

🍸 ✕

WALLY'S HOUSE OF EMBERS

▼▼▼▼

American

MC, VI.

Dinner: $10-$25 **Phone:** 608/253-6411
Location: I-90/94, exit 192 (US 12), 2.5 mi n. 935 Wisconsin Dells Pkwy 53940. **Hours:** 4:30 pm-10:30 pm, Sat-11 pm. **Closed:** 11/27, 12/24, 12/25. **Reservations:** suggested. **Features:** Casual dining in family owned restaurant since 1959. Famous for hickory smoked barbecue ribs. Also featuring Austrian veal and fresh fish. Private dining rooms are available. Dressy casual; cocktails. **Parking:** on-site. **Cards:** AX, DC,

🍸 ✕

WISCONSIN RAPIDS pop. 18,435

──── WHERE TO STAY ────

AMERICINN MOTEL & SUITES

▼▼▼▼

Small-scale Hotel

All Year 1P: $78-$90 2P: $78-$90 **Phone:** 715/424-3444
XP: $6 F18
Location: 1.4 mi s on SR 13. 3010 8th St S 54494. Fax: 715/424-3433. **Facility:** 65 units. 60 one-bedroom standard units, some with whirlpools. 5 one-bedroom suites ($94-$140), some with whirlpools. 2 stories (no elevator), interior corridors. *Bath:* combo or shower only. **Parking:** on-site, winter plug-ins. **Terms:** [ECP] meal plan available. **Amenities:** dual phone lines, hair dryers. **Pool(s):** heated indoor. **Leisure Activities:** Fee: game room. **Guest Services:** valet and coin laundry. **Business Services:** meeting rooms, fax (fee). **Cards:** AX, DS, MC, VI.

SOME UNITS
(A$K) (S☐) (🍴) (📶) (🏊) (👪) (📺) (DATA PORT) (💻) / (✕) (🛄) (🖥) /

BEST WESTERN RAPIDS MOTOR INN

SAVE

▼▼▼

Small-scale Hotel

5/16-10/18 [CP] 1P: $54-$65 2P: $60-$72 **Phone:** (715)423-3211
XP: $6 F12
4/1-5/15 & 10/19-3/31 [CP] 1P: $50-$60 2P: $58-$66 XP: $6 F12
Location: 0.5 mi s on SR 13 from jct SR 54. 911 Huntington Ave 54494. Fax: 715/423-2875. **Facility:** 43 one-bedroom standard units. 2 stories (no elevator), interior corridors. **Parking:** on-site. **Terms:** check-in 4 pm, pets (with prior approval). **Amenities:** irons, hair dryers. **Leisure Activities:** whirlpool. **Guest Services:** valet laundry. **Business Services:** fax (fee). **Cards:** AX, CB, DC, DS, MC, VI.

SOME UNITS
(S☐) (🐾) (🍴) (DATA PORT) / (✕) (🛄) /

HOTEL MEAD

AAA SAVE

▼▼▼

Large-scale Hotel

All Year 1P: $117-$159 **Phone:** (715)423-1500
XP: $10 F18
Location: Just e of downtown. 451 E Grand Ave 54494. Fax: 715/422-7064. **Facility:** 157 one-bedroom standard units, some with whirlpools. 5 stories, interior corridors. *Bath:* combo or shower only. **Terms:** check-in 4 pm, cancellation fee imposed, pets (with prior approval). **Amenities:** high-speed Internet (fee), dual phone lines, voice mail, irons, hair dryers. **Dining:** Cafe' Mulino, The Grand Avenue Grill, see separate listing. **Pool(s):** heated indoor. **Leisure Activities:** sauna, whirlpool, exercise room. *Fee:* game room. **Guest Services:** valet laundry. **Business Services:** conference facilities, business center. **Cards:** AX, DC, DS, MC, VI. **Special Amenities:** early check-in/late check-out and free newspaper.

SOME UNITS
(S☐) (🐾) (🍴) (🍸) (📶) (🏊) (✕) (📺) (DATA PORT) (💻) / (✕) (VCR) (🛄) (🖥) /

QUALITY INN

SAVE

▼▼▼

Small-scale Hotel

All Year 1P: $65-$75 2P: $72-$82 **Phone:** (715)423-5506
XP: $6 F18
Location: 1.5 mi s on SR 13. 3120 8th St S 54494. Fax: 715/423-7150. **Facility:** 36 one-bedroom standard units. 2 stories, interior corridors. **Parking:** on-site, winter plug-ins. **Terms:** [ECP] meal plan available. **Amenities:** voice mail. **Pool(s):** heated indoor. **Leisure Activities:** whirlpool. **Guest Services:** valet laundry. **Business Services:** meeting rooms. **Cards:** AX, CB, DC, DS, JC, MC, VI.

SOME UNITS
(S☐) (🍴) (🏊) (📶) (📺) (DATA PORT) (💻) / (✕) /

SUPER 8 MOTEL
Small-scale Hotel

Phone: (715)423-8080

All Year [CP]   1P: $49-$59   2P: $54-$64   XP: $5   F12
Location: 1.9 mi s on SR 13 from jct SR 54 W. 3410 8th St S 54494. **Fax:** 715/423-3595. **Facility:** 48 one-bedroom standard units. 2 stories, interior corridors. **Parking:** on-site, winter plug-ins. **Terms:** small pets only ($10 extra charge). **Amenities:** safes (fee). **Guest Services:** coin laundry. **Cards:** AX, CB, DC, DS, MC, VI.

SOME UNITS

—— WHERE TO DINE ——

CAFE' MULINO
Italian

Lunch: $6-$9   Dinner: $8-$17   Phone: 715/422-7000
Location: Just e of downtown; in Hotel Mead. 451 E Grand Ave 54494. **Hours:** 11:30 am-10:30 pm, Sun 10 am-10 pm. **Reservations:** suggested. **Features:** The lively, trattoria-style restaurant delivers regional specialties and traditional Italian cuisine, including pizza cooked in a wood-burning oven. Generous portions are an excellent value. The friendly, casual atmosphere is welcoming to families. Casual dress; cocktails. **Parking:** on-site. **Cards:** AX, CB, DC, DS, MC, VI.

FOUR STARS FAMILY RESTAURANT PANCAKE HOUSE
American

Lunch: $5-$8   Dinner: $5-$8   Phone: 715/424-4554
Location: 1.5 mi s on SR 13 from jct SR 54. 2911 8th St 54494. **Hours:** 5 am-10 pm. **Reservations:** accepted. **Features:** The popular restaurant's menu selections are vast and varied. Burgers, sandwiches, pitas, salads, pasta and Mexican specialties are featured. All-day breakfast selections include crepes, waffles, omelets and Swedish pancakes. Casual dress; wine only. **Parking:** on-site. **Cards:** AX, DC, DS, MC, VI.

THE GRAND AVENUE GRILL
American

Lunch: $5-$10   Dinner: $12-$20   Phone: 715/422-7000
Location: Just e of downtown; in Hotel Mead. 451 E Grand Ave 54494. **Hours:** 6:30-11 am, 11:30-1:30 & 5-9 pm, Fri & Sat-10 pm, Sun 6:30 am-2 pm. **Closed:** 12/25; also Sat & Mon for lunch. **Reservations:** suggested. **Features:** This traditional grill room offers time-tested favorites in a warm, relaxing atmosphere. Choice steak and seafood highlight the menu. Roast duck, smoked pork chop and Wisconsin venison stew are complements. The chef offers several new specials weekly. Desserts are made in-house and presented tableside on a tray. Service is attentive and capable. The white cloth covered tables, soft lighting and background music make for a comfortable dining experience. Dressy casual; cocktails. **Parking:** on-site. **Cards:** AX, CB, DC, DS, MC, VI.

WITTENBERG pop. 1,177

—— WHERE TO STAY ——

COMFORT INN & WILDERNESS CONFERENCE CENTER
Small-scale Hotel

Phone: (715)253-3755

6/1-8/31   1P: $59-$139   2P: $59-$139
1/1-3/31   1P: $69-$109   2P: $59-$109
4/1-5/31 & 9/1-12/31   1P: $59-$99   2P: $59-$99
Location: US 29, exit 189, just se. W17267 Red Oak Ln 54499. **Fax:** 715/253-3759. **Facility:** 64 one-bedroom standard units, some with whirlpools. 3 stories, interior corridors. **Bath:** combo or shower only. **Parking:** on-site. **Terms:** pets ($20 extra charge, must remain caged). **Amenities:** safes, irons, hair dryers. **Pool(s):** heated indoor. **Leisure Activities:** whirlpool, exercise room. **Guest Services:** coin laundry. **Business Services:** meeting rooms. **Cards:** AX, DC, DS, MC, VI.

SOME UNITS

WOODRUFF

—— WHERE TO DINE ——

PLANTATION SUPPER CLUB
American

Phone: 715/356-9000

Dinner: $7-$20
Location: 1.5 mi n on US 51, at jct SR 70. 54568. **Hours:** Open 4/1-2/14; 5 pm-10 pm. **Closed:** Mon. **Reservations:** accepted. **Features:** This traditional northern Wisconsin supper club is well-established, and was first constructed in 1938. The current owners have operated it since 1970. The service is friendly and attentive. The homemade onion rings and giant lobster tail are popular, as is the Friday night fish fry. Smoking in lounge. Casual dress; cocktails. **Parking:** on-site. **Cards:** AX, DC, DS, MC, VI.

Offices

Cities with main offices are listed in **BOLD TYPE** and toll-free member service numbers in *ITALIC TYPE*.
All are closed Saturdays, Sundays and holidays unless otherwise indicated.

The type of service provided is designated below the name of the city where the office is located:

+ Auto travel services, including books/maps, marked maps and on-demand Triptik maps
● Auto travel services, including books/maps, marked maps, but no on-demand Triptik maps
■ Provides books/maps only. No marked maps or on-demand Triptik maps available
▲ Travel agency services

NATIONAL OFFICE: 1000 AAA DRIVE, HEATHROW, FLORIDA 32746-5063, (407) 444-7000

MICHIGAN

ALLEN PARK—AAA MICHIGAN, 15220 SOUTHFIELD RD, 48101. MON-FRI 8:30-5:30, THU 8:30-7. (313) 386-7000, *(800) 222-8852.*+▲

ALPENA—AAA MICHIGAN, 2539 US 23 S, 49707. MON-FRI 8:30-5:30, THU 8:30-7. (989) 354-2151, *(800) 322-3014.*+▲

ANN ARBOR—AAA MICHIGAN, 1200 S MAIN ST, 48104. MON-FRI 8:30-5:30. (734) 930-2250, *(800) 447-5490.*+▲

ANN ARBOR—AAA MICHIGAN, 2650 CARPENTER RD, 48108. MON-FRI 8:30-5:30, SAT 8:30-12:30. (734) 973-2800, *(800) 833-4613.*+▲

BATTLE CREEK—AAA MICHIGAN, 778 W COLUMBIA AVE, 49015. MON-FRI 8:30-5:30, MON 8:30-7. (616) 962-2500, *(800) 435-0320.*+▲

BAY CITY—AAA MICHIGAN, 1111 S EUCLID AVE, 48706. MON-FRI 8:30-5:30, MON 8:30-7. (989) 686-2940, *(800) 322-4517.*+▲

BIRMINGHAM—AAA MICHIGAN, 34802 WOODWARD AVE, 48009. MON-FRI 8:30-5:30, THU 8:30-7. (248) 433-8200, *(800) 222-4419.*+▲

BRIGHTON—AAA MICHIGAN, 8350 W GRAND RIVER AVE, 48116. MON-FRI 8:30-5:30, THU 8:30-7. (810) 229-7100, *(800) 222-8801.*+▲

CANTON—AAA MICHIGAN, 2017 N CANTON CENTER RD, 48187. MON-FRI 8:30-5:30, THU 8:30-7. (734) 844-0146, *(800) 844-0424.*+▲

CENTER LINE—AAA MICHIGAN, 26522 VAN DYKE, 48015. MON-FRI 8:30-5:30, SAT 8:30-12:30. (586) 754-2200.+▲

DEARBORN—AAA MICHIGAN, 18800 HUBBARD DR #100, 48126. MON-FRI 8:30-5:30, SAT 8:30-12:30. (313) 336-0990.+▲

DETROIT—AAA MICHIGAN, 7800 W OUTER DR #120, 48235. MON-FRI 8:30-5:30, THU 8:30-7. (313) 255-9310, *(800) 222-4416.*+▲

DETROIT—AAA MICHIGAN, 719 GRISWOLD AVE STE 170, 48226. MON-FRI 7:30-5:30. (313) 237-5500, *(800) 934-8209.*+▲

DETROIT—AAA MICHIGAN, 9189 CADIEUX, 48224. MON-FRI 8:30-5:30, SAT 9-1. (313) 417-2393.+▲

FARMINGTON HILLS—AAA MICHIGAN, 38751 W 12 MILE RD, 48331. MON-FRI 8:30-5:30, SAT 8:30-12:30. (248) 994-4330, *(800) 224-1178.*+▲

FLINT—AAA MICHIGAN, G-5009 W BRISTOL RD, 48507. MON-FRI 8:30-5:30, SAT 8:30-12:30. (810) 230-8890, *(800) 552-5970.*+▲

GRAND RAPIDS—AAA MICHIGAN, 4650 PLAINFIELD NE, 49525. MON-FRI 8:30-5:30, TUE 8:30-7. (616) 364-6111, *(800) 442-8304.*+▲

GRANDVILLE—AAA MICHIGAN, 6305 KENOWA SW, 49418. MON-FRI 8:30-5:30, THU 8:30-7. (616) 457-8222, *(800) 258-6464.*+▲

GROSSE POINTE WOODS—AAA MICHIGAN, 19299 MACK AVE, 48236. MON-FRI 8:30-5:30, MON 8:30-7. (313) 343-6000.+▲

HOLLAND—AAA MICHIGAN, 587 E 8TH ST, 49423. MON-FRI 8:30-5:30, WED 8:30-7. (616) 392-5171, *(888) 544-9204.*+▲

JACKSON—AAA MICHIGAN, 1200 SOUTH WEST AVE, 49203. MON-FRI 8:30-5:30, MON 8:30-7. (517) 787-7300, *(800) 842-8999.*+▲

KALAMAZOO—AAA MICHIGAN, 2015 CROSSTOWN PKY W, 49008. MON-FRI 8:30-5:30, SAT 8:30-12:30. (616) 381-7100, *(800) 851-9692.*+▲

KENTWOOD—AAA MICHIGAN, 2560 E PARIS AVE SE, 49546. MON-FRI 8:30-5:30, SAT 8:30-12:30. (616) 957-4455, *(800) 222-3103.*+▲

LANSING—AAA MICHIGAN, 2829 E GRAND RIVER AVE, 48912. MON-FRI 8:30-5:30, SAT 8:30-12:30. (517) 487-6171, *(800) 222-9905.*+▲

LIVONIA—AAA MICHIGAN, 37383 SIX MILE RD, 48152. MON-FRI 8:30-5:30, WED 8:30-7. (734) 462-7000, *(800) 851-9691.*+▲

MACOMB—AAA MICHIGAN, 21851 HALL RD, 48044. MON-FRI 8:30-5:30, SAT 9-1. (810) 469-4050, *(800) 551-4311.*+▲

MARQUETTE—AAA MICHIGAN, WESTWOOD MALL, 49855. MON-FRI 8:30-5:30. (906) 225-6750, *(800) 526-4241.*+▲

MIDLAND—AAA MICHIGAN, 1900 S SAGINAW RD, 48640. MON-FRI 8:30-5:30, THU 8:30-7. (989) 832-6500, *(800) 322-4271.*●▲

MOUNT PLEASANT—AAA MICHIGAN, 913 E PICKARD SUITE L, 48858. MON-FRI 8:30-5:30. (989) 772-6001, *(800) 888-8850.*●▲

MUSKEGON—AAA MICHIGAN, 3575 HENRY ST, 49441. MON-FRI 8:30-5:30, WED 8:30-7. (231) 739-9363, *(800) 851-9689.*+▲

PETOSKEY—AAA MICHIGAN, 1321 SPRINGS ST, 49770. MON-FRI 8:30-5:30. (231) 347-8284, *(800) 294-6503.*■

PORT HURON—AAA MICHIGAN, 933 LAPEER, 48060. MON-FRI 8:30-5:30, MON 8:30-7. (810) 987-4800, *(800) 462-9968.*+▲

ROSEVILLE—AAA MICHIGAN, 25195 KELLY RD, 48066. MON-FRI 8:30-5:30, THU 8:30-7. (586) 774-7000.+▲

ROYAL OAK—AAA MICHIGAN, 27844 WOODWARD AVE, 48067. MON-FRI 8:30-5:30, THU 8:30-7. (248) 399-7100, *(866) 676-8757.*+▲

SAGINAW—AAA MICHIGAN, 3785 BAY RD, 48603. MON-FRI 8:30-5:30, MON 8:30-7. (989) 790-3240, *(800) 322-1120.*+▲

SOUTH LYON—AAA MICHIGAN, 558 N LAFAYETTE, 48178. MON-FRI 8:30-5:30. (248) 437-1729, *(800) 783-1729.*■▲

SOUTHGATE—AAA MICHIGAN, 15150 FORT ST, 48195. MON-FRI 8:30-5:30, THU 8:30-7. (734) 284-0800, *(800) 222-6612.*+▲

ST. JOSEPH—AAA MICHIGAN, 2090 NILES RD SUITE 200, 49085. MON-FRI 8:30-5:30. (616) 982-0033.▲

TRAVERSE CITY—AAA MICHIGAN, 940 N US 31 N, 49686. MON-FRI 8:30-5:30, SAT 8:30-12:30. (231) 947-8045, *(800) 442-1742.*+▲

TROY—AAA MICHIGAN, 25 E LONG LAKE RD, 48085. MON-FRI 8:30-5:30, SAT 8:30-12:30. (248) 879-2030, *(877) 349-1514.*+▲

UTICA—AAA MICHIGAN, 45700 MOUND RD, 48317. MON-FRI 8:30-5:30, THU 8:30-7. (586) 739-1400, *(800) 851-9690.*+▲

WATERFORD—AAA MICHIGAN, 5140 HIGHLAND RD, 48327. MON-FRI 8:30-5:30, THU 8:30-7. (248) 618-3440, *(800) 222-2661.*+▲

WISCONSIN

APPLETON—AAA WISCONSIN, 3215 W COLLEGE AVE, 54914. MON-FRI 8:30-5:30, SAT 9-1. (920) 738-4200, *(800) 236-1300.*+▲

BELOIT—AAA WISCONSIN, 2723 PRAIRIE AVE, 53511. MON-FRI 8:30-5:30, SAT 9-1. (608) 364-2740, *(800) 236-1300.*+

BROOKFIELD—AAA WISCONSIN, 12635 W NORTH AVE, 53005. MON-FRI 9-6, SAT 9-1. (262) 796-8960, *(800) 236-1300.*+▲

CEDARBURG—AAA WISCONSIN, W62 N208 WASHINGTON AVE, 53012. MON-FRI 8:30-5:30, SAT 9-1. (262) 376-8700.■

DELAFIELD—AAA WISCONSIN, 2566 SUN VALLEY DR, 53018. SATURDAY BY APPOINTMENT MON-FRI 8:30-5:30. (262) 646-6111.■

EAU CLAIRE—AAA WISCONSIN, 3436 OAKWOOD HILLS PKY, 54701. MON-FRI 8:30-5:30, SAT 9-1. (715) 836-8640, *(800) 236-1300.*✚▲

FOND DU LAC—AAA WISCONSIN, 504A N ROLLING MEADOWS RD, 54937. MON-FRI 8:30-5:30, SAT 9-1. (920) 923-4805.●

GREEN BAY—AAA WISCONSIN, 2285 S ONEIDA ST #1, 54304. MON-FRI 8:30-5:30, SAT 9-1. (920) 498-6120, *(800) 236-1300.*✚▲

GREEN BAY—AAA WISCONSIN, 2420 UNIVERSITY AVE, 54302. MON-FRI 8:30-5:30. (920) 406-2090.▲

JANESVILLE—AAA WISCONSIN, 2900 DEERFIELD DR STE 9C, 53546. MON-FRI 8:30-5:30, SAT 9-1. (608) 755-3960.✚▲

KENOSHA—AAA WISCONSIN, 10320 75TH ST SUITE D, 53142. MON-FRI 8:30-5:30. (262) 697-7280.✚▲

MADISON—AAA WISCONSIN, 8401 EXCELSIOR DR, 53717. MON-FRI 8:30-5:30, SAT 9-1. (608) 836-6555, *(800) 236-1300.*✚▲

MADISON—AAA WISCONSIN, 1701 THIERER RD, 53704. MON-FRI 8:30-5:30, SAT 9-1. (608) 242-6000.▲

MADISON—AAA WISCONSIN, 664 W WASHINGTON AVE, 53703. MON-FRI 8:30-5:30, SAT 9-1. (608) 251-0333, *(800) 236-1300.*✚▲

MADISON—AAA WISCONSIN, 1865 NORTHPORT DR, 53704. MON-FRI 8:30-5:30. (608) 246-5186.✚

MENOMONEE FALLS—AAA WISCONSIN, W176 N9352, 53051. MON-FRI 8-5:30. (262) 257-7555.✚

MILWAUKEE—AAA WISCONSIN, 4433 S 27TH ST, 53221. MON-FRI 9-6, SAT 9-1. (414) 423-2180, *(800) 236-1300.*✚▲

MILWAUKEE—AAA WISCONSIN, 200 W SILVER SPRING DR, 53217. MON-FRI 9-6, SAT 9-1. (414) 963-3060, *(800) 236-1300.*✚▲

MILWAUKEE—AAA WISCONSIN, 8333 W APPLETON AVE, 53218. SATURDAY BY APPOINTMENT MON-FRI 8:30-5:30. (414) 535-4040.▲

OAK CREEK—AAA WISCONSIN, 2333 W RYAN RD, 53154. MON-FRI 8:30-5:30.✚

ONALASKA—AAA WISCONSIN, 1220 CROSSING MEADOWS DR, 54650. MON-FRI 8:30-5:30, SAT 9-1. (608) 783-7412, *(800) 236-1300.*✚▲

OSHKOSH—AAA WISCONSIN, 1496 WEST SOUTH PARK AVE, 54902. MON-FRI 8:30-5:30. (866) 823-7665.■

RACINE—AAA WISCONSIN, 2310K S GREEN BAY DR, 53406. MON-FRI 8:30-5:30, SAT 9-1. (262) 554-4242, *(800) 236-1300.*✚▲

SHEBOYGAN—AAA WISCONSIN, 3104 S BUSINESS DR, 53081. MON-FRI 8:30-5:30. (920) 208-8900.✚▲

WAUKESHA—AAA WISCONSIN, 2020 E MORELAND BLVD, 53186. MON-FRI 9-6, SAT 9-1. (262) 548-1000, *(800) 236-1300.*✚▲

WAUSAU—AAA WISCONSIN, 4518 RIB MOUNTAIN DR, 54401. MON-FRI 8:30-5:30. (715) 241-7222.✚▲

WEST ALLIS—AAA WISCONSIN, 2251 S 108TH ST, 53227. MON-FRI 8:30-5:30. (414) 327-8880.✚

WEST BEND—AAA WISCONSIN, 910 GATEWAY CT, 53095. SATURDAY BY APPOINTMENT MON-FRI 8:30-5:30. (262) 338-0100.■

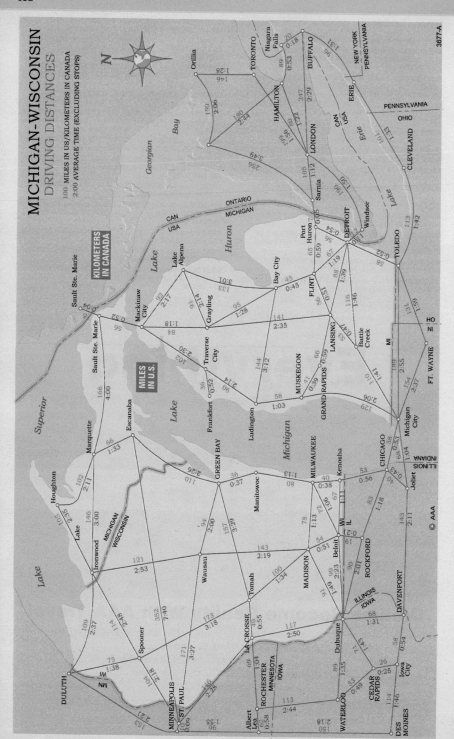

MICHIGAN-WISCONSIN
DRIVING DISTANCES

100 MILES IN US/KILOMETERS IN CANADA
2:00 AVERAGE TIME (EXCLUDING STOPS)

3677-A

© AAA

Border Information

FOR CANADIAN RESIDENTS

Entering the United States

PASSPORTS to enter the United States or return to Canada are not required for native-born citizens of either country. However, a Canadian passport remains the best internationally accepted evidence of Canadian citizenship. Proof of citizenship must be carried; a certified birth certificate, accompanied by a photo ID will usually suffice. Proof of residence also may be required. Unmarried parents who share custody of children should carry copies of the legal custody documents.

UNITED STATES CUSTOMS permits you to bring, free of duty, for personal use and not intended for sale: clothing, personal effects and equipment appropriate to the trip. Personal effects may include 200 cigarettes, 50 cigars or 4.4 pounds (2 kgs) smoking of tobacco or proportionate amounts of each, and 1 litre of alcoholic beverage. Cuban cigars are denied entry.

If you are planning to be in the United States at least 72 hours, you may bring gifts up to a fair retail value of $100 (U.S.), provided you have not claimed this exemption within the preceding 6 months. Family members may not combine their gift exemptions. Perfume containing alcohol and valued at more than $5 retail, tobacco products (except for 100 cigars) and alcoholic beverages are excluded from the gift provision.

Radio Communication Equipment: You may use your Family Radio Service Station (FRS) and cellular phone in the United States without any restrictions.

Returning to Canada

CANADIAN CUSTOMS allows you to bring, free of duty and taxes, goods valued up to $200 (Canadian) any number of times per year, provided you have been in the United States **48 hours or more.** All goods must accompany you; a written declaration *may* be required.

You may claim a $50 (Canadian) exemption on goods, excluding alcoholic beverages and tobacco products, if you are returning after an absence of **24 hours or more** and are not using any other exemption. If more than $50 worth of goods is brought back, the regular rate of duty and taxes will be levied on the entire value. This exemption may apply any number of times in a year. If your trip keeps you out of Canada for 48 hours or more, the exemption is $200.

If you are returning after **7 days or more** in the United States (not counting the day of departure from Canada), you may claim an exemption on goods valued up to $750 (Canadian). Goods, other than alcohol and tobacco products, are not required to accompany you; a written declaration *may* be required.

Permitted within the $200 and $750 exemptions are up to 50 cigars, 200 cigarettes, 200 tobacco sticks and 6.4 ounces (200 gm) of tobacco and up to 40 ounces (1.14 L) of liquor or 1.6 quarts (1.5 L) of wine or 9 quarts (8.5 L) of beer and/or ale (or its equivalent of 24 twelve-ounce bottles or cans). You must meet the minimum age requirement of the province entered to claim alcohol or tobacco products. Northwest Territories and Nunavut do not allow you to bring in more than the duty-free allowance of alcohol.

There is nothing to prevent you from importing any quantity of goods, even if you do not qualify for any kind of personal exemption, provided the goods you are importing are not restricted and you pay the full rate of duty and taxes.

Special Tariff: When you exceed your $200 or $750 exemptions, a special rate of 7 percent combined duty and taxes is levied on the next $300 value in goods (except tobacco and alcohol) in excess of maximum exemptible amounts, provided the goods are of U.S. origin. Regular duties apply on any amount over that. For detailed information concerning specific duty rates, consult Canadian Customs before leaving on your trip.

All exemptions are individual and may not be combined with those of another person. You may be asked to verify the length of your visit; dated receipts normally constitute proof.

GIFTS to the value of $60 (Canadian) may be sent from abroad, free of duty or taxes. These may not include alcoholic beverages, tobacco products or advertising matter. Gifts valued at over $60 (Canadian) are subject to duty and taxes on the amount in excess of $60. Gifts *sent* from abroad do not count against your personal exemption, but gifts brought back *must* be included as part of your exemption.

Bed & Breakfast Lodgings Index

Some bed and breakfasts listed below might have historical significance. Those properties are also referenced in the Historical index. The indication that continental [CP] or full breakfast [BP] is included in the room rate reflects whether a property is a Bed-and-Breakfast facility.

Country Inns Index

Some of the following country inns can also be considered as bed-and-breakfast operations. The indication that continental [CP] or full breakfast [BP] is included in the room rate reflects whether a property is a Bed-and-Breakfast facility.

Historical Lodgings & Restaurants Index

Some of the following historical lodgings can also be considered as bed-and-breakfast operations. The indication that continental [CP] or full breakfast [BP] is included in the room rate reflects whether a property is a Bed-and-Breakfast facility.

Resorts Index

Many establishments are located in resort areas; however, the following places have extensive on-premises recreational facilities:WISCONSINAccommodations

Many establishments are located in resort areas; however, the following places have extensive on-premises recreational facilities:552

The One For All

You know how AAA can simplify your life. Now make the lives of those you love the most a little easier—give them AAA associate memberships.

Associate members are eligible for the same security, services, and savings as primary members—emergency road service, valuable savings, access to travel services, and more. And all this protection is available for a reduced enrollment fee.

Help your family members simplify their lives with AAA associate memberships. Call or stop by your nearest AAA office today. And make AAA the one for you.

Points of Interest Index

Index Legend

⬇ GEM: Points of Interest Offering a *Great Experience for Members*

MUSIC HALLS & OPERA HOUSES

NATURAL BRIDGES

NATURAL PHENOMENA

NATURE CENTERS

NATURE TRAILS

OBSERVATORIES

PAINTINGS

PARKS, CITY; STATE; PROVINCIAL

SAVE *Attraction Admission Discount Index*

Comprehensive City Index

Here is an alphabetical list of all cities appearing in this TourBook® guide. Cities are presented by state/province. Page numbers under the POI column indicate where points of interest text begins. Page numbers under the L&R column indicate where lodging and restaurant listings begin.

COMPREHENSIVE CITY INDEX (CONT'D)

COMPREHENSIVE CITY INDEX (CONT'D)

COMPREHENSIVE CITY INDEX (CONT'D)

Photo Credit Index

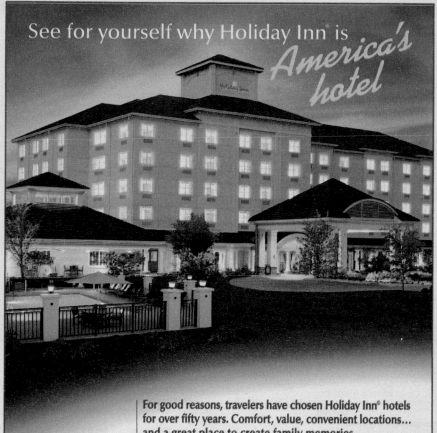

See for yourself why Holiday Inn® is *America's hotel*

For good reasons, travelers have chosen Holiday Inn® hotels for over fifty years. Comfort, value, convenient locations... and a great place to create family memories.

Here's what you can expect at every Holiday Inn hotel:*
- Kids Eat & Stay Free
- Swimming pools
- Restaurant, lounge, room service, and fitness center
- In-room amenities, including: dataport, iron/ironing board, coffeemaker, and hair dryer.

Holiday Inn hotels across the nation offer special AAA rates.

HOTELS · RESORTS

For Reservations:
Call **1-800-734-4275**,
your AAA Travel Professional
or visit **holiday-inn.com/aaa**

For more information on Holiday Inn hotels in the area you plan to visit, look for our hotel ads and "red" Official Appointment hotel listings.